# CONSUMER SALES LAW

## Second Edition

### Professor JK Macleod

Routledge·Cavendish
Taylor & Francis Group
LONDON AND NEW YORK

First edition published 2002
by Cavendish Publishing Ltd
Second edition first published 2007
by Routledge-Cavendish
2 Park Square, Milton Park, Abingdon, Oxon OX14 4RN

Simultaneously published in the USA and Canada
by Routledge-Cavendish
270 Madison Ave, New York, NY 10016

*Routledge-Cavendish is an imprint of the Taylor & Francis Group, an informa business*

© 2002, 2007 John Macleod

Typeset in Palatino and Gill Sans by
RefineCatch Limited, Bungay, Suffolk
Printed and bound in Great Britain by
TJ International, Padstow, Cornwall

Crown copyright material is reproduced with the permission of the
Controller of HMSO and the Queen's Printer for Scotland.

*British Library Cataloguing in Publication Data*
A catalogue record for this book is available from the British Library

*Library of Congress Cataloging in Publication Data*
A catalog record for this book has been requested

ISBN10: 0–415–41566–7 (pbk)
ISBN13: 978–0–415–41566–8 (pbk)

# CONSUMER SALES LAW

Consumer sales law involves the law relating to the supply of goods to consumers, in the last 50 years becoming a very significant part of the UK economy. Legally, it has become unnecessarily complicated because of the many strands of the law applicable. Much of this can be traced to the attraction consumer protection exerts over politicians, the last five years seeing an upheaval in consumer credit law, embodied in numerous heavyweight statutory instruments and a major new Consumer Credit Act in 2006. This book includes an attempt to equip the reader with an idea of how this fast-changing subject is likely to develop through the inclusion of those reform proposals which as at publication seem likely to take hold, including the draft Tribunals, Courts and Enforcement Bill 2006.

Additionally, it has recently embarked on a technical revolution. Whereas in the twentieth century the subject was firmly grounded in the common law of contract and tort, as amended by strict liability crimes fashioned in numerous traditional Westminster Statutes, in this century it is fast being taken over by the European Union. Already, important parts have been recast by the UK Parliament in obedience to EU Directives, much of the principle now being found in Statutory Instruments; but this is not always obvious because the outward form remains the traditional Westminster pattern. This development seems destined to continue at an accelerating rate. The Unfair Commercial Practices Directive 2005 is already being implemented here; and a major Consumer Credit Directive is presently being drafted in Brussels. It is not inconceivable that in another generation even the common law base of the subject will have been replaced.

At the same time, the subject shows signs of being prised from the grasp of the English legal profession as traditionally constituted. Even if much of the work continues to be done by those with legal training, this century has already seen an enormous escalation of the intervention of consumer advisers and debt advisers; official protection of consumers undertaken by public officials armed with the power to seek injunctions to protect consumers generally; and repair to the courts for the adjudication of particular disputes replaced by ombudsmen.

**John Macleod** retired from university in 2004, having taught sales and financing law to undergraduates for 40 years. Specialising in payment cards (including credit, charge and debit cards), he was for 20 years chief examiner in the finance industry. In retirement, he has at last found time to get to the bottom of the subject.

# CONTENTS

# PREFACE

The comparatively short space of time since the previous (2002) edition has marked a momentous change: a subject predominantly derived from English-originated law (whether statute or common law) has been replaced by one whose major inspiration is to be found in Brussels. The increasing trickle of EU-inspired consumer law observable in the twentieth century has swollen in the twenty-first century to one where the majority of developments nowadays emanate from Brussels. This will become increasingly obvious as the Unfair Commercial Practices (UCP) Directive (2005) is implemented in the UK; and the process is likely to continue with the Draft Consumer Credit Directive, which may (almost for the first time) begin to make significant changes in our Consumer Credit Acts 1974–2006. Much of this new Euro-derived law is likely to be implemented in the UK by statutory instrument: whereas in the twentieth century, an English lawyer could confidently concentrate on principles found in UK statutes, largely ignoring statutory instrument detail, in the twenty-first century much of the new general principles will be found in statutory instruments enacting EU Directives; and these new EU-inspired statutory instruments will have the power to override UK statutes—the first time since the seventeenth century that this has threatened on a wide scale.

Lesser changes include the following:

(1) The accepted meaning of 'consumer' is coalescing round that EU-inspired definition of supply by a business supplier to a private consumer. Further, under EU inspiration, there has been introduced, in 2002, an entirely new Pt 5A of the Sale of Goods Act 1979, establishing a new range of remedies for consumer-buyers, together with a new (non-SGA) scheme for enforcing manufacturers' guarantees. With these changes, it has been possible to reduce significantly the treatment of supplies from business to business, whilst international trade has been virtually excised from the work.

(2) The pre-Consumer Credit Act 1974 statutes are in most fields redundant and can be excised. Further, following the 2003 *White Paper*, the CCA 1974 has itself been the subject of major reform by a series of 2004 statutory instruments and the Consumer Credit Act 2006 (much due to come into force over the next few years). The 2006 Act has been fully integrated into the text, but largely without transitional provisions and sometimes without the dates upon which provisions will come into effect.

(3) The traditional scheme in the Companies Acts for regulating security granted by company debtors is about to be replaced, which should also allow the excision of much material relating to *Romalpa* clauses. The Companies Bill 2006 will lead to that scheme's replacement by a notice-filing system, based on Art 9 of the US Uniform Commercial Code and should also do away with the need to distinguish between fixed and floating charges. For the moment, there remains in force the nineteenth century system for the granting of security by individual debtors; but, in due course, this should also sweep away the Bills of Sale Acts 1878–82.

(4) When the twentieth century Consumer Credit Directives were promulgated, the UK consumer credit market was so far ahead of the continental systems

that the Directives largely followed UK ideas. However, the continental consumer credit systems are now much more sophisticated, so that any new Directive on the subject is likely to make significant changes to the UK system. The draft Consumer Credit Directive continues its seemingly endless debate: it now seems likely to include some maximum and some minimum provisions. Even here (and *a fortiori* as regards other draft directives) I have tried to avoid giving substantive details of the draft—the gestation period seems longer, and the results less certain, than with regard to Westminster legislation.

(5) So far as possible, I have tried to indicate the very many places where the UCP Directive will cause UK law to be replaced before the end of 2007.

(6) With the plethora of strict liability consumer protection provisions (both civil and criminal), there is now far less need for UK consumers to fall back on general common law principles of negligence; and to this extent, the position of UK consumers has strengthened. This has enabled me to cut to the bone treatment of the tort of negligence.

(7) There has been an observable trend for changes in the law to offer less by way of an action for damages by individual consumers and more by way of provisions designed to protect consumers generally, e.g. in Pt 8 of the Enterprise Act 2002. This is achieved by enabling the authorities to proceed for an injunction against traders who injure consumers generally, so that the individual consumer injured effectively faces a further hurdle: persuading the authorities that his case represents the general consumer interest before court action is taken. Further, in relation to the many strict liability criminal offences protecting consumers, a viable alternative route in the last century was to encourage the authorities to take criminal proceedings against the errant trader and ask the convicting court to grant a compensation order to the injured consumers; but in this century the Court of Appeal seems to have set its face against this tactic: see *R v Glen Adaway* (2004).

(8) From a consumer lawyer's point of view, a further worrying development has been the tendency to hive off individual consumer disputes to arbitration, e.g. by the Financial Services Authority, to Alternative Dispute Resolution and to administrative discretion, e.g. by the Office of Fair Trading unfair terms unit. As none of these systems produce records and precedent in the manner of the courts, it may become increasingly difficult to trace what decisions are in fact being made in relation to consumers and determine what 'rights' consumers in fact have.

(9) At the last moment, there was published the draft Tribunals, Courts and Enforcement (TCE) Bill 2006, relevant at paras 5.42; 6.10; 19.15–17; 27.04–05. Unfortunately, this proved too late to insert at paras 5.42 and 6.10, so the relevant material is to be found at para 27.04.

Only since my retirement in December 2004 have I had the opportunity to devote to this work the large amount of time required to follow through so many legal changes. My thanks are due to Robin Makin and Jez Marshall who, in their different ways, have supported the development of this edition; and as regards production, to my publisher and Bob Banbury and his colleagues at RefineCatch Ltd. However, any errors that remain in the text, tables or indices are my own responsibility.

In this edition, I have endeavoured to state the law in accordance with the authorities available to me on the date below.

JK Macleod
August 2006

# TABLE OF CASES

Note: Bold references indicate that a direct quote from the judgment has been used.

# TABLE OF STATUTES

N.B. Those sections set out in the text are denoted in bold print. Abbreviations found in the text for statutes are to be found here in square brackets.

# TABLE OF STATUTORY INSTRUMENTS

N.B. Statutory instruments made under the Consumer Credit Act 1974 have their titles abbreviated (CC = Consumer Credit) and the text of them will be found in the following; Goode, *Consumer Credit Law & Practice*; Guest, *Encyclopedia of Consumer Credit*. Most of the other statutory instruments lists below will be found in Thomas, *Encyclopedia of Consumer Law.*

# TREATY OF ROME

NB. Following a number of amendments, the articles of the Treaty were renumbered. The following table uses the new numbering, with the old numbers in brackets.

# TABLE OF EU DIRECTIVES

# PART 1

# THE NATURE OF CONTRACTS
# FOR THE SUPPLY OF GOODS

# CHAPTER 1

# INTRODUCTION

## SCOPE OF THE ENQUIRY

**[1.01]** This book is concerned with what laymen might term 'sales of goods' to consumers who are within England and Wales. Such transactions will normally be governed by English law (see para 18.13). The fundamental transaction in such activity must be that which is technically characterised as a sale of goods (see para 1.02).

This is a specialised area of the common law which largely developed in the eighteenth and nineteenth centuries, typically in relation to merchants purchasing for resale. It was first codified as a set of general rules in the Sale of Goods Act 1893. However, even in 1893 there may be observed some special rules fashioned for export sales; and, since then, export sales have become such a specialised area of law as to be beyond the scope of this work. For the UK,[1] the 1893 Act was subsequently re-enacted with amendments in the Sale of Goods Act 1979 (SGA). Unless otherwise stated, subsequent references to the SGA are to the SGA 1979:[2] the 1979 Act in fact only consolidated all the statutory amendments previously made to the 1893 Act.[3] Since then, Parliament has pursued a policy of piecemeal amendment.[4] Ignoring export sales, this body of legislation applied to goods bought for resale and those bought for consumption, whether the buyer be a business or a private person.

However, with the twenty-first century there has been introduced a further formal distinction in respect of goods bought for private consumption: these are to be found in the EU-led special developments in respect of consumer sales in the Sale and Supply of Goods to Consumers Regulations 2002 (SSG Regs).[5] So, it would seem that English law has at last reached a point where this book may consider alone a separate body of law relating to sales to private consumers (see para 1.02), where perhaps the single most important complicating factor is the need for 'buyers' to finance the acquisition of goods (see para 1.03). Additionally, such sales may bring into play a whole range of specialised statute-based rules of criminal law, largely introduced as ancillary supports for the civil law, e.g. the Consumer Credit Act 1974 (see para 1.03); and so the totality of the transaction must inevitably involve consideration of the interplay of civil and criminal 'remedies' (see paras 1.04 and 1.05). Sometime in the future, the common law of contract basis of the subject may be displaced by an EU Code.[6]

---

1    The modern American sales code is to be found in art 2 of the Uniform Commercial Code (UCC).
2    For the contracts to which the 1979 Act applies, see s 1 and Sched 1.
3    E.g. by the Supply of Goods (Implied Terms) Act 1973, the Unfair Contract Terms Act 1977.
4    By the Sale of Goods (Amendment) Act 1994; the Sale and Supply of Goods Act 1994; the Sale of Goods (Amendment) Act 1995.
5    2002 SI 3045; and see further, para 14.01.
6    Ridge (2006) 156 NLJ 902.

## The categories of contract

**[1.02] Basic sales**. In terms of legal analysis, no doubt the greater number of sales are achieved within the scope of the SGA by way of a simple sale of goods with payment on delivery (s 28: set out, para 23.16). The SGA 1893 purported to do no more than 'codify the law relating to the sale of goods' and expressly left the general principles of the common law untouched save insofar as they are inconsistent with the terms of the Act (now 1979 Act, s 62(2): set out, para 10.18). However, subsequent statutes have steadily reduced the role of the common law in the regulation of consumer sales (see below).

Within the context of sales of goods, the draftsman of the SGA 1893 (Sir Mackenzie Chalmers) endeavoured to capture the spirit of the common law rules, leaving alterations in the common law of England to be made by Parliament.[7] The underlying philosophy was to hold the ring between two equal parties whilst they achieved a true bargain,[8] the rules themselves being displaceable by contrary agreement: this attitude is often described as *laissez-faire*. Whilst Chalmers for the most part succeeded in embodying this philosophy in his draft, e.g. *caveat emptor* (see para 15.22), it may be questioned however, whether (a) the optimum moment was chosen for codification in terms of common law development, and (b) Chalmers was as successful in achieving his objective as is sometimes traditionally held. *A fortiori*, the continued universal use of the philosophy as regards sales of goods may itself be criticised.[9] The assumption of equality of bargaining power must clearly be erroneous in some cases, e.g. consumer standard-form contracts (see para 11.08); and it would seem an almost impossible task to formulate a set of even *prima facie* rules which would do justice to all parties in all the circumstances obtaining at the time of codification, let alone subsequently.[10] For consumer sales (see below), there are now considerable powers to insist that the express terms are consumer-friendly, both prospectively[11] and retrospectively.[12]

*Consumer sales.* English statute first introduced notions of consumer contracts in the context of exclusion clauses: there has since 1977 been a concept of 'dealing as consumer' (Unfair Contract Terms Act 1977 (UCTA), s 12: see para 18.18); and

---

7   See Chalmers' Preface to the 1894 Edition of his Commentary on the SGA. Some changes were made by Parliament, particularly during the course of extending the Bill to Scotland, e.g. the requirement as to notice in SGA, s 18, rr 2 and 3. See further Lord Diplock in *Ashington Piggeries Ltd v Christopher Hill Ltd* [1972] AC 441 at 501. See also Kerr (1978) 41 MLR at 17–18; Rodger (1992) 108 LQR 570; Mitchell (2001) 117 LQR 645, at 659–61.

8   Per Jessel MR in *Printing and Numerical Registering Co v Sampson* (1875) LR 19 Eq 462 at 465. See *Unfair Terms in Contracts* (2002, Law Comm 205), para 2.1; and standard form contracts, para 11.08.

9   Is it true to say that in modern consumer sales the SGA is still interpreted neutrally by the courts? See further, para 1.04; and generally *Chitty on Contracts*, 28th edn, Vol 1, para 1-010.

10  See Bridge [1991] LM & CLQ 52 at 53. For further discussion as to whether there are any general principles of commercial law and whether the subject should be codified as a whole, see Goode, *Commercial Law*, 3rd edn, Chap 40.

11  The OFT has wide powers to require suppliers to re-write their standard-form contracts (see para 11.08).

12  The courts have powers to strike down clauses in particular consumer contracts which are unfair or unreasonable (see paras 11.14 and 18.20).

this has, subsequently, been utilised in amendments to the SGA (see paras 11.05A and 11.12). Whilst there have, since, been other Westminster-inspired definitions of consumer,[13] in the twenty-first century, the dominant definition in our field has become the Euro-inspired one of the 'consumer', as meaning (SSG Regs, reg 2):

> 'any natural person who in the contracts covered by these Regulations, is acting for purposes which are not directly related to his trade, business or profession.'

As the Euro-version is compulsory, English law has begun to adapt the old 'dealing as consumer' concept to conform. The basic issues for parliamentary draftsman in the next few years are as follows:

(1) Whether we should retain a single code for all sales, or move to a separate consumer sales code.[14]

(2) Bearing in mind the pressures on the Parliamentary timetable, how should the new statutory provisions be kept up to date?[15] This appears to involve at least two major policy decisions: (a) whether any consumer sales code should be drafted in general or detailed form; and (b) to what extent (if any) the details should be fleshed out by statutory instrument.

**[1.03] Consumer supplies**. Whilst the basic transaction considered above rightly envisages the parties making a simultaneous exchange of the price for the goods, it is a fact of life that many consumers wishing to obtain goods in England and Wales do not have within their own resources the cash to pay for them on delivery. Broadly speaking, such consumers have available to them the following alternative methods of immediate acquisition:

(a) a cash *sale* (see para 1.07) financed by a *loan* (see para 7.01, *et seq.*); or

(b) an instalment contract, which may take any of these forms—

    (i)   a credit or conditional *sale* (see para 1.10) or

    (ii)  a simple *hiring*, rental or leasing (see para 1.17), or

    (iii) a *hire-purchase agreement* (see para 1.20).

It is submitted that it is unrealistic to look at the law relating to consumer sales without examining all these alternative forms of supply contract used to attain the same objective. It will be noted at once that the above forms of contract utilise two different types of contract to transfer the use-value of goods to consumers:[16] (1) sales (see para 1.06, *et seq.*); (2) hiring (see para 1.17, *et seq.*); and (3) loan (see para 7.01, *et seq.*).

For a long time it was a fundamental weakness of our law that these different solutions to the same problem were governed by disparate pieces of legislation, or in some cases were subject to no legislative control at all. However, this weakness

---

13  See Cartwright, *Consumer Protection and the Criminal Law*, 2–4; and generally, below Chap 4.

14  See Bridge (2003) 119 LQR 173. For a possible model, see the US Uniform Commercial Code, Art 2: see para 1.01.

15  See Brownsword & Howells (1999) 19 LS 287; and para 8.17B.

16  Besides the legal differences mentioned in the text, the different forms may have different financial implications, which the consumer should examine for the best deal.

was tackled by the Consumer Credit Act 1974 (CCA).[17] Whilst the SGA replaced the pre-existing common law of sale (see para 1.02), the CCA assumes the existence of the common law relating to supplies of goods and then makes detailed changes to it: so, to understand the CCA, the underlying common law must first be appreciated. The CCA, because it has to deal with a number of different legal transactions which may be used to achieve the same objective, is necessarily complicated. Indeed, it is a monument to the drafting skills of the author, Mr Francis Bennion,[18] who had planned to draft in layman's language (see below para 5.06) a comprehensive scheme built of brand-new concepts (see para 5.26). Whereas the SGA 1893 was in a sense typical of the nineteenth century in its reflection of the notion of freedom of contract,[19] the CCA is a leading example of post-1945 legislation with an axe to grind,[20] and increasingly reliant on criminal sanctions.[21]

With our accession to the EEC in 1973 (see para 1.03A), an entirely new factor has been introduced. In the 1970s, the EEC began the process of evolving its own community-wide policy on consumer affairs (see para 3.10); and of mixed EEC and domestic origins has been the enactment of the Consumer Protection Act 1987 (CPA) containing both civil and criminal provisions relating to three distinct aspects of consumer supplies.[22] By 1990, much of the centre of thinking and activity on reform of consumer law had passed to Brussels, with the EU-inspired SSG Regulations (see para 14.01). Apart from the potentially-significant domestic Deregulation Act 1994 (see para 5.10), the major UK-inspired development has been the Consumer Credit Act 2006 (see para 5.11).

**[1.03A] The European Union (EU).** In 1973, the United Kingdom became a member of the EEC, thereby undertaking all the rights and obligations arising, *inter alia*, from the Treaty of Rome, the articles of which have unfortunately been renumbered (old numbers in brackets where appropriate). Under this Treaty, the Community must strive towards the approximation of laws (Art 3(h)) and harmonise legislation (Art 94 [ex 100]), including the progressive approximation throughout the EEC of the different national policies and laws. Whilst the original Treaty of Rome did not lay down a clear basis for an EEC consumer protection policy, the EEC promoted a number of uniform consumer laws (see para 3.10) indirectly justified on the basis of various provisions of the Treaty.[23] The Maastricht Treaty 1991 introduced two relevant changes. *First*, it added to the Treaty of Rome a new objective of strengthening consumer protection to safeguard the 'economic interests of consumers' and provide 'adequate information to consumers' (Art 153 [ex 129A]). They do not necessarily preclude more stringent such national pro-

---

17  See the Preamble to the CCA. For the objectives of this Act, see further the Crowther Report upon whose recommendations it was substantially based: para 5.03.

18  He has produced a monumental loose-leaf commentary on the Act *Consumer Credit Control*—set out according to an entirely novel pattern.

19  It has been pointed out that the apparent simplicity of the drafting of the SGA is misleading: Goode, *Commercial Law*, 3rd edn, 192–93.

20  See Nicol (1981) 44 MLR 21.

21  For the interpretation problems to which this gives rise, see para 1.05.

22  (a) Consumer Safety (see para 4.31, *et seq.*); (b) Misleading Pricing (see para 8.09, *et seq.*): (c) Product Liability (see para 17.21, *et seq.*).

23  Mostly justified under old Arts 36, 100, 100A, 235. See generally Goode, *Consumer Credit Law & Practice*, Pt IJ.

tective measures as are compatible with the Treaty (see para 3.10). *Second*, it asserted the new principle of subsidiarity (so far seemingly little-used by the EU), which was supposed to restrict the organisation (now designated EU) from more enthusiastic intervention in fields so far occupied by national laws (Art 3B).

Under the EU Treaties, Member States must give effect to Community law, which takes precedence over English law, e.g. CPA, s 1(1) (see para 17.23). Those Community laws extant at the time of our accession were given the force of law within the UK by the European Communities Act 1972 (ECA), subsequent changes in the Treaties, and sometimes also laws,[24] being similarly incorporated. For our purposes, EU attempts to harmonise consumer law of Member States may be roughly divided into two types.

1. *Positive harmonisation*. Positive Community law is of two sorts:

   (a) 'Self-executing' laws which take direct internal effect in precedence to the domestic law of Member States.[25] These include provisions of the Treaties and Regulations,[26] which have general applications, whereas Decisions deal only with an individual case.[27] The Treaties and Regulations may be enforced in the UK by way of actions for breach of statutory duty (see para 3.21) and sometimes by the criminal law.[28]

   (b) Directives, which are only valid provided *intra vires* the article of the Treaty under which they are made.[29] The Directive will specify only the result to be achieved in domestic law, but leave to the national authorities the choice of form.[30] The UK has adopted the practice of fulfilling its Community obligations by the enactment of statutes or statutory instruments (see para 3.10), which should simplify public enforcement (see para 28.02).

   There are also EU Codes of conduct (see para 3.14).

2. *Negative harmonisation*. This comes into play where national measures ostensibly adopted to protect, say consumers, are incompatible with the Treaty. Theoretically, consumers adversely affected may complain to the EU Commission directly so that the latter may take up the matter before the European Court of Justice (Art 226 [ex 169]), in which case the decision of that Court is binding on the UK and overrides national legislation. In practice, such UK consumers are more likely to seek remedies within the UK courts, as the

---

24   *DEFRA v ASDA Stores Ltd* [2004] 1 All ER 268, HL (ECA referred to Community grading rules 'for the time being').

25   ECA, s 2(1). E.g. *Conegate Ltd v Customs and Excise* [1987] QB 254 CJEC (old Arts 30, 36); Sunday trading (see para 8.13). Directly applicable provisions of Community law should prevail over future Acts of Parliament: ECA, s 2(4); and see below.

26   E.g. Regulations (based on Art 95) are used to provide arrangements for co-operation between public authorities, e.g. cross-border enforcement institutions (see para 3.03A).

27   Art 249 [ex 189]. E.g. exempted from old Art 85 under Community Regulation 17. See generally Morris [1989] JBL 233; and para 2.13.

28   *Secretary of State for Environment v Asda Stores Ltd* [2002] 2 CMLR 66, DC.

29   *R (on the application of BAT) v Secretary of State for Health* [2003] All ER (EC) 604, ECJ (tobacco advertising: see para 8.06A); *R (ABNA Ltd) v Secretary of State for Health* [2004] 2 CMLR 39.

30   See Art 249 [ex 189] of the Treaty of Rome. For the process of making directives, see para 3.10.

Community treaties and law are directly enforceable in Member States, e.g. competition law (see para 2.12), taking precedence over domestic law: according to s 2(4), post-1972 UK legislation 'shall be construed and have effect subject to' UK statutes and statutory instruments incorporating EU law into UK law (see above).[31] The breach of Community law may be used as a cause of action, e.g. for breach of statutory duty (see above); or as a defence, where a party is sued in the UK courts, e.g. for breach of contract where relevant English statute contravenes Art 12 [ex 6] of the Treaty. Sometimes, it will be appropriate for the aggrieved consumer to apply for judicial review or damages against the State,[32] as where the State has neglected to implement a Directive,[33] so narrowing the distinction between Directives and Regulations (see above). However, it would seem that an aggrieved consumer cannot rely on Community law rights as against a private defendant in respect of an unimplemented directive.[34] In all cases, reference or appeal lies from the courts of the United Kingdom to the European Court of Justice (CJEC; Art 234 [ex 177]).

## Interpretation of the Acts[35]

[1.04] **Civil statutes**. In the preface to his commentary on the SGA 1893, Chalmers says that the pre-Act cases are only law insofar as they illustrate the words of the statute,[36] though the effect of this statement has since been complicated by the 1979 almost verbatim re-enactment of the SGA. In the nineteenth century, the typical judicial attitude to codifying Acts, such as the SGA, was that they should be interpreted according to the literal rule of statutory construction;[37] but in the twentieth century the courts have not in respect of all issues arising under the SGA maintained such a lofty impartiality.[38] *A fortiori*, it may be doubted whether the old impartiality will be visited upon the consumer protection legislation of later centuries, e.g. the Supply of Goods (Implied Terms) Act 1973 (SOGIT) and the

---

31  S 2(4) of the 1972 Act. This is an example of a 'Henry VIII clause' (see para 4.24) and has been used to overrule, e.g. Pt 2 of the CPA (see para 4.32).

32  *R v Secretary of State for Transport, ex p Factortame No 5* [2000] 1 AC 524, HL (damages); *Three Rivers DC v Bank of England* [2000] 3 All ER 1, HL (misfeasance in public office).

33  On such 'vertical direct effect' of directives, see Goode, *Op. cit.*, Pt X, para 4; Gordon and Miskin (1996) 146 NLJ 1055; Craig (1997) 113 LQR 67.

34  'Horizontal direct effect', e.g. *El Corte Inglès SA v Cristina Blezquez Rivero* [1996] CLY 1175, ECJ (Consumer Credit Directive); *R v Secretary of State for Employment, ex p Seymour-Smith* [1997] 2 All ER 273, HL. But there may be some help from the rules of interpretation where there is a relevant national provision (see para 1.04); and EU Regulations are directly enforceable: Consorzio Del Prosciutto Di Parma v Asda Food Stores Ltd [2002] 1 CMLR 43, HL.

35  See generally Interpretation Act 1978.

36  See Chalmers, *Sale of Goods*, 18th edn, vii. Cf. Atiyah, *Sale of Goods*, 10th edn, 1; Goode, *Commercial Law*, 3rd edn, 187, 190. See also per Lord Herschell in *Bank of England v Vagliano Brothers* [1891] AC 107, at 144–145, HL. For an application of this philosophy, see *Re Wait* (set out at para 20.22).

37  See generally, Allen, *Law in the Making*, 7th edn, 482–593; Willis (1938) 16 Can BR 1.

38  E.g. *caveat emptor* (see Chaps 13–14), the exceptions to the *nemo dat* rule (see Chap 21). See Goode, *Op. cit.*, 21–22, 192.

Supply of Goods and Services Act 1982 (SGSA),[39] where perhaps the evident bias of the legislation should lead to the adoption of the mischief rule of statutory interpretation.[40] Thus, in *Wilson v First County Trust Ltd* (set out para 3.09A) the House of Lords examined *obiter* the external permissible aids in interpreting s 127 of the CCA. In delivering the leading Judgment, Lord Nicholls pointed out that it is well-settled that the courts may look outside the statute in order to identify the 'mischief' Parliament was seeking to remedy (para 56), and even statements made in Parliament by the Minister or other promoter of the Bill;[41] and others of their Lordships gave the following additional examples of permissible external aids to interpretation: the additional background material found in published documents, such as a government White Paper, the explanatory notes published with a Bill, answers given to written parliamentary questions, issues explored by Select Committees, reports made and statistics collected (at paras 56, 118, 142). However, their Lordships unanimously rejected the Court of Appeal's reliance on the record of parliamentary debates on the ground that it involved 'questioning' what is said in Parliament contrary to Art 9 of the Bill of Rights 1689,[42] though drawing a clear distinction between that and the enquiry for incompatibility which the courts were bidden to conduct by s 4 of the Human Rights Act 1998 (at paras 65, 116, 141. See further below, para 3.09). In relation to the CCA, perhaps the most well-known external aid is the Crowther Report upon which it was based (see para 5.03); and its intention to protect consumers has been said to justify a purposive approach to interpretation.[43]

The interpretation of uniform statutes enacted or authorised by Parliament and derived from treaties or similar arrangements, e.g. EU Directives, is another matter entirely. In part, this is because these are more likely to be drafted according to the Continental, rather than the English model: indeed, especially in statutory instruments, there may simply be a copy-out by the English language version of Directives more or less verbatim, e.g. the Unfair Terms in Consumer Contracts (UTCC) Regulations (see para 11.12, *et seq.*) although it is not necessary to do so (see Art 249: see para 1.03A). Even in such cases, English courts could adopt their traditional English approach to interpretation, though perhaps at the risk of defeating the harmonisation intent lying behind the enactment.[44] In part, it seems

---

39   See respectively the following final Law Commission Reports: *First Report on Exemption Clauses* (Law Com No. 24, 1969); *Implied Terms in Contracts for the Supply of Goods* (Law Com No. 95, 1979).

40   Compare *Stevenson v Rogers* (set out at para 14.04); *R & B Customs Brokers Ltd v United Dominions Trust Ltd* (see para 18.18). See generally Atiyah (1985) 48 MLR 1.

41   At para 60, citing *Pepper v Hart* [1993] AC 593, HL. See also Lord Hope (at para 113); Lord Hobhouse (at paras 139–40) also noted the undesirable waste of resources involved.

42   Lord Nicholls at para 53; Lord Hope at paras 111, 116–7; Lord Hobhouse at para 143; Lord Scott at para 173; and Lord Rodger at para 178. See also Kavanagh (2005) 121 LQR 98.

43   *Broadwick Financial Services Ltd v Spencer* (set out at para 8.22), *per* Dyson LJ at para 21. In *OFT v Lloyds TSB* (see para 16.11), the CA looked at the long title of the CCA (at paras 18 and 76) and the Crowther Report which preceded it (at para 55: see para 5.03); whilst at first instance Gloster J adopted a purposive approach to interpretation (para 23) and mentioned the anomalies which might arise if four party transaction were not included in the CCA (para 33).

44   Unless such an approach is expressly excluded (e.g. CPA, s 1(1): see para 17.24). See generally Mann (1983) 99 LQR 376.

to follow from the ECA[45] and from a modern rule of interpretation applied by UK courts to try to interpret national legislation, where possible, consistently with EU rules.[46]

**[1.05] Criminal statutes**. Here, the matter of interpretation is further complicated because, particularly in recent years, Parliament has sought to put more effective teeth into its consumer protection statutes by imposing criminal sanctions for breach of their provisions in such profusion as almost to overshadow the civil law.[47] Some of these statutes, such as the Trade Descriptions Act 1968 (TDA) impose only criminal sanctions for breach of their provisions (s 35: set out at para 10.19); and it is a well-known maxim that penal provisions are to be interpreted restrictively in favour of freedom of the subject.[48] Yet this will not necessarily preclude the courts from looking at the mischief in need of a remedy[49] though such an approach has been explicitly rejected with regard to the CCA.[50]

Indeed, the CCA not only forbids the parties from contracting out of its provisions (s 173: see para 18.11), but contains a mixture of civil and criminal sanctions, sometimes even in respect of the same prohibited conduct[51] and expressly limits the sanctions to those specifically provided in the Act (s 170: see para 10.19). Yet another approach is to be found in the CPA, where some whole topics are regulated by civil obligations and others by criminal sanctions.

Finally, there must be borne in mind the possible effect on consumer protection statutes of the Human Rights Act 1998 and the 'convention rights' it introduces (see para 3.09A). Suppose the courts are faced with a UK statute or statutory instrument inconsistent with convention rights, whether passed before or after the 1998 Act. First, the 1998 Act requires the court to give effect to the consumer protection statute in a way that is compatible with convention rights 'so far as it is possible to do so'.[52] Second, it will try to do so even if this is inconsistent with a previous Court of Appeal interpretation.[53]

The basic categories of contract utilised to effect a consumer supply of goods (see para 1.03) are sale, hire and hire purchase (hp), all discussed below. Into which of these categories a particular transaction falls is a matter of substance, not form: see *Forthright Finance Ltd v Carlyle Finance Ltd* (set out at para 1.22).

---

45  S 2(4) and see *Three Rivers D C v Bank of England (No. 2)* [1996] 2 All ER 363; *U v V* [1977] Eu LR 342 (not a sale case; Hansard admitted).

46  E.g. UTCC Regs, reg 7; Enforcement Orders (see para 6.06). See also Maltby (1993) 109 LQR 301.

47  See Borrie, *The Development of Consumer Law and Policy* (1984), 45.

48  E.g. *Davies v Sumner* (set out at para 4.03A). See generally, Glanville Williams, *Criminal Law, The General Part*, 2nd edn, para 76; *per* McNeil J in *Miller v FA Sadd & Son Ltd* (set out at para 4.05) at 270c; *per* Ormrod LJ in *Westminster CC v Ray Allen (Alanshops) Ltd* [1982] 1 All ER at 774B.

49  *Attorney General's Reference (No. 1 of 1988)* [1989] 2 All ER 1, HL (insider trading); *R v Deegan* [1998] 2 Crim App R 121, CA (flick-knives); *Interfact Ltd v Liverpool CC* [2005] 1 WLR 3118, DC at para 19 (videos).

50  See *National Westminster Bank v Devon CC* (1996) 13 Tr LR 70, DC, esp. *per* Kennedy LJ at 75D; *Coventry City Council v Lazarus* [1996] CLY 1165. But compare *Scarborough BS v East Riding of Yorkshire CC* [1997] CCLR 47, DC.

51  E.g. entering into consumer credit agreements whilst an unlicensed trader: CCA, ss 39, 40. These provisions are discussed at para 6.28.

52  S 3(1). E.g. *Wilson v First County Trust Ltd* in the CA (set out at para 9.20).

53  See Emmerson (1999) 149 NLJ 1899 at 1900.

## DEFINITION OF A CONTRACT OF SALE

### Sales in general[54]

**[1.06] Introduction**. The contract of sale is defined by s 2 of the SGA,[55] and Chalmers suggests that this definition is merely declaratory of the common law (see s 62(2)). Traditionally, the contract of sale was rigidly distinguished from several other contracts which it resembled, but which had their own common law rules (see para 15.21, *et seq*.). Yet the distinction should not today be over-emphasised for the following reasons:[56]

(a) As the SGA 1893 was supposed to be a codification of the common law, the latter's rule for the analogous transaction may well be the same as the comparable SGA rule.[57]

(b) There is a modern tendency to enact statutory provisions for all transactions for the supply of goods which are virtually identical with those applicable to sales of goods: this has already happened in relation to the statutory implied terms in hire-purchase agreements in the SOGIT 1973 (see Chaps 12–16), the statutory restrictions on exclusion clauses in the Unfair Contract Terms Act 1977, ss 6–7 (see further Chap 18) and the statutory implied terms in quasi-sales and simple hirings in the SGSA (see further Chaps 12–16).

(c) There are a number of hybrid transactions which involve elements of both sale and an analogous transaction, e.g. sale and fitting of a carpet, installation of central heating, sale of patented goods under licence. Prima facie, the following analyses would appear possible: (i) there is a single contract, which may be categorised according to the predominant aspect;[58] (ii) there are two separate contracts, one of sale, and the other of, e.g. labour; (iii) there is a single hybrid contract, partly of sale or quasi-sale (see para 2.10) and partly of, e.g. labour[59] or hiring.[60] See further, para 15.26.

**[1.07] Definition**. Like most commercial law statutes, the SGA contains a definition section which describes the ambit of the Act (s 2), what may be termed its 'gateway'. A contract of sale is defined by s 2(1) of the SGA as follows:

---

54  See generally Atiyah, *Sale of Goods*, 11th edn, 2005; Benjamin's *Sale of Goods*, 6th edn, 2002: *Blackburn on Sale*, 3rd edn, 1910; Chalmers, *Sale of Goods*, 18th edn, 1981; *Chitty on Contracts*, 28th edn, 1999, Vol 2, Chap 41.

55  For the sale contracts to which the 1979 Act applies, see para 1.01; and for the definition of sales, see para 1.07.

56  Certain contracts for the supply of goods must still be evidenced in writing: see para 9.02.

57  E.g. *Young and Marten Ltd v McManus Childs Ltd* [1969] 1 AC 454, HL (implied term as to fitness in the unamended SGA); and see further paras 15.24–5.

58  E.g. *Vigers v Cook* [1919] 2 KB 475, CA (funeral); *Dawson (Clapham) Ltd v Dutield* (set out at para 2.10—sale); *Young & Marten Ltd v McManus Childs Ltd* (analogous transaction); *Common Services Agency v Purdie and Kirkpatrick* 1995 SLT (Sh Ct) 34 (photocopier rented at cost per copy).

59  E.g. *Watson v Buckley* [1940] I All ER 174, at 179–180. See further below, para 2.05; Atiyah, *Op. cit.*, 9; and generally Gearty (2002) 118 LQR 248. But see para 1.07. As to quasi-sale, see fn 73 para 2.10.

60  E.g. *The Saint Anna* [1983] 2 All ER 691 (charterparty held to include sale of oil on board at commencement of charter).

'A contract of sale of goods is a contract whereby the seller transfers or agrees to transfer the property in goods to the buyer for a money consideration, called the price.'

This definition requires that *all* the following components should be present before a transaction passes through the gateway and falls within the SGA:[61]

1.  *A contract.* The Act makes no attempt to interfere with the ordinary rules concerning the formation of contracts governed by English law. It just requires that there should be a contract (see Chap 10). But, even this apparently simple requirement may give rise to problems. *First*, what is the position of drugs supplied under the NHS? As between dispensing chemist and the patient there would appear to be no contract at all;[62] but would the court imply analogous terms as to the quality of the drugs supplied?[63] *Second*, account must be taken of the modern practice of franchising, which may make it difficult for the consumer to determine the identity of his retail supplier.[64] Even if the consumer is aware that he is dealing with a 'franchise', the expression covers a wide variety of business arrangements, including business-format franchising[65] and licences to supply[66] or to occupy premises. The fact situation may vary between (a) an entirely independent business-concession, e.g. shop-within-a-shop or a market hall, (b) a joint operation between the owner of the premises and the franchise-holder, and (c) the latter as a mere promoter of stock owned by the tenant of the premises. Is it significant who remunerates the salesman? *Third*, there is the problem of 'free gifts' (see below). *Fourth*, the parties may *prima facie* assign their contractual rights (see para 7.16).

2.  *Made in respect of 'goods'.* The meaning of the term 'goods' will be dealt with later (para 2.01 *et seq.*). However, the insistence on a supply of 'goods' distinguishes a sale of goods from a supply of services (see para 2.05). Nor is a contract for the supply of services turned into a sale of goods just because under that contract the general property in some goods is incidentally transferred from one to another.[67] There should also be distinguished pyramid sales (see para 1.09).

3.  *To transfer the 'property' in those goods.* The object of the contract must be to transfer the property in those goods (see para 1.08) from seller to buyer (see para 1.09), delivery not being an essential element. Thus, the Act provides that

---

61  Can a contract fall within the SGA definition where it contains all these elements, plus some additional ones, e.g. installation? See para 1.06.

62  *Pfizer Corpn v Ministry of Health* [1965] AC 512, HL (see further, para 4.29). *Contra* drugs supplied under private prescription, where a price is paid. The presence or absence of a retail supply contract may have implications for product liability: see paras 17.04 and 17.24. As to the supply of electricity, see para 3.07.

63  See para 15.25; and further Atiyah, *Sale of Goods*, 10th edn, 9; Treitel, *Law of Contract*, 11th edn, 97, fn 91; Woodroffe, *Goods and Services—The New Law*, para 2.06; and below, para 4.29.

64  As to franchising, see [1986] JBL 206. For the control of franchising by competition law, see para 2.13.

65  This type of franchising involves the sale of business knowledge and experience, coupled with a licence to use or sell a particular product, brand name, logo etc. See also para 1.09.

66  The supply may be of goods, e.g. motor trade distributorships, or of services, e.g. credit card franchises (see para 7.09).

67  E.g. *Appleby v Sleep* [1968] 2 All ER 265, DC (supply of drugs under NHS: see further para 4.30).

' "Sale" includes a bargain and sale as well as a sale and delivery' (s 61(1))[68] and sharply distinguishes between the contract and the transfer of property in the goods (see para 1.10).

4. *In exchange for the price*. Section 2(1) requires that the transfer of property be for 'a money consideration, called the price'. The concept of price is considered later (see para 2.06). Property and price must be exchanged, though not necessarily simultaneously (s 28: see para 23.22). Further, one who merely finances a sale by provision of the price does not thereby become a buyer of the subject-matter.[69] Normally, the insistence on consideration will clearly distinguish a sale from a gift (see para 2.08), though there may be difficulties in drawing the borderline in respect of so-called 'free gifts', and under the Unsolicited Goods and Services Acts 1971–5 the recipient of unsolicited goods may treat those goods as a gift rather than the offer to sell that their supplier intended (see para 8.18). Moreover, the requirement that the consideration for a sale be money, termed the 'price' (see para 2.06), distinguishes a sale from a barter or exchange (see para 2.10).

**[1.08] The object of the contract**. The substance of the contract[70] must be 'to transfer the property in goods' from the seller to the buyer, though the SGA does not insist on an immediate transfer of property (see para 1.10). The Act provides that 'property' means 'the general property in the goods, and not merely a special property'.[71] However, the general property in the goods is not always the most important consideration. Thus, the Act distinguishes between property and title (see Chap 19), and sometimes allows a person to pass a good title even though he does not possess the property in the goods (see Chap 21). Moreover, the Act contemplates that the parties may contract out of the implied obligation on the part of the seller that he will transfer a good title.[72] Particularly after the SOGIT in 1973 imposed obligatory implied terms as to title, there was a very real problem with regard to whether or not a contract which purported to oust completely the implied undertakings as to title was a contract for sale of goods at all.[73] However, the importance of this issue was lessened by the SGSA: if such a transaction is not a sale of goods, it may be an analogous transaction (quasi-sale) within the later Act.[74]

The insistence of the SGA on at least an agreement to transfer the general property in goods (see para 1.10), combined with its evident indifference as to whether there is any transfer of possession (see para 1.07), is underlined by s 62(4) (see para 1.02). Thus, there must be distinguished from sale all the following:

---

68  And see *Watts v Seymour* [1967] 2 QB 647, DC.

69  *Ebeling v Theo & Jos Van Der Aa, SA* [1955] 2 LIR 641. For financing of price, see further, paras 2.20–4.

70  *Contra* where the 'goods sold' are a mere token: see *Lipkin Gorman v Karpnale Ltd* [1991] 2 AC 548, HL (gambling chips). Are the chips a form of money (see para 2.02)?

71  S 61(1). As to 'special property', see below. This emphasis of English sales law on the passing of property has been described as 'obsessional': Goode, *Commercial Law*, 3rd edn, 194.

72  It will be argued later that the Act only insists that the seller promises to transfer the general property in the goods to the buyer insofar as he is able to do so: see para 12.17.

73  See the dispute between Preston and Carr: (1974) 37 MLR at 599–600. If the transaction could not be classed as a sale of goods, then it appeared to escape the statutory prohibition against contracting out of the implied terms as to title.

74  See para 2.10. *Quaere* whether SGSA, s 1 is subject to this same limitation as s 2 of the SGA?

(a) *Bailments*, e.g. hirings, where the essence of the transaction is the transfer of possession whilst the bailor retains the general property in the goods (see para 1.17).

(b) *Security transactions*, where the secured party will have something less than the unfettered general property in the goods.[75] But this exception does not include a sale with a reservation of title,[76] nor a genuine sale rather than a charge.[77]

[1.09] **The parties**. The essence of a sale is the transfer of the property in goods from one person (the 'seller') to another (the 'buyer').[78] Indeed, the common law rule was that a man could not purchase his own goods;[79] but this would seem to be amended to the extent that the Act allows one part-owner to sell to another.[80] Moreover, it is clear that the SGA will cover the situation where an owner of goods buys them back from one who has a legal right to dispose of them, such as a court Enforcement Officer (see paras 19.15–6). The requirement seems to be that the buyer must stand to gain some part of the general property in the goods from the seller; and for this reason it is essential to distinguish carefully a contract of sale from a contract of agency—one who sells from one who acts as an agent in effecting a sale.[81] Thus a franchise to sell goods may create just an agency, to which the SGA is inapplicable,[82] with separate contracts for the sale of goods made within that regime.[83] Alternatively, a franchise agreement may itself provide for the supply of goods to the franchise-holder (distributor).[84] One particular variant of franchising is pyramid-selling.[85] Such direct selling of goods, also known as 'Network Marketing', can be a legitimate form of self-employment, whereby participants earn both by recruiting other participants and selling goods to end-users. Unfortunately, such form of business can also be used to fleece participants, as where a participant's earnings

---

75 With a lien he will have only possession, with a pledge he will have possession plus a special property; and with a mortgage or charge his general property will he subject to an equity of redemption: see para 25.02.

76 *Armour v Thyssen* (set out at para 20.28).

77 *Welsh Development Agency v Export Finance Co Ltd* [1992] CLY 2541, CA; and see generally para 25.33.

78 According to s 61(1), ' "seller" means a person who sells or agrees to sell goods' and ' "buyer" means a person who buys or agrees to buy goods'.

79 Atiyah, *Sale of Goods*, 10th edn, 30, citing cases on the old liquor licensing Acts (see generally para 6.05).

80 S 2(2). As to whether a sale by a part-owner of his interest is a sale of goods, see para 20.22A.

81 *AMB Imballaggi Plastici SRL v Pacflex Ltd* [1999] 2 All ER (Comm) 249, CA. There may be practical difficulties, as where the alleged agent is a commission agent, or a *del credere* agent (one who guarantees performances by his principal), or acts in both capacities (e.g. mail order catalogue agent). Cf. *Potter v Customs and Excise Comrs* [1985] STC 45, CA (Tupperware parties); comp-u-card (1985 *Which?* 3).

82 E.g. *B Davis Ltd v Tooth & Co Ltd* [1937] 4 All ER 118, PC. See also Murdoch (1975) 91 LQR at 365; and generally, para 1.07.

83 *Rose and Frank Co v Crompton Bros* [1925] AC 445, HL (franchise agreement prevented from being a contract by the 'honourable pledge clause': see generally, para 10.01).

84 *Decro-Wall International SA v Practitioners in Marketing Ltd* [1971] 2 All ER 217, CA, esp. *per* Salmon LJ at 222.

85 The principal legitimate trade body is the Direct Selling Association, which has its own Code of Practice (see para 3.13). Distinguish direct selling from franchising (see para 1.07).

depend almost entirely on his recruitment of others. Attempts to control such abuses were first introduced in Part XI of the FTA; but, this proving inadequate, its provisions have been bolstered by the Trading Schemes Act 1996. These controls are based on the widely defined 'trading schemes' (FTA, s 118 (as substituted); on the power to make detailed regulations controlling such 'trading schemes';[86] and on the imposition of a number of criminal sanctions on scheme promotions.[87] In 2007, these rules for trading schemes may be overtaken by the UCP Directive (see below, para 4.20, item (j)).

**[1.10] Contract and conveyance**. It has already been pointed out that the two elements of *contract* and *conveyance* are both present in the one transaction of a contract of sale (see para 1.07). Indeed, the Act uses different terminology according to whether or not the property has passed under the contract. Section 2 says:

'(4) Where under a contract of sale the property in the goods is transferred from the seller to the buyer the contract is called a sale.

(5) Where the transfer of the property in the goods is to take place at a future time or subject to some condition thereafter to be fulfilled the contract is called an agreement to sell.

(6) An agreement to sell becomes a sale when the time elapses or the conditions are fulfilled subject to which the property in the goods is to be transferred'.

Thus, a sharp distinction is drawn between a sale and an agreement to sell: the one is an executed contract, the other executory.[88] The distinction is important, because the executory contract creates only personal rights between the parties whereas an executed contract gives the buyer an interest in the goods themselves.[89] Where it is convenient to avoid making such a judgment it is normal to use some neutral expression such as 'contract of sale'.

**[1.11] Absolute and conditional sales**. Section 2(3) of the SGA recognises that 'A contract of sale may be absolute or conditional'. 'Conditional' in this subsection does not refer to conditions in the sense of essential promises in the contract (see para 11.04), nor usually to conditions precedent to the existence of the contract (see para 15.21), but to conditions precedent or subsequent to *performance* of the contract itself.[90]

*(a) Conditions precedent*. These may suspend the passing of the property in the goods which are the subject-matter of the contract[91] until some act is performed either:

---

86  See the Trading Schemes Regulations, 1997 SI 30 (as amended), set out in Thomas, *Encyclopedia of Consumer Law*, Pt 2, para 1712, *et seq*.

87  FTA, ss 120 (1) (as amended), 120 (2), 122. There are the usual enforcement arrangements (see Chap 28), with special defences for an innocent advertiser or supplier (see para 28.16). Such schemes may also attract injunctions: OFT, *AR-2006/7*, 27.

88  For examples of the use of the dichotomy between 'sale' and 'agreement to sell', see SGA, ss 5(3), 6, 7.

89  For further consideration of the conveyancing effect of the contract, see Chap 19.

90  E.g. *Bentworth Finance Ltd v Lubert* (set out at para 15.23); *Financings Ltd. v Stimson* (set out at para 10.08).

91  The condition is normally precedent only to performance, but it could go further and be precedent to formation of the contract itself: see generally, para 15.21.

(i)   *by one of the parties.* This act may be a conditional performance,[92] but need not necessarily be so;[93] and the contract may make that act precedent to performance by the other party either expressly[94] or impliedly.[95]

(ii)  *by some third party.* Thus, in *Marten v Whale*:[96]

> M agreed to buy a plot of land from T, subject to M's solicitor's approval of title; and, in consideration of this agreement, T agreed to buy M's car. T took possession of the car 'on loan' and sold it to a *bona fide* purchaser. Subsequently, M's solicitor disapproved T's title to the land.

The Court of Appeal held that the two sales were interdependent, so that there was a conditional sale of the car within s 2(3); and that, even though the condition had never materialised, T was able to pass a good title as a buyer in possession (see para 21.46).

*(b) Conditions subsequent.* In *Total Gas Marketing Ltd v Arco British Ltd*[97]

> A operated a North Sea oilfield and T refined petrol from several such oilfields. A and T entered into an agreement for T to buy A's oil as from a given date. This agreement was made conditional on A before that date becoming party to an allocation agreement with other oil producers for the commingling of their oils at T's delivery terminal. By the given date, A had not entered into such an allocation agreement. T argued that this entitled him to terminate his agreement with A; but A claimed that their obligations under the contract were merely suspended until A entered the allocation agreement.

The House of Lords held that, particularly because A's entry into the allocation agreement was to happen before first delivery (see below, para 23.25), it was clearly intended to be a contingent condition; and A's failure to do so meant that T was no longer bound by the contract. Examples of such conditions subsequent in the retail trade may include some situations where the supplier grants an unfettered right to return goods without cause;[98] or direct financing where there is an initial contract of sale between dealer and consumer (see para 10.09).

One particular form of contract of sale whose performance is conditional is that where the seller's duty to transfer the *property* in the goods is made conditional upon the buyer's prior observance of all the terms of the agreement; and, in particular, his payment by instalments of part or all of the price. So common has this situation become that there has developed a tendency to describe only such situations as a 'conditional sale': they are dealt with below (see para 1.14).

---

92   E.g. *Trans Trust SPRL v Danubian Trading Ltd* (see para 27.35); or the type of 'conditional sales' considered below, para 1.14.

93   E.g. certificates of quality and inspection (see para 14.02); some prize competitions (see para 8.16).

94   E.g. the type of 'conditional sale' considered below in para 1.14.

95   E.g. a sale of goods not then in a deliverable state: see the SGA, s 18, r 2 (para 20.11).

96   [1917] 2 KB 480, CA: see further, paras 15.21 and 21.46.

97   [1998] 2 Lloyd's Rep 209, HL, where obligation to enter the allocation agreement was termed a 'contingent condition or a condition precedent'. See also Smith & Thomas, *Casebook on Contract*, 11th edn, 2000, 424.

98   For further discussion of express rights of cancellation, see para 10.28; and for sale or return transactions, see para 20.23, *et seq.*

## Instalment sales

**[1.12] Introduction**. The parties may enter into a contract (commonly by retail) which, whilst satisfying the definition of a contract of sale above considered, differs from an ordinary sale in some fundamental characteristics. *First*, it provides for payment of the price by (normally approximately equal) instalments and usually after an initial deposit. *Second*, it may oust the ordinary presumption that delivery and payment are concurrent terms (SGA, s 28: see para 23.16), providing for early delivery and subsequent payment of the price by instalments.[99] *Third*, the transactions are normally conducted by way of standard-form contracts.[100] Since 1938, the legislature has recognised that such sale contracts have much in common with hire-purchase (hp) agreements,[100] and accordingly the Hire Purchase Act 1938 (HPA 1938) sought to extend some hp controls to such sales. The Hire Purchase Act 1964 (HPA 1964) introduced a further refinement:[101]

(1) *Conditional sales*. Where the contract suspended the passing of property until such conditions as to the payment of instalments or otherwise as may be specified in the agreement are fulfilled, the transaction was to attract almost all the restrictions applicable to hp (see para 1.14).

(2) *Credit sales*. Where the property passed at latest on delivery, it attracted only a few of the restrictions (see para 1.13).

The result of this momentous innovation was as follows: henceforth, the crucial distinction in consumer instalment transactions was frequently no longer whether the customer had agreed to buy at the outset, but whether the property passed on, or before, delivery. Unfortunately, the position was not quite so simple as this.[102] Subsequently, the distinction between conditional sale and hp has begun to break down: see *Forthright Finance Ltd v Carlyle Finance Ltd* (set out at para 1.22).

**[1.13] Credit sales**. Where the property in goods passes on or before delivery, the buyer clearly has a good title which he can pass to another under the *nemo dat* rule (see para 19.11), or which might fall into his insolvency (see para 19.23). For the purpose of the statutory control of instalment contracts, the HPA 1938 (since replaced) introduced a category now termed a 'credit sale agreement' and defined in the CCA as:[103]

> 'An agreement for the sale of goods, under which the purchase price or part of it is payable by instalments, but which is not a conditional sale agreement'.

However, the purpose of this definition is not clear as the term 'credit sale' nowhere features in the body of the CCA, though it figures in Sched 2.[104] On the other hand, many 'credit sales' will amount to regulated consumer credit agreements (see

---

99 Distinguish instalment deliveries and matching payments where the rule in s 28 of the SGA is observed. For instalment contracts, see para 23.23, *et seq*.

100 For argument that, until the conditions are fulfilled, a conditional sale is a type of bailment, see para 1.14.

101 The HPA 1938 was itself consolidated in the HPA 1965: see para 1.24.

102 See Macleod, *Consumer Sales Law*, 1st edn, para 1.12.

103 See s 189(1). These agreements may be constituted by two or more documents: s 189(4). See also the Health and Safety at Work Act 1974, s 53; and CPA, s 45(1).

104 Example 5. As to the effect of these statutory examples, see para 5.06.

para 5.19), in which case they will be subject to restrictions as to the following matters: seeking business[105] and antecedent negotiations;[106] entry into the agreement;[107] cancellation;[108] during the currency of the agreement;[109] guarantees and indemnities;[110] preliminary notices before enforcement;[111] death of the buyer;[112] negotiable instruments;[113] and extortionate credit bargains (CCA, ss 137–40: see para 29.40). But, to save imposing burdens on suppliers out of all proportion to the monetary amounts involved, the provisions as to entry and cancellation do not apply to small agreements.[114]

## Conditional sales[115]

**[1.14] Introduction.** This paragraph is concerned with the situation where there is an instalment sale (see para 1.12) which satisfies the definition contained in the SGA (see para 1.07) but also contains a reservation of the property in the goods—usually until payment of the full price. In such circumstances, unless and until that condition is satisfied, the buyer obtains no general property in the goods to transfer to another,[116] whether for value (see para 1.15), or upon execution, bankruptcy or distress (see para 19.15, *et seq.*). Not only will the property remain in the unpaid supplier,[117] but the deposit[118] and payment terms will normally be arranged to confer throughout the contract a 'residual value' on the buyer.[119] The contract may also include two further provisions. *First*, in the event of the buyer's default, the seller would be granted an express right to recover possession of the goods (see below), which might be exercised either just to encourage the buyer to make good his default, or to enable the seller to resell the goods to recoup his loss;[120] and any such resale should be free of any interest of the buyer in the goods.[121] *Second*, to

---

105  CCA, ss 43–47: see further, para 8.21, *et seq.*
106  CCA, s 56: see further, para 16.08.
107  CCA, ss 55, 60–63: see further, para 9.06, *et seq.*
108  CCA, ss 67–73: see further, para 10.29, *et seq.*
109  CCA, ss 77, 81, 82, 94–97: see further respectively, paras 15.17, 15.16, 26.22 and 26.19.
110  CCA, ss 105–113: see further, paras 25.11–13.
111  CCA, ss 76, 89, 98: see further, paras 24.28–32 and 26.10.
112  CCA, ss 86(2): see further, para 24.47.
113  CCA, ss 123–125: see further, paras 25.08–9.
114  CCA, s 74(2). For 'small agreements', within the CCA, see para 5.17.
115  See generally Melville (1974) 124 NLJ 615; Jones, *Chattel Mortgages*, 6th edn, 1933, Chap 19; Goode, *Commercial Law*, 3rd edn, 709–13.
116  Whilst the buyer is in possession before the passing of property, it has been pointed out that the transaction is a form of bailment: Jones, *ibid*, para 932; and the *Romalpa* case (see para 25.29). *Contra* Bridge LJ in *Borden (UK) Ltd v Scottish Timber Products Ltd* [1981] Ch 25 at 35D.
117  The commercial principle is the same for hp: see para 1.20. The supplier's security in an unregulated agreement is ultimately recaption and resale: see para 27.02. For restrictions in respect of regulated agreements, see para 24.27, *et seq.*
118  The size of the deposit will normally be calculated to cover at least the drop in value on supply of the goods, e.g. the market price drop from new to second-hand.
119  See para 27.12. As to the supplier's interest in the goods, see para 24.22.
120  E.g. *Hewison v Ricketts* (set out at para 27.19).
121  Because the buyer (unlike a mortgagor: see para. 1.08) has no equity of redemption: see para 24.22.

preserve the market value of this right of repossession and resale, the agreement would contain provisions for the maintenance of the goods (see para 11.08).

*Licences to seize.* For some time, there were anxieties that this licence for the seller to repossess the goods (see para 1.14) might bring the transaction within the purview of the Bills of Sale Act 1882, which rendered void almost every chattel mortgage by an individual which was not in the statutory form (see para 25.26); and, as the statutory terms did not provide adequate security, creditors would normally seek to avoid the Act altogether.

However, in *McEntire v Crossley Brothers*,[122] the House of Lords held that such a conditional sale did not fall within the 1882 Act because Crossley as owner was not *granting*, but *reserving*, a licence to seize (see para 25.27). As we shall see later, this distinction is important for English law (see para 25.01); but it should be noted that US law has long foresworn such sophistry, treating conditional sales as a type of chattel mortgage.[123]

Fortunately, proposed reform of the English chattel mortgage law may remove entirely this arcane branch of the law, first from company law and then generally (see paras 25.28; 25.38).

**[1.15] Dispositions by the buyer.** Whilst the reservation of property by a conditional seller was a sensible first step to protect him against non-payment by the buyer (see para 1.14), an ever-present danger was that the conditional buyer might contract to dispose to a third party either of (i) the title to the goods or (ii) his interest in them.

1.  *Dispositions of title.* Suppose the conditional buyer sold or pledged the goods to a *bona fide* third party. It is true that, because the conditional buyer did not himself have a good title to the goods, as a general rule he could not pass one to that third party: this is because of the *nemo dat* rule (see para 19.11). However, he may be able to pass a good title to a *bona fide* purchaser or pledgee by way of one of the following exceptions to the *nemo dat* rule:

    (a) Buyers in possession (see para 21.43). The matter was litigated in *Lee v Butler*:[124]

    > Under an agreement made with a furniture dealer (A), B was to take immediate possession of some furniture in return for a promise to pay 'as and by way of rent' £1 on May 6th and £96 on the following August 1st. *Inter alia*, the agreement provided that, if B removed the goods, A might repossess them, and all sums previously paid should be appropriated to rent only; but, if B performed all the terms of agreement, the rent should cease, and the goods should then, but not before, become the property of B. Before all the instalments were paid, B sold the furniture to a *bona fide* purchaser (bfp). The Court of Appeal found that B had 'agreed to buy' the furniture, and therefore passed a good title to the bfp under s 9 of the Factors Act 1889.

    It was, of course, to meet this threat that the hp form of agreement was invented (see para 1.20), though subsequent case law has cast doubts on the

---

122 [1895] AC 457, [1895–6] All ER Rep 829, HL. See further Macleod, *Consumer Sales Law*, 1st edn, para 1.14A.

123 See Jones, *Chattel Mortgages*, 6th edn, 1933, Chap 19; and below, para 1.26.

124 [1893] 2 QB 318, [1891–4] All ER Rep 1200, CA.

ambit of the threat.[125] Nevertheless, it was thought that conditional sales had so much in common with hp agreements that this case-law distinction between the two types of contract was therefore partially destroyed by statute (see para 1.12): where a conditional sale falls within the CCA definition (see para 1.16) but not otherwise, the buyer is deemed not to be a person who has 'agreed to buy' within the meaning of s 9 (see para 21.46).

(b) A further limited exception to the *nemo dat* rule was created for dispositions of motor vehicles to 'private purchasers' (see para 21.55) made by one who was a conditional buyer or a hirer under an hp agreement (see para 1.22). In neither case does it matter whether or not the agreement is regulated by the CCA 1974 (see para 5.13).

Recognising that there will be some circumstances where a reservation of property may be insufficient to defeat the claim of a *bona fide* purchaser or pledgee to whom the conditional buyer has transferred the goods, the unpaid conditional seller may at this point attempt to transfer his claim to (or 'trace') the proceeds of that disposition (see para 27.14).

2. *Dispositions of his interest.* Suppose the conditional buyer (Z), instead of trying to dispose of a good title to the goods (see above), instead merely attempts to assign his interest in them to X.[126] He has contractual rights under the conditional sale; namely, to present possession of the goods and later acquisition of the property in them.[127] The result of such an assignment would be that X (the 'assignee') would *prima facie* 'stand in the shoes of' Z (the 'assignor'), taking over his position as conditional buyer (see para 2.22).

**[1.16] Statutory definition.** For the purposes of the statutory control of instalment contracts, there was introduced in 1964 a category termed a 'conditional sale' and now defined by the CCA as:[128]

'an agreement for the sale of goods or land under which the purchase price or part of it is payable by instalments, and the property in the goods or land is to remain in the seller (notwithstanding that the buyer is to be in possession of the goods or land) until such conditions as to the payment of instalments or otherwise as may be specified in the agreement are fulfilled'.

Typically, the contract will provide that the property is not to pass until the whole of the purchase price has been paid.[129] Further, it should be noted that the definition

---

125 See *Newtons of Wembley Ltd v Williams* (set out at para 21.51). It has even been suggested that a transfer by one who has only agreed to buy cannot be a sale within s 2 of the SGA: *Re Interview* [1975] Ir 382 at 395. *Sed quaere?* See further, para 21.49.

126 The rights of the conditional buyer may not be assignable: see the discussion of the similar issues which may arise with regard to a hirer under an hp agreement (para 1.23).

127 These contractual rights amount to a chose in action (see para 7.16), which may *prima facie* be assigned either in equity or under statute (see para 7.17, *et seq.*).

128 See s 189(1): these agreements may be constituted by two or more documents (s 189(4)). With the addition of a reference to land, this definition is taken verbatim from the HPA 1964, s 29(1). For an example, see Sched 2, Example 4. See also HPA 1964, s 29 (1); SOGIT, s 15(1); CPA, s 45(1).

129 Suppose the agreement provides that the property is to pass when part of the price has been paid. When that point is reached, does it become a 'credit sale agreement,' (see para 1.13); does it cease to be a 'conditional sale agreement'?

has been extended to include conditional sales of land,[130] though this jurisdiction has been largely transferred to the FSA (see para 3.02).

However, the CCA is not applicable to all conditional sales within the foregoing definition: for the most part, the provisions of the Act extend only to regulated agreements (see para 5.13). Where there is a regulated conditional sale, it is subject to all the same statutory restrictions as a credit sale agreement (see para 1.13) plus the following: first, it has already been seen that a buyer under such a conditional sale is not one who has 'agreed to buy' (see para 1.15); and second, such conditional sales have been largely assimilated to hp agreements (see para 1.24), being subject to the statutory restrictions in respect of the buyer's death (CCA, ss 86, 128: see para 24.44/5), his default,[131] his right to terminate[132] and the seller's right to repossess (CCA, ss 87–93: see para 24.27, *et seq.*).

## BAILMENT AND HIRING

**[1.17]  Bailment generally.**[133] In English law, bailment is the transfer (delivery) of *possession* of goods by one person (the bailor) to another (the bailee) on condition, express or implied, that the goods shall be returned to the bailor (or dealt with according to his instructions) as soon as the purpose for which they were bailed is ended.[134] It is distinguished from sale by reason of the fact that the normal objective of a bailment is to effect a transfer of the *possession* of goods, whereas the objective of a sale is to effect a transfer of the *general property* in goods.[135] Exceptionally, under a bailment the bailee may acquire the property in the goods from his erstwhile bailor, as where there is a hire-purchase agreement (see para 1.20) or perhaps a sale or return transaction (see para 20.23); or the bailee may have the right to mix and substitute other identical goods, e.g. in a grain store.[136] Moreover, where under a contract for the sale of goods the property and possession of goods are for some time separated, as English law allows (see para 19.01), for that space of time there may also be a bailment: if possession passes before property, the buyer will be in possession as bailee of the seller;[137] whilst if the property passes before possession, the seller will be in possession as bailee of the buyer. The separation of property and possession under a contract of sale may have implications for risk (see para 22.08).

---

130  Conditional sales of land are uncommon: Goode, *Consumer Credit Law & Practice*, para 38.5. Distinguish mortgages of land, in respect of which the CCA restrictions are considered at para 25.23.

131  CCA, ss 87–89, 90–93, 129–136: see below respectively, paras 24.30, 24.34 and 24.39.

132  CCA, ss 99–100, 102–103: see below respectively, paras 26.05 and 26.04. But not in the case of land after title has passed to the debtor: CCA, s 99(3).

133  See generally *Chitty on Contracts*, 28th edn, Vol 2, Chap 32; Palmer, *Bailments*, 2nd edn; Bell, *Personal Property*, Chap 5. For argument that the concept of bailment is redundant, see McMeel [2003] LMCLQ 169.

134  Winfield and Jolowicz on *Tort*, 16th edn, para 1.12. Distinguish a mere contractual licence to park a caravan on a site: *Hinks v Fleet* [1986] CLY 151, CA.

135  For the duty of delivery in relation to goods sold, see para 23.03.

136  *Mercer v Craven Grain Storage Co* [1994] CLC, HL (see 111 LQR 10); and Bridge, *Sale of Goods*, 54–7.

137  As under a conditional sale: see para 1.14. Nevertheless, that bailment will cease when some later event causes the property in the goods to pass to the buyer: see para 25.20.

There are many everyday transactions of bailment, such as the deposit of goods for safe custody or storage, the leaving of goods for the purpose of cleaning or repair, the hiring out of goods (para 1.18), a pledge (para 25.15), the carriage of goods, a supply of software on licence.[138] Whilst the relationship between bailor and bailee is frequently based on contract (see para 1.18); this is not necessarily the case,[139] as where a carrier or repairer acts gratuitously (without consideration), or goods are delivered before contract (see para 10.09). Indeed, there may also be a bailment where the bailee sub-bails the goods in such a way that there is no contract of bailment between bailor and sub-bailee.[140] The rights of the bailor and bailee to sue a third party in respect of the wrongful retention, destruction of, or damage to, goods will be dealt with later (paras 19.04, 19.06 and 19.10); but, whichever of the two recovers, he may have a duty to account to the other to the extent of that other's interest in the goods.[141] A bailee of goods from their apparent owner owes no duty of care in the tort of negligence to their true owner to investigate title, in the absence of anything to put him on enquiry.[142]

[1.18] Simple hiring agreements. The English contract to hire chattels may be defined as one whereby the hirer obtains a right to use the chattel hired, in return for a consideration (see para 10.01) which is normally, but not necessarily, the payment to the owner money,[143] this usually being termed 'rent' or 'hire-rent'. The commercial world has developed the practice of describing simple hiring agreements by different appellations according to context,[144] of which the following are examples:

(a) 'Charter' is the expression that has long been used in relation to the hiring of ships, and over the years a separate body of law has developed relating to charterparties which is beyond the scope of this work.[145]

(b) An 'equipment lease' is a contract between two commercial parties, lessor and lessee, giving the lessee possession and use of a specific asset on payment of rentals over a primary period: the lessor retains ownership of the asset, which will never pass to the lessee, unlike in hp.[146] Such leases are commonly divided according to whether or not the asset value is amortised (recovered) by the lessor over the primary period as: (i) finance (or full payout) leases,[147] are

---

138 *Watford Electronics Ltd v Sanderson CFL Ltd* (see para 18.21; unappealed point).
139 The obligations of the bailee to take care of goods is grounded in the tort of negligence: *Graham v Voigt* [1990] CLY 4310, Aust. See generally, Chap 17. Cf. involuntary bailees: para 8.18.
140 *The Pioneer Container* [1994] 2 AC 324, PC (see [1996] JBL 329). McMeel, *Op. cit.*, at 197–8.
141 *O'Sullivan v Williams* [1992] 3 All ER 385, CA.
142 *Marcq v Christie Manson & Woods Ltd* (set out at para 10.11), Tuckey LJ at para 50.
143 Distinguish sale of goods, where the consideration must be money: see para 1.07.
144 See Goode, *Hire Purchase Law & Practice*, 880–3; Soper & Munro, *The Leasing Handbook*, esp. Chap 19 for the terms of the leasing contract; Davies, *Equipment and Motor Vehicle Leasing and Hiring*.
145 'Large ticket' ship leases are properly 'demise charters'. As to the leasing of ships and oil rigs, see generally Soper & Munro, *Op. cit.*, 317–18.
146 See para 1.24. This ownership technicality is crucial for the tax-treatment of the two types of contract—particularly who is to claim the capital allowance of 'big-ticket' items (see below)—and as to the incidence of VAT between VAT-registered businesses.
147 See generally, Davies [1984] JBL 468; Goode, *Commercial Law*, 3rd edn, Chap 28; Soper & Munro *ibid*, 58 *et seq*. 319–21 (vehicle fleet management).

the most common type and have much in common with conditional sales (see para 1.14), hire purchase (see para 1.20) and chattel mortgages;[148] (ii) operating leases.[149]

(c) *'Contract hire'* (or car leasing) is a specialised form of operating lease, used for self-drive fleets of motor vehicles, where the lessor undertakes some of the responsibility for the management and maintenance of the vehicles.

(d) *'Rental agreement'* is the expression normally reserved for retail business and used in relation to the short-term hiring to private consumers of motor vehicles and the indefinite hiring of televisions, videos and furniture.

Leaving aside charterparties of ships, the common law rules are the same for all forms of simple hiring: basically, these will mostly be the same as for bailments generally (see para 1.17), of which simple hiring is but a species; but they may be varied or ousted by the terms of the contract of bailment and there will frequently be found a standard-form contract spelling out the obligations of bailor and bailee in considerable detail (see para 11.08)—and hence leaving little scope for the common law rules. Moreover, whilst the contract of hiring gives the hirer an interest which is *prima facie* assignable (see para 1.23), the absence of an option to purchase means that the hirer has no such interest in the goods which could be seized by way of execution or upon which distress can be levied;[150] and treatment of simple hiring agreements is likely to be materially different for the purposes of business taxation and grants. The terms statutorily implied in a 'contract for the hire of goods' in favour of the hirer will be dealt with later (see Chaps 12–15). Because the essence of a bailment is a transfer of possession (see para 1.17), the hiring, with its obligation to pay rent, does not commence until delivery and the bailee is *prima facie* under a duty to return the goods when the agreement is determined (see para 27.21).

*Distinguish simple hiring from hp.* Hire-purchase does, but simple hiring does not, include an option to purchase,[151] though this apparently simple distinction has given rise to difficulty with perpetual hiring agreements (see para 1.24) and has a number of consequences. *First*, the exception to the *nemo dat* rule is applicable in respect of motor vehicles let on hp, though not under simple hiring agreements.[152] *Second*, there are some differences in treatment as between simple hirings and hp as regards both minimum payment clauses (see paras 27.37 and 27.50) and the measure of damages in claims against the other party by a bailor (see para 27.31) or bailee (see para 29.25).

**[1.19] Statutory definition.** Relevant to this work, there are two different statutory definitions of bailment that are particularly important, depending on the purpose required.

---

148 Where there is an option to purchase, such transactions are sometimes termed 'industrial hp' or 'equipment leasing', or 'lease purchase', or 'personal leasing', regardless of legal niceties (see para 1.25). For sub-leasing, see para 1.17. Distinguish the (normally longer term) lease of land, governed by the law of real property: for fixtures, see para 25.23.

149 Such schemes are commonly used, together with a supply of services, for those types of goods which enjoy an active second-hand market, e.g. crane and driver; aircraft and crew, or for specialist equipment suffering high obsolescence rates, e.g. computers and software.

150 See Goode, *Hire Purchase Law and Practice*, 2nd edn, 633, 893.

151 The distinction may be vital: *Galbraith v Mitchenall Estates Ltd* (set out at para 27.21). For the option to purchase in hp agreements, see para 1.22.

152 As to the *nemo dat* rule, see para 19.11; and as to this exception thereto, see para 21.55.

1. *For statutory implied terms in bailments*, there is the definition to be found in the SGSA (see para 12.01A).

2. *For statutory control of instalment contracts*, there was introduced by the CCA a category termed 'consumer hire agreement' and defined (as amended in 2006) as:[153]

> 'an agreement made by a person[154] with an individual (the hirer)[155] for the bailment or (in Scotland) the hiring of goods to the hirer, being an agreement which
>
> (a)   is not a hire-purchase agreement (see para 1.24), and
>
> (b)   is capable of subsisting for more than three months'.[156]

This careful definition is aimed primarily at situations where a consideration is payable before the expiry of the bailment: typically, it will extend to periodic domestic rental/hire and the leasing of business equipment and vehicles (see para 1.18). Whether the lessor ('owner') is leasing office equipment to solicitors, medical instruments to doctors, plant and machinery to builders, cars to business-men or television sets to consumers, the Act and regulations will broadly apply if the agreement is not exempt and the lessee or hirer is not a company. Some further points may be noticed about this definition. *First*, it relates only to goods let as such and does not extend to leases of land.[157] *Second*, whilst it clearly comprehends all the types of simple hiring agreements considered above, in England it would also appear to cover gratuitous bailments.[158] *Third*, since the 2006 Act it is no longer limited by the value of the rentals at the time the agreement is made.[159] *Fourth*, in *Dimond v Lovell*:[160]

> D was an innocent driver in a road traffic accident. Whilst D's car was being repaired, she hired a replacement, for a period which turned out to be eight days, from accident hire company (A) upon the following terms: the rental period must not exceed 28 days; D would not have to pay the hire charges immediately; instead, A was given authority to sue the negligent driver (L) and recover its charges from him.

In the House of Lords, the case primarily concerns consumer credit (see para 5.13), but in relation to whether the accident hire agreement amounted to a consumer hiring within the above definition, the Court of Appeal held as follows: s 15 was also capable of applying to a single period of hiring and where the charges were paid upon completion of the litigation against D many months later; but the

---

153 Ss 15(1), 189(1): these agreements may be constituted by two or more documents—s 189(4). E.g. see CCA, Sched 2, Examples 20, 24. See generally Palmer and Yates [1979] 38 CLJ 180.

154 Presumably, the draftsman used the expression 'person' to cover both leasing and sub-leasing. But he then appears to deal with the same point again in his s 189(1) definition of 'owner'. Cf. the description of the transferor under s 8 as 'creditor' (see para 5.19); and as to 'creditor', see further, para 5.25. For contracts governed by foreign law, see para 18.13.

155 For the meaning of 'individual', see below, para 5.24. 'Hirer' is defined by s 189(1). For discussion of the similar definition of 'debtor', see para 5.24.

156 *Dimond v Lovell* (below).

157 *Contra* conditional sales: see para 1.15. As to 'goods', see para 2.01. Does 'goods' include credit cards (see para 5.30)?

158 As to which, see para 1.17. Could this lead to the application of the CCA rules as between bailor and sub-bailee?

159 S 15(1)(c) of the 1974 Act was repealed by s 2(2) of the 2006 Act.

160 [1999] 3 All ER 1, CA (see [1999] JBL 452, at 454–8).

accident hire agreement fell outside s 15 because the bailment was not capable of subsisting for more than three months (s 15(1)(b)).

*CCA provisions.* Where a 'consumer hire agreement' does fall within the ambit of the CCA, in which case it is termed 'regulated' (see para 5.13), the legislature has sought to reduce the advantages to be derived from utilisation of this form instead of an instalment sale or hp agreement. Accordingly, the CCA has made applicable almost all the same restrictions as obtain in the case of credit sales (see para 1.13), except that the unfair credit bargain provisions do not apply to consumer hirings (see para 29.46). However, despite the similar retention of ownership of goods let on hire, it was not possible to utilise all the further rules in respect of conditional sales (see para 1.16). Instead, the CCA introduced separate provisions as follows: the hirer is granted a special, more limited right of termination (s 101: see para 26.07); and there are limited restrictions upon the owner's right of recaption,[161] together with some financial relief to the hirer in that event (s 132: see para 27.50).

# DEFINITION OF A CONTRACT OF HIRE PURCHASE[162]

## Development of the common law form

**[1.20]  Background**. As will be seen below, the English contract of hire purchase (hp) started life as a form of sale, switched to a form of bailment towards the end of the nineteenth century, and has evolved into such a specialised form of bailment as now to be regarded as something *sui iuris*.[163]

Hp is in economic terms (see para 1.14), but perhaps not in legal theory, a fiction:[164] historically, evolution consists of increasingly sophisticated attempts by legal draftsmen to devise on behalf of suppliers under instalment contracts a form of contract which would preserve for the supplier such rights in the goods supplied as would provide adequate security for the subsequent payment of the 'price'. There are three major dangers which the supplier must face. *First*, he must secure his rights to the goods against the consumer and the latter's creditors (see para 1.21). *Second*, he must try to prevent the consumer overriding his possessory or proprietary interest in the goods in favour of a *bona fide* purchaser (bfp) or other transferee (see paras 1.22–23). *Third*, when the supplier has secured his legal interest in the goods, he must take steps to ensure that these rights continue to be of adequate value. Throughout the nineteenth century, the legal form of the contract

---

161  Recaption is subject to the notice procedure (see para 24.28) and time orders (see para 24.40) but not the protected goods rules (see para 24.35). Court actions for recovery of the goods are brought under the Torts Act 1977, s 3 (see para 24.26).

162  See generally, Diamond, *Commercial and Consumer Credit*; Dunstan, *Law Relating to HP*, 4th edn, 1939; Earengay, *Law Relating to HP*, 2nd edn, 1938; Goode, *HP Law & Practice*, 2nd edn, 1970; Guest, *Law of HP* (1966); Wild, *The Law of HP*, 2nd edn, 1965; Goode, *Commercial Law*, 3rd edn, 713–19; Cranston, *Consumers and the Law*, 3rd Edn, 232–4; and further, para 1.25.

163  See further, para 1.25. But see the persistent use of the terminology for 'industrial hp' (para 1.18) and consumer contracts termed 'option to own', or 'lease purchase' (see para 1.25).

164  Hp has been described as a legal fiction: the Crowther Report on *Consumer Credit* (Cmnd. 4596), para 5.2.3. But is it?

was evolving to meet these requirements;[165] and it was not until 1895 that the major characteristics of the form were settled.[166] By reason of its complicated nature, the transaction was almost always in writing[167] and commonly in standard form (see para 11.08).

**[1.21] Other creditors**. Any appropriate form of words will create a debt in the consumer, so that in the event of default the supplier may levy execution on any of the consumer's goods.[168] However, as the supplier also wishes to obtain a preferential claim to those goods as against the consumer's other creditors, one of the following forms was normally used:

(a)  A conditional sale; that is, an agreement to sell with a reservation of property until the price was paid (see para 1.14); or

(b)  An hp agreement; that is, a letting of the goods with an option to purchase.[169]

Because they both reserve the property in the goods to the supplier, either type of contract would usually keep the goods supplied out of the consumer's insolvency[170] or any execution levied on the consumer; and it might also give a right to trace.[171] However, the supplier's security might still be vulnerable because of the legislation relating to chattel mortgages[172] and landlord's distress.[173]

**[1.22] The *bona fide* purchaser or pledgee**. In the mid-nineteenth century, the conditional sale with a reservation of property was sufficient to defeat the claims of a *bona fide* purchaser or pledgee because of the rule *nemo dat quod non habet* (see para 19.11). However, an important exception to that rule was enacted in s 9 of the Factors Act 1889 (FA): this provided that, generally speaking, one who had 'agreed to buy' goods should be able to pass a good title to a *bona fide* purchaser or pledgee (see para 21.43). Almost immediately, the Court of Appeal decided that this new exception applied in the case of a conditional buyer (*Lee v Butler*: see para 1.15). This decision immediately threw the instalment credit trade into turmoil; and the new hp form of contract drafted with a view to avoiding this consequence was litigated in *Helby v Matthews*.[174]

---

165  Perhaps an early example was the Scots case of *Cowan v Spencer* (1828), as explained in the judgment of Lord Keith in *Armour v Thyssen* (set out at para 20.28).

166  The major characteristics of hp could be said to have been settled by the HL in 1895 with the following cases: *McEntire v Crossley Bros* [1895] AC 457, HL (see para 1.14); *Helby v Matthews* (set out at para 1.22).

167  The courts were reluctant to accept oral hp contracts: *Scammell & Nephew v Ouston* (set out at para 10.03). But see *Hitchens v General Guarantee Corpn* [2001] CLY 880, CA.

168  E.g. *Chubb Cash Ltd v John Crilley & Sons* [1983] 2 All ER 294, CA. For levying execution, see generally, para 19.15. To levy execution on the goods of a third party is an act of conversion: see para 19.06.

169  E.g. *Pearce v Brooks* (1866) LR 1 Ex 213; *City Motors (1933) Pty Ltd v Southern Aerial Super Service* (1961) 106 CLR 477, Aust HC, esp. *per* Kitto J at 486–7.

170  The rule extending the ambit of a bankruptcy beyond goods owned by a bankrupt to include also those of which he was the reputed owner has now been abolished: see para 19.15.

171  See Goode (1976) 92 LQR 360, at 376. Tracing is considered further, paras 27.13–14.

172  Bills of Sale Act 1882 (see generally, para 25.26).

173  Law of Distress Amendment Act 1908 (see para 19.17), countered by the verbose *Smart v Holt* clause (see para 26.09).

174  [1895] AC 471, [1895–9] All ER Rep 821, HL. The result is the same even if the customer gives a promissory note as collateral security: *Modern Light Cars Ltd v Seals* [1934] 1 KB 32.

The terms of the agreement between the dealer (A) and customer (B) were somewhat similar to those in *Lee v Butler*. B agreed to pay 10/6 per month as rent for hire of a piano, and the property was not to pass until 36 of these instalments had been paid. However, the agreement further provided that B might at any time determine the hiring by delivering the piano to A upon which B should remain liable for all arrears of rent. During the continuance of the agreement, B pledged the piano to C who took bf and for value, and pleaded title under s 9.

The House of Lords unanimously held, reversing the Court of Appeal, that C had not obtained a good title. Lord Macnaughten explained:[175]

> 'The contract . . . on the part of the dealer was a contract of hiring coupled with a conditional contract or undertaking to sell. On the part of the customer it was a contract of hiring only until the time came for making the last payment. It may be that at the inception of the transaction both parties expected that the agreement would run its full course, and that the piano would change hands in the end. But an expectation, however confident and however well-founded, does not amount to an agreement, and even an agreement between two parties operative only during the pleasure of one of them is no agreement on his part at law'.

Their Lordships distinguished *Lee v Butler* on the grounds that in that case, as soon as the agreement was made, there was a binding agreement to buy on the part of B and he had no option to return the goods,[176] though their Lordships might not have been so adamant if the *Helby v Matthews* agreement had contained a modern minimum payments clause.[177] Indeed, *Helby v Matthews* was itself distinguished in *Forthright Finance Ltd v Carlyle Finance Ltd*.[178]

> Forthright supplied a Ford Cosworth car to Senator Motors, a limited company dealer, under a contract described as a 'Hire Purchase Agreement': it required Senator to pay all the instalments of hire-rent and conferred the usual option to purchase on it when all the instalments had been paid; but it added that the option was deemed to have been exercised when all instalments had been paid, whereupon the property in the car passed to Senator, unless it told Forthright before completion of the payments that such is not the case. Before it had paid all the instalments, Senator sold the car to Cf. Ltd, who successfully claimed a good title under the above exception (see para 21.52).

Delivering the unanimous judgment of the Court of Appeal, Phillips LJ pointed out that Senator was bound to complete all the payments of hire-rent and held that it was a conditional sale agreement:[179] he distinguished *Helby v Matthews*, where the hirer was *not bound* to continue with the hiring for any particular number of months (at 97) and pointed out that (at 98)

---

175  At 482. The reasoning is criticised by Atiyah, *Sale of Goods*, 10th edn, 16.

176  See also *Hull Ropes Co Ltd v Adams* (1895) 65 LJQ 114.

177  The object of such a clause has been said to be to place the owner in at least as favourable a position as a conditional seller: Crowther Report on *Consumer Credit* (Cmnd. 4596), para 5.1.3.

178  [1997] 4 All ER 90, CA. The agreement was not regulated because Senator was a Limited company (see para 5.24); and the transaction was therefore capable of falling within the modern equivalent of s 9 of the FA, s 25(1) of the SGA (see para 21.45).

179  He cited the argument that it should be a conditional sale if the customer bound himself to complete all the payments in Goode, *Consumer Credit Legislation*, para 218.

The option not to take title, which one would expect only to be exercised in the most unusual circumstances, does not affect the true nature of the agreement.

His Lordship expressly refrained from deciding whether the agreement would have been a conditional sale if it had contained a positive nominal option, rather than a negative option.[180] The result is that, if the supplier wishes to enter an hp agreement, rather than a conditional sale, it would seem that he cannot legally bind his customer to complete the allotted span of the 'hiring' and hence pay an amount of rent which is equivalent to the deferred price:[181] all he can do is to so arrange the payment terms that it is in the customer's interest to complete the hiring (see para 1.25).

**[1.23]  Other *bona fide* transferees.** Besides an outright disposition of the general or special property in the goods by way of sale or pledge respectively (see para 1.22), the hirer under an hp agreement may seek to utilise such interest as he has by way of assignment or lien.

1.   *Assignment.*[182] The form of an hp agreement being a hybrid between bailment and sale, the hirer *prima facie* has two contractual interests each capable of independent assignment:[183]

   (a)  His right to hire the goods, which is similar to the right of a hirer under a simple bailment (see para 1.17).

   (b)  His option to purchase, which may be compared with the right of a conditional buyer (see para 1.13), though it is worth less because there is no guarantee that the hirer will exercise his option (see para 1.25).

   Despite the fact that the supplier will normally make careful enquiries into the character of the would-be transferee before entering the agreement (see paras 8.35–39), the courts have taken the attitude that this does not evince an intention to restrict the hirer's *prima facie* right of assignment. For this reason, most modern conditional sale and hp agreements expressly forbid assignment by the transferee of his rights under the agreement.[184] Such a clause may limit or exclude the rights which the assignee can acquire against the supplier (see para 7.26), which should render otiose the activities of Vehicle Transfer Agencies (see para 7.26A); but the purported assignee may have a remedy against the assignor.[185] In practice, the supplier will frequently relinquish his interest in the goods to the assignee on payment of the outstanding balance due under the agreement.[186]

---

180  This has significance for the drafting of the agreement: see para 1.25.

181  *Close Asset Finance v Care Graphics Machinery Ltd* [2000] CCLR 43. What would be the effect of an acceleration clause (see para 26.19)?

182  For assignments of choses in action generally, see para 7.16, *et seq.*

183  *Whiteley Ltd v Hilt* [1918] 2 KB 808, CA. See Goode, *HP Law & Practice*, 2nd edn, 525–6, 586–8.

184  Because the two rights of the hirer are independent, the clause must be carefully examined to see whether it has forbidden assignment of either or both the rights of hiring and option: see Goode, *ibid*, 526–9.

185  E.g. *Butterworth v Kingsway Motors Ltd* (set out at para 12.06). What if, at the time the agreement is made, the transferee makes it clear that he is obtaining the goods as a gift for a third party?

186  What is termed a 'settlement figure'; as to which, see further, paras 26.19 and 26.22.

2. *Liens.*[187] Essentially, a lien is just a right granted by common law or contract to retain possession of goods as security for the performance of particular obligations,[188] though lienees have been granted a special power of sale by the Torts Act 1977 (ss 12–13). In respect of goods supplied on conditional sale, simple hiring or hp, perhaps the most commonly claimed lien is that of a repairer.[189] Whilst no man can create a lien on goods of another without the other's consent, it has been held that a supply on conditional sale, simple hiring or hp normally gives the transferee an implied authority to create a lien for repairs,[190] but only whilst the instalment agreement remains in force (as to which, see paras 26.08–10). To counteract this, the agreement will normally expressly prohibit the transferee from creating any lien over the goods,[191] though the transferee may still be left with an ostensible authority to do so whilst the agreement continues, provided that the repairer knows that the goods are supplied on conditional sale, simple hiring or hp.[192]

## Statutory definition

**[1.24]** Upon this common law form of hp, a number of statutory definitions have been imposed. The leading modern definition is to be found in identical form in both SOGIT (s 15) and the CCA:[193]

' "hire-purchase agreement" means an agreement, other than a conditional sale agreement, under which—

(a) goods are bailed or (in Scotland) hired in return for periodical payments by the person to whom they are bailed . . ., and

(b) the property in the goods will pass to that person if the terms of the agreement are complied with and one or more of the following occurs—

   (i) the exercise of an option to purchase by that person,

   (ii) the doing of any specified act by any party to the agreement,

   (iii) the happening of any other specified event'.

This definition is more satisfactory than its predecessors in several ways: it makes it clear that the statutory category of hp cannot include credit sale (see para 1.13),

---

187 See generally Crossley Vaines, *Personal Property*, 5th edn, Chap 7. A contractual provision granting a lien may be an unfair term: OFT, *UCT Bulletin No 23*, case 21; and see below, para 11.14.

188 E.g. the lien of the unpaid repairer (below), auctioneer (see para 10.11) seller (see para 24.08) or cancelling debtor (see para 10.33).

189 *Tappenden v Artus* [1964] 2 QB 185, CA. *Semble*, the lien probably does not extend to towing and garaging charges: see *Re Southern Livestock Products Ltd* [1963] 3 All ER 801; *Hatton v Car Maintenance Co Ltd* [1915] 1 Ch 621. As to storage charges, see para 24.09.

190 *Green v All Motors Ltd* [1917] I KB 625, CA (hp).

191 Such a provision may be ineffective where contradicted by an express duty in the bailee or conditional buyer to keep in good repair. It may also amount to an unfair term under the UTCC Regulations: see above.

192 *Albermarle Supply Co Ltd v Hind* [1928] 1 KB 307, CA (hp). What if repairer does not know for certain that the goods are on hp, but merely that they are likely to be so?

193 S 189(1). The agreement may be constituted by two or more documents: *ibid* s 189(4). E.g. see Sched 2, Example 10. Cf. *Kay's Leasing Corpn Pty Ltd v Fletcher* (1964) 116 CLR 124, Aust HC. See also SOGIT, s 15(1); CPA, s 45(1).

pledges (see para 25.02) or deliveries on sale or return (see para 20.23). Moreover, it expressly excludes conditional sales (see para 1.14), which exclusion is considered later (see para 1.25).

*Perpetual hiring agreements.* In modern times, there has been a tendency to use simple hiring as an alternative to instalment sales (see para 1.12) or hp agreements (see para 1.20). If the agreement is truly a simple hiring agreement (see para 1.18), it will be treated as such by the courts.[194] In 1954, it was held that a hiring under which the option was not exercisable until the happening of a future uncertain event was not within an earlier statutory hp definition;[195] but it seems likely that such facts would fall within the above CCA definition.[196] However, the question is a matter of substance, not words, as witness the so-called 'perpetual hiring agreements', which provide that all the incidents of property[197] will pass to the bailee except the outward shell of ownership,[198] in which case the agreement might be regarded as hp or conditional sale.[199] If so, they are subject to much the same statutory restrictions (see para 1.16); but, if not, they are subject only to the lesser restrictions on consumer hire agreements (see para 1.19). There is presently debate as to whether more, or less, of these transactions should be regulated (see para 5.11).

**[1.25] Difficulties**. It is now possible to consider a number of the difficulties arising from the dual nature of hp.

1.  *As to the hiring*, there were two ways in which this might be arranged:

    (a) The hirer might agree to take the goods on hire from, e.g. month to month, what is termed a *'periodic hiring'*. From the viewpoint of the supplier, this form suffers from the disadvantage that the hirer might elect to return the goods.

    (b) The hirer might agree to take the goods on hire for a given number of months (a *'fixed-term'* hiring). From the viewpoint of the supplier, this has the attraction that he is sure to achieve the whole of his hp price, apart from the (usually nominal) option fee. However, this form was thought to be a conditional sale in *Forthright Finance Ltd v Carlyle Finance Ltd*.[200]

2.  *Turning to the option*, there were again two possible forms of contract:[201]

---

194  See *Galbraith v Mitchenall Estates Ltd* (set out at para 27.21); Cf. *Baker v Monk* (1864) 4 De GJ & SM 388.

195  *R v RW Profitt Ltd* [1954] 2 QB 35 (option exercisable 'subject to the enactment of the necessary legislation'; not within the definition in the HPA 1938, s 21): see the discussion by Turner in (1974) 48 ALJ 63. The contract might be regarded as a type of conditional sale: see Jones on *Chattel Mortgages*, 4th edn, para 960.

196  Within paragraph (b)(iii), not present in the 1938 definition: see Goode, *Consumer Credit Law & Practice*, para 23.144.

197  For the incidents of property which normally pass on sale, see para 19.10.

198  See *Domestic Electric Rentals Ltd v Dawson* [1943] LJNCCR 31; *Carroll v Credit Services Investments Ltd* [1972] NZLR 460; Goode, *HP Law & Practice*, 57–8.

199  See Jones on *Chattel Mortgages*, 4th edn, paras 952–9; and the Crowther Report, para 5.2.7.

200  Set out at para 1.22, *per* Phillips LJ at 98, without expressly deciding the point. *Contra Close Asset Finance Ltd v Care Graphics Machinery Ltd* [2001] GCCR 2617 (held hp).

201  Where the agreement falls within the CCA, form (a) may cause difficulty with the truth-in-lending provisions (see para 8.22). As to calculating the APR when levying documentation and option fees, see (1993) 48 CC3/2.

(a) The hirer was granted an *option* to purchase which he might exercise once he had paid a stipulated amount of hire rent, exercisable on payment of a further sum[202] (usually nominal),[203] which in practice was usually added to the last instalment.[204]

(b) The price of the *option* was paid at the outset, or included in the hire rent, so that the property in the goods would necessarily pass automatically but for the hirer's express power to terminate. However, the negative option in this form might now turn it into a conditional sale, following *Forthright Finance Ltd v Carlyle Finance Ltd* (above).

It seems to follow that the only safe form of hp remaining is the *periodic hiring* with a *positive option* (see further, para 1.26).

Because of the above dual nature of the hp agreement, the courts have frequently been faced with the problem of whether to apply to it the rules of sale or bailment. It purports to be a species of bailment; and the courts have so treated it when deciding such issues as the owner's measure of damages in contract (see para 27.37), who may maintain an action for wrongful interference with goods (see para 19.06), or whether to imply extra terms in favour of the hirer (see para 15.23). Yet the economic object of the traditional simple transaction is normally to effect a sale;[205] and the courts have looked exclusively at this element when determining such issues as the tort damages to which the owner is entitled as against the hirer or his assignee (see paras 27.22 and 27.31), or the hirer is entitled in respect of breach by the supplier (see para 29.34), or when the hirer may plead a total failure of consideration (see para 29.12). Similar inconsistencies of approach may be found in the decisions in relation to hp agreements in respect of such matters as risk (see para 22.01) and illegality (see para 10.20). As it is apparently impossible to decide whether hp has more in common with sale or bailment,[206] it has sometimes simply been labelled as a form of contract *sui generis*.[207] That this is a sensible way to view the transaction is, perhaps, confirmed by modern developments in, for example, motor finance by way of so-called 'Personal Contract Purchase' or 'Lease Purchase'.[208]

---

202 The amount should be kept within the 'exempt supply' limit (£10) so as not to attract VAT (see generally, para 2.06): (1989) 44 CC2/21. As to methods of payment, see para 23.13.

203 Alternatively, the hire-rent may be reduced by agreeing to make a substantial end option payment ('balloon payment'), e.g. to be paid for out of the proceeds of sale: see *Otis Vehicle Rentals Ltd v Ciceley Ltd* (set out at para 27.18). This type of contract is sometimes called 'lease-purchase': see para 1.18A.

204 Suppose a hirer announced during the currency of the agreement that he would not exercise his option when the time came, would he be bound by that announcement, perhaps as a waiver (see para 26.17) or election (see para 26.23)? Cf. *Marseille Fret SA v D Oltmann Schiffahrts GMBH & Co KG* [1981] Com LR 277, DC.

205 Recently, there have been developed variations under which the hirer in effect pays the rental appropriate to a simple lease for the duration of the agreement and is then given the choice of making a larger ('balloon') option payment: see [2000] *Which? Car* 11.

206 See the dicta of the CA in *Felston Tile Co Ltd v Winget Ltd* [1936] 3 All ER 473, CA, criticised *obiter* in *William Cory & Son v IRC* [1964] 3 All ER 66 at 71, 75. But see Goldberg (1972) 88 LQR 21.

207 E.g. *per* Goddard J in *Karflex Ltd v Poole* [1933] 2 KB 251 at 264, 265. See also para 27.31.

208 [2000] *Which? Car*, 11. These are (say) two-year leases under which during that two years the lessee pays rent calculated to be the depreciation of the vehicle. At the end of the period, the lessee may exercise an option to buy (the option fee being the capital value) or return the vehicle (cf personal leases: see para 1.18). See further (1995) 49 CC 5/20; and para 3.26.

*The hirer's interest in the goods.* The above problems are neatly illustrated by the difficulty of deciding the extent of the hirer's proprietary interest in the goods before he exercises his option to purchase. As we shall see later, the courts have decided that the hirer does not have an equity of redemption in the goods (see para 24.22). However, whilst he does not have an interest recognised by law, during the continuance of the hiring he has an interest whose economic value may be measured by the proportion of the hp price which has been paid: every instalment *pro tanto* reduces the value of the supplier's interest and increases that of the hirer. Yet this hirer's interest is of a peculiarly uncertain nature, inasmuch as the supplier by lawfully terminating the agreement in accordance with its terms, will automatically bring the hirer's interest to an end (see paras 26.08–10).

**[1.26] The future**. It has been seen that hp evolved as a hybrid form of contract, incorporating elements of both bailment and sale, in order to secure for the supplier the greatest possible amount of security that the 'price' will be paid as promised. In a sense, it typifies the nineteenth century attitude of freedom of contract (*laissez-faire*: para 1.02). Yet this hybrid has unsurprisingly given rise to a number of conceptual problems (see para 1.25). Moreover, subsequent case law has demonstrated that the creation of hp was largely unnecessary for the purposes for which it was created;[209] in the important area of implied terms, there has already been imposed an almost uniform statutory system (see Chaps 11–16); and the CCA treats bailment, hp and sale on credit in a very similar manner.[210] It has been suggested that these developments raise the following issues:[211]

(a) Should hire-purchase be abolished, by enacting that all hp agreements shall be deemed conditional sales? This would appear to have certain advantages and to be the way matters have gone in the United States of America[212] and Australia.[213] Within the CCA, it would make little substantive difference, whilst enabling a modest simplification of that Act; it would make possible the abolition of the separate rules for implied terms in hp agreements found in the SOGIT; and outside the CCA it would cut the Gordian Knot in the shape of the common law rules of damages. Or could we go even further and replace[214] both hire-purchase and conditional sale by a workable chattel mortgage system with a proper equity of redemption (see paras 25.20 and 25.38)?

---

209 E.g. *Newtons of Wembley Ltd v Williams* (set out at para 21.51); *Aluminium Industrie Vaassen BV v Romalpa Aluminium* (set out at para 25.29).

210 For the CCA treatment of conditional sales, see para 1.16. Such uniformity was recommended by the Crowther Report on *Consumer Credit* (Cmnd. 4596), paras 5.2 and 5.6.

211 Macleod and Cronin in Chap 22 of *Consumer Credit* (Ed Goode, 1978).

212 See paras 1.18 and 1.24. Except for Pennsylvanian 'bailment-leases': see Jones, *Chattel Mortgages*, 6th edn, 1933, para 960; but see *Op. cit*, para 955, note 72.

213 Australian Consumer Credit Code 1996, s 10.

214 Such a move was resisted on grounds of freedom of contract: the Crowther Report (above) para 5.2.15, though it did recommend that all the various forms of contract should be subject to the proposed chattel mortgage legislation (as to which see para 25.28).

(b) Should there be approved statutory forms of consumer instalment contract, instead of the present (largely theoretical?) Victorian *laissez-faire* arrangements (see para 1.02), mostly reversed by detailed statutory provisions later considered in this book, but beyond the wit of most consumers? We may be moving in that direction with the application by the Office of Fair Trading of the UTCC Regulations (see para 11.12, *et seq.*).

# CHAPTER 2

# SUBJECT-MATTER OF THE SUPPLY CONTRACT—GOODS AND PRICE

## THE GOODS

**[2.01] Introduction**. As a species of bailment (see para 1.17), the contracts of both hp and simple hiring (leasing) are only applicable to goods; and, of course, the term 'goods' is used in the SGA definition of a sale (s 2(1): set out at para 1.07) and in the CCA definitions of 'credit sale', 'conditional sale', 'hire purchase' and 'consumer hiring'.[1] Moreover, the expression 'goods' is also to be found in the Trade Descriptions Act 1968 and in Pt 8 of the Enterprise Act 2002 (see Chap 4). Whilst the last-mentioned Acts contain their own (non-exclusive) definition of 'goods',[2] the CCA expressly defines goods by reference to the SGA (s 189(1)), as does the Unfair Contract Terms Act 1977 (s 14), the Sale and Supply of Goods Regulations (reg 2: see para 14.01); and the SGSA sets out an almost identical definition (s 18(1)). Thus, the major definition for our purposes is the SGA one (see para 2.02), which distinguishes sales of services (see para 2.05).

**[2.02] SGA defintion**. Section 61(1) of the SGA (as amended by italicised words) provides that, unless the context otherwise requires,

> '"goods" includes all chattels personal other than thing in action and money . . .; and in particular 'goods' includes emblements, industrial growing crops, and things attached to or forming part of the land which are agreed to be severed before sale or under the contract of sale *and includes an undivided share in goods'*.

This definition may be analysed as follows:

1. *Chattels personal other than things in action and money.* The term 'chattels personal' covers all tangible,[3] movable[4] property,[5] and even water, oil, gas[6] and air, e.g. compressed air, though electricity is more doubtful (see para 3.07). In relation to supplies of computer software, the English courts have taken the following *prima facie* view:[7] sales of tangibles, viz the hardware, instruction manual and floppy discs carrying the software, are supplies of 'goods', whereas

---

1 These definitions are respectively set out at paras 1.13, 1.16, 1.24 and 1.19.
2 These two definitions also vary as between themselves: see Trade Descriptions Act 1968, s 39(1); Enterprise Act 2002, s 232; and see the criticism in Cmnd. 6628, para 68; and Bragg, *Trade Descriptions*, Chap 2. See also the (again different) definitions in the Factors Act 1889, s 1(3) (see para 21.29); and the Torts (Interference with Goods) Act 1977, s 14. Are all these differences in definition justifiable?
3 As to the controversy whether in the case of a motor vehicle, 'goods' includes the registration document, see para 21.29. As to supplies of services, see para 15.15.
4 *Contra* real (immoveable) property. For the distinction between the sale of goods and land, see para 9.03. For houseboats, see *Chelsea Yacht and Boat Co Ltd v Pope* [2001] 2 All ER 409, CA.
5 Including animals. As to human remains, see Benjamin's *Sale of Goods*, 6th edn, para 1-089.
6 E.g. the *Britvic & Bacardi* cases (see para 11.08). For the gas utility, see para 3.07.
7 *Watford Electronics Ltd v Sanderson CFL Ltd* (see para 18.21; unappealed point).

sales of the (intangible) software itself are not;[8] but this dichotomy has been criticised for paying too much attention to the medium of supply, viz whether the software is supplied on floppy disc or on-line.[9] The following types of personal property are excluded by the definition:

(a) *Things (or choses) in action.* The English law of property other than realty divides that property into two types: choses in possession, which can be enjoyed by taking possession of them, e.g. goods; and choses in action, which can be enjoyed only by court action, e.g. a debt (see para 7.16). The effect of this exclusion of choses in action from the definition is that an assignment (transfer) of a chose in action, e.g. a debt for the price of goods sold (see para 2.06), can never amount to a sale of goods.

(b) *Money.* This probably refers only to that which is transferred in the UK by way of legal tender for its face value at the time of contracting (see para 23.14). Thus, 'money' does not seem to include coins valued only by their substance,[10] or by way of their curio or rarity value,[11] or coins which have ceased to be legal tender,[12] or imitation or stage money. Payment cards are often inaccurately described as 'plastic money' when referring to their use by a card-holder (see para 2.27); but presumably the sale of blank plastic cards is a sale of goods.

2. *Emblements and industrial growing crops.* These are incorporated in the old term *fructus industriales,* and include growing crops of the soil which are produced by the labours of the cultivator, e.g. wheat, barley, potatoes.[13]

3. *Things attached to or forming part of the land.* This phrase covers both fixtures (see para 25.23) and what was known as *fructus naturales,* the latter expression comprehending natural products of the soil, such as grass and trees, provided the contract of sale intends their severance, e.g. hay, timber. As to the extent to which these may amount to sales of interests in land, see para 9.03.

4. *An undivided share.* Whilst a sale of a *divided* share of goods, e.g. half a lamb carcass by a food business, has long been regarded as a sale of goods, under the amendments introduced into the SGA in 1995 the sale of an *undivided* share in goods (see para 20.20A) is also to be regarded as a sale of goods, e.g. a half share of a racehorse to a punter.[14]

---

8 The *St Albans* case (see para 18.20), *per* Glidewell LJ at 493f–j; and see (1997) 16 TrL 387.

9 See *Beta Computers (Europe) Ltd v Adobe Systems (Europe) Ltd* 1996 SLT 604; and Atiyah, *Sale of Goods,* 10th edn, 66–71.

10 *Allgemeine Gold-und Silberscheideanstalt v Customs and Excise Comrs* [1980] QB 390, CA (Krugerrands), discussed [1985] JBL 97. But see the case cited in fn 12 below. Neither of these cases actually involved the SGA definition.

11 *Moss v Hancock* [1899] 2 QB 111, DC (1897 Jubilee £5 gold pieces).

12 *R v Thompson* [1980] QB 229, CA (half-crowns, sixpences). The case also dealt with Krugerrands as to which see above, fn 10.

13 Nowadays, the expression 'emblements' appears to add nothing to the definition: Benjamin *Op. cit.,* para 93. *Contra* Chalmers, *Sale of Goods,* 18th edn, 268.

14 Italicised words introduced into s 61(1) of the SGA (above) by the Sale of Goods (Amendment) Act 1995, s 2(c). See *Sale of Goods Forming Part of a Bulk* (1993, Law Com 215) paras 2.3–6, 4.2 and 5.3.

## Different categories of goods

[2.03/4]  One of the oddities in the drafting of the SGA lies in the manner in which it deals with the different categories of goods. The expressed scheme contained in s 5 refers to three 'types' of goods: *'existing goods'*; *'future goods'*; and *'a chance'*.[15] Nevertheless, very little will be found to turn upon the s 5 distinctions, whilst the all-important distinction between specific and unascertained goods receives scant mention in the Act. In practical terms, far more important than s 5 of the SGA is the dichotomy between 'specific' and 'unascertained' goods.

*'Specific goods'.* These are defined by s 61(1) (as amended), which lays down that, subject to a contrary intention:[16]

> ' "specific goods" means goods identified and agreed upon at the time a contract of sale is made *and includes an undivided share, specified as a fraction or percentage, of goods identified and agreed upon as aforesaid'*.

The key requirements are that the goods must be *identified and agreed upon* at the time of contracting. Further, the italicised phrase will bring within the definition of specific goods a sale of an undivided share (see para 2.02) of identified goods, e.g. a quarter share of an identified horse or boat.[17] As to identifiable goods, see para 20.03.

*'Unascertained goods'.* These are nowhere defined by the SGA, but the Act does use the expression by way of contrast to 'specific' goods, so that 'unascertained' goods must, *prima facie*, be goods which are *not identified and agreed upon* at the time when the contract is made, but will become identified and agreed upon (ascertained) at some later stage. 'Unascertained' goods may be of any of the following types: (a) To be manufactured or grown by the seller; (b) Generic goods, i.e. of a designated type; (c) An unascertained part of a specific bulk.[18]

The distinction between specific and unascertained goods is to be drawn at the moment of contracting, when it should be asked whether or not the contract goods are identified and agreed upon.[19] If yes, the goods are specific. If no, the goods are unascertained, regardless of how soon *after* contracting they become ascertained. Except by making a fresh contract of sale in place of an earlier one (a novation),[20] unascertained goods will *never* become specific, though they should become ascertained. On the other hand, the distinction between 'specific' and 'unascertained' goods will frequently only be one of degree: contracts for the sale of *any* hundred tons of wheat, for the sale of 99 tons out of a particular stock of 100 tons, or for

---

15   See further Macleod, *Consumer Sales Law*, 1st edn, para, 2.03.

16   Italicised words introduced by the Sale of Goods (Amendment) Act 1995, s 2(d).

17   *Sale of Goods Forming Part of a Bulk* (1993, Law Com 215), paras 2.26 and 5.4. This should remove such sales from the ambit of those SGA provisions based on possession or physical delivery (i.e. ss 18, 27–37): *ibid*, paras 5.5–7.

18   For a suggestion that this category might need special treatment, see Nicol (1979) 42 MLR 129, at 142. See further, paras 20.20 and 21.49.

19   The fact that a written contract or invoice contains a 'specification' is ambiguous for this purpose.

20   Discharge of the earlier contract by such subsequent mutual agreement is considered at para 26.18.

the sale of *that* 100 tons may look similar, but the first two are for the sale of 'unascertained' goods and the last for the sale of specific goods. The distinction is important in the contexts of the passing of property and impossibility of performance.[21]

**[2.05] Sale of skill and labour (services).**[22] The insistence that the transaction of sale, hp and hiring require that in exchange for money there shall be transferred *'goods'* theoretically enables these transactions to be distinguished from the supply of skill and labour. However, the importance of the requirement was substantially lessened by Parliament with the repeal of the rule requiring certain sales to be evidenced in writing (see para 9.02) and the enactment in 1982 of Pt 2 of the SGSA (see para 15.15). Furthermore, the common law has also contributed to this process by its tendency to apply the rules of sale of goods by analogy to supplies of services, e.g. in relation to delivery[23] and the implied term as to fitness (see para 15.26). Yet there would still appear to be differences, e.g. with regard to the passing of property[24] and the effects of frustration.[25] Assuming the parties have not settled by their contract the issue of whether or not a transaction is to be, or involve, a sale of goods (see para 1.06), the following points should be borne in mind:

(1) Where the work involves the 'seller' in affixing materials to the land or goods of the 'buyer', the position is as follows: if the seller (workman) supplies the materials, the issue is whether the contract is substantially to improve the 'buyer's' existing property,[26] or one of sale of goods with an incidental obligation to affix;[27] or one of quasi-sale (see para 2.10). But where the 'buyer' supplies the materials, it will normally be a contract only of skill and labour.[28]

(2) Where the work is substantially independent of the creation or supply of the goods, the position is this: ancillary services will not prevent a contract from amounting to a sale of goods,[29] and vice versa;[30] and where there is a supply of goods plus subsequent maintenance, there may be two separate contracts. In

---

21   See paras 20.01 and 22.14. *Contra* specific performance: see para 29.38.

22   See generally Benjamin's *Sale of Goods*, 6th edn, paras 1-041 to 47; Cranston, *Consumers and the Law*, 3rd edn, Chap 6.

23   *Charles Rickards Ltd v Oppenheim* (set out at para 26.25).

24   For the passing of property on the sale of goods, see Chap 20; for the passing of property on affixing one chattel to another (usually termed *'accessio'*), see para 19.05, and for the passing of property in goods becoming affixed to realty, see para 25.23.

25   Because the Law Reform (Frustrated Contracts) Act 1943 does not apply to certain contracts for the sale of goods (s 2(5)(c)): see para 22.18.

26   E.g. *Stewart v Reavell's Garage* [1952] 2 QB 545 (fitting new brake-linings to a car).

27   E.g. *Philip Head & Sons Ltd v Showfronts Ltd* [1970] I Lloyd's Rep 140 (sale and fitting of carpet); *Parsons (Livestock) Ltd v Uttley, Ingham & Co Ltd* (set out at para 27.42—sale and installation of a hopper). Cf. *Truk (UK) Ltd v Tokmakidis GmbH* [2000] 2 All ER (Comm) 594 (fitting lifting gear to a lorry).

28   What if some of the materials are provided by each party? See Benjamin, *Op. cit.*, paras 1-044 to 45.

29   E.g. *Lockett v A & M Charles Ltd* [1938] 4 All ER 170 (sale of meal in restaurant). What of a meal supplied to a lodger?

30   E.g. *Dodd v Wilson & McWilliam* [1946] 2 All ER 691 (vet making diagnosis and supplying drug). See Atiyah, *Sale of Goods*, 10th edn, 26.

this context, it may be significant whether the parties stipulate for one global consideration, e.g. a new car and post-deliver adjustments (see para 15.11); or two separate ones, e.g. TV plus tube insurance.

(3)  Where the work is wholly a component of the goods created and supplied, the courts appear to have changed their minds. The earlier relatively simple view was that there was a sale of goods so long as 'a chattel is ultimately to be delivered';[31] whereas the more recent view is that everything depends on the substance of the contract, the commissioning of a portrait from an artist being held as a supply of skill and labour, notwithstanding the incidental supply of a canvas.[32] A similar problem arises with the supply of computer software, where there may be a single package supply, e.g. of goods plus training.[33] In both cases, such transactions may now amount to quasi-sales (see para 2.10).

A contract to supply services may also attract criminal liability under s 14 of the TDA or Pt 2 of the CPA (see paras 4.16 and 8.09).

## THE PRICE AND CREDIT

**[2.06] The price of goods sold**. In order that the SGA can apply to a transfer of goods, the SGA requires that the property in those goods be transferred for 'a money consideration, called the price';[34] and it is clear that *prima facie* that price must be paid in legal tender[35] by, or on behalf of, the buyer.[36] Section 8 provides for the manner in which that price is to be determined, laying down the following rules:

(1)  Under s 8(1), the price in a contract of sale may be fixed by the contract,[37] or may be left to be fixed in a manner thereby agreed,[38] or may be determined by the course of dealings between the parties.[39]

---

31  *Lee v Griffin* (1861) 30 LJKB 252, at 253 (supply of false teeth by a dentist).

32  *Robinson v Graves* [1935] I KB 579, CA (criticised by Samek [1962] 36 ALJ 66); Benjamin, *Op. cit.*, para 1-041. Cf. *Cammell Laird & Co Ltd v Manganese Bronze & Brass Co Ltd* (set out at para 14.14). What of an undertaker?

33  *Watford Electronics Ltd v Sanderson CFL Ltd* (see para 18.21; unappealed point, at para 50).

34  S 2(1): set out at para 1.07. For the distinction between money and goods for the purposes of the SGA, see para 2.02. For price as a means of distinguishing sales of goods from certain other transactions, see para 2.08, *et seq*. These rules say nothing of the effect of inflation: as to which, see Downes (1985) 101 LQR 98.

35  As to which, see para 23.14; and as to decimalisation, see para 4.24. Distinguish the promise to pay money (legal tender) from the discharge of that promise, which may be accomplished by set-off, part-exchange, cheque or credit card (see para 23.14).

36  *Bennett v Griffin Finance* [1967] 2 QB 46, CA (see 92 LQR at 193). This is an aspect of the rule of privity of contract (see para 10.01).

37  E.g. *Anangel Atlas Compania Naviera SA v Ishikawajima—Harima Heavy Industries Co (No. 2)* [1990] 2 Lloyd's Rep. 526 ('most favoured customer' status). For express provisions as to price, see para 11.07.

38  The clause of the Sale of Goods Bill 1888 originally provided that the price might be 'left to be fixed by subsequent arrangement'; but these words were struck out in Committee. For the difficulties which price adjustment clauses may cause, see para 10.05.

39  E.g. *Finland Steamship Co v Felixstowe Dock Co* [1980] 2 Lloyd's Rep 287; *Agip SpA v Navigazione Alta Italia SpA* [1984] 1 Lloyd's Rep 353, CA.

(2) Under s 8(2), where the price is not determined in accordance with the fore-going provisions the buyer must pay a reasonable price.[40]

Thus, s 8 assumes that a contract has been made.[41] However, it must be borne in mind that the determination of the price is often an important factor in deciding whether a contract has been concluded, particularly if reliance is being placed on s 8(2) (see para 10.03). To the extent that s 8 is a codification of the ordinary common law rules, it will represent the *prima facie* rules applicable to other supply contracts, such as hp and simple hirings, where these rules may have less scope because of the standard form contracts.[42] Agreements to sell at a valuation are dealt with later (s 9: see para 10.05), as are lowest price guarantees (see para 11.07).

On top of the price as above defined there will *prima facie* have to be included value added tax (VAT) on most goods.[43] Payment of the price is dealt with later (see para 23.13, *et seq.*), as are restrictions on the pricing of goods and price variations (see para 26.21). In a consumer supply contract, the price *per se* is a core term and thus cannot be an unfair term.[44] There are also rules dealing with price displays (see para 8.08).

*Bar coding.* The code is a simple system of machine readable product identi-fication.[45] It is normally used by retailers in conjunction with a computer data-base, e.g. to enable check-out machines in supermarkets to register the sale automatically for the purposes of identifying and recording the price of the goods sold (as to mis-pricing, see para 8.09A).

*Electronic point of sale (EPOS).* This is an electronic till, that is, one connected to a telephone line, which can read bar-coding (see above). In its simple state, EPOS generates sales bills, records sales data and can be used to automatically order up replacement goods to the shelves and to trace goods for the purposes of safety (see para 4.35) and making delivery (see para 23.02). It can also be used to effect payment by plastic card (EFTPOS: see para 2.17).

**[2.07] Credit within the CCA.** The CCA 1974 is intended to protect private con-sumers and small businessmen; and, to do so, it employed a dual test of a financial ambit and exclusion of corporate consumers. The 1974 Act applies almost exclusively to regulated agreements (see para 5.13): these fall into two categories, consumer credit agreements (see para 5.19) and consumer hire agreements (see para 1.19). However, the major category is that of consumer credit agreement, the

---

40  What is a reasonable price is a question of fact (s 8(3)): see e.g. *British Coal Corpn v South of Scotland Electricity Board* 1991 SLT 302. For similar provisions in relation to the supply of services, see s 15 of the SGSA 1982 (see para 15.15).

41  If so, s 8(2) does *not* enable an aggrieved party to re-open the amount simply because he thinks the agreed price unreasonable; but he may be able to do so if it is extortionate or unfair: CCA, ss 137, 140A: see paras 29.41 and 29.44). For variation of contract, see para 26.21.

42  In regulated agreements, the issue is largely academic because of the requirement to state in writing the price or rent: see para 9.13.

43  See Value Added Tax 1994. For the effect on the price where the rate of VAT is changed between contract and delivery, see s 89. For the use of 'free insurance' to 'replace' part of price, see [2003] 7 *Which?* 7.

44  See para 11.12A–14; but a price increase clause may be unfair (Grey list (i): see para 11.18).

45  As from 2005, printed bar coding is likely to be replaced for back-of-store operations by radio frequency identification (RFID) tags: *Times* (18.11.04). Later use of RFID front-of-store is likely to raise privacy issues (see para 3.29): *Times* T2 (28.4.05, p 4).

ambit of which was largely regulated not by the 'price', but by the credit element in the transaction: the difference between the 'price' (plus VAT) and 'credit' may for the moment be thought of as likely to be the deposit and credit charge: both these items were excluded from the 'credit' within the CCA. However, the CCA 2006 has made a significant change: henceforth, the CCA applies without financial limit to private consumers; but a credit limit remains for small businesses (see para 5.23).

It should be borne in mind that there are statutory difficulties in supplying goods on credit to minors (see para 10.18).

*0% finance*. A popular marketing tool is the offer of credit at 0% finance,[46] though such deals are commonly hedged about with restrictions, either positive[47] or negative. The price charged for the credit, substantially made up of the interest rate, must for regulated agreements be quoted as an APR (see para 8.22). Absent a rate-ceiling (see para 6.09), the creditor may presently charge any rate of interest he wishes: this rate will not be caught by the Unfair Terms Regulations (reg 6(2): see para 11.14); and the creditor is also free to either charge the same rate for all of a particular type of business, or tailor the rate according to the risk presented by a particular debtor (risk-based pricing). On the other hand, it would seem misleading to advertise a deal as '0% finance' where the 0% is confined to some elements of the contract,[48] or lost if some conditions are not fulfilled by the debtor.[49] Moreover, a claim of '0% finance' must in a regulated agreement anyway comply with the Advertisement Regulations (see para 8.30).

## Price distinguishes other transactions

**[2.08] Gifts**. A gift involves an unconditional transfer of the property in goods without any consideration. It does not extend to unintended extras supplied with goods (*Wilson v Rickett Cockerell Ltd*: set out at para 14.03); nor to the packaging in which the goods may be supplied, even though both parties may expect that it will be thrown away (*Geddling v Marsh*: set out at para 14.03). If the contract provides for some sorts of packaging, e.g. a bottle, to be returnable, the bottle would appear to have been bailed (see para 1.17).

Unlike sales, hp and simple hiring agreements, a gift of goods is incomplete until delivery, unless accomplished by deed (see para 9.01) or declaration of trust.[50] Where a retail buyer obtains goods for the purpose of giving them to another, that gift cannot normally be effective until delivery, upon which the retail buyer's right to reject the contract goods used to be lost before any effective inspection (but see SGA, s 35(6): see para 29.06).

---

46   There are two common forms: (a) the price without interest is simply payable by instalments; or (b) the price plus interest is initially payable by instalments, but the interest subsequently refunded.

47   Frequently difficult for the consumer to fathom or execute, a high interest rate payable on default: see [2000] 12 *Which?* 10. Such limitations may be unfair terms (see para 11.12, *et seq.*).

48   E.g. balance transfers; '0% forever' (OFT, *AR-2003/4*, 34; 71 Quarterly Account 23). For the balance transfer trap, see paras 8.28 and 23.13.

49   This is misleading where interest is payable from the date of the agreement if the loan is not paid off in full by the end of the interest-free period (see OFT, *AR-2002/3*, 44; *AR-2003/4*, 35; and para 8.28). For the advertising rules as regards 0% finance, see para 8.30.

50   See *Milroy v Lord* (1862) 4 De GF & J 264; *Cochrane v Moore* (1890) 25 QBD 57, CA.

'*Free gifts*'. The question arises whether the so-called 'free gifts' commonly made in the course of retail business are genuinely gifts or are supplied for a consideration. If the 'free gift' or 'sample' is supplied without there being any obligation on the transferee to do anything, there will be no contractual relationship between transferor and transferee.[51]

However, in commerce, items described as 'free gifts' are frequently advertised as being available only where other goods or services are bought under a contract.[52] In some retail trades, such 'free gifts' can be of substantial value: they may take the form of either an immediate delivery of goods, e.g. a free portable TV with each car or bedroom suite supplied; or a voucher for a price reduction off a later purchase of goods or services.[53] The question of the status under which such 'free gifts' are delivered was considered in *Esso Petroleum Ltd v Comrs of Customs and Excise*.[54]

> Esso devised a 'World Cup coin' sales promotion for use by garages selling their petrol. Garages would advertise that, for every 4 gallons of petrol sold, it would supply a motorist with a coin bearing the likeness of a member of the English soccer team playing in the 1970 World Cup.

Two Law Lords, Lords Dilhorne and Russell, agreed with the Court of Appeal that the coins were of so little value that there was no intention to create legal relations, Lord Russell suggesting an analogy with a garage's offer of 'Free Air'; but this may be distinguishable where the 'gift' has a significant value.[55] However, the majority held that there was a contractual promise by the garage to transfer the coins in consideration for the motorist agreeing to buy the petrol (see para 8.05): according to Lords Wilberforce and Simon, as the consideration was not the price, but entry into the petrol sale contract, the coins were the subject of a collateral contract (see generally, para 11.06); but Lord Dilhorne held that the coins were the subject of a sale.[56]

None of these views affect the legal position with regard to the major goods or services purchased; that is, the petrol in the *Esso* case. However, suppose the 'free gift' supplied by the petrol-seller, e.g. World Cup coin, is not of satisfactory quality: if it is really supplied by way of gift, the supplier incurs no contractual liability; if it is supplied by way of sale, there may be liability under the SGA;[57] but, if it is supplied by way of collateral contract, any liability would be under the SGSA (see

---

51  For such promotional activities, see generally para 8.14. If 'free gifts' are offered at an auction, there may be an offence: see para 10.11.

52  It may amount to an offence as being an unfair commercial practice: see para 4.21.

53  Does this amount to the provision of a credit note? Is it *prima facie* assignable? Can any valid restrictions be placed upon its use? A 'free gift' coupon will not attract VAT *(Boots v Customs and Excise Comrs* [1991] CLY 3668, CJEC; and as to such vouchers generally, see para 15.18.

54  [1976] 1 All ER 117, HL. See generally Atiyah (1976) 39 MLR 335; Lawson, *Advertising Law*, 155–7.

55  See *Att-Gen v L D Nathan & Co Ltd* [1990] 1 NZLR 129, CA (criminal case; a 'free' bottle of wine offered with sales of 'family packs' of beef).

56  Within the Purchase Tax Act 1963, a view supported by Atiyah (1976) 39 MLR at 336. The Advertising Standards Authority now forbids the description of any offer as 'free' if there is any cost to the consumer beyond that of delivery: *Code of Advertising Practice* para 4.4 (generally, para 3.14).

57  See para 15.25. The 'free gift' would be supplied under the contract of sale: see para 14.03.

para 2.10). In some circumstances, there may be criminal liability, e.g. failure to supply the 'free gift',[58] or cause an advertisement so promising to amount to a misleading advertising (see para 8.12A). Furthermore, if the 'free gift' supplied to a consumer is dangerous, that may engender both civil and criminal liability.[59] Commonly, the 'free gift' will in fact be supplied by a third party:[60] unless the latter acts so as to create privity of contract (see para 17.08) in respect of that 'free gift' between the main supplier, e.g. petrol-seller, and consumer, there will in reality be two independent transactions, so that the consumer may be able to rescind one without rescinding the other.

**[2.09] Barter or exchange**. Section 2(1) of the SGA envisages that the consideration for the promise to transfer goods shall be money, for it calls that consideration 'the price'; and, in defining 'goods', s 61(1) explicitly excludes money.[61] Therefore, where each party merely promises to transfer goods to the other, then the contract is one of barter and hence outside the SGA; but it will instead amount to a quasi-sale (see para 2.10). The more difficult situation is where a money value is put by the parties upon the goods to be exchanged (valued barter). In *Dawson (Clapham) Ltd v Dutfield*,[62] there was a sale of two lorries for £475, of which £250 was to be paid in cash and the rest made up by two lorries taken in part-exchange; and Hilberry J held that there was an entire contract of sale. It is submitted that the case did not turn upon whether the greater proportion of the price was payable in cash or kind; but upon whether the parties intended the transaction to be a sale or barter. Indeed, it has been suggested that 'there is nothing to prevent the parties from expressly agreeing that what might have been a barter shall take the form of reciprocal sales, with a mutual set-off of prices and, if necessary, a cash adjustment'.[63]

*Part-exchange.* Particularly in respect of motor vehicles and other consumer durables, it is common for other goods (usually of a similar type) to be 'traded-in' in part-exchange, in which case a value will normally be assigned by the parties to the trade-in goods (the 'part-exchange allowance').[64] Further complicating factors often

---

58 If the 'free gift' is a service, e.g. free insurance, there may be an offence under s 14 of the TDA: *Kinchin v Ashton Park Scooters Ltd* (1984) 148 JP 540; and see para 4.16. If the free offer is to supply goods, there is no offence under s 20 of the CPA: Griffiths and McIntyre (1993) 14 Jo MLP 109 at 111; and see generally para 8.09.

59 As to civil liability, see CPA, Pt I (see para 17.24, *et seq.*); and as to criminal liability, see CPA Pt II and the GPS Regulations (see para 4.32, *et seq.*) .In the CPA, 'supply' is defined to catch not only sales, but also collateral contracts and gifts (CPA, s 46(1)); and the GPS Regulations define 'product' to include a gift (reg 2).

60 The 'free gift' may actually be supplied by a third party direct to the consumer, e.g. *Att-Gen v L D Nathan & Co Ltd* (above; wine owned by Nobilos and supplied on N's behalf to consumers as a promotion of a new brand).

61 See para 2.02. For other possible approaches, see Benjamin's *Sale of Goods* 6th edn, para 1-34, fn 30. What is the position with regard to hp and hiring agreements?

62 [1936] 2 All ER 232 (as to detinue, see para 19.04). See also *Aldridge v Johnson* (set out at para 20.16).

63 Benjamin, *Op. cit.*, para 1-037. But see *per* Lord Reid in *Chappel & Co Ltd v Nestle & Co Ltd* [1960] AC 87 at 109, HL.

64 E.g. *Oscar Chess Ltd v Williams* [1957] 1 All ER 325, CA. For what the CCA terms a 'part-exchange allowance': see *ibid*, s 73, discussed below at para 10.34. For a case where no such values were assigned, see *Flynn v Mackin* [1974] IR 101, noted 39 MLR 589. Systematic attribution of a nominal value to the trade-in goods has been treated by the OFT as an unfair term: *Bulletin No 23*, para 1.11.

found are: (i) that the goods traded-in were owned by a third-party finance company under an instalment credit contract (see para 1.03), it being envisaged that the third party's interest in the goods will (as part of the overall package) be bought out by payment to him of his 'settlement figure' (see para 26.19A); (ii) the balance of the part-exchange allowance will normally be utilised as the whole or part of the deposit; and (iii) the acquisition of the new goods may itself be on terms[65] financed by a fourth party (see para 2.20), in which case that deposit may be credited to the financier (see para 16.05). But it is clear that neither of these possibilities will necessarily interfere with the basic analysis of the transaction.[66] Returning to the central transaction, there would appear to be two plausible analyses:

(a) There may be one contract to supply the new goods, coupled with a subsidiary arrangement that the price may be partially satisfied (at an agreed amount) by delivery of the old goods.[67] If this is correct, it may be that the transaction should be regarded as a single quasi-sale (see para 2.10); but the difficulty with this view arises where the consumer has no title to the old goods or misdescribes them (see Chaps 12 and 13).

(b) There may be reciprocal contracts of sale with a set-off of prices: the consumer sells the 'trade-in goods' to the retailer; and the retailer sells the 'new goods' to the consumer. This view has the attraction that it is apparently easy to work out the respective rights of the parties by treating matters as two separate but interdependent sales of goods, each within the SGA.[68]

**[2.10/11] Quasi-sales**. Section 1(1) of the Supply of Goods and Services Act 1982 (SGSA) refers to a 'contract for the transfer of goods', which this gateway section defines as:[69]

'A contract under which one person transfers or agrees to transfer to another the property in goods, other than an excepted contract'.

The two major elements of this defintion are (1) a contract (2) under which A transfers the property in goods to B. This insistence on a transfer of goods is clearly apt to cover a barter transaction[70] and perhaps LETS.[71] Further, the definition does not say that B must only receive goods, so that it will also include his receipt of a

---

65   Those terms may be one of the basic types of instalment contract described at para 1.03. But they could be one of the modern variations, e.g. personal contract purchase (see para 1.25), personal loan (see para 2.17). The financial terms of these forms may vary.

66   E.g. *Bennett v Griffin Finance* [1967] 2 QB 46, CA. See also Palmer (1983) 46 MLR 621.

67   This analysis is preferred by Goode, *HP Law and Practice*, 2nd edn, 305. It is said to explain most of the cases: Benjamin, *Op. cit.*, para 1-039. It seems to have been adopted in the criminal law (see *Metsoja v Pitt & Co* (1989) 8 TRLR 155, DC.

68   Cf. *Marten v Whale* (set out at para 1.11); and see futher, para 10.09.

69   As amended, s 18 defines 'goods' and 'property' in terms identical to those employed in the SGA: as to which see respectively, paras 2.01 and 1.08. As to the SGSA generally, see para 15.02.

70   E.g. *Windenmeyer v Burn Stewart & Co Ltd* 1966 SLT 215. For the rules applicable to barter, see Benjamin's *Sale of Goods*, 6th edn, paras 1-035 to 36. For vouchers, see para 15.18; Woodroffe, *Goods and Services—The New Law*, paras 4.02–4.

71   L(ocal) E(xchange) T(rading) S(ystem). Under these systems, a locally-invented 'money' is used by groups whose members swap goods and services without cash necessarily changing hands. Each member holds an account which is credited or debited whenever an exchange takes place. See *The Times* (17.10.94 and 10.11.97).

combinations of goods and services (see para 2.05), such as goods made to order, e.g. a fitted suit, and goods to be installed, e.g. a fitted carpet. However, s 1(3) makes it clear that the consideration for the supply of goods does not, as in the case of a sale (see para 1.07), require a monetary price, but instead may be constituted by (or include) a supply of goods and services (see para 15.26). So the category might cover 'free gifts',[72] part-exchanges (see para 2.09) and the replacement of defective goods (see para 29.03A). The section draws the same distinction between contract and conveyance as the SGA (see para 1.10), though it contains no rules as to the passing of property equivalent to those found in the SGA.[73] On the other hand, the section is restricted to contracts involving the transfer of property in goods: whilst it may be applicable even where that transfer is conditional,[74] it is difficult to see how it can be applied to materials consumed in the course of their application by the supplier.[75] Further, s 1 expressly excludes all the following types of property-transferring ('excepted') contract:[76]

(i)   a contract of sale of goods (see para 1.07);

(ii)  a hire purchase agreement (see para 1.20);

(iii) a transfer or agreement to transfer which is made by deed and for which there is no consideration other than the presumed consideration imported by deed;[77]

(iv) a contract intended to operate by way of mortgage, pledge, charge or other security, this being an exemption identical to that employed in the SGA (s 62(4): see para 1.08).

In respect of quasi-sales, Pt 1 of the SGSA imports implied terms as to title, fitness, quality and sample which are closely modelled on those in ss 12–15 of the SGA (see Chaps 12–15). It also deals with hybrid contracts (see para 1.06), expressly stating that the transaction remains a quasi-sale, notwithstanding that services are also provided (s 1(3)), e.g. a plumber fitting a new tap (see para 15.15). On either view, it would seem that property and risk in the traded-in goods passes on delivery (see Chaps 20 and 22).

# STATUTORY CONTROL

**[2.12] Statutory control of prices**. At the outset, a distinction must be drawn between the following types of control in relation to prices.

---

72   'Free gifts' are usually supplied under contract: see paras 2.08 and 15.18. Do they fall within the SGSA or the SGA (see Woodroffe, *Op.cit.*, para 4.05)?

73   It may be that the passing of property depends on the intention of the parties (Benjamin, *Op.cit.*, para 5-032) or cannot pass until the job is completed (Woodroffe, *Op.cit.*, para 3.17). For the passing of property, see generally Chap 20.

74   As where the contract contains a *Romalpa* clause (as to which, see para 25.29). *Dubitante* Palmer (1983) 46 MLR at 622.

75   E.g. dyes, lotions, solvents, shampoos. It would appear that such transactions are still governed by the common law: see para 15.26.

76   S 1(2). Para (c) has been deleted: see para 15.17.

77   For gifts, see generally para 2.08. Note that there is no comparable exception in respect of the provisions of hire (see para 15.13) and services (see para 15.15).

1. *Price levels.* The Competition Act 1980 established the following scheme: as regards the private sector, prices were to be controlled indirectly by the competition rules (see below); but there were reserve powers to investigate pricing by public utilities.[78] This public/private divide was maintained by the modern system, which is largely contained in the Competition Act 1998 (CA) and the Enterprise Act 2002.[79] One of the themes of the 2002 Act is the empowering of consumers; and the Act in fact contains several independent topics, dealing with competition (see below), the OFT (Pt 1: see paras 3.01 and 3.03), consumer law (Pt 8: see paras 3.12 and 4.18), information disclosure (Pt 9: see para 28.06) and insolvency (Pt 10: see para 19.18); and it includes a sweeping new power for the Secretary of State to make consequential amendments to any statute or statutory instrument 'for the general purposes of this Act' (s 277).

2. *Price displays.* The power to control price displays is dealt with at para 8.08.

3. *Price discrimination.* Where a single supplier exercises price discrimination between his customers, this may amount to an anti-competitive practice (see below) or discrimination, e.g. on grounds of race or sex (see para 4.23).

4. *Restraints on trade/competition.* The earlier UK legislative scheme[80] has been largely replaced by the CA and the Enterprise Act 2002 (EA). Additionally, when the UK joined the EU (see para 1.03A), there was initiated here the EU system for regulating competition as between different Member States (ECA, ss 2 and 10). Accordingly, there was introduced the following dual system, detailed consideration of which is beyond the scope of this work.

   (a) *EU controls.* At the Community level, apart from State aid which may distort competition by conferring competitive advantage (Art 89 [ex 94]), economic activity between businesses which distorts competition or restricts the free movement of goods between Member States may contravene the EU Treaty itself (see para 2.13), or regulations made under it, e.g. the Merger Regulations.[81] The European Commission has broad powers to police these rules and impose fines of up to ten per cent of turnover, but tends only to investigate matters which raise issues significant at Community level; and in respect of these, local investigation within the UK would usually be conducted on behalf of the European Commission by the Office of Fair Trading (OFT).[82] Alternatively, civil action may be brought by third parties in the UK courts[83] for breach of statutory duty (see para 3.21).

   (b) *UK controls.* The earlier UK competition system has now been replaced by the CA (as amended), which is modelled on the EU system (see above): the UK system is outlined later (see para 2.14) and is to be interpreted so far as

---

78  Ss 11–13. Price increases by public utilities may also be challengeable in their own committee structure (see para 3.07) and subject to codes of practice (see para 3.14). As to the price of credit, see para 6.09.

79  The EA stems from the DTI White Paper, *Modern Markets: Confident Consumers* (1999).

80  Under the Restrictive Trade Practises Acts 1956–77 (RTPA) and Fair Trading Act 1973 (FTA).

81  See further *Chitty on Contract*, 27th edn, para 40-344.

82  Competition Act 1998, ss 61–5 (as amended). For enforcement, see further Chap 28.

83  *Garden Cottage Foods v Milk Marketing Board* [1984] AC 130, HL; and Chitty, *Op. cit.*, para 40-344.

possible consistently with the EU competition system,[84] which will include its case law. Subsequently, the RTPA and FTA system for dealing with monopolies, mergers and anti-competitive practices has been replaced by the EA, most of which is too specialist for this work.[85] Recent examples of competition enquiries within our scope include those into store cards (see para 2.24) and *MasterCard* fees.[86] The powers of the OFT were enhanced to give it (and the utility regulators) a domestic position in competition law similar to that of the European Commission at the Community level and dovetailed with the specific powers of the regulators of the utilities (CA, s 54: see para 3.07). The OFT has wide powers to carry out investigations and issue Decisions (CA, ss 25–31) and then issue directions and penalties (CA, ss 32–41). As regards enforcement, failure to comply is an offence (CA, s 42), enabling the OFT to impose fines on errant businesses of up to 10% of UK turnover (CA, s 36);[87] but it also seems likely that aggrieved third parties may take proceedings for breach of statutory duty.[88] Additionally, the EA has introduced a 'super-complaints' procedure, through which designated consumer bodies may initiate a fast-track procedure by the OFT and other regulators (EA, ss 11 and 205: see para 4.19), including the right to bring class actions for damages.[89]

**[2.13] EU controls on businesses**. Of particular relevance for our purposes are the following Community rules:

1. *The free movement of goods*. Government activity which restricts the free movement of goods between Member States, e.g. quotas, may contravene Art 28 [ex 30] of the Treaty of Rome, unless it is saved by Art 30 [ex 36] on 'grounds of public morality, public policy or public security'.[90] As EU rules *pro tanto* prevail in the event of conflict with UK legislation (see para 1.03A), the former have sometimes been pleaded with little justification simply to avoid (or delay the imposition of) UK legislation. For instance, it was sought to avoid UK Sunday trading laws (see para 8.13) as contravening the EU free movement provisions: but the European Court decided that this was a matter for national law; and the UK courts have confirmed that our Sunday trading laws are consistent with

---

84 CA, s 60 (as amended). This was intended to ensure so far as possible that the UK and EU prohibitions 'are interpreted and developed consistently with the Community competition system': Lord Simon, *Hansard*, HL, Vol 583, col. 960. For the overall Government intention, see *Modern Markets: confident consumers* (1999, Cm. 4410), paras 2.1–2.6.

85 EA Pts 3 (mergers), 4 (market investigations) and 6 (cartels). Transgressions may lead (s 204) to the disqualification of directors (see para 19.25) and for other remedies see below.

86 In the OFT Decision (see para 2.14), no directions or penalty were imposed.

87 The OFT claims to be able to use these powers to control indirectly the abuse of price levels, the so-called 'rip-off Britain' campaign: OFT, *AR–2000*, 11–2.

88 In Parliament, the Government stated that there would be such a right similar to that under the Treaty of Rome; but it refused to expressly so provide in the CA. As to statutory interpretation generally, see para 1.04. As to actions for breach of statutory duty, see para 3.21.

89 EA, s 19. This procedure was used in respect of a super-complaint about home credit: see [2004] CCA News, Autumn 6. For class actions, see generally, para 3.18.

90 E.g. *R v Henn* [1980] 2 All ER 166, CJEC & HL (import of pornography); *Quietlynn Ltd v Southend-on-Sea BC* [1991] 1 QB 454, CJEC (sex shops: see para 6.02); *Commission v Italy* [2003] CLY 1441, EC (food labelling).

the Treaty.[91] Further, any rules regarding 'selling arrangements' could go unchallenged, provided they apply to all traders within the territory of the Member State.[92]

2. *Competition controls.* Restrictive practices by businesses ('undertakings') which may affect inter-State trade may infringe the competition rules contained in Arts 81–2 of the Treaty of Rome, which are to be read in the light of the other policy objectives of the Treaty.[93]

   (a) **Art 81 [ex 85]** prohibits agreements or concerted practices (e.g. gentlemen's agreements) between undertakings which 'prevent, restrict or distort competition' insofar as they may affect trade between Member States and contains an indicative list of types of agreement which may be covered, e.g. price-fixing, control of production, market-sharing. Subject to a *de minimis* principle (see para 13.12), these provisions have been widely interpreted by the Commission and the courts to cover both horizontal and vertical agreements: 'horizontal' agreements are those between competitors at the same level in the distribution chain; and 'vertical' agreements are between those at different levels in the chain (see para 17.01). For instance, they have been invoked to strike down restrictions on the import of goods,[94] franchise agreements dividing markets,[95] territorial restrictions on manufacturers' guarantees,[96] advertisements (see para 8.06), dealers' rings (see para 10.13) and origin marking (see para 4.10); and in 2005-6 the EU announced an investigation into retail banking and credit card charges (see para 2.28). As this net is cast so widely, there is provision in the Treaty for the Commission to exempt agreements which meet certain criteria and are, on balance, beneficial (Art 81(3)): such agreements can be registered with the Commission with a view to obtaining individual exemption by Decision (see para 1.03A); and, even in advance of such application, the Commission has granted some block exemptions.[97]

   (b) **Art 82 [ex 86]** prohibits those who hold a dominant market position within the Community from abusing that position: the Treaty gives a number of examples of such abusive conduct, e.g. unfair buying or selling prices,

---

91  *Stoke-on-Trent City Council v B & Q plc* [1993] AC 900, HL. Cf. *Chisholm v Kirklees MBC* [1993] ICR 826 (no sex bias in Sunday trading law: see generally, para 4.23).

92  *Konsumentombudsman (KO) v Gourmet International Products AB* [2001] All ER (EC) 308, CJEC (advertisement for alcohol). As to alcohol advertising, see Tayleur (2001) 151 NLJ 859.

93  See generally Benjamin, *Sale of Goods*, 6th edn, para 3-041; Chitty on *Contract*, 28th edn, para 42-003, *et seq*. They may be enforced by injunction: see para 29.39.

94  *Ford Werke AG etc v EC Commission* [1985] 3 CMLR 528, CJEC (action to prevent Ford restricting the import of new Ford cars into the UK. Ford have subsequently given an undertaking to the OFT: see 1986 Annual Report, 77; and fn 97, below). See also *British Leyland v EC Commission* [1987] 1 CMLR 185, CJEC.

95  *Pronuptia de Paries GmbH etc v Schillgalis* [1986] I CMLR 414, CJEC. See generally Adams [1986] JBL 205, esp. 214–17.

96  See Twigg-Flesner, *Consumer Product Guarantees* (2003) 157–8; and generally para 17.09A.

97  E.g. EU Regulation 123/85 exempts new motor vehicle distribution agreements, which allow motor manufacturers to impose restrictions on competition between their dealers; but see *Modern markets: confident consumers* (1999, Cm. 4410) para 2.15. Block exempt agreements may still fall foul of Art 82, and were replaced by a narrower exemption in October 2003, allowing dealers to stock more than one brand of car.

predatory pricing, import/export bans. However, art 82 does not extend to refusing to supply an insolvent buyer.[98]

The above directly applicable rules (see para 1.03A) render automatically null and void not the whole agreement, but only those parts of agreements which restrict competition between Member States;[99] but they do not extend to agreements which affect trade exclusively (a) within one Member State,[100] or (b) outside the EU,[101] though these may be subject to the UK domestic rules (see para 2.14). Even where prosecution of breaches of Arts 81 and 82 does fall within EU competence, as from 2004 the EU (by Regulation 1/2003) has allowed enforcement by national authorities (see para 2.14).

**[2.14] UK competition controls on business**. At common law, as between the immediate parties to a contract for the supply of goods, the position is this. As regards vertical restrictions,[102] they may be binding insofar as they relate to the goods supplied but unenforceable as being in restraint of trade where it relates to goods other than those supplied under that agreement;[103] and as between the more remote parties in the chain of distribution, there is no privity of contract and the English Courts rejected the notion that contractual restrictions on the use of goods could run with those goods.[104] As regards horizontal restrictions,[102] such agreements were subject to the (now replaced: see para 2.12) restraint of trade doctrine,[105] though auction rings were upheld.[106]

*The Competition Act 1998 (CA)*. The CA provides a new set of competition rules modelled on the EU provisions (see para 2.13) and should be read consistently with them (CA, s 60).

(a) **Chapter I prohibitions (cf Art 81 [ex 85])**. The CA prohibits agreements which are implemented in the UK and whose purpose or effect is 'the prevention, restriction or distortion of competition within the UK' (CA, s 2(1)), e.g. the enquiry into *MasterCard* interchange fees.[107] Certain classes of agreement are excluded from the Act (CA, s 3 and Scheds 1–4, e.g. mergers), the Director has

---

98  *Leyland Daf v Automotive Products* [1993] BCC 389, CA. Cf. SGA, s 41(1): see para 24.10.

99  *Van Den Bergh Foods Ltd v Commission of the EU* [2004] 4 CMLR 1. UK courts will apply the familiar 'blue pencil' test to it: *Chemidus Wavin v TERI* [1978] 3 CMLR 514; and Chitty, *Op cit.*, para 42-065.

100  *Tepea BV v EU Commission* [1978] 2 CMLR 392.

101  Unless the agreement made outside Member States is to fix charges within Member States: *Re Wood Pulp Cartel* [1988] 4 CMLR 392.

102  See para 2.13.

103  See *Palmolive Co (of England) v Freedman* [1928] Ch 264, CA; *Esso Petroleum Co Ltd v Harper's Garage (Stourport) Ltd* [1968] AC 269, HL.

104  E.g. purported restrictions in wholesale contracts as to the retail get-up of goods: *Taddy v Sterious* [1904] 1 Ch 354; *McGruther v Pitcher* [1904] 2 Ch 306, CA. But consider the tort of wrongful interference with contract and industrial property rights, e.g. patents or trade marks (see para 12.03).

105  *Att-Gen of Commonwealth of Australia v Adelaide Steamship Co* [1913] AC 781, PC; trade codes of practice (see para 3.12).

106  *Rawlings v General Trading Co* [1921] I KB 635. However, such rings are now a criminal offence (see para 10.13), and therefore unenforceable.

107  CA98/05/05, involved an OFT enquiry under both Art 81 of the Treaty and s 2 of the CA into the interchange fees charged within the UK by MasterCard members entering four-party transactions (see para 2.28). The OFT issued a Decision that those fees infringed both provisions insofar as they recouped costs in excess of money transmission costs (see para 2.15).

power to grant individual exemptions[108] and there are also arrangements for block exemptions.[109]

(b) **Chapter II prohibitions (cf Art 82 [ex 86])**. The CA will prohibit the abuse by an undertaking of a dominant market position in the UK (s 18). Again, notification of abuses may be made to the DG (CA, ss 20–24) and certain cases are excluded (CA, s 19 and Scheds 1 and 3, e.g. mergers).

Having determined that the above rules have been broken, in the absence of compliance with its directions,[110] the OFT may apply to the court for an order to secure observance of his determination (CA, s 34). The Competition Commission of the OFT has two functions: (1) to act as an appeals tribunal for the enforcement of the above Chapter I and Chapter II provisions (CA, s 45 and Sched 7) under the mechanism laid down;[111] and (2) to replace the old Monopolies and Mergers Commission (see para 2.12). For our purposes, a good example of (2) is that the Commission may institute formal enquiries,[112] with a view to reporting monopolies to Parliament. Parliament may then make a statutory instrument: previously, these Statutory Orders were made under (the now repealed) s 91 of the FTA;[113] but thereafter they are to be made following market investigations under Pt 4 of the EA. Findings of fact by the OFT may be relied on in civil proceedings (CA, s 58). Accounts of enforcement are now to be found in the *Annual Reports* of the OFT.

# FINANCING THE PRICE

**[2.15] The consumer's obligation**. The consumer's need to pay the price in order to acquire legitimately the object of his desire gives rise to two different issues.

1. *Transmission of the price*. Assuming that the consumer has at his disposal sufficient money, he can safely enter into a cash sale under which he agrees to pay the price demanded (see para 23.01) by way of a lump sum at the moment the goods are delivered to him (see para 23.16). If the price is relatively small, it is likely to be so paid by handing over money (as to legal tender, see para 23.14), nowadays usually withdrawn from an ATM (see para 2.24). Alternatively, supermarket checkouts may offer cashback facilities: the consumer deliberately overpays for goods purchased, e.g. by plastic card, and is given the difference in cash from the till. In consumer transactions, larger sums were commonly paid by cheque (see para 7.24), but nowadays are more likely to be effected by

---

108 CA, s 4, provided they meet the criteria laid down in s 9. He may vary or cancel these exemptions.
109 CA, ss 6–9. These will automatically include all the EU block exemptions, and are known as 'parallel exemptions'.
110 E.g. undertakings (14.4.05) about their treatment of suppliers were given by supermarkets (under FTA, s 88; now repealed).
111 CA, as amended by Pt 5 of the EA. Appeals lie to the independent Appeals Tribunal (EA, Pt 2).
112 E.g. the 2004 enquiry into store cards (see OFT, *AR–2003/4*, 75; and para 2.24); the 2005 enquiry into home credit (see para 5.02) and PPI (see para 24.48) following super-complaints (see para 4.19).
113 E.g. credit card services (see para 2.28); the Supply of New Cars Order 2000 SI 2088; and the extended warranties order (see para 17.09).

payment card (see para 2.23) or BACS (see para 23.13): both of these are devices for transmitting money from the consumer's bank account to the supplier's bank account. The original providers of such money transmission services were the mainstream financial intermediaries described below (see para 2.17), whose activities are co-ordinated by APACS.[114] In an increasingly cashless society, the relatively small proportion of the population which does not have a money transmission account (the unbanked)[115] can find that makes life difficult.[116] But, spurred on by the Government, some banks are without much signs of enthusiasm experimenting with basic bank accounts (sometimes termed universal bank accounts), which are simple money transmission accounts operated through ATMs[117] and without overdraft facility or cheque-book.[118] Alternatively, the unbanked may obtain access to money transmission by way of a credit union (see below) or cheque-casher (see para 7.28) or the restructured Post Office.[119] Credit unions are financial co-operatives which also provide low interest loans (see para 15.19). In 2005, the EU published a draft Payments Directive.

2.  *Financing the price.* Particularly in relation to larger value items, consumers may not be able or willing to pay the price by way of a single lump sum at delivery of the goods (see above); and saving the price can be difficult for the unbanked.[120] For those consumers with a bank account,[116] it is possible to pay by regular instalments transmitted from that account by way of either standing orders or direct debits (see para 23.14). We have already examined the types of transaction which may then be used to facilitate immediate acquisition of the goods (see para 1.03). But somebody has to finance such arrangements: most consumers are likely to apply to one of the mainline financiers (see para 2.16), especially to pay by personal loan or credit card (see paras 2.17; 2.28); but the choice of low income consumers is likely to depend on whether or not they are waged.[121] The low full-time waged are likely to use mainstream credit,

---

114  The Association for Payment Clearing Services (APACS) *inter alia* oversees the clearing of paper cheques and plastic cards. The OFT has started an enquiry into payment systems (*AR–2003/4* 82) and sought to pressurise the banking industry into voluntary reform by setting up a four year Payment Systems Task Force: see its *Second Annual Progress Report* (May 2006: OFT 849).

115  The unbanked is usually estimated at about 15% of the population. Only about 10% of employees are now paid in cash. See OFT, *Vulnerable Consumers and Financial Services* (1999), 24–25; 51 Quarterly Account 4.

116  OFT, *Vulnerable Consumers and Financial Services* (1999), 6; 54 QA 1; OFT, *2000 AR* 21. For the difficulties of accessing money transmission and financing services in deprived areas, see: Dyson & Conaty, *The Case for a Community Banking Partnership Approach* (2005); Goff, McKillop & Ferguson, *Building Better Credit Unions* (2005).

117  For definition of basic bank accounts, see the Banking Code of Practice, para 17; 77 QA 18. For worries that the financially disadvantaged will in practice only have available to them charging ATMs (see para 2.24), see the *Fifth Report of the Treasury Committee of the House of Commons, Session 2004–5.*

118  Because of the legal constraints on minors repaying credit (see para 10.18), these facilities would also be more suitable for minors. By March 2004, there were 5.22M such basic bank accounts: [2004] 8 Credit Today 8. Of these, some 1.55M are 'Universal' accounts, which can also be operated through Post Offices (see below).

119  Under the Postal Services Act 2000. See Ryder [2001] JBL 510, at 519–21; Field (2001) 86 Adviser 44. They have since been renamed Post Office Card Accounts (POCAs). Take-up has been very slow; but in 2005 a loan facility was added. For Postal Orders, see para 23.14.

120  Kempson & Whyley, *Understanding and Combatting Financial Exclusion* (1999).

121  See Collard & Kempson, *Affordable Credit* (2005) 10–12.

especially credit cards, personal loans and store cards, but may use the following: agency mail order (see home shopping: para 8.19); credit unions (above), perhaps part-financed by the banks;[122] local Christmas clubs (see para 15.18); moneylenders (see paras 6.09 and 7.02–4A); cheque-cashers (see para 7.28); and borrowing from friends and family.[123] However, households dependant on state benefits and occasional earnings are presently most frequently financed as follows:[121] though often credit-impaired and so lacking access to mainstream financiers,[116] by commercial lenders, such as home collected credit (see para 5.02), home shopping catalogues (see para 8.19), sub-prime personal loans (see para 7.04A) and unlicensed moneylenders (loan sharks: see para 6.20); or by social lenders, such as the Social Fund,[124] other sources of social finance[125] and friends and family.[123] It is this category of borrowers who are particularly likely to be over-indebted (see para 6.10).

## The financiers

**[2.16] Introduction**. This section is concerned with the situation where the would-be consumer desirous of obtaining early enjoyment of goods does not wish to pay the full price on or before delivery of the goods.[126] From the viewpoint of that consumer, the necessary credit facilities may be extended to him by one of two persons:

1. *His goods-supplier*. If the goods-supplier seeks to provide such credit facilities to consumers in respect of a significant part of his turnover, he could raise the necessary capital from a third party[127] and provide what is here termed 'vendor credit' to the consumer (see para 2.19). Alternatively, he could simply act as agent for a third-party financier,[128] in which case although the situation may look the same to the consumer, the transaction does in fact fall within the second category (below).

2. *A financier*. A third-party financier may be invited to extend credit facilities **to** the consumer rather than to the goods-supplier in what is here termed 'lender credit' (see paras 2.20–24) by financiers whose normal economic function is to act as financial intermediaries (see para 2.17).

Surveying this field in 1971, the Crowther Report on Consumer Credit (see generally, para 5.03) made the following fundamental observations (para 1.2.2):

---

122 It is hoped that the Banks will provide or pay for a basic centralised infrastructure of the (voluntary) credit unions. This might replicate the infrastructure of the successful credit unions. The scheme would be regulated by the FSA (see para 3.02).

123 In CCA parlance, friends and family are non-commercial lenders (see para 5.18) and do not require a CCA licence (see para 6.12).

124 Under the Social Security Act 1986, the Social Fund Budgeting Loan Scheme provides interest-free loans deducted at source from benefits. See Which?, *Life After Debt* (2003); (2005) 76 QA 6; the White Paper, *Fair, Clear and Competitive: the Consumer Credit Market in the 21st Century* (Dec 2003, Cm. 6040), paras 5.47–8.

125 See the 2003 White Paper (above), paras 5.46 and 5.53–4; Collard & Kempson, *Op. cit.*, 4–5.

126 For the historical development of consumer credit see the Crowther Report on *Consumer Credit* (Cmnd. 4596), Chap 2.1.

127 The legal ramifications of raising finance mostly fall outside the scope of this work. But see indirect financing: para 2.22.

128 Either utilising one of the traditional forms of lender credit (see paras 2.20–4) or 'private label schemes' (see para 7.09).

(1) In respect of both vendor and lender credit,[129] there are two possible methods of financing: an instalment credit contract, or a cash sale plus loan (see para 1.03).

(2) Whilst some loans are entirely independent of the acquisition of goods (loan credit), e.g. bank overdraft, moneylender's or pawnbroker's loan, others are closely related thereto (sale credit),[130] this distinction being taken up later (see paras 5.29, 7.05 and 25.01).

(3) It may also be relevant to consider in relation to lender credit whether or not the goods and finance are being supplied as part of one single package, i.e. whether the vendor and financier are *connected* in what is really a joint enterprise, the financier then being described as a 'connected lender'.[131]

**[2.17/8] Financial intermediaries.** In the lender credit situation (see para 2.16), the financier is unlikely to finance such loans from his own resources, but may himself raise that money on the market.[132] All such deposit-taking will be supervised by the Financial Services Authority (see para 3.02). This paragraph is concerned with the most important types of such financial intermediary operating in our field,[133] the so-called 'prime lenders'.[134]

1. *The clearing banks.* Traditionally, these banks operated money transmission[135] through chequeing accounts and lent by way of overdraft on current account, sometimes with a provision for collateral security (see Chap 25). In modern times, they have sought to mechanise personal banking by the large-scale use of computers and telephones.[136] Thus, cash withdrawals are increasingly accomplished by automatic teller (ATMs: see para 2.24); the old paper-based transmission systems, e.g. cheques (see para 7.24) are being replaced by the electronic transfer of funds (EFT), e.g. debit cards, charge cards (see respectively, paras 2.25 and 2.27); and telephone and internet banking (see para 8.17) may displace branch transactions.[137] The banks have also sought to compete in

---

129 The expressions 'vendor credit' and 'lender credit' are here used in the sense seemingly utilised in para 5.2.1, *et seq.*, of the Crowther Report, and not that adopted when describing the pre-CCA law (paras 1.2.2 and 4.1.2).

130 E.g. bank personal loan, instalment credit contracts, all trade credit. Instead of sale or loan credit, the Crowther Report (para 5.2.12) uses the terminology 'purchase-money credit' and 'non-purchase-money credit', which is derived from the American UCC, Art 9–107.

131 See below, para 5.32. It has been pointed out that, whilst most loans by connected lenders will be purchase-money loans and most loans by independent lenders will not, this will not necessarily be the case: Crowther Report, para 6.2.23. For connected lenders, see para 16.11.

132 As to alternative methods of raising money by 'unitization', see Ferran, *Mortgage Securitisation*.

133 In relation to the quotation of interest rates by the financial intermediary, there is this difference: the quotation of rates to consumer-borrowers is carefully controlled by the CCA (see para 8.25); but the quotation of rates to consumer-depositors falls under s 32 of the Banking Act 1987.

134 For 'prime' and 'sub-prime' lenders, see para 7.04A. The distinction between the two sorts of lending is beginning to blur as the banks move into 'near-prime' lending: [2003] 11 Credit Today 35.

135 The use of money transmission services by criminals to conceal the criminal source of funds may now constitute the offence of money laundering, a topic beyond the scope of this work.

136 See generally the Jack Report on *Banking Services* (1989, Cm. 622), Chaps 9 and 10; and Arora, *Electronic Banking and the Law*, 2nd edn, Chap 5; Guest & Lloyd, *Consumer Credit Law*, para 2-188.

137 Telephone and internet banking particularly raise issues within the Data Protection Act 1998, such as the security of data: see further, para 8.17.

the business of financing the acquisition of goods for consumption by three means:[138]

(a) They instituted the Personal Loan, by which they meant an unsecured loan for a stipulated period made for the express purpose of, and tied to, the acquisition of goods. At the same time, the banks accepted the utilisation of overdrafts for similar purposes, though these are repayable on demand.

(b) They began to compete in the provision of payment cards (see para 2.24) and of finance for the acquisition of dwelling houses (see below).

(c) They made arrangements with supermarkets to set up banking operations within the supermarket halls, especially making deposits and granting loans.

(d) In the twenty-first century, many bank accounts have become accessible by telephone and then on-line banking (for internet sales, see para 8.17A).

2. *Finance companies.*[139] Such companies first developed in the nineteenth century to meet the needs of businesses to acquire on instalments plant and machinery, e.g. the wagon companies; and later similar companies were founded to satisfy the wants of consumers, e.g. for motor vehicles. The absence of a high-street branch network in the twentieth century contributed to their emphasis on doing business by way of direct financing (see para 2.21); and they have developed business lending (asset financing) on both fixed and current assets, e.g. factoring (see para 2.22) and equipment leasing (see para 1.18). The 1980s witnessed expansion into payment cards (see above), mortgages (usually second) of dwelling houses and unsecured personal loans, e.g. for white goods. In the 1990s, finance companies began to operate current accounts for consumers[140] and to issue cheque-book on them. This century, the wide range of credit services available on-line has significantly reduced the need for branch networks.

3. *Building societies.*[141] As recently as 1965, building societies were a specialist form of financial intermediary (with a mutual status) and high-street branch network, which concentrated on loans to finance the acquisition of dwellings: they were required by law to take security in the form of (in practice usually first) mortgages on land (see generally Chap 25). However, under the Building Societies Act 1986 (as amended), building societies are now able to make unsecured loans and offer almost a full range of consumer banking services, e.g. current accounts, overdrafts, money transmission; and many large building societies have turned themselves into banks.

4. *Credit unions*, at least one of which has begun to offer mortgages (see para 15.19).

---

138 Each bank now sets its own lending rates of interest; and for bankers duties, see para 7.03.

139 Finance companies have their own industry base interest rate, Finance House Base Rate (FHBR).

140 Insofar as finance companies allow consumers to accumulate credit balances on these accounts, they will also need banking licences (as to which, see fn 132, above): (1999) 53 CC5/37.

141 Although financial intermediaries, building societies are exempt from the Banking Act 1987 (s 4 and Sched 2 (as amended)), provided they fall within the Building Societies Act 1986 (as amended). The 1986 Act controls both the borrowing and lending of these institutions, though the latter is overridden by the CCA in respect of regulated loans (see para 5.13, *et seq.*).

5. *Collected (or home) credit* (see para 5.02).

## Vendor credit

**[2.19]** Where one person supplies both the goods and the 'loan' of their price (see para 2.16), that may be done in either of the following ways:[142]

(1) The supplier and consumer enter into one of the forms of instalment credit contract in relation to goods (see para 2.16). This form was commonly used by high street retailers (see below) and is still popular with mail-order houses (see para 8.19) and door-step sellers (see para 5.02).

(2) The supplier and consumer enter into both a cash sale of goods (see para 1.06) *and* a contract of loan.[143]

In the case of retail stores, it is becoming common for the retailer to supply the private consumer with a 'store card',[144] though, particularly with corner shops, there is still to be found instead the system of saving in advance through a club (see para 15.18). Where the retailer is making a loan to a private consumer, one of the following accounting systems is commonly used:[145]

(i) *An open account*, e.g. monthly, whereby the consumer pays the entire price for all the goods purchased during the preceding month on a designated day.[146]

(ii) *A revolving or budget account*, whereby the consumer agrees to make regular payments to the retailer of an agreed amount (e.g. £10 by monthly direct debit) and is then allowed to purchase goods from that retailer up to the value of a designated multiple (say 24 times) of that sum (e.g. £240), it being agreed that the credit shall never exceed that sum (the credit line), but that new purchases on credit may be made insofar as the outstanding credit falls below that amount.[147] Modern forms tend to utilise a 'budget card': it may involve loans of money to the consumer, or in some cases to the retailer.[148] This form of business will be discussed later (para 7.08).

(iii) *An option account*, which is an open account with a retailer whereunder the customer has the option, when presented with the (say) monthly statement, to

---

142 See generally the Crowther Report on Consumer Credit (Cmnd. 4596), Chap 2.5.

143 As to contracts of loan, see generally Chap 7. In the trade, it was customary to treat the sale and loan together, as giving rise to a credit sale, but it seems likely that English law would regard the transaction as a separate sale and loan: the trade view was prompted by urgent need to avoid the now repealed Moneylenders Acts (see para 6.09).

144 Store or budget cards tend to charge comparatively high rates of interest; and some stores will accept only their own cards for payments otherwise than in cash. This has led to a competition order (see para 2.24).

145 Under a private-label scheme, the loan is in fact provided by a third party: see para 2.24.

146 See the Crowther Report (above), para 2.5.1–2.

147 See *ibid*, para 2.5.3; Goode, *HP Law & Practice*, 896–8. This form of business is regarded as a useful way of keeping the customer psychologically tied to a particular outlet; but it is rigid in that the amount of the regular payment is fixed: compare credit cards (see para 7.09).

148 Some variants allow the consumer to continue making periodic payments even though his entire debt has been repaid ('save and borrow' accounts): at this stage, the consumer may become the creditor.

defer payment under the above revolving credit system.[149] Frequently, interest is not charged if the entire balance is discharged each month;[150] and, where most of the retailer's business is done on credit, any rate of interest charged may be nominally reduced by assimilating it into the cash price of the goods (but see para 8.27).

## Lender credit[151]

**[2.20] Introduction.** Where the goods and 'loan' are to be supplied by two separate people (see para 2.16), the obvious pattern would be for the goods supplier (dealer) to enter into a contract of sale of the goods for the price to be paid immediately by the consumer and for the financier to lend that price to the consumer.[152] However, this pattern had the disadvantage that it usually fell within the now-repealed Moneylenders Act 1900–1927: whilst this did not affect the clearing banks, which were exempt from those Acts,[153] it did deter other financiers who consequently adopted the following traditional forms of business:

1. *Direct financing*. For items of large unit value such as would justify the cost of setting up for each transaction a separate agreement directly with a customer, e.g. a motor vehicle, direct financing was used (see para 2.21).

2. *Indirect financing*. For items of smaller unit value, where it would be uneconomic to set up separate transactions but where the size of turnover would compensate for less individual control, it was common to bundle transactions together in what became known as block discounting or indirect financing (see para 2.22).

However, with the removal in 1974 of the artificial restriction represented by the Moneylenders Acts, financiers became free to conduct their business by way of their making loans to consumers (see para 2.23). This immediately threw into prominence the issue of security: was the financier prepared to make an unsecured loan to the consumer; or did he require the comfort of rights in some assets before parting with his money? In direct financing, the financier would automatically attain such security because he became the owner of the goods financed (asset financing); and thus direct financing has continued unabated for higher priced items, e.g. cars. However, the (albeit impaired) security of indirect financing has been largely relinquished for the (even cheaper to administer) simple loan,[154]

---

149 Goode, *Op. cit.*, 898. Cf. three-party credit cards: para 2.24. These are sometimes mistaken for fixed-sum credit: (1993) 48 CC 2/12.
150 This may produce up to five weeks' 'free credit' in respect of goods or services, but is unlikely to be offered in respect of cash advances.
151 In North America this is termed 'sales financing': see Geva: *Product Defences*, 3–4.
152 For the general rules as to the payment of the price and other debts, see para 23.13. The financier may himself finance this business by factoring the consumer debts: see generally, para 2.22.
153 The Moneylenders Act 1900, s 6(d) obviously exempted banks, but was shown to have no general application to even the largest finance company: *United Dominions Trust Ltd v Kirkwood* [1966] 2 QB 431, CA.
154 See para 16.03. For the mortgaging of land and goods, see generally, Chap 25. But see the comment at para 2.23.

commonly effected by credit card (see para 2.28), or less often by credit card cheque (see para 7.28).

**[2.21] Direct financing.**[155]

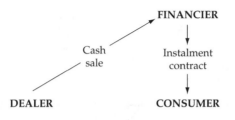

Under this system, the goods-supplier (dealer) makes a cash sale of the goods to the financier, who then enters into an instalment contract (see para 1.03) with the consumer.[156] The normal course of events is that the consumer selects his goods, typically a motor vehicle, from the dealer's stock and then completes an instalment contract and sometimes other[157] forms in respect of the goods.[158] In addition, the consumer may have to find a surety (see para 24.04, *et seq.*) and will normally have to pay a substantial deposit to the dealer.[159] The next step is for the dealer to forward the completed forms (plus any surety required) to the finance company, together with an invoice, which will contain details of the goods and their cash price, and will constitute an offer by the dealer to sell the goods to the finance company, commonly with full recourse.[160] If the finance company decides to accept the business, the agreement-form will usually be signed by one of its officers; and a copy dispatched to the consumer, which will normally amount to the company's acceptance (see para 10.08). At the same time, the finance company will notify the dealer that the proposal has been accepted, and that it is in order for him to deliver the goods to the consumer.[161] The result of this complicated transaction will thus be that: (a) the finance company will normally acquire title to the goods financed from the dealer (see para 16.03); and (b) there will be no primary contractual relationship between the dealer and the consumer, although there may be a collateral contract between them (see para 16.18). Sometimes, the dealer collects the instalments on behalf of the financier (agency collection);[162] and some financiers sell blocks of their debt by way of securitisation.[163]

---

155 See Goode, *HP Law & Practice*, 2nd edn, 124–51, 129–132b; *Commercial Law*, 3rd edn, 701–2, 723–9.

156 In the case of simple hiring, this will take the form of an equipment lease, such as sales-aid leasing (see para 1.18): see Goode [1981] JBL 239; Soper & Munro, *The Leasing Handbook*, 50–2.

157 The financier will usually require information about the consumer for their credit-vetting procedures (see para 8.35). Sometimes this information is included in the instalment contract form; but in others, a separate 'proposal form' is used.

158 For express terms, see generally, para 11.07. In law the consumer's signature thereon will usually amount to an offer to take the goods on those terms: see para 10.08.

159 For the liability of the finance company for the return of that deposit if the proposal is not accepted, see para 16.05.

160 For recourse provisions, see para 16.16. The invoice may contain the conditions of the proposed sale, or be subject to a Master Agreement (as to which see Macleod, *Consumer Sales Law*, 1st edn, para 16.21).

161 Normal finance company practice is to pay out the dealer only against the consumer's signed receipt.

162 Goode, *Op. cit.*, 125.     163 See generally Ferran, *Mortgage Securitisation* (1992).

**[2.22] Indirect financing**.[164] Here, the goods-supplier (dealer) enters into an instalment contract (see para 1.03) with the consumer,[165] typically in respect of a domestic appliance, so initially extending the credit to the consumer, just as in vendor credit (see para 2.19).

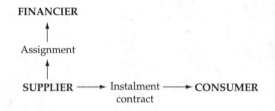

The dealer would then have two rights:

1. *His contractual right to the instalments*. Thus, the cash price due under a credit or conditional sale is a present legal chose in action (see para 2.02) in the hands of the dealer, as is the hire rent due under a fixed-term hiring; but the rent which may become due under a periodic hiring (see para 1.25), whether under a simple hiring or hp, is only a future chose (see para 7.18).

2. *His residuary proprietary rights to the goods*. A conditional seller, or one who supplies goods on hp or simple hiring *prima facie* retains the general property in the goods, which he may reclaim by suing in tort (see para 19.04).

The dealer would collect all his instalment agreements over a given period, e.g. a month, and then assign his interest in them to a financier in a block (hence the term 'block discounting'). That (monthly) assignment might be absolute, that is, a transfer of the dealer's entire interest; or it might be by way of security, i.e. by way of mortgage, charge or trust. Normally, this monthly assignment would be closely regulated by a complicated Master Agreement. Instalments are normally collected on behalf of the financier by the dealer unless and until the dealer defaults, so enabling the dealer to continue regular contact with the consumer.[166]

*Factoring*. Analytically similar to indirect financing, factoring is a form of business under which the dealer raises money on the debts owed to him by his trade customer ('accounts receivable') by selling them to a 'factor'.[167] Unfortunately, 'factoring' is one of those confusing expressions which has acquired several different meanings: a nineteenth-century factor would be a businessman who either sold goods (usually by retail) on his own behalf or as agent of another;[168] whereas the modern factor referred to here tends instead to specialise primarily in the sale and purchase of commercial debt (see para 2.27).

---

164 See Goode, *HP Law & Practice*, 2nd edn, 125–6; *Commercial Law*, 3rd edn, 702–9.

165 See Macleod, *Consumer Sales Law*, Butterworth edition, paras 16.22, *et seq.*

166 Where the dealer is a registered company, the system may be amended in the light of the proposed Companies Bill (see para 25.34).

167 E.g. *Re Charge Card Services Ltd* (set out at para 2.27). See generally, Goode, *Op. cit.*, 746, *et seq.* Adams, *Factoring*; Biscoe, *Law & Practice of Credit Factoring*; Salinger, *Factoring*, 3rd edn.

168 If entrusted with possession of his principal's goods. Compare a 'broker' who tended not to be entrusted with possession: see Fridman, *Agency*, 7th edn, 40–4. The 'factor' in this nineteenth century sense gave his name to a series of Acts of Parliament: see para 21.24.

Indirect financing and the similar factoring have become so specialised that they are now beyond the scope of this work.[169]

**[2.23] Loan financing and payment cards** This paragraph is concerned with the financing of consumer transactions by way of a loan to the consumer.

$$\textbf{FINANCIER}$$
$$\downarrow$$
$$\text{Loan}$$
$$\downarrow$$

**DEALER** $\xrightarrow{\text{Cash sale}}$ **CONSUMER**

Of all the various types of consumer loan financing (see para 15.17), by far the most important is payment cards,[170] which in the UK started with the launch of Barclay-card in 1966. The late twentieth century mushroom growth in the use of embossed plastic payment cards is part of the worldwide developments of retail banking.[171] There is a global technical specification for payment cards laid down by the International Standards Organisation (ISO), the ISO rules being embodied in British Standards (see para 3.08).

To try and combat counterfeiting, cards normally embody elaborate holograms. Nevertheless, the unscrupulous still seem to acquire supplies of blank cards and then persuade, e.g. a waiter, to run a customer's card through a swipe machine twice, so generating personal card details ('skimming') from which a card may be counterfeited; and there is substantial postal fraud.[172]

An important problem for bankers is to identify the person applying for payment by card, so reducing fraud.[173] Originally, reliance was placed on the human comparison of the signature which the card-holder was supposed to place on the card. Not only is signature comparison unreliable, e.g. the signature stripe may be replaced and depends on human recognition, but it can be entirely circumvented by the theft of blank cards and cannot be used for telephone and internet sales. So, there was introduced the personal identification number (PIN) system, where a machine compared the information on the magnetic stripe on a card with a matching PIN typed in by the card-holder: a unique four-digit number will be secretly issued to the card-holder, so that supposedly only the holder could type

---

169  For indirect financing, see Macleod, *Consumer Sales Law*, Butterworth edition, paras 16.22–8.

170  See Arora, *Electronic Banking*, 2nd edn, 108–9. There are EU Codes of Conduct relating to electronic payments (87/598/EEC) and systems (88/590/EEC): set out in Goode, *Consumer Credit Law & Practice*, Pt X, para 2.21, *et seq*.

171  See above, para 2.17. In 2005, plastic cards were used for 63% of all UK retail spending.

172  Card fraud increased by 20% in 2004. For counterfeit cards, see [2001] 5 *Which?* 14. Replacement cards tend to be posted out to consumers by card-issuers pre-activated, which enabled thieves to steal and use them to obtain some £80M in 2004: *Times* 11.3.05. Only if the card is regulated does the consumer have any statutory protection (CCA, s 66: see para 7.11).

173  For card-notification organisations, see the Jack Report on *Banking Services* (1989, Cm. 622), paras 11.13.17; and for counterfeit cards, see *ibid*, paras 11.18–22.

that number when inserting his card in a machine,[174] e.g. an ATM (see para 2.24). In the late 1990s card-issuers began to utilise 'smart-card' technology[175] to replace (insecure) magnetic stripes with information contained in a micro-chip embodied in the card. This micro-chip has been used to introduce from 2005 a complete replacement for signatures, under which a PIN is stored on the micro-chipped card, that card inserted in the retailer's till, the customer types his PIN on an attached key-pad (chip-and-pin cards) and the till authorises the transaction by comparing the two PINs.[176] This innovation should reduce EPOS (see para 2.06) card crime,[177] though not phone and internet (see paras 8.17; 8.17A; 8.17B) card-not-present crime; and it may shift some crime to identity fraud (see para 10.15). Still in development, there are other barametric identification devices, allowing machine comparison of, e.g. eye, voice or finger-print, digital signature; and devices to combat internet and other distance crime are planned.[178]

In a fast-developing market, e.g. affinity cards, UK payment cards now include various functions, sometimes combined on multi-purpose cards.[179] These cards fall into two groups:

(1) A two-party card issued by the supplier of the goods or services (see para 2.24);

(2) A three-party card issued by a third-party financier (see paras 2.25 and 2.28).

There are also systems helping retailers detect stolen ('hot') cards.[180] Modern payment cards tend to be marketed with a range of perquisites.[181] The EU is beginning to think in terms of introducing their own legislative control over such electronic payment mechanisms.[182]

**[2.24] Two-party cards**. The following types of two-party card may be noticed:

1.  *Cash cards* with which the card-holder can, by use with appropriate security

---

174 The card-user has the practical difficulty of remembering his PINs without writing them down: unlike a signature system, this tends to put the risk on the card-holder: see the Banking Code of Practice, para 12; and below, para 3.12.

175 Visa issued its first 'smart card' in 1998. 'Smart cards' contain a micro-processor and memory chip, so dispensing with human intervention: see the Jack Report, *Op. cit.*, paras 11.24–28; Banking Ombudsman, *Annual Report 1995/6*, para 12.4; (1998) 52 CC5/29; (1998) *CCA News*, Spring 24; *Times* 19.5.01. For Electronic Fund Transfer, see para 2.17.

176 (2002) 56 CC/6 32; BCCA, (2003) 26 *Newsletter* 5. The effect may be to shift the risk of crime from the card-issuer to card-holder (see *Times* 25.3.06; 15.5.06).

177 Unfortunately, there appears to be a security gap because the UK Clearing Banks have opted for the (cheaper) SDA system rather than the (safer) DDA system.

178 Devices planned would make use of chip-and-pin technology on-line to verify that the card being used belongs to the person placing the on-line order by internet or phone (*Times* 14.11.05). Consumer names and PINs are being remotely stolen from the computers of internet suppliers (*Times* 15.4.06).

179 See the Jack Report, *Op. cit.*, paras 11.10–12. From the viewpoint of consumer security, is a single all-purpose card desirable? The problem is compounded with high-value ('gold') cards.

180 Originally based on circulated lists, modern systems depend on lower floor levels and almost instantaneous telephone access by the retailer to the computerised records of credit bureaux: see para 8.36.

181 See [2000] 7 *Which?* 20.

182 See the draft Directive referred to at para 2.15.

(see para 2.23) withdraw cash from an Automated Teller Mechanism (ATM).[183] The debt will be electronically debited to the card-holder's current account by EFT (see para 2.17), usually immediately. Since the various ATM systems have been linked together so that customers of any bank may use any machine, ATMs have become an increasingly popular method of withdrawing cash,[184] including 'convenience ATMs'.[185] In effect, the cash card is a two-party debit card (see para 2.25), even if it can be used in ATMs owned by third parties.[186] ATMs are susceptible to fraud, both at the ATM[187] and where cards are posted to consumers (see para 2.23).

2.  *Pre-payment cards*, where the card-holder pays on issue for the value held on a disposable card: although it is not legal tender (see para 23.14), the card-holder is in effect paying in advance for services, so that the card may be considered as akin to cash, e.g. a payment card for minors.[188] There are also being introduced a new generation of rechargeable ('stored value') smart cards (see para 2.23): not only could these be used to obtain goods and services, but they would also enable the creation of so-called 'electronic' or 'digital' money, which operates as a sort of 'cashless purse' to be used by insertion into a card-reader;[189] and, if that reader is linked to a telephone, it could work like an ATM in reverse.[190]

3.  *Budget or store cards*, enabling the card-holder to charge purchases in the issuing store to his account there, the card functioning as a verification of the customer's signature.[191] Such cards are sometimes a form of vendor credit (see para 2.19). Alternatively, they may function as a three-party card (see para 2.25), as where the retailer operates the card through a separate company, e.g. jointly with a Bank; or that separate company is in fact run by a financier

---

183  E.g. Switch/Maestro cards. See Arora, *Electronic Banking*, 2nd edn, Chap 5; the Jack Report on *Banking Services* (1989, Cm. 622), para 9.08; Guest & Lloyd, *Consumer Credit Law*, para 2-015.

184  The pricing of this service has given rise to competition issues: see [2000] 8 *Which?* 12; and generally, para 2.14.

185  Whereas the earlier ATMs tended to be at bank premises (and do not charge customers fees for use), 'convenience ATMs' are likely to be at other retail premises or places of entertainment and to charge. Convenience ATMs will soon amount to 50% and are disproportionately being placed where the poor will be charged: see the Fifth Report of the Treasury Committee of the House of Commons, Session 2004–5; [2005] 3 *Which?* 8. As to charges, see the Banking Code of Practice, para 5.

186  The third party usually merely acts as agent: Goode, *Consumer Credit Legislation*, para 549.5.

187  The commonest fraud is 'skimming', where the criminal places devices over the ATM to record a user's details and can then manufacture, within the hour, a duplicate card to extract money from that account via an ATM; but chip-and-pin cards are more difficult to so duplicate: see *Times* 11.11.04.

188  E.g. the Splash Maestro MasterCard (see *Times* 26.1.06); the ICE Cash2Go card (see *Times* 25.3.06). For the legal difficulty with extending credit to minors, see para 10.18.

189  E.g. the Mondex card (see *Times* 5.9.94 and 24.2.97); APS pre-paid MasterCard with chip & pin ((2005) 35 BCCA Newsletter 2). The system is being developed for use on the internet (see *Times* 9.1.96). The issue of such electronic cheques has been brought within the FSMA (see para 3.02) registration system (2002 SI 682 and 2002 SI 765).

190  By extracting value from the card and passing it by phone to the supplier's bank account: see [1998] 6 *Which?* 41.

191  E.g. M&S, Dixons, Miss Selfridge. An attraction to retail issuers is that these cards have been shown to be a good way of enhancing customer loyalty: see (1994) 49 CC 1/27.

(private-label schemes), this being a disguised form of lender credit.[192] The OFT have conducted an enquiry into the high charges common on these cards;[193] and the Competition Commission has ordered that a wealth warning be placed on the product.[194]

**[2.25] Three-party cards.** These involve the introduction of a third-party financier (see para 2.17), who normally sets up a revolving credit account (see para 2.19) for the consumer, which the latter operates by way of a plastic payment card.[195] Such accounts may be divided according to whether or not the extension of credit is an integral part of the system. If so,[196] they are properly termed 'credit cards'[197] and considered later (see para 2.28).

However, in the following types of three-party card, any element of credit granted to the consumer is incidental:

1. *Cheque guarantee card*, first introduced into the UK in 1969 and for use where the card-holder pays for goods or services by modern cheque (see para 7.28). In exhibiting to the supplier of goods or services a cheque card with matching signature, the consumer is proffering the bank's promise that a cheque with that signature will be met up to the amount and on the conditions specified (see para 2.26).

2. *Debit card*, e.g. Maestro, which the card-holder presents at the point of sale (with either verifying signature or PIN), enabling the supplier of goods or services to debit electronically the sale to the card-holder's bank account within a pre-set limit.[198] First introduced in 1987, these will be examined later (see para 23.15), but for now may be thought of as a sort of electronic cheque.[199] For many years, it has been Bank of England policy to modernise money transmission by replacing (paper-based) cheques with (electronic-based) debit cards; and the usage of cheques has now declined sharply.[200]

3. *Charge card*, e.g. Diners, by production of which (with signature or PIN verification) the card-holder can obtain the immediate supply of the goods or services (see para 2.27); and the card-holder is normally expected to settle his bill to

---

192 See para 2.20. Cf. eponymous subsidiaries (see para 16.06). Distinguish loyalty cards: see para 8.13A.

193 Following a commitment to the Treasury Select Committee: (2003) 36 *Fair Trading* 5.

194 Under the *Store Market Investigation Order* (July 2006) of the Competition Commission acting under Pt 4 of the EA (see para 2.12), as from May 2007 a store card statement must contain the current APR, a wealth warning, the basis of insurance and other charges and provisions for payment by DD.

195 See para 2.24. Additionally, card-issuers sometimes also issue the consumer with a cheque book, so that the account may be operated like a traditional bank account: as to which, see paras 2.17; 7.28.

196 If so, use of that credit may be encouraged by the awarding of 'points' (see para 15.19).

197 In 2004, debit cards accounted for 56% (£12.9 billion) and credit cards 44% (£10.3 billion) of use.

198 E.g. Switch, Visa Delta. These cards may be used in conjunction with EFTPoS facilities at the cash-out, which machine-read the card and then debit the card-holder's bank account like an ATM. See further, para 23.15.

199 Campbell (1994) 13 Tr L 18 at 19.

200 Between 1993 and 2003, cheque usage fell by 40%; and, by 2003, only 6% of retail spending was still paid by cheque, as compared with over half by debit or credit card: APACS, *Cheques and cheque clearing* (2004) 5, 12.

the card-issuer in full at the end of each month,[201] though if he is entitled to roll over his debt it becomes a credit card.

**[2.26] Cheque guarantee cards.**[202] The commercial purpose of these cards is to persuade retailers to release goods against customer's cheques.[203] There are two dangers to the retailer in so releasing the goods: (a) the customer may have insufficient funds in his bank account to meet the cheque;[204] and (b) the customer may have forged the signature of the signatory to the bank account.[205] The question of whether a cheque guarantee card protected the retailer in event (b) was considered in *First Sport Ltd v Barclays Bank plc*:[206]

> A cheque book and cheque card issued by the Bank to a Mr Kahn were stolen from the latter. The trial judge found it likely that the genuine signature was removed from the card and replaced by the signature of the person who presented the cheque and card to the retailer. It followed that the alteration was probably undetectable. The Bank refused to meet the cheque when presented by the retailer on the valid grounds that the cheque had not been signed by Mr Kahn. Accordingly, the retailer sued the Bank on the cheque guarantee card.

The Court of Appeal held that the effect of the card was to convey a unilateral offer by the Bank to enter a collateral contract with the retailer. The terms of that contract were that, if the retailer complied with certain conditions,[207] the Bank would meet the cheque.[208] Accordingly, the court carefully construed the terms written on the card. The Bank argued that the cheque-form signed was not a cheque in the technical sense because the signature on it was a forgery; but the majority construed the conditions of the card as requiring only an apparently genuine signature.[209] The question is: How liberal will the courts be with the use of these cards?[210] The Banks are refusing to pay such cheques where the forgery is blatant. If the banks try to change the terms of the guarantee, these changes will have to pass the statutory tests of fairness and reasonableness.[211] Beyond that, the Banks may have to rely on the tort of negligent misstatement (see para 17.20).

---

201  E.g. American Express (Amex). Alternatively, these cards are sometimes described as 'Travel and Entertainment' (T&E) cards, e.g. Diners. Another variation is a bank budget account, under which the card-holder contracts to make regular payments (cf para 2.19).

202  See generally Chitty on *Contract*, 28th edn, Vol. 2, para 38-441. Partly because of the amount of fraud, some card-issuers have resisted increasing the upper limit of their obligation above the original £50: Jack Report on *Banking Services* (1989, Cm. 622) para 7.65.

203  I.e. to give up their right of lien on the goods until the cheque is met (see para 24.03).

204  In which case, the bank is usually entitled to refuse to meet the cheque: Bills of Exchange Act 1882, s 53(1).

205  In which case, that forged signature is a nullity: Bills of Exchange Act 1882, s 24.

206  [1993] 3 All ER 789, [1993] 1 WLR 1229, CA.

207  Unlike in this case, the conditions in a guarantee are usually read strictly: see para 25.06.

208  Evans LJ said that this was not strictly a 'guarantee' but 'a separate and independent obligation which is not dependent in any way on default by the customer' (at 795 c–d).

209  This crucial wording on Barclay's cheque guarantee cards has since been changed so as to give the retailer only protection (a): see (1993) 143 NLJ 430; 48 CC 2/20.

210  E.g. if the card is used to 'back' a cheque in excess (say £275) of the limit (say £50), will the guarantee be good for £50 if the card limit is circumvented by drawing several cheques for the card limit?

211  As to the current terms of the cheque guarantee scheme, see the APACS website (www.apacs.org.uk). As to fairness, see UTCC, reg 4 (see para 11.15); and as to reasonableness, see UCTA, s 3 (see para 18.21).

**[2.27] Three-party charge cards.**[212] The operation of these cards was judicially considered in *Re Charge Card Services Ltd*:[213]

> An unsuccessful charge card operation, CCS Ltd, was set up to operate a 'Fuel Card' Scheme as follows: account-holders could present a Fuel Card to a franchised garage exhibiting the logo and thereby pay for fuel by signing a sales voucher; one copy of the voucher was sent by the franchisee garage to CCS Ltd, who paid the franchisee the face value of the voucher less a commission; and CCS Ltd billed the account holder monthly. Because CCS Ltd would normally pay the franchisee before receiving payment from the account holder, the business was financed by factoring (see para 2.22).

The dispute was between the factor and franchisees over money collected by the liquidator of CCS Ltd from account-holders, technically the account-holders not being parties to the proceedings.[214] Nevertheless, Millett J carefully considered the whole legal structure of charge and credit cards, making the following points (in which he was broadly supported by the unanimous Court of Appeal):

(1)  The charge card operation involved three separate bilateral contracts between the account-holder (consumer),[215] CCS Ltd (card-issuer) and franchisee (retailer), each being a party to only two of the contracts (see para 7.09).

(2)  Goods were supplied by the retailer to the consumer under a supply contract concluded at the pump or till (see para 10.02). Rather than constituting a quasi-sale within the SGSA,[216] this supply contract probably amounted to a sale within the SGA (see para 1.07), the display of the logo simply adding a term allowing for payment by charge card.[217] Refusal by the retailer to accept a properly produced card is presumably a breach of contract and may amount to an offence under the TDA (s 14: see para 4.16).

(3)  *Prima facie*, use of the card constitutes absolute payment (see para 23.14), not conditional payment as would a cheque (SGA, s 38(1): see para 24.03). This reflects the popular perception of credit and charge cards as substitutes for cash, being frequently referred to as 'plastic money'.[218]

(4)  Thereafter, the retailer must look exclusively to the card-issuer for payment[219]

---

212 See generally Goode, *Consumer Credit Law & Practice*, Chap 39; Chitty on *Contract*, 27th edn, Vol. 2, para 36-388.

213 [1987] Ch 150, [1986] 3 All ER 289 (discussed (1987) 2 BFLR 119); affd [1989] Ch 497, [1988] 3 All ER 702, CA.

214 The propriety of the omission was confirmed by Millett J, who held that consumers were neither party nor privy to the relevant contracts.

215 The cards could be operated by the account-holder (commonly a registered company) or his authorised agents (usually employees). Millett J thought that for present purposes account-holders were liable as principals, disclosed or undisclosed, of card-holders.

216 See Tiplady [1989] LM & CLQ 22. For quasi-sales, see para 2.10.

217 See Dobson [1989] JBL at 341–2. This displaces the general rule requiring cash on delivery (s 28): see below, paras 23.16 and 23.22.

218 *Per* Browne-Wilkinson, VC, delivering judgment of the CA: at 705h–711d. Is this because the card company guarantee payment to the retailer? What if the card-holder resigns his card before the retailer presents his account to the erstwhile card-issuer?

219 It has been argued that if the card-holding contract were a regulated cancellable agreement (which it was not: see below) and cancelled, this could leave the franchisee without means of redress: Sayer (1986) 136 NLJ 1030.

and the latter was entitled to debit the consumer's account[220] in respect of all transactions of which he was notified of card use.[221]

(5) It follows that the consumer carried no risk of the card-issuer's insolvency, a matter of dispute wholly between the retailer and factor.[222]

**[2.28] Three- and four-party credit cards.**[223] Under this essentially three-party system of payment card (see para 2.25), a credit card is issued by the 'card-issuer' to a consumer (the 'card-holder') who uses that card to obtain goods or services from a merchant (retail-supplier) recruited by the merchant-acquirer (see below). Many card contracts allow for the issue of an extra card on the same account to an 'additional user' e.g. relative, employee. It is presumed that the legal analysis of the scheme is similar to that for charge cards (see para 2.27).

The retail-supplier will advertise his willingness to supply his goods or services on this system by displaying a logo; and the card-holder will initiate the system by signing a sales voucher, the basic security being provided by a signature test or PIN.[224] The card and card voucher will then be 'wiped' through a machine to transfer the details from the card onto the card voucher. In service industries, e.g. hotels, it is becoming common to wipe a card in blank before the service is provided. Does this provide the supplier with any security?

At the end of each accounting period (usually a month), the card-issuer presents an account to the card-holder who is automatically given a choice: he may make full payment within a set period, in which case probably no interest is charged, except perhaps for cash withdrawals;[225] or he may elect to defer payment and pay interest (account charges), in which case he may pay any amount he chooses in excess of a stipulated minimum. Meanwhile, the merchant-acquirer/card-issuer will reimburse the retail supplier (often at a discount: merchant fee) against presentation of sales vouchers; and, insofar as this is done before they are put in funds for that purpose by the card-holder, the card-issuer is probably lending money to the card-holder.[226]

In practice, the credit card system is a bit more complicated than above, involving up to four principal trade parties.[227] Besides the retail-supplier, these are:

---

220 Both charge and credit cards would appear to constitute a provision of credit (see para 5.22); but the fuel card scheme could not give rise to regulated agreements insofar as the debtors were registered companies (see para 5.24). The additional (e.g. employee) card-holders are irrelevant for this purpose in that they are not co-debtors (see para 7.08).

221 By the retailer presenting to the card-issuer a copy of the sales voucher signed by the consumer. Cf. *Customs & Excise Comrs v Diners Club Ltd* [1989] 2 All ER 385, CA (VAT case).

222 This unappealed issue is beyond the scope of this work.

223 See generally Chitty on *Contract*, 28th edn, Vol. 2, paras 38–433/6. The first credit card introduced into the UK was by American Express in 1963.

224 As to signature comparison, see para 2.24. The retailer should also check his 'stop list' and will have a 'floor-limit', i.e. if the transaction exceeds a nominated amount, he must phone the card-issuer for prior authorization. As to telephone sales see para 8.17.

225 About 25% of credit card debts are paid off during the interest-free period and are not generally regarded as borrowing ((2001) 29 *Credit Finance* 13). But technically it seems to involve the provision of credit under the CCA (see paras 5.21).

226 Goode, *HP Law and Practice*, 2nd edn, 902; Geva, *Financing Consumer Sales and Product Defences*, 11–16; Chitty, *Op. cit.*, para 3757. For the consumer's statutory protection, see para 17.09, *et seq*.

227 See Goode, *Consumer Credit Law & Practice*, paras 2.61–4; the OFT enquiry into Mastercard (see para 2.14). For the chain of indemnities between them, see (1994) 7 Fair Trading 14.

1. *Payment card organisations*, e.g. MasterCard, Visa. Their role is to set and administer internationally the scheme rules, hold the trade mark in the credit card and issue licences to merchant-acquirers and/or card issuers and charge fees to retailers per use.[228] Key rules imposed by card organisations have included to honour all cards, not to discriminate between retail purchasers by cash or credit card (surcharging) and minimum volumes.[229] They also have 'charge back' arrangements by which a payer on a queried transaction may obtain reimbursement, e.g. the card-issuer may credit the card-holder and then seek reimbursement from the merchant-acquirer, who may in turn seek reimbursement from the supplier. This mechanism may be used to operate the statutory indemnity, where applicable.[230]

2. *Merchant-acquirers*. These are intermediaries (see para 2.17) who obtain licences from the above organisation and then recruit (acquire) merchants (retail-suppliers) to the organisation under merchant agreements (see para 7.09).[231] The clearing banks have all become merchant-acquirers for both the major payment card organisations (see above). In *OFT v Lloyds TSB Bank plc* (see para 16.11), the Court of Appeal described the resulting four-party structure (at para 6) and held that the addition of a fourth party (the merchant-acquirer) made no difference to the operation of s 75 of the CCA. But that latter will usually pay an interchange fee to the card-issuer.

3. *Card-issuers*. Some card-issuers offer (either on a single or separate cards) the facilities of more than one card organisation, e.g. a card which is both a Master (previously Access) and a Visa card. Nowadays, many cards are issued in the UK in return for an annual charge: for the legal effect of this, see para 7.11. Besides making the card-holding (loan) contract with the consumer and collecting payments from him, card-issuers may also act as merchant-acquirers, sometimes for the very merchant to whom the credit card is presented.[232]

Conduct of these arrangements are subject to the Banking Code of Practice (see para 3.12). Further developments are that some card-issuers enable their card-holders to operate their accounts like bank accounts (see para 7.03) by supplying them with cheques which they can use to draw on the account.[233] In 2006, the EU

---

228 Known as 'interchange fees', these are typically less than 1% of each credit card transaction.

229 These terms were referred to the Monopolies and Mergers Commission (see para 2.14), who reported that the latter two were restrictive trade practices: *Credit Card Services* (1989, Cmnd. 718). Visa having unsuccessfully applied for judicial review (*R v MMC* [1991] Tr LR 97, CA) and refused to give voluntary undertakings (OFT, *1990 AR*, 81–2), the Commission's recommendations were implemented by two Orders: Credit Cards (Merchant Acquisition) Order 1990 SI2158; Credit Cards (Price Discrimination) Order 1990 SI 2159.

230 Under the Consumer Credit Act 1974, s 75(2): see OFT, *Connected Lender Liability* (1994), paras 3.16–19; and below, para 16.17.

231 For the retailer, there must be compared the cost of clearing cheques with the merchant charge on credit, charge, and debit cards.

232 Some UK card-issuers, e.g. Lloyds, Midland and NatWest, have collaborated to set up the Joint Credit Card Company to act as their merchant-acquirer (see above). Provisions in the merchant contract restricting card-issuers from acting as merchant-acquirers have now been declared unlawful monopolies: 1990 SI 2158.

233 These will be subject to all the rules for cheques: see para 7.28. Credit-issuers sometimes use them, together with 'teaser rates', to attract new consumer business by way of transferred balances: see [1999] *Which?* 12/44.

enquired into the charges and fees levied in connection with the use of payment cards.[234] In the case of a four-party (open card payment) system, these may be rendered diagrammatically as follows:

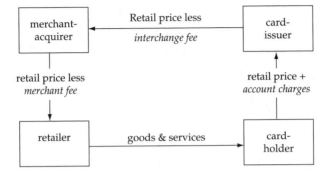

# PART 2

# CONSUMER PROTECTION

# CHAPTER 3

# REGULATION OF BUSINESS

**[3.01] Introduction.** In 1995, the United Nations passed a resolution setting out eight basic consumer rights,[1] against which the English system described in this book may be tested.

In Part 1 of the book, the nature of the contracts used for the supply of goods to consumers was examined. Part 2 is concerned with the different types of consumer protection that are available even before the parties start to negotiate a particular transaction. Chapter 3 deals with four topics: first, it outlines the various types of consumer watchdog (see paras 3.02–8); second, it looks at the statutory and voluntary control of supplies of goods to consumers (see paras 3.09–14); third, it outlines the means of achieving consumer redress (see paras 3.15–25); and fourth, it summarises the controls on the power of traders to accumulate personal information about consumers (see paras 3.26, *et seq.*).

However, from the outset, it must be borne in mind that any system of controls is really only as good as the understanding of the people using it. Thus, on the trader's side much of the effect of legislation is diluted if traders simply do not know of, understand or implement, the legal norms with which they are supposed to comply. Indeed, historically, one of the reasons for legislating has not been just to change the law, but to publicise it with the object of securing adherence.[2] On the other hand, a trader may simply decide to ignore consumer rights as a matter of policy.[3]

Turning to consumers, on the one hand there is considerable pressure for them to be provided with more information, whether as to their legal rights, product information at point of sale, or redress mechanisms;[4] and the next step is to make consumers more demanding. On the other hand, for even the ablest there is clearly a maximum limit of information that may be absorbed: it may be asked whether the English system of consumer protection is approaching that limit; and each extra protection should be weighed against the further complication it may introduce.[5] Furthermore, it is not the case that all consumers start from a basis of equal knowledge of their rights; and there are distinct limitations on the extent to which legislation can equalise differences between classes of consumers.[6] Indeed, it

---

1   The right to: safety; be informed; satisfaction of basic needs; choose; redress; consumer education; be heard; and a healthy environment (see OFT, *AR-96*, p 11).

2   OFT, *AR-2002/3* 85. For another example, see the work of the OFT in relation to traders and the UTCC Regulations: see OFT, *UCT Bulletin No. 5*, p 7; and generally, para 11.12A, *et seq.*

3   See *Modern markets: confident consumers* (1999, Cm. 4410) paras 3.1 and 3.4. Much government information is now published on the Internet.

4   See DTI, *Fair, Clear and Competitive: the Consumer Credit Market in the 21st Century* (Dec 2003, Cm. 6040), paras 5.26–9. For the techniques of regulation, see Cartwright, *Consumer Protection and the Criminal Law*, Chap 2.

5   Current government policy sees the present body of consumer law as broadly adequate: *Modern markets, Op. cit.*, para 6.2.

6   Cayne and Trebilcock (1973) 23 UTLJ 396, at 407–11; OFT, *Vulnerable Consumers and Financial Services* (1999) paras 200, 700; *Modern markets, Op. cit.*, paras 1.6 and 3.31; OFT, *AR-99*, 9.

may be that consumer protection legislation should therefore be limited in aim to remedying the imbalance in bargaining power between consumers and suppliers as a whole;[7] optimising simplicity and transparency in transactions; and educating against overindebtedness (see para 6.10). It should be remembered that virtually all measures of consumer protection have costs, which will have to be met—generally by way of higher charges for the relevant goods/services or taxation.

Complementary to this is the policy of putting the burden of enforcement of consumer rights on officialdom,[8] sometimes on behalf of consumers generally,[9] sometimes in respect of individual consumers.[10] Further, in modern times, steps have been taken to improve consumer awareness of their rights: the desirability of educating consumers as to their rights is being taken seriously, in relation to both children and adults.[11] The Office of Fair Trading has an important official function in this regard, as do the FSA directly sponsored bodies and local authorities (see para 3.02, *et seq.*); but there are also voluntary bodies concerned with consumer protection (see para 3.08) and education.[12] Finally, the traditional English obsession with redress by way of damages is at last being supplemented by the introduction of a continental-inspired system for injunctions and specific performance to be obtained on behalf of consumers against traders (see respectively, paras 28.03 and 29.02A); and, as against public bodies and private bodies carrying out public functions, consumers may sometimes be able to invoke the Human Rights Act 1998 (see para 3.09A).

# CONSUMER WATCHDOGS

## The Government

[3.02] **Whitehall**. 'The role of central government in consumer protection is to promote legislative policy, oversee the implementation of legislation and oversee the work of the various government agencies.'[13] However, within Whitehall, central government responsibility for consumer protection is spread between a number of different Departments of State, in a pattern which tends to change with the complexion of each government.[14] Hence, the usual draftsman's formula

---

7   Cayne and Trebilcock, *Op. cit.*, at 427.
8   For the officials concerned with consumer credit, see Goode, *Consumer Credit Law & Practice*, Directory.
9   E.g. Pt 8 of the EA: see para 6.06.
10  E.g. TDA: see para 4.02.
11  *Modern markets, Op. cit.*, paras 3.32–4; (2004) 39 *Fair Trading* 8; [2000] 5 *Credit Today* 21; NACAB, *Summing up: bridging the financial literacy divide* (2002); [2003] 7 *Credit Today* 16. For initiatives aimed at credit education for 14- to 16-year olds, see OFT, *AR-90*, 20, 27; [2004] 3 *Credit Today* 21–2; [2004] 5 *Credit Today* 41. As to financial education, see OFT, *AR-2001* 72 (roadshows); (2002) 66 *QA* 15; [2005] 3 *Credit Today* 29; (2005) 42 *Fair Trading* 19 (Alliance); *AR-2005–6*, 67–70. There seems to be some support for NVQ recognition for money advice.
12  E.g. DebtCred (see [2005] 2 *Credit Today* 16); Debt Test (see (2006) 60 CC5/41). The Government provides sporadic funding to bodies involved in consumer education.
13  Harvey and Parry, *Consumer Protection and Fair Trading*, 6th edn, 49.
14  Harvey and Parry, *Op. cit.*, 49–52.

in a statute that something shall be done by 'the Secretary of State' tends to refer even as regards consumer protection statutes to different Secretaries of State in respect of different functions and at different dates. Under this formal umbrella, there is likely to be a politician at Minister of State level responsible for day-to-day issues. For instance, the various Departments of State also sponsor a number of other functions[15] and bodies (see para 3.04). In 1994, the government empowered themselves to contract out certain ministerial functions under the deregulation initiative (see para 5.10); and, in the absence of new primary legislation, this procedure may be used to effect a number of statutory alterations beneficial to consumers.[16]

A good example of the division of departmental responsibility lies in the granting of credit to consumers. Where the credit is connected with the purchase of a dwelling house, the matter is overseen by the Treasury (see below), whereas other forms of consumer credit fall within the aegis of the Department of Trade and Industry (DTI: see para 3.02A). The DTI administers the relevant Act, the Consumer Credit Act 1974 (CCA, s 2), including regulated loans, whether unsecured or secured on houses ('second mortgages'), e.g. home improvement loans. Within the DTI, day-to-day responsibility is divided between a Minister of State[17] and an executive agency, the Office of Fair Trading (see para 3.03).

*The Treasury and the Financial Services Authority (FSA).* Since 2004, residential house-purchase loans, including non-status lending (see para 7.04A), has been controlled by the Treasury, overseeing the operation of the Financial Services and Markets Act 2000 (FSMA) and the activities of the FSA: whilst largely beyond the scope of this work, *inter alia*, the FSA controls deposit-taking by financial intermediaries (see para 2.17); promotes consumer financial education;[18] and ensures consumer protection, as by the ombudsman system (see para 3.25), the UTCCR[19] and extensive Codes of Conduct central to which is treating consumers fairly (FSA, Principal 6). So, ordinary residential mortgages will usually be outside (CCA),[20] being subject to different educational initiatives[21] and a different set of consumer protection rules, though the latter are likely in some respects to parallel those of the CCA.[22] Establishing the borderline between the operation of the FSMA

---

15  There should also be borne in mind the specialist functions in respect of such as discrimination, food, medicines and weights and measures. Co-ordination across government is promised: *Modern markets: confident consumers* (1999, Cm. 4410) para 9.2.

16  Including making some of the changes recommended in *Modern Markets* (above). Other alterations in commercial behaviour may be forced by use of the CCA licensing system: see para 6.18.

17  For the exercise of his functions under the CCA, see Goode, *Consumer Credit Law & Practice*, Directory.

18  S 4. In 2003, the FSA announced plans for a national strategy to raise the British public's financial awareness: [2003] 11 *Credit Today* 17.

19  The Unfair Terms in Consumer Contracts Regulations 1999 (UTCCR: see para 11.12, *et seq.*), reg 16, the FSA being a 'qualifying body' (see para 11.19).

20  Either because it exceeds the financial limit (see para 5.22) or is exempt from the CCA (see para 5.15).

21  Under FSMA, ss 4, 5. E.g. the booklets *Money Counts* (2000), *You and Your Money* (2001). See (2005) 60 CC2/10.

22  FSMA, s 428. The FSMA mortgage rules apply to mortgage activity undertaken after October 2004.

and the CCA is therefore likely to be vital.[23] Broadly speaking, the FSA applies
where the borrower is an individual owner-occupier and the lender takes a first
legal charge; but the CCA applies, irrespective of owner-occupation, where a
borrower-individual grants a second charge (see para 5.15). Nor do the two
organisations share a common regulatory approach: whereas the FSA operates
under a set of principles laid down in the FSMA and has extensive rule-making
powers not subject to parliamentary oversight, the OFT proceeds by secondary
legislation (sponsored by the DTI) and OFT-devised *Guidance*; and the distinction
has been characterised as that between FSA principles-based regulation and OFT
micro-management.[24]

**[3.02A] The Department of Trade and Industry (DTI).** Apart from the financing
of dwelling houses (see para 3.02), most governmental powers connected with
consumer protection are concentrated in the hands of the DTI, these powers
including oversight of product safety, fair trading (including credit) and weights
and measures (Paper, para 1.11). In June 2005, the DTI published a new strategy[25]
designed to produce a 'world-class regime' which was fair to both business and
consumers.[26] To achieve these goals, the Paper promised all the following:[27]

1.  *To promote open and competitive markets.* Besides maintaining the competitive
    regime in goods,[28] the Government promised to press the EU for the liberalisa-
    tion of services.

2.  *To empower consumers* by all the following:[29] (a) in 2006 to complete the national
    rollout of Consumer Direct, a telephone and internet service to help consumers
    sort out their consumer problems and, where that is not possible, to refer them
    on to specialist advice;[30] (b) expand the OFT Codes of Approval scheme (see
    para 3.13); (c) improve consumer education (see para 3.01) and the usefulness
    of consumer information/advocacy (see para 3.16); and (d) improve access to
    cross-border advice (see para 8.17B).

3.  *To simplify consumer law* by all the following:[31] (a) regulatory reform (see para
    5.10); (b) introducing a general duty not to trade unfairly (see para 4.20); and (c)
    to simplify EU consumer law (see para 3.10).

4.  *To make it easier to resolve problems* by:[32] (a) Consumer Direct (above) referring
    consumer problems to ADRs (see para 3.24); (b) consult on making it easier for
    victims to get evidence in civil cases (see para 17.05); (c) introduce representa-
    tive actions for consumers (see para 3.18); and (d) seek to return money from
    overseas scams and other improvements to cross-border redress systems.[33]

---

23  See the FSMA (Regulated Activities) Order 2001 SI 544. But all these calculations may be upset
    by the new definition of consumer credit in the Draft Consumer Credit Directive: see para 5.12.
24  See the debates on the Consumer Credit Bill: (2005–6) HL, 3R cols 146–7.
25  *A Fair Deal for All* (2005). This Paper set out what the DTI hoped to accomplish (Chap 2) and
    when the Government anticipated it would intervene in the market (Chap 3).
26  For the goals which the Government has set itself, see particularly paras 1.8–10 of the Paper.
27  See the Paper, Executive Summary (pp 4–5); and paras 1.2–6 and 1.9.
28  See the Paper, Chap 4. See further, paras 2.12–4.
29  See the Paper, paras 5.1–4.
30  For an account of this service in the Paper, see paras 5.5–8. For the National Debtline, see
    para 3.16.
31  See the Paper, Chap 6.      32  See the Paper, Chap 7.      33  See paras 3.03–03A.

5. *To ensure a fair and safe trading environment* by all the following:[34] (a) pilot Regional Standards Scambusters for those scams extending beyond local authority boundaries, but not nationally (para 8.13); (b) implement the Hampton Report on improving enforcement, in particular the setting up of a new national Consumer and Trading Standards Agency (para 3.03A); and (c) build strong and effective cross-border co-operation mechanisms (para 3.03A).

**[3.03] Office of Fair Trading**. Section 1 of the Fair Trading Act 1973 (FTA) created a new government agent to enforce competition and consumer protection.[35] This was the Director General of Fair Trading (the Director), who was supported administratively by the Office of Fair Trading (OFT) and subject to the control of the Secretary of State. The FTA envisaged two complementary major strands of consumer protection: prices and products. *First*, the OFT was to protect the economic interests of consumers by the promotion of economic efficiency and competition policy; but this large area of specialist law is mostly beyond the scope of this work (see paras 2.12–4). *Second*, it was to protect the economic and social interests of consumers *other* than in relation to the price of goods and services supplied; and, over the years the OFT collected a large number of such statutory functions (see para 3.03A).

Under Part 1 of the Enterprise Act 2002 (EA: see generally, para 2.12), as from April 2003 the office of Director has been abolished and his powers transferred to the OFT (EA, ss 2, 273), which has led to wholesale amendment of other statutes to replace references to 'Director' by 'OFT'. For instance, by the EA (Sched 25) in the Consumer Credit Act 1974, 'OFT' means Office of Fair Trading (see CCA s 189(1) (as amended)). The OFT has been turned into a statutory corporate body with a chairman and separate chief executive (the previous Director) and not fewer than four other members, who together will form the OFT Board.[36] Whilst all Board members will be appointed by the Secretary of State (see para 3.02), he will have less detailed control than under the FTA version (EA, s 9). Instead, the Board is responsible for the strategic direction of the OFT, its priorities, plans and performance;[37] but it is very unlikely that the Board will be involved in individual cases.

Under the EA, the OFT has the following general statutory duties:

1. *Annual Plan and Report*. Under the FTA, there was a duty at the end of each financial year to make annual and other reports to the Secretary of State in respect of the discharge of duties under the CCA[38] and any other enactment so requiring,[39] such reports to be published and laid before Parliament (FTA, s 125); and this duty has been re-enacted (EA, s 4, as amended). Additionally,

---

34 See the Paper, Chap 8.
35 See the OFT Statement of Purpose: *AR-2001* 11, 84; *AR-2002/3* 12, *et seq.*; *AR-2003/4* 12–5; *Annual Plan* 2006/7, 6. For a discussion of the extent to which market efficiency can achieve consumer protection, see Cartwright, *Consumer Protection and the Criminal Law*, 18.27.
36 EA, s 1 and Sched 1. See OFT (2003) 35 *Fair Trading* 9; 42 *Fair Trading* 9.
37 See the OFT Service Delivery Agreement: *AR-2001* 78–82.
38 FTA, s 125; CCA, s 5. Substantial Annual Reports (*AR*) have been published every year since 1974.
39 E.g. under the Courts and Legal Services Act 1990, ss 29, 31–3, 45–6, 105, 107 (as amended). Primarily, the OFT must report to the Lord Chancellor on the effect on competition of the provision of the Act as to legal services. It has defamation protection under s 69(2).

the OFT has been placed under a duty before each financial year to lay before Parliament an Annual Plan 'containing a statement of its main objectives and principles for the year' (s 3(1)). The Annual Report has begun to systematically list the extent to which the Annual Plan has been met, so allowing its progress to be politically monitored.[40]

2. *Acquisition of information*. Under the FTA, there was a duty to keep under review, and to collect, receive and collate information concerning commercial activities in the United Kingdom affecting the interests of consumers.[41] Since 1974, there has been an enormous expansion of the information services of the OFT. For instance, the OFT acts as the central collection point for information as to the consumer protection activities of local authority trading standards (see para 3.05); and the OFT has also been particularly active in publishing information[42] and advice to consumers,[43] including by website.[44] All these functions have been confirmed by the EA (ss 5 and 6); and the OFT sees its contribution to consumer education as important in empowering consumers to protect themselves.[45]

3. *Providing information and advice to ministers*. Under the FTA, there was a duty to make recommendations for action to the Secretary of State (s 2); and this duty to provide information and advice to Ministers has now been repeated (EA, s 7).

4. *Promoting good practice*. Under the FTA, there was a duty to encourage trade associations to prepare codes of practice for guidance in safeguarding and promoting the interests of UK consumers (FTA, s 124(3)). This has been enhanced by the EA (s 8), which imposes on the OFT a 'general function of promoting good practice in carrying out activities which may affect the economic interests of consumers in the United Kingdom' (s 3(1)), especially in encouraging consumer codes of practice (see para 3.13); and the Secretary of State is empowered to give financial assistance 'to any person' for the 'benefit of consumers' (s 274). By comparison with the promotion of best practice by codes, the OFT sees its issued Guidance Notes, e.g. on Debt Management (see para 5.42), as representing minimum standards and being enforced through the licensing regime, e.g. CCA licensing (see para 6.11).

In 2005, a Treasury Report[46] recommended further changes to the administrative structure, including the creation of a Consumer and Trading Standards Agency

---

40  See OFT, *Annual Plan 2003–04*, Annexe, esp. Objectives 1, 2, 6, 7, 8 (the draft Plan was subject to extensive consultation; *Annual Plan 2006/7*, esp. Objectives 1, 2, 6. E.g. note 46, below.).

41  FTA, ss 2(1), (2), 131; CCA, s 1(2). As to the classification of complaints, see OFT, *Annual Report*, Appendix K.

42  E.g. *Fair Trading* (a quarterly published digest for consumer protectors and advisers); and an OFT website (see below). As to restrictions on the disclosure of information, see ss 124, 133 (as amended); and para 28.06.

43  FTA, s 124; CCA, s 4. The OFT publishes a substantial number of leaflets and booklets: a current list is to be found in the latest *Annual Report*, e.g. *A Buyer's Guide*. For listening to consumers, see *AR-2002/3* 28; and for communicating with consumers, see *AR-2003/4* 88–97; *AR-2004/5* 70–7.

44  Ref: http://www.oft.gov.uk. See OFT (2002) 32 *Fair Trading* 5; *AR-2002/3* 37

45  See (2003) 36 *Fair Trading* 6; and generally above, para 3.01. For Consumer Direct, see para 3.16.

46  The Hampton Review, *Reducing Administrative Burdens* (2005). The FSA warned that it is not equipped to take over any OFT functions: see *The Times* (19.11.05); and the 2006 Budget retreated from the idea. For a new sense of urgency at the OFT, see its *Annual Plan 2006/7* (above).

(CTSA: see para 3.03A) and the possibility of transferring some OFT functions to the FSA (see para 3.02).

**[3.03A]** In 2005, the Hampton Review (see para 3.03) recommended that the consumer protection functions of the OFT should be grouped together under a new agency; but this recommendation has been rejected.[47] These functions are as follows:[48]

1. *Trading practices*. The erstwhile duty to keep under review commercial practices generally with a view to identifying trade practices which should be legislated against as adversely affecting the economic interests of consumers (EA: see below, para 4.19, *et seq*.); and to moniter the conduct of business by individual licensees.[49]

2. *Estate agency*. To superintend the working and enforcement of the Estate Agents Act 1979, a matter beyond the scope of this work.

3. *Rogue traders*. To seek assurances from traders and obtain court undertakings from rogue traders that they will mend their ways under what are now called Enforcement Orders (EA, Pt 8: see below, paras 6.06–8).

4. *Unfair contract terms*. Since 1994, to consider complaints that certain classes of standard contract terms are unfair. If so, as lead-enforcer to seek suitable undertakings from the *proferens* (see para 11.12, *et seq*.) or, failing that, take court action (see below).

5. *Licensing*. To administer the licensing system under the Consumer Credit Act 1974 (see para 6.11, *et seq*.) and in respect of estate agency (see above). The former powers have been extended in relation to European businesses (FSA, ss 203–4: see below, para 6.12). For all categories, lenders' behaviour is moderated by prosecution, licensing action and guidance.[50]

6. *Central co-ordinator*. To act as the central co-ordinator (see para 28.03) for enforcement of the Trade Descriptions Act 1968 (see para 4.02, *et seq*.), the Consumer Credit Act 1974 (CCA, s 161; and see Chap 5) and the EA (see above), e.g. Consumer Direct (see para 3.05) and the TSS service as a whole (see para 3.05).

7. *Enforcement*. By applying to court for Enforcement Orders (see above), to act as primary enforcer of the Unfair Terms Regulations (see para 11.19), long-stop enforcer of the Misleading Advertisement Regulations (see para 8.12A) and lead-enforcer for other consumer protection legislation (see below; and paras 6.06A; 29.39 and 29.39A), including under super-complaints (see para 4.19). In so doing, the OFT is under a duty to act proportionately under the Enforcement Concordat (see para 5.10). The OFT also co-ordinates enforcement by others, chiefly Local Authorities.[51]

---

47  See the DTI Consultation Paper, *Reducing Administrative Burdens—the Consumer and Trading Standards Agency* (July 2005), suggesting transfer to the FSA. Ownership appears to have been declined by the FSA, to the satisfaction of the OFT (*AR-2005/6*, 5). As to a joint action plan between the OFT and FSA, see (2006) 46 Fair Trading 8.

48  OFT, *AR-2001*, 19–20; *AR-2003/4*, 24–7.

49  CCA 1974, s 1 (as amended by s 62 of the CCA 2006).

50  OFT, *AR-2002/3*, 42.          51  OFT, *AR-2002/3*, 51.

8. *Registers of convictions.* To keep central registers of convictions which is available to local authorities, but not the public.[52]

9. *Distance selling.* To enforce the Distance Selling Regulations (see para 8.17) and publish information and advice about them (reg 29; and above).

10. *Cross-border provisions.* Over time, there has been built up an informal forum of national consumer protection agencies, ICPEN, of which the OFT is the UK representative.[53] There is also an across-border ADR system (see generally, para 3.24) called the European Extra Judicial Network (EEJ-Net).[54] In 2004, the EU adopted a Regulation (2006/2004: see generally, para 1.03A) designed to establish within the EU a formal network of public authorities to protect the collective interests of EU consumers, requiring each Member State as from 2007 to have at least one enforcement authority as regards any infringement of the Injunctions Directive (98/27). In the UK, this Directive is enacted by Part 8 of the EA (see above), which is mainly enforced by the OFT and LAs (see para 6.06A). Accordingly, the DTI is consulting as to whether to formally designate these bodies to implement the Regulation within the UK.[55] In enforcing the above powers, the OFT is bound to act proportionately.[56]

**[3.04] The National Consumer Council (NCC).**[57] The first Consumer Council was recommended by the Molony Committee.[58] After its demise in 1971, the present body was set up in 1975 with a government grant 'to give a vigorous and independent voice to consumers in the United Kingdom',[59] though not to give advice to the individual consumers.[60] Whilst the Secretary of State has a general responsibility for its work, the NCC is non-statutory and independent of the government. It seeks to influence policy affecting consumers by conducting research, making representations,[61] producing reports[62] and publishing general consumer advice.[63] Unfortunately, government thinking seems no closer to

---

52  See OFT (1995/96) 12 *Fair Trading* 4.

53  International Consumer Protection Enforcement Network (ICPEN). As to international co-operation, see generally OFT, *AR-2004/5* 40–1. For an example, see OFT (2006) *FT* 15, *AR-2005/6*, 8, 34.

54  NCC, *Seeking Resolution* (Jan 2004) pp 13–14, 69–70; and see (2004) NLJ 1396.

55  DTI, *Implementing the EU Regulation on Consumer Protection Co-operation* (July 2005).

56  Presently, this duty is contained in the voluntary Cabinet Office enforcement concordat (see para 5.10), but that 'duty' may be embodied in the Regulatory Reform Bill 2006 (2005/6) HL 3R col 143.

57  There is a statutory power to continue grants-in-aid: Competition Act 1980, s 20. See generally Harvey and Parry, *Consumer Protection and Fair Trading*, 6th edn, 56–8.

58  Committee on Consumer Protection (1962, Cmnd. 1781) Chap 20.

59  For the functions of the Council, see the statement 'About the NCC' in its Annual Reports. Reliance on a grant is, of course, relevant to its independence. See also Cranston, *Consumers and the Law*, 3rd edn, 17–18.

60  Though NCC gives much help to other consumer bodies which do advise individual con-sumers—see NCC, *Annual Reports*.

61  Sometimes supporting new legislation, e.g. the Credit Unions Act 1979 (see para 2.21); Supply of Goods and Services Act 1982 (see paras 15.12–14). It is also active in BEUC (see para 3.10).

62  E.g. *Report on Origin Marking* (1979); *Ordinary Justice* (1989).

63  It publishes a considerable range of very cheap or free publications advising consumers: see the list in the NCC Annual Report.

clarifying the relationship of this body to the OFT.[64] Whilst the OFT is a bottom-up organisation, whose campaigns are informed by the detailed complaints reported to it (see paras 3.03–03A), the NCC is a top-down organisation in search of a role.[65]

**[3.05] Local Authorities Trading Standards Service**. Over the centuries, legislators have found that it was necessary to call upon the criminal law to provide effective measures of consumer protection (see para 28.01). However, in developing that trading standards legislation (see Chap 4) it has been said that the UK was probably unique amongst EU Member States in relying upon enforcement by LA.[66] In modern times, the departments of local authorities administering these functions, of which there are over 200, have been called 'Consumer Protection' or 'Trading Standards' Departments and the government is trying to standardise these as the 'Trading Standards Service' (TSS),[67] co-ordinated by the OFT.[68] This Service (see para 28.02) has undertaken two distinct types of activity:

1. *Enforcement of the criminal law*. As it evolved, the above system developed two features: *first*, statutes increasingly imposed a **duty**, rather than a power, of enforcement on local authorities; and *second*, that duty tended to be exercisable by the local authority in its own right rather than simply as agent of the central government (see para 28.02). To encourage more uniformity of enforcement, central oversight has in recent times been entrusted to the OFT (see para 3.03A). The LAs and OFT also co-operate in the enforcement of the Unfair Terms Regulations (see para 11.19).

2. *Advice in relation to the civil law*. LAs have a discretion to seek an injunction on behalf of private citizens. However, leaving aside that unlikely possibility, LAs do have statutory permission to provide **advisory** services for the general public;[69] and encouraged by the Consumers' Association (see para 3.08), since 1969 LAs have been setting up Consumer Advice Centres[70] and have provided support for neighbourhood law centres (see para 3.16). In some instances, they also help consumers to obtain redress by guiding them through the County Court Small Claims Scheme (as to which, see para 3.22) and have offered advice where the complaint concerns 'misleading advertisements' which may be referred to the OFT (see para 8.12A). As ever, the availability of such discretionary services tends to be subject to the availability of local authority finance, a consideration which tends to reduce the stability of such service-provision. Under the deregulation initiative, Ministers are empowered to contract out designated non-judicial local authority functions (see para 5.10). Since 2005, much of this advisory work has been transferred to Consumer Direct (see para 3.16), a service operated by the OFT with TSA input.[71]

---

64 *Modern markets: confident consumers* (1999, Cm. 4410) paras 8.6–8.

65 See NCC Chairman Hutton in (2003) 34 *Fair Trading* 14.

66 Harvey and Parry, *Op. cit.*, 54.

67 See DTI, *Reducing Administrative Burdens—the CTSA* (July 2005): see above, para 3.03A.

68 See OFT, *AR-2005/6*, 18.

69 Local Government Act 1972, s 222; and see para 28.04.

70 Local Government Act 1972, ss 137, 142, 201(8).

71 See further Harvey and Parry, *Op. cit.*, 55–6. As to money advice, see para 3.08.

## Other watchdogs

**[3.06] Privatised utilities (1).** This paragraph introduces the privatised utilities concerned in the supply of goods to consumers, e.g. gas, electricity or water. It omits utilities wholly or largely concerned with the supply of services, e.g. telephony (see para 8.17), the Post Office (see para 2.15). Although gas, electricity and water may be 'goods' (see para 2.01), it has been held that their supply does not amount to the sale of goods (see para 1.07) because the terms of the supply do not depend on contract.[72] Instead, the methods by which citizens might seek to control the excesses of utilities were administrative, the terms of supply being laid down compulsorily by statute.[73] After 1945, the major public utilities were nationalised, with provisions to restrain their ability to employ their monopoly power over the supply of goods and services in a manner oppressive to consumers, e.g. pricing (see below), the special statutory powers to enter premises, and of gas and electricity utilities to disconnect unilaterally services for non-payment (see para 27.02). Parliamentary control of nationalised industries was later replaced by regulation of the privatised public utilities,[74] each industry being subject to oversight by a separate public official, now called a Regulator (see para 3.07), and a licensing system.[75] Among the common responsibilities of the Regulators in relation to the protection of consumer interests are the following: the level of prices charged to consumers generally are no longer regulated,[76] but are subject to the OFT and the Competition Commission;[77] the codes of conduct (see para 3.07); to make regulations prescribing standards of performance;[78] to direct suppliers as to the provision of information; and a complaints handling machinery.[79] Additionally, the utilities have been made subject to the following: in respect of their advertisements the ASA rules (see para 3.14); or, under the deregulation initiative, the Minister may instead accept an undertaking from the utility (see para 5.10). Because of the foregoing public accountability system, it was thought inappropriate to make these

---

72 *Norweb plc v Dixon* [1995] 3 All ER 952, DC; and hence a demand for payment cannot amount to unlawful harassment (see para 24.24); nor doorstep selling (see paras 10.21 and 10.29); nor perhaps an unfair term (see Elvin (2003) 14 KCLJ 39 at 50; and para 11.12A). In certain cases, there may be a deemed contract: Gas Act 1995, Sched 2, para 8.

73 See Harvey and Parry, *Op. cit.*, 71–3.

74 As to the efficacy of relying on large numbers of small shareholders to control public utilities, see Harvey and Parry, *Op. cit.*, 82.

75 Under the Utilities Act 2000, Pt IV (electricity licensing) and Pt V (gas licensing); Water Act 2003. The utilities may therefore be subject to public law remedies: see Cranston, *Consumers and the Law*, 3rd edn, 198. These rules do not apply to LPG: [2003] 9 *Which?* 8.

76 Utilities Act 2000, Pt II; but as to water, see below.

77 Competition Act 1998, s 54 (as amended), which grants concurrent powers to the OFT (see para 3.03); the EA, s 168; and the Energy Act 2004, ss 173–7. For the Competition Act 1998 and EA, see generally, para 2.12.

78 There are also standard-form offences of providing false information in the utilities statutes (Gas Act 1986, s 43; Electricity Act 1989, s 59; Water Industry Act 1991, s 207) and the consequent liability of corporate officers (1986 Act, s 45; 1989 Act, s 108; 1991 Act, s 210: and see generally, para 28.11).

79 The regulatory body for gas and electricity were combined as the Office of Gas and Electricity Markets (OFGEM); and that for water was the Office of Water Services (OFWAT). In 2004, OFGEM was supporting a move to simplify energy bills by means of a new BSI standard (see para 3.08): [2004] 8 *Credit Today* 13. The regulatory bodies have since been re-organised: see para 3.07.

utilities subject to the CCA licensing system (s 21(3): see para 6.12), but their equipment contracts with consumers (see para 3.07) remain regulated under the CCA transaction rules (see para 5.13).

**[3.07] Privatised utilities (2).** The privatised utilities (see para 3.06) include the following:

1. *Gas.* The Gas Act 1986 (as amended) made provision for the removal of the monopoly of supplying gas through pipes (ss 3, 5–8) and enacted a Consumer Code.[80] Statute established a dual system of control. First, it appointed a public official (the Regulator) to deal with matters affecting the public generally, now called GEMA:[81] under the Energy Act 2004, GEMA is required to produce Annual Reports (s 172); it has a duty to have regard to best practice (s 178); and it has the power to make regulations as to pre-payment meters (s 181: see para 27.02). Second, it created a consumers' council to deal with individual complaints, usually known as 'Energywatch'.[82]

2. *Electricity.* Under the Electricity Act 1989, there is laid down a Code of Practice.[83] Electricity is to be treated as goods for the purposes of UK competition law (1989 Act, s 100: see para 2.12); but it is not clear whether it is 'goods' within the SGA (see para 2.02). By the Utilities Act 2000, there was established a dual system of control modelled on that for gas (above); that is, a public Regulator, GEMA and a Consumers' Council to look into individual complaints, Energywatch.

3. *Water.* The water industry was privatised by the Water Act 1989, which introduced the notion of a public regulator. With powers subsequently re-enacted in the Water Industry Act 1991, the Regulator may make references to the Competition Commission (s 14). However, the entire scheme for the protection of private consumers was re-cast in Part 2 of the Water Act 2003 (substituting new provisions into the 1991 Act): this set up a new Water Services Regulatory Authority,[84] with a new independent Consumer Council for Water,[85] which must be consulted by the Authority (new s 30ZA); it enables the Secretary of State to issue guidance to the Authority on social and environmental matters and performance standards (new s 2A and amended s 39); and directs the Consumer Council to take into account the interests of listed types of vulnerable

---

80  Under the Gas Act 1986, Sched 2B (as amended). For disconnection, see para 27.02. Also bear in mind the Fuel Direct scheme administered by the DSS and the Benefits Agency.

81  Under the Utilities Act 2000, s 1, this is the Gas and Electricity Markets Authority (GEMA), which has disciplinary powers over the utilities by reason of the licensing system (see para 3.06) with which to enforce their codes of practice (see generally, para 3.14).

82  The consumer body for gas and electricity is known as GECC or 'Energywatch' (Utilities Act 2000, s 2). For its powers to make investigations and deal with consumer complaints, see ss 22, 23; and see (2003) 66 *Quarterly Account* 8; NCC, *Seeking Resolution* (Jan 2004) pp 39–40; [2004] 7 *Which?* 7; (2005) 78 *QA* 12. Unsatisfied complaints may be reported to GEMA.

83  Electricity Act 1986, Sched 6 (as substituted: the Electricity Code); Sched 7 (as amended: Meters Code). See also fn 78, above.

84  New s 1A (as inserted by s 34 of the 2003 Act). There are already plans to replace this body: DTI, *Extending Competitive Markets* (2004).

85  New s 27A and Sched 3A (as inserted by s 35 and Sched 2 of the 2003 Act). This consumer body is to be known as 'WaterVoice'.

consumer.[86] Unlike the above utilities, there is a public health consideration in the provision of water, which results in some different statutory controls, some of which are relevant for our purposes. For instance, it is an offence for a utility to supply water unfit for human consumption (s 70, as amended) or to unilaterally disconnect water supplies (s 63), without following the statutory procedure.[87]

With the increase of competition between utilities providing gas and electricity, the Government is intending to protect consumers by relying more on the ordinary competition rules (see para 2.12) and Consumer Direct (see para 3.16); and less on the special statutory rules (see para 3.06) and the HRA (see para 3.09A).

*Domestic equipment supplied by utilities.* There are circumstances where the utilities supply by contract domestic equipment, e.g. gas fires, electric cookers; and in respect of these transactions the supplier-utility will attract the transaction rules applicable to all suppliers, e.g. under the CPA, SGA, TDA, CCA (see above). In relation to the safety of domestic equipment supplied, the utilities are subject under the criminal law to some detailed safety regulations;[88] and the utilities are, of course, subject to the general safety requirement (see para 4.34). Moreover, the goods-supply agreements the utilities make with consumers are policed under the Regulations in respect of Distance and Doorstep Selling (see paras 8.17 and 10.36), Unfair Terms[89] and enforcement under the EA. Under Pt 8 of the EA, the Consumer Councils for the Utilities are empowered to bring consumer super-complaints (see para 4.19): in 2005, the Consumer Councils invoked these powers to make a super-complaint to GEMA about energy billing.[90]

**[3.08] Voluntary organisations.**[91] There are a number of organisations which offer information and guidance to consumers, either nationally or locally.

1. *Citizens' Advice Bureaux (CABx).* These locally-based bureaux, the first of which was set up in 1939, have a much wider remit than consumer protection in relation to the supply of goods with which we are concerned.[92] Their National Association (now called Citizens Advice) receives central government financial support, whilst autonomous local CABx are often grant-aided by local authorities, even though their functions overlap with Consumer Advice

---

86  1991 Act, new s 27C. The Council is required to acquire information about consumer matters (new s 27D); provide advice to public authorities (new s 27E) and consumers (new ss 27F, 38B and 95B); publish information about consumer matters (new s 27G); investigate consumer complaints (new s 29) and other matters relating to consumer interests (new s 29A).

87  Under s 62, must first follow a statutory code of conduct and then apply to the county court.

88  E.g. Electrical Equipment (Safety) Regulations 1994 SI 3260; Gas Appliance (Safety) Regulations 1995 SI 1629.

89  Whereas supplies of gas, electricity and water are probably not within the UTCCR because they are not supplied under contract (see para 3.06), supplies of goods by the Utilities are within the UTCCR.

90  *The Times* 7.4.05. See [2005] 2 *Which?* 8.

91  See generally, Harvey and Parry, *Op. cit.*, 58, *et seq*. As to other Marks of Approval, see [2001] 4 *Which?* 30.

92  See Cranston, *Consumers and the Law*, 3rd edn, 107. For the scope of their services, see the *Report of the Royal Commission on Legal Services* (1979) Cmnd. 7648, Chap 7. Only about one-fifth of their work is concerned with consumer problems: see the Annual Reports of the National Association of CABx; and NCC, *Seeking Resolution* (Jan 2004) pp 16–17.

Centres (see para 3.05). Besides referring individual consumers to solicitors or barrister as appropriate, the CAB also has an office in the Royal Court of Justice in London to help litigants in person (see para 3.17); and Citizens Advice provides a range of specialist support services[93] and makes super-complaints on behalf of consumers generally (see para 4.19).

2. *Which? (previously the Consumers' Association (CA)).* The CA was set up in 1957 as a company limited by guarantee, and it became a charity in 1987. The primary aim of the CA is to provide information to the consumer about products and services by reporting the results of its tests in its magazine, *Which?*[94] Besides numerous other publications[95] and an individual advice service,[96] it also lobbies on behalf of the consumer interest in Westminster, Whitehall[97] and Brussels, where it is a member of the European Office of Consumers' Unions (see para 3.10). The CA has spawned a network of local consumer groups.[98] It is a qualifying body under the UTCC Regulations (see para 11.19) and applies to court for Enforcement Orders on behalf of consumers (see para 28.03).

3. *British Standards Institution (BSI).* Under its present name, the BSI was incorporated by Royal Charter in 1929. Its objects include: the setting of standards for goods and services; setting dimensions and date-marking for manufactured goods; and the maintaining and promoting of a register of such 'British Standard' specifications, which now exceed 7,000 in number.[99] Whilst a manufacturer may simply claim that his goods comply with a certain British Standard,[100] the BSI also gave rise to a certification scheme, whose application to goods may be signified by application to them of a 'Kitemark'. Compliance with these standards by manufacturers is usually voluntary: but a false claim of compliance may be an offence under the TDA (s 2(1)(g): see para 4.02); and in some cases standards are compulsory, e.g. under some safety regulations (see para 4.35), or may be supported by the UCP Directive (see para 4.20, item (b)). Since 1972, the traditional work of the BSI in *laying down* standards has been to some extent side-lined by our entry into the EU, which has its own system of certified standards (CE marks);[101] but in recent years the BSI has acquired a

---

93 For the range of services bodies to which these services are provided, see (2005) 75 *Quarterly Account* 10. See the CAB reports *Deeper in Debt* and *Out of the Red* (2006).

94 Established in 1971, the CA Survey Unit provides a centralised system for conducting survey work and user trials about matters such as product safety and reliability. For a history of the CA, see [1987] *Which?* 106.

95 E.g. *Directory of Consumer Information Organisations; Handbook of Consumer Law; Which?* Guides, e.g. to car buying, the way to complain; legal advice leaflets on behalf of the Legal Services Commission (see para 3.17). These are increasingly available on-line.

96 The 'Legal Service' offers both subscription advice to individual members and an advisory service for local authority advice centres (see para 3.05). For criticism, see (2000) 150 NLJ 952.

97 E.g. it played a substantial part in promoting the Litigants in Person (Costs and Expenses) Act 1975; Unfair Contract Terms Act 1977 (see para 18.12, *et seq.*); Unsolicited Goods and Services Act 1971 (see para 8.18). A record of their campaigns is to be found in the *Annual Reports.*

98 Harvey and Parry *Op. cit.*, 61; Cranston, *Op. cit.*, 18–19.

99 E.g. the BSI for PINS and the ISO rules (see para 2.24); payment practice (see para 7.03A). For the BSI and Administration, see (1994) 6 *Fair Trading* 14.

100 E.g. the *Britvic* case (set out at para 11.08). Compliance may bring a tax advantage, e.g. zero VAT rating for safety boots (for VAT, see generally, para 2.06).

101 See para 8.06. For complaint that the CE marks are too voluntary, see [1998] 10 *Which?* 14.

new lease of life *testing* compliance with standards through the expansion of its Kitemarking scheme, e.g. operating a register of approved traders, and complaint-handling.[102]

4.  *Other organisations.* There are a large number of other organisations concerned with consumer guidance, including the following: the Design Council, a body established in 1944 in an attempt to improve the aesthetic, functional and engineering design of consumer products, e.g. safety (see paras 4.33, 14.20 and 17.28); the Advertising Standards Authority (see para 3.14); numerous trade and professional associations whose functions include an element of consumer protection (see para 3.11) and consumer advice bodies (see para 3.16).

## TYPES OF CONTROL

### Compulsory controls

**[3.09] Statutory.**[103] There are several major ways in which Parliament has sought to protect the consumer interest in the supply of goods. *First*, Parliament and government have played a substantial part in the creation and support of many of the consumer watchdogs (see above). *Second*, in legislating Parliament has made extensive use the techniques of strict liability criminal offences (see Chap 4) and the licensing of suppliers (see Chap 6), with special provisions for licensing money-lenders (see Chap 7). *Third*, there have been frequent statutory alterations made to the civil law relating to the supply of goods, all of them leaning one way:[104] they are designed to derogate from the even-handed, *laissez-faire* nineteenth century position (see para 1.02), instead giving the consumer some advantage to try to redress a real or imagined imbalance of bargaining-power.[105] *Fourth*, there are some statutory codes of practice, e.g. the pricing code (see para 8.10A), from which must be distinguished the ordinary voluntary codes (see para 3.11). *Fifth*, there is a growing amount of EU intervention (see para 3.10). *Sixth*, the Council of Europe has a membership which includes most other countries in Western Europe. Unlike EU legislation which is binding, proposals by the Council of Europe can only have national effect insofar as a State voluntarily ratifies its draft conventions, and implements these and other recommendations by national legislation.[106] From 1993, those European countries not members of the EU are pledged to adopt its conventions. *Seventh*, there is the possible effect on consumer law of the Human Rights Act 1998 (see para 3.09A).

---

102  As to the register, see (1998) 17 Tr L 52. As to complaint-handling, see OFT, *1998-AR 23; Modern markets: confident consumers* (1999, Cm. 4410) para 5.2.

103  The many statutes and statutory instruments are to be found in convenient up-dated form in Thomas, *Encyclopedia of Consumer Law*, Pts I and 2.

104  It is for consideration whether the present statutory provisions are both too elaborate and lacking in system. The further possibility of a Consumer Sales Act has already been mentioned (see para 1.01) and the UCP Directive will be considered later (see para 4.01A).

105  E.g. the Sale and Supply of Goods to Consumers Regulations 2002 (see para 14.01).

106  E.g. the Conventions on Product Liability (see para 17.23); Retention of Title (see para 24.21); and the Resolution on Access to Justice (14.5.81).

**[3.09A] The Human Rights Act 1998 (HRA).** This Act introduces into UK law the over-arching principles of the European Convention on Human Rights (Sched 1). Whilst largely beyond the scope of this work, the Act provides that English courts will be under a duty so far as possible to interpret UK legislation 'in a way which is compatible with Convention rights' (s 3(1): see para 1.04): if it cannot do this, under s 4 it is to make a declaration of incompatibility,[107] in which case a Minister may make a statutory order amending the offending legislation (s 10 and Sched 2). The HRA is primarily intended to give the private citizen rights against public authorities, providing that no 'public authority' may act in a manner incompatible with Convention rights:[108] it defines 'public authority' to include courts[109] and persons whose functions are 'of a public nature'.[110] The courts presumably extends to court officers, e.g. sheriffs or bailiffs collecting debt (see para 19.15), authorised officers entering premises (see para 28.05). It has also been interpreted to give private citizens justiciable rights against one another, the so-called 'horizontal effect'.[111] Amongst the convention rights possibly relevant to consumers are the following: a fair trial (Art 6: see paras 3.19, 3.22 and 3.24); privacy (Art 8: see paras 3.26 and 24.23); free speech (Art 10: see para 3.14)[112]; and protection of property (First Protocol, Art 1). In *Wilson v First County Trust Ltd (No. 2)*:[113]

> In 1999, Mrs W borrowed £5,000 from FCT by way of pawn. The loan was properly documented, except that the £250 documentation fee was misstated as part of the credit (stated at £5,250), rather than of the tcc (see para 8.25). After holding that the loan was permanently unenforceable under the now repealed s 127(3) (see para 9.21), the Court of Appeal adjourned the case, indicating that the effect of s 127(3) appeared to deprive FCT of its legal rights without a hearing, contrary to the European Convention of Human Rights; but the House of Lords confirmed that the loan was unenforceable under s 127(3) and held that, as a matter of interpretation (see para 1.04), s 3 of the Human Rights Act 1998 (implementing the Convention) did not apply to agreements made before it came into force (see para 3.09); and that the £5,000 was irrecoverable under the law of restitution (see para 10.19).

The Court of Appeal adjourned decision under s 4 of the HRA was unanimously reversed by the House of Lords on grounds of the presumption against retro-spectivity; namely that Parliament could not have intended the 1998 Act to have altered the existing substantive rights and obligations of the parties under the CCA 1974, which are to be enforced by the courts as the law applicable at the time the

---

107 See Bamforth (2001) 117 LQR 34; Loveland (2000) 150 NLJ 1595.

108 S 6(1): see *Lindsay v Customs & Excise* [2002] 3 All ER 118, CA (customs seizure of vehicle used for smuggling disproportionate). Can the Government effectively shake off the duties under the 1998 Act by contracting out its functions (see Craig (2002) 118 LQR 551)? For contracting out, see para 5.10.

109 S 6(3)(a). For 'public authority', see Burton (2002) 152 NLJ 1933.

110 S 6(3)(b). As to utilities (see para 3.07), see *James v London Electricity Plc* [2004] EWHC 3226.

111 See Beyleveld and Patterson (2002) 118 LQR 623.

112 *Interfact Ltd v Liverpool CC* [2005] 1 WLR 3118, DC (Video Recordings Act 1984), at paras 22–25 (leave to appeal to HL refused); *OFT v The Officers Club Ltd* [2005] EWHC 1080 (Ch), at paras 89–100, 128.

113 [2004] 1 AC 816; [2003] 4 All ER 97, HL. Rev the CA: [2001] 2 All ER (Comm) 134; [2001] 3 All ER 229, CA (see 118 LQR 203).

facts occurred.[114] This decision made it unnecessary for the House of Lords to consider a number of other issues raised by the case and important to us; but the majority of the House went on to give its *obiter* opinion on them as follows (at para 27):[115]

(1) The 1998 Act does have some retrospective effect as against the executive (at paras 13, 90, 130), e.g. disenabling a court bailiff from relying on earlier behaviour not compatible with a convention right, and also in respect of procedural rights (para 209).

(2) Art 6 of the Convention is concerned with procedural rights to a fair trial and did not touch now repealed s 127(3) of the CCA rendering some agreements unenforceable.[116]

(3) Art 1 of Protocol 1 (protecting private property) was concerned with the fairness of substantive law (at para 38; *contra* Lord Hope at 107); and that the effect of s 127(3) of the CCA was to deprive FCT of its property (at para 39), so engaging the Protocol.[117] In these circumstances, the court must identify the social policy ('mischief') behind s 127(3), namely the protection of debtors,[118] and compare that with the detriment to the creditor; and to comply with the HRA requires a 'reasonable relationship of proportionality between the means employed and the aim sought to be achieved' (*per* Lord Nicholls at para 69). However, the majority said that s 127(3) of the CCA did not infringe the Protocol because s 127(3) was proportionate to the problem of protecting debtors and so in the public interest.[119]

(4) In deciding this issue, the courts may only use Hansard as a source of background information, but cannot use parliamentary debates as an aid to construction (see above, para 1.04).

**[3.10] European Union directives**.[120] It has already been noted that the EU has begun to promote consumer interests generally; that at first it used indirect justifications for very specific interventions (see below); but that the Maastricht Treaty 1991 has given it a direct basis for such interventions (see para 1.03A). To administer this programme the EU has a Consumer Protection Directorate, advised by a Consumers' Committee and lobbied, *inter alia*, by the European Office of Consumers'

---

114 Lord Nicholls at paras 20, 22, 26; Lord Hope at paras 101–2, 124; Lord Hobhouse at paras 132–4; Lord Scott at paras 153, 157, 161–2; Lord Rodger at paras 187, 201, 210, 219–20. See also Lord Rodger in (2005) 121 LQR 57.

115 Lord Rodger offered no comment on these *obiter* issues.

116 At paras 36, 104, 165, 178, 215. What else is the concept of unenforceability (see paras 9.19–20)?

117 At paras 44, 136. Alternatively, Lords Hope and Scott argued that the Protocol was not engaged because the lender, by reason of s 127(3), only had a limited proprietary right from the outset (at paras 107 and 168).

118 At para 61. It is at this point that the extrinsic aids to interpretation become relevant: see para 1.04.

119 At paras 78, 109, 138, 169. Lord Nicholls expressly noted that this might sometimes penalise the blameless; pointed to a similar approach under the Moneylenders Act 1927 and HPA 1965; referred to the debtor's weak bargaining position; and even accepted the uncertainties over the legal definition of 'credit' (at paras 71–7).

120 For introductions, see Goode, *Consumer Credit Law & Practice*, Pt 1J; Harvey and Parry, *Consumer Protection and Fair Trading*, 6th edn, 39–45.

Organisations.[121] This Directorate has engendered a number of directives, in each
of which there has been a two-stage process: the first stage is to produce (usually
over a period of years) a draft directive;[122] and, if acceptable, this progresses to a
full Directive.[123] Early directives tended to involve detailed provisions as to harmonisation in the fields of safety, quality standards and weights and measures.[124]
However, the Single European Act of 1986 led to completion of the internal market
and has allowed a more generalised approach. Under the 1986 Act, purely national
laws can only apply to purely national goods, and not to those imported from
elsewhere in the EU.[125] The Commission has since undertaken an ambitious programme of reform,[126] including a scheme requiring each Member State to choose
national bodies which would be entitled to seek injunctions on behalf of consumers
in respect of infringement of relevant directives (see para 28.03). The UK Government have indicated a desire to see a reduction in the pace of change, with more
emphasis on enforcement and regular reviews of existing rules.[127] However, the
stream of draft directives shows no signs of abating and currently includes the
following: consumer credit (see para 5.12); consumer financial services; and payment card fraud.[128] Whilst the Commission remains the sole EU body which can
propose directives, in modern times its draft directives are also subject to the veto of
the EU Parliament: not only does this publicise inter-government deals, but it also
gives opponents a real opportunity to lobby for the rejection of undesired draft
directives, e.g. on Consumer Credit in 2003 (see para 5.12).

Up to the 1980s, the European Commission was anxious to optimise the assent
of Member States to new directives by drafting them as **minimum** directives; that
is, the rules embodied in directives was expressed as the minimum obligation of
Member States,[129] so enabling them to retain in force national legislation which
went further than the directives, e.g. the first (minimalist) consumer credit directive
did not affect the UK CCA.[130] However, more recently, greater confidence has led
the European Commission to put forward **maximum** directives; that is, the rules

---

121 Commission Decision (95/260/EEC). The early history is to be found in the Commission's First
   Report on Consumer Protection and Information Policy, set out in paras 5–751 of Thomas,
   *Encyclopedia of Consumer Law*. BEUC produces its own magazine, *BEUC Legal News*.
122 A Draft Directive is sometimes preceded by a Green Paper, e.g. proposing a replacement for the
   Misleading Advertising Directive (see OFT, *AR-2002/3* 52).
123 These include the following: consumer credit (see para 5.08); misleading advertisements
   (see para 8.06); product liability (see para 17.23); price displays (see para 8.08); unfair terms (see
   para 11.12); data protection (see para 3.27); distance selling (see para 8.19); consumer sales and
   guarantees (see paras 14.01 and 17.09A). The texts of relevant Directives will be found set out in
   Goode, *Consumer Credit Law & Practice*, Pt X.
124 These were designed from the industry standpoint to permit the free circulation of goods. For
   criticism of the old approach, see Cartwright, *Consumer Protection and the Criminal Law* (2001)
   134–5.
125 See (1992) Tr L 12. See the directives referred to in fn 123, above.
126 See the Consumer Policy Action Plan (COM/98/696). This was updated in May 2002, with the
   announcement of a new policy of consumer protection: (2002) 25 *Consumer Law Today* 8.
127 *Modern markets: confident consumers* (1999, Cm. 4410) paras 1.8 and 6.19. Except in relation to
   E-commerce: see para 8.17.
128 Documents 598PC0468; 599PC0438.
129 For 'Minimum Directives', see Stapleton (1994) 110 LQR 213.
130 Art 15. See also the following directives: Misleading Advertisements (see para 8.12A), Art 7;
   Distance Selling (see para 8.17), Art 8; Doorstep Selling (see para 10.21), Art 8; UTCC (see
   para 11.12), Art 8.

embodied in directives was expressed as the maximum obligation of Member States, so preventing them from retaining in force national legislation which went further than the directives.[131]

## Voluntary codes

[3.11] **Business self-regulation**.[132] A growth area in recent decades has been that of collective business self-regulation by voluntary codes of practice, which could be seen as a half-way house between the market forces and the statute book. Some businesses have even gone so far, usually under the aegis of a trade association, as to launch codes of ethical and social practice: this has commonly been done to create a good self-image for a trade, to distance its members from the more disreputable elements[133] and sometimes to stave off legislation, e.g. water disconnection code (see para 3.07); advertising codes (see para 3.14); tobacco advertising (see para 8.06); and Qualitas.[134] Official support for such codes started with the realisation of the limited capacity of traders to absorb new legislation (see para 3.01); that to take criminal or civil proceedings against a trader for acting in ignorance of the law was counter-productive; and that further effective changes in trading habits were more likely to be achieved through the medium of voluntary codes (see the *Second (1975) Annual Report* of the OFT). It is also a much cheaper and more flexible way of securing trader compliance.

An early supporter of voluntary codes of practice was the OFT; and statutory recognition of the value of this process came with the FTA, which imposed a duty on the Director 'to encourage relevant associations to prepare, and to disseminate to their members, codes of practice for guidance in safeguarding and promoting the interests of consumers in the United Kingdom' (s 124(3); now repealed). Accordingly, in the period 1974–2003 about 50 codes of practice were encouraged and approved by the OFT, concentrating on perceived problem sectors, such as electrical goods and the motor trade.[135] The OFT even went to the length of publishing guides for trade associations in drawing up their codes, e.g. for credit scoring (see para 8.39). According to the OFT, the key factors for the success of a code of practice are: the availability of a strong sanction; a plausible threat of statutory regulation; a clear wish by the good players in the industry to distinguish themselves from others; and obvious benefits to consumers, sufficient to affect their choice of trader.[136]

In persuading trade organisations to adopt them, the OFT has some powers: the carrot is that such codes have always been registrable with the OFT (see para

---

131 See also the GPS Directive 2001 (see para 4.32); Unfair Commercial Practices Directive (see para 4.21).

132 See generally, Harvey and Parry, *Op. cit.*, 360, *et seq.*: Cranston, *Consumers and the Law*, 3rd edn Chap 2.

133 E.g. the Finance Houses Association's *Credit Scoring* (see para 8.39) and the Visa Credit Code. See generally [2003] 3 *Which?* 47.

134 Following an OFT report of Feb. 1990, the furniture industry set up Qualitas as a company limited by guarantee to enforce a trade code of practice by hearing consumer complaints: OFT, *2000-AR*, 45; and para 23.22.

135 OFT, *Voluntary Codes of Practice* (1996) paras 2.3 and 2.5. For the 1996 Guidelines, see Appendix A.

136 *Ibid*, para 3.5.

3.12), which may recommend that approved codes be exempt from the competition rules; and the stick lies in his powers to recommend legislation[137] and that the local operation of codes can be monitored via the annual returns made by local authorities to the OFT (see para 3.05). Additionally, failure to observe other codes might lead the OFT to take one of the following types of action against the perpetrator: to seek Part 8 assurances (see para 6.06); to make issue of a credit licence depend on observance of a code (see para 6.19); to seek changes in standard-form terms (see para 11.08) by threatening use of the UTCC Regulations (see para 11.12).

The notion of a code of practice has proved so acceptable that in modern times it is also used in relation to statutory codes[138] and codes meant to guide the behaviour of the government bureaucracy[139] e.g. what the OFT terms its 'Guidelines'.[140] Nor is official sponsorship of codes of practice confined to the OFT (see para 3.14); but in our field the most important sponsors are the FSMA and the OFT (see paras 3.02 and 3.03). Concentrating on voluntary business codes of conduct, these may be divided as follows:

(a) Business-to-business codes, e.g. the business banking code,[141] the FLA Business Code,[142] the supermarket code.[143] These are beyond the scope of this work.

(b) Business-to-consumer codes, e.g. the EA Codes (see para 3.13), the Banking Code (see para 3.12). First, an assessment will be made of such codes (see para 3.12).

**[3.12] Assessment of business-to-consumer codes.** From an early stage the OFT realised that codes of practice could not directly raise the quality of products and so concentrated in relation to codes on the provision of information, the abandonment of unfair trading practices and the way complaints were handled (see paras 3.16 and 3.23). To some extent, the codes referred to above supplement gaps in the law.[144] For instance, these codes may supplement the law relating to the supply of goods and provide the flexibility so difficult to build into modern legislation: if a supplier fails to honour his previously announced adherence to a code, his supply contracts may have been induced by misrepresentation or amount to a breach of an express promise to abide by the code;[145] whereas the fact that a supplier has adhered to a code may help his defence to one of the strict liability offences

---

137 E.g. the codes of the privatised utilities (see para 3.07); or the pricing code (CPA, s 25: see para 8.10A); or general safety requirement (CPA, s 10(2)(b): para 4.33); or advertising (see para 8.12A); or any enforcement codes (see para 5.10). Reports on the monitoring of codes are made in the Annual Reports of the OFT.

138 E.g. the pricing code (CPA, s 25: see para 8.10A); or general safety requirement (CPA, s 10(2)(b): see para 4.33); or advertising (see para 8.12A); or any enforcement codes (see para 5.10).

139 E.g. the Deregulation Code (see para 5.10); the DPA Guidance Notes (see para 3.28).

140 See Goode, *Consumer Credit Law & Practice*, Vol 4, Division 8B.

141 See Goode, *Op. cit.*, Vol 4, Division 8A, Pt 5B.

142 See Goode, *Op. cit.*, Division 8A, Pt 1–III.

143 See [2003] 6 Farm Law 14. See further OFT (2003) 35 *Fair Trading* 4; *AR-2003/4* 59; *AR-2004/5* 69; and for undertakings given by supermarkets, see para 2.14.

144 By causing the courts to take into account any relevant code in establishing: (a) customary terms and trade usage (see para 15.11); (b) unfair terms (see UTCC Regulations, reg 4: para 11.15); (c) unreasonable terms (see UCTA, s 3: see para 18.24).

145 See *Bowerman v ABTA* [1995] Tr LR 246.

considered in Chapter 4, by supporting a general statutory defence,[146] or could be embodied in a Part 8 Assurance (see para 6.08). Moreover, codes may be useful for matters less appropriate to legislation, e.g. dealing expeditiously with complaints; conciliation by way of arbitration or ombudsman.[147]

However, it cannot be said that the voluntary codes adequately supplement the law in all respects. Such codes lack bite in the drafting and are sometimes adopted for less than altruistic motives, such as insulation from competitive forces. Indeed some codes have sometimes been dealt with by the courts as unreasonable restraints of trade.[148] Even where the rules of the relevant code do tend to favour the consumer, its operation may be less than satisfactory in practice. Whilst some codes recognise the possibility of the relevant trade association imposing sanctions for breach,[149] few associations seem prepared to invoke them; and in any event they cannot apply to non-members, a category which will usually include the more disreputable operators from whom the consumer is in greatest need of protection.

From 1993 the OFT begun to insist, as one condition of its support, that codes contain an element of independence in both redress and disciplinary procedures; from 1994 it started to require that codes expressly refer to the Unfair Terms Regulations (see above); and the OFT also required that such codes actively promote to their members model contracts compliant with the Regulations. By 1999 the Government had decided that codes of practice were a good thing and were once again encouraging their development,[150] so the OFT lobbied for its approval of codes to be put on a stronger statutory basis.[151] The effect is to be seen in the EA (see generally para 2.12), s 8 of which establishes a tougher two-stage process for the OFT formal approval of codes of practice (see para 3.13). At the same time, the OFT withdrew approval from all previous codes;[152] and this raises the issue of their continued legality (see para 3.11). What seems to be developing with voluntary codes is a two, perhaps overlapping, category situation.

(i)   Where the code promotes the supply of goods, perhaps on credit, this falls clearly within the ambit of the EA and its sponsors should apply for approval under that scheme (see para 3.13).

(ii)  Where the code promotes the supply of credit without any reference to goods, it may be that the originator of the code should seek approval under the FSMA (see para 3.02), e.g. the Banking Code (see below), the Mortgage Code.[153]

---

146  See Bragg, *Trade Descriptions*, 188–9; and generally, para 28.13.
147  See paras 3.24–5. E.g. *R (on the application of the Norwich and Peterborough BS) v Financial Ombudsman Service Ltd* [2003] 1 All ER (Comm) 65 (including principles for interpreting codes).
148  *Pharmaceutical Society of Great Britain v Dickson* [1970] AC 403, HL. See now the Competition Act 1998, s 2; and generally para 2.14.
149  A 'fine' was upheld in *Thorne v Motor Trade Association* [1937] AC 797, HL. For public enforcement under the UCP Directive, see para 4.20, item (a).
150  *Modern markets: confident consumers* (1999, Cm. 4410) paras 4.3–12; OFT *1999-AR*, 22. See also Cartwright, *Consumer Protection and the Criminal Law*, 53–60.
151  OFT, *2000-AR*, 8; (2001) 30 *Fair Trading* 15; [2001] 7 *Credit Today* 13.
152  OFT, *2001-AR*, 45. These were summarised in the 1st edn at para 3.13.
153  The Code is set out in Goode, *Consumer Credit Law & Practice*, Vol 4, Division 8, Pts 6 and 7. The mortgage industry has begun to lobby for replacement of that code by statutory regulation under the FSA; and the EU has accepted 'guidelines' for mortgage sales: [2001] 3 *Credit Today* 8.

*The Banking Code.*[154] Besides containing key commitments and information (paras 1–3 and 17), this Code deals with the following matters: interest rates (para 4); bank and cash machine charges (para 5); terms and conditions (para 6); moving accounts (para 7); advertising and marketing (para 8); statements, direct debits, standing orders, cheques and foreign exchange (para 9); credit and other payment cards, including PINs and credit card cheques (para 10); confidentiality (para 11);[155] customer protection of his accounts and liability for losses (para 12); lending, credit reference agencies and financial difficulty (para 13); complaints (paras 14–6).

**[3.13] OFT-sponsored EA codes of practice.**[156] Section 8(6) of the EA defines a 'consumer code' as

'A code of practice or other document (however described) intended, with a view to safeguarding or promoting the interests of consumers, to regulate by any means the conduct of persons engaged in the supply of goods or services to consumers (or the conduct of the employees or representatives)'.

The EA provides that the OFT 'may make arrangements for approving consumer codes and . . . give its approval or withdraw its approval from any consumer code' (s 8(2)). However, the OFT takes the view that s 8 only empowers it to operate in respect of industries which relate to the 'supply of goods or services to consumers' and/or are not within the aegis of any other statutory body: on this basis, it does not look at codes relating to broadcasting, utilities, advertising or finance (see para 3.14). From our point of view, perhaps the most important omissions are that the OFT does not deal with finance, e.g. pure consumer loans, nor with loans related to house purchase, e.g. mortgage code;[157] and these would all appear to fall within the ambit of the FSA (see para 3.02). The section is ambivalent in relation to codes relating to the supplies of goods on credit. Nor does the OFT really have any sanction to compel a party publishing a code to apply for OFT approval: not only is the EA silent on the matter, but the OFT is reluctant to apply the theoretic sanction of competition proceedings (see para 2.14) so long as the code on balance advantages consumers. The OFT has indicated that it will prioritise code applications from certain designated sectors of industry.[158]

The OFT s 8 arrangements are to be published (s 8(5)) and specify the criteria to be used (ss 8(3), (4)). The OFT have indicated that approval will involve a two-stage process as follows:[159]

*First stage.* Every code submitted must have a 'code sponsor', e.g. a trade association. The 'code sponsor' must draft and then submit to the OFT a code which it alleges meets all the OFT's core criteria,[160] is drafted in plain English and supplied

---

154 The Code is set out in Goode, *ibid*, Division 8, Pt 5A. For criticism that the Code is easy to circumvent, see [2005] 7 *Which?* 14–5.

155 See also para 7.03. For the Code rules on misuse of cards, see further para 7.07A.

156 See generally, OFT, *AR-2002/3*, 45–6; (2004) 38 *Fair Trading* 13.

157 The OFT is therefore not concerned with most of the codes appearing in Goode, *Consumer Credit Law & Practice*, Vol 4, Division VIIIA.

158 E.g. assistive products; car repair and servicing; computers; credit; direct marketing; domestic appliance repair; home furnishings; motor trade.

159 OFT (2003) 34 *Fair Trading* 12.

160 See OFT, *Core Criteria for Consumer Codes of Practice* (2002).

in a readable print size (see para 11.13). A conforming code must then be trialed over a number of months. The following stage-one achievers, who have not yet completed the second stage, have *inter alia* been announced: Retail Motor Industry;[161] Motor Vehicle Repairers Association; Debt Managers Standards Association. A number of other organisations are in discussions with the OFT.[162]

*Second stage.* This is the evaluation period, during which the 'code sponsor' must collect evidence so that it can demonstrate to the OFT that the code is working well on a day-to-day basis and delivering its promises to consumers, e.g. that any complaints have been satisfactorily handled. The 'code sponsor' may discharge his burden of proof by, for example complaints data, independent surveys, mystery shopping exercises. Only then will the 'code sponsor' achieve OFT approval and be able to exhibit the OFT approval logo.[163] The intention is that this logo will be marketed to consumers; and some small trade associations complain that the above elaborate procedure is too expensive for them.[164] Codes completing this stage include the following: the Direct Selling Association;[165] Society of Motor Manufacturers and Traders; Vehicle Builders and Repairers Association; British Healthcare Trades Association.

For the present, there remain a number of well-known voluntary codes of practice apparently within the scope of s 8(6) of the EA which have not yet achieved any recognition under the above process, although perhaps in negotiation with the OFT. This is particularly true of those industry codes relating to the supply of goods on credit,[166] where there is some feeling that the OFT is wearing two inconsistent hats: industry regulator and code-approver.[167] Some trade organisations continue to publish and promote, sometimes with OFT approval, new versions of old codes which have not gone through the EA procedure. The authorities then have to decide whether the codes have sufficient merit for consumers to justify official inaction, or whether to strike them down as in restraint of trade (see above). Codes may become enforceable under the Unfair Commercial Practices Directive (see para 4.21).

**[3.14] Other codes**. Those relevant to this work include codes relating to the following:

1.  *Broadcasting*. The communications industry, including both broadcasting and other methods of electronic communication, are governed by the Office of Communications (OFCOM): set up in 2002, OFCOM's functions are specified in Part 1 of the Communications Act 2003. As regards broadcast by television or radio, for our purposes the rules are only relevant insofar as they concern advertisements for the supply of goods. The BBC has long been forbidden by the terms of its licence to broadcast any commercial advertising or sponsored

---

161  The RMIF withdrew its application on 15.9.04.

162  OFT, *AR-2003/4*, 44–5; *AR-2003/4*, 42–5; *AR-2004/5*, 26; *AR-2005/6*, 23, 67.

163  See OFT (2005) 42 *Fair Trading* 6; *AR-2005/6*, 24.

164  (2003) BCCA Newsletter No. 25; (2002) 57 CC1/40; (2002) 9 CT 12.

165  (2005) 40 *Fair Trading* 10; Goode, *Op. cit.*, Division VIIIA, para 10.51; and see para 8.19.

166  See Goode, *Op. cit.*, Division VIIIA, the codes of the following Associations: Finance and Leasing; Consumer Credit Trade; Consumer Credit Trade of the UK.

167  E.g. FLA, *Lending Code AR 2004*, 11, where the disagreement is put in terms of code ownership.

programme without the permission of the Home Secretary.[168] However, under the Communications Act 2003, non-BBC broadcast advertising is subject to certain conditions: the Act itself sets out the general rules for programmes under a 'standards code': besides the impartiality requirement (s 320), this includes some restrictions on advertising (see below), including continuation of the ban on political and subliminal advertising (ss 319(2)(g) and (l)). This code extends to advertisements, so that there is a prohibition on 'the inclusion of advertising which may be misleading, harmful or offensive in television or radio' (s 319(2)(h)). Additionally, non-BBC advertising also has to meet the restrictions to be found in s 321. A statutory duty to secure observance of the code is placed on OFCOM,[169] which has farmed out performance of its duties to the ASA (see below). Misleading advertisements are within the broadcasting codes and also subject to Enforcement Orders (see para 28.04) in respect of repeated infringements. Under Part 2 of the 2003 Act, OFCOM also supervises electronic communications networks, e.g. telephones, which requires OFCOM to publish a policy on persistent misuse (s 131: see also para 8.16A).

2. *Privatised utilities.* Whether directly by statute, or as a condition of their authorisation, the public utilities are required to observe codes of practice in dealing with consumer debt, including water disconnections.[170]

3. *Advertising.* Under the threat of statutory intervention recommended by the *Molony Report on Consumer Protection* (1962, Cmnd. 1781), the non-broadcasting advertising industry set up the Advertising Standards Authority (ASA) to supervise and enforce a code of practice.[171] The essence is that 'All advertisements should be legal, decent, honest and truthful'.[172] The normal sanctions relied upon by the ASA are publicity and the agreement of the media to refuse publication to non-conforming advertisements.[173] Of course, as a back-up the OFT or other designated enforcer may exercise its powers with regard to advertisements misleading consumers (see para 8.12A); and it could take out an Enforcement Order (see below, para 6.08). The ASA administers these codes: the ASA British Codes of *Advertising Practice* and *Sales Promotion Practice*;[174] and the OFCOM Codes (see above). The ASA's decisions

---

168 For an unsuccessful attempt to obtain an injunction against broadcasting, see *Cambridge Nutrition Ltd v BBC* [1990] 3 All ER 523, CA.

169 Broadcasting Act 1996, s 325. This procedure is subject to the European Convention on Human Rights (see para 3.09A): *R v Broadcasting Standards Commission, ex p BBC* [2000] 3 All ER 989, CA. As to nuisance calls, see www.ofcom.org.uk/consult/condocs/misuse.

170 See generally Howells, *Consumer Debt*, Chap 8; and para 3.07.

171 As to the ASA, see Cranston, *Consumers and the Law*, 3rd edn, 55–60; [2004] 12 *Which?* 10. Does its jurisdiction extend to Internet advertisements?

172 Para 1.1, e.g. misleading bank advertising (see [1999] 10 *Credit Today* 6); Head & Shoulders Shampoo advertisement. See generally, Cranston, *Op. cit.*, 56. For mail order trading, see further, para 8.19.

173 The courts have indirectly supported this code by banning third parties from placing inserts (which may not be amenable to ASA control) in newspapers as amounting to passing-off: see para 17.17.

174 For the text, see Goode, *Consumer Credit Law & Practice*, Vol 4, Division VIIIA, Pt 10. See Circus, *Sales Promotion Law*, 2nd edn, 198; Pinto (2003/4) 135 MIP 38. There is also a media code in the newspaper industry: see (1994) 13 Tr L 246.

are subject to judicial review; but the court could interfere only on grounds of irrationality, illegality or procedural impropriety.[175] Nor can such judicial proceedings be used to temporarily gag the ASA, as the ASA will not usually be restrained from publishing its reports in the interim;[176] nor do its normal activities breach the European Convention on Human Rights.[177] Second and subsequent breaches of the ASA Codes may give rise to proceedings under the Misleading Advertisement Regulations (see para 8.12A). Additionally, newspaper advertisements are subject to the Mail Order Protection Scheme (MOPS).[178]

4. *Other codes.* The EU promulgates codes of conduct, e.g. relating to electronic payments (see para 2.24), home loans (see para 3.12) and eco-labelling (see para 8.06). The UK Government promotes codes on environmental claims[179] and national standards of enforcement for bailiffs (see para 19.15). The Consumers' Association co-sponsors the E-commerce code; and industry sponsors the credit scoring code (see para 8.39).

In 2007, much of the above may be overtaken by the UCP Directive (see para 4.20, item (g)).

# CONSUMER REDRESS[180]

## Information and advice

[3.15] **Introduction**. It is an old adage that before entering a transaction a consumer tends to suffer from 'buying fever' (when he may avoid thinking about the disadvantages of the transaction), whereas after the event this is replaced by 'buyer's remorse'.[181] At both stages, the consumer may need information and advice as to the product and any associated credit.[182]

1. *The pre-contract stage.* Broadly speaking, the role of consumer product information both generally and at the point of sale will be largely regulated by

---

175 *R v ASA, ex p The Insurance Service* [1990] TLR 169, DC (see 139 NLJ 1161); *R v ASA, ex p DSG Retail Ltd* [1997] CLY 3558; *R v ASA, ex p Charles Robertson Ltd* [2000] CLY 4146; *R (on the application of SKB PLC) v ASA* [2001] CLY 692.

176 *R v ASA, ex p Vernons Organisation Ltd* [1993] 2 All ER 202; *R (on the application of J) v A* [2005] EWHC 2609.

177 *R v ASA, ex p City Trading Ltd* [1997] CLY 3559 (claim that the Code contravened the free speech provisions of the European Convention on Human Rights failed). See also *R v ASA, ex p Matthais Rath* [2001] CLY 4409; and Lawson (2001) 151 NLJ 526.

178 This both vets advertisers and reimburses readers: see (2003) 59 *Magistrate* 266–7.

179 *Green Claims* (1998); and see *Modern markets: confident consumers* (1999, Cm. 4410) paras 3.17–8. For a voluntary green scheme for cars, see [2000] 1 *Which?* 7; and for dodgy green claims, see [2001] 1 *Which?* 17.

180 See generally Cranston, *Consumers and the Law*, 3rd edn, 102, *et seq.*; OFT, *Developments in Consumer Redress* (1996); Lowe and Woodroffe, *Consumer Law & Practice*, 6th edn, Chap 10.

181 For a survey by the OFT, see *Developments in Consumer Redress* (1995).

182 The case for information and advice in relation to consumer credit is put in Chapter 9.2–3 of the *Report on Consumer Credit* (1971, Cmnd. 4596). Codes of conduct (see para 3.11 *et seq.*) can also be seen as having a consumer redress function: OFT, *1984-AR*, 11.

the law relating to such matters as trade descriptions, labelling, packaging and pricing dealt with in Chapter 4, and that relating to advertising which is surveyed in Chapter 8.[183] Leading examples of such protection concerns the pre-contract disclosure of specified information required in respect of distance selling or in respect of regulated agreements under the Consumer Credit Act 1974 (see paras 9.05A–6). Independent providers of free advice to consumers generally include the NCC (see para 3.04), the OFT (see para 3.03), the Consumers' Association[184] and the media.[185]

2. *The post-contract stage.* Much of the remainder of this work is concerned with the rights available to the consumer in the event that the goods supplied do not meet his expectations. However, the mere existence of such rights is not enough in itself. *First,* a consumer unaware that one of his rights has been infringed is unlikely even to seek redress; and this has led to a sustained programme of consumer education (see para 3.01). *Second,* the consumer aware that his rights have been infringed should be encouraged in the first instance to approach his supplier with a complaint: this requires the supplier to have an adequate complaints procedure and the consumer to be taught how to use it.[186] Only if this fails does the dissatisfied consumer need specific legal advice relating to his particular problem (see paras 3.16–17). *Third,* armed with this information, for the enforcement of those rights (see para 3.18, *et seq.*) the consumer needs convenient,[187] cheap and efficient machinery:[188] this might include more *pro bono* legal advice (see para 3.16) and legal assistance by *McKenzie* friends (see para 3.17). *Fourth,* there is the very real problem of consumer over-indebtedness,[189] especially with regard to the prevalence of multiple indebtedness.[190] Effective total records of individual consumer credit industry indebtedness may be necessary (see para 8.36) and the need for money advice centres becomes greater (see para 3.16). To some extent, creditors can help by not over-lending[191] and pre-contract credit assessment (see para 8.35, *et seq.*), though the latter raises privacy issues (see para 3.26). Credit insurance helps (see para 24.44/5).

---

183 Many of the developments in the area were given significant impetus by the Molony Committee's *Report on Consumer Protection* (1962, Cmnd. 1781), especially Chaps 6–10, 15–18.

184 See [1984] *Which?* 22; *Getting action on complaints*. For the CA, see generally para 3.08.

185 One commentator even puts the media as the consumers' major source of advice and assistance: Cranston, *Op. cit*, 107.

186 See (1991) 8 Tr L 242–5; (1999) 54 CC 1/8; the regular consumer dissatisfaction surveys which appear in the *Annual Reports* of the OFT; and Twigg-Flesner, *Consumer Product Guarantees* (2003) 21–4. For an EU template complaints form for consumers, see OFT, *1998-AR*, 23. For a code on telephone call queuing, see [1998] 10 *Which?* 7.

187 This might include more consumer-friendly court/tribunal sittings, e.g. evenings: see Harvey and Parry, *Op. cit.*, 234.

188 This might include more trial by paper (Harvey and Parry, *ibid*) and easier enforcement of judgments (see para 27.04).

189 The remorseless increase in instalment credit (see para 5.01) is just one symptom of the increasing indebtedness *per capita*: see also Whitton (1998) 50 *Quarterly Account* 4; OFT, *Vulnerable Consumers and Financial Services* (1999) 5 and 16; and para 6.09.

190 It should be remembered that consumer indebtedness is likely to extend beyond the credit industry to include, e.g. Council Tax, debts to the Social Fund and utilities (see paras 2.15 and 3.07) and loans under the Education (Student Loans) Act 1990.

191 See the FHA Code: paras 3.13 and 6.10. For creditor in accessing such information, see para 3.29.

**[3.16] Consumer legal advice.**[192] Consumer sales law is a complicated subject; and it has proved difficult to ensure across-the-board, consistent, high level legal advice. Whilst some consumers are likely to receive adequate advice from organisations to which they belong, e.g. a trade union, or by paying an adviser,[193] there is undoubtedly a continuing consumer demand for local, readily accessible, free advice. In the first instance this tends to be met for the most part by the traditional local authority-funded organisations: Trading Standards Service (see para 3.05); and CABx (see para 3.08). To these should be added the utilities regulators (see para 3.07); and ombudsmen (see para 3.25); and the advice help-lines mentioned below.[194] Frequently, one of these services may be able to settle a problem between a trader and a consumer. But, if that proves impossible, then they may act as a filter for the forwarding of complaints to a solicitor, a step which immediately raises the question of cost. Of course, not all complaints follow this pattern: for instance, an advice centre will sometimes follow a dispute right through to litigation, e.g. the CAB office in the Royal Courts of Justice (see para 3.08); some CABx operate with a panel of solicitors on a rota scheme, commonly on a *pro bono* (law for free) basis;[195] or perhaps the more educated consumer may initially consult a solicitor privately, whilst the disadvantaged can do so on legal aid (see para 3.17) or may go to a neighbourhood law centre.[196]

Nevertheless, it is clear that there is never likely to be enough free advice to meet demands; and this is especially true in relation to debt advice. Accordingly, in recent years attention has been focused on other ways of financing further advice free to the consumer at the point of use[197] and subject to OFT licensing as ancillary credit businesses (see para 5.43). In the absence of sufficient public money being available, the income of advice agencies is likely to have to come from creditors and/or debtors. Broadly, there are three competing funding philosophies: first, industry support gathered centrally, as with the Money Advice Trust,[198] which in turn set up (with grant-aid) the telephone National Debtline and also a professional Institute of Money Advisers;[199] second, a US-style deduction from debts collected by the advice centre;[200] and third, there have developed businesses which charge debtors for advice. To bring together these varied debt advice schemes, there has

---

192 *Modern markets: confident consumers* (1999, Cm. 4410) para 5.1, *et seq.*; Twigg-Flesner, *Consumer Product Guarantees* (2003), Chap 4.

193 E.g. the *Which?* Legal Service (see para 3.08); the Citizens Debt Counselling Service (see (1997) CCA News, Summer 18).

194 The EU is also lauching a free advice helpline: [2002] *CCA News, Winter*, 9.

195 See Sweet (1999) 149 NLJ 1588; (2000) 150 NLJ 253; Boon and Whyte (2000) 150 NLJ 1564; (2002) 152, 1516 and 1795. For a *pro bono* protocol, see (2003) 153 NLJ 537.

196 *Law Centres: A Practical Guide* (1980) by the Law Centres Federation. See (2003) 151 NLJ 1726; and generally, Macleod, *Consumer Sales Law*, 1st edn, para 3.16. Some Law Centres are financially supported by the CLS (see para 3.17).

197 An early model was the Birmingham Settlement (see [2000] 8 *Credit Today*, Extra). As to how money advice works, see Chambers (1991) 46 CC 2/24; (1996) 17 CCA News 2/12.

198 The Money Advice Trust (MAT) was set up in response to an appeal by the Director of the OFT (see OFT, *1990-AR* 28 and continues to be supported by the OFT (OFT, *1997-AR*, 24). For the terms of membership, see (2001) 60 QA 1; (2004) 72 QA 1. MAT also trains non-lawyer money advisers. For the Pay Link Trust, see para 5.42.

199 One of the aims of the Institute is to offer professional accreditation and then seek audience for its members under the Courts and Legal Services Act 1990: see (2003) 58 CC2/38; and paras 3.17; 3.22.

200 E.g. the Consumer Credit Counselling Service (CCCS): see D'Ingeo (1995) 145 NLJ 190.

been set up the Money Advice Liaison Group.[201] Since the 2003 White Paper,[202] the DTI have now set up and funded Consumer Direct, a telephone and website consumer advice service operated by the OFT.[203]

**[3.17] Financing legal advice and proceedings**. Like the Ritz hotel, the legal system is open to everybody; but, obtaining legal advice and taking legal proceedings can be expensive. For many years, the State offered modest financial support under the Legal Aid Acts, though that system has been entirely replaced by the Access to Justice Act 1999.[204] This (perhaps misnamed) Act aims to restrict State financial support only to 'individuals' (s 7(1)), so that registered companies are not eligible for support. The State support is to be overseen by the Legal Services Commission (ss 1–3), which will have two arms: the Criminal Defence Service (CDS) and Community Legal Service (CLS). The CDS (ss 12–18, as amended) deals predominantly with the cost of **defence** in criminal proceedings, so that it is of little use to an aggrieved consumer (see para 3.19), but may be relevant to the small unincorporated trader charged with a strict liability offence (see Chap 4). The CLS (ss 4–11) is intended to ensure that the poor and disadvantaged can access the civil law services and benefits to which they are entitled on a means-tested basis (s 7): the individual may have to make a contribution (ss 10–11) and will be funded according to statutory criteria set out in a code (s 8). Initially, no more Government money was made available than under the previous legal aid scheme, which clearly circumscribed the services provided. As the criminal side rightly takes priority, the resources available to finance civil proceedings have steadily reduced: not only is this likely to circumscribe the amount of CLS support available to Law Centres (see para 3.16), but resultant squeeze on civil litigation makes it unlikely that legal aid will be available to owner-occupiers. Indeed, the CLS has been seen by the Commission as a welfare benefit focused solely on the poorest in society,[205] perhaps encouraging most consumers to use conditional fees and dispute resolution (see paras 3.18 and 3.24). However, in 2004 the CLS did introduce a free information and advice service available by telephone and website;[206] and in 2006 it added outreach projects.[207]

*Litigants in person.* Parallel to the development of the small claims procedure in the county court (see para 3.23), there has been a movement to encourage consumers to litigate in person. The Lord Chancellor's Office has produced an explanatory booklet for litigants in person;[208] and in practice considerable support

---

201 As to the Money Advice Liaison Group, see (1993) 48 CCI/26; (1994) 15 CCA News 1/21; (1996) 50 CC 6/20; (1998) 53 CC2/32; (2005) 75 QA 14.

202 *Fair, Clear and Competitive: the Consumer Credit Market in the 21st Century* (Dec 2003, Cm. 6040), paras 5.30–43.

203 See OFT (2005) 42 *Fair Trading* 4; (2006) 43 FT 9; *AR-2005/6*, 18.

204 The EU is proposing a draft directive on the provision of EU civil legal aid for cross-border disputes: (2002) 152 NLJ 1634.

205 (2004) 154 NLJ 1273 and 1673; (2005) 155 NLJ 347. As it is, the cost is some 10 × higher per capita than much of the rest of Europe: (2003) 153 NLJ 427.

206 Jones (2005) 77 QA 4; 78 QA 2. For other telephone advice, see para 3.16.

207 For areas of financial exclusion: see clspolicy@legalservices.gov.uk

208 See the leaflets produced by the Lord Chancellor's Office and widely available at CABx and Advice Centres. See also *How to Sue in the County Court* by the Consumers' Association. As to whether the legal aid of litigant-in-person statutes infringe the Human Rights Convention, see Birch (2001) 151 NLJ 162 and 277.

and advice in individual actions has been provided in recent years by organisations such as Consumer Advice Centres (see para 3.05). Furthermore, in those cases where costs are at issue, e.g. ordinary High Court or county court actions, the position of the consumer has been considerably improved in relation to costs by the Litigants in Person (Costs and Expenses) Act 1975. Prior to that Act, the litigant in person was not entitled to remuneration in respect of his time and labour,[209] whereas under the Act he may be.[210] Moreover, whilst solicitors and barristers have a right of audience in court, even if acting *pro bono* (see para 3.16), any litigant may instead represent himself.[211] Alternatively, it has long been clear that he may be represented by a friend without right of audience, usually known as a *McKenzie* friend.[212] However, it would seem that litigants-in-person remain unwelcome in the legal system.[213]

## Enforcement of consumer rights

[3.18] **Introduction**. Even when armed with advice as to his legal rights (see paras 3.15–17), the consumer faces a number of difficulties. If the trader against whom he is complaining refuses redress, he will need a considerable effort of sustained will-power to achieve his rights. Even more significant is likely to be the issue of financial resources. The basic assumption of the English Legal System appears to be that anybody seeking legal advice or participating in court proceedings is likely to utilise the services of lawyers; that costs will normally follow the event, i.e. the loser pays the costs of both sides; and, as such services are normally provided on the basis of an expensive piece-rate, it is usually very important to consumers to consider ways of cheapening the process.

Perhaps the most obvious solution to these problems might appear to be to look for a parallel criminal offence (see Chap 4), persuade another to undertake the prosecution of that offence,[214] and then seek compensation from the convicting court (see paras 3.19–20); but it must be remembered that the public authority is usually under no obligation to support an individual,[215] often being required only to support consumers generally, e.g. the EA, Part 8 (see para 6.07). Alternatively, or subsequently, the consumer may pursue civil proceedings through the courts (see para 3.22), perhaps using a prior conviction to cheapen the civil proceedings (see para 3.21). A policy of using civil test cases brought by public authorities might be helpful to consumers,[216] as may the wider availability of class actions,

---

209 *Buckland v Watts* [1970] 1 QB 27, CA.

210 *Hart v Aga Khan Foundation (UK)* [1984] 2 All ER 439, CA. Costs are not usually allowed in small claims in the County Court: see para 3.22.

211 See the Courts and Legal Services Act 1990, ss 27, 28, 29, 31, 31A, 31B and 31C (as amended, substituted and added by the Access to Justice Act 1999), e.g. *Wilson v Robertsons* (set out at para 5.22).

212 *McKenzie v McKenzie* [1971] p 33, CA (matrimonial case). See now the Courts and Legal Services Act 1990, s 27(2)(c).

213 See the account of a small claims court dispute in *The Times* (10.5.05).

214 In our context, that would commonly be the Local Authority: see para 28.03.

215 The availability of criminal test cases depends on the good of offices of the OFT or Local Authority (see para 3.19) and has budgetary implications.

216 Such schemes are widely available on the Continent. They were introduced here with the UTCC Regulations (see para 11.19).

which allow a whole class of persons severally injured by a defendant to sue that defendant together in a single action,[217] and super-complaints (see para 4.19). The Lord Chancellor announced[218] his intention to allow class actions by persons injured and representative actions by bodies such as consumer groups (see para 3.19). Further, a litigant in person may reduce his costs by use of advice centre support.[219] Alternatively, an aggrieved consumer may choose to pursue his complaint in an alternative forum which is likely to involve him in no or reduced costs, such as arbitration or an ombudsman (see paras 3.23–25); but, insofar as aggrieved consumers settle out of court, the law does not develop in the interests of consumers generally.

Having looked at all the above, an aggrieved consumer may find that the only effective avenue for redress is to employ lawyers to bring or defend civil proceedings on his behalf. In this context, there become relevant the game-plan of the Access to Justice Act 1999. This Act assumes the State financial assistance is unlikely to be available to the ordinary consumer (see para 3.17), who **instead** will finance the considerable financial costs of litigation by one or both of conditional fees (see below) and legal expenses insurance.[220] The consumer may have taken out such insurance before the event (BTE insurance), e.g. as part of his household or motor insurance; or, more likely, he may have to enter such a policy after the dispute has arisen (ATE insurance).[221]

*Conditional fees.* Traditionally, any arrangement by which a solicitor's entitlement to his fee was contingent on his client winning the case was considered reprehensible. So English common law treated any such solicitor-client contract as illegal on grounds of maintenance and champerty (see para 7.26), whether the agreement was that the solicitor recovered (a) some of his client's winnings, (b) his normal fee plus a success uplift, or (c) only his normal fee. However, in the 1980s perceptions of this public policy begun to change when it was appreciated that some form of conditional fee might facilitate access to justice by those earning too much to qualify for State financial assistance for litigation (see para 3.17). Accordingly, the outright statutory prohibition on solicitors entering any kind of conditional fee arrangement in the Solicitors Act 1974 (s 59(2)(b)) was first replaced by a provision in the Courts and Legal Services Act 1990, which enabled the Lord Chancellor by regulation to allow solicitors sometimes to charge what it called 'conditional fees' (s 58); and this provision has since been enhanced to become a central plank of the Access to Justice Act 1999, ss 27–8. The enhanced provisions

---

217 E.g. an action against a manufacturer in respect of a design fault: see paras 14.18 and 17.02. See Harvey and Parry, *Op. cit.*, 237, *et seq.*; Cranston, *Consumers and the Law*, 3rd edn, 121–33; Mildred, *Product Liability* (2000) Chap 10; Epstein (2003) 153 NLJ 153. Costs should be shared: *BCCI v Ali (Assessment of Costs)* [2001] CLY 479.

218 *Modern markets: confident consumers* (1999, Cm. 4410) paras 5.25 and 7.10. Multi-party action legal-aid funding has been extended: (2003) 153 NLJ 1089. See Group Litigation Orders.

219 E.g. by Local Authority Consumer Advice Centres (see para 3.05), or by Law Centres (see para 3.16). See the Money Advice Handbook on *Court Procedures*, 2nd edn.

220 The 1999 Act confirms that these insurance premiums are recoverable from the other side: ss 30–2.

221 *Callery v Gray (Nos 1 and 2)* [2002] 3 All ER 417, HL (ATE: see 152 NLJ 1058, 1098, 1099, 1439). These are recoverable as costs under s 29: see *Re Claims Direct Test Cases* [2003] 2 All ER (Comm) 788, CA. ATE insurance is not within the CCA: *Tilby v Perfect Pizza Ltd* (2002) 152 NLJ 397 (see 152 NLJ 417).

(1990 Act, ss 58, 58A), colloquially known as 'no-win-no-fee' arrangements, broadly allows arrangements of above types (b) or (c), but not (a);[222] and it extends to virtually any civil claim.[223] However, the Act expressly says that any other contingent fee arrangement shall remain 'unenforceable'.[224] It has been claimed that these statutory conditional fees 'are a halfway-house or hybrid grafted on to the existing litigation system by a Government determined to increase access to justice but too squeamish to go the whole hog and introduce US-style contingency fees'.[225]

**[3.19] Criminal proceedings.** Particularly in Chapter 4, there will be considered a large number of statutory provisions imposing criminal sanctions in attempts at consumer protection.[226] Many of these are offences of strict liability (see para 28.08) and must nowadays be consistent with the defendant's Convention Rights (see para 3.09A). Most of these offences are triable either on indictment (usually by jury) before the Crown Court or summarily (without a jury) by a magistrates' court,[227] frequently involving a heavier maximum penalty if trial is on indictment (see para 28.07). An analysis of the types of complaint and numbers of convictions are to be found in the Annual Reports of the Office of Fair Trading (see para 3.03). As State financial assistance is not available to prosecute such complaints (see para 3.17), a consumer is likely to wish to persuade somebody else to prosecute,[228] typically the local Trading Standards Department.[229] However, conviction is not normally the sole aim of the consumer: he may seek a compensation order from the convicting court (see para 3.20); or he may subsequently take civil proceedings (see para 3.21, *et seq*.). It is for consideration how far public authorities should go in bringing prosecutions where the primary objective is to make possible a compensation order or facilitate a civil claim (see para 3.18). In *R v Glen Adaway*[230] the Court of Appeal seemed to discourage such a policy. The case involved a conservatory installer making a false trade description within s 1(1)(b) of the TDA (see para 4.03), where the prosecutor ignored TSO Guidelines to prosecute only if the defendant was 'engaged in fraudulent activity' or 'deliberately or persistently breached legal obligations'.[231] Sadly for consumers, in quoshing the conviction, Rose LJ delivering the judgment of the court said (at para 21):

---

222  There is provision for the CLS (see para 3.17) to fund such conditional fee arrangements in what are called 'legal funding agreements': new s 58B. For consideration of some of the issues, see *Hollins v Russell* [2003] 4 All ER 590, CA.

223  For the steps to be followed in making a conditional fee agreement, see Harrison (2000) 150 NLJ 895; Marven (2004) 154 NLJ 1186. For subsequent and proposed amendments to the system, see Marshall (2003) 153 NLJ 833; and assessment from the litigant perspective, see [2004] 2 *Which?* 14.

224  New s 58(1). See *Awwad v Geraghty & Co* [2000] 1 All ER 608, CA (discussed 116 LQR 371).

225  See Bawdon (2000) 150 NLJ 1890. See also (2002) 152 NLJ 797; (2004) 154 NLJ 1468; (2005) 155 NLJ 155.

226  For a comparative survey within the EEC, see the Commission's *Consumer Redress* (12.12.84), Annex 2.

227  The procedure to be adopted is laid down in the Magistrates Court Act 1980, ss 17–28: see further, Harvey and Parry, *Op. cit.*, 246–8.

228  Private prosecutions are possible, but unlikely. E.g. *Donnelly v Rowlands* [1971] 1 All ER 9, DC (trade body); and see para 28.02.

229  See para 3.05. For prosecution by LAs, see Chap 28.

230  [2004] EWCA Crim 2831, CA. For another point, see para 28.13.

231  The TSO *Public Protection Enforcement Policy*, quoted at para 10. See further para 4.01.

The criminal law should not be mobilised to secure the settlement of private disputes which should more appropriately be determined in the county court or by arbitration or mediation.

However, if the criminal law is not to be so mobilised in favour of consumers, in 2006 the DTI consulted[232] on whether designated authorities (paras 21–3) should be empowered to bring representative actions (para 53) on behalf of groups of consumers aggrieved by the same or similar complaints against a business, e.g. a manufacturer of washing machines suffering a common fault, a promoter of a lottery scam.

**[3.20] Criminal compensation orders**. Assuming a supplier is prosecuted to conviction, it may be possible for any consumer injured by commission of the offence to obtain a compensation order from the convicting court. Such a general procedure was introduced in the Powers of Criminal Courts Act 1973; and, after many amendments, its powers were consolidated in the Powers of Criminal Courts (Sentencing) Act 2000. However, these statutory powers do not provide for any compensation where civil proceedings are concluded before conviction;[233] nor do they contain any interim power to freeze the defendant's assets pending conviction,[234] though there is power under the Supreme Court Act 1981 to apply for an injunction to this effect.[235]

Section 130(1) of the 2000 Act provides that:

'a court by or before which a person is convicted of an offence, instead of or in addition to dealing with him in any other way, may on application or otherwise make an order (in this Act referred to as 'a compensation order') requiring him—

(a) to pay compensation for any personal injury, loss or damage resulting from that offence or any other offence which is taken into consideration by the court in determining sentence; or

(b) to make payments for funeral expenses or bereavement in respect of a death resulting from any such offence, other than an offence due to an accident arising out of the presence of a motor vehicle on a road'.

Under this section, it is not strictly necessary that the person injured makes an application;[236] nor is the court bound to make an order.[237] However, it is necessary

---

232 DTI Consultation Paper, *Representative Actions in Consumer Protection Legislation* (July 2006). The DTI's preferred option would be a new statute empowering those bodies to bring self-funded (para 59) civil actions on behalf of named domestic consumers against business suppliers for breach of listed consumer legislation, giving the business the opportunity of offering replacement/repair rather than just paying financial compensation (paras 17–19).

233 *Hammerton Cars Ltd v London Borough of Redbridge* [1974] 2 All ER 216, DC. The order must be made by the convicting court: *R v Blackpool Justices, ex p Charlson* [1972] 3 All ER 854, DC. What, if any, is the effect on such powers of provisions in consumer protection statutes creating offences but forbidding any civil redress (see para 3.21)?

234 *Malone v Metropolitan Police Comr* [1980] QB 49, CA.

235 S 37(1): *Chief Constable of Kent v V* [1983] QB 34, CA. But see *Chief Constable of Hampshire v A* [1984] 2 All ER 385, CA.

236 Indeed, the Act does not even require the presence of an independent civil remedy to that person: *R v Chappell* (1984) 80 Cr App R 31, CA (criticised 48 MLR 706; Atiyah, *Sale of Goods*, 10th edn, 295).

237 The appellate courts have insisted that such orders are not to be made where the issues are complex or disputed: *R v Swan and Webster* (1984) 6 Crim App Rep (S) 22; *R v White* [1996] 2 Cr

that there be a conviction and loss:[238] the amount may include offences taken into account;[239] but there is a restriction on the maximum amount of compensation which a magistrates' court may order (s 131). Special rules apply in the case of injury or loss arising out of road accidents (ss 130(6)–(8)) or conviction under the Theft Act (s 130(5)); and where a court could, but declines to, exercise its powers under s 130, it must give reasons (s 130(3)). Under s 130(4), compensation[240]

> shall be of such amount as the court considers appropriate, having regard to any evidence and to any representations that are made by or on behalf of the accused or the prosecutor.

In making the order, the court is directed to have regard both to the means of the convicted person (s 130(11));[241] and where the courts considers it appropriate to impose both a fine and a compensation order;[242] but, if the convict has insufficient means to pay both, the court shall give preference to a compensation order.[243] The convict may appeal a compensation order (ss 132, 133); and, if there is subsequently any civil litigation in respect of the same damage, the damages awarded must be reduced by the amount of compensation paid.[244] The court has power to allow the convict time for payment or order payment by instalments (s 141); and this may be a real disadvantage to recipients needing to replace capital equipment. On the other hand, a compensation order can be recovered under the court bailiff system (see para 19.15).

## Civil proceedings

**[3.21]** **Prior convictions**. Notwithstanding that the consumer does not obtain any, or sufficient, compensation thereby, it may still be of advantage to a consumer to secure a conviction of his supplier for a criminal offence (see paras 3.18–20) before commencing civil proceedings.

---

App R(S) 58. As to presentation of claims by trading standards officers (see para 28.03), see (1993) 10 Tr L 187. As to Government encouragement for greater use of such orders, see *Modern markets: confident consumers* (1999, Cm. 4410) para 5.22.

238  *R v Boardman* [1987] CLY 892, CA (conditional sale; goods recovered undamaged). But distress may be sufficient (*Bond v Chief Constable of Kent* [1983] 1 All ER 456, DC); and the offence need not be the sole cause of the loss (*Rowlston v Kenny* (1982) 4 Cr App R(S) 85).

239  S 130(1)(a). As to where there are specimen charges, see *R v Crutchley and Tonks* (1993) 15 Cr App R(S) 627.

240  As to the special compensation rules where the offence leads to a death, see s 130(9) and (10).

241  S 130(11). As to determining the convict's financial circumstances, see s 126. An order should only be made where there is a realistic possibility of payment within a reasonable time: *R v Bagga* (1989) 11 Cr App R(S) 497.

242  It is still not possible for the court to make both a compensation order and a criminal bankruptcy order (s 39(1)); but it is possible to combine the latter with a restitution order (as to which, see para 24.25): *R v James* (1984) 6 Cr App R(S) 370, CA. For insolvency, see generally para 19.18, *et seq.*

243  S 130(12). It is unlikely that a compensation order can be combined with a custodial sentence. As to confiscation orders, see Proceeds of Crime Act 2002, ss 13–15.

244  S 134. *Quaere* whether the compensation order is evidence that the injury was caused by the offence, and what effect it may have on costs in the civil proceedings?

1.  *Evidential value.*[245] According to s 11(1) of the Civil Evidence Act 1968:

    > In any civil proceedings the fact that a person has been convicted of an offence
    > by or before any court in the United Kingdom ... shall ... be admissible in
    > evidence for the purpose of proving, where to do so is relevant to any issue in
    > those proceedings, that he committed that offence.

    Leaving aside defamation actions (s 11(3)), it is not conclusive evidence,[246]
    though the Act provides no guidance as to the standard of proof required to
    disprove the conviction, and little in identifying the conduct which is the
    subject-matter of the conviction (see s 11(2)(b)). However, it is clear that,
    following conviction, s 11 will tend to reduce the cost and increase the certainty
    of subsequent civil litigation.[247]

2.  *Statutory duties.* There are likely to be a significant number of cases where a
    person in the chain of distribution (see para 17.01) has committed a criminal
    offence by breaching one of the statutory provisions designed for the protection
    of consumers, see e.g. Chap 4, but it does not prove possible to obtain a
    compensation order (see para 3.20) and there is no privity of contract (see para
    10.01). In the foregoing circumstances, the consumer may wish to bring an
    action in tort for breach of statutory duty.[248] Thus, it has been said that:[249]

    > '*Prima facie* a person who has been injured by the breach of a statute has a right to
    > recover damages from the person committing it unless it can be established by
    > considering the whole of the Act that no such right was intended to be given'.

    A few statutes expressly grant such a right of action[250] whilst a number of
    others expressly rule out such an action.[251] Where statute is silent on the point,
    as regards domestic legislation the courts have usually preferred to refuse such
    a tort action on the grounds that a right of action was already available under
    the statute or some other rule of contract or tort: for instance that food is not of
    the nature and quality demanded or is unfit for human consumption;[252] or that
    a vehicle was supplied in breach of the construction and use regulations or in
    an unroadworthy condition (see para 4.37). Nor does it seem likely that such an
    action will lie for breach of the Trade Descriptions Act (see generally paras
    4.02–17): contrary to the recommendation of the Molony Committee,[253] s 35 of

---

245 See generally, *Cross on Evidence*, 9th edn, 96–9.
246 S 11(2)(a). See *J v Oyston* [1999] 1 WLR 694; *McCauley v Hope* [1999] 1 WLR 1977, CA.
247 E.g. under the Road Traffic Acts (see para 4.37), where conviction for supplying a vehicle
   contravening the regulations might then support a civil claim for unsatisfactory quality (see
   para 14.22).
248 See generally, *Street on Torts*, 10th edn, Chap 16; Winfield and Jolowicz, *Torts*, 12th edn, Chap 8;
   Buckley (1984) 100 LQR 204; Stanton, *Breach of Statutory Duty* (1986).
249 *Mark v Warbey* [1935] 1 KB 75 at 81, Greer LJ (Road Traffic Act 1930, s 35). The courts have been
   criticised as unnecessarily unhelpful to consumers in this regard: Harvey and Parry, *Op. cit.*,
   263, fn 12.
250 E.g. Mock Auctions Act 1961, s 3(6); Weights and Measures Act 1985, s 33(6); CCA, ss 92(3),
   72(11); CPA, s 41(1).
251 E.g. Medicines Act 1968, s 133(2)(a); CCA, s 170(1); CPA, s 41(2).
252 See *Square v Model Farm Dairies (Bournemouth) Ltd* [1939] 2 KB 365, CA; *Buckley v La Reserve*
   [1959] Crim LR 451, Cty Ct.
253 Report of the Committee on Consumer Protection (1962, Cmnd. 1781), para 459; and see
   para 3.15.

the Act is deliberately unclear on the point and it has subsequently been argued that an action should be denied because no personal injury is likely to be occasioned by breaches.[254] However, such tort actions have been allowed to give an individual damages for breach of EU law[255] and are sometimes described as 'eurotorts'.[256]

**[3.22] Litigation.** Assuming that a consumer does wish to proceed with a civil claim in the courts, the action is likely to be in contract or tort, or in respect of an unfair credit relationship under the CCA (see below); and the proceedings must nowadays be consistent with Convention rights (see para 3.09A). If such a claim involves a consumer and is worth less than (say) £10,000, it is likely to start in the County Court. These courts were first created in 1846 to try, on a local basis, claims involving a small sum of money, the jurisdiction of each court normally being limited to disputes in some way connected with its defined geographic area. However, it was recognised that this approach was unduly restrictive, particularly to large commercial or public bodies (some two-thirds of business of county courts) who were required to issue proceedings in all or most county courts and also where proceedings were undefended (see below): so the rules were altered to allow the plaintiff/claimant to choose a venue,[257] but with an automatic transfer to the defendant's local court on his filing a defence. The jurisdiction of the latter is laid down in the County Courts Act 1984 (as amended): this includes 'any action founded on contract or tort where the debt, demand or damage does not exceed' the 'county court limit' or any greater sum by agreement of the parties (s 18). The Courts and Legal Services Act 1990 gave the Lord Chancellor power (s 1) to adjust by order the jurisdiction limits of the High Court and County Court.[258]

As from April 1999, the Woolf reforms have made important changes to the court handling of **defended** claims: the High and County Court structure has been unified under a single system of Civil Procedure Rules (CPR);[259] the new system has been designed to encourage early settlement of disputes,[260] e.g. by offers to settle and payments into court, case conferences between parties; to minimise disputes by early openness, as by disclosure of documents, pre-action protocols (PANs)[261] and jointly-instructed experts; to make the proceedings proportional to

---

254 Review of the Trade Descriptions Act 1968 (1976, Cmnd. 6628), para 251. Cf. *Mid Kent Holdings plc v General Utilities plc* [1996] 3 All ER 132.

255 *Garden Cottage Foods v Milk Marketing Board* [1984] AC 130, HL; (2004) 120 LQR 324.

256 For their relationship to traditional English actions for breach of statutory duty, see Stanton (2004) 120 LQR 321.

257 This enables the plaintiff to take an undefended case through to judgment and enforcement (see para 27.03) in the venue of his choice. There has also been introduced the Northampton Bulk Centre to enable major plaintiffs to centralise their proceedings there; and an on-line service.

258 The system for non-CCA cases is as follows: the High Court has exclusive jurisdiction over a certain figure (currently £50,000); the county court has exclusive jurisdiction below a certain figure (currently £25,000); and both courts have concurrent jurisdiction in between.

259 For a summary of the rules, see Goode, *Consumer Credit Law & Practice*, Part XIIA; [2003] 2 *Which?* 50.

260 For speedy resolution of disputes, see Michaelson (2002) 152 NLJ 24. For offers to settle, see (2003) 153 NLJ 1116.

261 A formal pre-action system for identifying the issues in a particular type of dispute, which also allows binding admissions of liability (see Williams (2006) 156 NLJ 542). Four PANs are currently in force, more are in the pipeline. A debt PAN is under pilot in 2005 (see (2005) 78 *Quarterly Account* 2). For regulated agreements, the CCA 2006 requires formal arrears letters before action (see para 24.27A). Are both needed?

the dispute, e.g. choice of court, timetable, costs; and to encourage the parties to behave reasonably, e.g. when deciding costs. The objective is to achieve faster, cheaper justice by pushing defended claims as high up the following three litigation routes below High Court level as possible under the following unified structure:

(1) *Small claims* (CPR, Pt 27). The Small Claims Court will hear most straight-forward claims, e.g. for debt, under £5,000, frequently by litigants in person (see para 3.17). The procedure is relatively informal, with hearings in public, but with the possibility of written submissions. Disputes are heard by a District Judges, allow only lay (non-lawyer) representation,[262] further simplify pro-cedure and generally with a 'no-costs' rule. For practical purposes, his decision is final on the facts,[263] though there is a limited right of appeal on matters of law. The EU are proposing by way of an alternative to the foregoing a European Small Claims procedure for use in cross-border small claims.[264]

(2) *Fast track* (CPR, Pt 28). The Circuit Judge will hear the middle-value band of claims, which includes debt claims for £5–15,000. The procedure used includes a provision for entering judgment in default of appearance (default judgment: see below), the hearing of minor matters before the District Judge[265] and fixed scales of costs.[266] The big feature of this track is that the court will at an early stage set a trial date and allocate only one day: if the trial requires more than one day, it is transferred to the multi-track (see below).

(3) *Multi-track* (CPR, Pt 29). The greatest value claims will be distributed as appropriate between the County and High Court, except that all CCA disputes must go to the County Court (CCA, s 141: see para 24.39). There are procedures for transferring cases between multi-track trial before a Circuit Judge and trial in the High Court, including at the stage of execution of judgment (see para 27.04). A feature of multi-track trials is the case management conference: per-sonal attendance by the parties may be required; they will be encouraged to co-operate to minimise the issues; and the opportunity may be taken to try to settle the case. In some circumstances, only fixed costs will be awarded, e.g. claims for debt or under the CCA; but in any event multi-track costs are likely to be substantially less than those in the High Court.

(4) *Refer to ADR* (see para 3.24).

*Defended and undefended claims.* If no legally significant defence is put in, application may be made for default or summary judgment (CPR, Pts 12 and 24): for undefended claims, see para 27.03. Which court dealt with a claim, e.g. for debt (after judgment termed a 'judgment debt'), may have implications as to the

---

262 For the manner in which a solicitor may assist his client in small claims, see Frenkel (1998) 148 NLJ 623.
263 Harvey and Parry, *Op. cit.*, 231–4; Appleby, *A Practical Guide to the Small Claims Court*. For research into the operation of the system, see OFT, *1994-AR*, 24.
264 In a proposed Regulation 2005/87 (COD); criticised by Jack (2005) 155 NLJ 1135; sent to the European Parliament 2.6.06.
265 Below the small claims limit (see above), or where the defendant is not expected to appear. He also deals with the pre-trial review of cases expected to go before the Circuit Judge.
266 To combat the costs problems in, e.g. *Kasler and Cohen v Slovouski* [1928] 1 KB 78 (multiple parties).

methods of enforcing judgment (see para 27.04). In any event, any county court judgment (CCJ) against a debtor is likely to impair his credit rating.[267]

**[3.23] Arbitration.**[268] Arbitration involves an impartial, independent third party hearing both sides and issuing a binding decision to resolve the dispute: it is final and legally binding; and there are limited grounds for appeal. Whereas the courts (see para 3.22) may be a more suitable venue for the resolution of a test case, or to establish a precedent, the various forms of arbitration (see below) usually offer the advantages of relative speed, flexibility, cheapness and privacy. There should be distinguished from both the foregoing the various (normally much cheaper still) methods of resolving disputes which usually ultimately depend on the agreement of the parties for the efficacy of their solutions (see para 3.24).

1. *Commercial arbitration.* In the realms of formal commercial contracts, it has long been common for the parties to provide in their contract that any disputes between the parties should be settled by arbitration; and it is also competent for the parties to make an arbitration agreement to similar effect after a dispute has arisen.[269] At common law, the jurisdiction of the courts in matters of law could not be ousted; but under Part 1 of the Arbitration Act 1996, the parties may enter into an agreement excluding the jurisdiction of the High Court. Further discussion is beyond the scope of this work.

2. *Court arbitration.* In a High Court action, the Rules allow in particular circumstances the whole or any part of a case to be referred for trial to the referee or other official of the court, it being envisaged that this power should be used in particular when prolonged examination of documents or local examination is required or where matters of account are involved. Further, a judge in the Commercial Court now has power to postpone his hearings until the parties have attempted to settle their dispute through ADR or mediation (see para 3.24).

3. *Consumer arbitration.* Perhaps because of the deficiencies in the then county court small claims procedure (see para 3.22), there arose various voluntary trade arbitration schemes, either by geographical area or trade, and normally on a documents-only basis and instead of court action. These must all be consistent with Convention rights (see para 3.09A). A noticeable feature of many of the trade codes of practice (see paras 3.12–14) has been a provision for conciliation and arbitration in the event of dispute between trader and consumer. The envisaged first stage is usually an attempted conciliation by the trade association;[270] and, if that fails, traders supporting the code promise in advance to accept arbitration if requested.[271] Such arbitrations usually proceed on documentary evidence only to keep the cost to a minimum. Whilst some of

---

267 And hence the terms of subsequent loans. For such non-status loans, see para 7.04A. For credit-ratings, see para 8.39. For the first time in 14yrs, in 2005 there has been a 7% surge in CCJs.

268 Arbitration clauses are not within UCTA: (see s 13(2): para 18.16); but in relation to consumer supplies, they fall within the Unfair Contract Terms Regulations: see Grey List (q), para 11.18.

269 *Scott v Avery* (1856) 5 HLC 811; *Jones v Sherwood Computers* [1992] 2 All ER 170, CA.

270 Such conciliation tends to be free, but is not legally binding. E.g. FLA, *Lending Code AR-2004*, 12. See further Lowe and Woodroffe, *Consumer Law & Practice*, 6th edn, para 10.08; and para 3.24.

271 E.g. by codes of practice of FLA, CCTA (see para 3.13). As to the FLA Arbitration Scheme, see Goode, *Consumer Credit Law & Practice*, Vol 4, Division VIIIA, Pt 1.

the above schemes offer consumers definite advantages, it was found that others contained an agreement to submit to arbitration (a *Scott v Avery* clause), which bound consumers wishing to prosecute a claim to a high cost arbitration,[272] a problem dealt with directly by another statute (see below). However, the privacy of arbitration awards was thought inimical to consumers.[273]

4.  *Consumer arbitration agreements.* Since 1988 a consumer arbitration agreement (see above) has generally been unenforceable even with the consumer's consent. The present rules are to be found in the Arbitration Act 1996: whilst this Act is primarily concerned with commercial arbitrations (see para 3.23), ss 89–91 lay down special rules for consumer[274] 'arbitration agreements', meaning (s 89(2)) 'an agreement to submit to arbitration present or future disputes or differences (whether or not contractual)'. Section 89(1) provides that such consumer arbitration agreements are to be governed by the terms of the Unfair Terms Regulations,[275] whatever the law applicable to the arbitration agreement (s 89(3)). Moreover, the Act expressly deems unfair any arbitration agreement relating to small claims for amounts less than a specified figure (s 91, as amended), currently £5,000.[276] With regard to claims in excess of that figure, it may be expected that the provisions will catch, *inter alia*, unreasonable time limits on claims.[277]

**[3.24] Alternative Dispute Resolution (ADR).** The foregoing paragraphs set out the means by which disputing parties may reach a binding settlement of their dispute by way of court action or arbitration (see paras 3.22–3). However, the parties may prefer the much cheaper alternative methods by which the parties may settle their differences by way of a non-binding ADR, which has been described as a 'collective description of methods of resolving disputes otherwise than through the normal trial process':[278] the courts have jurisdiction to order mediation;[279] and, in any event, they may actively encourage mediation by use of the costs rules.[280] In August 2003, the DTI commissioned from the NCC (see para 3.04) a fact-finding report into the availability and usage of ADRs in consumer-to-business disputes.[281] Listed from the dispute resolution system least directive to the consumer to the system most directive to the consumer,

---

272  OFT, *Unfair Terms Bulletin No. 8*, 25.

273  NCC, *Seeking Resolution* (Jan 2004), p 69.

274  S 89(1) defines 'consumer' by reference to the UTCCR (see para 11.12A); but is extended to include not just natural persons, but also legal persons: s 90.

275  E.g. a clause granting the supplier a unilateral right to refer disputes to arbitration has been found unfair: OFT, *Bulletin No. 14*, case 4; *No 24*, case 14. See generally, para 11.18.

276  Unfair Arbitration Agreements (Specified Amount) Order 1999 SI 2167. For present dispute above that figure satisfactorily arbitrated, see [2005] 4 *Which?* 60.

277  As a Grey Term within the 1999 Regulations, Sched 2, para 1(q): see para 11.18.

278  The White Book. See further Michaelson and Maples (2005) 155 NLJ 725. For on-line dispute resolution, see Clark (2002) 152 NLJ 1710. For a court-based pilot, see (2004) 154 NLJ 946.

279  *Shirayama Shokusan Co Ltd v Danovo Ltd* [2004] CLY 941. Alternatively, the courts sometimes try to bring ADRs within our arbitration system (*Channel Tunnel Group v Balfour Beatty Construction* [1993] AC 334, HL).

280  See *Halsey v Milton Keynes NHS Trust* [2004] 1 WLR 3002, CA; and Sauter (2005) 155 NLJ 730.

281  NCC, *Seeking Resolution* (Jan 2004): for research definitions, see p 7. ADR is sometimes termed 'Proportionate Dispute Resolution' (PDR). For the EEJ-Net, see para 3.03A.

the NCC Report described the following systems (p 25): negotiation, including using the trader's internal complaints procedure (see para 3.16); mediation; conciliation; ombudsmen (see para 3.25); regulators (see para 3.07); arbitration (see para 3.23); litigation (see para 3.22). Both the litigation and arbitration systems are adversarial (meaning that the parties are responsible for producing their own evidence) and reach decisions binding on both parties, but are public, slow and expensive.[282] In recent years, the courts have begun to try to avoid these disadvantages by steering disputes into the ADR systems which are perceived as private, inquisitorial (the inquisitor produces the evidence), quicker and cheaper.[283] Indeed, it has been claimed that ADR sometimes succeeds where without prejudice (WP) negotiations have failed and in a sense may be seen as an extension of WP negotiations.[284] The NCC Report was most interested in the following ADR systems:

(a) *Conciliation.* The conciliator, commonly a trade association, 'gives factual information about rights and responsibilities and tries to resolve disputes' often over the telephone (p 18; and see Chap 5). There are examples in the consumer credit (see para 3.23) and second-hand car industries (pp 31–4).

(b) *Mediation.* An impartial, third-party mediator may help the parties to reach a 'voluntary, mutually agreed resolution', commonly involving some direct face-to-face contact between the parties (pp 22–3). This system has been described[285] as a structured form of negotiation assisted by a third party, the decision of which is not binding: there are no fixed procedures and the mediator may not necessarily be an expert in the field under review, but it has little formality and low costs.[286]

(c) *Ombudsmen.* This is an informal process (see para 3.25), which the consumer can use free of charge if the business does not resolve the complaint within a pre-set time. Any decision is not binding on the consumer, so that he is free to go to court if dissatisfied with it (p 24); but the decision is normally binding on the trader in the sense that he can be expelled for non-compliance (pp 68–9).

The NCC Report found that, whilst some ADR services were generic (covering any consumer dispute), most were sector-specific (p 48 and Chap 7). Thus, the availability of the above ADR services to consumers was very much a lottery (pp 52–3), depending on the type of goods, geographical provision and sometimes on the ability of the consumer to afford the fees (p 1) and consumer awareness of the scheme (pp 53–5 and 67–8); and that the best-known independent provider of

---

282  See Lightman J (2004) 154 NLJ 185; Partington 154 NLJ 624; 154 NLJ 1398. Besides the English consumer lobby and English courts, there has also been reform-impetus from the EU in respect of cross-border consumer transactions (p 5). As to the latter, see para 4.20.

283  *Cable & Wireless plc v IBM UK Ltd* [2002] 2 All ER (Comm) 1041. Unlike Ombudsmen schemes, other ADRs can commence before deadlock is reached between the parties.

284  Parkin [2004] 15 The Lawyer 23.

285  DTI, *Tackling Loan Sharks—and more!*, Consultation Document (March 2003), para 4.2.2. See also (2005) 155 NLJ 312, 728. As to court-sponsored pilot mediations, see (2004) 154 NLJ 484 and 604. A mediation hotline has been launched: (2005) 155 NLJ 312.

286  LCD, *Resolving Disputes* (1995); Trent (1999) 149 NLJ 410; Butterworth (2003) 153 NLJ 452; Nwagboso (2003) 153 NLJ 588; (2004) 154 NLJ 1394. Unlike arbitration clauses, mediation clauses are unlikely to inhibit litigation: *Halifax Financial Services Ltd v Intuitive Systems Ltd* [1999] 1 All ER (Comm) 303. But refusal of mediation may affect costs: Prince (2006) 156 NLJ 262.

ADR services is the Chartered Institute of Arbitrators.[287] The Report concluded that ADR is a good thing for consumers (p 66), but noted that the above deficiencies may have implications for the OFT Code of Practice scheme (p 2. For OFT Codes of Practice, see para 3.12-3). Further, the Report said that adequate funding was vital to ADR for low-value consumer disputes and recommended that the most effective funding model appears to be 'industry-funded but non-industry operated' (p 72).

As all the above schemes would seem inappropriate to regulated agreements,[288] the CCA 2006 introduced a new ADR scheme for consumer credit based on the Financial Ombudsman Service (see para 3.25). In 2005 the Lord Chancellor set up a National Mediation Helpline.

**[3.25] Ombudsman**.[289] The term 'ombudsman' comes from a Swedish word, loosely meaning 'grievance man'. The notion was originally imported into the UK to deal with complaints by private citizens against Government Departments under the Parliamentary Commissioner Act 1967 (as amended); and separate ombudsman schemes were subsequently set up for other public authorities, e.g. local authorities, public utilities (see paras 3.06–7), building societies[290] and legal services. More recently, this successful notion has been transplanted into the private commercial sector, e.g. insurance industry and banking industry.[291] Unlike public service arbitration schemes (see para 3.24), commercial sector ombudsmen have a dual role: they both investigate individual grievances and report their findings, e.g. in Annual Reports, so as to improve the services they monitor. Under the Financial Services and Markets Act 2000 (FSMA), all those Ombudsmen involved with financial services have been unified under a single statutory (s 226) scheme,[292] termed the Financial Ombudsman Service (FOS), to which has subsequently been added consumer credit (see below): this is compulsory to most businesses regulated by the FSA but has a common (cheaper) complaints-handling procedure; and it requires the Ombudsman to determine complaints 'by reference to what is fair and reasonable' (s 228(2)). Separately, an EU Ombudsman has been set up to deal with EU institutional maladministration[293] and is being considered to investigate cross-border consumer complaints.

Most of the English commercial Ombudsmen schemes work in a similar manner, being based in London with consumer access normally by post. They have carefully defined terms of reference, outside which the ombudsman will not step.[294] Within those terms of reference and subject to the complainant first

---

287 Page 20. A range of ADR providers is profiled in Chap 7 of the NCC Report.

288 By reason of CCA, s 141 (see para 24.39) and the risk that an agreement reached in ADR could of itself be a modifying agreement (see para 26.22). See *Fair, clear and competitive—the consumer credit market in the 21st century* (DTI, Dec 2003, Cm. 6040), paras 3.44–6.

289 See generally, Lowe and Woodroffe, *Consumer Law & Practice*, 6th edn, paras 10.61–8.

290 Under Pt IX of the Building Societies Act 1986. For the terms of reference of the Building Societies Ombudsman, see Goode, *Consumer Credit Law & Practice*, Vol 4, Division VIII, Pt 9.

291 See the Jack Report on *Banking Services* (1989), Cm. 622, Chap 15. For the terms of reference of the Banking Ombudsman, see Goode, *ibid*, Division VIII, Pt 8.

292 Pt XVI. Under a Chief Financial Services Ombudsman these replaced eight previous organisations, including those for banks and building societies. E.g. for FOS dealings with forged cheques, see para 7.24.

293 The remedy is intended to be political rather than judicial: see (1994) 144 NLJ 609.

294 For current Terms of Reference, see Goode, *Consumer Credit Law & Practice*, Pt VIII.

exhausting the businesses' internal complaints system (a 'deadlock' scheme), the scheme will provide a cheap (to the consumer) and informal method of providing redress for valid consumer complaints: this will normally apply any relevant code of practice[295] and try to put the consumer back into the position he was before the complained conduct, which is nearer to the measures of damages in tort than contract (see para 27.28). This whole service is paid for by the trade party to the dispute, so in effect by the extra overheads passed on to non-complaining customers of the trade party. In any event, any Ombudsman scheme must now comply with the individual's right to a fair trial;[296] but it has been held that under s 228(2) it does not have to follow the law so long as its decision was fair and reasonable.[297]

*Regulated consumer credit and consumer hire.* As from 2007, there is a new ADR scheme to hear disputes about consumer credit and hire matters (see generally para 3.24): it is voluntary for the consumer but compulsory for the trade party. To effect this, the FSMA was amended by the insertion of a new s 226A to extend its Ombudsman scheme (see above) on certain eligibility conditions (new s 226A(2)) to consumer complaints not within the above s 226 scheme, provided that the business concerns consumer credit and consumer hire agreements regulated under the CCA.[298] With details to be embodied in Regulations (see below), the new scheme allows such a debtor, hirer or his surety (an eligible complainant: new s 226A(4)) to bring before the FOS (see above) a complaint against a business holding a CCA standard licence (the respondent: new s 226A(3)):[299] as it will not apply to group licences, the scheme will not extend to the activities of consumer advice services (see para 3.16). The scheme is to be self-funding on the basis that it is free to consumers and wholly funded by CCA standard licensees (new s 234A of FSMA): there will be an annual levy on all licensees and a case fee payable by the respondent if the case is formally settled by the FOS. The standard licence-holder's conduct disclosed in the proceedings may be considered by the OFT in determining his fitness to hold a licence (see para 6.18); and the criteria for decision by the Ombudsman are those set out in the above-quoted s 228(2), which would appear to allow him to ignore consumer protection statutes.[297] Under s 61 of the 2006 Act, the scheme may specify the maximum amount recoverable (subs (5)). Draft FOS rules on this new jurisdiction suggest that it will operate in a manner comparable to the above compulsory scheme.[300]

---

295 *R (N & P) v Financial Ombudsman Service Ltd* [2003] 1 All ER (Comm) 65; and see generally, para 3.13. For resolving complaints, see (2002) 65 *QA* 5.

296 Human Rights Act 1998, incorporating into English law the European Convention on Human Rights Art 6 (see Sched 1 of the Act).

297 *IGF Financial Services Ltd v FOS* [2005] EWHC 1153 (Ombudsman not required to take into account the law of causation, so long as his decision is not perverse or irrational: para 13: see Aliker (2006) 156 NLJ 974).

298 The CCA 2006, s 59, inserts new s 226A into the FSMA (s 226A(1)). This is to be known as the 'consumer credit jurisdiction' (new s 226A(6)), with details set out in new Sched 17, Pt 3A (see Sched 2 of CCA 2006). Expressions used in the CCA also have the same meaning here (s 234A(15)).

299 It is intended to introduce the scheme for different classes of licensee on a staggered basis.

300 The new rules will be incorporated in the FSA Handbook in the chapter entitled 'Dispute Resolution: Complaints' (see the FOS Consultation Paper, *Rules for the new consumer credit jurisdiction* (June 2006).

# INFORMATION ABOUT CONSUMERS

**[3.26]** Amongst that segment of commerce and industry providing goods and services to individual consumers, the last quarter of the twentieth century saw an explosion of interest in the collection of information about those individuals. Such information is primarily required for three purposes: (1) to contact potential customers deemed likely to be interested and suitable for receipt of those goods and services; (2) to facilitate checks on those persons before supplying goods or services, e.g. credit; and (3) to trace defaulters. Many suppliers of goods and services themselves accumulate such information; but much of the information is collected on a commercial basis by third-party specialist credit bureaux for onward transmission to suppliers.

Originally, credit bureaux were very much a locally-based activity usually conducted by a manual card-index system. Their nature was transformed by the introduction of powerful computers: these are able not only to store vast amounts of information, but also to dispense it on-line (by telephone line to the trade customer's terminal). Since 1965, there have gradually been established nationwide computerised credit bureaux.[301] They hold personal records, such as the electoral roll (see below), county court judgments for debt (see para 3.22), disqualified directors (see para 19.25), other adverse and creditable information ('black' and 'white' data: see para 8.36) and the land registry records of titles to land.[302] Almost all the relevant finance companies, mortgage-providers, brokers and dealers subscribe to these services, supplying them with details of their own transactions,[303] and, before entering into any such transaction, they can for a small fee search (usually on-line) the register.[304] As they have become more confident in their systems, the credit reference agencies have expanded into related sectors, the assimilation by one of them of HPI being an early example (see above). The HPI service is also available to non-members, including the general public; and it is a matter for consideration as to whether its functions should be taken over by the government as the basis for a statutory title-registration system for goods (see para 21.60).

Because of their modern effectiveness, these credit bureaux and HPI have been made subject to special statutory control (see below): limited waivers to these controls have been granted in the interest of combating fraud, e.g. CIFAS;[305] and

---

301 For the leading agencies specialising in consumer credit, McNeil Greig, *The Growth of Credit Information* (1998) CCA News, Summer 8–13. There is now a routine exchange of information between the credit reference agencies, so improving the comprehensiveness of the data: FLA, *1998 Annual Report*, p 10.

302 The Land Registry has not made public mortgages on land.

303 Such data-sharing is by no means complete, e.g. the absence of student loans. What can happen when this practice is not adhered to was demonstrated in *Moorgate Mercantile Co Ltd v Twitchings* (set out at para 21.15).

304 Supplying information to bureaux for this purpose is not a breach of a bank's duty of confidentiality (see para 7.03): *Turner v Royal Bank of Scotland* [2001] 1 All ER (Comm) 1057, CA.

305 Launched in 1988 under the aegis of the CCTA (above), in 1991 the Credit Industry Fraud Avoidance System (CIFAS) became a separate company limited by guarantee and housed at the Registry Trust Ltd (see para 3.22). It provides a special reporting system by way of the ordinary credit reference agencies which creditors promise to trigger when fraud is suspected: see further, para 8.38.

such waivers are a matter currently particularly relevant to identity fraud (see para 3.29).[306] The first place where Parliament intervened in connection with the activities of credit bureaux was in the Consumer Credit Act 1974, which termed these bureaux 'credit reference agencies' (s 145(8): see para 8.36). Second, concern with the recording of information led to the wider statutory control of computerised records ('data') in the Data Protection Act 1984, which was intended to strike a balance between the free flow of information and individual privacy; and the 1984 Act was replaced by the Data Protection Act 1998 (see para 3.27). Third, in the Human Rights Act 1998, Parliament for the first time enshrined in English law the **right** of an individual to privacy.[307] Fourth, in the Representation of the People Act 2000, electors were given the option of indicating whether or not they wish registered information about them to be available for commercial purposes:[308] the 'full' register will continue to be available to credit reference agencies for credit applications (see para 8.35); but, when an elector chooses to be placed on the 'edited' register, his particulars will not be available to commercial organisations for other purposes, including purposes (1) and (3) above.[309] The proposed national identity cards might also be relevant (see para 8.36).

**[3.27] The Data Protection Act 1998 (DPA).**[310] The DPA is based on the Data Protection Directive, which requires Member States to protect the fundamental rights and freedoms of natural persons,[311] so that it follows that the 1998 Act must be read in the light of the Directive (see para 1.04). These rights may be linked up with the Human Rights Act 1998 (see para 3.26). As amended,[312] the DPA may apply to any 'personal data', meaning 'data which relate to a living individual who can be identified' (s 1(1)), e.g. customer lists.[313] The records comprising this personal data may be computerised or manual, because 'data' is defined by s 1(1) (as amended) in a manner which includes computerised records and also (unlike the 1984 Act: see above para 3.26) **some** manual (paper) records which fall within a 'relevant filing

---

306 The Government is considering release to CIFAS death register information, which would be the best source of information to combat a common form of identity fraud: (2004) 59 CC3/24; (2005–6) HL WS33.

307 Human Rights Act 1998, incorporating into English law the European Convention on Human Rights Art 8 (see Sched 1 of the Act); *Campbell v MGN Ltd* [2004] 2 All ER 995, HL; and generally, para 3.09A.

308 S 9. Implementation of the draft regulations was delayed by a court action alleging the commercial access to the electoral roll breached human rights (see above); but that allegation has now been rejected in favour of the public interest in fraud-control: see *R (Robertson) v First Secretary of State* [2003] CLY 2150.

309 A significant number of consumers (32% in 2005) have opted out (sometimes with LA encouragement), which worries the credit industry: see [2004] 3 *Credit Today* 11; 10 CT 7; [2006] 1 CT 7.

310 See the IC, *Guidelines*; and see further Charlton and Gaskill, *Encyclopedia of Data Protection*.

311 Directive (95/46/EC), Art 1. For the text of the Directive see Goode, *Consumer Credit Law & Practice*. For the junk mail directive, see para 8.17. The EU has begun to review the 1995 Directive and has also formally complained that the DPA does not fully comply with that Directive.

312 The DPA was significantly amended by the Freedom of Information Act 2000 as regards information held by a 'public authority'; but most of those amendments are beyond the scope of this work. For a relevant provision of the latter Act, see para 17.05.

313 See *Durant v FSA* (set out at para 8.38). Such data is protected by copyright: see generally, para 8.02.

system'.[314] However, the Act only applies to data concerning living persons ('data subjects') (s 1(1)): this requirement of living persons excludes from the DPA information about registered companies but includes that on sole traders and partnerships.[315] The Act gives special protection to 'sensitive personal data' (s 2), some of which is likely to be of relevance to commerce for the purposes outlined above (see para 3.26), e.g. racial origins, commission of any offence.

That data may be 'processed', which expression is widely defined to mean 'obtaining, recording or holding the information or data or the carrying out of any operation . . . on the data'.[316] This processing may be by any UK 'data controller';[317] that is, somebody who determines the processing, e.g. creditor or supplier; or somebody who executes that policy on his behalf and is termed a 'data processor',[318] e.g. computer bureau. For processing, see para 3.27A.

[3.27A] **Processing data**. Personal data concerning a data subject is usually processed for the data controller under licence by a data processor (see para 3.27). In doing so, the data controller and data processor must in relation to the data subject observe the Data Protection Principles (see para 3.28). Further, the Act grants the following rights to data subjects: access to the information held on them (ss 7–9: see para 3.28); to prevent processing likely to cause damage or distress (s 10), or for the purposes of direct marketing (s 11; see para 8.19); in relation to automated decision taking (s 12; see para 8.39); to compensate for damage caused by contravention of the Act by the data controller (s 13); to rectify, block, erase or destroy inaccurate data (s 14); and to request the Commissioner's help (see below). The foregoing principles are subject to various exemptions of different widths: the more important of these are contained in Part IV of the Act;[319] and lesser exemptions in Schedule 7.

The Act establishes (s 6) a public authority to promote and enforce the Act, the Data Protection Commissioner, who has since been renamed the Information Commissioner (IC):[320] *inter alia*, data controllers must register ('notification') with the IC specified particulars about themselves, the personal data that they hold and the uses to which that data may be put.[321] The IC must enquire into compliance with the Act at the behest of data subjects (s 42), e.g. those who believe that their

---

314  See *Durant v FSA* (above). Perhaps it covers default files? What about application forms?

315  Cf. CCA: see para 5.24.

316  S 1(1): see *Campbell v Mirror Group Newspapers Ltd* [2003] 1 All ER 224, CA (rev on other grounds). But this definition does not appear to fit with the common industry practice of delegating the collection of information locally: see [2001] 6 *Credit Today* 24.

317  'Data controller' is one who alone or with others 'determines the purposes for which and the manner in which any personal data are, or are to be, processed': s 1(1). For data controllers outside the UK, see s 5.

318  ' "Data processor", in relation to personal data, means any person (other than an employee of the data controller) who processes the data on behalf of the data controller': s 1(1).

319  They include data processed for the purposes of prevention of crime (s 29), e.g. CIFAS (see para 2.18); public watchdogs (s 31), e.g. the OFT and local authorities (see paras 3.03–6), OFGEM (see para 3.07), charities (see para 3.08), ombudsmen (see para 3.25); journalism (s 32); information available under public enactment (s 34, as amended), e.g. registries of company charges, court judgments, insolvencies; in connection with legal proceedings (s 35); domestic purposes (s 36).

320  Freedom of Information Act 2000, s 18. The Commissioner must promote good practice under the DPA (s 51), i.e. support the spirit of the Act, including taking account of the Human Rights Act 1998 (see para 3.26).

321  Ss 16, 18–20. This regularly renewable information to be held by the IC on a public register.

personal data has not been processed in compliance with the Act; he may serve on data controllers notices requiring information (ss 43–6); and to help enforce all this, the IC has powers of entry and inspection (s 50 and Sched 9: see para 28.05).

*Enforcement.* The major sanction available to the IC is to serve enforcement notices on data controllers contravening the data protection principles (ss 40–41), in which case an appeal lies to the Information Tribunal.[322] To give this process teeth, the Act creates a number of offences by a data controller: *inter alia*, these include the processing of data without notifying the IC (ss 17, 21); failure to notify the IC of changes in notifiable matters (ss 20, 21); failure to comply with an enforcement notice (s 47); obstruction of entry and inspection (Sched 9); unlawfully obtaining, procuring, disclosing or selling personal data (s 55), e.g. by tracing agencies; forcing a data subject to agree to access to his personal data (ss 56, 57); and unlawful disclosure of information by the IC or his staff (ss 58, 59). The IC is empowered to bring prosecutions against businesses contravening the Act (s 60), or their corporate officers (s 61: see para 28.11). Can information obtained in breach of the above rules be used in a court action?

**[3.28] The Data Protection Principles**. Like the 1984 Act (though in slightly different form), the DPA 1998 lays down eight 'data protection principles', applicable where data is 'processed'. Unless he falls within one of the exemptions and whether or not registered or exempt (see para 3.27), 'it shall be the duty of a data controller to comply with the data protection principles in relation to all personal data with respect to which he is the data controller' (s 4(4)). The Data Protection Principles are a curious mixture of generalisation and specific instance. They are as follows (s 4(1), Sched 1):

*First Principle.*[323] 'Personal data shall be processed fairly[324] and lawfully and, in particular, shall not be processed unless:

(i) In the case of ordinary personal data, it complies with one of the conditions set out in Schedule 2, e.g. the data subject has given his consent,[325] the processing is **necessary** for the administration of justice;[326] **and**

(ii) In the case of sensitive personal data (an expression which does not include financial data, except perhaps fines), it **also** complies with one of the conditions set out in Schedule 3, e.g. the data subject has given his **explicit** consent,[327] or

---

322 Ss 6, 48–9, Sched 6 (as amended). There is a right of further appeal on law to the appropriate court (s 49(6)). Cf. para 6.24.

323 The first Principle is particularly relevant to direct marketers and the finance industry, e.g. *British Gas Trading Ltd v DPR* [1999] CLY 823. As to proposal forms, see para 8.35.

324 The Act also contains a 'fair processing code': Sched 1, Pt II, paras 1–4, e.g. whether the data subject in giving the information was 'deceived or misled', or is himself notified of the identity of the data controller. As to third-party data, see fn 330, below.

325 It would appear to follow that information given in good faith and marked 'confidential' cannot be used.

326 This would justify the holding of public records as to, e.g. insolvency, court judgment.

327 The data subject must give **explicit** consent in relation to sensitive data; but presumably he can give implied consent in other cases. The Act does not define his 'consent'; but the Directive refers to 'any freely given specific and informed indication of his wishes by which the data subject signifies his agreement to personal data relating to him being processed'. As to third-party data, see fn 324, above.

the processing is **necessary** for the purposes of legal proceedings or equal opportunities'.[328]

*Second Principle.* 'Personal data shall be obtained only for one or more specified and lawful purposes, and shall not be further processed in any manner incompatible with that purpose or those purposes'.[329]

*Third Principle.* 'Personal data shall be adequate, relevant and not excessive in relation to the purpose or purposes for which they are processed'. This will exclude third-party data, e.g. adult children of the data subject.[330] For host mailing, see para 8.06.

*Fourth Principle.* 'Personal data shall be accurate and, where necessary, kept up to date' (see Sched 1, Pt II, para 7).

*Fifth Principle.* 'Personal data processed for any purpose or purposes shall not be kept for longer than is necessary for that purpose or those purposes'. This is relevant to the length of time for which a retailer may keep customers' payment card details.

*Sixth Principle.* 'Personal data shall be processed in accordance with the rights of data subjects under this Act',[331] so that he may access that information (ss 7–9: see para 8.38).

*Seventh Principle.* 'Appropriate technical and organisational measures shall be taken against unauthorised or unlawful processing of personal data and against accidental loss or destruction of, or damage to, personal data' (Sched 1, Pt II, paras 9–12). This requirement of security is particularly relevant as regards the reliability of the data controller's staff (para 10); or where one party is processing information on behalf of another, e.g. any computer bureau he uses (para 9), or in direct financing,[332] or sending only encrypted e-mails, or outsourcing (e.g. see below).

*Eighth Principle.* 'Personal data shall not be transferred to a country or territory outside the European Economic Area, unless that country or territory ensures an adequate level of protection for the rights and freedoms of data subjects in relation to the processing of personal data' (see Sched 1, Pt 2, paras 13–15. For exceptions, see Sched 4). This is particularly relevant in view of the propensity of the financial sector to set up satellite data operations in third world countries (outsourcing), e.g. India. The EU has served a formal notice on the UK that the DPA does not comply with the Directive in this context.[333]

---

328 As to legal proceedings, see Chaps 27 and 29. As to equal opportunities, see para 4.23. As to the use of payment cards by paedophiles, see 2006 SI 2068.

329 See Sched 1, Pt II, paras 5–6. As to using data, see *R v Brown* [1996] 1 All E R 545, HL. For the disclosure/sharing of data in relation to credit reference agencies, see para 8.38.

330 After prolonged negotiation with the industry, the IC has finally announced early implementation of a ban on third-party data: see (2004) 59 CC2/11; and see generally para 8.38.

331 A person will contravene this principle if, but only if, they fail to comply with ss 7, 10, 11, 12: Sched 1, Pt II, para 8.

332 There must be a suitable written contract between the controller and processor (paras 11–12). As to direct financing, see para 2.21. As to debt collection agencies, see para 5.42.

333 [2004] 8 *Credit Today* 5.

The DPC publishes a series of *Guidance Notes* on the application of the DPA to particular commercial activities.[334]

**[3.29] Reform**. The foregoing system of electoral roll and data protection for the most part carefully protects the privacy of the individual (see paras 3.26–8): but sometimes it protects data subjects too well by inhibiting data sharing,[335] whilst in other cases insufficiently.[336] It is subject to a number of exceptions, significant for our purposes being protection against fraud by the consumer. In this regard, fraudulent addresses may be checked on the voters roll (see para 3.26); whereas identity fraud may be combatted by the rule allowing access to 'black' data about a data subject (DPA, s 29: see para 3.27); and an ownership check will usually be made via a title ('asset registration') register (see para 21.01). Within the confines of the present system, the finance industry is making efforts to share both black and white data (see para 3.26) on the basis of reciprocity;[337] but the issue involves some legal uncertainty over white data[338] and is particularly troublesome where the debtor has multiple unsecured accounts, e.g. credit cards, on each of which the debt is apparently insignificant when taken in isolation.

Current debate concerns whether the above sophisticated anti-fraud system should be extended to combat over-indebtedness (see para 6.10), which would seem to require amendment to the DPA.[339] Currently, credit is both over-sold[340] and overbought (see para 6.10). The fact is that a small percentage (say 5%) of consumers is applying for too much credit. It would seem that the most likely way of curbing this problem would be for the credit-trader to be made aware at the moment of application of the applicant's existing heavy indebtedness so that the proposal may be declined.[341] This would require that the above fraud detection system be extended to disclosure of the existing indebtedness of all consumer-applicants, which amounts to a serious derogation from the financial privacy of 95% of consumers for the protection of the other 5%. The Government has rejected the possibility of including DPA-amending legislation in the CCA 2006, but is

---

334 E.g. the *Guidance Note for Direct Marketers* (see generally, para 8.19); *Guidance Note for Users of Document Image Processing Systems* (digitised storing of commercial records); *Guidance On Credit References* (see para 8.38); *Guidance Note on E-Mail Marketing* (see para 8.17A). Some of these notes are set out in Goode, *Consumer Credit Law & Practice*, Pt VIII.

335 E.g. much data on overdrafts, current accounts and credit card accounts is not shared, especially when the opening of the overdraft account precedes modern consent forms; employee loans; student loans; council tax data.

336 E.g. RFID (see para 2.06).

337 E.g. the Standing Committee of Reciprocity (SCOR): see (2005) 60 CC3/7. Not all creditors are anxious to make these checks: [2006] 5 Credit Today 25.

338 Under the First Data Principle (see para 3.28), the data must be processed 'lawfully'; and disclosure of data would appear to contravene the banker's common law duty of confidentiality (see para 7.03).

339 One claimed problem is that pre-DPA 1998 agreements with consumers do not contain wide enough file-sharing clauses (see FLA, *Lending Code AR-2004*, 9); but the Government has played this down ((2006) 60 CC5/43). It has been suggested creditors should be required to share full information as a condition of their credit licence, or should be obliged as part of their Code of Conduct to include appropriate consent clauses in all credit agreements.

340 Perhaps the Banking Code (see para 3.12) should be put on a statutory footing.

341 See Collard and Kempson, *Affordable Credit* (2005) 29.

consulting on other ways of relaxing restrictions on data-sharing.[342] The IC is pleading for tougher criminal sanctions to curb the burgeoning illegal trade in confidential personal information.[343]

The EU has begun to review the Data Protection Directive (see para 3.27) and may also include database access in a new Consumer Credit Directive (see para 5.12).

---

342 The Minister in debates on the CCA Bill 2005 (2005–6) HL Deb, R2, col. 1030. See also (2005–6) HC R3, cols.980–95; HL GC col.321. For the types of data likely to be under consideration, see above, fn 329. The Student Loan Company has asked the Government to change the rules so that it can pass on details of bad debtors: *The Times* 2.12.05.

343 IC, *What Price Privacy?* (2006).

# CHAPTER 4

# CONSUMER PROTECTION AND THE CRIMINAL LAW

**[4.01] Introduction**. This chapter is concerned with those parts of the criminal law which regulate the supply of goods to consumers.[1] Whilst the law of theft requires proof of *mens rea*,[2] it has long been recognised in this context that widespread effectiveness requires the imposition of strict criminal liability.[3] Consequently, since the Middle Ages there have been a series of such criminal UK measures;[4] and their scope was considerably enhanced as a result of the recommendations of the Molony Report in 1962,[5] especially the Trade Descriptions Act 1968 (TDA: see para 4.02) and the consumer safety legislation (see para 4.31). On the civil side, Molony led to a number of consumer protection statutes[6] and there are also a number of mixed civil and criminal statutes, e.g. the CCA (Chap 5), CPA (para 17.23). Many such statutes tend to regulate just information disclosure, reserving duties to take further steps to particular classes of dangerous goods (see para 4.26, *et seq.*); and, in relation to information disclosure, the preference is for prohibiting false information, rather than a positive duty to disclose, e.g. any unsafe goods.[7] But there are signs that the courts may be taking a different attitude to information disclosure, at least in relation to the TDA: see *Farrand v Lazarus* (set out at para 4.02). At the same time, the courts seem to prefer prosecution under the TDA to be confined to defendants with *mens rea*.[8]

It will be noticed that the statutory arrangements for the enforcement by public authorities of these strict liability offences to protect consumers in general have a substantial degree of similarity (see Chap 28). Further, considering redress for individual consumers, there are significant practical advantages in first examining the above criminal provisions, which frequently arise on the same facts as a civil right of action. *First*, it may be possible to persuade the appropriate public authority, e.g. the local authority (see para 3.05), to bring the criminal proceedings, so obviating costs and stress for the consumer (see para 3.18). *Second*, on conviction, it may be possible to persuade the criminal court to award compensation to the

---

1  See generally Cartwright, *Consumer Protection and the Criminal Law* (2001) Chap 3; Thomas and Clarke, *Encyclopedia of Consumer Law*. For statistics on supplier convictions and consumer complaints, see the *Annual Reports* of the OFT.

2  E.g. *R v Morris* [1984] AC 320, HL (consumer switching price labels in self-service store: *R v Lambie* [1982] AC 449, HL (abuse of credit card). See also Phillips [1982] JBL 377; Leigh (1985) 48 MLR 167; Goode, *Consumer Credit Law & Practice*, Division IE, para 70.1, *et seq.*; Law Commission, *Consultation Paper on Fraud and Deception* (1999, No. 155), which would reverse the burden of proof.

3  See Cartwright, *Op. cit.*, Chap 8.

4  Designed to regulate, e.g. weights and measures (see para 4.24) and food and drugs (see para 4.26).

5  Report of the Committee on Consumer Protection 1962, Cmnd. 1781. For a summary of its recommendations, see Harvey and Parry, *Consumer Protection and Fair Trading*, 6th edn, 22–3.

6  E.g. SOGIT, SGSA, UCTA (see paras 12.01; 18.12).

7  Cartwright, *Op. cit.*, 184–7.

8  *R v Glen Adaway* [2004] EWCA Crim 2831, CA; and see para 3.19.

consumer under the Powers of Criminal Courts Act 2000 (see para 3.20); but if not, the conviction may assist subsequent civil proceedings (see para 3.21).

However, the UK authorities can, for the protection of consumers, generally instead obtain injunctions to prevent continued infringement by minor offences (see paras 28.03 and 29.39); and this route is likely to receive encouragement from EU law (see para 4.01A), which would seemingly restrict the use of these laws to achieve individual redress.

**[4.01A] The EU dimension**. Nowadays, there is also an EU dimension to UK criminal law, designed to protect consumers, in that it must be compatible with the (general) provisions of the Treaty of Rome (see para 1.03A).[9] However, an entirely new dimension to EU intervention occurred with the promulgation in May 2005 of the Unfair Commercial Practices (UCP) Directive,[10] to be implemented in the Member States in 2007.[11] The general scope of the UCP Directive is that it applies to 'unfair business-to-consumer commercial practices ... before during and after a commercial transaction in relation to a product' (Art 3(1)), so that it extends to post-contractual behaviour; but it does not affect the law of contract (Art 3(2)), nor the law relating to the health and safety aspects of a product,[12] nor taste and decency (recital 7), nor hallmarking (Art 3(10): see para 4.23), nor special regimes (Art 3(8)) such as for the privatised utilities (see para 3.07) or regulated professions (see Art 2(1)). The Directive is confined to business dealings with 'consumers', which last expression it defines (Art 2) in the normal EU manner (see para 11.12A), so it does not affect business-to-business transactions (recital 6), nor transactions between private persons. It amends several other consumer Directives dealt with in this work[13] and, as a **maximum** directive,[14] should replace a complex patchwork of existing UK consumer law but, as it is only intended to plug gaps in the EU consumer protection framework, it does not override other EU rules regulating specific aspects of unfair commercial practices (Art 3(4)), nor competition law (Art 4: see paras 2.12–14).

Breach of the Directive does not give rise to specific rights for consumers individually; but enforcement of these strict liability provisions can be taken by public bodies for penalties to be specified nationally, which need not necessarily be criminal (Arts 11–13; cf. the EA: see para 6.06). The Directive not only pro-hibits some listed practices but also unfair commercial practices generally (Art 5: see paras 4.20–1A). In so doing, it is intended to grant consumers the same pro-tection against commercial sharp practice[15] and 'rogue traders' in relation to

---

9   E.g. Sunday trading (para 8.13); sex shops (para 6.02); and generally Bentil (1992) 9 Tr L 23.

10  2005/29. For the text of the Directive, see OJ L149/22.

11  It must be transposed into UK law by 12.6.2007, which law must come into force in Dec. 2007 (Art 19).

12  Art 3(3): so, it will not impinge on medicinal products (see paras 4.29–30), nor dangerous goods (see paras 4.31–7).

13  The Distance Selling and Distance Selling of Financial Services Directives (by Art 15: see para 8.17); and the Injunctions Directive (by Art 16: see para 3.03A).

14  Recitals 5 and 6: see para 3.10. There is a six-year grace period (Art 3(5)); and the maximum harmonisation rule does not apply to investor protection (Art 3(9)).

15  See the Art 2 definitions of 'business-to-consumer commercial practices' and 'to materially distort the economic behaviour of consumers'. See (2005) 7 EBL 1–2.

'products',[16] whether the consumers buy from the corner shop or a website in another country, and to make cross-border trading simpler, e.g. where a small trader wants to advertise by website in another Member Country. The practical consequences of this maximum harmonisation should be a considerable simplification of existing UK consumer protection law (see para 4.21B). In effect, it will introduce a general duty on traders not to trade unfairly with consumers: but, it should not add appreciably to the burdens on traders because it does not impose on traders a duty to show that they traded fairly. In relation to enforcement, the position is as follows: the Directive allows Member States to retain criminal law existing sanctions, e.g. the TDA (see para 4.02), whilst requiring the relevant substantive strict criminal law to be brought into alignment with the Directive, e.g. the addition of a transactional decision test;[17] in civil law, the Directive requires Member States to introduce an injunctive system for enforcement of the new general duty on behalf of consumers,[18] but is silent as to private law rights, e.g. action by consumers in respect of statutory implied terms (see Chaps 12–14); and the Directive allows Member States to encourage the use of codes of conduct (Art 10: see paras 3.11–4), even to the extent of requiring prior recourse to these before taking civil proceedings.[19]

With the enormous potential overlap with existing statutory rules of consumer protection, it is not surprising that the DTI are therefore studying the potential impact on existing UK legislation before the 2007 implementation.[20]

# TRADE DESCRIPTIONS[21]

**[4.02] Introduction.** The Trade Descriptions Act 1968 grew out of, but is much wider than, the old Merchandise Marks Acts 1887–1953, which it repealed. Whereas the primary purpose of the Merchandise Marks Acts was to protect businessmen against the passing-off as theirs of goods made by others, the chief objective of the Trade Descriptions Act (TDA) was the protection of consumers as against manufacturers and traders. The TDA is intended to deter misleading statements in the business supply of goods and services to consumers by making such statements criminal offences[22] without affecting the civil rights of the

---

16   Art 2 defines 'trader' in the normal EU manner (see para 11.12A); and 'product' to mean 'any goods or service including immoveable property, rights and obligations'.

17   For the transactional decision test, see para 4.21. The DTI have begun consultations on such alignment: see *The UCP Directive Consultation* (Dec. 2005: URN 05/1815), available at www.dti.gov.uk/consultations/consultation_1565.html.

18   Arts 11, 12, 13 and 16. The DTI is consulting (as above) to see whether it would be sufficient to apply to these new duties the existing scheme in Pt 8 of the EA (see paras 6.06–8); and whether to allow individual consumers to sue for breach of statutory duty (see para 3.21).

19   Art 11. As with the ASA Code and Misleading Advertising (see para 3.14 and para 8.12A).

20   The DTI commissioned an excellent academic report (202p) by Twigg-Flesner, *et al. An Analysis Of The Application And Scope Of The UCPD* (18 May 2005), available on the DTI website at /ccp/ consultpdf/final_report180505.pdf; and as to 'commercial practices', see 38–9. See also Howells *et al., European Fair Trading Law: The UCP Directive* (2006).

21   See generally Harvey and Parry, *Consumer Protection and Fair Trading*, 6th edn, Chap 12; Lowe and Woodroffe, *Consumer Law and Practice*, 6th edn, Chap 13; Bragg, *Trade Descriptions*.

22   About half the convictions under this Act tend to be against the motor trade: see the OFT *Annual Reports*. For enforcement of this Act, see Chap 28.

parties.[23] However, it contains this major difference in treatment: whereas there is strict criminal liability in relation to misstatements made in the business supply of goods (s 1: see para 4.03), the criminal liability in respect of the business supply of services was not intended to be so strict (s 14: see para 4.17). Notwithstanding some unforeseen judicial interpretation making the latter liability stricter, principally in *Wings Ltd v Ellis* (set out at para 4.17), there is still pressure for statutory amendment to impose 'the full measure of strict liability' on supplies of services,[24] though this would already seem to have been achieved where a service is performed on the bailor's goods.[25] Moreover, there are several other apparent inconsistencies in judicial interpretation as between offences under ss 1 and 14: for instance, as regards whether the defendant needs to know his statement is being made;[26] and liability for post-contractual statements.[27]

Meanwhile, control of false and misleading pricing has been removed to other legislation (see para 8.09, *et seq.*). Recently, it has become possible to have this legislation imposed by Enforcement Orders (see para 6.08). Despite the previously mentioned general statutory preference against positive disclosure (see para 4.01), in *Farrand v Lazarus*:[28]

> A car dealer, L, purchased at auction two Ford cars with mileage warranted at 151,105 and 115,679. As the odometers only had five figures, they therefore understated the mileage by 100,000 miles. L supplied the cars for sale with a disclaimer common in the motor trade saying the displayed mileages were incorrect. L was charged with an offence under s 1(1)(b) (see para 4.03).

Notwithstanding the disclaimer (see para 4.09), the Divisional Court held that L had committed offences under s 1(1)(b) by not disclosing the true mileages known to L. Simon Brown L explained (at para 28):

> 'I recognise, of course, that in the ordinary way dealers are under no positive duty to disclose the defects and disadvantages of their wares. Generally, they are entitled to be economical with the truth, although not, of course, to lie. With regard to inaccurate mileage readings, however, that, in my judgment, is not the law. In this limited respect they are required to volunteer the truth in so far as they know it'.

However, this offence would appear to be voluntary, in that L could have avoided its commission by not purchasing cars with warranted mileage; and, in any event it may not extend beyond odometers, e.g. where a previous owner had disguised a defect.[29] In 2007, the TDA will have to be aligned with the UCP Directive (see para 4.01A).[30]

---

23  S 35: see para 10.19. However, the power to make compensation orders (see para 3.20) is fairly widely used in TDA cases.

24  Bragg, *Op. cit.*, *Trade Description*, 171. Government action is promised: *Modern Markets: confident consumers* (1999, Cm. 4410) para 3.19.

25  *Formula One Autocentres Ltd v Birmingham CC* [1999] RTR 195, DC (car service; some promised items not checked. Held: s 1 offence by garage).

26  *Cottee v Douglas Seaton Ltd* (YES; see para 4.05); *Wings Ltd v Ellis* (NO; see para 4.17).

27  *Wickens Motors Ltd v Hall* (NO; see para 4.03); *Breed v Cluett* (YES; see para 4.16).

28  [2002] 3 All ER 175, DC.

29  In *Cottee v Douglas Seaton (Used Cars) Ltd* (set out at para 28.17) the judges *obiter* disagreed on the point.

30  See *An Analysis Of The Application And Scope Of The UCPD* (see para 4.01A), 132–149.

## False statements as to goods

*Prohibition of false trade descriptions*

**[4.03] The key offences**. The gateway provisions and principal offences to be found in the Trade Descriptions Act 1968 (TDA) are contained in s 1(1), which provides that:

'Any person who, in the course of a trade or business—

(a) applies a false trade description to any goods; or

(b) supplies or offers to supply any goods to which a false trade description is applied;

shall, subject to the provisions of this Act, be guilty of an offence'.

This section is designed to protect from the blandishments of errant traders both innocent private persons and innocent traders.[31] But it only applies to blandishments uttered in relation to '**goods**',[32] which expression probably does not include the price of goods;[33] nor does it include land. However, a false statement made in relation to the building of a house may amount to a supply of services within another TDA provision;[34] and such a statement made in respect of the contents of a built house may be within the above section as relating to goods.[35] There are entirely separate provisions designed to control the sale of houses by estate agents (see para 3.03) and misdescription of houses by them.[36]

It will be observed that s 1(1) actually creates two distinct classes of offence of strict liability:[37]

(a) *Applying* a false trade description to goods (see para 4.04), e.g. the offence of the actively unscrupulous;[38]

(b) *Supplying* goods to which a false trade description has been applied (see para 4.05), e.g. the offence of culpable failure to check what another said.[39]

Of these two offences, the former is the more heinous and therefore non-excludable (see para 4.09) and subject to less statutory defences (see para 28.17). Notwithstanding that the former offence can be committed innocently,[40] its prosecution

---

31  See *Shropshire CC v Simon Dudley Ltd* (set out at para 4.04); *R v Ford Motor Co Ltd* (set out at para 4.08). *Contra* misleading pricing: see below.

32  See the definition in the TDA, s 39(1). Compare the SGA definition of goods: para 2.02.

33  For offences in relation to false or misleading pricing, see para 8.09, *et seq*.

34  Under TDA, s 14 (see para 4.15): see *Beckett v Cohen* [1973] 1 All ER 120, DC; and further the *TDA Review* (1976, Cmnd. 6628), para 90. What of a meal in a restaurant?

35  E.g. fitted carpets sold with a house. What if the carpets are described as 'prizes' or 'gifts' (see para 2.08)? For fixtures and fittings, see para 25.23.

36  An offence is provided by the Property Misdescriptions Act 1991, s 1, which also grants power to make regulations.

37  See para 4.04. This may lead to some harsh results. What about the mechanic who innocently replaces a faulty odometer?

38  *Per* Lawton LJ in *R v Hammerton Cars Ltd* [1976] 3 All ER 758 at 765, CA.

39  *Per* Woolf LJ in *Lewin v Fuell* (1991) 10 Tr LR 126, at 128, DC. For s 6, see para 4.05.

40  E.g. *Clode v Barnes* [1974] 1 All ER 1166, DC (conviction of innocent partner with no knowledge or means of knowledge); and see para 4.09.

tends to be reserved for cases of dishonesty.[41] There are provisions allowing for substitute prosecution of the person really at fault (see para 28.11-2).

Both classes of offence are limited by a number of common requirements (see para 4.03A).

[4.03A] **The common ingredients.** Both principal offences (see para 4.03) are limited by **all** the following requirements:

(a) There must be a **false trade description** (see paras 4.06–8).

(b) That false trade description must be **applied** to goods (see para 4.04).

(c) The primary offence must be committed by a defendant '**in the course of a trade or business**', which apparently includes the professions.[42] So, private transactions are excluded *per se*,[43] though they may be caught indirectly, as where a private seller applies a false trade description and his buyer (a dealer) commits an offence by sub-selling under the same description: the private seller may be prosecuted under s 23 (see para 28.12). There are some doubts over unincorporated associations.[44] However, where the defendant has a business, the offence does not need to be part of the primary activity of that business.[45] Thus in *London Borough of Havering v Stevenson*:[46]

> The operator of a car-hire business usually sold vehicles for which he no longer had a use in his business. The odometer having under-represented the mileage in one such sale, he was held to have committed an offence under s 1(1)(b) because such sales were an integral (though secondary) part of the business.

On the other hand, in *Davies v Sumner*:[47]

> A self-employed courier purchased a car and used it almost exclusively in his business. When sold by the courier in part-exchange, the car had a false odometer reading. It was held that the courier had not committed an offence under s 1(1)(a).

Their Lordships had little difficulty in distinguishing the *Stevenson* case: whilst denying that the regularity of sales of stock-in-trade are necessarily required by the provision, they pointed out that this was the first such sale by Davies of his business equipment and would not necessarily be repeated.[48]

(d) That offence must be committed by a '**person**', i.e. personally, even if he is an employee (see para 28.08); and in the last case an offence may also be

---

41  Bragg, *Op. cit.*, 6–7.

42  *Roberts v Leonard* [1995] Tr L R 536, DC. As to the NHS, see Bragg, *Op. cit.*, 52.

43  *Blackmore v Bellamy* [1983] RTR 303, DC; and see Bragg, *Op. cit.*, 59–60. Cf. paras 4.19 and 14.04; and generally, Holgate [1984] JBL 263; Stephenson, *Criminal Law and Consumer Protection*, 3–6.

44  As to a member buying from an association, see *John v Matthews* [1970] 2 All ER 643, DC (doubted by Bragg, *Op. cit.*, 62–3). As to indirect offences, see Dixon (1994) 13 Tr L 297.

45  As to supply by a business agent (even without commission), see *Kirwin v Anderson* (1992) 11 Tr LR 33, 156 JP 301, DC (discussed 9 Tr L 151, at 152–3). For discussion of the situation where the defendant is not otherwise trading, see Bragg, *Op. cit.*, 57–62.

46  [1970] 3 All ER 609, [1970] 1 WLR 1375, DC.

47  [1984] 3 All ER 831, [1984] 1 WLR 1301, HL. Foll *Devlin v Hall* [1990] RTR 320, DC (D prosecuted in respect of first of several sales: acquittal criticised by comparison with the test in civil cases (see paras 14.04; 18.18) by Dobson in [1991] JBL 68).

48  Lord Keith (at 834) envisaged that a 'one-off adventure in the nature of trade' might fall within s 1(1); but he added that 'the occasional sale of some worn-out piece of shop equipment would not fall within the enactment'. As to reform, see Bragg, *Op. cit.*, 64.

committed by his employer (see para 28.10). There is no restriction that the goods must be supplied to a private consumer (see para 4.03).

(e) That offence can only be committed in relation to an **actual supply** of goods. Thus, the mere issue of an inaccurate test certificate in relation to goods will not amount to the offence; but, it may do so if the certificate is issued in connection with the supply of goods.[49] Further, mere preparatory acts showing only an intention to apply a trade description to goods is insufficient, though the description does not need to be uttered contemporaneously with the supply.[50] Once it has been shown that the trade description has been made in relation to a supply of goods, it is unnecessary to prove either dishonesty by the defendant or that anybody has actually been deceived. As to what amounts to a supply, see para 4.05. As to attempts to disclaim, see para 4.09.

(f) The prohibited acts must involve statements made to induce the customer to **enter** into the transaction relating to the supply contract for the goods:[51] it is insufficient that the customer returns the goods and the statement is then made to pacify him.[52] On the other hand, the offence can be committed by either transferor or transferee. In *Fletcher v Budgen*:[53]

> In negotiating the purchase of a car from a private seller, a car dealer stated that the car was only fit for scrap. He was then able to buy it for £2, repair it, and sell it at a large profit. Held: the car dealer committed an offence under s 1(1)(a).

**[4.04] Applying a false trade description to goods**. For a s 1(1)(a) offence to be committed, a false trade description must at the moment of supply be **applied** to goods, whether or not by their supplier. **Applying** is widely defined by s 4(1) as follows:

'A person applies[54] a trade description to goods if he—

  (a) affixes or annexes it to or in any manner[55] marks it on or incorporates it with—

    (i)   the goods themselves; or

    (ii)  anything in, on or with which the goods are supplied;[56] or

---

49 *Wycombe Marsh Garage Ltd v Fowler* [1972] 2 All ER 248, DC (inaccurate diagnosis of tyre defect led to refusal of an MOT certificate); *Roberts v Leonard* (above; veterinary certificate wrongly issued in respect of calves not inspected to allow their export).

50 *R v Haesler* [1973] RTR 486, CA. As to advertisements, see para 8.07.

51 *Norman v Bennett* [1974] 3 All ER 351, DC. It would appear that the test is wider than under s 13 of the SGA (see para 13.11): Dobson [1990] JBL at 436–7.

52 *Wickens Motors (Gloucester) Ltd v Hall* [1972] 3 All ER 759, DC. But compare the offence under s 14, which may be committed by statements made *after* the supply of services: see para 4.15; and Stephenson, *Criminal Law and Consumer Protection*, 9–10.

53 [1974] 2 All ER 1243, [1974] 1 WLR 1056, DC (criticised in 141 NLJ at 890 and 897).

54 For application by advertisement (s 5), see para 8.07.

55 This would appear to include attempts to disguise defects by repair (being a positive statement), but not sale of goods which another has so repaired because that would impose criminal liability for silence: see para 4.07.

56 *Swithland Motors v Peck* [1991] RTR 322, DC (goods themselves: odometer). Para (a) will include statements made on any label, packaging container or instructions: *Haringey LBC v Piro Shoes* [1976] Crim LR 462 (label on shoes); *R v Ford Motor Co Ltd* (set out at para 4.08—order form).

(b)   places the goods in, on or with anything which the trade description has been affixed or annexed to, marked on or incorporated with, or places any such thing with the goods;[57] or

(c)   uses the trade description in any manner likely to be taken as referring to the goods'.[58]

Of particular significance is s 4(2), which provides that 'An oral statement may amount to the use of a trade description'; and this clearly extends to oral misdescriptions by either seller or buyer.[59] Nor need the speaker be a party to the contract for the supply of goods. Thus, in *Fletcher v Sledmore*:[60]

D was a repairer of, and dealer in, cars. D sold a car to another dealer, X, on the basis that the car would remain on D's premises for repair. P, whom D knew to be a possible purchaser, was brought to D's premises to inspect the car; and D told P that the engine was all right. P, having purchased the car, found the engine to be defective. Held: D was guilty of the offence of applying by means of an oral statement a false trade description to the car.

One particularly common case is where the trade description is actually put forward by the transferee. To meet this case, s 4(3) provides:

'Where goods are supplied in pursuance of a request in which a trade description is used and the circumstances are such as to make it reasonable to infer that the goods are supplied as goods corresponding to that trade description, the person supplying the goods shall be deemed to have applied that trade description to the goods'.

The effect of this was considered in *Shropshire County Council v Simon Dudley Ltd*:[61]

The Council put out a specification for tender of a fire engine. On this basis, SD made the successful tender; but subsequently the parties agreed to amend the tender. The fire engine supplied complied neither with the original specifications, nor with the agreed modifications. The Divisional Court held that both the original and amended specification were trade descriptions and SD was convicted of offences under s 1(1)(b) in relation to both of them.

In relation to s 4(3), Phillips LJ pointed out that it was 'designed to cover the situation where the supplier made no express application of a trade description to goods, but made an *implicit trade description* by supplying them pursuant to a request for goods of their description' (at 81). As to the original specification, his Lordship had no difficulty in applying s 4(3), saying that the test was a simple test of fact and did not depend on whether or when the trade description became a term of the contract (at 79). In also bringing the modification within s 4(3),

---

57   E.g. *Roberts v Seven Petroleum & Trading Co* [1981] RTR 312, DC. Compare *Donnelly v Rowlands* [1971] 1 All ER 9, DC.

58   'Uses' is very wide: it presumably extends to a retailer just displaying in his window a poster which may be taken as a trade description of stock on the premises: see Lawson, *Advertising Law*, 206.

59   E.g. *Fletcher v Budgen* (set out at para 4.03A). There is a shorter time-limit for prosecutions in respect of an oral trade description (s 19(4)): see para 28.07.

60   [1973] RTR 371, (1973) 71 LGR 179, DC.

61   (1997) Tr L R 69, DC (no s 24(2) notice was served: see para 28.14). See Cartwright, *Op. cit.*, 188–9.

Phillips LJ admitted to a slight extension of its literal meaning; but he held that, where 'the trade description used in the original request was varied by a sub-sequent request, and the goods were supplied in circumstances such as to make it reasonable to infer that they correspond to the description as varied, the person supplying the goods had to be deemed to have applied to the goods the trade description as varied' (at 80). In this case, the Council had originally commenced a civil action and only later initiated a prosecution: Phillips LJ regretted the prosecution, on the grounds that the facts were not within the mischief at which the Act was aimed (at 82); but Hooper J was in no doubt that s 1(1) offences extended to express promises,[62] even as to the future.[63] For civil liability as to false descriptions, see Chap 13.

**[4.05] Supplying or offering to supply goods.** It is now settled that s 1(1)(b) creates two separate offences in respect of goods to which a false trade description is applied.

1. *Supplying goods.*[64] E.g. selling a vehicle on which another has replaced the odometer. In *Miller v FA Sadd & Sons Ltd*:[65]

   > D had made a successful tender to supply to the schools of a local authority such fruit and vegetables as might be ordered at the prices then quoted in the fruit trade journal. In response to an order, D supplied the fruit and vegetables to a particular school together with invoices quoting a higher price than those obtaining in the trade journal.

   The court held that no offence had been committed under s 1(1)(b): D's tender was a standing offer; and each order by the authority an acceptance, and hence, the court said, an actual supply.[66] Each invoice was merely a post-contract record of price which could not amount to a trade description (see para 4.06).

2. *Offering to supply.*[64] This expression was deliberately given a wide meaning by s 6, which laid down that 'A person exposing goods for supply or having goods in his possession for supply shall be deemed to offer to supply them'. Thus to facilitate enforcement, the Act has made it unnecessary to prove an actual offer to supply,[67] or even exposure for supply at business premises.[68] It is sufficient

---

62  At 74–5. This clearly comprehends express and logically implied terms (see paras 11.07 and 11.10); but does it extend to the statutorily implied terms (see para 11.11)?

63  At 72. Compare the s 14 offences, where the courts have confined the offence to promises of existing fact: see Milne (1997) 113 LQR 383; and para 4.15.

64  This will comprehend sale, hire and hire-purchase: *Cahalne v Croydon LB* (1985) 4 Tr L 199, DC. It has also been held to cover part-exchange: *Davies v Sumner* (set out at para 4.03A). Does it cover free samples/gifts or prizes (see paras 8.14–15) or supply under NHS prescription (see para 1.07)? See Bragg, *Op. cit.*, 18. Cf. 'supplying' in the CPA: see para 4.34.

65  [1981] 3 All ER 265, DC. See also *Formula One Autocentres Ltd v Birmingham CC* [1999] RTR 195, DC (car service; some promised items not checked. Held: s 1 offence by garage).

66  But in the uncited case of *Rees v Munday* [1974] 3 All ER 506, DC, it was held that 'supplied' in s 1(1)(b) refers rather to delivery. A similar view has been taken with regard to the Video Recordings Act 1984: *Interfact Ltd v Liverpool CC* [2005] 1 WLR 3118, DC, at para 16.

67  A window display is sufficient (cf. *Fisher v Bell* [1961] 1 QB 394, DC); or in some statutes a delivery (the *Interfact* case (above), at para 26).

68  *Stainthorpe v Bailey* [1980] RTR 7, DC (upon mere inspection of car at dealer's home). As to 'expose for sale', see para 4.27.

if the goods are in the defendant's possession in a stockroom. The result is that the *prima facie* offence may be committed very early in the negotiations,[68] so reducing the scope for disclosure (see para 4.09).

Note that the supplier of the goods does not himself need to apply the trade description to commit an offence under s 1(1)(b), though the offence overlaps with s 1(1)(a) insofar as the supplier himself does so.[69] Thus, in a typical case a retailer commits a s 1(1)(b) offence in supplying goods to which a manufacturer has applied a trade description, perhaps in an advertisement (see further, para 8.07). In recognition that the retailer has here committed a less heinous offence than if he himself had applied the trade description, the Act allows him a wider range of defences (see para 28.17); and it has been decided that the offence has only been committed where the supplier knows of the trade description,[70] though he does not need to be aware of its falsity.[71] Can the offence be committed by a retailer who has simply run out of the advertised goods?[72]

## False trade description

**[4.06] A trade description.** The TDA continues the policy of the previous Acts in that it provides an exhaustive list of those matters which are to be regarded as part of the trade description.[73] Section 2(1) provides that 'A trade description is an indication, direct or indirect, and by whatever means given, of any of the following matters with regard to any goods or part of goods':[74]

(a) 'Quantity, size or gauge' (see further TDA, s 2(3). Compare the undertakings as to quantity: see para 13.03, *et seq.*). An average weight (see para 4.25) is not a trade description.[75]

(b) 'Method of manufacture, production, processing or reconditioning', e.g. 'immaculate'; 'in excellent condition throughout'; 'home-grown'; 'rust-proof'; 'free-range'; 'organic'.

(c) 'Composition'.[76]

---

69  *Telford & Wrekin Council v Jordan* [2001] CLY 922, DC: see above, para 4.04.
70  *Cottee v Douglas Seaton (Used Cars) Ltd* (set out at para 28.17).
71  *Tarleton Engineering Co v Nattrass* [1973] 3 All ER 699, DC.
72  See Bragg, *Op. cit.*, 20; and para 4.16. What about switch selling?
73  *Cadbury v Halliday* (set out at para 4.08). But see TDA, s 3(3): para 4.08. However, trade descriptions do extend to approval marks made under the Road Traffic Act 1988, s 80: see para 4.37.
74  In relation to livestock, see also TDA, s 2(2). It has been claimed that most of the difficulties have concerned statements involving an element of subjectivity: Stephenson, *Commercial Law and Consumer Protection*, 11–12. See generally, Bragg, *Op. cit.*, 22–3.
75  Weights and Measures Act 1985, s 48(4). For overlap with the 1985 Act, see TDA, s 22(2): see para 28.16.
76  *British Gas Corp v Lubbock* [1974] 1 All ER 188, DC (discussed by Lawson, *Advertising Law*, 217–18); *Queensway Discount Warehouses v Burke* [1985] CLY 3112, DC (knock-down goods pictured assembled). Compare the undertakings as to quality: see para 13.09 *et seq*. As to the composition of textiles, see regulations made under ECA 1972, s 2(2); and see also TDA, ss 8 and 9: see para 4.10.

(d) 'Fitness for purpose, strength, performance, behaviour or accuracy'.[77] As to TDA liability for express and implied promises as to fitness, see para 4.07.[78]

(e) 'Any physical characteristics not included in the preceding paragraphs', e.g. misdescriptions as to components, such as a car being 'fitted with disc brakes' or having a 'tool-set'. Does it apply to garment washing instructions?

(f) 'Testing by any person and results thereof', e.g. 'MOT Certificate'; and see para 8.03. As to the information on an MOT certificate, see para 4.03A.

(g) 'Approval by any person or conformity with a type approved by any person', e.g. compliance with a British Standard (as to which, see para 3.08). It also overlaps with TDA, ss 12, 13 (see para 4.10). Non-existent standards are caught by s 3(4): see para 4.08. See also the Hallmarking Act 1973, s 1; Video Recordings Act 1984, s 14.

(h) 'Place or date of manufacture, production, processed or reconditioning'.[79] This overlaps with the special provisions in relation to imported goods, see para 4.10.[80]

(i) 'Person by whom manufactured, produced, processed or reconditioned'.[81] What about own-brand goods; or goods described generally by a manufacturer's name e.g. Biro, Hoover? In respect of counterfeit goods (see also paras 8.05 and 13.11), there are suggestions that this may not be an entirely appropriate form of control.[82]

(j) 'Other history, including previous ownership or use' (see UCP Directive: para 4.20, item (e)). In respect of motor vehicles, common complaints include the clocking of odometers or vehicles described as 'new', an expression capable of a number of meanings.[83]

Section 2(1) is discussed below (para 4.07), except for the special rules for advertisements (see para 8.07). As to misleading pricing, see para 8.09, *et seq*.

[4.07] To some extent the concept of a trade description is wider than 'direct or indirect' indications as to listed matters (see para 4.06), extending to anything

---

77  E.g. *Sherratt v Geralds, the American Jewellers Ltd* (1970) 68 LGR 256, DC ('Divers watch', 'waterproof'). Could s 2(1)(d) extend to misleading instructions for assembly or use (see para 18.29)? For a pessimistic view generally, see Stephenson, *Commercial Law and Consumer Protection*, 12–14. For unfit food, see para 4.28. As to unroadworthy vehicles, see OFT, *1987-AR*, 20; and paras 4.07 and 4.37.

78  Compare civil liability as to fitness: for such express promises, see para 14.01; and for implied promises, see Cartwright, *Op. cit.*, 189–93; and paras 14.07; 14.21.

79  *Routledge v Ansa Motors* (1979) 123 Sol Jo 735, DC (date of manufacture). See also UCP Directive: see para 4.20, item (i).

80  What about 'Cheddar cheese'? See also Anglo-Portuguese Commercial Treaty Acts 1914 and 1916 (port wine); Scotch Whisky Act 1988.

81  *Roberts v Severn Petroleum and Trading Co* [1981] RTR 312, DC (other petrol sold from an Esso station).

82  For civil claims in respect of passing off, see para 17.17. As to representations that goods have been made by disabled persons, see para 8.13. See generally, Bragg, *Op. cit.*, *Trade Descriptions*, 33–5.

83  E.g. meaning first retail sale, or current model, or new as opposed to old, used, damaged or second-hand. See *R v Inner London Justices* [1983] RTR 425 (car owned by a leasing company described as having had 'one owner'); Bragg, *Op. cit.*, 37–41; Andrew [1996] Tr Law 284; and para 4.08. As to the civil law, see para 13.11. What about returns (see [2004] 3 *Which?* 5; and para 10.28)?

likely to be taken as an indication of them (s 3(3): set out at para 4.08). Thus, it is well-established that an odometer reading is an indirect trade description;[84] and the widespread practice in the motor trade of winding back odometers ('clocking') has led to attempts to disclaim odometer readings (see para 4.09). Nevertheless, despite the generous wording of the Act, the courts have insisted that there will be no offence without a **positive statement**: this will avoid criminal liability for silence[85] and usually also for breach of promises as to the future.[86] With regard to express statements, mere puffs are probably outside the statute (see para 4.08), but not promises as to present facts. In *Denard v Smith*:[87]

> Dixons, an electrical retailer, advertised at the point of sale a computer package with certain specified computer games software. When the specified software was out of stock, Dixons continued to sell the package with different games without taking any steps to alert customers to that fact. Dixons and their manager were charged with an offence under s 1(1)(b).

The defence argued that the computer was accurately described and there was an intention to deliver the advertised software package at a later date, unless customers could be persuaded to accept substitute games, so that at most there was only a breach of promise to supply the software with the computer. However, the Divisional Court held that the advertisement (see generally, para 8.07) was to supply the computer and software as a package; that this amounted to a broken trade description; and that Dixons must have known that the software package was out of stock and therefore could not rely on the due diligence defence (see para 28.15). On the other hand, it seems that, if all the advertised goods (computer and software) had been sold out, Dixons would not have committed an offence.[88] However, it would appear to be a different story as regards implied promises. Except insofar as they amount to express promises as to present facts (see s 2(1)(d)), it follows that the concept of trade descriptions does not extend to implied terms (see Chaps 12–15).[89]

Whilst the court is looking for a direct or indirect indication of one of the listed matters of fact, the test is objective: the Act does not extend to subjective statements, e.g. of worth or value; but it does not matter if a particular consumer is not misled when an ordinary consumer would be. Thus, in *Holloway v Cross*,[90] the dealer's conviction for supplying a car to which a false trade description had been applied

---

84   Within s 2(1)(j): *Tarleton Engineering Co v Nattrass* [1973] 3 All ER 699, DC; *R v Hammerton Cars Ltd* (set out at para 4.09).

85   *Per* Widgery LCJ in *Cottee v Douglas Seaton (Used Cars) Ltd* [1972] 3 All ER 750 at 757a, DC. This supports the civil law rule *caveat emptor*: as to which, see para 15.22. Cf. misrepresentations: see para 11.01. For negotiations to require mileage statements, see OFT, *1987-AR*, 20.

86   *R v Lloyd* [1976] CLY 2472 (express warranty as to future performance).

87   (1991) 10 Tr LR 86, DC.

88   *Robins & Day Ltd v Kent CC* [1996] CLY 1168, DC.

89   *Per* Bridge J in *R v Ford Motor Co Ltd* (set out at para 4.08), at 491j–492a. It has been recommended that it remain so: *Review of the TDA* (1976 Cmnd. 6628) paras 140–5. As to unfit food, see para 4.28; and as to false implications of endorsement, see para 8.03.

90   [1981] 1 All ER 1012, [1981] RTR 146, DC. See also *Cadbury v Halliday* (set out at para 4.08); *Furniss v Scott* [1973] RTR 314, DC (actual private purchaser aware car not 'mechanically superb' as described); *R v Veys* (1993) 137 SJ 785 (football club coat of arms).

(see para 4.05) was upheld on the basis that his estimate was an indirect indication of mileage[84] by way of opinion.[91]

There is also power to exempt goods sold for export (s 32: see para 28.16); and the Act itself deems not to be trade descriptions certain descriptions properly made[92] under statutes relating to food and drugs[93] and some other cases.[94] Finally, it is for consideration whether it might not be more satisfactory to replace the specific list approach with a general misdescription clause.[95]

**[4.08] Falsity.** The Molony Report did not intend that every inaccurate statement relating to a supply of goods should amount to a trade description (Cmnd. 1791, para 634): mere statements of opinion of the character of a 'trade puff' were to remain outside the Act;[96] and there should only be an offence where the error was 'of such substance that it could fairly be regarded as capable of inducing a purchase'.[97] Parliament attempted to capture this distinction in s 3(1), which provides that 'A false trade description is a trade description which is false to a material degree'. Frequently, the issue of falsity will turn on the exact words used and the context in which they are used,[98] in which connection any disclaimer may be relevant (see para 4.09); and the court is not interested in whether the bargain is a fair one overall.[97] The words 'material degree' were considered by the Court of Appeal in *R v Ford Motor Co Ltd*.[99]

> A car manufactured by F was damaged whilst in the care of forwarding agents. It was repaired and supplied to the dealer as a 'new car'. Held: the damage was sufficiently limited and repairs sufficiently perfect for the car still to be a 'new car'.

Thus, it seems that 'material' relates to the degree of deception and that the test will usually be whether an ordinary man would be deceived, e.g. whether a trade term

---

91 It may be that the same view would not be taken of the same words spoken **to** a trade purchaser: see *Norman v Bennett* [1974] 3 All ER 351, DC. What of a DIY enthusiast? Cf. the civil law dichotomy between misrepresentations and terms: see para 11.02.

92 But if the description is not properly used within the statutes, there may be an offence under the TDA: *R v Inner London Justices, ex p Wandsworth LBC* [1983] RTR 425; *Benfell Farm Produce v Surrey CC* [1983] 1 WLR 1213, DC.

93 S 2(5), as amended by the following: (a) as to food, see para 4.27, *et seq.*; (b) as to drugs, see para 4.29; and (c) as to safety (see below).

94 S 2(4), as amended by the following: (a) as to agriculture, see the Agriculture Act 1970, and the European Communities Act 1972, Scheds 3 and 4; and (b) as to safety, see the CPA (see para 4.32, *et seq.*).

95 This suggestion was rejected by the *Review of the TDA* (above), which instead suggested a new order-making power (paras 119–39). As to the difficulty with vague and meaningless claims, see *Modern Markets: confident consumers* (1999, Cm. 4410) para 3.16.

96 E.g. *Cadbury Ltd v Halliday* (see below); 'best on the market'; and see Bragg, *Op. cit.*, 43. But for some cases which seem to bring puffs within the Act, see Bragg, *Op. cit.*, 27; and see s 3(3) (below).

97 *Furniss v Scholes* [1974] RTR 133, DC (car described as being in 'exceptional condition throughout').

98 E.g. *Donnelly v Rowlands* [1971] 1 All ER 9, DC (milkman using another's embossed bottles); *Farrand v Lazarus* (set out at para 4.01). Cf. the *de minimis* rule: see para 13.12.

99 [1974] 3 All ER 489, [1974] 1 WLR 1200, CA: discussed by Harvey and Parry, *Op. cit.*, 399–400; Lawson, *Advertising Law*, 214–17; and Bragg, *Op. cit.*, 39–40, 44. See also *Simmons v Ravenshill* [1983] Crim LR 749, DC. Distinguish *Cottee v Douglas Seaton (Used Cars) Ltd* (set out at para 28.17).

has acquired general usage.[100] Section 3 then seeks to plug three possible loopholes as follows:

1. *The literally true, but misleading, statement.* Section 3(2) provides that:[101]

   'A trade description which, though not false, is misleading, that is to say, likely to be taken for such an indication of any of the matters specified in section 2 of this Act as would be false to a material degree, shall be deemed to be a false trade description'.

   The effect of this subsection is illustrated by the attitude of the courts to disclaimers (see para 4.09) and has been held to include the situation where a car which had belonged to a leasing company was described as having had 'one previous owner', though not that goods were 'new' (see para 4.06).

2. *The indirect indication.* At common law, 'a nod or a wink, or a shake of the head, or a smile' may amount to a misrepresentation.[102] However, according to s 3(3):

   'Anything which though not a trade description, is likely to be taken for an indication of any of those matters and, as such an indication, would be false to a material degree, shall be deemed to be a false trade description'.

   In *Holloway v Cross*,[103] this was held to bring within the Act an 'estimate' given by a car dealer of the actual mileage and recorded as such on the invoice. Thus, s 3(3) may extend trade descriptions beyond the common law notion of misrepresentation (cf. s 14(2)(a): see para 4.15); injurious falsehood (see para 17.17). However, the courts have generally been cautious in applying the provision to indirect indications of trade descriptions. For instance, in *Cadbury v Halliday*[104] the Court held that a chocolate manufacturer had not committed that offence, because 'extra Value' stamped on wrappers was neither a trade description (see para 4.06), nor likely to be taken as an indication of one under s 3(3); and that in any event the manufacturers had a good defence under s 23 (see para 28.12). In a later case, it was said that the distinction between s 3(2) and s 3(3) is between 'an indication which tells a lie about itself' (s 3(2)) and 'one which, whilst accurate on its face, misleads by its associations in the mind of the customer' (s 3(3)).[105]

3. *Non-existent standards.* Section 3(4) enacts that 'A false indication, or anything likely to be taken as an indication which would be false, that any goods comply with a standard specified or recognised by any person or implied by the approval of any person shall be deemed to be a false trade description, if there is no such standard so specified, recognised or implied'.

---

100 See *Chidwick v Beer* [1974] RTR 415, DC; Lawson, *Advertising Law*, 208, 212–13; and see Bragg, *Op. cit.*, 44–5. What of credulous consumers?

101 E.g. *Robertson v Dicicco* [1972] RTR 431, DC ('beautiful car'); *Chidwick v Beer* (above) (car 'in exceptional condition'); *Dixons Ltd v Barnett Ltd* (1989) 8 Tr LR 37; *Lewin v Purity Soft Drinks* (2005) 169 JP 177 ('fruit burst'). But cf. *Kensington & Chelsea (Royal) LBC v Riley* [1973] RTR 122, DC.

102 *Per* Lord Campbell in *Walters v Morgan* (1861) 3 De GF & J 718 at 723–4. For misrepresentation, see para 11.01.

103 [1981] 1 All ER 1012, [1981] RTR 146, DC.

104 [1974] 2 All ER 226, [1974] I WLR 649, DC. See also Lawson, *Advertising Law*, 209–11; Bragg, *Op. cit.*, 42; Cartwright, *Criminal Law and Consumer Protection*, 174–6.

105 *Per* Taylor LJ in *Surrey CC v Clark* (above). As to whether the goods may tell a lie about themselves, see Cartwright, *Op. cit.*, 176–7.

**[4.09] Disclaimers**.[106] It has been decided that, where a party is charged with applying a false trade description to goods (s 1(1)(a): see para 4.04), he cannot escape conviction by a disclaimer on the grounds that he cannot disclaim his own fraud;[107] but it would seem that this ban on disclaimers applies even where the description was made innocently.[108]

On the other hand, a party may disclaim liability where he is charged with supplying goods to which another has applied a false trade description (s 1(1)(b): see para 4.05). The issue here is not quite the same as with the exclusion of civil liability (see para 18.04): for TDA purposes, constructive knowledge is insufficient and the issue has been said to be whether or not the disclaimer made before the goods are supplied is 'as bold, precise and compelling as the trade description itself'.[109] The point has most commonly arisen in connection with false odometer readings on motor vehicles. In *R v Hammertons Cars Ltd*:[110]

> The dealer (D) argued that, during the negotiations prior to the sale, the purchaser had been orally informed that the odometer readings were not guaranteed; and he further relied upon a printed 'guarantee' supplied at the time of delivery which included an express disclaimer. Held: if D wished to avoid conviction for 'clocking', he should have taken positive steps to negate the effect which such a reading might have upon the mind of a purchaser; and that neither a casual remark made in the course of oral negotiations nor the 'small print' in a contractual document were sufficient to save him from conviction under s 1(1)(b).

The TDA does not expressly permit disclaimers but there would seem to be two possible ways in which this judge-made rule may offer protection: *first*, it may be that it modifies the description that would otherwise relate to the goods;[111] or *second*, it may provide a defence once a trade description has been given.[112] There are important differences between the two views. Not only does the former view provide the supplier with a much wider protection because it is not limited to the terms of the defences;[113] but it also postulates that no offence has been committed so that

---

106  See generally, Bragg, *Op. cit.*, Chap 3; Roberts (1990) 7 Tr L 66.

107  *R v Southwood* [1987] 3 All ER 556, CA (odometer returned to zero). But see *Newham LBC v Singh* [1988] RTR 359, DC.

108  *May v Vincent* (1991) 10 TLR 1, DC (painting-auction catalogue); *Southend BC v White* (1992) 11 Tr LR 65, DC (damaged dashboard replaced: see 157 JP 294). For an unusual case, see *R v Shrewsbury Crown Court, ex p Venables* [1994] CLY 524, DC.

109  Per Widgery LCJ in *Norman v Bennett* [1974] 3 All ER 351 at 354a, DC. See also *Zawadskiv Sleigh* (below); *Holloway v Cross* (set out at para 4.07: 'estimate' overrode disclaimer); *Lewin v Fuell* (1991) 10 Tr LR 126, DC (being prepared to tell potential customers that the goods were fakes 'if they asked' was wholly inadequate). As to offences under s 6 (where there is no supply), see *Lewin v Fuell* (above; car boot sale: oral disclaimer too late).

110  [1976] 3 All ER 758, [1976] 1 WLR 1243, CA. See also *Waltham Forest LBC v TG Wheatley (Central Garage)* [1978] RTR 333, DC.

111  *Crook v Howells Garages Ltd* [1980] RTR 434 at 439, *per* Donaldson LJ; *Kent CC v Price* [1993] CLY 484, DC ('Brand copy'); decision affd by CA and described as 'counterfeiter's charter': see Whisson (1994) 13 Tr L 44); *Bury MBC v Real* [1994] CLY 523, DC; *R v Bull* [1996] CLY 1199, CA.

112  *Lewin v Fuell* (above).'The disclaimer is not one that negatives the description, but one that says enough to put a potential purchaser on guard': Bragg, *Op. cit.*, 75. The disclaimer must then be proved by the defendant to comply with all the requirements of a defence: see paras 28.13 and 28.17.

113  'A disclaimer' is not a defence at all in the strict sense of s 24(1), because a disclaimer is saying 'I am not making any representation at all': *per* Lane LCJ in *Wandsworth BC v Bentley* [1980] RTR 429 at 433H; and see Holgate (1990) 154 LGR at 571; Harvey and Parry, *Op. cit.*, 395.

nobody else, e.g. the person who 'clocked' the car, can be charged under the by-pass provision in respect of that supply (see para 28.12). Whatever the juristic basis, the actual decision in *Hammerton* with regard to clocking has since been limited to where the dealer is unaware of the mileage: *Farrand v Lazarus* (set out at para 4.02).

Presumably because of the easy profit to be made from misstating a vehicle's mileage (the price being normally based on that mileage) and the difficulty of detection, 'clocking' was widespread. This has led to attempts to control such a disclaimer on the basis that it might amount to a false trade description,[114] or an unfair term.[115] Whilst technical advances would seem to be reducing the problem of clocking motor vehicles, the effect of generalised disclaimers prominently displayed in retail establishments remains problematic.[116]

**[4.10/4]  Other offences in connection with the supply of goods.**

(a) *Definition and marking orders.*[117] The government has power by statutory order[118] to assign definite meanings to expressions used in relation to goods. Where such meaning is assigned to an expression it shall be deemed to have that meaning when used in a trade description or in such other circumstances as may be specified in the order.[119] There is also power to require by order that goods be marked with or accompanied by any information[120] or instructions[121] and to regulate or prohibit the supply of non-complying goods.[122] Similarly, an order may be made that an advertisement contain or refer to any information relating to the goods (s 9).

(b) *Imported goods.* The United Kingdom has a long history of trying to distinguish imported goods in the UK market-place. The TDA contains both negative and positive provisions to this effect, though some of these provisions are over-shadowed by EU rules (see para 2.13). On the negative side, s 2(1)(h) makes it an offence to state falsely the origin of goods (see para 4.06); the Act contains separate prohibitions against the importation into the UK of any goods bearing a false indication of origin (s 16) or an infringing trademark (s 17); and s 36 attempts to deal with the difficult problem of defining the origin of assembled goods.[123] On the positive side, attempts were made to specify that imported

---

114  See *Corfield v Starr* [1981] RTR 380, DC.

115  OFT, *Unfair Contract Terms Bulletin No. 4*, p 32; *Bulletin No. 27*, p 30; and see generally, para 11.12, *et seq*.

116  See *Zawadski v Sleigh* [1975] RTR 113, DC (auction-room notice insufficient); and generally, Bragg, *Op. cit.*, 72. Insofar as it purports to disclaim civil liability a disclaimer might amount to an offence under another provision: see para 4.22.

117  S 36(2). The OFT *Review of the TDA* (1976, Cmnd. 6628) reported that these order-making powers were too tightly drawn for widespread use, and that they should be amended to introduce greater flexibility (paras 289–94).

118  For the manner in which Orders should be made, see s 38. This has been criticised for causing potential difficulties with EU Directives by the OFT *Review* (above), paras 295–8.

119  S 7. There are similar powers to make definition orders in relation to the supply of services in s 15: see further para 4.15.

120  E.g. Trade Descriptions (Sealskin Goods) (Information) Order, 1980 SI 1150.

121  For the legal effect of instructions generally, see para 18.28.

122  Ss 8, 10. This power has been used to, e.g. require origin-marking of specified classes of goods. The EEC has successfully sued the UK before the European Court on the grounds that such orders interfere with free trade: see para 1.03A; and 138 NLJR 240.

123  S 16. Perhaps EU considerations have inhibited the use of powers under s 36(2) to make regulations: Bragg, *Op. cit.*, 31–2.

goods must be marked with their origin in both the TDA 1972 and orders made under s 8 of the 1968 Act; but the European Court forced revocation of the orders[124] and the 1972 Act was repealed after warnings by the Commission.[125]

(c) *False pricing* (see para 8.09).

(d) *False claims as to approval, etc.* In relation to the supply of both goods and services, it is an offence to give a false indication of royal approval or award (s 12) or to make a false representation that goods or services are of a kind supplied to any person.[126] It has been argued that these anomalous offences should instead be subsumed under ss 2 and 14;[127] but they should now be subsumed into the UCP Directive (see para 4.20).

## False statements as to service

**[4.15] Introduction**. Contrary to the recommendations of the Molony Report that the offences should be restricted to representations made in connection with the supply of goods, the gateway s 14 of the Act set out to regulate the supply of services.[128] However, in recognition that this was a new development, liability was made rather less strict. Leaving aside for the moment both the state of mind in which the representor makes his statement and also the subject-matter of the statement (see paras 4.16–17), it will be observed that the offences under s 14 are like those under s 1 in all the following matters: the statements must be made in the course of trade or business (see para 4.03A); they must be false to a material degree (s 14(4): see para 4.08); and liability may be avoided by an adequate disclaimer;[129] or by invoking the statutory defences even though, unlike the other provisions creating offences, s 14 is not expressed to be 'subject to the provisions of the Act'.[130] The nub of s 14 offences concerns 'statements made' as to the 'provision' of certain matters.

(a) *Statements*. Section 14 is primarily directed at 'statements', which expression is amplified by the following provision:[131]

> 'anything (whether or not a statement as to any of the matters specified in [s 14(1)]) likely to be taken for such a statement as to any of those matters as would be false shall be deemed to be a false statement as to that matter.'

---

124 S 13. E.g. see para 8.15. As contravening Art 28 [ex 30] of the Treaty of Rome (see para 8.06): *EEC v UK* [1985] 2 CMLR 259, CJEC.

125 CPA, s 48(2)(a). As to whether indirect attempts to preserve origin-marking under a new s 8 order effectively escapes the EU, see Bragg, *Op. cit.*, 225–7.

126 S 13. E.g. *R v Holland* [2002] EWCA Crim 2022, CA (false claim to be part of a large trading organisation).

127 See Bragg, *Op. cit.*, 175.

128 Cmnd. 1781 (1962) para 5. For TDA, ss 12 and 13, which apply to both goods and services, see para 4.10. For implied terms as to services, see para 15.15; and as to codes of conduct, see paras 3.11–14.

129 *Edward A Savory and Associates Ltd v Noel Dawson* (1976) 26.2, DC referred to in Cmnd. 6628, App. 3. Cf. para 4.09. See Bragg, *Op. cit.*, 158.

130 *Sunair Holidays Ltd v Dodd* [1970] 2 All ER 410, DC; cited by Lord Hailsham in *Wings Ltd v Ellis* (set out at para 4.17). For the defences, see Chap 28.

131 TDA, s 14(2)(a); *R v Bevelectric* (1993) 12 Tr LR 19, CA (servicer's policy to say replacement motor required). Cf. TDA, s 3(3): see para 5.08.

Unfortunately, the draftsman has not there made clear whether the test is subjective (likely to be taken by the addressee) or objective (likely to be taken by the reasonable man).[132] Further, the emphasis throughout s 14 is on false or misleading statements of existing fact, e.g. that a service has been provided: promises as to opinion or future performance *prima facie* fall outside the section;[133] but they may constitute offences where the speaker does not currently have that opinion or intention.[134] This dichotomy between present and future has caused particular difficulty in relation to the advertising of holidays at hotels and timeshares not then completed,[135] a subject beyond the scope of this work. Nor is it any defence that the service is offered subject to contract, so that alteration is no breach of contract.[135]

(b) *Made*. In *Wings Ltd v Ellis* (set out at para 4.17), the House of Lords explained that the expression 'statement made' does not necessarily import that a statement is communicated to anyone; but their Lordships affirmed that there will be an offence every time it is communicated to a different consumer.[136] Each communication is therefore a separate offence, allowing multiple prosecutions in respect of each statement 'made'. It has also been decided that the offence may be committed even though the statement is not made until after the parties have entered the contract.[137]

(c) *Provision*. The word 'provision' in s 14 is concerned only with the fact of providing services, etc.[138] The price at which they are provided is irrelevant for TDA purposes,[139] though it may amount to a pricing offence under the CPA (see para 8.09).

Subsequently, there have been introduced separate regulations to provide additional protection in respect of package holidays, a subject beyond the scope of this work. In 2007, much of the above may be overtaken by the UCP Directive (see para 4.20, item (g)).

**[4.16] The subject-matter**. In relation to the matters just discussed (see para 4.15), s 14(1) refers to statements made in the course of trade or business about the provision, nature, timing, evaluation or location of any 'services', 'accommodation' or 'facilities' (see below). Whilst none of the last three expressions is fully defined in the Act, there is power to make definition orders (s 15).

---

132 See Bragg, *Op. cit.*, 157–8.

133 *Beckett v Cohen* [1973] 1 All ER 120, DC (promise by builders as to completion date). *Contra* where it implies an assertion of existing fact: *R v Avro* (1993) 12 Tr LR 83, CA.

134 *British Airways Board v Taylor* [1976] 1 All ER 65, HL (double-booking, plane seats; see Cmnd. 6628, para 106); *James Ashley v Sutton* LBC (set out at para 4.16; and see the following note).

135 *R v Clarksons Holidays* (1972) 57 Crim App Rep 38, CA. Or a statement that a flight has been scheduled for a certain time: *R v Avro plc* (1993) 12 Tr L R 83, CA (subject to contract). See Lawson, *Advertising Law*, 222–5.

136 *R v Thompson Holidays Ltd* [1974] QB 592, CA. *Semble*, the statement may also be 'made' when the brochure is read by traders in the chain of distribution: *per* Lord Hailsham in *Wings Ltd v Ellis* [1985] AC at 285E, HL. See also *per* Lords Keith, Scarman and Brandon.

137 *Breed v Cluett* [1970] 2 QB 459, DC (NHRBC guarantee). *Contra* goods; see para 4.03.

138 This extends to false statements about services already provided: *R v Bevelectric Ltd* (above: see [1993] JBL at 46–7; 156 JPN 759; 13 Tr L 55).

139 *Newell and Taylor v Hicks* [1984] RTR 135, DC ('free' offer).

(a)  *Services.* The Act expressly extends the notion of 'services' to include the effect of any 'treatment, process or repair' (s 14(3)). However, it carefully distinguishes the provision of services, e.g. waterproofing, from anything done under a contract of employment (s 14(4)). The expression 'services' has been interpreted fairly widely to include not only a false statement that a guarantee existed,[140] but also a misdescription of the terms of the supplier's guarantee;[141] a mail order house's ambiguous offer to supply goods on approval 'carriage free';[142] a false claim that customers' monies would be held in a trust fund,[143] though not to promises of refunds;[144] and a s 14 offence is committed when the provider of a service falsely claims a relevant qualification.[145] On the other hand, it has been decided that a false claim as to the provision of a 'free gift' of goods with other goods cannot amount to the provision of a service within s 14(1) since the 'free gift' of goods is not a service.[146] However, a 'free gift' of services may be within the section. In *James Ashley v Sutton LBC*:[147]

> There was advertised at prices between £55 and £179 sales of a book containing a football pools formula with a money-back guarantee which the seller refused to honour.

It was held that there was both a sale of goods (the book) within s 1 (see para 4.03) and a service (the formula) within s 14; and that the blanket refusal to honour the money-back guarantee constituted a s 14 offence (see para 4.15). In 2007, these provisions may be overtaken by the UCP Directive (see para 4.20, item (k)).

(b)  *Accommodation.* As with the other two expressions, s 14(1) allows accommodation claims to be made in a number of respects, e.g. as to its nature or amenities.[148]

(c)  *Facilities.* Whereas 'services' connotes doing something for somebody, a 'facility' enables him to do it for himself. The expression 'facilities' was considered by the Divisional Court in *Westminster City Council v Ray Alan (Manshops) Ltd*.[149]

> A retailer placed a newspaper advertisement indicating that goods were on sale in his London shop at a lower price than previously charged, when the higher price had been charged at his Leeds branch. He also displayed a sign outside his London shop saying 'Closing Down Sale' when in fact the sale was not a closing down sale and the retailer continued to trade at the shop.

---

140  *Breed v Cluett* [1970] 2 QB 459, DC (NHRBC guarantee).

141  *Bambury v Hounslow LBC* [1971] RTR 1, DC (second-hand car); doubted by Bragg, *Op. cit.*, 169.

142  *MFI Warehouses Ltd v Nattrass* (set out at para 4.17). Does it extend to statements of adherence to Codes of Practice (para 3.11)? See also *R v Avro plc* (1993) 12 Tr L R 83, CA.

143  *R v Holland* [2002] EWCA Crim 2022, CA.

144  *Dixon Ltd v Roberts* (1984) 82 LGR 689, DC (retailer made a false claim that the difference would be refunded if goods could be bought more cheaply elsewhere). But see the CPA: para 8.09.

145  *R v Breeze* [1973] 2 All ER 1141, CA (architect); *R v Piper* [1995] CLY 1054 (master craftsman).

146  *Newell and Taylor v Hicks* [1984] RTR 135, DC. For the contractual effects of 'free gifts', see para 2.08.

147  (1995) 14 Tr LR 350, DC (see Clayson (1995) 14 Tr L 387; Cartwright [1996] JBL 58).

148  *Wings Ltd v Ellis* (set out at para 4.17); *R v Thompson Holidays Ltd* [1974] QB 592, CA.

149  [1982] 1 All ER 771, [1982] 1 WLR 383, DC (criticised 45 MLR 711–12).

The court held that the retailer had committed no offence in relation to his closure notice, as 'facilities' did not extend to shopping facilities. Ormrod LJ suggested that 'facilities' must be read *eiusdem generis* 'services' and 'accommodation', and Woolf J explained that the facts fell outside the mischief aimed at by the offence.[150] The expression 'facilities' has since been applied to the availability of 'cash back';[151] but it seems unlikely that 'facilities' extends to the availability of goods, though it would extend to free insurance[152] or willingness to accept credit cards by exhibiting the logo (see para 2.27).

The problem of price claims in relation to services, accommodation and facilities are now dealt with by the CPA (see para 8.09).

**[4.17] The representor's state of mind**. According to s 14(1) it is an offence in the course of trade or business (see para 4.03A) in relation to any of the matters there listed (see para 4.16) for a person: '(a) to make a statement which he knows to be false; or (b) recklessly to make a statement which is false'.[153] At one time, it was thought that this required *mens rea* for a s 14 offence; but that view has been shown to be too narrow.

(a) The expression 'make a statement which he knows to be false' was considered by the House of Lords in *Wings Ltd v Ellis*.[154]

> W Ltd, a holiday tour operator, mistakenly published a brochure describing certain accommodation in Sri Lanka as air-conditioned. In May 1981, W Ltd discovered the mistake and instructed all staff and agents to inform customers of the error. In 1982, a customer booked that holiday without being so informed. W Ltd did not plead any of the defences apparently available under the Act, but instead sought to show that they had not committed an offence under s 14.

The Divisional Court quashed the conviction under both paragraphs (a) and (b).[155] However, on appeal in respect of the s 14(1)(a) acquittal only, the House of Lords unanimously held that there might be a conviction where W Ltd had no knowledge of the falsity of the statement at the time of its publication,[156] but knew of its falsity at the time when the statement was read by the complainant.[157] On this reasoning, it would appear that there will still be an

---

150  All ER at 775, WLR at 388B, criticised by Cartwright (1992) 9 Tr L at 3–5. As to whether such conduct would now be caught by the CPA, see para 8.09.

151  *R v Killian; R v Lang* [2002] CLY 836, CA. For 'cash backs', see para 8.13A.

152  *Kinchin v Ashton* (1984) 148 JP 540, DC. See generally, Cartwright, *ibid*; Bragg, *Op. cit.*, 166–7.

153  It has been said that this creates two separate offences, which are not interchangeable: per Lords Wilberforce, Dilhorne, Simon, Edmund-Davies and Fraser in *British Airways Board* v *Taylor* [1976] 1 All ER 65, HL at 68, 71, 72, 74–5, 78. As to whose state of mind is relevant where the defendant is a corporation, see Cartwright [1997] JBL at 469–71; and generally, para 28.10.

154  [1985] AC 272, [1984] 3 All ER 577, HL (see 125 NLJ 160). As to which, see Chap 28.

155  [1984] 1 All ER 1046, DC. As to s 14(1)(a), it was held that there had been created a 'result crime', which only occurs where a defendant fails to take any available opportunity to counteract the effect of publication.

156  As to constructive knowledge of falsity through a servant, see Bragg, *Op. cit.*, 62–3.

157  'The subsection says not that it is an offence knowingly to make a false statement but that it is an offence to make the statement': *per* Lord Scarman at 295F. See also *per* Lord Hailsham LC at 289, who regretted his decision because of the absence of fault by W Ltd, and further (1985) 101 LQR 3. But see the criticism in (1985) 48 MLR 340; and (1991) 141 NLJ at 889.

acquittal where a defendant has not become aware of the falsity of the statement by the time it is made.[158] However, the effect is to introduce semi-strict liability: D did not need to know that the statement was made, nor need he be dishonest, before conviction; but he was required to know that the statement was untrue.[159]

(b) 'Recklessly made a statement which is false'. By itself, this phrase might be thought to refer to a *Derry v Peek* test of dishonesty (see para 17.18). However, it is amplified by s 14(2)(b), which provides that—

> 'a statement made regardless of whether it is true or false shall be deemed to be made recklessly, whether or not the person making it had reasons for believing that it might be false'.

Thus, a statement may be made 'recklessly' within s 14 whether or not there is any dishonest intent, so that the standard is much nearer to negligence.[160] In *MFI Warehouses Ltd v Natrass*:[161]

> D advertised the sale by mail order of louvre doors on fourteen days' free approval, after which the price and carriage charges were payable. The advertisement also offered folding door gear on approval 'carriage-free': D intended that the gear should be supplied only with the doors, and did not appreciate that the advertisement could be read so that the gear might be taken to be offered separately. Held: in refusing to supply the door gear alone carriage-free, D recklessly committed an offence under s 14.

In this case, Lord Widgery said that it sufficed for conviction that the advertiser 'did not have regard to the truth or falsity of the advertisement, even though it cannot be shown that he was deliberately closing his eyes to the truth' (at 313. Cf. CPA, s 20: see para 8.09). On the other hand, in *Wings Ltd v Ellis*[154] the Divisional Court held that there was no offence committed under s 14(1)(b) because there was no evidence that any one or more of the natural persons who constituted the directing mind and will of W Ltd were reckless.[162]

Whereas it had originally been envisaged that s 14 would only impose *mens rea* liability (see para 4.03) so that the general statutory defence (s 24: see para 28.13) would normally be ineffective, that does not now appear to be the case (*Wings Ltd v Ellis* (above)). Accordingly, once a semi-strict liability offence under s 14(1)(a) has been made out, the accused may plead the general statutory defence; but, where a *prima facie* s 14(1)(b) offence is shown, that will normally be inconsistent with the defence (see para 28.15). There is a proposal to make s 14 a straight-forward strict liability offence (see para 4.02).

---

158  *Coupe v Guyett* [1973] 2 All ER 1058, DC (sleeping partner).
159  Bragg, *Op. cit.*, 161.
160  Bragg, *Op. cit.*, 159. As to recklessness, see Smith and Hogan, *Criminal Law*, 11th edn, 102, *et seq.*
161  [1973] 1 All ER 307, DC; discussed in Lawson, *Advertising Law*, 219–20. See also *Dixons v Roberts* (1984) 82 LGR 689, DC.
162  Compare *Cowburn v Focus Television Rentals* [1983] Crim LR 563, DC; *Yugotours v Wadsley* (1989) 8 Tr LR 74, DC.

## FAIR TRADING

**[4.18] Introduction**. The Fair Trading Act 1973 (FTA) marked an entirely new departure in the field of consumer protection: the appointment of an officer of national status—the Director—backed by an adequate centralised Office of Fair Trading (OFT: see para 3.03). Whilst the Act had several principal objects, this book is interested only in the consumer protection provisions, which were encompassed by Pts II and III of the Act. If the Director/OFT discovered a business activity which he considers to be detrimental to consumers, he was given the following powers:

1. *Undesirable practices.* Where he considered that the type of conduct was not, but should be, regulated, the Director might initiate the process under Pt II of the FTA for the promulgation of a statutory order to deal with that conduct. After an initial burst of enthusiasm, the machinery fell into disuse and has now been abolished by s 10 of the EA 2002 (see generally para 2.12), except for two extant statutory instruments still considered to provide useful protection (s 10(2) of EA: see below, para 4.22). Both the general principle and these two statutory instruments are due to be replaced by the Unfair Commercial Practices Directive (see paras 4.20–1B).

2. *Undesirable traders.* Where the type of conduct was already regulated by law, but a particular business was finding it worthwhile to break that law persistently, the Director might under Pt III of the FTA obtain a court order requiring the cessation of that activity. Inspired by a Directive, this machinery was given a makeover by Pt 8 of the Enterprise Act 2002 (see para 6.06): this imposes no new obligations on business, but instead introduces a new tool for enforcing existing obligations owed to consumers generally. Further, it has been made more readily available to consumer organisations by the device of super-complaints (see para 4.19).

**[4.19] Super-complaints**. This new procedure is intended to encourage groups who represent consumers to make relevant collective complaints, primarily to the OFT, so that the OFT may exercise its powers (see para 3.03);[163] but certain other sectoral regulators may also be specified to deal with complaints within their field.[164] The procedure is contained within s 11 of the EA and may be invoked by any 'designated consumer body', meaning a body designated by the Secretary of State (s 11(5)) and there must be published criteria for determining acceptability (s 11(6)). 'Consumer' means an individual who is a consumer within Pt 4 of the EA (s 11(9)(b)), which adopts the modern standard test: namely, where a business supplies goods 'whether by way of sale or otherwise' (so it includes quasi-sale, hp and simple hiring) or services to one who does not take them in the course of business (EA, s 183(1)). Bodies so far designated[165] to make super-complaints are the NCC, CAB, CA and the consumer councils of the Utilities (see para 3.07).

---

163 OFT, *Super-complaints: guidance for designated consumer bodies* (2003) paras 2.5–6.

164 S 205. Under this power authority to deal with super-complaints within their field has been granted to, e.g. OFGEM, OFWAT (see para 3.07). See also OFT, *Super-complaint Concurrent Duties* (2003).

165 2004 SI 1517, 2004 SI 3366, 2005 SI 2340 and 2005 SI 2468. Cf. the 'qualifying bodies' under the UTCCR (see para 11.19).

Section 11 applies where (s 11(1))

'a designated consumer body makes a complaint to the OFT that any feature, or combination of features, of a market in the United Kingdom for goods or services is or appears to be significantly harming the interests of consumers'.

The expression 'feature of a market' has the same meaning as in Pt 4 of the EA (s 11(9)(a)); and this is a reference (s 184) to s 131(2). Expanded by s 131(6), this means (s 131(2)) '(a) the structure of the market concerned . . .; (b) any conduct . . . of . . . [any] person who supplies or acquires goods or services in the market concerned; or (c) any conduct . . . of [his] customers . . .' The result would appear to be that s 11 encompasses a wide selection of complaints: whilst the most obvious complaints may relate to competition issues (see para 2.12),[166] it would seem likely that it also comprehends recommending changes in legislation[167] or self-regulation (codes of practice: see paras 3.11–13) and offences within the purview of the OFT (see para 3.03A). However, as is usual with the OFT, the super-complaint process cannot apply to individual complainants, only to classes of complaint: in this respect, it would appear akin to class actions (see para 3.18), even sometimes extending to claims for damages (s 19); but, according to the OFT Guidance,[163] complaints about specific instances even of the above-listed behaviour will continue to be considered under other legislation (para 2.14).

Under that OFT Guidance,[163] the designated body must, of course, supply evidence to support its complaint (paras 2.11–3 and Annexe). Within ninety days of receipt of the complaint (or such other period as the Secretary of State may specify by statutory instrument (ss 11(4), (8)), the OFT must publish a reasoned response stating how it proposes to deal with the complaint (ss 11(2), (3)). The OFT may then exercise in relation to that complaint any of its powers considered elsewhere in this book.[168] The super-complaint is not to be given any sort of priority;[169] and, if it is unsuccessful, the trade party will be unable to recover any of his costs in connection with rebutting the complaint.[170] The first super-complaint was by the NCC with regard to doorstep selling, which led to a competition reference (see para 2.14); and there have since been a number of others,[171] including one by Energywatch (see para 3.07).

**[4.20] The UCP Directive: (1) Annexed practices.** Within its ambit (see para 4.01A), Art 5(5) of the Directive blacklists some 31 practices in Annex 1, which it deems to be unfair in all circumstances,[172] so that there is no need for them to come within the 'transactional decision' test considered below (para 4.21). The annexed list includes the following, some of which overlap with existing UK law (as indicated):[173]

---

166 At least initially, it seems that the OFT is likely to concentrate on this use: *AR-2001*, 28; *AR-2002/3*, 22.

167 E.g. the CAB has submitted a super-complaint that doorstep sales do not, but should, require the supplier to give notice of a right of cancellation at point of sale, rather than afterwards (see para 10.22).

168 See *Super-complaints: guidance* (above), para 2.25. As to publicity, see paras 2.28–30.

169 Hansard, HL Vol 637, respectively col 1199. So, how can it be 'fast-track' (para 2.15)?

170 Hansard, HL Vol 637, respectively col 746.

171 E.g. home credit; Northern Ireland Banks, PPI insurance.

172 Art 5(5). The list may only be amended by a further Directive (Art 5(5)).

173 See *An Analysis Of The Application And Scope Of The UCPD* (see para 4.01A), 47–8.

(a) As to codes of conduct, falsely claiming to be a signatory to a code of conduct, or that the code has an endorsement from a public or other body.[174]

(b) Falsely claiming that a trader or a product has been approved, endorsed or authorised by a public or private body or displaying a quality mark to that effect.[175]

(c) Misleading pricing (items 5 and 7: see para 8.09).

(d) Switch selling (item 6: see para 8.13A).

(e) Creating the impression that a product can legally be sold when it cannot (item 9: see para 4.06; and para 12.01).

(f) Not disclosing statutory rights and falsely pretending to be a private seller (items 10 and 22: see para 4.22).

(g) Misleading broadcast advertisements (item 11: see para 3.14) or other marketing (item 18: see para 4.15) and advertisements for sale aimed at children to buy advertised products or persuade their parents or other adults to buy advertised products for them (item 28: see para 8.06).

(h) Misleading claim of personal risk if the consumer does not purchase the product (item 12: see para 8.12).

(i) Misleading trade description as to manufacture (item 13: see para 4.06).

(j) Pyramid selling (item 14: see para 1.09).

(k) Closing-down sales, winning services, prize promotions and servicing availability (items 15, 16, 19 and 23: see para 4.16).

(l) Falsely claiming that a product is able to cure illnesses (item 17: see para 8.12).

(m) Misleadingly described 'free' gifts (item 20: see para 8.13A).

(n) Inertia selling of goods (items 21 and 29: see para 8.18).

(o) Creating the impression that the consumer cannot leave the premises until a contract is formed (item 24: see para 8.13A).

(p) Conducting personal visits to the consumer's home ignoring the consumer's request to leave or not to return (item 25: see para 8.16A).

(q) Unsolicited and persistent sales solicitations by telephone, fax, e-mail or other remote media (item 26: see para 8.16A).

(r) Requiring a consumer who wishes to claim on an insurance policy to produce documents which could not reasonably be considered relevant as to whether the claim was valid,[176] or failing systematically to respond to correspondence in order to dissuade a consumer from exercising his contractual rights (item 27: see paras 24.48 and 29.01).

(s) Explicitly informing a consumer that if he does not buy the product or service, the trader's job or livelihood will be in jeopardy (item 30: see para 8.13A).

---

174 Items 1 and 3. As to codes of conduct, see paras 3.11–14. 'Code of conduct' and 'code owner' are defined in Art 2.

175 Items 4 and 2. As to approvals, see para 4.10; and as to quality marks, see para 3.08.

176 This could be relevant to the operation of cashbacks (see para 8.13A) or PPI insurance (see para 24.48).

(t) Creating the false impression that the consumer has already won, will win, or will on doing a particular act win, a prize or other equivalent benefit (item 31: see para 8.15).

**[4.21] The UCP Directive: (2) Unfair Commercial Practices**. Besides explicitly banning within its ambit (see para 4.01A) the annexed practices in all circumstances (see para 4.20), the Directive also creates the general prohibitions discussed below in relation to 'unfair commercial practices'. These are practices by traders against consumers which satisfy all the following:

(a) 'It is contrary to the requirements of professional diligence' (Art 5(2)); meaning[177]

> 'The standard of special[178] skill and care which a trader may reasonably be expected to exercise towards consumers, commensurate with honest marketing practices and/or the general principle of good faith[179] in the trader's field of activity'.

This would seem to set the objective standard of reasonable behaviour expected by consumers of that trade: it does not require proof that the trader knew that he was engaging in an unfair commercial practice; nor does it condone poor standards prevalent in a particular sector.

(b) It does, or is likely to, materially distort[180] the economic behaviour with regard to the product of the average consumer whom it reaches, or to whom it is addressed.[181] So, the trader's conduct must adversely affect the decision-making of the average, typical consumer (see Recital 18) in making the transactional decision (see below), e.g. the man on the Clapham Omnibus.[182]

(c) The effect of (a) + (b) must be to make the consumer enter 'transactional decisions' (Arts 6(1), 7(1), 8(1)); which expression means (Art 2(k)):[183]

> 'Any decision taken by a consumer concerning whether, how and on what terms to purchase, make payment in whole or in part for, retain or dispose of a product or to exercise a contractual right in relation to the product, whether the consumer decides to act or refrains from acting'.

Note that it extends to post-sale decisions, e.g. to pay a debt as a result of aggressive debt collecting; and 'refrains from acting' covers actions deterring consumers from exercising contractual rights, e.g. 'no refund' signs.

---

177 Art 2(h). If the practice is directed at a particular group, or a particularly vulnerable group, the average consumer will be taken to be an average member of that group: Art 5(3); see DTI, *UCP Directive Consultation* (Dec. 2005) paras 72–6; and see *An Analysis Of The Application And Scope Of The UCPD* (see para 4.01A), 4–9.

178 Will 'special' be interpreted away in the same manner as in s 14(3) of the SGA (see para 14.10)?

179 See *An Analysis Of The Application And Scope Of The UCPD* (above), 8–11. Will 'good faith' be given the same meaning as in the UTCCR (see para 11.15)?

180 'Materially distort' is defined by Art 2(k) as 'using a commercial practice to appreciably impair the consumer's ability to make an informed decision, thereby causing the consumer to take a transactional decision that he would not have taken otherwise'. See *An Analysis Of The Application And Scope Of The UCPD* (above), 11–3.

181 Art 5(2)(b). Or, where it is directed to a particular group, the average member of that group (*ibid*), e.g. foreign language student, computer literates.

182 See *An Analysis Of The Application And Scope Of The UCPD* (above), 15–31.

183 See *An Analysis Of The Application And Scope Of The UCPD* (above), 13–14.

Where the above three conditions are satisfied, the Directive creates some general prohibitions in respect of 'misleading' and 'aggressive' unfair practices (see para 4.21A); but Art 5(4) makes it clear that these are simply the best examples, so that there may be other 'unfair commercial practices' which do not fit within those examples. This has been welcomed by the OFT as a move towards 'principle-based legislation' which will be less easy for rogues to circumvent.[184]

**[4.21A] The UCP Directive: (3) The General Prohibitions**. After defining 'unfair commercial practices' (see para 4.21), the Directive specifies two key types of unfair practice which cause the 'average consumer' 'to make a decision that he would not have taken otherwise':[185]

(1) **Misleading practices**. Whether 'before, during and after' the point of sale (Art 3(1)), commercial practices may mislead consumers either through act or omission.

    (i) *Misleading actions*. Limiting the present Misleading Advertisements Directive (by Art 14: see para 8.12A) to business-to-business advertising, Art 6 of the Directive explains when a practice is unfair because of what it contains.

    *General indicators*. Art 6(1) provides that:

> 'A commercial practice shall be regarded as misleading if it contains false information and is therefore untruthful in any way, including its overall presentation, deceives or is likely to deceive the average consumer, even if the information is factually correct, in relation to one or more of the following elements, and in either case causes or is likely to cause him to take a transactional decision that he would not have taken otherwise'.

    This seems to lay down two different ways in which a representation by a trader may mislead a consumer as to any of the seven listed matters: it contains false information; or true information which is likely to deceive him.[186] The listed matters are: (a) the existence or nature of the product; (b) its main characteristics;[187] (c) the extent of the trader's commitments, motives, sponsorship or approval of himself or the product; (d) the price or the manner in which it is calculated, or specific price advantage; (e) the need for a service, part, replacement or repair; (f) the nature or attributes of the trader;[188] or (g) the consumer's rights.[189]

---

184 OFT, *AR-2004/5*, 42. However, it has even been suggested that the Directive could reduce the protection of UK consumers: see Twigg-Flesner (2005) 121 LQR 386 at 388–9.

185 Arts 5(2)(b), 6(1), 7(1), 8(1). This objective test is modified by Art 5(3) to add some vulnerable groups, which are 'particularly vulnerable . . . because of their mental or physical infirmity, age or credulity' (Art 5(3)).

186 The DTI points to some doubt as to whether the following list relates to both false information and that likely to deceive: *The UCP Directive Consultation* (Dec. 2005) para 90.

187 E.g. 'its availability, benefits, risks, execution, composition, accessories, after-sale customer assistance and complaints handling, method and date of manufacture or provision, delivery, fitness for purpose, usage, quantity, specification, geographical or commercial origin or the results to be expected from its use, or the results and material features of tests or checks carried out on the product' (Art 6(1)(b)).

188 E.g. 'his identity and assets, his qualifications, status, approval, affiliation or connection and ownership of industrial, commercial or intellectual property rights or his awards and distinctions' (Art 6(1)(f)).

189 Under Art 6(1)(g), this includes the consumer rights to replacement or reimbursement under the Sale of Goods Directive 1999/44 (see para 29.02A).

*Specific instances.* Art 6(2) describes the following specific instances which were thought always to be deceitful: (a) confusion marketing;[190] and (b) misleading non-compliance with codes of conduct.[191]

(ii) *Misleading omissions.* According to Art 7(1),

> 'A commercial practice shall be regarded as misleading which, in its factual context, taking account of all its features and circumstances and the limitations of the communication medium, omits material information that the average consumer needs, according to the context, to take an informed transactional decision he would not have taken otherwise'.

This covers not just actual omissions of material information,[192] but also information which is hidden, ambiguous, or obscures its commercial purpose.[193] Art 7(4) makes special provision for where the trader makes an 'invitation to purchase' (Art 7(3)), this phrase being defined by Art 2 (cf. the common law concept of an invitation to treat (see para 10.02)). It does so by listing the 'material' information required as follows: the main characteristics of the product; the address and identity of the trader; the price and such as delivery charges; the arrangements for payment, delivery and complaints-handling; the existence of any right of withdrawal or cancellation; and Member States may specify additional material information (Recital 14). Material information is further extended by Art 7(5) to include all the information of other Directives listed in Annexe II.[194]

(2) **Aggressive practices**. According to Art 8,

> 'A commercial practice shall be regarded as aggressive if, in its factual context, taking account of all its features and circumstances, by harassment, coercion, including the use of physical force, or undue influence, it significantly impairs or is likely to significantly impair the average consumer's freedom of choice or conduct with regard to the product and thereby causes him or is likely to cause him to take a transactional decision that he would not have taken otherwise'.

These are commercial practices which significantly impair the average consumer's freedom of choice or conduct with regard to the product by harassment, coercion, including the use of physical force or undue influence; and undue influence is itself defined by Art 2 as exploiting a position of power in relation to the consumer so as to apply pressure, even using or threatening to use physical force, in a way which significantly limits the consumer's ability to make an informed decision.[195] Without prejudice to the width of all the

---

190 Art 6(2)(a). See para 8.12A.

191 For 'code of conduct' and 'code owner', see Art 2. It also includes breach of a desist commitment (Art 6(2)). The Directive does not interfere with UK consumer codes of conduct (Art 10), as to which see para 3.13.

192 E.g. a garden centre failing to say that a plant is a house plant, unsuitable for outdoor planting. However, the Directive does accept that some advertising mediums may have special constraints of time and space (Art 7(3)), e.g. TV. What about product placement in TV programmes?

193 Art 7(2), e.g. failing to make charges explicit. Art 7(2) also extends to failure to identify that the supplier is acting as a trader.

194 This includes the information requirements of the following Directives: medicinal products (see para 8.12); consumer credit (see para 9.03); price marking (see para 8.08); distance contracts, including of financial services (see para 9.05); E-commerce (see para 8.17A).

195 As to harassment, coercion and undue influence, see Art 9. As to how this may differ from the common law concepts, see Twigg-Flesner (2005) 121 LOR 386 at 387.

foregoing, Art 9 lists the following factors which may be taken into account in deciding whether they have been satisfied: its timing, location, nature or persistence; the use of threatening or abusive language or behaviour; exploitation of the consumer's specific disability; any onerous non-contractual barriers where a consumer wishes to exercise his contractual rights; any threat to take an action which cannot legally be taken. Examples of such aggressive practices would include the following: a plumber who obtains work by a low estimate, submits a high bill and then disconnects the water when the consumer objects; or a trader who implies that a consumer cannot leave his shop without paying; or misdescribing a product as 'free' (see para 2.08).

**[4.21B]  The UCP Directive: (4) UK Law Changes**. As part of its consultation on the UCP Directive (see paras 4.01A), the DTI have listed the following UK legislation which falls within the scope of this work and may require amendment or repeal to conform with the Directive:[196]

- Administration of Justice Act 1970, s 40 (see para 24.24).
- Business Advertisements (Disclosure) Order 1977 (see para 4.22).
- Consumer Credit Act 1974 (see para 5.12).
- Consumer Credit (Advertisements) Regulations 2004 (see para 8.30).
- Consumer Protection Act 1987, Pt III (see para 8.09).
- Consumer Protection (Code of Practice) Approval Order 2005 (see para 8.10A).
- Consumer Transactions (Restrictions on Statements) Order 1976 (see para 4.22).
- Food Safety Act 1990, s 14 (see para 4.28).
- Mock Auctions Act 1961 (see para 10.11A).
- Price Indications (Methods of Payment) Regulations 1991 (see para 8.08).
- Price Marking (Food and Drinks Service) Order 2003 (see para 8.08).
- Trade Descriptions Act 1968 (see para 4.02).
- Trade Descriptions (Sealskin Goods) Order 1980 (see para 4.10).
- Trading Representations (Disabled Persons) Act 1958 (see para 6.02).
- Trading Schemes Regulations 1997 (see para 1.09).
- Weights and Measures Act 1985, ss 29–31 (see para 4.25).

**[4.22]  Statutory orders made under Part 2.**[197]

(a) *Restrictions on statements*. Clauses purporting to limit or exclude the terms implied in favour of a consumer in a contract for the supply of goods are already avoided by the UTCCR[198] and UCTA (ss 6 and 7: see para 18.19). Nevertheless, such clauses continued to appear and to mislead consumers as to their rights, e.g. 'no cash refunds', 'credit notes only', 'sale goods may not be returned'. Accordingly, the Restrictions on Statements Orders made it an

---

196  See *An Analysis Of The Application And Scope Of The UCPD* (see para 4.01A), 88–132.
197  For the text of the orders currently in force, see Thomas, *Encyclopedia of Consumer Law*, Pt 2.
198  Under reg 7 (see para 11.13): OFT, *Unfair Contract Terms Bulletin No. 12*, case 16.

offence to include any of the following types of clause in a 'consumer transaction'[199] for most retail supplies of goods:[200]

(i)    A term rendered void by s 6 of UCTA, whether that term operates by way of display at his business premises, advertisement, statement on the goods or their packaging, or in any invoice or receipt.[201] On the other hand, it is not an offence to exclude undertakings in those sections in favour of a business transferee; nor to exclude undertakings not referred to in those sections, e.g. of a buyer to exchange goods on whim, or of a hirer to any of the implied terms granted by the SGSA, or any of the other exclusions rendered void by UCTA.[202]

(ii)   A written statement of his rights furnished to the consumer which does not also refer to his inalienable statutory rights (Art 4), e.g. an express guarantee of parts only, which would leave the consumer relying on his statutory rights as to the labour cost of any repair (see para 17.09).

(iii)  A statement on the goods or packaging of a business supply contract where that statement might be 'reasonably supposed' to be passed on to a consumer and does not refer to the consumer's inalienable statutory rights (Art 5). This was intended to apply to manufacturer's guarantees which might otherwise foster the common presumption amongst consumers that the guarantee was somehow instead of his rights against the retailer (see para 17.09).

(b)    *Mail order transactions*. This Order has been replaced by the Distance Selling Regulations (see para 8.17).

(c)    *Business advertisements*.[203] In contracts for the supply of goods certain terms are implied only where the supply is made in the course of business (see para 14.04); and the practice had developed in some trades, e.g. antique or car dealers, of advertising goods for sale in such a manner that there appeared to be a private sale, and hence misleading the consumer into believing that his contract did not contain these implied terms. Additionally, it will be less obvious that the transaction is regulated by the Trade Descriptions Act (see paras 4.03 and 4.15). Accordingly, the Business Advertisements (Disclosure) Order provides that a person 'seeking to sell goods. . . . in the course of a business' shall not for that purpose publish an advertisement unless it is there made reasonably clear that the 'goods are to be sold in the course of a business'.[204]

---

199  Consumer Transactions (Restrictions on Statements) Order 1976 SI 1813 (as amended), Art 2(1).

200  These provisions comprehend transactions by way of sale, or hp, but do not cover quasi-sales or simple hirings: Art 2 (as amended).

201  Art 3 (as amended). E.g. *Hughes v Hall* [1981] RTR 430, DC ('as seen and inspected' held capable of interfering with legal rights). Compare *Cavendish-Woodhouse v Manley* (1984) 82 LGR 376, DC ('bought as seen'), discussed by Dobson [1984] JBL 500. See further, Lowe and Woodroffe, *Consumer Law and Practice*, 6th edn, paras 17.10–15.

202  For the implied terms granted by the SGSA, see para 15.12, *et seq*. For the other exclusions rendered void by the UCTA, see para 18.22, *et seq*. Such exclusions may also amount to unfair terms: see para 11.15.

203  See generally Lowe and Woodroffe, *Op. cit.*, paras 17.16–7; and further, paras 8.19, 14.04.

204  1977 SI 1918, Art 2(1). It does not apply to advertisements of sale by auction or competitive tender, nor to some farm-gate sales: Art 2(3).

This offence may be committed without any resort to roguery[205] and should ensure that newspaper classified advertisements are properly categorised. It is rarely charged on its own, but normally added to other charges, e.g. under the TDA.[206]

In 2007, (a) and (c) will be overtaken by the UCP Directive (see para 4.20, item (f)).[207]

# OTHER STATUTORY PROVISIONS

[4.23] **Introduction**. Apart from the TDA (see para 4.02 *et seq.*) and fair trading rules (see para 4.18 *et seq.*), there are many other statutory provisions which seek to protect consumers of goods by the imposition of strict criminal liability. Leaving aside consumer credit (see Chap 5) and provisions relating to the seeking of business generally,[208] those dealt with in this chapter include the following: weights and measures (see para 4.24 *et seq.*), food and drugs (see para 4.26, *et seq.*) and other dangerous goods including motor vehicles (see para 4.31, *et seq.*). Apart from these, there are a host of miscellaneous provisions including those relating to the following:[209] selling to children, e.g. tobacco to persons under sixteen;[210] hallmarking;[211] energy consumption of motor vehicles;[212] mock auctions (see para 10.11); unlawful harassment of debtors (see para 24.24); discrimination in the supply of goods, facilities or services on grounds of sex,[213] race[214], disability[215] or religion,[216] matters also relevant to credit licensing (see para 6.19); the sale of some

---

205  *Blakemore v Bellamy* [1983] RTR 303, DC.

206  Bragg, *Op. cit.*, 58, fn 31.

207  See *An Analysis Of The Application And Scope Of The UCPD* (see para 4.01A), 158–62.

208  E.g. advertisement (see para 8.07), price displays (see para 8.08), false or misleading pricing (see paras 8.09–10), unsolicited goods (see para 8.18); circulars to minors (see para 8.33); age (see para 10.18).

209  See also the statutes mentioned later as rendering contracts illegal (see para 10.20) and those mentioned in the checklist in the *Encyclopedia of Forms and Precedents*, 5th edn, Vol 34, title Sale of Goods, paras 521–5.

210  Children and Young Persons Act 1933, s 7 (as amended). See *St Helens MBC v Hill* (1991) 11 Tr LR 94, DC; and for tobacco advertising generally, see para 8.06A. As to the general rule in contract law, see para 10.18.

211  Under the Hallmarking Act 1973; see *Chilvers v Rayner* [1984] 1 All ER 843, DC. This is the system for informing the public of the proportion of precious metal contained in alloys of gold, silver and platinum; see further, Harvey and Parry, *Op. cit.*, 284–5.

212  Energy Act 1976; Passenger (Car Fuel Consumption) Order 1983 SI 1486 (as amended, esp to meet EU Directive 93/116). For motor vehicles, see generally, para 4.37.

213  Sex Discrimination Act 1975, s 29. See *Quinn v Williams Furniture* [1981] I CR 328, CA (credit facilities); *Gill v El Vino* [1983] QB 425, CA (service in bar); and as to credit scoring, see para 8.39. As to sexual orientation, see the Equality Act 2006, s 81. See also DTI, *Getting Equal: Proposals to Outlaw Sexual Orientation Discrimination in the Provision of Goods and Services* (2006).

214  Race Relations Act 1976, s 20. See OFT, *Vulnerable Consumers and Financial Services* (1999) para 600.

215  Disability Act 1995, ss 19–21 (as amended). This extends to the provision of goods, facilities or services (s 19(2)), including banking, loans, credit or finance (s 19(3)(e)), e.g. a blind loan applicant. See also OFT, *Op. cit.*, para 500; and (2004) 59 CC2/35.

216  Equality Act 2006, s 46. To enforce all the Discrimination Acts, Part 1 of the 2006 Act establishes a Commission for Equality and Human Rights.

kinds of wildlife;[217] tampering with retail goods;[218] sale of human organs;[219] and health and safety.[220]

## Weights and measures

**[4.24] General.** From earliest times, Parliament has sought to protect both honest traders and consumers against the advantages conferred on unscrupulous traders by their giving short measure; and this included a system for ensuring that *minimum* weights were supplied, enforced locally.[221] However, from 1972 when we joined the EU (see para 1.03A), there has also been a stream of Directives on the matter. As has been seen (see para 3.10), early Directives in the consumer protection field tended to be very detailed and one of the areas covered was weights and measures.[222] Their main purpose was to require certain products to be sold by *average* quantity;[223] some pre-packed foods to be marked with an indication of quantity (see para 8.11); and to ensure that stated quantities can be relied upon as being accurate and not misleading. Moreover, as part of a Directive on price displays, there were promulgated rules on unit pricing, ie prices per kilogram, litre, etc (see para 8.08). Of course, these Directives overrule inconsistent UK provisions (see para 1.03A).

The two streams of rules on the subject have been brought together in the Weights and Measures Act 1985, which makes provision for their consolidation over a period of time by regulations, so enabling the UK government to introduce the EU aspects here slowly, and some would say, surreptitiously. The 1985 Act divides its operation between central and local government. The central government function is to set the primary and other standards of goods (ss 8–10) and coinage;[224] and to deal with matters such as the decimalisation of the currency[225] and metrication[226] and standardising of quantities of goods. For instance, central government will approve types of weighing and measuring machine and test pre-packed goods at the point of packing or import (Pts II, III and V). However, the

---

217 E.g. Wildlife and Countryside Act 1981, s 6 (as amended); Endangered Species (Import and Export) Act 1976, s 4 and see the Control of Trade in Endangered Species (Enforcement) Regulations 1985 SI 1155.

218 Public Order Act 1986, s 38. This is intended to cover actual or claimed contamination of goods at the point of retail sale.

219 Human Organ Transplants Act 1989, s 1. As to offences by corporate officers, see s 4; and para 28.11.

220 Health and Safety Regulations are made under s 15 of the Health and Safety at Work Act 1974 (as amended). For Health and Safety Regulations relevant to this text, see Thomas, *Encyclopedia of Consumer Law*.

221 See generally Harvey and Parry, *Op. cit.*, 2–7, 455.

222 E.g. Average Quality Packaged Goods Directives 75/106, 76/211; Food Labelling Directive 79/112.

223 For an account of the complicated method by which the Directive determined average weights, see Harvey and Parry, *Op. cit.*, 454–5.

224 See Pt I of the 1985 Act; the Coinage Act 1971 (as amended); and Harvey and Parry, *Op. cit.*, 443–4. For further discussion of the price of goods supplied, see para 2.06.

225 See the Decimal Currency Acts 1967 (repealed) and 1969 (as amended).

226 See the Units of Measurement Regulations 1995 SI 1804, implementing EU Directives: these regulations *pro tanto* overrule the provisions of the 1985 Act referring to imperial measurements. See further, Harvey and Parry, *Op. cit.*, 458–9.

essence of the Act is to be found in the functions placed upon local authorities, which have to ensure that retailers 'use for trade'[227] only approved types of machine[228] and also to test non-pre-packed goods (see para 4.25).

On paper, the result should be compulsory metrication of weights and measures on retail sales; but, the original text of the 1985 Act referred to imperial measures and the metrication provisions were only added to implement EU Directives under the European Communities Act 1972 (see para 1.03A) by subordinate legislation and codes of practice (some with statutory force).[229] So, opponents of metrication ('the Metric Martyrs') took advantage of this legislative confusion to defy the change. In *Thoburn v Sunderland CC*[230]

> Four separate retailers were convicted of failure to use metric weights as a primary indicator of weight for sale goods loose from bulk (the weights offences: see para 4.25) or failure to display such goods by reference to a kilogram weight (the price-marking offence: see para 8.08). The retailers argued that the 1972 Act had been impliedly repealed by the 1985 Act.

In supporting the convictions, the Divisional Court held as follows: (1) the 1972 Act had conferred on statutory instruments a Henry VIII power to amend statutes (see para 1.03A); (2) this Henry VIII power applied to both pre- and post-1972 statutes (see para 5.10); and, as a constitutional statute, the 1972 Act cannot be impliedly repealed.

The UK government hopes to improve the clarity of this branch of the law in due course;[231] and this might be achievable by statutory instrument under the Deregulation Act (see para 5.10), though the DTI insist that primary legislation is needed.

**[4.25] The local authority function: consumer protection offences**. Under the Weights and Measures Act 1985 (see para 4.24), the duty of local enforcement is placed upon the local authorities (see para 28.02). In particular, this relates to policing the use by retailers of weights and measures machines[232] for the supply of goods (Pt IV). This last function is of considerable importance to consumers. It involves the creation of a number of strict liability offences (see below), whilst allowing a defaulting retailer to plead several defences.[233] For weights, measures, food and drugs, special defences are created with regard to reliance on false warranties.[234] To some extent, consumer vigilance as to how a retailer uses equipment regulated by the Weights and Measures Act (see para 4.24) combined with the law

---

227 As to 'use for trade', see s 7, which effectively extends to all retail contracts for the supply of goods by quantity. For criticism of uneven enforcement, see the 2003 Report by the National Audit Office.

228 The use of unapproved weighing or measuring machinery is an offence (s 17).

229 See the Weights and Measures (Packaged Goods) Regulations 1986 SI 2049. This incorporates the Code of Practical Guidance for Packers and Importers and the Manual of Practical Guidance for Inspectors.

230 [2002] 4 All ER 156, DC (see 118 LOR 493). Leave to appeal to the HL was refused; and an appeal to the European Court of Human Rights dismissed (see para 3.09).

231 *Modern markets: confident consumers* (1999, Cm. 4410) para 3.11.

232 Or have in his possession for use: see *Bellerby v Carle* [1983] 2 AC 101, HL. Some of the requirements have been loosened under the deregulation initiative: 1999 SI 503; and see generally, para 5.10.

233 For the enforcement provisions and defences, see Chap 28.

234 See para 28.18. As to civil claims for breach of warranty, see para 11.06.

of theft will serve to protect consumers from dishonest traders. However, Pt IV of the 1985 Act goes much further, providing *prima facie* strict criminal liability as follows:

(a) *Selling goods by quantity.* The Act empowers the Secretary of State to impose by regulation requirements as to how particular goods (see Scheds 4–7) may be sold (s 22(1)) and to prescribe the manner in which such information is displayed.[235] In relation to goods sold loose, it contains alternative methods of satisfying the quantity provisions.[236] However, a more modern practice in many trades is to sell goods pre-packed: particularly with an eye to large-scale machine-packing, the Act therefore includes a system for average weights and measures.[237] 'Offering or exposing for sale' goods in breach of the above quantity rules will amount to a criminal offence.[238] Their pricing is dealt with later (see para 8.08).

(b) *Short weight.* According to s 28(1), 'any person shall be guilty of an offence who, in selling or purporting to sell any goods by weight or other measurement or by number, delivers or causes to be delivered to the buyer—

(a) a lesser quantity than that purported to be sold, or

(b) a lesser quantity than corresponds with the price charged'.

This offence is not confined to scheduled goods (see above), nor to retailers. Whilst not expressly so limited, this provision puts the primary liability in respect of goods that will be consumed by the public on the retailer;[239] and facts falling within it may also amount to the offence of applying a false trade description to goods[240] or give rise to civil liability under SGA, s 30 (see para 13.04). A contentious issue has been the quantity of beer supplied by publicans and, in particular,[239] whether to include the head (s 43: repealed by the Deregulation Act: see para 5.10). The Act also contains a number of other offences of misrepresenting the quantity of goods in connection with their sale or purchase,[241] such misrepresentations incurring strict criminal liability.[242]

## Food and drugs

**[4.26] Introduction.** Perhaps the two types of goods most obviously dangerous to the ordinary consumer are food and drugs. There has been criminal legislation[243]

---

235 Ss 23–4, e.g. *Thoburn v Sunderland CC* (set out at para 4.24). For the detailed provisions, see O'Keefe, *Law of Weights and Measures.*

236 Ss 44–6. Where the goods are not delivered at the time of sale, the quantity may have to be stated in writing (ss 26–7).

237 Ss 47–9; 1988 SI 2040 (as amended); and see para 4.24. For unit pricing, see para 8.08.

238 Ss 22(1), 25, 26(3). For defences and enforcement, see ss 32–40, 69–84; and generally, Chap 28.

239 E.g. *Bennett v Markham* [1982] 3 All ER 641, DC (head on glass of beer: see Clayson (1993) 137 SJ 1192).

240 E.g. *Kinchin v Haines* [1979] Crim LR 329, DC: for s 1(1) of the TDA, see para 4.03.

241 Ss 28(2), 29(1), 30(1), 31(1). As to misrepresentations by third parties, see *Collett v Co-operative Wholesale Society Ltd* [1970] 1 All ER 274, DC. Ss 29–31 may have to be amended to comply with the UCP Directive (see para 4.21B).

242 *Winter v Hinkley Co-Operative Society Ltd* [1959] 1 All ER 403, DC.

243 See generally Harvey and Parry, *Op. cit.,* 431, *et seq.*; Butterworth, *Law of Food and Drugs*; Baylis, *Food Safety—Law and Practice* (1994).

against the supply of impure food for human consumption since 1266.[244] The
increasing number of enactments on this subject were consolidated in the Food and
Drugs Act 1955. Yet these two aspects sat uneasily together in one statute: medicine
is supposed to do the consumer good; whereas food is expected not to do him
harm. Subsequently, the control of drugs was removed to the Medicines Act 1968
(see below) and the law relating to food re-enacted in the Food Act 1984.[245] From
our perspective, the more important parts of the 1984 Act were replaced in 1990 (see
below), but those parts of the 1984 Act still in force include those dealing with the
following: the regulation of markets (Pt 3) and some minor enforcement provisions
(ss 93–5; 121 (as amended)). In the late 1980s, there was a spate of food scares, e.g.
salmonella, listeria, botulism, and concern about the use in relation to food of certain
additives, ingredients, pesticides and irradiation. To deal with these issues, Parliament enacted the Food Safety Act 1990. Whereas earlier statutory definitions
proved inadequate, the 1990 Act contains no general definition of 'food', but merely
provides that it 'includes' (s 1(1))

'(a)  drink;[246]

(b)  articles and substances of no nutritional value which are used for human
     consumption;[247]

(c)  chewing gum and other products of a like nature and use; and

(d)  articles and substances used as ingredients in the preparation of food or any-
     thing falling within this subsection'.

According to s 1(2), it does **not** include: (a) live animals, birds or fish, unless consumed alive, e.g. oysters; (b) animal fodder and foodstuffs—which are governed
by the Agriculture Act 1970, etc; (c) licensed medicines and controlled drugs (see
para 4.29). From our viewpoint, the most important exception is (c): its effect is that
natural preparations which consumers ingest with the expectation that they will do
them good, but have no discernable therapeutic effect, are not medicines, but 'food',
e.g. vitamins, dietary supplements and herbal tea, slimming preparations and
perhaps chewing tobacco. These foods have historically been subject to far less, if
any, checks than medicines; but the EU is changing that (see below).

Apart from the major offences created by it (see paras 4.27–8), the 1990 Act
is largely an enabling measure, containing wide powers for the Minister (s 4) to
make regulations as to food safety and consumer protection,[248] whether inspired by
UK[249] or EU sources (s 17: see below); and the powers also include the registration

---

244  For civil action in respect of defective food, there may be an action under the SGA, e.g. *Frost v
     Aylesbury Dairy Co* (set out at para 14.08), for negligence, e.g. *Donaghue v Stevenson* (see para
     17.13) or under Pt I of the CPA (see para 17.24, *et seq.*).

245  There is a separate power to make statutory orders where there is an emergency threat of
     contamination to the food chain, e.g. by radioactivity or pesticides: Food and Environment
     Protection Act 1985 (as amended).

246  This will include water from the point of supply to premises (s 55: before this, it was governed
     by the Water Act 1989 (see para 3.07)).

247  E.g. slimming aids. As to 'human consumption', see s 53(1). For claims that preparations are
     food rather than drugs, see para 4.29.

248  S 13. These powers are extended (s 18(1)) to 'novel foods' (s 18(3)) or 'food sources' (s 1(3)), e.g.
     new slimming products, and to 'genetically modified food sources' (s 18(4)), e.g. yeast.

249  S 16 and Sched 1. UK-inspired regulations will usually first be referred to the Food Advisory
     Committee; and for irradiation, see [1991] JBL at 329.

and licensing of food premises[250] and the issue of codes of practice (s 40). The enormous volume of regulations made under earlier food legislation is to continue in force for the time being (s 59(3) and Sched 4).[251] Whilst Parliament took the opportunity of the 1990 Act to create a more systematic structure of enforcement powers and penalties (see Chap 28), further food scares in the 1990s, e.g. BSE (mad cow disease), led to the introduction of a Food Standards Agency to protect public health in relation to both human and animal food.[252] There is also an EU Regulation known as the General Food Law (178/2002), which has the effect of introducing directly into UK law (see para 1.03A) a general framework for food law operating throughout the EU. The EU Food Supplements Directive (2002/46) stipulates that any vitamin or mineral not on the EU 'positive list' will, in effect, be banned;[253] and the various EU rules concerned with food sampling and contaminants[254] have been implemented in England by Regulations (2006 SI 1464), dealing with contaminants in cereals, bread, breakfast cereals, biscuits, pasta and baby-food.

[4.27] **Food: composition and sale.** Part II of the Food Safety Act 1990 contains general provisions relating to the composition and sale of 'food' (see para 4.26). Repeated breaches may lead to proceedings under Pt 8 of the EA (see para 6.06). Any breach may also give rise to prosecution under the General Product Safety Regulations (see para 4.32) or a civil claim for breach of an implied term under the SGA (see Chaps 13–14). Besides widely defining 'sale',[255] the Act creates certain presumptions.[256] The principal provisions of the 1990 Act are as follows:

(i)   *Rendering food injurious to health.* Section 7 introduces a new offence for any person to 'render any food injurious to health' by the addition or use of any 'article or substance' (s 53(1)), the abstraction of any constituent (which will presumably cover abstraction from milk, but not its mere dilution), or subjecting the food to any other process or treatment.[257] To commit an offence under s 7, a person must **render** the food injurious: it is not sufficient that he merely sells injurious food, e.g. poisonous mushroom, though this may be an

---

250  S 19. The intention is to register all (including Crown) premises used for a 'food business' (s 1(3)), but largely confine the licensing to those food businesses which give rise to a risk to health (see *Greene King PLC v Harlow DC* [2004] 2 All ER 102). As to licensing of food markets, see above; and generally, para 6.02. As to enforcement powers, see para 28.05.

251  S 59(3) and Sched 4; and see *DEFRA v ASDA Stores Ltd* [2004] 1 All ER 268, HL (goodbye bendy bananas).

252  Food Standards Act 1999: see *de Prez* (2001) 13 ELM 311. In the light of BSE, is the Agency sufficiently able to disclose information? See also [2005] 1 *Which?* 19.

253  Implemented in England by 2003 SI 1387 (discussed 155 NLJ 1200). For provisions in relation to food-labelling, see para 8.11.

254  For enforcement, see EU Regulation No. 466/2001 and UK reg 4, which puts the responsibility on food authorities (see para 28.02). For EU Directives on GM foods, see O'Rourke (1997) 147 NLJ 1578; and for a failed challenge to a Directive, see *Ministry of Agriculture, etc v Webbs Country Foods Ltd* [1998] Eu LR 359.

255  According to s 2, 'sale' includes any supply of food in the course of a business, including food given, e.g. free meals or condiments, or offered as a prize or reward. S 2(1)(b) allows variation of the definition by statutory order; but there has been traced no order where a general variation has been made. Presumably, s 2 extends to auction and internet sales.

256  S 3(2). There are similar presumptions in respect of food or ingredients found on premises used for the manufacture, preparation, storage or sale of food (ss 3(3), (4)).

257  The section provides a useful benchmark for food control and may give rise to strict civil liability (see para 17.24): Harvey and Parry, *Op. cit.*, 433–4.

offence under s 8 (see below); and he must do something positive to the food.[258] In determining whether food is **injurious to health**, regard shall be had not only to the probable effect of that food on the person consuming it,[259] but also the cumulative effect of his consuming similar food in ordinary quantities (s 7(2)).

(ii) *Selling food not complying with safety requirements*. Section 8 makes it an offence for any person to sell, offer, expose or advertise,[260] food which 'fails to comply with the food safety requirements'. According to s 8(2), food fails this test if either:

(a) it has been rendered injurious to health by reason of any of the operations mentioned in s 7 (above); or

(b) it is unfit for human consumption;[260] or

(c) it is so contaminated (whether by extraneous matter or otherwise) that it would not be reasonable to expect it to be used for human consumption in that state.[261]

The test also *prima facie* taints any other food in the same 'batch, lot or consignment' (s 8(3)). Section 8 is in the course of being replaced by EU Regulation.[262]

(iii) *Selling food not of the nature etc demanded* (s 14: see para 4.28).

(iv) *Falsely describing or presenting food* (s 15: see para 8.11).

As will be seen later, powers are given to the authorised officers of a food authority to inspect, seize and condemn food which does not comply with the food safety requirements (see para 28.06). However, to try to intercept such food before it does too much harm, the 1990 Act introduces a new scheme of notices and orders (with criminal sanctions) in respect of any food business (s 1(3)):

(a) an *improvement notice* by an authorised officer, when it is suspected that an offence under certain regulations has been committed.[263]

(b) a *prohibition order* by the court following such conviction where there is a risk of injury to health, the order being mandatory as regards defective premises (s 11), but discretionary as to any human culprit.[264]

(c) a temporary *emergency order* without conviction where there is an imminent risk of such injury (s 12), which enables an *emergency prohibition notice* to be

---

258  Most additives and treatments are likely to be covered by the detailed regulations (see para 4.26); but s 7 should fill any gaps.

259  For definition of 'injury' and 'injurious to health', see s 7(3). This may also amount to an offence under the GPS Regulations (see para 4.32A): Cartwright (1995) 58 MLR 222 at 229–30.

260  As to 'advertise' and 'human consumption', see s 53(1). As to animals slaughtered in a knacker's yard, see s 8(4).

261  E.g. food which is mouldy, rancid or stale. Otherwise, it may be necessary to wait until an offence is committed under s 14.

262  EU Regulation 178/2002, Art 14. See (2005) 155 NLJ 1034.

263  S 10. For the regulations within this scheme, see s 10(3). For appeals, see ss 37 and 39.

264  S 11(4) talks of prohibiting the 'proprietor' (s 53(1)) from participating in the management of a 'food business' (s 1(3)); but the Act allows proceedings against any culpable manager (ss 11(10) and (11)): see [1991] JBL at 325.

issued by an authorised officer, usually to be followed quickly by an *emergency prohibition order* by the court. For more generalised food scares, s 13 allows the Minister to issue an *emergency control order* on any 'food source' (s 1(3)), e.g. substandard poultry farm, or 'contact materials' (s 1(3)), e.g. packaging or equipment.[265] Alternately, it may be possible to use the GPS recall system (see para 4.36A).

In 2007, s 14 may have to be amended to comply with the UCP Directive (see para 4.21B).

**[4.28]  Nature, substance and quality.**[266] Substantially repeating earlier legislation dating back to 1875, s 14(1) of the Food Safety Act 1990 provides that:

'Any person who sells to the purchaser's prejudice any food which is not of the nature or substance or quality demanded by the purchaser shall be guilty of an offence'.

An offence under this section will be committed by the person who in law is the seller, although on many occasions the sale will actually be conducted by an employee.[267] Its essence is to sell as food for human consumption (s 14(2)) to the **purchaser's prejudice**:[268] the Act expressly provides that 'it shall not be a defence that the purchaser was not prejudiced because he bought for analysis or examination' (s 14(2)); and earlier case law establishes that the offence includes sale of an inferior article, whilst having difficulty with disclaimers.[269] In fact, it would seem that s 14 creates three distinct but overlapping offences;[270] namely, as to compliance of the food with the demand[271] as regards:

1.  *The nature of the food.* This appears to refer to the type of food requested. So it is no answer to supply another sort of food or even something that is not food at all.[272]

2.  *The substance of the food.* Whilst primarily a reference to the constituents or ingredients of food,[273] this is also apt to cover the situations where food is adulterated or contains some foreign body[274] and alcohol is sold in short measure.[267]

---

265  As to ministerial use of s 13 powers, see *R v Secretary of State for Health, ex p Eastside Cheese Co* [1999] CLY 2590, CA.

266  See generally, Harvey and Parry, *Op. cit.*, 434–8. As to 'food' and 'sale', see paras 4.26–27.

267  *Nottingham CC v Wolverhampton & Dudley Breweries plc* [2004] 1 All ER 1352, DC. For liquor licensing, see further, para 6.05.

268  The prejudice is that of the ordinary hypothetical buyer, not the actual purchaser: *Pearks, Gunston & Tee Ltd v Ward* [1902] 2 KB 1 DC. See Gibbons (1993) 143 NLJ 515.

269  See Lawson (1991) 141 NLJ at 1103–4. Cf. disclaimers under the TDA: see para 4.09.

270  So separate charges should be laid where it is thought that the case falls under more than one head: *Bastin v Davies* [1950] 2 KB 579, DC; *Shearer v Rowe and Rowe* (1985) 4 Tr L 206, DC. For food fraud generally, see [1996] 4 *Which?* 26.

271  *McDonald's Hamburgers Ltd v Windle* (1987) 151 JP 333, DC (diet cola demanded; ordinary cola supplied).

272  *Meah v Roberts* [1978] 1 All ER 97, DC (lemonade ordered; caustic soda supplied). Cf. a false trade description: see para 4.06.

273  The standard to be applied is a reasonable one: *Goldrup v John Manson Ltd* [1982] QB 161, DC.

274  *Smedleys Ltd v Breed* [1974] AC 839, HL (caterpillar in tinned peas).

3. *The quality of food*. It would seem that this is not just a matter of description,[274] but relates to the essential characteristics of the food,[275] including its composition and water content.[276] Cf. SGA, s 14(2): see para 14.20.

**[4.29] Medicines and drugs**. The UK law relating to medicinal products was consolidated in the Medicines Act 1968 (as amended: see para 4.26); but an EU system is being introduced by Directive (2001/83, as amended). In the wake of the thalidomide tragedy, 'medical product' is broadly defined by s 130 with regard to potent substances. By ss 104–5, other articles not falling within s 130 may by statutory order be treated as medicinal products; and it is for consideration whether this power should be invoked to control (frequently highly priced, but imported) natural (herbal) medicines (see below). Parts II and IV of the 1968 Act relate to a licensing system for the manufacture of medicines and for retail pharmacies (see para 6.05). Parts V and VI are concerned with the packaging and labelling of medicinal products (see para 8.12). Part III of the Act regulates dealings with licensed medicinal products, making provision for the appropriate Minister to designate medicines as being available in one of the following categories:[277]

(a) *By doctor's prescription only*. Medicines on this list may be sold or supplied by retail[278] only by a registered pharmacy (see para 6.02) acting on prescription by an appropriate practitioner, contravention of this rule generally[279] being a strict liability offence.[280]

(b) *At a registered pharmacy*. If the item appears on the pharmacy only list, then generally speaking[279] it may be sold or supplied by retail[278] without prescription, but only by or 'under the supervision of' a registered pharmacist.[281] The opening hours of pharmacies are controlled.

(c) *As general sales list medicines*. Medicines on this list may be sold or supplied by retail[278] without prescription or the supervision of a registered pharmacist[282] from any premises meeting the prescribed conditions,[280] e.g. supermarkets or garage. Retail price controls ended in 2001 (see para 2.12).

Part III also contains provisions relating to the composition of medicinal products (see para 4.30) and there are separate provisions in relation to false warranties (see

---

275 As where the food includes extraneous matter: *Newton v West Vale Creamery Co Ltd* (1956) 120 JP 318, DC (dead fly in milk); *Lindley v GW Horner & Co Ltd* [1950] 1 All ER 234, DC (nail in sweet).

276 *Rodbourn v Hudson* [1925] KB 225 (general bar notice insufficient reference on sale of watered spirits). On water weight added to food, see [1996] 4 *Which?* 29.

277 S 51. *Sale* of unlicensed medicines is generally prohibited (ss 7, 43; and for offences, see s 45).

278 The expression is 'sell by retail . . . or supply in circumstances corresponding to retail sale': ss 53(1), 58(2)(a). This presumably covers both sales and dispensing under the NHS: see *Pfizer Corpn v Ministry of Health* [1965] AC 512, HL. For warnings, see para 8.12. For wholesaling, see ss 61, 62. For lax on-line pharmacies, see [2004] 3 *Which?* 9.

279 Ss 58, 59. For offences, see s 67; and *Pharmaceutical Society v Storkwein* [1986] 2 All ER 635, HL. There are exceptions for medical, dental and veterinary practitioners (s 55) and in respect of herbal remedies (s 56).

280 There are special provisions dealing with automatic vending machines (s 54) and herbal remedies (s 56); exemptions for doctors, dentists and vets (s 55); and a power to extend or modify exemptions (s 57).

281 S 52; and for offences, see s 67. E.g. *Pharmaceutical Society of GB v Boots* [1953] 1 QB 401, CA.

282 S 53 The proportion of licensed medicines included in this list has been expanded rapidly: see [1999] 4 *Which?* 22.

para 4.24). Under the central control of the Minister, the 1968 Act is to be enforced at a local level by the Pharmaceutical Society or local authority (s 108) and their powers of enforcement will be considered later (Chap 28). Where goods may be classified as food (see para 4.26) or medicine, there may be attempts to bring goods within the former category so as to escape the more rigorous controls of the Medicines Act.[283] However, as regards traditional herbal medicinal products, an EU Directive (2004/24) introduces a separate registration procedure and labelling system (see para 8.12), though it allows non-medicinal herbal products to be regulated under food legislation.[284]

*Drugs.* From those items classed as medicinal because of their therapeutic purpose (see above) are to be distinguished the law relating to the misuse of poisons[285] or drugs. The 'traditional' drugs are governed by the Misuse of Drugs Act 1971 (as amended): terming these 'controlled drugs',[286] e.g. heroin, cannabis, LSD, the 1971 Act places severe restrictions on their production, importation,[287] supply and possession;[288] and it imposes extensive criminal sanctions backed up by wide powers of search, seizure, forfeiture and arrest (ss 18–27).

[4.30] **Composition of medicines**. Under the Medicines Act 1968 (see para 4.29), there are a number of offences connected with the supply of medicines (s 67).

1. *Compliance with standards.* Section 65 prohibits the sale or supply in the course of a business of a medicinal product which does not comply with the standard laid down for a product of that name.[289]

2. *Safety prohibitions.* In the interests of safety,[290] Ministers are empowered by s 62 to make orders prohibiting the sale or supply[289] or importation of medicinal products of any kind, or animal feeding stuffs containing such products.[291]

3. *Adulteration.* Along the general lines of s 7 of the Food Safety Act 1990 (see para 4.27), s 63 creates several general prohibitions on the adulteration of medicines intended for sale or supply[292] in that state. However, unlike the 1990

---

283 E.g. *Optident Ltd v Secretary of Trade and Industry* [2001] 3 CMLR 1, HL (tooth-bleaching agent held a cosmetic).

284 See para 4.26. For herbal medicines, see [2001] 5 *Which?* 13.

285 Under the Pharmacy and Poisons Act 1933; Poisons Act 1972 (as amended). See also the Farm and Garden Chemicals Act 1967 (as amended).

286 S 10. See Jason-Lloyd (2000) 150 NLJ 1401. For an attempt to control 'glue-sniffing' by prohibiting the supply by retailers of intoxicants, e.g. typewriter correction fluid, aerosols, or varnish to minors, see the Intoxicating Substances (Supply) Act 1985.

287 S 3. But this limitation may contravene Art 3 of the Treaty of Rome (see generally, para 2.13): *R v Secretary of State for the Home Dept, ex p Evans Medical* [1995] All ER (EC) 481, ECJ.

288 Ss 3–9. Do the provisions extend to the 'mimic' drugs, e.g. heroin substitutes? The Secretary of State is also given power to make regulations and issue directions (ss 10–17). As to the meaning of 'supply', see *R v Maginnis* [1987] 1 All ER 907, HL (return to bailor).

289 For 'medicinal products', and for 'sale or supply', see para 4.29.

290 As to 'interest of safety', see s 132. See also the General Product Safety Regulations (para 4.33).

291 S 67(3) extends the offence to persons in possession of such goods and 'knowing or having reasonable cause to suspect that it was sold, supplied or imported in contravention of the order'. Exception to the prohibitions is generally made in favour of e.g. sales by doctors, or to a public analyst.

292 There is an express extension to 'supply' (s 64(5)), which increases the scope of the section to NHS prescriptions: see *Appleby v Sleep* [1968] 2 All ER 265, DC.

Act, s 63 requires that the adulteration must injuriously affect, not the consumer, but the 'composition of the product'.

4.  *Nature, substance and quality*. By way of close parallel to s 14 of the Food Safety Act 1990 (see para 4.28), s 64(1) provides that

> 'No person shall, to the prejudice of the purchaser, sell any medicinal product which is not of the nature or quality demanded by the purchaser'.

'Prejudice' is likewise extended to goods purchased for analysis or examination (s 64(2)). However, to the above offence (see s 67) there are two special defences:[293] first, insofar as the product contains some extraneous matter, it is a defence to show that this 'was an inevitable consequence of the process of manufacture';[294] or secondly, that there was an additional or subtracted ingredient which did not injuriously affect the composition of the product, that the operation was not done fraudulently and that the product carried an adequate notice.[295]

## Other dangerous goods

**[4.31] Introduction.** It will be seen later that the civil law regulating supplies of goods does enforce some general minimum standards, e.g. Pt 8 orders (see para 6.06); and, where there is a contractual nexus between the parties, there is compulsory strict liability in respect of both shoddy and unsafe goods (Chaps 14–15). However, the criminal law contains no counterpart for shoddy goods; and only in relation to unsafe goods has there been significant statutory intervention. Leaving aside licensing (see para 6.05), even here governments have been reluctant to fix too many compulsory detailed standards, preferring to leave the detail to voluntary standards.[296] Indeed, the Food Safety and Medicines Acts are perhaps unusual in prescribing in general terms minimum criminal standards as to product or performance only to safeguard human health or safety (see paras 4.26–30). Otherwise, UK governments have shown themselves willing to legislate only in relation to unusually hazardous activities or products, examples of the latter being motor vehicles (see para 4.37), explosives,[297] petroleum,[298] weapons[299] and, especially as supplied to young people, such as alcoholic liquor (see above) and tobacco (see paras 4.23 and 8.06A).

---

293  For the more general defences, see para 28.13, *et seq*. For discussion of the Food Act 1984, s 3 (now repealed), defences similar to s 64(3) and (4), see Stephenson, *Criminal Law and Consumer Protection*, 119–22.

294  S 64(3). Cf. *Smedleys Ltd v Breed* [1974] AC 839, HL (s 3(2) of 1984 Act; 'unavoidable consequences').

295  S 64(4). For what amounts to adequate notice, see s 64(4)(b); and cf. Stephenson, *Op. cit.*, 71–3; and para 4.09.

296  E.g. BSI standards (see para 3.08). See Cranston, *Consumers and the Law*, 3rd edn, 377–80; and *Modern markets: confident consumers* (1999, Cm. 4410) paras 4.18–9.

297  See the Explosives Act 1875; the Fireworks Act 2003 and 2004 SI 1836.

298  Petroleum (Consolidation) Act 1928 (as amended).

299  Firearms Acts 1968–1997; Crossbows Act 1987. Flick-knives were dealt with by the Restriction of Offensive Weapons Act 1959; but see *Fisher v Bell* [1961] I QB 394, DC (invitation to treat). See also the Criminal Justice Act 1988, s 141A (sale of offensive weapons); and the Violent Crime Reduction Bill 2006.

The major drawback to much of the foregoing legislation was that, each time a new standard was fixed or an old one revised, a fresh Act of Parliament was generally required.[300] This situation provoked the Consumer Protection Acts 1961 and 1971, which first gave the Secretary of State an extensively used general power to make regulations as to **any** class of **dangerous** goods, and allowed enforcement by local authorities (see Chap 28). In due course, these Acts were replaced by Pt II of the Consumer Protection Act 1987 (CPA), which introduced a general safety requirement (see below). However, the foregoing pattern has been substantially changed since 1987 in all the following respects:[301] (1) there have been a large number of directives imposing safety requirements on specific sectors of trade, the so-called sector-specific directives (see generally para 3.10) and these have usually been implemented in the UK by statutory order (see para 4.33); (2) as regards the general safety requirement; (3) the labelling of dangerous goods (see para 18.29); and (4) the introduction of Enforcement Orders by Pt 8 of the EA (see para 6.08).

**[4.32] EU Intervention**. In parallel to the above UK developments, from the 1980s the EU has developed its own rules to protect consumers from unsafe goods as follows.

1. *Civil law*. In 1985, the EU promulgated a Directive designed to ensure that the consumer injured by unsafe goods obtained adequate **civil** compensation (85/374). This was enacted into English law by Pt 1 of the CPA.[302]

2. *Criminal law*. Pt II of the CPA not only consolidated and enhanced the previous **criminal** safety provisions (ss 11–19: see para 4.31), but also introduced a general safety requirement according to the following game-plan: unless the goods conformed with some other statutory requirement as to safety, e.g. a sector-specific regulation, they had to comply with a 'general safety requirement'.[303] However, in 1992, there appeared an EU General Product Safety Directive (GPSD: 92/59) which attempted by way of **criminal** provisions to prevent injury to the consumer being caused by unsafe goods. This GPSD was incorporated into English law in 1994 by Regulations, which introduced an EU general safety requirement: it similarly gave way to sector- specific rules (see para 4.33) and was made under s 2 of the ECA and hence took precedence over the English law (see para 1.03A). The 1992 GPS Directive was repealed and replaced in 2001 by a revised GPS Directive (01/95),[304] which would appear to be a maximum directive.[305] The 2001 Directive has the same objectives as, but is an incremental improvement over, the 1992 Directive: it applies to all products (recital 5), however sold (including distance and electronic selling: recital 7), but not to civil liability for unsafe goods (recital 36; reg 44; and above); it confirms the general safety requirement (recital 6), but concentrates on safety

---

300 Interim Report of the Molony Committee on Consumer Protection (1961, Cmnd. 1010).
301 For statistics on modern dangerous consumer products, see DTI, *Consultation on GPS Regulations* (Dec. 2004) 76–7.
302 See para 17.24. Where the civil and criminal law overlap there should be borne in mind the advantages of first seeking criminal proceedings: see para 4.01.
303 CPA, s 10(3). See further Macleod, *Consumer Sales Law*, Butterworth edn, paras 10.33–4.
304 The text of the Directive is set out in Thomas, *Encyclopedia of Consumer Law*, Pt 5.
305 Recital 30; and see generally para 3.10. See also *Consultation on the GPS Regulations* (Dec. 2004), Appendix D, para 7.1.

problems which appear after products are placed on the market; it is not intended to apply to supplies of services *per se* (recital 1), but should cover products supplied in the course of a service (recital 9), e.g. hotel hair-dryers; and in particular, it extends to second-hand goods and introduces a last resort mandatory recall of unsafe products (see para 4.36A).

The 2001 Directive has been implemented in the UK in 2005 by Regulations[306] and refers to the Directive as 'the GPS Directive' (reg 2). The 2005 Regulations are a substantial technical improvement on those of 1994: whereas the 1994 Regulations keyed into the enforcement provisions of Part II of the CPA and entailed reading the UK and euro-processes side-by-side, the 2005 Regulations are self-contained;[307] so Part II of the CPA now applies only to UK Regulations made under the pre-GPS Directive system and should wither away as those Regulations are replaced by ones made under the Directive system.[308] The Regulations are claimed by the DTI to contain the following principles:[309] they encourage voluntary action by the trade; they penalise traders who save costs at the expense of safety; and are unlikely to have a detrimental effect on competition (see paras 2.12–4). Besides the detailed provisions considered in succeeding paragraphs, the Regulations also deal with market surveillance by enforcement authorities[310] and consumer complaints (reg 37).

**[4.32A] Definitions.** Both the CPA and the now-repealed 1994 Regulations are confined to consumers, albeit with different definitions of consumer: the 1994 definition (reg 2) was 'a consumer acting otherwise than in the course of a commercial activity'; but no such definition is to be found in the 2005 Regulations.[311] The key definitions in the Regulations are as follows.

1.  *Products.* The 2005 Regulations define 'product' as:[312]

> 'any product, including in the context of providing a service, which is intended for consumers or likely, under reasonably foreseeable conditions, to be used by consumers even if not intended for them and which is supplied or made available, whether for consideration or not in the course of a commercial activity and whether new, used or reconditioned'.

So, the primary definition is 'any product' which is 'supplied or made available . . . in the course of a commercial activity': 'supplied' connotes any contract of supply by a business', e.g. contracts of sale, hiring or hp (see Chap 1); and 'made available, whether for consideration or not' will cover sales ploys (see

---

306 The General Product Safety Regulations 2005 SI 1803. See the discussion in the above DTI, *Consultation*.
307 Pt 8 of the EA (see paras 6.06–8) is not intended to apply to these Regulations: the above DTI, *Consultation*, para 3.27.
308 For a list of the innovations, see the above DTI, *Consultation*, para 3.5 and Appendix D, para 3.3.
309 See respectively, DTI, *Consultation*, Appendix D, paras 5.1; 9.18; 17.1 and 19.1.
310 Recital 24. See reg 36. For Community surveillance, see recitals 25–32 (the RAPEX system).
311 The issue is whether the Regulations extend to business consumers: Preamble 10 of the Directive suggests not; but *contra* the *R & B Customs* case (see para 18.19).
312 Reg 2. This definition is taken verbatim from Art 2 of the Directive. It will cover any form of supply, e.g. sale, quasi-sale, and explicitly extends to free gifts and samples. 'Intended' is a subjective test and 'likely to be used' an objective one.

para 8.14). Further, the definition makes it clear that it extends to products, 'whether new, used or reconditioned'.[313] Whilst this primary definition seems intended to be restricted to consumer products, it does extend to products designed for the professional market which cause injury whilst in consumer use and are 'likely under reasonably foreseeable conditions' to 'migrate' to the consumer market, ie could be dangerous in amateur hands.[314] Somewhat like the CPA (s 10(7)), the Regulations contain specific restrictions regarding the types of product:

(a) *Second-hand products.* Whilst the Regulations *prima facie* apply to second-hand products (see above), under reg 3 they do not apply to second-hand products supplied 'to be repaired or reconditioned prior to being used', provided that that supplier so stipulates and transfers them to one in the business of repair or reconditioning, e.g. a second-hand car dealer with (adequate?) garage facilities, second-hand electrical goods retailer with workshop.

(b) *Sector-specific regulations.* By reg 4, the GPS Regulations do not apply to goods insofar as they are subject to sector-specific safety regulations (see para 4.33); but if a sector-specific regulation does not cover a particular safety risk which materialises, the GPS regulations will apply to it.[315]

2. *Safe products.* Regulation 2 produces a general definition of 'safe', followed by some specific instances. Thus, the opening words provide that

> '"safe product" means any product which, under normal or reasonably foreseeable conditions of use, including duration and, where applicable, putting into service, installation and maintenance requirements, does not present any risk or only the minimum risk compatible with the product's use, considered to be acceptable and consistent with a high level of protection for the safety and health of persons'.

The key to this definition (repeating the 1994 Regulations) is that products are only safe products where the risks to humans arising from use are **reduced to a minimum**, so that inherently unsafe goods, e.g. a kitchen knife, may be 'safe', balancing risk with utility (cf. para 17.02). However the injury might arise directly or indirectly from that risk, e.g. products which self-destruct; and the regulation explicitly extends 'use' beyond normal use to reasonably foreseeable misuse, e.g. superglue for children's play; sniffing correction fluid or aerosols. The Regulation limits this to risks which are (1) unacceptable and (2) consistent with a high level of protection for the safety and health of persons.[316] However, in an extension to the 1994 version, this definition also includes, 'where applicable', to 'putting into service, installation and maintenance': as the

---

313 Whilst the Directive excludes antiques or products to be repaired, etc (Art 2), the DTI included these to allow the complete repeal of s 10 of the CPA: *Consultation*, para 3.14, Appendix D, para 1.5.

314 See Recital 10. E.g. the DIY and tool hire markets. This should not proscribe migration, but may increase the use of labelling: DTI, *Consultation*, Appendix D, paras 9.12–3.

315 See also Recitals 11 and 12; Art 1(2). For further DTI suggestions, see *Consultation*, Appendix D, para 9.7.

316 Too high a standard may unduly disadvantage the low-income market: Cartwright, *Consumer Protection and the Criminal Law* (2001) 143.

regulations do not extend to supplies of services, so that it does not extend to unsafe installation, etc, *per se* (see above), it has been suggested that this extension only applies where the installation, etc is integral to the safety of the product.[317] As with the 1994 version, reg 2 then sets out the following list of non-exclusive factors to be considered in determining whether or not products are unsafe:

(a) the characteristics of the product, including its composition, packaging, instructions for assembly and maintenance (see also reg 7: para 4.35);

(b) the effect on other products, where it is reasonably foreseeable that it will be used with other products;[318]

(c) the presentation of the product, the labelling, any warnings and instructions for its use and disposal and any other indication or information regarding the product provided by the producer; and

(d) the categories of consumers at serious risk when using the product, in particular children[319] and the fact that higher levels of safety may be obtained or other products presenting a lesser degree of risk may be available shall not itself cause the product to be considered other than a safe product.

It will be noted that this list does not contain any explicit reference to **cost**.[320] Any product not satisfying the foregoing definition is termed a 'dangerous product' (reg 2).

**[4.33] Sector-specific safety regulations**. There are presently two streams of safety regulation.

1. *UK-inspired safety regulations.* Under earlier safety legislation (see para 4.31), there had been built up a considerable volume of safety regulations laying down compulsory minimum detailed standards of safety which retailed goods must meet.[321] Building on the previous legislation, s 11(1) of the CPA provides that 'safety regulations'[322] may be made for the purposes of securing 'that the goods to which this section applies are safe'.[323] For the time being, regulations made under earlier Acts continue in force (s 50(5)), contravention of both those and regulations made under the CPA[321] amounting to criminal offences (s 12(1)). Offences are also committed by failure to test goods for compliance with safety regulations, or to mark goods as required, or to give relevant information as required (ss 12(2), (3), 18). Finally, the CPA is particularly favourable to civil action by consumers injured through breach of safety

---

317 DTI, *Consultation*, Appendix D, paras 10.2 and 5.

318 See *Whirlpool (UK) Ltd v Gloucestershire CC* (1995) 159 JP 123, DC.

319 Presumably also the blind, elderly and illiterate in English.

320 E.g. that cost of safety features of a car. It is claimed that the regulations may be wide enough to include this factor: Cartwright, *Op. cit.*, 224.

321 See Thomas and Clarke, *Encyclopedia of Consumer Law*, Pt 2. For kitemarks, see para 3.08.

322 (As amended.) 'Safety regulations' are defined by s 45(1) of the CPA as those made under s 11, e.g. Pedal Bicycles (Safety) Regulations, 2003 SI 1101. For regulation relating to motor vehicles see para 4.37.

323 As to 'safe' and 'unsafe', see CPA, s 19(1): see 1st edn, para 4.32.

regulations: breach is expressed to give rise to an action for breach of statutory duty;[324] and any supply contract remains fully enforceable.[325]

2.  *EU-inspired safety regulations.* From an early stage, the EU begun to produce Directives in the field of consumer safety (see para 3.09) and had its own scheme for marking goods (the CE mark: see para 3.08). The normal way in which these Directives were enacted in the UK was by way of statutory instrument under s 2(1) of the ECA (see para 1.03A); and this has been true of both the 1994 and 2005 GPS Regulations (see para 4.32). However, when it came to enacting sector-specific safety regulations, it has been normal for the minister to do so by utilising the powers contained in the above s 11 of the CPA, whether or not the regulations were UK inspired or based on a Directive.[326] Leaving aside the special regime for road traffic regulations (see para 4.37), it will follow that enforcement of these sector-specific safety regulations will have to continue to follow the enforcement regime laid down in the CPA.[327] However, in due course the two streams of Regulations should coalesce, because the modern practice is to make new regulations under both sets of provisions.[328]

**[4.34] The general safety requirement.** The device of a general gap-filler to impose strict criminal safety standards in those areas not covered by sector-specific legislation first appeared in s 10 of the CPA (see para 4.32), now repealed by the GPS Regulations 2005 (reg 40). It has been replaced by the new 'general safety requirement' (see reg 2) to be found in reg 5, which is broadly similar to that under the 1994 Regulations. The key reg 5(1) of the 2005 Regulations provides that:

'No producer shall place on the market a product unless the product is safe'.

'Product' and 'safe product' have already been defined (see para 4.32A); and it will be noted that the primary obligation is here placed upon the 'producer', who is defined by reg 2 as falling within any one of the following three classes:

(1) the EU manufacturer of a product. When a manufacturer is based in the EU, he is the 'producer'; but the category is extended by reg 2 to two further classes: (i) own-branders or sub-branders of new goods, wherever manufactured; and (ii) reconditioners of old goods.

(2) In respect of goods manufactured elsewhere, the 'producer' is to be: (i) the manufacturer's EU representative where he has one; or (ii) in other cases, the importer into the EU.

(3) Subsidiary 'producer' liability is *also* to be placed on

'Other professionals in the supply chain, insofar as their activities may affect the safety properties of a product'.

---

324  S 41(1), (3), (5), (6). Is the civil action based on breach of s 11 limited to personal injury damage? This may provide an alternative to a civil action under Pt 1 of the CPA: see para 17.03. As to actions for breach of statutory duty, see para 3.21.

325  S 41(3): for illegality, see para 10.19. Apart from when a safety regulation so allows, it is forbidden to contract out of civil liability for breach of that regulation (s 41(4)); and see generally para 18.10.

326  See, e.g. the Cosmetic Products (Safety) Regulations, 2004 SI 2152 (as amended); 2003 SI 1101 (above). See *In the PINK Ltd v NE Lincolnshire Council* [2005] 11 CL 74.

327  See 1st edn, para 4.36.

328  E.g. 2004 SI 2152 (above).

E.g. a retailer misassembling a product. It is for consideration whether this includes inaction, e.g. a shopkeeper who fails to refrigerate perishables.

Not only does reg 5 place this general safety duty on one who '**places**' a product on the market (reg 5(1)), but it also stipulates that, unless a product is safe, the 'producer' shall not offer or agree to:[329]

(A) **offers** to place it on the market, or expose or possess any product for supply (reg 5(2)).

(B) **supply** it, or expose or possess any product for supply (reg 5(3)).

However, the general safety requirement is altogether inapplicable where the goods comply with EU specific safety rules (reg 4: see para 4.33); and the EU also intends to create a new class of European standards to help assess whether a product is safe.[330] Further, the above safety burden in relation to products in the UK is lightened by a 'presumption of conformity' in certain cases (reg 6).[331] *First*, in the absence of relevant specific EU safety rules, where the product complies with obligatory UK safety rules, 'the product shall be deemed safe so far as concerns the aspects covered by such rules'.[332] *Second*, lesser protection[333] follows where a product conforms to a voluntary UK national standard[334] giving effect to a relevant EU standard (recital 14), a protection which producers may welcome.[335] *Third*, in other cases, conformity of the product with the general safety requirement is to be similarly[331] assessed, taking into account (reg 6(3)):

(a) voluntary national standards of the UK giving effect to any other EU standard; e.g. CE Marks (see para 3.08);

(b) Other national standards drawn up in the UK, e.g. BSI standards (see para 3.08);

(c) recommendations of the EU setting guidelines on product safety assessment;[336]

(d) product safety codes of good practice in the sector concerned;[337]

(e) the state of the art and technology (cf. CPA, s 4(1)(e): see para 17.30);

(f) reasonable consumer expectations concerning safety.[338]

---

329 Reg 5(2) and (3). Cf. *Caerphilly CBC v Stripp* [2001] 2 CMLR 5. This is likely to be particularly relevant to retailers and mean that they may be *prima facie* liable, irrespective of their knowledge, for stocking dangerous goods.

330 Recital 15. See DTI, *Consultation*, para 3.5(ii) and Appendix D, para 11.1.

331 I.e. unless there is evidence that, despite such conformity, the product is nevertheless dangerous: DTI, *Consultation*, Appendix D, para 11.2.

332 Reg 6(1). E.g. the UK legislation for dealing with particular sorts of dangerous goods (see para 4.31).

333 Compliance with regs 6(2) and (3) is not an absolute bar to enforcement action: reg 6(4).

334 Reg 6(2). Such UK standards must be given an official published reference number by the Secretary of State.

335 The DTI also claim that such benchmarks are already widely used by producers: DTI, *Consultation*, Appendix D, paras 11.3–9.

336 E.g. EU rules on the manufacture of motor vehicles; or banning export from the EU of dangerous goods.

337 These will not be consumer codes of practice, but business-to-business codes (see para 3.11).

338 Suppose reasonable consumer expectations (an objective test?) differ from an established industry code?

**[4.35] Other obligation of producers and distributors**. The above general safety requirement must be supplemented by other obligations to prevent risks to consumers (recital 18). Here, the Regulations concentrate on the 'producer' of the product, whilst imposing only secondary responsibility on 'distributors'.

1.  *Obligations of producers alone.* Not only must a producer not place an unsafe product on the market (see para 4.34), but 'within the limits of his activities', he must also[339] undertake the following:

    (a) *Testing.* The producer must adequately test the product to inform himself of its risks: it would seem that he must adequately both test his product before distribution (reg 7(3)(a)) and continue to sample-test products thereafter (reg 7(4)(b)(I)).[340] No longer is it sufficient for a producer to rely on the testing and/or written warranty of his supplier (see paras 28.18–9): the producer is under a duty to himself conduct the above tests, which would also help him satisfy the general defence (see para 28.15).

    (b) *Traceability.* Except where it is unreasonable to do so, the producer must, as one of his 'appropriate actions' under reg 7(3), take adequate steps to make his products traceable (reg 7(4)(a)):[340] that is, he must mark his products, or their packaging with his name and address[341] and the batch number or product reference, e.g. in a bar code (see para 2.06).

    (c) *Warnings*[339] to consumer/shoppers (reg 7(1)): having conducted the above tests, the producer must give consumers sufficient relevant warnings to enable consumers to assess latent risks 'inherent in a product throughout the normal or reasonably foreseeable period of its use' and 'to take precautions against those risks';[342] if not, he can be made to do so (see para 4.36).

    (d) *Other measures.* The producer must[340] keep a register of complaints;[343] keep distributors informed of adverse results of such monitoring (reg 7(4)(b)(iii)); and, under reg 7(3) take appropriate action, including withdrawal of the product, further warnings and as a last resort recall. If the producer does not take these steps voluntarily, he can be made to do so (see para 4.36).

2.  *Obligations of distributors alone.* 'Distributor' means 'any professional in the supply chain whose activity does not affect the safety properties of a product' (reg 2); and it may be that this covers those who act as agents as well as those who act as principal.[344] Not all retailers will so qualify: sometimes he will be an own-brander or reconditioner (see para 4.34), and hence treated as a 'producer' (see above); sometimes he will not be acting by way of business, e.g. a charity or jumble sale. However, where he is such a 'distributor', he must 'act with due

---

339 Warnings alone do not exempt the producer from compliance with the Regulations: reg 7(2).

340 The duties under reg 7(4) are only to act insofar as it is reasonable to do so; but they must be 'commensurate with the risk' (recital 19).

341 With own-label products, is it sufficient if the product bears the name only of the own-brander?

342 Warnings cannot affect strict civil product liability to consumers (CPA, s 7): see para 17.30. For the effect of warnings on other civil liability, see para 18.28, *et seq.*

343 Reg 7(4)(b)(ii). This may be an important tool in identifying safety problems: DTI, *Consultation*, para 3.17.

344 DTI, *Consultation*, para 3.9.

care in order to help ensure compliance with the applicable safety requirements and in particular' is subject to the following measures (reg 8(1)): he must not supply a product which he should have known as a professional to be dangerous; and he must participate in safety monitoring 'within the limits of his activities'. For instance, he must keep adequate documentation to ensure the traceability of goods;[345] and he must co-operate in safety action by producers or enforcement authorities,[346] e.g. by producing relevant records. It is envisaged that the duty would be lessened on charity shops in respect of donated goods.[347]

3.  *Obligations of producers and distributors.* Except in the case of one-off dangers arising from second-hand products supplied as an antique or for repair/reconditioning (reg 9(2)), reg 9(1) imposes a new requirement that, where a producer or distributor knows that his product 'poses risks to the consumer that are incompatible with the general safety requirement', he shall forthwith notify the enforcement authority (see para 4.36) of both the risk[348] and the action taken to prevent it. So a reluctant producer/distributor can no longer take refuge in inertia and ignorance. On request, he must also co-operate with the enforcement authority to avoid such risks to consumers (reg 9(4)).

**[4.36] Enforcement of general safety requirement**. Where the 'producer' or 'distributor' contravenes the GPS general safety requirement (see para 4.34) he may commit an offence under reg 21.[349] There is the usual due diligence defence (reg 29: see para 28.13). However, it is a complete defence if he can show that he supplied or intended to supply the second-hand product as antique, or to be repaired/reconditioned prior to use (reg 30(1), (2)) and clearly so informed his transferee, whether trader or consumer (reg 30(3)). The Regulations also deal with the liability of persons other than the principal offender;[350] and enforcement is usually in the hands of the relevant local authority.[351] As the 2005 Regulations are stand-alone, the enforcement provisions of the CPA do not apply to these Regulations; but they will apply to enforcement of UK safety regulations.[352]

Simply to prosecute after the harm has been done is largely a stable-bolting exercise; and, over the years, first the CPA, and now the GPS Regulations have also developed a number of preventative mechanisms. The following powers

---

345  As to the sort of measures required, see DTI, *Consultation*, Appendix D, paras 12.1–6.

346  This includes the distributor taking 'measures enabling him to co-operate efficiently' (reg 8(2)). It is reckoned that the LAs already have adequate systems to discharge their part: DTI, *Consultation*, para 3.21.

347  Recital 20. But not in respect of bought-in goods? See DTI, *Consultation*, para 3.18.

348  In the event of a 'serious risk' (reg 2), the notification must include identification of (reg 9(3)): the product/batch; risk; tracing information; and actions taken to protect consumers.

349  'Contravention' includes a failure to comply and cognate expressions (reg 2). As to evidence, see reg 46.

350  There is a standard bypass provision (reg 31(1)): see para 28.12) and sanction for the prosecution of corporate officers (regs 31(2), (3): see para 28.11).

351  Reg 10: see para 28.03; but see the extended meaning of Enforcement Authority in reg 2. Notice must be given to the Minister (reg 33).

352  By reg 11, the following CPA provisions (see para 4.36) apply to products under the Regulations, sometimes with a reduced penalty (reg 11(d)): prohibition notices and notices to warn (s 13); suspension notices (ss 14 and 15); forfeiture orders (s 16); power to obtain information (s 18). See generally, 1st edn, para 4.36.

to be found in the Regulations are all triggered where the enforcement authorities have reasonable grounds for suspecting that a product is dangerous,[353] usually provided the authority acts in a proportionate way and first encourages voluntary action:[354]

1.  *Requirements to mark and warn.*[355] The enforcement authorities may serve one or both of the following 'notices' (meaning notice in writing: reg 2), requiring a person at his own expense:

    (i)   before the product is circulated (reg 11): (a) to ensure that the product is marked with the risks it may present;[356] and (b) to market the product subject to conditions specified in the notice to ensure it is safe.

    (ii)  after it has been circulated (reg 12): (a) to the extent that it is practicable to do so to ensure that individual purchaser/consumers receive a warning; (b) to publish a warning 'in such a form and manner as is likely to bring those risks to the attention of any such person'; and (c) to ensure that the product carries a warning 'as specified in the notice' ('a requirement to warn': reg 2).

    There is no counterpart of these powers in the CPA.[355] As to warnings, see generally para 18.29.

2.  *Suspension notices.* The enforcement authorities may serve a 'suspension notice' (reg 2) to cover 'the period needed to organise appropriate safety evaluations, checks and controls'. This notice may for the period of the suspension prohibit a person, without the consent of the authority, from (reg 13(1))

    (a)  placing the product on the market, offering to place it on the market, agreeing to place it on the market or exposing it for placing on the market;

    (b)  supplying the product, offering to supply it, agreeing to supply it or exposing it for supply.

    The notice may also require that the authority be kept informed of the whereabouts of the product (reg 13(2)). A less powerful suspension notice is available under the CPA.[357]

3.  *Withdrawal notices.* Under reg 14(1), the enforcement authorities may serve a 'withdrawal notice', meaning 'any measure aimed at preventing the distribution, display and offer of a dangerous product to a consumer' (reg 2). The notice is one permanently prohibiting the person on whom it is served from doing, without the consent of the authority, any of the things listed above in relation to suspension notices: this withdrawal notice may be issued whether or not the product is already on the market. Except in respect of products

---

353  Reg 10(4); recital 22. Lack of scientific certainty or consensus must not be used as a reason to postpone preventative action: DTI, *Consultation*, para 3.28.

354  These *caveats* are dispensed with where action is urgent (reg 10(4)). For voluntary actions, see para 4.35.

355  These new notices follow Arts 8.1(b) and (c) of the Directive. Hitherto, it has been normal to use Suspension notices for this purpose: see DTI, *Consultation*, para 3.31 and Appendix D, paras 14.1–6.

356  'A requirement to mark' (reg 2). This warning must be 'suitable, clearly worded and comprehensible': reg 11(2).

357  See 1st edn, para 4.36.

posing a serious risk which the authority deems to require urgent action (reg 14(3)), in respect of products 'already on the market', a withdrawal notice may only be served where 'the action being taken by the producer or distributor' to comply with these Regulations (see para 4.35) is 'unsatisfactory or insufficient to prevent the risks concerned'.[358] The notice may also require that the authority be kept informed of the whereabouts of the product (reg 14(4)); and the authority may also take action 'to alert consumers to the risks' (reg 14(5)). These powers had previously been exercised under the prohibition notices available under s 13 of the CPA.[359]

4.  *Recall notices.* (see para 4.36A).

5.  *Forfeiture notices.* (see para 4.36A).

A notice to mark, warn, suspend, withdraw or recall (collectively called a 'safety notice': reg 2) must contain certain prescribed information (reg 16(2)); and, for the purposes of deciding whether to serve such a notice, the Secretary of State has wide powers to obtain information (see para 28.07). Wherever feasible, prior to serving a safety notice (see reg 42), under reg 16(1) the enforcement authority 'shall give an opportunity to the person on whom the notice is served to submit his views to the authority'. Contravention of a safety notice *prima facie* amounts to an offence (reg 16(3)), subject to the rules discussed above; but, if there is no contravention under a suspension, withdrawal or recall notice, the authority shall be liable to pay compensation to the defendant (regs 16(4)–(7): see para 28.06). For appeals against safety notices, see reg 17.

**[4.36A] Product recall and forfeiture**. Where it is felt that consumers are insufficiently protected from circulating dangerous products by safety notices (see para 4.36), there are two other ways of ensuring that consumers no longer come into contact with these products.[360]

1.  *Recall.* Industry best-practice is that dangerous goods should be recalled from circulation;[361] and the GPS Directive is designed to promote co-operation by producers and consumers (recital 23; and see para 4.35). However, the expense of recall may lead industry black sheep to resist; and the enforcement authorities have finally been given a last-resort power (recital 23) in reg 15 to insist on 'recall', 'meaning any measure aimed at achieving the return of a dangerous product that has already been supplied or made available to consumers' (reg 2). Such compulsory recall is at the expense of the producer or distributor receiving the notice (reg 15(10)). The power of recall is usually only available where an authority has reasonable grounds for suspecting that a product is dangerous (reg 15(1)) and all the following circumstances are

---

358 Reg 14(2). It is anticipated that LAs will mainly use these powers where a particular producer 'has been reticent in resolving the matter or is less scrupulous than the majority of traders': DTI, *Consultation*, Appendix D, para 15.4.

359 As these CPA powers are no longer needed for the purposes of the Regulations, they are disapplied by reg 40(4); but these CPA powers of the Secretary of State are still needed for CPA safety regulations.

360 For statistics on the circulation of dangerous products, see DTI, *Consultation*, Appendix D, paras 7.5–7.

361 For an action for damages caused by a recall, see para 11.08. See generally, Mildred (ed.), *Product Liability Law and Insurance* (2000), 391–7.

present:[362] (a) other action would not suffice to prevent the risks; and (b) the action being taken by the producer or distributor with regard to such prevention 'is unsatisfactory or insufficient'; and (c) the authority has given seven days' prior notice to that person, who has not invoked the regulatory scheme for arbitration by the Institute as to whether the goods are dangerous.[363] In these circumstances, under reg 15(1) the authority may serve a 'recall notice' (reg 2), 'requiring the person on whom it is served to use his reasonable endeavours to organise the return of the product from consumers to that person or to such other person as is specified in the notice'.[364] Regulation 15(2) sets out a non-exhaustive list of measures that might be adopted: the recall notice may require recall to be in accordance with any applicable code of practice, specify direct and indirect measures of consumer contact and collection/return arrangements, together with other reasonable return arrangements.[365] The authority is also given powers to co-ordinate the actual recall (reg 15(3)); and it must give reasonable assistance to the producer/distributor in complying with the notice (reg 15(9)).

2. *Forfeiture.* An enforcement authority may in certain circumstances[366] apply to the magistrates court 'for the forfeiture of a product on the grounds that the product is dangerous' (reg 18(1)). The authority must serve a copy of the application on the apparent owner of the product to which it relates to enable him to appear in the proceedings.[367] On certain conditions (reg 18(5)), the court may make a forfeiture order,[368] in which case it may order that the product either be destroyed (reg 18(8)) or alternatively delivered at the defendant's expense to a named third party.[369] These powers may be compared with the forfeiture notices available under the CPA (s 16).

**[4.37] Road traffic.** Leaving aside licensing connected with the use of motor vehicles (see paras 6.02 and 6.05), this paragraph is concerned with their state. Among the many statutory requirements imposed on the manufacturer or importer of motor vehicles[370] are the construction and use requirements: under powers now embodied in the amended s 41 of the Road Traffic Act 1988 (RTA), the Secretary of

---

362 Reg 15(5). Where the matter is urgent, (b) and (c) may be omitted: reg 15(6).

363 The 'Institute' is the Chartered Institute of Arbitrators (reg 2; recital 17); and the applicant must pay the costs (reg 15(7)). For an explanation of the insertion of the arbitration system, see DTI, *Consultation*, para 3.36; and see generally, para 3.23.

364 The notice may also require that the authority be kept informed of the whereabouts of the goods (reg 15(8)).

365 In framing the recall notice, the authority 'must take into consideration the need to encourage distributors, users and consumers to contribute to its implementation' (reg 15(4)).

366 Under reg 18(2) an application may be made: (a) where criminal proceedings have been brought for contravention of the Regulations; or (b) where an appeal has been made under regs 17 or 26; or (c) otherwise by way of complaint.

367 Reg 18(3). He, and any other claiming to be the owner, have a right to appear in court to show why the product should not be forfeited (reg 18(4)).

368 Reg 18(6). There is a right of appeal: reg 18(7).

369 Reg 18(9). The third party could under reg 18(10) be one in the business of repairing or reconditioning goods, or treating them as scrap, or repaired on behalf of the defendant.

370 Under RTA 1988, s 63, there have been made regulations relating to the manufacturing specification of vehicles and making breach an offence under the TDA (see below). So the sale of a second-hand vehicle altered from that specification is an offence.

State has made extensive regulations as to the construction and use of motor cars[371] and equipment;[372] and there is also a comprehensive system for the annual testing of whether vehicles comply with those regulations (the MOT test).[373] More significant for our purposes are the provisions which make it an offence to supply a motor vehicle or vehicle parts which contravene the s 41 regulations.[374] In relation to an offending motor vehicle, the strict liability offence[375] may be committed by either a trade or private supplier (s 75(5)). In relation to offending spare parts, it is also made an offence to supply such parts either by way of fitting to a vehicle or where the supplier has reasonable cause to believe that it will be so fitted (s 76) and this is additional to any contractual liability (s 76(10)). Special provision is made for motor cycle helmets[376] and silencers (see the Motor Cycle Noise Act 1987). In some circumstances, the foregoing may overlap with TDA offences[377] or offences under safety requirement or regulations (see paras 4.33–5); or there may be infringements of Codes of Practice (see para 3.13). But still there are calls for yet more statutory protection for the consumer motorist.[378] As to driving licences, see para 6.02.

*Civil law rights.* Sometimes the injured consumer can obtain compensation by awaiting prosecution for one of the above offences and then asking the convicting court for a compensation order (see para 3.20). The consumer should be aware of the special rules concerning instalment contracts (see Chap 1), distance sales[379] and purchase by auction (see paras 10.10–13). All motor vehicles and spares must be as described (see Chap 13); in most cases the supplier will undertake to give a good title (see Chap 12) or a Pt 3 title may be obtained (see para 21.55); and where the car is paid for by credit card, the private consumer may also have a right of action against the credit card issuer (CCA, s 75: see para 16.11). As regards offences, the RTA also expressly saves the transferee's contractual remedies[380] and it would therefore seem that every breach of the construction and use regulations by a trade supplier is likely also to give rise to a civil claim for breach of the undertakings as to

---

371 According to RTA, s 185(1), 'motor car' means 'a mechanically propelled vehicle intended or adapted for use on roads'. See *Percy v Smith* [1986] RTR 262, DC.

372 Under RTA, ss 40A–42 (as inserted by RTA 1991, s 8), it is an offence both to construct vehicles contravening the regulations and to use such vehicles on the road. *Inter alia* these regulations require vehicles to comply with some British Standards (see generally para 3.08).

373 Under the Road Traffic Act 1988, ss 49–65 (as amended). A forged MOT would amount to an offence under the TDA, s 2(1)(f): see para 4.06.

374 RTA ss 75, 76 (as amended), which contain savings for vehicles sold as scrap. As to 'expose for sale', e.g. para 4.27; and as to 'supply', see *Devon CC v DB Cars* [2002] CLY 4661.

375 RTA, s 75(5) (as amended); *Sandford Motor Sales v Habgood* [1962] CLY 2730 (under RTA 1960). It is a defence to prove that the vehicle was supplied for export, or under a reasonable belief that it would not be used on the road: s 75(6).

376 RTA, s 17, e.g. *Loseix v Clarke* [1984] RTR 174, DC. There is no express saving for contractual rights.

377 E.g. TDA, s 1(a) offence (see para 4.03), as by applying a forged MOT certificate (see above), or clocking a vehicle (see para 4.09). See further, OFT (1999) 23 *Fair Trading* 10.

378 Especially in relation to purchaser of used vehicles: see (1991) 8 Tr L 171; OFT (1998) 18 *Fair Trading* 8.

379 See OFT, *Cars and other vehicles sold by distance means* (May 2005); and below, paras 8.17–17B.

380 RTA, s 75(7). This reverses the decision that such contracts were tainted with illegality (*Vinall v Howard* [1953] 2 All ER 515), so that a supplier might now recover on a stopped cheque; but it would not allow an action for breach of statutory duty (see para 3.21).

fitness and quality because the ordinary purpose for which a car is required is driving on the highway.[381] Manufacturer's and trade warranties may also provide significant protection (see paras 17.09–09A). For certificates of title, see para 21.60; and for Enforcement Orders, see para 6.08.

---

[381] Would it not be more satisfactory if the motorist could ascertain before his accident that he was driving a rebuilt car or on retrread tyres?

# CHAPTER 5

# CONSUMER PROTECTION AND INSTALMENT CREDIT

## INTRODUCTION

[5.01] **The background**. In the twentieth century, there was an explosive growth in the use made of instalment credit both by business (asset finance) and for private consumption. On the private consumption side, this seems to have been linked to the development of the affluent society and mass production of consumer durables. In 1971, the then shape of the credit market was surveyed by the Crowther Report (see para 5.03): in terms of loans outstanding, over 40% was vendor credit (see para 2.19) provided by retailers; whereas some 50% was lender credit (see para 2.20) supplied by banks and finance houses.[1] In the 1980s, lender credit increased to over 80% of the market: this was largely achieved by the expansion in the use of three-party payment cards in retail outlets at the expense of traditional forms of vendor credit, the latter falling below 5% of amounts outstanding.[2]

At the end of 2003, the temperature of the consumer credit market was again taken with a view to reform, this time by a White Paper entitled *Fair, Clear and Competitive*.[3] This reported that consumer credit was central to the UK economy (p 4) and that increased consumer credit was encouraged by record employment, low inflation and low interest rates.[4] It pointed out (paras 1.7–8) that the consumer credit market (£906bn) was comprised of the following: first-charge mortgages on dwelling houses was governed by the FSA (see para 3.02) and beyond the scope of this work; but most other credit was governed by the Consumer Credit Act 1974 (CCA: see para 5.05) and included second mortgages, credit cards and other unsecured loans, mail order, hp and store cards.[5] Within the category of CCA credit, there has since the enactment of the CCA been an enormous increase in credit cards (£49bn +).[6] The White Paper also analysed which types of consumer tended to use which forms of credit (paras 1.28–32). Whilst the banks, finance companies and building societies dealt mainly in large advances to prosperous customers (see above), other lenders, such as check traders, moneylenders and pawnbrokers (see para 15.17), more often lent modest amounts to poor families.[7] Vendor credit to poor families would typically be supplied by mail order (see para 8.19), or door-to-door traders. Developing out of the credit drapers and tallymen or 'Scotch drapers' of the eighteenth century,[8] these businesses provided goods on credit on a

---

1   OFT, Consultation Document on the Working and Enforcement of the Consumer Credit Act 1974 (1993), Annex 1. See also OFT, *Connected Lender Liability* (1994), para 3.1, *et seq*.

2   For a breakdown of ways in which members of that Association provide credit, see the Annual Reports of the FLA (see generally, para 2.18).

3   DTI, *The Consumer Credit Market in the 21st Century* (Dec 2003, Cm. 6040).

4   Para 1.2. See the details in paras 1.3–6.

5   Leaving aside second mortgages, this category (described as 'unsecured') amounted to £168bn.

6   Paras 1.15–16. For analysis of the usage of other types of consumer credit, see paras 1.9–14 and 1.17–27.

7   See Rowlingson, *Moneylenders* (1994) 17; OFT *Vulnerable Consumers* (1999) esp 16, 29.

8   Rowlingson, *Op. cit.*, 23, 81–99. For controls on peddling, see para 6.02.

door-to-door basis in low income areas. Providing small amounts of finance and flexible home collection, their services are relatively expensive[9] and disadvantaged by the APR rules (see para 8.23) and doorstep selling regulations (see paras 10.36–7). Whilst the White Paper reported increasing average indebtedness amongst households (para 1.33), most had no difficulty in meeting their commitments (para 1.35), but a minority experienced financial difficulties associated with overindebtedness (para 1.36: and see para 6.10).

**[5.02]  Pre-CCA legislative history**. The economic purpose of instalment credit is to advance the price of goods to the consumer for consumption before payment.[10] However, historically society's hostility to moneylending led to its being subject to legal restrictions (see para 6.09) and to the development of other legal forms of transaction which would achieve the same end whilst attracting less opprobrium, such as disguising the loan as a deferred sale (see para 1.03).

1.  *Tradesmen's credit.* Shopkeepers in the towns (credit or scotch drapers)[11] and itinerant pedlars in the countryside (tallymen) begun to supply goods on credit in a growing and systematic way. In the nineteenth century, this led to the evolution of sophisticated forms of instalment sales (see para 1.12) and the invention of hp (see para 1.20), with its many opportunities for technical default.[12] Eventually statutory controls were developed in the form of the Hire Purchase Act 1938 and its successors, until by 1970 there were extant the following: Hire Purchase Act 1964, Pt III (see para 21.55 *et seq.*); Hire Purchase Act 1965; Advertisements (Hire Purchase) Act 1967.

2.  *Moneylending.* Having experienced difficulty in collecting their debts,[13] shopkeepers supplying goods on credit began to take pledges (see para 25.15) and a series of Pawnbroking Acts were introduced from 1603 onwards in an attempt to provide regulation, culminating in the Pawnbrokers Acts 1872 and 1960. Meanwhile, in 1854 statutory control over the rate of interest charged by moneylenders was removed, though as regards restrictions on the form of security moneylenders might take over goods, widespread abuses eventually led to the Bills of Sale Acts 1878 and 1882 (see paras 9.02; 25.26). Moneylending itself remained uncontrolled until the end of that century, when the Moneylenders Acts 1900–27 introduced a system whose most notable facet was the total exclusion of banks from control (see para 6.09). Since the repeal of the Moneylenders Acts, credit-card business (see para 2.24) undertaken by the banks and others has boomed, whilst a shift towards non-purchase money lending secured by house mortgage[14] led to late amendments in what became

---

9   This has led to a Monopolies Committee Enquiry (see para 2.14).

10  The converse method is for the consumer to save in advance of delivery, e.g. by paying by instalments under a club scheme (see para 15.18).

11  See Goode, *HP Law & Practice*, 2nd edn, 900–1; Crowther Report (above), paras 2.5.9–15. For attempts to disguise pawnbroking as selling: see Macleod [1995] JBL 155; and below, para 25.17.

12  As to the sort of practice against which the 1938 Act was aimed, see the account of 'snatch backs', para 26.08.

13  What started as a 'secondary trade' frequently developed into a separate business: the Crowther Report, para 2.1.15.

14  In the case of building society and bank lenders, these loans have tended to be secured by tacking an additional loan onto a first mortgage, whereas finance companies particularly have expanded second mortgage lending. For purchase money loans, see generally, para 2.16.

the Building Society Act 1986. At the same time, there was a steady development of weekly home credit (see para 2.17), where it is relatively common both for the loan to be in default[15] and for loans to be rolled-over (see para 7.04A): this form of business has given rise to a Super-complaint.[16]

The net effect of the foregoing was a clear dichotomy of legislative control. If the supplier of goods chose to do business on credit, he should look to the Hire Purchase Acts for his controls; whereas, if the loan transaction was separate from the supply of goods, it might be governed by the Pawnbrokers Acts or the Moneylenders and Bills of Sale Acts. Eventually, the anomalous pattern of these statutory controls led to the creation in 1968 of the Crowther Committee (see para 5.03).

[5.03/4] **The Crowther Report**. The radical two volume Report of the Crowther committee was published in March 1971.[17] Besides commenting on the economic and social aspects of consumer credit[18] the Report pointed to serious deficiencies in the then existing law.[19] In the light of these findings, it opted for sweeping changes, resting on recognition of two points: *first*, that the extension of credit in sale or hp was in reality a loan, the reservation of title in conditional sale, hp and finance leases in reality being a chattel mortgage securing that loan; and *second*, that there should be introduced a uniform set of rules for all security devices. To implement this thesis, the Report proposed two new statutes **as a package** (para 5.2.20):

1.  *The proposed Lending and Security Act*. Other than loans secured on land, this was to apply to all credit transactions generally.[20] It would deal not just with the rights of the parties under the 'loan' contract, but also with registration of the security interest and conflicts between the secured party and any third party.[21]

2.  *The proposed Consumer Sale and Loan Act*. This would fuse together all the various forms of existing legislation relating to consumer credit into one rationally coherent enactment: whereas the proposed Lending and Security Act would apply to all transactions of the types mentioned, the proposed Consumer Sale and Loan Act was designed to catch only those types of transaction when applied to consumers.[22]

---

15   It is argued that this is not really default, in that technical default is normal, but not treated by either debtor or creditor as such: CCA, *Mirage or Reality* (1992) 20.

16   For the provisional findings of the Competition Commission (with the Final Report due Autumn 2006), see Ball [2006] 6 Credit Today 34. For Super-complaints, see generally para 4.19.

17   *Report of the Crowther Committee on Consumer Credit* (1971, Cmnd. 4596). It contains a mine of information on the then state of the industry, all carefully indexed and conveniently summarised in Chap 1.3. See the account in Goode, *Consumer Credit Law & Practice*, Division 1A, paras 1.41–3.

18   Paras 1.3.2–5. The matter is set out in more detail in Pt 3 of the Report.

19   Para 1.3.6. The then existing state of credit law is set out in Pt 4 of the Report.

20   Including unsecured loans; the loan aspect of all instalment sales, revolving credits, check trading and credit cards; hp and conditional sales; finance leases; mortgages and charges of goods, documents and intangibles; and pledges of goods and documents.

21   Paras 1.3.12–21. The details of these proposals are set out in Pt 5 of the Report.

22   Paras 1.3.23–47. The proposals are set out in some detail in Pt 6 of the Report.

Nevertheless, the government produced the following conclusions:[23] a Consumer Sale and Loan Bill should be introduced immediately (see CCA: para 5.05), but the proposed Lending and Security Bill should be shelved indefinitely (see para 25.37).

Finally, there should be noticed the important part played by the Crowther Report in the interpretation of the CCA (see para 1.04), a matter confirmed by the Court of Appeal in *OFT v Lloyds TSB Bank plc* (see para 55; and para 16.11).

## THE CONSUMER CREDIT ACT

**[5.05] Introduction**. Though amended substantially during its passage through Parliament, the Consumer Credit Act 1974 (CCA) was essentially a bi-partisan measure. Indeed, MP's almost killed the measure with kindness, as they competed with each other to give ever-more protection to their consumer-voters. The eventual Act was of very substantial proportions: 193 sections and five schedules, occupying some 174 pages in the Queen's Printer's copy; and a significant number of those provisions were simply enabling ones.[24] Indeed, it was the policy of the Act to confine itself to general principles, leaving the details to be filled out by statutory instruments;[25] and so great was the task that some of these instruments were not promulgated for ten years.[26] In *Dimond v Lovell* (set out at para 1.19) Scott VC confirmed the application of the orthodox canons of interpretation to this legislative scheme as follows (at 88g): the Act is to be construed as a whole; but it should not be construed in the light of the regulations (the 'Henry VIII' principle: see para 5.10).

The resulting body of legislation is compulsory (CCA, s 173; see para 18.11), being at once both radical and traditional (see paras 5.06–7). To some extent, the formidable bulk[27] is misleading, being derived from an attempt to cover every conceivable transaction and variation: if the individual provision is approached with particular examples in mind and the surplus words jettisoned, its general effect is frequently fairly easily apparent, even though the total weight of the legislation is undoubtedly formidable. In the 1990s, the Government undertook detailed simplification of the Act by way of the deregulation initiative (see para 5.10); and it introduced wholesale changes to the 1974 Act by way of the CCA 2006 (see para 5.11). Account must also be taken of the changes wrought by the EU, in particular through the consumer Credit Directives (see paras 5.12).

---

23  *Reform of the Law on Consumer Credit* (1973, Cmnd. 5427).

24  An unsuccessful attempt has been made to challenge some CCA regulations as being *ultra vires*: *First National Bank v Secretary of State* (1990) 10 TR LR 184, CA (advertising regulations made under s 44(1): see para 8.30).

25  The text of most relevant current statutory instruments will conveniently be found set out in the encyclopedias referred to below.

26  Unless otherwise stated, in the Regulations words have the same meaning as in the CCA: Interpretation Act 1978, s 11.

27  'An Act of extraordinary length and complexity': see Goff LJ in *Jenkins v Lombard North Central plc* (set out at para 8.29) All ER at 829e.

Moreover, because of its size, complexity and changing nature, the CCA can really only be satisfactorily consulted via one of the looseleaf encyclopedias,[28] or at very least a looseleaf annotated version of the statute,[29] though there are some monographs that attempt to put the Act in context.[30]

**[5.06] The radical aspect.** The CCA is self-consciously radical. Some idea of its scope may be gained from the list of enactments wholly or partially repealed (s 192 and Sched 5). The Act is certainly radical in the sense that it seeks to make a new start with newly-invented terminology. The purpose was to make it difficult for practitioners to ignore the new law by simply assuming that it only re-enacts previous law:[31] much of the new terminology will be found listed and explained by way of helpful examples in Sched 2;[32] and all the old Acts remaining in force are set out in the new terminology in Sched 4.[33] The CCA is also radical in that it extends its protection into fields hitherto uncovered e.g. the licensing of all credit-granters (see Chap 6), the restricting of canvassing of all credit (see para 7.05), and on second mortgages (see para 25.23).

**[5.07] The traditional aspect.** In another sense, the CCA is traditional. *First*, whereas the SGA 1893 was intended to embody the common law concepts by codifying them, the CCA merely assumes the basic common law concepts: so, whilst a coherent pattern of law can often be divined simply by reading the SGA and the previous common law largely discarded, with the CCA the reader must constantly bear in mind the underlying common law, to which the Act makes, often detailed, changes.

*Second*, at the statutory level many of the provisions in the CCA simply build on ideas found in previous legislation. Thus, many of the ideas of the old Hire Purchase Acts and Moneylenders Acts have simply been re-cast in the new terminology and adapted to cover a greater range of transactions, e.g. the provisions in relation to advertising (see para 8.27), cancellation (see para 10.29) and repossession (see para 24.27). Furthermore, the CCA does **not** do any of the following:

(a)  make chattel mortgaging easier (see para 25.25); nor

(b)  deal with the implied terms in contracts for the supply of goods (see Chaps 12–15); nor

---

28   See Bennion, *Consumer Credit Control* (see para 1.03); Goode, *Consumer Credit Law & Practice* (unless otherwise stated, all subsequent references are to Division 1); Guest and Lloyd, *Encyclopedia of Consumer Credit*. The last is the smallest of these works, and the one perhaps best suited to undergraduate needs.

29   A good working annotation is by Guest and Lloyd, *ibid*, Pt 2. See also Goode, *ibid*, Vol 2, Division II.

30   See Dobson's Concise College Text, *Sale of Goods and Consumer Credit*, 6th edn; Rosenthal, *Guide to Consumer Credit Law & Practice*, 2nd edn, 2002.

31   See the Crowther Report, para 5.2.20.

32   But see s 188: in the event of conflict, the CCA prevails over Sched 2; and see Lindgren (1977) 40 MLR at 163. If difficulty is experienced in locating any of the new concepts of the CCA, a good place to start is often the Act's definition section (s 189(1)).

33   What is the effect, if any, on the statutes set out in the Schedule insofar as they deal with unregulated agreements, e.g. Pt 3 of the HPA 1964 (see para 21.55); s 14(3) of the SGA (see para 14.12)?

(c) affect third-party rights (see Chap 21); nor

(d) interfere with the general fair trading rules (see Chaps 4 and 6).

**[5.08] The major areas of CCA control.** Leaving aside licensing (see Chap 6), the major areas in which the CCA imposes changes on the ordinary laws are as follows:[34]

(a) *The machinery of enforcement.* Breach of many of the provisions of the CCA (or regulations made thereunder) is a criminal offence of strict liability, imposed on an extended range of persons but subject to a number of defences.[35] Enforcement is placed in the hands of local weights and measures authorities (see para 3.05) working under a uniform system (see Chap 28) and subject to the centralised control of the OFT,[36] which also operates an all-embracing licensing system.

(b) *Truth-in-lending.* In attempting to force the disclosure of the true cost of credit, the CCA enables the Secretary of State to make regulations governing the components to be taken into account in calculating the 'total charge for credit' (see para 8.23). This concept is important for a number of reasons: to fix the low cost credit category of exempt agreement (see para 5.15); to decide whether or not a credit bargain is extortionate or a credit relationship unfair (see paras 29.41 and 29.44); and to publicise the total charge for credit.[37]

(c) *Transactional control prior to default.* Besides the truth-in-lending provisions (above), the CCA seeks to regulate all the following aspects of the transaction: advertising for such business (see para 8.20, *et seq.*); the formalities required in the making of agreements within its ambit (see Chap 9); the formation of the agreement, including cancellation[38] and contracting out;[39] the right to terminate the agreement;[40] and the persons liable for breach of undertaking or misrepresentation (see Chap 16).

(d) *Transactional 'default' control.* In favour of a defaulting debtor or hirer,[41] the CCA imposes the following restrictions on the freedom of action of his

---

34  There are also important provisions dealing with pawnbroking (see para 25.15), contracts of surety (see para 25.03) and consumer credit intermediaries (see para 5.36).

35  For strict liability crimes, see generally, para 4.01. However, the CCA criminal liability does not of itself lead to any further sanctions (s 170); and see para 10.19. For the defences, see para 28.13, *et seq.*

36  See para 3.03. For the OFT's current General Notices & Determinations, Circulars and Official Forms, see Goode, *Consumer Credit Law & Practice*, Division IV, XIII; Guest and Lloyd, *Encyclopedia of Consumer Credit*, Pt 4.

37  Expressed both as a sum of money and as a percentage by way of the advertisement and documentation regulations (see Chaps 8–10).

38  Under ss 67–73: see para 10.29, *et seq.*

39  Under s 173: see para 18.11.

40  Under ss 99–102: see further, para 26.05. As to accelerated settlement, see para 26.19.

41  Whilst the expression 'default' is used here, it will be seen later that the CCA provisions go far beyond the situation where the debtor or hirer is technically in default to include such as his death.

creditor or owner: obligatory preliminary notices;[42] and Enforcement[43] or Time Orders[44] by a court.[45]

**[5.09] Post-1974 credit practice**. In 1974 the greater amount of consumer credit was probably of finite sums, whether linked to a supply of goods in an instalment credit contract (see para 1.03), or by way of loan. However, in 2003 the White Paper *Fair, Clear and Competitive*[46] noted that since the enactment of the CCA there have been some major changes in the consumer market which require reforms of the CCA (see para 5.11). Changes in the general consumer credit market include the following:

1.  *Revolving credit*. The notion of revolving credit has long been familiar to consumers in this country in both the following contexts: the bank overdraft (see para 2.17) and store budget accounts (see para 2.19). However, the 1980s saw a significant switch in the forms of credit used. Whilst finite amounts of credit for higher value items is still likely to be granted by a way of a personal loan (see para 2.17) or instalment credit contract (see above), smaller items tend to be obtained through revolving credit based on a credit card (see para 2.28).

2.  *Bank accounts and other loans*. This move towards revolving credit has been linked with the spread of bank accounts and use of overdrafts. By the 1990s, over 80% of the population had bank accounts: such accounts have traditionally been operated by the use of cheque books (see para 7.28); but the authorities seem anxious to replace such a paper-based system by an electronic one, the debit card (see para 2.25). Consumers prefer to repay instalment credit by direct debit or standing order (see para 23.14) to minimise default.

3.  *Leasing*. As an alternative to bank overdraft to raise funds for purchase, there has been an increased willingness to lease goods (see para 1.18).

4.  *E-Commerce*. The wide-spread availability of shopping by internet in the twenty-first century and payment for such items by credit card has posed new problems (see para 8.17A), because the CCA assumed a paper-based system. However, since 2005, regulated agreements and most communications required by the Act can alternatively be made in electronic form.[47]

5.  *Low-income consumers*. There has already been encountered the two sources of finance available to low-income consumers (see para 2.15). Of these two sources, commercial lenders to low-income consumers are likely to be

---

42   Before a creditor or owner takes any of the specified major steps, e.g. to terminate the agreement, he is required to give the debtor or hirer a formal notice: ss 76, 87 and 98 (see paras 24.28–32 and 26.10).

43   In certain cases, before he can enforce an agreement, the creditor or owner must obtain from the court an enforcement order: ss 90–2, 96, 126, 127 (see paras 24.34–8, 24.44, 25.23 and 24.33). Distinguish Enforcement Orders under the EA (see para 28.03).

44   These orders will frequently be granted by the court in proceedings after 'default': see para 24.40.

45   Under s 189(1), in England and Wales 'court' in the Act *prima facie* means county court; as to which see generally, para 24.39.

46   See DTI, *the Consumer Credit Market in the 21st Century* (Dec 2003, Cm. 6040), the 'drivers for reform': see pp 4–5; and paras 1.37–46.

47   CC (Electronic Communications) Order 2004 SI 3236; and see para 9.05.

expensive,[48] largely because of the extra risk,[49] small loans for short periods and need for weekly cash payments.[50] Such consumers prefer to pay instalment debt by direct debit (if they have a bank account) or by home collection if they do not. Accordingly, it is these low income consumers who are seen as in greatest need of widened access to cheap credit[51] and greater transparency of lending terms. Whilst this may have been achieved under the 2004–5 reforms, it seems doubtful whether clear knowledge of their credit dilemma would aid the predicament of the poor, who seem already all too aware of the problem.

The formidable size of the CCA was partly based on the premise that there was so little parliamentary time likely to be granted for reform in this area that the opportunity should be taken to make sufficient changes to last a generation—what may be termed the 'big bang' theory. Besides changes to cope with market developments (see above), *Fair, Clear and Competitive* has been particularly concerned about the overindebtedness of the minority of consumers, particularly low income households (paras 1.46–51), a matter discussed later (see paras 6.09–10). Of the more general changes, some may eventually find their way into a new EU Directive (para 1.59; and see below, para 5.12); but the UK Government has itself made a substantial number of changes to UK law. Some were dealt with under the deregulation powers (see para 5.10); but the greatest number have been accomplished by changes to the CCA system by way of amendments to the Act and regulations made under it (paras 1.60–6; and see below, para 5.11). Non-legislative changes proposed included (pp 7–8): deliver financial eduction and advice to consumers (see paras 3.01 and 3.16); pilot an enforcement scheme to tackle loan sharks (see para 6.20); ensure the effectiveness of insolvency regimes (see para 19.19); and tackle overindebtedness (see paras 6.09–10).

**[5.10] Deregulation**. Government initiative in the 1990s to reduce red-tape across Whitehall led to the discovery that many of the desired changes could not be made because they required primary legislation. To try to reduce this Parliamentary bottle-neck, there was enacted the Deregulation and Contracting Out Act 1994.[52] The success of this Act led to the enhancement of the deregulatory powers in the Regulatory Reform Act 2001.[52]

Within Part 1 of the 1994 Act, Chapter 2 contains a list of miscellaneous statutory provisions whose requirements are simplified or removed, including those relating to the following: weights and measures (s 14: see para 4.25); licensed premises (s 19: see para 6.05); and shop opening hours (ss 23–4: see para 8.13). Of far wider significance are the two sorts of general power to be found in Part 1. *First*, whilst one statutory instrument can always be repealed or altered by another statutory instrument, it has been an accepted part of our constitutional law that primary legislation cannot generally be amended by a subsequent statutory

---

48  See Collard and Kempson, *Affordable Credit* (2005) 2–3, 12–13, referring to home credit, pawnbrokers, sale and buy back, payday loans and unlicensed moneylenders.

49  The risk-based pricing is increasingly assessed by credit scoring (see para 8.39): see Collard Kempson, *Op. cit.*, 22.

50  See Collard and Kempson, *Op. cit.*, 19–20.

51  See Collard and Kempson, *Op. cit.*, 17, 24, 27–8.

52  For valuable introductory notes on the 1994 and 2001 Acts, see *Current Law Statutes*. The first two years after enactment in 1994 saw a wealth of detailed change: [1996] 15 Tr L 343.

instrument, a 'Henry VIII clause' (see para 5.05), although there is already an exception as regards statutory instrument implementing EU laws.[53] However, under s 1 of the 2001 Act Ministers are empowered by statutory order to amend or repeal **existing** primary legislation (of any date) that imposes an unnecessary burden on business.[54] Unlike the powers under the 1994 Act, those under the 2001 Act can be used to impose burdens in limited circumstances (s 1(1) of 2001 Act); but the powers cannot be used to create an entirely **new** provision. Only some of the orders already made are relevant here;[55] and for us the most significant proposals are those in the field of consumer credit (see para 5.11). *Second*, the Act contains powers to 'improve' the 'fairness, transparency and consistency' of enforcement procedures,[56] which for our purposes is likely to be particularly significant in relation to the enforcement of consumer protection statutes by local authorities (see para 28.02). The 2001 Act enables the promulgation of statutory codes of practice:[57] these are mandatory on local authorities (LAs) in the sense that, where there is a local authority prosecution, any relevant code may be taken into account by the tribunal 'in deciding how to deal with the failure to comply with' the provision (s 9(3) of 2001 Act; and see para 28.06). Whilst the court or tribunal can take the LA's failure to comply with any relevant code into account at the sentencing and costs stage (see para 28.07), the provision seems unclear as to whether that failure is relevant before conviction.[58]

The Legislative and Regulatory Reform Bill 2006 would go much further in enabling the executive to amend or repeal statutes.[59]

**[5.11] Amendment of the Consumer Credit Act scheme**. Recognising that people's attitude to credit had changed dramatically since 1974, in 2001 the sponsoring Department (the DTI: see para 3.02) announced that a significant package of reform would be undertaken,[60] though it would bear in mind the parallel EU process to amend the Consumer Credit Directive (see para 5.12). Under the 2003 White Paper *Fair, Clear and Competitive*,[61] there were proposed amendments by all the following routes:

1.  *Statutory instruments (SIs)*. It has already been noted that, under the terms of the CCA 1974, many of its principles were fleshed out by SIs (see para 5.05); and, of

---

53  Under s 2(2) of the ECA: see *Thoburn v Sunderland CC* (set out at para 4.24); and see paras 1.03A; 4.24; 4.32.

54  Ss 1–3 of the 2001 Act. The manner in which order-making power may be exercised is dealt with in ss 4–8 of the 2001 Act which includes preliminary public consultation (ss 5 and 7).

55  E.g. unsolicited goods (see para 8.18); trading stamps (see para 15.17); credit unions (see para 15.19); truncation of cheques (see para 23.14A).

56  S 9(1)(b) of the 2001 Act. There is still in force an amended s 6 of the 1994 Act, empowering the Government to make model enforcement directions, e.g. that the enforcer must act proportionately. The Cabinet Office have put an Enforcement Concordat on the internet.

57  S 10 of the 2001 Act. For codes of practice, see generally, para 3.11.

58  E.g. to exclude evidence unfairly obtained; or a general defence, see para 28.14.

59  See Bohlander (2006) 156 NLJ 525; Burns (2006) 156 NLJ 787.

60  The Government 2001 Manifesto led to the following series of papers outlining the areas for reform: *Tackling Loan Sharks—and more!* (July 2001; Feb. 2002; March 2002; Aug. 2002; Nov. 2002; March 2003).

61  See DTI, *the Consumer Credit Market in the 21st Century* (Dec 2003, Cm. 6040). For co-ordinated implementation, see paras 5.83–5 and 5.87.

course, those SIs may be further varied by subsequent SIs.[62] The White Paper
proposed (p 6) new statutory instruments on the following subjects, all of
which have been implemented:[63] Advertising (see paras 8.22 and 8.30–1); Form
and Content of Agreements (see paras 8.25 and 9.10); Pre-contract disclosure
(see para 9.08) and Early Settlement Rebates (see para 26.19A). However, on
general principles, those SIs made under the CCA cannot vary the CCA itself
(a 'Henry VIII clause': see para 5.10). By way of exception, the following types
of SI may vary the text of the CCA:

(a) *Euro-SIs.* These are SIs implementing EU Directives generally (see para
    1.03A); and in particular amendments to the Consumer Credit Directive
    (see para 5.12). The SIs made to implement Directives may have both nega-
    tive and positive effect on the CCA: these euro-SIs may delete provisions
    of the CCA; and they may add new principles to the CCA (cf. Henry VIII
    clauses). However, from the standpoint of the DTI, euro-SIs suffer from the
    disadvantage that the DTI cannot directly control what goes into the Direct-
    ive and hence, what must appear in the SI.

(b) *The CCA 2006* (see below). The CCA 1974 may be amended by statutory
    instrument passed by Parliamentary affirmative resolutions 'in con-
    sequence of any provision of the CCA 2006, (s 68).

(c) *Deregulation SIs* (see para 5.10). It seems likely that these powers will be
    used in the current round, *inter alia*, to simplify the rules relating to Multiple
    agreements (see para 5.27). Of course, the deregulation powers are purely
    negative, in that they seek to derogate from an existing CCA provision: they
    cannot be used to create an entirely new provision. To do that, a statute is
    needed.

2.  *Statutes.* The CCA 1974 has served well for an entire generation, but is now
    beginning to show its age. Some changes to the CCA scheme have been effected
    by including amendments in a statute which is primarily designed to achieve
    some other purpose;[64] and significant changes to the CCA were introduced by
    the Enterprise Act 2002 (see generally para 2.12). However, after elaborate con-
    sultation,[61] in 2004–5 the DTI sponsored a major Consumer Credit Bill: during
    its completed passage through the House of Commons, the Minister rejected
    most attempted amendments,[65] whether on behalf of consumers,[66] or indus-
    try.[67] The seventy-section Bill included the following important areas of
    amendment:[68]

---

62   There is a general power to amend SIs made under the 1974 Act to comply with the changes
     made by the 2006 Act (s 68).
63   These all came into force between the end of October 2004 and May 2005.
64   E.g. CCA, s 74 (see para 9.07); s 187 (see para 5.33).
65   The Minister himself put forward a number of largely technical amendments, e.g. see the
     proceedings before HC Standing Committee E (Jan 2005; only two days).
66   E.g. the attempt at rate-capping (see para 6.09); credit-card cheques (see para 8.18).
67   E.g. the attempt to truncate CCA, s 99 (see para 26.05).
68   Others include: Statements (see para 15.16); Default Notices (see para 24.30); and Time Orders
     (see para 24.40). For transitional provisions, see Sched 3 of the 2006 Act.

- *Credit licensing regime* (see para 6.11). Thirty-five sections would 'strengthen the credit licensing regime to target rogue and unfair practices and provide enforcers with the powers they need to supervise a fair and effective credit market'.[69]

- *Unfair credit relationships* (see para 29.44). It would change the law to end unfair selling practices—replacing a limited 'extortionate' test with a wider 'unfairness' test.

- *Ombudsman* (see para 3.25). Under the aegis of the FSMA, there would be an effective dispute resolution mechanism without resort to court.

- *Financial limit* (see para 5.22). It would remove the £25,000 financial limit in respect of private debtors, but keep it for business debtors (see para 5.24).

The Bill fell in March 2005 when the General Election was called, but has been enacted in the Parliamentary Session 2005–6 in very similar form.[70] Most of it will probably be implemented in 2007,[71] but a longer timescale has been envisaged for the rules on unfair credit relationships (see para 29.43). The Consumer Credit Act 2006 is one of those curious provisions which has no independent life: it operates by inserting provisions into the CCA 1974; so all references in this work will still be to the 1974 Act (as amended): see s 67 of the 2006 Act.

**[5.12] EU developments**. Since the late 1970s the EEC has been moving towards the harmonising of consumer credit laws (see generally, para 3.10). The first Directive on this subject was dated 1987; and in 1990 that Directive was amended to add provisions on the computation of the annual percentage rate of charge.[72] The Directive was modelled on the CCA, but was short and general in character. It was a **minimum** directive,[73] in that it allowed Member States to 'introduce or retain more stringent provisions to protect consumers' (Art 15), so that it did not prove necessary to make any alterations to the CCA.[74]

However, the 1987 Directive did contain the (common) provision for the Commission to review its operation by the mid 1990s (Art 17). Accordingly, the EU promulgated further amendments to the Consumer Credit Directive,[75] which

---

69   See generally Stokes (2005) 155 NLJ 236, worried that the Bill might tend to replace the rule of law by whim of the regulator (the OFT). A Joint Committee of both Houses raised Human Rights (see para 3.09A) concerns in relation to the conduct of licensees and civil penalties.

70   The Act will come into force on dates to be appointed: s 71(2); and see 2006 SI 1508. For transitional provisions, see s 69 and Sched 3; and for repeals, see s 70 and Sched 4.

71   The Minister indicated in Parliament that different provisions would be likely to come into effect on different dates, largely on the basis of industry ability to assimilate the changes: (2005–6) HC Deb, R3, col. 1023. For the timetable, see the DTI website. As at August 2006, the DTI are issuing for consultation draft statutory instruments.

72   Directive 87/102/EEC, as amended by Directive 90/88.

73   For minimum and maximum directives generally, see para 3.10.

74   Goode, *Consumer Credit Law & Practice*, Pt IJ, para 125.2.

75   Directive 98/7/EC. The text of Directive 87/102, as amended by Directives 90/88 and 98/7 is set out in Goode, *ibid*, Pt X, para 1.91; Guest, *Encyclopedia of Consumer Credit Law*, para 9-126.

required some minor amendment to English law. In 2002, the EU Commission identified that the above Directives had engendered little of the intended cross-border credit transactions and in September of that year proposed a much more ambitious new Consumer Credit Directive:[76] the proposal was for a **maximum** consumer-friendly harmonisation measure[73] with limited exceptions relating to the position on burden of proof in relation to consumer information obligations and positive data exchange.[77] This was heavily criticised in the EU Parliament on the grounds that it placed undue burdens on business,[78] so much so that it was still with the European Parliament upon the 2004 enlargement of the Community. Subsequently, in October 2004, the EU Commission put forward a revised proposal, which then went out to consultation; this led in the UK to DTI *Consultation Documents*;[79] and the EU Council will try to reach a Common Position on the modified proposal during 2006.[80] UK practice is likely to significantly inform the proposals, because in 2005 the UK represented one quarter of the EU credit market and one half of the EU credit card market. As at March 2006, whilst the details are not yet finalised, the Commission proposal distinguishes the following three categories of credit agreement:[81]

(1) Outside the scope of the Draft Directive, in which Member States are free to introduce/maintain national provisions.[82]

(2) Inside the Draft Directive, but subject only to **minimum** harmonisation,[73] where there would be mutual recognition of national laws.[83]

(3) Inside the Draft Directive and subject to **maximum** harmonisation,[73] e.g. database access, information in the credit agreement, early repayment, APR.

In 2007, UK consumer credit law may also have to be amended to comply with the UCP Directive (see para 4.21B).

---

76   COM (2002) 0443. The Commission (DG SanCo) defended their Draft in *Questions and Answers on Consumer Credit* (dated 13.11.02), MEMO/02/252. The UK response is *UK Submission to Council—Directive concerning credit for consumers* (Feb. 2003).

77   The UK Government argued as above for much wider exemptions/minimum requirements, pursuant to the White Paper *Fair, Clear and Competitive: the Consumer Credit Market in the 21st Century* (Dec 2003, Cm. 6040) Chap 4.

78   As it would artificially constrain the availability of types of credit which have emerged in various countries to meet local needs. For the Parliamentary Draft for the Directive, see COM (2004) 747 final.

79   See DTI, *Consultation on a Proposed European Consumer Credit Directive* (Feb. 2005); *Proposal for an EC Consumer Credit Directive—Supplementary Consultation* (March 2006).

80   The Commission has issued a modified proposal (see COM (2005) 483 final).

81   The HL European Union Committee have produced an unenthusiastic Report on the Draft Directive: *Consumer Credit in the European Union: Harmonisation and Consumer Protection* (5 July 2006, HL Paper 210).

82   The Draft would not apply to: (a) any other than credit to private consumers; (b) where the amount of credit is above or below stipulated figures; (c) mortgages, pawns, simple hiring or hp; (d) short-term credit agreements and student loans; and (d) there is a partial exclusion of some overdrafts.

83   E.g. responsible lending, pre-contractual information, provision of advice, right of withdrawal, early repayment, overrunning of credit, regulation of creditors, obligations of credit intermediaries.

# The ambit of the Act

## *Regulated agreements*

**[5.13] Regulated agreements**. The CCA for the most part applies only to '**regulated agreements**'. To ascertain whether any transaction is regulated by the CCA, the first task is normally to identify any 'regulated agreement', this expression being defined by s 189(1) as follows:

> 'a consumer credit agreement, or consumer hire agreement, other than an exempt agreement, and 'regulated' and 'unregulated' shall be construed accordingly'.

This small section describes a vital two-stage intellectual process as regards **agreements**, whether actual or prospective (see below).

*Stage 1.* The draftsman has first identified for most purposes the permanent outer limits of the CCA by reference to the two key concepts of a **consumer credit** agreement (s 8) and a **consumer hire** agreement (s 15), both of which he deliberately defined too widely.

*Stage 2.* Then he has reduced their scope by introducing the, variable by statutory instrument, notion of **exempt** agreements (s 8(3), as amended: see para 5.14).

The result is that regulated agreements may be one of two sorts:[84]

(a)  non-exempt (s 8(3)) consumer credit agreements (see para 5.19, *et seq*.), which is usually thought of as the main category within the Act;

(b)  non-exempt (s 15(2)) consumer hire agreements (see para 1.19), which is aimed at finance leases (see para 1.18A), so that suppliers could not use that route to avoid the Act.[85]

Since the inception of the Act, most commentators have assumed that the above two categories are mutually exclusive; but this assumption was rebutted in *Dimond v Lovell*.[86]

> This case involved an accident hire agreement entered into by the innocent motorist (D) in a traffic accident, on terms previously described (see para 1.19). It had already been decided in a previous case that this form of agreement was not void as amounting to maintenance.[87] The present proceedings raised many issues; and the Court of Appeal decision in favour of the negligent driver (L) was affirmed on a narrower range of issues by the House of Lords. On an unappealed point, the Court of Appeal unanimously decided that in principle the agreement could amount to **both** consumer credit[88] **and** consumer hire, but was saved from the latter category by the 28-day restriction.[89]

Referring to the distinct danger that the two sets of CCA provisions may be incompatible, Scott VC said:

---

84  The agreement may be gathered from more than one document: s 189(4).
85  Goode, *Consumer Credit Law & Practice*, Pt 11B, para 5.25.
86  [1999] 3 All ER 1, CA (see [1999] JBL 452); affd [2002] 1 AC 384, [2000] 2 All ER 897, HL (see [2001] JBL 14; Goode, *ibid*, Pt 1C, para 24.63.
87  *Giles v Thompson* [1994] 1 AC 142, HL; see below, para 7.26.
88  Under s 9(1): see para 5.21.          89  Under s 15(1)(b): see para 1.19.

'If any genuine case of incompatibility were to arise, the Act provides a remedy via an application under section 60(3) for a waiver or variation of the requirements'.

*Dimond v Lovell* is a leading case concerned with the following two branches of the law:

(i)   The effect on the accident hire agreement of the CCA. On unappealed issues, the Court of Appeal held that the agreement amounted to running account-credit;[90] and that, because the agreement did not comply with the documentation rules,[91] it was unenforceable under s 65 (see para 9.19).

(ii)  The measures of damages recoverable by D because of L's admitted negligent damage to D's car, which led to the hiring of a replacement (see para 27.28). The issue was strictly *obiter*, because the agreement was unenforceable under the CCA (see above). However, the majority of the Court of Appeal would have allowed D to recover the sum claimed on the grounds that she had properly mitigated her loss by entering into the accident hire agreement (see para 27.44); but the House of Lords would have reduced the damages under the rules of causation (see para 27.29) and also refused a restitutionary remedy for unjust enrichment by reason of s 170 (see para 10.19).

*Prospective agreements.* The Act sometimes bites before there comes into existence what the common law would recognise as a binding contract, referring to a 'prospective agreement' (see para 5.20).

**[5.14] Exempt agreements**. Broadly, the draftsman has saved from the CCA agreements which he terms 'unregulated' because they are 'exempt' (see above). According to the Act (s 189(1)), an 'exempt agreement' means one specified in or under ss 16, 16A or 16B,[92] which in turn sets out different classes of exemption for the three main categories:

(a)  Exempt consumer credit agreements, a category in respect of which s 16 has been significantly amended over the years (see para 5.15).

(b)  Exempt consumer hire agreements as specified by statutory instrument.[93]

(c)  The exempt categories introduced by the 2006 Act (see para 5.15A).

Whilst the Act has little application to exempt agreements (see below), except in relation to the credit provisions which were or are extortionate[94] or unfair[95] and advertisements (s 43(1)(b): see para 8.29), in relation to regulated agreements it also creates some special categories (see para 5.16).

**[5.15] Exempt consumer credit agreements**. Even though a transaction amounts to a consumer credit agreement (see para 5.19), it may be an exempt agreement (see

---

90   Under s 10(1)(a): see para 5.28.
91   Under ss 60–61: see para 9.10.
92   2006 Act, s 5(1).
93   S 16(6). See Consumer Credit (Exempt Agreements) Order 1989 SI 869, Art 6.
94   S 16(7) was repealed by Sched 4 of the 2006 Act, so only applies to agreements made before the 2006 Act comes into force. See further generally, para 29.41.
95   New s 16(7A) of the 1974 Act (as inserted by s 22 of the 2006 Act): see para 29.44.

para 5.14) if it falls within one of the following categories under s 16 and its Regulations:[96]

1. *Short-term consumer credit.*[97] This exempt category covers consumer credit agreements for the supply of goods or services (dcs agreements: see para 5.34) within either of the following types:

    (a) *For fixed-sum credit* (see para 5.28) of up to 12 months' duration[98] in respect of goods supplied and where the number of instalments does not exceed **four**,[99] e.g. a 28-day trade credit for goods supplied, where the price is payable 28 days after delivery of the goods; a purchase from a department store of a bedroom suite by a deposit and not more than three post-delivery instalments. However, it was held that this category did not extend to *Dimond v Lovell* (set out at para 5.13) because the credit hire agreement for fixed-sum credit (see para 5.28) could last more than 12 months in that the payment of rental could be delayed beyond that time.

    (b) *For running-account credit* (see para 5.28) where the credit provided in each period e.g. weekly or monthly, *must* be repayable in **one** amount[94] e.g. the weekly milk bill; a purchase from a department store of a radio by a customer with an open monthly account, or using a charge card. As to open accounts, see para 2.19. As to charge cards, see para 2.24.

2. *Low-cost credit.* This category is restricted to pure loans (dc agreements: see para 5.35) extended on a non-commercial basis (see para 5.18) and does not apply to loans connected with the supply of goods or services, which will usually only be exempt under the above short-term category. It exempts only the following categories (s 16(5)(b); and Art 4):

    (a) loans by credit unions (see para 15.19) where as at June 2006 the rate of interest does not exceed 2% per month, or 26.99% APR.[100]

    (b) fixed loans which are not 'offered to the public generally', but only 'offered to a particular class, or particular classes, of individuals',[101] and the APR[101] does not exceed 1% more than the highest bank base rate as that rate varies. Confined to loans at below a commercial rate of interest, this category will cover such as low-cost loans to employees.[102]

---

96 The Consumer Credit (Exempt Agreements) Order, 1989 SI 869 (as amended). This account ignores some of the less common exempt classes.

97 S 16(5)(a) and Art 3(1)(a). This category does not include finance for the purchase of land, or conditional sales or hp or pledges of goods: Art 3(2). It does not apply to unsecured cash loans, which can only achieve exemption under category 2, below.

98 *Zoan v Rouamba* [2000] 2 All ER 620, CA; *Ketley v Gilbert* (2001) 151 NLJ 20, CA; *Thew v Cole* [2004] RTR 25, CA.

99 Art 3(1)(a). Only counted are repayments of capital (*contra* category 4, below) without option to extend the number of payments or without later variation to that effect.

100 As amended by 2006 SI 1273 (doubling the exempt rate from 1% to 2% per month). The proposition in the text is an over-simplification, because Art 4 gives a special meaning to the tcc (as to which, see para 8.24): see further Guest and Lloyd, *Encyclopedia of Consumer Credit*, para 3-338.

101 This requirement derives from Art 2(2) of the EU Consumer Credit Directive 87/102 and may be difficult to interpret: see Guest and Lloyd, *ibid*. Loans of variable amounts of capital are excluded by Art 4(2).

102 E.g. *Morris v Banque Arabe Internationale SA (No. 2)* [2000] CLY 675.

3.   *Finance for foreign trade.* Credit agreements made in connection with the export or import of goods or services are exempt,[103] but beyond the scope of this work. However, the fact that a UK credit transaction is used to finance the supply of goods or services abroad does not necessarily mean that it is exempt.[104]

4.   *House mortgages.* Where the lender is a body specified in or under s 16(1) (as amended) or s 16(6C) and the loan is by way of mortgage of a dwelling house, the transaction is governed by the Financial Services and Markets Act 2000 and beyond the scope of this work (see para 3.02).

5.   *Responsible mortgage lenders.* As they are assumed to be responsible lenders, second mortgages of dwelling houses remain within the CCA, but are automatically exempt by s 16(2) where the lender is a local authority (ss 16(1), (2)), or housing association (s 16(6A)). The 2003 White Paper (see para 5.11) suggests some tidying up (para 3.73).

**[5.15A] The exempt categories introduced by the 2006 Act**. The 2006 Act considerably extends the ambit of the CCA by removing the financial limit where the debtor or hirer is a private consumer (see paras 1.19 and 5.19). However, the 2006 Act then proceeds to save from the widened scope of the CCA the following two exempt categories, except in relation to unfair credit relationships (see para 29.44) to which they remain liable (2006 Act, ss 3(8) and 4(6)).

1.   *High net worth debtors and hirers.* The idea behind this so-called helicopter provision is that those well-heeled individual consumers (perhaps from overseas) who wish at very short notice to borrow large sums of money, to buy (say) a helicopter, without CCA impediments can do so with professional assistance. Under new s 16A(1) of the 1974 Act (2006 Act, s 3),

> 'The Secretary of State may by order provide that this Act shall not regulate a consumer credit agreement or a consumer hire agreement where—
>
> (a)   the debtor or hirer is a natural person;
>
> (b)   the agreement includes a declaration made by him to the effect that he agrees to forgo the protection and remedies that would be available to him under this Act if the agreement were a regulated agreement;
>
> (c)   a statement of high net worth has been made in relation to him; and
>
> (d)   that statement is current in relation to the agreement and a copy of it was provided to the creditor or owner before the agreement was made'.

The purpose of this provision is to allow the Secretary of State by Statutory Order to provide that a private[105] debtor under a consumer credit agreement or a hirer under a consumer hire agreement (see para 1.19) forgo almost all his protections under the CCA provided that the following two conditions are both satisfied:

---

103  S 16(5)(c) and Art 5: see Goode, *Consumer Credit Law & Practice*, para 49.92. But see Lindgren (1977) 40 MLR at 168–9. Compare s 27(2) of UCTA 1977: see para 18.14.

104  See *OFT v Lloyds TSB Bank plc* (see para 16.11) at paras 93–4.

105  Explanatory Note 19 draws attention to the fact that 'natural person' in s 16A(1) is intended to exclude partnerships and unincorporated associations.

(i)     The debtor or hirer who is a natural person signs a declaration in pre-scribed form in the credit or hire agreement making it clear that he forgoes those protections; and

(ii)    The lender or owner is in receipt of a statement in prescibed form of current 'high net worth'[106] made by a prescribed third party (new s 16A(3)), e.g. an FSA-approved solicitor or accountant, about the high net worth of the debtor or hirer.[107] This is seen as preventing lender abuse of the exemption.

2.   *Unincorporated business.* It will be seen later that the CCA extends to some business consumers who are sole traders, or small partnerships or unincorporated associations (see para 5.24). Whilst regulated credit or hire agreements with private consumers may after the 2006 Act be without financial limit (see para 5.23), Parliament intended to remove from CCA restrictions large business transactions, but to retain protection for small transactions, e.g. hp of a small car to an accountant, or a lease of a computer to a solicitor (see para 1.19). Accordingly, new s 16B(1) provides that it does not regulate:

'(a) a consumer credit agreement by which the creditor provides the debtor with credit exceeding £25,000, or

(b) a consumer hire agreement that requires the hirer to make payments exceeding £25,000,

if the agreement is entered into by the debtor or hirer wholly or predominantly for the purposes of a business carried on, or intended to be carried on, by him'.

The key to this exemption applicable to both credit and hire is thus the size and purpose of the transaction: the financial size of the transaction loan will be considered later (para 5.23); but there must here be mentioned the restriction of the exemption to the business of the unincorporated traders. If the businessman enters the transaction in his private capacity, any exemption should be considered under s 16A, above; but, if in it for business purposes (undefined), the 16B exemption should be considered. This test does not depend on whether a transaction goes through the books of the business debtor or hirer, but its purpose, which will be a matter of fact. To help in deciding the purpose of the transaction, the section offers the following two aids:

(i)     There is a presumption that it is a s 16B transaction where the debtor or hirer makes a declaration:[108]

'to the effect that the agreement is entered into by him wholly or predominantly for the purposes of a business carried on, or intended to be carried on, by him, the agreement shall be presumed to have been entered into by him wholly or predominantly for such purposes'.

(ii)    But there will be no such presumption if, 'when the agreement is entered into (s 16B(3)):

---

106  'High net worth' is defined by new s 16A(2) to refer to income or assets. Cf. the exemption under the FSMA 2000, by 2005 SI 270. The Minister indicated that this is intended to encompass a net income of £100,000 and net assets of £250,000 (HC, Standing Comm E, col.9).

107  See also ss 16A(6) and (7). Where there is more than one debtor or hirer, a separate statement is required in respect of each of them (new s 16A(5)). Under new s 16A(4), an Order may set out the details of this statement.

108  S 16B(2). By s 16B(4), the form and content of such declarations may be prescribed.

(a)  the creditor or owner, or

(b)  any person who has acted on his behalf in connection with the entering into of the agreement,

knows, or has reasonable cause to suspect, that the agreement is not entered into by the debtor or hirer wholly or predominantly for the purposes of a business carried on, or intended to be carried on, by him'.

The result is that, if a small trader through his business books takes on hp an expensive car above the financial limit, the transaction will remain governed by the CCA provided the car is intended for predominantly private purposes; but it will be unregulated hp or hire if he intends the car predominantly for the purposes of his business.

**[5.16] Special categories.** Whilst exempt agreements are, as their name suggests, almost wholly exempt from the provisions of the CCA (see para 5.15), the Act also contains a number of special regulated categories which are either exempted from particular (different) provisions, or additionally subject to some further ones.

1.  *Small agreements* (see para 5.17).

2.  *Non-commercial agreements* (see para 5.18).

3.  *Bank overdrafts.* These may be exempted by the Director (see para 3.03) from all the documentation provisions of the CCA (see para 9.07).

4.  *Mortgages to purchase land.* Instead of the regulated agreement being subject to the cancellation provisions, the debtor entering such (usually second) mortgages is given a special opportunity to withdraw before the agreement is concluded (s 58: see para 10.27).

5.  *Pledges of documents of title.* The CCA restrictions as to the taking of pledges[109] are designed to protect consumers rather than businessmen, and therefore do not apply to pledges of documents of title.[110]

6.  *Conditional sale and hp agreements.* As important types of consumer credit agreement (see para 5.19, *et seq.*), they are subject to many of the CCA controls. Additionally, there are some provisions which apply exclusively to regulated conditional sales and hp: they cannot be small agreements (see para 5.17); they may involve protected goods,[111] and also be subject to the prohibition on entering premises;[112] the buyer or hirer has a statutory right to terminate the agreement;[113] there is a special rule for showing adverse possession of goods let on hp;[114] and the court has special powers to make transfer or return orders (s 133: see para 24.43).

**[5.17] Small agreements.** According to s 17(1):

'A small agreement is—

(a)  a regulated consumer credit agreement for credit not exceeding [£x], other than a hire-purchase or conditional sale agreement; or

---

109  Ss 114, 122: see para 25.15, *et seq.*

110  S 114(3) (as amended). Such trust receipts are beyond the scope of this work (see para 25.16).

111  Within s 90: see para 24.35.

112  S 92: see para 24.34.

113  Ss 99–100: see paras 26.05–7.     114  S 134: see para 24.42.

(b)  a regulated consumer hire agreement which does not require the hirer to make payments exceeding [£x];

being an agreement which is either unsecured or secured by a guarantee or indemnity only (whether or not the guarantee or indemnity is itself secured)'.

This section extends to running-account credit with the same small credit limit;[115] and it includes an anti-avoidance device.[116] Overall, s 17 is drafted with three qualifications:

(1)  Its ambit is limited by a figure. Section 17 originally referred to £30, though like many of the Act's financial limits, it may be amended by statutory order;[117] and the figure has now been raised to £50.[118] However, in relation to the two types of regulated agreement the figure refers to different things: with regard to consumer credit agreements (see para 5.19, *et seq.*), it is speaking of the amount of credit, e.g. sum borrowed; whereas in respect of consumer hire agreements (see para 1.19), the important thing is the total amount the hirer is **required** to pay under the agreement, e.g. deposit, plus rentals and VAT. Nor is it possible to evade the financial limits by utilising running-account credit;[115] nor by splitting up the transaction into two or more agreements.[116]

(2)  It cannot include conditional sales (see para 1.16) nor hp agreements (see para 1.24). Such agreements may amount to consumer credit agreements (see para 5.23); but, however small the amount of credit, they cannot fall within s 17(1).

(3)  The agreement must be unsecured, or secured only by a guarantee or indemnity (see para 25.10). Thus, however small the amount of money involved, s 17(1) does not comprehend transactions supported by real security, e.g. a pledge for £5.

Examples of small agreements will include all the following: a credit sale (see para 1.13) where the credit does not exceed the designated figure;[118] bank overdraft or credit-card facility for less than that figure;[119] a consumer hire agreement for an indefinite period, but giving the hirer the option to terminate before his total payments reach the stipulated figure.[118] The major exemption enjoyed by small agreements is from most of Pt V of the CCA (s 74(2)), dealing with entry into credit or hire agreements (see para 9.07). Additionally, small agreements are exempt from provisions as to the following: the unsolicited mailing of credit cards,[120] copies of card agreements[120] and the duty to supply periodic statements of accounts.[121] The rationale of all these exemptions would appear to be that the relieved duties would amount to too great a burden on the creditor as against the advantage to the debtor.

---

115  S 17(2) (as amended), referring to s 16B(1)(a): see para 5.15A.
116  Ss 17(3) and (4): this is to prevent a transaction from being artificially split into two or more small agreements.
117  S 181. The intention behind the provision is to allow Parliament to inflation-proof the figure.
118  Consumer Credit (Increase of Monetary Limits) Order 1983 SI 1878.
119  See Sched 2, Examples 16 and 17. See also Example 22.
120  Ss 51(2) and 85(3). As to these duties, see para 7.12.
121  S 78(7). As to these duties, see para 7.08. Note that the creditor remains liable in respect of the other duties to supply information contained in ss 77 and 78.

**[5.18] Non-commercial agreements**. According to s 189(1), this expression:

'means a consumer credit agreement or consumer hire agreement not made by the creditor or owner in the course of a business carried on by him'.

Clearly, if the creditor carries on a business[122] of entering into regulated agreements, none of the regulated agreements which go through the books of the firm could be regarded as non-commercial. Equally clearly, a creditor not engaged in any business would have his regulated agreements classed as non-commercial.[123] But what of a creditor who is primarily engaged in some business not necessarily connected with entry into regulated agreements, e.g. a solicitor, but who does occasionally enter into regulated agreements?[124]

Non-commercial agreements not only obtain the same exemptions from the CCA as small agreements (see para 5.17), but are also totally exempt from the connected lender liability of s 75 (s 75(3)(a): see para 16.11). Additionally, non-commercial agreements are exempt from the following: the creditor or owner is exempted from the licensing requirements (see para 6.09, *et seq.*) so that by the absence of a licence he neither commits an offence (s 39) nor has his agreements rendered unenforceable (s 40); both parties are released from the duty to supply information during the continuance of the agreement as to respectively the state of accounts to debtor/hirer or surety,[125] or whereabouts of the goods,[126] or variation of the regulated agreement,[127] or termination statements;[128] and the transaction is saved from the restrictions in respect of the realisation of security,[129] and as regards pawn-tickets (s 114: see para 25.18).

## Consumer credit agreements

**[5.19] Consumer credit agreements**. This is one of the key concepts of the CCA, embracing all forms of contractual credit and including hp,[130] conditional sale,[131] credit sale,[132] check trading,[133] credit cards,[134] budget accounts,[135] overdrafts,[136] personal loans,[136] mortgages[137] and pledges (see para 25.15). The concept is defined in s 8: as with most of the CCA, s 8 applies only to regulated agreements,[138] which excludes exempt and certain other agreements (s 8(3), as amended: see para 5.15).

---

122 'Business' includes a profession or trade: s 189(1). Cf. SGA, s 61(1) (see para 14.04); UCTA, s 14 (see para 18.18).

123 Cf. Pt 3 of the HPA 1964: see para 21.56. What of internet person-to-person lending (ZOPA: see [2005] 10 *Credit Today* 22)?

124 See s 189(2), set out at para 5.36; and Goode, *Consumer Credit Law & Practice*, para 23.141. Does it matter whether or not the regulated agreements are put through the books of the practice? Cf. *Newton v Pyke* (1908) 25 TLR 127.

125 Ss 77–9, 107–10: see paras 7.08, 15.17.        126 S 80: see para 15.17.

127 S 82: see para 26.22.        128 S 103: see para 26.04.        129 S 112: see para 25.13.

130 See para 1.24.        131 See para 1.16.        132 See para 1.13.        133 See para 15.17.

134 See para 2.28.        135 See para 2.19.        136 See para 2.17.        137 See para 25.19.

138 But not the extortionate bargain/unfair relationship provisions (see para 29.40, *et seq.*). Why is s 8(3) needed in view of the definition of 'regulated agreement' in s 189(1)? In view of this, it is difficult to resist the inference that s 8 is unnecessarily complicated.

In respect of non-exempt agreements, the concept of a **consumer credit agreement** is defined by s 8(1) (as amended) in a simplified manner involving a number of constituent parts:[139]

> 'A consumer credit agreement is an agreement between an individual ('the debtor') and any other person ('the creditor') by which the creditor provides the debtor with credit of any amount'.

This contains the following four requirements:

(a)  there must be **an agreement** (see para 5.20);

(b)  for the **provision of credit** (see para 5.21);

(c)  between **the debtor** (see para 5.24); and

(d)  **the creditor** (see para 5.25).

**[5.20] An agreement.** A consumer credit agreement (see para 5.19) requires an **agreement**, meaning a binding contract between at least two parties made in accordance with the general law,[140] or a prospective agreement (see below); and it does not include non-contractual arrangements, e.g. supply of gas or electricity (see para 3.07). The CCA originally required a regulated agreement to be made in writing; but it may now also be made by E-Commerce (see para 9.05).

Furthermore, it must be an agreement to grant credit (see para 5.21): it is not sufficient that the agreement grants a **facility** under which its customer in breach of contract is able to obtain credit,[141] e.g. a universal bank account (see para 2.15); he must have the **right** under the agreement to obtain credit,[142] though it would seem sufficient if the bank simply honours a cheque which allows the account to go overdrawn.[143] Nor need the bank customer exercise immediately any right to an overdraft facility. The effect of this may be to bring within the CCA any payment cards issued on an account with an overdraft facility whether they be a debit card,[144] cash card,[144] cheque guarantee card,[145] or multi-function card.[146]

For the moment, we may ignore any formalities required of such a contract (see Chap 9) and any special rules required for its formation (see Chap 10), though we should note two special situations provided for by the Act. *First*, there are some circumstances where it is intended that the Act shall apply not just to actual

---

139  S 2 of the 2006 Act removes from the 1974 Act the expression 'personal credit agreement' (s 8(2)), which becomes redundant.

140  Goode, *Consumer Credit Law & Practice*, para 23.43. As to unregulated agreements treated by the parties as regulated, see Goode, *Op. cit.*, paras 23.4b–d.

141  Such as a building society account which expressly prohibits the holder from overdrawing. Cf. *Nejad v City Index Ltd* [2000] CLY 2597, CA.

142  The right to credit may be granted expressly, e.g. a Personal Loan Account (see generally, para 2.17); or it may be granted impliedly (see CCA, Sched 2, Examples 17, 18).

143  Goode, *Consumer Credit Law & Practice*, para 11.72.

144  See Dobson [1984] JBL 350; the Banking Ombudsman, Annual Report 1990/91, para 10.6; but contra Goode, *Op. cit.*, para 24.84.

145  Logically, it would seem that wherever the number of cheque forms issued to the customer times the card limit exceeds the credit balance in the account, the customer has a credit facility. See Sched 2, Example 21; Jones, *Credit Cards*, 10.

146  In the use of a multi-function card, each function may be treated as a separate agreement: s 18(2); and see para 5.27. See also the Banking Ombudsman, Annual Report 1990/1, para 10.7, case 10.

agreements, but also to inchoate ones:[147] in these situations only, the Act refers to 'prospective agreements' and the persons who will become parties to them.[148] This rule has special significance in relation to revolving credit agreements, e.g. an overdraft facility, where the alleged agreement may in fact only amount to a standing offer (see para 7.11). *Second*, the Act reinforces the common law (see para 10.03) and continues the general prohibition[149] previously found in the HPA against the consumer binding himself to enter into a regulated agreement. It provides that (s 59(1)):

> 'An agreement is void if, and to the extent that, it purports to bind a person to enter as debtor or hirer into a prospective regulated agreement'.

This prohibition does not extend to the creditor or supplier binding himself, so that s 59(1) does not avoid options to enter into a regulated agreement granted to the debtor or hirer;[150] nor does it extend to modified agreements (see para 26.12). For credit proposal forms, see para 8.35.

**[5.21] The provision of credit**. Credit is the amount of money of which the debtor has the use. According to s 8 (see para 5.19), what is required by that section is an agreement by which a prospective creditor binds himself to **provide** non-exempt credit,[151] which may be either of a fixed amount, e.g. a Personal Loan (see para 2.17), or a revolving credit, e.g. an overdraft (see para 5.28). The meaning of 'credit' under the CCA is to be found in s 9(1), which lays down that ' "credit" includes[152] a cash[153] loan and any other form of financial accommodation'. The 'cash loan' does not need to be paid direct to the debtor, for it may suffice that the money is paid at the debtor's request to a third party (see para 7.02). According to Goode, the ingredients of **credit** granted by a supplier/financier [A] to a consumer [B] are as follows:[154]

(a) *The receipt by B of a benefit*, e.g. goods. The CCA concentrates on the provision of credit under an agreement, as where **purchased** goods are delivered in advance of payment; but picking up goods in a self-service store does not involve credit because the contract is not made until the cash desk. Thus, in the ordinary cash sale, payment of the price and delivery of the goods are concurrent terms (SGA, s 28: see para 23.16), so that there is no element of credit; and this remains true where payment and delivery are by matching instalments, e.g. a book club (see paras 23.23 and 26.16).

---

147  E.g. ss 57, 58: see Chap 10. As to the ambit of 'prospective regulated agreements', see para 10.26.

148  See the warning against applying the concept of a prospective agreement too widely: Goode, *Op. cit.*, para 23.23; and para 5.24. At common law, such agreements may be difficult to achieve: see para 10.03.

149  S 59(2) contains a power to exempt by regulation to meet anticipated difficulties with business consumers: see further Guest and Lloyd, *Encyclopedia of Consumer Credit*, para 2-060.

150  It is another question whether the parties have finished agreeing: see para 10.03.

151  For criticism of the use of the word 'provides' in s 8, see Goode, *Consumer Credit Law & Practice*, para 23.50; Lindgren (1977) 40 MLR at 164. For the granting of credit to an undischarged bankrupt, see para 19.21.

152  However, s 9(1) is probably comprehensive: see Goode, *Op. cit.*, para 24.4.

153  According to s 189(1), ' "cash" includes money in any form'. Under s 9(2), it need not be money which is legal tender in England (see para 23.14).

154  Goode, *Op. cit.*, para 24.8, *et seq*. See also Guest and Lloyd, *Encyclopedia of Consumer Credit*, para 2-010.

(b) *Attracting to B a contractual duty of payment.* There is no credit if the recipient of the benefit is left under no contractual duty to pay for it, e.g. a gift (see para 2.08), or a sale of book-debts (see para 7.18) or bills of exchange,[155] or a quasi-contractual claim (see para 29.12). Payment by cheque is conditional payment (see para 24.03), so that notionally there is no credit, even though the cheque takes time to clear.[156] Credit and charge cards have been held to amount to absolute payment to the retail supplier (see para 2.25).

(c) *In money to A.* The contractual duty must be to pay money (a financial obligation),[153] not some other obligation.[157] Thus, actual payment before delivery of goods sold does not constitute credit to B, e.g. a Christmas club (see para 15.18); nor does an agreement to barter, though a part-exchange deal may involve credit (see para 2.09).

(d) *Contractually deferred.* As Goode explained:[158]

> 'Debt is deferred and credit is extended, whenever the contract provides for the debtor to pay, or gives him the option to pay, later than the time at which payment would otherwise have been earned under the express or implied terms of the contract . . . It is necessary . . . to ask when, but for [the express] stipulation, payment would have had to be made. It is the difference between the two dates that constitutes the credit'.

It is not sufficient that B delays payment beyond the provision of goods: for credit, there must be a contractual deferment of payment beyond the point at which it would otherwise be payable.[159] So, take a sale of goods, where a payment on delivery (a cash sale) involves a concurrent payment and no credit (see above). If payment is contractually delayed beyond delivery, leaving aside any deposit (see para 5.22) there is credit because payment is deferred, e.g. credit and conditional sale, and the same is true if the buyer receives a discount for cash, because this implies that he may otherwise delay payment; but, if payment is contractually made before delivery, there is no credit, e.g. mail order cash with order. Similarly, with a simple hiring agreement: on principle, at common law the hire rent is due at latest at the end of the period of bailment, which involves no credit; and the same would be true of a periodic hiring, e.g. from month-to-month. In *Dimond v Lovell* (set out at para 5.13), both the Court of Appeal and the House of Lords expressly approved the above passage from Goode.[160] Both courts then held that the accident hire agreement involved credit for the following reason:[161] the nub of the contract was for the

---

155 As to discounting bills, see Goode, *Op. cit.*, paras 11.76 and 24.47. Distinguish bills created as part of a credit transaction (CCA, ss 123–5: see para 25.09). But for pay-day advances, see para 7.28.

156 As to whether a cheque is nevertheless a credit token, see para 5.30. As to cheque cashing businesses, see para 7.28.

157 It must create a debt at the time of contracting: *McMillan Williams v Range* [2004] 1 WLR 1858, CA, at paras 20–3.

158 Goode, *Op. cit.*, para 24.25.

159 Might the mere non-enforcement of a creditor's rights amount to a granting of 'other financial accommodation' by him (see para 5.22)?

160 By the CA, at para 57; and by Lord Hoffmann in the HL at 903e.

161 The decision is vigorously, but not altogether convincingly, criticised by Goode, *Op. cit.*, para 24.62(1).

provision of services in the form of the hire of a car; leaving aside the terms of the agreement, the common law required that payment for those services be made at latest by the end of the hiring (see para 27.21); whereas clause 5 of the agreement allowed that payment to be deferred until damages had been recovered from L (see para 1.19).

(e) *Significantly contractually deferred.* On a common sense basis, there is only credit where the payment of the debt is significantly deferred. Presumably, the momentary deferment of payment for goods supplied does not amount to credit, as where a shopkeeper [A] hands goods to his customer [B] before B hands the price to A. Similarly, where B pays A by cash card or debit card,[162] there may be a momentary deferment before the sum is electronically debited to B's account, but this is not usually thought to amount to credit (s 187(3A): see para 5.33). Further, even a significant deferment of payment is disregarded if non-contractual, as where A delays sending out his bills or B is tardy in paying them: *contra* where A promises to delay sending out his bills, e.g. an open account (see para 2.19),[159] or a charge account (see para 2.24).

(f) *By way of financial accommodation* (see para 5.22)

**[5.22] Financial accommodation.** As explained above, credit is the amount of the price contractually deferred: so, to find the amount of credit, there must be deducted from the price the amount of any deposit. Whilst usually expressed in money,[163] this will commonly be a part-exchange allowance (see para 2.09). There is credit where A binds himself to **grant** credit, even where B does not bind himself to take it: it is sufficient that B has the option to take credit, e.g. a bank overdraft facility (see para 2.17), a budget or option account (see para 2.19) or a three-party credit card, the last being expressly caught by the Act;[164] and so may debit, cash, charge and cheque guarantee cards where there is the necessary **right** to an over-draft facility (see para 5.20).[165] Whilst charge cards allow up to a month's credit, they are exempt (see para 5.15). There have been Government proposals that cash, charge and debit cards be given their own consumer protection provisions.[166]

Wider still is the concept of '**other ... financial accommodation**' in s 9(1), which s 9(3) of the Act expressly extends to include the hire-rent in hp (see below). Although the expression 'financial accommodation' has been seen as an anti-avoidance device,[167] its essence would seem to lie in the capital sum which the debtor is **given time to repay**. This includes not only fresh capital made available to the debtor, but also earlier loans which the debtor is required to pay off out

---

162 Goode, *Op. cit.*, para 24.84.

163 'Deposit' is defined by s 189(1), but is of much reduced importance with the virtual removal from the CCA of any credit limit (see para 5.23). For crediting of the deposit to a financier in directly financed transactions, see para 16.05.

164 S 14(3): see para 5.30. This is so even if the debtor only uses his credit card as a charge card by paying it off in full each month: Jones, *Credit Cards*, 79.

165 It has been doubted whether a debit card on an account with an overdraft is within the definition: see Goode, *Consumer Credit Law & Practice*, para 24.84.

166 These recommendations of the Jack Committee were taken up by the 2003 White Paper (see generally para 2.17), para 4.6.

167 Goode, *Op. cit.*, II para 5.9. *Contra* Guest and Lloyd, *Encyclopedia of Consumer Credit*, para 2-010. Would it extend to activities within the (now repealed) Pawnbrokers Act 1872, s 6 (see Macleod [1995] JBL 155, esp at 170)?

of the new credit: this will cover old loans totally repaid from the old credit, i.e. refinancing (s 11(1)(c): see para 5.29); and also partial repayments, as where the debtor is required to use part of the new loan to pay off arrears on the earlier loan (see para 8.25). Further, s 9(4) provides that:

'For the purposes of this Act, an item[168] entering into the total charge for credit shall not be treated as credit even though time is allowed for its payment'.

The effect is illustrated by *Wilson v Robertsons (London) Ltd.*[169]

Among twenty seven pawnbroking agreements, W pawned a Cartier watch to R for a 6-month loan of £400, from which R deducted a documentation fee of £8, though stating in the regulated agreement that the loan was for £400. At the end of the 6 months, W was unable to find the money to redeem the pledge and was at risk that R would sell the watch. Accordingly, the parties agreed to re-pledge the watch for a further 6 months, that second agreement being back-dated 3 months. On a trial of preliminary issues, Laddie J found in favour of W on all the following grounds: (i) the documentation fee was not part of the credit (see below); (ii) the second agreement was an attempt to contract out of the Act (see para 18.11); and (iii) contravened the 6-month rule (see para 25.18). At full trial, the CA considered issues dealing with ss 170(1) and 106(d) (see below, paras 10.19; 25.13).

On the documentation fee, Laddie J explained that, because the documentation fee was part of the total change for credit (see para 8.24), s 9(4) required it to be ignored for the purposes of determining the amount of credit under s 9 (see paras 36, 40, 48).

*The special hp rule.* Section 9(3) provides that:

'Without prejudice to the generality of subsection 1, the person by whom goods are bailed . . . to an individual under a hire purchase agreement shall be taken to provide him with fixed-sum credit to finance the transaction of an amount equal to the total price of the goods less the aggregate of the deposit (if any) and the total charge for credit'.

We have seen that the essence of credit in s 9(1) is that the consumer is **given time to pay** (see para 5.21). On this analysis, s 9(3) was necessary because in hp the rental for each period is usually payable at latest by the first day of each period of hire so that, without s 9(3), there would be no 'financial accommodation' in hp.

For s 9(3), 'total price' is defined for the purposes of hp or conditional sale by s 189(1).[170] The effect of the foregoing rules on the computation of credit is illustrated elsewhere,[171] but may have unexpected results where there are multiple agreements (see para 5.27) and does not apply to credit limits under running account credit (as to which, see para 5.28).

**[5.23] The credit ceiling**. Under the CCA 1974, an agreement for the provision of credit (see paras 5.20–2) would only be a consumer credit agreement (see para 5.19)

---

168  This does not necessarily have to benefit the creditor, e.g. insurance premiums, survey fees. See *Humberclyde Finance Ltd v Thompson* (1997) Tr LR 242, CA.

169  [2005] 3 All ER 873 (preliminary issues); [2006] EWCA Civ 1088 (full trial).

170  See para 24.35. What if a dealer, as part of a promotion, agrees to pay the first instalment to the financier on behalf of the debtor?

171  CCA, Sched 2, Example 10; and Goode, *Op. cit.*, para 24.150.

where the amount of credit to which the debtor has a contractual right at the moment of contracting fell within a specified maximum[172] financial limit for the time being (see para 2.07). Originally, that upper figure was fixed at £5,000, perhaps aiming at a new family car. However, the CCA contains power to increase the limit by statutory order (s 181, as amended): in 1983 that power was utilised to increase the limit to £15,000; and in 1998 the limit was further raised to £25,000.[173] In 2003 the White Paper *Fair, Clear and Competitive*[174] proposed abolition of the credit ceiling altogether for private consumers, whether or not the loans were secured (paras 3.58–9), but to keep it for small businesses (see para 5.24). The CCA 2006 gave effect to this recommendation as follows: subject to the following two exceptions, as from April 2008 it abolished the financial ceiling in respect of all regulated agreements,[175] whether for fixed sum or running account (see para 5.28).

1.  *High net worth debtors and hirers.* Acting as a private consumer, by using s 16A such an individual can always enter into a credit or hire agreement outside the CCA (see para 5.15A).

2.  *Unincorporated business.* By entering a credit or hire agreement for business purposes, a debtor or hirer can utilise s 16B to take the agreement outside the CCA (see para 5.15A), provided the transaction exceeds the stipulated financial limit. Initially the CCA 2006 has fixed this limit at £25,000; but this is, of course subject to the above power to increase the limit. For business consumer credit, this retains the complicated two-stage process for determining the element of financial accommodation; but this is now beyond the scope of this work.[176]

Particularly important where a UK credit card is used to obtain goods or services abroad,[177] s 9(2) provides that,

'Where credit is provided otherwise than in sterling it shall be treated for the purposes of this Act as providing sterling of an equivalent amount'.

**[5.24] The debtor**. For our purposes, a consumer credit agreement is an agreement to extend credit to an individual (the debtor): see s 8(1), as amended.

*Individual.* The CCA has no application where the debtor is an artificial person, but may apply whenever the debtor is not a body corporate, this last expression meaning a company registered under the Companies Acts,[178] or created by Royal Charter or Act of Parliament.[179] The expression 'individual' obviously comprehends both a private consumer and a sole trader;[180] but the statutory

---

172  If the amount of credit falls below a minimum figure, there may only be a small consumer credit agreement: see para 5.17.

173  Consumer Credit (Increase in Monetary Limits)(Amendment) Order, 1998 SI 996.

174  See DTI, *the Consumer Credit Market in the 21st Century* (Dec. 2003, Cm. 6040), para 3.61.

175  For fixed sum agreements, the financial ceiling contained in s 8(2) of the 1974 Act was abolished by s 2(1)(b) of the 2006 Act; and for running account agreements, the financial ceiling mechanism contained in ss 10(2) and (3) of the 1974 Act is amended by s 5(2)(b) of the 2004 Act.

176  See Macleod, *Consumer Sales Law*, 1st edn, para 5.22.

177  See *OFT v Lloyds TSB Bank plc* (see para 16.11), 90 and 92.

178  E.g. *Re Charge Card Services Ltd* (set out at para 2.27).

179  See also para 1.19. Cf. 'dealing as consumer' within the UCTA: see para 18.18.

180  The Minister in (2004/5) HC Standing Committee E, col. 5.

definition in s 189(1) has been extended by the 2006 Act to both the following categories:[181]

(a) *Small partnerships.* Amended s 189(1) says that 'individual' 'includes a partnership consisting of two or three persons not all of whom are bodies corporate'. The effect is to exclude from the CCA all partnerships with more than three personal members, or where all the members are bodies corporate, e.g. international firms of lawyers and accountants. But small partnerships remain within the CCA on the basis that they have similar levels of credit expertise to ordinary consumers and their owners draw little distinction between their business and private lives.[180]

(b) *Unincorporations.* Amended s 189(1) also says that 'individual' 'includes an unincorporated body of persons which does not consist entirely of bodies corporate and is not a partnership', e.g. an unincorporated club, charity, or trade union. The justification is that the members of many of these bodies, which often perform valuable charitable and community work, are ordinary people.[180]

*Debtor* is defined as meaning (s 189(1)):

> 'the individual receiving credit under a consumer credit agreement or the person to whom his rights and duties under the agreement have passed by assignment or operation of law,[182] and in relation to a prospective consumer credit agreement includes the prospective debtor'.

Note that this definition of 'debtor' includes his assignees[183] and also extends to prospective agreements (see para 5.20).

Finally, s 185 contains special provisions to deal with the situation where there are joint debtors or hirers.[184] Notwithstanding that the CCA ordinarily applies only where the debtor or hirer is an 'individual', s 185(5) (as amended by the 2006 Act, s 5(8)) provides that:

> 'An agreement for the provision of credit, or the bailment or (in Scotland) the hiring of goods, to two or more persons jointly where:
>
> (a) one or more of those persons is an individual, and
>
> (b) one or more of them is not an individual,
>
> is a consumer credit agreement or consumer hire agreement if it would have been one had they all been individuals; and each person within paragraph (b) shall accordingly be included among the debtors or hirers under the agreement'.

Such cases are thus brought within the general CCA rule for co-parties (see para 25.08) that any right conferred on the debtor must be observed in relation

---

181 Following the recommendations of the White Paper, *Fair, Clear and Competitive: the Consumer Credit Market in the 21st Century* (Dec. 2003, Cm. 6040), paras 3.68–71.

182 E.g. personal representative; trustee in bankruptcy. For comment on 'and duties', see para 5.25. Cf. the definition of 'hirer': para 1.19.

183 For attempts by a debtor to assign his interest under an instalment credit agreement, see para 1.23. For assignment generally, see para 7.16, *et seq.*

184 The provision does not extend to joint and several debtors/hirers: see Goode, *Consumer Credit Law & Practice*, para 44.21.

to each of them,[185] whilst any duty cast on the debtor may be discharged by any of them.[186]

**[5.25] The creditor**. A consumer credit agreement is an agreement to extend credit within the requisite financial limitation by any other person (the creditor): s 8(1), as amended.

*Person.* Unlike the definition of debtor (see para 5.24), the creditor does not need to be an 'individual', and may therefore be either an artificial or natural person.[187] Except for the purpose of exempt agreements (see para 5.15), the Act is not concerned with the status of that person.

*Creditor.* According to the Act (s 189(1)):

> ' "creditor" means the person providing credit under a consumer credit agreement or the person to whom his rights and duties[188] under the agreement have passed by assignment or operation of law,[189] and in relation to a prospective consumer credit agreement, includes the prospective creditor'.

First, it should be noticed that, as with 'debtor', the definition extends to prospective creditors (see para 5.20). Second, by reason of the explicit extension to assignees,[190] the concept of creditor includes a financier to whom an assignment has been made by way of indirect financing.[191] Third, s 186 provides for the situation where goods are supplied by more than one person jointly in the following terms:

> 'Where an actual or prospective regulated agreement has two or more creditors or owners, anything required by or under this Act to be done to, or in relation to, or by, the creditor or owner shall be effective, if done to, or in relation to, or by, any one of them'.

Thus, any right conferred on the creditors may be exercised by any one of them,[192] whilst any duty cast on the creditors may also be discharged by any of them.[193]

---

185 E.g. pre-contract disclosure under s 55 (see para 9.08); personal signature of regulated agreements under s 61 (see para 9.13); the copies rules under ss 62–4 (see para 9.18); withdrawal and cancellation rights under ss 57, 60, 63 (see paras 10.26, 9.10 and 9.17); rights to information and documents under ss 77–9 (see paras 7.08 and 15.17); notices under ss 76, 87 and 98 (see para 24.28); statutory rebates under s 95 (see para 26.19A).

186 E.g. services of notices of cancellation under s 69 or termination under ss 99 or 101 (see paras 10.31, 26.05 and 26.07); early settlement under s 94 (see para 26.19); information as to the whereabouts of the goods under s 80 (see para 15.16); application to the court by the debtor or hirer under ss 129 or 132 (see paras 24.40 and 27.23). Can one act against the wishes of the other?

187 Interpretation Act 1978, s 5 and Sched 1.

188 It has been pointed out that 'and duties' departs from the HPA formulation 'or liabilities', and that the common law (see para 7.27) does not allow the assignment of duties: Goode, *Consumer Credit Law & Practice*, para 23.21; and see below, fn 190.

189 For involuntary assignment by operation of law, see para 7.27.

190 The CCA draftsman has acknowledged his misuse of the word 'assignees' because duties may not be assignable (see para 7.27): Bennion, *Consumer Credit Control* I: 920.

191 For voluntary assignments, see para 7.27, *et seq.* For factoring, see para 2.22.

192 See the other examples cited in para 5.24, fn 179, except in relation to ss 61 and 95.

193 See the examples cited in para 5.24, fn 180, except in relation to ss 80, 129 and 132.

# NEW CONCEPTS

**[5.26]** As already noted (see para 5.06), the CCA consciously introduced much new terminology. Its primary differentiation is between regulated and unregulated agreements (see para 5.13), though s 189(1) also defines a number of different sorts of agreement, e.g. conditional sale, credit sale, hire-purchase agreements.[194] Part 2 of the Act (ss 8–20) creates a number of new concepts, some of which have already been mentioned in this chapter. These include the following two key components of regulated agreements (see para 5.13). The first is consumer credit and consumer hire agreements.[195] The second is the system for exempting categories of agreement from the Act by introducing (i) a classification of almost wholly exempt agreements[196] and (ii) the partially exempt small agreements (s 17: see para 5.17). Additionally, Pt 2 also introduces a number of other important concepts (see paras 5.28–35): fixed-sum and running-account credit (s 10); restricted-use and unrestricted-use credit (s 11); debtor-creditor-supplier and debtor-creditor agreements (ss 12–13); credit-token agreements (s 14); and linked transactions (s 19). There is also the multi-concept of ancillary credit business (s 145: see para 5.36, *et seq.*). Many of these new concepts are modelled on the proposals contained in the Crowther Report (see para 5.03), and an explanation of them will be found there (see para 1.2.12).

With all these different classifications, it is not surprising that there is some overlap, where a single agreement falls simultaneously within more than one of the above categories, in which case the CCA christens it a 'multiple agreement' and deals with it in the very complicated, over-compressed and much criticised s 18 (see para 5.27). This notion of 'multiple agreement' does **not necessarily** refer to whether more than one item is supplied, e.g. a credit sale of a stereo system plus speakers. Instead, the draftsman intended this section to achieve the following two purposes:

(i) To prevent avoidance of the CCA by combining in one agreement transactions the Act intends to regulate with others it does not, e.g. contract-hire of a car with periodical maintenance included. However, in *National Westminster Bank plc v Story*,[197]

> Mr S and Miss P were joint owner-occupiers of a house from which Mr S carried on a carpentry business. In November 1986, the Bank agreed to lend a total of £35,000 on three separate credit facilities: an overdraft of £15,000 to Mr S to cover his business expenditure and secured by mortgage; a joint mortgage of £5,000 to Mr S & Miss P intended to refinance existing borrowing (separated to qualify for tax relief); and a joint loan of £15,000. On appeal, the issue was confined to the two joint loans: if they were provided under separate agreements, they were irrecoverable for non-compliance with the CCA, the then limit being £15,000.

---

194  For the definitions, see respectively paras 1.16, 1.13 and 1.24.
195  See respectively ss 8 and 15: see paras 5.19–25 and 1.19.
196  Ss 16, 16A and 16B: see paras 5.14–15A.
197  [2000] GCCR 2381, CA.

In this first case on s 18 to reach the Court of Appeal, the Court unanimously held that s 18 did not affect the common law position that the three facilities there formed part of one single agreement whose combined value fell outside the CCA.

(ii) To deal with the obvious fact that many regulated agreements will contain more than one 'parts' of an agreement and fall within more than one of the 'categories' mentioned in the Act; but s 18(1) does not define what it means by 'part' or 'category'. In *Story*, Auld LJ said *obiter*,[198]

> 'My inclination, without formally deciding the matter, is that the word 'part' in this context includes, but it is not restricted to, a facility that is different as to some of its terms from another facility granted under the same agreement or one that can stand on its own as a separate contract or bargain'.

Having held that under this test the two separate loan facilities (for £5,000 and £15,000) were separate 'parts' of the single agreement (see above), his Lordship continued, *obiter*,[199]

> 'there is then the question of whether they are placed within separate 'categories' of agreement in the [s 18] sense. My inclination here, influenced in part by the positioning of that provision in Part II of the Act, and again without needing to decide the matter, is that the word 'category' should be construed in the more narrow sense. That is, it applies to different 'categories' within Part II of the Act rather than as between every type of agreement for which the Act, in its various Parts, provides its own legal regime'.

## Part 2 Concepts

[5.27] **Multiple agreements**. According to its draftsman, s 18 is designed as an anti-avoidance and clarifying provision;[200] but unfortunately its drafting has caused much academic controversy. Under s 18(1), a 'multiple agreement' is one whose terms, as a matter of substance (not form), are such as:

'(a) to place a part of it within one category of agreement mentioned in this Act, and another part of it within a different category of agreement so mentioned, or within a category of agreement not so mentioned, or

(b) to place it, or a part of it, within two or more categories of agreement so mentioned'.

This highly compressed definition is not directed to whether the parties have drawn up their agreement on separate pieces of paper, nor does it refer to the layout of agreement. Instead, it relates to the legal effect of an agreement. It will be noted that s 18(1) contains two paragraphs which may be applied cumulatively so that an agreement creates the following four, perhaps overlapping, situations:[200]

198 At 2390. Bennion argues that the CA should have held this to be a multiple agreement within s 18: *Consumer Credit Control*, Release 50. For difficulties with payment protection insurance (see para 24.44), see Guest and Lloyd, *Encyclopedia of Consumer Credit Law*, para 2-019(I).
199 At 2390. In referring to s 19, the Report is clearly mistaken. Bennion argues that the restriction to Pt II categories is also mistaken: *Consumer Credit Control*, Release 50; and *Ocwen Ltd v Coxall* [2004] Unreported, Cty Crt.
200 Bennion, *Consumer Credit Control*, Release 49.

*Case 1: s 18(1)(a), first portion*. Part A of the agreement is within one CCA category, whilst Part B is within a different CCA category, e.g. two loan facilities under a regulated loan, one part of which (Part A) is to pay off existing indebtedness (restricted-use credit) and another part (Part B) which the borrower may spend as he likes (unrestricted-use credit).

*Case 2: s 18(1)(a), second portion*. Part C of the agreement is within a CCA category, whilst Part D is within a non-CCA category, e.g. a furnished letting;[201] bank savings account with overdraft facility (see Sched 2, Example 18); a credit card with points;[202] goods sold on credit sale with an extended warranty (see para 17.09).

*Case 3: s 18(1)(b), first portion*. The whole of the agreement is within two or more disparate[203] CCA categories, e.g. a single regulated loan may be restricted-use and debtor-creditor credit.

*Case 4: s 18(1)(b), second portion*. Part of the agreement is within two or more disparate[203] CCA categories, e.g. one of two loan facilities under a regulated loan is restricted-use and debtor-creditor credit.

Not every multiple agreement within s 18(1) is affected by that section, e.g. *Case 2*: so, in *Dimond v Lovell*, where an accident hire agreement amounted to a regulated consumer credit agreement (Part C: see para 5.21), the House of Lords held that, even though the agreement also amounted to a consumer hiring (Part D: see para 1.19), because it was exempt consumer hiring s 18 had 'no relevance' (*per* Lord Hoffmann at 905b).

On the other hand, *Cases 1, 3 and 4* will be affected by s 18. For these situations, s 18(2) provides as follows:

'Where a part of an agreement falls within subsection (1), that part shall be treated for the purposes of this Act as a separate agreement'.

Thus, in *Case 1* Part A of the agreement must obey the CCA rules for restricted-use credit, whereas Part B must follow those for unrestricted-use credit;[204] but there is some doubt as to how far this notion of treating each Part 'as a separate agreement' should be taken.[205] However, in *Story* (set out at para 5.26) s 18(2) had no effect because both the loan facilities were for fixed-sum, unrestricted-use credit.[206] For *Cases 3 and 4*, s 18(3) explains:

'Where an agreement falls within subsection (1)(b), it shall be treated as an agreement in each of the categories in question, and this Act shall apply to it accordingly'.

It has already been seen that a regulated consumer credit agreement will commonly fall within more than one category, e.g. *Case 3*: if so, s 18(3) is saying that it must comply with all the CCA requirements for each of them, e.g. all the requirements for restricted-use credit and all the requirements for debtor-creditor agreements. An

---

201  The lease of premises is outside the Act, whilst the lease of furniture is within it: see s 18(6).
202  As to a credit card, see para 2.28; and as to points, see para 15.18.
203  *Aliter*, if all the Parts fall within the same category, e.g. *Story* (see below).
204  For difficulties, see Guest and Lloyd, *Encyclopedia of Consumer Credit Law*, para 2-019(ii).
205  E.g. does it apply to documentation matters arising during the course of the agreement (see para 15.16); or exempt agreements (see para 5.15)?
206  Decision of fact by the Judge and accepted by the CA. Criticised by MacDonald (1999) 149 NLJ 962 at 964.

important instance of this for our purposes is a three-party credit card.[207] Special provision is made by s 18 for both the following cases: by s 18(4) for apportionment, e.g. in calculating the 'total price' to determine if there are 'protected goods' (see para 24.36); and by s 18(5) for running-account credit where the credit limit is temporarily exceeded (s 10(2): see para 5.28).

The OFT have canvassed reform[208] and the matter is under active DTI consideration following the 2003 White Paper, *Fair, Clear and Competitive* (see para 3.78).

**[5.28] Running-account credit**. It may be a positive advantage to a creditor (see para 5.25) to persuade a debtor to undertake revolving credit (see para 2.19) rather than a fixed amount of credit: he may thereby hope for repeat business without further separate credit checks.[209] Additionally, the creditor may take a personal security, e.g. guarantee (see para 25.08), but is unlikely to have any real security.[210] Section 10 seeks to ensure that both types of credit fall within the Act as being consumer credit (see para 5.19).

(a) *Revolving credit.* According to amended[211] s 10(1)(a):

> 'running-account credit[212] is a facility under a consumer credit agreement whereby the debtor is enabled to receive from time to time (whether in his own person, or by another person) from the creditor or a third party cash, goods and services (or any of them) to an amount or value such that, taking into account payments made by or to the credit of the debtor, the credit limit (if any) is not at any time exceeded'.

Whilst the notion looks complicated, the basic idea is simple, comprehending lines of credit, such as an ordinary bank overdraft,[213] some credit card arrangements, e.g. Master or Visa cards, and store and mail-order budget accounts (see para 2.19). It does not require that at any particular time the debtor be indebted: indeed, he may even be in credit; but the credit facility continues until terminated by the parties. However, it is crucial that the debtor is 'enabled to receive from time to time' credit, etc; that is, that the debtor 'has a facility on which he can draw at pleasure'.[214] For the special rules applicable to running-account credit, see para 7.08.

(b) *Fixed amount credit.* According to amended[212] s 10(1)(b):

> 'fixed-sum credit is any other facility under a consumer credit agreement whereby the debtor is enabled to credit (whether in one amount or by instalments)'.

---

207 See Sched 2, Example 16; and para 7.10. For difficulties, see Guest and Lloyd, *Op. cit.*, para 2-019(iii).

208 OFT Discussion Paper on *Multiple Agreement and section 18* (1995) Chap 7. Amendment of the Regulations, rather than the Act, has been supported: (1996) 50 CC5/29. As to difficulties with flexible mortgages, see Vaughan (2000) 55 CC 3/12.

209 There will, of course, be no need to credit score a new proposal, the creditor normally having the advantage of behavioural scoring: see generally, para 8.35. It also creates opportunities for enclosing mail advertising with (monthly) statements.

210 For real security, see para 25.01. It would seem possible to combine running account credit with a retention of title by way of conditional sale: *Armour v Thyssen* (set out at para 20.28); but not in respect of regulated agreements ((1985) 40 CC 2/21).

211 For criticism of the expression 'running-account credit', see Goode, *Consumer Credit Law & Practice*, para 25.24.

212 S 10 of the 1974 Act was amended by s 5 of the 2006 Act.

213 See Sched 2, Example 18 (authorised overdraft). As to overdrafts, see generally, paras 2.17 and 2.23, item 1.

214 Goode, *Op. cit.*, para 25.25. Does it include a milk account, or a newspaper account?

Into this category fall hp, conditional sales, credit sales, check and voucher trading and personal loans.[215] Even an overdraft may occasionally be fixed amount credit—as when the right to draw is exhausted; but, merely because the amount of the first loan is known, that will not necessarily render a facility fixed sum,[216] e.g. balance transfers. Unlike running-account credit, when the fixed-sum debt is paid off, the agreement normally terminates automatically, e.g. unauthorised overdraft (Sched 2, Example 17). Moreover, as fixed-sum credit is the residuary category, any consumer credit agreement which is not running-account must be fixed sum. This may have some unexpected results: so in *Dimond v Lovell* (set out at para 5.13), where an uncertain amount of credit was to be repaid all at once, the Court of Appeal held that it was fixed-sum credit.[217]

*The credit limit.* The 1974 Act dealt separately with running-account credit because, unlike fixed-sum credit, the amount of credit which will be utilised by the debtor is not known at the outset of an arrangement so that the Act could only refer to a credit ceiling. Section 10(2) provides that:

> 'in relation to running-account credit, 'credit limit' means, as respects any period, the maximum debit balance which, under the credit agreement, is allowed to stand on the account during that period, disregarding any term of the agreement allowing that maximum to be exceeded merely temporarily'.

Since the 2006 Act, the CCA has been applicable to private credit agreements without credit limit, but retained a credit ceiling for agreements by small businesses (see para 5.22). In the case of small businesses, by amended s 10(3)(a), running-account credit may amount to a consumer credit agreement where the credit limit does not exceed the amount specified in s 16B(1) (see para 5.19); or only does so temporarily.[218] As business credit is outside the scope of this work, there is no need to examine the complicated anti-avoidance devices found in s 10(3)(b).[219]

**[5.29]  Restricted use/unrestricted use credit**. A person who borrows cash may well be doing so to meet existing commitments, which will put him in a particularly vulnerable position. To offer him extra protection (see below), s 11 sets about identifying him by creating another dichotomy within the category of regulated consumer credit agreements (see para 5.19), this one being directed to the mechanism of payment.

1.  *Restricted use [RU] credit.* According to s 11(1):

> 'A restricted-use credit agreement is a regulated consumer credit agreement—
>
> (a)  to finance a transaction between the debtor and the creditor, whether forming part of that agreement or not, or
>
> (b)  to finance a transaction between the debtor and a person (the 'supplier') other than the creditor, or
>
> (c)  to refinance any existing indebtedness of the debtor's, whether to the creditor or another person, and 'restricted-use credit' shall be construed accordingly'.

---

215  For hp, see para 1.24; for conditional sale, see para 1.16; for credit sales, see para 1.13; for check and voucher trading, see para 2.23, item 2; and for personal loans, see para 2.17.

216  *Goshawk etc Ltd v Bank of Scotland* [2006] 2 All ER 610, at paras 91–103.

217  See [1999] JBL 452 at 459–60. Point conceded before HL.

218  Ss 10(2), 18(5) and 82(4); Sched 2, Examples 22, 23.

219  See Macleod, *Consumer Sales Law*, 1st edn, para 5.28.

The above three categories of RU credit are as follows:

(a) Both types of vendor credit (see Sched 2, Example 10; and para 2.19).

(b) This category is meant to deal with lender credit (see paras 2.20–28) and therefore introduces a third character, whom it terms the 'supplier'.[220] All three forms of lender credit can amount to RU credit within this category, provided only that the creditor controls the application of the credit, as by paying the supplier direct, e.g. in direct financing[221] or by furnishing the debtor with a redeemable token.[222] Perhaps the commonest example is the three-party credit card: it has always been accepted that s 11(1)(b) compre-hended the situation where there were three parties because the card-issuer also acted as merchant-acquirer (see para 2.28); but in *OFT v Lloyds TSB Bank plc* (set out at para 16.11) the Court of Appeal held that s 11(1)(b) also extended to the four-party situation where the card-issuer and merchant-acquirer were separate persons, on the grounds that in both situations 'the purpose of the credit agreement is to provide the customer with the means to pay for goods or services' (para 56).

(c) Refinancing (see para 7.04A), whether by way of rescheduling an existing debt between the parties[223] or not, e.g. Sched 2, Example 13. This category does not include credit hire because the charges are payable and the indebtedness created under the same transaction as provided for post-ponement of the time of payment.[224] Nor does it necessarily include paying off the arrears of any earlier loan.[225]

2. *Unrestricted-use [UU] credit.* According to s 11(2), this is 'a regulated consumer credit agreement not falling within subsection (1)'. The obvious example of this category is where money is passed to the debtor, whether by cash or cheque, e.g. Sched 2, Example 8, and whether or not the agreement under which it is passed is for fixed-sum credit.[226] A credit card can be RU or UU, depending on how it is used: if it is used to purchase goods, there is RU credit; but if it is used to obtain money, there is UU credit (see Sched 2, Example 16; and para 7.10).

However, to some extent the foregoing three categories of RU credit are overridden by the provision that (s 11(3)):

> 'an agreement does not fall within subsection (1) if the credit is in fact provided in such a way as to leave the debtor free to use it as he chooses, even though certain uses would contravene that or any other agreement'.

---

220  E.g. *Bank of Scotland v Truman* [2005] EWHC 583, at paras 80, 83 and 85. See the definition of 'supplier' in s 189(1): set out at para 5.34. Particularly significant for indirect financing, the Act confirms that it is irrelevant that, when the regulated agreement is first made, the identity of the eventual creditor may be unknown to the debtor (s 11(4)).

221  See para 2.21. Or perhaps to finance the provision of cash: see Guest and Lloyd, *Encyclopedia of Consumer Credit*, para 2-012.

222  Tokens may be redeemable only at designated outlets, as in check or voucher trading: see para 2.23, item 2.

223  E.g. *National Westminster Bank plc v Story* (see above).

224  *Dimond v Lovell* (set out at para 5.13), where the transaction was held to fall within s 11(1)(a).

225  See *McGinn v Grangewood Securities* (see para 8.24).

226  What of a cashback (as to which, see para 8.13A)?

In *National Westminster Bank plc v Story* (set out at para 5.26) the debtor expected that the £5,000 would be used to discharge his existing indebtedness; but the first instance Judge held that there was no term of the contract to that effect. So Auld LJ said that what mattered was the ordinary common law test of contractual intention (see para 11.07): whatever the debtor expected, because there was no contractual term restricting his use of the £5,000, it was unrestricted-use credit. Thus, the crucial thing is whether the debtor (see para 5.24) is **entitled** to get his hands on the money:[227] if he does, the transaction does not amount to RU credit even though it appears to fall within one of the three categories.

The effect of the RU/UU dichotomy. This is particularly relevant in deciding whether a credit facility can be canvassed: an RU facility can be canvassed with a special licence (s 23(1): see para 6.14) whereas a UU facility may not be canvassed in any circumstances (s 49: see para 7.07). There are also a number of situations where special treatment is given to RU credits: these include linked transactions (s 19(1)(c): see para 5.31), land mortgages (s 58(2): see para 25.23), cancellation[228] and exclusions from Pt V of the CCA (s 74(2): see para 9.07). The dichotomy also figures substantially in the debtor-creditor-supplier/debtor-creditor concepts (see para 5.32, *et seq.*).

**[5.30] Credit-tokens.**[229] The extension of credit by way of credit cards or check trading (see respectively para 2.28 and para 15.17) led to the creation of yet another category of consumer credit agreement (see para 5.19). Section 14(1) christens them 'credit tokens' and explains that:

'A credit-token is a card, check, voucher, coupon, stamp, form, booklet or other document or thing given to an individual by a person carrying on a consumer credit business, who undertakes—

(a)  that on the production of it (whether or not some other action is also required)[230] he will supply cash, goods and services (or any of them) on credit, or

(b)  that where, on the production of it to a third party (whether or not any other action is also required),[230] the third party supplies cash, goods[231] and services (or any of them), he will pay the third party for them (whether or not deducting any discount or commission), in return for payment[232] to him by the individual'.

'In essence a credit-token is a piece of paper or plastic which unlocks the door to credit'[233] and is 'given to an individual by a consumer credit business'.[234] Whilst widely defining what items might amount to credit tokens, to fall within s 14(1) the

---

227  E.g. overdrafts, whether of a fixed sum (Sched 2, Example 17) or running account (Sched 2, Example 18).

228  Ss 69(2) and 71: see respectively paras 10.32; 10.33.

229  See the recommendation of the Crowther Report, paras 6.12.1–12 and 6.13.10–11.

230  E.g. signing a receipt; entering a PIN (see para 2.24).

231  For 'goods', see s 189(1): see paras 2.01–2. Does 'goods' include a credit token, so arguably bringing credit tokens within consumer hirings (see para 1.19)?

232  'Payment' includes tender: s 189 (1). See generally, para 23.12 *et seq.*

233  Goode, *Consumer Credit Law & Practice*, para 25.68. It has been argued that the following are not credit tokens: (a) an application form (see para 8.35; Goode, *ibid*); (b) a cheque form, even where there is an overdraft agreement (Guest and Lloyd, *Consumer Credit Law*, para 2.015). *Sed quaere?*

234  For 'individual' and 'consumer credit business', see paras 5.24 and 6.12. But a 'credit token' need not be regulated, though a 'credit token agreement' (see below) must be: Guest and Lloyd, *ibid*.

giver of that item must on its 'production' 'undertake' either (a) or (b) above; but, as the agreement may be prospective (see para 5.20), there does not need to be a binding contract (see para 10.01). In *Elliott v DG*:[235]

> Retailers by way of an advertising scheme sent out unsolicited plastic cards, each expressed to be a credit card available for immediate use upon the recipient signing it. They did not disclose that, before honouring the card, a customer would have to enter into a credit sale with them and sign a direct debit mandate.

The retailers were convicted of supplying an unsolicited credit token,[236] notwithstanding that the 'undertaking' was intended to be conditional and to amount only to an invitation to treat which had no contractual force. A successful defence would have meant that the card amounted to a false statement as to the provision of services within s 14 of the TDA (as to which, see para 4.15).

Section 14 is designed to deal with both two- and-three party credit transactions (see para 2.19, *et seq.*); and it is expressed to be applicable whether the user presents the card to a person, or a machine (s 14(4)), e.g. an ATM (see para 2.24).

(a) *Two-party transactions* (s 14(1)(a)), where the issuer is the supplier. These will include store budget accounts (see para 2.19) and cards enabling the holder to draw cash from a bank dispenser (see Sched 2, Example 16). However, it may not include a cheque guarantee card, because of the express reference in the section to credit.[237]

(b) *Three-party transactions* (s 14(1)(b)), where the holder uses a card issued by a financier to obtain cash, goods or services from a third party. Section 14(1)(b) does not mention *credit* but s 14(3) deems him to obtain credit within s 9(1) when the item is supplied.[238] This had led to differing academic views as to whether or not a requirement of credit is to be read into s 14(1)(b):[239] this in turn has caused disagreement as to whether cash cards, debit cards, digital money and gift tokens (see paras 2.24–5 and para 15.18) can fall within s 14(1)(b) when there is no previously agreed credit arrangement.[240]

Credit token agreements (see para 7.10) will, of course, be subject to all the ordinary rules applicable to regulated agreements, plus some additional rules applicable even if there is no agreement at all (see para 7.09, *et seq.*).

**[5.31] Linked transactions**. The CCA, in interfering with freedom contract in relation to regulated agreements (see para 5.13), is drafted so that it also affects any satellite agreement. To do so, it creates in s 19 a new concept, for which it borrows[241] the expression 'linked transaction'. According to s 19(1):

---

235 [1980] 1 WLR 977, DC. Both the director and the company were prosecuted: see further, para 28.11.

236 S 51: see para 7.12. There was no offence under s 46 (see para 8.27) because the section was not in force at the time: Jones, *Credit Cards*, 40, 98.

237 Goode, *ibid*. *Contra* Guest and Lloyd, *ibid*, both citing Sched 2, Example 21. For credit generally, see para 5.12.

238 E.g. Master and Visa cards used to obtain goods (see Sched 2, Examples 3 and 16); trading checks and vouchers (see Sched 2, Example 14). As to charge cards, see Guest and Lloyd, *ibid*.

239 See Goode, *Op. cit.*, para 25.70 (yes); Guest and Lloyd, *ibid* (no).

240 See Goode, *Op. cit.*, paras 25.82–5 (no); Guest and Lloyd, *ibid* (yes)

241 The expression 'linked-on' agreement had previously been used in an entirely different context, which would now fall within s 82: see para 26.22.

'A transaction entered into by the debtor or hirer,[242] or a relative of his,[243] with any other person ('the other party'), except one for the provision of security,[244] is a linked transaction in relation to an actual or prospective regulated agreement (the 'principal agreement') of which it does not form part if . . . .'

any **one** of the three following criteria are satisfied:

(a) 'A contract entered into in compliance with a term of the principal agreement' (s 19(1)(a)), such as a contract for the maintenance of goods supplied under a credit or hire agreement. This can only be satisfied where the principal agreement is entered into first and makes the satellite agreements compulsory: it cannot extend to such contracts offered as an optional extra.

(b) Vendor or lender credit connected with the supply of goods or services, as in the case of budget accounts, loan financing or check trading: the contract for the retail supply of goods is a linked transaction if it 'is financed, or to be financed, by' that credit agreement.[245] However, this category cannot extend to direct financing, because the credit there 'forms a part' of the supply contract, and hence does not include the sale from dealer to financier.[246]

(c) This category involves three separate cases and looks rather complicated (ss 19(1)(c), (2)) but may be illustrated by the following examples:[247] where entry into a satellite agreement is **insisted** upon before the creditor or owner will enter the principal agreement; or is **suggested** by the creditor or owner; or is for a purpose **related** to the principal agreement.

The major restriction on linked transactions is to be found in s 19(3), which provides that generally[248] 'A linked transaction entered into before the making of the principal agreement has no effect until such time (if any) as that agreement is made.' Additionally, the category of a linked transaction is relevant for the following reasons: computing the total charge for credit;[249] withdrawal and cancellation;[250] rebates for early settlement (ss 95(1) and 96: see para 26.19A); to prevent the evasion of the Act by the use of security[251] or contracting out (s 113(8): see para 25.12); and unfair credit relationships (new s 140C(4)(b): see para 29.46). Although not

---

242 'Debtor' and 'hirer' are both defined by s 189(1): see respectively, paras 5.24 and 1.19.

243 See ss 184(1) and 189(1): see below, para 5.33.

244 E.g. contracts of surety, as to which see Chap 25.

245 S.19(1)(b); and *Goshawk etc Ltd v Bank of Scotland* [2006] 2 All ER 610, at para 81. It seems to follow that, if the parties agree a cash supply and only subsequently talk about credit, the cash supply is still within s 19.

246 Is this a drafting mistake? Does the reasoning necessarily prevent part-exchange goods from being supplied under a linked transaction? See the analysis of part-exchange goods, para 2.09.

247 Goode, *Consumer Credit Law & Practice*, paras 43.21–3. Particularly for the latter two, the fact that s 171(2) puts the burden of proof on the party mentioned in s 19(2), e.g. creditor, may be significant.

248 Subject to any transaction excluded by regulation: s 19(4) and the regulations made thereunder (1983 SI 1560), e.g. insurance (see para 10.32) or guarantee of goods (see para 17.09). See further, paras 10.32; 24.44 and 26.19A.

249 S 20(2): see para 8.24. As to the effect of the regulations made thereunder in narrowing the ambit of the concept of linked transactions, see Bennion [1986] JBL 294.

250 Ss 57(1) and 69(1): see respectively, paras 10.26; 10.32.

251 S 173: see para 18.11. Thus, the linked transaction cannot impose any greater liability than the regulated agreement.

expressly mentioned by the Act, linked transactions may be affected by connected-lender liability (s 75: see para 16.09), or the fact that a regulated agreement is improperly executed (s 65: see para 9.19), or terminated (s 99: see para 26.05) or otherwise discharged, e.g. for misrepresentation, or where the court exercises one of its powers under Pt IX of the Act (see para 24.27).

## Debtor-creditor-supplier/debtor-creditor agreements

**[5.32]** The Crowther Report (see para 5.03) defines a connected lender as 'one who, pursuant to a regular business relationship with one or more sellers, makes a loan which is used to buy goods or services from one such seller' (para 6.2.22). It will be observed that this definition contains two distinct elements. *First*, the 'connected' loan must be utilised to obtain goods or services. *Second*, assuming the financial accommodation (see para 5.22) is so utilised, the crucial matter is whether there is a business connection between the supplier of the goods to the consumer (the goods-supplier) and the financier. In a vendor credit situation (see para 2.19), the connection is obvious because the goods and finance are supplied by the same person; whereas in the case of lender credit (see paras 2.20, *et seq.*) it is necessary to define that business relationship, a task largely undertaken by s 187 (see below).[252] Building upon that s 187 connection, the Act seeks in ss 12 and 13 to distinguish whether a regulated agreement (see para 5.13) amounts to a connected or unconnected loan,[253] though it should be noted that the distinction is drawn between **two or three functions rather than two or three people**.[254]

(a)  *Debtor-creditor-supplier agreements* are elaborately defined by s 12 (see para 5.34). Here, the Act regards the s 187 connection as sufficient justification for interfering with the contract for the supply of goods or services by classifying that supply as a linked transaction within s 19(1)(b) (see para 5.31). This is particularly important to the goods-supplier upon withdrawal or cancellation of the regulated agreement[255] and to the financier with regard to connected-lender liability (s 75: see para 16.11).

(b)  *Debtor-creditor agreements* are likewise elaborately defined by s 13 (see para 5.35). The Crowther Report observed that 'where goods are bought for cash provided by an independent lender there is no reason to regard the sale as any different from a normal cash sale or to treat the loan as other than a normal loan' (para 6.2.24). In such a case, the pre-occupation of the Act is with the raising of the loan, and hence the prohibition on canvassing, approaching minors or supplying unsolicited credit-tokens.[256]

---

252  However, it has been held that s 187 does not define the only arrangements capable of falling within s 12(b): *OFT v Lloyds TSB Bank* (above), at para 65.

253  Additionally, the distinction between debtor-creditor-supplier and debtor-creditor agreements is significant for the following purposes: the criteria for exemption under s 16 (see para 5.15); and the disclosure requirements with regard to the formalities and formation of the agreement (see Chaps 9 and 10).

254  These definitions are a good example of the over-elaboration which detracts from the many merits of the CCA. For a diagrammatic explanation, see Bennion, *Consumer Credit Act Manual*, 3rd edn, 13.

255  Ss 57(1), 69(1): see respectively, paras 10.26 and 10.31.

256  See respectively, ss 49, 50 and 51, discussed paras 7.07, 8.33 and 7.12.

The scope of the three parties for the purposes of s 187 is extended to their 'associates'.[257] The debtor's associates include certain specified relatives[258] and also partners (s 184(2)). In the usual case, the supplier and creditor will be corporations, in which case the Act defines as an associate any interlocking company[259] and the controller of either company (s 184(4)). It has always been accepted that s 187 comprehended the MasterCard and Visa credit card schemes (see para 5.30), where there were three parties because the card-issuer also acted as merchant-acquirer (see para 2.28) and there is an 'arrangement' (usually contractual) between him and the supplier; but in *OFT v Lloyds TSB Bank plc* (set out at para 16.11) the OFT accepted before the Court of Appeal (para 61) that 'associate' in the above s 184(4) did not include a merchant acquirer in a four-party structure (see para 2.28).

**[5.33] The s 187 connection (business link).** The easiest way to understand this rather complicated concept is to bear in mind its object. It is concerned with the situation where goods or services are supplied to a debtor by two separate people as follows: the effective retailer of goods to the debtor is termed the 'supplier'; and the person who finances that supply on credit is termed the 'creditor' (see para 5.25). Section 187 defines whether the supplier and creditor are engaged in a joint venture (see para 5.33). Section 187 envisages two ways in which there may be a joint venture between them for the supply of goods or services to consumers.

1. *A pre-existing arrangement.* According to s 187(1):

   'A consumer credit agreement shall be treated as entered into under pre-existing arrangements between a creditor and a supplier if it is entered into in accordance with, or in furtherance of, arrangements[260] previously made between ... [them]'.

   Typically, this will cover the situation where a creditor has, before the appearance of the debtor, provided the supplier with a stock of his documentation.[261] This will obviously be satisfied in the case of credit cards; but does it extend to the credit card company issuing blank cheques to the consumer (as to cheques, see para 7.28)?

2. A contemplated future arrangement. According to s 187(2):

   'A consumer credit agreement shall be treated as entered into in contemplation of future arrangements between a creditor and a supplier if it is entered into in the expectation that arrangements will subsequently be made between ... [them] ... for the supply of cash, goods and services (or any of them) to be financed by the consumer credit agreement'.

---

257 S 187(4). The concept of an 'associate' is principally important for the purposes of licensing (s 25: see para 6.19).

258 Ss 184(1), (5) and 189(1), e.g. second husband of a businessman's divorced wife. The concept of a 'relative' is also important for the following purposes: linked transactions (s 19(1): see para 5.31); total charge for credit (s 20(2): see para 8.23); the return of goods on cancellation (s 72: see para 10.34); credit brokerage (see para 5.38); extortionate credit bargains (s 138(1): see para 29.41) and unfair credit relationships (new s 140B(1)(b): see para 29.47).

259 S 184(3). See the examples in Guest and Lloyd, *Encyclopedia of Consumer Credit Law*, para 2-185.

260 Does this extend to one-off transactions? And see Sched 2, Examples 8 and 16.

261 'Where the creditor is an associate of the supplier's, the consumer credit agreement shall be treated, unless the contrary is proved, as entered into under pre-existing arrangements between creditor and the supplier' (s 187(5)).

This will extend s 187 to the following credit card situation (see para 2.28): the card-holder uses his card at a retailer/merchant[262] who is not, at the time the card is issued, within the scheme, but joins it later.[263] Whilst s 187(2) refers only to 'future arrangements' for the reasons explained later (in para 5.34), it seems that 'arrangements' here refers to **credit** arrangements dealt with in s 12 (see paras 5.34-35), not **payment** arrangements between creditor and supplier referred to in s 11.[264]

By reason of s 187(3), s 187 has no application where the creditor holds himself out as willing to make payments to suppliers generally, e.g. debit and cheque guarantee cards.[265] Further, s 187(4) lists the persons between whom there must be a relationship in ss 187(1) and (2) as 'the creditor and supplier':[266] in *OFT v Lloyds TSB* (set out at para 16.11) the creditors argued that this expression did not extend in relation to credit card transactions to the merchant-acquirer in a four-party structure (at paras 61–2); but the Court of Appeal held that the words 'treated as' and 'arrangements' in ss 187(1) and (2) were wide enough to include the four-party structure.[267] There again, with the introduction of Electronic Fund Transfer (see para 2.17), the Banks were afraid that the arrangements set up to allow the operation of that system would be held to create a s 187 connection with the operator of the other terminal. Accordingly, they procured the passage of s 187(3A), which provides that:[268]

> 'Arrangements shall be disregarded for the purposes of subsections (1) and (2) if they are arrangements for the electronic transfer of funds from a current account at a bank'.

This will save banks[269] from a s 187 connection with the operator of an ATM or a retailer accepting a debit card (para 2.24): the result is that any credit arising because of an overdraft agreement will remain DC credit (see para 5.35) so that bank will escape any s 75 liability (see para 16.11) and the bank is exempted from documentation requirements by s 74(3A) (see para 9.07).

**[5.34] Debtor-creditor-supplier [DCS] agreements**. The DCS category is crucial to many important provisions of the Act, being its equivalent of Crowther's connected lender (see para 5.32). In looking for a joint venture as to the supply of goods (or services) and credit, s 12 identifies three separate types of regulated consumer credit agreement (see para 5.19, *et seq.*).

---

262 S 187(2) actually refers to a supply of cash by one other than the creditor. Is this a mistake? S 187(2) does not apply to s 12(c) (see para 5.34) and the draftsman obviously intended it to be DC credit where a credit card is used to obtain cash from an agent (see Sched 2, Example 16).

263 For an explanation of why s 187(2) is narrower than might at first sight appear, see Goode, *Consumer Credit Law & Practice*, para 25.63. *Contra* Howells, *Consumer Debt*, 8–9.

264 So that it does **not** include one-off RU agreements within s 11(1)(b) (see para 5.29), e.g. creditor promises to pay the supplier direct against his invoice, with no element of joint-venture between creditor and supplier: Goode, *Consumer Credit Law & Practice*, IIB, para 5.368.

265 See further, para 5.30; and Dobson [1988] JBL at 167.

266 S 187(4)(a). To these parties are added their associates (ss 187(4)(b) and (c): see para 5.32).

267 At paras 64–5, A similar analysis had already been applied where there were even more parties: see *Bank of Scotland v Truman* [2005] EWHC 583, at paras 94–100.

268 S 187(3A), inserted by the Banking Act 1987, s 89, e.g. a debit or cash card; see Guest and Lloyd, *Encyclopedia of Consumer Credit Law*, para 2-015.

269 Not every creditor who operates current accounts will amount to a bank: see *United Dominions Trust Ltd v Kirkwood* [1966] 2 QB 431, CA.

*Paragraph (a).* Section 12(a) covers:

> An RU[270] credit agreement to finance a transaction between the debtor[271] and the creditor, whether forming a part of that agreement or not.

This obviously comprehends all forms of vendor credit (see para 2.19), where the creditor and supplier are, of course, the same person; and it specifically deals with both variants of vendor credit, viz whether the goods and credit are supplied under a single instalment credit contract[272] or a cash sale and separate loan. Turning to lender credit, at first sight greater difficulty is caused by direct financing (see para 2.21), because of doubt as to the meaning of the word 'supplier'. The physical supplier of the goods or services to the debtor is the retailer, which might appear to take direct financing into paragraphs (b) or (c) below;[273] but the Act elsewhere makes it clear that 'creditor' for this purpose means the legal supplier,[274] from which it follows that direct financing falls within this category.[275]

*Paragraph (b).* Section 12(b) covers:

> An RU[270] credit agreement to finance a transaction between the debtor[271] and supplier and made by the creditor under a s 187 arrangement between himself and the supplier.

This paragraph appears to require the existence of three separate parties[276] and is essentially dealing with loan financing: it insists on a contract of loan[277] and a s 187 connection (see para 5.33), but also requires the creditor to make payment direct to the supplier (RU credit). Examples include credit cards used to purchase goods or services,[278] check or voucher trading and personal loans where the creditor makes out a cheque to the supplier.

*Paragraph (c).* Section 12(c) covers:

> A UU[270] credit agreement which is made by the creditor under a pre-existing arrangement between himself and the supplier[279] in the knowledge that the credit is to be used to finance a transaction between the debtor[271] and the supplier.

This is an anti-avoidance device, aimed at the situation where there is in reality a joint venture for the supply of goods (or services) within s 187 (see para 5.33), but the debtor is technically free to use the credit as he wishes (UU credit),[280] e.g. a

---

270 For RU and UU credit, see para 5.29.
271 For 'debtor', see generally, para 5.24.
272 Thus ordinary hp, conditional or credit sales within the Act will be properly described as: DCS agreements for RU fixed-sum credit within ss 10(1)(b), 11(1)(a) and 12(a). Is this degree of complication really necessary?
273 For the significance of this in relation to s 75, see para 16.12.
274 The definition of 'supplier' in s 189(1) for the purposes of s 11(1)(a) also includes his assignee (see below).
275 See Goode, *Consumer Credit Law & Practice*, para 25.48.
276 See the definition of 'supplier' in s 189(1), which for this purpose cross refers to s 11(1)(b): see para 5.29.
277 For loan financing, in general, see paras 2.23–8; and for contracts of loan, see para 7.01, *et seq.*
278 Whether there is a 3 or 4 party structure (see paras 5.32–3): see *OFT v Lloyds TSB Bank PLC* (see para 66; and para 16.11). See also Master and Barclay cards (see Sched 2, Example 16).
279 In defining 'supplier', s 189(1) here has yet another variant, this time referring back to s 12(c).
280 S 12(c) does not extend to credit agreements made in contemplation of future arrangements between creditor and supplier: for the reasons, see Goode, *Op. cit.*, para 25.50.

double-glazing company introduces the debtor to a creditor who makes an advance to the debtor for the purchase of windows (see Sched 2, Example 8).

**[5.35] Debtor-creditor [DC] agreements**. The DC category is required for a number of important provisions of the Act, being its equivalent of Crowther's 'unconnected lender' (see para 5.32). All that is really required is the absence of any joint venture between the creditor and any supplier, and thus something which is not a DCS agreement.[281] Unfortunately eschewing this simple course, s 13 identifies three[282] other types of regulated consumer credit agreement (see para 5.19, *et seq.*).

*Paragraph (a)*. Section 13(a) covers:

> An RU[283] credit agreement to finance a transaction between the debtor and the supplier[284] but not made by the creditor under a s 187 arrangement between himself and the supplier.

This comprehends the situation where the debtor searches out his own personal source of funds with which he intends to obtain goods (or services), but the creditor insists on paying the supplier direct, e.g. a personal loan. Even if there is co-incidentally an apparent s 187 connection between the creditor and supplier, the transaction is saved from that section because the creditor would be prepared to make a similar payment to any supplier (ss 187(3) and (3A): see para 5.33).

*Paragraph (b)*. Section 13(b) covers:

> An RU[283] credit agreement to refinance any existing indebtedness of the debtor's, whether to the creditor or another person.

This category deals with two situations, in neither of which does the debtor see any cash. *First*, it comprehends book transactions between debtor and creditor, as where a fixed-sum credit is converted into a running-account facility.[285] *Second*, it deals with refinancing (see para 7.04A), where a creditor agrees to take over one or more debts which a debtor already owes to third parties,[286] e.g. where the debtor transfers his credit card debts to another card issuer.

*Paragraph (c)*. Section 13(c) covers:

> A UU[283] credit which is not made by the creditor under a pre-existing arrangement between himself and the supplier[284] in the knowledge that the credit is to be used to finance a transaction between the debtor and the supplier.

This category covers all personal loans where the debtor is entitled to get his hands on the cash, so he may do with it as he pleases,[287] e.g. a bank overdraft or pledge

---

281 Goode, *Consumer Credit Law & Practice*, para 25.65. See also Guest and Lloyd, *Encyclopedia of Consumer Credit Law*, para 2-013. What should be done with a transaction which does not fit within any of the six categories of ss 12 and 13? Suppose a retailer wrongly exhibited a Visa logo?

282 What is the point of differentiating between these three categories?

283 For RU and UU credit, see para 5.29.

284 For the purposes of s 13(c), 'supplier' is defined by reference back to that provision: s 189(1). But what is to be done about the meaning of 'supplier' in s 13(a)?

285 See para 7.04A. For fixed-sum and running-account credit, see para 5.28. *Contra* a rescheduling of existing indebtedness? See Goode, *Ibid*.

286 This will amount to debt-adjusting within s 145(5): see further para 5.43.

287 S 11(3): set out at para 5.29.

(see Sched 2, Examples 8, 16, 17, 18). Does s 13(c) apply whether or not the supplier knows the credit is to be used, e.g. to buy goods?

# ANCILLARY CREDIT BUSINESSES

**[5.36/37] Introduction.** Whilst the major thrust of the CCA is to regulate the operations of creditors and owners under consumer credit and consumer hire agreements, it does not stop there. Instead, following the recommendations of the Crowther Report (see generally para 5.03), the CCA seeks to regulate a wide range of other types of business which participate in the credit and hire industry. The Act christens these others 'ancillary credit businesses', and s 145(1) (as amended) lists them:

> 'An ancillary credit business is any business[288] so far as it comprises or relates to:
>
> (a) credit brokerage[289]
>
> (b) debt-adjusting[290]
>
> (c) debt-counselling[298]
>
> (d) debt-collecting[290] or
>
> (da) debt administration[291] or
>
> (db) the provision of credit information services[291] or
>
> (e) the operation of a credit reference agency'.[292]

Note that s 145(1) places an emphasis on there being a business and s 189(2) explains that:

> 'A person is not to be treated as carrying on a particular type of business merely because occasionally he enters into transactions belonging to a business of that type'.

In *R v Marshall*,[293] the issue of when 'occasionally' becomes a 'type of business' was said to be a matter of fact and degree and not simply denote more than one transaction. A similar limitation is to be found in respect of non-commercial agreements (see para 5.18) and licensing (see para 6.12).

The types of business listed in s 145(1) are later defined in that section and must also be read in conjunction with the exceptions set out in s 146 (see paras 5.39; 5.43). All these ancillary credit businesses are subject not only to the licensing provisions (see para 6.27) but also to the CCA provisions relating to seeking business,[294]

---

288 'Business' includes a profession or trade: s 189(1), which also refers to s 189(2).

289 See para 5.38.

290 See para 5.43.

291 As inserted by ss 24(1) and 25(1) of the CCA 2006: see further, para 5.44.

292 See para 8.37, *et seq.*

293 (1989) 90 Cr App Rep 73, CA, *per* Taylor LJ at 77 (This case involved an unsuccessful prosecution for unlicensed credit-broking under ss 39 and 147(1): see para 6.28); *Hare v Schurek* [1993] CLY 456, CA. Cf. *Litchfield v Dreyfus* [1906] 1 KB 584; *Conroy v Kenny* [1999] 1 WLR 1340, CA (Moneylenders Acts).

294 Ss 151–2. See generally, paras 8.29 and 8.34.

canvassing[295] and formalities of the agreement (s 156. See generally para 9.09, *et seq.*). Additionally, there are some special rules relating to credit reference agencies[292] and one in respect of credit-brokers.[289] The 2006 Act has added two new categories for money advisers and administrators.[291]

## Credit brokerage

**[5.38] Introduction**. Of all the various types of ancillary credit business (see para 5.36), credit brokerage is probably the most important group. Pressure for the regulation of this type of business first arose in the 1960s from abuses by mortgage brokers operating in the second mortgage field.[296] The Crowther Report suggested a wider system of control for all persons carrying on business as brokers or other agents in connection with the making of consumer loans, whether or not connected with mortgages (para 6.4.25). The CCA went one better, and also included hire transactions. The result is most retailers and other dealers in consumer durables who do not carry their own credit rank as credit-brokers.[297] Thus, the prime mover in the retail supply of goods on credit or hire[298] will usually be a credit-broker (see para 5.39). He will require a category C standard licence[299] and be subject to several controls (see para 16.19). Unlicensed credit-broking attracts severe penalties.[300] Additionally, the express terms of the contract between the credit-broker and consumer may be unfair.[301]

**[5.39] The definition**. According to s 145(2) (as amended), subject to certain exceptions:[302]

'Credit brokerage is the effecting of introductions—

(a) of individuals desiring to obtain credit—[303]

    (i) to persons carrying on business to which this sub-paragraph applies,[304] or

    (ii) in the case of an individual desiring to obtain credit to finance the acquisition or provision of a dwelling occupied or to be occupied by himself or his relative,[305] to any person carrying on a business in the course of which he provides credit secured on land, or

(b) of individuals desiring to obtain goods on hire to persons carrying on businesses to which this paragraph applies,[306] or

(c) of individuals desiring to obtain credit, or to obtain goods on hire, to other credit-brokers'.

---

295 Ss 153–4. See generally, para 7.05, *et seq.*
296 See the Crowther Report, paras 2.4.47–53 and 6.4.22–4; and below, para 5.37.
297 Bennion, *Consumer Credit Manual*, 3rd edn, 150.     298 See Sched 2, Example 2.
299 See para 6.15. Is it of any legal effect for the creditor to require the broker to warrant that he is licensed?
300 (a) it is an offence under s 39—see para 6.28; (b) the agreement for the broker's services may be unenforceable under s 148—see para 6.27; (c) the credit agreement he introduces may be unenforceable under s 149—see para 6.28.
301 OFT, *UCT Bulletin No. 23*, case 38 and Annex B; *No. 29*, p 32; and see below, paras 11.15 and 11.19.
302 Ss 146(5) and (5A): see para 5.41.
303 For 'individuals' and 'credit', see respectively, paras 5.24 and 5.21.
304 This category is explained in s 145(3): see para 5.40.
305 For 'relative', see para 5.33.     306 This category is explained in s 145(4): see para 5.40.

This definition is complicated because it attempts to ensure that it catches all the desired categories of broker, but none of the ones it wishes to exclude: whilst primarily directed to introductions of agreements regulated by the CCA, it also catches some exempt agreements and certain other types of unregulated agreement. In essence, this form of ancillary credit business (see para 5.36) consists in making a business (see para 5.37) of effecting introductions (see para 5.41), an activity which may be broken down as follows:

1.  *The individual consumer introduced.* First, it is necessary to have an 'individual' (see para 5.24) who desires to obtain credit of any kind (see para 5.21), or to obtain goods on hire (see para 1.19). It should be noted that it is irrelevant whether or not the individual is consciously looking for credit—he may simply be looking for goods or services and not have considered the means of payment.

2.  *The credit or hire trader* to whom he is introduced (see para 5.40).

3.  *The intermediary* (credit-broker) effecting the introduction (see para 5.41).

**[5.40] The credit or hire trader**. Under the above seemingly unnecessarily complicated s 145(2) (as amended), introductions of an individual will only fall within the definition of credit-brokerage (see para 5.39) if they are introductions to a person carrying on at least one of the following categories of business:

1.  *A consumer credit business.*[307] The most common example is where a shopkeeper asks a finance company to finance a purchase by his customer under a regulated consumer credit agreement.[308]

2.  *An exempt DCS agreement business* (s 145(2)(a)(ii)). This is defined by s 145(3)(b) as a business which comprises or relates to exempt consumer credit agreements, otherwise than short-term credit (see para 5.15). The effect is that, whilst the credit trader who only enters exempt agreements largely escapes the Act (see para 5.15), a credit-broker who makes a business of introducing individuals to such traders is caught by the CCA, e.g. introductions to low-cost credit.

3.  *A mortgage to purchase a dwelling-house* granted by a mortgagee who does not have a s 16 exemption.[309] As such first mortgages have been removed to the FSA, there would appear to be little scope for this provision.[310]

4.  *An agreement with a foreign element.*[311] Caught under this anti-avoidance device may be introductions to foreign creditors, e.g. in Dublin, in circumstances

---

307 Ss 145(2)(a)(i), 145(3)(a). For consumer credit businesses, see para 6.12. It has been suggested that, because of the reference to 'persons' in s 145(2)(a)(i), introductions channelled through a single creditor are not credit-broking: Guest and Lloyd, *Encyclopedia of Consumer Credit*, para 2-146. *Sed quaere?*

308 For a debate as to whether this category extends to unregulated agreements, see Guest and Lloyd, *ibid*. *Contra* where a private supplier makes such a request **direct** to a financier, though not a 'private transaction' (explained in *Stoneleigh Finance Ltd v Phillips* [1965] 1 QB 537, CA).

309 S 145(2)(a)(ii). Compare the negative licensing power of the Director with regard to estate agents to be found in the Estate Agents Act 1979: see para 6.04.

310 See Goode, *Consumer Credit Law & Practice*, para 48.19.

311 Ss 145(2)(a)(i) and 145(3)(c), as amended; 145(4)(b). Little scope is seen for this provision: Goode, *ibid*, para 48.18.

under which, had the creditor been resident in England, he would have been carrying on a consumer credit business.

5. *A consumer hire business,*[312] except for an exempt consumer hire agreement.[313] For example, where an electrical dealer arranges the hire of a TV set from a rental company.[308]

6. *Another credit-broking business* (s 145(2)(c)). This is an anti-avoidance provision: a person who would be a credit-broker if he introduced the individual directly to the creditor or owner cannot avoid that label simply by doing such business indirectly through another credit-broker.[314]

**[5.41] The intermediary and his introductions.** A middleman (intermediary) will not be a credit-broker within the meaning of the Act (see para 5.39) unless he carries on a business of credit-brokerage, so that introductions by non-business friends or relatives will not do. The Act does not require the credit-broker to have a s 187 relationship (see para 5.33), but simply refers to 'the effecting of introductions' between an individual consumer (see para 5.39) and a credit or hire trader (see para 5.40), whether the consumer is introduced to the trader, or *vice versa*.[315] The sense of the provision is that the intermediary must not be the employee of either of the other two, but an independent conduit pipe, acting on his own account.[316] However, the introduction could be to another company in the same group.[317] The introduction may be direct or indirect: the Act does not specify how a direct introduction may be effected, e.g. by letter; or the introduction may be effected indirectly through another credit-broker (see para 5.40). Further, it should be noted that the individual must be introduced to the source of credit or hire: it follows that it is not credit-broking for a retailer simply to advertise credit or hire facilities, or even to stock the forms of the creditor or owner; but his forwarding a completed proposal form to the creditor or owner will amount to credit-broking.[318]

The Act (amended s 146) specially exempts some particular categories of intermediary:

1. *Lawyers involved in contentious business.* The difficulty here is for a lawyer wishing to rely on this category rather than a group licence (see para 6.16) to be certain at the outset that the matter he takes on will be contentious (s 146(1)–(4)).

2. *Housewife canvassers.* The foregoing definition would catch the army of housewives who, armed with a mail order catalogue, solicit business from neighbours and friends (see para 8.19). The Crowther Report recommended that they should be exempt even if carrying on a part-time business (para 6.4.20). Accordingly, s 146(5) provides that

---

312 s 145(2)(b), (4)(a). For consumer hire businesses, see para 6.12.
313 s 145(4), as inserted by s 5(4) of the CCA 2006. As to such exempt hirings, see para 5.14.
314 *Hicks v Walker* [1984] CLY 555, DC.
315 Goode, *Consumer Credit Law & Practice*, para 48.34.
316 Does s 146(5)(a) support or detract from this?
317 Guest and Lloyd, *Encyclopedia of Consumer Credit*, para 2-146. Or perhaps an in-house franchise (see para 1.07) offering business to his franchisor?
318 *Brookes v Retail Credit Cards Ltd* [1986] CLY 370, DC (discussed [1986] JBL 234; 40 CC3/12).

'For the purposes of section 145(2), introductions effected by an individual by canvassing off trade premises either debtor-creditor-supplier agreements falling within section 12(a) or regulated consumer hire agreements shall be disregarded if—

(a) the introductions are not effected by him in the capacity of an employee,[319] and

(b) he does not by any other method effect introductions falling within section 145(2)'.

Leaving aside consumer hire agreements, it should be noticed that the exemption is restricted to canvassing off trade premises[320] the supply of goods under DCS agreements within s 12(a): it does not exempt canvassing goods on trade premises, nor DC loans anywhere (see para 5.35); and with regard to goods, it does not save DCS agreements within s 12(b) or (c).[321]

3.  *Creditors, owners or dealers.* The object of this exemption is to save from the categories of debt-adjusting, debt-counselling, debt-collecting or debt administration (see paras 5.43–4) one who is already licensable under other provisions of the CCA as being: (i) the creditor or owner under the regulated agreement; or (ii) who in a directly financed transaction (see para 2.21) collects instalments under that agreement by reason of being the supplier of the goods or services, or credit-broker; or (iii) the canvasser (see para 7.06).[322]

4.  *An authorised person under the FSMA.* It is not credit-broking to introduce an individual consumer to a person who under the FSMA (see para 3.02) is an authorised person or qualifying broker.[323]

## Other ancillary credit businesses

**[5.42] Debt collectors and advisers.** There are a number of firms who make a business of collecting the debts of third parties, perhaps as an adjunct to other business, e.g. a credit reference agency (see para 8.37) or a firm specialising in repossessions (see para 24.23). Sometimes, the debt collector will act as agent for the creditor, e.g. trade protection societies, perhaps collecting on a 'no collection, no fee' basis, perhaps managing sales ledgers for creditors, tracing absconding debtors ('gone-aways'),[324] perhaps conducting legal action on behalf of creditors. In other cases, once a debt has reached a certain stage of default, it may be sold by

---

319  This exemption may also be available to some self-employed direct salesmen who would otherwise require their own credit-broking licence.

320  Ss 48, 153 and 189(1): see para 7.06. The words 'off trade premises' would appear to be tautologous; and the limitation to 'canvassing' leaves the housewife unprotected either when she is (a) invited to visit her customers in their own homes, or (b) taking orders in her own home: see Dobson (1980) 130 NLJ 528.

321  As to DCS agreements, see para 5.34. Hence, it cannot save agents for check traders. *Contra* Goode, *Op. cit.*, para 48.33.

322  Under s 146(6)(as amended) and new s 146(7).

323  s 146(5A), as inserted under the FSMA by 2003 SI 1475; 2005 SI 2967.

324  This may be controlled by access to the electoral roll (see para 3.26) and by the DPA (see para 3.28).

the creditor at a substantial discount to a specialist debt-collecting company,[325] which in practice runs a very different sort of business from the factor who buys good debts (see para 2.22). Parliament has attempted to curb the worst excesses by debt-collectors in attempting to recover debts from consumers by making them an offence under s 40 of the Administration of Justice Act 1970 (see para 24.24); and they may in future be brought within the Unfair Commercial Practices Directive (see para 4.21). Insofar as any collection document/letter may be mistaken for an official one emanating from the county court ('look-alikes'), it amounts to a specific offence under the County Courts Act 1984 (ss 135, 136). Insofar as any collection is attempted by telephone, there are another set of rules.[326] Further, such debt collectors also require a CCA licence (see para 6.11, *et seq.*), with significant further penalties for illegal loan sharks (see para 6.20). In the light of the foregoing, the Crowther Report recommended (para 6.12.15) and the CCA accepted that such activities should be regulated (see para 5.43). In practice, debtors with significant disposable income tend to be offered DMPs (see below), whilst others are sometimes recommended by debt collectors to an Individual Voluntary Arrangement (see para 19.20). The latter plans can last in excess of twenty years.[327]

*Money advice.* From those third parties who collect debts (above) may be distinguished those who merely advise consumers on the payment of debts (see para 3.16), an activity particularly relevant to overindebtedness (see para 6.10). Charitable organisations operating in this field tend to supply only advice and possibly offer to make arrangements with his creditors on the debtor's behalf,[328] under what are know as debt-management plans (DMPs),[329] e.g. CABx (see para 3.08), the Paylink Trust (set up by the Money Advice Trust: see para 3.16). On the other hand, businesses in this field sometimes go further and offer to take over from the multiple debtor responsibility for all his debts,[330] or otherwise re-finance his debts;[331] and their terms are subject to the UTCC Regulations.[332] Some of these activities fall within debt-collecting (see above) or one or more of the other existing categories of 'ancillary credit business' (see para 5.43): the significance of this is that only where the money adviser is an ancillary credit business is it subject to the

---

325 What have been termed 'dealers in the bad debts of others': the Crowther Report, para 2.6.12; see generally, para 5.03. Why is the debt worth more in the hands of the agency than in the hands of the creditor?

326 See further, para 8.16A. The OFT has issued a *Guidance Note on Debt Collection* (2003) which constitutes a set of rules which, if broken, can lead to loss of CCA licence: see [2004] 9 *Credit Today* 27; (2005) 77 *QA* 24.

327 DTI, *Improving IVAs* (2005), para 24.

328 Cranston, *Consumers and the Law*, 3rd edn, 267–8. A good first step may be to demand a copy of the regulated agreement under s 77 (see para 15.16).

329 [2003] 1 *Which?* 26; [2003] 3 *Credit Today* 15; [2006] 8 CT 22. The finance industry is adopting a Common Financial Statement. A DMP must be fair: [2005] *UTCCR Bulletin J/S, Sterling*; and para 11.15A. For a draft statutory plan to introduce approved debt management schemes, see para 27.04.

330 See Whyley and Collard, *Fee or Free?* (1999); [1999] 10 *Credit Today* 13; [2001] 5 *Credit Today* 31. Sometimes absconding with the debtor's payments: see the Crowther Report, para 6.12.14.

331 For re-financing, see para 7.04A. For an example of such activities, see the part played by Auto Finance in *Snook v London and West Riding Investments Ltd* [1967] 2 QB 786, CA: for criticism of this decision, see Cranston, *Op. cit.*, 268.

332 See OFT, *Unfair Contract Terms Bulletin No. 18*, case 8; and see para 11.12.

discipline of the OFT's powers over licensing (see para 6.15) and advertising (see para 8.20, *et seq.*).

Whether or not a money adviser is used, any default on re-scheduling of his debts by a consumer will normally be treated by the creditor as a default: this is likely to be registered with a credit bureau (see para 8.36); and it will probably result in the debtor being unable to obtain further credit under that name, except perhaps on impaired terms (called 'non-status' lending: see para 7.04A).

**[5.43] Other 1974 Act ancillary credit businesses.**[333] The activities described below were also brought within the rubric of 'ancillary credit businesses' by the CCA 1974.[334]

(i) *Debt-adjusting.* This is defined by s 145(5) as follows:

> 'Subject to section 146(6),[335] debt-adjusting is, in relation to debts due under consumer credit agreements or consumer hire agreements:
>
> (a) negotiating with the creditor or owner, on behalf of the debtor or hirer, terms for the discharge of a debt,[336] or
>
> (b) taking over, in return for payments by the debtor or hirer, his obligation to discharge a debt,[337] or
>
> (c) any similar activity concerned with the liquidation of a debt'.

The scope of debt-adjusting is wider than might appear at first sight.[338] *First*, it applies in relation to any consumer credit and consumer hire agreements, whether regulated or not.[339] *Second*, the activity need only be aimed at some rearrangement of a debt[340] arising from such agreements, whether or not the rearrangement is legally binding or the debts have yet accrued due, e.g. money advisers (see para 5.42).

(ii) *Debt-counselling.* This is defined by s 145(6) as follows:

> 'Subject to section 146(6)[335] debt-counselling is the giving of advice to debtors or hirers about the liquidation of debts due under consumer credit agreements or consumer hire agreements'.

Once more this extends to both unregulated agreements[339] and debts[340] not yet accrued due under existing agreements.[341] Not only does s 145(6) cover

---

333 See generally Goode, *Consumer Credit Law & Practice*, Pt 1, Chap 48.

334 See para 5.36. As to the types of standard licence ordinarily required, see para 6.15.

335 Under s 146(6) (as amended by s 24(3) of the 2006 Act and 2005 SI 2967), there is saved from these categories acts taken by: (i) the creditor or owner under the agreement; (ii) the supplier; or (iii) the credit-broker. Note that a housewife within s 146(5) (set out at para 5.41) is expressly saved from all these categories of ancillary credit business as well: s 146(6)(e).

336 E.g. the dealer taking goods in part-exchange (see para 2.09) who obtains a settlement figure from a finance house (see para 26.19A).

337 E.g. an overdraft granted to pay off existing obligations. Because the debtor does not pay the financier to take the assignment, s 145(5)(b) does not catch either indirect financing or the factoring of good or bad debts.

338 Goode, *Op. cit.*, para 48.36.

339 For exempt agreements, see para 5.15.

340 For debts, see para 7.04A. See also vehicle transfer agencies (see para 7.26A).

341 It does not extend to advice to those about to enter into such agreements: Goode, *Op. cit.*, para 48.39. For the formation of supply agreements, see generally, Chap 10.

persons who advise for reward,[342] but also those who do so as a 'profession', so that it would appear to extend to those organisations which offer free advice.[343]

*(iii) Debt-collecting*. This is defined by s 145(7) as follows:

> 'Subject to section 146(6),[335] debt-collecting is the taking of steps to procure payment of debts due under consumer credit agreements or consumer hire agreements'.

Again embracing unregulated agreements[339] and debts[340] not yet due, this category will comprehend not just commercial debt-collecting agencies (see para 5.42), but also professional collectors of debts owed to others,[344] e.g. repossession agents with authority to accept payments (see para 24.23); but, insofar as an activity does not amount to 'debt-collecting', it may be 'debt administration' (new s 145(7A): see para 5.44). 'Debt-collecting' does not include those who **buy** debts, e.g. factors (see para 2.22). Normally, debt collectors are not employed by the public, so that on principle the CCA should not be concerned with how they obtain their business from creditors. However, where a contract for his services is made by an unlicensed debt collector, it will be unenforceable without an OFT order (s 148): this is admittedly illogical, but is said to help re-enforce the licensing system.

**[5.44] Other 2006 Act ancillary credit businesses**. The activities described below were added to the 1974 list (see para 5.43) of 'ancillary credit businesses' by the CCA 2006 and are intended to fill gaps in the original scheme as from October 2008.

*(i)  Debt administration*. Subject to section 146(7),[345] this is defined by new s 145(7A) as follows:[346]

> 'debt administration is the taking of steps—
>
> (a)  to perform duties under a consumer credit agreement or a consumer hire agreement on behalf of the creditor or owner, or
>
> (b)  to exercise or to enforce rights under such an agreement on behalf of the creditor or owner, so far as the taking of such steps is not debt-collecting'.

This category covers two types of activity undertaken as agent on behalf of creditors or owners: paragraph (a) will apply where the agent performs **duties** which statute places on the creditor or owner, e.g. to supply documentation when the credit or hire transaction is set up (see Chaps 9 and 10) and subsequently (see para 15.16); and paragraph (b) will extend to the situation

---

342  E.g. solicitors, accountants, bankers, fee-charging debt counsellors. There are exemptions for the legal profession whilst engaged in contentious business: ss 146(1)–(4).

343  By reason of the definition of 'business' in s 189(1): Goode, *Ibid*. E.g. CABx (see para 3.08); neighbourhood law centres (see para 3.16); money advisers (see para 5.42). Group licences have been issued to CABx and Age Concern.

344  E.g. solicitors, receivers. Group licences for debt-collecting have been issued to solicitors. For the separate litigation exemption, see above, fn 337. A debt-collecting licence is not needed by one who was the credit-broker for a debt: (1992) 13 CCA News 5/11. See generally, [2000] 7 *Credit Extra*.

345  The exemption contained in new s 146(7) (as inserted by CCA 2006, s 24(4)), saves from debt administration the same persons who are saved from debt-adjusting by s 146(6): para 5.43.

346  As inserted by CCA 2006, s 24(2).

where the agent exercises or enforces some **right** short of debt-collecting, e.g. sending letters.[347]

(ii) *Credit information services.* These are businesses who help consumers to locate and correct records relating to their financial standing held by credit reference agencies (see para 8.36). By new ss 145(7B),[348] a person who would usually already be licensable under the CCA[349] provides 'a credit information service' if on behalf of an individual[350] he either takes any of the following steps, or gives advice to an individual in relation to the taking of such steps with a view (new s 145(7C)):[348]

'(a) to ascertaining whether a credit information agency (other than that person himself if he is one) holds information which is, or which the agency believes to be, relevant to the financial standing of an individual;

(b) to ascertaining the contents of such information held by such an agency;

(c) to securing the correction of, the omission of anything from, or the making of any other kind of modification of, such information so held; or

(d) to securing that such an agency which holds such information—

(i)   stops holding it; or

(ii)  does not provide it to another person'.

Whilst individual consumers already have a statutory right to insist that an inaccurate credit record relating to them be corrected,[351] where a credit information agency engages in sloppy or undesirable practices generally, the OFT may by reason of this new category use the licencing system to require improvement (see para 6.23A), e.g. credit repair firms (see para 27.03).

---

347 The Minister does not intend this to extend to retailers who retain cards on the instructions of card-issuers ((2005–6) HC Standing Committee D, cols.77–8) and does not believe that it does so ((2005–6) HC, R3, col.1028).

348 As inserted by CCA 2006, s 25(2).

349 By new s 145(7D), that person will usually be carrying on a consumer credit or consumer hire business (see para 6.12); but it also extends to some types of exempt agreement (see para 5.14).

350 For 'individual', see para 5.24.

351 Under the CCA and the DPA: see paras 8.36–8.

# CHAPTER 6

# LICENSING

## INTRODUCTION[1]

[6.01] This chapter is concerned with the use of administrative regulation to attain consumer protection. Even assuming all the ordinary consumer protection rules are enforced,[2] there are always likely to be situations where a trader may make a net profit by ignoring the rules and paying any fine or damages. Of course, there is a general power for the Attorney-General to seek an injunction to restrain persistent breaches of commercial law;[3] Pt 8 of the EA grants the OFT a similar power in respect of some breaches of both criminal and civil law (see paras 6.06–8); and the subsequent proliferation of ombudsmen to oversee various parts of commerce is intended to meet similar needs (see para 3.25). However, at best such proceedings are likely to remain a stable-bolting exercise, making no attempt to weed out the unscrupulous trader before he harms consumers. By contrast,[4] the technique of licensing has the advantage that it can be set up so that such traders may be precluded from lawfully trading before consumers can be harmed (see para 6.02). As always, there is the dilemma that too Draconian controls may simply divert consumer demand into the arms of illegal traders (see para 6.20).

[6.02] **Licensing**. For centuries, governments have used licensing as a technique for controlling the activities of their citizens, though its efficacy is in part dependent on the availability of resources to operate it.[5] Frequently, the objectives of a licensing system are economic, or a mixture of economic and political: for instance, licences to dispense NHS prescriptions (see paras 1.07 and 4.29); photocard licences for motor vehicles, issued by the Driving Licence Agency (DVLA: see generally para 4.37), this last being a useful identity check frequently used when granting retail credit (see para 8.35). The holding of markets and fairs is controlled in part by custom and the common law and in part by statute.[6] Sometimes, licences are a form of planning control, as with the licensing of public markets, e.g. car boot sales,[7] street traders,[8]

---

1   See generally Cartwright, *Consumer Protection and the Criminal Law* (2001) 41–4.
2   See the general protections offered by statutes in Chap 4; the special statutory protections in respect of consumer credit in Chap 5; and the rules of civil law enumerated throughout.
3   *Att Gen v Harris* [1961] 1 QB 74, CA; and see generally, para 29.39.
4   For a discussion of the advantages of licensing, see Borrie, *The Development of Consumer Law and Policy*, 90–97.
5   See generally, Goode, *Consumer Credit Law & Practice*, para 27.1; Cranston, *Consumers and the Law*, 3rd edn, 449.
6   See Hill (1985) 5 Legal Studies 320; e.g. Hereford Market Act 2003. Many of the private rights to hold markets have passed to local authorities; and the others are subject to planning permission. As to what is a market, see *Kingston upon Hull CC v Greenwood* (1984) 82 LGR 586; *Manchester Cty Council v Walsh* (1985) 50 p & CR 409, CA.
7   E.g. *Newcastle-upon-Tyne City Council v Noble* (1991) 89 LGR 618.
8   See the Local Government (Miscellaneous Provisions) Act 1982, s 3 and Sched 4; *Wandsworth LBC v Rosenthal* [1996] CLY 4142, DC; *Kempin v Brighton & Hove C* [2001] CLY 4317. A pedlar's certificate (see fn 12, below) is no substitute: *Watson v Malloy* [1988] 3 All ER 459, DC (see 132 SJ 1654); *Chichester DC v Wood* [1997] CLY 3534; *South Tyneside MBC v Jackson* [1998] EHLR 249, DC.

sex shops[9] or pharmacies.[10] Other control systems are introduced as a protection for public health[11] or safety (see para 6.05) or other interests of consumers, as with the door-to-door traders peddling goods,[12] e.g. home credit, or money (see para 6.09), or collecting donations for charity.[13] Plainly, many of these forms of licensing could in their operation tend towards restraint of trade (see para 2.12); and the administration of all such licensing systems is *prima facie* subject to control of the courts.[14] The various types of licensing are analysed below (para 6.04).

[6.03/4] **Licensing persons**. From the viewpoint of consumer supplies, perhaps the most significant form of licensing is that of persons, rather than of places or goods. Broadly speaking, a personal licensing system may belong to one of two types.

1.  *Positive licensing*. These are systems which require that a licence is obtained **before** undertaking the relevant activity. In fact, it is possible to distinguish between different types of positive licensing systems according to an ascending order of severity with which they interfere with activities within their ambit:[15]

    (a) registration,[16] frequently proved by way of a receipt;[17]

    (b) certification, which requires an applicant to demonstrate an appropriate standard before registration;[18] and

    (c) licensing proper. The last predicates that only those who meet the appropriate standard and are licensed may practice (see para 6.05); but its effectiveness depends on regular review,[19] whose cost implications sometimes make government reluctant to employ the technique.

---

9   See the Local Government (Miscellaneous Provisions) Act 1982, s 2 (see 45 MLR 676). These rules do not infringe the Treaty of Rome: see para 2.13.

10  Under the Medicines Act 1968, the retailer must hold a licence for dispensing medicines at those premises: see further, para 4.29.

11  E.g. the Public Health Act 1936, s 107 (offensive trades); Pet Animals Act 1951, s 1 (as amended). As to food premises, see para 4.26. As to damages, see 152 LGR 883.

12  See the Pedlars Act 1871 (as amended). For the scope of this provision, see *Murphy v Duke* [1985] 2 All ER 2744; *Stevenage BC v Wright* [1996] CLY 4144, DC; *R (on the Application of Jones) v Chief Constable of Cheshire* [2006] 2 CL 366. Special registration is required before one can purport to supply on behalf of blind or otherwise disabled persons: Trading Representations (Disabled Persons) Acts 1958 and 1972. See generally Bragg [1985] Jo of Social Welfare Law 103; and [1986] *op. cit.*, 302; Papworth (1998) 17 Tr L 201. For canvassing, see further, para 8.17. For proposals to licence street charity collections, see (2003) 153 NLJ 1331.

13  See the House to House Collections Act 1939 (as amended); and para 8.13.

14  *R v Wear Valley DC, ex p Binks* [1985] 2 All ER 699. See 102 LQR 24; and generally De Smith, *Judicial Review of Administrative Law*, 5th edn, ch 8. For injunctions see generally, para 29.39.

15  Cranston, *Consumers and the Law*, 3rd edn, 460–2.

16  Registration is where individuals need only list their names in an official register, e.g. Explosives Act 1875; Wildlife and Countryside Act 1981, s 6 (as amended); Scrap Metal Dealers Act 1964 (as amended); Data Protection Act 1998 (see paras 3.27–8).

17  E.g. the licences required by retailers of game (Game Act 1831, s 18; Game Licences Act 1860, ss 13–15: provisions under review).

18  E.g. Poisons Act 1972, s 3 (non-medicinal poison); Road Traffic Act 1988, Pt 3 (as amended: driver's licences; used in credit checks (see above)).

19  If positive licensing does not include regular review, the distinction from negative licensing is substantially lessened: see para 6.11.

2. *Negative licensing*[20]. The effect of these powers is negative in this sense: any businessman within the ambit of the system may act as he wishes unless and until an order is made against him that he 'cease and desist' from that activity. UK examples include estate agents,[21] food safety[22] and Pt 8 of the EA (see para 6.06). Whilst negative licensing has cost advantages both to businesses and government, it still requires for its effective implementation that a monitoring system be established to collect information[23] and may amount only to a stable-bolting exercise.[19]

**[6.05] Types of personal licensing.** Confining discussion to proper positive licensing systems relating to persons (see para 6.03), there are a number of different licensing systems of significance to consumers of goods.

1. *The Consumer Credit Act.* (See para 6.09, *et seq.*)

2. *Intoxicating liquor.*[24] Since medieval times, the troublesome subject of intoxicating liquor (now termed 'alcohol') has been the province of local magistrates, whose control has been partly exercised by means of a licensing system.[25] The current basis of the system is the Licensing Act 2003, which applies to most[26] 'licensable activities', which are defined as follows (s 1(a)): (a) sale by retail[27] of alcohol (s 191); (b) supply (s 14) of alcohol by or on behalf of a club (ss 1(2)–(3) and Pt 4); (c) provision of regulated entertainment (s 1(4) and Sched 1); (d) provision of late night refreshment (s 1(5) and Sched 2). Before they can lawfully be provided, these activities require authorisation (s 2) from the relevant authority, normally the LA (s 3).[28] Two kinds of licence are required, whether permanently or on a temporary basis (Pt 5): the premises[29] 'used' (s 1(6)) for licensable activities must be licensed (Pt 3), including opening hours (ss 17(4) and 172); and so must the person authorised to supply alcohol (Pt 6). It is a criminal offence to carry on or attempt to carry on a licensable activity without the requisite licences,[30] or to make a false statement to obtain a licence (s 158), or to sell alcohol to, or for, a drunk (ss 141–2). There is an array of offences connected with the sale of alcohol to children,[31] enforceable by the

---

20 Cranston, *ibid*, 448, 439–40.
21 Estate Agents Act 1979, s 3 (supervised by the OFT: see para 3.03A).
22 Food Safety Act 1990, s 19(1)(b) (see para 4.26).
23 Cranston, *ibid*.
24 Current laws have their origin in emergency powers introduced during the First World War to ensure that munitions workers were not drunk at work. See generally, (2005) 155 NLJ 1802.
25 'Alcohol' is defined by s 191 of the 2003 Act as being over 0.5% strength.
26 Certain licensable activities are saved from the Act (ss 1(7) and 173–5); and the supply of alcohol is banned from such as motorway service stations (s 176).
27 'Sale by retail' is defined by s 192. Cf. Medicines Act 1968, s 53(1): see para 4.29. S 190 extends the rules to those situations where the alcohol is delivered to a different location from that where the sale is made, e.g. e-mail or telephone orders. There is no specific reference to sale on credit.
28 Pt 2. The Magistrates Courts have lost their jurisdiction over licensing, except for appellate functions and supervision of the police closure of premises powers under Pt 8. There is an appeal system (s 181 and Sched 5).
29 The rules also extend to vessels, vehicles and moveable structures used for licensable activities: ss 156–7, 189 and 193.
30 S 136. This extends to exposing alcohol for unauthorised sale (s 137) or keeping it on premises for such purposes (s 138). There is a special defence of due diligence (s 139): see para 28.13.
31 Ss 146–53. The key offence of selling alcohol to children is not restricted to licensed premises.

LA Weights and Measures inspectors.[32] There are police powers of entry to investigate licensable activities and offences;[33] and prosecutions are generally in the hands of the LA.[34]

3. *Dangerous goods.* The supply of many types of dangerous goods are subject to licensing systems, e.g. petroleum,[35] firearms (Firearms Acts: see further para 4.31), explosives,[35] medicines (Medicines Act 1968, Pts I–IV: see para 4.29), food safety (see para 4.26). Previously considered and rejected was the licensing of garages to control vehicle servicing and repair.

4. *Privatised utilities.* (See para 3.07.)

5. *Driving licences.* (See para 4.37.)

# NEGATIVE LICENSING

**[6.06]** **Rogue traders**. To combat the situation where a trader finds it advantageous to break the law persistently and pay any fines or damages, there was introduced by Pt III of the FTA a system by which the Director-General of the Office of Fair Trading (see para 3.03) might seek a cessation of such activities. Without expressly repealing any of the sections of Pt III, Sched 2 of the Regulations introduced what was in effect an entirely new code, leaving the courts to piece together the two streams of legislation.[36] Mercifully, these two streams of legislation have now been repealed[36] and replaced by a single coherent scheme contained in Pt 8 of the Enterprise Act 2002 (EA: see generally, para 2.12).

Pt 8 gives no new rights to individual consumers, but only protects consumers generally; nor does it impose any new duties on businesses. This new injunctive scheme still amounts to civil proceedings (see para 28.04), but no longer requires a course of conduct detrimental to consumers. Instead, it is available as soon as there has been committed a single listed infringement, these infringements being divided into two sorts, domestic and Community.[37] However, the infringement must also satisfy **all** the following three requirements:

(1) A **supply** of goods or services, all of which expressions are given extended meanings (ss 232(1) and 234(1)). 'Supply of goods'[38] includes 'supply by way of sale, lease, hire or hp';[39] and extends to some supplies outside the UK,[40]

---

32 Ss 154 and 159; and see generally, para 28.02. As to offences by unincorporated associations, see s 188.
33 Ss 179–80; and see generally, para 28.05. As to the provision of information by the licensing authority, see s 185; and see generally, para 28.06.
34 S 186. For offences by corporate officers, see s 187; and generally, para 28.11.
35 See respectively: Petroleum (Consolidation) Act 1928 (as amended); Explosives Acts 1875 and 1923 (as amended).
36 The FTA, ss 34–42, and Stop Now Regulations, 2001 SI 1422 are repealed by EA, s 278 and Sched 26 from dates to be appointed (s 279).
37 This is to facilitate cross-border Community enforcement. See further, para 6.07.
38 ' "Goods" includes (a) buildings and other structures; (b) ships, aircraft and hovercraft': s 232(2). Otherwise, presumably the ordinary definition applies: see paras 2.01–2.
39 S 232(3)(a). In relation to buildings and other structures, 'supply' includes 'construction of them by one person for another' (s 232(3)(b)). 'Supplier' is widely defined by s 233.
40 Provided 'the person seeking the supply' (consumer?) **or** 'the person responsible . . . for effecting the supply' is in the UK (ss 232(4) and (5)).

e.g. supply by internet. 'Supply of services' covers various forms of supply[41] and extends to computer services (s 234(4)), specified land uses (ss 234(6)–(8)) and some supplies of services outside the UK.[40]

(2) A business[42] **supplier** (s 210(3): see para 6.07). Where there is a transaction regulated by the CCA (see para 5.13), references in Pt 8 to the supplier will include the person who conducted the antecedent negotiations (see para 16.08), so catching both the dealer and financier (s 233).

(3) To a **consumer**, which expression is given two different meanings according to context (see para 6.07). Where there is a domestic infringement (see para 6.07), '**consumer**' is defined as being where a business[43] supplies to an individual.[44]

However, given the requisite **supply** (see above) and where consumers generally are harmed by a listed infringement (see para 6.07), Pt 8 may be deployed against a business supplier/infringer by any enforcer (see para 6.06A).

**[6.06A]** **Enforcers**. Under the above scheme the OFT is just the lead-enforcer:[45] it is required to publicise the procedure (s 229), to provide advice as to the factors which should be taken into account in enforcing Pt 8[46] and is given power to control court proceedings (s 216: see para 6.08). According to s 213, there are to be three classes of enforcer as follows:

(1) *General enforcers*. These are (s 213(1)): (a) the OFT (see para 3.03), the lead-enforcer (see above); and (b) every local weights and measures authority (see para 3.05).

(2) *Designated enforcers*. These are bodies (whether or not incorporated) designated by the Secretary of State by Order, which he 'thinks has as one of its purposes the protection of the collective interests of consumers',[47] though its designation may be restricted to specified types of infringement (s 213(6)). Designated enforcers may fall within either of the following classes:

   (a) Public bodies, provided the Secretary of State is satisfied that it is independent (ss 213(3) and (9)); but such an Order is conclusive evidence that the body is a public body (s 213(6)). The Orders made include the

---

41  By s 234(3), supply of services includes: '(a) performing for gain or reward any activity other than the supply of goods; (b) rendering services to order; (c) the provision of services by making them available to potential users.' It excludes contracts of employment and apprenticeship (s 234(2)); but extends to supply by the Crown (s 236).

42  By s 210(8), 'business' includes (a) a professional practice; (b) any other undertaking carried on for gain or reward; (c) any undertaking in the course of which goods or services are supplied otherwise than free of charge.

43  S 210(3). It is immaterial whether or not the supplier's place of business is within the UK (s 210(5)).

44  By s 210(4), the individual must 'receive or seek to receive' the goods or services either privately or with a view to setting up a business.

45  S 216; and see further, para 6.08. The OFT has published *Enforcement of Consumer Protection Legislation* (2003), which sets out General Enforcement Principles (paras 3.67–92).

46  S 229(3). There are further comments on an OFT Consumer Regulations Website (Pt 4 of above Paper).

47  S 213(2). The Secretary of State must notify the EU of any changes in designated enforcer: s 213(11).

following:[48] the regulators of gas, electricity and water (see para 3.07), the Information Commissioner (see para 3.27) and the FSA (see para 3.02).

(b)  Non-public bodies or persons which satisfy the criteria published by Order (s 213(4)),[48] these including such criteria as independence, integrity, competence, expertise and experience. The Consumers Association has been specified (see para 3.08).

(3)  *Community enforcers.* These are enforcers from other EU States (s 213(5)), empowered to stop community infringements (see para 6.07).

To decide whether to initiate proceedings under Pt 8, general enforcers may 'give notice[49] to any person requiring the person to provide it with the information specified in the notice',[50] so as to enable the enforcer 'to exercise or to consider whether to exercise any function it has under' Pt 8 (s 224(2)(a)), or to ascertain whether any person is complying with an enforcement order.[51] Public designated enforcers have similar information powers (s 225(1)(b)), except that the power in relation to enforcement orders is here limited to orders made on application of that enforcer (s 225(3)). Private designated enforcers and community enforcers have not been given these information powers: instead, they must ask the OFT to obtain the information on their behalf (s 224(2)((b) and (c)). These information powers might be useful where, for example, the enforcer in receipt of a private complaint wishes to assess whether the conduct complained of is the result of accidental mistake or deliberate unfair conduct. In default of response, the enforcer can apply at the latter's expense for a court order.[52]

**[6.07]  Ambit.** The ambit of Pt 8 is confined to any act or omission which 'harms the collective interests of consumers' (ss 211(1) and 212(1)),[53] a phrase which appears to be a less restrictive version of the test previously found in the FTA (s 34(1)(a)); but it makes clear that Pt 8 still does not seek to provide a remedy for the individual consumer,[54] nor even a class action for consumers (see para 3.18). Whilst it is for the courts to decide its meaning, the DTI suggest that the phrase does not require that a large number of consumers have already been harmed, but simply that continued repetition could harm their interests.[55] The meaning of the expression **consumers** varies under s 210 according to whether there is a domestic or a Community infringement (see below).

1.  *Domestic infringements.* These are acts or omissions which 'harm the collective interests of consumers' (s 210(4): see above) *and* are of a description specified by

---

48   EA (Pt 8 Designated Enforcers, etc) Order, 2003 SI 1399; 2004 SI 935.

49   This requires a written notice as specified in s 226, which does not specify a reasonable time for compliance and may involve the recipient in considerable cost.

50   Ss 224(1) and 225(2). See generally, para 28.05.

51   S 224(2)(d). For enforcement orders, see para 6.08.

52   S 227. The court may require that person 'to do anything the court thinks it is reasonable for him to do for any of the purposes mentioned in ss 224 or 225 . . . to ensure that the notice is complied with': s 227(3).

53   *OFT v MB Designs (Scotland) Ltd* 2005 SLT 691, OH (including pre-EA conduct).

54   An individual consumer who wants to insist that his complaint be considered could proceed under the UTCCR: see para 11.19.

55   See the *Current Law Statutes* annotation to s 212(3). A single instance may be enough: (2004) 154 NLJ 1628.

the Secretary of State[56] by Order.[57] Statutes so specified include all the following: CCA; CPA, Pt III; Misrepresentation Act 1967; SGA; SOGIT; SGSA; TDA; and UCTA.[58] Statutory instruments specified include all those enacting EU directives listed as Community infringements (see below) plus a number of others relevant to this book, including the Restrictions on Statements and Business Advertisements Orders (see para 4.22). Moreover, the permissible scope of the Order extends to any of the following:[59] (a) criminal law, e.g. harassment (see para 24.24); (b) contract, especially contracts for the supply of goods and services; (c) 'non-contractual duties', especially the tort of negligence (see para 17.13); (d) any other duty 'enforceable by civil proceedings', e.g. breach of statutory duty (see para 3.21); (e) void and unenforceable contracts (see para 10.18); (f) attempted enforcement of supply contracts where this is 'restricted or excluded' by statute or statutory instrument;[60] (g) supply contracts where avoidance of liability is similarly 'restricted or prevented', e.g. UCTA (see para 18.12, *et seq.*). The coverage of the foregoing list is broadened by s 211(4).

2. *Community infringements.* These are acts or omissions which 'harm the collective interests of consumers' (see above) *and* contravene UK law giving effect to a listed Directive (s 212(1)(a)). In relation to Community infringements, a **consumer** is given a slightly different meaning (s 210(6): see above)[61] and public UK enforcers (see para 6.06A) may also take proceedings in other EU States (s 221). Primarily, community infringements are ones in respect of the Directives listed in the Injunctions Directive (s 235) and repeated in Sched 13 of the EA (as amended).[62] So, most qualifying supplies which take place wholly within the UK will amount to both domestic and Community infringements. However, the foregoing list over-simplifies the list for the following reasons:

(a) Minimum Directives. Specified Directives commonly express the minimum rules that Member-States (see s 212(5)) must enact, so that they are free to enact stricter rules (see para 3.10), which the EA terms 'additional permit-

---

56  S 211(2), though he is allowed to exempt acts or omissions of any description (s 211(3)). See further OFT, *Enforcement of Consumer Protection Legislation* (2003), paras 3.16–8 Annexe A.

57  See EA (Pt 8 Domestic Infringements) Order, 2003 SI 1593, which specified some 40 UK enactments.

58  Other statutes relevant to this book listed in Pt I include: Administration of Justice Act 1970, s 40; Cancer Act 1939; Explosives Act 1875; Hallmarking Act 1973; Intoxicating Substances (Supply) Act 1985; Mock Auctions Act 1961; Prices Act 1974; Road Traffic Act 1988, ss 75–6; Tobacco Advertising and Promotion Act 2002; Torts (Interference with Goods) Act 1977; Trade Marks Act 1994, s 92; Weights and Measures Act 1985, ss 21–3, 25, 28–32 and 50.

59  Ss 211(2), (6) and (7); and see the Order cited in fn 57 above, Pt III. Does the ambit extend to other matters within the EA, but not listed in Pt III, e.g. product liability under Pt I of the CPA?

60  S 211(5). E.g. CCA, s 173(1) (see para 18.11); UTCCR (see para 11.12, *et seq.*).

61  The inclusion of individuals setting up business was so worded to catch certain scams, home-working schemes: see OFT Paper (above), para 3.11.

62  By EA (Pt 8 Community Infringements) Order, 2003 SI 1374; 2004 SI 2095;2005 SI 2418. These include: Consumer Credit (see para 5.12); Distance and doorstep selling (see paras 8.17 and 10.21); Electronic commerce (see para 8.17A) and broadcasting (see para 3.14); Medicines (see para 8.12); Misleading Advertisements (see para 8.12A); Supply of goods to consumers (see para 14.01) and restrictions on statements (see para 4.22); Unfair Terms in Consumer Contracts and UCTA (see paras 11.12 and 18.12); junk calls and faxes (see para 8.16A). See *OFT v MB Designs (Scotland) Ltd* (above); and further OFT, *Enforcement of Consumer Protection Legislation* (2003), paras 3.19–23 and Annexe B; *AR-2003/4*, 38; (2004) 38 *Fair Trading* 1.

ted protections' (s 212(1)(b)). These last are also within the category of Community infringements;[63] and both classes may be specified by the Secretary of State by statutory order.[64] So, within the UK there will be some domestic infringements which do not amount to Community infringements, e.g. regulated connected lender liability (see para 16.11). Likewise, there may be some Community infringements, as in France, which do not amount to UK domestic infringements, e.g. a supply by a UK supplier via the internet.

(b) Member-State protection which is outside the scope of 'additional permitted protections' (above) because it cannot be said to stem from the minimum protection of a Directive. For instance, take the ambit of the CCA (see para 5.13): those parts of the CCA which relate to consumer credit agreements may be said to fall within the Consumer Credit Directive, even if they offer greater protection; but those parts of the CCA which relate to consumer hire are totally outside the Directive and can only qualify for Pt 8 as domestic infringements (see above).

**[6.08] Procedure**. Where the OFT or other enforcer considers that a trader is indulging in conduct within Pt 8 of the EA (see paras 6.06–7), the enforcer must usually 'engage in appropriate consultation[65] with' the trader (ss 214(1) and (7)). Such a consultation must take place before application for enforcement (s 214(1)), unless matters are too urgent or the trader absconded (s 214(3)), in which case the enforcer may immediately proceed with an interim enforcement order (s 218: see below). In any event, the above consultation process is time-limited (s 214(4)): ordinarily, the consultation process is limited to 14 days from when the trader receives the first request for consultation; but this is reduced to 7 days for an interim enforcement order.

Subject to the above, Pt 8 makes available an accelerated three-stage procedure.[66] Whilst the former FTA procedure had to be initiated by the OFT, it is hoped that many invocations of Pt 8 will be by other enforcers, e.g. the Local Authorities, who must first consult the OFT (s 214(1)), so that the OFT may perform its co-ordinating role (see s 216).

*Stage 1: A voluntary undertaking.* The enforcer's first choice, as being cheaper and quicker, is likely to be to seek a voluntary undertaking from the trader. There was a power to seek assurances under the FTA; and the gradually increasing number of assurances given annually is to be found in the OFT Annual Reports.[67] Renamed 'undertakings' by s 219 of the EA, these may be sought from a trader wherever the enforcer has power to apply for an Enforcement Order (s 219(1): see below) because he believes that the trader has engaged in the sort of conduct which would attract

---

63  S 212(2). The Explanatory Memorandum on the Bill gives an example where a Directive provides for a cooling-off period of, say 7 days, but the Member States' law allows 10 days.

64  Ss 212(3), (4) and 210(7). The list of Directives in Sched 13 has been modified: ss 210(9); 2003 SI 1374; 2004 SI 2095.

65  See s 214(2). As to Orders providing rules for this consultation, see ss 214(5) and (6); and 2003 SI 1375. For an explanation, see the above OFT Paper, paras 3.38–41 and 3.58–9.

66  See further OFT, *Enforcement of Consumer Protection Legislation* (2003), paras 3.34–7.

67  A consolidated set of texts is to be found in Pt 4 of the *Encyclopedia of Consumer Law* by Thomas. For illustrative cases, see Harvey and Parry, *Consumer Protection and Fair Trading*, 6th edn, 356–7.

an above s 214 consultation (s 219(3)). As against such a person, the enforcer may accept from that trader an undertaking that he (s 219(2) and (4)):

'(a) does not continue or repeat the conduct;[68]

(b) does not engage in such conduct in the course of his business or another business;[69]

(c) does not consent to or connive in the carrying out of such conduct by a body corporate with which he has a special relationship'.[70]

Whilst the FTA assurances were only negative in effect, it will be observed that the EA 'voluntary' undertakings are much more positive in tone.[71] Finally, any other enforcer must notify the OFT of the terms of an undertaking and the identity of the trader giving it (s 219(6)).

*Stage 2: Application to court.* Where it is satisfied that any conduct both breaches Pt 8 and 'harms the collective interests of consumers' (ss 211(1); 212(1): see para 6.07), any enforcer may apply to court for an Enforcement Order against the errant trader (s 215(1)) with this limitation in respect of the different types of enforcer and infringement (see paras 6.06A–7):

(a) A general enforcer (OFT or LA) may make application in respect of any infringement (s 215(2)).

(b) A designated enforcer may only make application within his designation (s 215(3)), e.g. the Information Commissioner in respect of a data protection infringement (see paras 3.27–8).

(c) A community enforcer may only make application in respect of a community infringement (s 215).

The proceedings are civil and so application will usually be made to the county court (s 215(5)); and the evidence may include any appropriate conviction[72] and civil judgment, e.g. for breach of contract or tort.[73] Any non-OFT enforcer must notify the OFT of both the Pt 8 application (s 214(1)(b): see above) and its result (s 215(9)).

*Stage 3: Court orders.* (See para 28.04).

## STATUTORY CONTROL OF MONEYLENDERS

**[6.09] The background: usury.**[74] Even before the time of Christ, usury was condemned as an evil practice, especially where the loan was not for some business

---

68  E.g. OFT, *AR-2003/4*, 7. This paragraph does not apply to Community infringements: s 219(5).

69  The reference to 'another business' will presumably prevent the trader from escaping the effect of his undertaking by establishing a phoenix business (see para 19.25).

70  The reference here is to a group of interconnected companies and their directors: s 223(3). See further, para 28.03.

71  E.g. [2006] *OFT Bulletin J/M, St Helens Glass.*

72  Ss 228(1)(a) and (3) and the Civil Evidence Act 1968 (see para 3.21). To help the OFT in its co-ordinating role, LAs must notify the OFT of intended prosecutions which are likely to be useful for this purpose (s 230; and 2003 SI 1376); and the courts must notify the OFT of such convictions (s 231).

73  Ss 228(2) and (3). The courts must notify the OFT of any appropriate judgments (s 231).

74  See generally, the Crowther Report (Cmnd. 4596) para 2.1.1, *et seq.*

purpose but to relieve poverty. However, in Tudor times, the medieval prohibition of usury was replaced by statutory regulation of maximum interest rates (what are today termed 'rate-ceilings'), even that control being removed in 1854. It was not until the twentieth century that a separate, statutory system was introduced for moneylenders in the (now repealed) Moneylenders Acts 1900–27.[75] Finding their desires balked (as was intended by these Acts), in the twentieth century lenders increasingly turned to the alternatives offered by the new forms of instalment credit contract (see para 1.03) and finance (see para 2.19, *et seq.*) which fell outside the ambit of those Acts. Contemplating the foregoing pattern, the Crowther Report (see generally, para 5.03) rejected rate-ceilings, but did recommend a new unified positive licensing system in respect of loans to consumers[76] that would be both wider and simpler in its control of lending.

In the twenty-first century, the apparently relentless tide of increasing house-hold debts is worrying some, but seen as a necessary evil.[77] The general picture seems to be that 95% of consumers manage their debt well, whereas difficulties are encountered by the other 5% with overindebtedness (see para 6.10). A background Report for the DTI found that the relatively small number of distressed debtors were from the most vulnerable in society and prey to the most unscrupulous lend-ers.[78] Of these borrowers, the first group is those on low income, who tend to use the alternative credit market,[79] where the main concerns relate to high-cost loans,[80] the unpleasant debt-recovery practices of loan sharks (see para 6.20) and debt-collectors (see para 5.42). The second group is those house-owners with a history of bad debt and county court judgments (the 'sub-prime' market), whose lack of choice frequently leads them to seek secured debt consolidation loans.[81] As to this 5%, *some* consumer groups called for the re-introduction of rate-capping,[82] as had been the case under the Moneylenders Acts (see above), or some variant of it,[83] partly to combat sales incentives to creditor's staff. However, the 2003 White Paper provisionally rejected such calls,[82] in part because of concerns that those too poor to qualify for the designated rate would otherwise be pushed into the hands of unlicensed loan sharks (see para 6.20) and in part because it would be too easy to hide the interest rate in other charges. Instead, the CCA 2006 took its lead from the

---

75   To prevent repetition of the activities of Isaac Gordon: see *Gordon v Street* [1899] 2 QB 641. For details, see Butterworths Edn, para 6.09A.

76   Paras 7.2.3–7. This system should be carefully distinguished from the regulation of the acceptance of deposit by financial intermediaries, e.g. borrowing by banks, now governed by the FSMA: see para 2.17.

77   See Collard and Kempson, *Affordable Credit* (2005) 5.

78   See Kempson and Whyley, *Extortionate Credit in the UK* (1999). For an indebtedness study under-taken for the EU, see (2002) 57 CC1/39. For the problems of accessing money transmission services, see para 2.15.

79   Principally, home-collected credit (see para 5.02), pawnbrokers (see para 25.15) and cheque-cashers (see para 7.28).

80   Especially roll-over of fixed-sum loans and store cards. As to interest-rate insensitivity by debt-ors, see para 8.21.

81   See a Report by the CCCS: (2004) 58 CC3/16.

82   E.g. Debt on our Doorstep, *Briefing on Consumer Credit Bill* ((2005) www.debt-on-our-doorstep.com). *Contra, Which?*, Citizens Advice, National Consumers Council (see paras 3.04; 3.08).

83   E.g. an interest-rate threshold, above which products must be licensed; OFT Guidelines; a responsible lending test; a reserve statutory power.

White Paper[84] as follows: besides the special proposals to protect the overindebted (see para 6.10), there are enhanced unfair credit relationship rules (see para 29.44), which are apparently not intended to extend to consumers accumulating relatively low amounts of debt on multiple credit cards.[85]

The 2003 White Paper also recommended the development of stronger codes of practice to tackle overindebtedness (paras 5.70–2).

**[6.10] Overindebtedness.** The DTI Debt Taskforce into overindebtedness was set up in 2000:[86] it faced both irresponsible lending, for instance by credit card issuers,[87] and irresponsible borrowing.[88] Under the CCA 2006, irresponsible lending may be curbed under the licensing provisions (see para 6.19) and possibly as amounting to an unfair credit relationship (see para 29.45); and there is special statutory protection for the mentally ill (see para 10.18).

In 2003, the Taskforce defined overindebtedness as: having 4+ current credit commitments and spending more than 25% of gross income on consumer credit.[89] It commented that the major causes were setting up home, having children and relationship breakdown (para 1.2). However, the Taskforce also observed that the problem could be minimised by stricter lender enquiries pre-contract (see para 8.35) or before increasing spending limits (paras 1.6–8; 1.12), e.g. by more effective credit scoring (see para 8.39); but, of course, there is a legislative trade-off to be made between the privacy of the credit-worthy majority and rejection of applications by the uncredit-worthy minority on the basis of data that could be held (see para 3.29). After credit problems materialised, the Taskforce suggested that they could be mitigated by better codes of practice for default management (see para 3.13) and more sympathetic court procedures (see para 27.01).

The 2003 White Paper *Fair, Clear and Competitive* (see para 6.09) considered the extent, causes and costs of overindebtedness (paras 5.7–19): it stated that the Government's objectives were to minimise the number of overindebted consumers and improve support for them;[90] and noted that many of the proposals considered elsewhere in the Paper were particularly likely to help the overindebted (para 5.2). Nevertheless, it recommended that the following further protections were desirable to help the overindebted (paras 5.22–4): measures to increase

---

84  *Fair, Clear and Competitive: the Consumer Credit Market in the 21st Century* (Dec. 2003, Cm. 6040), paras 3.49–52; Collard and Kempson, *Op. cit.*, 30. The White Paper also took note of a likely super-complaint on behalf of low income consumers (para 3.55: see para 4.19). See also the Minister (2005–6) HL Deb. R2, col. 1055.

85  The Minister (2005) HC Deb. 3R, col. 1161.

86  See DTI, *First Report of Task Force on Tackling Overindebtedness* (July 2001).

87  E.g. automatic increases in account limits, credit card cheques, reduced minimum payments and targeting the poor with direct marketing of specially high-rate cards (to reflect the increased risk?). See also the 2003 White Paper, paras 5.61–7; and the Banking Code, para 10 (see para 3.12).

88  E.g. card shuffling (monthly repayment of the minimum on a large number of cards), knowingly applying for credit that can't be repaid (as by overstating income). For overindebtedness by misjudgment, see Elliott (2005) 78 *Quarterly Account* 7.

89  Or more than 50% of gross income on consumer credit + mortgages: DTI, *Second Report of Task Force on Tackling Overindebtedness* (Jan 2003), paras 1.4 and 3.3. See also the 2003 White Paper, paras 5.5–6.

90  Para 5.21. The 2003 White Paper also mentioned improvements in the administration of Government support, e.g. Housing Benefit (paras 5.81–2) and monitoring (para 5.86).

financial literacy;[91] debt advice[92] and stronger codes of practice in relation to debt-collecting (paras 5.71–2). Meanwhile, the Lord Chancellor's Department (LCD)/Department of Constitutional Affairs (DCA) has been considering how to help the above overindebted and in summer 2004 issued some proposals.[93] Finding the existing procedures insufficient,[94] the LCD Consultation Paper makes the following additional proposals for those who cannot pay their debts (the 'can't pays'):[95]

(a) No Income No Assets (NINA). For those debtors with debts of less than £15,000 who have no disposable income or assets and cannot make worthwhile repayments in the foreseeable future, e.g. multiple debtors, the Paper recommends debt relief. It suggests that debt relief via the courts would be inappropriate (para 34) and recommends a NINA system administered by the Insolvency Service: the debtor would be discharged from the debts 12 months after a NINA Order (para 41). Acting on these proposals, the Insolvency Service has proposed the introduction of an administrative system of Debt Relief Orders[96], which has now reached the stage of a draft Bill (see para 27.04).

(b) Enforcement Restriction Order (ERO). For those 'can't pays' who are temporarily unable to pay their unsecured debts due to some unexpected change of circumstances, e.g. redundancy, divorce, illness,[97] the Paper recommends the introduction of EROs, which should give a judgment debtor time to recover from the short-term problem up to a maximum of 12 months (paras 44–56). During this time, the creditor could still obtain a judgment for debt, but would be unable to enforce it (see the draft Bill: para 27.04).

## The principles of the CCA system

[6.11] **Introduction.** The justification for selecting consumer credit for special treatment over other areas of consumer protection is said to be that it is particularly prone to abuses from which consumers can do little to protect themselves.[98] Following the 1973 White Paper,[99] an elaborate licensing system was established for creditors and owners in Pt III of the CCA, together with special licensing provisions for ancillary credit businesses (see below, para 6.27). Within its wide ambit (see para 6.12), the CCA establishes a system of different classes of licence (see para 6.13, *et*

---

91  Para 5.25. This includes: financial education and general financial advice (see para 3.01).
92  Paras 5.30–44. There are proposals for a new DTI-administered Financial Inclusion Fund. See further, para 3.16.
93  DCA Consultation Paper, *A Choice of Paths: better options to manage overindebtedness and multiple debt* (July 2004). For a summary of the DCA's aims, see (2004) 154 NLJ 1328; (2005) 75 *QA* 1.
94  Para 24. These are: bankruptcy (see para 19.21), IVAs (see para 19.20) and County Court Administration Orders (see para 27.04).
95  For the definition of 'can't pays', see paras 36–9. Distinguish the 'won't pays', who are to be left to the legal processes described in fn 94.
96  *Relief for the indebted—an alternative to bankruptcy* (Nov. 2005: see www.insolvency.gov.uk). Legislation is proposed by the Government and feared by creditors: [2006] 2 *Credit Today* 31.
97  Currently, these may be dealt with under the token offer procedure of the Banking Code (see para 3.12): see (2005) 76 *QA* 15.
98  Cranston, *Consumers and the Law*, 3rd edn, 465.
99  *Reform of the Law on Consumer Credit* (1973) Cmnd. 5427, paras 93–101 (see generally, para 5.03).

*seq.*) and lays down the businessmen's rights and duties with regard to that system (see para 6.17 *et seq.*). Control of the system is centralised in the hands of the Office of Fair Trading:[100] licensing is administered by this Office and is a matter of public record (see para 6.26); and in conducting this operation the OFT will have the benefit of the reports by local authorities and others (see paras 3.05; 3.08) on transgressions in relation to a whole range of statutes designed to protect consumers by means of the civil and criminal law.[101] The object was to ensure that, so far as practicable, only fit persons became and remained licensed to continue to operate in the consumer credit industry.

When the system was first set up, it was predicted that 50,000 licences would be requested but in the next twenty years the figure increased to over 300,000.[102] In the 1980s, these unexpected numbers threatened to overwhelm the system: it led to extensions in the licensing period (see para 6.14), computerisation of the OFT licensing administration and OFT reliance on other parts of the CCA;[103] and the unexpected cost made the Government wary of positive licensing (see para 6.04). However, by the early 1990s, the OFT began to feel comfortable with the computerised licensing system, in part because of the steady decline of licence applications. This led to a shortening of the licensing period; and the OFT began to favour the use of licensing rather than detailed new legislation.[104] In 1999, there was a Government review of licensing, which led to pressure on the OFT to tighten up administration of the system;[105] and in 2003 the White Paper *Fair, Clear and Competitive* [106] proposed a much more rigorous regime, including:[107] licences without time-limit (see para 6.14); more rigorous fitness tests (see paras 6.18–19); more flexible range of enforcement powers (see para 9.23); no appeal to Secretary of State (see para 6.25). A much more elaborate version of these proposals was enacted in the CCA 2006 (ss 23–58), granting the OFT, as from dates in 2008, significantly enhanced powers as explained below.[108]

The EU have begun to ponder improvements to the system (see para 5.12).

**[6.12] Ambit**. The key provision is s 21 of the 1974 Act (as amended by s 33 of the 2006 Act), which lays down as follows:

'(1) Subject to this section, a licence is required to carry on a consumer credit business or a consumer hire business or an ancillary credit business.

---

100 For the functions of the OFT, see generally, para 3.03. For administration, see the OFT Annual Reports.
101 For the setting up of this central register, see the *First Annual Report of the OFT*, 25–6.
102 OFT, *Consultation document on the Working and Enforcement of the CCA* (Aug 1993), para 2.10.
103 This seems to have suited the style of the second Director (Borrie), an academic lawyer, more aware of the legal issues of administrative discretion (see para 6.09).
104 The third Director (Carsberg), an accountant, was of this view: (1993) 14 CCA News 2/9. E.g. inertia selling of credit (see para 24.22).
105 By the National Audit Office, which pointed at the outmoded computer system: see OFT, *AR-1999*, 25; OFT, *AR-2000*, 16; OFT, *AR-2004/5*, 35.
106 See DTI, *the Consumer Credit Market in the 21st Century* (Dec 2003, Cm. 6040). For background, see the preceding DTI Summary of Consultation Responses (Dec 2003); and comment by Stokes (2004) 154 NLJ 660.
107 In 2005, there were already indications that the OFT is being more rigorous in applying the licensing rules.
108 The OFT plans to issue guidance as to how it will exercise these powers.

(2) A local authority does not need a licence to carry on a business.

(3) A body corporate empowered by a public general Act naming it to carry on a business does not need a licence to do so'.

Thus, the major thrust of the licensing provisions is aimed under s 21(1) at those who carry on 'consumer credit business' or a 'consumer hire business' within the amended definitions in s 189(1).[109] The obvious case involves a creditor or owner under regulated consumer credit or consumer hire agreements (see respectively paras 5.13; 1.19); but the definition has been expanded to make clear that it includes not just the original creditor or owner under the regulated agreement, but also one who subsequently becomes creditor or owner, e.g. by assignment;[109] and also one who administers agreements on behalf of a creditor.[110] Whilst this primary definition encompasses all those who enter into regulated agreements as creditor or owner, s 21 goes on to exclude creditors or owners falling into any of the following categories:

1. *Those outwith the industry*, so that the licensing provisions usually do not extend to those activities beyond the scope of the Act.[111] Moreover, the Act excludes those who do not make a business of entering into such agreements, e.g. private lenders, or businesses who only occasionally enter such transactions.[112]

2. *The usual exemptions.* Pt III of the Act excludes those who only supply credit or goods to companies,[113] or only under exempt agreements (see generally para 5.14), e.g. credit unions (see para 15.19); but small agreements are now caught.[114]

3. *Public bodies.* Local authorities (defined in s 189(1)) and public corporations,[115] e.g. the privatised utilities (see para 3.07). The reason for excluding both categories from licensing provisions has been said to be that Parliament has conferred powers on such bodies under separate Public General Acts.[116] Whilst local authorities also have the protection that their individual agreements with

---

109 See the definitions in s 189(1) of the 1974 Act (as inserted by s 23 of the 2006 Act). For examples of consumer credit business and consumer hire business, see para 6.15.

110 E.g. the unlicensed credit-broker in the *Meadows* case (set out at para 8.25), who would now be a debt-administrator (see para 5.44).

111 *Contra* credit-brokers, who must be licensed even though only introducing exempt agreements: see para 5.40.

112 S 189(2): set out at para 5.36 and cf. the Moneylenders Acts (see para 6.09). How infrequent is 'occasionally': see *Wills v Wood* (1984) 128 Sol Jo 222, CA (discussed by Palmer 26 Credit 47); *R v Marshall* (see para 5.36/7)? See further Goode, *Consumer Credit Law & Practice*, para 27.42; Guest and Lloyd, *Encyclopedia of Consumer Credit Law*, para 2-022.

113 Who are not 'individuals', as is required for debtors or hirers under regulated agreements. For 'individuals', see s 189(1): set out at para 5.24.

114 Small loans were originally exempt from licensing (Sched 3, para 5, as substituted). After several reports of such small loans (sometimes regularly topped up) by unlicensed lenders at upwards of 14 million % p.a. (say 40p in the £ per week), this exemption was removed for consumer credit business (1989 SI 1128). But the small loans licensing exemption remains for credit-brokers: see para 6.28.

115 S 21(3). Because they are not named therein, this formula does not extend to companies incorporated under the Companies Acts, or formed under such as the Friendly Societies Acts, Industrial and Provident Societies Acts, Building Society Acts or Trade Union Acts. Nor would the exemption appear to extend to chartered companies or those established by private Act.

116 Goode, *Op. cit.*, para 27.46. Is this a sufficient answer?

consumers are exempt (see generally, para 5.13), the actual credit agreements made by privatised utilities regulated (see generally, para 3.07).

4.  *EU Law*. The above CCA system has been amended by EU law as follows:[117] to enable banks and other financial institutions authorised in other EU Countries (EEA firms)[118] to carry on certain activities in the UK covered by the CCA without the need to obtain a CCA licence;[119] and in relation to UK-registered EU banks and building societies to require the OFT, before granting a CCA licence, to notify the FSA[120] and to comply with an amended version of the rules as noted below.

## The types of licence

**[6.13]** Where a business conducts activities which fall within the ambit of the licensing system (see para 6.12), amended s 22(1) makes available the following types of licence:[121]

'(a) a standard licence, that is a licence, issued by the OFT to a person named in the licence on an application made by him, which whilst the licence is in effect, covers such activities as are described in the licence, or

(b) a group licence, that is a licence, issued by the OFT (whether on the application of any person or of his own motion), which, whilst the licence is in effect, covers such persons and activities as are described in the licence'.

Thus, the Act formally envisages two major types of licence:[122] (a) standard licences (see para 6.14); and (b) group licences (see para 6.16). On the other hand, it might be more helpful to think of group licences rather as a delegation device: bearing in mind the huge number of businesses that require a standard licence, and the even greater number who operate at the periphery of the credit industry, the group licence scheme was devised to obviate the need for the OFT to undertake separate licensing of those peripheral categories. However, if a particular member of that peripheral class were engaged in a substantial amount of business within the Act, the OFT is empowered to exclude that named person from a particular group licence (s 22(6): set out para 6.16), so encouraging him to apply for a standard licence.[123] The 2003 White Paper recommended the granting of indefinite licences to enable the OFT to concentrate on 'those businesses and sectors which pose the greatest risk';[124] and the CCA 2006 accordingly introduced such indefinite licences,

---

117 By Directive 89/646, incorporated into UK law by regulation. See generally Goode, *Op. cit.*, Pt IIB, para 5.41.
118 New s 27A of the 1974 Act (as supplied by s 33 of the 2006 Act). 'Consumer credit EEA firm' is defined by CCA, s 189A, by reference to the FSMA: in effect, it covers EU countries plus some other European countries (the European Economic Area).
119 E.g. lending (para 7.04), issuing credit cards (para 7.10), credit reference services (para 8.37).
120 CCA, ss 25 (1A–1C; as inserted by s 29 of the 2006 Act). For the FSA, see para 3.02.
121 As amended by s 34 of the CCA 2006.
122 As amended by the Enterprise Act 2002, 'licence' and 'prescribed' are defined by s 189.
123 See s 22(5): set out at para 6.16. This power may also be used to weed out undesirables who only operate occasionally within the purview of the Act.
124 See DTI, *Fair, Clear and Competitive: the Consumer Credit Market in the 21st Century* (Dec 2003, Cm. 6040), paras 3.11–14.

with a special periodic charging regime.[125] Whilst the choice will normally be at the request of the OFT, the 2006 Act (s 34) assumes that a standard licence will usually be indefinite, a group licence will normally be time-limited.

**[6.14] Standard licences**. The characteristics of a standard licence, which requires individual application,[126] are as follows:

1. *It is issued to a named person only*. The licence does not authorise the licensee to carry on a business under any other than the specified name (s 24), to do so being an offence.[127] In the case of a sole trader or registered company, the licence shall not be issued to more than one person[128] and, in the case of a partnership or other unincorporated body of persons, the licence shall be issued in the name of the partnership or body.[129] It follows from these rules that, if a sole trader or partnership incorporates, a new licence is required; and, if the business is operated through a group of companies, each such company carrying on licensable activity requires a licence.[130] However, once a licence is issued to the principal in a business, it covers the activities of all persons, e.g. employees, acting on behalf of the licensee, including even part-time independent commission salesmen.

2. *It covers only the activities described*. As the licence is to carry on a particular type of business subject to the terms of the licence, it covers all lawful activities done in the course of that business, whether by the licensee or other persons on his behalf;[131] but, where the debtor is introduced to the creditor by an unlicensed credit-broker, the agreement is enforceable against the debtor only where the OFT so orders (s 149(1); and see para 6.28). The Act allows that the licence may limit the activities it covers by authorising the licensee to enter into certain types of agreement only; and the OFT has in fact specified seven different categories of business (see para 6.15). Additionally, there are the following limitations, which may be particularly relevant to the home credit trade:[132] first, whilst DC[133] agreements may not be canvassed at all off trade premises (s 49: set out at para 7.07), DCS[133] agreements and consumer hirings may be so canvassed—but only if, and to the extent that, the licence specifically so

---

125 New ss 28A–C of the 1974 Act, as supplied by ss 35–7 of the 2006 Act. See further, para 6.14.

126 S 22(1)(a) (as amended): set out at para 6.13. *Contra* group licences, which do not require (though they allow for) individual application.

127 S 39(2): see para 6.20. However, that would not appear to invalidate agreements made by the licensee other than under his licensed name (s 170(1): see para 10.19): Goode, *Consumer Credit Law & Practice*, para 27.187.

128 S 22(3) (as amended). Thus, even if operating under a franchise name (see para 1.07), each sole trader or company in the group requires a separate licence.

129 But where a change in the partnership results in a change in the partnership name, the licence shall cease to have effect: s 36(5). This rule appears to be a trap for a sole trader taking a relative into his business as a partner.

130 This is because each registered company is a separate legal person: see *Salomon v Salomon Ltd* (set out at para 19.25).

131 S 23(1) of the 1974 Act, as amended by s 33 of the 2006 Act. S 23(2) was repealed by Sched 4 of the 2006 Act.

132 For home credit, see para 2.18. This successor to the tallyman (see para 5.02) seems to depend largely on wages being paid weekly in cash. See Cayne and Trebilcock (1973) 23 UTLJ 396, esp at 404, 406, 423.

133 For DC and DCS agreements, see respectively, paras 5.35; 5.34.

provides;[134] and second, the OFT has power by general notice to specify other activities which may only be practised if covered by the express term of the licence.[135]

3. *It is operative only for the prescribed period.* Originally, it was envisaged that a normal standard licence would be granted for three years; and the OFT instituted the practice of carefully vetting applicants before licences were granted. However, the administrative burden proved so great (see para 6.11) that the OFT extended the licence period to fifteen years,[136] a matter which increased the significance of the provisions for suspending or revoking licences (see para 6.23); but, after computerisation of the system, the OFT were able to reduce the licensing period to five years. Indefinite licences were introduced by the CCA 2006 (s 34) as an alternative to time-limited licences (new s 22(1A)) of the 1974 Act: the time-limited licences shall be for the time prescribed by the OFT (new s 22(1B)); but 'a standard licence shall have effect indefinitely unless' the application requests a time-limited licence or the OFT has 'a good reason' to so limit it (new s 22(1C)). This should lift the burden from responsible lenders and allow the OFT to concentrate on rogue lenders.[137]

**[6.15] Types of standard licence.** The standard licensing (see para 6.14) is administered by what may be termed the driving-licence principle; that is, standard licences are divided into the following categories.[138]

Type A—Consumer credit businesses.[139]

Type B—Consumer hire businesses.[140]

Type C—Credit-brokerage.[141]

Type D—Debt-adjusting.[142]

Type E—Debt-counselling.[142]

Type F—Debt-collecting.[143]

---

134 S 23(3); and see the Crowther Report, para 6.4.20. The result is that a creditor must have such a separate endorsement on his licence before he can utilise door-to-door sales techniques, but may also require a pedlar's licence (see para 6.02). For other restrictions on door-to-door sales, see further para 10.21. As to whether door-to-door agents require a separate licence on their own account, see Guest and Lloyd, *Encyclopedia of Consumer Credit Law*, para 2-024.

135 S 23(4) of the 1974 Act, as amended by s 33 of the 2006 Act.

136 The three-year period put in the 1975 Regulations on the recommendation of the Crowther Report (para 7.2.10) was extended to 10 years by regulations made in 1979, and to 15 years by regulations made in 1986.

137 A new computer system installed in 2006 should help: OFT, *AR-2005/6*, 30, 80.

138 New s 24A(4) of the 1974 Act, as supplied by s 28 of the 2006 Act. The OFT must specify these categories by General Notice (new s 24A(5)–(6)).

139 E.g. retailers, finance houses, pawnbrokers, moneylenders, check traders, mail order firms, credit card companies, banks, building societies. For consumer credit businesses, see generally, para 6.12.

140 E.g. business leasing or hiring out TVs, cars, caravans, vending machines, office or factory equipment. For consumer hire businesses, see generally, para 6.12.

141 E.g. mortgage and insurance brokers, retailers who introduce customers to category A licensees. For credit brokerage, see generally, para 5.38.

142 E.g. accountants, solicitors, mortgage and insurance brokers, consumer agencies who advise about debt problems. For debt-adjusting and debt-counselling, see generally, para 5.43.

143 E.g. trade protection societies, finance houses which discount the debts of others. For debt-collecting, see generally, para 5.43.

Type G—Debt administration.[144]

Type H—Credit information services.[145]

Type I—Credit reference agencies.[146]

Applications may be made for one or more types of licence according to whether the applicant considers he may conduct business within that type and the relatively small fee and high penalty for unlicensed trading (see para 6.20) will normally indicate that the applicant should err on the side of applying for more, rather than less, types.[147] For instance, a retailer may need a licence covering the following types: insofar as he provides his own credit and hire facilities, types A and B, with or without a canvassing endorsement (see para 6.14); insofar as he introduces his customers to finance companies to provide credit, type C; insofar as he collects instalments and follows up arrears on behalf of a finance company, type E; and insofar as he takes goods in part-exchange, type D. Statistics and a report on licence applications will be found in the most recent Annual Report of the OFT.

**[6.16] Group licences.** To enable the OFT to delegate the supervision of those businesses on the fringe of the credit industry to their trade body (see para 6.13), the Act lays down that (s 22(6)):

> 'The persons covered by a group licence may be described by general words, whether or not coupled with the exclusion of named persons, or in any other way the Director thinks fit'.

Furthermore, a group licence differs from a standard licence (see para 6.14) in both the following ways: it does not **require** an individual application;[148] and it cannot include a special licence to canvass DCS agreements off trade premises.[149] Under the 2006 Act, a 'group licence shall have effect for a limited period only unless the OFT thinks there is good reason why it should have effect indefinitely'[150] and 'may limit the activities it covers in any way the OFT thinks fit' (s 22(5A)). On issuing a group licence, the Director must give a 'general notice'.[151] Whilst a group licence is in operation, the 2006 Act introduces a mechanism to deal with the situation where the OFT becomes dissatisfied with the manner in which that licence is operated (ss 39–43): it does so by introducing the notion of a 'responsible person in relation to a group licence', as being the original applicant who has accepted responsibility for it (new s 33B(6) of the 1974 Act). If the OFT is dissatisfied with the way in which that responsible person 'is regulating or otherwise supervising' persons acting under that group licence (new s 33B(1)), the OFT may by notice require him to do or cease doing certain things related to the group licence, which the Act terms

---

144 E.g. debt management plans (DMPs: see para 5.42).

145 E.g. helping individuals correct their credit reference files (see paras 8.37–8).

146 E.g. trade protection societies, one of a group of companies which supplies information to other members of the group. For credit reference agencies, see generally, para 8.37.

147 This policy now receives official encouragement: OFT, *1996-AR*, 26. As to applications for licences, see para 6.22.

148 But if there is an individual applicant for a group licence, the group licence shall be issued to that person: s 22(8).

149 S 23(3): for licensing to canvass, see para 6.14.

150 New s 22(1D) of the 1974 Act, as supplied by s 34 of the 2006 Act.

151 That means 'a notice published by the OFT at a time and in a manner appearing to it suitable for securing that the notice is seen within a reasonable time by persons likely to be affected by it': s 189(1) (as amended).

'requirements'.[152] These requirements may include a time specification (new s 33C(1)), e.g. a deadline or a period during which it is in force; but these cannot exceed the period of the group licence (new s 33C(2)), nor require any person 'to compensate, or otherwise make amends to, another person'.[153] The 2006 Act requires the OFT to issues guidance as to how it proposes to exercise its powers to issue requirements.[154]

The CCA envisages that a person may be covered by both a standard and a group licence, even in respect of the same activities (s 22(7)). Nevertheless the two types of licence are obviously designed for different sorts of situation; and it is clear that in the ordinary case a standard licence will be appropriate, for the Act provides that:[155]

> 'The OFT may issue a group licence only if it appears to him that the public interest is better served by doing so than by obliging the persons concerned to apply separately for standard licences.'.

The scope of this power would appear limited by the OFT's subjective view of the 'public interest'.[156] Group licences have already been issued to such as the Law Society, the Accountancy Institutes, Age Concern and the National Association of Citizen's Advice Bureaux.[157] However, in 2000 the Law Society was threatened with loss of its group licence because of concerns over its inability to deal with complaints,[158] a move which would force solicitors involved in regulated business to apply for individual standard licences (see para 6.14).

## The position of creditors and owners

[6.17] The underlying rule of Pt III of the CCA is that 'a licence is required to carry on a consumer credit business or a consumer hire business' (s 21(1): see para 6.12)). This rule will apply to both vendor and lender credit (see para 2.19, *et seq.*); and, as regards the latter, will apply to the financier (creditor), whether engaged in direct or loan financing. The basic step which the creditor will have to take is to apply under s 22 for a standard licence of the requisite categories, together with any desired specific authorisation to canvass (see paras 6.14–5). Unless the licence is expressly limited, it will cover 'all lawful activities done in the course of that business, whether by the licensee or other persons on his behalf' (s 23(1)). In applying for a standard licence to conduct such businesses (see below, para 6.22), a creditor or

---

152 New s 33B(2). For the limits of the OFT power, see new ss 33B(3)–(5). As to the procedure the OFT must follow in making requirements, see new s 33D.

153 New s 33C(3), e.g. a debtor. The OFT has power to vary or revoke any requirement on its own volition (new s 33C(4)) or at the request of the person on whom the requirement was imposed or his employee named in the requirement (new ss 33C(5)–(6)).

154 New s 33E of the 1974 Act, as supplied by s 42 of the 2006 Act. For appeals from requirements, see para 6.24.

155 S 22(5) (as amended). For the criteria utilised by the OFT in the issue of group licences, see *1976 Annual Report*, 22–3. Compare standard licences, in respect of which amended s 25(1) **requires** the OFT to issue a licence if satisfied of certain matters: see para 6.18.

156 Does 'public interest' include the minimising of a would-be licensee's overheads? On 'satisfied', cf. para 6.18.

157 For the terms of these licences, see Goode, *Consumer Credit Law & Practice*, Division IV.

158 See OFT (2000) 28 *Fair Trading* 4. In August 2003, its licence was renewed for the unusually short period of two years: see (2003) 153 NLJ 1258.

owner has to show that he is a 'fit person' (see paras 6.18–19). If he fails to do so and yet continues to operate within the ambit of the CCA, it lays down some Draconian penalties for unlicensed trading (see paras 6.20–21). However, there always remains the temptation to operate outside the law; and a typical example which is occasionally highlighted by the media is that of the back-street money-lender, perhaps illegally taking child benefit books by way of security.[159]

With regard to the conduct of a licensed, but not an unlicensed, business, s 26 allows the making of regulations as to the conduct of business,[160] a power which is extended by s 54 (see para 8.20). Insofar as regulations may be made under s 26 with regard to the seeking of business,[161] breach may constitute an offence.[162] Consideration has been given to use these powers in relation to the following: banning negative option insurance (see generally, para 8.20); strengthening the rules against sending credit circulars to minors (see paras 8.20; 8.33) and unsolicited credit circulars (see para 8.18); and unilaterally increasing the credit limit in relation to running-account credit (see para 5.28).

**[6.18] Fit persons.** There was a version of the requirement that a person be fit to hold a licence in the original 1974 Act, which put the emphasis on his past behaviour. In the 1990s there was criticism of the lax application of these criteria by the OFT.[163] The 2003 White Paper *Fair, Clear and Competitive*[164] therefore proposed a much more rigorous regime: this should include a strengthened fitness test (para 3.8; and see para 6.19); greater investigatory powers for the OFT (paras 3.15–6); assessment at the outset of the applicant's competence to run a licensed business (para 3.5); and thereafter his trading behaviour (para 3.6) and more flexible sanctions (para 3.7: see para 6.23). It is envisaged that different classes of trader should be considered separately, so that the process is proportionate to the risk, the system less onerous for competent businesses and more targeted for the OFT. Substituted s 25(1) of the 1974 Act (as inserted by s 29 of the 2006 Act) as from April 2008 provides that if an applicant for a standard licence—[165]

(a) makes an application within s 24A(1)(a) in relation to a type of business (see para 6.22), and

(b) satisfies the OFT that he is a fit person to carry on that type of business with no limitation,

> 'he shall be entitled to be issued with a standard licence covering the carrying on of that type of business with no limitation'.

---

159 See Borrie, *The Development of Consumer Law and Policy*, 86–7; OFT, *1983-AR*, 19.

160 Regulations have been made with regard to the conduct of credit reference agencies (see para 8.38) and pawnbrokers (see para 25.18).

161 A list of regulations made will be found in the loose-leaf encyclopedias (see para 5.05).

162 In the case of registered companies, such regulations might supplement those made under the Companies Acts. See generally, Gower, *Company Law*, 6th edn, Chap 19.

163 In the absence of serious convictions or insolvency, the OFT was likely to grant a licence ((2001) 61 *QA* 5); and the OFT computer has difficulty picking up convictions (see para 6.11).

164 See DTI, the *Consumer Credit Market in the 21st Century* (Dec. 2003, Cm. 6040).

165 The test no longer expressly refers to the name under which a licence is sought. For more limited licences, see new ss 25(1AA)–(1AD). There are special rules where there is an application for a consumer credit licence made by a business based elsewhere in the EU: new ss 25(1B)–(1C), as inserted by Order made under the FSMA (2001 SI 3649) and amended by Sched 4 of the 2006 Act.

Accordingly, it would appear that an applicant has a right to the issue of a standard licence[166] provided only that there are **satisfied** the above two conditions as to type of business and fitness,[167] rather than that issue being in the discretion of the OFT. However, this position is blurred by the fact that the OFT has to be **satisfied** as to those two conditions, a matter necessarily involving a value judgement on its part.[168] In reaching such a decision, it is not clear whether the OFT is acting in a manner which is executive, administrative, judicial or a mixture of these;[169] nor whether his duty is delegable.[170] Confirming previous practice,[171] by reason of the 2006 Act the OFT is required to issue to credit traders 'guidelines' as to how it will determine fitness,[172] with the implication that it will exercise its licensing powers if that advice is not heeded (see para 6.22, *et seq.*). The powers thus given to the OFT seem astonishingly wide, arbitrary and uncertain;[173] and it seems a matter for its discretion how much the OFT invokes these wide licensing powers rather than proceeding under some other (probably more limited) statutory power.

The 1974 Act laid down a number of negative criteria of unfitness; and the 2006 Act (s 29) has considerably strengthened these by adding some positive criteria of competence in substituted s 25(2) as follows:

'In determining whether an applicant for a licence is a fit person for the purposes of this section the OFT shall have regard to any matters appearing to it to be relevant including (amongst other things)—

(a) the applicant's skills, knowledge and experience in relation to consumer credit businesses, consumer hire businesses or ancillary credit businesses;

(b) such skills, knowledge and experience of other persons who the applicant proposes will participate in any business that would be carried on by him under the licence;

(c) practices and procedures that the applicant proposes to implement in connection with any such business;

(d) evidence of the kind mentioned in subsection (2A: see para 6.19)'.

However, to the extent that the OFT fails under the foregoing system to weed out unsuitable applicants at the outset (through timidity?), the system becomes more like negative licensing (see para 6.04) and greater emphasis is thrown on the system for dealing with existing licences (see para 6.23). Presumably, the OFT will continue its previous practice as to the dichotomy between licensing and Enforcement

---

166 There is no equivalent provision for a group licence. But compare ss 22(5) and (6): see para 6.13.

167 The OFT cannot refuse a licence on any other ground, e.g. that there is already a sufficiency of such services, or that the creditor is underfunded. See Cranston, *Consumers and the Law*, 3rd edn, 467. Can he grant one if he is not satisfied as to the listed matters?

168 See Guest and Lloyd, *Encyclopedia of Consumer Credit Law*, paras 2-004 and 2-026; Goode, *Consumer Credit Law & Practice*, para 22.22.

169 Presumably, s 170 (see para 10.19) precludes any action against the OFT by any customer of a miscreant licensee, claiming that the licence was negligently issued?

170 See *Vine v National Dock Labour Board* [1957] AC 488, HL (not a CCA case).

171 OFT, *2000-AR*, 7, 16. General Guidelines were issued Feb. 2001; e.g. the 'guidance' to debt collectors: see [2000] CCA News, Summer 14; 55 *QA* 2; and see generally, para 5.42.

172 New s 25A of the 1974 Act, as inserted by s 30 of the 2006 Act.

173 The power to impose requirements on licence-holders has been claimed to risk incompatibility with human rights (see para 3.09A).

Orders (see para 6.06): whilst the existence of such Orders will be relevant to the issue of fitness, the OFT sees a clear line between acting to stop a particular type of infringement and action to remove a trader from the market.[174]

**[6.19] Criteria of unfitness.** Whilst strengthening the positive criteria for fitness to hold a standard licence (see para 6.18), new s 25(2A) repeats from the previous Act a list of actions which are likely to disqualify an applicant from holding a licence (see s 29 of the 2006 Act). These are 'evidence[175] tending to show that the applicant, or any of the applicant's employees, agents or associates[176] (whether past or present) or, where the applicant is a body corporate, any person appearing to the OFT to be a controller of the body corporate or an associate of any such person, has':

(a) committed any offence[177] involving fraud or other dishonesty,[178] or violence;[179] or

(b) contravened any provision made by or under the CCA,[180] the FSMA Ombudsman Scheme (see para 3.25), or any other enactment regulating the provision of credit to individuals or other transactions with individuals,[181] or EU equivalent provision; or

(c) practised discrimination on grounds of sex, colour, race or ethnic or national origins in, or in connection with, the carrying on of any business;[182] or

(d) engaged in business practices appearing to the OFT to be deceitful, or oppressive;[183] or otherwise unfair or improper (whether unlawful or not).[184] At a late

---

174 OFT, *Stop Now Orders guidance* (April 2002), para A.11.

175 See s 170(2). This would appear to leave the OFT unfettered discretion as to the sources of his evidence. See Borrie, *The Development of Consumer Law and Policy*, 88. Including relevant evidence inadmissible in court: Borrie [1982] JBL at 95–6. What weight of evidence and standard of proof are required? What of an offence which has expired under the Rehabilitation of Offenders Act 1974?

176 For 'associates', see s 184: see para 5.33. For the purpose of this section, 'associate' includes a business associate (s 25(3), as amended), e.g. an undesirable credit-broker or controller.

177 See Guest and Lloyd, *Encyclopedia of Consumer Credit Law*, para 2-026. Effectiveness has been diminished by the fact that the OFT have been refused direct access to the Police National Computer: OFT, *AR-2003/4*, 36.

178 Thus, s 25(2)(a) does not include strict liability offences, as to which see below. For suggested tests of fraud and dishonesty, see Guest and Lloyd, *Op. cit.*, para 2-026. See also Borrie [1982] JBL at 95.

179 E.g. some of the acts which amount to unlawful harassment of debtors (see para 24.24), drug dealing (see para 4.29); and see OFT, *1981-AR*, 21; *AR-2004/5*, 35. Does the violence have to amount to an offence?

180 E.g. trading unlicensed. As to the CCA, see esp. s 170(2); but note the limitation suggested by Guest and Lloyd, *Op. cit.*, para 2-026.

181 The OFT take the view that this provision covers the strict liability offences protecting consumers, e.g. TDA: see *1979-AR*, 29–30; *1980-AR*, 33.

182 See further, para 4.23. It need not necessarily be a business connected with the credit industry. 'Practised' appears to require a degree of repetition and continuity: cf. s 189(2): see para 5.37.

183 Do the tests of 'deceitful' and 'oppressive' refer to the intention behind, or result of, the business practice?

184 E.g. persistently clocking cars (see para 4.09); selling credit to those who cannot afford it; driving extortionate credit bargains or unfair credit relationships (see paras 29.41 and 29.44); using high pressure sales techniques (see para 10.28); purporting to exercise contractual or common law powers they have not got; obtaining poor resale values on repossessed goods; taking customers' pension or allowance books; incompetence in the conduct of business; charging debtors for collecting their debts; failure to make refunds due (see para 29.04); inertia selling of credit insurance (see para 24.24); misleading advertisements (see para 8.12A); unfair terms (see para 11.12); eponymous subsidiaries (see para 16.06A).

stage, the Government acceded to impassioned pleas in Parliament to include here 'practices in the carrying on of a consumer credit business that appear to the OFT to involve irresponsible lending'.[185] Rather than introducing a duty on lenders to lend responsibly, the effect of this last provision is to allow the OFT to embody advice on this topic in its *Fitness Guidance* backed by the sanction of licence review:[186] hopefully, it should help to curb irresponsible lending and irresponsible borrowing (see para 6.10); but, if the criteria are too tight, this may tend to force too many sub-prime borrowers (see para 7.04A) onto the illegal market (see para 24.49).

If the OFT decides that the applicant is fit to carry out some types of activity but not others, the applicant is entitled to a licence for that or some lesser activity (new ss 25(1AA)–(1AC)), provided that the OFT is satisfied that the name under which he would be licensed is not 'misleading or otherwise desirable' (new s 25(1AD)).

**[6.20] Loan-sharking**. Where a person engages in activities for which a CCA licence is required, either standard or group (see para 6.13), without at that time being covered by such a licence, the Act imposes a number of cumulative criminal and civil sanctions. Leaving aside the situation where an unlicensed ancillary credit business has participated in a transaction (see para 6.27), this paragraph will concentrate on the situation where a creditor or owner has engaged in such unlicensed trading. Here, it will usually be the case that a category A or B standard licence (see para 6.15) is absent, or does not cover the requisite activity, e.g. canvassing without a specific endorsement, as required by s 23(3) (see para 6.14).

1.   *Criminal sanctions*. According to amended s 39:[187]

'(1) A person who engages in any activities for which a licence is required when he is not a licensee under a licence covering those activities commits an offence.

(2) A licensee under a standard licence who carries on business under a name not specified in the licence commits an offence.[188]

(3) A person who fails to give the OFT or a licensee notice under section 36 within the period required commits an offence.'[189]

Unlike under the old Moneylenders Acts,[190] unlicensed trading does not render the regulated agreements illegal and void: instead, it only has the additional civil effects referred to below,[191] and then probably only where there is a degree

---

185 New s 25(2B) of the 1974 Act (as inserted in the HL 3R by s 29 of the 2006 Act). This should apply to both new and existing licences: Minister (2005–6) HC Deb. col. 989. There is no statutory definition of 'irresponsible lending', which appears to rest wholly on OFT perception.

186 The Minister said that new s 25(2B) extended to all forms of lending, including hp ((2005–6) HL, 3R col. 139), but otherwise left the definition of 'irresponsible lending' to the OFT in its published *Guidance*. This has to be set with a view to the statutory powers of data sharing (see para 3.29).

187 For penalties, see s 167 and Sched 1. See *R v Carr* (1980) 2 Cr App R 153; *R v Priestly* (1983) 5 Cr App R 344, CA. For s 36, see para 6.26.

188 For trading name requirements, see s 24: see para 6.14.

189 S 36 deals with the licensee's duty to notify the Director of changes in his circumstances: see para 6.26.

190 E.g. *Cornelius v Phillips* [1918] AC 199, HL. For the Moneylenders Acts, see generally, para 6.09.

191 *Booth & Phipps Garages Ltd v Milton* [2000] CLY 2601, Cty Ct. See s 170(1); para 10.19. Does this prevent the contract being frustrated?

of repetition of the unlicensed activity. So, not only must the trader be carrying on a licensable activity (see para 6.12), but the drafting of s 39 would seem to require his entry into sufficient regulated agreements outside his licence to amount to an 'activity'. The 2003 White Paper[192] noted the low rate of prosecutions and announced a two-year pilot of special teams of investigators.[193]

2.  *Civil sanctions.* Replacement s 40(1)[194] provides that, if an activity requires a CCA licence (new s 40(1A)):

> '(1) A regulated agreement is not enforceable against the debtor or hirer by a person acting in the course of a consumer credit business or a consumer hire business (as the case may be) if that person is not licensed to carry on a consumer credit business or a consumer hire business (as the case may be) of a description which covers the enforcement of the agreement'.

Whilst this rule is not applicable to private creditors or owners, new s 40(1A)[194] explains that, subject to a validation order (see below), a regulated agreement is not enforceable against the debtor or hirer if:

> '(a) it was made by the creditor or owner in the course of a consumer credit business or a consumer hire business (as the case may be); and
>
> (b) at the time the agreement was made he was not licensed to carry on a business of a description which covered the making of the agreement'.

The effect is to *prima facie* render unenforceable by a business creditor or owner unlicensed for that type of agreement *at the time it was made* both the regulated agreement[195] and any security (s 113(2): see para 9.19). An elaborate machinery is provided for the making by the OFT[196] of such validation orders (see para 6.21), which it is his practice to make for specific agreements only.[197] Of course, faced with this situation a loan shark is more likely to employ illegal methods of debt collection[198] that will negate any defence of consent (see s 173(3): para 18.11).

**[6.21] Validation orders**. Suppose a licensable business activity (new ss 40(8)–(9))[199] is enforceable only by order of the OFT (see para 6.20). Replacement s 40(2)[199] provides that where—

> '(a) during any period a person (the 'trader') has made regulated agreements in the course of a consumer credit business or a consumer hire business (as the case may be), and
>
> (b) during that period he was not licensed to carry on a consumer credit business or a consumer hire business (as the case may be) of a description which covered the making of those agreements,

---

192 *Fair, Clear and Competitive: the Consumer Credit Market in the 21st Century* (Dec. 2003, Cm. 6040), paras 5.56–60. This is now operating: (2005) 77 *QA* 24.

193 For a report on the success of the Birmingham loan shark team, see (2006) 1 Quarterly Account 2.

194 Of the 1974 Act, as supplied by s 26 of the 2006 Act. For 'consumer credit business' and 'consumer hire business', see para 6.12. For EU businesses, see new ss 40(6) and (7).

195 See *Hertfordshire Investments Ltd v Bubb* [2000] 1 WLR 2318, CA.

196 Distinguish enforcement orders made by the court: see para 24.33.    197 OFT, *1990-AR*, 32.

198 Commonly systematic assault and intimidation. See also para 24.49. For difficulties of prosecution, see (1996) 51 CC 1/3. For the prevalence of loan sharks in low-income neighbourhoods, see Collard and Kempson, *Affordable Credit* (2005) 3. See generally, [2006] 1 *Credit Today* 20.

199 As supplied/replaced by s 26 of the 2006 Act.

he or his successor in title may apply[200] to the OFT for an order that the agreements are to be treated for the purposes of subsection (1A) as if he had been licensed as required'.

In such a case, amended s 40(5) says that:

'If the OFT thinks fit, it may in an order under subsection (2)—

(a) limit the order to specified agreements, or agreements of a specified description or made at a specified time;

(b) make the order conditional on the doing of specified acts by the applicant'.

Particulars of any such order are one of the matters recorded in the Public Register (see para 6.26) and do not prevent prosecution of that 'trader', e.g. of the broker (s 149: see para 6.28). According to amended s 40(4):[199]

'In determining whether or not to make an order under subsection (2) in respect of any period the OFT shall consider, in addition to any other relevant factors—

(a) how far, if at all, debtors or hirers under the regulated agreements in question were prejudiced by the trader's conduct,

(b) whether or not the OFT would have been likely to grant a licence covering the making of those agreements during that period on an application by the trader, and

(c) the degree of culpability for the failure to be licensed as required'.

Section 40(3) lays down a procedure to be followed where the OFT is minded to refuse such an application by a trader: there are rules governing representations that may be made to the OFT (see para 6.22); and there are also provisions relating to appeals (see paras 6.24–5). This has led to the characterisation of the whole process as judicial, rather than administrative.[201] The OFT receive a trickle of such applications.[202]

## The operation of the licensing system[203]

**[6.22] Applications for a licence**. Like any other application to the OFT under the CCA, an application for a licence[204]

'must be in writing, and in such form, and accompanied by such information and documents as the OFT may specify or describe in a general notice, and must be accompanied by the specified fee'.

This provision has been strengthened by the 2006 Act (s 44). *First*, under new s 24A(1) the application shall state whether the applicant is applying for: (a) all the

---

200 He may only apply on the designated form, and must then answer the questions indicated in Guest and Lloyd, *Encyclopedia of Consumer Credit Law*, para 2-041. Is this not to admit an offence?

201 Guest and Lloyd, *ibid*. Support may be found for this in s 170(3).     202 OFT, *1995-AR*, 25.

203 The EA 2002, Sched 25 made many verbal amendments to the CCA text in this part, substituting 'OFT' for 'Director'. For the operation of the licencing system, see generally the OFT Booklet, *Do You Need a Licence?* Used-car dealers attract the most adverse decisions: OFT, *1986-AR*, 21; *1989-AR*, 31.

204 S 6(2), as amended by s 44 of the 2006 Act. The Director has power to call for further and better particulars and require the information supplied to be verified (replacement s 6(3)) and also to require the applicant to publicise details of his application (s 6(4)). See further Goode, *Consumer Credit Law & Practice*, paras 27.106–7.

activities covered by that type of licence (new s 24A(3): see para 6.15); or (b) that type of licence 'only so far as it falls within one or more descriptions of business' there set out (new s 24A(2)). Licensees will be required to demonstrate fitness (see para 6.18) only for the sub-categories for which they have applied. *Second*, between application and determination, not only may the OFT require additional information (new ss 6(5)–(6)), but the applicant is required to update and correct information already provided and correct errors and omissions of which he becomes aware.[205] The provision of false information in such an application (or any other requirement) is an offence,[206] and the Act provides that (s 6(1)):

> 'An application to the OFT under this Act is of no effect unless the requirements of this section are satisfied'.

As the Act stipulates that a standard licence may only be granted on application with the appropriate fee,[207] an invalid application, e.g. by payment of the wrong fee, or giving incorrect information,[208] would appear to invalidate the licence thereby obtained,[209] so that the applicant will be operating as an unlicensed trader (see para 6.20).

Once the OFT has received a valid application, it has three choices:

(i)   To grant the application as requested, on the grounds that it is satisfied as to the matters referred to in amended s 25(2) (see para 6.19).

(ii)  To grant the application in terms different from those applied for.[210]

(iii) To refuse the application altogether.[211]

Unless the OFT takes the first choice, amended s 27(1) requires it to serve on the applicant a 'minded to refuse' notice, giving its reasons and inviting representations.[212] If still dissatisfied, the applicant may have recourse to the appeals procedure (see para 6.24).

The 2003 White Paper, *Fair, Clear and Competitive* (see para 6.18) proposed a new differential fee structure (para 3.25); and this was enacted in new s 6A.[213] As the fees are intended to make operation of the licensing system self-financing, it is to be hoped that they are set at a level which produces an income adequate for proper administration of the system,[214] including a crack-down on rogues. Moreover, there

---

205  New ss 6(7)–(8). However, the applicant is not required to include here changes subsequent to grant of the licence (s 36: see para 6.26), nor any 'clerical error or omission not affecting the substance of the information or document' (new s 6(9)).

206  S 7, as replaced by s 51 of the 2006 Act. For penalties, see s 167 and Sched 1. See further OFT, *1983-AR*, 19.

207  Ss 22(1), 25(1), new s 6(2A): set out respectively, paras 6.13 and 6.18.

208  This has even been interpreted by CCA adjudicators to include failure to specify convictions (even spent ones) unrelated to consumer credit, e.g. driving whilst disqualified and uninsured.

209  Borrie [1982] JBL at 92.

210  S 27(2), as amended. E.g. without the sought permission to canvass.

211  See the Crowther Report, para 7.2.11; and Borrie [1982] JBL at 94–100.

212  See the procedure set out in Goode, *Op. cit.*, paras 27.144–7. As to the raising of standards and quantity of information by the OFT, see para 6.11.

213  Of the 1974 Act, as inserted by s 27 of the 2006 Act.

214  Is that in itself enough to make fees charged proportionate?

has been detected a Goverment intention to mesh closely the new consumer credit regulatory regime with that of the FSA (see para 3.02).

**[6.23] Existing licences**. Where a licence has already been issued to an applicant (see para 6.22), there are, leaving aside the special rules for EU firms (new s 27A of the CCA),[215] a number of situations in which the licensing machinery may again be invoked in respect of licences.

(a) *Renewal*. Applications may be made to the OFT[216] for renewal of any standard licence of limited duration (s 29(1), as amended).[215] Generally speaking, all the previously discussed rules relating to first issue of a licence apply to renewals thereof (ss 29(3) and (3A)),[215] including the sweeping fitness powers granted to the OFT (see para 6.19). In the event of an application for renewal not being granted, the OFT no longer has power to authorise the licensee to continue with existing regulated agreements,[217] except as part of the winding up or transfer of the business (see below). On a refusal to renew, then until expiry of the 'appeal period' (see para 6.24) the licence continues in force (s 29(4)), leaving a period for negotiation.[218]

(b) *Variation*. This may be made by request, or compulsorily. Where there is an application to vary a standard licence,[219] the OFT may, if it thinks fit, grant the request;[220] but on refusal, the disappointed applicant has similar rights to reasons and representations as on original application (s 30(4), as amended: see para 6.24). Alternatively, the OFT is empowered to make a compulsory variation on the basis that[221]

> 'if the licence had expired at that time, he would, on an application for its renewal or further renewal on the same terms (except as to expiry), have been minded to grant the application but on different terms'.

For instance, this power may be used where the licensee is breaking the terms of his licence, employing undesirables, or has been convicted of relevant offences. But such a compulsory variation shall not take effect before the end of the appeal period (s 31(7)) and gives the OFT no power to validate agreements already made. There has also been introduced a new compulsory power for the OFT to time-limit an indefinite licence or shorten the duration of a limited licence.[222]

(c) *Suspension and revocation*. The OFT has power to suspend or revoke any licence on the basis that it (amended s 32(1))

---

215 As inserted by the CCA 2006, ss 31–4 (as amended); in force from April 2008.

216 S 6: see para 6.22. But the OFT may also renew any group licence of its own motion by giving general notice: ss 29(2) and (6). See the reports by the OFT in its *Annual Reports*.

217 S 32 of the 2006 Act, repealing ss 29(5) and 32(5) of the 1974 Act and amending s 32(2).

218 It has been pointed out that this period may be unmeritoriously used solely to prolong the legality of nefarious activities: Borrie, *The Development of Consumer Law and Policy*, 87.

219 It has similar powers to vary a group licence on application: ss 30(2), (3) and (5).

220 Ss 30(1), 31A and 31B, as substituted/inserted by s 31 of the 2006 Act. E.g. to add a new category of licensable activity or record a change of business name. Where a business changes its name and does not apply in time for variation or renewal of its licence, it would appear to be engaged in unlicensed trading (see para 6.20). Subject to any validation order (see para 6.21), for the effect of this see (1986) 41 CC 1/26.

221 Ss 31(1) and (1A), as amended/inserted by respectively ss 34 and 31 of the 2006 Act. This power exists in relation to both standard and group licences: ss 31(2)–(9) (as amended/inserted).

222 New ss 31(1B) and (1E) of the 1974 Act, as inserted by s 34 of the 2006 Act.

'is of the opinion that if the licence had expired at that time he would have been minded not to renew it'.

There is no longer any power for the OFT to validate agreements.[217] However, there is included a power to deal with the situation where there has been a change in the types of licence (see para 6.15) which may be issued (new s 32(9)).[215] The Act then makes some further provisions in respect of suspensions.[223] The suspension or revocation does not in any event take effect until expiry of the 'appeal period' (s 32(7)), leaving a period for negotiation.[218]

*(d) Termination.* The standard licence obtained by the successful applicant is clearly a very personal thing: it cannot be assigned, nor is it generally transmissible on death or in any other way.[224] There is also power by regulation both to specify other events causing automatic termination of a standard licence, and to defer such termination by up to twelve months.[225] Additionally, if the OFT decides to renew a licence on different terms, vary it compulsorily, revoke or suspend a licence, that may render conduct of the business no longer viable; and to meet this situation new s 34A[215] empowers the OFT to allow the licensee to carry on specified activities for a limited period pending transfer or liquidation of the business.

It was pointed out that it is a serious weakness of the 1974 Act that the only ultimate sanction available to the OFT is the slow but drastic and disproportionate procedure of revocation of licence;[226] and that it should be helpful if the OFT had the ability to impose fines as an intermediate sanction short of licence prohibition, perhaps accompanied by publicity (see para 6.23A).

**[6.23A] Civil penalties.** To meet the above problem, the 2003 White Paper *Fair, Clear and Competitive* (see para 6.18) proposed the introduction of special conditions on licence-holders, breach of which could lead to financial penalties (paras 3.21–2). In response, the CCA 2006 introduced into the licencing regime a system of civil penalties that may be imposed by a two-stage machinery: this is intended to allow the OFT as from April 2008 to impose proportionate sanctions less than licence interference (see para 6.23) in respect of minor breaches, e.g. problems within one branch of a national lender, or by one employee.

1.  *The imposition of licensing requirements.* New s 33A of the 1974 Act[227] empowers the OFT to impose requirements on the conduct of any licensee if 'dissatisfied with any matter in connection with' a business being carried on,[228] or proposed

---

223  For the effect of suspension, see s 32(8); and for applications to end a suspension, see s 33, as amended.

224  Ss 22(2) and 37, as amended. The licence generally terminates automatically if the licensee dies, is adjudicated bankrupt or becomes a mental patient: s 37(1). This section does not apply to group licences: s 37(4). On s 37, see generally Goode, *Consumer Credit Law & Practice*, paras 27.206–8; and the Crowther Report, para 7.2.11.

225  S 37(3). Thus, there may be a 'holding period', during which the licensee's representative could himself apply for a standard licence should he wish to continue the business. See further, Goode, *Op. cit.*, paras 27.215–16.

226  The OFT's attempt to revoke Colorvision's licence was disastrous for the OFT: see para 6.25.

227  As inserted respectively by ss 38 and 52 of the 2006 Act. Welcomed by the OFT: *AR–2004/5*, 35.

228  It is immaterial whether the matter arose before or after the licensee became licensee (s 33A(5)). Could the OFT impose a requirement that the creditor cease entering into unfair credit relationships (see para 29.45)?

to be carried on, by that licensee, associate or former associate, or any other conduct.[229] In these circumstances, provided the requirement relates to the business which the licensee is carrying on (new s 33A(3)), new s 33A(2) provides that:

> 'The OFT may by notice to the licensee require him to do or not to do (or to cease doing) anything specified in the notice for purposes connected with—
>
> (a)  addressing the matter with which the OFT is dissatisfied; or
>
> (b)  securing that matters of the same or a similar kind do not arise'.

The requirement 'may be framed by reference to a named person other than the licensee'.[230] In the case of a standard licence, the OFT must first listen to any representations by the licensee (new s 33A(6): see para 6.24); and an analogous procedure is available in respect of a 'responsible person' in relation to a group licence (new s 33B). In respect of both standard and group licences, the foregoing OFT powers are subject to the limitations set out in new s 33(C): see para 6.16.[231]

2.  *The levying of civil penalties for breach.* The OFT must first publish a (revisable) statement as regards its policy on levying such penalties.[232] Thereafter, the OFT may give a person notice that he is minded to impose such a penalty, what may be termed a 'yellow card' (new s 39B), so that the alleged defaulter may make representations to try to dissuade it (see para 6.24). If the defaulter fails and the default has not been adequately punished elsewhere (new s 39B(3)),[233] according to new s 39A(1),[227]

> 'Where the OFT is satisfied that a person (the 'defaulter') has failed or is failing to comply with a requirement imposed on him by virtue of section 33A, 33B or 36A,[234] it may by notice to him (a 'penalty notice') impose on him a penalty of such amount as it thinks fit'.

Under new s 39A(2), the 'penalty notice', or 'red card', must specify the amount of the penalty,[235] set out the OFT's reasons for imposing that penalty,[236] specify how payment may be made and the period within which it must be paid,[237]

---

229  S 33A(1). Presumably, 'other conduct' is to be read *eiusdem generis*. For 'associates', see s 184. For the purpose of this section, 'associate' includes a business associate (s 33A(7)), e.g. an undesirable credit-broker or controller.

230  New s 33A(4). E.g. that named employees undergo a specific type of training, or refrain from particular practices, or that a particular person not be involved in a business: see the Minister (2005–6) HL GC col. 311.

231  As these powers do not deprive the licensee of his licence, the Minister argued that the powers fall within the exception to Article 1, Protocol 1, of the Human Rights Convention (see para 3.09A): see (2005–6) HL GC col. 312.

232  Subject to the approval of the Secretary of State (new s 39C).

233  If the misconduct is serious enough, the OFT could issue an Enforcement Order (see para 6.08) or suspend a licence (see para 6.23).

234  For new ss 33A and 33B, see above; and for new s 36A, see para 6.26.

235  The maximum such 'penalty' is £50,000 per breach (new s 39A(3)); but that amount may be increased under amended s 181 (see new s 39B(3)).

236  These must be consistent with the above published statement of policy under new s 39C (new s 39C(6)); and the conduct must not relate to a period before publication (new s 39C(7)).

237  The period within which it is payable must not end before expiration of the 'appeal period' (new s 39A(4): see para 6.25).

and is subject to appeal by the defaulter (new s 39B(2): see para 6.25). Non-payment of the 'penalty' amounts to an interest-bearing debt recoverable by the OFT (new s 39A(5)).

**[6.24] Licence appeals.** The Crowther Report argued that, since it is protection of the individual debtor that is at stake, enforcement should not be made too difficult.[238] The Report therefore recommended that the licensing authority should be entitled to refuse to renew, revoke or suspend a licence (see para 6.23) if satisfied that 'the applicant has been conducting his business in repeated or flagrant breach of the law, or in such a way as to mislead the public, or that he has persistently made excessive charges, or that he has acted oppressively towards his debtors'.[238] However, the other side of the coin is that in so acting, the OFT can affect a businessman's livelihood. The CCA therefore lays down a careful system of appeals, being especially lenient to persons already engaged in an existing business. Thus, in every case where the OFT determines not to renew, to make a compulsory variation of, or to suspend or revoke, a licence, the Act provides that the licence shall continue in force until the end of the 'appeal period';[239] but this is not the case where the application is to start a business.

Where the OFT indicates by a minded to refuse notice (see para 6.22) to the applicant/licensee that it is contemplating making a decision in regard to any of the foregoing matters which that person will not like,[240] amended s 34(1) anticipates that the applicant/licensee may wish to make written and oral representations to the OFT.[241] Taking into account those representations, the OFT[242] shall reach a determination (s 34(2)); and then it will both give notice thereof to the applicant/licensee (s 34(3)) and enter its determination in the public register (see para 6.26). That determination is judicial in nature[243] and may then be challenged by the applicant/licensee. The 2003 White Paper, *Fair, Clear and Competitive* (see para 6.18) proposed that appeals be removed from the Secretary of State to the new Tribunals Service (para 3.23). It is envisaged that the appeals procedure would remain in similar form to that under the present system (see para 6.25).

**[6.25] Challenging a determination of the OFT.** Where a person is aggrieved by the final determination[244] of the OFT (see para 6.24), before the 2006 Act he used to resort to one of three courses:

(a) Follow the somewhat inadequate appeal procedure laid down in the CCA (see below); or

---

238 Para 7.2.11. Note the recommendation that the licensing procedure should allow for informal consultation to facilitate, e.g. changing business practices (para 7.2.13), something the OFT appears to be doing.

239 Amended ss 29(4), 31(7) and 32(7). For 'appeal period', see s 189(1). See the comment thereon in para 6.23.

240 To refuse a standard licence in the terms of the application (s 27(1)(b)); to exclude any named person from a group licence (s 28(b), as amended); to refuse an application to end a suspension (s 33(2)(b)), or validate unenforceable agreements (amended ss 40, 148 and 149).

241 Such representations may include undertakings as to future conduct: OFT, *1994-AR*, 28.

242 The work is done for it by adjudicating officers: see OFT, *1994-AR*, 14.

243 See para 6.21. It is accordingly subject to review by the Council of Tribunals: s 3 of the CCA was repealed and replaced by the Tribunals and Enquiries Act 1992, s 1 and Sched 1, Pt 1.

244 For inactivity by the OFT, see Goode, *Consumer Credit Law & Practice*, para 27.219.

(b) Apply to the court to exercise its inherent jurisdiction over administrative tribunals, a course of action which more properly belongs within the realms of administrative law, or perhaps complain to the ombudsman (see para 3.25); or

(c) Challenge the OFT by application to the Parliamentary Ombudsman: in one case, after a four-year investigation, that Ombudsman found the OFT had committed 'substantial maladministration'.[245]

The CCA 1974 envisaged a formal appeal to the Secretary of State by an aggrieved licensee/applicant only; but from April 2008, the 2006 Act has re-directed appeals to a new Consumer Credit Appeals Tribunal,[246] whose conduct is made subject to the Council on Tribunals (s 58 of the 2006 Act). Appeals against OFT decisions may be made to this Credit Appeals Tribunal,[247] with further appeals on points of law to the Court of Appeal and House of Lords.[248]

**[6.26] Miscellaneous**. Other licensing matters include the following:

1. *Publicity.* To ensure adequate publicity for the administration of the licensing system, the Crowther Report recommended a publicly available register of licences (para 7.2.10). Accordingly, such a register was set up by the 1974 Act.[249] Express right of public access to the register is laid down (amended ss 35(3)–(5)); and that register now includes minded to revoke or refuse notices, reasons for revocations, undertakings by traders[250] and civil penalties.[251] Further, it has been decided that publication in a newspaper that the OFT is minded to revoke a licence does not infringe s 174.[252] As the Act also requires the holders of standard licences to notify the OFT of various material changes (see below), the result is to provide a sort of publicly available compendium of current 'credit-drivers' licences'.[253] If acting for the debtor or hirer in a contentious regulated matter, it is usually advisable to make such a register check as a matter of routine: it may truncate the proceedings if the other side is unlicensed.

2. *Changes in information.* Under s 36 of the 1974 Act there is established a mechanism requiring each licensee to keep the OFT informed of changes in his particulars entered in the register (above). The 2003 White Paper recommended extension of the s 36 duties to require licensees to notify the OFT 'of any material changes in their circumstances relating to their fitness to hold a licence' and it is planned that this notifiable information should cover a much wider range of information than the then existing one (paras 3.17–8). In response, the

---

245 Failures included the breaching of the chinese walls between the investigators and the adjudicator; and passing incorrect information to the adjudicator: *The Times* 25.5.02; and see OFT, *AR–2002/3*, 45, 93.

246 New s 40A and Sched A1 of the 1974 Act, as inserted by s 55 and Sched 1 of the 2006 Act, which includes the nuts and bolts of how the tribunal should work.

247 New s 41 of the 1974 Act, as substituted by s 56 of the 2006 Act; and the Table in s 41 is amended by s 43 of the 2006 Act.

248 New s 41A of the 1974 Act, as inserted by s 57 of the 2006 Act.

249 By s 35(1) of the 1974 Act, as amended by ss 34, 38 and 43 of the 2006 Act. The OFT shall give general notice of matters required to be included in the register: s 35(2).

250 Goode, *Consumer Credit Law & Practice*, paras 22.62, 27.22 and 27.146.

251 New s 35(1)(ba) of the 1974 Act, as inserted by s 43 of the 2006 Act.

252 *Murtagh v Newspaper Publishing plc* [1990] CCLR 64 (see 44 CC 2/9). For s 174, see para 28.06.

253 It may only be inspected by personal callers, but postal and telex requests may be made for copies of clearly identified documents.

2006 Act strengthens the system as regards information not contained in the register in two ways. First, s 45 of the 2006 Act requires any standard licensee or applicant for a group licence (the 'relevant application') to notify the OFT where, after a licence has been issued (see para 6.22) and unless already covered by the above s 36 procedure (new s 36A(10)(a)), there have been new changes in specified information relevant to that licence application;[254] or where the licensee has become aware of any 'error or omission' in respect of information he previously supplied to the OFT.[255] Second, under s 46 of the 2006 Act the OFT may, by notice setting out its reasons (new s 36B(2)), require any licensee or third party to provide specified information or documents;[256] and, if there is any failure to comply with this requirement to supply information, the OFT may apply under new s 36E for a court order against the 'information defaulter' to enforce the requirement (failure to comply being a contempt of court).

Whilst the 2006 Act thus gives the OFT fairly sweeping new enforcement powers to implement the licencing system, it remains to be seen whether the OFT will continue to feel overly constrained by their view that such actions must be proportionate under the CPR.[257]

## Licensing ancillary credit businesses

**[6.27] Introduction.** Following the recommendations of the Crowther Report (para 6.4.25), s 147(1) explicitly made applicable to ancillary credit businesses[258] most of the above Pt 3 licensing provisions governing creditors or owners (see paras 6.11–26); but s 147(1) was repealed by the CCA 2006 (Sched 4), presumably leaving Pt 3 applicable to ancillary credit businesses as there stated, subject to the special rules below. Such businesses will mostly[259] require either a group licence (see para 6.16) or a standard licence of categories C- I (see para 6.15). There are some rules created specially with regard to the activities of unlicensed ancillary credit businesses:

1.   *Agreement for services.* Amended s 148 prevents the unlicensed ancillary credit business (UK trader)[260] from claiming under an agreement for his services[261]

---

254  New ss 36A(2) and (5). The duty is not to disclose all such changes, but only those specified by the OFT in a General Notice (new ss 36A(6), (7) and (9)) and which have not previously been supplied (new s 36A(4)). For 'relevant application', see new s 36A(11).

255  New ss 36A(8) and (9). This duty does not extend any 'clerical error or omission not affecting the substance of the information or document' (new s 36A(10)(b)).

256  New ss 36B(1) and (3). Such a requirement may only be imposed on a licensee if 'reasonably required for purposes connected with the OFT's functions under this Act' (new s 36B(4)); and there are even tighter restrictions on the OFT's powers to require information from a third party (new ss 36B(5) and (6)).

257  See the Deputy DGFT [2001] 12 *Credit Today* 9; and para 5.10. As to litigating proportionately, see para 3.22.

258  For ancillary credit businesses, see generally, para 5.36, *et seq.*

259  For exceptions see generally, para 6.12.

260  But EU traders are saved from this rule (s 148(6)) and instead fall within the FSA (see para 3.02).

261  Should this be restricted to agreements for the trader's ancillary credit services (Goode, *Consumer Credit Law & Practice*, IIB, para 5.288), so allowing him to recover commission on that part of his business which does not require a CCA licence? See Howells, *Consumer Debt*, para 3.04.

commission or other fees from a 'customer', e.g. a member of the public,[262] without an order of the OFT.[263] This rule will be particularly relevant to second mortgage brokers and commercial debt-adjusters.[264]

2. *Credit-brokers.* There are special rules with regard to canvassing endorsements[265] and business introduced (see para 6.28).

3. *Debt-collectors.*[266] There are special rules with regard to licensing (see para 5.43), canvassing endorsements[265] and entry into agreements.[265]

4. *Debt-adjusting, debt-counselling and credit information services.* There are special rules with regard to canvassing endorsements[265] and entry into agreements.[265]

5. *Debt administration.*[266]

6. *Credit reference agencies.* Amended s 147(2) contains a special power to make regulations with regard to the collection and dissemination of information by credit reference agencies[262] along similar general lines to that found in s 26 (see para 6.17).

As the first two rules both vest a discretionary power of validation in the OFT, they are both subject to the same rules relating to appeals as those which obtain with regard to his licensing powers generally (see paras 6.24–5), there being provided an express right of appeal by the disappointed applicant from the OFT to the Credit Appeals Tribunal (see para 6.25).

**[6.28] Unlicensed credit brokers**. If a trader carries on an unlicensed credit-broking business,[267] not only does he commit an offence,[268] but the business he introduces is tainted.[269] According to amended s 149(1):

> 'A regulated agreement made by a debtor or hirer who, for the purpose of making that agreement, was introduced to the creditor or owner by an unlicensed credit-broker is enforceable against the debtor or hirer only where—
>
> (a) on the application of the credit-broker, the OFT has made an order under section 148(2)[270] in respect of a period including the time when the introduction was made, and the order does not (whether in general terms or specifically) exclude the application of this paragraph to the regulated agreement, or
>
> (b) the OFT has made an order under subsection (2) which applies to the agreement'.

The effect of this important provision is to import a measure of trade policing:[271] no creditor or owner is likely to accept business introduced by a

---

262 'Customer' will be wide enough to include a creditor: Guest and Lloyd, *Encyclopedia of Consumer Credit Law*, para 2-149.

263 S 148(2). The validation procedure is very similar to that obtaining in respect of unlicensed consumer credit businesses (s 148(2)): see para 6.21.

264 For the limitation on fees in respect of licensed credit-broking, see para 16.19.

265 S 154 of the 1974 Act, as amended by s 25(4) of the 2006 Act. See para 16.19.

266 S 177 (registered charges: see para 25.24) does not apply to debt collectors or debt administrators: new s 146(7), as supplied by s 24(5) of the 2006 Act.

267 Even where exempt agreements are introduced: see para 5.40.

268 Ss 39 and 147(1): see *Brookes v Retail Credit Cards* [1986] CLY 370, DC.

269 E.g. if the broker is bankrupt (s 37(1): see para 6.23).

270 S 148(2): see para 6.27.

271 For a justification, see Borrie, *The Development of Consumer Law and Policy*, 86; Borrie [1982] JBL at 101. For credit-brokers, see generally paras 5.39–41.

credit-broker[272] without first satisfying himself that the latter is licensed.[273] If the creditor or owner does accept business from an unlicensed credit-broker,[274] any agreement[275] that the broker introduces is *prima facie* unenforceable,[276] regardless of how careful the creditor has been in accepting that business.[277] The regulated agreement may, however, become enforceable upon order of the OFT in either of two ways: either the credit-broker may successfully apply to the OFT,[270] or the creditor or owner may do so.[278]

---

272 *Aliter*, where the debtor makes the introduction: (1993) 48 CC2/28. But for EU traders, see new s 149(6).

273 To check the licence, see para 6.26. The creditor or owner aids and abets the credit-broker's offence, see *Brookes*, (above).

274 But what if the creditor or owner accepts business from a licensed credit-broker who has in turn obtained it from an unlicensed credit-broker? See Guest and Lloyd, *Encyclopedia of Consumer Credit Law*, para 2-150.

275 Is this limited to regulated and linked agreements? See Howells, *Consumer Debt*, para 3.05.

276 And any security will be unenforceable (amended s 113(2)): see paras 9.19 and 25.13.

277 This liability without fault has parallels with the creditor's liability under s 75: see para 16.11, *et seq*.

278 Under amended s 149(2). For suggestions as to what factors the OFT may take into account, see amended s 149(4). For the validation procedure, see para 6.21.

# CHAPTER 7

# MONEYLENDING

**[7.01] Introduction.** Whilst this book is primarily about the retail supply of goods, adult consumers frequently press for early delivery with subsequent payment, typically by instalments.[1] We have already seen (para 2.16) that payment may be financed by either the retail supplier of the goods (vendor credit) or by a third party (lender credit), using a number of different methods. Some of these methods are, or involve, what in law amounts to a loan of money; others do not, e.g. an instalment credit contract (see para 1.03).[2] If a loan contract is utilised, the two functions of a retail supply of goods and loan to the consumer may be separated.[3] Thus, a vendor credit transaction may be achieved by a cash sale and a separate loan contract between the same two parties (see para 2.19), whereas lender credit may involve a cash supply of goods financed by a loan from a third-party financier (see para 2.20). In either case, the funds under the loan contract (see para 7.02) may be transmitted in one of several ways:

(a) *By a delivery of cash to the consumer.* For security reasons, this method is likely to be used only in relation to relatively small sums of money. The consumer-borrower may go to the lender, as where the consumer goes to a bank, building society or pawnbroker;[4] or he may go to the lender's ATM (see para 2.24). Or the lender may go to the borrower, as in home credit (see para 5.02).

(b) *By delivery to the supplier of a cheque or other instrument* (see para 7.24), whether by hand or post. For instance, in loan financing the financier may post a cheque to the retail supplier.

(c) *By funding the consumer's existing current account* (see para 2.17). At simplest, this might involve a clearing bank providing its existing customer with a personal loan (fixed-sum credit) or an overdraft facility (running-account credit): the customer may then access that credit by:

    (i)   drawing cash, usually by inserting a cash card in an ATM (see below);

    (ii)  writing cheques, or utilising its modern equivalent, the debit card (see para 23.15).

(d) *By opening a new loan account for the consumer.* Funds in the loan account may be accessible by furnishing the customer with a cheque-book (as in (c) above); but a more popular modern alternative is for the account to be operable by way of a payment card (see para 2.24), e.g. a cash card for use in an ATM, credit card, debit card or store card. Such new accounts are particularly common for regulated loans (see para 7.04, *et seq.*).

---

1    There are further difficulties in supplying goods and/or money on credit to minors (see para 10.18), unless supported by an adult indemnifier: see para 25.06.

2    *Chow Yoong Hong v Choong Fah Rubber Manufactory* [1962] AC 209 at 216, PC.

3    See the Crowther Report, paras 4.1.3–4. For this Report, see generally, para 5.03.

4    As to bank and building society personal loans, see para 2.19. As to pawnbroking, see para 15.17.

**[7.02] Loans generally**. 'A contract of loan of money is a contract whereby one person lends or agrees to lend money to another, in consideration of a promise express or implied to repay that sum on demand, or at a fixed or determinable future time, or conditionally upon an event which is bound to happen, with or without interest.'[5] An executory contract to make a loan is not specifically enforceable,[6] but breach may give rise to an action for damages,[7] except perhaps where the borrower is a minor.[8] The obvious example of a loan is where B pays money to C, not intending to effect a gift or trust.[9] However, the notion of a loan from B to C also extends to where B pays money to A at the request of C.[10] Whether two or three parties are involved, the issue remains the same: whatever the legal form of the transaction, do the parties intend that its real **legal** nature shall be one of loan?[11] Or more shortly, is the transaction a mere cloak for a loan?[12]

*The general common law*. Where money is lent without any stipulations as to time of repayment, a present debt is created which is repayable immediately and without previous demand.[13] However, the parties may expressly or impliedly agree that the loan will only be repayable on demand, e.g. an overdraft on a bank current account,[14] or on some stipulated date, e.g. under a bank personal loan (see para 2.17). As to interest, see para 7.03A;[15] and as to the incorporation of the lender's standard terms into particular loan contracts, see para 18.04.

*Secured loans*. The fact that a loan is secured, as by mortgage (see below), pledge or surety (see para 25.02), does not mean that the lender is bound to look only to the security for repayment of the debt: the lender may nevertheless sue on the debt (see para 19.22). Now, the security offered by a (first) mortgage (see para 25.20) may justify a lower rate of interest (see para 7.03A); but first mortgages will usually be beyond the scope of this work (see para 3.02). Because of the priority rules (see para 25.22), a further advance from the same lender, e.g. for home improvements, may attract a similar rate because it may grant the same priority. On the other hand, a third-party mortgagee may require a higher rate to compensate for the lower priority, as where he is granting a second mortgage, e.g. for home improvements.

---

5   See *Chitty on Contracts*, 28th edn, Vol 2, para 38-221. For interest, see para 7.03A.
6   *South African Territories v Wallington* [1898] AC 309, HL.
7   See Chitty, *Op. cit.*, paras 38–228/9.
8   Minors' Contracts Act 1987, s 3: see generally, para 10.18.
9   *Prima facie* an obligation to repay arises from the fact of payment, and the onus is on C to prove B intended a gift: *Seldon v Davidson* [1968] 2 All ER 755, CA; and para 2.08. For trusts, see para 19.03.
10  *Law v Coburn* [1972] 3 All ER 1115. See further, para 7.15.
11  Chitty, *Op. cit.*, para 38-224. It is irrelevant that the **economic** purpose of the transaction is to effect a loan, e.g. direct financing (see para 2.21).
12  *Re Securitibank (No. 2)* [1978] 2 NZLR 136. See also the cases cited in para 7.03A.
13  *Re George* (1890) 44 Ch D 627. The action to recover the sum lent should be in debt, not quasi-contract: *Spargos Mining NL v Atlantic Capital Corp* [1996] CLY 772.
14  *Joachimson v Swiss Bank Corpn* [1921] 3 KB 110, CA; *Williams and Glyn's Bank Ltd v Barnes* [1980] Com LR 205. For overdrafts, see Goode, *Payment Obligations in Commercial and Financial Transactions*, 69.
15  For loans to students, see the Education (Student Loans) Act 1990 (as amended).

**[7.03] Bank loans**. If the lender is a bank, there are statutory requirements to maintain confidentiality with regard to information relating to the business or other affairs of any person, enforced by criminal sanctions (see Banking Act 1987, s 82; DPA: see para 3.27). Additionally, in the absence of any formal written agreement with its customer, the bank owes its customer certain well-established implied contractual duties: (i) to conform to the customer's mandate,[16] e.g. to honour/stop his cheques; only to debit a customer's account where appropriate, as on a cheque he personally signed; proper operation of a standing order or direct debit;[17] or insertion in an ATM of a card plus PIN;[18] (ii) to render accounts;[19] (iii) to act with proper care and skill (SGSA, s 13: see para 15.15); and (iv) a qualified duty of secrecy as laid down in *Tournier v National Provincial and Union Bank*,[20] the most important qualifications for our purposes being compulsion by law[21] and express or implied consent by the customer.[22]

In many cases the lender will not be content to leave his rights to the above common law presumptions, but will spell them out—often in a standard-form contract (see generally, para 11.08)—dealing with such matters as: the application process (see para 8.35); the amount loaned, which in the case of a business loan may bring it within the ambit of the CCA (see para 5.23); the rate of interest (see para 7.03A); the precise date(s) of repayment,[23] commonly making time of payment of the essence (see para 23.20), i.e. making it a condition of the contract (see para 11.07); and the position of any security.[24] Furthermore, where the loan is repayable by instalments, the agreement will commonly provide that, if the debtor makes default in respect of any instalment, all the instalments shall be repayable immediately, thus enabling the creditor to sue at once for the entire sum outstanding (an acceleration clause).[25] Normally, as an optional extra, insurance cover may be offered to the debtor (see para 24.44).

---

16  *Patel v Standard Chartered Bank* [2001] CLY 369 (ambiguous mandate); *RBS v Fielding* [2004] CLY 220, CA (joint ac).

17  The difference is that by a standing order a customer operates his account, whereas by a direct debit he authorises his creditor to do so. For payment by these systems, see further, para 23.14. For the pledge by banks of faster clearing, see OFT (2005) 41 *Fair Trading* 19–20; OFT (2005) 41 FT 19–20.

18  *Aliter*, if the underlying transaction is illegal: *Spector v Ageda* [1971] 3 All ER 417; and generally, para 10.20.

19  A banker may be estopped if he renders an inflated account upon which his customer acts. As to estoppel, see para 21.10, *et seq*.

20  [1923] 1 KB 461, CA; and see *Jackson v Royal Bank of Scotland* [2005] 1 All ER (Comm) 337, HL. Do the duties laid down in this case also apply to finance and leasing companies, whose dealings with customers are transaction-based rather than relationship-based (see (1994) 49 CC 3/21)? For further discussion, see generally, Howells [1995] JBL 343 at 348–50; and Paget's *Law of Banking*, 11th edn, Chap 10.

21  E.g. court orders for attachment of debt or earnings (see paras 27.04–5) and tracing (see para 27.13).

22  Including to a credit reference agency (see para 3.26). Is this consistent with the data protection principle (see para 3.28)? See the Jack's Report on *Banking Services* (1989, Cm. 622), Chap 5; (1989) 44 CC2/31.

23  For the risk in transmission of payments, see para 23.14. For the CCA right to complete payments ahead of time, see para 26.19.

24  Loans secured on realty may or may not be purchase-money (see para 2.16). For regulated loans, see para 7.04; for refinancing, see para 7.04A; and for security, see para 25.24.

25  E.g. cl.8 in *White & Carter (Councils) Ltd v McGregor* [1962] AC 413, HL (S). See further, para 26.19.

Such standard-form terms will be subject to two sets of rules in respect of burdensome contract terms, e.g. default interest (see para 26.19), default fees:[26] (i) the Unfair Terms Regulations (see para 11.16B); (ii) s 3 of UCTA (see para 18.20). Moreover, there may also be relevant the rules relating to undue influence (see para 29.40) and possibly also the Banking Code of Practice.[27] But the contract will contain none of the implied terms in favour of the customer found in contracts for the supply of goods (see Chaps 11–15). Only by using CCA, s 75, can such implied terms be used against the lender (see para 16.11).

**[7.03A] Interest.** This is the charge which the borrower pays for the use of the money borrowed. At common law,[28] the *prima facie* rule is that interest *per se* is not payable on a debt or loan by way of general damages,[29] though interest incurred as a result of default may be recoverable as non-remote special damage.[30] Whilst the SGA does not impede any such claim (s 54), as a general rule interest is not payable on the price of goods sold,[31] unless the buyer has given a cheque for the price (Bills of Exchange Act 1882, s 57: see generally, para 7.28).

Of course, it is otherwise where the agreement expressly provides for the payment of interest (see below), or where such an obligation may be inferred from the course of dealings or trade usage (see paras, 18.04 and 15.11). Further, compound interest is usually only payable at common law by agreement,[32] though this may be implied, as in the case of bank overdrafts;[33] and there is a special rule where a statutory rebate is available on early settlement (see para 26.19A). Two statutory powers to award interest on late payment of debts may be noted: (1) as to the late payment of **commercial** debts, which is beyond the scope of this work; (2) as to unregulated judgment debts.[34] With regard to the rate of interest chargeable under the loan agreement, the position is as follows: apart from the old equitable jurisdiction to re-open harsh and unconscionable bargains (see para 29.40), the general control is now to be found in the following: increased rates of interest payable on default may amount to a penalty at common law (see para 27.25); or it may be avoided by the CCA (s 93: see below); or in a consumer supply it may amount to an unfair term (see below). However, variable rates of interest according to a formula

---

26  Default fees may also amount to common law penalties (see para 27.25), but are common in the banking industry. The OFT has announced that it is prepared to take card issuers to court over penalty charges of £12 or more (*AR-2005/6*, 29). See also [2006] 5 *Which?* 7 and 31; [2006] 6 *Which?* 23.

27  Part B of the Code is addressed to banks, building societies and other card issuers. See generally, para 3.12.

28  Interest is sometimes payable in equity even in the absence of a promise to pay it, e.g. on a mortgage debt, or a surety's indemnity: see *Chitty on Contracts*, 28th edn, Vol 2, para 38-248; and generally Goode, *Payment Obligations in Commercial and Financial Transactions*, 79–89.

29  I.e. the damages claimable without proof of the real loss incurred. See *President of India v La Pintada Compania Navigacion SA* [1985] AC 104, HL. See further, Mann (1985) 101 LQR 30; Bowles and Whelan (1985) 48 MLR 229.

30  I.e. on producing evidence of the real loss incurred, e.g. interest charges suffered. See *Wadsworth v Lydall* [1981] 2 All ER 401, CA. As to remoteness of damage, see para 27.41.

31  Benjamin's *Sale of Goods*, 6th edn, para 16-006, *et seq*.

32  E.g. *Kitchen v HSBC Bank plc* [2000] 1 AER (Comm) 787, CA. See *Pre-Judgment Interest on Debts and Damages* (2004, Law Com 287) paras 2, 11–12.

33  Chitty, *Op. cit.*, para 38-250. As to the interest on bank overdrafts, see Paget, *Law of Banking*, 12th edn, para 13.6, *et seq*.

34  See Chitty, *Op. cit.*, paras 27-151 and 38-256; Law Com 287 (above), paras 2, 7–9.

are legitimate, e.g. x% over bank rate or FHBR for the time being, unless unreasonable.[35]

*Regulated loans.* In relation to **regulated** loans (see para 7.04), there is no statutory interest and it has become common for lenders to include in their loan agreement a provision under which contractual interest on the capital lent (**not** on the interest) does not merge in the judgment, but remains due until payment **after as well as before any judgment**. In a regulated agreement, such a clause might also be void under CCA, s 173 (see para 18.11), as contravening ss 93–5 (see paras 26.19–19A); and the debtor could apply for a variation of the clause under s 136 (see para 9.20). However, another avenue of attack was explored in *Director General of Fair Trading v First National Bank plc*:[36]

> Clause 8 of FNB's unsecured regulated loan for home improvements contained such a provision for contractual interest on the capital lent in respect of the period before and after judgment. This would have left the debtor liable to pay contractual interest even though he had satisfied any judgment, perhaps to pay by instalments with interest. If the debtor failed to pay, FNB would apply for a charging order on his house (see para 27.04); but, inexplicably, few debtors would invoke the above CCA defences, or ask for a Time Order (see para 24.40).

The DG applied for an injunction on the grounds that cl 8 was unfair under the 1994 version of the UTCC Regulations (see para 11.19). It was not in dispute that (i) those Regulations apply to regulated agreements and (ii) cl 8 was not individually negotiated (see para 11.14). Reversing the Court of Appeal, the House of Lords accepted that the effect of cl 8 was to prevent the interest provision merging in the judgment (see above: Lord Bingham at 1005, paras 3–4); and, whilst agreeing with the lower courts that cl 8 was not a core term (see para 11.14), but fell within the UTCC Regulations, the House held that it satisfied the fairness test there laid down (see paras 11.14–15). Bearing in mind the prevalence of versions of cl 8 in the industry (para 24) and of the availability to the courts of existing CCA provisions to control them (see above), their Lordships recommended various steps which might be taken to publicise these provisions to litigating debtors.[37] Accordingly, new s 130A of the CCA 1974 requires that as from April 2008 a business creditor or owner at his own expense to give regular written warnings to the debtor or hirer of the existence of such as cl 8;[38] and, whilst there is a default of s 130A, the debtor or hirer shall not be liable to pay such interest (ss 130A(2) and (3)). It follows that the direct effect of the *First National* case should be small.[39]

---

35  *Lloyds Bank plc v Voller* [2000] 2 All ER (Comm) 978, CA. For FHBR, see para 2.18; and for the CCA treatment of consensual variations, see para 26.21; and for possible dangers, see para 10.05. As to unreasonable terms, see Unfair Contract Terms Act 1977, s 3 (see para 18.20).

36  [2002] 1 AC 481; [2002] 1 All ER 97, HL (see 65 MLR 763, at 768–73).

37  Para 66. See *Fair, Clear and Competitive: the Consumer Credit Market in the 21st Century* (Dec. 2003, Cm. 6040), para 5.76.

38  Ss 130A(1), (4), (7) and (9), as inserted by s 17 of the 2006 Act. The 'first required notice' shall be given after the 'judgement sum' becomes payable and thereafter at six-monthly intervals (new s 130A(1)). As to the notices, see ss 130A(5) and (6). S 130A does not apply to non-commercial agreements (see para 5.18): s 130A(8).

39  But it may cause more debt-recovery actions to be defended and hence transferred to the debtor's local county court: see para 3.22.

# REGULATED LOANS

**[7.04] Introduction**. The circumstances in which a loan contract (see paras 7.02–3) amounts to a regulated loan within the CCA have already been examined (see para 5.13, *et seq*.). The CCA starts by comprehending all persons who make a business of lending money, and then granting exemption from particular provisions.[40] This it does as follows: all loans to private-consumer borrowers are consumer credit agreements (see para 5.19); but they are not regulated agreements if they are exempt (see para 5.14), and are saved from some of the provisions of the Act if they are non-commercial or small agreements (see paras 5.17 and 5.18). Additionally, some lenders, e.g. large banks, are expressly saved from much of Pt V of the Act[41] or the OFT empowered to exclude them.[42] Loans within the ambit of the CCA are further subject to the following (overlapping) classifications:

(1)  Restricted-use (RU) or unrestricted-use (UU) agreements;[43]

(2)  Debtor-creditor-supplier (DCS) or debtor-creditor (DC) agreements;[44] and

(3)  Credit-token agreements (see para 7.09).

Thus, the typical cash-loan under the CCA will be a regulated DC agreement for UU credit; and, if that loan is obtained through the medium of a credit card, it will amount to a UU loan obtained under a DC credit-token agreement (see para 5.30). However, a loan to refinance existing indebtedness is likely to amount to a regulated DC agreement for RU credit (see para 7.04A).

Whilst the rules applicable to regulated agreements generally are examined elsewhere,[45] there must here be considered certain special rules applicable only to regulated loans: these include interest provisions (see para 7.03A); canvassing (see para 7.05); revolving credit (see para 7.08); and credit-tokens (see para 7.09). Section 179 contains power to make regulations as to the form and content of secondary documents,[46] laying down that the effect of contravention shall from that moment be as if the regulated agreement had been improperly executed under s 60(1).[47] Additionally, s 83 saves the debtor from liability for misuse of a credit facility (see para 7.07A). Considered elsewhere are the very important connected lender provisions (see para 16.11, *et seq*.).

---

40  Occasional transactions are ignored and there must still be the requisite degree of repetition: see CCA, s 189(2); and para 6.12.

41  E.g. s 74(1)(b): see para 9.07.

42  E.g. ss 60(3) and 74(3): see paras 9.09 and 9.07.

43  This largely depends on whether or not the debtor *de facto* acquires freedom to use the credit as he wishes: see para 5.29.

44  This depends on whether or not there is a business connection between the suppliers of goods and finance: see para 5.32.

45  See especially the rules as to licensing (para 6.11, *et seq*.), advertising (see para 8.27, *et seq*.) and unfair credit bargains (see paras 29.44–7).

46  According to s 179(1), these secondary documents are 'credit cards, trading-checks, receipts, vouchers and other documents or things issued by creditors, owners or suppliers under or in connection with regulated agreements or . . . linked transactions'.

47  S 179(2). As to s 60(1), see para 9.10; and as to improperly executed agreements, see para 9.19.

**[7.04A] Refinancing and debt consolidation.** Amounting to RU credit (see para 5.28), the consolidation of a number of earlier debts, perhaps with statutory rebate (see para 26.19A), into one large debt is termed by the CCA 'refinancing', though without formal definition.[48] It may be achieved in two ways:

(a) the refinancing of credit agreements between the same two parties, as by a variation of one agreement (see para 26.22), e.g. granting more time to pay (roll-over loans; see below), top-up loans; or by a consolidation of several agreements,[49] which may offer cheaper monthly repayments by extending the loan period.

(b) the refinancing of one or more debts owed to third parties,[49] as where the creditor pays off the earlier creditors from one new loan to the debtor, e.g. where a credit card company attracts a new customer by paying off his existing card debts.

A particular problem has been the refinancing of existing debts in default, especially where (as is frequently the case) the debtor is no longer creditworthy, e.g. he lacks a steady income or has county court judgments (CCJs) against him. This is termed 'non-status' or 'sub-prime' lending and is made to borrowers who fail to meet the normal commercial test of creditworthiness and hence are legitimately charged much higher rates of interest.[50] It tends to be a specialist class of business, and lenders usually fall into one of the following groups:[51] first, those offering credit products tailored to the low-income market, such as home credit, pawn-brokers, sale and buy back, rental purchase; second, companies offering similar products to mainstream lenders, but at enhanced rates which reflect the increased risk, such as small banks, building societies, finance companies and money-lenders, often operating through a network of brokers. The average lending rate is 170% APR.

In this last class of business, it is common for the creditor to insist on credit insurance (see para 24.48) and a secured loan: the latter gives the creditor more effective remedies (see para 27.04); and the debtor may not understand that he is thereby moving from unsecured to secured debt. However, too much should not be made of this, because of (1) the ability of an unsecured judgment creditor to apply for a charging order (see para 27.04) and (2) the boundary between status and non-status loans is blurred. Where the refinancing includes a (usually second) mortgage on the debtor's home, it will normally be within the following CCA rules: the Advertising Regulations (see para 8.30); the Time Order procedure (see para 24.40); and the unfair credit relationship provisions (see para 29.44). Perhaps because of the financial pressure such debtors already face, in seeking refinance, they have shown themselves insufficiently conscious of the APR quoted (see para 8.22), the level of fees charged by brokers and lenders ('arrangement fees')[52]

---

48  Goode, *Consumer Credit Law & Practice*, para 25.65; and see OFT, *Debt Consolidation* (2004) AR-2003/4, 75.

49  This will usually amount to a novation (see para 7.27). See [2003] 7 *Credit Today* 15.

50  E.g. *Broadwick Financial Services Ltd v Spencer* (set out at para 8.22); *London North Securities v Meadows* (set out at para 8.25). For non-status lenders, see para 6.10; and for status lenders, see para 2.17.

51  See Collard and Kempson, *Affordable Credit* (2005) 1, 23.

52  For attempts to bring such fees within the APR, see para 8.24.

and that entry into secured financing puts their homes at risk.[53] The OFT has issued a code of practice for non-status lending,[54] backed up by the threat of credit licence revocation.[55] Moreover, whether or not regulated, the terms of such loans may also be attacked as unfair terms (see para 11.12), or on other grounds.[56] Indeed, it may sometimes be possible to wind up compulsorily an errant creditor or broker, e.g. broker who absconds with payments.[57]

Where available, a cheaper alternative for non-status debtors may be a credit union (see para 15.19) or social loans (see para 2.15).

## Canvassing credit

[7.05] **Introduction**. The Crowther Report sought to draw a distinction between the doorstep peddling on the one hand of goods on credit and on the other of money.[58] The Report recommended that the doorstep peddling[59] of money, already illegal under the Moneylenders Acts (see para 6.09), should continue to be banned, whilst the doorstep peddling of loans to purchase goods embraced many perfectly legitimate forms of business, e.g. check trading and mail order. However, foreseeing that the peddling of goods[60] might be used as a cloak for the peddling of money, the Report recommended that the former should only be allowable under a supplementary licence (see para 6.14). These recommendations were adopted by the CCA: it defined doorstep peddling as 'canvassing' (see para 7.06) and sought to prohibit most canvassing of DC agreements (see para 7.07). On behalf of consumers generally, breaches may also trigger injunctive proceedings under Pt 8 of the EA (see paras 6.06–8).

[7.06] **Definition**. Seeking to enact the Crowther recommendation (see para 7.05), s 48(1) provides:

> 'An individual[61] (the "canvasser") canvasses a regulated agreement[62] off trade premises if he solicits the entry (as debtor or hirer)[63] of another individual[61] (the 'consumer') into the agreement by making oral representations[64] to the consumer or

---

53  This is particularly the case with non-status borrowers (see paras 8.22 and 8.35): OFT, *Unjust Credit Transactions*, paras 1.6 and 4.11. Such consumers are sometimes encouraged to capitalise on the tremendously increased equity in their homes by taking out a second mortgage. As to foreclosure, see para 25.20; and as to second mortgages, see para 25.24. A much stronger warning to debtors is now required in such mortgage advertisements: see para 8.30.

54  *Guidelines for lenders and brokers in the non-status lending market* (1997); due to be reviewed: see Goode, *ibid*, VIII, para 16.1. For Codes of Practice, see generally, para 3.13.

55  As to renewal and termination of licences for creditors and credit-brokers, see respectively paras 6.23; 5.40.

56  E.g. as unenforceable for not stating the amount of credit or charges (see paras 8.24 and 9.21), or where the broker has a secret commission (see para 10.18), or the consolidation encourages overindebtedness (see para 6.10).

57  See CCA, new s 34A (see para 6.23).

58  Paras 6.4.17–20. For this Report, see generally, para 5.03.

59  But not postal advertising: *Op. cit.*, para 6.4.21.

60  Peddling goods may require a pedlar's licence and/or a street trader's licence: see para 6.02.

61  For 'individual' see the definition in s 189(1): set out at para 5.24.

62  For regulated agreements, see para 5.13, *et seq*.

63  For 'debtor' and 'hirer', see the definition in s 189(1): set out at respectively, paras 5.24 and 1.19.

64  'Representation' is defined in s 189(1) and discussed at para 16.08.

any other individual,[65] during a visit by the canvasser to any place (not excluded by subsection (2)) where the consumer, or that other individual, as the case may be, is, being a visit—

(a)  carried out for the purpose of making such oral representations to individuals who are at the place, but

(b)  not carried out in response to a request made on a previous occasion'.

Thus, the essence of canvassing is the oral soliciting of entry by the consumer into a regulated agreement by the individual canvasser during a visit to non-business premises. This is very carefully drafted and **none** of the following will amount to canvassing:

1.  Section 48(2) expressly excludes soliciting, etc, at any permanent or temporary **business premises** of the financier (creditor or owner), goods supplier, canvasser or consumer, e.g. stall at a trade fair, mobile display at roadside, retail premises. The exclusion here of the consumer's business premises may be compared with their inclusion within the cancellation provisions (see para 10.29).

2.  The soliciting, etc, involves **no oral communication**, thus excluding wholly written communications, whether delivered by post or otherwise. Mail drops offering credit facilities have become an increasingly common feature of modern life, e.g. junk mail, the sale of lists of potential customers being a substantial business. However, a circular sent to a minor may amount to an offence (see para 8.33). What about sign language to the deaf?

3.  The soliciting etc is not made during the course of a **visit** to non-business premises, as where a financier from his office telephones a consumer.[66]

4.  The visit must be **unsolicited**, so that it is not canvassing if the visit is made in response either to a reply-paid signed postcard sent in by the consumer[67] or even a prior[68] oral request. But a visit made in response to an oral request, whilst it will not amount to canvassing, may constitute an offence under s 49(2).[69]

5.  The visit is unrequested, but not carried out for the **purposes** of soliciting (s 48(1)(a)); for instance, where a discussion spontaneously develops about a loan either during a home visit to service a previous loan or at an independent party or round of golf.[70]

**[7.07] The prohibitions**. In accordance with the Crowther recommendations (see para 7.05), two acts are prohibited in relation to canvassing (see para 7.06).

---

65  E.g. spouse or other member of household.

66  For special cases, see Goode, *Consumer Credit Law & Practice*, para 28.87, item (c). For telephone selling generally, see para 8.16A.

67  S 48(1)(b). This does not stipulate by whom the request must be made: see Guest and Lloyd, *Consumer Credit Law*, para 2-049. The OFT would like to see this restriction removed: AR-2004/5, 64.

68  The request must be genuinely previous: it would be insufficient if on the doorstep the consumer signed a back-dated request.

69  See para 7.07. As to the delivery of unsolicited goods, see further, para 8.18.

70  *Aliter*, if the home visit or social event was set up or attended for the purpose of soliciting, a matter which may be difficult to prove. *Quaere*, if the visit was to solicit a DCS agreement?

1. *To canvass loans of money.* Section 49(1) provides that:

> 'it is an offence to canvass debtor-creditor agreements off trade premises'.

The effect of the restriction to DC agreements (see para 5.35) is to prohibit the unrequested doorstep peddling of cash, but not of trading checks or vouchers, nor any form of vendor credit.[71] It creates an offence in the canvasser,[72] but does not give rise to any further sanctions:[73] so any regulated agreement resulting from the canvassing is not affected. Moreover, the section expressly exempts the soliciting of overdraft facilities on existing current accounts;[74] nor does it apply to the doorstep peddling of goods on credit (DCS agreements) or hire (consumer hirings), though a canvassing endorsement is required on licences.[75] For many years, doorstep sellers have got round this prohibition by unsolicited canvassing of vouchers for goods (see para 15.17); but in Spring 2004 the DTI announced that it was proposed include a ban of this practice in the new legislation.

2. *Orally solicited visits.* Whilst not amounting to canvassing, s 49(2) enacts that:

> 'It is also an offence to solicit the entry of an individual (as debtor) into a debtor-creditor agreement during a visit carried out in response to a request made on a previous occasion, where—
>
> (a) the request was not in writing signed by or on behalf of the person making it, and
>
> (b) if no request for the visit had been made, the soliciting would have constituted the canvassing of a debtor-creditor agreement off trade premises'.

The draftsman could have simply amended the definition of canvassing to include under s 48(1)(b) only signed written requests; but, because he wished to use the definition of canvassing for other purposes as well, he chose to create this extra offence with the same limited sanctions[73] and banking exemption.[74] The effect of s 49(2) is that new home credit business can only be lawfully obtained by either (a) the consumer visiting the trader's business premises, or (b) indirectly at the consumer's house, e.g. by newspaper coupons or telephone calls.

Finally, it should be noted that just as the foregoing relate to the door-step soliciting of regulated agreements, the Act also seeks to control the doorstep soliciting of certain ancillary credit services. Section 154 (as amended) makes it an offence[72] to canvass off trade premises[76] the services of a person carrying on a business of credit-brokerage (see paras 5.38–41), debt-adjusting,[77] debt-counselling,[77] or credit information services;[78] but there is no prohibition in respect of orally solicited visits.

---

71   Because they are DCS agreements under s 12: see para 5.34.
72   For penalties, see s 167 and Sched 1. See further, Chap 28.
73   S 170(1): see para 10.19.
74   Amended ss 49(3)–(5), 183. For details, see Guest and Lloyd, *Consumer Credit Law*, para 4-4800; and for an explanation, see Bennion, *Consumer Credit Control*, para 4.10.
75   For the doorstep peddling of goods on credit, see para 6.14.
76   As defined by s 153, which contains a definition of canvassing slightly different from that in s 48 in relation to the type of premises involved.
77   See para 5.43. It is not made an offence to solicit the service of debt-collectors or credit reference agencies because these services are only likely to be employed by creditors and suppliers.
78   2006 Act, s 25. For such services, see para 5.44.

**[7.07A] Liability for misuse of credit facilities**. Whether the customer has a fixed or running account (see para 5.28) with a financier, there may be circumstances where a third party wrongfully withdraws money from that account. According to the general law, the financier can only charge that wrongfully withdrawn amount to the customer's account where he has a contractual right to do so.[79] However, s 83(1) of the CCA grants the consumer a special statutory immunity from such a contractual provision in the following terms:

> 'The debtor under a regulated consumer credit agreement shall not be liable to the creditor for any loss arising from the use of the credit facility by another person not acting, or to be treated as acting, as the debtor's agent'.

This general CCA rule is carefully limited as follows:

(1) The account between the consumer and financier must involve a **consumer credit agreement**,[80] so that it has no application as regards a simple customer's account containing a credit balance, e.g. a bank or building society account without overdraft facility which contains a £70 balance (see para 7.01). Section 83 is intended to give a customer/debtor an **immunity** from liability, not to protect a customer/debtor from **loss**:[81] so, if a thief pretends to be the account-holder to abstract that £70 balance, the section offers the account-holder no protection.

(2) This immunity applies only in respect of a **credit** facility, e.g. £100: it may be a fixed or running account, e.g. a bank Personal Loan (fixed-sum) or overdraft (running-account). It can have no application to consumer **hirings**, as where a third party impersonates another to hire goods.

(3) The indemnity is limited to loss arising from **use** of the credit facility, e.g. abstraction of £50 from the £100 facility. If the thief merely uses an ATM card (see para 7.01) to draw down a customer's balance, e.g. abstraction of £50 from customer's £70 balance, the matter is outside s 83,[82] but governed by the general law (see above). However, insofar as the thief utilises the customer's credit facility, e.g. sending him into unauthorised overdraft by abstracting £80 from an account £70 in credit, the matter may fall within s 83 as to the £10,[83] unless a credit token was used (s 84: see para 7.14).

(4) S 83 has no application where the withdrawal is made by a third party who is acting as the customer's **agent**, or to be treated as such; but the burden of proof lies on the creditor (s 171(4)(b)(i)). Thus, if the creditor can prove that the customer 'loaned' his ATM card and PIN to a spouse to make a withdrawal, the customer cannot claim the s 83 protection, even if the spouse drew more than was authorised.[84]

---

79  I.e. under the account mandate (see para 7.03). Or where the customer is estopped from denying this (see generally, para 21.10).

80  So it cannot apply where the third party misrepresents that there is a consumer credit agreement.

81  Goode, *Consumer Credit Law & Practice*, para 39.9.

82  It has been promised that all payment cards will be brought within ss 83 and 84: *Banking Services* (1990, CM 1026) paras 4.6, 8.3.

83  Goode, *Op. cit.*, para 39.10.      84  Goode, *Op. cit.*, para 39.8.

(5)  By s 83(2), the above indemnity does not apply to non-commercial agreements (see para 5.18); nor does it affect the bankers' statutory protection in collecting cheques,[85] an exception perhaps relevant in relation to credit-card cheques (see para 7.28).

*Banking code.* Issuers of payment cards who subscribe to the Banking Code of Practice (see generally, para 3.12) undertake, irrespective of ss 83 and 84 of the CCA, to pay the full loss incurred through use of a card: (a) when it has not been received by a customer;[86] (b) for all unauthorised transactions after the card issuer has been told that the card has been lost or stolen or that someone else may know the PIN (see generally, para 7.13), including money transferred to his electronic purse (see para 2.24); (c) if faults have occurred in the machine or other system used, causing customers to suffer direct loss, unless the fault was obvious or advised by a message or notice on display.[87] Customers will be liable for all loss so caused where they are shown to have acted fraudulently or with gross negligence.[88]

**[7.08] Revolving credit generally**. It has already been seen that a loan may be of either a finite sum or a revolving credit; and that these two types of loan are respectively christened by the Act 'fixed-sum credit' and 'running-account credit' (see para 5.28). In respect of all running-account credits, the CCA has to make some adjustments to bring them into line with fixed-sum credit with regard to the information to be supplied to the debtor during the currency of the agreement. The Act makes it clear that the running-account debtor is entitled not just (on payment) to comparable information **on request**;[89] but also *gratis* to **automatic** periodic statements of account,[90] typically a monthly statement showing the opening and closing balances, any movements (debits/credits) and the minimum payment due, which statement must now contain prescribed warnings as to the consequences of failing to make payments.[91] There are special rules for credit tokens (see para 7.09, *et seq.*); and, where more than one consumer is a party to the transaction, it may be a question whether they are co-principals[92] or one is just an additional permitted user of the other's facility.[93] Unfortunately, the Act does not appear to deal clearly

---

85   S 83(2). Under s 4 of the Cheques Act 1957: see para 7.28.

86   See generally, para 7.11. Would it be fairer if the burden of proof were transferred to the creditor (cf. s 171)?

87   Para 20.4. The burden of proof is on the issuer (para 20.5). For the concept of 'gross negligence', see the Banking Ombudsman, *Annual Report 1994/95* paras 10.4–6.

88   E.g. by writing a PIN on the card. See further the Banking Ombudsman, *1995–96 Annual Report*, paras 12.6, 12.7.

89   Ss 78(1)–(3): see generally, para 15.16.

90   Amended ss 78(4)–(5). The rule does not extend to small agreements (see para 5.17): s 78(5). The complicated regulations as to periodic statements are considered by Goode, *Consumer Credit Law & Practice*, paras 34.18–31. No sanction is prescribed for breach of s 78(4): s 170(1); and see para 10.19. As from 2007, there will be special requirements for store cards (see para 2.24).

91   New s 78(4A) of the 1974 Act, as inserted by s 7 of the 2006 Act and in force from April 2008. These could include warnings as to the effect of making only minimum payments. As to appropriation of payments, see para 23.13.

92   In the case of joint accounts (see generally, para 5.24), the Act allows the debtors to forego their right to one statement each by signing a 'dispensing notice' (new s 185(2)), which is effective in respect of the original and any modifying agreement (new s 185(2D)) until revoked or death (new ss 185(2A) and (2C)). It is not possible for all joint debtors to submit dispensing notices, the last in time being ineffective (new s 185(2B)).

93   For the effect of use by an 'additional card-holder', see para 7.09.

with 'application form agreements',[94] a form of business common in some types of running-account credit:[95] this may give rise to difficulties both as regards execution[96] and cancellation.[97]

Finally, and quite apart from the CCA, it should be borne in mind that, where goods are obtained through a running-account facility, there is no inherent right of recaption of goods (see para 24.23) as there would be if an hp agreement was utilised;[98] and credit balances on running-accounts may give rise to yet further problems.[99]

## Credit cards (tokens)

[7.09] **Introduction**. The three separate bilateral contracts in a credit or charge card operation (see para 2.27) may be analysed as follows:[100]

1. *Supply contract.* Between the retail supplier of goods or services and the consumer there will be a contract for the supply of those goods or services, the consideration being satisfied by means of a credit or charge card (plastic money). In the case of goods, this may amount to a sale with a special arrangement to pay by card; and with either goods or services the supplier may insist at the outset on either of the following:

   (a) taking an imprint of the card, which raises the question of whether there is then a preliminary contract; or have the parties not yet finished agreeing (see para 10.03)? If there is a preliminary agreement, does it contravene s 59 (see para 5.20)?

   (b) the card-holder signing in blank. It might be argued that there is (a) an open contract to pay whatever the supplier deems fit, or (b) a contract to pay only a reasonable price (see para 2.06). The supply contract follows all the ordinary rules as to express and implied terms and exclusions (see Pt 4). On the analogy of a cheque, is the card-holder under any tortious duty of care to ensure that the slip is so drawn that it is not possible afterwards for another to insert extra charges?

2. *Card-holding contract.* The credit or charge cards will have been issued to the account-holder (principal debtor) and any other card-holder, e.g. spouse, by

---

94 The practice of promoting schemes by way of a leaflet, part of which consists of an application form, the leaflet being available from a dispenser: (1984) 39 CC 1–19.

95 E.g. store budget cards (see para 2.19), credit cards (see para 7.09, *et seq.*). 'Application form' agreements for fixed-sum credit are effectively ruled out: Guest and Lloyd, *Encyclopedia of Consumer Credit*, para 2-062.

96 For the purposes of s 61(1)(c) (see para 9.12), is the leaflet extracted by the consumer from the dispenser 'presented' to him?

97 For the purposes of s 67 (see para 10.29), is the shop-assistant's direction of the consumer to the dispenser an 'oral representation'?

98 For alternative means of obtaining security, see Chap 25.

99 Where the consumer has a credit balance on his running-account, the question arises whether he has made a 'deposit' with the system-operator within s 5 of the Banking Act 1987. Whilst fixed-sum credits would seem exempted (s 5(2)), running-account credits would appear not to be so: see (1987) 41 CC 4/30.

100 See *Re Charge Card Services Ltd* (set out at para 2.27). Distinguish where there is a cheque card; or a debit card without overdraft facility (see para 5.21).

one of the following: with a two-party card, whether *simpliciter* or private label, the card-issuer will be the retail-supplier; whereas with a three-party card, the issuer (merchant-acquirer) will be a financier (see paras 2.24–5). In most cases, it would appear that the card contract will in essence be one of loan for revolving credit,[100] which the creditor should operate within the terms of the Banking Code (see para 3.12). Leaving aside the formation of that contract (see para 7.11), its terms are likely to include the following:[101] the time-limited card must be signed by the card-holder, is usually subject to an annual account fee (see para 7.11) and may only be used subject to the conditions for the time being in force (see para 11.07) and within the credit limit;[102] if the card is used above the limit, strictly the issuer is entitled to refuse to honour to the retailer that use, rather than honour it *pro tanto*;[102] the issuer will debit the holder's account[103] with the amount of all card transactions effected by him or his authorised agent (see paras 7.13–4); interest is payable on the balance outstanding after due date;[104] set out a payment hierarchy (see para 7.03); the card-holder must make a minimum specified payment each month,[105] as compared with the fixed regular payment under a budget account (see para 2.19), but in default of such minimum payment, there is likely to be an acceleration clause and a default charge (see para 7.03); or he may pay more at his option (cf. para 26.19); the card-issuer may issue to the holder (commonly unsolicited: see para 8.18) cheque forms on the account (see para 7.28); the card remains the property of the issuer[106] and the holder may terminate the agreement by surrendering the card to the issuer (cf. para 26.03); the card-issuer does not guarantee that the card will be honoured by any supplier and may disclose to its agents information about the card account, e.g. the retailer (as to consent to such disclosure under the DPA, see para 3.27). This contract will usually be regulated by the CCA (see para 7.10); and its express terms are subject to the statutory tests of reasonableness under UCTA 1977, s 3(1) (see para 18.24) and fairness under the UTCC Regulations (see para 11.15). Very profitable for issuers tend to be credit insurance (see para 24.44), 'administration fees' and 'penalty' charges.[107]

---

101 See Kiely [2001] 1 *Credit Today* 33; 2 *CT* 39. For some model forms, see Guest and Lloyd, *Encyclopedia of Consumer Credit*, paras 8–228, *et seq.*

102 The issuer may also attempt to enforce 'penalties' (see below). Card issuers have been criticised for being too quick to increase card limits for the over-indebted. The Minister is pressing the industry to deal with unsolicited increases in credit-card limits in the Banking Code: (2005–6) HC Deb, R3, cols. 1028–9.

103 Additional card-holders, e.g. employees or spouses, are sometimes made to underwrite their own card expenditure. This may make them personally liable as indemnifiers (see para 25.06) if the card-holder becomes insolvent (see para 19.12).

104 The account charge. For interest, see generally, para 7.03A. If the debt is not completely cleared by due date, interest is normally payable from billing. Cash advances may attract interest from the date of advance. A lower rate of interest may be obtained if the indebtedness is secured, e.g. by a mortgage.

105 By reducing the minimum payment sufficiently, the card-issuer can often trap the holder into a life-time debt. The issuer may also attempt to enforce 'penalties' (see below).

106 E.g. *Tony Mekwin MTV & Co v National Westminster Bank PLC* [1998] CLY 2512, CA. This may be advantageous where the issuer wishes to stop someone using the card, whether a holder or third party. For the action of conversion, see para 19.04.

107 See [2005] 1 *Which?* 10. These default charges may theoretically be curbed by the UTCCR or rule against penalties (see para 27.25); and the OFT has demanded that such charges be reduced (see para 7.03).

3. *Merchant contract*. Provisions commonly found in such franchise contracts between the supplier/merchant and the merchant-acquirer include the following: a derogation from the signed voucher provision for distance sales, where the sale is made telephone or mail-order; arrangements for refunds to account-holders (cf. para 29.04); and a commission payable to the card-issuer (merchant fee: see para 2.28). There also used to be a promise to supply card-holders at the same price as cash customers; but such provisions have now been rendered unlawful.[108] The contract will usually provide for termination on breach[109] and a 'charge-back clause', designed to put the risk of fraud on the merchant by relieving the merchant-acquirer of the obligation to pay out the merchant in respect of particular sorts of transaction,[110] e.g. where a fraudulent third party acquires goods or services by way of a card-not-present transaction, which is one where goods or services are ordered by telephone or mail order (as to which, see paras 8.17; 8.19). The express terms will usually be subject to the statutory test of reasonableness (UCTA, s 3: see above) which may cause difficulty, *inter alia*, as regards the application of 'charge-back clauses' to 'card-not-present' transactions.[111]

[7.10] **Application of the CCA**. Whilst both credit and charge card-holding contracts are in essence loans (see para 7.01), charge cards are exempt from the CCA (s 16: see para 5.21). On the other hand, a credit card contract is likely to amount to a regulated agreement within the CCA, being a loan to an 'individual'.[112] It will then amount to a regulated consumer credit agreement (see para 5.19) for the provision of running-account credit (see para 5.28) under which the account-holder is the debtor (see para 5.24), the card-issuer is the creditor (see para 5.25), the card-contract is a credit-token agreement[113] and the card issued under it a credit-token (see para 5.30). If such a card is used to obtain cash,[114] there will be a DC agreement for UU credit under ss 11(2) and 13(c) (see paras 5.29 and 5.35; and Sched 2, Example 16). However, if the card is used to obtain goods or services,[114] then there is RU credit (see para 5.29) and the position is as follows: in the case of a two-party card,[115] there is a DCS agreement[116] within s 12(a); whereas in the case of a three-party card,[115] there is a DCS agreement[116] within s 12(b) (see s 187(3), considered at para 5.33), the retailer being the supplier (see Sched 2, Examples 3, 16), and the supply contract a linked transaction.[117] The whole transaction is subject to all

---

108 As a monopoly: 1990 SI 2159; and see generally, para 2.12. It commonly results in retailers charging more for credit card purchases (a surcharge).

109 See, e.g. *Naheem v National Westminster Bank PLC* [1998] CCLR 10, CA.

110 E.g. *Bank of Scotland v Truman* [2005] EWHC 583, at paras 8–11, 103–26, 128, 137 (goods not delivered to consumers).

111 See Brownsword (1999) 19 LS at 311. Also (1997) 147 NLJ 1806; (1998) 148 NLJ 7 and 133.

112 But see *Re Charge Card Services Ltd* (see para 7.09).

113 S 14(2). Depending on whether or not a binding contract is made at the outset (see para 7.11), it will amount to either a prospective or actual credit-token agreement (see para 5.20). What if creditors dispense with plastic cards and merely require a number verbally repeated, e.g. telephone sales?

114 Because it falls within two categories, it is a multiple agreement: see para 5.27 and Sched 2, Example 16.

115 Two- and three-party cards are explained at para 2.24.

116 *OFT v Lloyds TSB Bank plc* (see para 16.11). As to DCS agreements, see para 5.34.

117 See para 5.31. As regards the exemption of insurance policies under s 19(4), see para 24.44.

the normal rules applicable to regulated agreements considered later,[118] and is additionally subject to certain special rules (see para 7.12). Normally, the card-issuer will require a category A licence (see para 6.15), whereas the retail supplier will not need any CCA licence.[119]

*Authorised users.* If the debtor accepts the frequently proffered invitation to add another member of his family as an 'authorised user' or 'additional card-holder' (usually with a separate card issued to that user), the legal position would be as follows: unless a co-debtor,[120] the authorised user has none of the CCA protections,[121] but the debtor remains liable for the latter's use of the card (see para 7.13).

**[7.11] Formation of card contract.** Whilst the terms of the card contract between the consumer and card-issuer have already been outlined (see para 7.09), there remains the issue of how that credit-token contract (see para 5.30) is made. Where the card-issuer charges a fee[122] there will be a bilateral contract, under which the credit card is then issued; and each replacement card, sent with a fresh set of terms (see para 7.12), will usually discharge the old contract by subsequent agreement (see para 26.18) and replace it with a new agreement on those fresh terms.[123] However, where no such fee is charged, the position would appear to be this:[124] if the antecedent card 'agreement' in fact amounts merely to an offer by the issuer to enter into a unilateral contract,[125] there is only a separate acceptance of the issuer's continuing offer each time the card is used by the holder,[126] a view which has been characterised as 'absurdly complicated'.[127]

Insofar as the credit-card contract may be regulated (see para 7.10), s 66(1) lays down the earliest moment at which the card-holder may become civilly liable under it.

> 'The debtor shall not be liable under a credit-token agreement for use made of the credit-token by any person unless the debtor had previously accepted the credit-token, or the use constituted an acceptance of it by him'.

Under this important provision, the burden of proof is on the creditor;[128] and s 66(2) goes on to explain that the debtor accepts a credit-token when: (a) it is

---

118 E.g. formalities (see Chap 9), s 56 liability (see para 16.08). See generally, Jones, *Credit Cards*, Chap 5.

119 Because he does not effect introductions, he is not a credit-broker (see para 5.41): Jones, *Op. cit.*, 15.

120 For co-debtors, see para 5.24. He may be required to indemnify the card-issuer: see para 7.09.

121 See Jones [1988] JBL 457. See generally, Jones *Credit Cards*, 106, 109.

122 To convert a card issued free into one for which a fee is charged may not be lawful: Borrie (1990) 44 CC 5/20.

123 OFT, *Equal Liability*, 7. See Campbell (1994) 13 Tr L 18 at 23–4. For the historical importance of this issue, see 1st edn, para 7.14.

124 For the burden of proof in respect of the lawful supply of credit-tokens, see s 171(4)(a). 'Lawful supply' seems to refer to s 51: see para 7.12.

125 It may be doubted whether this represents the reality of the transaction, because the offeree (consumer) is under an obligation to make payments as stipulated (see para 7.09A).

126 Is the reality a hybrid contract, under which the unilateral offer matures into a bilateral contract?

127 It may turn some uses of a card into small agreements (see para 5.17): Jones, *Credit Cards*, 64. It may convert each use of the card into fixed-sum credit (see para 5.28): Jones, *Op. cit.*, 74.

128 See s 171(4)(a); and Jones, *Op. cit.*, 146–7.

signed;[129] or (b) a receipt for it is signed;[130] or (c) it is first used, either by the debtor himself or by a person who, pursuant to the agreement, is authorised by him to use it. The effect is to protect the debtor in the event of the card being stolen in course of post to him and *pro tanto* overrides s 84 (see para 7.13); but it is not clear what happens if an additional card is stolen.[131] Aside from this statutory protection, similar rules may be applied to unregulated payment cards under the Banking Code (see para 7.13) and under regulations in respect of distance selling (see para 7.14).

**[7.12] Special CCA provisions**. Where the use of a credit card amounts to a regulated transaction (see para 7.10), it is subject to special CCA rules as follows:

1.  *Unsolicited mailing*. The early 1970s saw the launch of the two major three-party credit card systems in the UK by way of unsolicited mass mailing.[132] In s 51, an outraged Parliament sought to prevent repetition of this exercise by making it a criminal offence,[133] but made the rule subject to several exceptions: (a) small DCS agreements;[134] or (b) tokens given to companies in any event or to businesses for amounts above the CCA limit;[135] or (c) the credit token is given in response to a signed request by its recipient;[136] or (d) it is given for use under a credit-token agreement already made;[137] or (e) it is given in renewal or replacement.[138] In practice, new card-issuers have found these exemptions sufficiently generous to enable the effective marketing of new brands of card, despite tighter rules under the Banking Code of Practice (see para 3.13). Nor does the prohibition touch the over-relaxed issue of cards, nor the over-generous increase of credit limits on cards already issued, nor the issue of credit-card cheques. As to inertia selling, see para 8.18.

2.  *Copy of card-holding contract*. Unlike the general rule as to copies on execution of the regulated agreement, a copy of the credit-token agreement (see para 7.10) can be given to the debtor with the credit-token (see para 9.15). Except for small

---

129 Distinguish signature of the credit-token agreement: see para 9.13.

130 It is suggested that the receipt must be for the credit-token as such, and not merely for any package containing it, e.g. recorded-delivery letter: Goode, *Consumer Credit Law & Practice*, para 39.6.

131 As to theft of an authorised user's card, see Goode, *Op. cit.*, IIB, para 5.126. What of theft of one joint debtor's card?

132 Access and Barclaycards. Today, each are members of world-wide schemes: respectively the MasterCard and Visa networks.

133 *Elliott v DG* (set out at para 5.30). For the tariff see s 167 and Sched II; and see generally, para 28.07. ' "Give" means deliver or send by an appropriate method': s 189(1). S 51 does not preclude the giving of advertising literature.

134 S 51(2). For small agreements, see para 5.17. This exception is likely to save most trading-check operations: as to which, see generally, para 2.23.

135 Where the debtor is a company, the transaction is unregulated (see para 5.24); and where he is a businessman, there is a credit limit (see para 5.23).

136 S 51(2). Provided it does not amount to canvassing (see para 7.06), it is therefore possible to solicit the consumer in writing to apply for a credit card either by personal letter or general advertisement.

137 S 51(3)(a). This enables an unsolicited card to be sent to an authorised user, e.g. spouse, as an additional card-holder: see para 7.10.

138 S 51(3)(b). Is this consistent with s 82(2)(a)? S 53(1)(b) does not extend to 'replacing' a charge card by a credit card (OFT, *AR-2003/4*, 35).

agreements (see para 5.17), on each subsequent issue of a credit-token to the debtor (but not to an additional card-holder),[139] the creditor must give the debtor a further copy of any executed agreement and of any other document referred to in it (s 85). Further, during the life of the card, the creditor must also supply the debtor with information (see para 7.08).

3.  *Cancellation rights.* There are two variations from the ordinary cancellation rules (see generally, para 10.28, *et seq.*). First, notice of his right of cancellation may be given[133] to the debtor with the first credit-token (s 64(2)). Second, the debtor is not entitled to repayment of any sum payable for the issue of a credit-token until that token has been returned to the creditor or supplier.[140]

4.  *Use and misuse.* The Act establishes both the earliest moment at which a holder can become liable under a credit-token agreement (see para 7.11), and the extent to which he can be liable for misuse by another of the token (see para 7.13).

5.  *Reimbursement.* A consumer can achieve reimbursement by the charge-back mechanism (see para 7.09) or through connected lender liability (see para 16.11, *et seq.*).

6.  *Multiple agreements* (see para 5.27).

**[7.13]  Misuse of credit-tokens**. The general rule under s 83 is that a debtor cannot be made liable for another's **unauthorised** use[141] of his credit facility regulated by the CCA: in respect of **physical** misuse of credit cards, the rules are to be found in CCA, s 84 (see below); but as regards other payment cards, there are special rules to be found elsewhere (see para 7.14). Within the context of credit-tokens, s 84 provides that a debtor may within limits be liable for another's use of his card, though it should be remembered that this liability can only arise after acceptance of the credit-token (see para 7.11) and does not apply where the token is used in distance-selling.[142]

At common law, such liability for unauthorised user could arise either by virtue of the credit-token agreement (see para 7.09) or in the tort of negligence.[143] However, the Act provides that s 84 liability (see below) shall only last until 'the creditor has been given oral or written notice that [the card] is lost or stolen, or is for any other reason liable to misuse'.[144] Furthermore, that liability cannot arise unless the credit-token agreement prescribes details of the persons who must be notified of that loss, theft or misuse.[145]

---

139  For joint debtors, see s 185(2) as amended by s 38(3) of the Banking Act 1979. See generally, para 5.24; and para 25.08.

140  S 70(5). Note that this refers not to credit acquired by use of a credit-token, but only to sums payable for issue of the token.

141  This may amount to a *mens rea* criminal offence. As to where the card-holder signs a blank slip and an unauthorised amount is subsequently entered, see para 10.16.

142  S 84(3A), as inserted by reg 21(5) of the Distance Selling Regulations, 2000 SI 2334.

143  But see Goode, *Consumer Credit Law & Practice*, para 39.62; and generally, para 17.14.

144  S 84(3). The burden of proof is on the creditor: S 171(4)(b)(ii). 'Liable to misuse' might extend to a negligently disclosed PIN. Where oral notice is given, it must be confirmed in writing within 7 days (s 84(5)), which should protect the creditor against false assertions of oral notification: and see further Goode, *Op. cit.*, para 39.45. For card protection plans, see para 25.14.

145  S 84(4). For standards of legibility, see the Consumer Credit (Credit-Token Agreement) Regulations, 1983 SI 1555.

Within these limitations, s 84 distinguishes two cases for liability on a genuine credit-token:[146]

1.  *Unauthorised physical user.* Whilst the general rule in s 83 is that the card-holder is not liable for unauthorised use of his credit card by another (see para 7.07A), s 84(1) allows the credit-card agreement to provide for greater liability as follows:

    'Section 83 does not prevent the debtor under a credit-token agreement from being made liable to the extent of £x (or the credit limit if lower) for loss to the creditor arising from use of the credit-token by other persons during a period beginning when the credit-token ceases to be in the possession of any authorised person and ending when the credit-token is once more in the possession of an authorised person'.

    Suppose his card is lost or stolen from a card-holder.[147] By s 84(1), his maximum liability[145] for unauthorised user[148] of his genuine card is the **lesser** of his credit limit (see para 7.10), or the prescribed sum—which is currently £50[149]—per period of use.[150] However, this liability is only in respect of card transactions made whilst the card is not in the hands of any 'authorised person'.[148] The burden of proof as to timing lies on the creditor (s 171(4)(b)(ii)).

2.  *Authorised physical user.* Where possession or use of the card by another is authorised[148] by the debtor, his liability on ordinary agency rules is reinforced by s 84(2), which removes the above monetary limit protection, enacting that:

    'Section 83 does not prevent the debtor under a credit-token agreement from being made liable to any extent for loss to the creditor from use of the credit-token by a person who acquired possession of it with the debtor's consent'.

    The most obvious categories of authorised user within s 84(2) are: (a) the person to whom the debtor hands a credit card; and (b) the additional card-holder (see para 7.10), e.g. spouse. In neither situation does the card-holding debtor have any protection whatever against any transactions that third party initiates with the genuine card (see para 16.12); and he may have problems in cancelling the authority of the additional card-holder before the renewal date.[151] There may be real difficulties in proving whether or not the use is authorised, in which case the burden of proving the debtor's willing consent lies on the creditor.[152]

---

146 If two or more tokens are given under one credit-token agreement, each token is treated separately for the purposes of this section: s 84(8). See also s 84(6).

147 Distinguish where a genuine card is stolen in course of post to him: see para 7.11; or where a duplicate card is used: Banking Ombudsman, *AR 1994/5*, para 10.3.

148 The debtor, the creditor, and any person authorised by the debtor to use the credit-token, shall be authorised persons for the purposes of subsection (1): (s 84(7)). Does this apply to s 84(2)?

149 S 84(1) originally stipulated £30; but there is a power to alter the limit by regulation (s 181). The current figure of £50 was introduced in 1983: see now the Consumer Credit (Further Increase in Monetary Limits) (Amendments) Order, 1998 SI 997. In some cases, the consumer is offered insurance to cover this risk.

150 For illuminating examples of how this works, see the Banking Ombudsman, *Annual Report 1990/1*, para 10.3.

151 [1989] *Which?* 612. Can the card-holding contract be cancelled without returning to the card-issuer all cards issued under it? See the Banking Ombudsman, *AR 1990/1*, 24.

152 S 171(4)(b)(i). It seems likely that consent must be real consent (see para 24.37).

**[7.14] Other misuse of payment cards**. Where a credit card is physically misused, the rules are to be found in CCA, s 84 (see para 7.13). However, these rules do not extend to charge cards or debit cards. Whilst ss 83 and 84 have been informally extended to all payment cards by the Banking Code (see para 7.07A), subject to certain exceptions (see para 8.17) special rules have been introduced for other payment card unauthorised misuse as follows:

1. *Remote misuse of consumer credit cards*. Suppose the debtor retains physical control of his credit card, but his card details fall into the hands of another, who misuses them to make a purchase, e.g. armchair shoppers over the internet, by telephone or through the post. It has now been made clear that the situation does not fall within the CCA, s 84.[153] If the credit card is regulated by the CCA, s 83 of that Act applies;[154] but, if the credit card is not so regulated, e.g. a charge card, a similar result is produced by the Distance Selling Regulations 2000 (see para 8.17). So the card-holding consumer will be entitled to cancel the relevant item on his account (reg 21(1) and (2)), it being for the card-issuer to show that the transaction was authorised (reg 21(3)).

2. *Remote misuse of consumer payment cards*. Under the Financial Services Regulations (2004 SI 2095: see para 8.17), where a payment card issued to a private individual (the 'card-holder') is used to make a payment 'under or in connection with a distance contract' (reg 14(1)(a)), e.g. armchair shoppers (above), the position is as follows: if there is a credit card regulated by the CCA, s 83 of that Act applies;[155] but, if the credit card is not so regulated, and for all other payment cards, s 83 does not apply,[156] but a similar result is produced by the 2004 Regulations. Regulation 14 only applies where fraudulent use is then made of the payment card by a third person who 'is neither acting, nor to be treated as acting, as the card-holder's agent' (reg 14(1)(b)); and 'payment card' includes 'a credit card, charge card, a debit card and a store card' (reg 14(5)). Under reg 14(1), the card-holding consumer has similar rights to those under the 2000 Regulations (above), with a similar burden of proof on the card-issuer (reg 14(2)).

# TRIPARTITE TRANSACTIONS

**[7.15/17] Assignment of debts**.[157] It has already been seen that a chose in action is a type of personal property which can be enjoyed by the obligee [A] only by court action, e.g. a claim by a buyer [A] of defective goods under s 14 of the SGA (see para 14.01). However, by far the most common form of chose in action is a claim by a creditor [A] in debt (see para 2.02), e.g. by a seller of goods [A] for the price.

---

153 CCA, ss 84(3A) and (3B), as inserted by the Distance Selling Regulations, 2000 SI 2334 (see para 8.17), reg 21(5).
154 2000 Regulations, reg 21(4). For discussion of s 83 of the CCA, see para 7.07A.
155 2004 SI 2095, reg 14(3).
156 CCA, s 84(3C), as inserted by 2004 SI 2095, reg 14(4).
157 For assignments of choses in action, see generally, Treitel, *Law of Contract*, 11th edn, Chap 16; *Chitty on Contracts*, 28th edn, Vol I, Chap 20. For attornment of debts, see Oditah, *Accounts Receivable*, 88–90.

In practice, in our field transfer of debt is used in two very different situations: transfer of a good debt (where the debtor is willing and able to pay) is a method of financing (see para 2.22), whereas transfer of a bad debt is a method of collection (see para 27.02).

Transfer of a chose in action is usually by way of 'assignment' (see below), except in the case of negotiable instruments (see para 7.24). Whereas the common law refused to recognise attempts to transfer debts or other choses in action, equity would normally enforce such an assignment[158] from the creditor (the assignor) to a third party (the assignee), whether the chose be present or future (see para 7.18) and without the consent of the debtor.[159] To constitute a voluntary[160] equitable assignment, generally no particular form is required, since equity looks to the intent rather than the form; and in the commercial context that would generally[161] be accomplished simply by a contract to assign.[162] That contract would be made between assignor [A] and assignee [B]: in equity, notice to the debtor [C] was unnecessary to perfect an equitable assignment;[162] but such notice was necessary to constitute a statutory assignment[163] and may be needed for other purposes.[164] Both an equitable and statutory assignee will always take subject to the equities.[165]

Where the chose in action arises out of a regulated agreement, the CCA provides that the expressions 'debtor', 'creditor', 'hirer' and 'owner' shall include their assignees.[166] The rights of the debtor/hirer will normally be expressed not to be assignable (see para 7.26A), whereas the rights of the creditor/owner are likely to be expressed to be assignable, e.g. for indirect financing (see para 2.22). Both such assignment clauses may in a consumer supply be struck down as being unfair.[167]

**[7.18] Present and future chose.** Taking by way of example a debt, a chose in action may be classified as follows:

1. *Present chose.* This category will comprehend not just debts presently owing,[168] but also sums of money payable at a later date (perhaps conditionally) under a

---

158 For the exceptional case of non-assignable rights, see para 7.26.

159 It is thereby distinguishable from novation, a transaction to which the debtor must be a party: see generally, para 26.18. For other explanations of the effect of assignment, see Geva, *Financing Consumer Sales and Product Defences*, 61–4.

160 For compulsory assignment on death, see para 24.44.

161 Statute sometimes requires registration of assignment for the benefit of the assignor's other creditors: see Insolvency Act 1986, s 344 (for individual assignors: see para 19.24).

162 *Brandt's Son & Co v Dunlop Rubber Co* [1905] AC 454, HL; *Karsales (Harrow) Ltd v Wallis* (set out at para 18.07). Except that a disposition of an equitable interest must be in writing: see para 25.21. For perfection, see generally, para 25.19.

163 Law of Property Act 1925, s 136; and see further, Treitel, *Op. cit.*, 675, *et seq.*

164 E.g. the data protection rules (see para 3.28); to avoid harassment (see para 24.24).

165 See para 7.23. *Contra* negotiation: see para 7.24.

166 S 189(1). For debtor and creditor, see paras 5.24–5. For assignment of the burden of the contract, see para 7.27.

167 As to assignment by the debtor/hirer, see para 11.15A; and as to assignment by the creditor/owner, see para 11.18A.

168 E.g. *Brandt's Son & Co v Dunlop Rubber Co* [1905] AC 454, HL. (A purchased rubber with money provided by B and resold it to C; to repay B, A assigned to B the price due from C); and see para 16.19.

present contract.[169] Thus, the price due under a cash, credit or conditional sale is a present chose in the hands of the seller (A), as is hire rent due or growing due to the bailor (A) under a **fixed-term** hiring,[170] a category which seems no longer to include hp agreements (see para 1.25).

2.  *Future chose.* There will be a future chose in either of the following two circumstances:

    (a) the assignor (A) does not own the chose at the time of assignment, e.g. where A purports to assign a debt presently owed by C to X.

    (b) there is no presently existing chose, e.g. where A purports to assign future rentals which may become due to him under a **periodic** hiring[170] whether under a simple hiring or hp agreement.[171]

Whereas there can be an immediate equitable assignment of a present chose,[172] a purported assignment of a future chose can only operate as a contract to assign. In *Tailby v Official Receiver*[173] the House of Lords held that the assignment of future book-debts passed the equitable interest to B in debts arising after assignment: whilst it could not pass any interest immediately as the debt did not then exist, it operated as a contract to assign, which equity would regard as an assignment binding on the subsequent debt **from its creation** by way of a floating charge (see para 25.02).

[7.19/22] **Notice.**[174] Starting from the basic principle that equity is looking for an intention to assign (see para 7.17), it follows that the parties must have done every-thing which the law deems necessary to implement that intention. Normally, notice to the assignee (B) is necessary to perfect the assignment:[175] such notice could be by the assignor (A) or by someone with his authority, e.g. the debtor (C).[176] Once perfected, the assignment will bind not just A, but also all those who stand in his shoes, e.g. A's trustee in bankruptcy or judgment creditor.[177]

Whilst notice does not need to be given to C to perfect an equitable assign-ment,[177] it does need to be given for several other reasons.[178] First, notice to C is necessary to bind him: before receipt of notice, C may obtain a good discharge by

---

169 *Hughes v Pump House Hotel* [1902] 2 KB 190, CA (as security for an overdraft, A made an absolute assignment of all moneys due and becoming due under his existing building contracts); and see para 16.18.

170 The distinction is probably whether the hirer (C) is contractually bound to pay the hire-rent: see *Chitty on Contracts*, 28th edn, Vol I, para 20-028; Treitel, *Law of Contract*, 11th edn, 683; and para 1.25.

171 *Blakey v Trustees of Pendlebury* [1931] 2 Ch 255, CA (hp; case on s 38(c) of the Bankruptcy Act 1914, now repealed).

172 On the vexed question of the effect of a voluntary equitable assignment, see Treitel, *Law of Contract*, 11th edn, 682, *et seq.*

173 (1888) 13 App Cas 523, [1886–90] All ER Rep 486, HL. See also *Holroyd v Marshall* (1862) 10 HC 191, HL (involving after-acquired goods).

174 According to the rules of equity, notice may be given in any form, so that even oral notice of assignment, e.g. of a debt, is sufficient. But a written notice is necessary to secure priority over successive assignees of equitable interest (Law of Property Act 1925, s 137(3)).

175 *Morrell v Wootten* (1852) 16 Beav 197. For perfection, see generally, para 25.19.

176 Treitel, *Law of Contract*, 11th edn, 680.

177 *Gorringe v Irwell Works* (1886) 34 Ch D 128.

178 *Contra* negotiable instruments: see para 7.24.

paying his debt to A;[179] whereas, upon notice of the assignment, C ceases to be liable to A and may thereafter secure his release only by paying B.[180] Second, notice establishes priority (see below).

*Priorities.* Where there are successive transfers of the same property to innocent purchasers for value, it will be necessary to establish their order or priority to the property. For goods, priority is established by the historical order in which the transfers were made, the *nemo dat* rule (see para 19.11). However, in the case of equitable assignments of choses in action, priority is established by the order of notice to the debtor [C]: under the rule in *Dearle v Hall*,[181] generally speaking, the first assignee [B1] to give notice[174] to C is the one entitled to enforce the debt against C,[182] though in the case of assignment of a future chose, e.g. future hire rent under a periodic hiring agreement (see para 7.18), notice can only be given as from the time the chose comes into existence.[183]

**[7.23] Subject to the equities**. Whether the assignment be equitable or statutory (see para 7.17), it is a general principle that the assignee (B) takes 'subject to the equities';[184] that is, the debtor (C) may plead against B claims that C had against the creditor/assignor (A).[185] The object of the rule is that C shall not be prejudiced by the assignment;[186] and it has a number of effects. *First*, B takes subject to any defect in A's title to the chose which may have existed at the time of the assignment, which may be seen as an aspect of the doctrine *nemo dat* (see para 19.11): if no money ever became due from C to A, B takes nothing;[187] and the same will follow if a contract of debt between C and A is void for mistake[188] or illegality, or voidable for misrepresentation.[189] *Second*, there are the notice rules (see para 7.19). *Third*, C may *prima facie* plead by way of set-off, that is, as mutual debts between B and C, all claims arising out of the chose in action,[190] whether arising before or after assignment,[191] and whether liquidated or unliquidated,[192] and whether arising before or after C has notice of the assignment.[193] *Fourth*, C may also plead as against

---

179 *Bence v Shearman* [1898] 2 Ch 582; *Warner Bros Records Inc v Rollgreen Ltd* [1976] QB 430 (assignment of option).

180 *Brice v Bannister* (1878) 3 QBD 569 (Oditah, *Accounts Receivable*, 241); *The Attica Hope* [1988] 1 Lloyds Rep 439. *Contra* UCC, Art 9–318(2).

181 (1828) 3 Russ 1.

182 *Marchant v Morton* [1901] 2 KB 829.

183 *Johnstone v Cox* (1880) 16 Ch D 571. This makes life difficult for factors (see para 7.28).

184 *Security Trust Co v Royal Bank of Canada* [1976] AC 503, PC. See generally Geva, *Financing Consumer Sales and Product Defences*, 50–4; Oditah, *Legal Aspects of Receivables Financing*, 224–5.

185 *Contra* negotiable instruments: see para 7.24. Distinguish the 'mere equities' considered here, from equitable interests in property (e.g. para 7.16): see Goode, *Commercial Law*, 3rd edn, 27.

186 The rule seems to apply to both present and future choses: Oditah, *Op. cit.*, 239–40.

187 *Tooth v Hallett* (1869) LR 4 Ch App 242.

188 For the relationship of this rule to the doctrine of *non est factum* (see para 10.16), see Geva, *Op. cit.*, 54–8.

189 *Graham v Johnson* (1869) LR 8 Eq 36 (no consideration). As to why C cannot recover sums mistakenly paid to B, see Geva, *Op. cit.*, 72–80.

190 See generally Goode, *Legal Problems of Credit and Security*, 3rd edn, Chap VII; Oditah, *Op. cit.*, 227–31. But see cut-off clauses (see para 7.25); and distinguish counter-claims, e.g. under the SGA, s 53(1) (see para 29.26), and running-account credit (see para 7.08).

191 *Roxburghe v Cox* (1881) 17 Ch D 520 (before); *Laurence v Hayes* [1927] 2 KB 511 (after).

192 *Young v Kitchen* (1878) 3 Ex D 127. For liquidated and unliquidated debts, see para 27.24.

193 *Government of Newfoundland v Newfoundland Railway* (1888) 13 App Cas 199, PC.

B even claims arising *dehors* the chose in action, provided that such claims arose before C had notice of the assignment;[194] but, because C is essentially setting up against the innocent B a claim he has against A, C's set-off can then never exceed his debt to A.[195]

**[7.24] Negotiability**. Mercantile custom has recognised certain categories of choses in action by written contract as amounting to negotiable instruments, including the following important categories, none of which amount to 'goods' within the SGA (see para 2.02):

1.  *A bill of exchange*. The rules relating to these instruments were codified in the Bills of Exchange Act 1882.[196] It defines a bill of exchange as an unconditional[197] order in writing, addressed by one person (A: the drawer) to another (C: the drawee),[198] signed by A, requiring C to pay on demand or at a determinable future time[199] a sum certain in money to or for the order of a specified person [B1], or to bearer [B2] (s 3(1)). However, where the bill contains words prohibiting transfer, it is valid between the parties but not negotiable (s 8). A forged signature on a bill is a nullity.[200]

2.  *A cheque* is defined as 'a bill of exchange drawn on a banker [C] payable on demand' (s 73) and is generally subject to the same provisions as bills of exchange,[201] except where the 1992 Act applies (see para 7.28).

3.  *A promissory note* is an unconditional promise in writing made by one person [C] to another [A] signed by the maker [C], engaging to pay, on demand or at a fixed or determinable future time, a sum certain in money, to, or to the order of, a specified person [B1] or bearer [B2] (s 83). Generally speaking, a promissory note is subject to the same rules as a bill of exchange.[202]

4.  *A bank note* is a promissory note made by the Bank of England [C] payable to the bearer [B2] on demand.[203] It amounts to legal tender (see para 23.14).

Besides having special rules as to consideration (ss 27–30), negotiable instruments have two important characteristics:

**(a) Transfer**. The manner in which a negotiable instrument may be transferred (negotiated) from A to B depends on the manner in which it is currently

---

194  *Bennett v White* [1910] 2 KB 643, CA.

195  For the non-assignability of the burden of a contract, see para 7.27.

196  Unless otherwise stated, all subsequent references are to the 1882 Act, which (like the SGA 1893) was drafted by Sir MacKenzie Chalmers (see para 1.02).

197  Distinguish travellers' cheques, which are conditional: see Paget, *Law of Banking*, 12th edn, para 15.43.

198  If the drawee signifies his acceptance of the order, he becomes the 'acceptor' (s 17) and incurs the special liability of an acceptor (s 54).

199  A 'time bill' is one which the drawee/acceptor must pay at the time stipulated, e.g. a 90-day bill (s 11). The holder of a time bill may always discount it (i.e. sell it at less than its face value) to obtain payment before due date. And see further, para 23.14.

200  1882 Act, s 24. Distinguish fraudulent alteration in the body of the bill, which is dealt with by s 64. A consumer whose signature has been forged on a cheque may take proceedings under the FSA Ombudsman Service (FOS: see para 3.25), the FOS publishing a policy on forged cheques.

201  It has special rules as to crossings (1882 Act, ss 76–81) and the protection of the paying and collecting banker (Cheques Act 1957). As to payment by cheque, see para 23.14.

202  1882 Act, s 89, with the modifications necessary because the maker is promising to pay (ss 83–9).

203  Currency and Bank Notes Act 1954, s 3.

expressed to be payable:[204] if it is payable to order, it may be transferred by indorsement on the back and delivery by the transferor [A]; whereas, if it is payable to bearer [B2], it may be transferred by his mere delivery.[205]

(b) **Defects of title**. Whilst an ordinary assignee [B] takes subject to the equities (see para 7.23), under certain conditions the transferee (B: holder) of a negotiable instrument takes free from any defect of title of prior parties,[206] as well as from more personal defences available to prior parties amongst themselves (s 38(2)). B will take free of such equities and is termed a 'holder in due course': every holder is presumed to be a holder in due course unless the instrument is affected by fraud, duress or illegality.[207]

**[7.25] Cut-off devices**. The rule (see para 7.23) that claims by the debtor [C] against the assignor [A] arising before notice of the assignment can be set off against the assignee [B], may *prima facie* be excluded in either of two ways:

1. *By negotiation*. As payment for the supply of goods could easily be made by the supplier [A] taking a cheque or other bill of exchange (see paras 23.14 and 24.03), an obvious means by which A might both finance the transaction and shake off C's equities would be for A to negotiate the bill to a holder in due course (see para 7.24). To combat this, the CCA has introduced special rules to restrict the circumstances in which a bill taken in a regulated supply can come into the hands of a holder in due course (ss 123–5: see paras 25.09–10).

2. *By cut-off clause*. At common law, C's equities could be excluded by the express provisions of the contract creating the debt, e.g. credit card contracts (see para 7.09). Such provisions are already common form in English debentures.[208] In North America cut-off clauses have appeared in instalment credit contracts in terms that the buyer [C] agrees not to raise against an assignee [B] of the seller [A] any defences he may have under the agreement,[209] so seeking to confer on B something approaching the status of a holder in due course.[210] However, where a UK transaction is regulated, it would appear that s 113(1) of the CCA will prevent the enforcement of such cut-off clauses.[211]

---

204 S 31. Compare assignments of choses in action (see para 7.17) and delivery orders (see para 23.03). As no notice to C is required, negotiations are free of the rule in *Dearle v Hall*: as to which, see para 7.19.

205 Compare gifts of chattels (see para 2.08), sales of goods (para 19.01) and hp (para 15.22). Transfer may not in practice be possible where the cheque is crossed 'a/c pay' (see above), which may cause problems to payees who do not have bank accounts (see para 7.28).

206 E.g. misrepresentation, breach of contract, or total failure of consideration. Except where a party's signature to the instrument is wholly void under the doctrine of *non est factum* (see para 10.16) or under statute. See further, Geva, *Financing Consumer Sales and Product Defences*, 88–93.

207 Ss 29–30. For the position of a holder **not** in due course, see Geva, *Op. cit.*, Chaps. 5 and 6; *Lipkin Gorman v Karpnale Ltd* [1991] AC 548, HL.

208 See Pennington, *Company Law*, 8th edn, 580, *et seq*.

209 For ways in which such clauses may surmount the privity problem, see Geva, *Financing Consumer Sales and Product Defences*, 93–103.

210 Goode and Ziegel, *Hire Purchase and Conditional Sale*, 111–12; Geva, *Op. cit.*, 103 *et seq*. Often they include a title retention clause (see para 25.30), which causes considerable difficulty as to whether the expressed promissory notes are sufficiently unconditional to amount to bills of exchange: see now UCC, Arts 9–206(1), 318(1); and Geva, *Op. cit.*, Chap. 6.

211 See para 25.11. It would seem to have this effect by reason of the wide definition of security: see para 25.10.

**[7.26] Non-assignable rights**. Notwithstanding the general rule that contractual rights are *prima facie* assignable (see para 1.23), there are the following exceptions.

1. *A bare right of action.* At common law, a chose in action was not assignable if it savoured of maintenance or champerty:[212] maintenance is supporting litigation in which one has no legitimate interest; and champerty is financing litigation in which one has no legitimate interest in return for a share in the proceeds. However, this rule did not apply to assignment of a debt, nor where the assignee [B] had a legitimate interest in the rights assigned,[213] nor to an agreement to assign the proceeds of litigation.[214] Notwithstanding the abolition of the crimes and torts of maintenance and champerty by the Criminal Law Act 1967 (s 14), these rules against trafficking in litigation may still attack the assignment of a bare right of action, i.e. a claim for unliquidated damages;[215] but they do not preclude the assignment of a liquidated debt, even if the assignment is of a bad debt at a heavy discount,[216] nor an accident hire agreement (see para 5.13).

2. *Personal contracts.* A contractual right cannot be assigned if it is clear that the intention was to grant a purely personal right. This principle has been applied to contracts for the sale of goods so as to save a supplier [C] from having to give his buyer's [A's] business successor [B] either credit[217] or enough goods to satisfy all needs.[218] On the other hand, any such presumption of non-assignability will be rebuffed where the contractual right is expressly or impliedly made assignable.[219]

3. *Contracts expressed to be not assignable.* (See para 7.26A).

**[7.26A] Contracts expressed to be not assignable**. Suppose a particular type of contractual right is *prima facie* assignable; for instance, a debt (see para 7.17), hp rights (see para 1.23), a guarantee (see para 25.06). Nevertheless, at common law a provision in the contract may render it non-assignable.[220] Thus, an instalment credit contract frequently provides that the rights of the buyer or hirer [A], but not of the supplier, shall **not** be assignable; and, if the buyer or hirer [A] nevertheless

---

212 A bare right of action may be made assignable by statute: see *Ramsey v Hartley* [1977] 2 All ER 673, CA (now Insolvency Act 1986, s 314).

213 See the *Stocznia No. 2* case (set out at para 26.16A).

214 *Fitzroy v Cave* [1905] 2 KB 364, CA (for conditional fees, see para 3.18); *Glegg v Bromley* [1912] 3 KB 474, CA. See also *Giles v Thompson* [1994] 1 AC 142, HL (credit hire; as to the CCA, see para 5.13; *Stocznia No. 2* (see para 29.16A)); and see McCormack [2000] JBL 422. As to hiring a replacement, see generally, para 27.28).

215 It is clear that these restrictions on assignment have survived: *Trendtex Trading Corporation v Credit Suisse* [1982] AC 679, HL; *Brownton Ltd v Edward Moore Inbucon Ltd* [1985] 3 All ER 499, CA; and see generally, Tan (1990) 106 LQR 656.

216 *Camdex International Ltd v Bank of Zambia* [1998] QB 22, CA; *Factortame Ltd v Secretary of State for the Environment* [2002] 4 All ER 97, CA. What about contingent fees (see para 3.15)?

217 *Cooper v Micklefeld Coal & Lime Co Ltd* (1912) 107 LT 457 (on the grounds that credit was granted on the basis of business experience).

218 *Kemp v Baerselman* [1906] 2 KB 604 (where the buyer sold his business to a large company).

219 *Tolhurst v Associated Portland Cement Co* [1903] AC 414, HL (promise to supply); *Re Charge Card Services Ltd* (set out at para 2.27; promise to pay); promises to pay under instalment supply contracts (see para 1.23); and generally, Treitel, *Law of Contract*, 11th edn, 695.

220 *Linden Gardens Trust Ltd v Lenesta Sludge Disposals Ltd* [1994] 1 AC 805, HL, esp. *per* Lord Browne-Wilkinson at 428–9 (110 LQR 42; [1994] JBL 129). See also *Bawejem Ltd v MC Fabrications Ltd* [1999] 1 All ER (Comm) 377, CA.

purports to assign them, his assignee [B] cannot enforce the assignment as against the supplier.[221] In this event, it seems that the contract of assignment may nevertheless be effective as between the assignor [A] and assignee [B],[222] with the result that the supplier should logically recover the entire value of the goods. Perhaps not surprisingly, this has caused confusion as to whether the supplier can sue the assignee [B] in conversion for the full value of the goods, this being the seemingly logical answer (see para 27.30), or must deduct the value of the hirer's [A's] option, perhaps the fair answer (see para 27.31). In a consumer supply agreement (see para 11.12A), a prohibition on assignment may be unfair.[223]

*Vehicle transfer agencies*. First appearing about 1990, these purport to arrange such assignments for impecunious hirers,[224] though this service causes difficulty by reason of the standard prohibition against assignment normally found in conditional sale and hp agreements (see para 1.23) and of the failure by the agency to keep up the promised payments.[225] To pursue a transaction in the face of such a prohibition may render the Agency unfit to hold a CCA licence:[226] sometimes, the Agency may succeed in passing a good Part 3 title if the assignee is in fact a 'private purchaser' (see above); but, in most cases the original owner is likely to be entitled to repossess the vehicle.[227]

**[7.27] The burden of the contract**. Whilst the benefit of a contract is *prima facie* assignable (see para 7.17), the position is different in relation to the burden of a contract. Suppose C supplies goods to A under an instalment contract which makes C responsible for their servicing; and subsequently C wishes to retire from business. Can C assign to B both the right to collect the price and the burden of the servicing? It would appear that the servicing obligation can be passed to B in a number of ways, unless the contract expressly or impliedly provides for personal service by C:[228]

1. C may delegate performance to B, though this is not a true assignment because C will remain liable to B for the servicing.[229]

---

221 *United Dominions Trust (Commercial) Ltd v Parkway Motors Ltd* [1955] 2 All ER 557; doubted by two members of the CA in the *Wickham Holdings Case* (set out at para 27.31). As to attempts by vehicle transfer agencies to do this, see below. Could such an attempt take effect as a declaration of trust under the rule in *Re Turcan* (1888) 40 Ch D 5 (suggestion by JWA Thornely)?

222 *Chitty on Contract*, 28th edn, Vol 1, para 20-044; and para 1.23.

223 UTCC reg 4: see OFT, *UCT Bulletin No. 17*, cases No. 13 and 21; and para 11.15A.

224 Such Agencies tend to advertise (wrongly) that for a commission the hirer/lessee is relieved of any further obligation to keep up the payments, whereas in law the hirer/lessee can only be so released with the consent (normally withheld) of the owner/lessor. The advertisements also attract would-be hirers who would be unlikely to obtain finance facilities.

225 Over 90% of such Agencies have been found to fail to make the payments.

226 These Agencies may be licensable as debt-adjusters or credit information services. As transfer will normally interfere with the original hp or lease agreement, there will usually be reasons for doubting the fitness of the Agency to hold a licence (see generally, para 6.18): see (1992) 46 CC 6/11.

227 Even if the vehicle were 'protected goods' under a regulated agreement, the hirer will have lost protection under the CCA by voluntarily parting with possession: see para 24.37.

228 *Robson and Sharpe v Drummond* (1831) 2 B & Ad 303 (hire: C entitled to refuse performance by B). Cf. *British Waggon G v Lea* (1880) 5 QBD 149, CA (hiring contract allowed vicarious performance).

229 *Stewart v Reavell's Garage* [1952] 2 QB 545; and see fn 234, below.

2.    A, B and C may by novation agree to discharge the old contract between A and C, replacing it with a new one between B and C.[230] This process may be streamlined by securitisation.[231] It would seem that the concept of novation does not include situations like that in *Alpha Chauffeurs Ltd v Citygate Dealership Ltd* (set out at para 14.12; at para 32), where Alpha ordered a new Rolls Royce from Citygate on the following basis: there was initially a conditional sale between the two of them; but, before delivery, Alpha had under clause 10 an option, which it exercised to have that supply contract replaced with a directly financed transaction under which Citygate sold the car to a financier, who in turn let it to Alpha under an hp agreement (there termed a 'lease purchase agreement': para 36).

3.    Payment of the debt may be conditional on performance of the servicing, in which case B may not enforce the debt without seeing that the servicing is performed;[232] and B will in any event take subject to the equities (see para 7.23).

4.    C may make the contract as undisclosed principal for B;[233] but the agency must be created before the supply, because an undisclosed principal cannot ratify (see para 10.06). Beyond that, at common law the burden of a contract cannot be voluntarily assigned.[234] Different rules apply to involuntary assignments[235] and possibly to assignments of regulated agreements.[236]

[7.28] **Modern cheques**. Under the scheme contained in the Bills of Exchange Act 1882 (see generally, para 7.24), an ordinary cheque would be a document in which the holder of a bank account (A: the drawer) directed his bank to pay a specified sum from that account to a named payee [B] '. . . *or order*', this last expression being the authority for the instrument to be transferred by endorsement and delivery (see para 7.24). If the instrument were stolen, the thief could forge the endorsement of the payee and present the cheque for payment: normally, such a forged indorsement would be of no effect (s 24). To protect himself from loss, A was likely to cross the cheque 'not negotiable': the effect of this was that the cheque remained transferable, but could not transfer a good title free of the equities.[237] At common law, the innocent bank [C] would thus be liable to the payee as true owner in the tort of conversion (see para 19.04); but, provided he acts in good faith and without negligence, the collecting banker of a cheque 'or other document' is protected by s 4 of the Cheques Act 1957.

*The Cheques Act 1992*. With the prevalence of the habit of paying debts by posted cheque, there was a wave of theft of cheques in course of post, in which case A or B lost his money. The *Jack Report* recommended that this problem be dealt with

---

230 E.g. *Harbinger UK Ltd v GE Information Services Ltd* [2000] 1 AER (Comm) 166, CA. For the distinction between assignment and novation, see para 7.17.

231 Which removes the need for B's consent on transfer: Goode [1991] LM & CLQ 177 at 187.

232 Diamond (1956) 19 MLR 498 at 500.

233 See Reynolds [1984] JBL 260.

234 A purported assignment of the burden has been struck down as an unfair term: OFT, *Bulletin No. 22*, case 16; and see further, *Chitty on Contracts*, 28th edn, Vol 1, paras 20-075/8.

235 E.g. on death or insolvency, where there is statutory provision for automatic assignment.

236 The issue is whether the statutory definition in s 189(1) of 'creditor' and 'owner' includes an assignee of their duties: compare Goode, *Consumer Credit Law & Practice*, para 23.21; Guest and Lloyd, *Encyclopedia of Consumer Credit Law*, para 2-190.

237 1882 Act, s 81; *Sutters v Briggs* [1922] 1 AC 1, HL.

by the creation of a new non-transferable 'Bank Payment Order'.[238] Instead of creating a new instrument, the Government preferred to amend the existing law in the Cheques Act 1992 so that the effect of the crossing 'account payee' became that (1882 Act, s 81A(1), as inserted by the 1992 Act, s 1):

'the cheque shall not be transferable, but shall only be valid as between the parties thereto'.

Almost immediately, the clearing banks [C] altered their ordinary printed cheque forms: first, they printed them with an 'account payee' crossing to bring them within the 1992 Act;[239] and second, they deleted the 'or order', so that the cheque was expressed to be payable to a named payee [A] only.[240] The combined effect of the 1992 Act and the new payee-only cheques seems to be this: not only will a transferee [B] always take subject to the equities,[241] but such cheques cannot be 'negotiated' and can only be assigned.[242] In effect, this has turned the modern cheque into a Bank Payment Order. It is for consideration whether or not the other rules relating to bills of exchange (see para 7.24) apply to payment made by such modern cheques, e.g. the rules relating to the effect of payment by cheque. Further, payment by such an essentially old-fashioned paper-based system may be compared with payment by modern electronic transfer by debit card (see para 23.15).

*Cheque cashing businesses.* In the course of time, the above developments led to the setting up of cheque cashing businesses doing two very different types of business, both of which may be within the UTCCR:[243]

1. *Third-party cheque cashing.* Whilst the above 1992 Act safeguards the interests of payees of cheques who have bank accounts, it created something of a dilemma for those payees who do not have a bank account (up to 9% of the population: see para 2.15), e.g. the unemployed receiving an insurance cheque. To meet the needs of this group of customers, there soon sprung up 'cheque cashing' businesses to cash for the payee cheques drawn in their favour by third parties. The cheque-casher cannot take title to an 'account payee' cheque by negotiation (see above); but they may obtain title to the underlying debt by way of assignment.[244]

2. *Pay-day advances.*[245] This type of facility has only developed since 1997: it is designed to meet the short-term financial needs of those customers in employment who have a bank account, but wish to acquire relatively small sums of money in advance of payment of their wages. It is achieved by the customer

---

238 *Banking Services* (1989, Cm. 622), para 7.35.
239 Bankers collecting for the wrong person bearing the name of the payee still have the protection of s 4 of the Cheques Act (see above): 1992 Act, s 3.
240 It may be that the instrument is then not a bill of exchange within the meaning of s 8 of the 1882 Act: Wheatley (1992) 142 NLJ 607.
241 As to assignment subject to the equities, see para 7.23. For the prohibition on taking a negotiable instrument by way of payment under a regulated agreement, see para 25.09.
242 *Plimley v Westley* (1835) 2 Bing NC 249. For assignment, see para 7.17.
243 OFT, *UCT Bulletin No. 17*, case No 14; and see generally, para 11.12, *et seq.*
244 Macleod (1997) 113 LQR 133; Cooke (1998) 52 CC 6/35.
245 See generally, Dominy and Kempson, *Pay Day Advances* (2003); (2002) 64 QA 12; [2003] 3 *Credit Today* 36; 69 QA 5; Collard and Kempson, *Affordable Credit* (2005) 3. The British Cheque Cashers Association has issued a code of practice (2003).

being granted an immediate loan in return for his making out a cheque to the cheque-casher for a larger sum, that cheque only to be drawn upon at the end of the agreed period of borrowing;[246] and the system is commonly used where the cheque-casher's charges are less than those of a bank overdraft or credit card. Technically, this transaction probably amounts to discounting of cheques rather than moneylending (see para 5.21). However, perhaps to avoid further legislation, the industry has agreed with the OFT that it shall be treated as regulated lending within the CCA, that is, as a regulated fixed-sum loan;[247] and there is pressure on cheque-cashers not to make repeated extensions of time by then taking new cheques for the same debt.

*Credit card cheques.* Since 1995, credit card-issuers have begun to shower their card-holders and others with unsolicited 1992 Act cheque-forms (see above): these credit card cheques are particularly used where a supplier may not accept payment by credit card, e.g. a plumber, or retailer; by writing the cheque out to another credit card-issuer to effect a balance transfer; or by writing it to self to raise a loan. If used by the card-holder, the sum drawn will be debited to his card-account, provided it is within his credit-limit; and, if used by a non-customer, may be used by the issuer to open a credit card account, which amounts to inertia selling (see para 8.18). Either way, the sums drawn will be treated as cash advances, i.e. the card-issuer will charge interest (usually at the higher rate applicable to cash advances) from the moment the cheque is cashed. Further, it would seem that a misuse by a third party of a credit card cheque is outside the protection afforded to debtors by s 83 (see para 7.07A); and also use of the cheque by the debtor would be treated as a dc drawing outside s 75 protection (see para 16.12). Whilst the unsolicited issue of credit card cheques already falls within the Banking Code (see para 3.12), the Government presently regard banning as disproportionate, but have it in mind to introduce a statutory instrument to insist on transparency.[248]

---

246 There is a temptation for the lender to enhance the security of the cheque by also requiring production of a cheque guarantee card (see para 2.26); but to do so breaches the code of conduct laid down by APACS. It would also appear to contravene Art 18 of the Draft EU Directive on Consumer Credit (2002).

247 Insofar as that cheque is furnished by way of security, it will amount to a regulated surety: see para 25.11. The cheque itself may be guaranteed under the Transax system: see para 25.05.

248 DTI, *Credit Card Cheques: A Discussion Paper* (Nov. 2005), e.g. to insist on a written statement to the consumer prior to his use of the cheque of: the interest rate, any rate-free period, any charges and what happens if the credit limit is exceeded.

# PART 3

# NEGOTIATING SUPPLY CONTRACTS

# CHAPTER 8

# SEEKING BUSINESS

## ADVERTISING GENERALLY

**[8.01/4] Introduction**. This section deals with the legal rules relating to seeking business by advertising as it concerns persons outside the advertising industry.[1] To maximise its effectiveness in promoting the distribution of goods, commercial advertising of products will normally be aimed at a target group (see para 8.05, *et seq*). However, such advertising also has a powerful effect on third parties, though this too is outside the scope of this work.[2]

Besides this substantial body of legal rules, in recent years significant attempts have been made at the self-regulation of the advertising industry. Thus, the broadcasting of advertisements is strictly controlled by OFCOM, whilst other forms of advertisement fall within the purview of the ASA (see para 3.14). The OFT (see generally, para 3.03) has also been active in promoting voluntary codes of practice, e.g. mail order advertisements (see para 3.11, *et seq*.), recognising that what is needed is a judicious mixture of legal controls[3] and self-regulation;[4] and the OFT's representatives on the ground are the trading standards officers of the local authority (see para 3.05).[5] Some such codes are easier to police than others, as where the code is produced by an advertising medium[6] or approved by it.[7] To the foregoing may be added the effect of numerous EU-generated rules, such as that relating to public procurement,[8] data protection (see paras 3.26–8) and misleading advertisements.[3] There seems to be little general legal control as regards the misleading packaging, as opposed to labelling, of goods.[9]

**[8.05] The common law of contract**. Except in the field of misrepresentation (see para 17.10), English law has traditionally seen little need for the imposition of general restrictions upon negotiations leading up to a contract for the supply of goods. However, in the famous case of *Carlill v Carbolic Smoke Ball Co*[10] it was made clear that the manufacturer's advertisement may amount to an offer of a reward to the whole world, which could be accepted so as to complete a binding

---

1 For the legal relationships within the industry, see Lawson, *Advertising Law*, Chaps 2 and 3; Circus, *Sales Promotion Law*, 2nd edn; Shears (1995) 145 NLJ 1682.
2 See Macleod, *Consumer Sales Law*, 1st edn, paras 8.02–4. For counterfeit goods, see [2006] 1 *Which*? 16.
3 See the OFT powers in relation to misleading advertisements: see para 8.12A.
4 OFT, *1982-AR* 11. For the OFT sponsored codes, see para 3.13.
5 The OFT and LAs have begun to systematically monitor newspaper advertisements: OFT, *AR-2004/5*, 7.
6 E.g. the ASA code (above); the ICSTIS code for premium-rate phone services; the codes of British Advertisers and Institute of Purchasing (set out in Circus, *Op. cit.*, 211, *et seq*).
7 E.g. the schemes applying to the mail order trade, such as MOPS (see para 3.14).
8 See Singleton (1994) 13 Tr L 414; Bovis [1994] JBL 615.
9 For examples, see [2001] 5 *Which*? 6.
10 [1893] 1 QB 256, [1891–4] All ER Rep 127, CA (discussed by Simpson [1985] *Jo of Legal Studies* 345). For the formation of contracts, see generally, para 10.01, *et seq*.

contract on the basis of its terms by any of that target group who knowingly fulfils them. In this case, a consumer purchased the goods to which the advertisement related from a retailer, so that the £100 contract with the manufacturer is what would today be described as collateral to the retail supply contract;[11] but in other cases it may be a question whether a manufacturer's advertisement might also form part of the retail supply contract.[12] Alternatively, the advertisement may be published by the retail supplier; and it may be possible to spell out that he thereby intends only, e.g. a personal quotation.[13]

However, not every advertisement amounts to an offer: it is a question of fact whether the advertisement lacks any intention to create legal relations (see para 10.01) and is simply an invitation to treat[14] or a mere puff (statement not independently verifiable). This may be the case with a manufacturer's advertisement, e.g. sales literature.[15] It is also commonly the case with advertisements by or on behalf of a retailer.[16] If the advertisement does not amount to an offer, then it may be a question in civil law whether it is devoid of all contractual effect as being a mere puff;[15] or whether it amounts to a misrepresentation[17] or induces a mistake (see paras 10.14, *et seq.*; 17.11), so affording certain remedies to the disappointed reader obtaining goods from the advertiser on the faith of it.[18]

**[8.06] Statutory intervention**. Against the foregoing background as to the contractual effect of advertisements (see para 8.05), there has also been significant statutory intervention, primarily concerned with ensuring the truthfulness of claims made.[19]

1. *Trade descriptions*. In Chapter 4, the general TDA rules relating to false statements as to goods and services were considered. However, the TDA makes special provision to deal with false trade descriptions when they are found in advertisements for goods (see para 8.07), whilst saying nothing specific about the advertisement of services.

---

11 E.g. the Hoover fiasco: see Shears (1995) 145 NLJ 1754. For collateral contracts by manufacturers, see generally, para 17.09.

12 See *Esso Petroleum Ltd v Commissioners of Customs and Excise* (set out at para 2.08). This could be either alternatively, or as well as, making a contract between the manufacturer and consumer; but it has been argued that the case does not represent a change in the attitude of the courts towards advertising (Cranston, *Consumers and the Law*, 3rd edn, 51–2). For express terms, see generally, para 11.07; and for counterfeiting, see para 4.06 and para 13.11.

13 *Philp & Co v Knoblauch* 1907 SC 994. But see *Boyers v Duke* [1905] 2 IR 617.

14 E.g. circular requesting tenders (*Spencer v Harding* (1870) LR 5 CP 561). For offers and invitations to treat, see generally, para 10.02.

15 *Lambert v Lewis* (set out at para 17.06); *Bowerman v ABTA* [1995] Tr LR 246; *Alpha Chauffeurs Ltd v Citygate Dealership Ltd* (set out at para 14.26) at para 28; and see generally Treitel, *Law of Contract*, 11th edn, 162, 330–2. As to whether a puff can be a false trade description, see para 4.08; and as to statutory consumer guarantees, see para 17.09A.

16 It has been so held in the case of advertisements for auctions, catalogues and price lists, displays of goods in a shop window or on a self-service shelf; see further, para 10.02.

17 E.g. *Moorehouse v Woolfe* (1882) 46 LT 379 (moneylender advertising 'easy terms'; 125% interest charged); *Word v Stevens* [1993] CLY 1993, Cty Ct (car advertised as 'absolutely immaculate'). For misrepresentation, see generally, paras 11.02 and 17.10.

18 *Contra* where the advertiser is not privy to the retail supply and does not make the advertisement as agent of the retail supplier.

19 See generally Harvey, *Consumer Protection and Fair Trading*, 6th edn, Chap 2; Cranston, *Consumers and the Law*, 3rd edn, 51–5.

2. *Credit advertising* (see para 8.20, *et seq*).

3. *Pricing.* Regulations sometimes require the display of prices (see para 8.08); and, in any event, there are prohibitions on misleading price indications (see para 8.09).

4. *Food and drink* (see para 8.11).

5. *Medicines and drugs* (see para 8.12).

6. *Community law.* Article 28 [ex 30] of the Treaty of Rome prohibits all restrictions to the free circulation of goods as well as any measure having equivalent effect. This rule has been used to encourage a negative harmonisation[20] by striking down some discriminatory regulation of advertising by Member States.[21] Additionally, the Community felt the need for a measure of positive harmonisation[20] to control the growing volume of cross-border advertising, notably on television. Accordingly, the Misleading Advertisements Directive was adopted to lay down minimum standards (see para 8.12A) and a more far-reaching effect obtained under the UCP Directive (see para 4.20, item (g)). Moreover, as part of the 1992 initiative, there has been adopted Article 95 [ex 100A], which for some purposes allows harmonisation by majority vote, instead of the previous rule of unanimity in all cases, e.g. the directives on tobacco advertising (see below).

7. *Tobacco advertising* (see para 8.06A).

8. *Miscellaneous.* Among the miscellaneous statutory powers concerned with the protection of target groups in the advertising of goods may be included those relating to the following matters: weights and measures (1985 Act, s 23(1): see para 4.25); mail order transactions and business advertisements (see para 4.22); printed material;[22] indecent or obscene advertisments;[23] petrol consumption;[24] discrimination (see para 4.23); 'host mailing', where a trader inserts a third party's leaflet in his mailings;[25] and the general power to obtain Part 8 undertakings (see para 6.08). Additionally, there are substantial voluntary controls sponsored by: the EU, e.g. eco-labelling;[26] and within the UK by the Advertising Standards Authority and the indirect controls of the Broadcasting

---

20 As to positive and negative harmonisation, see para 1.03A.

21 Art 28 (see generally, para 2.13) has been applied to strike down national regulations concerning the advertisement of alcoholic beverages: *Cassis de Dijon Case* [1979] ECR 649 (liqueurs); *Commission v France* [1980] ECR 2799 (wine); and see Tayleur (2001) 151 NLJ 859. For a table of restrictions on sales promotions in different EU countries, see Circus, *Sales Promotion Law*, 2nd edn, App 8. These may be struck down by EU law: *GB-INNO-BM v Confederation du Commerce Luxembourgeois* [1991] 2 CMLR 801, Eu Ct.

22 Any paper or book must contain the name and business address of the printer: Newspaper, Printer and Reading Rooms Repeal Act 1869 (as amended).

23 Indecent Displays (Control) Act 1981: see Stone (1982) 45 MLR 62. For indecent advertisements communicated by post or telephone, see para 8.16A. See generally Lawson, *Advertising Law*, 301–4.

24 See the Energy Act 1976, s 15(1), and the Passenger Car Fuel Consumption Order, 1996 SI 1132. For the display of petrol prices, see the orders made under the Prices Acts (para 8.08).

25 See (1994) 49 CC4/32. This may infringe the DPA (see para 3.27): DPR, *Personal Data Held Within The Finance Industry* (1994), para 19.

26 Regulation 1980/2000 establishes a voluntary labelling scheme for manufactured products designed to highlight their low environmental impact: see Twigg-Flesner, *Consumer Product Guarantees*, 2003, 164–5.

Authorities (see para 3.14). There is pressure for control of labelling claims relating to green matters and energy consumption.[27]

**[8.06A] Tobacco advertising.** Previously only children had been protected by English law from tobacco sales (see para 4.23), though there were health warnings and restrictions in codes of practice from 1962 onwards, e.g. TV (see para 3.14). However, in 1997 the Government made a first-term manifesto commitment to ban tobacco advertising generally, which it attempted to honour by introducing regulations to implement EU Directive 98/43;[28] but this failed when the European Court held that that Directive was invalid as based on the wrong article of the Treaty of Rome.[29] Accordingly, the Government tried the Parliamentary route: the first Bill failed when a General Election was called in 2001; but a similar provision was enacted as the Tobacco Advertising and Promotion Act 2002.[30] Whilst this was happening, the EU promulgated another tobacco advertising Directive; and this Directive was implemented in the UK by Regulations, which principally concern maximum tar yields and product packaging.[31] The purpose of the 2002 Act is to curtail the consumption of cigarettes and other tobacco products by making it an offence to promote them to consumers, whether by way of sponsorship[32] or other advertisements. As to the latter point, the key provision is s 2(1), which provides that:

'A person who in the course of business publishes a tobacco advertisement, or causes one to be published, in the United Kingdom is guilty of an offence'.[33]

An advertisement could be by way of billboard, newspaper or website, etc: a 'tobacco advertisement' is one whose purpose or effect is to promote a 'tobacco product'; and the latter expression means 'a product consisting wholly or partly of tobacco and intended to be smoked, sniffed, sucked or chewed'.[34] The s 2(1) offence covers two types of businessman:[33] (a) one who 'publishes', which is defined as any

---

27 See NCC, *Green Claims*, 1996. For the EU-inspired compulsory energy labelling scheme (eco-labelling), see: [2004] 7 *Which?* 14.

28 Even though the Government defeated an attempt to secure an injunction to prevent implementation of the Directive before the ECJ ruling (see below): *R v Secretary of State for Health, ex p. Imperial Tobacco Ltd* [2000] 1 All ER 572, CA (unsuccessfully appealed to the HL: [2001] 1 All ER 850). For injunctions, see para 29.39.

29 *R v Secretary of State for Health, ex p Imperial Tobacco Ltd* [2000] All ER (EC) 769; and see para 1.03A.

30 The Government Bill which fell in 2001 was re-introduced after the election as a private member's Bill in virtually identical form and later adopted by the Government: so the parliamentary debates on its various provisions are to be found in a number of places in Hansard.

31 See Council Directive 2001/37 (held valid in *Swedish Match AB v Secretary of State for Health* [2005] 1 CMLR 26, ECJ); implemented in the Tobacco Products (Manufacture, Presentation and Sale)(Safety) Regulations, 2002 SI 3041. See also Directive 2003/33.

32 Leaving aside transitional provisions (s 20), s 10 prohibits sponsorship by tobacco companies, e.g. of motor racing; and s 11 enables the Secretary of State to prohibit attempts to get round the Act by 'brandsharing' (undefined), e.g. tobacco brand name on clothing or luggage: see 2004 SI 1824.

33 'Course of business' is not defined, but cf. para 4.03A; 'advertisement' is also undefined, but cf. para 8.27; and for the strict liability offences, see s 16 and para 28.08. Can a tobacco manufacturer advertise his name in Yellow Pages?

34 S 1. 'Purpose' includes one of a number of purposes (s 21); but 'product' is undefined, cf. para 17.25.

means of publishing including electronic means, e.g. by internet (s 21); and (b) one who 'causes to be published', which would include advertisers. Both offences (a) and (b) are extended to any business which 'prints, devises or distributes' a tobacco advertisement (s 2(2)), e.g. printers or retailers, and distribute includes in electronic form (s 2(3)), e.g. internet advertising.[35] Further, the s 2 offences extend to 'displays' of tobacco products,[36] free distributions (s 9: see para 8.13A) and advertisements appearing in 'a newspaper, periodical or other publication' (s 3); but broadcasting is to be left to the indirect controls of its own bodies (s 12; and below). On the other hand, all the offences are confined to public advertisements:[37] they do not apply to advertisements within the tobacco trade; nor where a consumer has privately requested the information; nor where the principal market objective for the advertisement is not the UK (s 4(1) and (2)). Moreover, the offences do not extend to some specialist tobacco retailers in respect of advertisements which are not for cigarettes or hand-rolling tobacco (s 6); there are provisions allowing the exemption of some classes of advertisement by regulation;[38] and granting a defence to some innocent advertisers (ss 5 and 17: see para 28.16). Enforcement is placed in the hands of local authorities (s 13; and see para 28.02), subject to the usual controls on entry to premises (ss 14–15; and see para 28.05) and power to convict corporate officers (s 18; and see para 28.11).

**[8.07] Trade descriptions by advertising**. The Trade Descriptions Act 1968 makes special provision to deal with the situation 'where in an advertisement[39] a trade description[40] is used in relation to any class of goods'. If the advertisement is for a specific item, application of a false trade description may be clear;[41] but, where the reference is to a class of goods, s 5(3) helpfully explains that:

> 'In determining for the purposes of this section whether any goods are of a class to which a trade description used in an advertisement relates regard shall be had not only to the form and content of the advertisement but also to the time, place, manner and frequency of its publication and all other matters making it likely or unlikely that a person to whom the goods are supplied would think of the goods as belonging to the class in relation to which the trade description is used in the advertisement'.

---

35  But the s 2 internet offences are confined to those carrying on a business in the UK (s 2(4)), whose advertisement is aimed at the UK public (s 4(1)(c)). S 7 empowers the Secretary of State to amend the Act in the light of later electronic technology (see further, para 9.05).

36  S 8(1), e.g. the shelves in retail shops where packets of cigarettes are displayed or cigarette vending machines, though websites are excluded (s 8(2)). There is clearly an overlap between the two undefined expressions 'advertisement' and 'display'; but it is hoped that any problems can be dealt with by the power to make regulations (s 8(1), (3) and (4)).

37  ' "Public" means the public generally, any section of the public or individually selected members of the public' (s 21).

38  S 4(3) and (4); and see 2004 SI 765, which are not incompatible with the manufacturer's human rights (*R (on the application of BAT) v Secretary of State for Health* [2005] CLY 2740). As to specialist tobacconists, see 2004 SI 1277.

39  'Advertisement' includes a catalogue, a circular and a price list: s 39(1). Compare the CCA definition: see para 8.29.

40  For trade descriptions, see para 4.07. S 5 does not apply to the advertisement of services: see para 8.06.

41  Eg *Rees v Munday* [1974] 3 All ER 506, DC.

It has been said that this enables a court to take into account **all** of the following:[42]

(i)    that the advertisement was contained in an out-of-date periodical, e.g. the 'shelf-life' prescribed in the Pricing Code (see para 8.10A);

(ii)   that publication of the advertisement was recent, whilst the goods were supplied and offered as old stock;[43] and

(iii)  that the advertisement had not circulated in the area in which the goods were supplied or offered.[44]

In the foregoing circumstances and for the purposes set out in paragraphs (a) and (b) considered below, s 5(2) introduces the presumption that:

> 'The trade description shall be taken as referring to all goods of the class, whether or not in existence at the time the advertisement is published'.

The effect of s 5 is thus that any trade description contained in an advertisement is 'used' in relation to goods of a class and thus 'applied' to them by virtue of s 4(1)(c).[45] In these circumstances, s 5(2) carefully distinguishes according to whether a retailer is advertising his own wares, or a manufacturer is advertising his products to promote sales of them by retailers. Thus, the presumption introduced by s 5(2) distinguishes between the two section 1 offences (see para 4.03) as follows:

> *Paragraph (a) offences.* Section 5(2) presumes application of the trade description for the purpose of deciding whether the person who both manufactures and sells has applied a false trade description.[46] However, it also extends to the person who innocently advertises goods supplied by another, and s 25 therefore contains a special defence for such advertisers (see para 28.16) and s 39(2) makes it clear that the s 5 offence does not extend to editorial comment.

> *Paragraph (b) offences.* Section 5(2) presumes application of the trade description contained in, e.g. the manufacturer's advertisement, to goods supplied by another, e.g. a retailer.[47] As both the s 1 offences are ones of strict liability, the Act provides a number of defences to them (see para 28.13, *et seq.*) and contains power to specify the information to be contained in the advertisements (see para 4.10).

**[8.08] Price displays.** Whilst the presentation of the weight of goods sold is controlled by the Weights and Measures Acts (see para 4.25), there are two different

---

42    Current Law Statutes, Annotation to s 5(3). Misleading advertisements as to prices are now dealt with elsewhere: see para 8.10.

43    But see Bragg, *Trade Descriptions*, 17.

44    Is the test subjective (referring to the particular consumer misled) or objective (referring to the generality of consumers)?

45    For s 4(1)(c), see para 4.04. It may be that comparative advertising can be brought within this provision: Lawson, *Advertising Law*, 253–4.

46    *British Gas Corp v Lubbock* [1974] 1 All ER 188, DC (accessories). It would appear that in some of the cases referred to in note 47 below, the charge could have been laid under s 1(1)(a).

47    E.g. *Rees v Munday* (above); *Chidwick v Beer* [1974] RTR 415, DC; *Furniss v Scholes* [1974] RTR 133, DC.

types of control in relation to the **display** of prices, which should both be distinguished from the **level** of prices (see para 2.12).

1.  *The Prices Acts 1974 and 1975.* Section 4 of the 1974 Act (as amended)[48] contains wide powers enabling the Secretary of State to make **positive** regulations as to the accurate display of the prices of goods and services being sold[49] or supplied by retail; and s 7 and the Sched makes contravention a criminal offence and contain wide, almost common-form, powers of enforcement (see Chap 28). Over the years, extensive use has been made of these powers; for instance, there are regulations requiring the price of food and drink to be indicated at premises where it is supplied for consumption on the premises.[50] Further, since 1991 the s 4 powers have been utilised to implement a series of EU Directives (see generally, para 3.10). The present powers are to be found in the Price Marking Order, 2004 SI 102 which reflect an EU Directive (98/6/EC), and contain two distinct strands for the protection of 'consumers'.[51] *First,* reg 4(1) imposes a general obligation[52] on retailers (which it calls 'traders'[53]), whether by terrestrial sale or e-commerce (reg 3(2): see para 8.17A), to show a rounded (regs 12–13) 'selling price' (reg 1(2)), unless the product is sold from bulk (see below), or except in the case of a separate 'advertisement'.[54] *Second,* reg 5 requires most such 'traders'[53] to indicate 'unit prices'[55] for all 'products sold from bulk',[56] or under Pts IV or V of the Weights and Measures Act, or pre-packaged (see para 4.25). However, there are exempted from this unit-pricing rule all advertisements which do not indicate a price (reg 5(4)) and all the following (reg 5(3)): items listed in Sched 2, e.g. shown on TV; goods sold at a unit price identical to the selling price, e.g. goods sold in a 1 kilo pack exhibiting a price per kilo; bread sold in a 'small shop'; and pre-packaged goods in a constant quantity and sold in a 'small shop', by an 'itinerant trader',

---

48  As substituted by s 16(1) of the Price Commission Act 1977. Without prejudice to the generality of these powers, s 4(2) of the 1974 Act (as amended) spells out some examples.

49  The expression 'sale of goods' may include any conditional sale or hp agreement: Counter-Inflation Act 1973, s 21(5). Curiously, this provision does not appear to have been amended so as to refer to the CCA.

50  See the Price Marking (Food and Drink Services) Order, 2003 SI 2253. For overlap with the UCP Directive, see para 4.21A.

51  'Consumer' means 'any individual who buys a product for purposes that do not fall within the sphere of his commercial or professional activity' (reg 1(2)). Cf. para 1.02. For overlap with the UCP Directive, see para 4.21A.

52  It does not apply to goods supplied during the course of a service, e.g. a plumber supplying a new tap (see para 2.05); nor to sales by auction (see para 10.10); nor of works of art or antiques (reg 3).

53  'Trader' means 'any person who sells or offers for sale products which fall within his commercial or professional activity' (reg 1(2)).

54  Reg 4(2). 'Advertisement' means 'any form of advertisement which is made in order to promote the sale of a product but does not include any advertisement by means of which the trader intends to encourage a consumer to enter a 'distance contract' [also defined in reg 1(2): cf. para 8.17], a catalogue, a price list, a container or a label' (reg 1(2)).

55  'Unit price' means the final price, including VAT and all other taxes (e.g. petrol tax), for one kilogram, etc, or in respect of the products specified in Sched 1, the final price for the corresponding unit of quantity set out in that Sched, or, where products are sold by number, the final price for one individual item of the product (reg 1(2)).

56  'Products sold from bulk' means 'products which are not pre-packaged and are weighed or measured at the request of the consumer' (reg 1(2)). As to pre-packaged solid food presented as a liquid, take the 'net drained weight' (reg 1(2)): see reg 8. As to 'Metric Martyrs', see para 4.24.

or from a vending machine (see the definitions in reg 1 and reg 15). In respect of both types of control, the price must *prima facie* be shown in sterling (reg 6) and clearly includes VAT (regs 7 and 11); and there are special provisions relating to general reductions (reg 9) and precious metals (regs 10 and 1(2)).

2.   *Consumer Protection Act 1987 (CPA), s 26.* Whilst the above provisions are generally positive in flavour, specifying how prices shall be displayed, amended s 26 contains a power to make regulations which seems rather more **negative**. Section 26 mentions two purposes for which regulations may be made: first, as regards price indications for the retail supply of any goods, services or accommodation; and second, to facilitate enforcement of s 20 (see para 8.10). Under s 26, there have been made the Price Indication Regulations, 1991 SI 199 to deal with traders who chose to charge a different price when the customer pays for goods, services or accommodation by different payment methods, e.g. payment by cash, as against cheque or payment card. The Regulations apply whenever such a 'price'[57] is stated generally either orally or in writing by a trader who does not intend that price to apply to all acceptable methods of payments: they do not apply where the price discrimination consists only of a charge made for instalment credit (reg 2(4)); nor to supplies by a club to its members (reg 2(5)); nor to private sales (reg 2(6)); nor to supplies of motor fuel (reg 2(1)). The duty is for that trader to provide before contract a statement in a specified manner either of the difference in price or percentage difference.[58] Reg 8 makes contravention an offence and also employs the CPA defences, etc, to misleading price indications under ss 24(3), 39 and 40 (see Chap 28).

Enforcement of s 26 regulations is placed in the hands of the local weights and measures departments;[59] and compliance with the regulations will be a defence to s 20 proceedings (see para 8.09). For mistake as to price in civil law, see para 10.16.

**[8.09] Misleading price indications**. Attempts were first made to tackle false or misleading prices in the TDA (s 11) and then the also now-repealed Bargain Offer Order 1979. These unsatisfactory provisions have now been replaced by Pt III of the CPA, of which s 20 creates new offences where a trader 'in the course of any business of his' (see below) gives to any private consumer (see para 8.10) a misleading (see para 8.09A) indication as to the price at which any goods,[60] services,[61]

---

57   'Price' is defined (by reg 2(2) and (3)) by reference to s 20(6) of the CPA: see para 8.09. As to ticket tout regulations, see Clayson (1995) 14 Tr L 321.

58   Reg 3; and for the specified manner of price displays, see regs 5–7. Alternatively, the trader can give actual prices to the individual consumer (reg 3(3)); or generally by notice at public entrances, with special provisions for petrol stations and restaurants (reg 4).

59   Weights and Measures Act 1985 (see para 4.24); Prices Act 1974, s 7 and Sched, para 6; CPA, s 27. See further, Chap 28. It has been pointed out that the prosecution has a lesser burden of proof under s 26 regulations than as regards misleading price indications: OFT (1992) 1 *Beeline*, 8.

60   As to 'goods', see s 45(1); and further, para 4.33. For a history of Pt III, see Bragg, *Trade Descriptions*, 113–15.

61   'Services' includes the provision of credit, banking or insurance services (s 22(1)(a)), but not when provided under a contract of employment (s 22(2)). 'Credit' has the same meaning as in the CCA (s 22(5)): see para 5.21. It does not extend to Euro-services: 1992 SI 3218, Sched 9. What of low-income consumers?

accommodation,[62] or facilities[63] are available, whether from himself or another.[64] These pricing offences are clearly restricted to trade supplies to consumers;[65] and they concentrate on the 'price', defining this as 'the aggregate of the sums required to be paid by a consumer . . . in respect of the supply'.[66] In *R v Kettering Magistrates' Court, ex p MRB Insurance Brokers Ltd*:[67]

> M Ltd arranged a contract of motor insurance and also entered into a regulated consumer credit agreement to facilitate payment of the insurance premiums. In making the latter, M Ltd quoted a substantially inaccurate APR (see para 8.21). The court held that the fact that the APR became a term of the credit agreement did not preclude its being an 'indication' within s 20(1).

Douglas Brown J pointed out that the inaccurate APR was quoted in the contract and said that 'every term is an indication for the purposes of the Act; not every indication is a term of the contract' (at 356j).

The scope of the offence was considered in *Warwickshire County Council v Johnson*.[68]

> J was employed as a branch manager of Dixons. With Dixon's authority, he placed a notice outside the shop stating—'We will beat any TV, HiFi and Video price by £20 on the spot'. Whilst that notice was displayed, a customer saw a TV offered for sale elsewhere in the area for £159.95. The customer demanded to purchase an identical set from J's shop for £139.95 (£159.95 – £20). J refused to sell it at the reduced price, his normal price being £179.95, but was prepared to sell for £159.95 (£179.95 – £20). J was prosecuted under s 20(1) of the CPA.

There were only two issues before the House of Lords; namely, (1) whether for the purposes of s 20(1) the notice was misleading (yes: see para 8.09A); and (2) whether J could commit a s 20(2) offence. Section 20(2) says that a person shall be guilty of an offence if, 'in the course of any **business of his**', he gives a misleading price indication.[69] The Divisional Court construed this phrase in the sense of the occupation of J,[70] bearing in mind the CPA definition of 'business' as including 'a trade or profession' (s 45(1): see para 4.33). The court worried that, if an employee could not

---

62  As to 'accommodation', see s 23. Cf. TDA, s 14: see para 4.16. As to misdescriptions of real property, see para 4.03.

63  This would catch shopping facilities, e.g. a closing-down sale, cf. *Westminster CC v Ray Alan (Manshops) Ltd* (set out at para 4.16): Bragg, *Op. cit.*, 142.

64  S 20(3)(b). So it is an offence to misstate the price charged by another trader: *Denard v Burton Retail Ltd* [1997] CLY 973, DC (franchise). Similarly, it is irrelevant whether the indication is misleading to all consumers or only some of them: s 20(3)(c).

65  But not to any particular consumer: *MFI v Hibbert* [1995] CLY 741, DC. As to 'consumers', see para 8.10. Cf. the TDA, which also protects traders and penalises purchases by traders (see para 4.03A). Regrettably, it is not entirely clear whether there must be an actual supply; and it does not deal expressly with mixed use (cf. para 18.18).

66  As to price, see s 20(6), including any method to determine an aggregate. What of a manufacturer's advertisement 'up to 50% off'; or an 'estimate'?

67  [2000] 2 All ER (Comm) 353, DC.

68  [1993] AC 583, [1993] 1 All ER 299, HL.

69  The certified question from the Divisional Court concerned the same phrase in s 20(2)(a)—presumably because the claim only became misleading after it was given (see para 8.09A): but see Scott [1993] JBL at 492, note 6.

70  (1991) 11 Tr LR 76, DC. Popplewell J argued that this must have been the intention of Parliament, bearing in mind the existence of multiple retailers (as here) and the by-pass procedure (see below): Oughton [1993] JBL at 47–8; Holgate (1993) 10 Tr L at 24–5.

be convicted under s 20, he could not be convicted under the by-pass provision (s 40: see para 28.12). An argument that this could be avoided by construing 'business of his' in s 40 as business of the employer (see below) was rejected by the House (at 303g–304j: see further para 28.12). However, the House of Lords unanimously held that J was not guilty of the offence charged for two reasons. *First*, s 20 was designed to replace s 11 of the TDA, under which both an employer and employee could probably be strictly liable for a pricing offence and this remains the position under s 1 of the TDA (see para 4.03A); whereas the different wording of s 20(1) must refer to a business of which the defendant is 'either the owner or in which he has a controlling interest' (at 304). *Second*, they found decisive an explanation of the s 20 wording given when the Bill was before Parliament (see para 1.04). Nevertheless, their Lordships found it strange 'that the person actually responsible for what happened, as [J] clearly was, should be immune from conviction' (at 304). But was J 'responsible' when he appears to have been carrying out Dixon's policy? It has been said that the Divisional Court followed the traditional criminal law policy of attributing responsibility to the actor, whereas the House of Lords looked instead to the policy of the legislation.[71] In 2007, the CPA, Pt III will have to be aligned with the UCP Directive (see para 4.20, item (c)).

**[8.09A] Misleading**. For the purposes of determining whether there has been a misleading price indication within s 20 (see para 8.09), the CPA lays down in s 21 an extensive definition of what is 'misleading'. It provides that (s 21(1)):

> 'an indication given to any consumer is misleading as to a price if what is conveyed by the indication, or what those consumers might reasonably be expected to infer from the indication, includes'

certain listed matters. It is to be noted that this formula makes it clear that the test of price **given**[72] is objective[73] and extends to omissions;[74] but it does not mention disclaimers and it remains to be seen whether they will be effective.[75] The list is as follows, dealing with both the price itself and any method of determining the price (s 21(1)):—

(a) The price is less that it in fact is, e.g. overcharging.[76]

(b) The applicability of the price does not depend on circumstances on which it does depend, e.g. quoted price only available to cash customers.[77]

---

71  Scott [1993] JBL at 494; Cartwright, *Consumer Protection and the Criminal Law*, (2001), 168.
72  As to when the price indication is 'given', see *Toys 'R' Us v Gloucestershire CC* (1994) 13 Tr LR 276, DC (where goods displayed on retailer's shelf; see Holgate (1994) 13 Tr L 410).
73  *Holman v CWS Ltd* [2001] CCLR 2777, DC. Cf. TDA, s 3: see para 4.08. But does this combat confusion marketing (see para 8.12A)?
74  E.g. a compulsory extra charge. What about an optional charge? As to VAT, see Bragg, *Trade Descriptions*, 127–8. As to the difficulty with mail order catalogues, see Bragg, *Op. cit.*, 124.
75  See Bragg, *Op. cit.*, 118. If it can be disclaimed, is the test of disclaimer the same as for the TDA (see para 4.09)?
76  S 21(1)(a). E.g. *R v Kettering Justices, ex p MRB Insurance Brokers Ltd* (set out at para 8.09). On overcharging: see Bragg, *Op. cit.*, 120–1; *contra* Fidler (1989) 139 NLJ 943. Bar-coding (see para 2.06) may differ from shelf pricing: see [1996] 6 *Which?* 20. Discrepancies from bar-coding can be obviated by instructing the cashier always to charge the lower price: *Toys 'R' Us v Gloucester CC* (1994) 13 Tr LR 276, DC.
77  S 21(1)(b). As to the cash customer example, cf. CCA, s 45: set out at para 8.27. Similarly, if the quoted price does not apply to part-exchange deals (see generally, para 2.09); or misleading 'free' offers (Bragg, *Op. cit.*, 129–30).

(c) The price covers matters for which an additional charge is in fact made, e.g. delivery charges.[78]

(d) That a person expects the price to change when in fact he has no such expectation, e.g. that a manufacturer's recommended price is to increase.[79]

(e) The facts upon which a consumer draws a price comparison are not what in fact they are, e.g. never knowingly undersold.[80]

Section 21(2) applies the same rules to the method of determining or calculating the price, e.g. price per pound, stating a weight.[81]

In *Warwickshire CC v Johnson* (set out at para 8.09), the question arose whether promises later dishonoured could be misleading. The Divisional Court treated the statement in the advertisement as a continuing offer[82] and concluded that it was therefore misleading when taken up by a consumer. The House of Lords approved the decision that a notice could be rendered misleading by refusal to honour it without reference to any other provisions, saying that to hold otherwise would restrict the efficacy of this part of the consumer protection legislation (at 302g–j). See further, para 8.10.

**[8.10] Offences.** Giving a misleading price indication (see para 8.09A) is only an offence where it is given by a person in the course of his business (see para 8.09) to one or more (s 20(3)(c): see below) consumers. A **consumer** in relation to goods means one who takes 'for his own private use or consumption';[83] and in relation to services, accommodation or facilities one who takes 'otherwise than for the purposes of any business of his'.[84] For the purposes of a s 20 offence, it is immaterial whether (s 20(3)): (a) the person giving the indication is acting as principal or agent, e.g. the second-hand shop selling goods as agent for private sellers; (b) he is the person from whom the services, etc, are available (see below); (c) the indication misled some or all consumers, e.g. withdrawal of a pensioner discount.

At this point, s 20(1) in laying down the offences distinguishes according to whether or not the price indication was misleading when given (see para 8.09A). Suppose a retailer's advertisement is accurate when published, e.g. as to a manufacturer's recommended price, which later becomes inaccurate, e.g. because the

---

78  S 21(1)(c). E.g. *Toyota (GB) Ltd v North Yorkshire CC* (1998) 162 JP 794, DC. Cf. *MFI Warehouses Ltd v Nattrass* (set out at para 4.17).

79  S 21(1)(d). E.g. falsely indicating fore-knowledge of a price change to be recommended by the manufacturer on future stock deliveries.

80  S 21(1)(e). E.g. *MGN Ltd v Ritter* [1997] CLY 974, DC; *DSG Retail Ltd v Oxfordshire CC* [2001] 1 WLR 1765, DC. See further s 21(3).

81  An example which may also fall within the Weights and Measures Act 1985 (see paras 4.25 and 8.08).

82  It clearly is not an offer in the contractual sense (see para 10.20). Nor does the CPA contain any provision giving an extended meaning to 'offer'; cf. TDA s 6 (see para 4.05). However, the case law on s 14 has developed a similar notion of a continuing statement: see *Wings Ltd v Ellis* (set out at para 4.17).

83  S 20(6)(a). *Contra* the TDA, which also protects traders and penalises purchasers: see para 4.03. As to part-exchange, see Bragg, *Trade Descriptions*, 122. 'Consumer' includes a tso (see para 28.03): *Toys 'R' Us v Gloucestershire CC* (1994) 13 Tr LR 276, DC.

84  S 20(6)(b), (c). What about the businessman who, to the knowledge of the supplier, puts his private purchases through the books of his business, or of the private consumer who shows a trade card to get a trade discount?

manufacturer alters his recommendation. Bear in mind that an indication is **given**, according to *Wings Ltd v Ellis* (set out at para 4.17) every time the advertisement is read. So, offences may be committed as follows:

1.  *Misleading when given*. According to s 20(1):

    'Subject to the following provisions of this Part, a person shall be guilty of an offence if, in the course of any business of his, he gives (by any means whatever) to any consumers an indication which is misleading as to the price at which any goods, services, accommodation or facilities are available (whether generally or from particular persons)'.

    If the manufacturer changes his recommendation *before* a consumer reads the advertisement, there may be a s 20(1) offence.[85] A defendant charged with this offence[86] is granted two special defences not available under s 20(2) (below): he may escape conviction by proving (a) due diligence (ss 24(5) and 39(5): see para 28.13); or (b) that he was a prior party in the chain of distribution, e.g. importer, recommending a price which he reasonable believed 'was for the most part being followed'.[87]

2.  *Subsequently misleading*. Section 20(2) provides that a person shall also be guilty of an offence if:

    (a) in the course of any business of his, he has given an indication to any consumers which, after it was given, has become misleading as mentioned in subsection (1) above; and

    (b) some or all of those consumers might reasonably be expected to rely on the indication at a time after it has become misleading; and

    (c) he fails to take all such steps as are reasonable to prevent those consumers from relying on the indication.

    This provision may apply where there is a brochure with a long life expectancy, or a pretended closing-down sale. It should be noted that there is no due diligence defence available under s 20(2): this is because lack of diligence is part of the offence. So, if the above manufacturer changes his recommended price *after* the consumer has read the advertisement, but before the consumer enters the transaction, there may be a s 20(2) offence. This has caused difficulty where a retailer does not honour his price promises. *Warwickshire CC v Johnson* (set out at para 8.09) appears to suggest that there might be a s 20(2) offence. However, it has been strenuously argued that s 20(2) refers only to a change of **external** circumstance, not a change of mind; that s 21(1)(d) was not contravened because J always intended the price reduction (which he granted on other goods) right up until the moment of confrontation with this customer (see para 8.10); and that the offence should not extend to broken promises.[88] It may be

---

85  *DSG Retail Ltd v Oxfordshire CC* [2001] 1 WLR 1765, DC (display notice did not contain the limitations to which it was subject). See further, the Pricing Code, para 1.6: see para 8.10A.
86  It may extend to overcharging, by combining s 20(1) with s 21(1)(b): Bragg, *Trade Descriptions*, 126.
87  S 24(4). Is the manufacturer precluded from relying on this defence if he knows at the time his advertisement is read of a discount war between retailers of his product? See s 24(4)(d) and Bragg, *Op. cit.*, 145.
88  See Oughton [1993] JBL at 45–6, commenting on the DC judgment; and Bragg, *Op. cit.*, 125, writing in 1990.

that this issue simply was not considered in *Warwickshire CC v Johnson*; and that on this basis there can be supported later cases denying the application of s 20(2) to broken price promises.[89]

Subject to a time limit (s 20(5): see para 28.07), a person acting in the course of his business may *prima facie* commit either of the above offences,[90] whatever his function in the chain of distribution (s 20(3): above). However, under s 24 it is a defence for the defendant to show any of the following:[91] he is an advertiser innocently taking an advertisement (s 24(3): see para 28.16); or the indication was given through the media but not in an advertisement;[92] or that he complied with pricing regulations.[93] Other provisions make relevant compliance with the price code (see para 8.10A).

**[8.10A] Pricing codes of practice**. To increase the flexibility of the above misleading pricing rules, s 25(1) gives the Secretary of State power to introduce a pricing code with statutory backing.[94] The Bill originally envisaged that compliance with the code should be a complete defence, but this was subsequently modified by s 25(2) so that non-compliance with the code 'shall not of itself give rise to any criminal or civil[95] liability', whereas compliance may be relied on by a person charged with a s 20 offence (see para 8.10). Thus, it has a status like that of the Highway Code and has the effect of putting the burden of proof on the defendant, so making it more readily enforceable.

*The Code.*[96] Addressed to the retailer, the Code gives advice on all the following matters:[97] express comparison with his own previous price;[98] introductory offers and special promotions intended whilst stocks last (para 1.3); comparisons with prices related to different circumstances (para 1.4), e.g. special prices for 'seconds' or kit-form; comparisons with other traders' prices (para 1.5), e.g. 'If you can buy for less, we will refund the difference'; comparisons with recommended prices;[99] flash, sale and free offers;[100] quoted prices misleading because of other

---

89 See *Link Stores Ltd v Harrow LBC* [2001] 1 WLR 1479.

90 As to offences, see s 20(4): see generally, para 28.04. They give rise to no civil right of action nor render the contract illegal: see para 8.10A.

91 The burden of proof is clearly cast on the defendant. As to the weight of that burden, see para 28.13.

92 S 24(2). E.g. an author misstating the price of his book during a TV interview. Even if he did so knowingly?

93 S 24(1). Unlike the general safety requirement (see para 4.33), compliance is not an automatic defence unless the trader follows the practices designated in the regulations (see para 8.08).

94 As to such statutory orders, see s 25(4). There is power for the Minister to modify or withdraw his authority from a code (s 25(3)).

95 Non-compliance gives rise to no civil right of action (s 41(2): see generally, para 3.21), nor does it render any contract illegal (s 41(3): see generally, para 10.19). Cf. the food code: see para 4.26.

96 The 1988 Code was replaced by the Consumer Protection (Code of Practice for Traders on Price Indications) Approval Order 2005 SI 2705. The Code is set out in Thomas, *Encyclopedia of Consumer Law*, para 2-1035. The 2005 Code adds provisions for websites.

97 The Code also contains separate sections dealing with Price Indications which have become misleading after being given (Pt 3) and Sale of New Houses (Pt 4).

98 Para 1.2.2 introduces a test of offering the goods for at least 28 consecutive days during the previous 6 months at the same premises. See generally, Bragg, *Trade Descriptions*, 136–7.

99 Para 1.6. Where such recommended prices are particularly out of touch with retail prices charged, such comparisons are 'banned'. See Bragg, *Op. cit.*, 132–4.

100 As to reductions already printed on packaging ('flash offers') see para 1.7; as to special sale prices, see para 1.9; and as to 'free offers', see para 1.10; and para 2.08.

factors;[101] and the price of credit (para 2.2.20), which refers to regulations made under the CCA (see para 8.27). The Code is to be enforced by Trading Standards Officers;[102] and in 2007 it may have to be amended to comply with the UCP Directive (see para 4.21B).

The end result of Pt III of the CPA should thus be a flexible, three-tiered scheme as to what constitutes misleading pricing: the general principles are enshrined in the Act (see para 8.09); but more detailed matters are confined to regulations (see para 8.08); and practical guidance for traders set out in plain English (see para 11.08) in the codes. Some breaches of the Code may amount to the offences of misleading pricing[103] or misleading advertising. For instance, in *OFT v The Officers Club Ltd*,[104]

> A multiple retailer devised a '70% off' sales strategy which attempted to comply with the letter of the above Code by previously offering a very small amount of the so-labelled goods at a few of its 159 stores and adding to its '70% off' notices:
>
> > 'All discounted goods have been for sale at the higher price at six or more of our branches for a minimum of 28 days in the preceding six months.'
>
> Presumably because of doubts as to whether a Code-compliant notice could breach s 20 of the CPA (see para 8.09A), the OFT sought an enforcement order under Pt 8 of the EA (see para 28.04) for breach of the Misleading Advertisements Order (see para 8.12A).

Rejecting any breach of the HRA (see para 3.09A), Etherton J held that the retailer had made an implied representation in breach of the (above) Code (at paras 156, 159, 166) and hence a misleading advertisement (at para 185). The retailer subsequently gave an undertaking to the court.[105]

**[8.11] Food and drink.** Leaving aside the special rules concerning the advertising of alcoholic beverages,[106] the Food Safety Act 1990 (see generally, para 4.26) creates several offences connected with the advertising of food or drink for human consumption.[107]

(a) *Food safety requirement.* It being an offence to sell food not complying with the food safety requirement (see para 4.27), the Act prohibits the 'advertising' (see s 53(1)) of food which fails to comply with that requirement (s 8(2)), though providing a special defence of innocent publication (s 22. See further, para 28.16).

(b) *False descriptions.* Section 15(1) makes it an offence to provide a label in connection with the sale or display of any food which either (i) falsely describes

---

101 Para 2.2. E.g. prices which do not mention optional extras, postage and packing, VAT, service charges.

102 Arts 5 and 6. For its effect in court proceedings, see Arts 4 and 7.

103 E.g. *AG Stanley Ltd v Surrey CC* [1996] CLY 1166, DC (Clayson 15 Tr L 229).

104 [2005] EWHC 1080 (Ch). This Decision led the OFT to produce draft guiance, *Advertising Own Price Discounts* (June 2006).

105 (2005) 42 Fair Trading 1.

106 See the Customs and Excise Act 1952, ss 162–4 (as amended).

107 For offences, see s 35; and for presumptions, see s 3. For offences by corporations (s 36) and the defences of another's default (s 20) and due diligence (s 21), see para 28.07, *et seq.*

the food[108] or (ii) is likely to mislead the ordinary man[109] as to the nature or substance or quality of the food (see para 4.28). A separate offence is committed by anyone who publishes an advertisement (see above) which does either of those things (s 6(2)). Nevertheless, many such false descriptions are likely to continue to be prosecuted under the TDA (but see s 2(5)(as amended): see para 4.07); and it may also give rise to an action for breach of contract, either for breach of an express term (see para 8.05) or statutory implied term as to description (see para 13.11), or the special rights in respect of distance contracts (see para 8.17).

(c) *Positive labelling.* Besides not being untruthful, Parliament has also been concerned that labelling should be positively required to state matters connected with food.[110] As under the previous Food Acts, regulation-making powers have been utilised to make the Labelling of Food Regulations.[111] A second stream of food labelling requirements is to be found in the Food Labelling Directives.[112] In fact, the 1990 Act contains sweeping new regulation-making powers, which extend to, for instance, antibiotic residues in meat, food irridation, the implementation of EU obligations and GM foods.[113] Inevitably, there will always be those who want labels to contain more information;[114] and, if a food label makes a medicinal claim,[115] it is dealt with as a medicine (and para 8.12). However, it may be that, rather than increase the foregoing **positive** requirements, it might be more satisfactory to adopt the US **negative** position that nothing may be claimed on a food label without prior official authorisation. As to restaurant price lists, see para 8.08.

**[8.12] Medicines and drugs.** Leaving aside the prohibitions of advertisements relating to remedies for certain specific diseases[116] and controlled drugs under the Misuse of Drugs Act 1971 (s 4:), Pts V and VI of the Medicines Act 1968 are concerned with the promoting, labelling and packaging of 'medicinal products'

---

108 But see *Cheshire CC v Moonflake* (1993) 157 JP 1011 (can help cut down heart disease: DC acquitted as ambiguous). The statement may also fall within the TDA: see para 4.07.

109 E.g. *R v AF Pears Ltd* (1982) 90 ITSA MR 142. The Act expressly states that mere accuracy is not necessarily a defence (s 15(4)) and also extends the section to include misleading presentation (s 15(3)).

110 E.g. *Hackney LBC v Cedar Trading Ltd* [1999] CLY 2603 (Coca-Cola labelled in Dutch; DC convicted; see 149 NLJ 1111). Positive labels will have little impact in the absence of consumer education: Cayne and Trebilcock (1973) 23 *Univ. of Toronto LJ* 396 at 406.

111 1996 SI 1499 (as amended), e.g. 'use by', 'best before' dates; Holgate (1995) 14 Tr L 408; [2004] 4 *Which?* 18. See generally O'Keefe, *Encyclopedia of Food and Drugs*.

112 The general Food Labelling Directive (2000/13) is supplemented by a Nutrition Labelling Directive (90/496) and a Food Supplements Directive (2002/46), which last contains some labelling requirements (Arts 6–8; and see generally, para 4.26).

113 E.g. 2002 SI 1817 on nutritional additives; and see generally, Lawson (1993) 143 NLJ 520 and 557; and fn 115, below. For language requirements, see *Geffroy and Casino France SNC's Reference* [2001] All ER (EC) 222, ECJ.

114 E.g. as to food claims ([2005] 3 *Which?* 16; [2005] 12 *Which?* 10); eco-labels; as to GM foods ([2004] 9 *Which?* 11). The government is committed to clear labelling: *Modern Markets: confident consumers* (1999, Cm. 4410) para 6.8. The Food Standards Agency (see para 4.26) is developing labelling guidelines for industry, e.g. 'fresh', 'natural', 'fat-free'. As to nutrition labelling, see [2006] 8 *Which?* 3 and 6.

115 See *Cheshire CC v Morningflake Oates* (above). There is a voluntary code: see [2001] 2 *Which?* 4.

116 E.g. Cancer Act 1939, s 4 (as amended); Health and Medicines Act 1988, s 23 (AIDS test kits).

(see generally, para 4.29). However, under a Directive (2004/24) traditional herbal non-medical products may be treated as food.

The 1968 Act distinguishes in its treatment of statements between those made (a) on any label attached to the medicine, or its container or package, or leaflet to accompany products[117] and (b) promotions independent of the goods by advertisement or representation.

(a) *Labels*. Pt V empowers the Minister to make regulations for the purpose of ensuring that medicinal products are correctly described and readily identifiable, contain any appropriate warning or instruction, and to promote safety.[118] The Act makes it an offence[119] in the course of business to have in one's possession for the purposes of sale or supply a medicinal product which contravenes any such regulations (s 85(3)), or which is falsely or misleadingly described by that labelling.[120]

(b) *Promotions*. Pt VI of the Act seeks to control false or misleading advertisements[121] and representations.[122] Section 93 makes it an offence for a 'commercially interested party'[123] to issue or cause to be issued a false or misleading[124] advertisement relating to medicinal products (s 93(1)); or for a person carrying on a 'relevant business' (s 93(4)) to make a false or misleading[124] representation relating to a medicinal product (s 93(3)). Section 95 contains powers to regulate advertisements and representations; and there are also powers to impose further controls on advertisements directed at practitioners[125] and for the licensing authority to require copies of advertisements (s 97).

More modern regulations tend to be made jointly under the 1968 Act and s 2 of the ECA to implement Directives;[126] and these provisions may be enforceable by Enforcement Orders (see para 6.08), but do not give rise to actions for breach of statutory duty (see para 3.21). The OFT has proposed to remove the restrictions as

---

117 'Label', 'container', 'packet' and 'leaflet' are all defined by s 132(1) of the Medicines Act 1968.

118 Ss 85(1) and (2), which have been extensively used. There are special powers to make regulations with regard to leaflets (s 86), containers (ss 87 and 88), automated machines (s 89) and medicated animal foodstuffs (s 90). As to instructions generally, see para 18.28, *et seq*.

119 For offences, see s 91. For the special defences of default of another (s 121) and warranty (s 122), see para 28.13, *et seq*.

120 S 85(5). As TDA criminal liability and contract liability, the position is as in para 8.11.

121 'Advertisements' are elaborately defined by s 92. Compare the other statutory definitions: see para 8.11 and paras 8.12A and 8.29. For counterfeit medicines, see [2006] 1 *Which?* 16.

122 'Representations' are defined in s 92(5) as meaning 'any statement or undertaking (whether constituting a condition or a warranty or not) which consists of spoken words other than words falling within subsection (2)'. Compare the CCA, s 189(1): see para 16.08.

123 A 'commercially interested party' is defined by s 92(4), and includes a manufacturer, wholesaler or retailer.

124 The 1968 Act is really only interested in misleading descriptions of medicinal properties: s 93(7); *R v Roussell* (1989) 88 Crim App R 140.

125 S 96: as to the effect of such warnings on such liability, see paras 17.30 and 18.28, *et seq*. This is quite apart from the separate statutory controls over trade publications found in Pt VII of the Act: see [2003] 1 *Which?* 5.

126 Medicines (Advertising) Regulations, 1994 SI 1932 (as amended), implementing Directives establishing a common framework for all pharmaceutical advertising. For an overlap with the UCP Directive, see para 4.21A.

to which pharmacies may dispense NHS prescriptions and is policing the internet for misleading health claims.[127] In 2007, the above rules may have to be brought into line with the UCP Directive (see para 4.20, items (h) and (k)); and food labels making medical claims may be referred to the European Food Safety Authority.

**[8.12A] Misleading advertisements.** Pursuant to EU Directives,[128] there have been introduced the Control of Misleading Advertisement Regulations[129] with the object of curbing, by use of the criminal law, the following:

1.  Most misleading 'advertisements'[130] carried by the media to promote trade in the supply of goods and services 'Misleading' is defined by reg 2(2) as an advertisement that both (a) 'deceives or is likely to deceive' consumers and (b) therefore affects the economic behaviour of consumers.[131] Even the truth could be couched so that it is 'likely to deceive', as in the *Officers Club* case;[132] but the category would not seem to extend to 'confusion marketing', that is, where marketing is conducted so as to make comparisons between different suppliers as difficult as possible, e.g. selling by different quantities from competitors.

2.  Some 'comparative' advertising, which is designed to protect businesses against other businesses and are there beyond the scope of this work.

In implementing these Directives,[128] Government policy that nothing should hinder the work of the existing procedures for the control of advertising (see below) led to the formulation of the new powers as a long-stop. The regulations divide misleading advertisements as follows (reg 4):

(a)  Where there is an established and effective system of regulation, the complaint will be referred to that body. Thus, in the case of a 'broadcast advertisement',[131] a duty is cast upon OFCOM (see para 3.14) to consider any such complaint (reg 4(2)). Similarly, as regards a medical advertisement (see para 8.12), the scheme set up by the Medicines Act will be used (see para 4.29).

(b)  With regard to other advertisements,[131] the complaint must first be considered by the appropriate body, which is likely to be the local trading standards authority (see para 3.05) or the Advertising Standards Authority (ASA: see para 3.14), but could in the last resort be the OFT (see para 3.03), e.g. internet advertisements (see para 8.17A). The OFT have since 2000 increased their activity in this field.[133]

---

127 *AR-2002/3*, respectively 21 and 47. For the civil law rules concerning buying medicines over the internet, see para 8.17A.

128 Misleading Advertisements Directives 84/450/EEC and 97/55/EC.

129 1988 SI 915 (as amended by 2000 SI 914), made under the ECA, s 2 (see para 1.03A). There have since been further amendments to take account of OFCOM.

130 'Advertisement' and 'broadcast advertisement' are defined in reg 2(1). Cf. other statutory definitions referred to at para 8.12. The Regulations do not apply to 'investment advertisements': reg 3.

131 Cf. CPA, s 21 (see para 8.09); TDA, s 3 (see para 4.08). For examples, see *Modern Markets: confident consumers* (1999, Cm. 4410) 19. For civil action, see para 11.01.

132 *OFT v The Officers Club Ltd* (set out at para 8.10A), at para 192. Retailer advertised goods '70% off everything', when the advertised price was the standard price and the goods had not previously been advertised at the higher price in significant quantities over significant periods. In proceedings under the Regulations and the EA, after HC judgment against him, the retailer gave an undertaking.

133 See OFT, *AR-2001*, 42; 33 *Fair Trading* 10; *AR-2002/3*, 41, 49; *AR–2004/5*, 34.

Only where the above procedure has failed to deal adequately with the complaint (reg 4(3)) do the regulations require the OFT to consider any reasonable complaint as to misleading advertising;[134] for instance, a complaint by the ASA of repeated publication of a misleading advertisement notwithstanding ASA warnings.[135] As a first resort, the OFT has adopted the practice of seeking suitable assurances from the advertiser.[136] However, if appropriate,[134] the OFT[137] may institute High Court proceedings for an Enforcement Order[138] to prohibit that or further publication (regs 6(1), (2) and (6)), as in the *Officers Club* case.[132] Thus, only repetition of injuncted advertisements will amount to an offence.[139]

There may be some overlap between these rules and the following: (i) trade descriptions (see para 4.02, *et seq.*); (ii) misleading pricing (see para 8.10); (iii) the CCA advertising regulations (see para 8.30) and (iv) the UTCC Regulations (see para 11.12); but this overlap is due to be removed because the Misleading Advertisements Directive (above) has been amended to restrict it to business-to-business advertisements by the Unfair Commercial Practices Directive (Art 14: see para 4.20).

# PARTICULAR TYPES OF RESTRICTION

**[8.13] Shops**. Because so many retail sales take place at the retailer's premises, significant control of sales is indirectly provided by planning restrictions, especially on the siting of shops and markets (see para 6.02) and discrimination legislation (see para 4.23). Apart from special controls for particular types of business (see para 6.05), general controls were consolidated in the Shops Act 1950, which dealt with two matters within the scope of this work:

1. *Hours of closing*. Pt 1 of the 1950 Act laid down hours of closing and early closing, but has now been repealed by the Deregulation Act 1994, s 23 (see para 5.10).

2. *Sunday closing*. Pt 4 contained some long-standing restrictions on Sunday closing,[140] but has now been replaced by the much less restrictive Sunday Trading Act 1994 (as amended), likewise imposing criminal sanctions.[141]

---

134 Reg 4(1) and (2). The OFT must have regard to the public interest and to the desirability of encouraging control by self-regulation (reg 4(4)). As to its obtaining and disclosing information, see reg 7.

135 See OFT, *1994-AR*, 31; *1998-AR*, 28–9; *1999-AR*, 27–9; *2000-AR*, 37, 44; *AR-2003/4*, 32; and generally, (2001) 29 *Fair Trading* 19.

136 See OFT, *1994-AR*, 31; *1998-AR*, 28–9; *1999-AR*, 27–9; *2000-AR*, 37, 44; and generally, (2001) 29 *Fair Trading* 19.

137 In some Member States consumer associations have been given the right to proceed at law against misleading advertisements. For class actions, see generally, para 3.18.

138 See para 6.08. Except where an interlocutory injunction is concerned, the court must first be satisfied that the advertisement is misleading (reg 6(1)). For a shift of the burden of proof, see regs 6(3)–(5). For injunctions, see para 29.39.

139 *Director General of Fair Trading v Tobyward* [1989] 2 All ER 266. *Contra*, price indications: see para 8.09.

140 It has been decided that these restrictions did not infringe Art 28 [ex 30] of the Treaty of Rome (see para 2.13).

141 See generally, Askham, *The Sunday Trading Act 1994*, Chap 1; Envis (1994) 144 NLJ 1176.

Central to the 1994 Act is the definition of a 'shop' as meaning 'any premises where there is carried on a trade or business consisting wholly or mainly of the sale of goods' (Sched 1, para 1). This looks to a number of elements. *First*, it requires **premises** on which designated activity is carried on: there is no definition, which may cause difficulty with forecourts, markets, and telephone mail order businesses.[142] *Second*, on those premises there must be carried on a **trade or business**.[143] *Third*, the business activity on those premises must consist wholly or mainly[144] of a **sale of goods**, e.g. auction houses. It does not include the service sector, such as shops specialising in the hiring out of goods or the supply of services, e.g. video and equipment hire shops; and this would also exclude travel agents, launderettes, shoe repairers and dry-cleaners. Further, there are specific exemptions for shops selling food, whether to be consumed on the premises (e.g. restaurant, public house) or taken away (e.g. off-licence, take-away shops).

The basic scheme of the 1994 Act is to be found in Sched 1, though it has since been loosened by a Regulatory Reform Order:[145] it is to control only large retail shops,[146] but not small ones. The Schedule defines a 'large shop' by floor area[147] and provides that in general[148] 'a large shop shall not be open on a Sunday for the serving of retail customers' (para 2(1)), breach of this rule being an offence.[149] However, a large shop may trade for up to six hours on a Sunday, but not on Christmas Day,[150] and some such shops are pressing for liberalisation.[151] Responsibility for enforcing the Act is laid on the LAs (Sched 2: see Chap 28).

Apart from these general restrictions, there are special rules with regard to contracts with minors (see para 10.18), sales promotions (see paras 8.13A–16) and home sales (see para 8.16A–19).

## Sales promotions

**[8.13A] Introduction.** Enhancement of the effect of advertising is commonly sought by the use of sales promotion devices such as the following:[152]

---

142 Askham, *Op. cit.*, paras 2.56–62.

143 There is no definition in the Act of 'trade or business'. Cf. s 1 of the TDA: see para 4.03. Does it extend to outdoor car-boot sales (see para 8.13A)?

144 It has been suggested that this requires at least 50% of the turnover to consist of sales of goods: Askham, *Op. cit.*, 2.32–41.

145 Regulatory Reform (Sunday Trading) Order, 2004 SI 470 (and see generally, para 5.10); and see the Christmas Day (Trading) Act 2004, s 4.

146 But not wholesalers. This may cause difficulty at the borderline, e.g. DIY stores: see Askham, *Op. cit.*, 2.21–3.

147 E.g. *Haskins Garden Centres Ltd v East Dorset DC* [1998] CLY 836, DC. There is no definition of a small shop. For the difficulties of applying this yardstick, see Askham, *Op. cit.*, 3.7–18.

148 Sched 1 contains two exceptions of large shops which may open on a Sunday without restriction: (a) exempted shops, e.g. chemists, filling stations, farm shops, exhibition stands; (b) shops instead closing on the Jewish Sabbath.

149 Sched 1, para 7. Under the 1950 Act, it has been repeatedly held that the offence consists of the **personal** serving of customers: see Askham, *Op. cit*, 4.4–15.

150 Christmas Day (Trading) Act 2004, ss 1 and 3.

151 The DTI have rejected the liberalising proposal (*Times* 7.7.06).

152 See generally Lawson, *Advertising Law*, Chap 8; Circus, *Sales Promotion Law*, 2nd edn, 1995. There are EU proposals for a sales promotions Regulation: (2003) 58 CC1/19; 58 CC2/40

1. *Free samples and gifts.* These may either be supplied directly (see para 8.14), or indirectly by way of trading stamps (see para 15.17). Both these transactions must be carefully distinguished from inertia selling (see para 8.18).

2. *Pricing ploys.* Apart from trading stamps, vouchers and loyalty cards (see para 15.17), perhaps the most common pricing ploy is the loss leader, whose promotion must avoid contravening the misleading pricing rules (see para 8.09) and the rules relating to pricing displays (see para 8.08). However it must be borne in mind that *prima facie*[153] the mere fact of a price reduction will not deprive the transferee of his ordinary rights with regard to the goods, e.g. the statutory implied terms (see Chaps 12–15), though it may reduce the value of those rights, as where a price reduction or specified defect reduces their burden (see para 14.15, *et seq.*), or the supplier later becomes insolvent (see para 19.19).

3. *Games and competitions.* A sale of a chance is unlikely to amount to wagering,[154] but there must also be mentioned the issue of whether certain games and competitions are illegal (see para 8.16). In 2007, these rules will have to be aligned with the UCP Directive (see below). From such games and competitions which actually take place must be distinguished wholly bogus ones (scams).[155]

4. *Trading representations.* Naturally, these must comply with the TDA, both as regards goods and services (see para 4.02, *et seq*). Additionally, a recurring sharp practice has been the promotion of goods by the false representation that purchase will benefit a charity or particularly deserving class.[156] Accordingly, it has been made an offence for an unregistered person in the course of a business to sell or solicit orders for goods by representing in the course of a visit from house to house that blind or otherwise disabled persons are either employed in the production of the goods or will benefit from the proceeds of sale.[157]

5. *Mail shots.* Advertising material is frequently delivered to the homes of actual or prospective customers. Computerised lists of customers may be obtained from loyalty cards,[158] or obtained by purchasing lists compiled by third parties (usually) for other reasons. In any event, these lists are subject to the data protection rules (see para 3.27); and, if the material is delivered by mail, it is subject to the rules referred to later (see para 8.16A). A modern mass-market scam[159] might be to embody the information on a CD-Rom or unsolicited e-mail (spam: see para 8.17A) and amount to a misleading advertisement (see para 8.12A).

6. *Promotional credit*, such as 'interest-free credit' and 'buy now, pay later' offers are considered elsewhere (see para 8.20, *et seq*).

---

153  *Aliter* if the goods are marked, e.g. 'shopsoiled', or 'seconds' or 'rejects'.

154  *Ellesmere v Wallace* [1929] 2 Ch 1, CA.          155  See OFT, *AR-2005/6*, 27, 28 and 67.

156  This requires a licence under the House to House Collections Act 1939 (see para 6.02): *Cooper v Coles* [1987] 1 All ER 91, DC.

157  Trading Representations (Disabled Persons) Act 1958, s 1 (as amended); regulations made under s 64 of the Charities Act 1992. The enforcement of the provisions is in the hands of local authorities, and there are special rules for offences by corporations: see further, Chap 28.

158  Plastic identity cards issued by retailers to customers and commonly offering some perk, such as a discount off future purchases.

159  See OFT, *AR-2004/5*, 8, 32, 103. For an OFT campaign against scams, see (2006) 43 *Fair Trading* 6; *AR-2005/6*, 28; (2006) 44 *Fair Trading* 4–7.

7. *Car boot sales.* Commonly held at special venues on a Sunday, car boot sales must avoid infringing the territorial rights of local markets (see para 6.02) and may be subject to the Sunday trading laws (see para 8.13). Particular hazards identified are: misdescriptions and fakes;[160] stolen goods;[161] dangerous new goods and shoddy old ones.[162]

8. *Mock auctions* (see para 10.11).

9. *Switch selling.* This is where sales staff criticise the advertised product and recommend the purchase of a more expensive alternative. The practice may lead to the commission of a TDA offence (see para 4.05) and is likely to contravene the British Codes of Advertising and Sales Promotion (see para 3.14). In 2007, this will be overtaken by the UCP Directive (see para 4.20, item (d)).

10. *Cashbacks.* These schemes are usually offered to the consumer, e.g. of furniture or financial services, by a third party.[163] Under them, the retail buyer is provided with a post-dated 'cashback cheque' redeemable in (say) 5 years, subject to stringent terms and conditions, e.g. presentation by post to the third party of the receipt for the retail purchase within a week of the fifth anniversary of purchase. One such set of conditions on a loan has been modified under the UTCC Regulations.[164] If the goods are obtained on credit, this may give rise to additional claims against the creditor under ss 56 or 75 of the CCA (see Chap 16).

11. *Tobacco advertising* (see para 8.06A).

12. *Imprisonment or livelihood.* In 2007, the UCP Directive may forbid the creation of the impression that a consumer may not leave trade premises without contracting (see para 4.20, item (o)); or from explicitly informing a consumer that, if he does not make a purchase, the trader's livelihood will be in jeopardy (*ibid*, item (s)).

**[8.14] Free samples and gifts.** The purpose of a free sample is to encourage the transferee subsequently to enter a contract to obtain more of the same sort of goods;[165] whereas in commerce a 'free gift' is more often used as a bait to sell different goods and may actually be supplied under a contract (see para 2.08).

1. *Free samples.* Where a free sample is supplied gratuitously, as in door-to-door promotions,[166] it will amount to a gift in law and thus only be complete on

---

160 It may be possible to invoke the TDA, if it can be shown that the supplier is a trader (see para 4.03A); or the misleading advertisements regulations (see para 8.12A).

161 For implied undertakings as to title, see para 12.01.

162 For dangerous goods, consider criminal and civil claims (see para 4.32; and para 17.21); and for food, see para 4.27. For shoddy goods, see the implied terms (see Chaps 13, 14 and 15).

163 See generally (1997) 15 *Fair Trading* 6; and *Elida Gibbs Ltd v Customs and Excise Cmmrs* [1996] CLY 5908, Eu Ct (a VAT case); [2004] 3 *Which?* 8. Distinguish satisfaction guarantees by the seller (see para 10.28).

164 See OFT, *Unfair Contract Terms Bulletin No. 21*, paras 1.8–9; No. 22, case 14; and para 11.12.

165 As to the function of a sample, compare contracts by sample: see para 15.03. What if the freebie is of higher quality than the goods promoted?

166 Because the supply is intended to be gratuitous, the Unsolicited Goods and Services Acts are inapplicable: as to these Acts, see para 8.18.

delivery;[167] and any action would have to be at common law for the tort of negligence (see para 15.25) or under the ASA Code (see para 3.14). However, free samples given away for the purposes of advertisement may fall within particular statutory restrictions: for instance, they may consist of unfit food,[168] or medicines and drugs,[169] or other unsafe goods may contravene the GPS Regulations (see para 4.32). What of trade descriptions?[170] A promise of expensive goods as a free gift in return for buying a low-value product (a matrix scheme) may amount to an unlawful lottery.[171]

2.   *Free gifts.* Where a so-called 'free gift' of goods is in fact supplied under a contract,[172] the transferee is likely to have the benefit of the implied terms imported by the SGA or SGSA (see Chaps 13–15); but those provisions have no application where the transfer in fact amounts to a gift,[167] matters then being governed by the law of negligence (see above). Nor may any valid conditions be attached to the completed gift.[173] Subject to the same particular statutory restrictions as free samples in respect of food,[168] medicines or drugs[169] and the TDA,[170] free gifts supplied by retailers to promote other goods are sometimes objectionable on those grounds to their manufacturer.[174] A 'free offer' with other goods sold may contravene the misleading pricing rules (see para 8.09), whereas an 'extra value pack' may breach the weights and measures rules.[175] In 2007, the rules will have to be aligned with the UCP Directive (see para 4.20, item (m)).

**[8.15/16] Games and competitions**. In civil law, entry in compliance with its terms into a game or competition for which a prize is offered may constitute the formation of a *prima facie* binding contract.[176] If that is so, and if the prize offered is goods, it maybe that such a transaction amounts to a conditional contract for the sale of goods within the SGA (see para 1.11). However, Parliament has long rendered certain such contracts illegal, in which case the winner cannot enforce his claim to a prize,[177] but any entry contributions may be recoverable from the holder of the fund.[178] The law relating to lotteries, prize competitions and amusements with

---

167 see para 2.08. Gifts are expressly taken outside Pt I of the SGSA by s 1(2)(d): see para 2.10. See *The Second Report on Exemption Clauses* (Law Com 69) para 35.

168 Food Safety Act 1990, s 2(2). By this section, the unfit food comes within the s 8 prohibition against sale: as to which, see para 4.27.

169 In the case of both medicines and drugs, 'supply' would seem wide enough to cover free samples and gifts: see para 4.29.

170 Does 'supply' in TDA, s 1(1)(b) require consideration (see para 4.05)?

171 OFT, *AR-2005/6*, 27; and see para 8.15.

172 E.g. under a credit or charge card agreement, 'free' gifts or insurance may be offered on card use (see para 15.18).

173 E.g. 'not to be sold': *R v Cording* [1983] Crim LR 175 (selling not theft).

174 Agreements not to supply may be anti-competitive: see para 2.12.

175 This is where a manufacturer increases the size of a pack. It may infringe the weights and measures rules on declarations of quantity (see para 4.25): See Circus, *Op. cit.*, 70–3.

176 E.g. *Hall v Cox* [1899] 1 QB 198, CA (competition). Cf. *Rooke v Dawson* [1895] 1 Ch 480 (exam). *Contra* if there is insufficient skill to amount to consideration; or if the arrangement is expressed to be binding 'in honour only'; or is discriminatory (see para 4.23). For a consumer satisfaction survey, see OFT, *1996-AR*, 20.

177 *Blyth v Hulton & Co Ltd* (1908) 72 JP 401, CA. See generally, Lawson (1991) 13 Tr L 41.

178 *Barclay v Pearson* [1893] 1 Ch 154. See generally, para 10.20.

prizes are frequently encountered by the advertising and promotions industries; and the enactments relating to them were consolidated in the Gambling Act 2005.

1.   *Lotteries.* Hopefully to be more successful than the preceding case-law in defining lotteries,[179] s 14(1) of the 2005 Act provides that there will only be a 'simple lottery' where **all** the following three elements are present:[180]

(a)   Persons are 'required' to pay in order to participate;[181] and

(b)   One or more 'prizes' are allocated (see s 14(4) and (5) and Sched 2); and

(c)   Those prizes are allocated 'by a process[182] which relies wholly on chance'.[183]

The rules governing 'lotteries' are to be found in Pt 11 of the 2005 Act, which does not apply to the National Lottery (s 264); nor exempt lotteries within Sched 2, which effectively draws a distinction between a commercial lottery and the free prize draws so common in promotions. Where there is a lottery within Pt 11, any person commits an offence (s 263) if he promotes (s 258) or facilitates (s 259) a lottery.[184]

2.   *Prize gaming.* Whereas a person may commit offences by helping to organise commercial gaming (ss 33 and 37),[184] he does not do so where he only organises 'prize gaming' within Pt 13 of the 2005 Act. Unlike the preceding law relating to prize competitions,[179] s 288 defines 'prize gaming' as where neither the nature nor the size of the prize is determined by reference to the number of players or amount raised. Recognising that prize gaming is not designed for commercial profit, Parliament in Pt 13 allow 'prize gaming' if the organisers obtain a permit (s 289 and Sched 14),[185] satisfy certain conditions[186] and fall within one of the following categories: (a) adult gaming and family entertainment centres (s 290);[185] (b) bingo halls (s 291); (c) travelling fairs offering equal chance prize gambling only as 'ancillary amusement' (s 292).[185] Competitions should be run in conformity with the rules set out in the British Code of Sales Promotion Practice (see para 3.14); but they persistently give rise to scams.[187]

In 2007, the UCP Directive will forbid the creation of the false impression that the consumer has won a prize (see para 4.20, item (t)).

---

179   Under the Lotteries and Amusements Act 1976 (now repealed), which did not define the concepts. See *Readers Digest Association Ltd v Williams* [1976] 3 All ER 737, DC (prize entries via the 'No' envelope); *Imperial Tobacco Ltd v Att-Gen* [1981] AC 718, HL (prize tickets included in each cigarette packet); *Express Newspapers plc v Liverpool Daily Post and Echo plc* [1985] 3 All ER 680 (newspaper bingo; free entry); *Russell v Fulling* [1999] CLY 587 (scratchcards; few free entrants did not save scheme).

180   S 14(2). There is a power to amend by regulation (s 14(7)).

181   'Required' is probably not satisfied where there is a genuine open free route available to participate: see s 14(6) and Sched 2.

182   Where there are two or more processes of which the first is a matter of chance, there is a 'complex lottery' within s 14(3).

183   As defined by s 14(5). Where a significant element of skill is introduced, there may instead be a 'prize game' (see below).

184   There is also a provision for corporate offences (s 341); and see generally, para 28.10.

185   Under s 294, there is power by regulations to remove some or all prize gaming entitlements.

186   Under s 293 the conditions are: (i) a maximum prescribed charge to participate; (ii) the gaming takes place on premises during the course of one day; (iii) the prize does not exceed the maximum prescribed value; and (iv) participation is free-standing, self-contained and not linked to other gaming.

187   See (2005) 40 *Fair Trading* 7.

## Home sales

**[8.16A] Introduction.** In attempting to effect sales to people in their own homes, suppliers may make use of a number of techniques, abuse of which may fall within Pt 8 of the EA (see para 6.06) and the DPA (see para 3.27). Sometimes, the technique may result in contracting with minors (see para 10.18)):

1.  *Leaflets and circulars.* If the sender is a registered company, they may have to contain prescribed identifying information.[188] Where such matter ('junk mail') is delivered by post, it will usually have been generated by computerised address lists and hence be subject to the DPA (above) and the British Code of Sales Promotion Practice (see para 3.14). Further, offences which may be committed by the act of sending the leaflet include[189] advertising to minors the availability of credit or hire (see para 8.33), or to anyone an unsolicited credit token (see para 7.12).

2.  *Canvassing.* Selling goods from door-to-door may amount to peddling within the Pedlars Act 1871 (see para 6.02). Cash sales may fall within the doorstep selling rules (see para 10.36); but unfortunately these rules do not protect the householder who solicits the salesman's visit, e.g. by following up advertisements or mail-shots, or where the cash price is less than £35.[190] In respect of sale on credit, the CCA makes it an offence to canvass DC agreements in any circumstances (see para 7.07), or to canvass DCS agreements without a special canvassing indorsement (s 23(3): see para 6.14); and a regulated agreement so canvassed may be cancellable (s 67: see para 10.29). There are special restrictions where the trader represents that he is selling on behalf of disabled persons (see para 8.13A).

3.  *Telephone selling.* Systematic unsolicited telephone calls ('junk calls') is a modern phenomenon, e.g. of goods[191] or services.[192] Frequently, the supplier cold-calls, his telephone lists raising privacy problems (see para 3.27); but sometimes advertisements entice consumers into phoning suppliers.[193] Repeated calls by traders might lead to liability under the general law;[189] and there is a ban on sending to 'individuals' unwanted[194] 'junk' telephone calls[195]

---

188 Companies Act 1985, ss 349 and 351 (correspondence).

189 For some further offences, see the 1st edn, 2002, para 8.17.

190 The OFT is considering a super-complaint about door-step selling (see para 4.19).

191 Pretence at surveys ('sugging') is now curbed by reg 7(4): see para 9.05A. As persistent misuse of electronic communications, see para 3.14.

192 Such junk calls fall within Pt 2 of the Communications Act 2003. Under s 131, OFCOM (see para 3.14) has made a Statement of Policy: persistent misuse in breach of the policy may give rise to civil enforcement and prosecution (ss 128–130). Complaint should now be made to OFCOM.

193 As to pricey premium-rate numbers and prize scams, see [2005] 6 *Which?* 16; [2006] 1 *Which?* 10; OFT, *AR-2005/6*, 27.

194 There are several Preference Service enables consumers by registering to opt out of receiving marketing communications, e.g. by telephone, fax, mail. For details, see [2005] CCA News, Autumn, 19.

195 A powerful modern version is power-dialling: the seller buys a list of potential customers and then feeds them into a computer programme which telephones them automatically with number withheld; and, if the subscriber answers, then a salesman may come on the line: see James [2004] SJ 1233. These calls are controlled by OFCOM (see para 3.14). See [2006] 3 *Which?* 18.

and faxes.[196] At any event, such communications will usually fall within the Distance Selling Regulations (see below). It is possible for the consumer to complete the transaction during that telephone call (see para 10.02); but, in that case any incorporated terms may be unfair, as being hidden terms within the UTCC Regulations (Grey Term 1(i): see para 11.17). Payment may be effected by oral direct debit (see para 23.14) or by giving a credit card number: the latter form gives the consumer the advantage of s 75 protection (see para 16.11); but it does facilitate 'card-not-present' fraud at retailer's risk.[197] Some such telephone contacts are likely to be followed up by a personal visit, so possibly bringing any resulting transactions within the present CCA definitions of canvassing (s 48) and cancellable agreements (s 67: see above). For debt-collecting by phone, see para 5.42.

4.  *Sales parties*. Housewives may be persuaded to sponsor in their own home parties for the sale of goods, the housewife hostess to invite her friends and frequently being rewarded by a commission.[197] Unless the invitation makes it clear that the seller is a trader, an offence may be committed under the Business Advertisements Order (see para 4.22), and where the goods are supplied on credit the agreements might arguably be cancellable (see above). In any event, the transaction may fall within a code of practice (see para 3.13).

5.  *Mail order* (see further, para 8.19).[194]

6.  *Pyramid selling* (multi-level marketing) (see para 1.09).

7.  *Distance selling* (see para 8.17).[194]

8.  *Sales by e-commerce*. Since 2000, this has become a popular method for selling new goods to the end-consumer, whether the business-supplier is a manufacturer, wholesaler/importer or retail shop.[194] Additionally, both new and second-hand goods are sold by internet auction (see para 10.10),[198] including by private seller.[199] Besides the ordinary rules applicable to sales, e-commerce is a form of distance contract (see paras 8.17A–B); it is possible to make credit agreements by e-commerce (see para 5.20); the making of e-sales is subject to some special formalities (see paras 9.04–5); delivery risk will be on the supplier (see para 22.02A); and delivery normally by independent carrier, so attracting the transit rules on buyer's insolvency (see para 24.17).

9.  *Refusal to leave*. In 2007 the UCP Directive may prohibit a salesman invited to enter the consumer's home from refusal to leave (see para 4.20, item (p)).

Much of the above area may see provisions made under the Unfair Commercial Practices Directive (see paras 4.20, item (q); 4.21).

---

196 Under Directive 2002/58, replacing Directive 97/66, will enhance protection of personal data in the digital age, esp. with reference to e-mails (see para 8.17A) and mobile phones; and it is implemented in the UK by 2003 SI 2426: see Riach (2003) 153 NLJ 379; Hart (2003) 153 NLJ 1333; and para 8.17A–B.

197 Even if resulting transactions are on credit, the housewife is saved from several of the classes of ancillary credit business (amended s 146(6) of the CCA: see paras 5.43–4) and therefore does not require a CCA licence.

198 This will be under a charge-back clause in the merchant agreement: see para 7.09. For a new PIN scheme to reduce on-line fraud, see [2003] 7 *Credit Today*, Extra, p II.

199 Particularly with private sales, e.g. on eBay, there are real problems combatting fraud: see [2005] 12 *Which?* 8.

**[8.17] Distance selling.** The EU has super-imposed two Directives relating to:

A.  *The distance selling of goods and services.* Following an EU Directive (97/7/EC), additional consumer protection has been introduced by the Distance Selling Regulations.[200] These generally[201] apply to **'distance contracts'** (reg 4), meaning (reg 3(1)):

> 'any contract concerning goods or services concluded between a supplier and a consumer under an organised distance sales or service provision scheme run by the supplier who, for the purposes of the contract, makes exclusive use of one or more means of distance communication up to and including the moment at which the contract is concluded'.

'Means of distance communication' is itself defined by reg 2(1) as 'any means which, without the simultaneous physical presence of the supplier and the consumer, may be used for the marketing of a service between the parties'. This covers armchair shoppers buying goods or services, including energy (see para 3.07) and services connected with the supply of goods, e.g. most simple hiring,[202] sales agents (see para 10.06) for sale or purchase, such as sourcing agents. These contracts must be **made exclusively** at a distance from home, whether by telephone, internet or mail order, even if there is a later meeting perhaps to effect delivery; but it does not apply to those who make a distance enquiry followed by a visit to the retailer's premises.[203] Excepted contracts are the following (reg 5, as amended): sale of an interest in land (see para 9.03), other than short-term rentals; 'financial services',[204] which excludes matters falling within the separate rules for financial services (see below); and contracts concluded by means of a 'vending machine or automated commercial premises', or by public payphone (*contra* private phone: see above), or by public auction, whether terrestrial or e-Commerce (see para 10.09A). In respect of distance contracts made pursuant to an 'organised . . . scheme' (undefined) by a business 'supplier' (reg 3(1)), the Regulations provide some protections to 'consumers'.[205] These compulsory (reg 25) protections in distance contracts are as follows: usually the provision of listed pre-contract particulars (regs 7–9: see para 9.04);[201] a right of cancellation (regs 10–18: see para 10.38);[201] a requirement that the contract be performed within 30 days (reg 19: see para 23.18);[201] protection where a payment card has been misused (reg 21: see paras 7.07A

---

200  Consumer Protection (Distance Selling) Regulations, 2000 SI 2334. The OFT has published *Guidance* (2002).

201  Under reg 6 (as amended), the regulations do not apply to supplies of certain perishable consumer goods, e.g. food, beverages, by a regular roundsman, e.g. milk; nor to 'transport' services (see fn 202, below). Nor do they apply to certain types of contract beyond the scope of this work, e.g., timeshares and certain service contracts.

202  It has been held that 'transport' in reg 6(2)(b) extends to transport services, such as internet car hire, which is therefore excluded from much of the regulations: *EasyCar (UK) Ltd v OFT* [2005] All ER (EC) 834, ECJ.

203  What if, following enquiries at a branch, the consumer then contracts by phone with head-office?

204  Sched 2 of the 2000 Regulations was removed by reg 25(5) of the 2004 Regulations, which substitutes the definition used in the 2004 Regulations (reg 25(2)b: see below).

205  'Any natural person who, in contracts to which these Regulations apply, is acting for purposes which are outside his business' (reg 3(1)). See also the definition in the UTCC Regulations: para 11.12A.

and 7.14); and some new rules as regards inertia selling (see para 8.18). These Regulations are to be enforced (reg 26) by the 'enforcement authorities',[206] who must consider complaints (reg 26), may extract undertakings from errant business suppliers (reg 26(4)) and apply for Enforcement Orders against them (reg 27: see para 6.08). The OFT issues detailed guidance to suppliers making IT consumer goods contracts both generally and with regard to motor vehicles.[207]

B.  *The distance selling of financial services.* The EU Parliament having been per- suaded that the above regime was not suitable for financial services, there has since been promulgated a separate Directive relating to the selling of consumer financial services exclusively by distance means,[208] which has been imple- mented in the UK by the Financial Services (Distance Marketing) Regulations, 2004 SI 2095. Using a similar definition of 'distance contract', 'means of dis- tance communication', UK 'supplier'[209] and 'consumer',[205] the Directive defines a 'financial service' as 'any service of a banking, credit,[210] insurance, personal pension, investment or payment nature'. So, the 2004 Regulations will apply where a consumer uses the internet or phones round to find the best such deal; but it is not clear whether the 2004 Regulations will apply where the finance is arranged through face-to-face discussion with a retailer or broker and the consumer never meets the financier.[211] Ignoring those types of contract beyond the scope of this work, it will be noted that the definition of 'credit' is wide enough to cover consumer credit, money transfers, insurance and mort- gages; but it is disputed whether hp is a supply of goods within the 2002 Regulations or a financial service within the 2004 Regulations; and it is uncertain whether leasing (which is outside the 2002 Regulations) can be brought within the 2004 Regulations.[211]

Where there is a series of transactions between the parties, e.g. in respect of a bank account or credit card, the Regulations only apply to the 'initial service agreement' (reg 5); and, where the financial services are marketed through 'an intermediary', e.g. a broker, the obligations laid on the 'supplier' (see above) are sometimes also applied to that intermediary (reg 6). In relation to all these contracts, the Regu- lations makes compulsory provision (reg 16) as follows: inertia selling (reg 15: see para 8.18); listed pre-contract particulars (regs 7–8: see para 9.06); right of withdrawal (regs 9–13: see para 10.39); and payment cards (reg 14: see para 7.14). Enforcement responsibilities are split between the FSA and DTI (regs 17 and 23: see paras 3.02–3): that body must consider complaints (reg 18); obtain injunctions to secure compliance (regs 19–21); and prosecute offences (reg 22).

---

206  Meaning the OFT (see para 3.03) and Local Authorities (see para 28.03): reg 3(1). LAs taking action under these Regulations must notify the OFT (reg 28).

207  Reg 29. See the OFT Consultation Paper, *IT consumer contracts made at a distance* (Oct 2003). As to proposed OFT Guidance on distance supplies of motor vehicles, see OFT, *Consultation* (Feb 2004).

208  2002/65, set out in Goode, *Consumer Credit Law & Practice*, Vol 5, para XA2.461.

209  Where the supplier is based in another EEA country and hence also subject to the Directive there, the UK regs do not apply (reg 4(1)).

210  'Credit' includes a cash loan and any other form of financial accommodation, and for this purpose 'cash' includes money in any form' (reg 2(1)). Cf. CCA, s 9(1): see para 5.21.

211  See Bowden (2004) 59 CC4/12.

**[8.17A] E-commerce and the EU**. Attracting customers for goods and services by electronic means (e-commerce) is burgeoning, as in respect of internet auctions (see para 10.10) and retailing, e.g. groceries, including products more traditionally bought by mail order (see para 8.19), or over the telephone, e.g. books, music, banking (see paras 2.17 and 8.17). Despite the comparatively small proportion of retail sales of good and services conducted on the internet, the EU has invested much effort in devising for them an effective legislative framework,[212] with more promised,[213] though it should be remembered that e-customers are, of course, for the most part limited to those who have payment cards and computers.

Perhaps the most important of these for our present purposes is the E-Commerce Directive (00/31), enacted in the UK by Regulations.[214] According to reg 4(1), the Regulations apply to the business providers by electronic means (termed 'service providers') of an 'information society service', which expression generally[215] covers any commercial on-line service[216] made 'at the individual request of' the consumer, which excludes public broadcasts (as to which, see para 3.14). The service may be provided to business or private consumers; and, whilst it does not require consideration (see para 10.01), it must be of a commercial nature. Examples of such on-line services include on-line newspapers, financial services, e.g. banking, entertainment services, such as video-on-demand, and on-line selling of goods (direct marketing: see para 8.19). Nor do these Regulations apply to the goods or services themselves: the distinction would be between on-line selling a book delivered by post, where the Regulations do not apply to the delivery or title of the book itself; and down-loading a book in electronic form, which is covered.[217] In relation to such e-services, the Directive draws a fundamental distinction as follows:

(A) **'Inbound'** e-commerce services. The Directive is intended to encourage the free flow of information society services across the EU by reducing the extent to which service providers are exposed to the laws of other Member States. Hence, the Regulations provide that the service provider must comply with the national law of the Member State where it is established (reg 10), the 'country of origin principle', e.g. Germany. Thus, UK public law requirements as such for e-commerce (what is termed the 'coordinated field' (see reg 2)) cannot be imposed on 'inbound' e-commerce services, e.g. from Germany; so, upon an

---

212  For the institutional framework, see the Communications Act 2003 (para 3.14). Besides the Directives below, others include: the distance selling of goods and services (97/7; 2002/65: see para 8.17); junk calls (2002/58: see para 8.16A); electronic signatures (see para 9.05).

213  The EU Commission's 2002 e-Europe Action Plan promises high quality e-commerce codes; ADRs; and clear and consistent laws and enforcement. For details of these Commission Recommendations, see Goode, *Consumer Credit Law & Practice*, Vol 4, Division X, Part B.

214  Electronic Commerce (EC Directive) Regulations, 2002 SI 2013. The main objectives of the Directive are to be found in Recital 5. See generally Smith and Hand (2003) 153 NLJ 1579. For overlap with the UCP Directive, see para 4.21A.

215  Reg 3 excludes, *inter alia*: data protection (see para 3.27); cartel law (see para 2.12); betting and gaming (see para 8.15). What does reg 3(2) mean?

216  The complicated definition in reg 2 cross-refers to the Directive, recital 17 and Art 2(a). Any terms not defined in reg 2 have the same meaning as in the Directive (reg 2(3)). What about faxes?

217  See Hornle (2004) 12 *IJ of Law & IT* 333 at 336. But where a hard-copy book is ordered on-line, the Regulations would apply to the on-line advertisement: Hornle, *Op. cit.*, 336.

on-line sale of medicines, German labelling law would apply. But it has been argued that this does not interfere with the ordinary private conflict laws as to the contract made.[218] Nor do the Regulations apply to service providers in third countries, e.g. USA.

(B) '**Outgoing**' e-commerce services. The Directive was seemingly drafted to dovetail with national laws where possible; and this approach is embodied in reg 4, which makes it clear that UK law 'requirements'[219] generally apply to 'outgoing' service providers established in the UK, irrespective of whether the service is provided in the UK or another Member State,[220] e.g. the Distance Selling Regulations (see para 8.17B). This rule does not apply to the scheduled services,[221] nor to e-mails (regs 9(4) and 11(3)).

In relation to **outgoing** e-commerce services, the Regulations provide as follows:

(1) Service providers shall make available to consumers (whether business or private) 'in a form and manner which is easily, directly and permanently accessible', e.g. on his web-site, his name and stated particulars (reg 6(1)); and, where he refers to prices, these 'shall be indicated clearly and unambiguously', including 'whether they are inclusive of tax and delivery costs' (reg 6(2)).

(2) 'Commercial communications' (defined in reg 2) which form part of an information society service (see above), such as electronic advertising, e.g. as part of direct marketing activities, must clearly identify its nature, the person on whose behalf it is made and any promotional offer or competition (reg 7). This rule will extend to all unsolicited electronic messages where the recipient's identity is irrelevant (spam: see below), whether by e-mail, fax or text messaging.

(3) Spam is unsolicited electronic communications (cf. junk mail) sent for direct marketing purposes and costs the sender nothing: it may disclose the sender's identity (soft-core spam), or hide his identity (hard-core spam). Under the E-Commerce Regulations, spam sent by e-mail (but not text messages sent to a mobile phone) must be 'clearly and unambiguously identifiable as such as soon as it is received' (reg 8). Further Regulations containing additional prohibitions concern spam generated within the EU and sent to private addresses, which are enforceable by the Information Commissioner.[222] What about spam generated outside the EU?

(4) Where a business concludes a contract with a consumer via a web-site, but not by e-mail (regs 9(4) and 11(3)), reg 9 requires that the supplier before contracting explain certain matters (see para 9.05).

---

218 Hornle, *Op. cit.*, 354–5; and for the Conflict of Laws relating to contracts, see generally, para 10.01.

219 It is argued that 'requirements' is broader than mere licensing or regulatory requirements and can extend to, e.g. some aspects of liability: see Smith and Hand, *Op. cit.*, 1598.

220 But see the derogations in regs 4(3), 4(5) and 5, especially where the service provider is established in another Member State, or on grounds of public policy. This may make cross-border trading more difficult for e-suppliers: see Hornle, *Op. cit.*, 345–8.

221 Reg 4(4). These exemptions include: choice of laws; contractual obligations concerning consumer contracts; and unsolicited e-mails.

222 Privacy and Electronic Communications (EC Directive) Regulations, 2003 SI 2426, which also deals with junk telephone calls and faxes (see para 8.17): see Room (2003) 153 NLJ 1780; the IC's *Guidance* (see para 3.28).

(5) Where a consumer places an order by web-site, but not by e-mail (regs 9(4) and 11(3)), there are some rules dealing with the formation of the contract (see para 10.09A), but none as to the terms of the contract, nor the goods themselves.

Consumers may enforce the above duties by action for breach of statutory duty (reg 13: and see generally, para 3.21); and the authorities may secure compliance by Enforcement Orders (reg 16; and see generally, para 28.04). Where the service provider plays a passive role as a mere conduit of third-party information he is generally exempted from liability for the content that he unwittingly carries or stores, though injunctive relief against him may still be possible.[223]

[8.17B] Internet sales.[224] In considering the legal position of English and Welsh consumers who obtain goods over the internet, a distinction must be drawn according to whether or not the internet trader is within the jurisdiction.

1.  *Internet traders within the jurisdiction.* Internet shopping within the jurisdiction would appear to behave legally much like mail order sales (see para 8.19), so that it would seem to attract the ordinary rules as to the formation of contract (see para 10.01, *et seq.*), e.g. pricing mistakes;[225] but internet sales attract some extra regulatory provisions concerning formalities and formation (see paras 9.05 and 10.09A). Payment can be effected by payment card in a manner similar to telephone selling (see para 8.16A) at retailer's risk (see below), so enabling the consumer to seek redress from the creditor instead of the internet trader where the consumer uses a credit card;[226] but this is probably not the case where the consumer uses another payment card.[227] Under the Distance Selling Regulations, delivery must be made within 30 days; but delivery risks will usually be upon the seller (SGA, new s 20(4): see para 22.02) and fraud (a particular problem with internet auctions) minimised in the same way as in mail order (see above). If a document is **desired**, it may be obtained by getting the website to generate a hard-copy order, which the consumer signs and posts to the supplier: this would seem to attract the ordinary rules considered elsewhere in this work, including Enforcement Orders (see para 6.08). However, a document may be **required** by statute (see para 9.02): the CCA 1974 originally required a written signed document, but that is no longer the case (see para 9.05), so that it is now permissible to make on-line regulated agreements. The OFT have been conducting sweeps of websites for compliance with all the following regulations:[228] Enforcement Orders (see above); Data Protection (see para 3.27); Misleading Advertisements (see para 8.12A); Distance Selling (see para 8.17); E-Commerce (see para 8.17A); and Unfair Terms.[229]

---

223 See regs 17–22; Anassutzi [2002] 1 CCLR 337 at 338; and see generally, para 29.39.
224 See generally Atiyah, *Sale of Goods*, 10th edn, Chap 5; *Modern markets: confident consumers* (1999, Cm. 4410) 7. As to shopping on-line, see OFT, *2000-AR* 30; [2004] 9 *Which?* 46.
225 For detailed consideration of internet supplies of motor vehicles, see the OFT website, *Cars and other vehicles sold by distance means* (May 2005).
226 Under the CCA, s 75: see para 16.11, *et seq.*
227 Because of the effect of reg 21 of the Distance Selling Regulations: see Goode, *Consumer Credfit Law & Practice*, Vol 4, P VI, the commentary to para 1.770.
228 OFT, *AR-2002/3*, 40–41.
229 See OFT, *UCT Bulletin No. 18*, case 15: see para 11.12.

Does a website amount to an 'advertisement'? Compare the definitions for trade descriptions (TDA, s 39(1): see para 8.07); and for regulated agreements.[230] May the website owner (if different) be engaged in credit-brokerage (see para 5.38)?

2. *Internet traders outside the jurisdiction.* The parties may in their transaction agree to be subject to a particular set of courts and legal system in a choice of laws clause (see para 18.13). However, if not, where an English or Welsh consumer deals over the internet with a trader from outside the jurisdiction, the legal position depends on the location of the internet trader (see para 10.01). Cross-border sales promotions within the EU may in the future be subject to special controls.[231]

**[8.18] Inertia selling.** Suppliers frequently capitalise on consumer inertia.[232] Strictly speaking, at common law the practice of sending unsolicited goods produced this result: the involuntary bailment did not give rise to the usual bailee's duty of care (see para 1.17); and, where delivery amounted to an offer (see para 10.02), the bailee/consumer was under no obligation to accept,[233] though his use of the goods might amount to an implied acceptance[233] or conversion (see para 19.04). Parliament intervened generally in both aspects of inertia selling by businesses with the Unsolicited Goods and Service Acts 1971 and 1975. These Acts mostly apply to the delivery of goods; and, by reason of the subsequent distance selling regulations (see para 8.17), it is necessary to distinguish according to whether there is supplied to a consumer goods or services.

1. *Supplies of goods to consumers.* These are now dealt with wholly by the Distance Selling Regulations, which presumably apply to any attempt to make a **distance contract**, whereby (reg 24(1)):

    '(a) unsolicited goods are sent[234] to a person ('the recipient') with a view to his acquiring[234] them;

    (b) the recipient has no reasonable cause to believe that they were sent with a view to their being acquired for the purposes of a business; and

    (c) the recipient has neither agreed[235] to acquire nor agreed to return them'.[236]

The key notion is that the goods are '**unsolicited**', an expression whose definition enables the Regulations to be avoided by acting only on a prior

---

230 CCA, s 189(1): see para 8.29. As to designing regulated web advertisements, see Patrick [2000] 9 *Credit Today* 21.

231 EU Green Paper on Consumer Protection (2001).

232 (2004) 39 *Fair Trading* 9; [2005] 7 *Which?* 11.

233 *Felthouse v Bindley* (1862) 11 CBNS 869; *Capital Finance Ltd v Bray* (see para 24.25); and generally, para 10.02. Could it amount to a sale or return transaction (see para 20.24): see Ping-fat, (1991) 8 Tr 267 at 208. For implied acceptance, see *Weatherby v Banham* (1832) 5 C & P 228.

234 'Acquire' includes hire: reg 24(6). As to 'sender', reg 24(6) says that it includes '(a) any person on whose behalf or with whose consent the goods are sent; (b) any other person claiming through or under the sender or any person mentioned in paragraph (a); and (c) any person who delivers the goods'.

235 Does it also include the situation where the recipient so agrees, in ignorance of his legal rights? There is an obligation to draw the recipient's attention to these rights in the documentation (reg 24(7)): see below.

236 Does the recipient have a lien for expenses, even though a rejecting buyer does not (see para 24.03)? Does the notice operate from posting or receipt? Any express terms agreed will be subject to the UTCCR: see [2005] *Bulletin O/D, US Euro Link*; and see para 11.15A.

request: so a mail order trader may avoid the Act by sending out goods only in response to a returned newspaper reply coupon. Once given, a written request endures until retracted, e.g. annual subscriptions, though such a request may be an unfair term (see para 11.15).

(i)   *The actual delivery.* Any rights of the business sender to the goods are immediately extinguished (reg 24(3)) and the recipient may treat the goods as if they were an unconditional gift.[237]

(ii)  *Any demand for payment.* The regulations make criminal[238] any **direct** demand, provided that 'in the course of business a person[239] makes a demand for payment, or asserts a present or prospective right to payment,[240] for what he knows are' **unsolicited** goods or services 'sent to another with a view to his acquiring them for purposes other than those of his business' (reg 24(4)). Nor may he **indirectly** pressure a consumer to pay for unsolicited goods: this too is an offence where he (reg 24(5)):

(a)   threatens to bring any legal proceedings, or

(b)   places or causes to be placed the name of any person on a list of defaulters or debtors or threatens to do so, or

(c)   invokes or causes to be invoked any other collection procedure, or threatens to do so.

2.  *Supplies of services to consumers.* Leaving aside the specialist CCA rules in respect of the unsolicited issue of credit tokens (CCA, s 51: see para 7.12), under the Financial Services (Distance Marketing) Regulations, 2004 SI 2095, the UK has introduced rules dealing with the unsolicited supply by a business to a consumer of 'financial services' (see para 8.17); and 'unsolicited' means 'that they are supplied without any prior request made by or on behalf of' the consumer (reg 15(4)). The private recipient of unsolicited financial services is not 'subject to any obligation (to make payment or otherwise)' for those services (reg 15(1)); but this is not to affect the automatic renewal of the distance contract itself (reg 15(8)). Any demand for payment amounts to an offence (see para 28.07, *et seq.*), whether included with that supply or not (regs 15(2) and (3)), 'demand for payment' being defined (reg 15(5) and (6)) by reference to the Unsolicited Goods Act (see above). This should at least partially address inertia selling of credit insurance (see para 8.20) or extended warranties (see para 17.09). What about unsolicited credit card cheques (see para 7.09)?

---

237  Reg 24(2). Might this provision be struck down as a contravention of human rights: see *Wilson v First County Trust Ltd* (set out at para 3.09A)? For gifts, see para 2.08.

238  The offences are not confined to the 'sender' of the goods, so it includes such as a debt-collecting agency or solicitor. Cf. unlawful harassment of debtors: see para 24.24. As to reasonable cause, see Ping-fat, *Op. cit.*, at 211.

239  Cf. *Reader's Digest Association Ltd v Pirie* 1973 SLT 170 (knowledge of a junior member of staff not to be imputed to the Association: see further, para 28.10). For offences by corporations, see s 5 of the 1971 Act, but there is no equivalent in the Regulations; and generally, para 28.11.

240  'Asserting a right to payment' 'includes any invoice or similar document which (a) states the amount of a payment, and (b) fails to comply with' regulations referred to below: see s 6(2), as substituted, and reg 6(7). See Lawson, *Advertising Law,* 163. Is a pre-payment invoice (see [1996] 5 *Which?* 6) a 'demand' for payment? There may also be an offence under s 40 of the AJA: see para 24.24. For Enforcement Orders (see para 6.08), see OFT, *AR-2002/3,* 48.

3.  *Supplies of goods to businesses.* These are still governed by the Acts and leave the business recipient of unsolicited goods an unfettered choice between paying for, or returning, the goods.[241]

    The Secretary of State for the purpose of these Acts and the Regulations may make 'regulations as to the contents and form of such notes of agreement, invoices and similar documents' (s 3A; reg 24(8)).[242] In 2007, the above rules for the protection of consumers will have to be aligned with the UCP Directive (see para 4.20, item (n)).

**[8.19] Direct Marketing (home shopping).** This form of business developed during the Victorian era and at first serviced consumers by way of the post office. Today, it tends also to accept orders by telephone and internet. To reach individual consumers by advertisement, direct market suppliers must obtain their names and addresses: as the acquisition of such data can only proceed with the consent of the subject under the DPA, the consumer is in a position to block such direct marketing and is entitled to compensation in default.[243] Some seek custom *via* inertia selling (see para 8.18), or junk mail or e-mails (see paras 8.16A and 8.17). As direct marketing houses offer delivery direct to the door, typically *via* an independent carrier, normally the two principals will never meet face-to-face: so, this form of business will be subject to the Distance Selling Regulations (see para 8.17); and, whereas in a shop the consumer will choose and normally take delivery immediately, with direct marketing the consumer will have to choose and await delivery (for delivery rules, see para 23.04).

Direct marketing houses tend to fall into one of two categories:

1.  *Direct sales houses.* Traditionally, such businesses advertised extensively in the press, which made them particularly susceptible to the voluntary codes of practice.[244] Modern techniques include advertisement by spam, bringing them within the E-Commerce and other Regulations (see para 8.17A). Many such advertisements tend to be on the terms cash-with-order, so avoiding any unpaid seller's transit problems (see para 24.17, *et seq.*): if sent by post, there are a number of means of effecting payment (see para 23.14); but a telephone order will usually be made by a payment card (see para 2.23). Other types of mail order are frequently conducted by instalment deliveries.[245] To help the public seek redress from mail order traders, the latter must disclose both their business character and address;[246] delivery to the consumer must be made within 30 days (reg 19: see para 23.04); the supplies will be subject to a right of cancellation by the consumer;[247] and there is special protection against payment card

---

241 S 2 of the Unsolicited Goods and Services Act 1971 Act, as amended by reg 22(3).

242 See the Unsolicited Goods and Services (Invoices etc) Regulations, (1975 SI 732).

243 For controls on such lists, see the DPA, s 11 (para 3.27).

244 See the Mail Order Code; the Advertising Standards Authority Code and MOPS (see para 8.16A); the British Code of Sales Promotion Practice; and the Code of the Direct Marketing Association (paras 3.13–14)

245 E.g. book or record clubs. For instalment contracts, see para 23.23, *et seq.* Consumers should be careful over the minimum obligation, as the small print will usually avoid the inertia selling rules (see para 8.18).

246 Distance Selling Regs 8 and 9: see paras 9.04–05. But see OFT, *AR-2002/3*, 40.

247 Regs 10–18: see para 10.38.

misuse.[248] However, unless the goods are supplied on sale or return (see para 20.23), in the absence of a right of cancellation, the property (but no longer the risk) in them is likely to pass on posting:[249] this may cause difficulty over pre-payments on the traders' insolvency (see para 23.22); but not where goods are lost in the post (see para 22.01). Despite the consumer's signature on an acceptance note (see para 23.10), he retains the right to reject defective goods (see para 29.05). However, there remains a continuing difficulty with card-not-present fraud (see para 8.17).

2.  *Catalogue houses.* The crucial thing here is the production of an elaborate catalogue,[250] copies of which are distributed either direct to private consumers or *via* an agent. The agent is commonly a housewife supplying family or friends on commission: if the agent recruits other agents, it may amount to pyramid selling (see para 1.09). Supplies are likely to be on credit sale (see para 1.13): as a form of distance sale, this is likely to attract most of the above sale rules applicable to direct sales houses. Moreover, most such business is conducted with a money-back guarantee; that is, the consumer is granted an express right to rescind without cause: this may amount to a sale or return transaction (see above). Further, whether or not a credit sale is used, there will almost certainly be some form of credit, so that there is likely to be a regulated consumer credit agreement (see para 5.19) under which the mail order trader is the creditor (see para 5.25) and his business is susceptible of control by the credit licensing system (see para 6.11, *et seq*). Any housewife agent is specially saved from being a credit-broker or other ancillary credit business (see paras 5.41 and 5.43). The industry should no longer have difficulty complying with the CCA documentation rules.[251] Moreover, the agreement will be cancellable: whilst it is unlikely to be cancellable under the CCA,[252] it will be cancellable under the Distance Selling Regulations.[248] However, if payment were made by payment card, the transaction will usually give the consumer rights against the card-issuer: if a credit card is used, this will be under the CCA (s 75: see para 16.11, *et seq.*); and if a debit or charge card is used, this will be under the Distance Selling Regulations.[248]

## SUPPLIES ON CREDIT OR HIRE

[8.20] **Introduction**. Whilst some classes of credit business prefer word-of-mouth recommendation,[253] where it is sought to obtain credit or hire business by way of writing, Parliament has long felt the need to impose statutory restrictions. Early

---

248  Reg 21: see paras 7.07A and 7.13.

249  These rules may be ousted by a contrary intent: see paras 20.06 and 22.02. With regard to risk, is a trade custom developing that the trader will bear the risk in course of post? For trade custom, see generally, para 15.11.

250  Cf. *The Littlewoods Organisation Ltd v Harris* [1978] 1 All ER 1026, CA.

251  Consumers are normally sent a credit agreement and asked to return it; but, if they do not, there may be a breach of the documentation rules (CCA, s 63(2)). After the 2006 Act, it will no longer be automatically unenforceable: see para 9.19.

252  Because there are no face-to-face dealings: CCA, s 67 (see para 10.29).

253  Such as low-income credit: see Collard and Kempson, *Affordable Credit* (2005) 20.

controls on the advertising of credit or hire were to be found in the (now repealed) Moneylenders Act 1927 and Advertisements (Hire Purchase) Act 1967.[254]

These two veins of legislation have now been amalgamated and extended in the CCA. The greater part of these provisions are to be found in Pt IV of the Act, which restricts both the information which may be supplied to the debtor or hirer (see para 8.21 *et seq.*) and that which may be obtained about him (see para 8.35, *et seq.*). Additionally, the compulsory licensing system in Pt II enables the Director to curb undesirable advertising practices (see para 6.19); s 26 empowers the minister to control by regulation the conduct of licensees;[255] and the canvassing[256] and cancellation (see para 10.28, *et seq.*) provisions are likely to have a substantial effect on the manner in which a creditor or owner will go about seeking business.[257] Additionally, where any lending is secured on land (see para 7.04A), advertisement of that facility must carry a special warning (see para 8.30).

## Information supplied to the debtor or hirer

[8.21] Following the recommendations of the Crowther Report,[258] a major feature of the CCA is the importance attached to the disclosure to the consumer of information concerning the terms and cost of credit.[259] An important objective is to enable the consumer to make an informed choice between different credit packages available in the market place.[260] Nowhere is this more obvious than in the rules designed to ensure that the cost of credit is uniformly expressed as an Annual Percentage Rate (APR: see para 8.22). The Act provides for pre-contract disclosure of this information at **all** the following stages of consumer credit:

1. In advertisements, which will typically be aimed at a segment of the market (see para 8.27). Even this may mislead where the quoted rate is for prime customers, but later adjusted before contract for actual credit rating (risk-based assessment), often portrayed in 'from' advertisements.[261]

2. Personal quotations or other pre-contract information, which will be directed to a particular consumer (see paras 8.32 and 9.08).

3. In the copy of the agreement-form which the consumer must always obtain when he first signs it (see para 9.14).

---

254 For analysis of the reasons why consumers in credit transactions are particularly in need of protection by way of pre-contract controls, see Goode, *Consumer Credit Law & Practice*, para 28.1.

255 See para 6.17. This power is expressly extended by ss 54 and 152(1)(as amended) to regulations relating to the seeking of business by a licensee: see para 9.08.

256 See paras 7.05–7. In commercial terms, the canvassing of consumers (loan financing) and persuading dealers to proffer credit terms at point of sale (direct financing) are alternative ways of attracting business.

257 As to the control of credit-brokers' fees, see s 155; and para 5.37.

258 Paras 6.5.15–21. For the Report, see generally, para 5.03. See also the subsequent White Paper, *Reform of the Law on Consumer Credit* (1973, Cmnd. 5427) paras 28–30.

259 What is termed 'truth-in-lending': see generally, para 5.08. Contrast the position of the cash seller who does not have to reveal his mark-up.

260 Nevertheless, there continues to be evidence that debtors remain insensitive to the cost of credit: [1986] *Which?* 449; (1988) 138 NLJ 589, 657; OFT, *1989-AR*, 102; Howells, *Aspects of Credit and Debt*, 36–7, 84.

261 See [2003] 5 *Which?* 13.

Failure to disclose accurately, or at all, the cost of the credit at **all** the above stages will usually amount to a CCA offence.[262] However, the whole edifice is predicated on rate sensitivity being the crucial thing for consumers considering which credit proposal to accept,[263] whereas there is persistent evidence that they are more interested in the size of the deposit and repayment.[264] Moreover, even where consumers are attuned to this issue, the present APR system does not always assist in choosing a bargain:

(a) Suppose several types of credit might meet his purposes. The APR rules require differing elements, e.g. administrative costs, to be taken into account, so that it is difficult to make rate comparisons in a segmented market (see para 8.23).

(b) In relation to the most popular form of credit, credit cards, there are up to 11 different legal ways of calculating the APR:[265] card issuers have fought vigorously to maintain this state of affairs on competition grounds; but this does seem to allow confusion marketing (see para 8.12A). On the other hand, the credit card industry now seems to have accepted that a low rate for the first x months ('introductory' or 'teaser' rates), e.g. on credit card offers, is not an APR.[266]

In 2003 the White Paper *Fair, Clear and Competitive*[267] proposed substantial amendments to the above Regulations to ensure greater consistency and transparency in credit advertising; and it also noted much greater public awareness of APRs (White Paper, para 3.9); and these changes were introduced by Regulations (see para 8.30-1). The FSA has taken control of house mortgage advertising (see para 3.02); but, as regards advertising remaining within the CCA, the CCA has allocated to the OFT a central co-ordinating role (see para 3.03A).

## Expression of credit charge

**[8.22] Introduction.** The Moneylenders Acts 1900–27 (now repealed) contained some restrictions both as to the rate of interest which might be charged (rate ceilings: see para 29.40) and the manner in which that rate might be expressed. Taking over the latter function only, s 20 of the CCA breaks the process down into two stages:

---

262 Giving an inaccurate interest rate may also amount to misleading pricing (see para 8.09A); and it may contravene ASA codes (see para 3.14).

263 See Dominy and Kempson, *Pay Day Advances* (2003) 21–2; [2003] 12 *Which?* 16. There is even the suggestion that some consumers think that the crucial notation APR (see para 8.25) stands for 'always pay regular'.

264 E.g. Cayne and Trebilcock (1973) 23 *Univ. Tor. LJ* at 403, 423–6; Howells, *Op. cit.*, 48; Cartwright, *Consumer Protection and the Criminal Law* (2001) 51; (2002) 57 CC4/16 and 28; Collard and Kempson, *Affordable Credit* (2005) 15. Would consumers pay more attention if it was expressed in cash terms?

265 E.g. to charge interest on cash withdrawals from outset (plus perhaps a cash handling charge), rather than from the statement date normally used for goods. See [2003] 8 *Credit Today* 5 and 13.

266 OFT, *AR-2002/3*, 43.

267 See DTI, *the Consumer Credit Market in the 21st Century* (Dec 2003, Cm. 6040), paras 2.8–10.

*Stage 1.* To identify all the items which are to be included in the credit charge—what it termed the 'total charge for credit' (tcc: see para 8.23).

*Stage 2.* To turn that total charge for credit from a sum of money into a rate of interest—what it termed the 'annual percentage rate' (APR: see para 8.25).

For greater flexibility, s 20 did not itself set out those two steps in detail, but instead empowered the Secretary of State to make regulations to this end. To simplify and standardise the processes so far as possible, these very technical regulations make a series of assumptions and allow certain tolerances (see para 8.26); and for this purpose, the Regulations (see para 8.24) employ two important dates: (i) the agreement date, which is the date upon which the regulated agreement is made (see para 9.12); and (ii) 'the relevant date', which is the date upon which the debtor is entitled to begin enjoyment of the contract, e.g. delivery of the hp goods, or draw upon the credit.[268] Therefore, in approaching those regulations, 'the key point to bear in mind is that the [calculation of the APR is] based on what the consumer credit agreement stipulates is to happen and what . . . the regulations deem to happen, not in what in fact happens'.[269]

The effect of the above provisions for identifying the tcc may be illustrated by reference to the treatment of an undeserving debtor pleading technicalities: in *Broadwick Financial Services Ltd v Spencer*[270]

> The borrower (S) had a history of serious mortgage arrears and was therefore considered a 'non-status borrower' (see para 7.04A). S's broker negotiated a regulated loan from A, secured by a first charge on S's house and at a rate of interest variable by A; but S does not seem to have taken any steps to read or understand the documentation. Before the loan was signed, A sent S a 'concession letter', reducing the rate of interest to be charged 'by way of *ex gratia* concession only'. After the loan was made, A transferred the benefit of the agreement to B, who had the following undisclosed policy: not to reduce interest rates even if market rates fell.

S tried to escape from the agreement, but found early settlement (see para 26.19A) too expensive and fell into arrears. Before the Court of Appeal, S sought to avoid loss of his house by unsuccessfully challenging the possession order on all the following grounds:[271]

(a) The 'concession letter' was held not to amount to a contractual term requiring inclusion in the agreement by reason of the Agreement Regulations (see para 9.12), nor to be considered part of the 'credit bargain' (see para 29.41). It also successfully circumvented the s 93 prohibition on default interest (see para 26.19).

(b) So there was no 'dual interest rate'; but, even if there were, the difference between the two rates should be disregarded as being insignificant (at para 60).

(c) The actual credit bargain was not extortionate (see para 29.42).

---

268 Reg 1(2). See Goode, *Consumer Credit Law & Practice*, paras 29.126–39.
269 Goode, *Op. cit.*, para 29.124.
270 [2002] 1 All ER (Comm) 446, CA.
271 S did not raise the UTCC Regulations (at para 81): see para 11.12.

**[8.23] Stage 1: total charge for credit (tcc).** Basically, these are the additional payments which a cash purchaser would not have incurred. In seeking to define what items are to be included as part of the cost of credit, s 20 of the CCA makes it clear that what matters is the cost to the debtor rather than the net return to the lender, thereby disadvantaging those forms of credit which have high administrative costs.[272]

Which items are given statutory recognition as part of the cost of credit is essentially a matter of legislative policy: at the minimum, it could be confined to pure interest; but at the maximum it might embrace everything the debtor has to pay other than the capital sum 'borrowed'.[273] The Act attempts to steer between these two extremes: it starts by naming the items collectively 'total charge for credit' (tcc) and defining this (s 189(1)) by reference to the regulations made under s 20 (see para 8.24). Exactly where that (arbitrary) line is drawn may have implications for the relative fairness of the system as between different sectors of the finance industry.[274] Particularly noticeable are differences produced by the statutory rules as between the following different types of credit: mortgage credit as opposed to (shorter term) personal loans;[275] bank overdrafts;[276] credit cards[277] as opposed to weekly collected credit;[278] small loans for short periods.[279] In *Huntpast v Leadbetter*,[280] the Court of Appeal said that, in construing and applying the regulations, courts should have regard to the substance and reality of the transaction rather than the form, as the whole point of the regulations is the determination of the true cost of the credit to the debtor.

The TCC is significant in a number of contexts (see para 5.08); and the EU is proposing reform (see para 5.12). However, the very complication of the system makes for both loopholes and difficult policing; and the government is trying to plug the gaps with the 2003 White Paper *Fair, Clear and Competitive*.[281] In June 2004, the DTI indicated that, in the interests of competition, it would not force all APR

---

272 E.g. the cost of money to the creditor, something likely to vary greatly as between the different types of lender; home collection costs. For explanation of the segmented market, see Lamiday (2004) 58 CC5/13. See para 2.17.

273 Goode, *Consumer Credit Law & Practice*, para 29.4.

274 E.g. with credit cards, the low interest rates charged for an initial period in respect of balance transfers.

275 A first mortgage may be fixed rate: see *National Westminster Bank v Devon CC* (1994) 13 Tr L 70, DC (Whisson 14 Tr L 304; 48 CC 4/21; OFT, *1997-AR*, 24). A second mortgage is also secured (see para 7.04A); and it only has to quote the rate to one decimal place (Goode, *Op. cit.*, Pt VII, para 3027), a concession the more valuable the longer the repayment period.

276 If charges were included, an unauthorised bank overdraft could cost in the order of 9,000% APR. For examples, see CCA (UK) *Mirage or Reality?* 31, 58, 60.

277 The previous freedom for card-issuers to make different assumptions as to card use in calculating the APR has now been reduced by Regulations made in 2004 (see para 8.25), but still leaves 14 different methods of calculation: [2006] 2 *Which?* 16.

278 Which has heavier administration charges and rarely charges for late payment. For the effect of this, see CCA (UK), *Op. cit.*, 28, 30, 57.

279 Whereas a personal loan may have a minimum loan size over which to spread costs, the small lender does not. For the effect of this see CCA (UK), *Op. cit.*, 29.

280 [1993] GCCR 1631, CA (a case on an earlier version of the regulations).

281 See DTI, *the Consumer Credit Market in the 21st Century* (Dec 2003, Cm. 6040), para 2.28.

calculations into a single formula,[282] but instead require consumers to be informed in a preliminary document (see para 9.08) of the formula used.[283] Would it help if the creditor had to show his charges on a common scenario in terms of pounds and pence?

**[8.24] The TCC Regulations.**[284] These simply state which items are to be included and which will be excluded from the TCC.[285] According to Lloyd LJ, the first task is to ascertain 'whether the amount in question is a charge specified in Regulation 4. If it is, it is then necessary to consider whether it is taken out of the [tcc] by being included in regulation 5(1)'.[286]

1.  *Items included.* The TCC Regulations apply to the costs of the credit, which, according to reg 4 (as amended) includes items, unless expressly excluded by reg 5 (below), which are any of the following:

    (i)   All interest charges, e.g. bank interest.[287] This does **not** include repayments of the capital sum borrowed (see para 5.22).

    (ii)  All premiums for compulsory credit insurance solely against the debtor's death, invalidity, illness or unemployment (reg 4(c)), what is termed PPI Insurance (see para 24.48), but only where it is compulsory (see below). A good example is the compulsory insurance premium in the *Meadows* case (at paras 45, 58 and 67).[286]

    (iii) Other charges:

    > 'at any time payable under the transaction by or on behalf of the debtor or a relative of his whether to the creditor of any other person'.[288]

    This last formula is very wide, extending to charges paid by the debtor or a relative of his under the credit agreement itself, e.g. hp finance charges and probably option fees, credit card fees, survey fees, legal fees, stamp duties.[289] It also extends to charges arising under any other contract which the creditor insists on the debtor or his relative making or maintaining as a condition of being granted the credit,[290] which will usually be a linked transaction (see generally, para 5.31), e.g. compulsory installation or most maintenance contracts in respect of the subject matter of the credit agreement (which may extend beyond the period of the credit agreement). Additionally, it

---

282  The Government have also justified continued ability for card-issuers to calculate their APR on different bases to allow product differentiation: (2005–6) HL GC col.154.

283  A proposal criticised by the HC Treasury Select Committee as 'silly': *The Times* 30.6.04.

284  Consumer Credit (Total Charge for Credit) Regulations, 1980 SI 51, Pt 2 (as amended). There are helpful annotations in Pt 3 of Guest and Lloyd, *Encyclopedia of Consumer Credit.*

285  Art 3. For a serious drafting slip, see Goode, *Consumer Credit Law & Practice*, para 29.141.

286  *London North Securities Ltd v Meadows* (set out at para 8.25), at para 43.

287  Reg 4(a). As to interest, see generally, para 7.03A. What if the rate of interest is variable, whether automatically or consensually (see para 26.21)? See Goode, *Payment Obligations in Commercial and Financial Transactions*, 81–2. *Sed quaere?*

288  Reg 4(c). As to 'debtor', 'creditor' and 'relative', see respectively paras 5.24, 5.25 and 5.33.

289  See *Humberclyde Finance Ltd v Thompson* (1997) Tr LR 242, C A (payment waiver policy).

290  See *McGinn v Grangewood Securities Ltd* (see para 8.25).

comprehends any security agreement,[291] brokerage fees[292] and documentation fees.[293]

2.  *Items excluded.* According to reg 5 (as amended), this excludes from the TCC all the following classes of items which would otherwise fall within reg 4: (i) default charges, as for late payment (reg 5(1)(b));[294] (ii) charges payable by cash and credit customers alike, e.g. car delivery fees, voluntary maintenance contracts (reg 5(1)(c)); (iii) previously incurred charges for incidental services or benefits, e.g. membership fees for an organisation which offers *inter alia* cheap credit facilities, but not brokerage fees (reg 5(1)(d));[292] (iv) bank charges, as charges for operating a current account which are unrelated to any overdraft facility (reg 5(1)(f)), e.g. for standing orders; and (v) voluntary insurance (reg 5(1)(i)), e.g. PPI insurance (see above).

[8.25] The task is to distinguish between on the one hand the credit/financial accommodation (see para 5.22) and on the other the tcc (see para 8.23). The difficulty in deciding whether an item falls within or outside the TCC Regulations (see para 8.24) is illustrated by three similar Court of Appeal cases where the consumer applied for a second secured loan; that regulated loan was granted on condition that it was first applied to pay off first charge arrears, with only the balance being paid to the consumer; and the debtor defaulted on the second loan. In all cases, the documentation of the second loan described the arrears as part of the credit, but the debtor pleaded that the agreement was improperly executed because it was a prescribed term that the arrears should have been included as part of the tcc within reg 4 (see para 8.24). Everything appeared to turn on the meaning of the ambiguous word 'charge' in reg 4. In *Watchtower Investments Ltd v Payne*,[295] the borrower gave genuinely informed consent to part of the second loan being applied to the arrears on the first charge: the Court of Appeal unanimously held that payment of the arrears (£1,777) was not an 'other charge' within reg 4, but part of the credit, 'because it was not of the nature of a charge for credit as distinct from being part of the credit itself' (para 55). On the other hand, in *McGinn v Grangewood Securities Ltd*[296] another Court of Appeal unanimously held that the payment of arrears on the first charge (one monthly instalment of £359) did fall within reg 4, with the result that the agreement did not accurately state the amount of credit, so that the agreement was unenforceable under s 127(3) (see para 9.20). In delivering the leading judgment, Clarke LJ distinguished the *Watchtower* case on the following basis: in *Watchtower* part of the borrower's purpose in the second loan was to pay off the arrears of the first loan (at para 58); whereas in *McGinn* it was no part of the borrower's purpose for the second loan to pay off arrears (at para 61), which seems to have been just an accounting adjustment (made in reliance on the small print and

---

291  See para 25.11. It will also include any survey or valuation fees paid by a surety.

292  *Huntpast v Leadbetter* [1993] GCCR 1631, CA (on an earlier version of the regs).

293  *Wilson v Robertsons (London) Ltd* (set out at para 5.22).

294  E.g. unauthorised overdraft. If a default is made good, the right to any default charge is avoided (see para 24.32); and, if a default is not made good, the default charge may amount to a penalty (see para 27.46).

295  [2002] GCCR 3055, CA.

296  [2002] GCCR X/251, CA (see 57 CC2/4). There was also a side-letter, deferring the payment of legal fees and expenses on the same terms as to credit: see Say (2004) 72 QA 7 at 9.

without the borrower's prior awareness) to take account of the period of time over which the second loan was being negotiated and comparable to the broker's fee (at paras 62–3) or legal fees.[297] The foregoing cases were considered in *London North Securities v Meadows*.[298]

> M, having mortgage arrears of some £2,600, in 1989 approached a mortgage-broker (B) for a further loan of about £2,400 to make home improvements. B in turn approached a non-status lender (L),[299] whose terms of business always required the discharge of all arrears of prior mortgages before completion of their mortgage loan. L sent M documents for a fifteen-year regulated loan of £5,750 at a variable 34.9%APR. The loan documents detailed that the loan of £5,750 was made up of: arrears of £2,600; a loan of £2,400; and an (unrequested) insurance of £750. Following a crucial phone call between them, M returned the signed documents to L and the transaction was completed.[300] After two or three monthly payments, M fell into arrears, upon which he was liable to pay compound interest at the above rate; and a suspended possession court order was made in 1990. By 2004, M owed £144,760, of which £104,708 was interest.

The County Court Judge found in favour of M on a number of grounds,[301] of which the Court of Appeal only pursued the argument that the loan was unenforceable because of a failure to comply with the CCA as regards the mortgage arrears (£2,600) and the insurance premium.[302] A unanimous Court of Appeal held that the mortgage arrears were part of the credit (see para 8.24), following *Watchtower* (para 32: see above), but that the insurance premium was indeed part of the tcc (para 69). In delivering the judgment of the court, Lloyd LJ pointed out that in the crucial phone call L had told M that the real purpose of the insurance (which M had not requested and did not want) was to provide for L's remuneration, without which the loan would not go through (para 41); and he emphasised the importance of looking at the reality of the transaction (para 33).

**[8.26] Stage 2: annual percentage rate (APR).** Even when the tcc has been fixed (see paras 8.23–4), it is clear that this sum of money may be translated into a percentage rate in a number of different ways having very different mathematical results.[303] Further, the regulations made under s 20 have to cover the many very different types of regulated agreement, including fixed-sum and running-account credit (see para 5.28). Moreover, whilst the purposes for which the APR scheme is set up (see para 8.22) require that the APR be quoted at the outset of a transaction, it will be obvious that many of the factors required to calculate the APR will not be

---

297 Clarke LJ said, *obiter* (at para 80), that, as the lender always intended by subsequent agreement with the debtor to add the legal fees to the amount to be repaid, that also should have been included of the credit. See (2004) 72 *QA* 7, at 8–9.

298 [2005] GCCR 5381, [2005] EWCA Civ 956, CA.

299 For non-status loans, see generally, para 7.04A. In fact, the agreement was administered on behalf of L by an unlicensed broker (see para 6.12). See [2006] 3 *Which?* 5.

300 L did not sign them, but immediately passed the loan to X (later re-named LNS), who made the advances.

301 The loan was extortionate (see para 29.42); the provision for compound interest was void as a penalty (see para 27.25); he would exercise his discretion under s 127 to overlook the creditor's failure to sign the loan (see para 9.20); but he would make a Time Order (see para 24.41).

302 *Per* Lloyd LJ at para 70.

303 See the Crowther Report, paras 6.5.18–21.

settled at that point; so, with running-account credit, it will then be unknown for how long the agreement is to run and how much will be drawn down. To cope with these issues, the TCC Regulations, 1980 SI 51 (as amended), take matters in two stages.

1.  *Assumptions.* The Regulations make certain assumptions about factors unknown **at the date of contracting**.[304] There are two different classes of assumption:

    (a) *Overriding assumptions* (reg 2), which are applicable irrespective of the terms of the consumer credit agreement, include the following: the creditor will not accelerate payment under an acceleration clause;[305] if the agreement allows for variation of the rate upon the happening of an uncertain event, e.g. the interest rate is linked to FHBR (Finance House Base Rate), that the uncertain event, e.g. a change in FHBR (see para 2.18), will not occur;[306] where the provision or repayment of credit is to be made 'on or before' a specified date, it is assumed that that date is the 'relevant date' (see para 8.22), so ignoring the fact that payment/repayment may be delayed (reg 2(2)(a)); where the agreement is for running-account credit so that the amount repayable at the end of each billing period is uncertain, e.g. an overdraft or credit card, the charge is calculated on the debit balance at the beginning of the billing period, e.g. month;[307] and, if the debtor has a choice as to the amount of payment, e.g. under a credit card, he is assumed to make only the minimum payment (reg 2(2)(c)).

    (b) *Gap-fillers* (Pt IV). Unlike those above, the Pt IV assumptions are to be employed only where the regulated agreement is silent as to some matter relevant to the computation of the APR. These include the following: where the amount of credit is unascertainable, that the debtor will borrow up to the credit-limit if there is one (reg 15), e.g. a bank overdraft, and that the credit is provided for one year (reg 14); where the interest rate is index-linked, the prevailing rate at the date of agreement will be taken;[308] where the agreement is of uncertain duration and the rate charged will increase after a specified period, the higher of the two rates is to be taken (reg 16); where the earliest date as to the provision of credit is unascertainable, e.g. on delivery, the date of contract is to be taken (reg 17); where a charge is payable on an uncertain date, it will usually be assumed to be payable on the 'relevant date' (above), e.g. date of provision of credit; and where there is running-account credit, e.g. credit cards, a 2004 amendment introduces a number of assumptions designed to reduce the number of ways in which the APR may be calculated.[309]

---

304  See Goode, *Consumer Credit Law & Practice*, paras 29.20–27.

305  Reg 2(1)(c). For acceleration clauses operating on the debtor's default, see para 7.03.

306  Reg 2(1)(d). As to what amounts to uncertainty for this purpose, see *Scarborough BS v Humberside TSD* [1997] GCCR 2165, DC (discussing the applicability of reg 2(1)(d) of 1980 SI 51 to a low-start mortgage). As to interpretation, see para 1.05. As to the special rule for land mortgages, see reg 2(1)(e).

307  Reg 2(2)(b). Thus, the calculation is simplified by ignoring any payments made during the month.

308  Reg 15. There is a special rule for index-linked mortgages: reg 15A.

309  Consumer Credit (Agreements)(Amendment) Regulations, 2004 SI 1482, reg 15. See also the Advertisements Regulations, where the matter is discussed (para 8.31).

2.  *Formulae for computation.* The cumbersome UK system[310] has now been replaced by the revised Consumer Credit Directive (98/7/EC: see para 5.12), which prescribes a single equation which will be satisfied if the APR is correctly stated.[311] Whilst the original UK regulations disregarded anything after the first decimal place, reg 6A requires a rounding up or down. Regulation 7 embodies the euro-formula for calculating the APR.[312]

The above assumptions and formula are simply programmed into industry calculators, so that it should be relatively simple for those within the industry in any given situation to calculate the appropriate APR.[313]

## Advertising

**[8.27]  Introduction**. There are a large number of statutory controls relating to the advertising of goods which apply whether the supply is intended to be on cash terms or credit.[314] However, where the advertising relates to a credit supply, there also existed some pre-CCA statutory controls (see para 8.20). Following its normal pattern, Pt IV of the CCA sought in the main to take the earlier statutory controls and make them systematically applicable across the full range of 'advertising', an expression widely defined by s 189(1) 'to catch almost any form of activity designed to attract custom',[315] e.g. web-sites. As will be seen, s 43 starts from the premise that all 'advertising' of credit or hire facilities is within Pt IV, regardless of whether the resulting credit or hire agreements would be within the ambit of the CCA (s 43(1): set out at para 8.29), e.g. credit to a corporate debtor, and then excluding some situations (s 43(2)–(5): see para 8.29). For cases within its ambit, Pt IV lays down the following types of restriction in relation to credit or hire businesses:[316]

1.  *Detailed stipulations* in regulations made under s 44 as to the form and content of advertisements (see para 8.30, *et seq.*), which can also be the subject of Enforcement Orders (see para 6.08).

2.  *Availability of cash terms.* Section 45 provides that:

> 'If an advertisement to which this Part applies indicates that the advertiser is willing to provide credit under a restricted-use credit agreement relating to goods or service to be supplied by any person, but at the time when the advertisement is published that person is not holding himself out as prepared to sell the goods or provide the services (as the case may be) for cash, the advertiser commits an offence'.

---

310  See 1st edn, para 8.26.

311  See Goode, *Consumer Credit Law & Practice*, para 29.140.

312  See Goode, *Op. cit.*, paras 29.206a–b.

313  Because it determines the ambit of the Act, the APR has to be calculated more strictly in the case of exempt agreements, whereas some tolerances are allowed by the regulations in the other cases: Goode, *Op. cit.*, para 29.123.

314  E.g. trade descriptions (see para 8.07); price displays (see para 8.08); misleading pricing (see para 8.10); misleading advertising (see para 8.12A).

315  Goode, *Consumer Credit Law & Practice*, Vol 2, para IIB, para 5.369.

316  They are also applicable to credit-brokers: s 151(1); *R v Munford and Ahearne* [1995] CCLR 16, CA.

The object is to prevent effective avoidance of s 44 (above) in relation to restricted-use credit (see para 5.29) in the following manner: an 'advertiser' who did not supply the goods for cash[317] could assume an inflated notional cash price,[318] so enabling him to advertise his goods with no credit charge or a very low one in a manner which literally conformed with the rules as to the contents of advertisements.[319] However, this restriction has done little to curb the popularity in financed transactions of 'interest-free' credit, often advertised as '0% APR' (see para 2.07). In this class of business, the cash and credit retail customer will both pay the same price for an item, thus satisfying s 45;[320] but the creditor will deduct the cost of the credit from the amount it pays the supplier, which may mean that cash customers unwittingly contribute towards another customer's credit. Again, it would appear that the traders who deals on both cash and credit terms could seek to avoid s 45 by stocking separate brands/ models for cash and credit customers.

3.  *False or misleading advertisements* (see para 8.28).

Contravention of any of the above advertising rules *prima facie* amounts to a criminal offence;[321] but that fact does not in itself lead to any further sanctions (s 170: see para 10.19). The primary offence is committed by the 'advertiser', to which the expression refers, not to the publisher of the advertisement, but (s 189(1))

> 'means any person indicated by the advertisement as willing to enter into transactions to which the advertisement relates'.

For example, if a car dealer places an advertisement indicating the willingness of XYZ Finance Ltd to enter hp agreements in relation to that dealer's cars, XYZ Finance Ltd is 'the advertiser'; and it has been suggested that there may be more than one 'advertiser' in relation to a single advertisement, so that the car dealer is also the 'advertiser'.[322] Moreover, s 47 extends the scope of the notion of 'advertiser' to the following cases:

*Case (a).* One who publishes the advertisement in the course of business,[323] e.g. a newspaper proprietor, though he is given a special defence (s 47(2): see para 28.16).

*Case (b).* One who in the course of business[323] devised the advertisement, e.g. an advertising agency.

---

317  Cash sales will be uncommon for ghetto merchants: Cayne and Trebilcock (1973) 23 *Univ of Toronto LJ* 396 at 412–13.

318  E.g. *Metsoja v Norman (H) Pitt & Co* (set out at para 8.28).

319  See Cayne and Trebilcock, *Op. cit.*, at 398, 405. Some mail order firms (see generally, para 8.19) are geared exclusively to credit transactions; but they are saved from this rule by an exemption order under s 43(5): see para 8.29.

320  And the advertising regulations (see para 8.30). Any brokerage fee charged would fall within the tcc regulations (see para 8.24).

321  Ss 167(2), 45 and 46. For penalties, see s 167(1) and Sched 1; and generally, Chap 28. For the defences, see s 168: see para 28.13.9. There have been complaints about significant amounts of illegal credit advertising and uneven enforcement: (2003) 58 CC4/7.

322  By straining the meaning of 'transaction': See Goode, *Consumer Credit Law & Practice*, Pt IIB, para 5.87.

323  As to course of business, cf. SGA, s 14: see para 14.04.

*Case (c).* One who procured the publication of the advertisement. This will cover the situation where a person is the advertiser, not because he placed the advertisement, but because he is named in it as the person willing to enter into a transaction within Pt IV of the Act,[324] e.g. dealers named in a list published by XYZ Finance Ltd.

**[8.28] False or misleading credit advertisements**. Section 46(1) provides that

'If an advertisement to which this Part applies conveys information which in a material respect is false or misleading the advertiser commits an offence'.

Although restricted to Pt IV advertisements (see para 8.29), the offence is applicable to both creditors/owners and brokers (amended s 151: see para 16.19). Section 46 is widely drawn. Thus, in *Metsoja v Norman H Pitt & Co*,[325]

A car dealer's advertisement referred to '0% finance deal' 'payments over 24 months without paying a penny in interest' and '0% APR'. In practice, the dealer allowed a higher part exchange allowance to cash customers than to credit customers.

The Court held that, besides infringing the Advertising Regulations (see para 8.29), the advertisement was *prima facie* false in that it clearly indicated that a purchaser using the finance scheme would pay the same as a cash purchaser. The test has been said to be whether the advertisement would mislead an 'ordinary member of the public';[326] but this does not seem to have stemmed the profusion of confusing 'interest-free' deals advertised,[327] e.g. the balance transfer trap (see para 23.13).

Nor is the s 46(1) offence confined to credit information:[328] it extends to **any** information in a Pt IV advertisement,[329] including that a broker was providing his own credit.[330] The provision speaks of information which is false or misleading 'in a material respect'. This is reminiscent of the language of the TDA (s 3(1): see para 4.08); and it may be that there is some overlap between the provisions. Whilst at common law a false statement of intention would not amount to an offence,[331] s 46(2) adds that

'Information stating or implying an intention on the advertiser's part which he has not got is false'.

This provision will catch out-of-date sales literature;[332] and, in relation to prices quoted, may overlap with the misleading prices rules (CPA, s 21(1)(d): see para 8.09).

---

324 Goode, *Op. cit.*, para 28.69.
325 [1990] CLY 620, DC (see 43 CC6/2). See also *National Westminster Bank v Devon CC* (1994) 13 Tr LR 70, DC.
326 *Dudley MBC v Colorvision plc* [1997] CCLR 19, DC.
327 See [1998] 11 *Which?* 49; [1998] 12 *Which?* 7. As to 'instant credit', see (1986) 41 CC 1–4.
328 E.g. Where the advertisement does not mention that it applies only above a minimum amount of credit (47 CC1/14); nor that in a low-start mortgage the interest shortfall would be capitalised (48 CC5/25); cashbacks with unstated early redemption penalties (51 CC 2/21).
329 *Rover Group Ltd v Sumner* [1995] CCLR 1 (quoted price did not include road tax and other items).
330 *R v Munford & Ahearne* [1994] CCLR 16, CA (advertisement also false in that it referred to fixed-rate loan without disclosing that fixed rate only for 12 months).
331 *R v Dent* [1955] 2 QB 590, CCA. *Contra* civil law: see para 17.18.
332 E.g. *Home Insulation v Wadsley* [1988] CCLR 25, DC (outdated promotional literature).

The CCA lays down that breach of one of its requirements attracts no other sanctions (s 170(1): see para 10.19). However, it is thought that this does not affect civil liability arising independently of the Act:[333] so the false or misleading statement may amount to a material misrepresentation (see para 17.10), or a breach of term of any supply contract thereby induced, whether as an express (see para 11.07) or implied term, e.g. as to description (see para 13.11). It may also be the subject of an Enforcement Order (see para 6.08).

[8.29] Credit and hire advertisements. Part IV of the CCA applies to 'advertisements' (see s 189(1): para 8.27). However, s 43 proceeds to limit the ambit of Pt IV to certain classes of 'advertisement'. Section 43(1) provides that:

> 'This Part applies to any advertisement, published for the purposes of a business carried on by the advertiser, indicating that he is willing:
>
> (a)  to provide credit, or
>
> (b)  to enter into an agreement for the bailment . . . of goods by him'.

Thus, the essence of s 43(1) is that the 'advertisement'[334] must be an indication: (i) 'published';[335] (ii) for the purposes of a credit or hire business, whether regulated or not;[336] (iii) carried on by the 'advertiser'[337] (see para 8.27); (iv) indicating a willingness to provide credit. In *Jenkins v Lombard North Central plc*:[338]

> The defendant national finance company, LNC, supplied a car dealer with stickers to be placed on cars offered for sale. The stickers were vertically divided: the cash price was to be indicated in ink by the dealer on the right-hand side; and on the left-hand side were printed the name and logo of LNC. The prosecution argued that, because it was well-known that LNC offered credit for the acquisition of motor cars, the stickers amounted to an indication within s 43 that the advertiser (LNC) was willing to provide credit and thus fell within the advertisement regulations.

However, the Divisional Court held that corporate advertising which merely kept LNC's name in the public eye did not amount to such an indication, even if members of the public might infer such a willingness from LNC's reputation. It seems to follow that *corporate* advertising by itself is not an 'indication' within s 43.[339] On the other hand, *service* advertising 'indicating' an express willingness to grant credit or hire facilities is within s 43.[340]

---

333  Goode, *Consumer Credit Law & Practice*, Pt IIB, para 5.86; and see para 10.19.

334  There have been attempts to distinguish mere information, e.g. notification of interest-rate changes, from statements promoting new business: Goode, *Consumer Credit Law & Practice*, para 28.10. See also Jones, *Credit Cards*, 38–9.

335  It will be observed that the definition is not confined to visual advertisements but extends to oral ones, and even to sales patter in a shop. Does it include the supply of a complimentary diary or pencil? See generally, Goode, *Op. cit.*, para 28.21. Two or more documents may constitute an advertisement: s 189(4).

336  As to which, see Goode, *Op. cit.*, para 28.23.

337  Or a credit-brokerage business (amended s 151: see para 16.19). As to which, see generally, para 5.38. For regulated and unregulated agreements, see para 5.13; and for credit and hire businesses, see para 6.12.

338  [1984] 1 All ER 828, [1984] 1 WLR 307, DC.

339  *Quaere* with MasterCard and Visa logos, which appear to guarantee the provision of credit.

340  Goode, *Op. cit.*, Pt III, para 44. Or perhaps the distinction lies in the difference between an express or implied indication: see Goode, *Op. cit.*, Pt I, para 28.27.

*Exceptions.* Even where an advertisement *prima facie* falls within s 43(1), the Act exempts certain types of advertisement from Pt IV (s 43(2) and (5)):

1.  As regards the business of the advertiser, where either (a) that business does not amount to a consumer credit or consumer hire business (s 43(2)(a), e.g. the advertiser only places such advertisements occasionally; or (b) the advertiser does not provide credit to individuals secured on land (s 43(2)(b)).[341] So, if the advertiser is lending on mortgage, he must rely on one of the exemptions below.

2.  Even where the advertiser carries on a business within the scope of Pt IV, he can still issue particular advertisements to which the Act does not apply if he makes it plain in that advertisement that:

    (a)  as to credit facilities, credit is available only to a body corporate;[342]

    (b)  as to hiring facilities, he is not willing to enter into consumer hire agreements (s 43(4)), e.g. an advertiser carrying on a consumer hire business who issues an advertisement for the hiring of commercial plant.

3.  Exempt agreements. Some agreements are generally exempt from the CCA (see paras 5.14–15A), e.g. first mortgages of land (now within the jurisdiction of the FSMA). Most such cases have also been exempted from Pt IV of the CCA by statutory order:[343] e.g. agreements exempt as short-term credit, low-cost credit, finance for foreign trade or hire. However, there remain some circumstances where Pt IV mostly applies to otherwise exempt agreements:[344] in particular, first or second mortgages of land and other dc loans.[345]

**[8.30] Form and content**. Different detailed controls of both the content (amount and type of information) and form (the way in which the information is presented) of credit advertisements was previously to be found in both the Moneylenders and Advertisements (HP) Acts (see para 8.20). However, for flexibility, s 44 of the CCA chose to allow the control of 'advertisements' to be introduced by regulation, breach of which amounts to an offence (s 167(2): see para 8.28). It also gave the following indication of what is expected: the regulations should be designed to ensure that 'an advertisement conveys a fair and reasonably comprehensive indication of the nature of the credit or hire facilities . . . and of their true cost to the person using them' (s 44(1)). In 2003 the White Paper *Fair, Clear and Competitive*[346] proposed substantial amendments to the above Regulations to ensure greater consistency and transparency in credit advertising.

---

341  S 43(2)(c) (as amended) attempts to prevent circumvention of Pt IV by the use of ingenious 'off-shore' operations. But is there a drafting slip in that it contains too many negatives? Does the amendment achieve this?

342  Amended s 43(3) of the 1974 Act, as further amended by s 2 of the 2004 Act.

343  Made under s 43(5), the Consumer Credit (Exempt Advertisements) Order 1985, SI No 621.

344  See Goode, *Op. cit.*, para 28.46.

345  But the advertising regulations do not apply to certain types of agreement, including first mortgages: see para 8.30.

346  See DTI, *the Consumer Credit Market in the 21st Century* (Dec 2003, Cm. 6040), para 2.7. This is to bring them into line with the FSA regime on first mortgage regulation (para 2.8: see para 3.02).

The subsequent Advertising Regulation[347] apply to credit and hire advertisements[348] within Pt IV of the Act published by the creditor, lessor or credit-broker
(see para 8.29); and the person who causes the advertisement to be published shall
ensure that it complies.[349] The Regulations contain a list of the types of information
which must be included in credit or hire advertisements (see para 8.31) and also
contain the following general rules as to any information required or permitted
to be included in any advertisement. *First*, even where that information varies
from one transaction to another, the advertiser is no longer allowed to state 'representative terms', except as to APRs.[350] *Second*, the required information must
use plain and intelligible language, be easily legible (or audible) and specify the
name of the advertiser (reg 3): clarity refers to substance, whilst legibility is directed
at the ability to read it.[351] *Third* that information must generally be 'shown together
as a whole' (reg 4(2)), except for split advertisements, where the statement of
'cash price'[352] may be split off from the other required information in a dealer's
catalogue (reg 5) or showroom (reg 6). *Fourth*, special prominence must be given
to the current APR (reg 8), especially as compared with any other rate statement,
e.g. flat rate. *Fifth*, the use of certain types of statement is restricted.[353] *Sixth*, in
all mortgage advertisements, there is required a prominent wealth warning in
statutory form that the debtor's home is at risk if he defaults;[354] and that warning
must be repeated in the agreement (see para 9.11). *Seventh*, the regulations do not
apply to advertisements to (a) most business consumers, nor (b) domestic first
mortgage advertisements within the FSMA.[355]

Finally, an advertisement contravening the Advertising Regulations may also
be the subject of an Enforcement Order (see para 6.08) or proceedings under the
ASA Code (see para 3.14). The OFT has explicitly agreed that enforcement will be
proportionate (see para 3.09A). In 2007, CCA advertising law may have to be
amended to comply with the UCP Directive (see para 4.21B).

[8.31] **The types of advertisement.** The foregoing Regulations require that an
advertisement for credit or hire facilities to consumers which falls within Pt IV of
the CCA must comply with the above general rules (para 8.30); and must be drawn

---

347  Consumer Credit (Advertisement) Regulations, 2004 SI 1484 (as amended). Whilst the Regula-
     tions contain some definitions (reg 1), in other cases reference should be made to the CCA
     definitions (see generally, para 5.05). The OFT have published *Frequently Asked Questions* (2005)
     and plan a booklet on credit advertising about the Regulations. These go beyond the letter of the
     law.
348  Reg 1(2) defines 'credit advertisement' and 'hire advertisement' by reference to CCA, s 43(1).
349  Reg 2. Contravention is an offence: see para 8.27. The OFT and TSS carry out newspaper, etc,
     sweeps to catch defaulters: OFT, *AR-2005/6*, 29.
350  Old reg 3 of the 1989 is not repeated in the present regulations. But for representative APRs, see
     para 8.31.
351  This may also infringe UTCC, reg 7: see para 11.13.
352  Reg 4(3). 'Cash price' and 'cash purchaser' are defined by reg 1(2).
353  Reg 9. This refers to: 'overdraft' (see regs 1(2) and 2(3)); comparative advertising (10 Tr L 46; cf.
     para 8.06); 'interest-free' (see 57 CC1/34); 'no deposit' ('deposit' defined CCA, s 189(1): set out at
     para 5.22); 'loan guaranteed' or 'pre-approved'; 'gift' or 'present'; 'weekly equivalent'. See
     *Holman v CWS Ltd* [2001] CCLR 2777, DC (now reg 9(c): co-op divi).
354  Reg 7; and there is a totally new warning required for advertisements enticing debtors under
     unsecured loans to consolidate them into a secured loan (reg 7(2)(b): see para 7.04A). Cf. *First
     National Bank plc v Sec of State for Trade and Industry* (1990) 9 Tr LR 184, CA. As to the prominence
     of this warning, see Goode, *Op. cit.*, para 9.33.
355  Reg 10; and for the FSMA, see para 3.02. But most of Pt IV of the CCA applies: see para 8.29.

within one of the several categories.[356] Whereas the old regulations were drawn to distinguish in considerable detail between three types of advertisement (simple, intermediate and full), in 2003 the White Paper *Fair, Clear and Competitive*[357] proposed substantial amendments to the above Regulations to ensure greater consistency and transparency in credit advertising. In effect, the new Regulations have dispensed with intermediate advertisements and distinguish credit and hire advertisements according to whether or not they contain any of the listed financial information: the result has been to reduce the amount of required detail and cast more emphasis on the general duty not to publish misleading advertisements (CCA, s 46: see para 8.28).

1. *Simple advertisements* are designed just to keep the name of a business in the public eye,[358] e.g. a brief advertising message at sponsored event; 'give-away' items such as a book of matches. The credit or hire information which can be given is limited by reg 4(1) so that it cannot include any of the trigger credit/ hire information listed below.[359] As before, there is no objection to the advertisement including non-credit related information, e.g. 'established 1861'; non-trigger credit information, e.g. the fact that credit is available, its type, amount or period, creditor logo; and, another change from the old regulations, this may include the cash price.[360] These advertisements only have to obey the following rules: they must not be false or misleading (CCA, s 46: see para 8.28); nor use certain prohibited expressions (reg 7: see para 8.30); but must comply with the general requirements of reg 3 (see para 8.30).

2. *Advertisements containing credit/hire information.* The rules as to the content of credit or hire advertisements apply only where the advertisement contains **any** of the following trigger information (reg 4(1)):[359] the frequency, number and amounts of 'repayments of credit', or 'hire payments';[361] other payments and charges;[362] and, in the case of credit advertisements, the total amount payable by the debtor (Sched 2, para 7), including the amount of the 'total charge for credit' (para 7(c); reg 1(2)), e.g. 'cheaper loans', 'lowest rates ever'. Not only does this list of triggers include the APR (see para 8.22), but there is in reg 8 a wider list of triggers which themselves trigger the APR requirement, e.g. 'CCJs no problem'. Where a credit or hire advertisement contains **any** of these amounts, not only must it comply with same rules as simple advertisements (see above), but reg 4(1) requires it to contain **all** that financial information, together with **all** the following information as listed in the appropriate

---

356 The detailed rules for credit advertisements and hire advertisements are contained respectively in Scheds 2 and 3.

357 See DTI, *the Consumer Credit Market in the 21st Century* (Dec 2003, Cm. 6040), paras 2.11–13.

358 The name must be that on any standard licence (reg 1(6)): as to such licences, see generally, para 6.14.

359 The listed financial information varies according to whether it is a credit or hire advertisement: compare Sched 2, paras 5–7 and Sched 3, paras 4 and 5.

360 See Sched 2, para 3; Sched 3, para 3.

361 See Sched 2, para 5; Sched 3, para 4. 'Hire payment' and 'repayment of credit' are defined by regs 1(2) and (5).

362 See Sched 2, para 6; Sched 3, para 5 (as amended).

Regulatory Schedule and usually[363] the postal address of the advertiser: the amount of credit (Sched 2, para 1); any deposit (Sched 2, para 2; Sched 3, para 1); any 'advance payment' (Sched 2, para 4; Sched 3, para 2), though that expression does not include an insurance payment or tcc (reg 1(2)); and any variable payments or charges for hiring.[364] Additionally, the Regulations deal specially with two types of information. *First*, if a credit advertisement specifies the APR or any other rate of charge,[365] by reg 8(1) it must also specify a 'typical APR', meaning an APR at which the advertiser reasonably expects to enter at least 66% of agreements made as a result of the advertisement (reg 1(2)), which may cause difficulty in respect of risk-based credit.[366] Regulation 8 also requires that the result shall be specified at greater prominence than other Sched 2 information as '%APR' (or range of APRs), listed with those other items and described as 'variable' where it is subject to change; but there is a special dispensation for banks to instead continue to use their own formula (AER) for the cost of overdrafts (reg 8(6)). In advertisements for running-account credit, the APR must be calculated on the assumptions set out in Sched 1:[367] these differ from the old regulations as regards the amount of credit taken as having been advanced, the interest rate applied and the manner in which the credit is repaid. *Second*, reg 7 contains special provisions for statutory wealth warnings where the debtor puts his house at risk (see para 8.30).

## Miscellaneous

[8.32] Apart from the extensive control of advertising (see paras 8.27–31), Pt IV of the CCA also contains a number of other restrictions upon a creditor or owner seeking business with regard to information that he may supply to the debtor or hirer.

1. *Canvassing dcs credit* (see paras 7.05–7).
2. *Issuing unsolicited credit-tokens* (see para 7.12).
3. *Quotations.* A quotation is a document giving a particular prospective debtor or hirer information about the terms on which any one of the following persons are prepared to do business (s 52(1)(a)): one who carries on a consumer credit or consumer hire business (see para 6.12); or a credit-broking business (s 152(1): see para 16.19); or a business in the course of which he provides credit to individuals, even if outside the financial limit of the CCA

---

363 Exempt from the address requirement are broadcast advertisements, fixed advertisements on the premises of the advertiser, advertisements which include the name and address of the 'dealer' (reg 1(2)) or credit-broker (reg 4(1)(b)).

364 Sched 3, para 6. Does 'charges' include liquidated damages (see para 24.27)?

365 Or if the advertisement indicates that credit is available to non-status borrowers, or includes any incentive to apply for credit: reg 8(1)(c) and (d).

366 Consider the dilemma of a creditor who properly devises his advertisement for a particular segment of the market for which the advertised APR is appropriate, but unexpectedly receives responses from consumers outside that market segment, where to accept them at an appropriate APR would falsify the APR advertised. He can avoid this by relying on simple advertisements; but this may make it difficult for consumers to make rate comparisons.

367 This is the effect of the reference in reg 8(1) to 'total charge for credit' and its definition, and that of 'APR' in reg 1(2). Sched 1 would appear to be in terms virtually identical with the assumptions for running-account credit contained in the Agreement Regulations (see para 8.25).

(see para 5.23). Section 52 allows regulations to be made as to the form and content of any quotations,[368] which power extends to ancilliary credit businesses.[369] Under the deregulation initiative (see para 5.11) the general regulations were replaced by some restricted to mortgages secured on the customer's home.[370] However, s 52 has since been used to introduce a general alternative to quotations, based on Schumer boxes (see para 9.08).

4.  *Circulars to minors* (see para 8.33).

5.  *Display of information.* Section 53 empowers the making of regulations[368] requiring the display of prescribed information at his place of business about consumer credit or consumer hire or second mortgage business.[371]

6.  *The licensing rules* (see para 6.11, *et seq.*).

**[8.33/4] Circulars to minors.** Besides the **civil** protection to minors offered by ordinary contract law (see para 10.18), there has long been some special **criminal** protection as regards credit contracts.[372] This policy was continued in the CCA, s 50(1) of which provides as follows:

'A person commits an offence[373] who, with a view to financial gain, sends to a minor any document inviting him to:

(a)  borrow money,[374] or

(b)  obtain goods on credit or hire,[375] or

(c)  obtain services on credit, or

(d)  apply for information or advice on borrowing money or otherwise obtaining credit, or hiring goods'.

The offence consists of the **sending**[376] to the minor of a document inviting him to do any of the four listed things,[377] there being a special exemption for student loans.[378]

Besides the ordinary defences available under ss 168–9 (see Chap 28), s 50 provides a special defence to s 50(1): the sender is protected if he proves that he did not know and had no reasonable cause to suspect that the recipient was a minor;[379] but, if he sends the document to a minor at an educational establishment

---

368  Breach would amount to a criminal offence: s 167(2) and Sched 1; and see generally, Chap 28.

369  S 152, as amended by s 25 of the 2006 Act.

370  Consumer Credit (Content of Quotations) etc Regulations, 1999 SI 2725.

371  It seems that the previous voluntary quotations failed because consumers did not ask for them, perhaps partly because of the credit footprint engendered (see para 8.36). Hence the new compulsory rules for pre-contract disclosure: see para 9.08.

372  The Betting and Loans (Infants) Act 1892 (now repealed).

373  For penalties, see s 167(1) and Sched 1; and see generally, Chap 28. As to the effect of minority on any subsequently formed contract, see para 10.18.

374  For contracts of loan, see Chap 7.

375  For credit and hire contracts, see Chaps 1 and 5.

376  'Send' may extend beyond sending by post: Guest and Lloyd *Encyclopedia of Consumer Credit*, para 2-051. What if it is re-addressed to a minor? What if it is not a 'document', but a disc?

377  *Alliance & Leicester BS v Babbs* [1993] CCLR 77, DC (circular stated loans not available to minors). See also the Code of Banking Practice (see para 3.12).

378  Education (Student Loans) Act 1990, Sched 2, para 3(8).

379  S 50(2). Cf. *Tesco Stores Ltd v Brent LBC* [1993] 2 All ER 718, DC (decided under a similar defence in the Video Recordings Act 1984, s 11).

for minors, he is deemed to know the recipient was a minor (ss 50(3) and 171(5)). Curiously, there would appear to be no offence committed under s 50 when a person **hands** (instead of sends) such a document to a minor,[380] or complies with a request to permit a minor to become an 'additional' credit card holder.[381] The offence has no civil effect on any contract made with the minor (s 170(1): see para 10.19).

## INFORMATION ABOUT THE DEBTOR OR HIRER

**[8.35]** The consumer has no right to credit; it is a privilege granted by the creditor only when satisfied that the loan is a commercial proposition, provided only that in reviewing the matter the creditor does not indulge in unlawful discrimination (see para 4.23). If credit is refused, lenders' codes of practice (see para 3.12) normally say that the lender should give an indication of any problem; but this is not an obligation.[382] In considering whether to enter into agreements, the fundamentals of risk assessment are Character, Capacity and Collateral.[383] To apply these three Cs, creditors or owners will normally seek information about the prospective debtor or hirer from either or both of two sources.[384]

*First*, information is likely to be sought from the prospective debtor or hirer himself; and and this is commonly done through the device of a signed Application Form for him to complete,[385] together with the production of some identification,[386] upon which a credit check can be run (see below). *Inter alia*, the Application Form is likely to ask about his address (to trace), income and outgoings (to establish capacity to pay), his credit record (to assess willingness to pay) and whether he is a home owner;[387] and it may seek to make all this information the basis of the contract (see para 26.08).[388] For the creditor or owner to run an effective credit check, the proposal form must give him effective permission to search for the purposes of the DPA (Sched 3, para 1: see para 3.27).

*Second*, applications may be made to third parties for information (see para 8.36). However, it should be remembered that most debt problems are not caused by consumers initially borrowing too much, but because later life changes disrupt their income.[389]

---

380 It might amount to unlawful canvassing (see generally, paras 7.05–7): Guest and Lloyd, *Encyclopedia of Consumer Credit*, para 2-051).

381 The request must come from the adult account holder, be signed by the minor and sent to the adult. See generally, para 7.09, *et seq*.

382 But, if a credit bureau has been consulted, this must be disclosed: see paras 8.37 and 8.38.

383 See the Chairman of the NCC, reported in (1990) 45 CC 4/4–6; and see also the OFT, in *Credit Scoring* (1992) paras 2.1 and 7.7; and see para 8.39.

384 These expensive enquiries necessary for new business can be avoided with regard to on-going running-account business: see para 8.39.

385 For the effect of misrepresentation by the customer in the proposal form, see para 17.10.

386 E.g. the production of a photocard driving licence (see para 6.02); Master or Visa Card (so relying on the credit-check of that card-issuer).

387 Home ownership would indicate the availability in default of a charging order (see para 27.04); tenancy suggests possible reliance on distress (see para 19.17).

388 Some of these clauses may amount to unfair terms (see para 11.12): Adams [2000] JBL 203. Cf. the basis of the contract clauses in insurance policies.

389 Especially family breakdown, long-term illness or job loss. For credit insurance, see para 24.48.

**[8.36] Information from third parties**. Such information may be sought to check the identity of the applicant,[390] or his address, e.g. the electoral roll (see para 3.26). Particularly with a non-status loan secured on a house, a valuation is likely to be important.[391] With regard to any motor vehicle traded in, the financier is likely to have recourse to HP Information Ltd;[392] and, with an eye to the prospective credit or hire agreement, the most significant sources of information about the debtor or hirer, after any county court judgments (CCJs),[393] are likely to be his existing[394] or past creditors.[395] The last can either be approached individually[394] or the information can be sought from credit bureaux (see para 8.36). Techniques have been developed for dealing systematically with all the computerised information thus obtained by what are known as credit scoring and behavioural scoring (see para 8.39). Since it became common for retailers to have on their premises terminals with on-line connection to credit bureaux, it has been possible for them to offer more safely 'Instant Credit', which is essentially an offer to undertake the above credit-vetting within a few minutes whilst the customer waits.[396] If the applicant is turned down for credit,[397] it is likely to be for one of the following (perhaps overlapping) reasons: the applicant is a minor (see para 10.18); he is not the sort of applicant with whom the creditor wishes to do business, e.g. too good a credit risk,[398] so likely to make early settlement (see para 26.19A); he is not a good enough credit risk (see paras 8.36–8); fraud is suspected.[399] The Government did consider requiring creditors, if they wish their credit agreements to be enforceable,[400] to make adequate pre-contract checks as to the applicant's

---

390 For the all too prevalent identity fraud, see [2005] 3 *Which?* 10; [2005] 2 *Credit Today* 15 and 21. For the fraud exemption from the Data Protection Act, see s 29 (para 3.27); and for the national ID card scheme, see the Identity Card Act 2006, ss 1(3)(b), (4)(b). The credit industry would welcome gaining access to the National Death Register (see para 3.26).

391 E.g. *Platform Home Loans Ltd v Oyston Shipways Ltd* [1996] EG LR 112 (valuer liable in negligent misstatement: see generally, para 17.19). As to 'non-status loans', see para 8.36.

392 As to which, see para 2.18. What, if any, redress does the prospective debtor or hirer have if HP Information Ltd (HPI) erroneously state that they have an interest registered against his vehicle?

393 CCJs (see para 3.22) are held on computer by the Registry Trust Ltd (see para 27.03). Unpaid CCJs are one of the main bars to obtaining credit.

394 If the prospective creditor is already the applicant's banker or building society, they will have the advantage of already-available internal information. Similar considerations favour applications to increase revolving credit limits.

395 For the lender's contractual duty of confidentiality to the borrower, see para 7.03. For the bankers' Code of Practice as to confidentiality, see para 3.13. This is in effect what happens in the CIFAS system: see para 8.38. For improvements in data-sharing, see para 3.29.

396 Too long a delay for further checks might risk breaching the TDA, s 14 (see para 4.15) or the CCA, s 46 (see para 8.28).

397 The fact that an applicant has unsuccessfully applied for credit is likely to leave a footprint on his credit record, from which adverse inferences may be drawn by a subsequent credit-searcher. To the debtor, this is a disadvantage in obtaining multiple quotes (see para 8.32).

398 This may be indicated by a credit score which shows too low a 'profitability' score (see para 8.39).

399 E.g. identity thieves, as by card skimming (see para 2.23); long-firm frauds ([2003] 6 *Credit Today* 15); the dead (2005) 59 CC6/32); and see generally, para 10.15. The proposed National Identity Card (as above) and access to the death roll might help creditors, as may more vigorous application of the DPA, to obtain information (see para 3.27).

400 So far, the only government step in this direction is to allow the OFT to consider affordability enquiries in renewing credit licences (see CCA, new s 25(2B): see para 6.19).

ability to pay,[401] this already being a 'duty' under some codes of practice (see para 3.12).

**[8.37] Credit reference bureaux**. These bureaux are in business to provide information about the financial standing (credit status) of credit-seekers,[402] whether businesses or individuals.[403] Their effectiveness has been enhanced by the advent of major computers, which has rendered feasible in this field the collection of an enormous amount of information about credit status on a nationwide basis.[404] The capacity to store much fuller information, both favourable and adverse ('white' and 'black' data: see para 3.26), has led to the development of what are called 'payment profile services' (see para 8.39). This has three results. *First*, credit-seekers are effectively allowed under a single identity a maximum of one free bite at the credit industry: the registration of sufficient adverse information with such a bureau will normally ensure that further credit is virtually never granted to that name;[405] and a favourable payment record is likely to have the opposite effect.[406] *Second*, it enables creditors to stratify applicants according to credit risk: a good credit risk is said to establish credit 'status'; and a bad credit-risk is said to be 'non-status', e.g. those with outstanding CCJs and a poor employment history. This status helps determine whether credit will be granted and on what terms.[407] *Third*, the acquisition of information clashes with the *Tournier* rules (see para 7.03), whilst its storage raises the following issues.

The consequent power wielded by these credit bureaux was responsible for the inclusion of some special provisions in the CCA (see below) and later for some more generalised controls in the DPA 1984. When the DPA 1998 came into force, the statutory duties to disclose data held on individuals (not corporate bodies) was divided as follows: partnerships and unincorporated bodies will be dealt with under the CCA (see below); private individuals and sole traders will fall under the DPA (see para 8.38). There is, of course, a contradiction between the following two policies: requiring the creditor to make sufficient pre-contract checks to discourage overindebtedness (see para 6.10); and protecting the privacy of consumers against disclosure of their personal information to creditors, by way of the Human Rights Act and CCA/DPA.[408]

---

401  See paras 5.11–12. For affordability metrics, see [2004] 5 *Credit Today* 20. But for current legal impediments to this, see para 8.38.

402  Hence, many offers/advertisements are expressed to be 'subject to status'. For conditional offers, see para 10.02.

403  Only non-profit-making bureaux may be protected by qualified privilege: Clerk and Lindsell on *Tort*, 18th edn, para 22-128. See further, Crowther Report, para 9.1.23.

404  Perhaps that information should include DMPs (see para 5.42) and consolidation loans (see para 7.04A).

405  E.g. unsatisfied judgments (see para 3.22). These do not fall within the purview of the Access to Personal Files Act 1987. For credit repair firms, see para 3.23.

406  There seems to be a consensus on the sharing of adverse information to check actual credit applications (but not as a marketing tool—termed 'pre-screening'), though less willingness to share favourable information. See FLA, *1995 AR* 16.

407  For non-status loans, see para 7.04A. For the different types of contracts likely to be offered to applicants of different financial status, see para 24.49. By 2003, about 20% of UK adults had been barred by the credit industry: (2003) 57 CC5/40.

408  The HRA was used to restrict access to the electoral roll: see para 3.26. See also [2004] 2 *Which?* 25.

*Credit reference agencies.* Following the recommendations of the Crowther Report (paras 9.1.16–23), the CCA placed some controls on what it termed a 'credit reference agency'.[409] Any agency which satisfies these criteria requires a Category F licence (see para 6.15). Where a credit reference agency is involved in any transaction, ss 157–60 of the CCA (as amended) stipulate a number of steps, whose details are elaborated by regulations.[410]

1. *Discovering the agency.* One of the greatest difficulties of the disappointed individual seeking credit or hire facilities is to discover why he has been turned down. Whilst he has no right to such facilities (see para 8.35), his rejection may be caused by information from the agency. To meet this case, s 157(1) provides the debtor or hirer with a statutory right to know of any credit reference agency consulted during the antecedent negotiations.

2. *File disclosure.* Armed with the foregoing information, the disappointed applicant for credit or hire can approach the identified agency and obtain a copy of the information held on him.[411]

3. *File rectification.* Upon disclosure of the agency's file, the 'objector' may discover that it contains inaccurate information. If he considers this to be prejudicial to him,[412] then amended s 159 affords him a procedure for having the inaccurate information removed or amended.

Failure to comply with these rules amounts to an offence;[413] but otherwise the state of affairs gives rise to no statutory right of action (s 170(1)), though there may sometimes be a possible action in defamation or negligence (see para 8.36).

**[8.38] Data Protection Act 1998 (DPA): individuals.** Not only has the consumer no right to credit (see para 8.35), it is plainly desirable to minimise over-indebtedness amongst consumers.[414] To do this, the prospective creditor needs to be aware of the prospective debtor's existing commitments, a matter controlled by the DPA where the 'personal data' relates to a 'living individual' (see para 3.27). Under the 1998 Act, data on partnerships, etc, will be dealt with under the CCA provisions (see para 8.37); and the administration of both sets of provisions will be conducted by the Data Protection Commissioner, now the Information Commissioner (IC).

The IC takes the view that both credit reference bureaux and the financiers who use their services are 'data controllers' within the 1998 Act (see para 3.27). Information submitted by creditors and collected by bureaux must comply with the

---

409 The complicated expression is defined in ss 145(8) and 189(1): for discussion, see 1st edn, para 8.37.
410 Consumer Credit (Conduct of Business) (Credit Reference Agency) Regulations, 1977 SI 330 (as amended); Consumer Credit (Credit Reference Agency) Regulations, 2000 SI 290.
411 Under ss 158 (private individuals) and 160 (small traders). The latter may not be entitled to know the source of filed information.
412 E.g. record of a CCJ which has been paid (is this defamatory?).
413 Ss 157(3), 158(4), 159(6), 160(6), 167 and Sched 1; and see further, Chap 28.
414 The Younger Committee concluded that checking creditworthiness prevented reckless or dishonest people from obtaining credit, kept down overheads and prices by reducing bad debts and stimulated trade by facilitating the ready granting of credit in appropriate cases: *Report on the Committee on Privacy* (1972, Cmnd. 5012) 78.

Data Protection Principles.[415] This is particularly relevant to credit scoring (see para 8.39). An example of the effectiveness of the DPA concerns the industry practice of filing information by address: because this may result in the disclosure of information about third parties, e.g. persons previously living at the address, the Data Protection Tribunal prohibited such practices as breaching the *First Data Protection Principle*.[416] The IC has also forcefully argued that the collection of favourable and adverse information (see para 8.36) are both within the DPA.[417] But, in practice, these rules are not used against industry systems designed to combat fraud.[418] The following Data Protection Principles also seem particularly relevant to credit bureaux (see para 3.28):

> *The fourth principle* requires a bureau to correct any errors in the data held of which it becomes aware.[419] In case of doubt, use could be made of a credit information service (see para 6.15) or an approach could be made to the IC.

> *The sixth principle* grants a right of access by the data subject to all personal data held on him.[420]

In *Durant v FSA*,[421]

> D, having been in unsuccessful litigation with a bank (B) and complained about B to the FSA (see para 3.02), sought disclosure under s 7 of the DPA from the FSA of 'personal data' (see para 3.27) about him revealed to it by B and held on both computerised and manual files with a view to re-opening the issue of B's conduct. The FSA resisted disclosing such information on its manual files on the grounds that the information was not 'personal', nor the file 'part of a relevant filing system'.

The Court of Appeal unanimously refused D's application, holding that not all information retrieved against an individual's name was 'personal data':[422] it accepted that a purpose of the DPA was to apply the same standard of accessibility to manual filing systems as to computerised records; but it applied its discretion under s 7(9) to reject what it saw as a misguided attempt to use s 7 as a means of third-party discovery against B rather than of establishing the accuracy of the information held on D. On the basis of this decision, the IC has issued guidance that, where an individual's name appears in information, the name will only be 'personal data' where its inclusion in the information affects the named individual's

---

415  See para 3.26. On the application of those Principles, see DPC, *Guidance Notes on Default*.

416  The Tribunal amended the enforcement notices issued by the DPR: see *CCN Systems Ltd v DPR* (1992) and the subsequent cases set out in Charlton and Gaskill, *Encyclopedia of Data Protection*, Pt 6, para 030, *et seq.*

417  The Registrar argues that both may only be obtained with the subject's consent; and that consent is subject to the UTCC Regulations (see para 11.12): DPA, *Guidance on Credit Referencing*, 1996.

418  The 'Principle of Reciprocity'. E.g. the Gone Away Information Network (GAIN), the Credit Industry Fraud Avoidance System (CIFAS: see (1994) 49 CC 2/23, 31; (2002) 4 *Credit Today* 7; and para 3.26).

419  More than one in ten files contained errors: [2000] 9 *Which?* 9; [2003] 9 *Which?* 5.

420  See DPA 1998, Sched 1, Pt 2, para 8. See further ss 7, 10, 11 and 12: para 3.27.

421  [2004] CLY 1551, [2004] EWCA Civ 1746, CA (see 59 CC1/19). Whilst the HL has refused leave to appeal (see (2005) 60 CC4/41), the EU has issued a notice of intended proceedings against the UK for failure to implement the Data Protection Directive (94/46: see para 3.27): see (2005) 155 NLJ 1870.

422  Since then, there has come into force the wider provisions of the Freedom of Information Act 2000 as to the meaning of 'personal data' (see para 3.27).

privacy, ie he is the focus of the information; and that the DPA will only extend to manual files (a 'relevant filing system') where they are sufficiently sophisticated to provide similar accessibility as computerised files and hence the DPA will extend to few manual files.

*The seventh principle* requires the user or bureau to take appropriate security measures against (a) unauthorised access or (b) accidental loss of the data.[423]

**[8.39] Credit Scoring.**[424] Traditionally, lenders tried to minimise bad debt by finding out as much as they could about individual applicants, concentrating on 'the three Cs' (see para 8.35). This was done on the premise that the behaviour of new applicants will closely resemble that of similar previous applicants (see below). Its weakness was the inability to predict extraneous events closely associated with default, e.g. family break-up, redundancy, serious injury.[425] To cope with huge increases in volume, modern lenders have standardised these procedures into a process known as 'credit scoring', which is inevitably more remote and impersonal. Large volume lenders usually computerise the process, normally on the back of computer-based accounting and management systems.

*The technique.* In essence, credit scoring seeks to harness two streams of information as a credit-granting tool:

(a) A statistical analysis of a large number of existing accounts, with numerical values assigned to pieces of information found significant in determining payment record, e.g. age of debtor, deposit percentage, householder or tenant.[426] This body of data has the advantage of objectivity. Yet, it only deals in probability, whilst ignoring the applicant's willingness to pay.

(b) Personal information about the applicant. Much of this he will supply on an Application Form (see para 8.35). But more about his personal credit history will be obtained from a credit reference agency (see paras 8.36–8); and lenders of large sums may also run checks with other third parties, e.g. bank (see para 7.03), or employer. Most checks will so far as possible usually be done by the lender's computer automatically and on-line calling up the agency's computer. If accurate,[427] this will say much about the applicant's ability to pay; but there remains a reluctance to ask too many questions as to the affordability of the proposal to the applicant.[428] The lender's system then constructs a score card for the applicant from the points he achieves in respect of each scoring piece

---

423 See DPA 1998, Sched 1, Pt 1, para 7. See further, para 3.28.

424 See generally the OFT document, *Credit Scoring* (2000): see Goode, *Consumer Credit Law & Practice*, VIII, Pt A, para 7.

425 Some of these risks can be reduced by credit insurance (see para 24.48). But this does create a problem in detecting over-indebtedness, as to which see para 6.10.

426 For maximum effectiveness, each lender needs to assess his own (unique) lending experience; and then keep that assessment updated (monitoring).

427 The agency file on the applicant may be inaccurate from fraud (despite CIFAS and GAIN) or from innocent input, or insufficient e.g. where a judgment debt was paid, or manipulated, e.g. by credit repair (see para 27.03).

428 The industry tends to regard too many detailed questions about the applicant's income and expenditure as over-intrusive ((2006) 60 CC5/9: see para 3.29), which may contribute to over-indebtedness (see para 6.10).

of information and hence whether he attains an overall pass score.[429] Too harsh a scheme leads to rejection of too many good credit risks, whereas too lenient a scheme would tend to produce too many bad debts, e.g. the over-indebted (see para 6.10).

*Credit and behaviour scoring.* A lender will undertake 'application scoring' at the outset of a fixed-sum transaction, e.g. direct selling, hp, mail order, personal loan. However, with regard to running account credit, the lender can also take advantage of the continuing credit characteristics of the debtor, e.g. his payment record or average balance in what has become known as 'behaviour scoring', e.g. credit cards, charge cards, overdrafts. This is a 'statistically derived assessment of the future risk of a current customer'[430] and has been found to be highly predictive of future performance.

*Control of scoring systems.* Generally, the law is in favour of such systems because they are so effective in minimising fraud and over-indebtedness.[431] Yet that very effectiveness has led to statutory intervention with regard to the construction and operation of scoring systems. Controls on construction of the system deal with direct or indirect discrimination;[432] and data protection rules control both the lender and credit reference agency whose automatic processing 'significantly' affect the applicant (DPA, s 12(1)(d) and (1)), which expression presumably includes credit-granting. Controls on the operations of the system are aimed at the following: providing individuals with a general description of how the credit-scoring system works (DPA, s 7); granting the applicant the right to see, and if necessary correct, his credit record;[433] ensuring that the automatic scoring process is subject to review by a human being;[434] and the entire regime for the storage of personal data on a computer, e.g. third-party information (see para 8.38). Additionally, the OFT have inspired *The Guide to Credit Scoring*, which covers a large number of other matters in the operation of credit scoring systems.[435] The new Draft Directive may require the creditor to undertake adequate pre-contract credit scoring (see para 5.12).

---

429 For a simple explanation of the complicated mathematical system of creating a score-card, see [2002] 11 *Credit Today Extra*, p XVII.

430 OFT, *Op. cit.*, para 4.10. Thus, it is both a credit-granting and management tool, so it can also be used after default to predict the recoverability of judgment (see para 27.04) and to detect stolen cards from uncharacteristic spending patterns.

431 As to fraud, see CIFAS and GAIN (para 8.38); and as to overindebtedness, see above.

432 E.g. red-lining (see OFT, *Op. cit.*, paras 5.35–47). For a word of caution, see OFT, *Vulnerable Consumers and Financial Services* (1999) para 612. As to discrimination, see para 4.23; and as to the unfitness to hold a credit licence, see para 6.18.

433 See CCA, ss 157–60 (see para 8.37); and the Sixth Data Protection Principal (see para 8.38).

434 DPA, s 12. But the decision whether to grant credit is exempt: ss 12(4)–(7).

435 This 1993 code is set out in Annex C of the OFT *Credit Scoring* (see above).

# CHAPTER 9

# FORMALITIES OF THE AGREEMENT

**[9.01] Introduction**. With regard to the formalities required in a simple contract for the supply of goods, a sharp contrast may be observed between the SGA and the CCA. As to ordinary sales within the SGA, required formalities are the exception (see para 9.02, *et seq*.); but, in the case of regulated transactions, compliance with extensive formalities is seen as an essential measure of consumer protection and is therefore the norm (see para 9.06, *et seq*.). In the absence of the consideration necessary for a simple contract,[1] ownership of goods may be transferred by gift[2] or deed.

*Deeds*. Whether or not supported by consideration,[1] a formal promise made in a deed will be enforced by the courts,[3] subject to the defence of *non est factum* (see para 10.16) and a special limitation period (see para 26.17). However, the law relating to the formalities required of a deed was amended by statute in 1989. First, the requirement of a seal has been partially abolished: for the execution of a deed by an individual, statute now requires only that the instrument makes it clear on its face that it is intended to be a deed and that it be signed and witnessed;[4] whereas, for execution of a deed by a registered company, another statute requires the deed to be described as such and signed or sealed.[5] Second, there has been repealed the famous s 40 of the LPA requiring the sale or other disposition of an interest in land to be evidenced in writing (see para 9.03).

## ORDINARY SUPPLIES

**[9.02] The SGA**. The common law required no special formalities in the conclusion of a contract of sale,[6] but the SGA 1893 mentioned two such cases; namely, where one of the parties was a corporation[7] or the price was £10 or more.[8] The modern rule is to be found in s 4(1) of the SGA and provides as follows:

---

1    See para 10.01.
2    As to gifts, see para 2.08.
3    See generally *Chitty on Contracts*, 28th edn, Vol 1, para 1-042, *et seq*.
4    By the Law of Property (Miscellaneous Provisions) Act 1989, s 1. See (1989) 105 LQR 553–5.
5    Ss 36 and 36A of the Companies Act 1985, as substituted by s 130 of the Companies Act 1989.
6    But the parties may seek to impose special formalities, as where one indicates that he will only contract by signature on standard terms: as to standard terms, see generally, para 11.08; and as to formation by signature, see para 10.02.
7    SGA 1893, s 3, itself imposed no formalities whatsoever but simply referred to other legislation which has required no formalities for some time: Companies Act 1948, s 32 (now CA 1985, s 36); Corporate Bodies' Contracts Act 1960 (as amended).
8    SGA 1893, s 4, which embodied the old Statute of Frauds rule requiring such sales to be evidenced in writing. It was repealed by s 1 of the Law Reform (Enforcement of Contracts) Act 1954.

'Subject to this[9] and any other Act,[10] a contract of sale may be made in writing (either with or without seal), or by word of mouth, or partly in writing and partly by word of mouth, or may be implied from the conduct of the parties'.

Certain formalities are, however, required for sales of goods which also fall within the following categories:[11]

1. Regulated conditional or credit sales (see para 9.06, *et seq*.).

2. Sales of an interest in land (see para 9.03).

3. Documentary sales to individuals are caught by the Bills of Sale Acts and must also comply with the rules there laid down, subject to the following distinction:

    (a) In essence, the Bills of Sale Act 1978 applies to documentary sales; that is, sales recorded in writing (a bill of sale) where there is no transfer of possession from seller to buyer. Such absolute transfers fall within the SGA (SGA, s 62(3)) and must also comply with the formalities of the 1878 Act). They are relevant to insolvency of the seller (see para 19.22).

    (b) The Bills of Sale Act 1882 applies only to sales by way of mortgages, or non-absolute transfers. Such transactions are outside the SGA (s 62(4)). However, they must currently comply with the archaic 1882 Act, which is intended to protect the buyer/borrower (see para 25.26).

4. Sales of a ship. Under the Merchant Shipping Act 1995, sale of an interest in a British ship must be in the prescribed form and registered, there being a simplified system for small ships.[12]

5. Sale of an aircraft. There are special rules for the sale of an interest in an aircraft, which must be registered with the Civil Aviation Authority.[13]

6. Caravans. Site licences for touring and holiday caravans are subject only to the ordinary rules[14] but there are special provisions governing licences to park residential caravans.[15]

7. Auctions. Auctioneers are required to display at auctions their name and addresses, and also copies of the Auctions (Bidding Agreements) Acts.[16]

8. Pyramid selling. Regulations made under the FTA require that each distributor enter a written contract and be given a copy of it (see para 1.09).

9. Goods subject to special statutory regimes, such as firearms (see para 4.31) or motor vehicles.[17]

---

9 The reference is otiose: *Benjamin's Sale of Goods*, 6th edn, para 2-021.

10 'Nothing in this section affects the law relating to corporations' (s 4(2)); as to which, see fn 7, above.

11 The blind and partially sighted have protection in respect of documents by the Disability Discrimination Act 1995 (see para 4.23).

12 Likewise a mortgage of a ship, so that there is a registration system for ship sales and mortgages.

13 See further, Goode, *HP Law & Practice*, 132D. These rules do not apply to very small aircraft, e.g. models.

14 Principally, that site licences and ancillary contracts are governed by the UTCCR: see OFT, *Guidance on unfair terms in holiday caravan agreements* (2005); and see para 11.12, *et seq*.

15 Caravan Sites etc. Act 1960 (as amended); Mobile Homes Act 1983 (as amended); and see *Howard v Charlton* [2002] CLY 3641, CA. Such parking does not constitute a bailment (see para 1.17).

16 Auctioneers Act 1845, s 7; and as to the Auction (Bidding Agreements) Acts, see para 10.13.

17 The DVLC (see para 6.02) requires the submission of signed transfer forms.

10. Consumer supply contracts (see para 11.12A) must be drafted legibly in plain English (UTCC, reg 6: see para 11.13) and may be unfair if important terms are given insufficient prominence (Grey Term 1(i): see para 11.17).

11. Distance sales (see paras 9.04–5) and doorstep sales (see para 10.36).

**[9.03] Goods and land.** In place of the old rule requiring dispositions of an interest in land (see para 19.02) to be **evidenced** in writing (LPA 1925, s 40; repealed), the Law of Property (Miscellaneous Provisions) Act 1989 now requires that the 'sale or other disposition of an interest in land can only be **made** in writing' and must incorporate or refer to all the terms which the parties have expressly agreed.[18] 'Disposition' extends to contracts to grant a mortgage or charge,[19] so that it is no longer possible to have a valid charge created by a mere deposit of deeds.[20]

As there is now no similar rule in relation to sale of goods (see para 9.02), this requires a line to be drawn between sales of interests in land (within the LPA) and sales of goods (within the SGA).[21] One view is that there is no overlap between the LPA and SGA because a contract in respect of something which is attached to, or part of the land, is always a sale of goods because it is sold with a view to its ultimate severance. Another view is that the word 'goods' may have a different meaning under the SGA from that under the LPA, so that one transaction may be both a sale of goods within the SGA and a sale of an interest in land within the LPA.[22] For the present purposes, the definitions of 'goods' (see para 2.02) give rise to several problems:

1. *Crops, trees, etc.* It is said that, for the purposes of the SGA, sales of such emblements and industrial growing crops will almost always be sales of goods, 'since the agreement between the parties must be that they shall be severed (from the land) either "before sale" or "under the contract of sale" as provided by s 61(1)'.[23]

2. *Fixtures.* As will be seen later (see para 25.23), where a chattel is annexed to land so as to become a fixture, at common law it generally becomes the property of the owner of the land and the title of its previous owner is extinguished.[24] If the owner of the land agrees with X that X shall build, e.g. a wall, or attach a fixture, e.g. central heating, on terms that no property is to pass until affixed, for most purposes this is not a sale of goods to the landowner,[25] but a contract for work and materials (see para 2.05) annexed to the land (see above). However, if the landowner subsequently severs either a fixture, or part of the building, which he then sells, it is a sale of goods, e.g. an old boiler, or slate roof.

---

18 S 2. See *Benjamin's Sale of Goods*, 6th edn, para 1-092; Annand (1989) 105 LQR at 555–8; Greed (1990) 140 NLJ 296.

19 S 2(6). As to fittings sold with land, see *Wright v Robert Leonard (Developments)* [1994] NPC 49, CA (lease of show-flat to include furniture and fixtures); and see below.

20 *United Bank of Kuwait v Sahib* [1996] 3 All ER 215, CA (see 113 LQR 533).

21 There is also a difference in the application of UCTA: see para 18.17.

22 Atiyah, *Sale of Goods*, 10th edn, 71–2.

23 See *Benjamin, Op. cit.*, para 1-093. Is this the explanation of 'pick-your-own-strawberries'?

24 *Reynolds v Ashby & Son* [1904] AC 446, HL (hirer of machinery fixed it to floor).

25 See *Benjamin, Op. cit.*, para 1-096, suggesting that some SGA provisions may nevertheless apply to the transaction.

3.  *Minerals, gravel, soil, etc.* These are not merely 'attached to' the land, but part of it. If the landowner has himself already severed the minerals, etc, before contracting to sell them, or if he agrees to do so before the property is to pass, there is a sale of goods.[26] However, the courts have had more difficulty if the severance is to be done by the buyer: in the case of trees, it has been held to be a sale of goods;[27] but in the case of cinders and slag, there has been held not to be a sale of goods, but a sale of an interest in land.[28]

**[9.04] Distance supplies of goods and services**. Whether the private consumer is dealing by phone, internet or mail order, the Distance Selling Regulations may apply (see para 8.17). Leaving aside internet supplies (see para 9.05) and sales of financial services (see below), the Distance Selling Regulations require that the distance supplier shall provide to the consumer information divided into two distinct waves, which the Directive describes as 'prior information' and 'written confirmation' (Arts 4 and 5).

*First wave (prior) information.* 'In good time prior to the conclusion of the contract',[29] he will supply all the following information (reg 7(1)(a)) in a medium unspecified (see below):

(i)     the identity of the supplier and, where the contract requires payment in advance, the supplier's address.[30]

(ii)    a description of the main characteristics of the goods or services.[31]

(iii)   the price of all goods or services including all taxes.[32]

(iv)    delivery costs where appropriate.[33]

(v)     the arrangements for payment, delivery or performance.[34]

(vi)    the existence of any[35] right of cancellation (see para 10.38).

(vii)   the cost of using the means of distance communication where it is calculated other than at the basic rate, e.g. premium-rate telephone call.

(viii)  the period for which the offer or the price remains valid.

---

26  See *Benjamin, Op. cit.*, para 1-097.

27  *Kursell v Timber Operators Ltd* (set out at para 20.04).

28  *Morgan v Russell & Sons* [1909] 1 KB 357, DC; *Mills v Stockman* (1966–7) 116 CLR 61 (Aust HC: waste dumped from a slate quarry).

29  'In the case of a telephone communication, the identity of the supplier and the commercial purpose of the call shall be made clear at the beginning of the conversation with the consumer': reg 7(4).

30  For the problems of advance payment, see para 23.22.

31  How, if at all, does this differ from the identity test for the implied term as to description (see para 13.13)?

32  As to price, see para 2.06. 'Services' originally included credit; but there are separate provisions for financial services (below). A provision allowing price increases after contract breaches this rule and is unfair: OFT, *Bulletin No. 24*, case 48; and see para 11.16.

33  This is because delivery will usually be at the consumer's home. As to the delivery rules, see para 23.04.

34  Why only one of these arrangements? Performance must be within 30 days (reg 19: see para 23.04). As to payment cards, see reg 21 (see paras 7.07A and 7.13). A delivery estimate may be unfair: OFT, *Bulletin No. 24*, case 48.

35  Following the Directive, this is ambiguous: what is to happen if there is no right of cancellation? For reform proposals, see DTI, *Consultation* (Jan 2004), paras 2.6–9.

(ix) where appropriate, the minimum duration of the contract, in the case of a contract for the supply of goods or services to be performed permanently or recurrently, e.g. a book club.

Further, if the supplier proposes, in the event of non-availability, to supply substitute goods or services, the consumer must be informed of this fact (reg 7(1)(b)) and that the supplier will bear the return-cost of returning the substitute (reg 7(1)(c)). Moreover, under reg 7(2) all this information must be provided in an appropriate 'clear and comprehensible manner' with due regard to the principles of commercial good faith (see para 11.15) and the protection of minors (see para 10.18).

*Second wave of information (confirmation).* Usually at a later stage (see below) 'the supplier shall provide to the consumer in writing or in another durable medium[36] which is available and accessible to the consumer' (reg 8(1) and (3)) certain stipulated information (see below) either:

'(a) prior to the conclusion of the contract, or

(b) thereafter, in good time and in any event—

(i) during the performance of the contract, in the case of services; and

(ii) at the latest at the time of delivery where goods not for delivery to third parties are concerned'.

So, in the case of goods, the second stage durable-medium information could be supplied either before acceptance (see para 10.02), e.g. a catalogue, or before delivery, e.g. in a posted acceptance or delivery note. The specified information is listed in reg 8(2) (as amended) as follows: items (i)–(vi) in reg 7(1) above; details of any right of cancellation;[37] the supplier's business address to receive complaints; and information about after-sales service and guarantees (see para 17.09), frequently in addition to that required under the SSG Regulations (see para 17.09B). However, the foregoing second wave rules do not apply where there is a one-off supply of services invoiced by means of distance communication (reg 9(1)), e.g. a service provided by telephone: in this case, the supplier must take 'all necessary steps' to ensure the consumer has his address so that he is able to make any complaints (reg 9(2)).[38]

*The distance supply of financial services.* There is contained in the Financial Services (Distance Marketing) Regulations, 2004 SI 2095 a separate scheme of pre-contract information to deal with the distance selling of financial services, e.g. credit (see para 9.06).[38]

**[9.05] Internet sales.** Commercial sales to consumers via the internet is a form of distance sale, but requires special consideration by reason of all the following (perhaps overlapping) legislation.

---

36 As to 'durable medium', cf. consumer guarantees, reg 15(3) (see para 17.09A).

37 Under regs 10–18: see para 10.38. The consumer must also be told the conditions and procedures for exercising any statutory right of cancellation, any obligation to return the goods and consequent cost he should bear (reg 8(2)(b)); any conditions for exercising any contractual right of cancellation (reg 8(2)(e)). As to cancellation of a contract of services, see reg 8(3); and reg 8(2)(b)(iii), inserted by 2005 SI 89, reg 1.

38 For overlap with the UCP Directive, see para 4.21A.

1.  *The Distance Selling Regulations.* Where a business concludes a contract with a consumer *via* a website (but not by e-mail: regs 9(4) and 11(3)), the transaction will usually be subject to the same first- and second-wave information requirements as ordinary distance supply of goods or services, or of financial services (see para 9.05). Thus, the website must contain the first-wave information; but, if the supplier wishes his internet offer to be available in more than one Member State, there may be difficulty in adequately stating the information. The second-stage information is likely to be provided by fax or letter; but an internet supply of services will fall within the reduced information requirements in reg 9(2).

2.  *E-Commerce Regulations.* The transaction must not only follow the general rules in the E-Commerce Regulations (see para 8.17A), but reg 9 requires that the supplier before contracting explain all the following matters to private consumers 'in a clear comprehensible and unambiguous manner' (reg 9(1)):

    (a)  The different technical steps to follow to conclude the contract.

    (b)  Whether or not the concluded contract will be filed[39] by the service provider and whether it will be accessible.[40]

    (c)  The technical means for identifying and correcting input errors prior to the placing of the order (see para 10.09A).

    (d)  The languages offered for the conclusion of the contract.

    (e)  Any relevant code of conduct to which the service provider subscribes and how it may be consulted electronically (reg 9(2)). For codes of conduct, see generally para 3.12.

3.  *Electronic signatures.* From the early 1990s, some Member States began to develop rules dealing with on-line authentication of signatures. Wishing to harmonise this field to prevent the proliferation of incompatible rules, the EU produced the Electronic Signatures Directive.[41] The UK implemented its minimum requirements in the Electronic Communications Act 2000,[42] which introduced two changes relevant to this work: s 7 clarifies that electronic signatures are admissible in court;[43] and ss 8–10 permits the 'appropriate Minister' by statutory order to modify the requirement of any statute or subordinate legislation that certain documents be in writing, replacing it with 'electronic communications or electronic storage';[44] and this has been used to allow the making of regulated agreements electronically.[45] This has achieved

---

39   The 'filing' referred to is a legal concept in other Member States. It would only apply in the UK where a UK consumer makes a website contract with a service provider established in those States.

40   It must be possible for the consumer to download the terms and conditions (reg 9(3)).

41   99/93. Set out in Goode, *Consumer Credit Law and Practice*, para 2.241. See Treitel, *Law of Contract*, 11th edn, 186–7; Wright (2006) 8 EBL 7.

42   See the Electronic Signature Regulations, 2002 SI 318 (see Anassuti, [2002] 1 CCLR at 338–9).

43   This would seem to be consistent with the provisions of the EU Electronic Signatures Directive (1999/93/EC). What if an electronic signature is stolen?

44   By s 15, 'electronic communication' is widely defined to include communication by phone or internet.

45   CCA (Electronic Communications) Order, 2004 SI 3236, reg 2, which so amends the CCA: see the definition of electronic transmission in new s 176A.

the following changes provided the consumer is computer-literate:[46] references in the CCA to sending documents 'by post' are replaced by 'an appropriate method';[47] written signatures will not be required where the agreement is made by electronic means;[48] electronic communications will *prima facie* be deemed to be delivered on the next working day after transmission; and in a number of CCA regulations,[49] though not those concerned with default notices, where it was thought important that the notice be in paper form (see para 24.28).

The maintenance of credit card security, both in terms of identifying the consumer and protecting his credit card details, should be enhanced by smart cards (see para 2.23) and through encryption.[50]

# REGULATED AGREEMENTS

## Introduction

**[9.06] The scope of controls**. The elaborate safeguards developed by owners ensured that hp agreements would usually be in writing (see para 1.20, *et seq.*); and in respect of hp, credit and conditional sale (see paras 1.13 and 1.14) the HP Acts 1938–65 developed a series of consumer safeguards relating to the formalities of the agreement. Most of these ideas, now extend to loans as well, are to be found in Pt V of the CCA, and may be classified as follows:

1.  Pre-contract disclosure (see para 9.08).

2.  The form and content of regulated agreements (see para 9.09).

3.  The execution of regulated agreements (see para 9.12, *et seq.*).

4.  Copies of regulated agreements (see para 9.14, *et seq.*).

5.  The withdrawal from prospective regulated agreements and cancellation of actual regulated agreements (see paras 9.17; 10.26, *et seq.*).

The Act provides some exemptions from the above rules (see para 9.07) and makes special provision for the situation where a regulated agreement is subsequently varied: even if the modifying agreement would not be regulated taken by itself, if it is for fixed-sum credit it will always be taken as regulated,[51] whereas this will not necessarily be the case with running-account credit;[52] and, if the earlier agreement

---

46   Under s 176A(1), the consumer must have agreed to e-communication and have the capacity to store such communications (inserted by reg 2(7)).

47   In CCA, s 63(3) (copies rules: see para 9.15); ss 64 and 69(7) (cancellation rights: see paras 9.17 and 10.31); s 176 (service of documents).

48   This is particularly important for signature boxes in CCA, s 61 (reg 2(2): see para 9.13).

49   E.g. Regulations on the Termination of Licences, (1976 SI 1002, reg 3: see para 6.24); Agreements (reg 4: see para 9.10); CNC (reg 6: see para 9.17).

50   Controlled by the Regulation of Investigatory Powers Act 2000.

51   S 82(3). E.g. if the amount of a fixed sum loan to a small business is increased beyond the ambit of the Act. As to variation of commercial agreements, see further, para 26.22.

52   See s 82(4): para 9.07. If the credit limit permanently exceeds the ambit of the Act, the agreement is no longer regulated and falls outside Pt V; but, if the credit limit is only temporarily exceeded, it remains regulated and within Pt V. How temporary is 'temporary'?

was cancellable, any modifying agreement made within the cancellation period will also be cancellable.[53] The effect of non-compliance with all these rules is considered later (para 9.19). In 2003 the White Paper *Fair, Clear and Competitive*[54] proposed substantial amendments to the Regulations to ensure consumers are aware of the small print (see para 9.09, *et seq.*); to require key financial particulars to be given to consumers before contracting (see para 9.08); and to enable the making of agreements in electronic form (see para 9.05).

*The distance supply of financial services.* As has already been seen (see para 8.17), there is contained in the Financial Services (Distance Marketing) Regulations, 2004 SI 2095, a separate scheme of pre-contract information to deal with the distance selling of financial services, e.g. credit. In such cases, the required pre-contract information is very similar to that required for distance supplies of goods (see para 9.04) and likewise stipulates for two waves of information:

(1) First wave (prior) information (reg 7(1)) must include certain extra information specified in Sched 1. All this must be done in a clear, comprehensible and appropriate manner to the means of communication and with due regard for the principles of good faith (reg 7(2)). The supplier must make his commercial purpose clear (reg 7(3)), though there are special rules for 'voice telephone communication' (reg 7(4) and Sched 2). The information supplied must accurately reflect the contractual obligations which would arise (reg 7(5)).

(2) Second wave (additional information). Either before or immediately after the formation of the contract, all the prior information, together with the terms of the contract, must be communicated to the consumer on paper 'or in another durable medium' (reg 8(1)). On request, for the duration of the contract the supplier must usually communicate to the consumer subsequent paper copies,[55] except where a copy has previously been sent and the terms have not changed.[56]

As many, but not all, such transactions may be governed by the amended CCA (see para 5.11), it is intended to dovetail the two sets of requirements.[57] For overlap with the UCP Directive, see para 4.21A.

[9.07] **Exemptions from Part V**. According to s 74 of the CCA (as amended), the following categories of regulated agreement (see para 5.13) are not caught by any of the provisions of Pt V of the Act except for those as to pre-contract information (s 55: see para 9.08) and agency (s 56: see para 16.08).

1. *Non-commercial agreements* (s 74(1)(a): see para 5.18).

2. *Small DCS agreements for RU credit.* Thus, regulated transactions such as small credit sales (£50: see para 1.13) may be made wholly orally (s 74(2)); but, insofar

---

53  S 82(5). But not necessarily otherwise: s 82(6). As to cancellable agreements, see para 10.29.

54  See DTI, *the Consumer Credit Market in the 21st Century* (Dec 2003, Cm. 6040), paras 2.18–21.

55  Reg 8(2). *Prima facie*, the consumer may request a change in the means of distance communication (reg 8(4)). For subsequent copies of regulated agreements generally, see para 15.16.

56  Reg 8(3). So, in a running-account contract where the terms may change from time to time, a copy of each changed term must be sent.

57  DTI, *Review of the CCA: Electronic Agreements*, 2002, 8–9.

as any part of them is expressed in writing, that part must comply with the Pt V rules as to form and contents.[58]

3.  *Small cancellable agreements*. Whereas the Doorstop-selling Regulations provide for the cancellation of **cash** transactions in excess of a lower limit on the doorstep (see para 10.36), the CCA, s 74(2A), provides a matching lower limit (£35) for the application to doorstep **credit** transactions of the CCA cancellation provisions.[59]

4.  *Overdrafts*.[60] These will be exempt from Pt V only if the OFT so determines,[61] though a distinction is now drawn according to whether or not it is a bank overdraft:

    (a) Bank overdrafts. There is a presumption in favour of such a determination unless it thinks it would be against the public interest.[62] Further, there is an outright exemption where a bank on one occasion honours a cheque above an agreed overdraft limit (s 82(4)).

    (b) Other overdrafts, e.g. in-store budget accounts, finance company revolving credit schemes. These may be exempted only if the OFT is of the opinion that this is not against the interest of debtors.[63]

5.  *Agreements to finance payments on death*. Insofar as made orally,[58] these rather specialised agreements[64] may be exempted from Pt V, but only if the OFT so determines[61] and it is not against the interest of debtors.[63]

Finally, there should be noticed the effect of this system on modifying agreements[65] and house mortgages. House-purchase mortgages are outside most of the CCA other than the advertisement rules (see s 43(1): para 8.29); but regulated mortgages can only escape Pt V by reason of the rules of this paragraph (see also para 10.27).

**[9.08] Pre-contract disclosure**. In pursuance of the objective of truth-in-lending (see para 5.08), the CCA took steps to make creditors and owners disclose the costs charged for their services (APR) at three separate stages (see para 8.21). Because some creditors and owners were refusing to disclose their terms before

---

58  S 74(4) (as amended). Subject to the ordinary dispensing power under s 60(3): see para 9.09. For the special cancellation rule, see s 74(2A) and para 10.29.

59  See para 10.28, *et seq*. There is no lower limit as regards the cancellation of distance contracts (see para 10.38).

60  This term is not defined in the CCA, but should perhaps be read as referring to running account credit (as to which, see para 5.28): Karpinski and Fielding, *Consumer Credit Agreements*, para 7.11. Was this a drafting slip? Some such overdrafts will also fall within the Doorstep-selling Regulations: see para 10.36.

61  It may exempt on such conditions as it sees fit: s 74(3)(a). For such determinations, see *Coutts & Co v Sebestyen* [2005] EWCA 473, CA; and Goode, *Consumer Credit Law & Practice*, Division IV.

62  S 74(3A), inserted by the Banking Act 1979, s 38. Even if that contradicts the interests of debtors. The consequent lack of written record of a loan may cause later difficulties: see Banking Ombudsman, *Annual Review 1990/91*, para 4.3.

63  Amended ss 74(3) and 183. Thus, the Act discriminates with regard to test and burden of proof against overdrafts offered by, e.g. building societies, department stores and smaller finance companies.

64  E.g. for court fees for probate. For the scope of this exemption, see Goode, *Op. cit.*, para 30.17.

65  S 82(3). See also s 82(4) (above). As to the CCA restrictions on modifying agreements, see generally, para 26 22; and as to cancellation of modifying agreements, see para 10.32.

the prospective debtor or hirer signed, in 2003 the White Paper *Fair, Clear and Competitive*[66] proposed an increase of these requirements, including 'Schumer' boxes (see below), a 'wealth warning' on secured loans (see para 8.30), examples of early settlements (see para 26.19A), information about the right to cancel (see para 10.28) and all the information required on a distance supply of financial services (see para 9.06).

*The pre-contract information document.* This is an idea from the United States that, before entering the credit agreement, the consumer should be presented with the key financial information so that he may compare a proposal with others being offered: they are termed *'Schumer'* or *'honesty'* boxes. In 2004, the UK adapted it in the form of a separate compulsory[67] document by Regulations.[68] These apply in respect of all regulated agreements except those where a separate pre-contract document is already required; namely (reg 2):

(a)  land mortgage advance copies (see para 10.27); and

(b)  'distance contracts' (reg 1(2): see para 8.17) prior information (see para 9.06).

**Before** the making of a regulated agreement within these rules, the creditor or owner must disclose to the debtor or hirer in the manner set out below 'the information[69] and statements of protection and remedies' that are required to be given as follows:[70]

1.  *Consumer credit agreements.* There must be set out all the information required to be included in such a regulated agreement under reg 2 of the Agreement Regulations (see para 9.11), e.g. certain examples of early settlement rebates (see para 26.19A).

2.  *Consumer hire agreements.* There must be set out all the information required to be included in such a regulated agreement under reg 3 of the Agreement Regulations. According to reg 4, this information must be easily legible, not interspersed with any other information,[71] of equal prominence and contained in a document[72] which 'is separate from the document embodying the' prospective or actual regulated agreement,[73] is headed *Pre-contract Information* and may be taken away by the debtor or hirer. Accordingly, this document

---

66  See DTI, *The Consumer Credit Market in the 21st Century* (Dec 2003, Cm. 6040), paras 2.20–3. The White Paper also wishes to encourage consumers to shop around without impairing their credit status by leaving 'credit application footprints' (see para 2.24).

67  Distinguish the old voluntary quotations (see para 8.32). APACS had already gone some way to voluntarily introducing Schumer boxes in marketing literature: [2003] 12 *Which?* 16.

68  Consumer Credit (Disclosure of Information) Regulations, 2004 SI 1481.

69  The information will usually be that which must be included in the prospective agreement; but, where that information is then unknown 'the creditor or owner shall disclose estimated information based on such assumptions as he may reasonably make' (reg 3(2)).

70  Reg 3(1). There are special rules for modifying agreements (see para 26.22): see reg 3(1)(c) and (d).

71  So it cannot be the Application Form (see para 8.35).

72  The document must be 'on paper or on another durable medium' (reg 4(d)(iv)); and 'durable medium' is defined (reg 1(2)) as a medium which allows him to store and access it, e.g. his home computer.

73  What reg 4(d) terms the 'relevant agreement' and reg 3 makes clear is to be the prospective or actual regulated agreement (depending on which side is to sign first).

(which need not be signed)[74] must be separate from the executed agreement (CCA, s 63(1): see para 9.14) and signature copy (CCA, s 62(1) and (2): see paras 9.15–16). But it would appear that there is nothing to inhibit instant credit: a consumer may on the same occasion be given the *Pre-contract Information* and the signature copy (see paras 9.15–16) in the same pack.

Unless this *Pre-contract Information* is so provided, the CCA says that the consequent regulated agreement is not properly executed (s 55(2)), with the consequences considered later (see para 9.19), but no others (s 170(1): see para 10.19). However, on behalf of consumers generally, it may also be possible to obtain an Enforcement Order (see para 6.08).

## Form and content of agreements

**[9.09]** Following its usual strategy, the CCA does not itself spell out any requirements. Instead, s 60(1) enables the Secretary of State to 'make regulations as to the form and contents of documents embodying[75] regulated agreements' (see para 9.10). However, such regulations will not extend to agreements exempted from Pt V of the Act (see para 9.07). Additionally, the OFT is empowered (s 60(3)) upon application of any consumer credit or consumer hire business (see para 6.12) to relieve[76] by notice[77] that business from any such regulations insofar as it appears to the OFT to be impracticable[78] for the applicant to comply with any requirement 'in a particular case'.[79] If a document falling within their ambit does not comply with the regulations, it is not properly executed (s 61(1)(a): set out at para 9.12), with the effects considered below (para 9.19) but no others (s 170: see para 10.19).

Additionally, agreements are likely to contain a ('notification') clause, warning consumers that information about them may be registered with a credit reference agency.[80]

**[9.10] Agreement regulations.** Section 60(1) provides that the Secretary of State may make regulations as to the form and content of regulated agreements (see para 9.09), which

> 'shall contain such provisions as appear to him appropriate with a view to ensuring that the debtor or hirer is made aware of—
>
> (a) the rights and duties conferred or imposed on him by the agreement,

---

74 Is there any advantage to the creditor in requiring the debtor to sign for this?

75 'A document embodies a provision if the provision is set out either in the document or in another document referred to in it'—s 189(4).

76 The statute speaks of the requirement being 'waived or varied'. This relief only extends to regulations made under s 60, so that the successful applicant must still comply with s 61: as to which, see para 9.12.

77 Only if the OFT 'is satisfied that to do so would not prejudice the interests of debtors or hirers': amended s 60(4).

78 As to the meaning of 'impracticable', see Goode, *Consumer Credit Legislation*, para 1221.

79 Not only is this in no sense a general dispensing power, but it can only be exercised on behalf of the applicant to cover specific circumstances.

80 The form of clause has been agreed as complying with the First Data Protection Principle: see para 3.28.

(b)  the amount and rate of the total charge for credit (in the case of a consumer credit agreement),

(c)  the protection and remedies available to him under this Act, and

(d)  any other matters which, in the opinion of the Secretary of State, it is desirable for him to know about in connection with the agreement'.

These powers have been utilised to introduce Agreement Regulations,[81] which lay down detailed rules to govern the content and form of regulated agreements, subject to any prior waiver by the OFT.[82] Significant additional requirements were introduced by the 2004 Regulations,[83] which also revised the format of agreements to make them clearer and more transparent, including APRs for credit cards (see para 8.23). These rules will also apply indirectly to the documents which will become regulated agreements when signed by all parties[84]—what the Act terms 'prospective agreements' (as to which see para 5.20).

1.  *Content of agreements.* Section 60(2)(a) explains that the regulations may:

'require specified information to be included in the prescribed manner in documents, and other specified material to be excluded'.

In fact, the Agreement Regulations specify different rules for different permutations as follows (regs 2 and 3): the two types of regulated agreement, consumer credit and consumer hire agreements (as to which, see para 5.13); the time at which the agreement becomes executed;[85] and whether or not the agreement is cancellable (as to the prescribed notices in cancellable agreements, see para 9.17). Leaving aside multiple agreements,[86] the rules generally speaking[87] require all the different permutations to display prominently at their commencement the type of agreement,[88] to identify the parties,[89] to set out the statutory statement of protection and remedies available to the debtor or hirer (Scheds 2, 3 and 4), to show the other financial and related particulars (see further, para 9.11) in a strictly designated order without interspersal

---

81  Consumer Credit (Agreements) Regulations, 1983 SI 1553 (as amended). There are separate rules covering cancellation notices and copies: see para 9.17. For criticism, see (2005) 155 NLJ 770.

82  Under amended s 60(3) and (4) and s 183 (as substituted by s 64 of the 2006 Act). A s 60(3) application must be made before an agreement is entered into: *Dimond v Lovell* (set out at para 5.13); and Macleod [1999] JBL at 462–3.

83  Consumer Credit (Agreements) (Amendment) Regulations, 2004 SI 1482 (as amended). See the DTI White Paper, *Fair, Clear and Competitive: the Consumer Credit Market in the 21st Century* (Dec 2003, Cm. 6040), paras 2.25–7.

84  See Goode, *Consumer Credit Law & Practice*, para 30.47. The rules also apply to security instruments signed by the debtor or hirer: see para 25.12. What is the effect of using CCA documentation for transactions outside the Act?

85  This may or may not be when the document is signed by the debtor or hirer: see further, para 9.13.

86  As to multiple agreements, see para 5.27; and as to the regulatory requirements for multiple agreements, see Goode, *Op. cit.*, paras 1312–18.

87  For further details, see Goode, *Op. cit.*, paras 30.161 and 30.260.

88  Sched 1, para 1; Sched 3, para 1. E.g. 'Hire-purchase agreement regulated by the CCA'.

89  Sched 1, para 2; Sched 3, para 2. The names and postal addresses of the parties. Can the creditor use an accommodation address or PO Box number (see 13 CCA News 1/24)?

(regs 2(4), 3(4) and 7(4)), to embody any security provided by the debtor or hirer[90] and to give information about early settlement (see para 26.19A).

2.  *Form and layout of agreement.* According to s 60(2)(b), the regulations may:

> 'contain requirements to ensure that specified information is clearly brought to the attention of the debtor or hirer, and that one part of a document is not given insufficient or excessive prominence compared with another'.

Usually, the specified information (prescribed terms) is contained together on the signature side of the document, whilst the desired standard terms (the required terms) are on the back (see para 9.13). The Agreement Regulations used to provide simply for legibility;[91] but the 2004 amendments now also stipulate as to equal prominence of most of the material (reg 6(2)(b): see para 9.11), which should banish small print.

Entirely separate from the foregoing rules are those dealing with the information which must be provided by the parties during the continuance of the agreement (ss 77–80: see para 15.16) or at its termination.[92]

**[9.11] A consumer credit example**. The Agreements Regulations (see para 9.10) provide a set of detailed instructions to the draftsmen of regulated agreements within their ambit as to the information which must be included, its layout and the order in which the information must appear. For instance, such a conditional sale or hp agreement must always contain at the prescribed prominence the prescribed headings and terms (see para 9.10), the signature boxes[93] and statutory wealth warnings to keep up payments as follows (reg 2(3) and Sched 2, Pt 1): a general warning for all agreements:

> 'Missing payments could have severe consequences and make obtaining credit more difficult';

and a special warning to mortgagors:

> 'Your home may be repossessed if you do not keep up repayments on a mortgage'.

Further, the agreement must also embody the statutory statements of repossession and termination rights,[94] together with the special cancellation notice (see para 9.17) if the agreement is cancellable (see para 10.29), and certain insurance particulars, if applicable (reg 2(8) and (9)). For CPI insurance, see para 24.48.

Additionally, under what has been termed the 'holy ground rule',[95] the agreement must show 'together and as a whole' the following financial and related

---

90  CCA, s 105(9): Agreement Regulations, reg 2(10). As to 'embody', see para 9.12.
91  Reg 6(2). See also s 61(1)(c): para 9.12. The OFT has had cause to make public complaint at the small print used in some credit and charge card applications (*The Times* 15.8.85). Cf. *L 'Estrange v Graucob Ltd* [1934] 2 KB 394, DC (small print).
92  As to settlement figures (s 97), see para 26.19A; as to termination statements (s 103), see para 26.04; and as to notices (ss 76, 87 and 98), see para 24.28.
93  Reg 2(7) and Sched 5, Pt 1. There are similar requirements for consumer hire agreements: Art 3(6) and Sched 5, Pt 2. As to signing within such boxes, see para 9.13.
94  Reg 2(3) and Sched 2, Pt 1. There are similar rules for consumer hirings: see Art 3(3) and Sched 4. As to rights of termination, see paras 26.05–7; and as to protections against repossession, see para 24.34.
95  So-called because of the requirement to separate it from other information: Goode, *Consumer Credit Law & Practice*, paras 30.223–25.

particulars: a description of the goods,[96] their cash price,[97] any advance payments,[98] the amount of credit,[99] rate of interest,[100] the total amount payable,[101] the duration of the agreement (Sched 1, paras 8A and 8B), the timing and amount of repayments (Sched 1, paras 12–14A) and the tcc/APR,[102] with special provision for where the rate is variable.[103] This, combined with the requirements of s 61 considered below (para 9.12) and of the copies rules (see para 9.14) ensures a substantial similarity in appearance between the documentation of different consumer credit businesses as regards documentation which fall within the Agreement Regulations. Which categories of document each business produces will depend on its types of business.[104] In practice, the larger businesses tend to produce their own documentation in most categories, whilst smaller businesses commonly use trade association documentation, perhaps over-printed with their individual logo. What if there is a mathematical error made when completing the form?

## Execution of the agreement

[9.12] Section 61(1) embodies the primary requirements[105] as to the execution of all regulated agreements within its ambit.[106] It provides that:

'A regulated agreement is not properly executed unless—

(a) a document in the prescribed form itself containing all the prescribed terms and conforming to regulations under section 60(1) is signed in the prescribed manner both by the debtor or hirer and by or on behalf of the creditor or owner; and

(b) the document embodies all the terms of the agreement, other than implied terms; and

---

96 Sched 1, para 3. There is a similar rule for consumer hire agreements but no such requirement in respect of DC loans (see para 5.35) or running-account credit (see para 5.28), and a special rule where both goods and services are supplied.

97 Sched 1, para 4, requiring just one cash price in respect of each 'list' of items. 'Cash price' is defined as 'the price or charge at which the goods . . . may be purchased by, or supplied to, the debtor for cash': Art 1(2); and see *R v Baldwins Garage (Warrington)* [1988] Crim LR 438.

98 Sched 1, para 5. This rule extends to DC loans and running-account credit, and there is a similar rule for consumer hirings (Sched 3, para 4). 'Advance payment' includes any deposit and any part-exchange allowance: see Art 1(2); and for the statutory definition of a 'deposit', see s 189(1).

99 Sched 1, paras 6 and 7. In the case of running-account credit, the credit **limit** must be shown (para 8); but it seems that the credit **rate** may be unilaterally variable: *Lombard Tricity Finance Ltd v Paton* (set out at para 26.22); and generally, para 10.05.

100 Sched 1, paras 9 and 10. As to uncertainty as to the basis of calculation, see Goode, *Op. cit.*, para 30.184.

101 Sched 1, para 11: as this includes any option fee, it is the same as the 'total price' defined by the CCA (see para 24.35). A separate rule exists for consumer hirings (Sched 3, para 5); and there can be no such requirement for running-account credit, nor for fixed-sum variable rate credit.

102 Sched 1, paras 15–17. For the tcc and APR, see paras 8.22–5. In a genuinely interest-free agreement, this could be shown as '0% APR': see para 2.07.

103 Sched 1, paras 18–19. These have been held to apply only to external varying factors (see para 10.05), leaving intact variations at the absolute discretion of one party: *Lombard Tricity Finance Ltd v Paton* (above). For notice of variation, see para 26.22.

104 See Goode, *Op. cit.*, Division XI, Pts D and E.

105 As to the additional requirements in respect of land mortgages, see para 9.17A.

106 For exemptions from these rules, see para 9.07. For the position where there is more than one debtor or hirer, see para 9.18.

(c) the document is, when presented or sent to the debtor or hirer for signature, in such a state that all its terms are readily legible'.

By s 61(2) (as amended), a regulated agreement within Pt V (see para 9.07) is not properly executed[107] unless it complies with all the following requirements:

*Paragraph (a)*. See para 9.13.

*Paragraph (b)*. It requires that the regulated agreement[108] contain or refer to all the express terms[109] of that agreement.[110] This does not include mere puffs which have no legal significance (see para 11.01), nor those which have only non-contractual legal significance.[111] Indeed, the paragraph does not even extend to all contractual statements, omitting both implied terms (see para 11.10) and collateral contracts.[112] It is thus confined to the express terms 'embodied'[110] in the regulated agreement:[113] most of these are likely to be in printed standard-form; but insofar as the form contains blanks to be filled in by hand, the paragraph would appear to render documents signed in blank improperly executed.[114] Where the regulated agreement also amounts to a consumer supply contract, the express terms must also comply with the UTCC Regulations as to both legibility and fairness, except insofar as prescribed by the CCA (UTCC, Sched 1, para (e)(i): see para 11.12A): so, the UTCC is inapplicable to CCA-prescribed terms (see para 9.13), but may attack express terms which are not CCA-prescribed.

*Paragraph (c)*. It has already been pointed out that the other formalities rules are only expressly referrable to actual agreements (see para 9.10). However, paragraph (c) is applicable to prospective agreements. It covers indistinctly printed forms (and see para 9.10) and also requires that the blanks on the form are completed legibly[115] and not presented in such a way as to hide any information from the consumer.[116]

---

107 With the effect considered later (para 9.19) but no others (s 170: see para 10.19).

108 This will normally be in standard-form: as to which, see generally, para 11.08.

109 As to express terms, see generally, paras 11.07–9. Presumably, parol evidence may be tendered to show that the written terms do not include all the terms expressly agreed: Goode, *Consumer Credit Law & Practice*, para 30.127. As to clerical errors, see Guest and Lloyd, *Encyclopedia of Consumer Credit*, para 2-062.

110 By s 189(4), one document is 'embodied' in another if referred to in it (see para 9.09). But, bear in mind that certain information must be exhibited 'together as a whole' (see paras 9.10–11).

111 *Broadwick Financial Services Ltd v Spencer* (set out at para 8.22; *ex-gratia* concessions). See also misrepresentations (see para 11.02); or conditions precedent and subsequent which do not acquire promissory status (see paras 15.21, 26.01). E.g. that the consumer must furnish a guarantor before the deal is finalised.

112 Collateral contracts (outside the paragraph) should be carefully distinguished from collateral terms (within it): see generally, para 11.06.

113 It has been claimed that this does not extend to 'mere items of information': Goode, *Op. cit.*, para 30.125. *Sed quaere?*

114 See also s 61(1)(a): paras 9.13. E.g. *PB Leasing Ltd v Patel and Patel* [1995] CCLR 82, Cty Ct (and see further, para 9.20).

115 It is therefore normal for the information inserted in such blanks to be carefully printed. Signatures are an exception: see para 9.13. For a possible difficulty with dispensers, see para 7.08.

116 In the sense of impede by physical difficulty, e.g. by stapling pages together. See *Reform of the law on Consumer Credit* (1973, Cmnd. 5427), para 47.

**[9.13] Paragraph (a).** This paragraph of s 61(1) (see para 9.12) clearly requires that a regulated agreement, including a credit token agreement (see para 7.10), within its ambit (see para 9.07) must comply with **all** the following requirements:[117]

1. *Prescribed form.* The agreement may be either in writing or electronic (described in amended s 61(2)(b) as 'by appropriate method': see para 9.05), but must in any event accord with the layout prescribed by the Agreement Regulations (see para 9.10).

2. *Prescribed terms.* On the same side as the signatures, the agreement **itself** must contain the terms **prescribed** in the Agreement Regulations (reg 6(1)). According to Sched 6, these will vary according to the type of agreement, but broadly deal with the following:[118] the amount of the credit or credit limit; in some cases the rate of interest; and a term stating how the financial obligations of the debtor or hirer are to be discharged. To the extent that these rules refer to information falling into the category of that which must be stated 'together and as a whole' (see para 9.11), that will ensure that the larger list is included in the actual agreement rather than any document referred to in it. These terms are no longer outside the dispensing power of the court as set out in s 127 (see para 9.21).

3. *Required terms.* Commonly on the non-signature side of the form, the agreement must **'embody'** (s 189(4)) the terms required by the Agreement Regulations so that they must be included either in the agreement itself or a document referred to in it (see paras 9.10–11), which makes the post-contract correction of errors difficult;[119] and there would appear to be no compliance where the debtor or hirer signs in blank.[120] It would appear to be a matter of judgment as to whether these rules are so complicated that it would not on balance be more satisfactory to lay down compulsory statutory forms of agreement (see generally, para 11.08).

4. *Signed by the parties.* Paragraph (a) requires the agreement to be **'signed** . . . both by the debtor or hirer and by or on behalf of the creditor or owner':[121] the signatures need not be legible (reg 6(2)); and in the case of a registered company, the company seal will suffice (s 189(3)). Unlike the common law (see para 10.02), the CCA thus requires formation of the agreement by actual or electronic signature of the parties conforming with the requirements of the Act and the Agreement Regulations. This requirement is no longer outside the dispensing power of the court as set out in s 127 (see para 9.21).

---

117 It is clear that s 61(1)(a) is referring to the prospective regulated agreement, so that its requirements must be fulfilled by that document and not just by another document to which it refers: Goode, *Consumer Credit Law & Practice*, paras 30.102–3.

118 The regulations probably deal with the substance of the terms, rather than the terminology: see the County Court cases referred to at (2003) 153 NLJ 700; and (2004) 72 *QA* 7 at 8, n 1.

119 Use of the common law methods of contract variation (see para 26.21) would render the regulated agreement unenforceable under s 65; and a modifying agreement is required (see para 26.22).

120 Goode, *Op. cit.*, para 30.108. As to the effect at common law of signing documents in blank, see para 16.05.

121 Where there is more than one debtor or hirer (see para 5.24), generally speaking all of them must sign personally, e.g. spouses (s 185(3)); but signature by agent is allowed where the joint debtors or hirers are either a partnership (s 61(4)) or in respect of the one of them which is a body corporate (s 185(6)) or presumably under a power of attorney.

5. *Signed in the prescribed manner*. To protect consumers so far as possible from unwittingly signing hp agreements, the HPA 1964 devised a successful scheme whereby consumers sign in a special signature box. This scheme is adopted by the Agreement Regulations, which require that the debtor or hirer sign within the signature box whilst the creditor or owner signs outside it (reg 6(3)); and it is presumably intended that this rule extend to agreements made electronically.[122] Furthermore, that signature box must be in the form laid down in Sched 5 appropriate for the type of agreement, including the date of signature by the debtor or hirer, warnings against the binding effect of signature[123] and sometimes resale.[124] The 2004 amendments have further utilised the idea to require an additional signature box and signature where the agreement includes PPI insurance.[125]

It is for consideration whether a prospective agreement complying with all the above rules contains too much information for optimum effect.

## Copies of the agreement

**[9.14] Introduction**. The hp legislation slowly evolved two principles; and the key to understanding them is to bear in mind that normally in this field a transaction will be effected by document, which will only take legal effect when signed (see para 10.08). The *first* principle was that consumers should be sent a copy of the signed agreement within seven days of the agreement being made (the agreement copy) and subsequently further copies on demand (see para 15.16). The *second* principle, as the first rule might leave a gap of up to seven days between a consumer signing and obtaining a copy of what he signed, sought to ensure that the consumer was never without a copy of what he signed (the signature copy). The Crowther Report gave enthusiastic support to these two principles and recommended that they be extended to all types of transaction within the scope of the legislation (para 6.5.14). The CCA has done just that, adding the gloss that in the case of joint consumers the copies rules must be observed in relation to each of them.[126] The CCA has sought to implement the principles by formulating rules requiring that generally speaking[127] the two copies[128] be dealt with on one of the following bases:

---

122 There is power to do so in the Electronic Communications Act 2000; and it is consistent with the changes to the CCA introduced by 2004 SI 3236 (see para 9.05). But nowhere does it seem clearly stated that s 61(1)(a) of the CCA may be satisfied by an electronic signature: see McCaffrey & Nash (2006) 61 CC1/3.

123 E.g. 'This is a Hire Purchase Agreement regulated by the Consumer Credit Act 1974. Sign it only if you want to be legally bound by its terms.'

124 E.g. for hp 'The goods will not become your property until you have made all the payments. You must not sell them before then.'

125 Agreement (Amendment) Regulations 2004 (see para 9.10), reg 2(7)–(9) and Sched 5. For PPI insurance, see para 24.48.

126 S 185(1)(a): see para 5.24. However, in relation to periodic copies of running accounts (s 78(4)), the Act provides a dispensing procedure (amended s 185(2)): see para 7.08.

127 As to the variations for cancellable agreements, and land mortgages, see paras 9.17–17A; and as to the situation where there is more than one debtor or hirer, see para 9.18.

128 As to the contents of copies and documents referred to therein, see para 9.18.

(a) Documents **presented personally** to the debtor or hirer for signature (see para 9.15); or

(b) Documents **sent** to the debtor or hirer for signature (see para 9.16).

In each of these two cases the CCA principles usually require that the debtor or hirer obtain two copies as follows: the first copy was of the 'unexecuted agreement';[129] and the second copy was of the 'executed agreement'.[130] However, if the document becomes an executed agreement on the occasion upon which the debtor or hirer signs,[131] it would be pointless to require two copies.[132] Accordingly, the CCA dispenses with the signature copy in some cases as follows (s 63(1)):

> 'If the unexecuted agreement is presented personally to the debtor or hirer for his signature, and on the occasion when he signs it the document becomes an executed agreement, a copy of the executed agreement, and of any document referred to in it, must be there and then delivered to him'.

This will cover vendor credit situations (see para 2.19) where the creditor or owner is prepared to make an instantaneous decision as to whether to supply on credit ('instant credit'); but it is not particularly common, because most creditors or owners will prefer to forward the document signed by the debtor or hirer to their credit department for processing;[133] but it is commonly employed with weekly collected credit (see para 10.17). However, even leaving aside any difficulty over the meaning in s 63(1) of 'there and then' (see para 9.15), this rule would appear to leave a hiatus when the debtor does not sign in the presence of the creditor's representative a form already signed by the creditor.[134] A similar position is taken by the Act where the debtor or hirer obtains documents from some impersonal source, e.g. from a dispenser or a trade display stand, or by cutting it out from a newspaper, so that it would be impracticable to require the creditor or owner to supply then a first completed copy signed by the debtor or hirer.[135]

Unless it complies with all the applicable copies rules, a regulated agreement is not properly executed (ss 62(3), 63(5) and 64(5)), with the effects considered below (para 9.19), but no others (s 170: see para 10.19).

**[9.15] Unsigned document presented personally**. This paragraph deals with the common situation where the document is 'presented personally' to the

---

129 This is defined as 'a document embodying the terms of a prospective regulated agreement, or such of them as it is intended to reduce to writing': s 189(1). As to prospective agreements, see generally, para 5.20. For a deficiency in this definition of 'unexecuted agreement', see Goode, *Consumer Credit Law & Practice*, para 30.301.

130 This 'means a document, signed by or on behalf of the parties, embodying the terms of a regulated agreement, or such of them as have been reduced to writing': s 189(1).

131 This formula avoids any difficulty that might arise in deciding whether the document was signed first by the debtor or hirer, or first by the creditor or owner.

132 Any notional delay between the signature of the debtor or hirer on the document and when he obtained a copy of the executed agreement is thus ignored, e.g. instant credit.

133 For such enquiries about the debtor or hirer, see para 8.35, *et seq*.

134 How will the creditor know when to supply a s 63(1) copy? If the debtor signs in his home, is this a cancellable agreement so as to require a s 64 notice (see para 9.17)?

135 See Goode, *Op. cit.*, para 30.302. But why should the debtor or hirer not have to be supplied with two copies initially, so that he can complete, sign and return one whilst retaining the other?

prospective[136] debtor or hirer for his signature,[137] but does not on that occasion become a regulated agreement because it is not 'there and then' signed by or on behalf of the prospective creditor or owner.[138] In this situation, the CCA requires that the prospective debtor or hirer obtain two copies as follows:

*Signature copy.* Section 62(1) provides that:

> 'If the unexecuted agreement is presented personally to the debtor or hirer for his signature, but on the occasion when he signs it the document does not become an executed agreement, a copy of it, and of any documents referred to in it,[139] must be there and then delivered to him'.

It has been persuasively argued that 'there and then' refers to the time of presentation to the debtor or hirer, not of signature by him: otherwise, if the debtor or hirer took the document away for signature, it would be impossible for the creditor or owner to comply with s 62(1).[140] What if the prospective debtor or hirer leaves his copy of his offer behind on trade premises?

*Agreement copy.* Except in the case of credit tokens (see below), s 63(2) requires that, in the circumstances covered by this paragraph:

> 'A copy of the executed agreement, and of any other document referred to in it, must be given to the debtor or hirer within the seven days following the making of the agreement'.

The agreement is actually made by signature by or on behalf of the creditor or owner (see para 10.08). As 'give' means 'deliver or send by appropriate method',[141] it is common for the agreement copy to be posted to the debtor or hirer; and in the case of cancellable agreements that second copy must be sent by post.[142] With regard to credit-token agreements (see para 5.30), the creditor can send the second copy by post as above but is alternatively permitted to 'give' it to the debtor before or with the credit-token.[143]

**[9.16] Unsigned documents sent for signature.** This would typically be the case with distance contracts, e.g. internet or mail order (see paras 8.17A and 8.19). Unless the signature of the debtor or hirer at home were preceded by oral representations made by the negotiator in his presence (s 67: see para 10.29), agreements sent to the consumer for his signature no longer automatically give him a right of

---

136  By s 189(1) 'debtor', 'hirer', 'creditor', 'owner' here mean prospective parties: see para 5.20.

137  Presentation to the prospective debtor or hirer will usually be made by an agent of the creditor: this may be an employee, as in DC loan financing (see para 5.35); but it is more likely to be made by a credit-broker, as with DCS arrangements (see para 5.34).

138  For the situation where it becomes an executed agreement 'there and then', see para 9.14. Does this category extend to dispenser agreements—are they 'presented personally'?

139  As to 'documents referred to in it', see para 9.18. Is a photocopy produced quickly enough?

140  Goode, *Consumer Credit Law & Practice*, para 30.304.

141  S 189(1). Cf. *Skuce v Cooper* [1975] 1 All ER 612, CA. Is posting sufficient during a postal strike?

142  S 63(3). As to the special documentation rules for cancellable agreements, see paras 9.17 and 10.30.

143  S 63(4): see para 7.12. As to cancellable credit-token agreements, see para 9.17.

cancellation. Unless it does so,[144] the CCA copies rules are as follows for documents sent:[145]

*Signature copy.* Section 62(2) provides that:

> 'If the unexecuted agreement is sent to the debtor or hirer for his signature, a copy of it, and of any other document referred to in it,[146] must be sent to him at the same time'.

So, the initial step required is for the debtor or hirer to receive two copies:[147] one to be signed and returned by him to the creditor or owner; and the other to be retained by him as a record.[148]

*Agreement copy.* Exceptionally, the creditor or owner may sign the document[146] before sending it to the debtor or hirer, e.g. British Telecom telephone rental contract, in which case the signature of the debtor or hirer may be the acceptance[149] and no further copy need be initially supplied to him.[150] However, in the normal case, the returning of a copy 'signed' by the debtor or hirer (either by actual or e-signature) will be an offer and a second copy of the document 'signed' by the creditor or owner (now an executed agreement) must be sent to the debtor or hirer within seven days (s 63(2): set out at para 9:15), a rule which may cause difficulty with direct marketing (see para 8.19). There appears to be nothing to prevent the creditor or owner including advertising material with this copy.

**[9.17] Documentation of cancellable agreements**. As will be seen later, the debtor or hirer under a regulated agreement in some cases has a statutory right of cancellation (see para 10.28, *et seq.*). The CCA is usually anxious that the debtor or hirer is aware of this right so that he may exercise it within the statutory time limit. This s 64 seeks to achieve by two additional steps.[151]

1.  *Prescribed notices.* Whilst the original cancellable form signed by the debtor or hirer must contain a short boxed cancellation notice as prescribed by the Agreement Regulations, Sched 2 (see para 9.10), s 64(1) lays down that copies must include:

    > 'a notice in the prescribed form indicating the right of the debtor or hirer to cancel the agreement, how and when that right is exercisable, and the name and address of a person to whom notice of cancellation may be given'.

---

144 In the case of cancellable agreements (see above), the second copy must be sent by an appropriate method (s 63(3), as amended). As to the special documentation rules for cancellable agreements, see para 9.17.

145 As it amounts to a distance contract (see para 8.17), there must also be supplied the documentation required by the distance selling regulations (see paras 9.04–5).

146 As to 'documents referred to in it', see para 9.09.

147 It has been suggested that this should be read to include an agent, e.g. solicitor or spouse, of the debtor or hirer: Goode, *Consumer Credit Law & Practice*, para 30.305. *Sed quaere?* Cf. s 185(1)(a).

148 Suppose the debtor carries his copy to the creditor's premises and signs there. Does the creditor have to comply with s 62(1) as well?

149 For offer and acceptance by signature, see para 10.02.

150 S 63(2)(b). Did the draftsman intend this only to operate where the offeror dispensed with communication of acceptance?

151 The documentation must, of course, otherwise comply with the ordinary rules considered in this chapter: see para 9.06, *et seq.* As to the comparable rules for doorstep and distance selling transactions, see paras 10.36–9.

These powers have been utilised to introduce the CNC Regulations,[152] specifying in detail the precise type of boxed notice of cancellation rights to be included in each different type of agreement and situation.[153] These boxes should not only alert the debtor or hirer to any cancellation rights,[154] but also tell him how he should exercise those rights (see para 10.31). To make it easier for the debtor or hirer to exercise this right, the notice must be accompanied by a cancellation form (CNC Regulations, reg 5(2)(b) and Pt IV of the Sched: see further, para 10.31).

2.  *Copies rules.* Under s 64(1)(a), these prescribed notices will usually[155] have to be included in each of the two copies required and the second copy must always be sent to him (see paras 9.15–16) by an 'appropriate method', e.g. by post or e-mail. In those cases where only one statutory copy need be supplied to the debtor or hirer (see paras 9.14–15), a separate notice of cancellation must generally be sent[156] to the debtor or hirer.[157] To avoid this expense, in the home credit industry (see para 2.18) it is common for the creditor to sign the agreement before the debtor, so bringing the case within s 63(1) (see para 9.14), with the cancellation notice to be delivered on a subsequent visit.[158] However, dispensations from sending this separate notice may be granted under regulations (amended s 64(4)); and these have been utilised to allow the OFT to grant dispensations in respect of certain mail order consumer credit (but not hire) agreements.[159]

**[9.17A] Documentation of land mortgages.** Of course, the CCA will not usually apply to first mortgages of dwelling houses (see para 3.02); but for mortgages within its scope, principally second mortgages, the CCA wished to give the debtor or hirer a special regime of protection (see para 10.27). Accordingly, it introduced an additional third tier of copies, usually applicable 'where the "prospective regulated agreement" (see para 5.20) is to be secured[160] on land (the "mortgaged land")'.[161]

---

152  Consumer Credit (Cancellation Notices and Copies of Documents) Regulations, 1983 SI 1557 (as amended).

153  See further, Goode, *Consumer Credit Law & Practice*, paras 31.114–17.

154  To cover the situation where the creditor or owner gives his customer a contractual right of cancellation, the amended CNC Regulations treat the agreement as if it were cancellable: reg 5(4).

155  In the case of credit-tokens, the notice can be sent by an appropriate method before or with the credit-tokens: s 64(2), as amended.

156  It has been suggested that it is sufficient if the notice be sent by some independent carrier: Goode, *Op. cit.*, para 30.306.

157  S 64(1)(b), as amended. S 64(3) allows regulations to require that a further copy of the executed agreement be included; but this power has not been exercised.

158  Does this comply with s 64(1)(b)?

159  Consumer Credit (Notice of Cancellation Rights) (Exemptions) Regulations, 1983 SI 1558. Such dispensations must he individual, not general, and are recorded in the public register (as to which, see para 6.26). See further Goode, *Op. cit.*, para 31.118.

160  The test is thus as to the common intention of the parties prior to the formation of the regulated agreement that it will, when concluded, be secured on the mortgaged land. This may give rise to factual disputes: see Goode, *Consumer Credit Law & Practice*, para 31.54.

161  S 58(1). The rules are applicable whether the land mortgage is to be given by the debtor/hirer or by a third party. For the exceptional cases within s 58(2), see para 10.27.

1.  *Advance copy.* According to s 58(1):

> 'Before sending to the debtor or hirer, for his signature, an unexecuted agreement in a case where the prospective regulated agreement is to be secured on land (the 'mortgaged land'), the creditor or owner shall give the debtor or hirer a copy of the unexecuted agreement which contains a notice in the prescribed form indicating the right of the debtor or hirer to withdraw from the prospective agreement, and how and when the right is exercisable, together with a copy of any other document referred to in the unexecuted agreement'.

It will be noted that the debtor or hirer must be given[162] copies of both the prospective regulated agreement and any other document referred to in it.[163] These copies must be true copies;[164] and the advance copy of the prospective regulated agreement must also contain a notice of this right to withdraw in statutory form[165] and comply with the CNC Regulations (see para 9.18).

2.  *Signature copy.* Section 61(2) provides that:

> 'In addition,[166] where the agreement is one to which section 58(1) applies, it is not properly executed[167] unless—
>
> (a)  the requirements of section 58(1) were complied with, and
>
> (b)  the unexecuted agreement was sent, for his signature, to the debtor or hirer by appropriate method not less than seven days after a copy of it was given to him under section 58(1)'.

Thus, service of the advanced copy (above) does not absolve the creditor or owner from his duty to supply separate copies of both the agreement form and any document referred to in it[163] in accordance with the ordinary rules for documents sent for signature (see para 9.16).

Further, it will be noticed that there is a compulsory time-gap between the sending of the advance and signature copies, this being known as the 'consideration period' (see further, para 10.27). These two copies of the unexecuted agreement will differ in that **only** the advance copy will contain the notice of right of withdrawal.[168]

3.  *Agreement copy.* After the debtor or hirer signs and returns the signature copy,[169] that document must be signed by or on behalf of the creditor or owner (see para 9.12) and a copy of the now-executed agreement, together with any document referred to in it,[163] sent to the debtor or hirer within seven days.

---

162 ' "Give" means deliver or send by appropriate method': s 189(1). It does not need to be given to the debtor personally: Goode, *Op. cit.*, para 31.56.

163 E.g. the intended mortgage. However, no copy need be served of documents referred to in the 'other document', e.g. referred to in the mortgage. See further, para 9.18.

164 CNC Regulations (see para 9.17), reg 3(1). It has been reasoned that the copies must therefore be complete, except for execution: Guest and Lloyd, *Encyclopedia of Consumer Credit*, para 2-059.

165 CNC Regulations, reg 4. There is a statutory warning that a debtor's home will be at risk: see para 8.30.

166 This will ensure that land mortgages also comply with the requirements of s 61(1): see para 9.12.

167 With the effects considered later (paras 9.19 and 10.27) but no others (s 170): see para 10.19.

168 This should preclude the production of a single document to comply with both ss 58 and 62.

169 What if he mistakenly signs and returns the advance copy?

In the normal case within s 58, the agreement form will refer to the mortgage, so that if the transaction is undertaken by a couple as a joint debtor or hirer, the above rules will require the creditor or owner to serve at least 12 documents![170]

**[9.18] Contents and copies**. The CCA requires that, when a transaction is set up, the debtor or hirer and any surety, obtain not only the required copies of the agreement form but also copies of 'any other document referred to in it' (ss 62, 63, 105(5): see paras 9.14–16 and para 25.12). As it was appreciated that some limitation should be placed on this duty, the CCA provides for derogation by regulation (s 180(3)). Accordingly, the CNC Regulations (see para 9.17) contain a list of excluded classes of documents, such as the following:[171] documents obtained by the debtor or hirer from a third party, e.g. a survey report, catalogue or document of title; or to be kept by him under the terms of the agreement, e.g. receipts for insurance premiums, rent or rates; entries in public registers, e.g. copies of birth certificates or entries in the CCA register (as to which, see para 6.26); enactments, which presumably includes subordinate legislation, both UK and EU; or any earlier agreement being modified (see generally, para 26.22).

Not content with stipulating the documentation to be supplied, the CCA also requires the creditor or owner to supply copies of it to all the debtor(s) or hirer(s) and any sureties: this applies to copies of the unexecuted agreement (ss 62, 185(1)(a): see generally, paras 9.15–16), initial copies of the executed agreement (ss 63 and 185(1)(a): see generally, paras 9.14–16), subsequent copies of that agreement[172] and notices.[173] In relation to copies of the unexecuted and executed agreement, the CNC Regulations require that every copy shall be a 'true copy' (reg 3). In relation to the original documentation, it is now common practice for creditors or owners to satisfy this requirement by printing their agreement forms in three copies.[174] Whilst extra copies can be photocopied, the CNC Regulations in fact permit some information to be omitted from copies.[175]

## Effect of non-compliance

**[9.19] Improperly executed**. The concept of unenforceable contracts has long existed under the Statute of Frauds (see para 9.02). When the documentation rules under the CCA are infringed, the 1974 Act provides that the regulated agreement 'is not properly executed'. This is the sanction expressed in respect of breaches of all the following documentation rules: pre-contract disclosure (s 55(2): see para 9.08); land mortgage rules (ss 58 and 61(2): see para 10.27); signing agreements in proper

---

170 Six on each debtor or hirer. No dispensing notice would appear available under s 185: but see the suggestion in Guest, *Op. cit.*, para 2-062.

171 See further, Goode, *Consumer Credit Law & Practice*, paras 30.309–26.

172 Ss 77–9, 107–10 and 185(1)(a). See generally, paras 15.17 and 25.12.

173 Ss 64, 76, 87, 98, 111 and 185(1)(a). See para 9.17 and para 24.28.

174 An original (for retention by the creditor or owner); a first copy (to be handed or sent to the debtor or hirer as the unexecuted agreement); and a second copy (to be sent to the debtor or hirer as the executed agreement). Carbonizing or photocopying will ensure that most of the blanks will be identically completed and required printed variations between first and second copies can be ensured. An extra copy may be needed for land mortgages: see para 9.17A.

175 E.g. material in the section 'For Office Use Only'. See further, Goode, *Op. cit.*, para 1338.

form (s 61(1): see para 9.12); supply of copies (ss 62(3) and 64(5): see para 9.17); and for sureties (s 105(4) and (5): see para 25.12). The key provision is s 65, which gives the following explanation:

'(1) An improperly-executed regulated agreement is enforceable against the debtor or hirer on an order of the court only.

(2) A retaking of goods or land to which a regulated agreement relates is an enforcement of the agreement'.

It follows that an improperly executed agreement will still exist:[176] it can be enforced by the debtor or hirer if he so wishes as against anybody;[177] or by the creditor or owner as against a third party.[178] On the other hand, the agreement cannot be enforced by the creditor or owner against the debtor or hirer by judicial process[179] or self-help (see para 24.33), except by court order (see para 9.20) or with the consent of the debtor or hirer (s 173(3): see para 18.11). This position is reinforced by s 142(1), which allows parties other than the creditor or owner[180] to seek a declaration of unenforceability in the following circumstances,[181] unless the agreement is unenforceable 'on technical grounds only':[182] where either the court dismisses an application for an enforcement order[183] or on application by 'an interested party',[184]

'the court may if it thinks just make a declaration that the creditor or owner is not entitled to do that thing, and thereafter no application for an enforcement order in respect of it shall be entertained'.

Whilst the creditor is not subject to any further sanctions (s 170: see para 10.19), he cannot avoid the above rules by the devices of either a preliminary agreement (s 59(1): see para 5.20) or taking security.[185] Additionally, the OFT can apply for an Enforcement Order on behalf of consumers generally (see para 28.04).

**[9.20] Enforcement orders.** In a number of cases, the CCA provides that a regulated agreement can be enforced 'on an order of the court only', whether because that agreement was improperly executed (see para 9.19) or otherwise (see para 24.33); and the same result follows as regards any security (s 113: see para 25.14). Section

---

176 It is not void, or even voidable (as to which, see para 10.14); nor is it illegal (as to which, see para 10.19): *Carlyle Finance Ltd v Pallas Industrial Finance Ltd* (set out at para 10.08).

177 In *Wilson v First County Trust Ltd (No 2)* [2004] 1 AC 816, HL, Lord Nicholls said, *obiter*, that a debtor could insist on making further drawdowns (para 30). Can the debtor recover sums already paid by him to the creditor on grounds of mistake?

178 *Wilson v First County Trust Ltd* [2001] 2 All ER (Comm) 134, CA, *obiter* at para 25.

179 *Dimond v Lovell* (set out at para 5.13); [1999] JBL 452 at 464. For enforcement by judicial process, see para 24.27, *et seq.*

180 Guest and Lloyd, *Encyclopedia of Consumer Credit*, para 2-143; Goode, *Consumer Credit Law & Practice*, Division IIB, para 5.282.

181 S 142(2) also makes provision for declarations of cancellation (s 69(1) and (2): see para 10.32) or of termination (s 91: see para 24.38), though in these cases the creditor or owner may, as 'an interested party' be seeking the declaration. Outside s 142, the power to seek a declaration rests on the ordinary procedure under the rules of court.

182 See s 189(5); and the discussion of 'technical grounds' by Goode, *Op. cit.*, para 37.222.

183 As where the creditor or owner seeks to enforce the agreement by judicial process: see above.

184 E.g. a party standing in the shoes of the debtor or hirer, such as a personal representative or trustee in bankruptcy, afraid that the creditor or owner will resort to self-help: as to which see above.

185 See para 25.11. Do the above rules also apply to s 124 (see para 25.09)?

127 then deals with applications to the court for an 'enforcement order' (defined in s 189(1)). Section 127(1) instructs the court to grant an enforcement order unless it considers it just to refuse such an order, having regard **only** to the following of its powers:

(a) *Prejudice.* 'Prejudice caused to any person by the contravention in question and the degree of culpability for it.'[186]

(b) *Reduction of debt.* The power contained in s 127(2) that:[187]

> 'if it appears to the court just to do so, it may in any enforcement order reduce or discharge any sum payable by the debtor or hirer, or any surety, so as to compensate him for prejudice suffered as a result of the contravention in question'.

(c) *Condition or suspension.* The powers contained in s 135(1) that the court may, if it considers it just to do so, include in its order provisions:

(a) making the operation of any term of the order conditional on the doing of specified acts by any party to the proceedings;[188]

(b) suspending the operation of any term of the order either—

(i) until such time as the court order subsequently directs, or

(ii) until the occurrence of a specified act or omission.[189]

The court may feel inclined to exercise this power if, for instance, the infringement is technical only (as to 'technical grounds', see para 9.19); or the consumer parties can be safeguarded by varying or suspending the agreement. It may subsequently vary such an order (s 135(4)). There are two qualifications to the suspending power in s 135(1)(b): the court shall not suspend an order for the return of the goods (see para 24.26) by any person, unless satisfied that the goods are in his possession (s 135(2)); nor may the power be used to extend the period of a consumer hiring (s 135(3)).

(d) *Amendment.* Under s 136,[187] the court has the following power to amend any agreement:

> 'The court may in an order made by it under this Act include such provision as it considers just for amending any agreement or security in consequence of a term of the order'.

Provided only that it is 'in consequence of a term' of an order, s 136 empowers the court to vary the contractual rate of interest.[190]

Thus, in cases falling within amended s 127(1), the court is instructed to refuse an enforcement order only if it cannot do justice as between the parties under one of the powers (a)–(d) above.[191] For the special cases within s 127(3), see para 9.21.

---

186  S 127(1)(i). Note the extension beyond prejudice to the debtor or hirer to 'any person', e.g. surety.

187  Compare *Nissan Finance UK v Lockhart* [1993] CCLR 39, CA with *National Guardian Mortgage Corp v Wilkes* [1993] CCLR 1.

188  E.g. the return of certain property to the debtor or hirer.

189  E.g. an order to return goods to the creditor or owner (see para 24.43) can be made conditional on further default by the debtor or hirer. But see s 135(2).

190  *Southern and District Finance plc v Barnes* (set out at para 24.41).

191  By Sched 4 of the 2006 Act. See *London North Securities v Meadows* (where the creditor had not signed the agreement, but this caused no prejudice to the debtor: set out at para 8.25) Cty Ct at para 72.

Without an enforcement order, any goods would appear to fall into a legal black hole: the creditor cannot repossess them and the debtor cannot sell them.[192]

**[9.21] Special cases.** In the following cases only, the 1974 Act deemed the infringement to be so prejudicial to the debtor, hirer or surety that the court was given no discretion to order enforcement, so that the agreement remained permanently unenforceable:

1. *An unsigned document.* A regulated agreement remained perpetually unenforceable if either it did not contain the prescribed terms or it was not signed by the debtor or hirer (s 127(3)).

2. *A cancellable agreement.* Under s 127(4), the court had no dispensing power where a cancellable agreement either did not comply with the copies rules (ss 62–3: see above) or contain the prescribed notices of the right of cancellation (s 64: see para 9.17).

3. *Any security.* This was, and is, enforceable to no greater extent than the regulated agreement (s 113(1): see para 25.11).

In *Wilson v First County Trust Ltd* (set out at para 3.09A),[193]

> The court found a breach of s 61(1)(a), so that the agreement was not properly executed. W defaulted and FCT sought to sell the car. In an interim judgment,[194] the Court of Appeal held that the result was that both the agreement and the pledge were permanently unenforceable under ss 127(3) and 113(2), so that FCT had to hand back the car to W and forgo the debt. The House of Lords held that this was compatible with the HRA (see para 3.09A).

The view of the House is therefore that s 127(3) extinguished the creditor's contractual rights both to recover the debt and retain the security, an outcome against which the HRA offers him no protection.[195] What is worse for the creditor, the application of s 127(3) depended on correctly allocating the documentation fee of £250 as between credit and the tcc; and it has already been seen that that may be a very difficult exercise, which apparently turns on the facts (see para 8.25). To resolve this problem, s 15 of the CCA 2006 therefore repealed prospectively[196] s 127(3)–(5) of the CCA 1974, so making s 127 more proportionate to the problem.[197]

---

192 Might the creditor obtain a s 134 declaration to demonstrate adverse possession (see para 24.43) and then sue in tort (see para 24.25)?

193 Foll. In relation to s 106: see *Wilson v Howard Pawnbrokers* [2005] EWCA 147, CA; and para 25.13. Foll. in relation to s 69(1) in *Goshawk etc Ltd v Bank of Scotland* [2006] 2 All ER 610; and para 10.32.

194 [2001] QB 407, CA (see Dobson 150 NLJ 1815).

195 Similarly inflexible would appear to be CCA, s 127(4) (cancellable agreements: see above); s 91 (protected goods: see para 24.38); s 125(1) (negotiable instruments: see para 25.09).

196 CCA 2006, Sched 3, para 11. So ss 127(3)–(5) will continue to apply to all agreements made before April 2007.

197 Minister (2005–6) HL Deb, R2, col. 1029. As to the use of Hansard to determine the intention of Parliament, see para 1.04.

# CHAPTER 10

# FORMATION OF THE AGREEMENT

## GENERAL PRINCIPLES

**[10.01] Introduction**. This book is concerned for the most part with contracts for the supply of goods[1] and loans taken out to finance such acquisitions.[2] Apart from the special rules for auctions (see para 10.10), in the fundamentals of contract the SGA simply refers back to general contractual principles (s 62(2)); most related Acts do not even bother to include such a cross-reference, e.g. SOGIT; CCA; UCTA; SGSA; but there are some special rules for website sales (para 10.09A). The general rules as to the formation of contract will be found in the standard works[3] but their application in the present context requires mention as follows:

1. *Agreement*. There will be considered below the process of agreeing (see para 10.02, *et seq*.), mistake (see para 10.14) and invalidity (see para 10.18). Into that agreement, written terms may be incorporated (see para 18.04): if a party is foolish enough to accept (say) harsh standard terms (see para 11.08), *prima facie* at common law he is bound by them;[4] but he may be able to escape those terms under the Unfair Terms in Consumer Contracts (UTCC) Regulations (see para 11.12, *et seq*.). In a supermarket, where the contract is usually made at the check-out,[5] the price is likely to be charged according to a bar code (see para 2.06). As to advertisements, see para 8.05.

2. *Consideration*. Whilst consideration is not required for a deed (see para 9.01), in the case of a simple contract to supply goods, consideration is likely to take the form of price, rent or goods taken in part exchange (see respectively paras 2.06, 1.18 and 2.09). At common law, only one who provides that consideration will be privy to the contract. This rule has two aspects:

   (a) *The burden of the contract*. Only a person who is a party to the contract is subject to its burdens, a rule which will be relevant as regards restrictions on the use of goods which purport to bind a sub-buyer (see para 2.14) and exemptions (see para 18.05).

   (b) *The benefit of the contract*. Whilst at common law, disregarding agency (see para 10.06) and assignment (see para 7.17), usually only the promisee can enforce the benefit of a contract against the promisor, for our purposes there are three important statutory exceptions: (i) deemed agents (see para 10.24); (ii) connected lenders (see para 16.11); and (iii) named beneficiaries (see para 17.08).

---

1   The principal forms of contract for the supply of goods (sale, hiring and hp) are explained in Chap 1.
2   For contracts of loan, see generally, paras 7.02–3A.
3   *Chitty on Contracts*, 29th edn, Vol I, Chaps 2–3; *Halsbury's Laws*, 4th edn, Reissue, Vol 9, para 601 *et seq*.; Treitel, *Law of Contract*, 11th edn, Chaps 2–4; Goode, *HP Law & Practice*, 2nd edn, Chap 7.
4   *Per* MacKinnon LJ in *South Bedfordshire Electrical Finance Ltd v Bryant* [1938] 3 All ER 580, at 584, CA. On 'sugging', see (1992) 142 NLJ 888.
5   *Pharmaceutical Society of GB v Boots* [1953] 1 QB 401, CA.

3.  *Intent to create legal relations*. Where an agreement is made between business-
    men, it is presumed that they intend to enter a binding contract,[6] though this
    may be negatived.[7] At the other end of the scale, a domestic arrangement
    to exchange goods for cash is more likely to constitute reciprocal gifts (as
    to gifts, see para 2.08). Advertisements may fall either side of the line.[8]
    Further, goods supplied under a statutory obligation may not give rise to
    contractual obligations, e.g. drugs dispensed under the NHS (see paras 1.07 and
    4.29–30).

4.  *Governed by English law*. Where a contract has an international flavour, it will not
    necessarily be enforced by English law, but perhaps by another legal system,
    e.g. of Scotland, Germany or the United States. This issue is determined by the
    Conflict of Laws rules governing (i) the courts and (ii) the law applicable, which
    may differ where one of the parties is outside the jurisdiction. In the consumer
    context, these Conflict rules are most likely to affect supplies where the contract
    is made by way of the internet.[9] On the other hand, these Conflict rules may be
    ousted where the parties show a contrary intention (see para 18.13); and many
    suppliers to consumers are likely to take advantage of such an opt-out in a
    consumer contract, as by a standard-form provision (a choice of laws clause)
    that a contract with a Scottish consumer is to be governed by English law.[10]
    Such a choice of laws clause in a consumer contract may be struck down as
    being an unfair term.[11] For reform proposals, see para 18.27.

## The process of agreeing

[10.02] **Offer and acceptance**. Generally speaking, for the formation of a contract
between A and C what the law is looking for is a declaration of their willingness to
be bound to each other on identical terms. Leaving aside those unusual cases where
it is difficult to identify the offer and acceptance,[12] the first such declaration will be
the offer and the second the acceptance, it being possible for either A or C, or both,
to act through an agent (B1; B2: see para 10.06). For auctions, see para 10.10.

*The offer*. The first question which arises is whether the statement by A is intended as
a declaration of willingness to be bound (an offer),[13] or only an invitation to make

---

6   *Rose & Frank Co v Crompton & Bros Ltd* [1925] AC 445, HL (sales contract).
7   *Ibid* (franchise contract); *Baird Textiles Holdings Ltd v Marks & Spencer plc* [2002] 1 All ER (Comm)
    737, CA. Letters of comfort or intent between businesses are beyond the scope of this work.
8   Compare *Carlill v Carbolic Smoke Ball Co* (para 8.05) and *Bowerman v ABTA* [1995] Tr LR 246
    (113 LQR 47). For a suggestion that the issue should be treated differently with regard to
    consumers, see Twigg-Flesner, *Consumer Product Guarantees*, 2003, 180–1, esp. n 18. *Sed quaere?*
9   See para 8.17B. For contracts made by e-commerce, see Atiyah, *Sale of Goods*, Chap 5.
10  As to an unsuccessful attempt to contract by English *and* Islamic law, see *Shamil Bank of Bahrain
    EC v Beximco Pharmaceuticals Ltd* [2004] 2 All ER (Comm) 312, CA.
11  Grey term (q): see OFT, *UCT Bulletin No. 22*, case 13; and para 11.18. As to cross-border actions
    by consumer protection organisations, see *Verein etc v Henkel* [2003] 1 All ER (Comm) 606, Eu Ct.
12  E.g. where the parties continue to negotiate terms during performance (see para 10.03); in a
    battle of forms (see para 10.04). For pre-incorporation contracts, see para 19.25.
13  E.g. *Great Northern Railway Co v Witham* (1873) LR 9 CP 16 (standing offer); *Financings Ltd v
    Stimson* (set out at para 10.08; hp proposal form). For advertisements and quotations, see
    para 8.05.

an offer (an invitation to treat).[14] Any offer may be absolute or conditional,[15] e.g. 'subject to availability', 'subject to credit status', 'whilst stocks last'; and all the express terms of an offer must either be stated expressly in the offer or incorporated by reference.[16] These may be standard-form terms (see para 11.08). For instance, if the terms expressly granted the consumer an initial period for reflection, whether by way of warming up or cooling off (cf. para 10.23), that might assist in equalising the relative bargaining position of the parties for the purposes of the UTCC Regulations (reg 4(1): see para 11.15). For contracting by signature, see para 18.04.

*The acceptance.* An offer may only be accepted before its termination, as by revocation by the offeror, rejection by the offeree, lapse of time, occurrence of condition, impossibility. In some trades, the process of acceptance can be accelerated by use of a computer-link, e.g. credit applications, e-mails[17] or internet sales (see para 10.09A). Assuming an existing offer by A, the next question is whether C has accepted it. Of course, C can only accept where the offer is made to him (see para 10.15) and acceptance by C is then his declaration of willingness to be bound on identical terms: if C attempts to introduce any new or different terms or conditions, he will be making a counter-offer.[18] Usually, the offer will require communication of acceptance by C to A before a binding contract is made,[19] though acceptance may be implied, e.g. a confirmation of order by e-mail or website. The precise moment of formation is *prima facie* when C's acceptance is communicated to A;[20] but the parties may dispense with communication of acceptance and provide that some act is to constitute the acceptance,[21] e.g. cashing a cheque.[22]

The resulting contract may be absolute or conditional; and the latter may be subject to conditions precedent or subsequent (see para 1.11). Moreover, leaving aside agency (see above), there may be more than three separate principals

---

14  E.g. *Spencer v Harding* (1870) LR 5 CP 561 (circular requesting tenders); *Pharmaceutical Society of GB v Boots Cash Chemists (Southern) Ltd* [1952] 2 QB 795, CA (self-service shop); *Fisher v Bell* [1961] 1 QB 394, DC (shop-window display); *Partridge v Crittenden* [1968] 2 All ER 421, DC (magazine classified advert); *Esso Petroleum Ltd v Comrs of Customs and Excise* (set out at para 2.08; petrol station promotion). For the difficulty of classifying 'quotations' and 'estimates' in respect of the supply of services, see OFT, *A Buyer's Guide*, pp 21, 43 (defining a quotation as a firm price; and an estimate as an informed guess).

15  Distinguish promissory conditions: see para 11.04.

16  E.g. price adjustment clauses (see para 10.05). See also the battle of the forms (para 10.04). For the incorporation of exclusion clauses, see para 18.04; and for express and implied terms, see paras 11.07 and 11.10.

17  *Pretty Pictures Sarl v Quixote Films Ltd* [2003] EWHC 311; and generally, Capps (2003) 153 NLJ 906.

18  *Hyde v Wrench* (1840) 3 Beav 334 (not a goods case). Distinguish attempts to put additional terms in A's mouth: *Stevenson v Maclean* (1880) 5 QBD 346.

19  *Felthouse v Bindley* (1872) 11 CBNS 869; and as to inertia selling, see further, para 8.18. It would seem that the offeror may waive his right to communication of acceptance: *Robophone Facilities Ltd v Blank* [1966] 3 All ER 128, CA; and for direct financing, see para 10.08.

20  *Brinkibon Ltd v Stahag Stahl etc mbH* [1983] 2 AC 34, HL (telex); *Holwell Securities Ltd v Hughes* [1974] 1 All ER 161, CA (post; manner of communication specified). An offer cannot be revoked after acceptance: *Byrne v Van Tienhoven* (1880) 5 CPD 344.

21  E.g. *Carlill's* case (above; unilateral contract); *Financings Ltd v Stimson* (above; bilateral contract); *Byrne v Van Tienhoven* (above; the pf postal rule of acceptance on posting); *Re Charge Card Services Ltd* (set out at para 2.27). See also CCA, s 66 (para 7.11).

22  *IRC v Fry* [2002] CLY 722.

involved in what appears to be a single transaction, as where the transaction is financed (see Chap 16). For the Unfair Commercial Practices (UCP) Directive, see para 4.21.

**[10.03/4] Incomplete agreements**. 'To be a good contract, there must be a concluded bargain; and a concluded contract is one which settles everything that is necessary to be settled and leaves nothing to be settled by agreement between the parties'.[23] The objection is that the parties only agreed in outline,[24] whilst showing that they still intended to negotiate the detail.[25] Similar decisions have been reached where the following remained to be settled: price and delivery;[23] detailed written terms to be supplied,[26] subject to *force majeure* conditions (see para 22.13A); or there was a contract to negotiate.[27]

On the other hand, the agreement between the parties may be completed, although not worked out in meticulous detail,[28] and the SGA itself provides for the price 'to be fixed in a manner agreed by the contract'.[29] Thus, the parties have been held to have finished agreeing in the following cases: where a contract was made on auction particulars;[30] where the missing detail was left to be supplied by the law, as by way of implied terms (see para 11.10); or on the basis of what is reasonable, e.g. SGA, s 8(2) (see para 2.06); or supplied by a third party, e.g. agreements to sell at a valuation (see SGA, s 9: see para 10.05); or where the apparently uncertain terms were meaningless.[31]

Whilst everything therefore turns upon the attitude of the courts to whether the parties have shown they have finished agreeing, this has not obviated difficulties such as the 'battle of the forms',[32] or price escalation formulae (see para 10.05), or letters of intent (see para 10.01), or forms signed in blank (see para 16.05), or even non-land agreements made 'subject to contract'.[33]

---

23  *May and Butcher Ltd v R* (1929) [1934] 2 KB 17a at 21, HL, *per* Lord Dunedin. See *Jordan Grand Prix Ltd v Vodafone Group plc* [2003] 2 All ER (Comm) 864 (not a sale case).

24  *Scammell & Nephew Ltd v Ouston* [1941] AC 251, [1941] 1 All ER 14, HL.

25  The result is the same where the agreement itself is subject to a condition precedent: *Astra Trust v Adams & Williams* [1969] 1 Lloyd's Rep 81 (purchase of ship 'subject to a satisfactory survey'); and see generally, para 15.21. Similarly, mere standing orders: see para 10.02.

26  *JH Saphir (Merchants) Ltd v Zissimos* [1960] 1 Lloyd's Rep 490. See also *Manatee Towing Co v Oceanbulk Maritime SA* [1999] 2 All ER (Comm) 306 ('subject to details').

27  *Walford v Miles* [1992] 1 All ER 453, HL (sale of business). For argument that this decision is wrong and that there is a duty to negotiate in good faith see: Brown [1992] JBL 353; Neill (1992) 108 LQR 405; Jamieson [1992] LM & CLQ 186; Berg (2003) 119 LQR 357.

28  They may intend a binding provisional agreement to be later replaced by more elaborate terms negotiated between them: *Brogden v Metropolitan Railway Co* (1877) 2 App Cas 666, HL; *The Blankenstein* [1985] 1 All ER 475, CA; *Pagnan SpA v Feed Products* [1987] 2 Lloyd's Rep 601, CA. E.g. an open credit card contract (see para 7.09).

29  SGA, s 8(1): set out at para 2.06; *Masport Ltd v Morrison Industries Ltd* [1996] CLY 1252, PC. For argument as to whether the 'manner' might include subsequent agreement between the parties, see Atiyah, *Sale of Goods*, 10th edn, 31. This would not appear to be what Parliament intended: see the amendment to the Bill referred to at para 2.06. What is the effect of 'Our offer is made on the basis of our current price list'?

30  *Filby v Hounsell* [1896] 2 Ch 737 (not a goods case; as to auctions, see para 10.10).

31  *Nicolene Ltd v Simmonds* [1953] 1 QB 543, CA ('usual conditions of acceptance').

32  *Butler Tool Co Ltd v Ex-Cell-O Corpn (England) Ltd* [1979] 1 All ER 965, CA (discussed Adams 95 LQR 481; Rawlings 42 MLR 715; Parris, *Retention of Title on Sale of Goods*, 18–21).

33  *ProForce Recruitment Ltd v Rugby Group Ltd* [2006] EWCA Civ 69, CA (service-cleaning contract).

**[10.05] Price adjustment formulae**. Particularly if there is likely to be any significant delay between formation of a supply contract and delivery/payment, it is common to find that the supplier seeks to include in his contract a price escalation clause.[34] A similar position is likely to obtain in respect of loans of substantial sums of money. In such cases, suppliers of goods or money frequently embody their price/rate escalation clause in standard form contracts (see generally, para 11.08).

If such an adjustment clause is accepted by the buyer, hirer or borrower and does not amount to the offence of misleading pricing (see para 8.10), there is the danger that it will result in a court finding that the clause negatives the existence of any contract on the grounds that the parties have not finished agreeing.[35] Even if the clause is part of the contract, there may be an implied term that the interest rate adjustment clause should not be exercised for an improper purpose, dishonestly, capriciously, arbitrarily or unreasonably;[36] and, in a consumer supply it may be found not binding on the consumer because it is unfair (Grey term 1(l): see OFT, *UCT Bulletin No. 22*, case 13; and para 11.17). It is common for a loan agreement to contain a variable rate of interest clause (see para 7.03A). To reduce this danger, such a clause will usually provide for the price/rent/interest rate to be fixed by some third party or objective formula.

1.  *Third-party pricing*. Where there is an agreements to sell at a valuation set by a third party[37] s 9 of the SGA lays down two rules:

    (a) Where such third party cannot or does not make such valuation, 'the agreement is avoided; provided that if the goods or any part thereof have been delivered to and appropriated by the buyer he must pay a reasonable price for them' (s 9(1)). This assumes that such a contract is void, though it is conceivable that the seller or buyer may **promise** that the third party will make the valuation.[38]

    (b) Where such third party is prevented from making the valuation by the fault of the seller or buyer, the party not in fault may maintain an action for damages against the party in fault.[39]

    Do the same rules apply by analogy to quasi-sales, hp and simple hiring agreements?

---

34  With the almost continuous inflation of modern times, these clauses have become common in commercial contracts, e.g. *Hillas & Co Ltd v Arcos Ltd* (1932) 147 LT 503, HL. Mistaken beliefs that a contract contains a price escalation clause will not necessarily amount to a repudiation: see para 26.15. For VAT charges, see s 89 of the Value Added Tax Act 1994.

35  *May & Butcher Ltd v R* (1929) [1934] 2 KB 17n, HL. It may be evidence that the terms are just an invitation to treat: see para 10.03. Compare *Queensland Electricity GB v New Hope Collieries* [1989] 1 Lloyd's Rep 205, PC.

36  *Paragon Finance plc v Staughton & Nash* (set out at para 11.10) *per* Dyson LJ at para 36, *obiter*.

37  For the effect of an erroneous valuation, see *Burgess v Purchase & Sons (Farm) Ltd* [1983] Ch 216 (sale of shares). Cf. auctions: para 10.11.

38  See Atiyah, *Sale of Goods*, 10th edn, 34. Compare the discussion on s 6 of the SGA (para 22.10) and on s 22(2) of the SGA (para 22.03).

39  S 9(2). Does the action sound in contract or tort? 'Fault' is rather unhelpfully defined by the SGA as 'wrongful act or default' (s 61(1)), but presumably comprehends breach of contract or tort. Cf. 'fault' in another statute: para 27.40.

2.   *Objective formula.* The clause may only give the supplier/lender **power** in designated circumstances to vary the price/rent/rate;[40] but more commonly it provides for **automatic** variation by reference to some outside criteria of price or interest rate. Assuming the variation is not so great in relation to market value as to turn the transaction into a wager,[41] an automatic variation clause will generally be effective.[42] In respect of regulated agreements, see the CCA rules as to documentation (para 9.11) and variation (para 26.22).

**[10.06] Agency**. Under the ordinary common law rules of agency, which are expressly saved by the SGA (s 62(2)), any party (A) who can make a contract personally with C in the manner considered above (paras 10.01–05) may alternatively make that contract through his agent (B) in a number of ways:[43]

*(1) Actual authority.* Where A confers actual authority on B, whether expressly or by implication,[44] and whether disclosed or undisclosed to C.[45] However, an undisclosed principal cannot ratify.[46]

*(2) Apparent authority.* Notwithstanding that there is no actual authority, where A clothes B with the appearance of authority.[47] This rule requires a representation from A to C[48] that B has A's authority to act as A's agent.[49] It is closely related to estoppel (see para 21.10, *et seq.*), and shares with it a number of rules, including the rule that a mere handing over of possession of goods to B generally will not, without more, confer an apparent authority on B to dispose of them (see para 21.13).

*(3) Usual authority and ratification.* Notwithstanding that there is no actual or apparent authority, where it is in the usual course of B's business to make such a disposition,[50] or A subsequently ratifies that transaction.[46]

*(4) Necessity.* Notwithstanding that there is no actual, apparent or usual authority, there may be an agency of necessity, though the courts are today reluctant to

---

40   *Lombard Tricity Finance Ltd v Paton* (set out at para 26.22). For the effect of the CCA on such powers, see para 26.22.

41   *Brogden v Marriott* (1836) 5 LJCP 302 (horse sold for £200 if within a month it trotted 18 miles in an hour; but for 1 shilling if it failed to do so).

42   Under the doctrine *Certum est quod certum reddi potest*: see *per* Viscount Dunedin in *May Butcher Ltd v R* (above).

43   For the ways in which an agent may bind his principal, see Treitel, *Law of Contract*, 11th edn, Chap 17.

44   *Lloyds and Scottish Finance Ltd v Williamson* [1965] 1 All ER 641, CA; *SMC Electronics Ltd v Akhter Computers Ltd* [2001] CLY 109, CA.

45   *Rolls Royce Power Engineering plc v Ricardo etc Ltd* [2004] 2 All ER (Comm) 129, at paras 56–8.

46   *Keighley Maxted & Co v Durrant* [1901] AC 240, HL; *Secured Residential Funding PLC v Douglas Hendeles & Co* [2000] CLY 2607, CA (loan on house mortgage) But an unnamed principal can: *Sui Yin Kwan v Eastern Insurance Co Ltd* [1994] JBL 260.

47   As to where an employee/agent changes employers, see *Discount Kitchens v Crawford* [1989] CLY 51, CA; the *Bacfid* case (set out at para 16.06). See also *Charrington Fuel Oil v Parvant Co* [1989] CLY 58, CA (order by new owner of property).

48   Distinguish the consent exception (paras 21.04–5) where A tells B that B may dispose of the goods on his own account.

49   This overlaps with the estoppel exception, where A may represent to C either (i) that B has A's authority to sell on behalf of A, or (ii) that B is the owner: see para 21.10.

50   *Watteau v Fenwick* [1893] 1 QB 346; *Kinahan Ltd v Parry* [1910] 2 KB 389, CA. It has been argued that this rule may extend to all agents exceeding their actual authority whilst acting within the scope of their employment as agent: Atiyah, *Sale of Goods*, 10th edn, 381–2; Brown [2004] JBL 391. But see *Chitty on Contracts*, 29th edn, Vol 2, para 32-063.

find such an agency.[51] The principle has been applied in the case of the sale of perishable goods by a carrier,[52] but not to a sale of furniture by a voluntary bailee;[53] and Parliament has extended the list of bailees who have authority to sell by reason of the bailor's failure to collect the goods (Torts Act 1977, ss 12, 13 and Sched 1).

For the CCA provisions as to how the agent (B) may affect relations between the principal (A) and third party (C), see para 10.24. In consumer contracts, the relationship between A and B is governed by the common law (see SGA, s 62(2): set out at para 10.18); but it may be unfair to amend the above common law rules (OFT, *UCT Bulletin No. 21*, case 9, referring to reg 7; and see para 11.13).

**[10.07] Direct financing**. The effect of the foregoing principles must now be examined in those circumstances where a third party provides the finance. The first question is: to whom does the retail supplier sell? In loan financing, there is a simple sale from goods-supplier to consumer with the price provided by the financier lending that sum to the consumer.[54] Alternatively, the transaction may be directly financed, in that the supplier sells the goods to the financier, who himself supplies them to the consumer under an instalment contract (see para 2.21), in which case there will be two supply contracts as follows:[55]

1. *Dealer/financier*. The three parties will envisage the dealer selling the goods chosen by the consumer to the financier. In *North West Securities Ltd v Alexander Breckon Ltd*[56] the Court of Appeal held that as a result there were two entirely separate supply contracts: viz a contract of sale from dealer to financier and a contract of hp from financier to consumer (at 522 H–K; 523J; 524G).

2. *Financier/consumer*. Between the financier and consumer, it is envisaged that there will be an instalment contract (see para 1.03). 'The conventional manner in which offer and acceptance takes place ... is for the proposed ... (retail customer), as offeror, to sign the agreement for forwarding to the finance company and for the finance company to accept it by signing the agreement itself, subsequently communicating that acceptance to the offeror, usually by post'.[57] At any moment before then, at common law the consumer can back out of the transaction and recover his deposit (see para 16.05) or perhaps any part-exchange goods); but the position may be significantly different if the agreement is regulated.[58]

---

51 See *Prager v Blatspiel, Stamp and Heacock Ltd* [1924] 1 KB 566 (but see McMeel [2003] LMCLQ 169 at 184–6).
52 *Springer v Great Western Railway Co* [1921] 1 KB 257, CA.
53 *Sachs v Miklos* [1948] 2 KB 23, CA. See para 21.06. For wagers, see para 8.15.
54 See *Edmond Murray v BSP International Foundations* [1994] CLY 548, CA. For loan financing, see para 2.23.
55 For collateral contracts between dealer and consumer, see para 16.18.
56 [1981] RTR 518, CA.
57 *Carlyle Finance Ltd v Pallas Industrial Finance Ltd* (set out at para 10.08), *per* Potter LJ at para 35, accepting the analysis of counsel at para 21.
58 If the debtor or hirer exercises either of his statutory rights of withdrawal or cancellation (see respectively, paras 10.26 and 10.29) the CCA then allows him certain cancellation rights (ss 57(1) and 69): these rights are discussed at para 10.31. Where the CCA applies, that procedure will satisfy the rules as to copies (see paras 9.14–18).

*(a)  The offer.* In *Financings Ltd v Stimson*:[59]

> On March 16th S signed an hp proposal form produced by a dealer; and
> two days later the dealer allowed him to take away the car to which that
> document related. On March 20th, S returned the car to the dealer, saying
> that he did not want it and (believing himself to be bound by a contract)
> offered to forfeit his deposit. During the night of March 24th/25th the car
> was stolen from the dealer's premises and recovered badly damaged.
> On March 25th, the finance company (not having been informed that S had
> returned the car to the dealer) signed the agreement.

The finance company's action against S for breach of the hp agreement
failed before the Court of Appeal. Their Lordships unanimously took the
view that S's completed proposal form constituted an offer (see para 10.02),
but that offer had come to an end before the finance company purported to
accept in on 25 March for the following reasons:

(i)   (Pearson LJ, dissenting) the return of the car by S to the dealer on
      March 20th amounted to a revocation of his offer (see generally, para
      10.02) as the dealer had an ostensible authority to accept the revocation
      of the offer on behalf of the finance company;[60]

(ii)  (unanimously) the offer was conditional on the car being in substan-
      tially the same condition at the time of acceptance as at the time
      of offer, and therefore the offer terminated on the night of March
      24th/25th.[61]

*(b)  The acceptance* (see para 10.08).

**[10.08]  Acceptance in direct financing**. To try to ensure that the contract is made in
the manner outlined above (para 10.07), the proposal form will usually contain
some clause such as the following to be found in *Financings Ltd v Stimson* (set out at
para 10.07):

> 'This agreement shall become binding on the (finance company) only upon accept-
> ance by signature on behalf of the (company) and the hiring shall be deemed to
> commence on such date of acceptance'.

Their Lordships therefore took the view that the offer contained in the proposal
form had not been accepted before 25 March; and they also rejected the argument
that there was a preliminary oral contract containing most of the terms embodied
in the proposal form.[62] The early release of the goods by the dealer to the retail

---

59   [1962] 3 All ER 386; [1962] 1 WLR 1184, CA; and see also *Eurodata Systems PLC v Michael Gerson
     (Finance) PLC* [2004] CLY 669 (finance lease). Distinguish *Hitchens v General Guarantee Corpn Ltd*
     [2001] CLY 669, CA (directly financed agreement made orally).

60   As to an agent's ostensible authority generally, see para 10.06; and as to variations in the
     authority of an agent to accept communications on behalf of the financier, see para 10.24. As
     to regulated agreements, see para 10.25.

61   An alternative view is that there is a contract breached by delivery of goods in a different
     condition from that obtaining on the consumer's prior inspection: *Karsales (Harrow) Ltd v Wallis*
     (see para 18.07); *Bentworth Finance Ltd v Lubert* (set out at para 15.23).

62   Presumably because of the clause cited above. Alternatively, acceptance may be implied
     at common law from delivery of the goods: *Carlyle Finance case* (see below). Cf. *NWS Ltd v
     Alexander Breckon Ltd* (see para 10.07).

customer 'does not in the ordinary way amount to more than a preliminary bailment pending formal acceptance . . .'[63] Whether or not the transaction is regulated, the common motor trade practice of delivering new cars against a mere offer seems dangerous (see para 10.09). In *Carlyle Finance Ltd v Pallas Industrial Finance Ltd*:[64]

> The customer (V) and dealer agreed that V should purchase a car under a directly finance regulated conditional sale agreement with a finance company (C). C approved the transaction in principle, paid the price to the dealer and authorised delivery of the car to V. Before C could sign the conditional sale, V sold the car, which eventually passed to P, another finance company. It was accepted that P would obtain a good Part 3 title if, at the time of V's sale, a conditional sale existed between C and V (see para 21.55).

The Court of Appeal distinguished *Financings Ltd v Stimson* on the basis that the *Carlyle* (C) contract contained no such acceptance provision (at para 32) and ascertained that, whilst the agreement envisaged the normal formal signed acceptance,[65] C had made up its mind to accept the proposal and authorised the dealer to deliver the goods (at para 27). On the basis that V had no reason to suppose that the delivery of the car was not an acceptance by the dealer on behalf of C (see para 10.06) of V's offer to enter a conditional sale, the court held that at common law the dealer on behalf of C had accepted that offer by conduct[66] in delivering the car to V (at para 33: see para 16.06). The court said that the fact that the regulated agreement was not properly executed (see para 9.19) for breach of s 61 (see para 9.12) did not prevent that unenforceable agreement passing title (*per* Potter LJ at para 30).

**[10.09] Delivery before acceptance**. This paragraph is concerned with the situation where the parties are negotiating a directly financed transaction (see para 2.21) but the dealer delivers the 'new' goods[67] to the consumer before the financier accepts the transaction, seemingly a fairly common situation (see paras 10.07–8), perhaps in return for delivery to the dealer of part-exchange goods (see para 2.09).

1. *The new goods*. Generally speaking, in the period before the financier accepts the proposal the consumer is likely to hold the new goods as a bailee at will from the dealer;[68] but it is possible that an agreement between the consumer and financier may be inferred, so that the consumer may pass a Pt III title to a bfp.[69] On the other hand, the parties may intend a provisional contract of sale

---

63  *Carlyle Finance Ltd v Pallas Industrial Finance Ltd* (below), *per* Potter LJ at para 35, accepting the analysis of counsel at para 21. See further, para 10.09.

64  [1999] 1 All ER (Comm) 659, CA.

65  Potter LJ argued that the formal provision for acceptance by signature had been waived under the rule that a party inserting a provision for his own benefit may do so: at para 34.

66  *Aliter* where either (i) C had not already bought the car from the dealer, or (ii) the dealer made delivery to V on his own account without C's authority: *per* Potter LJ at paras 31 and 33.

67  The expression 'new' is used only to identify the goods the consumer is acquiring (which may be new or second-hand) from those traded in by him.

68  Will the consumer have to pay for that use? What if the consumer is injured by the defective state of the goods? See generally, para 1.17; and further, Goode, *HP Law & Practice*, 2nd edn, 146–8.

69  *Hitchens v General Guarantee Corpn Ltd* [2001] CLY 880, CA; and see para 21.55.

between dealer and consumer, to be set aside if the financier subsequently accepts the proposal.[70] In the latter event, if the financier subsequently declines the proposal, the consumer may have a better right to the new goods than the dealer.[71] Whether the consumer initially holds as bailee or buyer, there will be discussed later the liability of the financier after his acceptance of the proposal for any misrepresentations by the dealer (see para 16.03 *et seq.*) or breach of implied terms (see para 14.13).

2. *The part-exchange goods.* In effect, the consumer sells the part-exchange goods to the dealer for the amount of the part-exchange allowance, which sum the dealer holds as the deposit payable in respect of the new goods.[72] Suppose the financier declines the proposal. It is conceivable that there is an independent unconditional sale of the part-exchange goods,[73] but much more likely that the parties intended the two transactions to be interdependent (see para 2.09). However, there would appear to be several possible analyses of the nature of that interdependence:[73] first, in relation to the transfer of the part-exchange goods to the dealer, formation of the contract to supply the new goods was a condition precedent (see para 1.11) either to its formation[74] or performance;[75] or second, that there is an immediate sale of the part-exchange goods to the dealer, subject to a condition subsequent that it is determinable if the financier does not accept the transaction in respect of the new goods (see para 1.11). Which analysis is adopted might be important, as where the part-exchange goods are damaged in the meantime,[76] or the consumer has only a defective title to them,[77] or the part-exchange goods are defective.[78] A standard-form contract may well seek to deal with these matters (see para 11.08).

**[10.09A] Contracting by website**.[79] Where a consumer places an order on an English web-site, the ordinary common law rules of offer and acceptance (see para 10.02) would seem to produce the following position: the web-site might be an invitation to treat and the consumer's order the offer; or the website might be an offer and the consumer's order the acceptance.[80] In the former case, the ordinary

---

70  The sale between dealer and consumer may thus be subject to a condition subsequent (see generally, para 1.11); but it may infringe the Bills of Sale Acts: *Polsky v S & A Services Ltd* [1951] 1 All ER 1062, CA; and see para 25.27.

71  *City Motors v Southern etc Service* (1961) 106 CLR 477, HC (criticised Goode, *Op. cit.*, 148–9).

72  Goode, *Op. cit.*, 309–10.

73  Goode, *Op. cit.*, 311–13.

74  It would follow that the dealer had not agreed to buy the goods (see fn 76 below). But what if the dealer had meanwhile settled any outstanding balance due to a fourth party in respect of the part-exchange goods?

75  The dealer would have agreed to buy the goods (see fn 77 below). Does it also follow that the consumer has conditionally agreed to take the new goods in breach of CCA, s 59 (set out at para 5.20)?

76  E.g. *Clarke v Reilly* (1962) 96 ILTR 96. For the passing of property, see further, Chap 20.

77  Has the dealer 'agreed to buy' them within s 9 of the Factors Act 1899 (as to which see para 21.45)? See Goode, *ibid*, 305–6. For the position as between the contracting parties, see below.

78  Does the supply attract the implied terms from ss 12–15 of the SGA or ss 2–5 of the SGSA (see Chaps 12–15)? See generally, Law Com. 95, paras 52–3.

79  See generally, Nicoll [1998] JBL, esp. at 42–9.

80  If the website quotes a ridiculously low price, the law of mistake as to terms may prevent formation of any contract (see para 10.16).

confirmation of order is *prima facie* an implied acceptance; but the terms exhibited on the website may vary this so that, for instance, the dispatch of the goods is the acceptance.[81] However, the E-Commerce Regulations (see para 8.17A) lay down that in respect of contracts made by website,[82] not only must the consumer be provided with certain pre-contract information (see para 9.05), but there are also some variations of the ordinary rules of contract.[83] Suppose a consumer reacts to a website advertisement by placing an order on-line, e.g. by proffering his payment card and clicking on the 'Order Now' button.[84] Seemingly, the Regulations do not alter this as regards the following provisions:[85] the supplier must by electronic means acknowledge receipt of that order 'without undue delay' (reg 11(1)(a)); and the order and acknowledgment will be deemed received when either the addressee is able to access it or the service provided (reg 11(2)(a)), except where the acknowledgment takes the form of the provision of the ordered service (reg 11(2)(b)). However, it is a different matter as regards the following rules, in respect of which the consumer's order 'shall be the contractual offer':[86] he must then be allowed to correct any input errors before 'the placing of the order' (reg 9(1)(c): see para 9.05); and, if the consumer's order is an acceptance, he must likewise by allowed to correct any input errors before 'the placing of the order' (reg 11(1)(b)). The drafting of reg 12[86] seems to suggest that the draftsman thought that the website would have to be an invitation to treat; but why could it not be an offer subject to a condition precedent (see para 1.11) that the consumer could correct input errors? This last would be consistent with reg 15 (see below).

If the supplier fails to provide this reg 11(1) facility for the consumer to correct his order, reg 15 provides that the consumer

> 'Shall be entitled to rescind the contract unless any court having jurisdiction in relation to the contract in question orders otherwise on the application of the service provider'.

This provision would appear to be ill-drafted: Why can the consumer not make an application? Is the right rescission *ab initio* (see para 26.12)? For how long does the right of rescission last? When should a court deny rescission?

Even after formation of the contract, there may be a statutory right of cancellation (see para 10.28, *et seq*.); and any clause allowing the supplier to vary the specification or price after contract may be unfair,[87] as may one excluding liability for fraudulent use of stolen payment card details posted to the website.[87]

---

81  This gives the supplier an opportunity to correct (say) any pricing errors on his website: [2005] 7 *Which?* 7.

82  But not where the contract is concluded exclusively by e-mail: regs 9(4) and 11(3).

83  Where neither of the parties are consumers, they may agree to dispense with these rules: reg 11(1).

84  A term on the website that the supplier may vary the specification or price without notice would appear to be unfair: OFT, *UCT Bulletin No. 23*, case 16; and see para 11.17.

85  Regs 9(1) and 11 generally apply whether or not the order amounts to an offer: reg 12, last phrase.

86  Reg 12, opening phrase.

87  UTCCR, Grey term (k); [2005] *Bulletin A/J, Micro*.

# Auctions[88]

**[10.10] Introduction**. An auction normally involves a sale to the highest bidder by public[89] competition,[90] conducted on behalf of the seller by his agent, the auctioneer (see para 10.11). Even if the auction is advertised in advance, the auctioneer is *prima facie* not bound to hold the auction;[91] and, if he is commissioned to sell a number of items, the SGA provides that 'each lot is *prima facie* deemed to be the subject of separate contract of sale' (s 57(1)). Almost inevitably, an auctioneer will apply some sort of description to each lot, perhaps in a catalogue and/or when he puts each lot up; and this may cause that description to be incorporated into the buyer's contract (see para 18.04).

Where a consumer bids at an auction, particularly an internet auction,[92] the first matter to consider is the sale of counterfeit goods, e.g. DVDs, perfume, clothes: this may amount to an offence (see para 8.02) and so may render the contract illegal and void (see para 10.20). Second, a bidder in an internet auction, e.g. eBay, will inevitably have to supply electronically his payment card details, which allows an opportunity for these particulars to be fraudulently abstracted to defraud either sellers[92] or buyers.[93] These considerations aside, in any auction, including an internet auction,[94] the position is as follows: a buyer of second-hand goods will not usually be dealing as consumer for the purposes of UCTA (see para 18.18), so that statutory implied terms may be excludable (see para 18.19); but the express terms of any contract he makes at the auction will be subject to the UTCC rules with regard to legibility and fairness, e.g. events when commission payable (OFT, *UCT Bulletin No. 15*, case 6); and any attempt to deny the auctioneer authority to make representations, or giving the auctioneer an absolute authority to determine disputes may be an unfair term.[95] Of course, if the goods are purchased by on-line auction there may be further problems (see para 10.09A), especially for a buyer who has not paid by credit card with the protection of CCA, s 75 (see para 16.12).

Once the bidding on a particular lot has commenced, s 57(2) describes how a contract for its sale comes into existence:

---

88  See generally Harvey and Meisel, *Auctions*, 2nd edn, 1995. In relation to goods, auctions are frequently used to achieve sales at market value of commodities, plant and machinery and motor vehicles: see Harvey and Meisel, *Op. cit.*, 9–12.

89  Distinguish competing for a contract by sealed bid: see *Harvela Investments Ltd v Royal Trust Co of Canada (CI) Ltd* [1986] AC 207, HL, *per* Lord Templeman at 230.

90  The concept of an auction is not defined by the SGA. Does s 57 extend to the descending-price system (Dutch Auction)? As to the different types of auction, see Harvey and Meisel, *Op. cit.*, 1–4.

91  *Harris v Nickerson* (1873) LR 8 QB 286.

92  A stolen payment card may be used to pay for goods ordered to an accommodation address and the genuine card-holder subsequently reclaims the payment: *The Times* (19.3.05). For sales on eBay, see [2006] 4 *Which?* 18.

93  The particulars supplied by a bidder may be used to empty the bidder's account or otherwise defraud him: see *The Times* (17 and 19.1.05).

94  OFT, *UCT Bulletin No. 23*, case 31. Distinguish internet notice-boards, which only result in private sales. For internet sales, see (2005) 16 *Computers & The Law* 34–6; and para 9.05.

95  Grey Terms 1(b) and 1(n): see paras 11.16 and 11.18. For many other auctioneer's terms attacked by the OFT, see [2005] *UCT Bulletin O/D, Christie's; Society of Auctioneers*.

'A sale by auction is complete when the auctioneer announces its completion by the fall of the hammer, or in other customary manner; and until the announcement is made any bidder may retract his bid'.

Thus, the auctioneer's request on behalf of the seller for bids amounts only to an invitation to treat;[96] each successive bid is an offer,[97] revocable until acceptance;[98] and the auctioneer is, on behalf of the seller, *prima facie* free to accept or reject that bid. Bidders sometimes go to some lengths to conceal their bid from other bidders.[99]

There may be attempts to manipulate the system of selling by auction to their own advantage by any of the three parties involved: the seller may or may not reserve a price or right to bid (see para 10.12); the seller/auctioneer may conduct a mock auction (see para 10.11); and the bidders may form a ring (see para 10.13). Goods unsold in an auction may be sold by the auctioneer privately thereafter, in which case the ordinary rules of offer and acceptance apply (see para 10.02).

**[10.11] Auctioneers.** In selling goods,[100] the auctioneer acts primarily as the agent of the seller,[101] *prima facie* having a lien over the goods sold[102] and a right to sue the purchaser for the price.[103] As he is not normally a party to the sale, the auctioneer is not usually himself liable for the statutory implied conditions (see para 14.04); but he may be liable to the buyer in respect of statements at the auction, either on the basis of negligent misstatements[104] or collateral contract (see para 11.06); or if he conducted a mock auction (see para 10.11A). If, in selling the goods, an auctioneer exceeds his authority, as a mercantile agent he may nevertheless pass a good title (see para 21.24, *et seq.*). Suppose an auctioneer's principal (the seller) is not the true owner of goods sent for auction: in the case of a motor vehicle, the auctioneer commissioned to sell by the debtor under an hp agreement may pass a good Pt 3 title to the buyer (see para 21.55, *et seq.*); or any kind of goods may be sold with foreign title acquired abroad (see para 21.05). However, in knocking down those goods to the highest bidder, the auctioneer (albeit innocently) may

---

96 *British Car Auctions Ltd v Wright* [1972] 3 All ER 462, DC (criminal case: see para 4.37).

97 Perhaps each bid falls when superseded by a valid higher bid: Treitel, *Law of Contract*, 11th edn, 11.

98 *Payne v Cave* (1789) 3 Term 148. It seems to follow that in 'taking' a bid, the auctioneer is not accepting that offer, but merely indicating that he has no objection to treating with that bidder (suggestion by JWA Thornely).

99 See Harvey and Meisel, *Op. cit.*, 129–30. In the event of a disputed bid, the conditions frequently allow the lot to be put up again, e.g. *Richards v Phillips* [1969] 1 Ch 39 (sale of land).

100 Whether he actually knocks the goods down in the auction (see para 10.10) or sells them privately (perhaps because the goods have failed to find a buyer at auction). The agency contract may contain an implied term that the auctioneer will carefully value the goods: *Luxmoore-May v Messenger, May, Baverstock* [1990] 1 All ER 1067, CA (see 107 LQR 28) (painting).

101 For the circumstances in which, and the extent to which, he may also act as the agent of the buyer, see Harvey and Meisel, *Auctions*, 2nd edn, 115–18. For the auctioneer's authority as agent of the seller, see Harvey and Meisel, *Op. cit.*, 24–6; 36–8. For a situation in which the auctioneer buys and resells as principal, see Harvey and Meisel, *Op. cit.*, 294–6.

102 The lien is good against both seller and buyer and is for the auctioneer's charges and the price respectively; see Harvey and Meisel, *Op. cit.*, 62–7. The lien is free of any claim for distress by the seller's landlord (as to distress, see generally, para 19.18): Harvey and Meisel, *Op. cit.*, 77–9.

103 *Chelmsford Auctions Ltd v Poole* [1973] QB 542, CA; *Pollway Ltd v Abdullah* [1974] 2 All ER 381, CA. As to actions for the price, see paras 27.16–18.

104 *Thomson v Christie, Manson & Woods Ltd* [2005] EWCA Civ 555, CA; and see generally, para 17.20.

commit conversion of the goods[105] and is then in difficulty as to the proceeds.[106] *Contra* where the goods fail to sell: in *Marcq v Christie Manson & Woods Ltd*[107]

> The claimant was the owner of a stolen painting, which some years later came into the hands of S. S placed the painting in the hands of an auctioneer, who attempted unsuccessfully to sell it, and then returned the painting to S. The claimant sued the auctioneer (1) as a negligent bailee (see para 1.17) and (2) in the tort of conversion (see para 19.04).

The Court of Appeal unanimously held the auctioneer not liable, saying that, with regard to lesser ('ministerial') acts which do not deny the claimant's title (as here), where an auctioneer proves that he acted in good faith and without notice of the claimant's title, he does not commit conversion.[108] However, their Lordships said, *obiter*, that an auctioneer would be liable in conversion (para 24: see para 19.06) if he succeeded in selling and delivering the goods to a buyer (as opposed to just intending/hoping to do so); but that the auctioneer had no duty in the law of bailment to investigate the title of the seller (para 54: see para 1.17).

**[10.11A] Mock auctions.**[109] These are a form of elaborate and long-established confidence trick which Parliament has sought to contain by the Mock Auctions Act 1961. The major difficulty faced by the draftsman was to catch all such mischievous activities whilst not hindering genuine auctions. The Act makes it a criminal offence to sell or 'to promote or conduct or to assist in the conduct of, a mock auction'[110] by way of competitive bidding[111] any lot which includes prescribed articles, e.g. plate, linens, china, jewellery (s 3(2)), using any of the following techniques, there being provisions to lighten the burden of proof on the prosecution (ss 3(3)–(5)): the goods are knocked down to a person at a price less than his highest bid or part of the price is repaid to him (s 1(3)(a)), there being an exemption if the reduction in price/repayment was on account of a 'defect' or 'damage sustained after the bid was made' (s 1(4)); or the right to bid is restricted to persons buying more than one article;[112] or there are free gifts (s 1(3)(c). For 'free gifts', see generally, para 2.08). The OFT have sought to discourage such offences by utilising their powers under Pt 8 of the EA (see para 6.07). In 2007, the Act may have to be amended to comply with the UCP Directive (see para 4.21B).

---

105 *Unicorn Transport Finance Ltd v British Car Auctions Ltd* [1978] 2 All ER 385, CA (car on hp); and see para 19.05.

106 See Harvey and Meisel, *Op. cit.*, 104–8. The safest course may be to interplead.

107 [2003] 3 All ER 561, CA. See Harvey and Meisel, *Op. cit.*, 136–9; and para 19.06.

108 At para 24, adopting the reasoning of Jack J: [2002] 4 All ER 1005, at paras 40–41. A ministerial act has been defined as one which merely changes possession of goods and not the property in them (para 34, quoting the Law Reform Committee). As to the burden of proof being upon the auctioneer as being in possession, see Jack J at para 59; and cf. para 21.36.

109 See generally, Harvey and Meisel, Auctions, 2nd edn, 206–9; and Cranston, *Consumers and the Law*, 3rd edn, 418–9.

110 S 1(1). For offences, see s 1(2); and para 28.01. For offences by corporate officers, see s 2; and para 28.11. Other criminal proceedings, e.g. theft, or civil actions are expressly saved (s 3(6)): see para 3.21. For a list of convictions see Thomas, *Encyclopedia of Consumer Law*, para 1-334.

111 See s 3(1). It will extend to English and Dutch Auctions (see para 10.10): see *Allens v Simmons* [1978] 3 All ER 662, DC; *R v Pollard* [1984] CLY 664, CA.

112 S 1(3)(b). E.g. *Clements v Rydeheard* [1978] 3 All ER 658, DC.

**[10.12] Seller's reserve/right to bid**. There are several permutations as to whether the seller may impose a minimum price.[113]

1.  *Express reserve/right to bid.* The SGA expressly recognises that (s 57(3)):

    'A sale by auction may be notified to be subject to a reserve or upset price, and a right to bid may also be reserved expressly by or on behalf of the seller'.

    Notification will usually be by way of announcement in the conditions of sale and/or auctioneer's oral announcement before opening the bidding. Both types of notification are means of informing bidders that the authority of the auctioneer is limited to selling at above a (usually undisclosed) figure, so limiting the auctioneer's actual, apparent and usual authority (as to which, see generally, para 10.06). The Act also explains that (s 57(6)):

    'Where, in respect of a sale by auction, a right to bid is expressly reserved (but not otherwise) the seller or any one person on his behalf may bid at the auction'.

    The effect is to convert each bid into a conditional offer. It follows that, if by mistake the auctioneer knocks the goods down to the highest bidder below the reserve price, there is no contract of sale and the auctioneer is not liable for breach of warranty of authority.[114] However, assuming that the auctioneer remembers his reserve, or the highest bid is made by the **one** person authorised to do so on behalf of the seller,[115] that seller has failed in his objective of disposal of the goods by way of public auction. In such a situation, the auctioneer will frequently be able to negotiate a subsequent private sale below the reserve between the seller and highest *bona fide* bidder.[116]

2.  *Seller's instruction unannounced.* Where the seller instructs the auctioneer to place a reserve on his goods but that instruction is unannounced, the auctioneer may still execute the seller's wishes by refusing to accept any bid below the reserve, because bids are only offers (see para 10.10). However, he may not do so by accepting a bid on behalf of the seller. Section 57 lays down that:

    '(4) Where a sale by auction is not notified to be subject to a right to bid by or on behalf of the seller, it is not lawful for the seller to bid himself or to employ any person to bid at the sale, or for the auctioneer knowingly to take any bid from the seller or any such person.

    (5) A sale contravening subsection (4) above may be treated as fraudulent by the buyer'.

    The effects are as follows: (a) to prohibit the seller or his agent from bidding or the auctioneer from accepting any such bid;[117] and (b) if he does so, to enable

---

113  Or a modern practice is for the auctioneer to guarantee a minimum price. As to guarantees, see para 25.06.

114  *McManus v Fortescue* [1907] 2 KB 2, CA.

115  It has been argued that, where the auctioneer accepts bids by more than one person on behalf of the seller, the transaction is invalid: *Benjamin's Sale of Goods*, 6th edn, para 3-009.

116  E.g. *RH Willis & Son v British Car Auction Ltd* [1978] 2 All ER 392, CA (discussed Harvey and Meisel, *Auctions*, 2nd edn, 278–9).

117  The seller and/or auctioneer may be liable in tort (see below). But is the auctioneer strictly liable for breach of warranty of authority? Are they both liable for breach of statutory duty (see generally, para 3.21)? What if the auction conditions expressly permit such a bid?

the buyer to rescind the contract of sale *ab initio*, claim damages for deceit[118] and perhaps treat the contract as illegal.[119]

3. *Sale announced without reserve*. Notwithstanding the announcement, the auctioneer is not bound to put the goods up; but if he does so the auction may be completed by his knocking the goods down to the highest *bona fide* bidder (see para 10.10). However, the SGA leaves obscure what is to happen if, in contravention of the announcement, the seller intervenes after the auction has started either to revoke the auctioneer's authority or buy in the goods;[120] or if the auctioneer seeks to promote the bidding by taking an imaginary bid 'off the wall'.[121] In *Barry v Davies*:[122]

> Two new condensing engines worth about £14,000 were put up for sale 'without reserve'. The auctioneer refused to accept P's bid of £200 each, because he considered it far too low. Presumably because he felt that the owner could not be compelled to accept his bid and enter a contract of sale (see para 10.10), P sued the auctioneer for damages.

The Court of Appeal held the auctioneer liable for damages under a separate collateral contract for breach of warranty of authority, awarding P the same measure of damages as if the seller had been sued for non-delivery (see para 29.19, *et seq*.). Could any attendee or bidder sue?

**[10.13] Buyer's bidding ring.**[123] Whilst a seller will normally auction his goods with a view to obtaining their market price (see para 10.10), this expectation may be defeated if prospective buyers form a ring to operate as follows: before the auction a group of prospective buyers agree not to compete against each other but appoint one of their number to bid for the goods on behalf of the ring; and, if successful, the ring subsequently hold their own private auction ('knockout') for the goods, the difference between the two prices then being divided between members of the ring. This practice is not illegal at common law[124] but may fall within the Auction (Bidding Agreements) Acts 1927 and 1969.[125] These Acts apply only where one or more of the members of a 'ring' are 'dealers',[126] in which case the conduct is made criminal[127] unless the prior agreement between the prospective buyers was to purchase at the auction on *bona fide* joint account and a copy of that agreement was deposited with the auctioneer. In practice, it may be difficult to distinguish an illegal ring from a genuine joint account, hence the requirement that a copy of

---

118 As to rescission *ab initio*, see para 26.12; and as to the tort of deceit, see para 17.18.

119 *Benjamin's Sale of Goods, ibid*. As to illegality, see generally, para 10.19.

120 US law will not permit this: Uniform Commercial Code, art 2-328(3).

121 As to the criminality of such behaviour, see Harvey and Meisel, *Op. cit.*, para 1-334., 219, *et seq*.

122 [2001] 1 All ER 944, [2000] 1 WLR 1962, CA. See further *Benjamin's Sale of Goods*, 6th edn, para 2-005; Harvey and Meisel, *Op. cit.*, 29–33.

123 See generally Harvey and Meisel, *Auctions*, 2nd edn, 209, *et seq*.

124 *Cohen v Roche* [1927] I KB 169.

125 The auctioneer's name and copies of these Acts must be exhibited at auction sales: 1927 Act, s 3; 1969 Act, s 4.

126 ' "Dealer" means a person who in the normal course of his business attends sales by auction for the purposes of purchasing goods with a view to reselling them': 1927 Act, s 1(2); 1969 Act, s 3(5).

127 Triable summarily or on indictment (1927 Act, s 1(1)); 1969 Act, s 1), but only with the consent of the Attorney-General (1927 Act, s 1(3)).

the latter agreement be deposited with the auctioneer. However, whilst safeguarding *ad hoc* joint agreements, the proviso may pose a trap for genuine long-term partnerships. Not only are persons convicted of belonging to rings (an infrequent occurrence) banned from subsequently attending auctions for a stipulated time,[128] but the seller has the right to treat the auction sale as voidable,[129] the parties to the ring then being jointly and severally liable for any loss to the seller (1969 Act, s 3(2)). The major difficulty in enforcing the Acts has been found to be proving the existence of a ring. It has been argued that the Acts should be repealed, leaving the seller to the protection of his reserve (see para 10.12) and trade self-regulation (see generally, para 3.11); or that it would be more effective to require registration of ring agreements with the auctioneer (what if he participated in the ring?). Dealers' rings may also be impugned under Art 81 [ex 85] of the Treaty of Rome.[130]

## Mistake

**[10.14] Introduction**. Apart from the circumstance where mistake raises the question of impossibility of performance (see para 22.09, *et seq.*), s 62(2) of the SGA expressly saves the common law rules relating to the effect of mistake which includes the rules of equity (see para 1.02); and the other major statutes regulating the supply of goods are entirely silent on the matter, e.g. SOGIT; CCA; SGSA; CPA. If mistake operates at common law at all, it operates so as to negative or in some cases nullify consent to a contract.[131] Mistake negatives consent when it prevents the parties from reaching agreement, e.g. mistake as to person (see para 10.15), mistake as to terms (see para 10.16); and it nullifies consent where the parties reach agreement, but that agreement has no legal effect because it is based on a fundamental mistaken assumption, e.g. mistake as to quality (see para 10.18). The general rules on mistake can safely be left to the standard works on contract[132] and what follows is only a summary of those rules which are particularly important for our purposes. They should be distinguished from the recovery in quasi-contract of money paid under mistake[133] and mistakes in operating contractual arbitration machinery.[134]

**[10.15] Mistake as to person**.[135] Leaving aside the rules of agency (see para 10.06), *prima facie*, an offer can only be accepted by the person to whom it is made.[136] To

---

128 1969 Act, s 2, under which contravention of such a ban is itself an offence.

129 1969 Act, s 3(1): as to voidable contracts, see para 10.15. The 1927 Act had made such sales 'fraudulent' (cf. SGA, s 57(5): see para 10.12); but this provision was repealed by the 1969 Act, s 3(4).

130 *Per* Webster J (*obiter*) in *Shearson Lehman Bros v Maclaine Watson & Co Ltd* [1989] 2 Lloyd's Rep. 570 at 621. For Art 81 [ex 85], see para 2.13.

131 *Per* Lord Atkin in *Bell v Lever Bros Ltd* [1932] AC 161 at 217, HL.

132 See *Benjamin's Sale of Goods*, 6th edn, para 3-011, *et seq.* and the authorities cited at the outset of that section.

133 *Kleinwort Benson Ltd v Lincoln CC* [1999] 2 AC 349, HL (not a goods case).

134 *Soules CAF v Louis Dreyfus Negoce SA* [2000] 2 All ER (Comm) 154.

135 See generally *Halsbury's Laws of England*, 4th edn, Reissue, Vol 9, paras 704–6; *Benjamin's Sale of Goods*, 6th edn, paras 3-012/15.

136 *Boulton v Jones* (1857) 2 H & N 564 (sale of business). As to the difficulties inherent in this test, see para 10.16.

determine that person, the offer is normally construed objectively;[136] but, where the person receiving the offer is aware that the offeror is mistaken and did not intend to contract with him, the test is subjective—with whom did the offeror actually intend to contract?[137] In the latter case, there is said to be a 'void contract', though this is really a contradiction in terms.

In many of those cases where the offeree is aware that the offeror has mistakenly directed an offer to him, the offeree will have fraudulently induced the offer, it being the essence of the fraud that the offeror does not realise that his offer was internally contradictory.[137] If the alleged contract is in writing, it was decided by the House of Lords in *Cundy v Lindsay* that it is a matter of interpretation for the court to decide which of the two contradictory intentions predominates;[137] but where the parties are dealing face-to-face it is helped by a presumption that the offeror intended to deal with the person in front of him.[138] In modern case law, this issue has given rise to disputes as to whether the mistake of the offeror relates to:

(a) the **identity** of the person addressed, in which case the alleged contract between them is wholly void under the rule in *Cundy v Lindsay*;[139] or

(b) the **attributes** of that person, e.g. his financial standing, in which case the contract is only voidable,[140] i.e. valid at common law, but in equity capable of being rescinded *ab initio* for misrepresentation (see para 26.12). As will be seen later (see para 21.19), in the interim the apparent purchaser can pass a good title to a *bona fide* purchaser (bfp), because of the ordinary equitable rule that the innocent party's equitable right to rescind gives way to the rights of a bfp.

In *Shogun Finance Ltd v Hudson*:[141]

> A rogue went to showrooms and selected a Shogun car he wished to acquire on directly financed hp. He told the dealer that he was Mr Patel and produced a stolen driving licence. The dealer faxed the hp proposal and stolen driving licence, both in the name of Patel, to the financier. Having conducted a credit search in the name of Patel, the financier accepted the proposal; and the car was released to the rogue, who immediately sold it to H, a bfp. The financier unsuccessfully sought to recover the car and H pleaded a Pt III title (see para 21.55).

At common law, everything depended on whether the financier had contracted with the rogue. Before the House of Lords, H made a frontal assault on whether *Cundy v Lindsay* was good law: but, by a bare majority (Lords Hobhouse, Phillips[142] and Walker), the House confirmed *Cundy v Lindsay*, so retaining the above dichotomy between identity and attributes and holding that the present facts fell within case (a), above. A strong minority, Lords Nicholls and Millett, would

---

137 *Cundy v Lindsay* (1878) 3 App Cas 459, HL (whether to sell to Blenkiron (the genuine firm) or the addressee (the rogue Blenkarn)).

138 *Phillips v Brooks Ltd* [1919] 2 KB 243 (shop sale where rogue purported to be Sir GB).

139 *Cundy v Lindsay* (above: written negotiations); *Ingram v Little* [1961] 1 QB 31, CA (3 old ladies deal face-to-face with rogue).

140 *King's Norton Metal Co Ltd v Edridge, Merrett Co Ltd* (1897) 14 TLR 98, CA (written negotiations); *Lewis v Averay* [1972] 1 QB 198, CA (face-to-face dealings).

141 [2004] 1 AC 919; [2004] 1 All ER 215; [2004] 1 All ER (Comm) 332, HL (see Macdonald 120 LQR 369; McLauchlan 121 LQR 9; Chandler and Devenny [2004] *Jo of Obligations & Remedies* 7).

142 Lord Phillips (at para 170) was 'strongly attracted' to the minority view, but 'unable to adopt it'.

have preferred to set the law on a completely new course, reversing *Cundy v Lindsay* and treating all identity fraud as falling within case (b).[143] The issue is an important one in view of the prevalence of identity fraud:[144] this decision puts the risk on the innocent consumer in directly financed transactions,[145] notwithstanding that it is far easier for the finance and motor trades, rather than the innocent buyer, to make pre-contract identity checks (*per* Sedley LJ in the CA, at para 12); but, in the longer term, it may be that identity cards may reduce the problem (see para 8.35).

None of the majority of Lordships commented on the grounds upon which the Court of Appeal decided the case: namely, the capacity in which the dealer acted as agent of the finance company; the CA majority thought that the finance company only authorised the dealer to convey its acceptance (so that case (a) applied), but Sedley LJ, dissenting, thought that the dealer was authorised to act as agent of the finance company for the purposes, *inter alia*, of making the contract (see generally, para 16.06), so that the face-to-face principle applied (case (b), above).[146]

**[10.16] Mistake as to terms**. Although there is no agreement without the assent of both parties, in most cases each party will look as though he is assenting to the proposed terms; and on the objective test[147] will therefore be precluded from denying the formation of an agreement on terms which an objective bystander would have thought the parties were agreeing.[148] Whilst the agreement may purport to enable the supplier to cancel the contract if his quotation contains an arithmetical or clerical error (see para 10.28), in a consumer supply this may amount to an unfair term (OFT, *Bulletin No. 15*, case 9). On the other hand, there are bound to be a few cases where the objective bystander would conclude that the parties had never reached agreement, so that there was no contract between them, as where they are genuinely at cross-purposes as to the subject-matter,[149] or in a battle of the forms (see para 10.04) or where the agreed terms are ambiguous.[150]

The situation is entirely different where one party (A) is aware that the intentions of the other party (B) are not the same as his own. There will then be no justification for imposing an agreement in an objective sense or, if different, in the sense understood by A: the cases do not distinguish whether in this situation there is an agreement in the sense understood by B or no agreement at all.[151] If a dealer mistakenly completes a non-Act form in respect of a regulated agreement, it would

---

143 For thinly disguised criticism of the minority position, see Lord Hobhouse at para 55.

144 As to trade mechanisms for establishing the identity of customers, see [2003] 2 *Credit Today* 15 and 16; and see generally, paras 8.35–6.

145 *Contra* where a stolen credit card is used at point of sale, where the sale would be void within case (a) above.

146 At para 18. However, Lord Hobhouse expressly rejected this possibility on the facts (at para 51). See further Elliott [2004] JBL 381 at 385–7.

147 This test is also applied in mistake as to person: see para 10.15. For the difficulties inherent in this test, see Howarth (1984) 100 LQR 265; Vorster (1987) 104 LQR 274.

148 *Tamplin v James* (1880) 15 ChD 215 (not a goods case). Distinguish mistake as to quality: see para 10.17.

149 *Scriven v Hindley* [1913] 3 KB 564 (auction). As where there is a mistake at a supermarket check-out as to the item sold: see [1996] 6 *Which?* 20.

150 *Falck v Williams* [1900] AC 176, PC (patent ambiguity); *Raffles v Wichelhaus* (1864) 2 H & C 906 (latent ambiguity).

151 *Smith v Hughes* (set out at para 10.17); *Hartog v Colin & Shields* [1939] 3 All ER 566 (price per piece/pound).

seem safer to start again with CCA documentation.[152] But it is another matter where an Act form is completed in respect of an unregulated agreement, as it is usually thought that the effect is that the financier has contracted to give his customer all the CCA protections;[153] or where the dealer and consumer collude to defraud the financier.[154]

*Non est factum.* The ancient common law defence of *non est factum* (literally—it is not my deed) originally developed as a defence by one who could not read (whether through blindness or illiteracy) to a claim based on a promise made by him in a deed under seal (see para 9.01); but by the nineteenth century it had been extended to persons who could read and to all kinds of signed contract.[155] Whilst the general common law rule remains that a man is bound by his signature (see para 18.04), the basis of this defence is that the signatory is mistaken as to the nature of the document he signed (see para 18.04), so that his signature is a nullity and cannot be relied upon by anyone into whose hands the document may have come, though it is not normally applicable to documents mistakenly signed in blank (see para 16.05). The modern ambit of the plea of *non est factum* was laid down by the House of Lords in 1970: it is an exceptional defence in which the burden of proof falls on the signatory to show that in signing he acted with reasonable care in making a fundamental mistake as to the nature of what he signed.[156] If the plea was successful in relation to a regulated agreement, it would presumably render that agreement not properly executed under the CCA (see para 9.13) and void at common law. What if a credit card slip signed in blank is subsequently completed in an unauthorised manner (see para 7.09)? If regulated, the position depends on the CCA, ss 83 and 171(4)(b) (see para 7.13).

**[10.17] Mistake as to quality**. It has long been recognised that a common mistake as to the **existence** of the subject-matter of a sale at the time of contracting will normally render the contract void.[157] In *Bell v Lever Bros Ltd*,[158] Lord Atkin accepted that the doctrine of mistake was not limited to the foregoing and that a contract is void if there is a mistake such as to nullify 'a foundation essential to its existence' (at 225–6). However, where the mistake relied upon is as to the **quality** of goods bought, Lord Atkin said that 'such a mistake will not affect assent unless it is the mistake of both parties, and is as to the existence of some quality which makes the thing without the quality essentially different from the thing as it is believed to be'.[159] Whilst this common law doctrine is clearly a very narrow one, attempts to supplement it by an equitable doctrine relating to mistakes as to quality have now

---

152 Because the agreement will be not properly executed under s 61(1): see para 9.12.

153 See (1991) 46 CC4/30.

154 E.g. by inflating a deposit or trade-in: see *Royscot Trust Ltd v Rogerson* (set out at para 27.28); and (1992) 46 CC 5/5.

155 *Foster v Mckinnon* (1869) LR 4 CP 704 (not a sale of goods case).

156 *Saunders v Anglia Building Society* [1971] AC 1004, HL (not a sale of goods case). Doctrine applied in *Lloyds Bank v Waterhouse* (1991) 10 Tr LR 161, CA (guarantee: see para 25.06).

157 *Res extincta*: see para 22.10. A similar view is taken where a man mistakenly purports to buy his own goods (*res sua*).

158 [1932] AC 161, [1931] All ER Rep 1, HL (not a goods case; see (2003) 119 LQR 625).

159 At 218. For the narrow range of such operative mistakes, see *Harrison and Jones Ltd v Bunten and Lancaster Ltd* (set out at para 17.11); and generally, *Benjamin's Sale of Goods*, 6th edn, para 3-020.

been firmly rejected.[160] Nevertheless, its existence gives rise to the rule *caveat emptor* (see para 15.22) and makes it important to distinguish carefully between mistakes as to (i) quality and (ii) warranties as to quality. In *Smith v Hughes*:[161]

> B, a farmer, invited A, a trainer of racehorses, to buy some oats from him, and showed a sample to A. A wrote to say he would take the whole quantity but later complained that the oats were useless to him because they were new, whereas he needed old oats to feed his racehorse. B knew they were new oats—he had no old oats—but refused to take them back and sued for the price. There was a crucial conflict of evidence as to how B described the oats at their meeting: B said he described them as 'good oats'; but A said B described them as 'good **old** oats'.

As the court pointed out, assuming B had not in fact used the word 'old',[162] the difference in A's perception of what B had said was crucial:

(i)   If A had actually realised that B had described them as 'good oats' but A had mistakenly thought them old, then A's unilateral mistake as to quality would not avoid the contract (see above) for 'good oats'.[163] This is the common law principle known as *caveat emptor*.[164]

(ii)  If A had thought mistakenly that B had described them as 'good **old** oats', then the contract would be void for lack of *consensus*, because A would be mistaken as to the terms of the offer, believing them to include a warranty of quality (see para 10.16).

## Invalidity

**[10.18] Introduction**. Leaving aside insolvency (see para 19.13, *et seq.*) and restraint of trade (see para 2.13, *et seq.*), this paragraph attempts to draw together the various rules which may invalidate a contract for the supply of goods. Where a transaction falls within it, the SGA lays down that (s 62(2)):

> 'The rules of the common law,[165] including the law merchant,[165] except in so far as they are inconsistent with the provisions of this Act,[166] and in particular the rules relating to the law of principal and agent[167] and the effect of fraud,[168]

---

160  *The Great Peace* [2002] 4 All ER 689, CA (but see 119 LQR 177 & 180; 153 NLJ 1654; [2004] JBL 34); *Champion Investments Ltd v Ahmed* [2004] EWHC 1956 (loan terms).

161  (1871) LR 6 QB 597, [1861–73] All ER Rep 632.

162  If he had, B would have given an express warranty of quality. As to express promises, see generally, para 11.07.

163  B's 'passive acquiescence' in the 'self-deception' of A will not entitle A to avoid the contract: *per* Cockburn CJ at 603. But see Friedmann (2003) 119 LQR 68 at 80.

164  See para 15.22. But in 2007 it will sometimes be reversed for consumers by the UCP Directive, Art 7: see para 4.21A.

165  As to the rules of equity and law merchant, see para 1.02; and generally, Goode, *Commercial Law*, 3rd edn, 192.

166  Whilst Chalmers attempted to capture the spirit of the common law in his draft Bill of 1890, some substantive changes were made during its passage through Parliament (see below; and para 1.02).

167  Where an agent is given a secret commission by the lender, the loan may be fraudulent and voidable: see *Re A Debtor (No. 229 of 1927)* [1927] 2 Ch 367, CA. As to the common law rules of agency, see para 10.06.

168  As to the action in tort for deceit, see para 17.18; and as to rescission *ab initio*, see para 26.12. As to actions for damages for misrepresentation, see paras 17.10 and 26.12. As to mistake, see para 10.14, *et seq.*

misrepresentation,[168] duress or coercion,[169] mistake,[168] other invalidating cause, apply to contracts for the sale of goods'.

No counterpart to this section is to be found in the other major statutes governing the supply of goods, e.g. the CCA; but the position is presumably the same. 'Invalidating causes' has been said to cover illegality;[170] and there are a number of offences, mostly statutory, which may be committed in the course of completing a contract for the supply of goods, e.g. the offences referred to in Chaps 4 and 5. The difficulty is to know what is the effect of transgression on the supply agreement (see para 10.19). There must be distinguished from illegal contracts those made unenforceable by statute. This category includes all the following: unevidenced guarantees (see para 25.06 *et seq.*); improperly executed regulated agreements (see para 9.06, *et seq.*); and supplies made in contravention of the distance or doorstep selling rules (see para 8.17; paras 10.36–9). Further, there may be relevant here the Mental Capacity Act 2005, which provides a statutory framework to empower and protect vulnerable people who *may not be able to make their own decisions*. Starting with a presumption of capacity (s 1(2)), the 2005 Act stipulates that 'a person is not to be treated as unable to make decisions unless all practical steps to help him do so have been taken without success' (s 1(3)), nor because 'he has made an unwise decision' (s 1(4)). Where a contracting party satisfies the definition of incapacity found in s 2,[171] the Act makes him liable only for 'necessary goods or services' in a similar manner to a minor (s 7: see below). This may particularly help those with mental ill-health entering pressure-sold loans.[172]

*Contracts with minors.*[173] Capacity to buy and sell is governed by the general law concerning contracts to transfer and acquire property (SGA, s 3(1)): the general rule was that a contract made by a minor was voidable at his option; but he was liable to pay a reasonable price for necessaries actually supplied.[174] Contracts under which a minor acquires property with obligations are voidable by the minor during minority, but bind him whilst he retains the property.[175] Loans

---

169 'Coercion' was added when the 1890 Bill was extended to Scotland. As to duress and undue influence, see generally Treitel, *Law of Contract*, 11th edn, Chap 10; and as to economic duress, see *CTN Cash and Carry Ltd v Gallagher* [1994] 4 All ER 714, CA.

170 *Benjamin's Sale of Goods*, 6th edn, para 3-027; and it presumably also extends to contracts void on 'grounds of public policy'; fraudulent auctions (s 57(5): see para 10.12); and contracts with minors (see below). What about sales of human body parts by live persons (see 139 NLJ 159)? Or a credit card used to obtain the services of a prostitute?

171 'A person lacks capacity in relation to a matter if . . . he is unable to make a decision for himself in relation to the matter because of impairment of, or a disturbance in the functioning of, the mind or brain' (s 2(1)). That lack of capacity may be temporary (s 2(2)), but the subject must be over 15 (s 2(5)). See further, s 3.

172 As to the problem area, see (2004) 71 *Quarterly Account 5*; (2005) 76 QA 9.

173 Minors are persons under 18 years of age (formerly 'infants' until 21): Family Law Reform Act 1969. For the law relating to contracts with minors, see generally Treitel, *Law of Contract*, 11th edn, Chap 13. For co-principals, see para 25.05. For case examples, see (2006) 1 QA 8.

174 SGA, s 3(2). For the definition of 'necessaries', see s 3(3); and *Nash v Inman* [1908] 2 KB 1, CA. It is presumed that the same rule applies to hp and hiring of necessaries: Goode, *HP Law & Practice*, 2nd edn, 134, n 10. It is not clear whether or not a minor is liable on an executory contract for necessaries.

175 There are cases on leases of land; and it is thought that similar principles apply to non-necessary leases and hp of goods. See Goode, *Op. cit.*, 135–7.

which a minor uses to obtain necessaries would seem to be recoverable, though possibly involving criminal offences (see para 8.33); but other loans do not bind a minor, though any agreement by the minor after achieving his majority to repay the loan (and any negotiable instrument made in connection with it) is now enforceable (Minors' Contracts Act 1987, s 1(b)). A minor is not liable in tort for obtaining goods or a loan by fraudulently misrepresenting his age;[176] but under the Minors' Contracts Act 1987 he may be liable to restore the property obtained where he refuses to pay for it (s 3) and a guarantee of the minor's contractual obligations is enforceable, whether or not the minor's contract was regulated (1987 Act, s 2). For guarantees of unregulated agreements, see para 25.06; for guarantees of regulated agreements, see para 25.11; and for student loans, see para 3.15. The foregoing special rules for minors would not appear to inhibit contracts for those forms of payment card which do not include credit (see paras 2.24–5).

**[10.19] Illegality**. Where a contract for the supply of goods gives rise to a criminal offence (see para 10.18), attention must first be turned to the statute creating the offence. Sometimes the statute spells out the effect of that offence on the supply contract, e.g. the Discrimination Acts.[177] Conversely, the TDA provides that[178]

> 'A contract for the supply of any goods[179] shall not be void or unenforceable by reason only of a contravention of any provision of this Act'.

The effect is that a civil action does not lie merely for breach of the TDA. However, where (as will commonly be the case) the breach **also** amounts to a civil wrong, e.g. for misrepresentation or breach of contract, or for the return of goods subject to a cancelled agreement (see para 10.34), the injured party may institute proceedings in respect of that separate civil wrong. Even more far-reaching, the CCA lays down that (s 170(1)):

> 'A breach of any requirement[180] made (otherwise than by any court) by or under this Act shall incur no civil or criminal sanction as being such a breach, except to the extent (if any) expressly provided by or under this Act'.

Apart from expressly preserving the functions of the OFT[181] and any judicial controls thereon,[182] the intention of s 170 might appear to be to deprive breaches

---

176 *Leslie Ltd v Sheill* [1914] 3 KB 607, CA.

177 See para 4.23. See also the Prices Act 1974, Sched, para 5(2); Auctions (Bidding Agreements) Act 1969 (see para 10.13); Scotch Whisky Act 1988.

178 S 35. See also the Weights and Measures Act 1985, s 72; Road Traffic Act 1988, s 75(7); Courts and Legal Services Act 1990, s 106(7); Property Misdescription Act 1991, s 1(4).

179 What about a supply of services in contravention of s 14 (as to which, see para 4.15 *et seq*.)? See the annotation in Current Law Statutes.

180 Presumably, 'requirement' does not extend to provisions conferring enforceable rights on debtors or creditors, e.g. ss 69, 70(1), 71(2), 73(2), 75, 94, 95, 99, 100 and 101. Exclusion of these rights is prevented by s 173(1): see para 18.11. But what of the following sections: s 81(2) (see para 23.13); s 113(1) (see para 25.14)?

181 CCA, amended s 170(2). In particular, in relation to his licensing function (s 25): see para 6.18.

182 CCA, s 170(3). This leaves open the question of which functions of the OFT are judicial acts amenable to judicial review.

of the CCA of any legal consequences[183] other than those provided by the Act itself,[184] except where the actions contravening the CCA give rise to separate civil[185] or criminal[186] wrongs. Thus, in *Wilson v Robertsons (London) Ltd*:

> After the preliminary hearing had decided that the replacement contracts were not properly executed (see para 5.22), at the full trial the CA unanimously held that the pawns were ineffective security (s 106(d): see para 25.13)., so that the replacement cost of some goods was recoverable in tort (see para 27.30), notwithstanding s 170.

On this last point, Carnwath LJ observed that s 170(1) is dealing simply with the consequences of a breach of the Act and says nothing about remedies for common law wrongs outside the Act (para 41). Furthermore, it has been decided that s 170 should be restricted to common law consequences, so that s 170(1) does not preclude reliance on statutory offences,[187] or wrongs, e.g. enforcement orders under the EA (see para 6.07). Finally, the CPA provides different rules for its separate criminal parts:[188] breach of safety rules or regulations (Pt II) does not render any agreement void or unenforceable (s 41(3): see paras 4.33–4) and only infringement of the regulations gives rise to an action for breach of statutory duty (s 41(1), (5) and (6): see para 4.34); whereas contravention of the misleading pricing provisions (Pt III) has none of these civil effects (s 41(2) and (3): see para 8.10A).[187]

Where statute does not spell out the effect of the offence on a supply contract, recourse must be had to common law principles (see para 10.20).

**[10.20/2] Illegality at common law**. The standard works consider contracts rendered illegal at common law. Insofar as statutory offences arising during the supply of goods do not spell out the extent (if any) to which that offence taints the supply contract (see para 10.19), recourse must be had to common law principles. Now, these criminal offences may be committed at the following different stages in the life of the transaction for the supply of goods:

(i)  the offence may occur prior to the formation of contract;[189] or

---

183 See s 39(2) (see para 6.20); ss 44–6 (see para 8.28); s 78(4) (see para 7.08); s 105(7) (see para 25.12); s 126 (see para 24.33); s 91 (see para 24.38).

184 E.g. the further penalty for unlicensed trading (s 39) is limited to unenforceability under s 40 (see para 6.20); there is no action for breach of statutory duty (see para 3.21), except where the Act so provides (e.g. s 92(3): see para 24.34); and repossession of protected goods (s 90) gives rise only to the sanctions in s 91 (see para 24.38). What if the party subject to the duty finds it profitable to ignore the duty and pay any statutory penalty? See Goode, *Consumer Credit Legislation*, Pt III, para 171.

185 'Civil sanction' includes unjust enrichment: *Dimond v Lovell* (set out at para 5.13; and Macleod [2000] JBL 14); *Wilson v First County Trust Ltd* (set out at para 3.09A) at paras 50, 123, 145, 172 and 178.

186 *Hicks v Walker* [1984] Crim LR 495, DC; *Brookes v Retail Credit Cards Ltd* [1986] Crim LR 327, DC.

187 *R v Kettering Justices, ex p MRB Insurance Brokers Ltd* [2000] 2 All ER 353, DC (CCA, s 170(1); CPA, Pt III).

188 The statutory product liability (Pt I) imposes only civil sanctions: see para 17.24.

189 E.g. under the Business Advertisements Order (see para 4.22); Wildlife and Countryside Act 1981, s 6(1)(b); Children and Young Persons (Harmful Publications) Act 1955 (as amended); Highways Act 1980, Pt IX (as amended: obstruction); Knives Act 1997, s 1.

(ii)  the formation of the contract may constitute the criminal offence, examples being found elsewhere in this work,[190] or otherwise;[191] or

(iii)  the contract may be legal in its formation, but the illegality occur subsequently in performance[192] or use.[193]

Leaving aside the question of severance of an illegal contract and illegality of performance (case (iii)) which is adequately dealt with in the ordinary contract books, we must consider the effect of the statutory illegality in cases (i) and (ii). Whilst it is clear that the illegality taints the contract in case (ii), this is by no means so clear in case (i): the illegality may be totally unconnected with the contract, in which event the contract presumably may not be tainted; but, where the statute is intended to protect one party in his entering into such transactions, it is arguable that the illegality should taint the transaction.

*The effect of illegality.*[194] Assuming that a contract is tainted with illegality, the effect may be as follows:

(a)  As a general rule, to prevent either party relying on the illegal contract in any litigation,[195] though it may be that a party who entered into the transaction under an innocent mistake as to the facts which constitute the offence can sue on the contract or in tort[196] or under a collateral contract[197] or where there is no affront to public conscience.[198]

(b)  By way of exception, to allow a claim in respect of transferred money or other property, notwithstanding the illegality. Usually that title passes under an illegal contract notwithstanding the illegality, so that goods or money[199]

---

190  E.g. the sale of some kinds of wildlife (see para 4.23); sales which contravene the Misuse of Drugs Act 1971 (see para 4.29); supplying unsafe goods, such as crossbow bows and other offensive weapons (see para 4.31); intoxicating liquor (see para 6.05); out of hours and Sunday sales (see para 8.13); Unsolicited Goods and Services Acts 1971–5 (see para 8.18).

191  E.g. the tobacco products (see Children and Young Persons Act 1933, s 7 (as amended)); sales only by approved persons (Pharmacy and Poisons Act 1933, s 17; Opticians Act 1989, s 27); sale of pet animals in street (Pet Animals Act 1951, s 2 (as amended)); Motor Cycle Noise Act 1987; supplies of AIDS test kits (Health and Medicines Act 1988, s 23); human organs (Human Organ Transplants Act 1989, s 1(1) and (2)); tobacco to children (Children and Young Persons (Protection from Tobacco) Act 1991); Breeding and Sale of Dogs Act 1999, s 8.

192  E.g. the supply of an unroadworthy vehicle which the supplier had promised to put in good order before delivery (see para 4.37); sale of a solvent-based product; Video Recordings Act 1984, as interpreted in *Interfact Ltd v Liverpool CC* [2005] 1 WLR 3118, DC, at para 21. Does this category include sales contravening the Anatomy Act 1984, s 5(2), and cocaine-snorting kits? Does a recaption which amounts to a contravention of s 40 of the AJA 1970 (discussed at para 24.24) fall within this category?

193  E.g. Wireless Telegraphy Act 1949, Pt 2 (surveillance equipment); Powers of Criminal Courts (Sentencing) Act 2000, s 143 (property used for purposes of crime); inflated invoice to make insurance claim (112 LQR 545).

194  See *Benjamin's Sale of Goods*, 6th edn, paras 3-028/033.

195  *Pearce v Brooks* (1866) LR 1 Ex 213; *Snell v Unity Finance Ltd* [1964] 2 QB 203, CA; *Birkett v Acorn Business Machines Ltd* [1999] 2 All ER (Comm) 429, CA.

196  *Archbolds Ltd v Spanglett Ltd* [1961] I QB 374, CA (contract); *Belvoir Finance Co Ltd v Stapleton* [1971] 1 QB 210, CA (tort).

197  *Strongman (1915) Ltd v Sincock* [1955] 2 QB 525, CA; *Southern Industrial Trust v Brooke House Motors* (1968) 112 Sol Jo 798, CA.

198  *Howard v Shirlstar Container Transport Ltd* [1990] 3 All ER 366, CA.

199  *Kingsley v Stirling Industrial Securities Ltd* [1967] 2 QB 747, CA (goods); *Belvoir Finance Co Ltd v Stapleton* (above; goods; see Treitel, *Law of Contract*, 11th edn, 502); *Berg v Sadler and Moore* [1937] 2 KB 158, CA (money).

transferred cannot be recovered by the transferor from the transferee; but exceptionally property may be recovered, either by one who belongs to a class that the statute infringed was intended to protect (for lotteries, see para 8.16), or that the illegal transfer was for a limited interest which has expired.[200]

# REGULATED AGREEMENTS

[10.23] **Introduction**. Generally speaking, all the rules as to the formation of contract previously considered in this chapter apply to the formation of a regulated agreement (see para 5.13, *et seq.*). However, over the years it was found that, if the formation of agreement was left to the common law rules, these would be manipulated by the stronger party to his advantage. Particularly in the field of what are now regulated agreements, this was thought to be undesirable. The common law rules have therefore been statutorily amended in the following areas concerned with the formation of such agreements:[201] (1) agency (see para 10.24); (2) withdrawal by debtor: a warming-up period (see para 10.26); (3) right of cancellation: a cooling-off period (see para 10.28).

## Deemed agency

[10.24] It will be seen later (para 16.06) that it is sometimes a difficult question at common law whether a dealer in a directly financed transaction is the agent of either the financier, or the consumer, or both of them.[202] Between the two World Wars, it therefore became common for the proposal form to provide expressly that the dealer was to be regarded as the agent of the consumer. This was thought to be unfair,[203] and such deemed agency clauses were avoided by the HPA 1938 in a provision now re-enacted in s 56(3) of the CCA (set out at para 16.05). This section introduces the wide concept of the 'antecedent negotiations' which precede the making of a regulated agreement and of the 'negotiator' who conducts them; but for the time being, it is sufficient to think of the 'negotiator' as the dealer setting up a financed transaction.

The effect of what is now s 56(3) is simply to avoid any deemed agency clause and to allow the court to apply the common law to the true facts. However, the HPA 1964 went further and actually **increased** the liability of the financier by making the dealer (negotiator) the agent of the financier for certain purposes. These compulsory[204] deemed agency provisions are now to be found in the CCA and cover the following purposes:

---

200 *Bowmakers Ltd v Barnet Instruments Ltd* [1945] KB 65, CA. This case has been severely criticised by academic writers seeking to maintain a rule that such an action can only be supported where recovery can be made without reference to the illegality: Treitel, *Op. cit.*, 496–7. For another view, see Enonchong (1995) 111 LQR 135.
201 The Act takes special measures to deal with the situation where there is more than one creditor/owner (s 186: see para 5.25) and/or debtor/hirer (s 185: see para 25.08).
202 As to basic common law agency, see generally, para 10.06.
203 It might now amount to an unfair term under the UTCC Regulations: see para 11.18.
204 The parties cannot contract out of these provisions (s 173(1)): see further, para 18.11.

(a) to receive notices from the consumer of withdrawal of his offer contained in the proposal form or, where that offer has been accepted, the cancellation or rescission of the agreement (see para 10.25); and

(b) to receive notice from the consumer of the particular purpose for which the goods were required so that the consumer might invoke the implied undertaking as to fitness (see para 14.12); and

(c) for any representations made by the dealer to the consumer in the course of negotiating the transaction (see para 16.06).

**[10.25] To receive notices.** As part of its general deemed agency provisions (see para 10.24), the CCA deems the 'negotiator' (dealer) to be the agent of the creditor or owner for the purpose of receiving notices from the debtor or hirer in **all** the following respects:

(1) The debtor or hirer is withdrawing his offer to enter a regulated agreement. Where the debtor or hirer has such a right of withdrawal (see para 10.26), s 57(3) provides that each of the following shall be deemed to be the agent of the creditor or owner for the purposes of receiving such notice of withdrawal:

> '(a) a credit-broker or supplier[205] who is the negotiator in antecedent negotiations,[206] and
>
> (b) any person who, in the course of a business carried on by him, acts on behalf of the debtor or hirer in any negotiations for the agreement'.[207]

Apparently to protect the creditor or owner in circumstance (b),[208] s 175 places that deemed agent 'under a contractual duty to the creditor or owner to transmit the notice . . . to him forthwith'.[209]

(2) The debtor or hirer is cancelling a cancellable agreement. Where the debtor or hirer has such a right of cancellation (see para 10.29), s 69(6) deems exactly the same person to be the agent of the creditor or owner as in the case of withdrawal (see above).

(3) The debtor or hirer is exercising any common law right of rescission. Where the debtor or hirer has such a right (see paras 26.11–16), s 102(1) deems exactly the same persons to be the agent of the creditor or owner as in the case of withdrawal (see above).

## Withdrawal of offer (a warming-up period)

**[10.26] The ordinary case.** Except in the case of those regulated agreements exempted from Pt V of the Act (see para 9.07) and the special rules for land mortgages (see para 10.27), s 57 enables either side to withdraw from a 'prospective

---

205 As to 'credit-broker', see para 5.41; and as to 'supplier', see para 5.34.

206 This effectively enacts the decision in *Financings Ltd v Stimson* (set out at para 10.07).

207 So a debtor can effectively serve a notice on his creditor by physically sending it to his (the debtor's) own agent, e.g. spouse or solicitor!

208 As to whether this affects service of notice of cancellation, see para 10.31.

209 'Forthwith' presumably means at the earliest available moment: Goode, *Consumer Credit Law & Practice*, para 52.5.

regulated agreement', wherever made.[210] At common law, an offer may ordinarily be revoked or rejected at any time before acceptance (see para 10.02); and this rule achieves statutory confirmation in s 57(2), which provides that:

> 'The giving to a party of a written or oral[211] notice which, however expressed, indicates the intention of the other party to withdraw from a prospective regulated agreement operates as a withdrawal from it'.

The Act thus does not mind which party made the offer to enter a regulated agreement,[212] nor whether the withdrawal is technically a revocation or rejection of offer; but it does make three alterations in the common law rules. *First*, whilst at common law a revocation or rejection is generally[213] ineffective unless and until communicated,[214] withdrawal from a prospective regulated agreement probably takes effect on posting.[215] *Second*, in favour of the debtor or hirer only, the common law rule that one may contract not to revoke an offer (= an option) is generally void (s 59(1): see para 5.20). *Third*, in favour of the debtor or hirer only, an extension is made of the deemed agents upon whom such notice may be served (see para 10.25), though no steps are taken to ensure that the debtor or hirer is aware of this right of withdrawal. Compare the case of a cancellable contract, where the debtor or hirer is entitled to a statutory notice of his right of cancellation (s 64: see para 9.17).

Turning to the effect of withdrawal, because of the above alterations to the common law rules, the right of withdrawal may sometimes be exercisable where on common law principles there is a binding contract; and so in some cases the CCA recognises that a prospective agreement in respect of which both sides have a right of withdrawal may also be cancellable by the debtor or hirer (see para 10.29). Even where that is not the case, the Act directs that the **effect** of withdrawal shall be as if the prospective agreement were cancellable (s 57(4)). Section 57(1) explains that:

> 'The withdrawal of a party from a prospective regulated agreement shall operate to apply this Part[216] to the agreement, any linked transaction and any other thing done in anticipation of the making of the agreement as it would apply if the agreement were made and then cancelled under section 69'.

---

210 *Contra* cancellable agreements, which depend on the place of negotiation (s 67): see para 10.29. As to 'prospective regulated agreements', see generally, para 5.20; but as to the earliest moment when such an agreement exists, see below.

211 This ousts the s 189 (1) definition of 'notice'. Compare notices of cancellation under s 69(1): see para 10.31.

212 Or even whether the parties have got as far as either of them making an offer. Goode, *Consumer Credit Law & Practice*, Division IIB, para 5.107, suggests that s 57 does not apply to conditional offers which lapse under the condition.

213 Except in the case of revocation of offers to the whole world, or unilateral contracts, or perhaps where reliable indirect evidence of revocation is acquired.

214 This rule extends to the revocation of offers made by post: *Byrne v Van Tienhoven* (1880) 5 CPD 334.

215 By s 189(1), which defines 'give' as 'delivers or sends by appropriate method': cf. s 69(7) (see para 10.31); and Goode, *Op. cit.*, para 3377. *Contra* Guest and Lloyd, *Encyclopedia of Consumer Credit* para 2-058; Goode, *Op, cit.*, Division IIB, para 5.107.

216 The effect of this reference would seem to be that, if the creditor or owner breaches s 57, the agreement will also be improperly executed with the effects described in s 65: see para 9.19. For what purpose is this extra protection necessary?

The effect of withdrawal is summarised as cancelling (see para 10.32) all the following: (a) the prospective regulated agreement;[217] and (b) any linked transaction, e.g. maintenance contracts, which in any event have no effect until the regulated agreement is made (s 19(3): see para 5.31);[218] and (c) any other thing done in anticipation of the making of the agreement, e.g. paying survey or brokerage or legal fees. Any security given is rendered ineffective (s 113(6): see para 25.13).

**[10.27] Land mortgages**. It was felt that special protection was needed by householders who entered into second mortgages of their homes to secure regulated agreements, e.g. credit agreements to finance home improvements such as central heating, double-glazing or kitchen refits, or refinancing agreements.[219] However, application to such transactions of the cancellation provisions was ruled out (s 67(a): see para 10.29) on grounds of administrative difficulty.[220] Accordingly, it was decided to protect this group by re-enforcing the ordinary withdrawal provisions (see para 10.26) with the introduction of an advance copy procedure together with its 'consideration period' (see below).

Where a second land-mortgage falls within s 58(1),[221] the Act provides the debtor or hirer with the following three additional protections against undue pressure to commit himself, which makes the whole procedure extremely long-winded.

(1) An additional 'advance copy' notifying him of his right of withdrawal (see para 9.17A).

(2) Thereafter an isolation period, termed 'the consideration period'.[222] Section 61(2)(c) stipulates that during that period:

> 'the creditor or owner refrained from approaching the debtor or hirer (whether in person, by telephone or letter, or in any other way)[223] except in response to a specific request made by the debtor or hirer after the beginning of the consideration period'.[224]

---

217 How soon will negotiations amount to a 'prospective regulated agreement'? It is suggested that this concept is narrower than 'antecedent negotiations' (see para 16.08) and requires a 'clear prospect' that a regulated agreement will ensue: Goode, *Op. cit.*, para 31.31.

218 Suppose after the apparent conclusion of a cash sale contract a customer inquires about the possibility of paying by credit card? When (if ever) does that enquiry become a prospective regulated agreement (see above), so turning the cash sale into a linked transaction? It has been suggested that a communicated offer is required: Goode, *Op. cit.*, Division IIB, para 5.107. *Sed quaere?*

219 First mortgages of dwelling houses are exempt from the CCA (see para 5.15) and instead within the FSMA (see para 3.02).

220 Goode, *Consumer Credit Law & Practice*, para 31.53. What about additional secured home improvement loans? Nor is there a right of cancellation under the distance selling rules (see para 10.39).

221 The following categories of transaction were excluded from this procedure: (a) totally exempt agreements (see para 5.15); (b) those agreements exempt from Pt V of the Act (see para 9.07); and (c) agreements specially exempted from these rules by s 58(2), effectively remortgages and bridging loans.

222 This is defined by s 61(3)(a) as effectively a minimum seven day period between service of the advance and first copies. For the possible meanings of s 61(3)(b), see Goode, *Consumer Credit Law & Practice*, IIB, para 5.121.

223 Is the prohibition restricted to matters related to the prospective regulated agreement and to the debtor/hirer personally? See Guest and Lloyd, *Encyclopedia of Consumer Credit Law*, para 2-059.

224 As to the practice of obtaining the written request of the debtor/hirer to such an approach, see Guest and Lloyd, *ibid*.

It has been suggested that, if the creditor or owner does break this rule, he can save himself by starting the procedure again and sending a new advance copy.[225]

(3) Subsequent pestering. The creditor or owner may not send the signature copy after he has received notice of withdrawal (s 61(2)(d)).

Breach of any of these requirements will render an agreement not properly executed (s 61(2)). This has the effects considered above (see para 9.19) but no others (s 170: see para 10.19), which may be useful if the creditor or owner has thereby inveigled the debtor or hirer into completing a regulated agreement.

## CANCELLATION OF AGREEMENT (A COOLING-OFF PERIOD)

**[10.28] Introduction**. At common law, there is nothing to prevent a contract from expressly allowing one side a unilateral right of cancellation subsequent to its formation and before it is fully executed, with[226] or without cause,[227] possibly on terms.[228] For example, mail order (see para 8.19) may provide a 28-day money-back guarantee 'if not entirely satisfied' (a satisfaction guarantee).[229] In a consumer supply contract such an express right of cancellation may nowadays be unfair under the UTCC, e.g. if unbalanced,[230] as in respect of a cancellation fee (Grey Term 1(e): see para 11.16); but, if there are 'hidden terms', an express right of cancellation, e.g. in a telephone sale (see para 8.17), might avoid the supplier's standard terms being unfair (Grey Term 1(i): see para 11.17). Whether or not the consumer is an individual, the cancellation clause may be unreasonable (UCTA, s 3(2): see para 18.20).

However, whilst the matter remained voluntary, such a right was seldom accorded to the consumer without cause,[231] perhaps because of possible legal difficulties with reselling returned goods as new.[232] For this reason, the Molony Report recommended that, in order to protect the consumer from unfair selling practices exercised against him in his home, a person signing consumer instalment credit documents otherwise than at a retail establishment should be allowed a compulsory 'cooling-off period' of 72 hours within which he could withdraw from

---

225 Goode, *Op. cit.*, para 31.59.

226 E.g. *Hyundai Heavy Industries Co Ltd v Papadopoulos* [1980] 2 All ER 29, HL. In such cases, the express right to cancel tends to merge with the common law right to rescind for breach: see the *Stocznia No. 1* case (set out at para 26.16A).

227 This may be the explanation of sale or return transactions: see para 20.23. See also price adjustment clauses: para 10.05. Does this extend to where a CCA cancellable agreement form is mistakenly used? See (1991) 46 CC 4/30.

228 E.g. as to proof of purchase, exchange, credit voucher. For a table of the policy of retailers, see [1996] 1 *Which?* 17.

229 Satisfaction guarantees are probably not 'consumer guarantees' (see para 17.09B).

230 OFT, *UCT Bulletin No. 21*, case 17.

231 If the supplier is in breach, the consumer has the remedies considered in Chap 29.

232 This may give rise to difficulty with the TDA (see para 4.07) and the SGA (see para 13.15). Cancellation without any right to do so will amount to a breach of contract, giving the supplier a right of action (see para 27.27, *et seq.*).

the transaction.[233] This idea was taken up in the HPA, but limited by the CCA to those circumstances where there is personal contact between the salesman and consumer.[234] On the other hand, it has not proved possible to escape the place-of-signature test which first appeared in the HPA, even though this allowed an unscrupulous salesman to escape the cancellation rules by enticing the customer to return to trade premises to sign the relevant documents.[235] But at least a positive act is required of the consumer before the restrictions are avoided: he has the journey time to business premises to repent. Reputable traders should keep two sets of documentation (applicable where the transaction is/is not cancellable) and ensure the correct documentation is used (see paras 9.10; 9.17). Nevertheless, for the scrupulous trader the cancellation rules amount to a serious restriction on trade. Indeed, it is a common precaution for traders not to deliver goods until the cooling-off period has expired, nor to customise them,[236] though the home credit trade tends to be an exception.[237]

**[10.29] Cancellable agreements**. Following the recommendations of the Crowther Report (paras 6.7.1–4), the CCA provides that a 'cancellable agreement' is one which may be cancelled by the debtor or hirer by virtue of s 67 (s 189(1)). Section 67 lays down that, with the exceptions set out below:

> 'A regulated agreement may be cancelled by the debtor or hirer in accordance with this Part if the antecedent negotiations included oral representation made when in the presence of the debtor or hirer by an individual acting as, or on behalf of, the negotiator'.

Pt V thus grants the debtor or hirer (as to 'debtor' and 'hirer', see respectively, paras 5.24 and 1.19) a compulsory (s 173: see para 18.11) statutory right of cancellation (see para 10.31) during a cooling-off period (see para 10.30) which satisfies **all** the following requirements:

1. The result was a regulated agreement (see para 5.13). However, a cash supply on the doorstep may give rise to a different cancellation right (see para 10.36).

2. It was made during antecedent negotiations.[238] This formula appears to exclude agreements solicited by the army of housewives acting as catalogue agent, because of the combined effect of ss 56(1)(b) and 146(5) (see para 5.41).

3. By an individual salesman acting 'as, or on behalf of, the negotiator'. In the case of consumer credit, this means salesmen acting on behalf of the creditor or credit-broker, but in the case of consumer hirings, it does not extend to the credit-broker.[238]

---

233 *Final Report of the Committee on Consumer Protection* (1962, Cmnd. 1781), paras 525–9. E.g. Code of Practice of the Direct Selling Association (see generally, para 3.13).

234 See para 10.29. For modified agreements, see para 9.06.

235 Adherence to the letter and spirit of these rules is reinforced by the licensing powers of the OFT: see para 6.19. To some extent, the OFT can also utilise their powers under Pt 8 of the EA: see para 6.07

236 What is the trader to do with a customised fitted garment or furniture?

237 Whatever the risks (see paras 10.33–4), such suppliers tend to take the view that commercially they need to hand over the goods/money immediately.

238 E.g. *Goshawk etc Ltd v Bank of Scotland* [2006] 2 All ER 610, at paras 40–1. As to 'antecedent negotiations' and 'negotiator', see s 56, discussed at para 16.08.

4. This included oral representations before contracting (see below).

5. These were made in the presence of the debtor or hirer, though they do not need to be addressed to him.[239] If not preceded by a face-to-face sales pitch, it may be a distance contract giving another right of cancellation (see paras 10.38–9).

An example within s 67 is provided by *Moorgate Services Ltd v Kabir*.[240]

> K and M wished to obtain a refrigerated cabinet from their food business. A directly financed regulated credit sale was arranged by the supplier's employee, Fowler. When the financier (MS) sued for unpaid instalments, K successfully pleaded that the agreement was cancellable and should therefore have been made on cancellable documentation (see para 9.17).

Everything turned on whether the statements uttered by Fowler at the business premises of K and M amounted to 'representations' within s 67, this expression being defined by s 189(1) as including 'any condition or warranty, and any other statement or undertaking, whether oral or in writing'. The Court of Appeal thought that this apparently wide definition must be restricted to statements 'of fact or opinion or an undertaking as to the future which is capable of inducing the proposed borrower to enter into the agreement', though it does not need to actually induce K's entry into the agreement (*per* Staughton LJ). Nevertheless, the Court unanimously held that Fowler's statements did so amount to representations: the statement that the amount of credit would be £7,000 was a 'representation', whereas the statement that Fowler would have to phone his office for the APR was not.

*Exceptions.* Even where an otherwise regulated agreement satisfies *all* the above four requirements, it will not be cancellable under this Act (though it may be cancellable under other Acts (see paras 10.35–9)) if it falls within *any* of the following categories:

(a) Exempt (see para 5.14) or some small agreements.[241]

(b) Agreements outside Pt V of the Act (s 74: see para 9.07).

(c) Agreements secured on land,[242] or re-mortgages or bridging loans.[243]

(d) Unexecuted agreements signed by the debtor or hirer at 'business premises',[244] which are (s 67(b)):

---

239 So long as it was made in his presence, e.g. to a spouse: see Goode, *Consumer Credit Law & Practice*, para 31.96. It follows that distance selling is normally outside the CCA cancellation provisions.

240 [1995] GCCR 1947, [1995] CLY 722, CA (Lawson 14 Tr L 525).

241 This will exclude small credit sales and unsecured loans where the credit in either case does not exceed £35: s 74(2)(A), inserted by reg 9 of the Doorstep-selling Regulations (see para 10.21). Hp and conditional sales remain within these rules without bottom limit. For an explanation of the convoluted manner in which this is achieved, see Goode, *Op. cit.*, para 31.78.

242 These may instead be subject to the mortgage withdrawal rules: see para 10.27.

243 S 67(a). Remortgage and bridging loans are also outside the withdrawal rules: see para 10.27.

244 As s 67(b) refers to the signing by the debtor or hirer of an 'unexecuted agreement' (see para 9.14), does it follow that, if the creditor or owner signs first, an agreement signed by the debtor or hirer on business premises remains cancellable?

'premises at which any of the following is carrying on any business (whether on a permanent or temporary basis)'[245]

(i)   the creditor or owner;

(ii)  any party to a linked transaction (other than the debtor or hirer or a relative of his);[246]

(iii) the negotiator in any antecedent negotiations.[238]

It should be noted that these exemptions do *not* include the business premises of the debtor or hirer, e.g. a partnership,[240] nor unconnected trade premises, e.g. a public house; and that, where there are joint debtors or hirers, e.g. spouses, the exception at first sight appears confined to the situation where both sign at the listed 'business premises'.[247] The formula may cause difficulty where there is a directly financed consumer hire transaction signed at the premises of the supplier, in which case it is arguable that such a transaction is cancellable, which seems surprising;[248] or where a consumer credit agreement is signed by the debtor at the premises of an agent of the creditor, because s 56(1) may not include such business agent within the term 'negotiator' (see para 16.08); or if the debtor takes the form home to sign, though there may then be trouble with the copies rules (see para 9.14) and cancellation notice (see para 9.17).

**[10.30] Cooling-off period**. Where there is a cancellable agreement (see para 10.29), the debtor or hirer has a right of cancellation (see para 10.31) only during the statutory cooling-off period This period is defined by s 68 as the applicable one of the following, each of which runs from the date of signature by the debtor or hirer on the agreement form:

(a)  Where the unexecuted agreement does not become executed on the occasion when the debtor or hirer signs it then he must normally receive two copies, whether the agreement form was presented to him personally (see para 9.15) or sent to him,[249] each copy containing the prescribed notice of cancellation.[250] This will be the usual case and s 68(a) then gears the cooling-off period to the date upon which the debtor or hirer received the signature copy, providing that the agreement may be cancelled 'until the end of the fifth day following the day on which he receives' the signature copy.[251]

(b)  Where the agreement is executed on the occasion when the debtor or hirer signs it, then he need only receive **one** copy of the agreement, whether it was presented to him personally (see para 9.14) or sent to him.[249] In this situation, a separate notice of cancellation must normally within seven days be sent to the debtor or hirer[250] and s 68(a) sets the five days running from receipt of

---

245  Temporary business premises would include a stand at an exhibition, a mobile sales caravan. What of a company car in a car park; or even where parked outside the consumer's house?

246  As to 'linked transactions', see generally, para 5.31; and as to 'relative', see para 5.33.

247  Cf. canvassing: see para 7.06. But what if the spouse signing at home was **not present** during the face-to-face sales pitch?

248  See Dobson [1983] JBL at 317–18; Goode, *Op. cit.*, para 31.111 and Division IIB, para 5.106.

249  As to service of documents sent by post or 'electronic communication', see amended s 176 and new s 176A (and para 9.05).

250  See para 9.17.

251  E.g. second copies/notice **received** on Monday, agreement may be cancelled until end of following Saturday. As to where the notice is detained or lost in the post, see below.

that notice.[251] However, in those cases where the OFT has dispensed with that notice,[250] the cooling-off period runs until 'the end of the fourteenth day following the day on which he signed the unexecuted agreement'.[252]

Except where the OFT has dispensed with a notice of cancellation,[252] it will be observed that time runs from receipt by the debtor or hirer of a second copy or notice. Suppose that copy or notice is never received.[253] Unless a fresh copy or notice can be served within the seven days, it would appear that the agreement remains binding[254] and enforceable[255] but perpetually cancellable.[256]

**[10.31] The right of cancellation.** According to s 69(1):

> 'If within the period specified in s 68 the debtor or hirer under a cancellable agreement serves on—
>
> (a)  the creditor or owner, or
>
> (b)  the person specified in the notice under section 64(1), or
>
> (c)  a person who (whether by virtue of subsection (6) or otherwise) is the agent of the creditor or owner,
>
> a notice (a 'notice of cancellation') which, however expressed and whether or not conforming to the notice given under section 64(1), indicates the intention of the debtor or hirer to withdraw from the agreement'

that notice shall take effect (see para 10.32). The provision thus contains the following requirements, which must **all** be satisfied before the right of cancellation can be exercised in respect of a cancellable agreement (see para 10.29) during the cancellation period (see para 10.30):

1.  *Form of notice of cancellation.* The Act is here unclear, although a Cancellation Form is provided in the regulations (see para 9.17). Whilst it explicitly allows the debtor or hirer to use any form of words to indicate his[257] intention,[258] that notice must be in writing (s 189(1)). A posted notice must be properly addressed and stamped;[259] but s 69(7) adds that 'Whether or not it is actually received by

---

252  S 68(b). For those cases where the OFT has dispensed with a notice of cancellation, see para 9.17.

253  The evidential problems this may cause for the creditor/owner are examined later (para 10.31). However, it would seem possible to avoid them in the case of a cancellable credit-token agreement by sending the token with the second copy/notice: use of the token then proves receipt.

254  For the definition of agreement, the CCA relies on the common law (see para 5.20). As to the common law rules for formation of agreement, see para 10.02, *et seq*. To this extent, the cancellation rules are not as advantageous to the consumer as those on inertia selling (see para 8.18).

255  It is properly executed since 'service' by post does not require receipt (see s 176 and the s 189(1) definition of 'service') so that posting complies with ss 63 and 64. Even during a postal strike?

256  Subject to the dispensing power of the court (see para 9.21). How can the creditor or owner counter a simple denial by the debtor or hirer that he ever received the second copy/notice, bearing in mind s 173(1) (see para 18.11)?

257  In the case of joint debtors or hirers, it would appear that one of them may give a cancellation notice which will then bind both (s 185(1)(b): set out at para 25.08). So a spouse who signs at business premises can give notice of cancellation even though his/her spouse who signed at home does not.

258  Compare the tightly controlled form of words which the creditor or owner must use to give the debtor or hirer notice of his right of cancellation: see para 9.17.

259  Interpretation Act 1978, s 7. What if there is a postal strike? Compare creditors' notices, which must arrive: see para 10.29.

him, a notice of cancellation sent by post to a person shall be deemed to be served on him at the time of posting.'[260]

2. *On whom served.* Section 69(1) provides that a notice of cancellation (as above) may be served on[261] any of the following:

(a) the creditor or owner (see respectively, paras 5.25 and 1.19); or

(b) the person specified in the cancellation notice (see para 9.17); or

(c) any person who is the agent of the creditor or owner, being either their statutory agent (s 69(6): see further, para 10.25), or common law agent (see para 16.06).

In the common case,[262] this will enable service of a notice of cancellation on the dealer[263] or financier by post[260] or other transmission[264] which will take effect immediately on posting, even if never received. It has been said to be 'scarcely conceivable' that s 69(7) would be confined to the creditor/ owner, not applying to notices posted to his agent.[265] But would not such a construction avoid the dilemma posed above, confining deemed receipt to the situation where a creditor/owner could himself arrange for mail to be forwarded, though it would have the drawback of not then covering genuine loss in course of post to dealer?

**[10.32] The effect of cancellation.** Where a debtor or hirer properly exercises a right of cancellation (see para 10.31), s 69(1) lays down the general rule that the notice shall operate:

'(i) to cancel the agreement, and any linked transaction, and

(ii) to withdraw any offer by the debtor or hirer, or his relative, to enter into a linked transaction'.

The general effect[266] of cancellation thus extends over all the following matters:

(a) *The regulated agreement.* Since a notice of cancellation may be sent by the debtor or hirer at any time after he has signed the unexecuted agreement (see para 10.30), its effect depends on whether or not a contract then exists:[267]

(i) if not, s 57(1) operates to withdraw any offer (see para 10.26);

---

260 How does the creditor or owner rebut a claim by the debtor or hirer that he posted such a notice in due form or time? See further below.

261 Even to an address known to be vacated (38 MLR 728)?

262 For the position with regard to check-trading, see Goode, *Consumer Credit Law & Practice*, para 31.120.

263 Even if the agent is known to have severed his connection with the creditor; or to be worthless, so nullifying the statutory indemnity under s 175 (see para 10 25): Adler (1975) 38 MLR 8.

264 By amendment to s 69(7)(b), where notice is transmitted by internet, at the time of transmission; and transmission is defined by new s 176A (see para 9.05B).

265 Goode, *Op. cit.*, para 52.5.

266 The ordinary rules as to the effect of cancellation are ousted (s 69(3)) and some special ones applied in the following cases (s 69(2)): (a) goods or work supplied under a DCS agreement for RU credit to meet an emergency, e.g. gas cooker in winter; or (b) goods supplied which the debtor or hirer has incorporated in any land or unassociated thing, e.g. new engine for car, washing machine plumbed in. As to an unfortunate omission from (a), see Goode, *Consumer Credit Law & Practice*, para 31.138.

267 Any interested party may apply to the court for a declaration to this effect: s 142(2)(a); and generally, see para 9.19.

(ii)   if so, s 69(1)(i) cancels the agreement and s 69(4) adds that:

> 'Except as otherwise provided by or under this Act, an agreement or trans-action cancelled under subsection (1) shall be treated as if it had never been entered into'.

The exercise of this right of cancellation makes the regulated contract void *ab initio*[268] and is in addition to any common law right of rescission[269] or statutory right of termination (see paras 26.05–7). The cancellation also cancels any modifying agreement made during[270] the cooling-off period.[271] For the further effects of cancellation on money and goods, see paras 10.33–4.

(b)  *Any linked transaction.* The meaning of the expression 'linked transaction' has already been examined (see para 5.31), where it was seen that a linked transaction has no effect until the principal agreement is made (s 19(3)). If the principal agreement is cancelled, the linked transaction generally[272] falls as well:[267] if still an offer, it is withdrawn; or, if an agreement, it is cancelled; for instance in loan financing the contract for the supply of goods; or in a second mortgage, the life insurance cover. Whilst applying to a consumer sale which is loan financed, this rule does not apply to the sale to a financier in a directly financed transaction;[273] but it could extend to a foreign supply financed by a UK credit card.[274]

(c)  *Any security.* Security given by the debtor or hirer entering a regulated agreement is not a linked transaction (s 19(1)), but it is elsewhere provided (s 113(3) (a)) that the security shall automatically be invalidated under s 106 (see para 25.13) and that any duty to return, e.g. property lodged by the debtor or hirer, must be completed before the debtor or hirer has to repay any credit or restore any goods (s 113(5)). As to these duties, see paras 10.33–4.

**[10.33] Further effects.** Where an agreement is cancellable (see para 10.29), it may be that the parties prudently defer performance of any part of the transaction until after expiry of the cooling-off period (see para 10.30): if the agreement is cancelled, it will then have only the effects above-mentioned (para 10.32). However, the Act also seeks to deal with the possibility that before cancellation the parties may have transferred money or goods thereunder.

1.   *Money paid.* Under the cancelled agreement, money may have been paid by either side as follows:

---

268  *Colesworthy v Collmain Services* [1993] CCLR 4, Cty Ct.

269  By either side either *ab initio* or *de futuro*: see paras 26.12–16. Exactly the same persons are made deemed agents for this purpose (s 102): see para 26.04. What if the agreement is frustrated?

270  But the cancellation provisions do not apply to modifying agreements (see para 26.22) made **after** expiry of the cooling-off period: s 82(6).

271  Even if the modifying agreement would not otherwise be cancellable, e.g. because signed on business premises: s 82(5).

272  There is power to save classes of linked transaction by regulation (s 69(5)). See 1983 SI 1560; and *Goshawk etc Ltd v Bank of Scotland* [2006] 2 All ER 610, at paras 52–67. See further, Bone and Rutherford [1985] JBL 209; and Goode, *Op. cit.*, paras 31.177–9.

273  So cancellation of a directly financed transaction will leave the sale from dealer to financier standing (see para 5.31); and the best way for the financier to divest himself of the goods would appear to be under a repurchase provision (see para 16.21).

274  *OFT v Lloyds TSB Bank plc* (see para 16.11), *obiter* at paras 99–102.

(a) If the debtor or hirer or any relative[275] has **paid** any money under the cancelled agreement, e.g. deposit, s 70 generally makes it recoverable[276] from the person to whom it was paid.[277] Thus, in direct financing the deposit will under the CCA normally be recoverable from the supplier-dealer whilst subsequent instalments are recoverable from the creditor. If the debtor or hirer has any goods in his possession under the terms of the cancelled agreement, the debtor or hirer has a lien on them for that repayment (s 70(2). For liens, see generally, para 25.02). But there are special provisions for loan financing,[278] credit-tokens,[279] brokerage fees[280] and cases falling within s 69(2),[281] whilst the common law deals with deposits in direct financing (see para 16.05).

(b) As regards any credit **received** by the debtor, the Act is deliberately designed to discourage the creditor from making any cash loan to the debtor before either expiry of the cooling-off period for cancellation or time for withdrawal of offer (see para 10.26), because of the likelihood that it will be immediately spent so making repayment difficult.[282] Accordingly, s 71(1) provides that such a cancelled agreement 'shall continue in force so far as relates to repayment of credit and payment of interest'; but any obligations with respect to future advances, linked transactions or security are extinguished (see para 10.32). In making these payments,[283] the debtor is given a choice:

(i) Take one month's free credit before repaying without interest the whole or any part of the credit already advanced.[284]

(ii) Insofar as he cannot repay the capital as above, repay it with interest as follows: if the loan was repayable in a lump sum, repay with the contract interest provisions; if the loan was repayable by instalments, repay the capital with an advantageous pro-rating rule as to interest.[285]

---

275 As to 'debtor', see para 5.24; as to 'hirer', see para 1.19; and as to 'relative', see paras 5.31 and 5.33.

276 S 70(1)(a); but see s 113(5) (para 10.32). And any sum payable ceases to be payable: s 70(1)(b).

277 S 70(3); *Colesworthy v Collmain Services* [1993] CCLR 4.

278 S 70 does not apply to credit already extended to the debtor under a cancelled loan falling within s 71 (s 70(5): see below). In other cases, both the creditor and supplier are liable to repay such sum (s 70(3)), e.g. the deposit in loan financing is recoverable from either creditor or supplier. If the sum is recovered from the creditor, he has a right of indemnity against the supplier (s 70(4)).

279 The token must be returned before money payable for its issue is recoverable (s 70(5)), e.g. some charge cards and trading checks.

280 As the Act restricts broker's commission to a nominal figure, if no credit or hire agreement results from his introduction (see para 16.19), a similar ceiling is imposed in respect of brokerage fees for cancelled agreements (s 70(6)) or sums so deemed (s 70(7)).

281 S 70(8). For cases falling within s 69(2), see para 10.32.

282 Goode, *Consumer Credit Law & Practice*, para 31.180.

283 Payments may be made to any person upon whom a notice of cancellation could have been served (see para 10.31), except one who was the agent of the debtor (s 71(4)).

284 S 71(2). Insofar as the debtor has not spent the advance, he can therefore return it without further obligation.

285 S 71(3). E.g. under a personal loan. See explanation in Goode, *Op. cit.*, paras 1480–3; and also Howells, *Consumer Debt*, para 4.51.

2.   *Property transferred.* (See para 10.34.)

**[10.34] Property transferred.** Under a cancelled agreement (see para 10.32), property may have been transferred either way as follows:

1.   *Part-exchange goods.* In some cases the debtor or hirer[286] will at any early stage have tendered to the negotiator goods in part-exchange (see generally, para 2.09) in respect of a transaction which is subsequently cancelled[287] or from which he has withdrawn (see para 10.26). Under s 73(2) the primary entitlement of the debtor or hirer is to recover the part-exchange allowance[288] from the negotiator, e.g. dealer, except in the case of loan financing;[289] and, where that allowance is recovered by the debtor or hirer, his title to the part-exchange goods vests in the negotiator (s 73(6)). This will be so regardless of from whom the allowance is recovered, so a loan financier paying the allowance will need the above indemnity. However, within a period of 10 days from the date of cancellation, the above duty to pay the part-exchange allowance may be discharged by the return of the part-exchange goods to the debtor or hirer in a condition substantially as good as when they were delivered to the negotiator.[290] For the foregoing purposes, the debtor or hirer is given a lien over any goods (s 73(5)) to which the cancelled agreement relates (see below).

2.   *Agreement goods.* If the debtor, hirer or any relative[286] has acquired possession of goods under a cancelled transaction, e.g. under a credit sale, but not otherwise,[291] s 72 generally[292] places him under a legal duty, actionable as a breach of statutory duty,[293] to redeliver[294] those goods,[295] subject to his lien for

---

286  As to 'debtor', 'hirer' and 'relative', see respectively, paras 5.24, 1.19 and 5.33. To the extent that the dealer in a directly financed consumer hire transaction is not the 'negotiator' (see para 10.29), s 72 covers the agreement goods but the part-exchange goods are outside s 73 (see s 73(1): below).

287  S 73(1). See further the definition of when goods are taken in part-exchange in s 73(7)(a). What rules are to govern consumer hirings (see above)?

288  The part-exchange allowance is defined in s 73(7)(b). It assumes the part-exchange goods are not supplied under a linked transaction (see para 5.31).

289  When the dealer and financier will be jointly and severally liable for payment of the part-exchange allowance (s 73(3) and (8)). But in this case the creditor is entitled to an indemnity from the dealer (s 73(4)).

290  S 73(2). As to attempts by the debtor or hirer to insist on return of the part-exchange goods, see Goode, *Consumer Credit Law & Practice*, Division IIB, para 5.143. If both sides agree, any deterioration or delay can be ignored (s 173(3): see para 18.11).

291  So, if DC credit is used to buy goods, the sale contract continues despite the cancellation of the credit: Howells, *Consumer Debt*, para 4.55.

292  S 72(1)–(2). Except in the case of perishable or consumable goods or those supplied to meet an emergency or incorporated in land (s 72(9)) and subject to s 113(5) (see para 10.32). See further, Goode, *Op. cit.*, paras 31.157–71.

293  S 72(11). For such duties, see generally, para 3.21.

294  Redelivery is to the 'other party' (s 72(4)), meaning the person from whom the consumer acquired possession (s 72(2)(b)). Physical possession will usually have been acquired from the dealer; but it has been argued that the required redelivery is to the financier: Goode, *Op. cit.*, para 1460. *Sed quaere?*

295  S 72(4). Goods can actually be taken or posted back; but redelivery need only be made at the address of the debtor/hirer (s 72(5) and (10)); and it may be made to anyone upon whom a notice of cancellation could have been served (see para 10.31), except one who is the agent of the debtor (s 72(6)).

any part-exchange goods (see above) and the recovery of any security (see para 10.32). Meantime, the debtor, hirer or any relative is under the following duties:[296]

(a) To retain possession of the goods. Whilst the consumer need ordinarily only hold the goods awaiting collection (see above), what if he moves house?

(b) To take reasonable care of the goods for 21 days after cancellation,[297] thereafter usually becoming an involuntary bailee, with a duty only to refrain from wilful damage. This is designed to encourage the other side to make early collection of the goods and hence relieve the consumer of their inconvenience.

## OTHER STATUTORY RIGHTS OF CANCELLATION

[10.35] The above cancellation without cause[298] device has proved so effective that it has also been adopted as a consumer protection measure in other statutory provisions,[299] including the Distance Selling Regulations (see paras 10.38–9) and the Doorstep-selling Regulations (see paras 10.36–7). With so many different cancellation regimes, the EU proposed harmonisation in its 2002 e-Europe Action Plan (see para 8.17A); and in 2002 a DTI Minister expressed herself in favour of a 14-day cancellation period for all consumer credit agreements, however concluded.

[10.36] **Doorstep-selling for cash.** The Government has chosen to implement the EU Doorstep-selling Directive[300] by statutory instrument.[301] The intention of the Directive is to neutralise the element of surprise available to a trader who knocks on the door of the consumer's home and to allow the consumer time to make a comparison between the trader's offer and other offers available elsewhere. The ambit of the regulations is generally[302] restricted by reg 3(1) to a doorstep 'supply': this is not defined, but presumably covers any contract under which the possession and/or property in goods is transferred, e.g. sale, hp or simple hiring.

---

296 S 72(3). This makes the duties retrospective to include the period before cancellation, and is to deal with the time when, e.g. the buyer under a credit sale, had a perfect common law right to damage or sell goods. It then links up with s 72(11): see above.

297 S 72(8). This obligation ceases on redelivery (s 72(7)) but may be indefinitely extended by unreasonable failure to redeliver (s 72(8)). As to the duty of a bailee to take reasonable care of goods, see generally, para 1.17. What if the debtor drives a hired car, e.g. 3,000 miles before redelivery?

298 If the supplier is in breach, the consumer has the remedies considered in Chap 29.

299 E.g. Insurance Companies Act 1982, ss 75–7 (life insurance: see para 24.48); Timeshare Act 1992 (as amended) (which extends to both timeshare and timeshare credit agreements: see Goode, *Consumer Credit Law & Practice*, para 31.241, *et seq.*).

300 Council Directive 85/577/EEC. As to the text of this Directive, see Guest and Lloyd, *Encyclopedia of Consumer Credit*, para 9024, *et seq.*; Thomas, *Encyclopedia of Consumer Law*, para 5-184, *et seq.*; Goode, *Consumer Credit Legislation* X, para 22.01. As to the background to this Directive, see *Consumer Law in the EEC* (Ed Woodroffe) 73–4. As to Directives generally, see para 1.03A.

301 Consumer Protection (Cancellation of Contracts Concluded away from Business Premises) Regulations, 1987 SI 2117 (as amended). In 2005, the DTI consulted on reform.

302 Under reg 3(2), the following classes of contract are excepted: (a) those concerned with the purchase of land; (b) perishables, such as milk or bread delivery; (c) mail order business (see para 10.38); (d) insurance contracts; (e) investment agreements. As to (a), cf. *Heiniger v Bayerische* [2002] GCCR 4351, Eu Ct.

The supply must be for **cash** by a trader[303] of goods[304] or services[305] to a consumer[306] which is made during an **unsolicited visit** (see below) to the consumer's home for a VAT inclusive price of £35 or more: if the goods or services are s-pplied on **credit**, the transaction escapes these Regulations (reg 3(2)(g)), but will usually fall within the cancellation rules of the CCA (see para 10.28, *et seq.*); but, if the goods are supplied for **cash** (and that will include goods supplied against a payment card: see *Re Charge Card Services Ltd*: set out at para 2.27), they may fall within the present Regulations. However, it would seem that the remainder of reg 3(1) is to be read disjunctively, so that the regulations also extend to the following: a **solicited** visit which is used for switch-selling (reg 3(1)(b)); or a visit made after an order is placed by a consumer (reg 3(1)(c)); or a sale made during an excursion organised by the trader.[307]

In relation to a doorstep supply for cash, the Regulations apply only where the transaction is conducted during an **unsolicited visit** to the consumer's home[308] or place of work (reg 3(1)(a)). According to reg 3(3), '**unsolicited visit**'

> 'means a visit by a trader, whether or not he is a trader who supplies goods or services, which does not take place at the express request of the consumer;'[309]

and this basic definition has subsequently been enhanced as an anti-avoidance device to include a visit which is arranged by telephone or during another unsolicited visit.[310] The likely effect of the regulations is this: *prima facie*, they will catch cash doorstep supplies of goods, such as vacuum cleaners, and building services, such burglar alarms, double-glazing, roof repairs and tarmacking; and to avoid the regulations these businesses will have to solicit business by such as newspaper advertisements and leaflet drops. The OFT is pressing for an extension of the rules to solicited visits.[311]

**[10.37]** Where a transaction falls within the ambit of the Doorstep-Selling Regulations (see para 10.36), reg 4 provides the consumer with a compulsory[312] seven-day right of cancellation, which must be notified to him in the prescribed

---

303 'Trader' means a person who, in making a contract to which these regulations apply, is acting for the purpose of his business, and anyone acting in the name or on behalf of such a person: reg 2.

304 'Goods' has the same meaning as in the SGA (reg 2): see para 2.02. For doorstep-selling of energy, see para 3.07.

305 'Service' includes a guarantee, but only of a private debt: *Bayerische Hypotheken-und Wechsel-bank AG v Dietzinger* [1998] All ER (EC) 332.

306 ' "Consumer" means a person, other than a body corporate, who, in making a contract to which these regulations apply, is acting for purposes which can be regarded as outside his business': reg 2.

307 Reg 3(1)(d). This follows the Directive and is apparently aimed at malpractices more familiar on the Continent. However, it could catch UK time-share operators and also act as an anti-avoidance device. See *Travel-Vac SL v Sanchis* [1999] All ER (EC) 656.

308 The extension by reg 3(1)(a)(i) to 'the home of another person' will bring in sales parties (see para 8.17).

309 *Havair Ltd v Vile* [2000] CLY 848, Cty Ct (leafleting). For telephone sales pitches, see para 8.17. An example of an 'express request' may be returning an advertising coupon. What of a letter informing a consumer he has 'won a prize' and inviting him to phone?

310 Holgate (1999) 18 Tr L 33.

311 (2004) 38 *Fair Trading* 5. In July 2004, the DTI published a Consultation Paper on reform of the Regulations.

312 Reg 10. For contracting out prohibitions, see generally, paras 18.09, *et seq.*

form[313] at the time of the offer or contract (reg 4(4)). The regulations also seek to deal with potential overlap with other rights of cancellation by excluding them from the present regulations as follows (reg 4(2)):

(a) An agreement which is a cancellable regulated agreement within the CCA (see para 10.29). The effect of this is to leave within the present regulations both unregulated consumer credit,[314] and also most regulated non-cancellable agreements where the total payments exceed £35.[315]

(b) 'An agreement which may be cancelled by the consumer in accordance with terms of the agreement conferring upon him similar rights as if the agreement were such a cancellable agreement.' The test seems to be whether the contractual cancellation rights are 'similar' to those for regulated agreements.[316]

*The doorstep-selling provisions.* The Regulations now contain both civil and criminal provisions.

(i) *Civil provisions.* Reg 4(1)) provides that:

> 'No contract to which these Regulations apply shall be enforceable against the consumer unless the trader has delivered to the consumer notice in writing [of his right of cancellation and a Cancellation Form]'.

There is an express prohibition on contracting out[312] and no dispensing power, unlike the CCA (see para 9.20). It should be observed that such transactions remain fully enforceable **against** the trader; but, within seven days of the making of the contract,[317] the consumer may give notice of cancellation 'however expressed' which 'shall operate to cancel the contract' (reg 4(5)), in which event it 'shall be treated as if it had never been entered into by the consumer'.[318] The regulations then proceed to deal with the civil consequences of such a cancellation in a manner which closely resembles that of the CCA: they provide for the recovery by the consumer of money paid by him[319] or goods given in part-exchange (reg 8. Cf. CCA, s 73: see para 10.34); and his subsequent redelivery of the goods subject to the cancelled contract (reg 7. Cf. CCA, s 72: see para 10.34) and repayment by the consumer of any credit (reg 6, as amended. Cf. CCA, s 71: see para 10.33).

---

313 As to the contents of the notice, see regs 4(3), (4) and the Sched; and as to service of the notice, see regs 4(7) and 11; and the Interpretation Act 1978, s 7. Compare the different requirement for notices of cancellation under the CCA: see para 10.31. Documentation is also subject to the Unfair Terms Regulations: *Bulletin No. 23*, para 1.11; *No. 24*, case 6; [2005] *Bulletin* J/M, *Amex* case. If no notice is given, there is no time limit on the right of cancellation: *Heiniger v Bayerische* [2002] GCCR 4351, Eu Ct.

314 E.g. credit agreements exempt from the CCA; regulated agreements signed on trade premises after a home visit by the trader (reg 3(1)(c)). See further, Guest and Lloyd, *Encyclopedia of Consumer Credit*, para 2-068.

315 Reg 3(2)(f), unless under an hp or conditional sale agreement (reg 3(2)(g)). The minimum figure for the CCA cancellation provisions is reduced to the same figure: see para 10.29.

316 For express contractual rights of cancellation, see para 10.28. Does this extend to other statutory rights of cancellation, e.g. under the Timeshare Act 1992?

317 Compare the time limit for cancelling CCA cancellable agreements: see para 10.30. Will it lead to much difference in practice? And is it sensible to have slightly differently worded rules?

318 Reg 4(6). Unlike the CCA (see para 10.32), this would leave any linked transaction standing. Is this satisfactory?

319 Reg 5, which gives the consumer a lien on goods delivered to him as well as cancelling any security. Cf. CCA, s 70: see para 10.33.

(ii) *Criminal provisions.* Under the amended Regulations, a trader commits an offence if he fails to deliver to the consumer a cancellation notice[320] and a duty to enforce the Regulations is placed upon the local authority,[321] who may apply for an Enforcement Order (see para 6.08). Or a designated body may make a super-complaint to the OFT (see para 4.19).

**[10.38] Distance selling of goods**. The Government has chosen to implement the EU Distance-selling Directive[322] by statutory instrument.[323] As has already been seen (para 8.17), these Regulations grant a consumer certain rights when he enters a distance contract for the supply of goods; for instance, one made by telephone, internet or mail order. Among these rights is a right of cancellation. Even if the transaction is regulated by the CCA, the consumer will not have a CCA right of cancellation, because there are no face-to-face negotiations (see para 10.29); but he may have such a right under these Regulations in respect of both regulated and unregulated distance contracts (see below). The OFT have used the Unfair Terms Regulations to make distance suppliers amend their express terms to comply with the Regulations.[324]

*The right of cancellation.* Starting with a requirement that the consumer receives at an appropriate time notice of his right to cancellation (reg 8(2)(b) (as amended) and (3): see para 9.05) and a prohibition on contracting out (reg 25(1): see para 18.10), reg 10(1) generally[325] grants the consumer of goods[325] or services[326] a right of cancellation within a cancellation period, exercisable by giving 'a notice of cancellation[327] to the supplier, or any other person' to whom a notice of cancellation may be given (see reg 8: above). The cancellation period begins when the contract is concluded (regs 11(1) and 12(1)) and ends at times which differ according to whether there are supplied goods or services:[328] in the case of goods, if the supplier complies with the documentation rules in reg 8 (see above), it ends on the

---

320  Reg 4A. For the liability of other persons, see reg 4C; and paras 28.11–12. This is subject to a defence of due diligence: reg 4B; see para 28.13.

321  The duty is cast upon the local Weights and Measure Authorities (regs 4D, 2(1); and see para 28.03), who have powers of investigation (regs 4E and 4F; and see para 28.05) and duties of confidentiality (reg 4G; and see para 28.06).

322  Council Directive 97/7/EEC. As to the text of this Directive, see Thomas, *Encyclopedia of Consumer Law*, para 5-495/1, *et seq.*

323  Consumer Protection (Distance Selling) Regulations, 2000 SI 2334 (as amended). For discussion of the return policy of distance sellers, see [2003] 1 *Which?* 34.

324  OFT, *UFT Bulletin No. 21*, case 9; *No. 22*, case 13; *No. 23*, cases 16 and 44; *No. 24*, cases 46 and 48. See also Miller (2003) 147 NLJ 1361.

325  *Prima facie*, the consumer has no right to cancel in any of the following cases (reg 13(1) (as amended)): (a) supply of services satisfying reg 8 and begun with the consumer's consent before expiry of the cancellation period; (b) goods or services supplied at a price fluctuating with the financial market; (c) customised goods or those likely to deteriorate rapidly; (d) audio or video recordings or computer software unsealed by the consumer; (e) newspapers, periodicals or magazines; (f) gaming, betting or lottery services.

326  The absence of a right of cancellation in respect of services (see reg 13(1) above) is particularly significant for the hire of vehicles by phone. For financial services, see para 10.39.

327  The notice may be given in writing or 'another durable medium' and takes effect however expressed: reg 10(3). As to extra forms of cancellation, see DTI, *Consultation* (Jan 2004), paras 2.21–6.

328  On a supply of non-financial services, there are similar expiry rules in regs 12(2)–(4) (as amended). As to financial services, see para 10.39.

expiry of seven working days after goods-delivery (reg 11(2)); if within a three-month period of goods delivery, so that the supplier complies late with reg 8, it ends seven working days after the consumer received the information (reg 11(3)); otherwise, it expires three months plus seven working days after goods-delivery (reg 11(4) and (5)). When due notice of cancellation is given (see reg 10(4) and (5)), that notice 'shall operate to cancel the contract' (reg 10(1)) and any 'related credit agreement',[329] upon which 'the contract shall be treated as if it had not been made' (reg 10(2)) and any security given is 'treated as never having had effect' (regs 14(4) and 15(4)). The regulations then proceed to deal with the civil consequences of such a cancellation in a manner which closely resembles that of the CCA: they provide for the recovery by the consumer of almost all[330] money paid by him[331] or goods given in part-exchange (reg 18. Cf. CCA, s 73: see para 10.34); and his subsequent redelivery of the goods subject to the cancelled contract (reg 17. Cf. CCA, s 72: see para 10.34) and repayment by the consumer of any credit (reg 16. Cf. CCA, s 71: see para 10.33). Restrictions on the consumer's rights after cancellation may be unfair.[332]

For online signature, see para 9.05.

**[10.39] Distance selling of financial services**. Distance selling by way of phone, fax, internet or mail of financial services, e.g. credit or credit insurance, are now governed by their own cancellation rules under the Financial Services (Distance Marketing) Regulations, 2004 SI 2095 (see para 8.17). Presumably to be without prejudice to any express right of cancellation or termination (see para 10.28), reg 9(1) grants consumers a general statutory right of 'cancellation', which may apply whether or not an agreement has been made. However, reg 11 lists certain types of contract which normally may not be cancelled,[333] of which the following may be relevant to this work: (i) contracts already completed; (ii) credit secured by a legal mortgage of land;[334] (iii) contracts cancellable under the Distance Selling Regulations (see para 10.38); (iv) restricted-use credit agreements secured on land or for a bridging loan (see para 10.29).

Widely defining the medium in which a notice of cancellation may be given (reg 9(3)), the place to which it may be sent (reg 9(4)–(6)), and the person to whom it may be given (reg 9(7)), the Regulations go on to specify the cancellation period (reg 10) in a manner similar to that for distance selling of goods (see para 10.38). Where the consumer exercises the foregoing right of cancellation of the 'main contract' for

---

329 Reg 15(1). 'Related credit agreement' is defined by s 15(5) and (6). In lender credit (reg 14(8)), the supplier must notify the creditor of the cancellation (reg 15(2)), upon which charges paid under the credit agreement must usually be returned to the consumer (reg 15(3)).

330 Except that, if previously agreed by a term which is not unfair (reg 14(6)(b): see para 11.12, et seq.), the supplier is entitled to make a re-delivery charge for the goods supplied, but not substitutes (reg 14(5) and (7)). The re-delivery charge is not available where the consumer is exercising a right to reject defective goods (reg 14(6)(a)).

331 Reg 14(1). This includes sums paid by the consumer under any 'personal credit agreement' (reg 14(2) and (8)).

332 OFT, *Bulletin No. 24*, case 48.

333 By reg 11(2)–(3), even those exempted categories may sometimes be cancellable under reg 9 where the supplier has not served the second-wave information required by reg 8, but has served first-wave information required by reg 7 (see para 9.05).

334 For a drafting difficulty, see Susman (2005) 155 NLJ 770–1.

418          Consumer Sales Law

the provision of financial services, this *prima facie* operates to also cancel any 'secondary contract' (reg 12(3) and (4)), whether supplied by the same person or a third party (reg 12(1)), provided that the secondary contract is attached to the main contract in a manner similar to that of a linked contract under the CCA.[335] Regulation 13 then provides for the consequences of cancellation (reg 13(1)), whether it is of a distance contract for financial services by notice under reg 9 or of a secondary contract automatically under reg 12 ('a cancellation event': reg 13(2)). These consequences are similar to those in respect of a regulated agreement cancelled under CCA, s 67 (see paras 10.32–4). The supplier must refund any sums received (reg 13(3) and (4)), less a proportionate charge for any services already supplied (reg 13(6) and (7)) of which the consumer was forewarned (reg 13(8)–(10)); and return any security taken (reg 13(5)). The consumer must repay any money received and return any property acquired (reg 13(11)), on pain of an action for breach of statutory duty.[336] The enforcement authorities are (reg 17(1): see paras 3.02–3 and 3.05):

(a) the Financial Services Authority in respect of breaches of 'specified contracts', which includes (reg 17(2)) debit cards, electronic money, first mortgages of land.[337]

(b) the OFT in respect of non-'specified contracts', where the supplier is a local authority.

(c) every local authority weights and measures department (reg 17(4)), in relation to any other breach.

For on-line signature, see para 9.05.

---

335 Reg 12(2). For linked CCA transactions, see para 5.31.
336 Reg 13(12). For actions for breach of statutory duty, see generally, para 3.21.
337 Reg 17(4). See respectively, paras 2.25, 2.24 and 3.02.

# PART 4

# THE CONTENTS OF A CONTRACT
# FOR THE SUPPLY OF GOODS

# CHAPTER 11

# CONTRACTUAL TERMS

## REPRESENTATIONS AND TERMS

**[11.01] Pre-contractual statements**. In the course of the negotiations which precede a contract, it is common for the parties to make some statements either by words or conduct, or occasionally by silence. Sometimes those statements are of no legal significance to that contract, as where the 'statement' says nothing of relevance or is not intended seriously (mere puffs: see para 8.05); but at other times they may amount to representations—statements of fact inducing the contract.[1] Perhaps even more potent than words in selling to consumers is pictures. Suppose a misleading picture, e.g. an advertisement for a pictured car in untrue colour/shade, the eye being distracted by the human model draped over it, or the computer-enhanced representation of goods in a catalogue, as where a plant has an increased number of flower-heads.

The common law refused to grant damages for innocent misrepresentation,[2] but would do so in the tort of deceit if the representation were fraudulent (see para 17.17), or in contract if the representation became a term of a contract between the parties.[3] Whilst deceit required the plaintiff to discharge the heavy burden of proving that the defendant did not honestly believe his statement to be true (always a difficult matter), liability in contract was strict, and fraud need not be proved (see para 17.18). This relative attractiveness of the contractual action led litigants to frame actions based on misrepresentation in contract rather than tort, so that the vital question was frequently whether the representation had attained contractual status (see para 11.02). However, modern reform has widened the scope of actions for innocent misrepresentation: not only are more such actions now available, either in tort (see para 17.19) or under the Misrepresentation Act 1967 (see para 17.10); but the list of potential defendants extends beyond the scope of the doctrine of privity of contract, either by suing in tort (see above) or under s 56 of the CCA (see para 16.08). Attempts to exclude liability for misrepresentation may be both unfair (UTCC, reg 5: see para 11.15) and unreasonable (Misrepresentation Act 1967, s 3: see para 18.17).

Further, there may now also be criminal liability under the TDA (see paras 4.07–8) or other statutes;[4] and, where a business deals with a consumer, silence may sometimes render the business liable under the UCPD in wider circumstances than would amount to misrepresentations at common law (Art 7: see para 4.21A).

---

1   E.g. *Watford Electronics Ltd v Sanderson CFL Ltd* (see para 18.21; unappealed point). See further, Treitel, *Law of Contract*, 11th edn, 330–43.

2   *Hopkins v Tanqueray* (1854) 15 CB 130 (auction: see para 10.10); *Oscar Chess Ltd v Williams* [1957] 1 All ER 325, CA (car log book misled parties); *Humming Bird Motors v Hobbs* [1986] RTR 276, CA (seller's statement to best of knowledge and belief). Perhaps this applies to car manufacturers' warranties: as to trade usage, see para 15.11.

3   *Harling v Eddy* [1951] 2 KB 739, CA (auction: see para 10.10).

4   E.g. Weights and Measures Act 1985, s 29 (see para 4.25).

**[11.02] Misrepresentation or contractual term**. The courts had to decide whether a statement remained a mere representation, in which case it attracted only the remedies for misrepresentation (see para 17.10); or became a contractual term, express or implied (see para 11.03, *et seq*.), in which case it **also** attracted the remedies for breach of contract (see Chap 26), though without any double recovery (see para 27.39). This issue turned on the intention of the parties.[5] Where it was expressly stated that the defendant warranted the truth of the statement, then it was easy to infer such an intention,[6] but in many other cases the enquiry led the courts into considerable difficulty, because the parties may not have adverted their minds to the question.[7] Alternatively, they may not have exhibited any clear intention, or may have exhibited contrary intentions.[8] In view of such possibilities, the criterion of the intention of the parties may be criticised as elusive, artificial and almost useless. However, the persistence of the litigants has forced the courts to return to the question time and again, though the amount of light shed has been slight.[9] All that can be said is that, in the field of consumer transactions,[10] the courts in modern times appear to be making a determined effort to impose on a dealer contractual liability for the representations he makes[11] to private consumers. Fortunately, it may be that the extension of liability for misrepresentation (see para 11.01) will shift attention away from the dichotomy of contractual term and mere representation.

## THE NATURE OF THE TERMS

**[11.03] Introduction**. Having distinguished contractual terms from mere representations (see para 11.02), this section concentrates on the promissory effect of the former. The nature of contractual terms is subject to considerable confusion, largely because of the nomenclature involved: the appellations 'condition' and 'warranty' have been used by the courts without any precise definition and the same expressions have been used to explain different phenomena.[12]

(a) *Warranty*. Whilst starting life as an action in tort for deceit (see para 17.18), towards the end of the eighteenth century the action began to be declared in *assumpsit*, and soon came to be thought of in a contractual rather than a tortious context.[13] This process had particular repercussions in the law relating to the sale of goods, then fast-developing; and the legacy is to be seen in Chalmers' definition of a 'warranty' in what is now s 61(1) of the Sale of Goods Act 1979 (SGA) as:

---

5   See Burrows (1983) 99 LQR at 251.
6   E.g. *Liverpool and County Discount Co Ltd v AB Motor Co (Kilburn) Ltd* [1963] 2 All ER 396, CA.
7   What if a manufacturer by advertisement 'guarantees' his product? See Twigg-Flesner, *Consumer Product Guarantees* (2003) para 2.6; and generally, para 17.09A.
8   See Gilmore and Axelrod (1948) 57 Yale LJ 517, 518, fn 3.
9   See *Heilbut, Symonds & Co v Buckleton* [1913] AC 30, HL (not a goods case).
10  As to where both parties are in the same trade, see *Harlingdon & Leinster Enterprises Ltd v Christopher Hull Fine Art Ltd* (set out at para 13.11).
11  E.g. *Dick Bentley Ltd v Harold Smith (Motors) Ltd* [1965] 2 All ER 65, CA. *Contra* a private supplier to a trade buyer: *Oscar Chess Ltd v Williams* [1957] 1 All ER 325, CA.
12  Stoljar (1952), 15 MLR 425; (1953) 16 MLR 174.
13  See para 17.18. As to criminal proceedings in respect of breach of warranty, see para 4.24.

'an agreement with reference to goods which are the subject of a contract of sale, but collateral to the main purpose of such contract, the breach of which gives rise to a claim for damages, but not to a right to reject the goods and treat the contract is repudiated'.

Leaving aside for the moment the meaning of collateral (see para 11.06), it will be observed that Chalmers in part defined a warranty according to the effect of its breach (see para 11.04).

(b) *Condition*. By the nineteenth century, English courts were familiar with the notion of what are today known as conditions precedent: namely, non-promissory conditions to which a contractual promise by B to A might be made subject (see para 1.13). However, reflecting recognition by the courts that B may sometimes promise that that condition will occur, Chalmers in the SGA 1893 employed the expression 'condition' in both its promissory and non-promissory senses.[14] In s 2 of the SGA, it is utilised in the sense of condition precedent,[15] whereas in ss 11–15 it means an important contractual promise. In the latter sense, 'condition' is also defined in terms of the effect of its breach (see para 11.04).

**[11.04] Conditions and warranties**. After a breach of warranty by the seller, a buyer might, in theory, wish to reject the goods tendered and affirm the contract; but it would seem that the meaning of the SGA (see para 11.03) is that he may neither reject nor rescind,[16] no matter how serious the effects of the breach of warranty.[17] On the other hand, the SGA defines a promissory condition in s 11(3) as a term, breach of which will give rise not only to the right to damages, but also to reject goods and repudiate the contract.[16]Thus, under the scheme adopted by the SGA, a condition in the sense of an essential stipulation is clearly superior to a warranty, the relationship between them being partly explained by s 11(2) (set out at para 26.24). In view of the rigid distinction between the two types of term, it may therefore be important to determine whether a particular term is a condition or a warranty. Section 11(3) of the SGA says that in each case it depends on the construction of the contract, and adds unhelpfully that[18] 'A stipulation may be a condition, though called a warranty in the contract'. In many cases, the SGA avoids the problem by expressly assigning a status to a particular term; and this approach has been continued in those later statutes which imply terms into other types of contract for the supply of goods: namely, the Supply of Goods (Implied Terms) Act 1973 (SOGIT); and the Supply of Goods and Services Act 1982 (SGSA).

However, in the absence of such statutory specification the question can only be determined on common law principles. Perhaps the most widely accepted

---

14  It has been convincingly demonstrated that the nineteenth century common law development was itself based on a misconception: see Stoljar (1954) 69 LQR 485. See further, Montrose (1937) 15 Can BR 303, 323; Treitel (1990) 106 LQR 185; Goode, *Commercial Law*, 3rd edn, 279–83.

15  See para 1.11. Conditions precedent are further discussed below, paras 15.21 and 26.01.

16  For rejection, see para 29.03; and for repudiation for breach, see further, para 26.15. In contracts for the supply of services, as opposed to goods, the courts have been willing to temper this right to rescind by the doctrine of substantial performance: as to which, see para 26.02.

17  See *Benjamin on Sale*, 8th edn, 1950, 983.

18  Perhaps in recognition of the lack of consistency in nomenclature used by the courts. Was it also designed to enable the courts to restrict exemption clauses (see para 18.06)?

test is that laid down by Fletcher Moulton LJ in *Wallis, Son and Wells v Pratt and Haynes*.[19]

> There was a sale by sample of a quantity of seed described as 'common English sainfoin'. Seed equal to sample was delivered and planted by a sub-buyer. When it came up, it was found to be not common English, but giant sainfoin, a seed which is indistinguishable but of inferior quality. Reliance was placed on a clause 'Sellers give no warranty . . . as to description'.

Notwithstanding that the seed was equal to sample, the House of Lords held that there was **also** an undertaking that the goods complied with their description (see para 15.06); that the undertaking was an implied condition of the contract (see para 13.11); that the implied condition did not lose this status simply because the buyer was reduced to claiming damages, by reason of the subsale under s 11(4) (see para 29.04); and that the sellers were therefore not protected by a clause excluding liability for breach of warranty (see para 18.06). In drawing the vital distinction between a condition and a warranty, the House adopted the dictum of Fletcher Moulton LJ in the Court of Appeal (dissenting) that the issue turned on whether the term went to the substance of the contract, or was:[20]

> 'so essential to its very nature that [its] non-performance may fairly be considered by the other party as a substantial failure to perform the contract at all'.

So classifying terms as conditions or warranties has the advantage of certainty, but that certainty is obtained at the expense of rigidity.[21] Modern English law offers several methods by which a court can escape having to classify the term as a condition and hence give the innocent party the excessive right of treating the contract as repudiated for slight breach of condition, so reducing the significance of the condition/warranty dichotomy (see para 11.05).

**[11.05] Modern developments**. Suppose the retail purchase of a new motor vehicle which, on delivery and unknown to the seller, is found by the buyer to have a defective trafficator bulb. This will amount to an offence by the seller under the Construction and Use Regulations (see para 4.37) and also a breach of the statutory implied conditions as to fitness and satisfactory quality (see Chap 14). Under classical English law, the buyer will be entitled to rescind the contract, so pushing onto the seller the reduction in price as the vehicle went from new to second-hand (say one third the price). Yet the defect is easily curable by changing the bulb and the modern law has developed several means of ameliorating that injustice to the seller.

(1) By the courts classifying the breach instead of the term under the doctrine in the *Hong Kong Fir* case, a doctrine beyond the scope of this work.[22] Yet that

---

19　[1911] AC 394, [1911–13] All ER Rep 989, HL.

20　[1910] 2 KB 1003 at 1012. Compare this test with that for innominate terms (see para 11.05) and for the doctrine of frustration (see para 22.14).

21　A rejecting buyer does not in classical English law have to act reasonably in choosing rejection rather than damages or cure: *Clegg v Olle Anderson* (set out at para 14.18).

22　*Hong Kong Fir Shipping Co v Kawasaki* [1962] 2 QB 26 (not a sale case); *Cehave v Bremer, The Hansa Nord* [1976] QB 44, CA; *Northern Foods PLC v Focal Foods Ltd* (set out at para 26.26), at paras 7.12–16. See further, 1st edn, para 11.05; and the standard works on contract.

approach is unlikely to be available on the above facts, because the status of the breached term is specified by statute.

(2) By statute, where a business supplies goods to another business, *prima facie* the commercial buyer is only allowed damage for 'slight breach' of condition. This defence would be available in the above circumstances; but, as a business-to-business sale, it is beyond the scope of this work.[23]

(3) By statute, in a consumer supply the consumer's remedy of rescission is now a last resort, as he will usually now first have to consider replacement or repair (see SGA, Pt 5A: para 29.02A).

**[11.06] Warranties and collateral contracts**. Returning to the warranty, it will be recalled that the SGA defines the warranty as being 'collateral to the main purpose of' a contract of sale (see para 11.03). No doubt, this formula faithfully reflects case law developments in the nineteenth century; and it still reasonably describes the common situation where the agent makes a promise to a customer to induce him to contract with the agent's principal.[24] However, it has been pointed out that the ordinary warranty in the contract of sale certainly is not a separate agreement as distinct from the rest of the contract, since no further consideration is required.[25] Indeed, we must carefully distinguish the collateral term from the collateral contract, the latter being supported by its own consideration.[26] The collateral contract may be of one of the following types:

(1) A makes a representation to B, as a result of which B enters into a contract with C;[27] or

(2) A makes a representation to B, as a result of which B enters into a contract with A.[28]

In *Wells (Mersham) Ltd v Buckland Sand and Silica Co Ltd*,[29] the facts fell within case (1) and Edmund Davies J said:

> 'As between A . . . and B . . . two ingredients, and only two are . . . required in order to bring about a collateral contract containing a warranty: (1) a promise or assertion by A as to the nature, quality or quantity of the goods which B may reasonably regard as being made *animo contrahendi* and (2) acquisition by B of the goods in reliance on that promise or assertion'.

It is submitted that this dictum should also be applied to case (2), and the cases treated in the same manner, though case (2) does involve an additional factor in that it may circumvent the parol evidence rule.[30]

---

23  New s 15A(2) (as inserted by the 1994 Act, s 4(1)); SGSA, new s 5A (as inserted by the 1994 Act, Sched 2, para 6(5)); SGSA, new s 10A (as inserted by the 1994 Act, Sched 2, para 6(9)); SOGIT, new s 11A (as inserted by the 1994 Act, Sched 2, para 4(6)). See further, 1st edn, para 11.05A; and the standard works on contract.

24  E.g. *Barnett v Peter Cox Group Ltd* [1996] CLY 3406, CA.

25  Stoljar (1952) 15 MLR 425, 430–432.

26  E.g. agent's warranty of authority: *Barry v Davies* (set out at para 10.12).

27  E.g. *Andrews v Hopkinson* (set out at para 16.18); *Wake v Renault UK Ltd* [1996] CLY 1250.

28  E.g. *Webster v Higgin* [1948] 2 All ER 127, CA; *Esso Petroleum Ltd v Comrs of Customs and Excise* (discussed at para 2.08).

29  [1965] 2 QB 170, at 180. Contrast *Inntrepreneur Pub Co Ltd v East Crown Ltd* [2000] 2 Lloyd's Rep 611 (entire agreement clause).

30  See Treitel, *Law of Contract*, 11th edn, 192–201.

In our context, the collateral contract has been particularly useful in respect of statements by a dealer in a directly financed transaction (see para 16.18); but has been less successful when pleaded by consumers against manufacturers (see para 17.09) and other advertisers (see paras 8.05 and 10.01). As to the formalities required of a contract collateral to the sale of an interest in land, see para 9.03.

## EXPRESS AND IMPLIED TERMS

**[11.07] Express terms**. Where express stipulations are put forward, some statements are designed to prevent any contract coming into existence at that stage, perhaps by making them only an invitation to treat (see para 10.02); or to preclude particular words becoming part of that contract, e.g. mere puffs (see para 8.05). Where words spoken[31] or written are intended to be contractual,[32] they may range from the barest essentials to an elaborate written contract. Examples include express warranties,[33] conditional offers, e.g. 'whilst stocks last' (see para 10.02), price statements,[34] limitations on supplier's liability,[35] e.g. entire agreement clauses (see para 11.09), all variations in signed writing (see para 26.24), performance by words, e.g. instructions for use (see para 18.28, *et seq.*), provisions assigning to terms the status of conditions or warranties (see para 11.04), e.g. making time of the essence (see para 23.20) and restrictions on remedies.[36] Particularly significant in this context may be the implied terms imposed by law.[37] For instance, an express warranty as to description may be converted by statute into an implied condition (see para 13.11).

At the other end of the scale, there may be elaborate written contracts (see para 11.08) and terms incorporated by reference (see para 18.04), both of whose construction may involve the factual implication of terms.[37] These may be freshly drafted for the particular contract or standard terms, the latter usually being printed beforehand.[38] There may even be the rules of a trade association (as subsequently amended) incorporated into a contract by reference:[39] and these may be registrable as a restrictive practice (see para 2.12). Commercial documents

---

31  The spoken word inevitably raises problems of proof and possibly also the parol evidence rule (see para 11.06).

32  For the common law rules concerning the incorporation of terms in any contract, see para 18.04.

33  E.g. *Cehave v Bremer* [1976] QB 44, CA; *Harling v Eddy* [1951] 2 KB 739, CA (see para 11.01); *Mendelssohn v Normand Ltd* [1970] 1 QB 177, CA (see para 18.05); *Thomas Witter Ltd v TBP Industries Ltd* (set out at para 26.14). A forged MOT certificate (see para 4.37) might amount to false trade description (see TDA, s 2(1)(f): see para 4.06).

34  E.g. 'guaranteed lowest prices—or we will refund the difference'. Does 'never knowingly undersold' give a contractual right to the refund of any difference (see [2000] 12 *Which?* 9)? For an express promise, see para 8.17; and for offences, see para 8.10.

35  E.g. 'bought as seen' (limiting description: see para 13.16); 'E & OE' (errors and omissions excepted: but see UCTA, ss 6–7: see para 18.19); express guarantees for a finite period (see paras 14.06 and 17.09).

36  E.g. 'no cash refunds' (but see the Restrictions on Statements Order, 1976 SI 1813: para 4.22).

37  For the distinction between terms implied in fact and those implied in law, see para 11.10.

38  For standard terms, see para 11.08. If there are both written and standard terms, the written terms may give rise to criminal liability, e.g. it may amount to a false statement as to services prevail: *Indian Oil Corpn v Vanol Inc* [1991] 2 Lloyd's Rep. 634.

39  *Shearson Lehman Hutton Inc v Maclaine Watson & Co Ltd* [1989] 2 Lloyd's Rep 570 (see [1990] LM & CLQ at 308–9).

and contracts should be construed in a manner which makes good commercial sense and not by a detailed semantic and syntactical analysis if that would defeat the commercial purpose of the document or contract.[40] The rules for interpreting exclusion clauses, disclaimers and indemnities are considered later (see para 18.06) though more flexibility may be obtainable by treating them as unfair terms (see para 11.12).

In all cases, any promises are only worthwhile to the consumer whilst the promisor-supplier continues in existence/business (see para 19.25), or is insured. However, his promises may sometimes give rise to criminal liability, e.g. it may amount to a false statement as to services (see para 4.15), or save from that liability, e.g. a defence of words of another person (see para 28.18).

[11.08] **Standard form contracts**. If both parties try to impose their own, different standard terms on a transaction, this may give rise to the 'battle for the forms' (see para 10.04); and the expression 'written standard terms' has now received statutory recognition.[41] They have considerable advantages to a party engaged in numerous transactions.[42] *First*, this saves the cost of individual drafting and hence time and money. Where documents commonly used contain particular phrases and expressions which have a clear and well-established meaning among commercial lawyers, it is important that those expressions should be construed consistently with that meaning, unless there are compulsive surrounding circumstances or a context strongly suggestive of some other meaning. It may be extremely convenient to businessmen to be able to make a contract, perhaps orally, merely by reference to one of the standard forms well known in their particular trade.[43] Thus, the standard-form contract is a useful device for allocating the many risks of a transaction between the parties.[44] *Second*, the standard-form contract has been used to exploit economic advantage, e.g. entire agreement clauses (see para 11.09), *Romalpa* clauses (see para 25.30), consumer contracts (see below).

At common law standard-form contracts are made under the incorporation and *contra proferentem* rules (see paras 18.04–6); and by statute they are subject to the notices required by the DPA (see para 3.28) and to the reasonableness test in s 3 of UCTA. For example, litigation arose out of the unexpected contamination with benzine of carbon monoxide gas (goods: see para 2.02) intended for human consumption, whilst being manufactured by Terra: this contamination was insufficient to amount to a health hazard; but public perception made it commercially necessary for trade parties who had used that carbon monoxide to make bottled drinks to withdraw all contaminated products. In the *Britvic* case,[45] a unanimous Court of Appeal held that under the wholesale contract: (a) the

---

40  *The Antaios* [1985] AC 191, HL (not a sale case); *Sinochem International Oil (London) Co Ltd v Mobil Sales and Supply Corpn* [2000] 1 All ER (Comm) 474, CA. See also *per* Lord Hoffman in *Investor's Compensation Scheme Ltd v West Bromwich BS* [1998] 1 All ER 98 at 114–15, HL (not a sale case).

41  UCTA, s 3 (see para 18.20). For general discussion of standard-form contracts, see: Treitel, *Law of Contract*, 11th edn, Chap 7.

42  See Elvin (2003) 14 KCLJ 39 at 41–2.

43  E.g. *British Crane Hire Corpn Ltd v Ipswich Plant Hire Ltd* [1975] QB 303, CA (operating lease).

44  E.g. price variation clauses (see para 10.05); *Romalpa* clauses (see para 25.30); acceleration clauses (see para 7.03); risk in transfer of the goods (see para 22.02) or payment (see para 23.14). See generally, *Encyclopedia of Forms and Precedents*, 5th edn, Vol 34 (1991).

45  *Britvic Soft Drinks v Messer UK Ltd* [2002] 2 All ER (Comm) 321, CA.

wholesaler's promise that the gas complied with a BSI (see para 3.08) did not amount to a promise that the gas was free from benzine; but (b) an exclusion clause was struck down as unreasonable under s 6 of UCTA (see para 18.19). In the *Bacardi* case,[46] the same court unanimously allowed a wholesale buyer to recover the loss occasioned by the recall and destruction (see para 17.02) in two ways:

(a) A claim in contract against the wholesale seller (M). *Prima facie* liability for breach of s 14 of the SGA being admitted, M relied on clause 12(2), which was struck down as being unreasonable, the court refusing to interfere with the trial judge's decision (para 26; and see para 18.19).

(b) A claim in the tort of negligence against the manufacturer of the gas (see para 17.13) and by way of a contribution.[47]

*Consumer contracts*[48]. Use of a standard-form contract to disadvantage the weaker party is particularly the case in respect of those enterprises doing business with the consumer: the terms and price are rigidly laid down, and the only choice available to the individual consumer is whether or not to contract at all.[49] A good example is provided by instalment credit contracts,[50] and the maintenance of security clauses many of them contain.[51] Besides all the above general common law and statutory rules, if the contract is regulated by the CCA, it must contain the prescribed terms and notices (see para 9.11). Moreover, if it amounts to a consumer supply contract it is subject to the UTCC test of fairness (see OFT, *UCT Bulletin No. 21*, cases 10, 19, 21: see para 11.15): for instance, struck down as unfair may be terms which use small print or jargon (reg 7: see para 11.13); or grant the supplier automatic extensions of time (Grey Term 1(h): see para 11.17); or deny the salesman's representations any effect unless embodied in writing (Grey Term 1(n): see para 11.18), which are termed 'entire agreement' clauses (see para 11.09).

**[11.09] Entire agreement clauses**.[52] Such a clause may have the following two components:

(1) A statement that the present contractual document contains 'the whole agreement of the parties and supersedes all previous agreements'.[53] This may be effective to exclude liability for things said orally or in writing during negotiations and may also rule out alleged implied terms based on custom or usage.[53] But, it will not necessarily oust liability for rectification or misrepresentation (see paras 17.10–11).

---

46  *Bacardi-Martini Beverages Ltd v Thomas Hardy Packaging Ltd* [2002] 2 All ER (Comm) 335, CA.

47  Under the Civil Liability Contribution Act 1978: see [2002] 1 LLR 20 at 62; and generally, para 12.10.

48  See Cranston, *Consumers and the Law*, 3rd edn, 74–78.

49  E.g. motor trade sales of new or used cars; loans (see para 7.03); credit-card contracts (see para 7.09); auction conditions of sale (see para 10.10).

50  E.g. deemed agency clauses (see para 10.24); snatch-back clauses (see para 24.25); required terms (see para 9.12). As to model forms of instalment credit contract, see Goode, *Consumer Credit Law & Practice*, Pt X111; Guest and Lloyd, *Encyclopedia of Consumer Credit*, Pt 8.

51  See 1st edn, para 11.09.

52  As to entire agreement clauses, see generally, Thomas (2002) 152 NLJ 1898.

53  E.g. *Exxonmobil Sales and Supply Corpn v Texaco Ltd* [2004] 1 All ER (Comm) 435. As to custom and usage, see generally, para 11.10.

(2) An acknowledgment that the parties 'have not relied on any representation that is not set out in the agreement'.[53] The conditions on which this might be effective at common law were laid down in *Lowe v Lombank Ltd* (set out at para 18.06).

However, modern statute has restricted the efficacy of entire agreement clauses. In a consumer supply contract, any such clause may be unfair (Grey List 1(n): see para 11.18); but in other cases, it is less likely to be struck down as being a standard-form term (UCTA, s 3(2): see para 18.24) or exclusion of misrepresentation (1967 Act, s 3: see para 18.17) which is unreasonable.[54]

**[11.10] Implied terms**. It has been pointed out that the expression 'implied terms' covers two distinct categories:[55]

1.  *Logically implied terms* are those terms which, though unenunciated by the parties, may be logically deduced from the terms expressly agreed,[56] as where there is no delivery date for the supply of goods or services and the law will imply a reasonable one (SGA, s 29(3); SGSA, s 14).

2.  *Non-logically implied terms*. At one end of the scale are terms implied by custom,[57] course of dealings (see para 18.04) or trade usage (see para 15.11), such as the banker's duty of confidentiality.[58] From there, the expression 'implied terms' extends to those necessary to give business efficacy to a transaction,[59] e.g. adequate supplies of spare parts for a reasonable time,[60] or replacements on the same terms as the originals.[61] At the other extreme are the situations where the terms are said to be 'implied' whatever the actual intention of the parties, as with the statutory implied terms imported into contracts for the supply of goods (see para 11.11). Indeed, in consumer supplies UCTA makes such implication compulsory (ss 6 and 7: see further, para 18.19): in such circumstances, the 'implied terms' cannot be grounded in the intention of the parties at all.

In *Paragon Finance plc v Staughton & Nash*[62]

> A mortgagee (P) specialising in non-status loans (see para 7.04A) claimed possession for arrears due under two agreements containing variable interest rate clauses.

---

54  See the *Watford Electronics* case (see para 18.21).

55  See Glanville Williams (1945) 61 LQR 384, 401–6.

56  E.g. *Northern Foods PLC v Focal Foods Ltd* (set out at para 26.26), CA, at para 1.5 (see page 732). Where a seller tenders non-conforming goods, he may be deemed to offer the goods actually tendered (SGA, s 30): see para 13.02. See generally, Treitel, *Law of Contract*, 11th edn, 201–6.

57  There are two types of customary term: (i) common law customs, which are supposed to date back to 1189, e.g. market overt (now repealed: see para 21.05); and (ii) commercial customs, or trade usage, e.g. *Goodwin v Robarts* (1875) LR 10 Ex. 337 (Ex Ch) (see paras 15.11 and 18.09).

58  See para 7.03. This rule probably extends to any borrower/lender relationship: Ferran, *Mortgage Securitisation*, 130–4; and see paras 3.13 and 8.35.

59  *The Moorcock* (see para 15.22); *Bank of Scotland v Truman* [2005] EWHC 583, at para 120. But the courts tend to be sparing in their finding of such terms, e.g. *Ultraframe (UK) Ltd v Tailored Roofing Systems Ltd* [2004] 2 All ER (Comm) 692, CA. See generally, Peden (2001) 117 LQR 459.

60  See [2003] 1 *Which?* 27. This will be necessary to make sense of the buyer's right to a cure: see para 29.03A.

61  *VAI Industries (UK) Ltd v Bostock & Bramley* [2003] BLR 359, CA, at para 40.

62  [2001] 2 All ER (Comm) 1025, [2002] 2 All ER 248, CA (discussed 62 QA 9; 145 Sol Jo 1158). Foll. *Paragon Finance plc v Pender* [2005] GCCR 5331, [2005] EWCA Civ 760, CA, at para 120.

P was committed to charging above market rates to retrieve its serious financial position. The mortgagors admitted the arrears, but unsuccessfully claimed relief on the following grounds: breach of an implied term (see below); s 3 of UCTA (see para 18.20); and the extortionate bargain rules (see para 29.42).

In delivering the judgment of the Court of Appeal, Dyson LJ said that the right of P to vary interest rates from time to time was not completely unfettered. His Lordship stopped short of implying a broad term that the lender would not act unreasonably, but said that the existence of all the CCA protections did not preclude the implication of any term (paras 28 and 34). He thought that there was a negative implied term in the mortgage (not breached here) that P would not set interest rates 'dishonestly, for an improper purpose, capriciously or arbitrarily';[63] nor do so unreasonably.[64] The court has since refused in a similar case to imply a positive term that the lender was under a duty to reduce interest rates from time to time as market rates fell.[65] This development has been seen (wishfully?) as part of an 'indication that English law is (slowly) moving towards the adoption of a good faith standard in the exercise of contractual discretion'.[66]

**[11.11] Statutorily implied terms**.[67] There must first be identified the type of transaction to determine which statute is applicable, e.g. for sales, look in the SGA. The major obligations[68] imposed on the parties to a contract for the supply of goods by common law or statute[69] are as follows:

1.  *Identification of the goods*.[69] The law imports a condition that the goods delivered will correspond with their contract description. This undertaking will be examined in Chap 13.
2.  *Title to goods*.[69] Recognising that the object of the transferee is normally to acquire title to the goods, the law imports certain undertakings by the supplier as to title. These will be examined in Chap 12.
3.  *Quality and fitness*.[69] As the 'use-value' of goods is perhaps the most important aspect of the transaction to the buyer or hirer, English law imports certain obligations designed to ensure the usability of the goods. These will be examined in Chaps 14 and 15.

---

63  At para 32. For reasons, see paras 34–5. The implication seems to be on the *Moorcock* basis (para 36).

64  In the *Wednesbury* sense ([1948] 1 KB 223: a well-known administrative law test): see paras 38–41. The CA found the rates reasonable because P was committed to paying high rates of interest on the loan capital it employed (para 2).

65  *Sterling Credit v Rahman No. 2* [2003] CCLR 13.

66  Twigg-Flesner, *Consumer Product Guarantees* (2003) para 8.3. Cf. UTCC reg 5 (see para 11.15).

67  These were first codified in the SGA 1893 (now re-codified in the SGA 1979). Similar terms were implied into hp agreements by SOGIT 1973; and into quasi-sales and simple hirings by the SGSA 1982.

68  It will be noted that categories 1–3 are called 'implied terms' whereas categories 4–5 are not. This probably accurately reflects 1893 usage derived from their common law origins. But does it accurately reflect the modern position?

69  As will be seen, the supplier is strictly liable for breach of these implied terms (Chaps 12–14). Some commercial suppliers have adopted the practice of insuring this liability under group insurance—and even sometimes the performance of express promises, e.g. extended guarantees.

4. *Delivery and payment*. As the primary object for the supplier is the transfer of goods for a sum of money, the obligation to deliver will be considered together with payment of the price in Chap 23.

5. *Risk*. Because of the importance of deciding which party bears the risk of loss of goods, the law deals carefully with this issue. The passing of risk will be discussed in Chap 22.

On behalf of consumers, these above rules may now be enforceable by Enforcement Orders (see para 6.08)[70]. These implied terms (items (1)–(3)) apply to a contract for the supply of goods even before the property in the goods passes;[71] and as against consumer buyers they are not excludable.[72] Moreover, in a consumer supply, the risk remains with the supplier until delivery (see para 22.02A); whereas any attempt to make the price payable before delivery may be unfair.[73]

# UNFAIR TERMS

**[11.12] Unfair Terms Regulations**.[74] Whilst our (inaccurately named) Unfair Contract Terms Act 1977 primarily deals with exclusion clauses (UCTA: see para 18.12), the Unfair Contract Terms Directive[75] has initiated substantial **minimum** (Recital 12; Art 8: see para 3.10) compulsory changes (see para 1.03A) to the effectiveness of a wide range of express (and possibly some implied) terms, though without prejudice to more stringent national rules.[76] Unfortunately, the Directive was implemented in 1994 (by 1994 SI 3159) without any change to the overlapping s 3 of UCTA (see para 18.24); and this point was still not met when the provisions were re-enacted 'to reflect more closely the wording of the Directive' in the Unfair Terms in Consumer Contracts (UTCC) Regulations 1999.[77] Further, in some places the UTCC Regulations follow the Directive verbatim ('copying-out'),[78] despite the fact that the latter is expressed in the continental form of drafting, perhaps clouding its meaning for English lawyers.[79] These provisions may be re-enacted in the proposed Unfair Terms Bill (see para 11.21).

In the *First National Bank* case (set out at para 7.03A), Lord Steyn noted that the Directive was the 'dominant text' (para 31) and continued:

---

70 E.g. [2006] *OFT Bulletin J/M, St Helens Glass*.

71 *Alpha Chauffeurs Ltd v Citygate* (set out at para 14.26) at para 31.

72 UCTA, ss 6 and 7: see para 18.19.

73 Grey Term (o): see para 11.18A.

74 See generally, Treitel, *Law of Contract*, 11th edn, 267, *et seq*.; Goode, *Consumer Credit Law & Practice*, Pt IJ, para 124.31, *et seq*.; *Chitty on Contract*, 28th edn, Chap 15.

75 93/13/EEC, based on Art 100A of the Treaty of Rome. For the text of the Directive, see Goode, *ibid*, X, para 1.181.

76 Art 8. E.g. the Restrictions on Statements Order (see para 4.22).; UCTA, s 2 (see para 11.16).

77 1999 SI 2083 (as amended), made under s 2(2) of the ECA 1992 (see para 1.03A). For an explanation of the intention of the sponsoring Department, see DTI, *Guidance Notes* (1995: set out in Goode, *ibid*, Pt VIII, para 1006, *et seq*.). The OFT has also issue extensive written *Guidance* (see www.oft.gov.uk/Business/Legal/UTCC/guidance.htm); and below.

78 For a discussion on copying-out, see Bright (2000) 20 LS 330 at 338–9.

79 As to interpretation, see the DTI, *Guidance Notes*, para 2.

'The purpose of the Directive is twofold, viz, the promotion of fair standard contract forms to improve the functioning of the European market place and the protection of consumers throughout the European Community. The directive is aimed at contracts of adhesion, viz, 'take it or leave it' contracts. It treats consumers as presumptively weaker parties and therefore fit for protection from abuses by stronger contracting parties. This is an objective which must throughout guide the interpretation of the directive as well as the implementing regulations'.

The Regulations are enforced by the OFT and other bodies (see para 11.19); and the OFT publishes frequent detailed *Bulletins* on its operation.[80] The purpose of the *Bulletins* is administrative, namely to: (i) provide a systematic record of all cases taken up under the Regulations; (ii) enable the OFT to set out its views and procedures (*Bulletin No. 4*, p 5); and (iii) enable the monitoring of whether businesses are honouring agreed changes (*Bulletin No. 12*). Until there appears a greater number of court-decided cases, the *Bulletins* provide the best indications of the practical effect of the Regulations and will therefore be so used below.

*Effect of the Regulations.* In 2002–3, as a result of OFT enforcement action 1,477 terms were amended or abandoned.[81] So, for transactions within their ambit (see para 11.12A), the Regulations in a sense represent the death of freedom of contract (see para 1.02): whilst the Regulations contain no power to specify what terms a contract must contain, they can determine what may not be included, a good starting point being the so-called 'Grey-list' of suspect terms.[82] Henceforth, lawyers drafting contracts for such suppliers may best serve the interests of their client not by maximising his position (the traditional objective), but by producing a balanced draft in plain English (see para 11.13). Sometimes it will be the case that the consumer is best protected by complete removal of all the previous express terms, leaving the consumer to rely on implied terms; or the express terms may be limited to business-to-business contracts.[83] It will be observed that the effect of these Regulations is to transfer some of the emphasis in the contracts covered from judicial intervention after breach to administrative intervention before contract. Or, to put it another way, the Regulations have to work at two different levels: on contractual terms before utilisation to make specific contracts; and on particular contracts made on those terms.[84]

**[11.12A] The ambit of the Regulations.** This is confined to **consumer supply contracts**, which may be analysed into the following requirements:[85]

---

80  OFT, *1998 AR*, 29–30. As from late 2004, *Bulletins* are only available electronically (www.crw.gov.uk); and the EU have announced that they will do something similar.

81  OFT, *AR–2002/3*, 38.

82  See para 11.16, *et seq*. See the above OFT *Guidance*, which is divided into groups of issues, noted in later paragraphs as relevant.

83  E.g. OFT, *UCT Bulletin No. 20*, cases 14 and 21; *No. 22*, case 33.

84  See Macdonald (2004) 67 MLR 69 at 91–2.

85  See DTI, *Guidance Notes* (Goode, *Consumer Credit Law & Practice*, para 1009). Cf. the definition of 'dealing as consumer' within s 12 of UCTA: see para 18.18. As to whether it is possible to contract out of the Regulations, see Brownsword and Howells [1995] JBL at 244–5.

(1) There must be a contract for 'sale or supply'. In relation to goods (see para 2.01), this presumably covers sales of goods (see para 1.07), quasi-sales (see para 2.10) and other contractual[86] supplies, as on simple hiring or hp (see paras 1.18; 1.20). The expression also seems apt to extend to supplies of services.[87]

(2) That contract must be governed by the law of a Member State (see para 10.01), and this requirement cannot be side-stepped by a choice of non-EU law clause (reg 9. See DTI, *Guidance Notes*, para 8). Do the Regulations apply to a contract governed by English law under a choice of laws clause (see para 18.13) where the parties have no other connection with the EU?

(3) There must be a 'seller or supplier', which expression means (reg 3(1)):

> 'any natural or legal person who, in contracts covered by these Regulations, is acting for purposes relating to[88] his trade, business or profession, whether publicly owned or privately owned'.

So contracts between two private persons are outside the Regulations, as may be contracts with unincorporated associations, e.g. Clubs, because of the difficulty of distinguishing the consumer from the supplier (*Bulletin No. 5*, p 18. But see para 1.09). However, so long as the 'seller or supplier' is conducting a trade, etc, it matters not whether it is a natural person, a business corporation[89] or a public authority.[90] Does the rule extend to private sellers to business buyers, e.g. trade-ins?

(4) The person obtaining the goods or services must be a 'consumer'; that is, 'a natural person who, in making a contract . . . is acting for purposes which are outside his trade, business or profession' (reg 3(1)). So, contracts between two businessmen are outside the Regulations.[90] Thus, in *Cape Snc v Idealservice Srl*[89] there was an Italian standard-form supply of automatic drinks dispensers to an employer for use by his employees; and the European Court held that it was outside the scope of the Unfair Terms Directive (compare the English rule for UCTA: see para 18.18). Where a supplier deals with both business and private consumers, he may therefore develop two different sets of documentation. What if, for example, a car is being supplied for a mixture of business and pleasure?

---

86  As to whether the Regulations extend to non-contractual statements, see Law Commission, *Unfair Terms in Contracts* (2002, Law Com Consultation Paper No. 166), para 3.106; and above, para 3.07.

87  See para 2.05. The Regulations seem to apply to insurance contracts; but *contra*, UCTA: see para 18.17. *Quaere* whether the Regulations apply to sale and mortgage of land? See Bright and Bright (1995) 111 LQR 655; Bright (1999) 115 LQR at 361; Elvin (2003) 14 KCLJ 39 at 50.

88  'Purposes related to' in reg 2(1) may be wider than 'dealing in the course of' in UCTA, s 12: Beatson [1994] CLJ at 236; and see para 14.04.

89  *Cape Snc v Idealservice Srl* [2005] QB 37, Eu Ct (Italian case). Compare Elvin, *ibid*, at 49.

90  *Khatun v Newham LBC* [2005] QB 37, CA. The same formula of a business seller and private buyer is to be found in the Doorstep and Distance Selling Regulations: see paras 10.35 and 10.38. Cf. *R & B Customs* case (set out at para 18.18).

91  Three different interpretations of 'mandatory' have been identified: DTI, *Consultation Paper* (July 2000), paras 3.11–13; Elvin, *ibid*, at 46. It could (wrongly) refer to the rules of other EU countries: Law Commission, *ibid*, para 3.36.

(5) Exemptions. From the above, reg 4(2) excludes altogether contractual terms which reflect:

'(a) mandatory[91] statutory[92] or regulatory[93] provisions (including such provisions under the law of any Member State or in Community legislation having effect in the United Kingdom without further enactment);[94]

(b) the provisions or principles of international conventions to which the Member States or the Community are party'.[95]

On the other hand, the Regulations may catch terms which **mislead** consumers as to their rights under that other legislation, e.g. the right of cancellation under the Doorstep-selling Regulations (as to which, see para 10.36). The Unfair Terms Bill would repeat the above definition of consumer (see para 11.21).

In respect of such **consumer supply contracts** as satisfy the above requirements, the Regulations contain two classes of rule protective of the consumer, irrespective of whether or not he had legal advice before entering the transaction. Most transactions are likely to fall within both; but it is not clear whether the Regulations are so confined.

A.   *Written terms.* (See para 11.13).

B.   *Terms which have not been individually negotiated* (see para 11.14) which are, or may be, unfair (see para 11.15). With this category must now be included some provisions in distance contracts for financial services (see para 10.39), which are deemed unfair as follows:[96]

'Any contractual term providing that a consumer bears the burden of proof in respect of showing whether a distance supplier or an intermediary complied with any or all of the obligations placed upon him resulting from the Directive and any rule or enactment implementing it shall always be regarded as unfair.'

**[11.13] Any written terms: transparency.** Regulation 7 provides two rules applicable to any 'written terms' in a *consumer supply contract* (see para 11.12A), designed to enhance their transparency in content, style and presentation, whether on hard-copy or web-site.[97] Whilst it does not apply to statutory implied terms (reg 4(2)(a): see para 11.12A), reg 7 does not appear to be restricted to terms 'not individually negotiated' (see para 11.14).

---

92   E.g. the statutory implied terms (see Chaps 12–15) made mandatory by ss 6 or 7 of UCTA: see para 18.19. What about other implied terms (see para 11.10)? The OFT suggests that, in casting future statutory implied terms, the Government must ensure that they comply with the Directive: OFT, *Bulletin No. 1*, para 1.21. The DTI have asked whether this exemption should be removed: *Consultation Paper* (July 2000), para 3.14.

93   E.g. contractual provisions reflecting the Doorstep Selling Regulations (see para 10.21); *Bulletin No. 13*, case 23 (Parcelforce terms when trading under s 28 of the Post Office Act 1969); services supplied by utilities (see para 3.07).

94   The words in brackets refer to such EU provisions as have direct effect in the UK: see para 1.03A.

95   This would cover international conventions which have not (yet) become part of national law.

96   UTCCR, reg 5(6), imported by the Financial Services (Distance Marketing) Regulations, 2004 SI 2095, reg 24; and for definitions, see new regs 1A and 1B. 'Directive' means the one implemented in the foregoing regulations; and 'rule' means one made under the FSMA (reg 5(7)).

97   See OFT, *Guidance*, Group 19 (see generally, para 11.12); and *Bulletin No. 18*, case 7; *No. 20*, case 9; *No. 21*, case 9.

## A. According to reg 7(1).

'A seller or supplier shall ensure that any written term of a contract is expressed in plain intelligible language'.

The effect would appear to be to encourage the Plain English Campaign (see *Bulletin No. 17*, case 22; and para 11.08). *First*, the OFT have interpreted 'plain ... language' to mean that a consumer supply contract must be intelligible to ordinary consumers without recourse to legal advice,[98] e.g. in short, simple sentences, not too vague[99] or imprecise (*Bulletin No. 29*, pp 13, 14). Thus, a contract drafted in technical language must, under reg 7, at very least contain a definition clause explaining technical terms in plain English;[100] and it may be safer not to use technical terms at all. *Second*, the contract must be expressed in 'intelligible language'. So, it would seem insufficient to say 'this does not affect your statutory rights' without giving a flavour of those rights, as these may be unfamiliar to the average consumer.[101] This rule should also attack all the following: unreadably small print;[102] ambiguity;[103] implying that a contract could not be cancelled after supplier's breach without his consent (*Bulletin No. 18*, case 5); unclarity in contract price;[104] by signing, the consumer was agreeing the terms overleaf;[105] omission of the fact that the price quoted does not include VAT;[106] the inclusion of terms probably only applicable to business buyers (*Bulletin No. 26*, p 71; *No. 27*, p 34); and contradictory terms *Bulletin No. 27*, p 14). Moreover, if a *core* term (see para 11.14) is hidden away in small print as if it were unimportant when in fact it is potentially burdensome, then it is considered as potentially unfair.[107] *Third*, the foregoing are of little value to consumers unless they have a **real** opportunity to read and understand the terms before contracting (*Bulletin No. 23*, case 24) and may be compared with the (frequently only theoretical) opportunity available at common law (see para 18.04). The Regulations have to be interpreted so as to achieve the purpose of the Directive they implement. Recital 20 of the Directive makes clear that the

---

98  OFT, *Bulletin No. 2*, paras 2.19–20; *No. 3*, paras 12.2–5; *No. 27*, p 105; Elvin (2003) 14 KCLJ 39 at 48–9.

99  *Bulletin No. 24*, case 26; *No. 24*, cases 24 and 26; *No. 27*, pp 16–7.

100  E.g. 'ad idem', 'assigns', 'bailee', 'condition precedent', 'consequential loss', 'credit rating', 'E&OE', 'ex-factory', 'forbearance', 'force majeure', 'indemnify', 'joint and several', 'lien', 'liquidation', 'nett', 'offer', 'of the essence of the agreement', 'representations and warranties', 'repudiation', 'risk', 'passing of title', 'time of the essence', 'Trade Standards', 'warrants', 'waiver', 'without prejudice'. See OFT, *Bulletin No. 2*, paras 2.14–8; *Bulletin No. 5*, Pt 6, Group 19; *No. 21*, case 25; *No. 22*, cases 13 and 26; *No. 23*, case 2; [2005] *Bulletin J/M, Ebuyer*.

101  DTI, *Consultation Paper* (July 2000), para 5.4; *Bulletin No. 15*, cases 1, 19; *No. 17*, cases 10, 16, 19 and 28; *No. 21*, case 25; *No. 22*, cases 6 and 24; *No. 23*, cases 6 and 24; *No. 24*, cases 20, 24, 27, 40, 46 and 48; *No. 26*, pp 43, 74; *No. 27*, pp 30, 107; [2005] *Bulletin J/S, Forthright Finance*; [2005] *Bulletin O/D, Carpetright*. Some of these rights will be non-excludable (see para 18.19) and to purport to exclude them may be an offence (see para 4.22).

102  OFT, *Bulletin No. 1*, para 1.16; *No. 2*, paras 2.27–8; *No. 17*, case 12; *No. 23*, case 3. See also DTI, *Consultation Paper* (July 2000), para 5.6.

103  *Bulletin No. 17*, case 21; *No. 22*, case 14; *No. 27*, pp 103–4, 108.

104  *Bulletin No. 21*, case 2; *No. 26*, p 91; *No. 27*, p 12. See also price displays: para 8.08.

105  *Bulletin No. 20*, case 8. Cf. *L'Estrange v Graucob Ltd* [1934] 2 KB 394. See also Grey Term (i): see para 11.17.

106  *Bulletin No. 17*, cases 1 and 12; *No. 21*, case 20; *No. 27*, p 13. See also price displays: para 8.08.

107  *Bulletin No. 6*, para 1.25; *No. 26*, pp 21, 70; *No. 27*, p 103, *No. 29*, pp 12, 14 and 15.

aim is not just the substitution of plain words for legal jargon but rather that consumers are given a real chance to read and understand contracts before becoming bound by them. So, this regulation links up with the requirement that consumers be given a pre-contract opportunity to examine all contractual terms (Grey list (i): see para 11.17). Small wonder then, that the OFT claims that the demands of the Regulations will displace the long-standing precedents and that the very process of re-writing a standard form in intelligible language in itself helps to make contracts fairer (*Bulletin No. 4*, p 26).

B.   Regulation 7(2) says that:

> 'If there is doubt about the meaning of a written term, the interpretation which is most favourable to the consumer shall prevail but this rule shall not apply in proceedings brought under regulation 12'.

The objective is to give the consumer the benefit of the doubt in respect of language of doubtful meaning: it seems to invite the mischief rule of interpretation (see para 1.04), avoid any defence of supplier's innocent intention and appears to mirror the English *contra proferentem* rule (see para 18.06). Not only will this provide a sanction that may be deployed in any consumer litigation relying on the principles in A (above) or unfairness (see para 11.15), but the OFT also claim that it entitles it to consider any ambiguous clause according to its least favourable meaning.[108] However, the concluding phrase excludes proceedings for an injunction (reg 12: see para 11.20) from reg 7(2); in such a case, the plaintiff, e.g. the OFT, will have to prove according to the ordinary rules of interpretation the meaning for which it contends; but this would appear to make little difference in the light of the common law *contra proferentem* rule.

Whilst the Regulations mention no direct sanction for breach of reg 7, it may be that breach will bring any term within the sanctions regarding an 'unfair term' (see para 11.17). The DTI *Consultation Paper* (July 2000) questioned whether it should be possible for the enforcement authorities to act against terms breaching reg 7 regardless of fairness (para 2.7). The Unfair Terms Bill would include both the above rules A and B (see para 11.21).

**[11.14]  Terms not individually negotiated**. The Regulations apply to *'unfair terms'* (see para 11.15) in *consumer supply contracts* (see para 11.12A) 'which have not been individually negotiated' (regs 2(1) and 5). The rationale seems to be that the consumer should have a genuine opportunity to influence the substance of contract terms; that this rarely happens with the *small print*; but that the consumer is likely to address the *core* of the contract. The Regulations address both notions.

1.   *The small print*, which is described in reg 5 as 'terms not individually negotiated'. Typically, such a term will be found in a signed standard-form contract (see para 11.08); but the Regulations do not require such terms to be in writing, let alone signed[109] and reg 5(2) presumes that:

---

108  *Bulletin No. 2*, paras 2.9–10; *Bulletin No. 7*, case 7 (consumer declaration that terms have been fully understood). (2002) Law Commission, *Unfair Terms in Contracts* (2002, Law Com Consultation Paper No. 166), para 3.74.

109  Reg 3 does not stipulate that the agreement must be signed; and the recitals to the Directive clearly include an oral contract. For the incorporation of standard terms by notice or signature, see para 18.04.

'A term shall always be regarded as not having been individually negotiated where it has been drafted in advance and the consumer has not been able to influence the substance of the term'.

Thus, reg 5(2) is drawing a distinction familiar to English law in respect of written contracts between **standard terms** printed in advance (see para 11.08) and **customised terms**;[110] that is, those blanks which are filled in when the contract is made, e.g. a proposal form for a regulated agreement.[111] The distinction refers to **terms**, not contracts, because it will frequently be the case that a written (mixed) contract will contain some of each; and the burden of proving that a term has been individually negotiated lies on the seller or supplier.[112] Where there is a mixture of standard and 'individually negotiated' terms, reg 5(3) provides that:[113]

'Notwithstanding that a specific term or certain aspects of it in a contract have been individually negotiated, these Regulations shall apply to the rest of a contract if an overall assessment of the contract indicates that it is a pre-formulated standard contract'.

Whilst reg 5 does not apply to individually negotiated terms in a mixed contract, the effect of reg 5(3) is that the Regulations will usually apply to the standard terms,[114] for which purpose the contract must be considered **as a whole**, including the individually negotiated terms.[115]

2.    *The core terms.* (See para 11.14A).

**[11.14A]  Core terms**. As regards such standard terms, reg 6(2) provides that, 'insofar as it is expressed in plain intelligible language', 'the assessment of fairness of a term shall not relate' to terms which in effect encompass the vital interests of the trader and may be described as the **core** terms of the contract. The effect of these opening words is that, insofar as a core term itself satisfies reg 7 (see para 11.13) and is fairly brought to the notice of the consumer (see Grey Term (i): see para 11.17), the court cannot interfere with it in on grounds of unfairness (see para 11.15). According to reg 6(2), core terms are those which relate to either:

*Para (a)* 'the definition of the main subject matter of the contract': for instance, terms in our context stating the description of the product (colour, model, etc), the price or the delivery date, the expiry date on gift vouchers.[116] Of the

---

110  Both standard and customised terms will also have to satisfy the statutory test of reasonableness in s 3 of UCTA: see para 18.22.

111  As to the formalities and formation of which, see Chaps 9 and 10. The European Commission is worried that this dichotomy can be circumvented by a business never pre-printing standard terms, the whole contract being computer-generated each time: see DTI, *Consultation Paper* (July 2000), p 14.

112  Reg 5(4). See further DTI, *Guidance Notes*, para 5 (Goode, *Consumer Credit Legislation*, Pt VIII, para 1010). What if a consumer simply did not realise that there was an opportunity to negotiate (see Elvin (2003) 14 KCLJ 39 at 45)?

113  The reference in reg 5(3) to 'standard' seems to introduce an extra requirement that was not present in Art 3(2) of the Directive, which makes it clear that this is just an example: see Watson and Bone (2002) 1 Jo of Remedies and Obligations 29 at 38.

114  Unless on 'an overall assessment' it is not a standard-form contract, in which case the effect of reg 3(4) seems to be that the Regulations will not apply to any standard terms. *Quaere?*

115  This seems to be pointing to the interaction of terms: Dean (1995) 145 NLJ 28 at 29.

116  OFT, *Bulletin No. 6*, case 56. As to gift vouchers, see para 15.18.

two classes of core terms, these may give rise to the greater difficulty: as the Regulations do not extend to the statutory implied terms,[117] will this category be limited to the ambit of the statutory implied condition as to descriptive quality; or does it extend to descriptive quantity, title and fitness (see generally, para 11.11)? Moreover, para (a) seems to require a distinction to be drawn between those terms which **define** the contract and those which do not;[118] and the OFT argue that this must be viewed from the perception of the consumer.[119] What is the effect of a clause purporting to make any term part of the core of the contract (see para 8.35)?

*Para (b)* 'the adequacy of the price or remuneration, as against the goods or services sold or supplied'; that is, the 'value-for-money' equation. This dove-tails with the English law dismissal of the adequacy of the consideration (see para 10.01), so that the Regulations should not touch the bad bargain cases (see para 27.28); but it should be remembered that there are circumstances where statute imports an obligation to pay a reasonable sum,[120] or the sum stipulated is unfair (see para 29.45). However, the UTCC Regulations may defeat, for instance, the following variations in price: variations allowed in quotations (see *Bulletin No. 23*, case 24); interest rate variations and price escalation clauses (see Grey List, paras (j), (l): para 11.17); insufficiently prominent charges (see para 11.13); and perhaps dual interest rates (see para 8.22).[121]

The meaning of both these categories of core term were considered in *DG v First National Bank plc* (set out at para 7.03A), where the courts had to decide whether clause 8 was unfair, or escaped the Regulations as being a core term. At first instance, the judge held that clause 8 was **not** a core term: its effect was only to deprive a defaulting borrower of the statutory prohibition on interest from judgment until payment; and this was not amongst the important terms which a borrower would have under consideration when deciding whether or not to accept an advance.[122] After listening to the Bank's argument that the purpose of the Directive upon which the Regulations were based was to harmonise the position in Member States and receiving evidence of their disparate law, the Court of Appeal unanimously agreed (at para 25), as did the House of Lords (at paras 12, 34, 42–3, 53 and 62). Pointing out that reg 3(2) gives effect almost verbatim to the words of Art 4(2), Lord Bingham explained (at para 12) that the object was to protect consumers, which 'would plainly be frustrated if reg 3(2)(b) were so broadly interpreted as to cover any terms other than those falling squarely within it'. He concluded that clause 8:

---

117 Reg 4(2)(a): see para 11.12A.

118 For the difficulty of identifying terms which 'define the main subject matter of the contract', see Macdonald [1994] JBL at 460–2; Brownsword & Howells [1995] JBL at 248–52.

119 *Bulletin No. 2*, para 2.26 and example at p 26.

120 E.g. SGA, s 8(2); SGSA, s 15 (see paras 2.06 and 15.15).

121 *Bairstow Eves London Central Ltd v Smith* [2005] CLY 721 (estate agency case); but see the *Spencer* case (set out at para 8.22).

122 [2000] 1 All ER 240; Law Commission, *Unfair Terms in Contracts* (2002, Law Com Consultation Paper No. 166), paras 3.27–33. Price levels would be controlled under only the competition rules (see paras 2.12–14).

'does not concern the adequacy of the interest earned by the bank as remuneration but is designed to ensure that the bank's entitlement to interest does not come to an end on the entry of judgment'.

The Unfair Terms Bill would amend these provisions (see para 11.21).

**[11.15] Unfair terms (1).** It has been seen that the UTCC Regulations strike at non-core standard terms in *consumer supply contracts* (see para 11.13) which are 'unfair'; or which are deemed unfair (see para 11.12A). The concept of 'unfair' is explained thus (reg 5(1)):[123]

> 'A contractual term which has not been individually negotiated shall be regarded as unfair if, contrary to the requirement of good faith, it causes a significant imbalance in the parties' rights and obligations arising under the contract, to the detriment of the consumer'.

As Lord Bingham said (at para 17) in the *First National Bank* case (set out at para 7.03A):

> 'The member states have no common concept of fairness or good faith, and the directive does not purport to state the law of any single member state. It lays down a test to be applied, whatever their pre-existing law, by all member states. If the meaning of the test were doubtful, or vulnerable to the possibility of differing interpretations in differing member states, it might be desirable or necessary to seek a ruling from the European Court of Justice on its interpretation'.

Thus, a non-core standard-form term is 'unfair' if it satisfies **all** the three following tests,[124] which are to be read in the light of the Directive (see para 11.12) by the national courts;[125] but the Unfair Terms Bill would delete *good faith* (see para 11.21).

A. *Lack of good faith.* Now, an English lawyer will already be familiar with the concept of good faith, both at common law[126] and under statute.[127] Whilst the cynical common law largely confines good faith to lack of proven dishonesty (see para 21.19), ignoring further protestations as likely to be self-serving, civil law starts from the idealistic standpoint that all contracting parties will do their utmost to make, perform and break their contract in an even-handed manner.[128] Unlike the 1994 version of the Regulations,[129] the 1999 version of

---

123 If the term is ambiguous, it may also fall within both limbs of reg 7 (see para 11.13).

124 The OFT look at the term itself, any balancing provision, the context and good faith: *Bulletin No. 4*, pp 22–3. As to the burden of proof, see the Law Commission, *Unfair Terms in Contracts* (2002, Law Com Consultation Paper No. 166), paras 3.79–80.

125 This is not a matter for the ECJ: *Freiburger Kommunalbauten GmbH v Hofstetter* [2004] 2 CMLR 13, ECJ.

126 E.g. in applying the exceptions to the *nemo dat* rule (see Chap 21); or the rules for the incorporation of terms (see para 18.04); or the notion of contracts *uberrime fidei* (see para 11.01). See *per* Bingham LJ in *Interfoto Picture Library Ltd v Stiletto Visual Programmes Ltd* [1988] 1 All ER 348, CA, at 352–3, 357.

127 SGA, s 61(3): see paras 21.19 and 21.41.

128 As developed by the European court, it seems good faith is required 'at all times': see DTI, *Guidance Notes*, para 7 and Annex 2; McNeil [1995] JR at 148; *Halsbury's Laws*, 4th edn rev, Contract, paras 612–14.

129 The 1994 version of the Regulations (1994 SI 3159) contained a definition of 'good faith' (Sched 2): the first three factors bore a considerable resemblance to three of the reasonableness factors in Sched 2 of UCTA (see para 18.26); and the last factor read '(d) the extent to which the seller or supplier has dealt fairly and equitably with the consumer'. See Treitel, *Law of Contract*, 11th edn, 259; Elvin (2003) 14 KCLJ 39 at 53–7.

the Regulations does not contain a definition of good faith; but Recital 16 of the Directive does, so presumably this should be taken into account. In the *First National* case (above), Lord Bingham said:[130]

> 'The requirement of good faith in this context is one of fair and open dealing. Openness requires that the term should be expressed fully, clearly and legibly, containing no concealed pitfalls or traps. Appropriate prominance should be given to terms which might operate disadvantageously to the customer. Fair dealing requires that a supplier should not, whether deliberately or unconsciously, take advantage of the consumer's necessity, indigence, lack of experience, unfamiliarity with the subject matter of the contract, weakness of bargaining position or any other factor listed in Sched 2 of the regulations. Good faith in this context is not an artificial or technical concept; nor, since Lord Mansfield was its champion, is it a concept wholly unfamiliar to British lawyers'.

The Directive may lead to a dichotomy in English law: consumer contracts to be governed by good faith and perhaps also reasonableness (see below), whilst commercial contracts are only subject to the reasonableness test (ss 2(2) and 3 of UCTA: see paras 18.20–1). Good faith would seem to have both a substantive and a procedural aspect: that is, it may relate to (i) the substance of a term, in which respect it may overlap with the imbalance of rights (see below); and (ii) procedural matters, such as whether the consumer has notice of the term.[131]

Is this EU concept of 'good faith' in fact wide enough to comprehend also both the following factors?[132]

B.  *A significant imbalance of rights* (see para 11.15A).

C.  *To the detriment of the consumer* (see para 11.15A).

**[11.15A] Unfair terms (2)**. As well as a lack of good faith (see para 11.15), reg 5(1) requires both the following:

B.  *A significant imbalance of right.* Reg 5(1) says that an 'unfair term' is one which 'causes a significant imbalance in the parties' rights and obligations'; and it seems that the OFT's starting point tends to be to ask itself what would be the position of the consumer if the suspect clause was not there (the 'default position').[133] At the substantive level, 'significant imbalance' is obviously aimed at contractual terms under which the supplier has a **right** to do something, but the consumer does not (the 'mirror image' rule): for instance, the seller has a price escalation clause (see para 10.05), whereas the consumer has no counter-balancing right to cancel the contract without penalty (*Bulletin No. 1*, para 1.05; *No. 5*, p 34), or the two sides have uneven rights of cancellation or assignment (*Bulletin No. 15*, cases 1, 17; *No. 22*, case 13); terms which refer to out-of-date consumer protection legislation or transfer the risk to the consumer (*Bulletin No. 17*, cases 22 and 27). It also applies to terms which impose an

---

130  At para 17. See also Lord Steyn at para 36. As to the common law position, see Mason (2000) 116 LQR 66.

131  See *per* Peter Gibson LJ in *DG v First National Bank plc* (above) at 769, paras 28–30; and Law Commission, *ibid*, paras 3.57–69.

132  It has been suggested that a term does not have to satisfy all three criteria to be 'unfair', so long as it fails the good faith test: DTI, *Guidance Notes*, para 7.2.

133  See Elvin (2003) 14 KCLJ 39 at 52.

**obligation** on the consumer but not on the supplier (Grey term (o): see para 11.18). No doubt, many breaches of the mirror-image rule will involve clauses which embody an important interest of the supplier, but are simply drafted too widely. Regulation 5(5) provides that Sched 2 contains a list of the terms which may be regarded as unfair and is known as the Grey List (see paras 11.16–18). However, this does not preclude the existence of other unfair terms which are not mentioned in Sched 2 and the *Bulletins* mention the following categories of such unfair terms:

(i)     Allowing a supplier to impose an unfair financial burden (OFT, *Guidance*, Group 18(a); *Bulletin No. 24*, case 26).

(ii)    Transferring unfair risks to consumers, e.g. by requiring him to insure against the supplier's negligence (*Bulletin No. 24*, case 27), or to obtain official permission ([2006] *Bulletin J/M, Oakland*) or requiring supplier's approval to his insurance ([2005] *Bulletin J/S, Forthright Finance*). See *Guidance*, Group 18(b).

(iii)   Onerous enforcement clauses.[134]

(iv)    Excluding consumers' rights to assign.[135]

(v)     Consumer declaration about contractual circumstances (*Bulletin No. 24*, cases 19 and 27; *No. 26*, pp 42, 76; *No. 27*, p 12), e.g. that he understood that a deposit was not refundable (*Bulletin No. 27*, p 30), or orders cannot be cancelled (*Bulletin No. 27*, p 35). See *Guidance*, Group 18(e).

(vi)    Excluding consumers' non-contractual rights (*Guidance*, Group 18(f); *Bulletin No. 26*, pp 12, 21).

(vii)   Delivery at suppliers' discretion, or by instalments (see para 23.23). See *Guidance*, Group 18(g).

(viii)  Other: terminate without notice for late payment or minor breaches ;[136] enter the consumer's premises to recapt (see para 24.24); prevent claims on behalf of a third-party beneficiary (see para 17.08); exclude rights under the DPA (see para 3.28); allow deduction of payment from consumer's card without notice (*Bulletin No. 26*, pp 28, 89); making the consumer the insurer of the goods (*Bulletin No. 26*, p 71); requiring a bailee to immediately inform his bailor of any damage;[137] allowing the supplier to retain prepayments (*Bulletin No. 27*, p 17); incorporation of terms by reference (see para 18.04); an all monies clause (see para 20.28).

But all this is to be done without taking into account the price (see para 11.14). On the other hand, whilst the Regulations do not formally transfer the burden of proof to the trader, the OFT consider that this requirement produces a similar effect (*Bulletin No. 4*, pp 24–6). Further, at the procedural level, it would seem that this requirement extends to clauses which may be fair in substance, but

---

134 See OFT, *Guidance*, Group 18(c) (see generally, para 11.12); and *Bulletin No. 24*, case 26; *No. 29*, p 15.

135 *Guidance*, Group 18(d); and *Bulletin No. 24*, cases 20, 40, 44; *No. 26*, p 78; *No. 27*, pp 29 and 105; [2005] *Bulletin J/M, Flogas*; [2005] *Bulletin A/J, Pratt*; [2005] *Bulletin J/S, BP Oil*.

136 *Bulletin No. 24*, case 27; [2005] *Bulletin J/S, Forthright; LloydsTSB*.

137 *Bulletin No. 26*, p 91; *No. 29*, p 15.

tucked away in the small print so that they are not drawn to the attention of the consumer.[138]

C. *To the detriment of the consumer.* At the obvious level, this requirement excludes from the regulations contracts where the imbalance of rights is to the detriment of the supplier.[139] Examples of detriment to the consumer include the following: allowing the supplier to charge for collecting parts when this should not have been necessary; introducing uncertainty into charging; unfairly restricting the consumer's power to assign the contract; unfair power to enter consumer's premises to repossess goods (see para 24.23); consumer agreed to contract out of one of the statutory protections, e.g. under the CCA, or the distance selling regulations; consumer declaration of matters which he was not qualified to assess; allowing the supplier excessive discretion to suspend supplies; supplier to refuse refund where the goods do not fit into consumer's home; automatic renewal of membership; internet sale required full advance payment and no refunds.[140] However, in determining whether a non-core term in a consumer contract contrary to the requirement of good faith causes such a significant disadvantage to the consumer, reg 6(1) lays down that, without prejudice to reg 12 (see para 11.19),

> 'An assessment of the unfair nature of a term shall be made taking into account the nature of the goods or services for which the contract was concluded and referring, as at the time of the conclusion of the contract, to all circumstances attending the conclusion of the contract and to all the other terms of the contract or of another contract on which it is dependent'.

Notice the emphasis in reg 6(1) on surveying matters 'as at the time of the conclusion of the contract': like s 11(1) of UCTA (see para 18.24), it would seem that the Regulations do not bite on terms fair as made, but which are, or may be, applied unjustly.[141] On the other hand, reg 6(1) is wider than s 11(1) in that 'it places emphasis on the interaction of terms, both in the particular contract and any related to it'.[142] The reference to 'all circumstances attending the conclusion of the contract' seems to direct the emphasis more towards procedural matters, such as drawing core and other important terms to the attention of the consumer (OFT, *Bulletin No. 3*, para 13); and it may also focus attention on any applicable Code of Practice (see para 3.13). Within that context, a consumer pleading the regulations must show actual detriment arising from the unfair term. Is this wide enough to catch clauses which are void under other legislation,[143] or at common law, e.g. the rule against penalties (see para 27.25), simply on the grounds that the presence of the clause might mislead consumers as to their rights?[144]

---

138  Bright (2000) 20 LS 331, at 348–9. But see Elvin, *ibid*, at 53.

139  It has been suggested that the detriment requirement has the further purpose of allowing recourse to *de facto* detriment to consumers outside the scope of the contract: Brownsword & Howells [1995] JBL 243 at 254.

140  Respectively *Bulletin No. 17*, cases 12, 13, 16, 19 and 21; *No. 18*, cases 4, 7 and 13; *No. 20*, case 3.

141  *Per* Lord Bingham in the *First National Bank* case, at para 24: see para 11.15B.

142  Dean (1995) 145 NLJ at 30.

143  Such as fraud, duress, undue influence, misrepresentation, non-disclosure and sharp practice: Beatson [1995] CLJ at 237.

144  See Elvin (2003) 14 KCLJ 39 at 52–3.

**[11.15B] Unfair terms (3).** The first reported judicial consideration of the above concept of an unfair term occurred in *DG v First National Bank plc* (set out at para 7.03A), where the disputed and widely used clause 8 was neither mentioned in the Grey List, nor within UCTA. The first-instance judge accepted the Bank's argument that, because in a regulated loan the court has jurisdiction under s 136 of the CCA to adjust clause 8 to prevent interest accruing after judgment (see para 9.20), clause 8 was not unfair just because the court had not exercised that jurisdiction and the debtor was unaware of it.[145] However, the Court of Appeal disagreed, explicitly rejecting the view of the first-instance judge. Peter Gibson LJ explained that clause 8 was unfair because:[146]

'The bank with its strong bargaining position as against the relatively weak position of the consumer, has not adequately considered the consumer's interest in this respect. In our view the relevant term in that respect does create unfair surprise and so does not satisfy the test of good faith, it does cause a significant imbalance in the rights and obligations of the parties by allowing the bank to obtain interest after judgment in circumstances when it would not obtain interest under [the ordinary law: see para 7.03A] and no specific benefit to compensate the borrower is provided, and it operates to the detriment of the consumer who has to pay the interest'.

The House of Lords unanimously restored the first-instance decision.[147] In delivering the leading judgement, Lord Bingham reasoned as follows: the Bank would not lend unless the agreement allowed it to recover in full the capital and interest (para 20); following the Crowther Report (see para 5.03), the CCA does not prohibit recovery of post-judgment interest, so clause 8 cannot 'be stigmatised as unfair on the ground that it violates or undermines a statutory regime enacted for the protection of consumers' (para 22); the Regulation (now 5) is 'directed to the unfairness of a contract term, not the use which a supplier makes of a term which is in itself fair' (para 24); and, in any event, there already exists powers under the CCA to apply to a court for a variation of clause 8 (para 24: see paras 7.03A; 9.20).

Perhaps on the other side of the line is the continued inclusion of clauses rendered void by statute.[148]

**[11.15C] The effect of unfair non-core provisions.** The effect of the UTCC Regulations is to strike at non-core standard terms which are 'unfair' (see para 11.15). Thus, reg 8(1) lays down that:

'An unfair term in a contract concluded with a consumer by a seller or supplier shall not be binding on the consumer'.

This postulates that, *prima facie*, the contract will remain binding on both contracting parties,[149] even in respect of unfair terms imposing burdens on the seller or supplier. However, insofar as the unfair term burdens the consumer, 'it shall not

---

145 [2000] 1 All ER 240, at para 51.
146 [2000] 2 All ER 769, at para 35, CA. See Mitchell (2000) 116 LQR 557.
147 The other Law Lords expressly agreed with Lord Bingham's reasoning at paras 39, 40, 53 and 62.
148 See para 18.09, *et seq*. A fortiori, where the exclusion is a criminal offence (see para 4.22)?
149 The Regulations do not seem to protect third parties: Law Commission, *Unfair Terms in Contracts* (2002, Law Com Consultation Paper No. 166), para 3.104.

be binding on him', cf.unregulated guarantees (see para 25.06). At first, the DTI interpreted this neutral phrase to mean 'voidable'.[150]

However, the effect seems more like that of improperly executed regulated agreements (CCA, s 65: see para 9.19); and it has been likened to the English blue pencil rule.[151] The effect of this is spelt out in reg 8(2):

> 'The contract shall continue to bind the parties if it is capable of continuing in existence without the unfair term'.

Clearly, two situations are envisaged; and in practice there may be scope for argument as to which side a particular term falls. *First*, perhaps in the majority of cases, the standard-form contract can continue without the unfair term. *Second*, if the contract is not capable of continuing in existence without the unfair term, the contract falls[152] and the position of the parties is presumably governed by quasi-contract.[153] Suppose the consumer suffers financial loss as a direct result of the supplier's use of the unfair term: are damages recoverable?[154]

The Unfair Terms Bill adopts both the above rules (see para 11.21).

**[11.16] The Grey List (1)**. To help decide whether a non-core standard term in a consumer contract is unfair (see para 11.14), Sched 2 of the UTCC Regulations 1999 contains what it terms an '**indicative and non-exhaustive** list of terms which may be regarded as unfair'.[155] So, Sched 2 (which repeats verbatim Sched 3 of the 1994 Regulations) is not a black-list, but 'simply illustrates a selection of overlapping *types* of term whose use might cause unfairness:'[156] whether they do so or not is a matter of substance, not form (*Bulletin No. 5*, p 10). Absence from the list does not indicate that a term is fair;[157] and appearance on the list does not necessarily mean that it is unfair, though it raises a substantial suspicion (*Bulletin No. 4*, p 22). A list of specimen terms for each Grey List category is to be found in the *Bulletins*.[158] Subject to some savings (Sched 2(2)), Sched 2 lists some (possibly overlapping) 'terms which have the object or effect of' the following:[159]

---

150 DTI, *Consultation Document on the UTCC Directive* (Oct 1993). As to voidable contracts, see para 10.15.
151 Bright (2000) 20 LS 331, at 350. But see *Bankers Insurance Co Ltd v South* [2003] CLY 2456 (unfair insurance notification condition treated as innominate term so that insurer retained some protection).
152 Is it discharged *ab initio* or *de futuro* (see para 26.11)?
153 Is there a total failure of consideration (see para 29.12)?
154 *Consultation Paper* (July 2000), para 2.9; Elvin (2003) 14 KCLJ 39 at 57–8.
155 The EU has some doubt as to the wisdom of the List approach: see *Report on Implications of UTCC Directive* (April 1993), para 3 (set out in DTI, *Consultation Paper* (July 2000)).
156 DTI, *Guidance Notes*, para 6; OFT, *Briefing—Unfair Standard Terms* (1995) 4. For example, see OFT, *Bulletin No. 2*, Pt 4.
157 For examples of unfair terms not in Sched 2, see OFT, *Bulletin No. 3*, para 11: indemnification; unfair enforcement; signed statements; instalment deliveries.
158 The OFT have found the following gaps in the list (DTI, *Consultation Paper* (July 2000), para 4.7): allowing a supplier to impose an unfair financial burden; transferring unfair risks (e.g. by indemnities) to consumers; onerous enforcement clauses; excluding consumers' right to assign; consumers' declarations about financial circumstances; excluding consumers' non-contractual rights; delivery at supplier's discretion. See also above, para 11.15A.
159 The '**object**' is the intention behind the wording; the '**effect**' is the practical outcome of inclusion of the term as worded, even if different from what was intended: OFT, *ibid*. This analysis is used to limit the operation of restrictions: *Bulletin No. 5*, p 10.

(a) *No liability for death or injury*[160]. These are terms 'excluding or limiting the legal liability of a seller or supplier in the event of the death of a consumer or personal injury to the latter resulting from an act or omission of that seller or supplier'. Unlike UCTA (s 2: see para 18.17), this rule comprehends (*Bulletin No. 27*, pp 104–5), but is not limited to, injury caused by negligence.[161]

**[11.16A] The Grey List (2).**

(b) *No liability for breaches of contract.* These are terms '**inappropriately** excluding or limiting the legal rights of the consumer *vis-à-vis* the seller or supplier or another party in the event of total or partial non-performance or inadequate performance by the seller or supplier of any of the contractual obligations, including the option of offsetting a debt owed to the seller or supplier against any claim which the consumer may have against him'. Unlike s 3 of UCTA (see para 18.20), this category is confined to consumer contracts and the *Bulletins* break this down into the following sub-categories:

(i) excluding liability for defective or misdescribed goods,[162] or breach of the TDA (see para 4.09), or delivery of the wrong quantity (see para 13.07). This clearly also extends to attempts to exclude other implied terms, that is, those which are not within reg 4(2) (see para 11.12A). The category will include clauses giving the supplier the right to determine the type of redress,[163] or to deny redress if any adjustments have been made to the goods by a third party (*Bulletin No. 26*, pp 72 and 77).

(ii) excluding liability for poor services, or work and materials, e.g. excluding the duty to take reasonable care and skill under statute (see para 15.15) or common law (see paras 17.14).[164]

(iii) restricting the amount or type of liability, e.g. allowing an additional charge to remedy defective work, deeming any alterations to be a separate contract, 'confirmation of satisfaction' declaration (see para 18.06), consumer to pay x% of invoice value on rejecting defective goods, restricting retailer's liability to that of the manufacturer (*Bulletin No. 26*, p 72), consumer to pay cost of inspecting defective goods at his own premises (*Bulletin No. 27*, p 34), excluding liability for defects not inspected at the time of delivery (*Bulletin No. 27*, p 35). See generally *Guidance*, Group 2(c).

(iv) time limits on claims,[165] as where there is a time limit for a consumer of running-account credit to challenging his regular statement, e.g. 30 days.

---

160 See generally the OFT *Guidance* (see para 11.12), Group 1.

161 E.g. OFT, *Bulletin No. 1*, cases 7 and 13 (cl 6); *No. 4*, pp 9–10; *No. 18*, case 9; *No. 22*, case 33; *No. 24*, cases 40 and 46; *No. 26*, p 30; *No. 29*, p 13. Cf. product liability (CPA, s 7: see para 17.30). Any more stringent liability in UCTA, s 2, is saved by Art 8 (see para 11.12: DTI, *Guidance Notes*, para 6.3).

162 See OFT, *Guidance*, Group 2(a) (see generally, para 11.12). E.g. *Bulletin No. 17*, case 28; *No. 24*, case 46; *No. 26*, pp 10 and 76; *No. 27*, pp 16, 26, 30 and 31.

163 *Bulletin No. 26*, pp 72 and 78; *No. 27*, pp 21, 26 and 33. An attempt to modify the consumer remedies available is already void: see para 29.09A.

164 See *Guidance*, Group 2(b); and *Bulletin No. 17*, cases 12 and 13; *Bulletin No. 18*, case 13; *No. 24*, cases 6 and 46; *No. 26*, pp 42, 76, 90 and 105; *No. 26*, p 91; *No. 27*, pp 14–15; *No. 27*, pp 16 and 108; *No. 29*, p 13.

165 See *Guidance*, Group 2(d); and *Bulletin No. 24*, case 48; *No. 26*, pp 42 and 69; *No. 27*, pp 21 and 33; [2005] *Bulletin A/J*, *Micro*.

(v)    excluding consumers' right of set-off (see para 29.26), so depriving the
       consumer of a lever to secure performance and requiring him to take
       court action, such as where a business tries to prevent the consumer
       offsetting the balance of the price against a defective delivery, as by
       requiring payment before delivery,[166] or allowing the supplier to deduct
       late payments from a credit card (*Bulletin No. 24*, case 40), or denying any
       deductions from the price.[167]

(vi)   excluding or restricting liability for delay.[168] For instance, a deemed
       delivery clause; allowing delivery to an unattended property, or beyond
       an estimated delivery date,[169] or by stating that delivery times are only
       estimates (*Bulletin No. 24*, case 24).

(vii)  excluding or restricting liability for the supplier's non-performance, as
       by denying the ordinary remedy for non-delivery (*Bulletin No. 27*, p 26)
       or other breach of condition (see para 11.04), e.g. 'no refunds', 'credit
       notes only', 'colour shading excluded', 'E & OE' ([2005] *Bulletin O/D,
       Carpetright*); supplier protected where consumer cancels for supplier's
       default (*Bulletin No. 27*, pp 106 and 110); limiting damages, as by exclud-
       ing consequential loss.[170]

(viii) excluding or restricting liability *via* a guarantee, or insurance.[171]

(ix)   other cases, such as a swingeing *force majeure* clause (as to which, see para
       22.13A), or passing the risk to the consumer (see para 22.02), or requiring
       the consumer to insure (*Bulletin No. 27*, pp 28–9) or bear the risk (see para
       22.02A); deeming any notice by the consumer only to be served on the
       supplier if complying with certain formalities, e.g. by recorded delivery
       letter, or in writing within 7 days; or by requiring the consumer to pay the
       return carriage on defective goods or return goods in their original pack-
       aging/unopened;[172] directing any consumer complaints to a prior party
       in the chain;[173] allowing replacement goods to be inferior (*Bulletin No. 26*,
       p 71); unclear service charges (*Bulletin No. 26*, p 77); claiming that the
       consumer is under a duty to inspect the goods (*Bulletin No. 27*, p 27);
       excluding liability for loss to the consumer resulting from information
       supplied (*Bulletin No. 27*, p 34).

**[11.16B] The Grey List (3).** Further to the foregoing paragraphs, the Grey List
continues:

(c)    *Right not to provide services.* These are terms 'making an agreement binding on
       the consumer whereas provision of services by the seller or supplier is subject

---

166  See *Guidance*, Group 2(e); and *Bulletin No. 17*, cases 10, 12 and 13; *No. 18*, cases 5, 9 and 17; *No. 24*,
     case 6; *No. 26*, pp 11, 41 and 72; *No. 27*, pp 13–14, 20.
167  [2005] *Bulletin J/M, GIS Windows* case.
168  See *Guidance*, Group 2(f); and *Bulletin No. 26*, pp 73, 75 and 77; *No. 27*, pp 16, 28, 30 and 34; *GIS
     Windows* case (above).
169  *Bulletin No. 18*, case 9; *No. 26*, p 12; *No. 27*, p 32.
170  See *Guidance*, Group 2(g); and *Bulletin No. 18*, case 4; *No. 24*, case 6; *No. 26*, pp 68 and 75; *No. 27*,
     pp 27–8: see paras 29.23, 29.31 and 29.35.
171  See *Guidance*, Group 2(h); and *Bulletin No. 17*, case 27; *No. 26*, p 21.
172  As to return carriage, see *Bulletin No. 24*, case 48; *No. 26*, p 70; but see SGA, s 36 (para 23.09). As
     to original packaging, see [2005] *Bulletin A/J, Micro*.
173  See *Bulletin No. 18*, cases 5 and 17; *No. 24*, case 48.

to a condition whose realisation depends on his own will alone', e.g. that the trader may on a whim cancel the contract or will repair any goods he deems defective. See generally *Guidance*, Group 3.

(d) *Retention of pre-payments*. These are terms 'permitting the seller or supplier to retain sums paid by the consumer where the latter decides not to conclude or perform the contract, without providing for the consumer to receive compensation of an equivalent amount from the seller or supplier where the latter is the party cancelling the contract'.[174]

(e) *Penalty clauses*. These are terms 'requiring any consumer who fails to fulfill his obligation to pay a disproportionately high sum in compensation', such as: excessive compensation[175] or rate of interest (*Bulletin No. 26*, p 41); payment of interest after judgment (see para 7.03A); no duty on the supplier to mitigate (see para 27.44); harsh minimum payment clauses (see para 11.08); indemnities (*Bulletin No. 24*, case 40); recaption (see para 24.23); clogs on the equity of redemption (see para 25.20); retention of title clause (see para 25.29); default clauses (see para 27.37) and fees on unauthorised overdrafts (see paras 7.02 and 7.09); penalties (see para 27.25); administration fees (*Bulletin No. 26*, p 74); high charges for dishonoured cheques or collection expenses on cancellation by the consumer (*Bulletin No. 27*, pp 14 and 22); a consumer in breach must anyway pay the full price (*Bulletin No. 27*, p 29); or continue making payments after impossibility (see para 22.13A). It has even been extended to clauses which simply had the potential to allow unspecified, and therefore potentially unreasonable, charges.[176] A good example of the application of this clause is *Falco Finance Ltd v Gough*;[177] and there are many others.[178]

(f) *General opt-out clauses*. These are terms 'authorising the seller or supplier to dissolve the contract on a discretionary basis where the same facility is not granted to the consumer, or permitting the seller or supplier to retain the sums paid for services not yet supplied by him where it is the seller or supplier himself who dissolves the contract'. This deals with, first, a supplier's right to cancel for minor breaches[179] or none;[180] or make refunds discretionary.[181]

---

174 See OFT, *Guidance*, Group 4 (see generally, para 11.12). E.g. a non-returnable deposit (see *Bulletin No. 3*, para 3; *No. 17*, cases 22 and 30; *No. 24*, case 40; [2005] *Bulletin A/J, Pratt*; and para 23.27); *Hartman v P & O Cruises Ltd* [1998] CLY 3732, Cty Ct.

175 See *Bulletin No. 23*, case 3; *No. 27*, p 106; [2005] *Bulletin J/M, GIS Windows & Flogas* cases.

176 *Bulletin No. 26*, p 28; *No. 27*, p 106; *No. 29*, pp 12, 14 and 15.

177 (1998) 17 Tr LR 526 (dual interest rates; the rule of 78): see OFT, *1998-AR* 30–1; Bright (1999) 115 LQR 360.

178 See *Guidance*, Group 5; and also *Bulletin No. 13*, case 15; *No. 17*, cases 12 and 14 (dishonoured cheques), case 16 (non-APR), case 27 (late payment penalty); *No. 18*, cases 5 and 7 (allowing supplier to retain a fixed sum), case 17 (where consumer delayed delivery); *No. 20*, case 6 (to pay supplier's legal fees on indemnity basis); *No. 22*, case 13 (unlimited interest on overdue payments), case 14 (fraud or misrepresentation), case 16 (if consumer's particulars incomplete), case 17 (termination fees); [2006] *OFT Bulletin J/M, Log Book* (late payment interest), *Oakland* (fees).

179 See *Guidance*, Group 6(a); and *Bulletin No. 15*, cases 4 and 8; *No. 26*, p 90; *No. 27*, pp 26 and 109; [2005] *Bulletin J/S, BP Oil*.

180 See *Guidance*, Group 6(b); and *Bulletin No. 23*, case 26; *No. 24*, case 6; *No. 27*, pp 21–2.

181 *Bulletin No. 15*, case 8. See also termination provisions in instalment contracts (see para 26.08); retention of sums paid in advance for installation or services not supplied (*Bulletin No. 2*, p 18).

Second, it covers denial of cancellation by the consumer where the supplier's breach would entitle repudiation at common law (*Bulletin No. 29*, p 25). Third, it attacks unequal cancellation rights,[182] or cancellation fees (*Bulletin No. 21*, case 31).

(g) *Right to terminate.* Except in the case of financial services contracts,[183] these are terms 'enabling the seller or supplier to terminate a contract of indeterminate duration without **reasonable notice**,[184] except where there are serious grounds for so doing', e.g. to terminate a periodic hiring or running-account credit without notice where there are no serious grounds for doing so; snatch-back clauses (see para 26.08).

(h) *Automatic renewal.* These are terms 'automatically extending a contract of fixed duration where the consumer does not indicate otherwise, when the deadline fixed for the consumer to express this desire not to extend the contract is **unreasonably**[184] early'.[185]

**[11.17] The Grey List (4).** Further to the foregoing paragraph, the Grey List continues:

(i) *Hidden terms.* These are terms 'irrevocably binding the consumer to terms with which he had no real opportunity of becoming acquainted before conclusion of the contract'. This covers two principal areas: first, where terms are not physically available to the consumer at the time he enters a contract, which would appear to impinge on the common law rule of incorporation of terms by reference;[186] and second, the phrase 'no real opportunity' may extend to vital terms 'buried' in small print of even signed contracts,[187] including core terms and the lack of plain language (*Bulletin No. 4*, pp 21–2). The OFT consider that this extends to rendering unfair a declaration that the consumer's signature signified his acceptance of the terms of the document;[188] but it does suggest that a trader may be able to avoid such a result by giving the consumer an express right to cancel the contract (see para 10.28) when he discovers the terms (*Bulletin No. 7*, para 1.12).

(j) *Variation clauses.* Except in the case of financial services contracts,[183] these are terms 'enabling the seller or supplier to alter the terms of the contract

---

182  *Bulletin No. 17*, cases 10 and 11; *No. 18*, case 9; *No. 22*, case 17; *No. 23*, case 6; *No. 26*, pp 40, 70 and 75; *No. 27*, pp 25 and 108.

183  [2005] *Bulletin A/J, Micro.* By Sched 2, para 2(a), there is saved the supplier's 'right to terminate unilaterally a contract of indeterminate duration without notice where there is a valid reason, provided that the supplier is required to inform the other contracting party or parties thereof immediately', e.g. termination of an overdraft facility. (See also para 2(c)). For an explanation of the purpose of Sched 2 para 2, see DTI, *Guidance Notes*, para 6.7.

184  See *Guidance*, Group 7. E.g. *Bulletin No. 24*, cases 40 and 46. It has been suggested that 'the practical effect' of this reasonableness test is similar to the UCTA reasonableness test (see para 18.20): DTI, *Guidance Notes*, para 6.6.

185  See *Guidance*, Group 8. As where an annual service agreement provides for automatic renewal unless the consumer cancels 'unreasonably early' (*Bulletin No. 2*, case 18); inertia selling (see *Bulletin No. 17*, case 4; *No. 24*, case 39 (by direct debit): para 8.18; and para 24.44); *Interphoto Picture etc Ltd v Stiletto Ltd* [1988] 1 All E R 348, CA.

186  See OFT, *Guidance*, Group 9 (see generally, para 11.12). Such as other written terms held elsewhere, e.g. lodged at head office of the business (*Bulletin No. 2*, case 25; *No. 17*, case 7; *No. 18*, case 17; *No. 20*, case 8; *No. 26*, pp 43 and 89).

187  See reg 6 (para 11.13); OFT, *1995-AR* 10. E.g. *Bulletin No. 2*, 16–17; *No. 15*, case 19.

188  *Bulletin No. 13*, case 8. This will substantially reverse the rule in *L'Estrange v Graucob Ltd* [1934] 2 KB 394, DC (see para 18.04).

unilaterally without a valid *reason*,[184] which is specified in the contract'. This strikes at a business power of arbitrary alteration (*Bulletin No. 15*, case 22), including changes to core terms (see para 11.14), retrospective early redemption penalties; and the power for the supplier to replace it with others terms found unenforceable[189]. Not only must there be a valid reason for the alteration, e.g. the manufacturer has altered the specification or the goods are in need of urgent repair[190], but this reason must be 'specified in the contract'. It does not apply to variation by the consumer, e.g. early settlement (see para 26.19A). However, the special treatment of financial services is here extended in the following circumstances, provided the consumer is subsequently given notice and 'is free to dissolve the contract':[191] to variations of interest rate and other charges;[192] and to unilateral alterations to 'the conditions of contracts of indeterminate duration'.[193]

(k) *Switch sales and hirings.* These are terms 'enabling the seller or supplier to alter unilaterally without a valid reason any characteristics of the product or service to be provided'. This obviously covers not just criminal switch-selling (*Bulletin No. 24*, case 6: see paras 4.05; 8.13A), but also sales by sample in which the goods do not comply with the sample,[194] e.g. where there is significant product development between contract and delivery,[195] or where the consumer agrees in advance to modifications (*Bulletin No. 26*, p 43). The consumer must be allowed an adequate right to cancel the contract (*Bulletin No. 21*, case 25; *No. 22*, case 26). The paragraph also applies to powers to unilaterally vary the terms of payment card contracts.[196]

**[11.18] The Grey List (5).** Further to the foregoing two paragraphs, the Grey List continues:

(l) *Price increases.* Except in the case of price indexation clauses,[197] these are terms 'providing for the price of goods to be determined at the time of delivery or allowing a seller of goods or supplier of services to increase their price without in both cases giving the consumer the corresponding right to cancel the contract if the final price is too high in relation to the price agreed when the contract was concluded'. This refers to two types of term: sales of goods where the price is

---

189  *Bulletin No. 27*, pp 107–9.
190  See *Bulletin No. 23*, case 24
191  As to whether this is consistent with the CCA Regulations permitting variation by newspaper advertisement (see para 26.22), see Guest and Lloyd, *Encyclopedia of Consumer Credit Law*, para 2-083.
192  Provided the supplier gives notice 'at the earliest opportunity' (Sched 2, para 2(b)). E.g. changes of interest rate or other charges on a personal loan, e.g. OFT, *1999-AR* 31. Distinguish the power to vary a regulated agreement by notice (CCA, s 82(1): see para 26.22). See *Guidance*, Group 10.
193  'On reasonable notice' (Sched 2, para 2(b)). E.g. unilateral variation of terms of an overdraft, such as the credit limit. As to whether the 'reasonable' notice requirement is consistent with the CCA procedure under s 82, see Guest and Lloyd, *ibid*.
194  See para 15.07: *Bulletin No. 2*, cases 17 and 21; *No. 20*, case 15. For the implied term as to correspondence with sample, see para 15.06. See *Guidance*, Group 11.
195  *Bulletin No. 3*, para 6; *No. 5*, p 38; *No. 13*, case 1; *No. 15*, cases 1, 4 and 8; *No. 17*, cases 7, 11, 19 and 27; *No. 18*, cases 7, 9 and 17; *No. 23*, cases 3, 6 and 27; *No. 24*, case 6; *No. 26*, p 76; *No. 27*, p 21.
196  [2005] *Bulletin J/M, GE Capital*.
197  This 'is without hindrance to price indexation clauses, where lawful, provided that the method by which prices vary is explicitly described' (Sched 2, para 2(d): see also para 2(c)).

left to be settled on delivery;[198] and price escalation clauses,[199] including hidden charges.[200] In both cases, it requires that the consumer[201] have a contractual right of cancellation (see para 10.28).

(m) *Exclusive jurisdiction.* These are terms 'giving the seller or supplier the right to determine whether the goods or services supplied are in conformity with the contract, or giving him the exclusive right to interpret any term of the contract'. This deals with three ways in which the supplier may seek exclusive jurisdiction over the contract: first, by controlling the evidence;[232] second, having the final say in the meaning of any term, which, being a matter of law, would anyway be void at common law (see para 3.23); and third, giving the supplier sole discretion over refunds and credit notes.[203]

(n) *Agents and formality.* These are terms 'limiting the seller's or supplier's obligation to respect commitments undertaken by his agents or making his commitments subject to compliance with a particular formality'. The *Bulletins* break this down into the following sub-categories:

(i)   Clauses disclaiming liability for statements of his employees' or other agents. This attacks clauses saving the supplier from the acts of his agents, e.g. denying the agent power to make any representations on the part of the supplier.[204] Such 'entire agreement' clauses (see para 11.09) have already been the subject of careful OFT scrutiny, on the grounds that they encourage salesmen to increase sales by misrepresentations;[205] and it is for consideration whether this will avoid limitations on the agent's power to contract.[206] Moreover, the prohibition may also extend to clauses deeming, e.g. a salesman, to be the agent of the consumer (see para 16.07).

(ii)  Formality requirements. This deals with the supplier's attempt to make his liability dependent on difficult conditions, as where the consumer must comply with onerous formalities before the supplier becomes liable to

---

198  See OFT, *Guidance*, Group 12 (see generally, para 11.12). E.g. a term in a double-glazing contract that the price will be determined when the assembled windows are delivered (DTI); OFT *Bulletin No. 2*, 28 and 32. *Contra* supplies of services: see SGSA, s 15(1): see para 15.15.

199  *Bulletin No. 24*, case 48: see para 10.05. Evidently, this is not to be a core term (see para 11.14). See OFT, *Bulletin No. 2*, case 27; *No. 3*, para 7; *No. 15*, cases 4 and 16; *No. 17*, cases 13, 27 and 28; *No. 18*, case 17; *No. 23*, case 21; *No. 27*, p 105. For price escalation clauses, see para 10.05.

200  *Bulletin No. 27*, p 13; *No. 29*, p 14; [2005] *Bulletin J/S, Newquest.*

201  *Bulletin No. 19*, case 9; *No. 24*, case 27; *No. 26*, p 105; [2005] *Bulletin J/S, BP Oil.*

232  *Guidance*, Group 13; and *Bulletin No. 3*, para 8.2; *No. 17*, cases 12 and 13; *No. 19* case 13; *No. 27*, pp 15 and 33; *No. 29*, p 12. Cf. *Lowe v Lombank Ltd* (set out at para 18.06).

203  *Bulletin No. 24*, case 46. For credit notes, see para 29.02.

204  *Guidance*, Group 14(a). E.g. *Watford Electronics Ltd v Sanderson CFL Ltd* (see para 18.21). See OFT, *Bulletin No. 2*, 37; *No. 15*, case 4; *No. 17*, cases 10, 11, 13, 19 and 27; *No. 18*, cases 5, 7 and 17; *No. 20*, case 19; *No. 21*, cases 9 and 25; *No. 22*, cases 13, 17 and 26; *No. 24*, cases 6 and 14; *No. 26*, pp 10 and 68; *No. 27*, pp 12–13, 25; [2005] *Bulletin A/J, Micro*; [2005] *Bulletin J/S, BP Oil; Newquest*; [2006] *Bulletin J/M, Oakland*; and see Beatson [1995] CLJ at 236; and para 10.24.

205  *Bulletin No. 1*, paras 2.5–6 and 2.7–21; *No. 3*, paras 9.2–6; *No. 13*, case 2; *No. 15*, cases 16, 17, and 20; *No. 17*, case 7; *No. 24*, case 44; *No. 27*, pp 105 and 110.

206  *Bulletin No. 18*, cases 7 and 17; *No. 19*, cases 9 and 13; *No. 20*, case 15; *No. 22*, case 14; *No. 24*, cases 27 and 48. Cf. *Overbrooke Estates Ltd v Glencombe Properties Ltd* [1974] 3 All ER 511 (not a goods case: see para 18.17). For agent's actual authority, see para 10.06.

perform one of his promises, e.g. give notice in a particular manner or within a certain time;[207] or where all variations must be in writing and/or signed by an authorised officer,[208] or where the consumer must send all correspondence by recorded delivery (*Bulletin No. 24*, cases 12 and 27); or requiring a consumer to produce his copy of a guarantee, or a defective part, before he can claim on it (*Bulletin No. 26*, pp 71 and 90).

(iii) Other, as where the consumer must first perform all his minor promises (*Bulletin No. 24*, case 20); automatic termination on the consumer's insolvency (see para 26.09).

**[11.18A] The Grey List (6).** Further to the foregoing paragraphs, the Grey List continues:

(*o*) *Unequal obligations.* These are terms 'obliging the consumer to fulfil all his obligations where the seller or supplier does not perform his', e.g. obligations to pay a service charge, but with exclusions of the service-provider's liability for interruptions of the service;[209] consumer to pay 90% of price, even where the work is not completed (*Bulletin No. 17*, case 13) or goods not delivered (*Bulletin No. 27*, p 106). See *Guidance*, Group 15.

(*p*) *Assignability.* These are terms giving the seller or supplier the possibility of transferring his rights and obligations under the contract, where this may serve to reduce the guarantees for the consumer, without the latter's agreement, e.g. where the supplier subcontracts the installation of goods; or gives a non-assignable guarantee.[210] As to non-assignability by consumers, see para 11.15A.

(*q*) *Restrictions on remedies.* These are terms 'excluding or hindering the consumer's right to take legal action or exercise any other legal remedy, particularly by requiring the consumer to take disputes exclusively to arbitration not covered by legal provisions, unduly restricting the evidence available to him or imposing on him a burden of proof which, according to the applicable law, should lie with another party to the contract'. This provision attacks a number of restrictions on the consumer's legal remedies. First, it deals with impediments of the right to sue, e.g. setting a short time limit for complaints, restricting the supplier's liability to English law,[211] preventing proceedings in

---

207 *Guidance*, Group 14(b); and *Bulletin No. 3*, para 9.7; *No. 13*, case 13; *No. 14*, case 23; *No. 15*, case 4; *No. 20*, case 9; *No. 27*, p 15; *No. 29*, p 20; [2005] *Bulletin J/M, Flogas* case. Cf. UCTA, s 13(1)(a): see para 18.16.

208 *Bulletin No. 23*, cases 6 and 24; *No. 24*, cases 6 and 27; *No. 26*, pp 43 and 74; *No. 27*, p 20; [2005] *Bulletin J/S, BP Oil*.

209 Newstead [1994] Lawyers' Europe at 4. Also restrictions on the borrower's power to pay off a loan, including clogs on the equity of redemption (see para 25.20); demands for full payment before supply (OFT, (1999) 22 *Fair Trading* 3; 1999-AR 30).

210 See OFT, *Guidance*, Group 16 (see generally, para 11.12); and *Bulletin No. 22*, case 17. Obligations cannot be assigned (see para 7.27); but rights under an instalment contract are *prima facie* assignable (see para 7.26).

211 See OFT, *Guidance*, Group 17; and *Bulletin No. 24*, cases 46 and 48; *No. 15*, case 22; *No. 27*, pp 105 and 110. Cf. UCTA, s 13(1)(b): see para 18.16. See also examination clauses (para 18.06).

consumer's local court.[212] Second, it covers exclusive jurisdiction clauses,[213] compulsory arbitration,[214] increasing his burden of proof[215] and delivery acknowledgments.[216]

The Unfair Terms Bill would allow the addition of further categories to the Grey List by statutory order (see para 11.21).

[11.19] **Enforcement of UTCC Regulations**. Following the usual English pattern, the individual consumer can plead the Regulations in an action concerning a consumer supply contract (see para 11.12); but, of course, his supplier cannot do so. Further, the court has power to evaluate the fairness of terms of its own motion.[217]

Now, there have already been pointed out (see para 3.15) the difficulties caused by consumer inertia and aversion to costs. However, this problem is reduced by the Directive, which follows the continental pattern of designating a public official as able to litigate on behalf of consumers generally. In responding to this lead, the DTI drafted the UTCC Regulations so as to confer the enforcement powers on the OFT,[218] though without any power of initiative.[219] Whilst the Directive makes provision for representative actions,[220] all reference to such actions was omitted from the 1994 version of the Regulations. However, in the 1999 Regulations by giving a subsidiary enforcement power to the 'qualifying bodies' set out in Sched 1 (as amended),[221] including the Consumers' Association (see para 3.08). To streamline the administration, the OFT has entered into concordats with these qualifying bodies (*Bulletins 12 and 13*).

The powers of the OFT and the qualifying bodies under the Regulations are as follows:

(i)    *Consider complaints.* The OFT **must** consider any complaint made to it that any contract term drawn up for general use is unfair, unless (a) the complaint appears to be frivolous or vexatious, or (b) a qualifying body has agreed to

---

212  *Bulletin No. 26*, p 89; [2005] *Bulletin J/M, GIS Windows*; [2005] *Bulletin A/J, Micro*; [2005] *Bulletin J/S, BP Oil*. See para 3.22.

213  *Bulletin No. 17*, case 19; *No. 18*, case 13; *No. 20*, case 6; *No. 21*, case 9; *No. 27*, p 30. If there is no international element in the transaction, the clause may fall within UCTA (see para 18.13); but, if it is a genuine cross-border transaction, the clause may be unfair: *Bulletin No. 5*, p 35; *No. 15*, cases 17 and 21.

214  E.g. OFT, *Bulletin No. 2*, case 24; *No. 15*, case 9; *No. 22*, case 13; *No. 24*, case 14. As to arbitration agreements, see paras 3.23–24.

215  Cf. UCTA, s 13(1)(c): see para 18.16.

216  *Bulletin No. 15*, cases 15 and 21. For delivery notes, see para 23.10; and for acceptance notes, see para 29.06.

217  See *Oceano Grupo Editorial SA v Quintero* [2002] GCCR 4451, Eu Ct. *Contra* DTI, *Consultation Paper* (July 2000), para 6.8.

218  'OFT' has been substituted for 'Director' by reason of s 2 of the EA; and see generally, para 3.03. In practice, matters are considered within the OFT by the Unfair Contract Terms Unit.

219  E.g. *Bulletin No. 20*, cases 6 and 15. The OFT believe that it must wait until a complaint is made to it: *Briefing—Unfair Standard Terms* (1995) 3. As to complaints by consumers in other Member States, see Brownsword and Howells [1995] JBL 243, at 262–3.

220  Art 7(2) refers to this power being granted to 'persons or organisations having a legitimate interest under national law . . . in protecting consumers'. See para 3.18.

221  Reg 3(1). These also include the following: the Information Commissioner (see para 3.27); the Utilities regulators (see para 3.07); the LA weights and measures authorities (see para 28.03); the Financial Services Authority (see para 3.02).

consider it.[222] The qualifying bodies would appear to have a **discretion** as to whether or not to consider complaints; but, if they so notify the OFT, they must do so (reg 11(1)). To help them consider complaints, the OFT and qualifying bodies have been given a new power to require any person, e.g. the trader, to produce copies of their standard contracts and give information about their use (reg 13). The purpose of considering **complaints** is for the OFT or qualifying body to consider whether to take injunctive action (see (iii) below).

*(ii) Obtain undertakings.* In deciding whether or not to apply for an injunction (see below) in respect of a term considered unfair, the OFT or qualifying body (regs 10(3), 11(2))

> 'may, if it considers it appropriate to do so, have regard to any undertakings given to it by or on behalf of any person as to the continued use of such a term in contracts concluded with consumers'.

'Continued use' covers the continued inclusion of the objectionable term in future contracts and also continued enforcement in existing contracts. So, ignoring any continued use of the unfair term in contracts with business consumers, the OFT or qualifying body **may** accept a suitable **undertaking**;[223] and, if a qualifying body accepts such an undertaking, it must so notify the OFT (reg 14(a)). Both the OFT and any qualifying body must give reasons for applying or not applying for an injunction (regs 10(2) and 11(2)). Undertakings are the OFT's preferred course of action, even after breach of undertaking (e.g. *Bulletin No. 24*, case 19); and sometimes the most effective course of action is to agree 'model terms' with a trade association, which will then agree to encourage their usage by its members.[224] There is now a very considerable number of informal undertakings,[225] and a few formal ones:[226] their terms are set out for the guidance of traders, trade associations and Local Authorities in the *Bulletins*.[227] However, the OFT has always made it clear that it has no power to give formal 'clearance' of replacement terms (*Bulletin No. 1*, paras 1.8–10 and 1.12–13). Nor would it wish to do so: it must and does reserve the freedom to take further action against any term shown as having been revised, in the light of complaints and experience (*Bulletin No. 5*, p 51; *No. 17*, paras 2.2 and 2.4, case 18). Nor may a business receiving OFT clearance claim OFT approval for its term (*Bulletin No. 12*, paras 1.9 and 2.2); and such a claim may amount to a misleading advertisement (see para 8.12A).

---

222 Reg 10(1). For summaries and analysis of the level and origin of complaints, see the *Bulletins*.

223 E.g. *DG v First National Bank plc* (set out at para 7.03A); undertaking given in the CA (overturned on appeal) set out in *Bulletin No. 9*, Appendix A. Sometimes the undertaking is to obey trade association terms agreed with the OFT, e.g. *Bulletin No. 20*, case 6; *No. 29*, paras 1.4–12.

224 *Bulletin No. 17*, case 18: (National Pawnbrokers' Association): *No. 26*, paras 1.6–13: (Glass and Glazing Federation); Auctioneers and Valuers: ([2005] *Bulletin J/S, Lyon*).

225 The OFT have reported over 2,000 unfair terms have been dropped/improved so far: (2000) 28 *Fair Trading* 10. The OFT may reserve their position in respect of some terms; and may allow the use of existing documentation until exhausted, but without reliance on unfair terms: see respectively *Bulletin No. 17*, cases 13, 17.

226 Under reg 13(6). E.g. *Bulletin No. 12*, Appendix C; *No. 13*, Annexes; *No. 15*, para 1.7; *No. 21*, Annexe; *No. 23*, case 18 and Annexe C; *No. 29*, paras 1.4–9; [2005] *Bulletin A/J, Micro*. See AR-2004/5 37.

227 *Bulletins No. 5*, p 13; *No. 6*, paras 1.16–18; *No. 7*, para 1.11. For accounts of the OFT process, see *Bulletin No. 4*, p 20, *et seq.*; 1999 AR, 31; AR-2003/4, 30.

*(iii) Seek injunctions.* There may be sought an injunction under the UTCCR (see para 11.20) or an Enforcement Order.[228]

Besides the above powers, the OFT may arrange for the dissemination of information and advice to the public concerning the operation of these Regulations (reg 15(3)). The OFT attach considerable importance to this (*Bulletin No. 1*, paras 1.22–3): besides issuing **guidance** for the general public and answering **enquiries**, the OFT **negotiates** extensively with traders to 'improve' their contracts[223] and with trade associations over the production of model terms.[227] Additionally, the 1999 Regulations require the OFT to arrange for publication of all undertakings given to him or a qualifying body, or to the court in injunction proceedings (reg 15(1)); and he must inform any person upon request whether any particular term has been the subject of an undertaking or court order (reg 15(2).

The Unfair Terms Bill adopts all the above provisions (see para 11.21).

**[11.20]  Court action.** If judged by him to be unfair, the OFT or qualifying body:[229]

> 'may apply for an injunction (including an interim injunction) against any person appearing to the OFT or that body to be using or recommending use of, an unfair term drawn up for general use in contracts concluded with consumers'.

Notice that there is no duty to apply for an injunction,[230] but that one **may** be applied for against 'any person': this will include not just the trader using the unfair clause, but also the trade organisation recommending it, e.g. in a code of practice (see paras 3.11–4). Further, the expression 'use' seems apt to extend to terms which are ineffective under the general law, e.g. penalties (see para 27.25), or unincorporated in the contract (see para 18.04).[231] Reasons must be given for applying, or not applying, for any such injunction (see above). The OFT consider this power to be exercisable not only where there is **actual** detriment, but also where the term has the **potential** to be unfair to consumers; but it sees this power very much as one of the last resort.[232]

Upon application by the OFT or a qualifying body (see para 11.19), the court is empowered to grant an injunction[233] on such terms as it thinks fit[234] and (reg 12(4)).

> 'An injunction may relate not only to the use of a particular contract term drawn up for general use but to any similar term, or a term having like effect, used or recommended for use by any party to the proceedings'.

---

228  See para 6.07. The list of designated enforcers may differ: for UTCCR, see above; for EO, see para 6.06A.

229  Reg 12(1); and see also reg 12(2). If the practice was sufficiently widespread in a trade, could the OFT use this as a basis for a new trade Code of Practice (see para 3.11)? Can the OFT bring proceedings without a prior complaint (see Elvin (2003) 14 KCLJ 39 at 62)?

230  The OFT could just ask for another undertaking: OFT, *Bulletin No. 19*, No. 17; and see para 11.19.

231  See Law Commission, *Unfair Terms in Contracts* (2002, Law Com Consultation Paper No. 166), para 3.122.

232  *Guidance*, Group 13; and *Bulletin No. 3*, para 8.2; *No. 17*, cases 12 and 13; *No. 19* case 13; *No. 27*, pp 15 and 33; *No. 29*, p 12. Cf. *Lowe v Lombank Ltd* (set out at para 18.06).

233  The first High Court action was the *First National Bank case* (set out at para 11.14), which was unsuccessful. For injunctions, see generally, para 29.39. Cf. Pt 8 of the EA: see para 6.06.

234  Reg 8(5); e.g. *Bulletin No. 15*, case 13. As to possible difficulties with the jurisdiction of the court, see Brownsword and Howells [1995] JBL 243, at 261–2.

Whilst the injunction need not be confined to the precise formula of words used by the supplier, it can only be granted against 'any party to the proceedings', so, the injunction can have no effect against any third party using similar provisions in his contract. Further, the OFT takes the view that it is not intended that the OFT should litigate for the purpose of obtaining a direct civil law remedy for a particular aggrieved consumer, but rather that action will only be taken in the more general interests of consumers and competitors.[235] This presumably means that, when seeking an injunction, the OFT will not also claim damages on behalf of the aggrieved consumer. But could the consumer intervene in the proceedings himself to request damages?

**[11.21] Reform (1): The draft Unfair Terms Bill.** The Government were troubled by the obvious difficulties arising from the fact that the UTCC Regulations embodying the UTCC Directive (see para 11.12) overlapped to such an extent with the home-grown Unfair Contract Terms Act 1977 (see para 18.12). Accordingly, in January 2001 the DTI referred to the Law Commission the following issues:[236] (a) replacing them with a 'unified regime'; (b) extending the scope of the Regulations to protect small businesses; and (c) making any replacement legislation clearer and more accessible to readers. In its first attempt to comply with the above DTI reference, unfortunately the Law Commission proposed that the two legislative streams be weaved together in a proposed new Unfair Terms Bill.[237] However, as the Regulations are based on a Directive and the UK are committed by the ECA not to contradict EU Directives (see para 1.03A), the Regulations cannot be so dismissed. In February 2005, the Law Commission attempted to meet this difficulty in their Final Report,[238] which includes a complete draft Bill (Appendix A). This draft Bill would bring together in one place the statutory control of both express and implied terms (see para 11.07, *et seq.*) and make sweeping changes to UCTA (see para 18.27). The changes proposed to the UTCC Regulations are as follows:[239]

(1) *Unified legislation.* There should be a single piece of legislation for the whole UK (para 3.9), embodying the UTCC Regulations, UCTA and the Sale and Supply of Goods Regulations 2002 (see para 14.01), but not other statutory or common law rules applying to unfair terms in consumer contracts (para 3.18).

(2) *Definition of consumer.* The definition of consumer should be broadly limited to natural persons (para 3.24) who are private consumers (para 3.22) within the UTCCR rules and *pro tanto* rejecting the UCTA concept of dealing as consumer (see para 18.19).

(3) *Maintained consumer protection.* There should be no significant reduction in consumer protection (para 3.13),[240] subject to the following exceptions:

---

235 DTI, *Guidance Notes*, para 9.2.

236 See *Unfair Terms in Contracts* (2002, Law Com Consultation Paper No. 166), para 1.1.

237 *Unfair Terms in Contracts* (2002). For review of this Consultation Paper and of the proposed Bill, see Macdonald (2004) 67 MLR 69.3.

238 *Unfair Terms in Contracts* (2005, Law Com No. 292).

239 See Pt 3: 'A Unified Regime for Consumer Contracts'.

240 The present UTCCR exemption of matters required by enactment, rule of law, international convention or competent authority should be retained (para 3.72).

(i)   The UCTA test of 'reasonableness' and the UTCCR test of fairness should
      be combined so contractual clauses must be *both* 'fair and reasonable'
      (para 3.90); this should be tested at the time of contracting taking into
      account (paras 3.96 and 3.101–2) matters of substance, procedure and
      transparency (para 3.159). See further (4), below.

(ii)  The burden of proof should lie on the business supplier as against the
      consumer (para 3.130), but not as against an Authorised Body taking
      preventative proceedings (para 3.163).

(iii) The effect of a clause being found to breach the rules should be much as in
      reg 8 of the UTCCR (paras 3.138 and 3.140: see para 11.15C).

(iv)  Noting that both the UTCCR and the Enterprise Act 2002 (see paras 6.06–8)
      contain powers enabling authorised bodies to bring proceedings in respect
      of breaches of the UTCCR, the UTCCR provisions should be retained[241]
      and extended to: (a) terms which have never been incorporated in the
      consumer's contract;[242] and (b) the UCTA-derived provisions (para 3.153).

(v)   The UCTA rules concerning consumer indemnities and product liability
      (ss 4 and 5: see paras 18.25–6) should not be replicated because they are
      unnecessary (paras 3.164–5).

(4) *Increasing the ambit of UTCCR*. The source of the Regulations is a minimum
Directive (see para 11.12), which in theory means that there is nothing to
stop the UK conferring extra benefits on consumers (see para 3.10). The Law
Commission has sought to take advantage of this in the following respects:[243]

(i)   The business supplier to a consumer should include the activities of
      government departments, or local or public authorities (para 3.34).

(ii)  Where a consumer obtains goods partly for business and partly for private
      purposes, in such a 'mixed purpose' transaction it should be left to the
      courts to determine the predominant purpose (para 3.38).

(iii) With the exception of core terms (see below), the new rules should apply
      whether or not a term is individually negotiated,[244] a proposal which is
      claimed to be likely to have little effect (para 3.53).

(iv)  The core terms exclusion from the UTCCR (see para 11.14) should be
      re-defined (paras 3.65 and 3.66), claiming that the Directive permitted this
      (para 3.57).

(v)   The rules should also apply where the consumer is the seller or supplier
      (paras 3.76 and 6.19), e.g. part-exchange goods.

---

241 Para 3.149: this was so that the injured consumer would have a right to require the authorised
body to act (para 3.147(3)); but they are not needed with regard to omissions (para 3.161). The
detailed enforcement powers recommended are set out at para 3.151; and they are contained in
Sched 1 of the draft Bill.

242 Para 3.155: these are terms which fail to be incorporated in the contract under the common law,
or mere non-contractual notices (see para 18.04).

243 This could be confounded were the EU to revise the Directive as a maximum Directive: see
para 11.22. As to gratuitous supply, see para 3.40.

244 Para 3.55. It recommended that the authorised bodies' injunction powers extend to other types
of term which suppliers usually include in that sort of contract (para 3.157).

(vi) The UTCCR test of fairness (see para 11.15) should be widened by deletion of the requirement of good faith (para 3.91), but fleshed out in the body of the Bill by rules as to transparency (para 3.102) and *contra proferentem* (para 3.107), together with 'substantive guidelines' (para 3.105) termed a non-exclusive Indicative List (para 3.109).[245] The List should be expandable by statutory order (para 3.112) and supported by a Grey List (see below).

(vii) The UTCCR Grey List (see para 11.16, *et seq.*) should also be capable of expansion by statutory order (para 3.112); it should be reformulated in language more likely to be understood by UK consumers (para 3.116); and include examples in the Explanatory Notes accompanying the Bill (paras 2.53 and 3.119).[246]

**[11.22] Reform (2): EU Directive**. Besides the suggestions already noted, the DTI have canvassed a number of other suggested changes to the Regulations.[247] These relate to problems encountered with the judicial system which the European Commission believes may thwart the goal of the Directive.[248]

1. *Paucity of sanctions*. The Commission argues that the existing sanctions leave business virtually free to trade with unfair terms until injuncted; and that what is needed are strengthened sanctions, e.g. punitive damages or fines (Chap 6).

2. *Slowness of judicial process*. The Commission's desire for an accelerated procedure (para 7.3) would seem to be satisfied in the UK by Enforcement Orders (see para 28.04).

3. *Injunctions bind only the parties*, not other traders using identical terms. The Commission suggests a new special procedure to apply injunctions industry-wide (para 7.6). Yet a third party may already be guilty of contempt of court where, having notice of an injunction, he acts so as to diminish its effect.[249]

In 2004, the European Commission announced that it planned to review eight directives, including the UTCC Directive;[250] and this may have repercussions on the proposed Unfair Terms Bill (see para 11.21).

---

245 This Indicative List is largely built on s 11 and Sched 2 of UCTA (see para 18.21).
246 But the exceptions from the Grey List, e.g. financial services contracts, should continue, but be reformulated (para 3.123).
247 *Consultation Paper on the UTCC Directive* (July 2000).
248 Para 2.10. The goal is to be seen in the Recitals to the Directive.
249 Elvin (2003) 14 KCLJ 39 at 61.
250 COM (2004) 651 final on 11 October 2004.

# CHAPTER 12

# UNDERTAKINGS AS TO TITLE

**[12.01] Introduction.** Section 12 of the SGA 1893 provided for an implied condition as to the seller's title to the goods sold, and two implied warranties by him of quiet possession and freedom from encumbrances. It seems probable that these three implied undertakings were largely declaratory of the common law;[1] and, subsequently, the courts implied similar undertakings in hp agreements. To do so, they rejected the (now abolished) common law rule of bailment that a bailee was estopped from denying his bailor's title,[2] and introduced a presumption to the opposite effect.[3]

In modern times, these three undertakings have been re-enacted for sales in s 12 of the SGA 1979, for quasi-sales (see para 2.10) in s 2 of the SGSA and for hp[4] in s 8 of SOGIT (as amended). A necessarily different version for simple hiring agreements has been embodied in s 7 of the SGSA (see para 12.01A). In 1973, a further statutory refinement was introduced by SOGIT to limit the supplier's power to exclude the undertakings as to title; and this has made it necessary to distinguish those contracts where there is no attempt to limit the supplier's statutory obligations to transfer title (clean contracts: see para 12.02) from those which contain such an exclusion clause (see para 12.17). The Sale and Supply of Goods Act 1994 rechristens each of the undertakings in s 12 of the SGA 'terms' and then provides[5]

> 'As regards England and Wales and Northern Ireland, the term implied by subsection (1) above is a condition and the terms implied by subsections (2), (4) and (5) above are warranties'.

Similar amendments have been made for hp,[6] but not quasi-sales.[7]

This is the first time there has been encountered the difficulty that the statutory terms implied in favour of the transferee as to title, identification, quality and fitness, and sample (see generally, para 11.11) are to be found in different statutes according to the legal nature of the supply contract. So, to apply these statutory implied terms, the type of supply contract must first be identified: if it is a sale, these implied terms must be found in the SGA; if it is hp, they must be found in SOGIT; and if it is a quasi-sale or simple hiring, they must be found in the appropriate part of the SGSA. Remember, it is now possible to obtain Enforcement Orders in respect of breaches of these terms (see para 28.04); that these implied terms cannot be unfair (see para 11.12A); and that there may be overlapping criminal provisions.[8]

---

1   S 12 largely followed s 7 of the Conveyancing Act 1881. For conditions and warranties generally, see para 11.04; and for implied terms, see generally, para 11.10.
2   Abolished by the Torts Act 1977, s 8: see para 19.06.
3   *Karflex Ltd v Poole* (see para 12.17).      4   For a statutory definition of hp, see para 1.24.
5   S 12(5A) of the SGA 1979 (as inserted by SSGA 1994, Sched 2, para 5(3))).
6   See SSGA 1994, Sched 2, para 4(1).
7   *Sed quaere?*
8   See TDA, s 2 (see para 4.06); and the UCP Directive (see para 4.20, item (e)).

**[12.01A] Contracts of simple hiring**. In 1973, Parliament imported into hp agreements by SOGIT implied undertakings closely modelled on those in sales,[9] as for example in the undertakings as to title (see para 12.01). The next step was taken in 1982, when Pt 1 of the SGSA attempted to import into simple hirings undertakings as closely modelled on sale as the circumstances permitted:[10] with regard to the undertakings as to description, quality and fitness, the similarity is very great;[11] and such undertakings are considered together with those of sale in Chaps 13–15. However, the undertakings as to title are necessarily different (see para 12.03A).

The ambit of the statutory implied terms in hirings is fixed by amended s 6(1) of the SGSA, which provides that:[12]

> 'In this Act a 'contract for the hire of goods' means a contract under which one person bails or agrees to bail goods[13] to another by way of hire, other than an [hp agreement]'.

The essence of this category is a bailment for value, which will include some of the common law transactions termed here simple hirings (see para 1.18) and all regulated consumer hire agreements (see para 1.19). As with quasi-sales,[14] the category 'contract for the hiring of goods' includes (by reason of s 6(3), as amended)[12] both transactions under which services are also supplied[15] and whatever the nature of the consideration.[16] But this time, hp agreements are excluded by s 6(2).[12]

# CLEAN CONTRACTS

## Implied conditions as to title

**[12.02] The rule**. Where there is a sale of goods, the amended s 12(1) of the SGA provides that, unless a contrary intention appears,[17] there is:

> 'An implied **term** on the part of the seller that in the case of a sale he has a right to sell the goods, and that in the case of an agreement to sell he will have a right to sell the goods at the time when the property is to pass'.

This implied term is designated as a condition (SGA, new s 12(5A): see para 12.01).

---

9   This gave effect to the proposals of the Law Commission: see its *First Report on Exemption Clauses* (1969, Law Com No. 24).
10   This gives effect to Law Com No. 95: see para 15.02. See generally Palmer [1983] 3 LMCLQ 377.
11   But do ss 6–10 extend to replacement parts added to leased chattels by the lessor under a repair obligation?
12   Amended by 2005 SI 871, reg 5(b).
13   S 18 defines 'goods' in terms identical to those employed in the SGA: as to which, see para 2.01.
14   See para 2.10. Does the present category extend to sales whilst there is a reservation of property, e.g. conditional sale, sale or return.
15   Does this category include use of a washing machine at a launderette? For terms imported by the SGSA as regards the service element, see para 15.15.
16   For examples, see Woodroffe, *Goods and Services—The New Law*, para 5.05.
17   S 12(3), emphasis supplied. As to where there is a contrary intention, see para 12.17, *et seq*.

In respect of quasi-sales, there is an almost identical provision, except that the supplier is there described as the 'transferor'[18] and his duty is to have 'the right to transfer the property'.[19] However, in the case of hp the supplier will, by definition (see para 1.21), never transfer his title immediately the contract is made, so s 8(1)(a) of SOGIT simply provides that there is:[20]

'an implied **term**,[21] on the part of the creditor[22] that he will have a right to sell the goods at the time when the property is to pass'.

On the other hand, SOGIT also saves the common law undertaking that the supplier is capable of conferring a good title at the time the hiring commences (see para 12.04).

Two matters must be considered: first, what right must be transferred (see para 12.03, *et seq*.); and second, the effect of a breach of this obligation (see para 12.05, *et seq*).

**[12.03] The 'right to sell'.** It is clear that, leaving aside simple hirings (see para 12.03A), the nub of the implied condition, both at common law and under the statutory formulations, is a 'right to sell' (see para 12.02). In 1895, Lord Russell CJ drew the (apparently logical) deduction that the duty was merely to pass the general property in the goods;[23] but a more extended view of the transferor's obligations has since been taken by the Court of Appeal. In *Niblett v Confectioners' Materials Co*,[24] the facts were as follows:

The seller agreed to sell 3,000 tins of condensed milk, to be shipped from America to England. The price was paid on tender of the shipping documents; but, what those documents did not reveal was that the tins were labelled 'Nissly' brand, which was a colourable imitation of *Nestle's* trade mark, and gave the latter company the right to restrain their sale in England by injunction. The buyer therefore had to strip off the labels, and sell the tins of milk unbranded for the best price obtainable. He then sued the seller to recover the difference between the price obtained, and that which the milk would have fetched as a branded article, alleging breach of the implied undertakings of (1) the right to sell, (2) quiet enjoyment and (3) merchantable quality.

At this point, we are only interested in the right to sell (the other pleas are considered at paras 12.14 and 14.16). Upon this matter, the trial judge followed Lord Russell's view. However, his decision was unanimously reversed by the Court of Appeal and Atkin LJ commented (at 402):

---

18  'Transferor' is defined by s 18(1) and (2) of the SGSA as '(depending on the context) a person who transfers the property in the goods under the contract, or a person who agrees to do so or a person to whom the duties under the contract of either of those persons have passed [by assignment, operation of law or otherwise]'.

19  SGSA, s 2(1). For the situations where the undertaking is implied, see para 2.10.

20  As amended and set out in para 35 of Sched 4 of the CCA, emphasis supplied. Does the amended version apply even to unregulated agreements?

21  This term is designated a condition (SOGIT, new s 8(3)): see para 12.01.

22  By s 15(1) of SOGIT (as amended), 'creditor' means—'the person by whom the goods are bailed . . . under a hire-purchase agreement or the person to whom his rights and duties under the agreement have passed by assignment or operation of law'. Cf. para 5.25.

23  *Montforts v Marsden* (1895) 12 RPC 266, at 269. This could be done by a principal himself, or by an agent on his behalf (see generally, para 10.06).

24  [1921] 3 KB 387, [1921] All ER Rep 459, CA. Compare *Lloyds and Scottish Finance Ltd v Modern Cars and Caravans Ltd* (set out at para 12.14).

'The Lord Chief Justice is using the right to sell in two different senses. The right to pass the property is one thing, and no doubt the [seller] could have passed the property in the milk but for the intervention of the Nestle Company; but the existence of a title superior to that of the vendor, so that the possession of the vendee [buyer] may be disturbed is another thing . . . The owners of the patent had no right or ability to pass the property, but they had a right to disturb the possession of the [vendee/buyer] in that case'.

It would appear from this decision that 'right to sell' must be read as meaning 'power' or 'ability' to sell: as the vendors could have been prevented by injunction from selling, they had no power or ability to sell.[25]

Plainly, if the vendor does not possess the unencumbered general property in the goods and cannot pass it,[26] there is a breach of both the undertakings of a right to sell or transfer the property.[27] What if the supplier can pass a good title under one of the exceptions to the *nemo dat* rule (see Chap 21)? From the viewpoint of what the buyer obtains, it might seem that, as the buyer has lost nothing, there is likely to be no breach,[28] or an insignificant one.[29] However, it was decided in *Barber v NWS Bank Plc* that a buyer who obtained a Pt III title could still plead breach of an express condition as to title.[30]

Further, does the rule in the *Niblett* case extend to the SGSA undertaking to transfer the property in goods?[31] The position with regard to sale, quasi-sale and hp may be contrasted with that for simple hirings, where the obligation is just to transfer rightful possession (see para 12.04A).

**[12.04] The time factor**. When must the supplier have the right to sell? In *Barber v NWS Bank Plc*:[32]

CC was the hirer on hp of a Honda car owned by Mercantile. In breach of the hp agreement, CC disposed of the car, which subsequently came into the hands of NWS under a directly financed conditional sale to Barber. When Barber, some twenty months later, sought to trade-in the Honda, HPI (see para 8.36) was consulted, revealing Mercantile's title. Barber sought to rescind the conditional sale and recover all monies paid on grounds of total failure of consideration.

---

25  Does this rule extend to any common law or statutory prohibition on selling? What of sale of a book published in breach of copyright?

26  In some cases it will be possible to check whether or not any third party owns the goods or has a security interest in them: if the supplier is a natural person such interest may be registrable as a bill of sale (see para 25.26); if he is a registered company, it may be registrable under the Companies Acts (see para 25.28); and in the case of a motor vehicle a financier's interest may be registered with HPI (see para 8.36).

27  What if he can pass the general property, but subject to the special property of, e.g. a pledgee? As to the situation where title is doubtful, see Goode, *Commercial Law*, 3rd edn, 285.

28  See *per* Atkin LJ in the *Niblett* case (above), at 401; and *per* Mustill J in *The Elafi* (set out at para 20.05A) at 215; *Benjamin's Sale of Goods*, 6th edn, para 4-004. Compare Atiyah, *Sale of Goods*, 10th edn, 104–5; the Crowther Report, para 5.7.32; Goode, *ibid*, 298; Brown (1992) 108 LQR 221; and para 21.58.

29  Even in a sale to a business buyer, that would not reduce the claim to one for breach of warranty: see para 11.05.

30  See para 12.04. Is this justifiable on the grounds that the bfp can only prove title by the expense and uncertainty of litigation?

31  SGSA, s 2(1). The actual language might appear closer to *Montforts v Marsden* (above); if so, the SGSA undertaking would not be as extensive as the SGA one.

32  [1996] 1 All ER 906, CA (Macleod 15 Tr L 223 (pages transposed)). But see *Freeman v Walker* [2002] GCCR 3025, CA (which seems to have been decided *per incuriam*).

The Court of Appeal unanimously held that there was an **express** condition that NWS was the owner of the car at the time it contracted with Barber; that this condition had been broken, *prima facie* entitling Barber to rescind;[33] and that this right had not been lost by Barber's acceptance of the goods[34] or Pt III title (see para 21.58).

*Implied title terms*. In the case of a sale of goods or quasi-sale, statute provides that the crucial time is when the property in the goods is to pass.[35] However, when a similar obligation was imported by the courts into hp agreements, they rejected the existing rule as to time, and decided that the transferor must have a right to sell at the time of delivery.[36] Statute restored the test of the time when the property is to pass (see now SOGIT, s 8(1)(c)); but it also preserved the common law rule (see now SOGIT, s 15(4)). Thus, unless the hp agreement effectively ousts the common law term, the result will be that in an hp agreement the supplier must have a right to sell both at the time of delivery and when the property is to pass.[37] The position is similar with regard to contracts of hiring (SGSA, s 7(1): see para 12.03A).

**[12.04A] The right to transfer possession.** In the case of a simple hiring agreement (see para 1.18), it would be inconsistent with the nature of the transaction to introduce statutory implied terms that the bailor impliedly undertook to make an out-and-out transfer of a good title to the bailee in the manner of the undertakings in sale (see para 12.03). To the contrary, it has been necessary to modify the sale undertakings in two important respects before analogous terms could be imported into a 'contract for the hire of goods' (see para 12.01A) by s 7 of the SGSA:

(a) The undertakings had to be limited to the period of the hiring contract; and

(b) There had to be an express saving of the contractual right of the bailor to repossess the goods under the express or implied terms of the hiring contract.[38]

Subject to this, s 7 of the SGSA follows the model of sale and imports into contracts for the hiring of goods undertakings as follows, though allowing their reasonable exclusion (see para 18.19):

1.   *Implied condition as to title*. Section 7(1) provides that:

---

33   NWS paid out to Mercantile at some unspecified time. If this had been before Barber rescinded, Barber should have thereby lost his right to rescind by the feeding of title to him: see *Butterworth's* case (set out at para 12.06).

34   It would appear that a *prima facie* right to rescind for breach of s 12(1) is not lost by acceptance of the goods (s 11(4)): see para 12.06A.

35   SGA, s 12(1); SGSA, s 2(1): see para 12.02. However, in practice this rule may be displaced in effect where the supplier can subsequently make good the defect, as by cure (see para 29.03), or where the title is fed (see para 12.06).

36   *Mercantile Union Guarantee Corporation Ltd v Wheatley* [1938] 1 KB 490.

37   If the impediment to title arises only after the passing of property, there will be no breach of the implied condition, but there may be a breach of the implied warranty of quiet possession: see *Microbeads A G v Vinhurst Road Markings Ltd* (set out at para 12.16). But there will be no breach of the warranty of freedom from encumbrances: see para 12.13, *et seq*.

38   S 7(3). For contractual termination of the bailment, see para 26.09; and for actions to repossess the goods bailed, see para 24.25. What if such repossession breached the CCA provisions (see para 24.27)?

'In a contract for the hire of goods there is an implied condition[39] on the part of the bailor that in the case of a bailment he has the right to transfer possession of the goods by way of hire for the period of the bailment and that in the case of an agreement to bail he will have such a right at the time of the bailment'.

Just as in relation to sales, there is a distinction drawn on the basis of when the transaction is executed: if there is to be an immediate transfer of possession, the undertaking is to be tested at once; whereas, if there is only an agreement to bail goods in the future, it is tested when possession is transferred.[40] However, it will be noted that, whereas in the case of sales the implied condition is of a 'right to sell' (see para 12.03), here it is only a 'right to transfer possession'. It has been suggested that the rule in *Rowland v Divall* (set out at para 12.05) is here inapplicable,[41] from which it would follow that a hirer who has to relinquish possession to a third party with a better title has to bring into account the use obtained with regard to both the claims for rescission and damages.[42]

2.  *Implied warranties as to title* (see para 12.13).


## Breach of the undertaking

Where the supplier is in breach of the undertaking/condition that he has the right to sell the goods, the buyer or hirer *prima facie* has two courses of action open to him: he may elect either to rescind or affirm the agreement.[43]

**[12.05] Rescission.** *Prima facie*, the transferee under a contract of sale, quasi-sale or hp agreement has a right to rescind where his supplier has no 'right to sell' (see para 12.03). If the buyer or hirer takes this course, it has been said that the proper method of recovering the price is by an action in quasi-contract on the grounds of total failure of consideration (see para 29.12). Ordinarily, a party who brings such a claim will not have obtained any benefit at all; but, in the present context, it would seem that the buyer or hirer may sometimes have his cake and eat it as well. Thus, in the leading case of *Rowland v Divall*:[44]

> The plaintiff dealer bought a car from the defendant for £334, repainted it and two months later sold it to X for £400. After a further two months, it was discovered that the car had been stolen by the person who sold it to the defendant. The plaintiff refunded the £400 to X,[45] and then sought to rescind his contract with the defendant, and to recover his price (£334) on the grounds of total failure of consideration.

---

39  Compare the modern two-stage process in sale for making the terms conditions.

40  E.g. if a leasing contract is made in respect of goods not at the moment owned by the lessor, as where there is a directly financed transaction. Compare hp, where the implied term does not have this second leg: see para 12.02.

41  *Sed quaere*? See Woodroofe, *Goods and Services—The New Law*, para 5.23.

42  See the criticism by Palmer (1983) 46 MLR at 624–5.

43  These remedies are considered further in Chap 26.

44  [1923] 2 KB 500, [1923] All ER Rep 270, CA. See also *Karflex Ltd v Poole* [1933] 2 KB 251, DC. It has been argued that this rule also applies to quasi-sales: Woodroffe, *Goods and Services—The New Law*, para 3.14.

45  It has been suggested that the plaintiff could now reduce his liability to X by any increase in value attributable to the repainting under the Torts (Interference with Goods) Act 1977, s 6(3) (see para 27.30): Treitel, *Law of Contract*, 11th edn, 1053, fn 92. But are there 'proceedings for wrongful interference with goods'?

Bray J found that there had not been a total failure of consideration (see para 29.15) because the plaintiff had had the use of the car for a considerable time, so that there was a deemed acceptance (see para 29.07) and the breach of condition could only be treated as a breach of warranty. This decision was unanimously reversed by the Court of Appeal, who held that, as the buyer had not received any part of that for which he bargained, his use of the car was immaterial[46] and there had been a total failure of consideration, so that he could recover the £334 price.[47] The majority ignored the problem of whether the condition was converted into a warranty by the plaintiff's resale and delivery (see para 12.06A). On the facts of this case rough justice may have been done in favour of the plaintiff dealer.[48]

**[12.06]  The effect.** The implications of *Rowland v Divall* (see para 12.05) were spelt out in *Butterworth v Kingsway Motors Ltd*,[49] where the plaintiff was not a dealer, but a consumer.

> X let a car to Miss R under an hp agreement. Mistakenly thinking that she had a right to sell the car subject to her continuing to pay the instalments, Miss R sold the car to K before she had completed payments. K resold to H; H resold to the Kingsway Motors; and the latter resold the car to Butterworth for £1,275. After making full use of the car for eleven months, Butterworth was notified by X of his title, and immediately wrote to the Kingsway Motors claiming the return of his price. About a week later, Miss R paid the remaining instalment due to X and exercised her option to purchase, upon which X notified Butterworth that he, X, had no further interest in the car. Nevertheless, Butterworth continued his action against the Kingsway Motors; and H, K and Miss R were joined in the action. Owing to the fall in the market values, the car which Butterworth had bought for £1,275 was only worth about £800 when he repudiated, and £400 by the date of the hearing.

Pearson J held that the sale by Miss R to K was a clear breach of s 12(1), as was each succeeding sale in the chain,[50] but observed that a great deal of trouble would have been saved if Butterworth had merely bought off X, and recovered the sum from Miss R.[51] His Lordship agreed that the Kingsway Motors, H and K were reduced to claiming damages for breach of warranty, but held, on the authority of *Rowland v Divall* (set out at para 12.05), that Butterworth was entitled to rescind notwithstanding his use of the car for 11 months, because the issue of total failure of consideration (see para 29.15) was to be tested at the date Butterworth purported to rescind. Pearson J further held that, in assessing the value of what Kingsway Motors received for the purposes of mitigating their loss as against H, the material date was when Miss R exercised her option and her newly-acquired title thereupon 'fed down the line' to the Kingsway Motors (see para 12.10). Accordingly, Butterworth recovered his £1,275 from Kingsway Motors; and the latter recovered

---

46   This might have been material if he had held onto the car with knowledge of the facts, and thereby affirmed: see para 29.13.

47   A reasonable outcome as the plaintiff was a dealer buying for resale: Treitel, *ibid*, 1053–4.

48   But, in fact, the plaintiff acquired the car for £260: Atiyah, *Sale of Goods*, 10th edn, 106. Compare the reasons given in fn 47, above with those of Bridge, *Sale of Goods*, 393.

49   [1954] 2 All ER 694; [1954] 1 WLR 1286.

50   Nowadays, it would seem that Butterworth would get a good Pt III title: see para 21.59. As to whether there would nevertheless be a breach of s 12, see para 12.03.

51   As in *Whiteley Ltd v Hilt* [1928] 2 KB 808, CA. In fact, X offered to allow Butterworth to acquire for a settlement figure of £175: for settlement figures, see para 26.19A.

£475 from H.[52] Thus, Kingsway Motors, as owners, lost £400.[53] The other £475 was the amount of damages arising from the breach of warranty of title; and this was passed back up the line to Miss R, together with cumulative costs (see para 29.36). The decision has subsequently been followed in a line of cases involving defective title to goods supplied on hp,[54] but has been restricted to lack of title: once a valid option to purchase has been conferred, there is no total failure of consideration where the hirer is for some reason prevented from exercising the option,[55] or where defects make the goods virtually unusable.[56] Presumably the rule in *Rowland v Divall* has no application to simple hirings (see para 12.04A), because it is not a title-transferring transaction.[57]

**[12.06A] The right to rescind.** There is an obvious injustice (see para 12.11) in allowing the plaintiff consumers in *Butterworth* (see para 12.06) and *Barber* (see para 12) 11 and 20 months' free use of the cars respectively. Further, there is also an illogicality in applying the quasi-contractual rule in *Rowland v Divall* (see para 12.05) in the *Butterworth* and *Barber* cases to a person who bought for use rather than resale: the prime motive of a dealer-buyer is presumably resale, so that he has lost that prime objective if he cannot sell because he has no title; but a consumer-buyer presumably buys for enjoyment, which Butterworth and Barber achieved, although the court ignored this by treating **enjoyment** as confined to **lawful enjoyment**.[58]

Even leaving these issues aside, the immediate problem is to know why a buyer is not in these circumstances reduced to claiming damages by his acceptance of the goods. As will be seen later (see para 29.04), acceptance of goods by the buyer will usually have such a result by reason of s 11(4) of the SGA.[59] In *Rowland v Divall*, Bray J would seem to have based his decision at least in part on the application of the forerunner of s 11(4); but, in the Court of Appeal, only Atkin LJ referred to this provision, and he merely said that it had no application to breaches of the implied condition as to title, without offering any convincing reason (at 506–7).

On the other hand, it has since been accepted that, if the buyer were to take delivery with knowledge of the seller's lack of title, he would be reduced to claiming damages;[60] and in *Butterworth* none of the intermediate parties was allowed to rescind.[61] Whilst there would appear to be no logical reason why s 11(4)

---

52  The price repaid to Butterworth (£1,275) less the value of the goods when Kingsway Motors acquired title to them (£800).

53  The depreciation of the car from the moment Kingsway Motors acquired title to the judgment on grounds of *res perit domino*: as to which, see further, para 22.01.

54  E.g. *Karflex Ltd v Poole* [1933] 2 KB 251, DC; *Warman v Southern Counties Finance Corpn Ltd* (set out at para 12.07; where the point arose on a counter-claim against the hirer); *Barber v NWS Bank Plc* (set out at para 12.04: see Treitel, *Law of Contract*, 11th edn, 1054–5).

55  *Kelly v Lombard Banking* [1958] 3 All ER 713, CA: see para 29.15.

56  *Yeoman Credit Ltd v Apps* (set out at para 29.25).

57  But Atiyah seems to suggest otherwise: *Sale of Goods*, 10th edn, 106, fn 16.

58  See the cases cited by Bridge, *Sale of Goods*, 392, fn 28.

59  But not a hirer under an hp agreement. Nor would this provision have been applicable if Butterworth had been a conditional buyer within SOGIT, s 14(1) (as amended): see para 29.04.

60  See *per* Devlin J in the *Kwei Tek Chao* case, as reported in [1954] 1 All ER 779, at 788. See also the *Warman* case (para 12.07).

61  But the plaintiff in *Rowland v Divall* was an intermediate party.

should never apply to breaches of the implied condition as to title,[62] a similar view has unanimously been taken by the Court of Appeal as regards breach of an express condition as to title.[63] As s 11(4) only applies to some sales as opposed to other types of disposition (see para 29.04), this position at least has the merit of avoiding distinctions between, e.g. cash sale and hp.

**[12.07] Affirmation**. The buyer or hirer may elect, with knowledge of the breach, to affirm the agreement,[64] as occurred in *Warman v Southern Counties Finance Corpn Ltd*.[65]

> In pursuance of a directly financed hp transaction, the plaintiff agreed to hire a Hillman car from the defendants. Before payments were completed, the plaintiff received notice from the true owner, X, of his claim to the hired car. Nevertheless the plaintiff continued to pay the instalments due and eventually exercised the option to purchase on the very day that X served a writ on him claiming the return of the car. The plaintiff returned the car to X, and sued the defendants for damages for breach of the implied term as to title, claiming all the sums paid under the hp agreement, together with the cost of insurance, repairs and legal expenses.[66]

Following *Karflex Ltd v Poole* (see para 12.17), Finnemore J held that there was an express condition that the defendants were the owners of the car. He added that that condition was to be tested on delivery (see para 12.04), and that any knowledge gained by the hirer thereafter was therefore irrelevant.[67] By way of damages, the court awarded the sum claimed.[68] The defendants, however, counter-claimed for a reasonable sum for hire of the vehicle for the seven months during which the plaintiff hirer had had the use of it, and thereby raised a point which Goddard J had expressly left open in *Karflex Ltd v Poole*. The counter-claim was rejected by Finnemore J, who said:[69]

> 'If [the plaintiff] wanted to make an agreement merely to hire a car he would make it, but he enters into a hire purchase agreement because he wants to have the right to purchase the car; that is the whole basis of the agreement . . . I should have thought that, even on broad principle, if the defendants break their contract or are unable to carry it out they are not entitled to claim on a sort of *quantum meruit*'.

Actually, the loss in this case did not fall on the defendant finance company, because the company brought in the dealer as third party, pleading breach of warranty of title; and Finnemore J held that the dealer must indemnify the company for all loss arising from the breach.[70]

---

62  See Atiyah, *Sale of Goods*, 10th edn, 110; Samek (1960) 33 ALJ 392; Bridge, *Sale of Goods* 393.

63  *Barber v NWS Bank plc* (set out at para 12.04).

64  As to whether it is more advantageous to rescind and reclaim the price (see para 12.05), a claim in debt, or to affirm and claim damages, see Treitel, *Law of Contract*, 11th edn, 1056–7; and generally, para 27.15A.

65  [1949] 2 KB 576, [1949] 1 All ER 711. See also *Bowmaker (Commercial) Ltd v Day* [1965] 2 All ER 856; *Rubicon Computer Systems Ltd v United Paints Ltd* [2000] CLY 899, CA.

66  The action for damages is further considered at para 29.27.

67  The answer might have been different if the plaintiff had made the agreement with knowledge of the defect in the defendants' title.

68  Criticised by Bridge, *Sale of Goods*, 394; Treitel, *ibid*, 1057.

69  At 582. The language reported in the All ER is slightly different (at 714a–b).

70  For such recourse provisions, see further, para 16.22.

## The effect of the undertaking

**[12.08]** Let us take a typical example, where the goods are stolen from O by a thief (X), who sells and delivers them to A, who resells and delivers them to B, who resells and delivers to C, who resells or lets on hp to D:

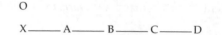

O

X———— A———— B———— C———— D

In the normal case, there will be at least three innocent parties involved in breach of the undertaking as to title; namely, the original owner (O), the intermediate buyer (A) and the ultimate buyer or hirer (D). Besides the complication necessarily arising from the number of parties involved, certain other factors must be borne in mind. *First*, the value of the goods may rise, fall or fluctuate as they pass down the chain; and there must be brought into account any improvements to the goods any of the parties may make.[71] *Second*, O may, though he will not necessarily, sue any or all of the parties in the chain in conversion because any of the acts of selling, buying, letting or hiring is sufficient ground for such actions.[72] *Third*, satisfaction of an action in conversion transfers the claimant's title to the defendant;[73] and, depending on the circumstances and the actions taken by the parties, the property in the goods may at the end of the day still reside in O, e.g. *Rowland v Divall* (set out at para 12.05); or it may be found in any one of the subsequent innocent parties, e.g. *Butterworth* (set out at para 12.06). *Fourth*, each of the parties back up the chain will be able to recover damages from his supplier: this will include any damages he has to pay his own buyer for breach of the undertaking as to title;[74] and any costs he has to pay his buyer, provided the sale was non-remote.[75] *Fifth*, in addition to the ordinary remedies of rescission and damages for breach, the transferee may be able to reclaim all monies paid in quasi-contract on grounds of total failure of consideration (see para 29.12); but, because the last claim can only be made where the failure of consideration is total (see para 29.15) this will **not** normally lead to his unjust enrichment, except insofar as the quasi-contractual claim is obtainable notwithstanding that the transferee has obtained a benefit (see para 12.11). *Sixth*, a party may seek a declaration as to his ownership of goods; and, from the moment of judgement that declaration will bind the parties as in *Powell v Wiltshire*.[76]

> After E apparently sold a light aircraft to a trust represented by W, a dispute arose as to its ownership. W sought a declaration of ownership (see para 29.01); but, before trial, E sold and delivered the aircraft to X, who re-sold to a bfp. Thereafter, the

---

71 Torts (Interference with Goods) Act 1977, s 6(3); Benjamin's *Sale of Goods*, 6th edn, para 4-007; and para 27.30.

72 For the statutory tort of wrongful interference with goods, see para 19.05. The effect of breach of the undertaking does not appear to be circumscribed by the doctrine of acceptance (SGA, s 35): see para 29.05.

73 Torts (Interference with Goods) Act 1977, s 5; and see para 26.17.

74 *Butterworth's* case (above), the intermediate parties; and see para 12.10.

75 Benjamin's *Sale of Goods*, 6th edn, paras 4-015/6; and para 27.41.

76 [2004] 3 All ER 235, CA.

trial judge granted W a declaration of ownership. W argued that, by reason of the declaration, under the *nemo dat principle* (see para 19.11), E had no title to pass to X or the bfp.

The Court of Appeal unanimously found for the bfp: it accepted that in principle a judgment in relation to goods could bind the parties and their privies[77] but held that it could only bind a party who acquired title after the date of judgment.[78]

In a typical case, the owner (O) will be suing in the tort of conversion (see para 19.04) any of the later parties in the chain of dispositions of the goods (A, B, C, D: see para 12.09); and we must then consider the position of both the intermediate parties (A, B, C: see para 12.10) and the ultimate buyer or hirer (D: see para 12.11).

**[12.09] The original owner (O).** Assuming that at the beginning O has the property in the goods, it may be that he will recover possession and still have the best title to the goods.[79] On the other hand, it may be that either A or B or C or D has acquired the best title either by buying off O[80] or by satisfying a judgment in conversion obtained by O (see para 26.17); and, on acquisition, such title is immediately fed down the chain to each party in succession, stopping only when and where the chain has been broken by rescission.[81] On principle, it would seem that the risk of any change in the value of the goods should be borne by the transferee in whom the title is vested.[82]

**[12.10] The innocent intermediate parties (A, B or C).** Each may complain that his seller is in breach of the undertaking as to title, and recover non-remote damages on this ground, such damages being passed back up the chain, so that the loss is suffered by the first innocent party, e.g. *Warman's* case (set out at para 12.07). Such a result follows the normal pattern of the law that the party (A), who bought from the thief (X), should be left to seek his remedy from X; but it is a little harsh when X is instead an innocent hirer under an hp agreement, e.g. Miss R in *Butterworth's* case (set out at para 12.06). Three particular problems arise with the intermediate parties:

(1) Can they be made to pay for any use of the goods which they may have had? It has been shown that at common law whoever is sued by O in conversion, the loss is passed back up the line from that person, no allowance being made for any use of the goods by the intermediate parties, e.g. *Butterworth's* case (above). However, whilst the common law has no power to apportion, the person sued in conversion can always claim a contribution from any other

---

77 'Privies' for this purpose includes persons deriving title from the person estopped (E): *per* Latham LJ at paras 14–23.

78 Under the doctrine *estoppel per rem judicatem*: see *per* Latham LJ at para 25. Distinguish issue estoppel: see para 21.09

79 E.g. *Rowland v Divall* (set out at para 12.05); *Warman's* case (set out at para 12.07).

80 E.g. *Karflex Ltd v Poole* (see para 12.17); *Butterworth's* case (set out at para 12.06).

81 E.g. *Butterworth's* case (above), sale by Kingsway Motors to B (see para 29.12); and see *Benjamin's Sale of Goods*, 6th edn, para 4-011.

82 It is on this ground that the Kingsway Motors had to bear the loss of £400 in the *Butterworth* case. On risk, see generally, Chap 22.

tortfeasor under the Civil Liability (Contribution) Act 1978:[83] whether or not they are joint tortfeasors,[84] each defendant[85] 'liable in respect of the same damage'[86] is *prima facie*[87] liable to make a contribution[88] because he has converted the goods;[89] and that contribution may reflect any use made of the goods.[90] Opinions seem to differ as to whether the parties in the chain are 'liable in respect of the same damage': where they commit the same act of conversion by selling and buying to one another, e.g. B and C, it would seem the provision can be used;[91] but where this is not the case, e.g. A and C, it has been argued that the provision is not available.[92]

(2) Can each intermediate party rescind and claim the price he has paid as on total failure of consideration? Such a possibility would seem to follow from *Rowland v Divall*[93] but gives rise to a number of legal problems. Can a contract be rescinded after resale and delivery (see para 29.06)? Is the quasi-contractual claim dependent on the ability to rescind (see para 29.13)? Must a breach of the condition as to title necessarily amount to a total failure of consideration (see para 12.11)?

(3) There may be difficulty in applying the notion of feeding title propounded in *Butterworth* (see para 12.06) where the person in the position of Miss R makes two successive dispositions to K1 and K2 and then acquires title.[94]

**[12.11] The ultimate buyer or hirer (D)**. The major problem here is whether D can be made to pay for his use of the goods. At common law, this involves the issues of his right to rescind, and the relationship of the quasi-contractual claim to rescission (see respectively, paras 29.06 and 29.13). However, sometimes such

---

83  Following the recommendations of the Law Commission, *Report on Contribution* (1977, Law Com. 79), the 1978 Act replaced the contribution rules previously found in the Law Reform (Married Women and Tortfeasors) Act 1935, s 6. The 1978 Act is wider than s 6 in that it is not restricted to the situation where both parties are joint tortfeasors (e.g. see para 17.04); but the 1978 Act does not seek to deal with the apportionment rules on contributory negligence (as to which, see para 27.40).

84  This will depend on whether they committed the same or different acts of conversion. For separate acts of negligence, see paras 17.15.

85  Compare the situation where the claim for 'apportionment' is between plaintiff and defendant: e.g. below, paras 12.12, 27.30 and 27.40.

86  *Royal Brompton Hospital NHS Trust v Hammond No. 3* [2002] 1 All ER (Comm) 897, HL (not a goods case).

87  Subject to any effective contractual arrangement between them for exclusion or indemnity (s 7(3)). As to where there is a contractual provision covering the risk, see *Co-Operative Retail Services Ltd v Taylor Young Partnership* [2002] 1 All ER (Comm) 918, HL (not a sale case). As to exclusion, see UCTA, ss 6(1) and 7(4): para 18.19.

88  Even after the other tortfeasor has settled: s 1(3) and see *Logan v Uttlesford DC* (1986) 136 NLJ 541, CA.

89  S 1(1): see Treitel, *Law of Contract*, 11th edn, 1056. For discussion of the 1977 Act, see generally *Street on Torts*, 10th edn, 594–601.

90  S 2. It could even amount to a complete indemnity if, say, one of the parties had enjoyed possession of the goods for virtually the whole of their useful life.

91  See Atiyah, *Sale of Goods*, 10th edn, 108.

92  Benjamin's *Sale of Goods*, 6th edn, para 4-014.

93  Set out at para 12.05. But see the *Butterworth* case (above).

94  Compare *West Ltd v McBlain* [1950] NI 144 (buyer after title fed prevailed) with *Patten v Thomas* (1965) 66 SR (NSW) 458 (first in time prevailed). The latter solution may be defeated by SGA, s 24: see para 21.38.

dilemmas can be avoided by use of the Civil Liability (Contribution) Act 1978 (see para 12.10), as in the famous problem where the goods consumed are whisky rather than a car.[95]

The ordinary rule in quasi-contract is that he who seeks the return of any benefit given, must *prima facie* restore any benefit gained (see para 29.16). In *Rowland v Divall*[96] the car had been returned to the true owner, and the defendant therefore argued that the plaintiff could not maintain his claim because he could not return the car to the defendant; but this argument was rejected by the Court of Appeal, who pointed out that the very reason for the plaintiff's inability to return the car to the defendant was that of which he was complaining, namely, the defendant's lack of title. The defendant also argued unsuccessfully that the plaintiff's use and enjoyment of the car made restitution impossible; but Atkin LJ replied (at 507):

'To my mind [the use] makes no difference at all ... The buyer has not received any part of that which he contracted to receive namely, the property and right to possession—and, that being so, there has been a total failure of consideration'.

This might be considered a reasonable argument on the facts because, although the plaintiff dealer had had four months use of the car, he had purchased for resale (see para 12.05); but it would appear unrealistic as applied to the consumer Butterworth, who thereby obtained 11 months' free use of the goods.[97] It came about because the court confined enjoyment to lawful enjoyment (see para 12.06A).

Now, it is well settled that the quasi-contractual remedy requires that the failure of consideration be total, not partial (see paras 29.15–16). Yet, despite the fact that the transferee in these circumstances will be bargaining for title **and** possession, it has been held that if he gets possession but **not** title there is a total failure of consideration, e.g. *Rowland v Divall* (above); *Butterworth* case (above). It is difficult to know how far this principle extends. *First*, does it apply to any breach of the undertaking as to title, e.g. such as occurred in the *Niblett* case, (set out at para 12.03); or merely to inability to transfer the property in the goods? *Second*, would the answer be the same if the buyer or hirer acquired a good title, but the goods were never delivered to him?[98] *Third*, suppose the transferor does not initially pass a good title, but the transferee subsequently acquires one: he may buy off the true owner;[99] or an intermediate party may do so, e.g. *Butterworth* case (above). It has been held that D could still claim total failure of consideration.[100] Would it make any difference if D did not discover the defect in title until after it

---

95 The problem was invented by Atiyah: see his *Sale of Goods*, 10th edn, 107. It has been argued that a fair result can be achieved by using the 1978 Act: Treitel, *Law of Contract*, 11th edn, 1056.

96 Set out at para 12.05. See generally Goff and Jones, *Law of Restitution*, 6th edn, paras 20.014–23.

97 Treitel, *Law of Contract*, 11th edn, 1054. *A fortiori Barber* (set out at para 12.04), who had had 20 months' free use.

98 It has been suggested that it follows from *Rowland v Divall* (above) that there will be no total failure of consideration—Atiyah, *Sale of Goods*, 3rd edn, 39 (point dropped from later editions). *Contra* Samek (1959), 33 ALJ 392, 397.

99 E.g. *Whiteley Ltd v Hilt* [1918] 2 KB 808, CA.

100 *Barber v NWS Bank Plc* (above; Pt 3 title).

had been cured by an intermediate party?[101] A Commonwealth court has held that it would then be too late to rescind.[102]

**[12.12] Reform proposals and conclusions**. Many of the difficulties outlined above flow from the disregard of substantial enjoyment of tortious possession in an action for the return of the price.[103] If the action were merely for damages for breach of the implied condition as to title, any net benefit obtained could be taken into account in assessing the overall position,[104] though that might sometimes be outweighed by expenses incurred[105] and consequential loss.[106] In 1975 the Law Commission proposed that the innocent party should be entitled to rescind and get his money back, subject to a deduction for his use and possession of the goods.[107] Certain problems were shown to arise from this approach;[108] so in 1983 the Commission canvassed opinion on the merits of restricting a claim to damages;[109] but in 1987 it concluded that it was so difficult to devise a satisfactory scheme to preclude the buyer's unjustified enrichment that matters were best left as they are.[110] This unsatisfactory result has been characterised as 'title obsession'.[111] Apparently despairing of finding a precise solution fair in all circumstances, *Atiyah* has suggested that 'the answer may well lie, not in abandoning all attempt at reform, but rather in abandoning the attempt to reform the law by working out detailed rules in advance'.[112] *Bridge* proposes that the problem may be mitigated by utilising the new right of the contract-breaker to effect a cure (see para 29.02A);[113] but unfortunately, those rules only extend to designated breaches, which category does not extend to the undertakings as to title (see para 29.02).

In view of these many difficulties, it is sometimes suggested that *Rowland v Divall* was wrongly decided (see para 12.06A): if s 12(1) were made subject to the acceptance rule (s 11(4): see para 29.04), the disappointed buyer after that acceptance would be left to rely on *Warman* (set out at para 12.07). More radically, it has been suggested that the implied condition as to title should be excised from this branch of the law.[114] A third possibility would be to allow the ultimate buyer a common law right to reclaim his price on grounds of total failure of consideration, but make this subject to the statutory contribution rules as regards his use of the goods (see para 12.11).

---

101 In the *Butterworth* case (above) Pearson J felt some difficulty on this point. Compare Samek (1959) 33 ALJ 392, 398; Treitel, *ibid*, 1056; Goode, *HP Law & Practice*, 2nd edn, 590.
102 See *Patten v Thomas Motors Pty Ltd* [1965] NSWR 1457; and Bridge, *Sale of Goods*, 397, 398.
103 *Karflex Ltd v Poole* [1933] 2 KB 251, DC: see para 12.07.
104 E.g. *Charterhouse Credit Co Ltd v Tolly* [1963] 2 QB 683, CA (hirer's net benefit valued at only £5 in view of serious defects in car).
105 E.g. *Mason v Burningham* [1949] 2 KB 545.
106 E.g. *Farnworth Finance Facilities Ltd v Attryde* [1970] 2 All ER 774, CA (inconvenience).
107 *Pecuniary Restitution on Breach of Contract* (1975, Law Com WP No. 65) para 78.
108 See Treitel, *Law of Contract*, 11th edn, 1055.
109 *Sale and Supply of Goods* (1983, Law Com WP No. 85), para 6.12. See also the further possibility canvassed in that Paper at para 6.13.
110 *Sale and Supply of Goods* (1987, Law Com. 160) para 6.5.
111 Bridge [1991] LMCLQ 52 at 66.
112 *Sale of Goods*, 10th edn, 109.
113 Bridge, *Sale of Goods*, 397.
114 Atiyah, *Sale of Goods*, 3rd edn, 40 (point dropped from later editions); Law Reform Committee, *Twelfth Report* (1966) Cmnd. 2958, para 36.

## Implied warranties as to title

**[12.13] The rules.** Where there is a clean sale of goods, amended s 12(2) of the SGA provides that, unless a contrary intention appears,[115] there are implied **terms**[116] that:

> '(a) the goods are free, and will remain free until the time when the property is to pass from any charge or encumbrance not disclosed or known to the buyer before the contract is made, and
>
> (b) the buyer will enjoy quiet possession of the goods except so far as it may be disturbed by the owner or other person entitled to the benefit of any charge of encumbrance so disclosed or known'.

These implied terms are designated as warranties.[117] In the case of quasi-sales, virtually identical undertakings are to be found in s 2(2) of the SGSA.[118] Similarly, almost identical undertakings[119] are imported into hp agreements by s 8(1)(b) of SOGIT. However, as regards contracts for the hiring of goods (see para 12.01A), s 7(2) of the SGSA provides that:

> 'In a contract for the hire of goods there is also an implied warranty that the bailee will enjoy quiet possession of the goods for the period of the bailment except so far as the possession may be disturbed by the owner or other person entitled to the benefit of any charge or encumbrance disclosed or known to the bailee before the contract is made'.

This limited implied warranty in hire is similar to that found in sales (see para 12.20); but it will be noted that there is no implied warranty of freedom from encumbrances—that is because the essence of the transaction is a transfer only of possession.[120]

It will be observed that all these implied warranties are expressed *de futuro*, from which it would follow that the limitation period does not begin to run until breach.[121] Leaving aside for the moment the precise details of the two separate warranties (see paras 12.15–16), it must first be asked to what extent the warranties overlap with the implied condition (see para 12.14), and whether they should only be warranties however serious the breach.[122]

**[12.14] Relationship of undertakings.** Not only will a breach of the implied condition as to title frequently involve a breach of one or both of these warranties,[123] but

---

115 S 12(3): as to where a contrary intention appears, see para 12.17.

116 As amended by SSGA 1994, Sched 2, para 5(3)(a).

117 SGA, new s 12(5A): see para 12.01.

118 Substituting 'transfer' for 'sale'. 'Transferor' is defined in s 18 of the SGSA: see para 12.02. Why did the 1994 Act not substitute 'term' for 'warranty'?

119 But substituting the language of bailment for that of sale. The SSGA 1994 also substituted 'term' for 'warranty' and added a new provision designating them warranties (Sched 2, para 4).

120 See the criticism by Palmer (1983) 46 MLR at 624–5.

121 See Atiyah, *Sale of Goods*, 10th edn, 112.

122 *Sale and Supply of Goods* (1983, Law Com WP No. 85), para 6.22. As to conditions and warranties generally, see para 11.04. The suggestion was not repeated by the Law Commission in their Final Report (Law Com. 160).

123 E.g. *Niblett* case (set out at para 12.03). The buyer pleaded s 12(1) and (2): only Atkin LJ referred to s 12(2) and he thought that there had also been a breach of that subsection.

it has sometimes been doubted whether the warranties cover any cases which do not also amount to breaches of the implied condition as to title. However, the usefulness of the warranties was demonstrated in *Lloyds and Scottish Finance Ltd v Modern Cars Ltd*.[124]

> In pursuance of a writ of execution, a sheriff took 'walking possession' of a caravan occupied by the judgment debtor.[125] But subsequently, the debtor sold the caravan to the defendant dealer, who removed it, and resold it to the plaintiff finance company as part of a directly financed hp transaction with W. By the dealer's invoice to the finance company, he expressly warranted that 'the goods are . . . our sole property unencumbered and that we have the right to sell such goods free from any lien'. Later, the sheriff seized the caravan, and W repudiated the hp agreement. The plaintiffs claimed damages from the defendant for breach of warranty of title.

Edmund Davies J held that the sheriff had effectively seized the caravan by taking 'walking possession'[126] of it and he concluded that (at 781):

> 'although the defendants transferred a good title in the caravan to the plaintiffs, they did so in breach of the express warranty in their dealer's invoice that it was unencumbered, and also in breach of the warranties as to quiet possession and freedom from encumbrance implied by s 12 of the [SGA]'.

He therefore held that the plaintiffs were entitled to recover the price they paid for the caravan, the hp charges that were irrecoverable from the hirer, and also the expenses to which they had been put in asserting title to the caravan.[127]

**[12.15] Freedom from encumbrances**. It would seem probable that this warranty was originally derived from land law, but differs therefrom in that it is broken by the mere existence of an encumbrance over the goods supplied.[128] However, in practice, this warranty is likely to be of limited utility to buyers because of the comparatively rare circumstances in which a third person not in possession can have an encumbrance binding on a purchaser,[129] e.g. a sheriff taking walking possession,[130] a pledgee taking a trust receipt.[131]

The implied undertaking is not absolute, but only that there are no encumbrances 'not disclosed or known' to the transferee **before** the supply contract was made:[132] it follows that, if the supplier knows of any such encumbrance, it would be prudent to disclose it—and preferably to record this fact in any written supply agreement. How specific should the disclosure be?

---

124 [1966] 1 QB 764, [1964] 2 All ER 732. It has been suggested that there was also a breach of s 12(1) in this case: *Benjamin's Sale of Goods*, 6th edn, para 4-030, fn 89.
125 For 'walking possession', see para 19.16.
126 For seizure by a sheriff in execution, see para 19.15.
127 The measure and mitigation of damages are discussed at paras 29.27 and 27.44.
128 *Benjamin's Sale of Goods*, 6th edn, para 4-023.
129 Atiyah, *Sale of Goods*, 10th edn, 112. But a third party in possession may have an encumbrance, e.g. the lien of a prior unpaid seller or of an unpaid warehousekeeper.
130 Cf. the *Lloyds & Scottish* case (set out at para 12.14).
131 Cf. *Mercantile Bank of India Ltd v Central Bank of India Ltd* [1938] AC 287, PC.
132 Any disclosure after the moment of contracting is mere evidence of breach.

Insofar as the supplier does not make disclosure of encumbrances unknown to the transferee,[133] the implied undertaking covers not just encumbrances existing at the time the supply contract is made, but also amounts to a promise that none will attach at any time after contract and before the property is to pass.[134] It does not apply to encumbrances arising thereafter.[135]

**[12.16] Quiet possession.** Normally, this warranty will be broken where the transferee suffers some physical interference with his possession either by his supplier,[136] e.g. a computer installer secretly fitting a 'time-lock' to ensure payment;[137] or some third party acting lawfully, as where wrongly sold goods are repossessed by a third party who has a better title,[138] or where the transferee's use and enjoyment of goods could be restricted by virtue of a right vested in a third party such as a copyright, design, patent or trade mark.[139] In *Microbeads AG v Vinhurst Road Markings Ltd:*[140]

> In spring 1970, the English buyer (VRM) bought from a Swiss seller (Microbeads) some machinery for marking white lines on roads. Unbeknown to the parties, at that time, a third party had already applied for a patent which would cover such machinery: such applications were confidential; but, when the patent specification was granted in 1972, statute back-dated the patent-holder's rights to cover the Spring sale, so that he was able to claim patent infringement against VRM.

The Court of Appeal held that the Swiss seller had unwittingly breached the undertaking as to quiet enjoyment, so establishing that the undertaking includes events occurring after the supply contract is made.[137] Two questions arise.

(1) For how long after the supply contract does the supplier's obligation last? It has been suggested that, unless and until he resold or the goods cease to exist, the transferee should be entitled to the benefit of the undertaking for the entire limitation period.[141]

(2) Is the supplier liable for all third-party interference? Clearly, the supplier is liable where a private third party is entitled to interfere under the law of the supply contract;[138] but perhaps this does not extend to private third-party rights under other systems of law.[142] Further difficulties arise where the interference is by lawful act of State.[143] What about a third party who unlawfully but

---

133 It would be unwise to rely on the knowledge of the transferee unless he signs a written acknowledgement to this effect.

134 See Yates [1973] JBL 136, at 137.

135 *Contra* quiet possession: see para 12.16.

136 *Industria Azucarera Nacional SA v CUBAZUCAR, The Playa Larga* [1982] Com LR 171 (first instance). He would also have a right of action in tort: see para 19.05.

137 *Rubicon Computer Systems Ltd v United Paints Ltd* [2000] CLY 899, CA.

138 *Mason v Burningham* [1949] 2 KB 545; *Lloyds and Scottish Finance Ltd v Modern Cars Ltd* (set out at para 12.14).

139 E.g. *Niblett* case (trade mark: set out at para 12.03); *Microbeads A G v Vinhurst Road Markings Ltd* (see below; patent).

140 [1975] 1 All ER 529, [1975] 1 WLR 218, CA.

141 Bridge, *Sale of Goods*, 407.

142 *Time-Life International (Netherlands) BV v Interstate Parcel Express Co Pty Ltd* (1976) 12 ALR 1, Aust (Aust supply contract; US copyright); and see Chandran [1999] Tr L 14.

143 See *The Playa Larga* (below); and Chandran [1999] Tr L 14.

forseeably interferes, e.g. a third-party owner defeated by one of the exceptions to the *nemo dat* rule (see Chap 21)?[144]

Once more the implied warranty is not absolute; there is no undertaking in respect of any disturbance of the transferee by 'any person entitled to the benefit of any charge or encumbrance . . . disclosed or known' **before** the contract was made (see para 12.15).

## CONTRACTS CONTAINING EXCLUSION CLAUSES

**[12.17]  The problem**. Can the implied undertakings as to title be excluded at common law? Obviously, such a result could only be achieved by an unmistakable contractual intention and even clear words to this effect may be struck out on grounds of repugnancy (see para 18.06) if a supplier also gives an express guarantee as to title. Thus, in *Karflex Ltd v Poole*[145] the courts were able to ignore such an exclusion clause on the grounds that the references in the hp agreement to 'the owner' amounted to an express term that the person named as 'the owner' was the true owner. For this reason, it is unlikely that a purported exclusion of all the undertakings as to title in an hp agreement will be effective at common law.[146]

In relation to sales, one view was that, despite the fact that the 1893 Act allowed contracting out, a contract of sale without any express or implied undertakings as to title would amount to a sale of a chance (see para 8.13A), and not to a sale of goods within the SGA on the grounds that such a sale cannot be brought within the then statutory definition of sale of goods.[147] On the other hand, it was argued that that definition (see para 1.08) did not require an absolute promise to transfer the general property in the goods, and a conditional promise to do so would be sufficient.[148] Certainly, the language of the 1893 Act would appear to favour the latter view[149] and it seems likely that the position was as follows: there was a sale within the meaning of the SGA 1893 where the seller agreed to transfer such title as he had; but not where he did not promise to transfer even such title as he had.[150] The Law Commission accepted this, but recommended that the implied condition as to title should only be excludable where it was clear that this is what was intended, and that the implied warranties as to title should never be totally excludable.[151] These recommendations have been implemented (see para 12.18) and should facilitate

---

144 *Empresa Exportadora de Azucar v IANSA, The Playa Larga* [1983] Com LR 58, CA (see Bridge, *Sale of Goods*, 408–9).

145 [1933] 2 KB 251, DC. Followed in *Warman v Southern Counties Finance Ltd* (set out at para 12.07).

146 Should the new CCA terminology of 'creditor' and 'debtor' make any difference to this argument? Cf. *Barber v NWS Bank plc* (set out at para 12.04).

147 E.g. Atiyah, *Sale of Goods*, 3rd edn, 40; Guest (1961) 77 LQR 98. Whilst these authors placed reliance on *Rowland v Divall* (set out at para 12.05), the plea was not raised therein, and it does not appear that the decision necessarily supports their conclusion.

148 E.g. Hudson (1957) 20 MLR 236 and (1961) 24 MLR 690; Samek (1959), 33 ALJ 392 and (1961) 35 ALJ 437; Reynolds (1963), 79 LQR 534; Coote, *Exception Clauses*, 61–69; Battersby and Preston (1972) 35 MLR 268 at 272–5.

149 See ss 1(2) and 5(2) and the opening words of s 12 of the 1893 Act. See also *per* Atkin LJ in *Niblett v Confectioners Materials Co* (set out at para 12.03) at 401.

150 See Thornely (1958) CLJ 123, at 125; Reynolds (1963) 79 LQR 534, 542.

151 *The First Report on Exemption Clauses in Contracts* (1969, Law Com No. 24), paras 16–18.

dealings with such as abandoned vehicles and rebuilt insurance write-offs; and presumably they would allow exclusion of such non-title breaches as found in *Niblett v Confectioners Materials Co.*[152]

Has UCTA made any difference in those circumstances where the supplier does not even promise to convey such title as he has? At first sight, this looks like a breach of UCTA's prohibition on a supplier denying title (ss 6(1) and 7(3A): see para 18.19). However, it is submitted that the reality is that the transaction is one of bailment with the appropriate *prima facie* implied terms (see para 12.04A), in which case UCTA only makes the exclusion of title subject to the reasonableness test (s 7(1) and (4)).

**[12.18] The rules**. Nowadays, the statutory provisions dealing with the undertakings as to title expressly make provision for the situation where:[153]

> 'there appears from the contract or is to be inferred from its circumstances an intention that the [supplier] should transfer only such title as he or a third person may have'.

In such cases, statute will import no implied condition as to title, but only two qualified warranties as to freedom from encumbrances and quiet possession (see paras 12.19–20). Thus, it has been clearly spelt out that a supplier may explicitly or impliedly promise to supply goods subject to all or any defects of title. It has been said that the true consideration would seem to be the assignment of the right, whatever it is, that the supplier or the third party has at the time of the supply.[154] In all such cases, the combined effect of the statutory undertakings and the prohibition on contracting out seems to be this: the supplier may contract to transfer only such title as he or a third party may have; but he may not enter into a sale, quasi-sale or hp agreement promising less than that.[155] If the supplier contracts to transfer possession only, the contract is one of simple bailment, whose statutory implied terms as to title were considered above (see para 12.13).

**[12.19] Freedom from encumbrances**. Except in the case of simple hirings, in supply contracts containing an appropriate exclusion clause (see para 12.18), there is:[156]

> 'an implied warranty that all charges and encumbrances known to the seller and not known to the buyer have been disclosed to the buyer before the contract is made'.

The concept of encumbrances has already been explained, where it was seen that the warranty was broken by the mere existence of such an encumbrance (see para 12.15). However, where the contract contains an appropriate exclusion clause, there is no such absolute promise in respect of all encumbrances not disclosed or known to the transferee: the promise is only to disclose[157] such encumbrances existing at the time of contracting which are **both** known[158] to the supplier[159] **and**

---

152  Set out at para 12.02. *Contra* Atiyah, *Sale of Goods*, 10th edn, 110.
153  SGA, s 12(3). See also SOGIT, s 8(2); and SGSA, s 2(3).
154  *Benjamin's Sale of Goods*, 6th edn, para 4-032.
155  *Contra* Yates [1973] JBL 136, 137.
156  SGA, s 12(4). See also SGSA, s 2(4); and SOGIT, s 8(2)(a).
157  How specific must disclosure be?
158  What has to be **known**: the facts or the law or both?
159  Will stupid ignorance be a sufficient defence?

not known[158] to his transferee.[160] In practice, there is thus likely to be a substantial area where, notwithstanding the existence of an encumbrance, the supplier is not in breach, and this will certainly be the case with regard to all encumbrances coming into existence after formation of the supply contract.

**[12.20] Quiet possession.** In supply contracts containing an appropriate exclusion clause (see para 12.18), there is an implied warranty that none of the following will disturb the buyer's or hirer's quiet possession of the goods; namely:[161]

'(a)  the seller;

(b)  in a case where the parties to the contract intend that the seller should transfer only such title as a third person may have, that person;

(c)  anyone claiming through or under the seller or that third person otherwise than under a charge or encumbrance disclosed or known to the buyer before the contract is made'.

The concept of quiet possession has already been explained, together with the fact that in a clean contract the warranty of quiet possession was only as against interference by encumbrancers not disclosed or known to the transferee (see para 12.16). However, where the contract contains an appropriate exclusion clause, there is no such absolute promise in respect of all encumbrancers not disclosed or known to the transferee: the warranty is only in respect of such disturbance by the supplier, or other person whose title is being transferred, or any person claiming 'through or under' either of them; and there is no undertaking that quiet possession will not be disturbed by any other person.[162]

---

160 For argument that the buyer's knowledge should be irrelevant, see *Goode, Commercial Law*, 3rd edn, 289.

161 SGA, s 12(5). See also SGSA, s 2(5); SOGIT, s 8(2)(b). There is no comparable provision for simple hiring.

162 Even where the supplier knows that such a person has a right to disturb the transferee's quiet possession?

# CHAPTER 13

# UNDERTAKINGS AS TO QUANTITY AND QUALITY

## INTRODUCTION

**[13.01]** Suppose the supplier tenders goods which do not comply with the contract description in a manner which is not *de minimis*; that is, 'microscopic deviations which businessmen and therefore lawyers will ignore'.[1] Two explanations of his conduct may be possible. *First*, his act may suggest that he has no intention of performing the existing contract, but is offering to enter into a new contract to deliver the goods tendered, this new contract to discharge the old one.[2] The supplier is then making an entirely new offer, which the offeree has complete freedom to accept or reject:[3] if he accepts it, the old contract is at an end;[2] but, if he rejects that offer, he may sue for breach of the existing contract.[4] *Second*, it may be clear that in tendering goods which do not comply with the contract description the supplier does not intend to make a new offer, but is merely trying to perform, albeit defectively, the existing supply contract. In such a case, acceptance of the goods tendered will neither create a new supply contract nor discharge the old one: it will merely limit the remedies available to the transferee for breach of contract,[4] for it will operate as an election to forego the right to repudiate so that he can thereafter only claim damages in respect of that breach (see para 29.04). Thus, in *Albright & Wilson UK Ltd v Biochem Ltd*:[5]

> A Ltd, a chemical producer, had two different plants (A & B) on the same site. A Ltd placed two orders with different suppliers as follows: (i) with Berk for 23 tons of sodium chlorate for delivery to their plant A; and (ii) with X for 23 tons of EPI for delivery to their plant B. Both sellers engaged the same delivery agent, who mixed up the two orders. As a result, 23 tons of sodium chlorate was delivered by tanker to plant B, together with a delivery order saying it was EPI from X. The tanker discharged into existing stocks of EPI, causing an explosion.

On a trial of preliminary issues, and confirming the decision of Eady J, the Court of Appeal held that the delivery was at one and the same time a purported performance of the two entirely separate contracts with Berk and X.[6] However, the House of Lords unanimously disagreed:[7] it held that, A Ltd was entitled to assume the delivery documents presented are relevant to the load to which they purported to relate (see para 23.03); so that the misdelivery objectively amounted to

---

1   *Per* Lord Atkin in *Arcos Ltd v Ronaasen Ltd* (set out at para 13.12). See further, para 13.03.

2   For discharge by subsequent agreement, see para 26.18.

3   *Hart v Miles* (1836) 15 M & W 85. At common law, it has been held that a buyer cannot exercise such an option until he knows the true facts: see para 13.05. However, by statute, he may be able to treat it as an unsolicited gift: see para 8.18.

4   For the transferee's remedies, see Chap 29.

5   [2002] 2 All ER (Com) 753, HL.

6   [2001] 2 All ER (Comm) 537, CA.

7   The CA held that the delivery firm was acting as agent for both sellers. But the HL distinguished acts of agency in (i) contract formation (see para 10.06), from (ii) agents for delivery (see para 23.03): at paras 6, 8, 14, 36 and 53.

a purported performance by Berk. It followed that Berk was in breach but X not liable. As to Berk, their Lordships confirmed the Court of Appeal as follows: in a case giving rise to potential claim in contract and tort, A Ltd may elect to sue in contract;[8] this amounted to a breach of the undertakings as to description,[9] quality and fitness, the delivery note being part of those undertakings (see para 14.02); and the contract incorporated A Ltd's terms (see para 10.06), those of X being proffered too late (see para 18.04). For criminal liability as to false descriptions, see para 4.04.

**[13.02] Quantity and Quality.** Where the supplier tenders a different **quantity** of goods from that stipulated by the contract,[10] the ordinary inference is likely to be that he is offering to enter into a new contract; whereas, if he tenders goods which only deviate from the contract description in **quality**, the inference is more likely to be that this is merely a defective performance of the existing contract. Whilst the difference between these two situations is merely one of degree, in practice it is sufficiently marked to merit separate treatment.[11]

In respect of transactions falling within the SGA, the undertaking as to descriptive quality are to be found in s 13, located within Pt II of the Act headed *'Formation of the Contract'*, whereas delivery of the wrong quantity is dealt with by s 30, located within Pt IV of the Act headed *'Performance of the Contract'*; and it was one of the oddities of the SGA 1893 and 1979 that these headings appeared to suggest exactly the opposite inference on offer and acceptance from that suggested by the facts and set out above. Under those two Acts, the only area of overlap between ss 13 and 30 was to be found in the now repealed s 30(4), which purported to deal with the situation where there was a delivery of the contract goods 'mixed with' goods of a different description.[12] Moreover, the SSGA 1994 has further lessened the gap between ss 13 and 30 by providing that in a business-to-business sale *prima facie* the buyer should not be able to reject the goods where the breach 'is so slight that it would be unreasonable for him to do so'.[13] A similar change has been made in respect of undertakings as to quality (see para 11.05). Remember, it is now possible to obtain Enforcement Orders in respect of these breaches (see para 28.04) and that these implied terms cannot be unfair (see para 11.12A).

# UNDERTAKINGS AS TO QUANTITY

**[13.03] Introduction.** Neither in relation to quasi-sales, hp nor simple hiring agreements are there any provisions dealing with delivery of the wrong quantity (see SGSA, Pt I and SOGIT respectively). However, in relation to sales, s 30 of the

---

8   See para 26.17. So the Law Reform (Contributory Negligence) Act 1945 (see para 27.39) was not applicable: CA at 13; HL at paras 3 and 19.

9   See para 13.12. There may also be hybrid terms which escape SGA, s 14 (see para 15.22).

10  Unless the excess is obviously delivered in error. As to mistake, see generally, para 10.16.

11  Is 'acceptance' in s 30 to be taken in the offer and acceptance sense (see para 10.02), or does it have the s 35 meaning (see para 29.05)? The latter view has been suggested: *Benjamin's Sale of Goods*, 6th edn, para 8-046.

12  Compare *Barker Ltd v Agius Ltd* (1927) 33 Com Cas 120 with *Re Moore Ltd* at [1921] 1 KB 73 (affd on other grounds). For an explanation of the difficulties caused by s 30(4), see Atiyah, *Sale of Goods*, 9th edn, 473–5.

13  SGA, new s 30(2A) (as inserted by SSGA 1994, s 4(2)). See further 1st edn, para 13.02.

SGA makes it clear that it is the seller's duty to deliver the exact quantity of the goods specified and, as regards breaches which are more than *de minimis*, spells out the results of his failure to do so in a manner which suggests that delivery of the wrong quantity is being treated as a new offer (see para 13.02). Insofar as this is simply a formulation of the common law rules of offer and acceptance, then it presumably applies by analogy in the case of quasi-sales, hp and simple hiring agreements; and insofar as the scheme is not all-embracing even for sales, then it may be complemented by reference to the common law.

Section 30 of the SGA thus insists on strict compliance, but subject to the following exceptions. *First*, s 30(5) lays down that:

'The provisions of this section are subject to any usage of trade, special agreement, or course of dealing between the parties'.

Whilst allowing for the importation of a special trade meaning (see para 13.11) or an agreed tolerance,[14] this provision also envisages that the parties may contract beforehand as to what is to happen if the seller is in breach of his duty under s 30.[15] *Second*, the strict duty of performance is qualified by the *de minimis* rule in a manner similar to that of s 13.[16] *Third*, it should be borne in mind that the strict rules of s 30 will not be applicable where the seller elects to treat the contract as repudiated by reason of the buyer's breach before the time for delivery arrives.[17] *Fourth*, the effect of the rules in s 30 may be varied where the contract is severable or divisible (see para 23.24-5). *Fifth*, where the wrong quantity is delivered, it may sometimes be possible to construe this as a new offer allowing the buyer to accept just part of the goods delivered.[18]

Subject to the foregoing, s 30 deals separately with the following situations: delivery of too little (see para 13.04); and delivery of too much (see para 13.05). However, in respect of some retail sales, there are also special provisions to ensure minimum quantity enforced by criminal law.[19]

**[13.04] Delivery of too little**. Section 30(1) provides that:

'where the seller delivers to the buyer a quantity of goods less than he contracted to sell, the buyer may reject them, but if the buyer accepts the goods so delivered he must pay for them at the contract rate'.

In *Behrend & Co v Produce Brokers Co*:[20]

There was a contract for the sale of 700 tons of cotton seed ex the *Port Inglis*. The ship discharged 37 tons in London, and then left for Hull in order to discharge there other goods which had been loaded on top of the remainder of the seed.

---

14   E.g. *Shipton Anderson & Co v Weil Brothers* [1912] I KB 574; *The Elafi* (see para 20.05B).

15   Such clauses are outside ss 6 and 7 of UCTA (see para 18.19) but may be within s 3 of UCTA (see para 18.24).

16   Compare *Shipton Anderson & Co v Weil Brothers* (above) with *Wilensko Slasko Towarcy Stwo Drewno v Fenwick & Co Ltd* [1938] 2 All ER 429. And see *per* Diplock LJ in *Margaronis Navigation Agency Ltd v Peabody & Co of London Ltd* [1965] 2 QB 430, CA, at 448. See further *Benjamin's Sale of Goods*, 6th edn, paras 8-050/58. Cf. TDA, s 3(1): see para 4.08.

17   *Gill & Duffus SA v Berger & Co Inc* (set out at para 23.06). As to repudiation, see para 26.15.

18   *Hart v Mills* (1846) 15 M & W 85; and Hudson (1976) 92 LQR 506.

19   E.g. Weights and Measures Acts; alcoholic beverages; food; and under the TDA: see Chap 4.

20   [1920] 3 KB 530, [1920] All ER Rep 125.

Bailhache J held that the buyer was entitled to keep the part actually delivered and pay for it at the contract rate,[21] and to reject the balance of the goods and reclaim the remainder of the price as on total failure of consideration.[22] This rule has been subject to a number of refinements. *First*, in a subsequent case, Wright J held that the buyer could not be taken to have exercised the option conferred on him by s 30 unless and until he knew the true facts.[23] *Second*, the strict duty of performance is slightly relaxed in respect of microscopic deviations under what is known as the *de minimis* principle (see paras 13.01 and 13.04). *Third*, a seller accused of short delivery cannot usually justify himself by claiming that he will deliver the remainder later, because *prima facie* the buyer is not bound to accept delivery by instalments (s 31(1): see para 23.24). However, where there is a short delivery in one instalment in an instalment contract (see para 23.24), s 30(1) is inconsistent with s 31(2): here the more flexible s 31(2) is to be preferred on the issue of repudiation[24] whilst a claim for damages may lead the buyer to accept the balance in mitigation.[25]

**[13.05/6]  Delivery of too much**. Section 30 provides that:

'(2) Where the seller delivers to the buyer a quantity of goods larger than he contracted to sell, the buyer may accept the goods delivered in the contract and reject the rest, or he may reject the whole.

(3) Where the seller delivers to the buyer a quantity of goods larger than he contracted to sell and the buyer accepts the whole of the goods so delivered, he must pay for them at the contract rate'.

Thus, if the seller sends too many goods of the contract type, this rule saves the buyer from the trouble and expense of separating the contract goods from the others, whilst allowing him to do so if he wishes.[26] Alternatively, s 30(3) allows the buyer to accept the whole and pay *pro rata*; but, presumably on the basis that this is a counter-offer, it has been argued that this is not the case where it is obvious that the seller did not mean to supply the excess.[27]

**[13.07]  Conclusion**. It has already been observed that in one sense s 30 merely deals with an aspect of the undertaking to be found in s 13. Yet there is good reason for distinguishing between the two situations. The availability of the right to reject may vary according to whether the goods tendered constitute merely a defective performance or a counter-offer: if the latter, the 'buyer' must always have a right to reject the offer; but, in the former situation, the availability of the right to reject the goods and rescind the contract may be restricted by the terms

---

21  He cannot accept only part of that which is delivered: Hudson (1976) 92 LQR 506.
22  See para 29.12. An alternative explanation is that recovery was made on the basis of money had and received.
23  *Barrow, Lane and Ballard Ltd v Phillips & Co Ltd* (set out at para 22.12). Compare rescission: para 29.06.
24  *Regent OHG Aisenstadt Und Barig v Jermyn St Ltd* [1981] 3 All ER 327: see further, para 23.25.
25  Goode, *Commercial Law*, 3rd edn, 359. See generally, para 27.44.
26  E.g. *The Elafi* (set out at para 20.05A). Even if he is not asked to pay for the excess?
27  See *Sale and Supply of Goods* (1987, Law Com 160), para 6.23. For mistake as to terms, see para 10.16.

of the contract or the general law.[28] Since 1994, matters have been further complicated by the need to distinguish according to whether or not the buyer deals as consumer:[29]

(1) *Consumer buyers.* By expressly giving the buyer a right to accept or reject the whole of the goods delivered, s 30 seems to envisage that the delivery will constitute a counter-offer. Unlike many other provisions of the SGA, the rules contained in s 30 are not expressed to give way to a contrary intention;[30] but neither is s 30 subject to the UCTA prohibition on exclusion (s 6: see para 18.19), though exclusion may be unfair.[31] Can it be inferred that breaches of s 30 will **always** constitute a counter-offer (but see below)? Or is it possible to choose instead the consumer remedies found in new Pt 5A of the SGA (see para 29.02A)?

(2) *Commercial buyers.* The buyer who does not 'deal as consumer' nowadays only retains his s 30 right to accept or reject the goods delivered where the amount delivered is more than a 'slight' deviation from the contract quantity (see para 13.02). If there is only a slight deviation, the matter is treated as a defective performance and the buyer must accept the amount delivered and claim damages (cf. para 11.05).

Despite the apparently mandatory wording of s 30(1) and (2) (see above), the SGA does contain a general rule that its provisions give way to a contrary intention,[30] which might point to the conclusion that s 30 does, after all, only embody a *prima facie* rule.

## UNDERTAKINGS AS TO DESCRIPTIVE QUALITY

**[13.08] Introduction.** In a sense, the SGA 1893 marked the beginning of the movement away from *caveat emptor*.[32] It is true that the common law had to some extent modified its attitude where this was found to be excessively inconvenient or unfair; but the SGA as subsequently amended may have taken the process somewhat further when it laid down a number of implied terms. Sections 13 and 14 of the SGA 1979 now include three major implied conditions:[33] that in all sales the goods are as described (s 13); and that in a 'trade sale'[34] they are of satisfactory (previously merchantable) quality under that description (s 14(2)); and are fit for the

---

28  For the restrictions imposed by law, see para 29.04.

29  This phrase is to be construed in accordance with Pt I of UCTA (see para 18.18): SGA, s 61(5A), inserted by Sched 2, para 5(9)(c), of the 1994 Act.

30  But could the reference in s 30(5) to 'special agreement' (see generally, para 13.03) be used to achieve such a result? Cf. the problem in SGA, ss 6 and 7, where the omission also causes uncertainty: see para 22.11.

31  *Bulletin No. 27*, p 103; and UTCCR, Sched 1(b) (see para 11.16).

32  Let the buyer beware. For the modern extent of the doctrine *caveat emptor*, see para 15.22. It does not apply where the supplier fraudulently induces the contract: *Gordon v Selico* [1986] CLY 1877, CA.

33  For conditions generally, see para 11.04; and for implied terms generally, see para 11.10.

34  Where goods are supplied in the course of a business: see para 14.04.

particular purpose for which they are supplied (s 14(3)).[35] These provisions have since been more or less consistently interpreted by the courts in favour of the buyer and are also to be found in the other supply statutes (see para 12.01). Particularly important has been the gradual extension of the scope of 'sales by description'. Today it covers most if not all contracts for the supply of goods, with the result that all three implied conditions may today apply to almost any 'trade sale' (see para 13.09), though of course the undertaking as to compliance with description alone of the three extends to private sales.[36]

## Supplies by description[37]

**[13.09] History.** The common law attempted to draw a sharp distinction between sales of specific goods and sales by description, and this dichotomy was adopted by Chalmers when he drafted the SGA 1893.[38] At its simplest, the dichotomy depended on the idea that a buyer would know the subject-matter of his contract either by acquaintance or by description. However, perhaps because there are many cases which do not fall neatly into one or other of the two categories, the ambit of each of them was never clearly defined. The two categories were these:[39]

(1) Sales 'of unascertained or future goods, as being of a certain kind or class, or to which otherwise a "description" is applied'. Here, it is essential that the contract is by description, for in no other way can the parties achieve certainty of subject-matter.[40]

(2) Sales 'of specific goods, bought by the buyer in reliance, at least in some part, upon the description given or to be tacitly inferred from the circumstances, and which identifies the goods'. The law had already recognised that sales by sample fitted within this category (see para 15.03).

Category (2) does not fit easily into any simple dichotomy of goods known **either** by acquaintance **or** by description; and it has been within this category that the crucial developments have taken place. The first step was to interpret the concept of sales by description to cover all sales of specific goods where the buyer had not seen the goods either before or at the time of contracting, but was relying on the description alone.[41] Then, the concept was extended to cover those situations where

---

35   For the basic undertaking as to description, see para 13.11; but for the undertaking in respect of goods supplied as in accordance with both description and sample, see para 15.06. The undertakings as to fitness and suitability will be considered in Chap 14, but for samples, see also, para 15.10.

36   E.g. *Varley v Whipp* (set out at para 13.14). *Contra* the undertakings as to fitness and quality: see above.

37   See generally, Montrose (1937) 15 Can BR 760; Stoljar (1952) 15 MLR 425, at 441–445; and (1953) 16 MLR 174; Feltham [1969] JBL 16.

38   In respect of sales by description, Chalmers also separated the common law undertaking into two separate statutory terms: (1) the goods must comply with their description; and (2) they must be merchantable under it. For the two modern implied terms, see respectively, paras 13.11 and 14.15.

39   *Benjamin on Sale*, 8th edn, 1950, 615. This dichotomy was approved in *Harlingdon & Leinster Enterprises Ltd v Christopher Hull Fine Arts Ltd* (set out at para 13.11).

40   See *per* Channell J in *Varley v Whipp* (set out at para 13.14), at 516.

41   *Varley v Whipp* (above). See Goode, *Commercial Law*, 3rd edn, 292.

the buyer was contracting in the presence of goods which he had no opportunity to inspect before purchase, such as beer bought in a public house.[42] From this point, it broadened to cover virtually all retail sales (see para 13.10). However, the fact that a sale of specific goods **may** be a sale by description does not prove that it **must** be so (see para 13.11).

**[13.10] Retail sales.** With the gradual erosion of the restrictions on the concept of sales by description (see para 13.09), the courts soon became indifferent as to whether or not the parties were negotiating in the presence of the goods. Thus, in *Grant v Australian Knitting Mills Ltd* Lord Wright said:[43]

> 'It may also be pointed out that there is a sale by description even though the buyer is buying something displayed before him on the counter: a thing is sold by description, though it is specific, so long as it is sold not merely as the specific thing but as a thing corresponding to a description, e.g. woollen undergarments, a hot-water bottle, a second-hand reaping machine, to select a few obvious illustrations'.

In that case, the Privy Council decided that a retail sale of undergarments conducted across a shop-counter was a sale by description.[44] A striking case is *Beale v Taylor*:[45]

> The seller advertised a 1961 Herald car for sale. The buyer inspected the car and agreed to buy it, but subsequently discovered something the seller had never realised all the time he had owned the car: that the rear half of the car was a 1961 Herald but the front half was part of an earlier model, the two halves having been welded together.

The buyer succeeded before the Court of Appeal in his claim for damages for breach of the implied condition that the goods correspond with their description (see para 13.11). In delivering the judgment of the Court, Sellers LJ said that, even if there were no other terms as to the state of the goods, fundamentally the seller was selling a 1961 Herald car. However, his Lordship did adopt one limitation to be found in Chalmers,[46] namely that the rule be confined to non-apparent defects (see para 13.11).

Today, the position would appear to be that almost every sale, whether of specific or unascertained goods, can be a sale by description, e.g. oven-proof glaze on china; and the concept is particularly likely to be useful where contracts are concluded at a distance, e.g. mail order and internet purchase (see para 8.19). Even if the seller does not himself describe the goods to the buyer, either orally or in writing, it may be that any label attached to the goods may form part of the description and that the physical shape of the goods may itself amount to a description.[47] Just to clarify matters, statute now provides that the supply or hiring may be

---

42  *Wren v Holt* [1903] I KB 610, CA. See also *Thornett v Beers* [1919] I KB 486 (buyer declined invitation to inspect contents).

43  [1936] AC 85, at 1001, PC.

44  In *Godley v Perry* [1960] 1 All ER 36, Edmund Davies J accepted that a retail sale of a plastic catapult by a newsagent to a six-year-old boy was a sale by description.

45  [1967] 3 All ER 253, [1967] 1 WLR 1193, CA.

46  *Sale of Goods*, 15th edn, 1967, 57; but cf. the 18th edn, 120. See further, para 13.11, fifth point.

47  E.g. the rear of the car in *Beale v Taylor* bore the inscription '1200'; but compare the monogrammed painting in the *Harlingdon* case (see para 13.11). See also Diamond (1960), 23 MLR 200; Feltham [1969] JBL 16, at 21.

by description, notwithstanding that the goods are selected by the buyer or bailee (SGA, s 13(3); SGSA, ss 3(3) and 8(4); SOGIT, s 9(2)): this will cover retail outlets using the self-service system[48] and auctions.[49]

## Undertakings as to the description

**[13.11] The undertakings**. The new s 13(1) of the SGA lays down that:[50]

'Where there is a contract for the sale of goods by description, there is an implied term that the goods will correspond with the description'.

In English law, this implied term is a condition.[51] A virtually identical undertaking is implied into quasi-sales, except that the supplier is there described as the 'transferor'.[52] Similarly, where goods are bailed by description, there is an implied condition that the goods will correspond with their description, whether the contract be one of simple bailment[53] or hp.[54]

Several points may be made at the outset. *First*, the nature of the supply contract must be identified in order to apply the appropriate statutory implied term (see para 12.01). *Second*, it is rather misleading of the Act to speak of **implying** such conditions when the condition will often be an express term of the contract,[55] e.g. as to a motor vehicle, the model, its mileage (odometer), previous ownership or use. *Third*, whilst it is not possible to challenge the unfairness of the statutory implied term itself,[56] there are limitations on the supplier's ability to exclude or restrict this undertaking (see para 13.16), though it is questionable whether these limitations extend to certificates of compliance.[57] *Fourth*, unlike the major conditions as to the state of the goods (see para 14.04), the undertaking as to correspondence with description is implied whether or not the supplier is a dealer; but, like those conditions, a business transferee will only be able to treat a 'slight breach' as a breach of warranty (see para 11.05A). *Fifth*, if the description has a special trade usage, the goods may have to comply with that specialised meaning, rather than the ordinary one, but only if it is possible to spell out an agreement by the parties to the term

---

48  As to the manner in which the contract is made in a self-service store, see Treitel, *Law of Contract*, 11th edn, 12–13; and generally, para 10.02.

49  This brings in any catalogue description: Harvey and Meisel, *Auctions*, 2nd edn, 162. As to the manner in which the contract is made by auction, see para 10.10.

50  As amended by the SSGA 1994, Sched 2, para 5(4)(a). See generally, para 11.11. For EU changes, see para 14.01.

51  New SGA, s 13(1A): see SSGA 1994, Sched 2, para 5(4)(b).

52  SGSA, s 3(1) For 'transferor', see para 12.02. The SSGA does not amend the status of the term as in the SGA.

53  SGSA, ss 8(1) and (2). See *Woodroffe, Goods and Services—The New Law*, para 5.15. The SSGA does not amend the status of the term as in the SGSA.

54  SOGIT, s 9(1), as amended: see para 12.02. The SSGA here amends the status of the implied term as in the SGA: see SSGA, Sched 2, para 4(3).

55  E.g. goods counterfeiting (see paras 4.06 and 8.05); *Wallis, Son & Wells v Pratt and Haynes* (set out at para 11.04); *Andrew Brothers, Ltd v Singer Ltd* [1934] 1 KB 17, CA. Compare the *First Report on Exemption Clauses* (1969, Law Com No. 24), paras 21–2.

56  UTCC Regulations, Sched 1, para (e)(i): see para 11.12.

57  E.g. *Toepfer v Continental Grain Co* [1974] I Lloyd's Rep 11. See generally, para 14.02.

being used in the sense ascribed to it by the trade usage,[58] as perhaps where it is a requirement of the criminal law that the goods are of a certain description (see para 4.23, *et seq*). However, particularly if the trade usage was not known to one of the parties, it may be that there is no contract because the parties were never *ad idem* as to the description of the goods;[59] or that they are actually using the description in a general sense.[60] *Sixth*, in a sample contract (see para 15.04), the goods also have to comply with the sample (see para 15.06). *Seventh*, notwithstanding that a description has been used, it is another question whether the contract is **by** description (see para 13.11A) or sample (see para 15.04). *Eighth*, for consumer sales (see para 14.01), another version of this undertaking is to be found in the SGG Directive (arts 2(1), (2)(a) and (5): see para 13.11A). *Ninth*, it is now possible to obtain Enforcement Orders in respect of these breaches (see para 28.04).

**[13.11A] The description**. Suppose that in negotiating the supply contract, the supplier describes the goods. Leaving aside any criminal law liability for mis-description,[61] the descriptive words may give rise to civil liability in ascending order of legal significance: (1) for mistake;[62] (2) for misrepresentation;[63] (3) for breach of contract. Concentrating on the last possibility, there may be liability for breach of an express promise as to description (see para 11.07) or an implied condition (see para 13.11), e.g. a sale of counterfeit goods.

Attention has already been drawn to the ordinary rules by which a representation becomes a contractual term and in particular the attitude of the courts where one party was in trade, whereas the other was not (see para 11.02). However, in a later case between two private parties, Sellers LJ seemed to suggest that s 13 of the SGA somehow converted all descriptive statements into contractual terms.[64] However, this view was impliedly rejected in *Harlingdon & Leinster Enterprises Ltd v Christopher Hull Fine Art Ltd*:[65]

> D was an art dealer. In 1984, he was asked to sell two monogrammed oil paintings which had been described in a 1980 auction catalogue as being by Münter, an artist of the German expressionist school. As D specialised in British contemporary art, he

---

58  E.g. *Grenfell v EB Meyrowitz Ltd* [1936] 2 All ER 1313, CA. *Compare Andrews Ltd v Singer & Co Ltd* (above) and *Morris Motors Ltd v Lilley* [1959] 3 All ER 737 (new cars). See also an auctioneer's system of painting attribution: Harvey and Meisel, *Auctions*, 2nd edn, 341. What is the effect of dealers registering new cars as sold by them simply to qualify for a manufacturer's bonus? Or when he has already contracted to supply the goods to another on sale or return? See also OFT, *1992-AR*, 13. As to implied terms annexed by trade usage, see para 15.11.

59  See *Peter Darlington Ltd v Gosho Ltd* [1964] 1 Lloyd's Rep 149. What about 'low-alcohol beer' supplied in response to a request for 'alcohol-free' drink? See further, the discussion on mistake, para 17.11.

60  E.g. Hoover (for vacuum cleaner); Biro (for ball point pen). What about 'woollies' as a mere description of knitted garments, regardless of fibre?

61  As to when words may amount to a trade description for the purpose of criminal liability under the TDA, see para 4.07.

62  For mistake as to identity of subject-matter, see para 10.16; and for mistake as to quality, see para 10.17 and para 17.11.

63  E.g. *Harrison v Knowles and Foster* [1918] 1 KB 608, CA. For misrepresentation, see para 17.10.

64  *Beale v Taylor* (set out at para 13.10) It has even been suggested that all express statements which 'constitute a substantial ingredient in identity' are conditions: *per* Scott LJ delivering the unanimous judgment of the CA in *Couchman v Hill* [1947] KB 554 at 559.

65  [1991] 1 QB 564, [1990] 1 All ER 737, CA (see Brown 106 LQR 561; Snaith 140 NLJ 1672; Bentil 8 Tr L 25; Adams [1990] JBL 433).

took the paintings to P, who ran a gallery specialising in the German expressionist school. D made it clear to P that he was not an expert in this class of painting. P bought them for £6,000 without further enquiries, D's invoice describing the paintings as by Münter. The paintings were subsequently discovered to be forgeries. P sought to recover the price on grounds of breach of ss 13(1) and 14(2).

On the s 13(1) issue[66] the Court of Appeal found for D, holding that for a s 13 undertaking to arise, the parties had first to evince a common intention that the description was part of the contract under the ordinary rules,[67] whereas here D's disclaimer of expert knowledge helped to show that P was not relying upon him and hence did not intend the seller's description[68] to become part of the contract.[69] *A fortiori*, a patent misdescription by a seller of goods which are in the presence of the parties will not normally become part of the contract because the parties will have evinced an intention to contract for *those* goods, regardless of description, e.g. goods sold 'as seen'.[70] On the other hand, it has been argued[71] that such mere representations may fall within Art 2(2)(a) of the SGG Directive, so rendering the goods not 'in conformity with the contract' (see generally, para 14.01) and attracting the SGG Regulation remedies applicable to breaches of contract (see para 29.02).

**[13.12] The extent of the duty.** Assuming the descriptive words amount to a contractual promise, the extent of that duty is dependent on the degree of precision of description:[72] if the description is vague, the duty may be minimal;[73] and the better the description,[74] the more onerous the duty.[75] Thus, in *Arcos Ltd v Ronaasen & Sons Ltd*:[76]

There was a contract for the sale of a quantity of staves of ½inch thickness. The buyer purported to reject the staves delivered on the grounds that they did not comply with

---

66   As to the s 14(2) issue, see paras 14.19; 14.21. As to *caveat emptor* see para 15.22. No claim for misrepresentation was possible because (i) D reasonably believed the paintings were by Munter and (ii) P had resold them.

67   See para 11.03. Is this another facet of the identity test (see para 13.13)? See Brown, *ibid*. If so, then presumably the description amounted to a mere puff (see para 11.01). As to mistakes as to quality (see para 17.11), see Snaith, *ibid*.

68   The CA do not seem to have addressed the point that the monogram described the painting. Nor did they mention *Beale v Taylor*, when the goods also described themselves (see para 13.10).

69   Stuart Smith LJ dissented on the inference of intention to be drawn from the facts (QB at 580 D–F). It follows from the majority rules (supported by *Adams, ibid*, Bentil, *ibid* at 30) that there could be no question of any misrepresentation (see para 11.02) because of the absence of reliance by P, nor of an express warranty as to description. Cf. the apparently much more easily satisfied reliance test in the undertaking as to fitness: see para 14.13.

70   See *Benjamin's Sale of Goods*, 6th edn, para 11-011 ('as such').

71   Willett, Morgan-Taylor & Naidoo [2004] JBL 94 at 106–7.

72   This may particularly be the case with contracts for work and materials, e.g. servicing a car, as it may not be known in advance what needs to be done: Woodroffe, *Goods and Services—The New Law*, para 3.18.

73   A statutory minimum description has been suggested for used cars: Borrie [1987] JBL at 440. As to where a supplier offered to supply his choice from a list, see [1995] 11 *Which?* 6.

74   E.g. auction catalogues (see para 10.10). Many commercial sales are made against detailed specifications or according to elaborate definitions, e.g. of chemical composition or engineering characteristics.

75   E.g. 'new car': see *Andrews Bros Ltd v Singer & Co Ltd* [1934] 1 KB 17, CA; *Raynham Farm Co Ltd v Symbol Motor Corpn Ltd* [1987] CLY 447; and cf. TDA, s 2 (see para 4.08). The contract itself may expressly provide for changes in description, e.g. 'subject to alterations in our supplier's specifications'. See also Mildred, *Product Liability Law and Insurance*, 2000, paras 7.65–79.

76   [1933] AC 470, [1933] All ER Rep 646, HL.

the contract description. The arbitrator found that only 5% of the staves were of ½inch thickness, but that the rest were nearly all less than 9/16 inch thick. Moreover, the staves were required, to the knowledge of the seller, to make cement barrels; and the arbitrator found that they were fit for this purpose, and that they were commercially within and merchantable under the contract description. He therefore held that the buyer was not entitled to reject.

The decision was reversed by Wright J, who was unanimously upheld by the Court of Appeal and the House of Lords. Lord Atkin said (at 479–80):

> 'It was contended that in all commercial contracts the question was whether there was "substantial" compliance with the contract: there must always be some margin; and it is for the tribunal of fact to determine whether the margin is exceeded or not. I cannot agree. If the written contract specifies conditions of weight, measurement and the like, those conditions must be complied with. A ton does not mean about a ton, or a yard about a yard. Still less when you descend to minute measurements does ½ inch mean about ½ inch. If the seller wants a margin he must, and in my experience does, stipulate for it . . .
>
> No doubt there may be microscopic deviations which businessmen and therefore lawyers will ignore . . . But, apart from this consideration, the right view is that the conditions of the contract must be strictly performed'.

The net effect is that, in relation to contractual descriptions (see para 13.11A), there are now three classes of misdescription.

1. *De minimis rule (microscopic deviations)* which the courts will ignore (see above). Whilst primarily used in relation to undertakings as to quantity (see para 13.04), in principle the law ought to be willing to ignore microscopic deviations as to descriptive quality,[77] though much should depend on the degree of accuracy reasonable in that contract.[78]

2. *'Slight breaches'* can only be treated by a commercial buyer as grounds a claim in damages (see para 11.05): this might reverse the actual decision in the *Arcos* case (see above). A similar result may be achievable at common law by the doctrine of substantial performance (see para 26.02).

3. *Other cases.* The implied condition that goods comply with their description may well in practice overlap with the undertakings as to fitness and quality (as to which, see Chap 14)[79] and any relevant sample provisions (see para 15.06). However it is likely to be particularly important where there is no such overlap, as where there is a private supplier;[80] or the desired quality is not within the undertakings of fitness or quality;[81] or where those undertakings are excluded whilst the implied condition as to description is not (see para 13.16). In practice, the misdescription cases tend to fall into one of two categories: (a) where

---

77  *Steels & Busks Ltd v Bleeker Bike Co Ltd* [1956] 1 Lloyd's Rep. 228 (sale of crepe rubber; preservation chemical ignored). In the consumer context, this might apply to small discrepancies in the size of vegetables or garments. See generally Atiyah, *Sale of Goods*, 10th edn, 133, 153–5.

78  *The Troll Park* [1988] 2 Lloyd's Rep 423, CA. In this a test of fitness for the purpose supplied?

79  Examples given by *Benjamin's Sale of Goods*, 6th edn, para 11.017 include unsuitable 'baby food', 'cough mixture', 'cold cure'.

80  E.g. *Beale v Taylor* (set out at para 13.10).

81  E.g. *Arcos Ltd v Ronaasen & Sons Ltd* (above). Atiyah, *Sale of Goods*, 10th edn, 151 gives the example of a suit sold as 'pure wool'.

the misdescription alters the identity of the goods (see para 13.13); (b) non-identifying misdescriptions (see para 13.15).

**[13.13] The identity test.** The leading case on the scope of the implied statutory condition that the goods comply with their description is *Ashington Piggeries Ltd v Christopher Hill Ltd*:[82]

> The plaintiff manufacturers habitually undertook the compounding of animal feedstuffs to customers' formulae. The defendants asked the plaintiffs to compound a vitamin-fortified mink food, to be called King Size, in accordance with a formula to be supplied by the defendants. The plaintiffs made it clear that they knew nothing about mink, but did suggest that herring meal should be substituted for one of the other ingredients. After making satisfactory deliveries for about 12 months, the plaintiffs began to make up the compound with herring meal purchased from N, under a contract which stipulated that it was 'fair average quality of the season' and was to be taken 'with all faults and defects . . . at a valuation'. Unknown to any of the parties, that meal contained DMNA, a chemical produced in the meal by chemical reaction. DMNA was found to be harmful in some degree to all animals but particularly toxic to mink. The plaintiffs sued for the price, the defendants counter-claimed for breach of what is now the SGA, ss 13(1), 14(2) and (3); and the plaintiffs brought in N.

At this stage, we need consider only the argument on s 13.[83] The decision of Milmo J that each seller was liable to his buyer under s 13 was reversed by the Court of Appeal,[84] whose judgment was affirmed by the House of Lords.

1. *King Size.* As between the plaintiffs and defendants, their Lordships held that the compound did correspond with its description, the contract description being 'King Size, meaning thereby a food compounded in accordance with an agreed formula'. Davies LJ delivering the judgment of the Court of Appeal made the following points: first, the description did not include the suitability of the compound as a food for mink; and second, that DMNA was a condition of the herring meal, and not an additional unauthorised ingredient.[85] This view was followed by the majority of the House of Lords,[86] who contrasted this case with those where so much of a different ingredient was added as to make the goods a different commodity.[87] As Lord Wilberforce put it, the defendant's formula for King Size was commercial, not chemical.

2. *Norwegian Herring Meal.* Nor did the Court of Appeal think that there was a breach of the undertaking as to description as between the plaintiff and N: they held that the contract description was 'Norwegian Herring Meal, fair average quality of the season'; and that the goods complied therewith, because that description related only 'to such qualities as are apparent on an ordinary

---

82   [1972] AC 441, [1971] 1 All ER 847, HL.

83   These other issues are considered in Chap 14, especially at paras 14.04, 14.09 and 14.14.

84   [1969] 3 All ER 1496, CA.

85   At 1510–13. But see Patient (1970) 33 MLR 565, at 566.

86   Lords Hodson (at 853), Guest (at 858), Wilberforce (at 872), Diplock (at 884). Lord Dilhorne, dissenting, agreed that the matter was one of degree, but thought that the facts had crossed the line (at 868).

87   *Pinnock Bros v Lewis and Peat* [1923] I KB 690 (castor oil added to copra cake); *Munro & Co Ltd v Meyer* [1930] 2 KB 312 (cocoa husks added to meat and bone meal).

examination or analysis of the goods, such as is usually done in the trade in relation to such goods' (at 1519–22). The House of Lords agreed, explaining that the goods complied with their description 'Norwegian Herring Meal', whereas the contractual description 'fair average quality of the season' was not part of the s 13 implied condition because it was not needed to identify the goods.[88] Lord Guest distinguished *Arcos Ltd v Ronaasen Ltd* (discussed at paras 13.14–15), where he explained that the full description was necessary to identify the contract goods.[89]

**[13.14]** It is interesting to consider the *Ashington* case (set out at para 13.13) in the light of Benjamin's two categories of sales of goods by description (see para 13.09).

*(1) Sales of unascertained or future goods.* The courts had previously applied the strict test of breach of the undertaking as exemplified in *Arcos Ltd v Ronaasen & Son Ltd* (set out at para 13.12) to contracts for the supply of goods to consumers and trade buyers: as in a sale of 'common English sainfoin grass seed';[90] or a 'new Singer car'.[91] Further, in the case of trade buyers, the courts had previously shown themselves willing to extend the undertaking beyond the physical state of the goods: as to the size of bags containing goods;[92] the average weight of parcels;[93] the date of the arrival of a ship in which the goods were being transported;[94] and that the goods have been shipped under-deck[95] or packed in the wrong multiples.[96]

*(2) Sales of specific goods.* In *Varley v Whipp*:[97]

> The defendant agreed to buy a second-hand reaping machine then owned by a third party, which the defendant had never seen, but which the plaintiff seller stated to have been 'new the previous year' and very little used. On discovering that the machine did not comply with this description, the defendant returned the reaper to the plaintiff. Channell J held that there was a breach of s 13.

A similar approach was taken with an advertised '1961 Triumph Herald'[98] and is presumably applicable to such mundane consumer matters as the sizing of clothing, domestic equipment or furniture.[99]

---

88  Lords Hodson (at 856), Guest (at 860), Wilberforce (at 877), Diplock (at 890). Lord Dilhorne, dissenting, agreed that for the purposes of the undertaking, the description was only 'Norwegian Herring Meal', but thought that the goods did not comply with that description by reason of the presence of DMNA (at 869).

89  He expressly agreed that a qualitative description could be within the undertaking, as in *Varley v Whipp* (set out at para 13.14).

90  *Wallis Son & Wells v Pratt and Haynes* (set out at para 11.04).

91  *Andrews Brothers (Bournemouth) Ltd v Singer & Co Ltd* [1934] 1 KB 17, CA.

92  *Manbre Saccharine Co Ltd v Corn Products Ltd* [1919] 1 KB 198.

93  *Ballantine & Co v Cramp and Bosman* (1923) 129 LT 502.

94  *Macpherson Train & Co Ltd v Ross & Co Ltd* [1955] 2 All ER 445.

95  *White Sea Trust Timber Ltd v North Ltd* [1933] 148 LT 263. See also *Fisher, Reeves & Co v Armour Co* [1920] 3 KB 614, CA (ex-store).

96  *Re Moore Ltd* [1921] 2 KB 519, CA.

97  [1900] 1 QB 513. It is difficult to reconcile this decision with ss 11(4) and 18 of the SGA: see para 20.08. For other points raised by this case, see paras 20.02 and 20.03.

98  *Beale v Taylor* (set out at para 13.10).

99  Cf. TDA, s 2(1)(a): see para 4.06.

In the light of the *Ashington* case, the difficulty is to judge the extent to which the foregoing cases are still good law (see para 13.15).

**[13.15]** Of course, a contractual description may always amount to an **express condition** under the ordinary rules for classifying terms (see para 11.04). However, where this is not the case, the *Ashington Piggeries* case (set out at para 13.13) clearly establishes an identity test as to whether or not an **express term** amounts to an **implied condition** (see para 13.11).

Descriptive words may identify the contract goods with different degrees of precision (see para 13.12), though it does seem from that case that the test is a commercial one,[100] with the courts ignoring an obscure chemical reaction, albeit a disastrous one.[101] On the one hand, it might be argued that only those elements in the description which delineate the **commercial class or kind** within which the goods belong should be within the undertaking (e.g. a garment with a wrong size label), in which case a small amount of another ingredient would not breach it.[102] On the other hand, **any matter** delineating the contract goods might be within the undertaking, so that even a small amount of another ingredient would, unless *de minimis*, breach the undertaking.[103] A third possibility is that the former test applies to specific goods, whilst the latter is apposite to unascertained goods.[104] Yet this last distinction seems undermined by the wide view of identity taken by Stuart-Smith LJ:[105]

> 'Every item in a description which constitutes a substantial ingredient in the "identity" of the thing being sold is a condition ... That the identity of the artist who painted a picture can be a substantial ingredient in the identity of the thing sold seems to be beyond question'.

Even if the former, narrow view, of the undertaking is taken, this does not necessarily deprive other descriptive statements of all effect.[106] The words may amount to an express condition (see above) or warranty as to description;[107] or an express or implied undertaking as to fitness or quality;[108] or a remedy may be available on grounds of misrepresentation.[109]

---

100  E.g. the way the courts approach samples: see para 15.06. What about returns (see para 10.28)?

101  Atiyah, *Sale of Goods*, 10th edn, 154.

102  This narrower test seems to be supported by *Benjamin's Sale of Goods*, 6th edn, para 11.018, citing *Reardon Smith Line Ltd v Hansen-Tangen* [1976] 3 All ER 570, HL, *per* Lord Wilberforce at 576f (describing some of the authorities as 'excessively technical and due for fresh examination in this House'). See also *Tradex Export SA v European Grain & Shipping Ltd* [1983] 2 Lloyd's Rep 100.

103  This wider test seems to be supported by Atiyah, *Sale of Goods*, 6th edn, 94–5; but compare his 10th Edn 152.

104  See further Goode, *Commercial Law*, 3rd edn, 291, *et seq.* As to specific goods, see generally, para 20.02.

105  In *Harlingdon & Leinster Enterprises Ltd v Christopher Hull Fine Arts Ltd* (set out at para 13.11A) at All ER 747b.

106  See generally Atiyah, *Sale of Goods*, 10th edn, 147.

107  E.g. the statement 'fair average quality of the season' in the contract between the plaintiff and N in the *Ashington Piggeries* case (above); *Trasimex Holdings SA v Addax BV, The Red Sea* [1991] 1 Lloyd's Rep 28, CA.

108  See Atiyah, *ibid*, 151; Benjamin, *ibid*, para 11-016, *et seq.*

109  E.g. *Harrison v Knowles and Foster* [1918] 1 KB 608, CA; *Howard Marine & Dredging Co v Ogden (Excavations) Ltd* (set out at para 17.10); and see para 13.11.

**[13.16] Exclusion**. In the case of supplies falling within Pt 1 of UCTA, there are severe statutory limitations on the supplier's power to exclude or restrict statutory implied undertakings as to compliance with description: where the transferee deals as consumer, any exclusion or restriction is void; and in other cases the clause is subject to the test of reasonableness.[110] Suppose the contract labels express terms as to description as only being warranties in the technical sense. Insofar as that express description is within both the statutory undertakings as going to the identity of the subject-matter (see para 13.13) and UCTA (see above), the foregoing statutory consequences obviously apply,[111] though there remains the issue of the effect of designating other parts of the contractual description as a warranty. In a consumer contract, it might be possible to ignore such a non-core express provision as being an unfair term;[112] but in a non-consumer contract the position is as follows. Where there is a slight breach, the express provision merely re-enforces the amended SGA (new s 15A: see para 11.05); and, in other cases, matters seem to be left to the common law.[113] Thus, the clause will be construed strictly as against the *proferens*;[114] but a distinction must also be drawn between those clauses which exclude and those which limit liability: the clause may either prevent any obligation from arising or merely limit liability for breach of an obligation once it has arisen (see para 18.03). If the contract goods are unascertained, an attempt to **exclude** all undertakings as to description would destroy any certainty of subject-matter;[115] but this argument would not obtain where the contract goods are specific.[116] Thus, if the only objection to clauses excluding undertakings as to description was on grounds of certainty of subject-matter,[117] the position would appear to be as follows: the seller could always **limit** his liability; he could **exclude** it where the contract was for the sale of specific goods;[118] and, even where the contract was for the sale of unascertained goods, he could probably **exclude** liability for such trivial breaches as those which occurred in *Arcos Ltd v Ronaasen & Son Ltd*.[119]

---

110  UCTA, ss 6(2)(3), 7(2) and (3): see further, para 18.19.

111  Because the designation as 'warranty' is intended to 'restrict . . . a remedy' (s 13(1)(b)): see para 18.16.

112  UTCC Regulations, reg 5 (see para 11.14); [2005] *UTCCR Bulletin J/S, Forthright Finance*; and Grey List terms (b) and (q) (see paras 11.16A; 11.18A).

113  The general common law rules for dealing with exclusion clauses are considered at para 18.02, *et seq.*

114  See *Munro & Co v Meyer* [1930] 2 KB 312; *Harrison v Knowles and Foster* [1918] 1 KB 608, CA; *Nicholson and Venn v Smith-Marriott* (1947) 177 LT 189; *Christopher Hill Ltd v Ashington Piggeries Ltd* [1969] 3 All ER 1496, CA, at 1522–1523 (the exclusion clause in the contract between the plaintiffs and N). For the *proferens*, see para 18.06.

115  See *Benjamin on Sale*, 8th edn, 1950, 622–3. *Contra* Yates and Hawkins, *Standard Business Contracts*, 231.

116  *Hughes v Hall* [1981] RTR 430 at 437F, *per* Donaldson LJ (sold as seen and inspected); *Cavendish-Woodhouse v Manley* (1984) 82 LGR 376, DC (bought as seen).

117  See *First Report on Exclusion Clauses in Contracts* (1969, Law Com No. 24), para 21: see further, para 18.07.

118  Goode, *Commercial Law*, 3rd edn, 297.

119  See Atiyah, *Sale of Goods*, 10th edn, 148. As to the manner in which auction houses deal with deliberate forgeries, see Harvey and Meisel, *Auctions*, 2nd edn, 163, *et seq.*

# CHAPTER 14

# UNDERTAKINGS AS TO FITNESS AND SATISFACTORY QUALITY

## SCOPE OF UNDERTAKINGS

**[14.0A] Introduction**. As to express promises, there has never been anything to prevent the parties from inserting in their contract terms as to fitness and quality **more** onerous than the statutory implied terms;[1] and this category is likely to be increased by the provision making the retailer liable in some circumstances under manufacturers' guarantees (see para 17.09A). But any attempt to insert **less** onerous terms is likely to amount to an exclusion clause (see para 14.02). As to criminal liability in relation to trade descriptions, see para 4.02, *et seq.*

In relation to implied promises, the SGA 1893 probably narrowed the scope of the common law maxim *caveat emptor* (see para 13.08) by providing that, subject to a contrary intention and leaving aside sales by sample (see paras 15.03–10), there shall be implied into a contract of sale three conditions[2]—as to description, merchantable quality and fitness for the purposes supplied[3]—and an implied warranty as to trade usage (see para 15.11). It has been pointed out that these three implied conditions represent a series of graduated duties.[4] The undertaking as to correspondence with description offers the buyer only minimal statutory protection, but applies to almost all sales (see para 13.09–10), whereas the other two undertakings apply only to trade sales (see para 14.04). Further, all three implied undertakings leave open some issues of policy. Thus, the level at which each of them should be pitched is a matter of judgment,[5] including such factors as nationally desired standards of quality control by manufacturers.[6]

**[14.01] The modern law**. At a later date, the above national undertakings were re-enacted for sale in an amended form in the SGA 1979; and similar undertakings have been imported by statute into quasi-sales, simple hirings and hp (see para 12.01). The EU have adopted a Sale of Goods (SGG) Directive designed to harmonise the laws of Member States, so encouraging consumer confidence in cross-border shopping and creating a level playing-field between sellers and buyers: this it seeks to do by giving additional compulsory[7] **minimum** protections[8] to consumers over

---

1    See [1999] 8 *Which?* 6. Express detailed specifications are common in large engineering contracts. For express terms, see generally, para 11.07, *et seq.*; paras 15.13 and 15.22; and Atiyah, *Sale of Goods*, 10th edn, 140.

2    As to the content of the conditions (as opposed to when they were applicable) it would seem that the SGA 1893 largely reproduced the common law: see para 13.09.

3    See *per* Lord Buckmaster in *Manchester Liners Ltd v Rea Ltd* [1922] 2 AC 74, HL, at 79. For conditions generally, see para 11.04; and for implied terms, see generally, para 11.10.

4    Atiyah, *Op. cit.*, 138.

5    The undertakings cover both new and second-hand goods: *Bartlett v Sidney Marcus Ltd* [1965] 2 All ER 753, CA.

6    See *Sale and Supply of Goods* (1983, Law Com Working Paper No. 85), para 3.3.

7    Art 7: see para 18.10.

8    Art 8: see para 3.10.

and above the ordinary national ones.[9] With some exceptions,[10] this has been implemented in the UK by the SSG Regulations[11] made under the ECA (see para 1.03A). The implementation was delayed until the DTI were able to achieve it largely by using those Regulations to make amendments to the relevant UK statutes,[12] though some of these rules are still found only in the Regulations (regs 2 and 15). These changes will make a substantial difference for private 'consumers' (see para 1.02) as follows:

(1) *Statutory implied promises.* The Directive requires goods to be 'in conformity with the contract' (Art 2(1)) and lists four cases where the goods 'are presumed to be in conformity with the contract (Art 2(2)). The DTI took the view that, except in the case of 'public statements' (Art 2(2)(d)), the level of protection offered by the existing English implied terms in general already exceeded that required by this minimum directive: having defined 'in conformity with the contract',[13] the Regulations therefore make special provision only for 'public statements'.[14] Accordingly, the changes made by the Regulations are largely confined to the following: special provisions as to the durability of the undertakings (see reg 5; and para 14.06); suing back up the chain of distribution (see para 17.07); exclusion clauses (see reg 14; and para 18.18); risk and delivery (see regs 4 and 9; and paras 22.02A and 23.09A); and additional remedies (see regs 5 and 9; and para 29.02A) to a private consumer (see above).

(2) *Express statements.* The Regulations define breach of an express term as being not 'in conformity with the contract' (see above), so attracting to such breaches all the remedies offered for breach of the statutory implied terms (see para 29.02); and the same should be true of any incorrect installation of the goods by the supplier.[15] As regards non-conformity with express statements made by the manufacturer, the Regulations have enhanced the remedies available to the consumer as against (a) his supplier (see regs 3, 7 and 13; and para 14.19) and (b) that manufacturer ('guarantees': see para 17.09A).

Remember, besides the ordinary remedies available to the injured consumer (see Chap 29), it is now possible for public authorities to obtain Enforcement Orders in respect of these breaches on behalf of consumers generally (see para 28.04) and that these implied terms cannot be unfair (see para 11.12A).

---

9 *Directive on the Sale of Goods and Associated Guarantees* 99/44/EC, Arts 1(1) and 8. As to publicity, see Art 9. As to the purposes of the Directive, potentially so important in interpretation (see para 1.04), see Oughton and Willett (2002) 25 Jo of Consumer Policy 299, at 302–3.

10 The following optional provisions in the Directive have not been introduced into English Law (Art 8(2): secondhand goods sold at auctions (Art 1(3): see para 10.10); requiring notice of lack of conformity within two months (Art 5(2)); shorter liability period for secondhand goods (Art 7(2)). The Directive is to be reviewed in 2006 (Art 12). See generally Twigg-Flesner (2002) 12 Consumer Policy 88 at 92; Willett, Morgan-Taylor and Naidoo [2004] JBL 94 at 100–2.

11 Sale and Supply of Goods to Consumers Regulations, 2002 SI 3045 (the SSG Regs). The following provisions in the Directive were not specifically included because they were already thought to be part of English law: Arts 1(4), 2(5), 4 and 5(1).

12 As to the position during the fifteen months when the changes should have been implemented, but were not, see para 1.03A.

13 SGA, new s 48F; SGSA, new s 11S(1)(a): see para 29.01A.

14 SGA, s 14(2)(F): see para 14.19A.

15 SGSA, new s 11(S)(1)(b) is presumably intended to implement Art 2(5) of the Directive. As to whether or not it does so, see Willett, etc [2004] JBL at 104–6.

**[14.02] Scope of the undertakings: common limitations**. In this Chapter, the two undertakings as to fitness and quality will be considered separately below. However, before so doing, it is convenient to mention several points which they have in common.

(1) *Exclusivity of implied undertakings*. Apart from undertakings already mentioned (see para 14.01), there are no other statutory implied undertakings applicable to any supply of goods (see para 15.22), though there is nothing to prevent the supplier giving an express promise to similar effect (see para 14.0A).

(2) *Goods supplied*. This phrase in the statutory implied terms extends beyond the subject-matter of the contract to include any goods supplied under the contract (see para 14.03) and any label[16] or instructions for use (see below).

(3) *Trade suppliers*. The undertakings are limited to contracts made by trade suppliers (see para 14.04), but indifferent as to whether or not their customers are in business—a matter relevant to exclusion clauses (see below) and remedies.[17]

(4) *Unprepared goods*. If it is contemplated that something be done to the goods by the transferee before use, e.g. assembly, the goods must conform with the statutory undertakings after, though not necessarily before, this has been done.[18] However, in that circumstance, it may be that any instructions for preparation or assembly of the goods themselves become part of the goods for the purposes of the undertakings, e.g. cooking or assembly instructions (see further, para 18.28, *et seq*).

(5) *Partial non-compliance* (see para 14.05).

(6) *Congeries of defects*. In the Scottish case of *Pollock v Macrae*[19] the marine engine supplied was held to have 'such a congeries of defects as to destroy the workable character of the machine' and took the goods outside the ambit of an exclusion clause.[20] This notion that minor defects, each in themselves insubstantial, may be taken together and the effect of the total considered was subsequently imported into English law to support the development of the doctrine of fundamental breach.[21] This last doctrine having been subsequently set aside (see para 18.08), the concept of a congeries of defects ought for English law to be relevant only as follows: bearing in mind that partial non-compliance breaches the undertakings (see para 14.05), whereas any matters *de minimis* are to be ignored (see para 13.12), presumably a congeries of defects can only be a collection of minor matters, individually *de minimis*, but cumulatively amounting to a partial breach,[22] perhaps outside the construction of any exclusion clause (see below).

---

16  *Niblett v Confectioners' Materials Co* (set out at para 12.03); the *Albright and Wilson* case (set out at para 13.01), CA para 35.

17  See new Pt 5A: set out at para 29.02A.

18  *Heil v Hedges* [1951] 1 TLR 512 (sale of partly-cooked pork chops). As to the possible overlap with SGSA, s 13, see para 15.15.

19  1922 SC (HL) 192. In Scots, but not English law, there is a rule preserved by SGA, s 11(5) that the right of the innocent buyer to treat the contract as repudiated depends on whether or not there is a failure by the seller to perform any 'material part' of the contract.

20  See *Benjamin's Sale of Goods*, 6th edn, para 13-051.

21  E.g. *Yeoman Credit Ltd v Apps* (set out at para 29.25).

22  This argument may be relevant in relation to the undertaking as to satisfactory quality: see para 14.23.

(7) *Durability and the burden of proof.* On ordinary principles, a buyer or other transferee alleging that his goods are defective must prove his case.[23] This is particularly a problem where the defect is only discovered some time after delivery. However, in favour of private consumers a defect discovered within six months is deemed to have existed on delivery (see para 14.06).

(8) *Consumer contracts.* In a consumer supply contract, it is possible to challenge the fairness of **express terms**;[24] and there may be some enhancement of the statutory **implied terms** (see para 14.01).

(9) *Exclusion.* Restrictions on the power of the supplier to exclude or limit his liability under these implied statutory undertakings by UCTA will be considered later (Chap 18), though in a consumer supply contract such exclusions may also be unfair.[25] It is doubtful whether the UCTA restrictions extend to certificates of compliance.[26]

**[14.03] Goods supplied.** The two implied conditions are expressed to be applicable not just to the contract goods, but also any other goods **supplied under** the contract.[27] Thus, in *Geddling v Marsh*:[28]

> The plaintiff shopkeeper purchased bottles of mineral water from the defendant manufacturer on the basis that one penny was refundable on every bottle the shopkeeper returned to the manufacturer. Whilst the plaintiff was handling a bottle, it burst and injured her.

Despite the fact that the contract in respect of the bottles seems to have been one of hire rather than sale, the plaintiffs successfully claimed damages before the Divisional Court: Bailhache J pointed out that the goods could not be supplied except in some sort of container; and Bray J found support in the fact that the opening words of the relevant provision of the SGA (s 14) speak of 'goods supplied under the contract of sale'. A spectacular application of those statutory words by the Court of Appeal is to be found in *Wilson v Rickett Cockerell Ltd*:[29]

> The plaintiff purchased a ton of Coalite from the defendant coal merchant. Subsequently, the plaintiff was injured when there was an explosion in the grate by reason of the inclusion of an explosive substance (a detonator) in the consignment.

The Court of Appeal unanimously rejected the defendant's plea that there was nothing wrong with the Coalite as Coalite. If the rules apply to (presumably) unintended extras, perhaps it also applies to 'free gifts' supplied under a contract of

---

23  *Leicester Circuits Ltd v Coates Bros Plc* [2003] EWCA Civ 290, CA (see 58 CC2/41).

24  See para 11.12. *Contra* the statutory implied terms: UTCC Regulations, Sched 1, para (e)(i).

25  Grey Term 1(b): see para 11.16A.

26  See generally Schmitthoff, *Export Trade*, 10th edn, 4-012/4. Distinguish arbitration agreements: see para 3.23. As to liability in deceit under a compliance certificate, see para 17.18.

27  SGA s 14(2) and (3). Identical language is employed in the other enactments applicable to supplies of goods: see SOGIT, s 10(2) and (3); SGSA, s 4(2) and (5), 9(2) and (5). Cf. CPA, s 46(1): see para 4.34.

28  [1920] 1 KB 668, [1920] All ER Rep 631, DC. See also *Niblett's* case (set out at para 12.03).

29  [1954] 1 QB 598, [1954] 1 All ER 868, CA.

supply (see para 2.08), in which case they too would attract the benefit of the implied undertakings as to fitness and quality under the SGA[30] or SGSA.[31]

[14.04] **Trade suppliers**. The two statutory undertakings now apply only to goods supplied 'in the course of a business':[32] leaving aside trade agents (see para 14.04A), the undertakings provide a definition of 'business'.[33] In relation to sales, this represented an extension in the ambit of the undertakings. The apparently restrictive wording of the SGA 1893 (suggesting just supplies of stock-in-trade) had already been extended in the *Ashington Piggeries* case[34] to any across-the-counter supply.[35] It would seem that trade supplies include both the last sale in a business[36] and supplies by part-time traders.[37] Indeed, it has since been held that the present statutory formulation has extended the ambit still further to any goods which go through a dealer's business books.[38] In *Stevenson v Rogers*[39]

> R had been a fisherman for some 20 years. In 1988, he sold his sea-going fishing boat, the *Jelle*, which he had owned for some three years. Finding the *Jelle* defective, the buyer (S), as a preliminary issue, had to show that the sale was a sale 'in the course of a business' within s 14(2) of the SGA. The trial judge held that the *Jelle* was not sold 'in the course of a business', relying on *Davies v Sumner* (set out at para 4.03) and the *R & B Customs Brokers* case (set out at para 18.18).

In the Court of Appeal, the leading judgment allowing S's appeal was delivered by Potter LJ. Having reviewed the legislative history of s 14(2), his Lordship applied the mischief rule (at 624e: see para 1.04) to find that the words were simply used 'to distinguish between a sale made in the course of the seller's business and a purely private sale of goods outside the confines of the business (if any) carried on by the seller' (at 623j). He explained the narrower interpretation of sales of stock in *Davies v Sumner* as being appropriate in a criminal case (at 624h); and he distinguished the civil *R & B Customs* case as involving another statute, UCTA (at 625d). He explained (at 625–6):

> 'As to the proper construction of s 14(2), given the clear view which I have formed, I do not consider it right to displace that construction simply to achieve harmony with a decision upon the meaning of s 12 of UCTA 1977. Section 14(2) . . . was itself a piece of consumer protection intended to afford wider protection to a buyer than that provided in the 1893 Act. Indeed, there is a sense in which the decision in *R & B*

---

30  See the *Second Report on Exemption Clauses* (1975, Law Com No. 69) para 35.

31  It could amount to a quasi-sale (see para 2.10) or be left to the common law (see para 15.25).

32  This phrase is also found in UCTA s 12(1)(b): see para 18.18. Cf. the TDA, CCA: see respectively, paras 4.03 and 5.18; and Lunn and Miles (1996) 15 Tr L 120. *Contra* trade usage: see para 15.11.

33  'Business' is defined so that it 'includes a profession and any activities of any government department or local public authority': SGA, s 61(1); SOGIT, s 15(1); SGSA, s 18(1). See further *Benjamin's Sale of Goods*, 6th edn, para 11-046. Is the effect that the SGSA now extends to faulty devices fitted by a surgeon?

34  Set out at para 13.13: the supply of King Size by P.

35  Benjamin, *Op. cit.*, para 11-045.

36  *Buchanan-Jardine v Hamilink* [1983] SLT 149 (stock sold off as part of a sale of business).

37  For moonlighters, see Woodroffe, *Goods and Services—The New Law*, para 3.23.

38  Cf. the test under UCTA, s 12(1)(a): see para 18.18.

39  [1999] 2 QB 1028, [1999] 1 All ER 613, CA (Brown 115 LQR 384, who asks whether this case extends to some amateur sellers, e.g. a car-boot sale, a bring-and-buy sale?).

*Customs* case can be said to be in harmony with that intention. It dealt with the position of consumer **buyers** and the effect of adopting the construction propounded in *Davies'* case in relation to s 12(1)(a) of UCTA 1977 was to further such buyers' protection.'

In EU-derived law, the width of the concept of 'seller' seems to vary:[40] the SGG Directive seems to accord with English law, so that the above rules apply; but the UTCC Directive (Art 2(c)), rendered into English law as reg 3(1), does not, so that the meaning may differ (see para 11.12A).

**[14.04A] Trade agents.** It is clear that the undertakings as to fitness and quality will not normally attach to a supply by a person in his private capacity (see para 14.04), though it should be remembered that it is an offence to disguise a business sale as a private one.[41] By way of exception to that trade-supplies-only rule, the undertakings are applicable if a private supplier-principal chooses to use a business agent, e.g. an auctioneer, to find a client. Thus, s 14(5) of the SGA provides:

'The preceding provisions of this section apply to a sale by a person who in the course of a business is acting as agent for another as they apply to a sale by a principal in the course of a business, except where that other is not selling in the course of a business and either the buyer knows that fact or reasonable steps are taken to bring it to the notice of the buyer before the contract is made'.

A similar provision is to be found in the case of quasi-sales, hp and simple hirings.[42] It has been argued that, in the above provision, the phrase 'sale by a person' makes the agent liable for breach of the implied terms in the supply contract;[43] but this view was rejected in *Boyter v Thomson*.[44]

T was the owner of a cabin cruiser. T instructed HML to sell the cruiser under their brokerage scheme. The cruiser was sold by HML in the course of their business to B, but was found to be unseaworthy and the parties agreed she was unfit for the purpose for which she was purchased. It was found as a fact that B thought HML was the seller, so that it was a sale by an undisclosed private principal (T) through a business agent (HML).

Now, if the private seller (T) had sold the cruiser himself, he could not be liable under s 14; but the House of Lords held T liable by reason of the above s 14(5).[45] In delivering the judgment of the court, Lord Jauncy said:[46]

'In my view, subs. (5) is applicable to any sale by an agent on behalf of a principal, whether disclosed or undisclosed, where the circumstances giving rise to the exception do not exist.'

---

40   Compare the UTCC Directive 93/13, Art 2(c), with the Sale of Goods Directive 99/44, Art 1(2)(c).
41   E.g. a business selling bankrupt stock at a car-boot sale (see para 4.22).
42   SOGIT, s 10(5); SGSA, ss 4(8) and 9(8). The SOGIT amended provision refers to 'credit-broker'. Does the amended version apply even to unregulated agreements?
43   Atiyah, *Sale of Goods*, 10th edn, 160.
44   [1995] 2 AC 629, [1995] 3 All ER 135, HL(S) (see Brown 112 LQR 225).
45   On the basis that T had given express authority to sell to HML: see generally, para 10.06.
46   At 138d. Because HML was contracting for an undisclosed principal, B could have sued HML under s 14 of the SGA. *Contra*, if T had been disclosed, but unnamed. See generally Fridman, *Law of Agency*, 7th edn, 253, *et seq*.

Thus, the fact that the supplier-principal putting his goods up for auction is acting as a private person will not relieve him from the undertakings,[44] except where:

(a)  he is not in fact supplying in the course of business, **and**

(b)  prior to contracting the transferee knows this fact or reasonable steps have been taken to bring it to his notice.[47]

In view of the uncertainty as to what will amount to sufficient notice to take a case outside s 14(5), it has been argued that, at least for a consumer-buyer, it would be preferable if an auctioneer were liable on the statutory implied terms.[48]

**[14.05]  Partial non-compliance**. The buyer will *prima facie* be able to reject the goods where only part of them do not comply with the undertakings, except in the following circumstances: (a) the contract is severable; or (b) the *de minimis* rule applies. Both exceptions were considered in *Jackson v Rotax Motor and Cycle Co*:[49]

> A contract for the sale of about 600 motor horns allowed for delivery in 19 cases at varying dates over a period of two months. Upon delivery of the last case, the buyer inspected the goods, and he thereupon determined to reject the whole of them, except for one case which he had legally accepted by reason of his having resold it. The buyer alleged that 364 horns were defective; but the official referee found that the horns were substantially in accordance with the contract, and that 'most if not all . . . could at a very slight cost have been made merchantable'.

The Court of Appeal unanimously held that the contract was divisible (see para 23.24), so that acceptance of one case did not bar rejection of the others (see para 29.08), and that the goods were not of merchantable quality so that the buyer might reject them. Their Lordships rejected the attempt to apply the *de minimis* rule (see para 13.12) and said that if the buyer had to expend money on the goods to make them saleable, albeit a trifling amount, there was a breach of the undertaking.[50] Subsequently, doubt would appear to have been cast on this last finding.[51]

**[14.06]  Durability**. The common law took the view that the goods ought to comply with the undertaking for long enough for the buyer to deal with them in the ordinary way of business;[52] but, for some time after the passage of the SGA 1893, there was a view that there was a clear requirement of durability in the undertakings.[53] It was recommended that the matter be put beyond doubt by statute.[54] Accordingly,

---

47  As to the extent to which auctioneers do this, see Harvey and Meisel, *Auctions*, 2nd edn, 153. As to where the private seller forbids the agent from disclosing his status, see Brown (1996) 112 LQR at 228–9.

48  Brown (1996) 112 LQR at 229. As to auctioneers, see generally, para 10.11.

49  [1910] 2 KB 937, CA.

50  See Cozens Hardy MR at 943. The contract price was £450 and the repairs cost £35 (= 7.7%).

51  *Cehave v Bremer, The Hansa Nord* [1976] QB 44, CA. The issue would appear to need HL resolution.

52  *Beer v Walker* (1877) 46 LJQB 677.

53  *Mash & Murrell Ltd v JE Emmanuel Ltd* [1961] 1 All ER 485 (rev. on facts); *Lambert v Lewis* (set out at para 17.06); *Crowther v Shannon Motor Co* [1975] 1 All ER 139, CA; and see Atiyah, *Sale of Goods*, 10th edn, 181–2. *Contra* Hudson (1978) 94 LQR 566.

54  *Implied Terms in Contracts for the Supply of Goods* (1979, Law Com No. 95) paras 113–14; *Sale and Supply of Goods* (1987, Law Com No. 160), paras 3.47–61.

in 1994 it was enacted that, *inter alia*, the quality of the goods includes their durability.[55] Two issues arise:

(1) At what moment in time should the undertakings be tested? A test of the time when property passes might suit sale and quasi-sale, whilst relating the test to the time of delivery would suit also hp and simply hirings.[56]

(2) For how long must the goods last? According to Benjamin,[57]

> 'In principle durability is an aspect of quality on delivery: goods are not of satisfactory quality at that time unless they are capable of enduring for a period reasonable in the circumstances, and the fact that they seriously deteriorate or (for example) break down during such a period is evidence that they were not of satisfactory quality.'

Plainly, this is a question of fact, which will vary from one circumstance to another, e.g. it may depend on the price of the goods, whether or not they are second-hand, a declared 'shelf-life', the availability of spare parts (see para 17.09). Moreover, in some cases further uncertainty may be caused by the supplier arguing that the lack of durability is due to the way in which the goods have been treated after delivery, e.g. the outdoors use of bedroom slippers.

*Special protection for consumers.* These uncertainties have been thought to be inimical to the consumer interest. Accordingly, in compliance with the SGG Directive as to lack of conformity with the contract (Art 5(3): see para 14.01), where the buyer deals as consumer, compulsory new s 48A(3)[58] provides that *prima facie*[59]

> 'Goods which do not conform to the contract of sale at any time within the period of six months starting with the date on which the goods were delivered to the buyer must be taken not to have so conformed at that date'.

Similar rules have been introduced for consumer quasi-sales, simple hirings and hp,[60] but not for non-consumer transactions.[61] The *prima facie* formal effect should be to reverse the burden of proof over the state of the goods during the first six months after purchase, so that the onus is on the supplier to prove that the goods were not faulty on delivery: after that six months, it is for the consumer to prove the delivery non-conformity within the remainder of the limitation period (see below). To the extent that courts may already informally give the consumer the

---

55  SGA 1979, s 14(2B)(e), as inserted by the SSGA 1994, s 1: set out at para 14.20. In respect of hp, quasi-sales and simple hirings, the 1994 Act also inserted identical provisions in SOGIT, s 10(2B)(e); and the SGSA, s 18(3)(3).

56  See *Benjamin's Sale of Goods*, 6th edn, para 11.062. Cf. *Vikase Ltd v Paul Kiefel GmbH* [1999] 3 All ER 362, CA, esp *per* Chadwick LJ at para 16 and 20; *VAI Industries (UK) Ltd v Bostock & Bramley* [2003] BLR 359, CA, *per* Carnworth LJ at paras 18–36 (120 LQR 214).

57  *Benjamin, Op. cit.,* para 11.052; [2001] *Which?* 6.

58  As introduced by SSG, reg 5. Clothing retailers fear that consumers will use this to wear new goods and then return them, claiming a fault: DTI, *Impact Assessment* (4.1.2001), Annex D, para 2; Annex E, para 3. See also SGSA, s 11M(3).

59  The rule does not apply if it is (a) established that the goods did so conform on delivery, or (b) incompatible with the nature of the goods or the nature of the lack of conformity (new s 48A(4)).

60  SGSA, new s 11M(3) and (4), as introduced by SSG, reg 9. For the explanation, see para 29.10.

61  A state of affairs which has been regretted: Willett, Morgan-Taylor and Naidoo [2004 JBL 94 at 110.

benefit of the doubt, the change should not be too great;[62] but it may help to level the playing field between legitimate and rogue traders.

Additionally, there may sometimes be offered optional product insurance for an extended period (see para 17.09) or a money-back guarantee (see para 10.28). Further, there must be distinguished from the durability of the implied terms the length of time during which the transferee may rescind for breach (see paras 29.04–10) and the limitation period within which an action must be brought, usually six years (see para 26.17).

## UNDERTAKINGS AS TO FITNESS

[14.07] **The undertakings**. In the absence of any express undertaking as to the fitness of goods supplied, such an undertaking may only be imported by operation of law. In the case of sales, s 14(3) (as amended) of the SGA provides as follows:[63]

'Where the seller sells goods in the course of a business and the buyer, expressly or by implication, makes known—

(a)  to the seller, or

(b)  where the purchase price or part of it is payable by instalments and the goods were previously sold by a credit-broker to the seller, to that credit-broker,[64]

any particular purpose for which the goods are being bought, there is an implied term that the goods supplied under the contract are reasonably fit for that purpose, whether or not that is a purpose for which such goods are commonly supplied, except where the circumstances show that the buyer does not rely, or that it is unreasonable for him to rely, on the skill or judgment of the seller or credit-broker.'

In English law, this implied term is a condition.[65] Similar obligations are imported into quasi-sales,[66] hp[67] and simple hiring.[68] Certain common limitations have already been considered (see para 14.02); and, in the next two subsections, there will be explained (a) the content of the undertakings (see paras 14.08–9) and (b) the further special limitations on them (see paras 14.10–14). The requirements of the criminal law as to the fitness of goods supplied are dealt with elsewhere.[69] For consumer sales (see para 14.01), a simpler version of this undertaking is to be found in the SGG Directive (Arts 2(2)(b) and (5)), though this has not been transposed into the SSG Regulations.

---

62  But see the worrying Scottish case of *Thain v Anniesland Trade Centre* 1997 SLT (Sh.Ct.) 102, discussed by Ervine [2004] JBL 684, at 700–2.

63  As amended by the SSGA 1994, Sched 2, para 5(5)(a). See generally, para 11.11.

64  As to the meaning of 'credit-broker', see para 14.12.

65  New SGA, s 14(6): see SSGA 1994, Sched 2, para 5(5)(b).

66  SGSA 1982, s 4(4), (5) and (6). The SSGA 1994 does not amend the status of the term as in the SGA. Section 4 of the SGSA makes use of the expression 'transfer' instead of seller (see para 12.02).

67  SOGIT 1973, s 10(3). The SSGA 1994 here amends the status of the implied term as in the SGA: SSGA, Sched 2, para 4(4)(b) and (c). S 10 of SOGIT uses the expression 'creditor', which it defines as including any assignee therefrom (s 15(1)).

68  SGSA 1982, s 9(4), (5) and (6). The SSGA 1994 does not amend the status of the term as in the SGA. S 9 of the SGSA uses the term 'bailor' and is said to represent a significant tightening of the previous law: Woodroffe, *Goods and Services—The New Law*, paras 5.14–19 and 5.27.

69  E.g. TDA (see para 4.07); Food Act 1984 (see para 4.28); Construction and Use Regulations (see para 4.37).

## Content of the undertakings

**[14.08] Strict liability**. The foregoing statutory undertakings (see para 14.07) all require that the goods be 'reasonably fit for the purpose for which they are supplied'. This is not to say that the supplier's liability is founded on carelessness. On the contrary, his liability is strict, as may be seen from *Frost v Aylesbury Dairy Co*:[70]

> Typhoid germs were found in milk sold by a dairy for 'family use'. As these germs could only be discovered by prolonged scientific investigation, the sellers argued that they could not reasonably have discovered the defect by the exercise of reasonable care.

Notwithstanding this, the Court of Appeal unanimously held the dairy liable for breach of the undertaking as fitness. Nor is it any answer for the seller to plead that he promised two contradictory things, so that in *Baldry v Marshall Ltd*[71] the seller was held liable for breach of the undertaking in promising to sell (1) a Bugatti car that (2) was suitable for touring.[72] Nor is it even any answer that the transferee was himself unaware of the possibility of harm. Thus, in the *Ashington Piggeries* case (set out at para 13.13) there was no dispute that the meal was toxic to mink, and the House of Lords found that each buyer had made known to his seller that he required the goods as animal feeding stuffs, rather than as fertiliser (see para 14.10). Accordingly, their Lordships held each seller liable to his buyer for breach of the undertaking as to fitness because, not only was DMNA highly toxic to mink, but it was in some degree toxic to all other domestic animals and poultry.[73] It would seem the answer would have been otherwise if DMNA had only been toxic to mink—because neither buyer had asked for food suitable to feed to mink.[74]

The result is that, in the law of contract,[75] the supplier is under a strict liability[76] to ensure that the goods are 'reasonably fit' (see para 14.09) for the purpose supplied (see para 14.10).

**[14.09] Reasonably fit**. Whilst strict (see para 14.08), the statutory undertaking that the goods be 'reasonably fit' is not absolute: it must be tested in relation to the purpose for which the goods are supplied and must depend on the degree of precision with which that purpose is specified. In *Griffiths v Peter Conway Ltd*:[77]

---

70  [1905] 1 KB 608, [1904–7] All ER Rep 132, CA. See also *Preist v Last* [1903] 2 KB 148, CA; *Henry Kendall & Sons Ltd v William Lillico & Sons Ltd* (set out at para 14.10).

71  [1925] 1 KB 260, [1924] All ER Rep 155, CA. Cf. *Lynch v Thorne* [1956] 1 All ER 744, CA.

72  Greer J held that the Bugatti car ordered was not suitable for touring. Perhaps a modern equivalent might be a car to be suitable for motorway driving.

73  Actually, it was held that once it was proved that DMNA was toxic to mink, the onus (which they had not discharged) was on the sellers to show that the meal could have been fed with impunity to all other types of livestock. See further, para 14.10.

74  See also *Henry Kendall & Sons Ltd v William Lillico & Sons Ltd* (above); *Sumner, Permain & Co v Webb* (set out at para 14.16), where the CA decided against the buyer on other grounds.

75  Compare the supplier's liability in tort, which is substantially based on negligence: see para 17.12, *et seq*.

76  In the case of hp and simple hiring, this would appear to represent a clear increase in the supplier's liability beyond the common law position: as to which, see Macleod, *Sale and HP*, 1971, 86.

77  [1939] 1 All ER 685, CA.

P contracted dermatitis from a Harris Tweed coat which she had bought from D. It was found as a fact that P had an unusually sensitive skin and that the coat would not have harmed an ordinary person.

In finding the retail seller not liable for the unfitness of the coat for P, Lord Greene MR explained that, if a person suffering from such an abnormality desires to obtain the benefit of the implied condition:[78]

'The essential matter for the seller to know . . . consists in the particular abnormality or idiosyncrasy from which the buyer suffers. It is only when he has that knowledge that he is in a position to exercise his skill or judgment . . . The fact that those essential characteristics are not known . . . to the buyer does not seem to me to affect the question.'

Certainly, if the buyer does make clear to the seller the **particular purpose** for which he requires the goods, the seller **may** be strictly liable,[79] notwithstanding that he could not reasonably have prevented the harm.[80] A case where neither party was aware that a particular characteristic was needed was *Slater v Finning Ltd*.[81]

The owner of a fishing vessel engaged a marine engineer to repair the vessel's engine, including replacing the camshaft. Neither party was aware that the vessel had an abnormal tendency to produce excessive torsional resonance. The engineer fitted a new type of camshaft, which failed.

The House of Lords unanimously held that there was **no** breach of the implied condition as to fitness, Lord Keith saying that in the course of argument there was (405j–406a)

'put the illustration of a new front wheel tyre being purchased for a car which, unknown to the buyer or seller, had a defect in the steering mechanism as a result of which the tyre wore out after a few hundred miles of use, instead of the many thousands which would normally be expected. In these circumstances it would be totally unreasonable that the seller should be liable for breach of s 14(3).'

This links up with the presumption that, if nothing is said, the implication is that the goods are required for an ordinary purpose (see para 14.11); but it seemingly makes no allowance for those circumstances where an inexpert buyer presents the circumstances in which the goods are to be used to an expert seller so that the latter may exercise his expertise in advising what goods should be supplied as suitable for the buyer's purpose.[82] Alternatively, it may be that in the circumstances the seller's duty is merely to warn the buyer of possible hazards connected with the purpose for which the goods are required.[83]

What is the ambit of strict liability? According to Lord Greene in *Griffith v Peter Conway Ltd*, it might seem that the seller should be liable for any injury to the buyer

---

78   At 691. But could the buyer realistically expect the seller to know about the effect of the garment on her skin? Compare the case in fn 81 with the discussion of reliance at paras 14.13–14.

79   But that might amount to unreasonable reliance: as to which, see para 14.13.

80   E.g. *Frost v Aylesbury Dairy Co* (set out at para 14.08); *Henry Kendall & Sons Ltd v William Lillico & Sons Ltd* (set out at para 14.10).

81   [1996] 3 All E R 398; 15 Tr LR 458, HL(S).

82   E.g. a parent buying shoes for a child expecting the shop assistant to measure the child's foot: see Gullifer (1997) 16 Tr L 29.

83   E.g. *Vacwell Engineering Co Ltd v BDH Chemicals Ltd* (set out at para 18.29).

which flows from the range of 'essential characteristics' made known. Yet it is submitted that there must be some limitation on the rule. The burden of the rule ought to be limited by the circumstances of the transaction: A, who buys a thirty-year-old car for £150 cannot expect it to be as fit for driving as the three-year old car purchased by B for £5,500;[84] and B cannot expect his car to be as fit as the new car purchased by C for £15,500.[85] It may be that this is the proper meaning of the words 'reasonably fit': the goods must be as fit for the purpose supplied as goods of that description and in those circumstances usually are.[86]

## Qualification of the undertakings

*Knowledge of particular purpose*

**[14.10]** The undertakings as to fitness (see para 14.07) are expressed to apply only where the transferee, expressly or by implication, makes known to certain stipulated persons (see para 14.12) the 'particular purpose for which the goods are being' bought or hired. Since the SGA 1893 where they first appeared, the quoted words have consistently been interpreted by the courts in favour of the buyer: *first*, they refused to read 'particular' in the sense of special, as opposed to ordinary, purpose;[87] *second*, they did not insist that the buyer gave the information as to his purpose to the seller, but held it to be sufficient that the seller was aware of the purpose for which the goods were required;[88] and *third*, that purpose might be made known either expressly[89] or impliedly. For instance, in *Kendall v Lillico*:[90]

> K and G Ltd were both wholesale dealers and members of the London Cattle Food Trade Association. K sold to G Ltd a quantity of 'Brazilian ground nut extraction' knowing that G Ltd required the goods for resale for compounding as food for cattle and poultry. However, the goods contained a toxic substance (unsuspected at this time) which resulted in their being fit for use as food for cattle, but not for poultry. G Ltd orally agreed to sell part of the goods to one of their long-standing customers, SAPPA Ltd, a dealer, and subsequently sent SAPPA Ltd one of their ordinary 'sold notes' which stated that the buyer took liability for latent defects.[91] SAPPA Ltd then

---

84  Distinguish cars purchased as vintage or for scrap. Would an MOT test certificate affect the position?

85  Compare *Bartlett v Sidney Marcus Ltd* [1965] 2 All ER 753, CA (second-hand) and *Rogers v Parish Ltd* (set out at para 14.23: new car).

86  And see Lord Pearce in *Henry Kendall & Sons Ltd v William Lillico & Sons Ltd* (above) at 115. For the possible relevance of instructions for use, see para 18.34.

87  E.g. *Frost v Aylesbury Dairy Co* (set out at para 14.08; milk). See also *Wallis v Russell* [1902] 2 IR 585 (crabs 'for tea').

88  *Ashington Piggeries Ltd v Christopher Hill Ltd* (set out at para 13.13) as between N and P. CA decision reversed by HL, who held that N was aware that the herring meal was required for compounding for animal feedstuffs: see Lords Hodson (at 857), Guest (at 862–3), Dilhorne (at 869–70), Wilberforce (at 877–8); and Diplock dissenting (at 891).

89  *Ashington Piggeries Ltd v Christopher Hill Ltd* (above) as between P and D. The decision of the CA on this point was not in dispute before the HL.

90  *Henry Kendall & Sons Ltd v William Lillico & Sons Ltd* [1969] 2 AC 31, [1968] 2 All ER 444, HL. See generally Davies (1969) 85 LQR 74.

91  The CA explained that, whilst the 'sold note' became part of the contract between G Ltd and SAPPA Ltd (see para 18.04), it did not protect G Ltd from liability for breach of the undertaking as to fitness (see para 18.06).

compounded the goods bought from G Ltd into food for birds, and sold some to the Hardwick Game Farm. Many of their pheasants having died as a consequence of being fed the compound, the farmers sued SAPPA Ltd for breach of the undertakings as to fitness and quality (see para 14.19), who brought in G Ltd, and G Ltd brought in K, each buyer alleging similar breaches of s 14 against his seller.[92]

The House of Lords agreed with the Court of Appeal that the purpose for which each buyer required the goods, even though their normal and obvious purpose, was a sufficient particular purpose made known to the seller. Lord Morris said:[93]

'The degree of precision or definition which makes a purpose a particular purpose depends entirely on the facts and circumstances of a purchase and sale transaction. No need arises to define or limit the word 'particular' . . . There is no magic in the word 'particular'. A communicated purpose, if stated with reasonably sufficient precision, will be a particular purpose . . .

The next question that arises is whether that particular purpose was made known so as to show that the buyers relied on the skill and judgment of the sellers . . . Again, there is no magic in any particular word in the section.'

**[14.11] Single and multi-purpose goods.** It has long been settled that the undertaking as to fitness (see para 14.07) applies to goods which have only one ordinary purpose.[94] The difference between goods capable of ordinary use for many purposes and those ordinarily used for only one purpose was explained by Collins MR in *Priest v Last*,[95] where he said that in the multi-purpose case:

'in order to give rise to the implication of a warranty, it is necessary to show that, though the article sold was capable of general use for many purposes, in the particular case it was sold with reference to a particular purpose. But in a case where the discussion begins with the fact that the description of the goods by which they were sold points to one particular purpose only, it seems to me that the first requirement of the sub-section is satisfied . . . The sale is of goods which, by the very description under which they are sold, appear to be sold for a particular purpose'.

The effect of the cases would appear to be as follows: if the goods have only one ordinary use, the supplier is impliedly promising that the goods are fit for that use;[96] whereas, if the goods have more than one ordinary use, there is no implication that they are fit for any one of their particuilar ordinary uses[97] unless the buyer specifies for which ordinary use he requires the goods,[98] though there will be a

---

92 The CA held that there had been no breach of the undertaking as to merchantability (see para 14.20): *sub nom Hardwick Game Farm v Suffolk Agricultural Poultry Producers Association* [1966] 1 All ER 309, CA.

93 At 93–4. See also *per* Lord Pearce, at 114–15.

94 E.g. *Priest v Last* [1903] 2 KB 148, CA (hot-water bottle); *Grant v Australian Knitting Mills Ltd* [1936] AC 85, PC (underpants); *Griffiths v Peter Conway Ltd* (set out at para 14.09; clothing); *Wilson v Rickett Cockerell Ltd* (set out at para 14.03; Coalite); *Lowe v Lombank Ltd* (set out at para 18.06; car); and the cases cited in 87.

95 [1903] 2 KB 148, CA at 153.

96 E.g. *Wilson v Rickett Cockerell Ltd* (above; Coalite is bought for burning); *Lowe v Lombank Ltd* (above; car for driving).

97 E.g. *Sumner Permain & Co v Webb* (set out at para 14.16; sale in particular country).

98 E.g. *Kendall v Lillico* (set out at para 14.10); *Baldry v Marshall Ltd* [1925] 1 KB 260, CA (Bugatti car suitable for touring). In the *Ashington Piggeries* case (set out at para 13.13), it was made clear meal required for animal feed rather than fertiliser (see at para 14.09).

breach of the undertaking unless the supplier proves that the goods are fit for at least **one** of their ordinary uses.[99] Whilst the undertakings are expressly made applicable to extraordinary use,[100] if the transferee wishes to obtain the benefit of the undertaking in relation to an extraordinary use, he must specify that use.[101] In *Jewson Ltd v Boyhan*:[102]

> K, a developer, acquired a former school building to turn into 13 self-contained flats for sale, rather than rent; and he wished to instal a separate boiler in each flat. Ruling out gas as too expensive and time-consuming to instal, K consulted J, builders' merchants, as to whether there were any available electric boilers. After making enquiries, J reported to K that the new Amptec boilers appeared suitable; and K purchased from J 12 Amptec boilers for about £7,500 + VAT. After completion of the flats, K was invited by the LA to have the flats rated for SAP, the government energy-rating, a system unfamiliar to both K and J. The boilers had never been rated for SAP purposes and the flats therefore achieved a disastrous default rating. K counter-claimed under SGA, s 14, on the grounds that this would make the flats unsaleable.

The Court of Appeal unanimously rejected K's argument that the boilers were not of satisfactory quality (s 14(2): see para 14.21) and unfit for the purpose supplied (s 14(3)). Accepting that there was a considerable overlap between the two undertakings (see para 14.21), the Court unanimously held that J was not liable under s 14(3), because, although he had made clear that the boilers were required for installation in the building, K had not thought to ask any questions about the SAP rating of the boilers. Thus, K had given J no information about the nature of the building conversion such that J could have calculated the SAP rating so as to exercise relevant skill and judgment; nor did K rely on J's skill and judgment for this purpose (see para 14.13).

**[14.12]  Recipient of knowledge**. The modern statutes have tackled one particular problem which arose from the form of directly financed transactions (see para 2.21): at common law, it was sometimes difficult to say that a particular purpose made known by the consumer to the dealer was necessarily communicated to the financier, who in law supplied the goods to the consumer.[103] The HPA 1965 sought to overcome this difficulty by allowing the consumer to make his purpose known to **either** of the two following parties; and this formula was adopted (with suitable amendment) by the CCA:

(a)  the supplier (the financier), **or**

(b)  the dealer, which the CCA termed the 'credit-broker' (Sched 4, paras 3 and 35).

---

99  The *Ashington Piggeries* case (above): although the meal could have been intended for a range of animals, it was toxic to all of them (see para 14.09). See further Goode, *Commercial Law*, 3rd edn, 318–19.

100  'Whether or not that is a purpose for which such goods are commonly supplied': SGA, s 14(3); SOGIT, s 10(3); SGSA, ss 4(5) and 9(5).

101  *Griffiths v Peter Conway Ltd* (see above); *BS Brown Ltd v Craiks Ltd* 1969 SLT 107 and 357 (the subsequent appeal to the HL was only based on the undertaking as to merchantable quality: as to which, see para 14.21).

102  [2004] 1 Lloyd's Rep. 505, [2003] EWCA 1030, CA.

103  E.g. the householder's special requirements will obviously be made known to a double-glazing contractor, but not necessarily to the financier; a finance lease (see para 1.18); and see generally, para 16.03.

The solution was accepted by s 14(3) of the SGA (set out at para 14.07), s 61(1) of which appears to have lifted, without acknowledgment,[104] the definition of 'credit-broker' from the CCA.[105] A similar approach is to be found in relation to the undertakings as to fitness in relation to quasi-sales,[106] hp[107] and simple hiring.[108] Where the consumer is an 'individual' within the meaning of the CCA (see para 5.24), the effect would appear to be similar to that first introduced by the HPA 1965. However, where the sole consumer is a registered company (and hence not within the CCA category of 'individual'),[109] it might appear that such a transferee-company has unintentionally been put back in the pre-1965 position of having to show that he has made his purpose known to his supplier (the financier). In *Alpha Chauffeurs Ltd v Citygate*:[110]

> Alpha, an up-market driven car hire firm, decided to obtain a new Rolls Royce as a flagship for their fleet. Unfortunately, Alpha chose from the dealer a Monday morning car (see para 14.23) and then signed a conditional purchase agreement giving Alpha the option under clause 10 to switch to a directly financed transaction (see para 7.27). After Alpha exercised the option, the defective car was delivered to Alpha on Sept. 27; but the hp agreement with the financier was not executed until Oct 6. Eventually, Alpha lost patience with the car; and on May 11 wrote to the dealer purporting to cancel the transaction. Not until November 25 did Alpha notify the financier that it rejected the car and was stopping further payments. Alpha then sued both the dealer and financier.

The High Court Judge said that the car was neither fit for the purpose supplied, nor of satisfactory quality and held the defendants liable for this as follows:

(i)    There being no novation (see para 7.27), the dealer was in breach of the SGA, s 14(2) and (3) (para 34); but the dealer's liability was reduced to nominal damages after the exercise of clause 10.

(ii)   The financier was not liable for breach of the undertaking as to fitness in SOGIT, s 10(3) (paras 37–8), because the dealer not being a credit-broker, the financier was not infected with the dealer's knowledge of the purpose for which the goods were required and further, Alpha did not rely on the financier's skill and judgment, or it was unreasonable to do so (see para 14.14). However, the financier was liable for the unsatisfactory quality of the car (see para 14.26) and could in turn make the same claim against the dealer (see para 16.22).

---

104  Does this mean that the CCA requirement that the transferee is an individual (see para 5.245) does not apply here?

105  For a 'credit-broker' within the CCA, see para 5.38. Presumably the effect is to apply that learning to both regulated sales, e.g. credit sales and unregulated sales, e.g. cash sales.

106  SGSA, s 4(4), 'credit-broker' being defined in s 18(1).

107  SOGIT, s 10(3), 'credit-broker' being defined in s 10(6).

108  SGSA, s 9(4), 'credit-broker' being defined in s 18(1).

109  *Contra* where the company is joint consumer with an individual: see para 5.24.

110  [2002] GCCR X/301 (case rev. by CA wholly on grounds of costs).

*Reliance*

**[14.13]** At common law, the undertaking as to fitness was ousted by the mere opportunity on the part of the buyer to inspect the goods;[111] the undertaking in the SGA 1893 did not apply where the goods were sold under a trade name (e.g. *Webb's* case: set out at para 14.16) and required the buyer to show that he relied on the seller's skill and judgment. However, the courts decided that such reliance might be in part only. In *Cammell Laird Ltd v Manganese Bronze and Brass Ltd*:[112]

> The buyer of ship's propellers stipulated for certain specifications. The propellers supplied were found to be unfit for the purpose supplied because they were not thick enough, a matter not covered by the specifications. The House of Lords held that in respect of matters not specified the buyer was relying on the seller's skill and judgment.

The next step was taken in 1973, when statute appeared to shift the burden of proof to the supplier;[113] once the transferee showed that he had made his purpose known, the undertaking was imported unless the supplier could show either non-reliance (see para 14.14) or unreasonable reliance[114] on the supplier **or** credit-broker.[115]

These 1973 changes were reproduced in the present legislation. Where the transferee can show that he expressly or impliedly made known to the supplier or credit-broker the purpose for which the goods were required (see paras 14.10–12), there is an implied undertaking that the goods are reasonably fit for that purpose except where the circumstances show that the transferee 'does not rely, or that it is unreasonable for him to rely, on the skill or judgment of' the supplier or credit-broker.[116] This provision represents a further step in the statutory protection of the transferee; and it would seem that a supplier may be liable even though he in turn relies exclusively on his supplier (see para 11.08). As to implied reliance, see para 14.14.

*Ousting the undertaking.* Not only are there restrictions on the ability of the supplier to exclude the undertaking (see para 18.19), but it is clear that the mere recitation in a standard-form agreement that the transferee does not rely on the supplier's skill and judgment will not necessarily oust the undertaking;[117] and such a term may also be attacked under the UTCC Regulations (see para 11.12) and the UCTA (s 3: see para 18.24). Nor will even the fact that the goods have been delivered

---

111  Compare the present position in relation to the suitability of goods supplied by reference to a sample: see para 15.10.

112  [1934] AC 402, [1934] All ER Rep 1, HL. See also *the Ashington Piggeries* case (set out at para 13.13), where all the parties had different areas of expertise: if the DMNA had been toxic only to mink, D would have relied on his own skill and the CA would have been correct (see para 14.14). See also *Jewson Ltd v Boyhan* (set out at para 14.11), at paras 62–3.

113  SOGIT, ss 3 and 10(3). Did this transfer the legal or only factual burden of proof?

114  Consider the extent to which this requirement may have reversed the previous decisions mentioned in para 14.09. The change was based on the First Report on *Exemption Clauses in Contracts* (1969, Law Com No. 24), para 37. But see the *Aswan Engineering* case (set out at para 14.14).

115  This formula was first introduced in SOGIT, s 10(3), to deal with directly financed hp transactions, where the dealer was likely to be an expert in the type of goods supplied: see para 14.12.

116  SOGIT, s 10(3); SGA, s 14(3); SGSA, ss 4(6) and 9(6); *Anglo Group PLC v Winther Browne & Co Ltd* [2002] CLY 708; and generally, para 14.07.

117  *Lowe v Lombank Ltd* (set out at para 18.06). See Goode, *Commercial Law*, 3rd edn, 323.

and the defect discovered before the contract is made necessarily do so.[118] On the other hand, if the transferee insists on the supply of unsuitable goods, there remains the obligation that those goods must be of satisfactory quality.[119]

**[14.14]  Reliance**. In the *Ashington Piggeries* case (set out at para 13.13), the House of Lords held as follows:

(1) *As between P and D*. The Court of Appeal had held that D did not rely on the manufacturer (P) in respect of the suitability of any of the ingredients of King Size for feeding to mink, but D relied on his own skill. This was reversed by the House of Lords on the following grounds: even though D had relied on his own skill and judgment to ensure that the formula King Size was suitable for feeding to mink, D relied on P's skill to ensure that the ingredients were of a quality suitable for compounding into animal foodstuffs.[120]

(2) *As between P and N*. The Court of Appeal did not have to consider the question of reliance,[121] whereas the House of Lords held that there had been reliance[122] and Lord Guest commented that, once knowledge of particular purpose had been shown, it was an 'easy step' to infer reliance.[123]

With this case may be compared *Aswan Engineering Etc Co v Lupdine Ltd*:[124]

> A was a construction company carrying on business in Kuwait. A bought from L a quantity of liquid waterproofing packed in heavy duty plastic pails manufactured and supplied by TB. On arrival at Kuwait, the pails were stacked in the sun on the quayside. The pails collapsed in the heat and the compound was lost, though if the pails had been stacked in a particular way they would not have done so. Neill J's decision that L was liable to A for breach of s 14(3) of the SGA was not appealed.

As between L and TB,[125] the Court of Appeal held that there was no liability for breach of the undertaking as to fitness in supplying the pails because 'the circumstances showed positively that the buyers did not rely on the seller's skill or judgment in any relevant sense'.[126]

---

118  *R & B Customs Brokers Co Ltd v UDT Ltd* (see para 18.18). *Sed quaere?*

119  *Young & Marten Ltd v McManus Childs Ltd* [1969] 1 AC 454, HL. As to satisfactory quality, see para 14.15, *et seq.*

120  *Per* Lords Hodson (at 468–9), Guest (at 473), Dilhorne (at 485), Wilberforce (at 490), Diplock (at 507–8). Lord Diplock appeared to be saying that, at least where there was partial reliance, it was for the supplier to prove that the defect lay within the transferee's area of responsibility.

121  Because the CA had held that N had no knowledge of the particular purpose for which P required the herring meal; but they were reversed on this point by the HL: see para 14.10.

122  *Per* Lords Hodson (at 471), Guest (at 477), Dilhorne (at 486–7), Wilberforce (at 496); Lord Diplock dissenting on the grounds that it is not sufficient for the buyer to show that the seller knew only that the goods may be used for such a purpose before the inference can be drawn (at 513).

123  See also *Manchester Liners Ltd v Rea* [1922] AC 74, HL; *Henry Kendall & Sons Ltd v William Lillico & Sons Ltd* (set out at para 14.10).

124  [1987] 1 All ER 135, [1987] 1 WLR 1, CA.

125  For the merchantability chain between A and L, see para 14.21; and for the product liability claim between A and TB, see para 17.14. L being insolvent, for A's claim against L's insurers, see para 17.02. See also *Alpha Chauffeurs Ltd v Citygate* (set out at para 14.12), at para 39; *Jewson Ltd v Boyhan* (set out at para 14.11), at paras 60–61.

126  After the supply of both a sample and a trial order: *per* Lloyd and Fox LJJ at 149d, 159f. See also *per* Nicholls LJ (at 157f), who held that the fitness claim failed because the merchantability claim failed. Where is the evidence here of a burden of proof on TB (see para 14.13)?

A number of other examples may be given of factors which may be taken into account in deciding whether to infer reliance. *First*, there is the relative expertise of the parties, though this is not conclusive;[127] and, bearing in mind the introduction of the supplier's defence of unreasonable reliance (see para 14.13), it remains to be seen whether this consideration will play any significant part in relation to goods supplied for consumption.[128] For instance, might it oust the undertaking where the transferee probably knows more about the suitability of the goods for his purpose than the supplier, as in *Griffiths v Peter Conway Ltd* (set out at para 14.09); or perhaps is a self-declared know-all? *Second*, there may be relevant any instructions which the supplier may have provided as to the use of the goods (see para 18.32).

## UNDERTAKINGS AS TO SATISFACTORY QUALITY

**[14.15] The undertakings**. In the absence of any express undertakings as to the quality of goods supplied, an undertaking as to quality might be imported at common law: this required that goods sold by description be merchantable under that description; and in 1815 Lord Ellenborough defined 'merchantable' as meaning that the goods:[129]

> 'shall be saleable in the market under the denomination mentioned in the contract'.

In codifying the subject, Chalmers wrote into s 14(2) of the SGA 1893 the requirement that the goods must be of 'merchantable quality', thus introducing the word 'quality' (see para 14.16), but not defining 'merchantable'.[130] Following the recommendation of the Law Commission,[131] 'merchantability' has been replaced by a new undertaking of 'satisfactory quality'. Accordingly, new SGA, s 14(2) provides[132]

> 'where the seller sells[133] goods in the course of a business, there is an implied term that the goods supplied under the contract are of satisfactory quality'.

In English law, this implied term is a condition.[134] Similar terms are imported into quasi-sales,[135] hp,[136] and simple hiring.[137] Some limitations have already been considered (see para 14.02); and, in the next two subsections, there will be explained

---

127 Thus, reliance has been found even as between two wholesale-dealer members of the same trade association: *Henry Kendall & Sons Ltd v William Lillico & Sons Ltd* (above). But see para 14.26.
128 Cf. *Priest v Last* [1903] 2 KB 148, CA; *Grant v Australian Knitting Mills Ltd* [1936] AC 85, PC; *Ashford Shire Council v Dependable Motors Ltd* [1961] AC 336, PC.
129 *Gardiner v Gray* (1815) 4 Camp 144 at 145.
130 In the nineteenth century, there was no need to define this commercial man's notion, which would be readily understandable to commercial courts and juries: *Benjamin's Sale of Goods*, 3rd edn, para 800.
131 *Sale and Supply of Goods* (1987, Law Com. 160), Pt 3.
132 As inserted by the SSGA 1994, s 1. See generally Bridge [1995] JBL 398.
133 'Sells' presumably includes agreement to sell (see para 1.10): Goode, *Commercial Law*, 3rd edn, 300.
134 New SGA, s 14(6): see SSGA 1994, Sched 2, para 5(5)(b).
135 SGSA 1982, s 4(2). The SSGA 1994 does not amend the status of the term as in the SGA. Section 4 of the SGSA makes use of the expression 'transferor' instead of seller (see para 12.02).
136 SOGIT 1973, s 10(2). The SSGA 1994 here amends the status of the implied term as in the SGA: SSGA Sched 2, para 4(4)(b), (c).
137 SGSA 1982, s 9(2). The SSGA 1994 does not amend the status of the term as in the SGA. S 9 of the SGSA uses the term 'bailor'.

(a) the content of the undertaking (see paras 14.16–24) and (b) the other limitations on them (see paras 14.25–26).

For consumer sales (see para 14.01), another version of this undertaking is to be found in the SGG Directive (Art 2(2)(c), (d) and (4)).

## Content of the undertakings

**[14.16] Quality.** Section 61(1) of the SGA 1893 provided that the **quality of goods** 'includes their state or condition'. Unfortunately, in the two leading cases on the point, the same Court of Appeal appears to have come to opposite conclusions as to the meaning of the word **quality**. In *Niblett's* case (set out at para 12.03), the majority held that there had been a breach of s 14(2), as well as of the implied condition as to title, and Bankes LJ said (at 395):

> 'Quality includes the state or condition of the goods. The state of this condensed milk was that it was packed in tins bearing labels. The labels were as much a part of the state or condition of the goods as the tins were. The state of the packing affected the merchantable quality of the goods.'

On the other hand, in *Sumner, Permain & Co v Webb*[138] the same Court of Appeal found that there had been **no** breach of s 14(2):

> S was the manufacturer of a product known as 'Webb's Indian Tonic Water'. As S knew, the buyer (B) purchased some of this tonic water from him for the purpose of shipment to the Argentine. However, S was unaware of two vital facts: (1) his product contained a small quantity of salicylic acid; and (2) the sale of any article of food or drink containing salicylic acid was prohibited in the Argentine. After the Argentine authorities had seized and condemned his tonic water, B claimed damages for breach of the undertakings as to fitness and quality.

In respect of s 14(2),[139] the Court of Appeal were clear that the fact that the goods were unsaleable in the Argentine did not prevent their being of merchantable quality: a subsequent change in the law would now reverse that decision (see para 14.21). Atkin LJ sought to explain his decision in the earlier case as follows:[140]

> 'nobody would buy those tins, because, if they did, they would probably be buying a law-suit, and the tins in that state and condition were unsaleable, not merely in this country by reason of a law peculiar to this country, but unsaleable anywhere'.

The distinction seemed to be this: the condensed milk with those labels was treated as not being saleable anywhere, and not merely by reason of the law peculiar to this country;[141] but the tonic water could be sold almost anywhere as such, except in the

---

138 [1922] 1 KB 55, [1921] All ER Rep 680, CA.

139 In relation to the undertaking as to fitness, the argument turned on what significance should be attached to the use of the trade name, a matter specifically mentioned in the 1893 Act, but now dropped: see para 14.13.

140 At 65–6. See also Banks LJ at 61. In *Buchanan-Jardine v Hamilink* [1983] SLT 149 (cattle sold held of merchantable quality, even though subject to a Ministry 'stop notice' because another cow not subject to the sale reacted positively to a tuberculosis test).

141 Is this so? Did Atkin LJ have in mind the conflict rule that, if no evidence of foreign law is produced, it is assumed to be the same as English Law? Does this rule apply to statute law? Would there have been a reasonable distinction if Atkin LJ had said 'not saleable anywhere by **reason of English Law**'?

Argentine.[142] The same definition of 'quality' now appears as part of a much larger definition in new s 14(2B): see para 14.20.

**[14.17] Merchantability.** This concept was not defined in the SGA 1893.[143] However, over the course of time the persistence of litigants repeatedly forced the courts to examine the meaning of 'merchantable'[144] and two distinct judge-made formulations of the concept appeared:

(1) *Acceptability.* The formulation of Farewell LJ in *Bristol Tramways Carriage Co v Fiat Motors Ltd* stressed whether the goods were **acceptable** to the buyer.[145] This test addressed itself to the needs of a commercial buyer. However, not only was it circular,[146] but the test also assumed a particular level of demand for the goods in question.[147]

(2) *Usability.* Particularly to meet the situation where goods were bought for consumption rather then resale, there was developed the test of **usability** of the goods based on a dictum of Lord Wright in *Cammell Laird Ltd v Manganese Bronze and Brass Ltd*.[148]

Usually, whichever of the above tests was selected was entirely suitable for the circumstances in which it was applied. The trouble was that it seemed inconsistent with the other test. By 1970, an impasse appeared to have been reached[149] and attention switched to statutory reform.

After a false start,[150] in 1987 the Law Commission returned to the subject. *First*, the Commission proposed the introduction of a brand new concept to replace merchantability (see para 14.18). *Second*, the Commission recommended a multiple definition to meet the different circumstances in which the concept would have to be used (see para 14.20).

**[14.18] The statutory definition of *satisfactory*.** In 1987, the Law Commission recommended that the old concept of 'merchantability' should be replaced by a positive adjective,[151] whilst retaining much of the rest of the definition (para 3.12:

---

142 This would fit in with the general maxim that the undertaking as to merchantability is not usually an undertaking that the goods will be fit for any particular purpose—see para 14.21.

143 As with the undertaking as to fitness (see para 14.08), liability is strict: *Daniels and Daniels v White & Sons Ltd* (set out at para 17.13).

144 Whilst a nineteenth-century term of general use (see para 14.15), in the twentieth century it fell into disuse: *Cehave v Bremer, The Hansa Nord* [1976] QB 44, CA, at 80.

145 [1910] 2 KB 831, CA, at 841, as elaborated by Dixon J in *Australian Knitting Mills Ltd v Grant* (1993) 50 CLR 387, HC (affd [1936] AC 85, PC).

146 A reasonable buyer would only accept the goods if he were legally bound to do so: *per* Salmond J in *Taylor v Combined Buyers Ltd* [1924] NZLR 627, at 646. *Contra* Benjamin, *Sale of Goods*, 6th edn, para 11-035, speaking of the amended version.

147 *Per* Scrutton LJ in *Webb's* case [1922] 1 KB 55, CA at 63.

148 [1934] AC at 430: case set out at para 14.13.

149 *BS Brown & Sons Ltd v Craiks Ltd* (above) at 825, *per* Lord Reid, see para 14.20; and Benjamin, *Op. cit.*, para 11-037.

150 *First Report on Exemption Clauses in Contract* (1969, Law Com No. 24), para 43.

151 *Sale and Supply of Goods* (1987, Law Com 160), paras 3.14–18.

see below, para 14.19); and the draftsman chose in new s 14(2) to employ the expression 'satisfactory' (see para 14.15). This notion he explained in new s 14(2A), which provides as follows:[152]

> 'For the purposes of this Act, goods are of satisfactory quality if they meet the standard that a reasonable person would regard as satisfactory, taking into account any description of the goods, the price (if relevant) and all the other relevant circumstances.'

Similar provisions are to be found in quasi-sales, hp and simple hirings[153] Such a generalised standard has the merit that it is applicable to all cases, but the demerit that, without going to court, a consumer will not know whether it has been met in his case.[154] To some extent, this disadvantage is counter-balanced by the fact that the modern definition also specifies a number of relevant factors (see para 14.19).

The essence of the new definition is the standard of the reasonable man. The Law Commission intended (see paras 3.25–6) that the test should be whether the goods would be acceptable to the reasonable man with hypothetical knowledge of the defects, from which should be distinguished both the following situations where the buyer himself knows of the defects: (i) because he has actually examined the goods (see para 14.26); and (ii) where he is assumed to know of the defects because the sale is by sample, which he is presumed to have examined (see para 15.10). Earlier decisions on defective goods may provide some guidance;[155] but the first substantial reported case on the new concept was *Clegg v Olle Andersson*.[156]

> In 1999, B agreed to buy a new yacht from S, with 'keel in accordance with the manufacturer's standard specification' for a price of £236,000. It was delivered in August 2000. S then informed B that the keel was substantially heavier than the above specification and indicated that he would make reasonable alterations. B sought from S information as to the safety consequences, which he did not receive until 2001. Three weeks later, B sought to rescind on grounds that the yacht was unsatisfactory and reclaimed his price. The Court of Appeal unanimously held that the yacht was unsatisfactory (see below) and that B was entitled to rescind and recover his price, not having lost his right to rescind by acceptance (see paras 29.05–7). There was no suggestion that B was a business-buyer[157] and it should be noted that the case was decided under the old law (see para 29.06) before there came into force the new consumer remedies (see para 29.02A).

In the Court of Appeal, it was found that the effect of the heavier keel was not to render the yacht unsafe, but to shorten the life of the rigging.[158] S argued that the

---

152  As supplied by the SSGA 1994, s 1.
153  As supplied by Sched 2 of the SSGA 1994: see respectively SOGIT, new s 10(2A) (hp); SGSA 1982, new s 4(2A) (quasi-sale); SGSA 1982, new s 9(2A) (hiring).
154  See Twigg-Flesner, *Consumer Product Guarantees*, 2003, para 1.6.
155  Ervine [2004] JBL 684 at 689–90, 692–3; and see 1st edn, para 14.18.
156  [2003] 1 All ER (Comm) 721, CA. The CA did not proceed with a first instance finding for the seller with regard to the s 13 claim.
157  At para 50. So, distinguish the issue of whether S's breach was so slight as to affect B's remedy (see para 11.05).
158  At para 45. The CA did not pursue B's arguments as to the statutory definition of 'quality' (at para 48): as to which, see para 14.20.

yacht was of satisfactory quality because it only required remedial work costing some £1,680; but the Court of Appeal did not accept this because more than minimal remedial work was required.[159] As Hale LJ pointed out, under the above statutory definition of satisfactory quality, the choice of reasonable remedial work did not lie with S, but with B (at para 70). Her Ladyship repeated the above quote from the Law Commission and continued in relation to the buyer:[160]

'A reasonable person is not an expert. If a reasonable person had been told in September 2000 that the seller himself had realised that a very large quantity of lead would have to be removed in some as yet unspecified way from the keel of a brand new boat costing nearly a quarter of a million pounds with as yet unspecified consequences for its safety and performance he or she would have had little difficulty in concluding that the boat could not be of satisfactory quality.'

She concluded that, once this question had been answered, B 'does not have to act reasonably in choosing rejection rather than damages or cure':[161] this may represent a change in the law[155] and would seem to bring English law closer to what it is claimed the SGG Directive requires.[162] In *Jewson Ltd v Boyhan* (set out at para 14.11) Sedley LJ rejected K's attempts to introduce his personal agenda to make the flats saleable and explained (at para 78):

'The reasonable person in s 14(2A) is a construct by whose standards the Judge is required to evaluate the quality of the goods. So, for example, the safety and durability of a soft toy would ordinarily need to be judged in relation to how a toddler may handle it—not in relation to the possibility of its being given to a dog. . . . unless the toy were bought in a pet shop . . . [which] . . . might well be a relevant circumstance.'

In *Bramhill v Edwards* (set out at para 14.21), the Court of Appeal confirmed that, although the test is objective, 'the reasonable buyer must be attributed with knowledge of all relevant background facts'; viz the vehicle was of illegal width and that the authorities were turning a blind eye (para 39).

**[14.19] *Satisfactory*: the specified factors.** The new statutory notion of when goods are satisfactory (s 14(2A): see para 14.18) includes express reference to the following factors:

1. *Any description of the goods.* The Law Commission argued that 'goods of a different description may well be expected to be of different quality.[163] Thus, the quality of goods must usually be judged in the light of the contractual description. For instance, in *Harlingdon* (set out at para 13.11A), the majority of the Court of Appeal decided that a miss-attributed painting was merchantable, though they disagreed as to whether a non-contractual description could be

---

159 At paras 47–8, 71 and 77, disagreeing with the first instance judge. See also *Jackson v Rotax Motor & Cycle Co* (on merchantability; set out at para 14.05; not cited); *Lamarra v Capital Bank* 2005 SLT 21, Sh. Ct.
160 At para 73; and Dyson LJ expressly agreed with both judgments. Hale LJ was a Law Commissioner at the time of this Report.
161 At para 74. As to the possibility of cure under the old law, see para 29.02.
162 Willett, Morgan-Taylor and Naidoo [2004] JBL 94 at 102–31.
163 *Sale and Supply of Goods* (1987, Law Com 160), para 3.27.

taken into account in assessing merchantability.[164] Other examples would be the retail sale of goods described as 'new',[165] an expression which may presumably be subject to any trade usage (cf. para 13.11), or luxury goods.[166]

2.  *The price (if relevant)*. In *Kendall v Lillico*, Lord Pearce argued that the price could be a relevant factor in assessing merchantability, e.g. the regular retail market for 'seconds' with a price discounted to reflect the defect;[167] and the same may be true of inferior quality,[168] or superior quality.[166] Whilst a useful indicator of standards in some circumstances,[169] care is required in the inference to be drawn from the price, which might instead reflect market price fluctuations, e.g. seasonal sales, or that the supplier is a discount store, or errors of judgement. Thus, in *Harlingdon* the majority thought that, although the painting was bought by a dealer for resale and its price depended on its attribution, it was still merchantable as not unfit for 'aesthetic appreciation'.[170] What if the price reduction reflects that the goods are unsafe?[171]

3.  *All the other relevant circumstances*. The Commission suggested (para 2.12) that the 'relevant circumstances' may include any inadequate instructions as to the use of the goods (see paras 18.32–3), but probably not any manufacturer's repair warranties.[172] Whilst the undertaking obviously applies to second-hand goods, even in the absence of specified defects (see para 14.25), goods described as 'second-hand' or 'demonstration model' only have to reach a lower standard,[173] both as to major defects[174] and minor or cosmetic ones (see paras 14.23–4). The Regulations (see para 14.01) have since explicitly added the category of 'public statements' (see para 14.19A). Judicial pronouncement has added the shop in which a soft toy is purchased (toy shop or pet shop: see para 14.18).

4.  *The guidelines as to quality* (see para 14.20).

**[14.19A] Public statements.** Public statements made or utilised by the seller are already taken into account by English law as regards the undertakings as to description (see para 13.10); and the SGG Directive (Art 2(2)(d) and (4): see para

---

164 Of the majority, Slade LJ (at QB 586F) said that a non-contractual description should be ignored, whilst Norse LJ conceded (at QB 576F) that the description was 'applied to' the painting within the definition of merchantability (old s 14(6)). Stuart-Smith LJ (dissenting) held that the court was 'entitled and required' to take that description into account (at QB 583A).

165 See *Andrews Ltd v Singer & Co Ltd* [1934] 1 KB 17, CA. Cf. TDA s 2(1)(j): see paras 4.06–7.

166 E.g. *Rogers v Parish* (set out at para 14.23), *Clegg v Olle Andersson* (set out at para 14.18).

167 [1969] AC, at 118; set out at para 14.10. The Law Commission enthusiastically endorsed this suggestion: *First Report on Exemption Clauses* (1969, Law Com No 24), para 42.

168 *Feast Contractors Ltd v Ray Vincent Ltd* [1974] 1 NZLR 212.

169 E.g. *Rogers v Parish* (set out at para 14.23); *Shine v General Guarantee Corpn Ltd* [1988] 1 All ER 911, CA (for another point, see para 14.22).

170 Even though it could only have been resold for £50–100 as against the contract price of £6,000 (see Norse LJ at QB 576D). See criticism by Brown (1990) 106 LQR at 563–4; and para 14.20.

171 Cf. *Godley v Perry* [1960] 1 All ER 36. Safety is now an expressed feature of quality: see para 14.20.

172 *Rogers v Parish* (set out at para 14.23), *per* Mustill LJ at All ER 237e–h. It might be more accurate to distinguish manufacturers' guarantees (to replace initially faulty parts) from repair warranties (after-sales service, replacement parts to prolong the life of the goods): Twigg-Flesner, *Consumer Credit Guarantees*, 2003, paras 5.11.3 and 8.10.1; and see below, paras 17.09–09A.

173 *Benjamin's Sale of Goods*, 6th edn, para 11.061.

174 *Thain v Anniesland Trade Centre* 1997 SLT 102, Sh. Ct. (5-yr-old automatic car, the buyer accepted the risk that the gearbox might fail at any time).

14.01) contains a similar rule as regards the undertakings as to the fitness and quality which has been embodied in the SSG Regulations.[175] By way of an additional rule (compulsory new s 14(2F)), new s 14(2D) of the SGA,[176] adds to the list of specified factors (s 14(2A): see para 14.19) that, where the buyer **deals as consumer,**[177] *prima facie*

> 'the relevant circumstances mentioned in subsection (2A) above include any public statements on the specific characteristics of the goods made about them by the seller, the producer or his representative, particularly in advertising or on labelling'.

It has been argued that such 'public statements' do not extend to mere sales puffs (see para 8.05), but that they otherwise apply to statements made prior to the retail supply in 'brochures, notices, labelling and general advertising'.[178] It would seem that the public statements may be made by: (1) the retailer to the consumer; (2) the manufacturer in statements which the retailer passes on to the consumer; (3) the manufacturer direct to the consumer.[178] The first two categories would seem to be simply helpful confirmations of existing English law (see above); but category (3) would appear to open up a new field of retailer supply contract liability, which could even extend to statements made by a manufacturer, e.g. by way of media, billboard advertising, direct mailing, text messaging, long after he has supplied goods to the retailer.[178]

However, there are a number of 'defences' available to a retailer faced with such a claim. Public statements will not give rise to liability where either (SGA, new s 14(2E)):

> '(a)  at the time the contract was made, he was not, and could not reasonably have been, aware of the statement, or
>
> (b)  before the contract was made, the statement had been withdrawn in public or, to the extent that it contained anything which was incorrect or misleading, it had been corrected in public, or
>
> (c)  the decision to buy the goods could not have been influenced by the statement'.

(a) might save a retailer reasonably unaware of a manufacturer's advertising campaign; presumably (b) will be confined to a public withdrawal sufficient to alert consumers; and (c) should be limited to statements unknown to the consumer or known sales puffs.

A similar rule is to be found in the case of quasi-sale, simple hiring and hp.[179]

**[14.20]  Statutory definition of quality**. Following the recommendation of the Law Commission,[180] the hitherto largely statutorily undefined[181] notion of 'quality' has

---

175  As to criticism of Art 2(2), see Twigg-Flesner, *Consumer Product Guarantees*, 2003, 8.

176  As inserted by SSG, reg 3.

177  By SGA, s 61(5A), 'dealing as consumer' has the same meaning as in UCTA: see para 18.18.

178  Willett, Morgan-Taylor and Naidoo [2004] JBL 94 at 97–8.

179  SGSA, new ss 4(2B–D), 9(2B–D) and SOGIT, s 10(2D–F), as introduced by SSG, regs 7, 10 and 13.

180  *Sale and Supply of Goods* (1987, Law Com 160), para 3.37, *et seq*.

181  The short definition of 'quality' (see para 14.16) was previously found in SGA, s 61. That definition was repealed by the SSGA 1994, Sched 2, para 5(9)(a): this follows the recommendation of the Commission (*ibid*, para 3.37).

been expanded by the Sale and Supply of Goods Act 1994 (SSGA). New s 14(2B) of the SGA provides as follows:[182]

'For the purposes of this Act, the quality of goods includes their state and condition and the following (among others) are in appropriate cases aspects of the quality of goods—

(a)  fitness for all the purposes for which goods of the kind in question are commonly supplied,

(b)  appearance and finish,

(c)  freedom from minor defects,

(d)  safety, and

(e)  durability.'

A similar provision is introduced as regards hp,[183] quasi-sale and simple hiring.[184] Besides rendering more prominent the 'state or condition' of the goods (see para 14.16), the provision also draws attention to the following non-exhaustive list of guidelines to be taken into account in assessing the quality of the goods 'in appropriate cases':

(a)  *Fitness for purpose.* The present extent of this guideline is discussed in relation to defective and unsuitable goods (below, paras 14.21–2). However, it is to be noted that the above new s 14(2B) refers to 'commonly supplied'; whereas the SGG Directive (see para 14.01) refers to 'normally used' (Art 2(2)(c)): Does this mean the same?[185] For criminal liability for unfit goods, see para 4.02, *et seq.*

(b)  *Appearance and finish* (see para 14.24).

(c)  *Freedom from minor defects* (see para 14.23).

(d)  *Safety.* It is already a criminal offence where goods do not comply with the general safety requirement or safety regulations (see paras 4.32–5); or as regards food which is unsafe to eat or motor vehicles to drive.[186] Whilst breach of such provisions might already sometimes give rise to a civil right of action, whether under the supply contract[187] or otherwise,[188] the Law Commission recommended that this aspect should constitute a clear breach of the supply contract (paras 3.44–6). A reduction in safety factor which does not make the goods criminally unsafe may still render them unsatisfactory;[189] and goods may be rendered unsafe where the retail supplier does not provide adequate safety instructions as to their installation or use.[190] As to the safety aspects of work by the Design Council, see para 3.08.

---

182  Inserted by s 1 of the Sale and Supply of Goods Act 1994. See Ervine [2004] JBL 684 at 693–6.

183  SOGIT, new s 10(2B): see SSGA 1994, Sched 2, para 4(4)(a).

184  SGSA 1982, new s 18(3): as inserted by the SSGA 1994, Sched 2, para 6(10).

185  See Ervine [2004] JBL 684 at 702–3.

186  See paras 4.27 and 4.37. As to genetically modified organisms, see Waldron [1999] JBL 395.

187  *Godley v Perry* [1960] 1 WLR 9, CA.

188  It directly does so as regards breach of the safety regulations (see para 4.35), but not for breach of the general safety requirements or GPS regulations (see above).

189  *Clegg v Olle Anderson* (set out at para 14.18).

190  E.g. [2004] 6 *Which?* 6 (inadequate instruction on installation of child car seat). As to instructions for use, see generally, para 18.28, *et seq.*

(e) *Durability* (see para 14.06). For instance, an oil filter would generally not last longer than a year; but that would not mean that it was not of satisfactory quality; similarly food beyond its use-by date (see para 8.11). Further, the buyer cannot complain where the deterioration of the goods is due to fair wear and tear, or his own accidental damage of the goods.

**[14.21] Fitness for purpose (1): defective goods.** Under the previous test, these might be rendered unmerchantable by one major defect,[191] or a congeries of minor ones (see para 14.17; para 14.23); and the defect might be substantive or cosmetic (see para 14.24). Examples of one physical defect rendering goods unmerchantable were beer contaminated with arsenic,[191] lemonade contaminated with acid,[192] underpants impregnated with sulphate,[193] a power boat going into self-destruct within 27 days of delivery[194] and Coalite packed with a detonator.[195] Alternatively, the single major defect might be a legal one, as where labels contained an infringing trademark,[196] or a motor vehicle contravened the construction and use regulations,[197] or did not carry a rust warranty.[198]

After the replacement of the merchantability test by satisfactory quality (see para 14.18), the courts seemed to continue on the same tack as regards goods with one major physical defect,[199] or a congeries of defects.[200] However, with respect to goods with a single major legal defect, it may be that the courts are adopting a more restrictive interpretation. In *Bramhill v Edwards*,[201]

> The buyer (B) in 1999 purchased from a dealer (D) a second-hand motor-home imported from the United States. The width of the motor-home was 102 inches, which exceeded the maximum 100-inch width permitted in the UK by the Construction and Use Regulations (see para 4.37); but illegality was not argued. B adduced evidence that it was technically uninsurable. But D pleaded that the excess was so small as to be immaterial and that authorities knew of that 2 inch breach, but turned a blind eye to it—the 'Nelson touch'. The Judge held that the risk of B's prosecution for use on the roads rendered the goods unsatisfactory; but that D had a good defence on the basis of s 14(2C)(b) (see para 14.26).

The Court of Appeal unanimously held that the sale of the motor-home did not breach the undertaking as to satisfactory quality (s 14(2)), when read with s 14(2(A)

---

191 *Wren v Holt* [1903] 1 KB 610, CA. Not every contaminant would necessarily render goods unmerchantable: there might be permitted and even desirable levels of what may in higher concentration be toxic: *Cehave v Bremer, The Hansa Nord* [1976] QB 44, CA.

192 *Daniels and Daniels v White & Son Ltd* (set out at para 17.13).

193 *Grant v Australian Knitting Mills Ltd* [1936] AC 85, PC.

194 *Rasbora Ltd v JCL Marine Ltd* [1977] 1 Lloyd's Rep 645. See also *Bernstein v Pamson Motors Ltd* [1987] 2 All ER 220.

195 *Wilson v Rickett Cockerell Ltd* (set out at para 14.03).

196 *Niblett's* case (set out at para 12.03).

197 *Farnworth Finance Ltd v Attryde* [1970] 2 All ER 774, CA; *Yeoman Credit Ltd v Apps* (set out at para 29.25); *Charterhouse Credit Ltd v Tolly* (set out at para 29.34); *Lee v York Coach and Marine* 1977] RTR 35, CA.

198 *Shine v General Guarantee Corpn* [1988] 1 All ER 911, CA (mistakenly referring SOGIT: for another point, see para 14.19).

199 *Clegg v Olle Andersson* (set out at para 14.18).

200 *Alpha Chauffeurs Ltd v Citygate* (set out at para 14.26).

201 [2004] 2 Lloyd's Rep 653, CA (see 121 LQR 205).

(see para 14.18). Deliberately ignoring the issue of illegality on the grounds that it was not pleaded,[202] Auld LJ held that, as the excess width was known among UK enthusiasts who nevertheless bought such motor-homes without complaint or prosecution, B had not proved unsatisfactoriness (para 42); nor was the technical breach relevant to insurability because the evidence showed that insurers ignored it (para 48). Worryingly, the result seems for the first time to apply a *de minimis* test (see para 13.01) to legal breaches on the basis that reasonable buyers ignore small chances of prosecution. As to damages, see para 29.33.

**[14.22] Fitness for purpose (2): unsuitable goods**. Where the goods are not in any way defective, the real complaint may be that the goods delivered comply with the contract description but do not have the specific qualities required. However, if the transferee has not expressly or impliedly specified the required qualities and therefore cannot plead the undertaking as to fitness (see para 14.10), he may attempt to frame his complaint in terms of quality. This raises the issue of the relationship of the undertakings as to fitness and quality.[203] In *Jewson Ltd v Boyhan* (set out at para 14.11), the Court of Appeal pointed out that the two subsections performed different functions: it held that the boilers were fit to instal in flats for sale generally (the general standard of s 14(2)), there being nothing wrong with their quality (*per* Clarke LJ at para 70); but K gave J no information about his flats by which J could judge whether or not the boilers were suitable for those flats (the higher standard of s 14(3)). As Sedley LJ explained:[204]

> 'Section 14(2) is directed principally to the sale of substandard goods. This means that the court's principal concern is to look at their intrinsic quality, using the tests indicated in subsection (2A), (2B) and (2C); [whereas s 14(3) is concerned with] factors peculiar to the purposes of the particular buyer.'

The extent of the overlap with s 14(3) depends on the number of ordinary uses to which the goods may be put.

1.  *Single-user goods*. Where the goods have only a single ordinary use, the undertaking as to satisfactory quality requires that the goods be fit for the purpose 'for which goods of the kind in question are **commonly** supplied'.[205] At its simplest, the difference between the two undertakings is this: the undertaking as to quality requires that the goods be fit for their **common** purpose;[206] whereas only the undertaking as to fitness demands that the goods

---

202  At para 27, even though it was common ground at trial that the motor-home could not be driven on UK roads (para 15). This does not seem to accord with usual practice: see *Chitty on Contract*, 27th edn, 1994, para 16-174. As to the effects of illegality at common law, see para 10.20.

203  E.g. *Amstrad plc v Seagate Technology Inc* [1988] CLY 4384 (agreement by correspondence not reduced to formal contract: disc drives should not be subject to random and unpredictable failure).

204  At para 77. See also Clarke LJ at 67–9. And see Ervine [2004] JBL 684, at 691, 697–9.

205  SGA, new s 14(2B)(a): set out at para 14.20.

206  *Rogers v Parish* (set out at para 14.23); *Danka Rentals Ltd v Xi Software Ltd* (1998) 17 Tr LR 74; *Brocket v DSG Retail Ltd* [2004] CLY 3269, Cty Ct (new computer programme incompatible with buyer's existing programme: retailer under no liability under SGA; but liable in tort for failure to warn—see para 17.14).

be fit for any particular **(in the sense of special)** purpose made known.[207]
However, it has already been seen that the courts extended the notion of
'particular purpose' to include ordinary purpose (see para 14.10), so
establishing an overlap between the two undertakings. The courts have
accepted that, if single-user goods are not so usable, they are neither fit for the
purpose supplied nor of the requisite quality.[206]

2. *Multi-user goods.* Where the goods have more than one ordinary use, it would
   seem that the SSGA 1994 has changed the law. The pre-1994 position is
   exemplified in *Kendall v Lillico* (set out at para 14.10). The evidence showed
   that buyers who only compounded poultry food would not be prepared to buy
   the contaminated goods at any price; but that compounders of cattle food
   would be prepared (with complaints) to pay the full price, test the goods and
   use the less highly contaminated groundnuts in their cattle feedstuffs. The
   majority of the House of Lords held that, if the goods were fit for **any** ordinary
   purpose, they were merchantable.[208] This decision may be contrasted with the
   post-1994 position, which requires that, to be of satisfactory quality, the goods
   must be fit for '**all** the purposes for which goods of the kind in question are
   commonly supplied'.[205] So, if feeding to poultry was **one** of the ordinary
   purposes for which groundnuts were ordinarily sold, presumably a court
   would now find that the groundnuts were not of satisfactory quality.[209]
   Similarly, an aesthetically pleasing fake painting would presumably now
   fail the undertaking as genuine paintings are bought at least in part as an
   investment.[210]

**[14.23] Minor defects**. Bringing the text of the statute into line with case-law
development, the new expanded definition of 'quality' now explicitly includes
'freedom from minor defects' (see para 14.17). Suppose the goods supplied have a
congeries of minor defects (see para 14.02) collectively too great to be dismissed as
*de minimis* (see para 13.12), e.g. the Monday morning car (the first manufactured on
a Monday). In *Rogers v Parish*:[211]

> The parties treated the issue as concerning the sale of a 'new' yellow Range Rover by
> the dealer for a price of £16,000.[212] The vehicle was found to be unsatisfactory and
> underwent a series of repairs by the dealer. However, after driving 5,500 miles in
> some 6 months, the consumer-buyer gave notice of rejection.[213] The judge found that

---

207 *Brown v Craiks* [1970] 1 All ER 823, HL (s) (sacking required for unusual purpose not
    unmerchantable); *Slater v Finning* (set out at para 14.09).
208 Lords Reid (at 76–9), Morris (at 96–8) and Guest (at 108). It is worth noting that Lords Reid and
    Morris applied the usability test (see para 4.18) whilst the majority preferred the acceptability
    test (see para 4.18).
209 Similarly reversed would be: *Summer, Permain & Co v Webb* (set out at para 14.16); *Aswan
    Engineering Establishment Co v Lupdine Ltd* (set out at para 14.14).
210 Cf. the *Harlingdon* case (set out at para 13.11A).
211 [1987] QB 933, [1987] 2 All ER 232, CA (discussed 138 NLJ 6). See also *Danka Rentals Ltd v Xi
    Software Ltd* (1998) 17 Tr LR 74 at 83B; *Alpha Chauffeurs Ltd v Citygate* (see para 14.26) at
    para 34.
212 The facts were actually more complicated in all the following respects, none of which the parties
    relied on: the original supply was of a green Range Rover by way of a directly financed con-
    ditional sale; but after a few weeks use, the green car proved unsatisfactory and was replaced by
    the yellow one; and no issue of lack of privity was taken.
213 The dealer did not plead that the buyer was precluded by his conduct from rejecting the car. See
    further, para 29.04.

the car was merchantable because it was roadworthy and the defects had been repaired under the manufacturer's warranty.

However, the Court of Appeal unanimously held the dealer in breach of old s 14(2) and explained that the judge had applied the wrong test.[214] The fact that the defects were repairable did not prevent the car being unmerchantable on delivery;[215] the presence of the manufacturer's warranty did not assist the dealer;[216] and the fact that the car was safely driveable did not necessarily suffice. Mustill LJ explained the statutory definition of merchantable (old s 14(6)) as follows:[217]

> 'Starting with the purpose for which 'goods of that kind' are commonly bought, one would include in respect of any passenger vehicle not merely the buyer's purpose of driving the car from one place to another but of doing so with the appropriate degree of comfort, ease of handling and reliability and, one may add, of pride in the vehicle's outward and interior appearance. What is the appropriate degree and what relative weight is to be attached to one characteristic of the car rather than another will depend on the market at which the car is aimed.'

His Lordship noted that the buyer of a new Range Rover was entitled to expect a standard in all respects higher than that of a second-hand Range Rover or of a new ordinary family saloon, and to what the judge termed 'value for money'.[218]

Of course, this case was argued on a rather artificial basis: whilst irrelevant to the issue of merchantability, retention and use of the car might go to the right to reject;[213] and in any claim for damages, submission or otherwise of the car to post-delivery adjustments might go both to the measure of damages[219] and acceptance (see para 29.05). Moreover, the case suggests a test for new goods which is plainly more onerous for the supplier than would be the case with second-hand goods. Whilst the latter must *prima facie* be free of major defects,[220] minor ones are to be expected 'sooner or later'.[221] Finally, the effect of the 1994 statutory definition of quality is to make minor defects part of the implied condition (see para 14.20). Taken together with other changes in the remedies available for breach, the effect is that a consumer will only be able to rescind for minor defects and cosmetic defects where the goods are not replaceable or repairable (see para 29.02A).

---

214 Compare the following decisions there cited: *Cehave v Bremer* [1962] QB 44, CA; *Bernstein v Pamson Motors Ltd* [1987] 2 All ER 220.

215 The CA dismissed as irrelevant to the issue of merchantability the normal post-delivery adjustments: see below; and para 15.11.

216 Mustill LJ suggested that, insofar as the manufacturer's warranty was advanced to exclude the contractual liability of the retail supplier, it would infringe s 6 of UCTA (see para 18.19); and he denied that that warranty could be a 'relevant circumstance' under s 14(6) such as should reduce the reasonable expectations of the buyer (see para 14.19).

217 At 237a. His Lordship actually thought there might have been an express undertaking as to merchantability but noted that the parties were content to rely on s 14 of the SGA.

218 As to the relevance of price, see generally, para 14.19.

219 Submission of the car for cure might amount to a variation or waiver of claim (see para 26.21, *et seq.*), whilst non-submission might breach the duty to mitigate (see para 27.44).

220 *Shine v General Guarantee Corpn* [1988] 1 All ER 911, CA (second-hand car insurance write-off because submerged in water for over 24 hours; see 104 LQR at 522–3).

221 *Business Application Specialists Ltd v Nationwide Credit Corpn Ltd* [1988] CLY 3169, CA, applying a dictum by Lord Denning MR in a 1965 case. See also *Benjamin's Sale of Goods*, 6th edn, para 11-061; Stephenson (1988) 6 Tr L 172.

**[14.24] Appearance and finish.** In *Jackson v Rotax Cycles* (set out at para 14.05), the Court of Appeal held unmerchantable motor horns bought for resale which were slightly dented and discoloured; and this would seem correct, because the goods in that condition were unsaleable by the buyer under the contract description. This case involved goods bought for resale and, it may be that the courts had already reached a similar position in respect of goods bought for consumption.[222] However, the Law Commission recommended that the matter be put on a clear statutory footing.[223] Accordingly the new definition of 'quality' now explicitly includes 'appearance and finish' (see para 14.17), so expanding the notion of 'satisfactory quality' (see para 14.15).

There may now be a breach of the undertaking where goods with a cosmetic defect are obtained for consumption, e.g. the stained fur coat or consumer durable with chipped or discoloured paint.[224] Not only are cosmetic defects more likely to be taken into account in respect of new rather than second-hand goods,[225] but it seems more likely to apply to manufactured rather than natural produce.[225] As to the Design Council, see para 3.08.

## Qualification of the undertakings

**[14.25] Specified defects.** The Sale and Supply of Goods Act 1994 transfers the previous qualifications on the undertaking as to merchantability to the new one as to 'satisfactory quality' (see para 14.15). Thus, new s 14(2C) of the Sale of Goods Act provides as follows (as supplied by the 1994 Act, s 1):

> 'The term implied by subsection (2) above does not extend to any matter making the quality of goods unsatisfactory—
>
> (a) which is specifically drawn to the buyer's attention before the contract is made,
>
> (b) where the buyer examines the goods before the contract is made, which that examination ought to reveal, or
>
> (c) in the case of a contract for sale by sample, which would have been apparent on a reasonable examination of the sample.'

There are similar qualifications as regards the undertaking as to satisfactory quality in contracts of hp, quasi-sale and simple hiring.[226]

1. *Specified defects*, e.g. goods marked 'shop soiled' or 'seconds'.[227] As the Law Commission pointed out on an earlier occasion,[228] in one sense this defence was already comprehended within the statutory definition of the undertaking;

---

222 *Rogers v Parish* (set out at para 14.23): the judge found the bodywork of the yellow car defective; and Mustill LJ expressly included this in the items rendering the goods unmerchantable in his reference to 'appearance' in the *dicta* quoted at para 14.23.

223 *Sale and Supply of Goods* (1987, Law Com), para 3.39.

224 But compare supplies of services: see para 15.15.

225 E.g. *Clegg v Olle Anderson* (set out at para 14.18).

226 SOGIT, s 10(2C) (hp); SGSA, s 4(3) (quasi-sale) and 9(3) (hiring) (as substituted by the 1994 Act, Sched 2, paras 4(4), 6(3) and 6(7)).

227 Cf. *Crowther v Shannon Motor Co* [1975] 1 All ER 139, CA. Examples might be goods expressly sold as 'seconds' or 'damaged' or 'imperfect', or 'display models'.

228 *First Report on Exemption Clauses* (1969, Law Com No 24), para 49.

but this mode of expressing it makes available to the supplier a clear-cut defence in law, even in those circumstances where he is prohibited from contracting out of his liability for breach of the implied terms.[229] *Prima facie*, a supplier may save himself by specifically drawing the attention of the transferee to enumerated defects before the contract is concluded,[230] as for instance in a warning as to use (see para 18.32). How effective such a defence is to the supplier perhaps depends on how precisely he specifies the defect: it is presumably not enough for the supplier to use some general phrase such as 'bought as seen',[231] though the matter would seem one of degree; and any attempt to utilise this provision to achieve a blanket exclusion of the undertaking is likely to meet a fate similar to that of clauses 8 and 9 in *Lowe v Lombank Ltd*.[232] Where goods are supplied by a trader to a consumer, it is for consideration whether such specified defects are saved from the UTCC Regulations by these provisions.[233]

2.    *Examination*. (see para 14.26).

3.    *Sample*. (see para 15.10).

**[14.26] Examination**. At common law, the undertaking as to merchantability was excluded from a sale by the mere opportunity for pre-contract examination. Whilst this rule was retained for sales by sample (see para 15.08), the SGA 1893 brought about two changes: (1) the exclusion of the undertaking was made to rest on an examination in fact; and (2) even if there was an examination, the undertaking was only ousted in respect of defects which such examination ought to have revealed. After difficulties with a case where a buyer, pressed for time, wrongly told the seller that he had made an examination,[234] the Law Commission recommended a verbal alteration of the qualification with the following object:[235] to put beyond doubt that this qualification will only exclude the undertaking in respect of such defects as the examination actually made ought to have revealed.[236] That change was made in 1973 by SOGIT (ss 3(2)(b) and 10(2)(b)) and is now to be found in all the current undertakings:[237] a thorough examination or a cursory examination will each oust the undertaking as regards defects they respectively would have revealed,[238] possibly making something of a trap for the consumer who takes possession before contract and discovers the defect before contract without realising its gravity.[239]

---

229  UCTA, ss 6 and 7: see para 18.19.

230  SGA, s 14(2)(a); SOGIT, s 10(2)(a); SGSA, ss 4(3)(a) and 9(3)(a). It would be a wise precaution to note these defects on the invoice.

231  *Cavendish-Woodhouse v Manley* (1984) 82 LGR 376, DC. See also Woodroffe, *Goods and Services: The New Law*, para 3.30; OFT, *UCT Bulletin No. 4*, 32, 37; No. 5, 47.

232  Set out at para 18.06. See also Goode, *Commercial Law*, 3rd edn, 302.

233  Sched 1, para (e)(i): set out at para 11.12A.

234  *Thornett v Beers* [1919] 1 KB 486. It may be that in such circumstances the buyer would be estopped from denying he had made the examination represented, and that the undertaking is ousted in respect of defects which that represented would have revealed. Alternatively, the case has been explained on grounds of waiver: Goode, *Commercial Law*, 3rd edn, 303.

235  *First Report on Exemption Clauses* (1969, Law Com No 24), para 48.

236  But see Yates [1973] JBL at 139, fn 12.

237  SGA, s 14(2)(c), as supplied by the Sale and Supply of Goods Act 1994, s 1. For similar undertakings, see the 1994 Act, Sched 2, paras 4(4), 6(3) and 6(7).

238  But might deliberate failure to inspect be a 'relevant circumstance' within the definition of satisfactory quality (see para 14.19) making the goods satisfactory?

239  *Per* Dillon LJ in *R & B Customs Brokers Co Ltd v UDT Ltd* (set out at para 18.18), at 851c, CA.

Indeed, the provision would seem to both reward the careless buyer who does not examine the goods before contract and penalise the careful buyer (who perhaps obtains an expert pre-contract report), and one who brags as to his expertise when making an examination.[240] In *Alpha Chauffeurs Ltd v Citygate* (set out at para 14.12) on the issue of satisfactory quality the Judge held as follows: in using the car from delivery Alpha had discovered some of the defects before execution of the contract with the financier (Oct 6) so that the financier was not liable for those discovered defects under s 10(2C)(b); but the financier remained liable for those defects Alpha discovered after Oct 6 (para 41). Accordingly, Alpha had a *prima facie* right to rescind the hp for breach of s 10, which right had not been lost (see para 26.16); and, upon rescission, the car was returned to the financier and Alpha was entitled to recover all the hire-rent paid (para 67), subject to a counter-claim for damages (see para 29.10). However, this distinction would appear to have been obliterated by the Court of Appeal in *Bramhill v Edwards* (set out at para 14.21). Even if the motor-home were of unsatisfactory quality, Auld LJ said *obiter* (para 49) that, knowing of the legal relevance of 100-inch external width and having the opportunity to do so, B ought to have measured its external width; that such an examination ought to have revealed its width (para 51); and that his failure to do so gave D a good defence under s 14(2C)(b) (para 54). This argument seems to flatly ignore the wording of the provision: all that should be relevant is any inspection actually made; but the case might just be reconciled with the statutory wording on the basis that B did measure the internal width at 100 inches, so must have known that the external measurement exceeded that.

---

240 See generally Atiyah, *Sale of Goods*, 10th edn, 165.

# CHAPTER 15

# OTHER IMPLIED TERMS, TRANSACTIONS AND OBLIGATIONS

[15.01] The statutory obligations as to delivery and payments will be dealt with in Chap 23; and it remains to consider here the residue of undertakings[1] as to the character and quality of goods implied by statute (see para 15.02) or common law (see para 15.21). Furthermore, discussion of all the express and implied terms and obligations considered in Chaps 11–15 for the most part assume a two-party transaction. In Chap 16 there will be considered the effect upon these terms and obligations of the fact that the transaction is financed by lender credit. The wider ramifications of liability back up the chain of distribution will be discussed in Chap 17. Lastly, attempts to avoid or reduce this liability by suitable wording is the subject of Chap 18.

## TERMS AND OBLIGATIONS DERIVED FROM STATUTE

[15.02] Chapters 12–14 considered the major terms implied into contracts for the supply of goods. The original statutory formulation of these undertakings was to be found in the SGA 1893. A series of Hire Purchase Acts gradually introduced increasingly similar undertakings in respect of hp agreements;[2] and the undertakings reached almost common form in respect of sale and hp agreements with the enactment of SOGIT in 1973.[3] The provisions in relation to sales were subsequently re-enacted in the SGA 1979, whilst those in respect of hp are still to be found in SOGIT. As a result of further recommendations of the Law Commission,[4] Part I of the SGSA[5] imported similar undertakings into quasi-sales (see para 2.10) and simple hiring agreements (see para 1.18); and modification of the remedies was made by SSGA 1995 (see para 11.05A). It remains to consider here the following types of special case: the undertakings as to sample and trade usage imported into all four types of contract for the supply of goods (see respectively, paras 15.03 and 15.11); the undertakings in supplies of services (see para 15.15) embodied in Part II of the SGSA;[5] the undertakings in regulated agreements (see para 15.16); the variations

---

1 Some are implied conditions and some are implied warranties. For conditions and warranties see generally, para 11.04; and for implied terms, see generally, para 11.10.

2 These provisions of the HPA 1938 and HPA 1964 were consolidated in the HPA 1965, ss 17 and 19.

3 SOGIT gave effect, with modifications, to the First Report of the Law Commission on *Exemption Clauses in Contracts* (1969, Law Com No. 24).

4 *Implied Terms in Contracts for the Supply of Goods* (1979, Law Com No. 95).

5 Whereas Pt I of the SGSA gives effect, with minor modifications, to the proposals in Law Com No. 95 (see fn 4, above), Pt II of the SGSA has its origins in the NCC publication, *Service Please* (1981). On the SGSA generally, see Palmer (1983) 46 MLR 619; James [1982] JBL 10; Woodroffe, *Goods and Services—The New Law* (1982); and for an annotated text, see Thomas, *Encyclopedia of Consumer Law*.

with regard to other sorts of transaction (see paras 15.17–20); and terms derived from the common law (see paras 15.21–60).

## Undertakings in contracts by sample

[15.03] **Background**. The classic exposition of the legal function of a sample is that of Lord Macnaghten in the commercial case of *Drummond v Van Ingen*,[6] where he said:

> 'The office of a sample is to present to the eye the real meaning and intention of the parties with regard to the subject-matter of the contract which, owing to the imperfections of language, it may be difficult or impossible to express in words. The sample speaks for itself.'

A sample may be utilised in the supply of specific or unascertained goods, in which case the sample will be taken respectively from the contract goods, or bulk from which it is to be drawn; or there may be a supply of future goods as corresponding with a particular sample.[7] In either case, the function of the sample is similar to that of the description of the goods supplied, and might almost be regarded as a special type of supply by non-verbal description. Yet it is normal to distinguish between the two, because statute makes separate provision for supplies by sample,[8] and even contemplates that supply may be both by description and by sample (see para 15.06).

[15.04] **Sample contracts**. When does a sample become part of the contract? Just as with supplies by description (see para 13.11), it is a question of intention whether the sample (non-verbal description) becomes part of the contract.[9] Therefore, s 15(1) provides:

> 'A contract of sale is a contract for sale by sample where there is an express or implied term to that effect in the contract.'

Of course, the provision as to a sample may be express.[10] However, s 15(1) may cause more difficulty where such a term is to be implied, as it would appear to import all the pre-1893 learning on the matter. The position at common law seems to have been that, just because a sample is exhibited at the time of sale,[11] there is not necessarily a sale by sample: the seller may decline to sell by sample, and require

---

6 (1887), 12 App Cas 284, HL at 297.

7 If the contract goods are yet to be manufactured, the contract may provide that they are to be manufactured according to a model. If the contract is for goods yet to be grown, notorious variations in crops of different seasons may affect the legal significance of the sample: Murdoch (1981) 44 MLR 388, at 389–90.

8 It has been argued that this separate treatment is of little practical value and could be abolished: Murdoch, *op. cit.*, at 388.

9 If the sample does not become part of the contract, it has been suggested that it may nevertheless take effect as a misrepresentation: Murdoch (1981) 44 MLR 388, at 392–3. As to the effect of misrepresentation, see para 17.10.

10 E.g. *Re Walkers, Winser & Hamm and Shaw Son & Co* [1904] 2 KB 152 (barley: 'as per sample'); *Champanhac & Co Ltd v Waller & Co Ltd* (set out at para 15.07).

11 It has been argued there may also be a sale by sample where, in accordance with the contract, the sample is to be exhibited only after the formation of the contract: Hudson [1982] JBL 485. But see *Benjamin's Sale of Goods*, 6th edn, para 11-094.

the buyer to inspect the bulk; or the parties may in some other way show that in their contract they are not relying on the sample.[12] On the other hand, there are many retail sales where the customer closely inspects a 'demonstration model', e.g. a new car, a household appliance; and in some cases the consumer has no realistic opportunity to inspect the purchased item until some time after its delivery, e.g. shrink-wrapped electronic appliances. It therefore seems puzzling that it has been said to be 'less likely' that a consumer sale is by sample.[13]

On the other hand, the more modern provisions dealing with quasi-sales, hp and simple hiring speak rather of goods being supplied 'by reference to a sample'.[14] It has been said that goods will be let or sold by reference to a sample:[15]

'where a sample is exhibited or supplied . . . during the negotiations for the contract, and there need be no term in the contract, express or implied to this effect'.

For example, if a car dealer takes a customer for a demonstration run in a new car, it would seem that if a similar new car is subsequently let to the customer it may be let by reference to the demonstration car, even if the transaction is directly financed. If so, the effect of the difference in terminology in the Acts would appear to be that a sample is more likely to become part of a transaction which falls within the other statutes than part of one which is within the SGA.[16]

**[15.05] Title.** Section 15 of the SGA, which sets out the terms which are to be implied into sales by sample, makes no mention of undertakings as to title, but presumably s 12 is wide enough to cover such transactions (see Chap 12). A similar omission is to be found in those statutes dealing with the terms to be implied into sample contracts by way of quasi-sale, hp and simple hiring (SOGIT; SGSA).

**[15.06] Correspondence with sample.** In the case of a sale by sample, s 15(2)(a) of the SGA provides that there is an implied condition that:[17]

'the bulk will correspond with the sample in quality'.

Identical provisions are to be found in relation to quasi-sales, hp and simple hirings,[18] except for the following: the SGA contains a definition of 'bulk', introduced in 1995 for another purpose, and thought inapplicable here.[19] None of the enactments specifically refers to the question of quantity; and the rules concerning quantity have been considered above (see paras 13.03–7). The position in relation to exclusions is examined below (see para 15.07).

---

12   Benjamin, *Op. cit.*, para 11-091.
13   *Ibid*, para 11-092.
14   SOGIT, s 11; SGSA, ss 5(1) and 10(1). See the warning about applying the appropriate statute: see para 12.01.
15   Guest, *Law of HP*, para 302. It has been argued that a transaction is unlikely to be by sample unless the sample is released to the transferee: Goode, *Commercial Law*, 3rd edn, 324. *Sed quaere?*
16   Does it make any difference whether (a) there is being supplied more than one of the item, (b) the contract goods include the sample (see note 15)?
17   As with the other implied terms, s 15(2) reduces the undertaking to an implied 'term', but a new provision (here new s 15(3)) gives it the status of a condition for English law: SSGA 1994, Sched 2, para 6.
18   SOGIT, s 11(a); SGSA, ss 5(2)(a) and 10(2)(a). In the case of SOGIT, all subsequent references are to s 11(a) as amended by the CCA: see further, para 12.02.
19   SGA, new s 61(1), introduced by the SGAA 1995: see para 20.22B.

The undertaking that the goods will correspond with the contract sample in quality is closely related to the undertaking that goods shall correspond with their description (see paras 13.08, *et seq.*). A strict attitude used to be taken to compliance with the undertaking: for instance, it has been held insufficient that it might be possible to make the bulk conform with the sample by a simple process.[20] However, even where a contract sample is involved,[21] compliance will be subject to the *de minimis* rule[22] and the following: if the normal trade practice is that a sample be subjected only to a visual examination, there may be no breach of the undertaking if the bulk does not correspond with the sample in some manner not discoverable by such examination;[23] a trade certificate of compliance may be conclusive;[24] and there may also be a breach of the undertaking as to satisfactory quality (see para 15.10).

The obvious close similarity of this undertaking with that as to compliance with description raises the question of whether to apply to the former the *Ashington* rule (see para 13.14): if so, there would only be a breach where the non-compliance of the bulk with the sample amounts to a difference in kind.[25] On the other hand, both the SGA and the other statutory undertakings stipulate in almost identical terms that in this situation:[26]

'it is not sufficient that the bulk of the goods correspond with the sample if the goods do not also correspond with the description'.

These would appear to reflect the common law,[27] where the undertaking of compliance with description appears to have been paramount.[28] However, it may suggest that s 15(2)(a) is wider than s 13 and extends to non-identifying contractual description (see para 13.12), which would give some separate meaning to each provision.

**[15.07] Exclusion clauses.** Where a transaction falls within Pt I of UCTA, there are substantial restrictions on the power of the supplier to exclude the statutory undertakings implied in supplies by sample (see para 18.19); but no further restrictions are imposed by the UTCC Regulations (see Sched 1, para (e)(i): see para 11.12A). Outside those provisions, the problem was illustrated in *Champanhac & Co Ltd v Waller & Co Ltd*,[29] where on delivery, the goods were found to be perished and unmerchantable. Slade J held that there was a sale by sample; and that the goods did not correspond with their sample, which was neither perished nor

---

20  *F & S Ruben Ltd v Faire Brothers & Co Ltd* [1949] 1 KB 254. Has this survived the rule in the *Ashington Piggeries* case (see below)?

21  Not every sample will be a contract sample: see para 15.04.

22  *Joe Lowe Food Products Ltd v JA and P Holland Ltd* [1954] 2 Lloyd's Rep 70. As to the *de minimis* rule, see para 13.12.

23  *Hookway v Isaac* [1954] 1 Lloyd's Rep 491; *Steels & Busks Ltd v Bleeker Bik & Co Ltd* [1956] 1 Lloyd's Rep 228. *Contra*, where the trade usage is not part of the contract (see para 13.11).

24  *Gill & Duffus SA v Berger & Co Inc* (set out at para 23.06). For certificates of inspection, see generally, para 14.02.

25  *Polenghi Brothers v Dried Milk Co* (1904) 92 LT 64.

26  SGA, s 13(2). See also SOGIT, s 9(1); SGSA, ss 3(3) and 8(3). E.g. *Wallis, Son & Wells v Pratt & Haynes* (set out at para 11.04).

27  See *Nichol v Godts* (1854) 10 Exch 191.

28  For what appears to be an exceptional case, see *Joseph Travers & Sons Ltd v Longel Ltd* (1947) 64 TLR 150.

29  [1948] 2 All ER 724.

unmerchantable. In considering the exclusion clause, his Lordship thought that the cases under s 13 of the SGA were in *pari materia*, and held that the seller was not protected in respect of breach of the undertaking that the goods should correspond with their sample.[30] In this case, the undertaking was express, so that it may be that any exclusion clause must be otiose; but it has been suggested on the basis of this case that the undertaking as to correspondence with sample can never be excluded.[31] The problem would seem to be the same as that considered in relation to attempts to exclude the undertaking that the goods comply with their description (see para 13.16).

**[15.08/9] Opportunity for inspection**. By the SGA, s 15(2)(b), there was an implied condition that the buyer shall have 'a reasonable opportunity of comparing the bulk with the sample'. The result would appear to have been that, where there was a sale by sample the buyer had two rights to examine the goods: he had the ordinary right to examine under s 34 (see para 23.10) and the special right now under discussion. These two rights imposed on the buyer different duties; and attempts to exclude this special right were subject to UCTA (ss 6 and 7: see para 18.19).

Whilst similar statutory rights of inspection were introduced into hp, quasi-sale and simple hirings,[32] it was difficult to justify two statutory rights of inspection. Accordingly, such a right was deleted from sales by the SSGA 1994,[33] though the Act inexplicably left standing the parallel rights in hp, quasi-sale and simple hiring.[34]

**[15.10] Satisfactory quality and fitness.**

1.   *Satisfactory quality.* In *Drummond v Van Ingen,*[35] the House of Lords accepted that there was ordinarily a presumption that, if the bulk corresponded with the sample it satisfied the contract, but that this presumption was rebutted by proving that the goods contained a latent defect rendering them unmerchantable. For sales, this rule was embodied in s 15(2)(c) of the SGA,[36] which provided that there is an implied condition:[37]

> 'that the goods will be free from any defect, making their quality unsatisfactory, which would not be apparent on reasonable examination of the sample'.

A virtually identical provision is to be found in relation to quasi-sales, hp and simple hiring.[38] In all cases, the expression 'satisfactory' is to be construed in accordance with the concept of satisfactory quality already considered.[39]

---

30   He suggested *obiter* that the clause might have protected the seller if there were latent defects in the goods and sample which rendered the goods unmerchantable.

31   Chalmers, *Sale of Goods*, 15th edn, 57, note(t)—suggestion dropped from subsequent editions.

32   SOGIT, s 11(b); SGSA 1982, ss 5(2)(b), 10(2)(b).

33   SSGA 1994, Sched 2, para 5(6)(a).

34   Presumably, such deletion should have been listed in Sched 2, paras 4(5) & 6(8).

35   (1887) 12 App Cas 284, HL.

36   As supplied by the Sale and Supply of Goods Act 1994, s 1(2). There is an identical limitation in new s 14 of the SGA: see para 14.25.

37   As with the other implied terms, s 15(2) reduces the undertaking to an implied 'term', but a new provision (here new s 15(3)) gives it the status of a condition for English law: SSGA 1994, Sched 2, para 6.

38   SOGIT, s 11(c); SGSA, ss 5(1)(c) and 10(1)(c).

39   SGA, s 15(3); SOGIT, s 15(2); SGSA, ss 5(3) and 10(3): see para 14.19.

However, it will be observed that the provisions currently being discussed differ from the ordinary undertakings as to satisfactory quality in **all** the following respects: there is no requirement as to supply in course of business (see para 14.04); there is no express defence of specified defects (see para 14.25); and the undertaking is ousted in respect of defects which would be apparent on reasonable examination of the sample (see para 14.26), so the undertaking is thus confined to latent defects.[40] What should happen, therefore, if the supply is both by description and by sample? It is submitted that in those circumstances the ordinary undertaking as to satisfactory quality can have no application: this would appear to reach an answer consistent with the common law; and, if the latter were applicable in these circumstances, the more severe limitations of the undertakings applicable to supplies by sample would be pointless.[41]

2.  *Fitness.* Neither the SGA nor the other statutes applicable to supplies of goods makes any special reference to an undertaking that the goods are fit for the purpose for which they are supplied where the transaction is by sample;[42] and in all cases the statutory language of the ordinary undertaking appears to be wide enough to cover this situation.[43] Support for the application of the ordinary undertakings as to fitness to transactions by sample is to be found in the common law.[44]

For exclusion of these two undertakings, see para 18.19.

## OTHER STATUTORY UNDERTAKINGS

**[15.11/3]  Trade usage.** Section 14(4) of the SGA provides that:[45]

'An implied term as to quality or fitness for a particular purpose may be annexed to a contract of sale by usage.'

This undertaking is not limited to trade sales (compare the undertakings as to quality and fitness: see para 14.04). A virtually identical undertaking is imported into quasi-sales, hp agreements and simple hirings.[46] These rules are statutory formulations of what is perhaps the best-known example of implied terms at common law.[47] The alleged usage must fulfil all the normal tests of a commercial[48]

---

40  The latent defect may be in the sample, or in the bulk, or in both: see Goode, *Commercial Law*, 3rd edn, 325.

41  But see Murdoch (1981) 44 MLR 388, at 398–9. It has been recommended that the law should be so clarified: *Sale and Supplies of Goods* (1987, Law Com No. 160) para 6.27.

42  SGA, s 15; SOGIT, s 11; SGSA, ss 5 and 10.

43  SGA, s 14(3); SOGIT, s 10(3); SGSA, ss 4(4)–(6) and 9(4)–(6): see further, para 14.07.

44  *Drummond v Van Ingen* (1887) 12 App Cas 284, HL. See especially *per* Lords Macnaghten and Herschell, at 295 and 293.

45  As amended by the SSGA 1994, Sched 2, para 5(a). As the term could be a condition or warranty, there would appear to be no substantive change.

46  See SOGIT, s 10(4) (as amended by the 1994 Act, Sched 2, para 4(4)(b); SGSA, ss 4(7) and 9(7). Inexplicably, the terms implied by the SGSA were not amended by the 1994 Act.

47  See *per* Lord Blackburn in *Tucker v Linger* (1883) 8 App Cas 508, at 511. See Allen, *Law in the Making* 7th edn, Chaps 1 and 2.

48  Distinguish common law customs: see para 11.10.

custom;[49] but, provided that it does so,[50] it will become part of the contract so long as it is reconcilable with the express and implied terms of that contract.[51]

Hitherto, most of the cases on trade usage have involved contracts between businessmen; but there would appear to be no reason why the rule should not also apply to retail sales to private consumers, given that the consumer has the requisite degree of knowledge of the trade custom, cf undertakings as to description (see para 13.11). Thus, in respect of a retail sale of a new car this undertaking may be used to import the following obligations:

(a) the retailer will make the pre-delivery checks and adjustments as per the manufacturer's specifications or express terms;[52]; and

(b) the retailer is entitled to make reasonable post-delivery adjustments **before** it is decided whether the vehicle meets the statutory implied obligations,[53] or under the cure rule (see para 29.02). Similarly, it may be possible to import by means of this undertaking common-form warnings and instructions as to the use of goods supplied after the contract is made (see para 18.33), and possibly trade voluntary codes of practice (see para 3.12).

**[15.14] Supplies of services**. Part 2 of the SGSA[54] applies where there is a 'contract[55] for the supply of services',[56] whether or not goods are also transferred or bailed under that contract.[57] In such a case, unless the contract is one of employment (s 12(2)), or of a type exempted by the Secretary of State,[58] there are implied the following innominate[59] statutory terms (see para 15.15), subject to the usual restrictions on exclusions (s 16: see para 18.09). In a consumer contract, it may be that breach of any of these implied terms is susceptible to an Enforcement Order on behalf of consumers generally (see para 28.04).

---

49   E.g. *Peter Darlington Ltd v Gosho Ltd* [1964] 1 Lloyd's Rep 149; *Three Rivers Trading Co v Gwinear and District Farmers* (1967), 111 Sol Jo 831, CA. That which is insufficiently established to amount to a trade custom may become part of the contract by reason of the course of dealings between the parties: see para 18.04.

50   If the custom extends to private sales, so may the implied term. Cf. the restriction of the undertakings of quality and fitness to trade sales (see para 14.04).

51   See *Produce Brokers Co Ltd v Olympia Oil and Cake Co Ltd* [1916] 1 AC 314, HL; and further litigation under the same name, [1917] 1 KB 320, CA. See generally, para 13.11.

52   For express promises to make repairs prior to delivery, see [2006] 5 *Which?* 72.

53   But see *Rogers v Parish* (set out at para 14.23).

54   As to Pt II, see generally, fn 5; and Thomas, *Encyclopedia of Consumer Law*, para 1-1269. As to codes of conduct in relation to the supply of services, see paras 3.11–14; and as to criminal offences, see paras 4.15–17. See generally Murdoch [1983] 4 LMCLQ 652.

55   Pt II will not apply where liability in respect of the provision of a service lies **only** in tort (e.g. negligence: see para 17.13, *et seq*.). *Contra* where the action lies in contract or tort: Woodroffe, *Goods and Services—The New Law*, paras 6.09–10.

56   SGSA, s 12(1) and (3): see generally, para 2.05. Does Pt II extend to the provision of facilities for self-service, e.g. launderette, petrol, super-market, (cf. para 4.16)? What of the provision of computer software?

57   S 12(3). Examples of contracts of service frequently linked with a supply of goods are the following trades: plumbing; building; electrician; roofing; installation of double-glazing, central heating and cavity-wall insulation.

58   For exemptions, see s 12(4) and (5); and see Thomas, *Op. cit*. Note that the reference is only to implied terms, without any attempt to classify them as conditions or warranties: see further, para 11.04.

59   They are all described simply as 'implied terms'. For innominate terms, see generally, para 11.05.

**[15.15]** **Undertakings in supplies of services**. Where there is a supply of services (see para 15.14), there are the following implied terms.

1. *Care and skill*. Where the supplier is acting in the course of a business,[60] it is implied that 'the supplier will carry out the service with reasonable care and skill'.[61] Whilst the common law only required the supplier of the service to carry it out with reasonable care and skill,[62] it has been claimed that s 13 requires the contractor to achieve a satisfactory result,[63] an argument which might be useful where the supplier fails to collect an instalment of his fee by direct debit (see para 23.13); or a restaurant prepares an inedible meal.[64] Further, s 16(3) saves any stricter duty imposed by the contract, common law or statute, e.g. TDA, s 14 (see para 14.15). Thus, if a plumber supplies and fits a tap which thereafter leaks, the position is probably this: if the defect is in the tap, the householder must look to the implied undertakings as to quality and fitness in quasi-sales;[65] whereas if the defect is in the fitting he must look to the present rule (SGSA, s 13).

2. *Time for performance*. Where the supplier is acting in the course of a business,[60] and no time is specified, that 'the supplier will carry out the service within a reasonable time', which is a question of fact (s 14). This provision could be applicable both to simple service contracts, e.g. of repair, and also where the service was linked with a supply of goods, e.g. a supply of goods upon which a service is to be performed before delivery.[66] It has been recommended that in the case of supplies to consumers time can be made of the essence,[67] but even where it is not, an action for damages will lie (cf. para 29.28).

3. *Consideration*. Whether or not the supplier is in business, if no consideration is agreed, 'there is an implied term that the party contracting with the other party will pay a reasonable charge'.[68] The drafting here appears to follow the provisions as to price in s 8 of the SGA (see para 2.06): it only applies where there is a contract between the parties,[69] in which case it in effect directs the court to

---

60  For supply in the course of business, see para 14.04; and for a survey, see [1992] *Which?* 492. Does this extend to 'foreigners' and 'moonlighting'?

61  SGSA, s 13; and see Bell, *Personal Property*, 104. This does not appear to extend to cosmetic defects: *CRC Flooring v Heaton* (1984) Tr L 33, CA; but compare supplies of goods (see para 14.24). For other criticisms, see Borrie, *The Development of Consumer Law and Policy*, 22; and Palmer (1983) 46 MLR at 628–30.

62  E.g. *Eyre v Measday* [1986] 1 All ER 488, CA (sterilisation); *Wilson v Best Travel Ltd* [1993] 1 All ER 353 (travel operator). There are also some relevant provisions in Codes of Practice: see para 3.13.

63  *Rolls Royce Power Engineering plc v Ricardo Consulting Engineers Ltd* [2004] 2 All ER (Comm) 129, at para 85. See Bragg and Lowe, *The Business of Licensing*, 55. Cf. the right of cure: see para 29.02.

64  *Aliter*, where the food is unfit for human consumption: see SGA, s 14(2B)(d), para 14.20.

65  SGSA, s 4: see paras 14.07 and 14.15. In this case, the goods will not be 'in conformity with the contract' (SGSA, s 11S): see para 29.01A.

66  As with the pre-delivery inspection of a motor vehicle (see generally, para 15.11). Cf. *McDougal v Aeromarine of Emsworth Ltd* [1958] 3 All ER 431 (contract to build and supply yacht).

67  Thomas, *Encyclopedia of Consumer Law*, para 1-1273, citing *Charles Rickards Ltd v Oppenheim* (set out at para 26.25). Cf. *Peregrine Systems Ltd v Steria Ltd* [2005] EWCA 239, CA, para 15; and the SGA delivery rule: see para 23.04. See also Woodroffe, *Op. cit.*, paras 6.33–6.

68  SGSA, s 15(1). 'What is a reasonable charge is a question of fact': s 15(2). If the consumer wished the service to be performed under the terms of a guarantee (see para 17.09), it would thus be safer to say so.

69  *Russell Brothers (Paddington) Ltd v John Lelliott Management Ltd* (1996) 11 Const LJ 377 (OR).

apply the industry standard. It does not preclude express agreement to a charge which proves exorbitant.[70]

Thus, where a consumer orders a meal in a restaurant, in the absence of sufficient express terms, there may be implied terms that the meal is produced with reasonable skill (s 13),[64] within a reasonable time (s 14) and at a reasonable charge (s 15). In a consumer supply contract, exclusion of any of the above terms may be unfair (*UCT Bulletin No. 18*, case 13: see para 11.16).

**[15.16] Undertakings in regulated agreements**. The major terms implied in favour of a debtor or hirer are to be found elsewhere (see Chaps 12–14), the CCA having little to say on the subject. It remains to draw together here those other obligations arising under regulated agreements (see para 5.13).

The common law right of the creditor or owner to refuse to accept instalments of price or rent tendered after a breach by the debtor or hirer is modified in relation to regulated agreements by the default notice procedure considered later (see para 24.30); and, where there is more than one debt due from the debtor or hirer to one person under two or more regulated agreements, the common law right of the supplier to appropriate payments to a particular debt is excluded (see para 23.13). On the other hand, the common law duty of a bailee to take reasonable care of the goods bailed receives statutory reinforcement under the termination provisions (see para 27.50).

The CCA also seeks to avoid a fertile source of misunderstanding and even oppression by ensuring that both parties can ascertain their rights and duties under a regulated consumer credit agreement at any time during its currency. Most such compulsory provisions (s 173: see para 18.11) are in favour of the debtor or hirer and any surety:[71]

(1) *At the outset*, i.e. before entry into the agreement (ss 44, 52, 55 and 62–3: see paras 8.21 and 9.08).

(2) *Annually*. In 2003, the White Paper, *Fair, Clear and Competitive*[72] said that it was particularly important for debtors in arrears to receive regular statements. The CCA 2006 translated this into a requirement[73] for debtors under fixed-sum credit agreements with a duration of more than one year to be provided *gratis* with annual statements in a specified form:[74] this should be self-enforcing, because 'non-compliance' (new s 77A(7)) by the creditor entails that during the period of non-compliance the creditor 'shall not be entitled to **enforce** the agreement' and the debtor shall not in respect of the period of non-compliance have to pay any interest or default sum;[75] but it will not help debtors with loans

---

70  It is exempt from the UTCC Regulations as being a core term: see para 11.14. It has been argued that there should be a statutory power to re-open such charges: Woodroffe, *Op. cit.*, para 6.39.

71  As to the rights of any surety to similar statements, see ss 105–10: see para 25.12.

72  See DTI, *the Consumer Credit Market in the 21st Century* (Dec 2003, Cm. 6040), paras 3.38–9.

73  New s 77A of the 1974 Act, as inserted by s 6 of the 2006 Act. In force as from April 2008.

74  New s 77A(1)–(3): the statement could be in writing or sent electronically. These rules do not apply where: (a) there is no sum payable under the agreement either now or in the future (new s 77A(4)); or (b) the agreement is a non-commercial or small one (new s 77A(8)): see paras 5.17–18.

75  New s 77A(5) and (7). As to 'enforce', see below. As to 'default sum', see new s 187A: see para 24.27A.

of less than a year, perhaps rolled-over. There is a similar provision requiring periodical statements in the case of running-account credit (s 78(4A): see para 7.08).

(3) *Upon request*. During the currency of most regulated agreements, the debtor or hirer is entitled to receive from the creditor or owner[76] at minimum intervals and upon tender of the prescribed fee a copy of the executed agreement;[77] and a statement setting out the prescribed information appropriate to that type of agreement.[78] If the creditor or owner fails to supply such a statement, he commits a criminal offence;[79] and the agreement is **unenforceable** whilst default continues.[80] Any statement he supplies is *prima facie* binding on him (s 172). Thus, if the creditor or owner understates the amount owed, the debtor or hirer is then entitled to a termination statement at that figure (see below).

(4) *Settlement figure* to discharge the agreement (s 97: see para 26.19A).

(5) *Termination statement* that agreement has been discharged (s 103: see para 26.04).

Almost as a *quid pro quo* for the creditor, s 80 requires the debtor or hirer to inform the creditor or owner of the whereabouts of any goods supplied under the agreement.[81] On behalf of consumers generally, it may be possible to bring injunctive proceedings under the EA (see paras 6.06–8).

## Other transactions

**[15.17] Loan financing**. Where the goods-supplier (dealer) makes a cash sale to the consumer with the price of those goods being loaned to the consumer by the financier (see para 2.20), the lender credit may take any of the following forms:

1. *Ordinary loan*. Since the 1960s, the clearing banks, finance companies and building societies have undertaken a substantial amount of lending by way of overdraft and personal loan to finance the acquisition of goods for consumption (see para 2.17). Retailers have developed their budget accounts.[82] At the same time, the business of the eighteenth century tallyman (see para 5.02) has developed into the modern weekly collected credit trade for the bottom end of the market (see para 2.18).

---

76  Ss 77 (fixed-sum credit), 78(1)–(3) (running-account credit), 79 (consumer hire). The rules do not apply to non-commercial agreements (see para 5.18): ss 77(5), 78(7) and 79(4).

77  This has implications for the creditor/owner as to the storage of agreements, e.g. microfilming, computerising. Consumer advisers tend to routinely use this provision to check whether an agreement is properly executed.

78  The detailed information required by the Regulations is set out in Goode, *Consumer Credit Law & Practice*, para 34.11, *et seq*.

79  Ss 77(4)(b), 78(6)(b) and 79(3)(b). For offences, see Sched 1. But the offence in itself gives rise to no further sanctions: s 170, set out at para 10.19.

80  Ss 77(4)(a), 78(6)(a) and 79(3)(a). However, the agreement and interest *prima facie* continue to run and may be claimable after the default has been cured. As to the effect of a more permanent type of unenforceability, see para 9.19.

81  A removal of the goods by the debtor from a nominated place may amount to a breach of an express term of the agreement.

82  See para 2.19. For the converse situation, where the consumer in effect lends money to, or is granted a credit by, the supplier, see para 15.18.

2. *Check or voucher trading.*[83] Developing about 1880, the traditional check-trader (financier) issues a 'trading check' to the customer,[84] which check will be accepted in lieu of payment to its face value by any retailer with whom the check-trader has an arrangement: the retailer can redeem (at a discount) these checks with the check-trader; and the consumer will subsequently pay the face value of the check (plus a service charge) to the check-trader by subsequent instalments.[85] It seems clear that check trading is a form of lending.[86] A modern variant are vouchers carrying the name of the retailer. Where they are issued to the consumer by the retailer, the position may be as follows: if the consumer pays at issue the face value of the voucher to the retailer and that voucher is subsequently 'cashed' in return for goods, the consumer is lending money to the retailer, as in a Christmas Club (see para 7.02); whereas, it is a form of vendor credit (see para 2.19) if the consumer takes delivery of the goods before completing the payments[86]. Another variant is for a financier to buy the voucher at face value (less discount) from the retailer[84] and then 'sell' it to a consumer either for cash,[87] or on credit, which will usually be for weekly collected credit (above).

3. *Pawnbroking.* This is making a business of lending money on the security of the transfer of possession (pledge) of goods (see para 25.15). Flourishing from the seventeenth century, traditional pawnbrokers have recently seen revival, partly on a weekly collected credit basis.

4. *Trading stamps.* This scheme of sales promotion basically works as follows: a retailer enters into a 'franchise' agreement with the trading stamp company, which agreement will not itself fall within the SGA (see para 1.09); the retailer will supply to each consumer a number of 'stamps' in proportion to 'purchases' made;[88] and the consumer, normally after collecting these stamps in a book, exchanges the stamps for goods, usually at one of the stamp company's distribution centres. These forms of transaction received separate treatment by the legislature in the Trading Stamps Act 1964 as amended (TSA). However, trading stamps are no longer issued as a promotional device; and the TSA has therefore been mostly repealed.[89]

5. *Credit unions* (see para 15.19).

---

83  See *Mason v Provident Clothing* [1913] AC 724, HL; and generally the Report on Consumer Credit (1971, Cmnd. 4596), paras 2.4.1–7; Goode, *HP Law & Practice*, 2nd edn, 898–900; *Chitty on Contracts*, 28th edn, Vol 2, para 38-442; Rowlingson, *Money Lenders*, 25–6. The expression 'voucher' is sometimes used for respect of larger amounts over longer periods: see Goode, *Consumer Credit Law & Practice*, para 2.35.

84  This amounts to a promise by the check-issuer to pay the face value of the check to the presenter: it is thus a form of chose in action; as to which, see para 7.15.

85  A home collection agent may also use the opportunity to sell new checks: as to the restrictions on such canvassing, see CCA, ss 48–9, considered at para 7.05.

86  Chitty, *Op. cit.*, para 38-225, fn 9.

87  See (1990) 11 CCA News 6/11; (1992) 13 CCA News 1/7; Griffiths and Howells (1991) 42 NILQ 199. It then acts like a gift stamp: see para 15.18.

88  The retail franchise-holder is supposed to benefit from increased sales to consumers addicted to collecting the stamps: for sales promotions generally, see para 8.13.

89  By the Regulatory Reform (Trading Stamps) Order, 2005 SI 871. S 10(1) is kept alive for the purposes of the Restriction on Statements Order 1976 (see reg 2; and para 4.22).

6. *Other forms*. These include loans by friendly and loan societies, life assurance offices and building societies.[90]

**[15.18] Vouchers, stamps and other perks**. Some such items may be part of promotion competitions,[91] or are methods of financing the price (see para 2.16), or are simply receipts for payment, as with payment in advance of delivery, e.g. Co-op milk tokens. Leaving these aside, any of the following types of item may be connected with a supply of goods:

(1) A stamp or voucher separately purchased by consumers from, e.g. a retailer, whereunder the stamp-supplier (retailer) undertakes to exchange the stamp for goods to its face value on subsequent presentation. Such schemes would appear to sub-divide as follows:

(a) 'Christmas Club' stamps (see para 15.17).

(b) 'Gift' stamps, where it is contemplated that the stamp purchaser will donate the stamp (frequently mounted on a fancy card) to a third party.[92] Such a stamp would appear to be a credit note transferable by delivery.[93] It is for consideration whether the donee's redemption of this stamp for goods from a retailer amounts to a quasi-sale by the retailer (see para 2.10).

(2) By way of promotional scheme, a retailer or manufacturer[94] may promise a consumer a reduced price in respect of his next purchase from that retailer or of that manufacturer's goods.[95] When the coupon is supplied free to the consumer, it is simply an advertisement of price reduction and may fall within the CPA (see para 8.10). However, where the consumer gives value for the coupon, e.g. coupons printed on product or in newspapers purchased, he may also have a collateral contract with the coupon issuer.[96] What is the effect where retailer A accepts for value the vouchers issued by retailer B; or where A accepts vouchers issued by manufacturer X against supplies of goods manufactured by Y?[97]

---

90  See Goode, *Op. cit.*, paras 2.37–9.

91  E.g. in newspapers or magazines, or on products. Prize competitions are governed by the Gambling Act 2005 (see para 8.15).

92  There is also a variation whereunder the voucher is provided by a third party, being sold to the public and redeemed from them by any participating retailer, e.g. book tokens. Cf. check-trading (see para 15.17).

93  This would be a form of chose in action: as to which, see generally, para 7.17. It is neither a bill of exchange within the Bills of Exchange Act 1882 (s 3), nor a promissory note (*ibid*, s 83): see generally *Chitty on Contract*, 28th edn, Vol 2, para 34-020.

94  E.g. retailers' coupons delivered from door-to-door, or in a 'newspaper'; manufacturer's coupons printed on goods, in newspapers or magazines, or delivered from door-to-door. Sometimes these are just promotional schemes, e.g. by two manufacturers.

95  See the Institute of Sales Promotion, *Recommended Best Practice*, set out in Circus, *Sales Promotion Law*, Appendix 3.

96  *Taylor v Smetten* (1883) 11 QBD 207 (illegal lottery); *Scott & Co Ltd v Soloman* [1905] 1 KB 577 (statutory licence). Cf. the *Esso* promotion scheme discussed at para 2.08. *Quaere* whether a coupon 'issued' by a manufacturer will bind the retailer? As to the fairness of Air Miles, see *UCT Bulletin No. 29*, p 8.

97  Have the vouchers then become transferable, as with some gift vouchers (above)? As to whether such actions by A infringe the British Code of Advertising Practice (see para 3.14), see Lawson (1992) 142 NLJ at 1274.

(3) Stamps, vouchers, etc issued by the supplier at the time of supply and to be exchanged for goods or services at a later date so that value is given for the stamp, voucher, etc. Usually, the stamp, voucher, etc is of small face value and is meant to be collected over repeated purchases. The original versions of such an idea were Co-op Dividend stamps and then Trading Stamps, both forms of promotion which fell into disuse.[92] Instead modern promotions tend to offer for collection 'points' on a payment card,[98] e.g. 'loyalty cards';[99] or 'cash back' vouchers on goods (see para 8.13A). Can a stamp-supplier *bona fide* redeeming a stolen stamp, voucher, points etc take free of the equities (see para 7.24), perhaps on the basis that it is 'negotiable by estoppel'?[100]

The foregoing schemes may be subject to the Sales Promotion Code (see para 3.14). At common law, the supplier of the vouchers may attach to them whatever terms he wishes; but their terms may be subject to the Unfair Terms Regulations (see para 11.15).

**[15.19] Credit unions**. In essence, a credit union is a non-profit-making loan society formed on a co-operative basis.[101] This concept has flourished abroad, but has been more reluctant to take root in the UK.[101] Here, they have mutual status like building societies (see para 2.17) and are developing within the framework of the Credit Unions Act 1979.[102] They have two basic functions: (i) they act as savings clubs, in which capacity they typically pay rates of interest which exceed the commercial rate for size of savings and are now controlled by the FSA;[103] and (ii) make loans to members (usually of 2–3 times savings and free life insurance), which because of their low interest charges have been exempted from the CCA (see below). The essence of credit unions is the common bond between members, e.g. neighbourhood, association, or workplace; but experience saw a divergence between the more successful industry-based unions and the less successful area-based unions.[104] From the viewpoint of low-income groups, the crucial potential area of development is neighbourhood credit unions in areas from which commercial banks have withdrawn; but for some reason these proved particularly

---

98 The terms on which points are awarded may be subject to the UTCCR: [2006] *Bulletin J/M, American Express.*

99 E.g. Tesco Clubcard; Nectar: see [1998] 1 *Which?* 16; [2003] 3 *Which?* 24. What is the point if customers hold multiple loyalty cards? E.g. Nectar; Boots Advantage; Tesco Clubcard; WH Smith Clubcard; Marks & Spencer and More. See generally *The Times* 4.6.2005.

100 *Easton v London Joint Stock Bank* (1886) 34 Ch D 95 at 113–14; see *Paget on Banking*, 12th edn, para 31.30; and Jacobs, *Bills of Exchange*, Chap 6. Cf. travellers cheques, as to which see Chitty, *Op. cit.*, para 34-173. For stolen points, see [2003] 9 *Which?* 5; [2004] 10 *Which?* 7.

101 The 1971 Crowther Report (see para 5.03), paras 2.4.28 (v); 9.2.12–3.

102 (As amended). See generally Griffiths and Howells (1991) 42 NILQ 199 at 204–15; (1992) 142 NLJ 235; Howells, *Aspects of Credit and Debt*, 15–17, 51, Chap 8; (1993) 14 CCA News 4/12. As to how to set up a credit union, see the Open University, *An Introduction to Credit Unions*; NCC, *Saving for Credit: The Future of Credit Unions in Britain* (1994); [2004] 8 *Which?* 24.

103 2002 SI 704. Deposits are protected by the Financial Services Compensation Scheme and complaints may be taken to the FSA ombudsman (see para 3.25). For the FSA, see generally, para 3.02.

104 Area-based unions lack confidentiality and the resources to institute the (frequently) desired weekly collected credit: (1990) 11 CCA News 2/17; *Mirage or Reality*, Appendix C. Howells, *Op. cit.*, 48–9. Compare commercially-based weekly collected credit: see para 2.18.

reluctant to develop, despite Government support.[105] Accordingly, the 1979 Act has been substantially amended through Deregulation Orders (see para 5.10), principally to relax the common bond requirement[106] and ease loan conditions,[107] which has led to an increase in the popularity of credit unions. The Government has plans to support these local unions by the introduction of a Central Service Organisation:[108] this should help unions to offer current accounts with access to the clearing bank system (see para 2.15), with cash machines, direct debits and standing orders.[109] The Government has called for the encouragement of credit unions (see para 6.09) and the Consumers Association has also supported them with a positive review.[110] As of June 2006, two changes have been introduced with the object of increasing the potential group of customers who could borrow from a credit union:

(1) The CCA exemption has been increased to 2% per month, with the object of restricting the costs of unions at the expense of statutory protection to their borrowers.[111]

(2) The maximum rate of interest chargeable by credit unions has been doubled to 2% per month,[112] so making them more financially viable and allowing them to lend to even lower income consumers.

**[15.20] Miscellaneous cases.** Apart from the cases above considered, there are a number of other statutes which impose obligations on the contracting parties. Often these provisions are aimed at a particular type of transaction or a transaction involving a specified type of goods, or both.

In imposing such an obligation, three techniques are available to the Legislature. *First*, terms may be imported into a contract, breach of which will give the innocent party civil law rights by statute[113] or statutory instrument.[114] *Second*, the agreement may be rendered unenforceable or terminated in the event of non-compliance.[115] *Third*, a statute may refuse[116] or impose criminal sanctions in respect

---

105 There are concerns with the size of Unions, their administration, economic viability and the inflexibility of the legislation. See OFT, *Vulnerable Consumers and Financial Services* (Jan 1999); Liverpool JMU Report for Joseph Rowntree, *Keep Out or Opted Out* (Mar 1999); Social Exclusion Unit, *Access to Financial Services* (Nov 1999); [1999] CCA News, Winter, 3. See also the White Paper, *Fair, Clear and Competitive: the Consumer Credit Market in the 21st Century* (Dec 2003, Cm. 6040), paras 5.52; and Collard and Kempson, *Affordable Credit* (2005) 35.

106 S 1(4), as amended by the Deregulation (Credit Unions) Order, 1996 SI 1189 art 3. See further Ryder [2003] JBL 45 at 57. There has even been a suggestion to allow postal applications.

107 Ss 11 (as amended), 11A–D. See further Ryder [2003] JBL 45 at 57–60.

108 See Ryder [2001] JBL 510. Cf. the Michigan Credit Union League, USA.

109 See further Ryder [2003] JBL 45 at 60–62; and Jones [2003] 9 *Credit Today* 26.

110 See [2004] 8 *Which?* 24.

111 In particular, this would save credit unions from having to comply with CCA regulations relating to: agreements; pre-contract information; advertisements; information disclosure; credit licences; and default, termination or early settlement.

112 S 11(5) of the 1979 Act; and the Credit Unions (Maximum Interest Rate on Loans) Order 2006 SI - 1276.

113 E.g. Hops (Prevention of Frauds) Act 1866, s 18; Anchors and Chain Cables Act 1899, s 2; Agriculture Act 1970, s 72; Plants and Seeds Act 1964, s 17.

114 E.g. the SSG Regulations (see para 14.01). Remember that English statutes can be amended by regulations made under the ECA or Deregulation Acts (see paras 1.03A and 5.10).

115 E.g. CCA, s 65 (see para 9.19); CCA, s 90 (see para 24.35).

116 This may be the effect of the obscurely worded SGA, s 60: see Chalmers, *Sale of Goods*, 18th edn, 261. What then is the effect of SGA, s 57(5)?

of the prohibited act (see the statutes considered in Chap 4). This last course tends to be more favoured nowadays as it is more likely to be effectively enforced, but it does give rise to certain problems: (1) does it render the agreement illegal;[117] (2) if so, to what extent does this prevent the parties from relying on the agreement; and (3) does contravention give rise to an action for breach of statutory duty?[118]

# TERMS AND OBLIGATIONS DERIVED FROM COMMON LAW

[15.21] There is nothing in any of the Acts relating to supply contracts to oust any express or implied condition precedent, e.g. SGA, s 2(3) (para 1.11). Conditions in the sense of essential stipulations have already been distinguished from conditions precedent (see para 11.04); and in relation to conditions precedent it is further necessary to distinguish between those precedent to the existence of a contract[119] and those precedent only to performance of some or all of its obligations.[120]

We are now in a position to consider the terms implied by common law into supply transactions, whether they are terms within the contract, or conditions precedent of one sort or the other.

## As to quality and fitness

[15.22] **Caveat emptor**. Where a transaction falls within the SGA (see para 1.07, *et seq.*), then the SGA appears to re-affirm the basic tenet of freedom of contract (see para 1.02) by re-stating the old *caveat emptor* rule in s 14(1) (as amended by the SSGA 1994, Sched 2, para 5(5)):

> 'Except as provided by this section[121] and by section 15 below[122] and subject to any other enactment,[123] there is no implied term about the quality or fitness for any particular purpose of goods supplied under a contract of sale'.[124]

There is a very similar provision in respect of hp, quasi-sales and simple hirings.[125] These words might appear to confirm the full severity of the common law attitude of *caveat emptor*,[126] but they have been said not to prevent any implication of terms

---

117  See generally, para 10.20.
118  See generally, para 3.21.
119  Ie the offer may be conditional, e.g. *Financings Ltd v Stimson* (set out at para 10.08).
120  E.g. *Marten v Whale* (set out at para 1.11); *Bentworth Finance Ltd v Lubert* (set out at para 15.23); and para 26.01.
121  For the terms implied by s 14, see Chap 14, and para 15.11. For a summary of the historical development of the implied terms, see Goode, *Commercial Law*, 3rd edn, 187.
122  For the terms implied by s 15, see paras 15.03–10.
123  See the examples referred to at para 15.20.
124  For discussion of the phrase 'goods supplied under a contract of sale', see para 14.04.
125  See respectively: SOGIT, s 10(1) as amended by SSGA 1994, Sched 2, para 4(4)(a); SGSA, s 4(1); SGSA, s 9(1). In the case of the SGSA, the 1994 Act has not replaced 'condition or warranty' by 'term'—is this a mistake?
126  See *Smith v Hughes* (see out at para 10.17). But have the implied terms now developed so far that this traditional introduction is now misleading? See Goode, *Op. cit.*, 298; and compare Brown (2000) 116 LQR 537; Hedley [2001] JBL 114.

as to quality or fitness under the doctrine of the *Moorcock*.[127] In the *Harlingdon* case, the disclaimer by the seller of any expert knowledge was held by the majority of the Court of Appeal to rule out any implied promise by him as to the description or merchantability of the goods.[128]

However, there are a number of ways in which the full severity of this rule may be mitigated. *First*, the section says 'there is no warranty or condition', which seems to imply that 'condition' is here used in the sense of essential stipulation. If so, the sections do not prevent the implication of conditions precedent (see para 15.21). *Second*, the sections do not prevent the prudent buyer or hirer from securing an express contractual promise by the seller or owner as to the quality or fitness of the goods supplied (see para 14.0A) or as to some related matter.[129] Does such an express promise oust the terms which would ordinarily be implied? At common law this turned on whether the parties intended the term to be in addition to the implied term or to replace it;[130] and statute now provides (SGA, s 55(2). See also SOGIT, s 12; SGSA, s 11(2), with a slight variation in wording):

'An express warranty or condition does not negative a warranty or condition implied by this Act unless inconsistent therewith.'

This subsection would appear to be merely an example of the ordinary rule as to the exclusion of implied terms set out elsewhere (see para 18.09). *Third*, it may be possible for the buyer to bring an action in the tort of negligence, though such an action will not usually be as likely to succeed as a claim in contract (see para 17.12, *et seq*.). *Fourth*, it has been suggested that a person who buys (or hires?) goods with a latent defect may be able to rescind the contract on the grounds of non-disclosure.[131] *Fifth*, there may be particular statutory offences concerning the quality of goods supplied, e.g. motor vehicles, where the provisions extend to private sales (see para 4.37). Bear in mind compensation orders (see para 3.20). *Sixth*, there may be other implied terms which are not exclusively about quality and fitness.[132] *Seventh*, as from 2007 it may sometimes be reversed for consumers by the UCP Directive (Art 7: see para 4.21A).

## Other terms in hire purchase

In contrast to the situation with regard to sales, the courts have been able to import into hp agreements a considerable number of implied terms for the benefit of both owners and hirers: there is express permission to do so contained in SOGIT, s 15(4).

---

127 (1889) 14 PD 64, CA. See *St Albans DC v International Computers Ltd* (see para 18.20), *per* Glidewell LJ at 494b–d; *Watford Electronics Ltd v Sanderson Ltd* (see para 18.21; unappealed point). This may be important in relation to the common law terms in bailment and hp: see paras 15.23–4.
128 The first instance judge had rejected evidence of a custom that sales in the art market are on a *caveat emptor* basis. But the CA achieved the same result, thereby depriving the buyer of the protection of the implied terms by way of UCTA (see para 18.12, *et seq*). See Smith (1990) 140 NLJ at 1675. Thus, the ruling may not apply to a private art buyer: see Bentil (1991) 8 Tr L at 32–3, 36.
129 Such as that the goods would be supplied with any necessary warning: *Vacwell Engineering Ltd v BDH Chemicals Ltd* (set out at para 18.29).
130 See *Bigge v Parkinson* (1862) 7 H & N 955.
131 E.g. motor vehicles, where the provisions extend to private sales (see para 4.37).
132 The *Albright & Wilson* case (set out at para 13.01), CA at paras 34 and 35.

Many of these implied terms obviously owe their inspiration to the law of bailment (see generally, para 1.17).

**[15.23] For the benefit of the hirer.** It has been decided that the hiring does not commence until delivery,[133] and that the goods have not been delivered until they have been accepted by the hirer so as to pass into his possession.[134] Furthermore, the courts have implied conditions that the goods should remain in substantially the same condition from the time when the offer is made up to the time of acceptance;[135] and from then until the time of delivery[134]. In *Bentworth Finance Ltd v Lubert*:[136]

> The plaintiff finance company agreed to let a car to L under a directly financed hp transaction under which M agreed to act as surety for L. The dealers left the car unlicensed and untaxed, outside L's house, and L neither used the car nor paid any instalments.

The Court of Appeal unanimously dismissed the plaintiff's action against L and M for arrears of instalments on the following grounds:

(1) It was an implied condition of the hp agreement that the log-book should be supplied, and until it was supplied 'there was no contract of hp at all', and no instalments fell due;[137]

(2) M was not liable because the plaintiff's loss did not arise from the contract of hp being unenforceable, but from the 'plaintiff's allowing the dealers to hand over the car without the log-book' (see further, para 25.06).

Now, in all the cases so far cited in this paragraph the owner was suing the hirer, and the courts did no more than hold that performance of a particular act by the owner was a condition precedent to his enforcement of the agreement.[138] It is, however, usually thought that the owner impliedly promises to deliver the goods, and to deliver them in substantially the same condition as they were when inspected by the hirer. In *Karsales (Harrow) Ltd v Wallis*:[139]

> The consumer (C) entered into a directly financed transaction in respect of a Buick car. Prior to signing the agreement, C had inspected the car, and found it to be in good order. Shortly after the date of the agreement, the 'car' was (apparently) towed into position outside C's premises at night; and on inspection the following morning it was found to be in a deplorable condition, and incapable of self-propulsion.

The Court of Appeal unanimously found for C on the grounds that the object delivered was not the car contracted for, and that such a breach disentitled the plaintiff[140] from relying on the exclusion clause[134]. Alternatively, the majority

---

133  *National Cash Register Co v Stanley* [1921] 3 KB 292, DC.

134  *Karsales Ltd v Wallis* (set out below). As to what amounts to a delivery, see generally, para 23.03.

135  *Financings Ltd v Stimson* (set out at para 10.08).

136  [1968] 1 QB 680, [1967] 2 All ER 810, CA.

137  For conditions precedent, see generally, para 15.21.

138  Were they conditions precedent to contract or performance? See Lord Denning MR in *Lubert's* case (above), at 685; and *Financings Ltd v Stimson* (above).

139  [1956] 2 All ER 866, [1956] 1 WLR 936, CA. See Goode, *HP Law & Practice*, 2nd edn, 227.

140  The finance company assigned their rights to the plaintiff dealer under a repurchase provision: see para 16.21.

were prepared to decide the case on the further ground that delivery of the car had not been accepted.[141]

**[15.24] In favour of the owner**. The terms which the common law will imply into simple bailments in favour of the **owner** have already been considered (para 1.17). Similarly, the courts have implied in favour of the owner under an hp agreement obligations that the hirer will accept delivery of goods tendered in performance of the contract;[142] that he will take reasonable care of them during the currency of the agreement;[143] that he will not do any act in relation to the goods which is totally repugnant to the terms of the bailment (see para 26.09); and that he will pay the sums stipulated in the agreement subject to the ordinary common law rules of payment (see para 23.26, *et seq.*). Furthermore, where the agreement is determined, the hirer is under a common law duty[144] to redeliver the goods;[145] but, should redelivery become impossible through no fault of his own, the hirer is *prima facie* discharged from this duty (see para 22.10, *et seq.*).

## Analogous transactions[146]

**[15.25]** Goods are sometimes supplied on a commercial or quasi-commercial basis under transactions which do not fit easily within the established categories of contract for the supply of goods. Of course, the supplier will be subject to the obligations of the law of tort applicable to such circumstances; but this will normally mean only liability towards his transferee in the tort of negligence (see Chap 17). The question is this: in view of the business basis of the transaction, can the supplier be subjected to the more onerous strict liability of contract?

At the outset, a distinction must be drawn according to whether or not there is any contractual basis to the supply.[147] Transactions where there is **no** such basis are outside the SGSA[148] and may fall into one of the following categories:

(1) Where there is a simple transfer of possession, the supplier retaining the property in the goods. This will amount to a bailment at will, and the obligations of such transactions have already been examined (para 1.14), the bailor probably only being liable to the bailee in the tort of negligence (see para 8.14). If there were liability at common law for negligence, does s 2 of the Unfair Contract Terms Act 1977 (see para 18.17) prevent its exclusion?

---

141 It would follow that the plaintiff's only possible remedy would be for damages for non-acceptance (see para 27.24), which right had not been assigned to him (see para 7.17).

142 *National Cash Register Co v Stanley* [1921] 3 KB 292 DC.

143 The extent of this common law duty is uncertain; and it is unlikely to be settled as the agreement will almost always impose strict liability on the hirer. See paras 1.14 and 1.15.

144 In the absence of any contractual provision to the contrary, the common law duty is merely to hold the goods ready for the owner to fetch them: see para 24.25.

145 Failure to comply with his duty to redeliver will render the hirer liable to an action for breach of contract or in tort for conversion (see para 19.04).

146 See generally Miller and Lovell, *Product Liability*, 115–22; Waddams, *Product Liability*, 87–100; Cranston, *Consumers and the Law*, 3rd edn, Chap 6.

147 For transactions where there is a contractual basis to the supply, see para 15.26.

148 Because of the absence of a contract: see the SGSA, s 1(1), considered at para 2.10.

(2) Where there is a transfer of possession and property with the requisite intent, this will amount to a gift (see para 2.09), the donor's only liability being in the tort of negligence. Leaving aside drugs supplied under the NHS (see para 1.07), perhaps the most obvious difficulty here concerns 'free gifts'. Some transactions so described are clearly sales of goods, e.g. 'three for the price of two'; whilst in others the 'free' goods are in fact supplied under a quasi-sale (see para 2.10), as where goods are supplied in return for coupons, wrappers or points, with[149] or without[150] some additional monetary consideration.[151] On the other hand, some free gifts or samples are clearly gifts, probably attracting to the supplier only liability towards the donee in the tort of negligence (para 8.14).

(3) Where the intending purchaser is injured by the goods before the formation of the contract for their supply.[152] Whilst this may amount to a 'prospective regulated agreement' within the CCA,[153] there is no contract, and hence no possibility of any express or implied promises, so that the tort of negligence is the supplier's only other possible liability to the injured consumer.[154]

[15.26] **Contract basis**. Where goods are supplied on a commercial or quasi-commercial basis under a contract, before the SGSA it was sometimes difficult to decide how to treat such transactions. Some transactions were found on closer inspection to fall within the SGA (see para 1.06, *et seq.*): for instance, goods sold in a hired container;[155] or a 'three for the price of two' constitutes a sale of all three units; or where an apparent barter turns out to amount rather to reciprocal sales;[156] or a sale of goods-to-be-fitted.[157] On other occasions, there may be found to be two contracts within one transaction, a contract for the sale of goods supplied plus an installation or fitting contract (see para 2.05); and in these cases the rules of sale or hire purchase or hiring can clearly be applied to the supply of goods, and Pt II of the SGSA to the supply of services (see para 15.15). However, there remained the difficult cases where goods were supplied under a collateral contract (is this the proper analysis of the sale of a fully furnished house?); or where there was only one hybrid contract under which there was a supply in part of goods and in part of services.[158] Presumably, the fact that the details of a pure contract to provide

---

149 *Chappell & Co Ltd v Nestle Co Ltd* [1960] AC 87, HL.

150 *Esso Petroleum Ltd v Cmrs of Customs and Excise* (see para 2.08).

151 Or the transferee may supply some consideration in kind, e.g. by submitting an entry to a competition for a prize.

152 E.g. a supermarket customer injured by goods before reaching the check-out; or where goods are at the time of injury being demonstrated to, or examined by, a customer before purchase. Does this category include goods on sale-or-return before purchase (see para 20.23)?

153 E.g. Pts IV and V of the CCA, discussed at Chaps 8, 9 and 10.

154 *Lasky v Economy Grocery Stores* (1946) 65 NE (2nd) 305, 163 ALR 235.

155 See *Geddling v Marsh* (set out at para 14.03).

156 See para 2.09. But what if the supplier agrees to replace defective goods 'free of charge'?

157 E.g. *Phillip Head and Sons Ltd v Showfronts Ltd* [1970] 1 Lloyd's Rep 140 (fitted carpets).

158 E.g. *Young and Marten Ltd v McManus Childs Ltd* [1969] 1 AC 454, HL (roofing sub-contractor supplying defective tiles); *Watson v Buckley Ltd* [1940] 1 All ER 174 (hairdresser applying dye); *Dodd v Wilson* [1946] 2 All ER 691 (vet inoculating with defective serum); *Samuels v Davis* [1943] 1 KB 526 (dentist supplying dentures).

services are set out in writing and that document handed to the other party does not make the contract a hybrid one.[159]

In some hybrid contracts, the courts have applied the rules of sale by analogy.[160] However, s 1(3) of the SGSA provides that (subject to the exclusions in s 1(2): see para 2.10):

'For the purposes of the Act a contract is a contract for the transfer of goods whether or not services are also provided or to be provided under the contract, and . . . whatever is the nature of the consideration for the transfer or agreement to transfer.'

It follows that the category of quasi-sales within Pt I of the SGSA (see para 2.10) clearly includes both the following categories:

(a) the first limb of s 1(3) brings in hybrid contracts;[161] and

(b) the second limb extends the category to barter or exchange,[162] some 'free gifts'[163] and other title transferring transactions,[164] including perhaps collateral contracts.[165]

In a consumer supply contract, any exclusion clause may be an unfair term.[166]

---

159  What about the provision of computer software? See *per* Norse and Glidewell LJJ in *St Albans DC v International Computers Ltd* (see para 18.25), at 487j, 494a.

160  *Per* Lord Diplock in the *Ashington Piggeries* case (set out at para 13.13) at 501. E.g. *Ingham v Emes* [1956] 2 QB 366, CA (hairdresser applying dye); *Andrews v Hopkinson* (set out at para 16.18). See further, para 1.04.

161  E.g. *Stewart Gill Ltd v Horatio Meyer & Co Ltd* [1992] 2 All ER 257, CA (decided on another point: see para 18.16); *Watford Electronics Ltd v Sanderson CFL Ltd* (see para 18.21; unappealed point).

162  This includes part-exchange. For contracts of barter or exchange, see generally, para 2.09.

163  Notwithstanding the terminology, the 'free gift' of goods may amount to a collateral contract (see para 15.25), under which goods are supplied subject to all the ordinary implied terms. But see Law Com No. 95, para 32; and further Woodroffe, *Goods and Services—The New Law*, paras 2.11–15.

164  E.g. prizes award in competitions. See further, Palmer (1983) 46 MLR at 621–2.

165  Distinguish collateral contracts which do not transfer the property in goods: see paras 16.14 and 17.09.

166  OFT, *UCT Bulletin No. 13*, case 8: for Grey Term 1(b), see para 11.16A.

# CHAPTER 16

# FINANCED TRANSACTIONS

**[16.01] Introduction.** The express and implied terms which may be found in contracts for the supply of goods have been examined in Chaps 11–15, together with the effect of any misrepresentation inducing entry into the supply contract. In the present chapter, the extent to which that scheme may be amended where the retail supply is financed is considered, whilst product liability and exclusion clauses are respectively left over until Chaps 17 and 18. Particularly important in lender credit are the rules concerned with the financier's liability for the dealer's acts (see para 16.04, *et seq.*) and the liability of the dealer to the consumer (see para 16.18, *et seq.*).

However, before embarking on these topics, it may be helpful to summarise the circumstances in which the SGA, the SOGIT, the CCA and the SGSA are applicable to the various forms of vendor and lender credit (see respectively, paras 16.02–03).

## STATUTORY ANALYSIS

**[16.02] Vendor credit** (see para 2.19). This involves the retail-supplier himself financing the transaction and may take either of the following forms:

(a) *A single instalment credit contract* (see para 1.03), to which all the rules previously considered in Chaps 11–15 apply. Which statutes are applicable will vary according to the form of instalment credit contract utilised as follows:

  (i) a credit[1] or conditional[2] sale, whose 'supply' element will be **within** the SGA[3] or SGSA,[4] and whose 'credit' element may also amount to a regulated DCS agreement **within** the CCA;[5] **or**

  (ii) a hp agreement,[6] whose 'supply' element falls **outside** the SGA,[3] but within SOGIT,[7] and which may have a 'credit' element which amounts to a regulated DCS agreement **within** the CCA;[5] **or**

  (iii) a simple hiring agreement,[8] whose 'supply' element falls **outside** both the SGA[3] and SOGIT,[7] but **within** the SGSA,[4] and which may amount to a regulated consumer hire agreement **within** the CCA.[9]

---

1 For credit sales, see para 1.13.
2 For conditional sales, see paras 1.14–15.
3 For the ambit of the SGA, see 1.07. For the implied terms, see Chaps 12–15.
4 The SGSA introduced some new implied terms for quasi-sales and simple hirings: see Chaps 12–15.
5 For DCS agreements, see para 5.34.
6 For hp agreements, see paras 1.20, *et seq.*
7 The SOGIT introduced some new implied terms for hp agreements: see Chaps 12–15.
8 For simple hiring agreements, see paras 1.18–19.
9 For consumer hiring agreement, see para 1.19.

(b) *Two associated transactions* as follows:

    (i)    a contract of loan (see para 7.02), which may amount to a regulated DCS agreement **within** the CCA;[5] **and**

    (ii)   a cash sale, whose 'supply' element will fall within the SGA[3] or SGSA,[4] and which may amount to a linked transaction **within** the CCA (see para 5.31).

**[16.03] Lender credit.** This involves a third party financing the transaction and may take either of the following forms, each of which requires **two** major contracts:

(a) *Direct financing* (see para 2.21), where there is **both**:

    (i)    A cash sale of the goods **within** the SGA[10] or SGSA[11] from the dealer to the financier;[12] **and**

    (ii)   An instalment contract between the financier and consumer, which contract will follow the same analysis as in the case of vendor credit (see para 16.02).

(b) *Loan financing* (see paras 2.23–4), where there is **both**:

    (i)    A cash sale of the goods **within** the SGA[10] or SGSA[11] from the dealer to the consumer; **and**

    (ii)   A loan by the financier to the consumer, which loan may amount to a regulated consumer credit agreement **within** the CCA.[13]

If the regulated loan is independent of the sale,[14] the loan will then be a DC agreement;[15] but, if the loan and sale are both part of a single package,[14] the loan will be a DCS agreement[16] and the sale a linked transaction (see para 5.31).

## FINANCIER'S LIABILITY FOR THE DEALER'S ACTS

**[16.04] Introduction.** The matter to be considered here is the effect which the form of the financing may have on the personal obligations of the parties.[17] Where a binding transaction is financed by the dealer—vendor credit (see para 2.19)—there will always be a contract for the supply of goods between the dealer and consumer, so that all the rules previously considered in Chaps 11–15 will apply to the dealer's conduct. The same will be true if the transaction is loan financed (see para 2.23). However, if the transaction is directly financed (see para 2.21), there will be no primary contractual relationship between the dealer and consumer;[18] and, if the

---

10   For the ambit of the SGA, see para 1.07. For the implied terms, see Chaps 12–15.

11   The SGSA introduced some new implied terms for transactions analogous to sales: see Chaps 12–15.

12   This is **not** a linked transaction: see paras 5.31 and 10.32.

13   For regulated consumer credit agreements, see para 5.13.

14   See the CCA, s 187: discussed at para 5.33.

15   For DC agreements, see para 5.35.

16   For DCS agreements, see para 5.34.

17   The security element of instalment credit transactions will be considered later: Chaps 24 and 25.

18   Though there may be a collateral contract between them (see para 16.18). For some special difficulties caused by this absence of any primary contractual relationship, see para 16.05.

transaction is financed by way of loan of the price to the consumer, there will be no contract for the supply of goods from the financier to the consumer.

For these reasons, the insolvency of the dealer in a directly financed or loan financed transaction has caused problems; and the feeling has developed that some attempt must be made to help the consumer to find a solvent defendant by giving him rights against the financier in respect of wrongdoing by the dealer,[19] on the basis that the financier should in some way be 'responsible' for the dealer.[20] This has led to three different (overlapping) veins of statutory intervention:[21]

(a) interference with the common law rules of agency as between the dealer and financier;[22]

(b) the dealer in directly financed transactions has been made the agent of the financier as regards his misrepresentations;[23]

(c) the financier in loan financing has been made liable for misrepresentations and breaches of the supply contract by the dealer.[24]

**[16.05] Direct financing**. The absence of any primary contractual relationship between dealer and consumer in direct financing (see para 16.04) has caused some special difficulties at common law.

(1) *The deposit.* On signing the proposal form, the consumer will usually hand over a deposit to the dealer. This deposit may be either cash or goods taken in part-exchange (see para 2.10).

(a) If the financier does not accept the proposal or the agreement is void *ab initio*, it is a question of intention whether the deposit is recoverable by the consumer from the dealer: normally, it is intended simply to form part of the consideration for the contemplated contract,[25] in which case it is recoverable by the consumer from the dealer on grounds of total failure of consideration;[26] but, if it is intended to be by way of security for completion of the transaction by the consumer, then in the event of his default it cannot be recovered at common law, though equity may offer relief against forfeiture (see para 27.20), or that agreement may be avoided by the CCA (s 59: see further, para 5.20), or the UTCC Regulations may offer relief.[27]

(b) Where the financier accepts the proposal, the dealer will credit the financier with the amount of the deposit or part-exchange allowance, in which case

---

19  This has given financiers a real sense of grievance: see, e.g. *Instalment Credit* (Ed Diamond) 27–9.

20  At common law, this 'responsibility' argument is usually conducted in terms of whether the dealer is participating in the transaction as agent of the financier: as to which, see below.

21  Whilst (a) leads into (b), it is perhaps unfortunate that (b) and (c) have been drafted in ss 56 and 75 of the CCA so that there may be considerable overlap between them. But in loan financing, liability under (b) and (c) is not co-extensive: Jones, *Credit Cards*, 215–17.

22  This intervention is now to be found in s 56(3) of the CCA: see para 16.07.

23  This rule is now to be found in s 56(2) of the CCA: see para 16.10.

24  This liability has been introduced by s 75 of the CCA: see para 16.11.

25  *Chillingworth v Esche* [1924] 1 Ch 97, CA—a real property case cited in a 1951 edition of *Benjamin on Sale*, 8th edn, 947, fn (e).

26  As to which, see generally, para 29.13. Is the deposit alternatively recoverable from the financier under s 56(2) of the CCA? See para 16.10.

27  See the Grey list, term (o): see para 11.18A.

that amount will be regarded as being given by the consumer indirectly to the financier. In *Branwhite v Worcester Finance Ltd*[28] the majority of the House of Lords decided that the dealer was not the agent of the financier;[29] but their Lordships unanimously held that, as the dealer had credited the financier with the deposit as against the price to be paid by the financier to him, this was equivalent to an actual payment of the deposit to the financier on behalf of the consumer in respect of a transaction which had wholly failed so far as the consumer was concerned;[26] and so the financier must return the deposit to the consumer (at 572, 582 and 590). This rule will apply wherever the consumer elects to treat as discharged for breach his instalment credit contract with the financier (as to which, see para 26.15).

(2) *Documents signed in blank.* Particular difficulty has arisen where the consumer has signed the proposal in blank and then the dealer has subsequently fraudulently completed and forwarded the documents to the financier.[30] In *Mercantile Credit Co Ltd v Hamblin*,[31] A sought a loan from a dealer (B), who persuaded A to sign in blank a document which turned out to be an hp proposal. B then persuaded a financier (C) to accept the proposal. As against C, A unsuccessfully claimed that she could deny her signature on grounds of *non est factum*,[32] though nowadays, if regulated, she would be able to plead that the agreement was not properly executed.[33]

(3) *Defective goods.* Whilst the goods are physically supplied to the consumer by the dealer (see para 2.21), in law they are supplied to him by the financier (see para 16.11). Statutory alteration to this pattern has made the financier additionally liable for the dealer's representations (see para 16.07); but the dealer may alternatively be liable as 'supplier' under the safety legislation.[34]

## Agency of the dealer

**[16.06] Common Law.** The question of whether the financier can be made 'responsible' for the acts of the dealer on the basis that the latter acted as the former's agent has caused particular difficulty in relation to directly financed transactions.[35] There are two diametrically opposed judicial views of the matter. In *Financings Ltd v Stimson*,[36] Lord Denning MR argued that the dealer is the financier's agent on the basis of ostensible authority (see para 10.06). On the other hand, there is considerable authority for the rejection of any general proposition that the dealer is the

---

28  [1969] 1 AC 552, [1968] 3 All ER 104, HL. In this litigation, it had been decided in previous proceedings (and was so binding by issue estoppel) that the hp agreement was void *ab initio*, the customer having signed in blank: but it has now been shown that this may be wrong, see below.

29  Per Lords Morris, Guest and Upjohn, at 573 and 578. Lords Reid and Wilberforce dissented, at 589. See further, para 16.06.

30  See generally Allcock (1982) 45 MLR 18.

31  [1965] 2 QB 242, [1964] 3 All ER 592, CA.

32  See also *United Dominions Trust Ltd v Western* [1976] QB 51, CA; and generally, para 10.16.

33  *PB Leasing Ltd v Patel and Patel* [1995] CCLR 82, Cty Ct; and generally, para 9.13.

34  CPA, s 46(2): see further, para 4.34 and para 17.27.

35  As to directly financed transactions, see generally, para 2.21 For further discussion of the agency issue, see Goode, *HP Law & Practice*, 2nd edn, 286–96.

36  [1962] 3 All ER 386, CA, at 388. He was supported in this case by Donovan LJ (at 389); but Pearson LJ disagreed (at 392).

agent of the financier.[37] No doubt, the above two positions are strictly reconcilable; but they were accepted as involving rival views in *Branwhite v Worcester Finance Ltd*,[38] a case involving a directly financed hp transaction. Three members of the House of Lords there expressly adopted the latter view.[39] In practice, the courts seem to be very reluctant to accept that at common law the dealer has acted as agent of the financier. For instance, it has been held that the dealer had implied authority neither to accept the consumer's offer contained in the proposal form;[40] nor to receive the consumer's offer to the finance company for the purposes of the *inter praesentes* rule;[41] nor to receive instalments of hire rent;[42] nor to fix the financier with knowledge that the transaction was a disguised bill of sale;[43] nor that the dealer's title to the goods was defective;[44] nor in paying a settlement figure (see para 26.19A); nor probably for the purposes of making representations. In *Woodchester Leasing Equipment Ltd v BACFID*:[45]

> Black was employed as a salesman by Magnum, an office equipment supplier. Black persuaded BACFID, a trade association, to sign an hp agreement for a fax machine, leaving the supplier's name blank. Black then changed employers and submitted the proposal to a financier in the name of his new employers. Meanwhile, Magnum sent another salesman, Marco, to retrieve the business: by misrepresentation, Marco persuaded BACFID to complete a separate proposal to lease from Woodchester. When two fax machines were delivered, BACFID declined to continue with the transaction.

Woodchester sued BACFID for breach of the lease and the latter sought to rely on Marco's misrepresentation. Following the *Branwhite* case (above), the Court of Appeal held that Woodchester were not responsible for the misrepresentation of Marco. Contrast the position of eponymous subsidiaries;[46] and for statutory intervention, see para 16.07.

**[16.07] Statutory intervention**. To obviate the difficulties at common law described above (see para 16.06) of determining whether or not the dealer has acted as agent of the financier, the financier in an instalment credit transaction governed wholly by the common law will usually expressly deny the dealer any authority to commit him by acting as his agent, so preventing any possibility of actual authority; and he will normally take steps to notify the consumer of this fact,[47] so as to preclude any

---

37 *Mercantile Credit Ltd v Hamblin* [1965] 2 QB 242, CA, at 269. See also Holroyd Pearce LJ in *Campbell Discount Co Ltd v Gall* [1961] 1 QB 431, at 441, CA.

38 [1969] 1 AC 552, [1968] 3 All ER 104, HL.

39 *Per* Lords Morris, Upjohn and Guest, at 573 and 576.

40 *Financings Ltd v Stimson* (set out at para 10.07). But compare *Carlyle Finance Ltd v Pallas Industrial Finance Ltd* (set out at para 10.08).

41 *Shogun Finance Ltd v Hudson* (set out at para 10.15).

42 *Bentworth Finance Ltd v White* (1962) 112 LJ 140, Cty Ct. For actions for arrears of rentals, see generally, para 27.21.

43 *Spencer v North County Finance Ltd* [1963] CLY 212, CA.

44 *Car and Universal Finance Ltd v Caldwell* (set out at para 21.22).

45 [1995] CCLR 51, CLY 1193, 49 CC6/2, CA. See also *Williams & Co v McCauley* [1994] CCLR 78, CA.

46 *Lease Management Services Ltd v Purnell Secretarial Services* (1994) 13 Tr LR 337, CA. See generally, Macleod, *Consumer Sales Law*, 1st edn, para 16.06A.

47 The instalment contract will usually recite that the dealer is not the agent of the financier, making it difficult to advance an ostensible authority argument on the basis put forward by Lord Denning MR in para 16.06. See generally, Goode, *HP Law & Practice*, 2nd edn, 283–5.

apparent authority.[48] If so, it follows that at common law the financier can normally only be rendered contractually liable on the basis that he has done something which overrides the disclaimer and clothes the dealer with some apparent or ostensible authority to act as his agent.[49] However, where the transaction falls within one or both of the following statutory protections it is a different matter altogether.

1.  *The CCA*. Following the precedent in the HPA 1965, where such deemed agency clauses occur in regulated agreements, they may be attacked under s 56 of the CCA. This provision christens the dealer the 'negotiator' in the 'antecedent negotiations' (see para 16.08). Compulsory[50] s 56(3) provides 'An agreement is void, if and to the extent that, it purports in relation to an actual or prospective regulated agreement[51]

    (a)  to provide that a person acting as, or on behalf of, a negotiator is to be treated as the agent of the debtor or hirer, or

    (b)  to relieve a person from liability for acts or omissions of any person acting as, or on behalf of, a negotiator.'

    It will be observed that this provision is entirely **negative**: it does not make the dealer the agent of the financier for any purpose, but simply precludes the parties from ousting the ordinary common law rules for determining the extent, if any, to which the negotiator[52] is the agent of the financier, or the latter vicariously liable for the former.[53] However, other CCA provisions do **positively** deem the dealer to be the agent of the financier for certain purposes (see para 10.24), including for the purpose of making representations during the 'antecedent negotiations' (see para 16.08).

2.  *The UTCC regulations*. Where there is a 'consumer supply contract' (see para 11.13), the deemed agency clause may be an 'unfair term' and hence not binding on the consumer (see paras 11.14–15). This is because such deemed agency provisions are probably within the Grey List (para (n): see para 11.18).

**[16.08]  Antecedent negotiations.** According to s 56(1) of the CCA:

'In this Act "antecedent negotiations" mean any negotiations with the debtor or hirer—

(a)  conducted by the creditor or owner in relation to the making of any regulated agreement, or

(b)  conducted by a credit-broker in relation to goods sold or proposed to be sold by the credit-broker to the creditor before forming the subject-matter of a debtor-creditor-supplier agreement within section 12(a), or

(c)  conducted by the supplier in relation to a transaction financed or proposed to be financed by a debtor-creditor-supplier agreement within section 12(b) or (c),

---

48  *Overbrooke Estates Ltd v Glencombe Properties Ltd* [1974] 3 All ER 511 (not a goods case: further, para 17.10); and generally, para 10.06.

49  *Mendelssohn v Normand Ltd* [1970] 1 QB 177, CA.

50  The parties cannot contract out of this provision (s 173(1)): see further, para 18.11.

51  This 'agreement' may or may not be the regulated agreement. For actual and prospective regulated agreements, see para 5.20; and para 16.12.

52  Because of the drafting of s 56(1), s 56(3) will not usually extend to a directly financed lease: see para 16.08.

53  See further Goode, *Consumer Credit Law & Practice*, para 32.32.

and "negotiator" means the person by whom negotiations are so conducted with the debtor or hirer.'

This provision concentrates on the 'negotiator' (including his servant or agent), meaning the person who conducts the 'antecedent negotiations' leading towards a regulated agreement in any one of three scenarios:

*Para (a): creditor or owner as negotiator.* Negotiations conducted by the creditor or owner[54] in relation to the making of any regulated agreement, e.g. a money-lender's employee negotiating a DC loan, or a dealer negotiating a directly financed transaction as agent of the financier.[55] Might this extend to a directly financed lease (see below)?

*Para (b): dealer as negotiator.* Negotiations conducted by the credit-broker[56] in relation to a directly financed consumer credit agreement, e.g. Sched. 2, Example 2; but this cannot include a housewife mail-order agent.[57] In the appropriate circumstances, these negotiations may render the agreement cancellable, e.g. Sched. 2, Example 4; and see generally, para 10.29. Two problems have arisen. *First*, the consumer may arrange with the credit-broker to trade-in an existing model upon which there is outstanding finance which the credit-broker undertakes to discharge. In *Forthright Finance Ltd v Ingate* (set out at para 16.10) it was held that the second finance company (the creditor) can be made liable under s 56 for any such undischarged finance: the issue turns on whether the credit-broker's undertaking is made 'in relation to the goods sold or proposed to be sold'. *Second*, because of the reference to s 12(a), *para (b)* cannot include directly financed leases, which are consequently unlikely to be cancellable (see para 10.29), or leave the financier liable for the dealer's misrepresentations.[58]

*Para (c): supplier as negotiator.* Negotiations conducted by the supplier[59] in a financed transaction, as where it is loan financed.[60] Note that this paragraph overlaps with s 75 (see para 16.12): so, by using s 56(1)(c) it may be possible to avoid the limitations in s 75(3) (see para 16.13).

As all regulated agreements must inevitably be preceded by some prior communications between the parties, they must always be preceded by 'antecedent negotiations', and the effect of s 56(1) is that a wide variety of persons may amount to the 'negotiator'. Further, s 56(4) provides that:

---

54  By the s 189(1) definitions, this expressly includes any prospective creditor or owner (see para 5.25), which is important here because the negotiations must take place before formation of the regulated agreement.

55  See respectively CCA, Sched 1, Example 1; and for the exceptional agency case see para 16.04.

56  As to 'credit-broker', see para 5.38. It is suggested that he does not need to be acting as a credit-broker in that particular transaction: Guest and Lloyd, *Encyclopedia of Consumer Credit*, para 2-057.

57  See para 5.41. So, she will not be a 'negotiator': Goode, *Consumer Credit Law & Practice*, para 31.91.

58  *Moorgate Mercantile Leasing v Isobel Gell* [1986] CLY 371, Cty Ct; *Contra Woodchester Leasing Equipment v Clayton* [1994] CLY 500, Cty Ct. *Aliter*, in respect of the implied undertakings as to fitness: see para 14.12.

59  This will in effect be the dealer who in law and fact supplies the goods to the consumer: see para 5.34.

60  See s 12(b). E.g. goods bought with a credit card (Sched 2, Example 3). As to an example within s 12(c), see Goode, *Op. cit.*, para 31.92.

'For the purposes of this Act, antecedent negotiations shall be taken to begin when the negotiator and the debtor or hirer first enter into communication (including communication by advertisement), and to include any representations made by the negotiator to the debtor or hirer and any other dealings between them'.

The effect of s 56(4) is twofold. *First*, negotiations are made to include: (i) any 'representation', which expression is widely defined to include 'any condition or warranty, and any other statement or undertaking, whether oral or in writing' (s 189(1); see further, para 10.29); and (ii) 'other dealings'.[61] *Second*, s 56(4) extends back in time the commencement of 'antecedent negotiations' to the time when the debtor or hirer reads any 'advertisement'[62] put out by the 'negotiator', e.g. point-of-sale advertising poster by dealer, such as a windscreen sticker, or a newspaper advertisement placed on the dealer's behalf by an advertising agency; or a manufacturer's advertisement adopted by the dealer, as on packaged goods. What if the advertiser is independent of the dealer and the advertisement is not adopted by the dealer? Whilst the Act is silent on the point, it would appear that 'antecedent negotiations' terminate on formation of the regulated agreement: this may have different effects according to whether the agreement is for fixed-sum credit[63] or running-account credit.[64]

## Misrepresentation by the dealer

**[16.09]** Where a dealer induces a consumer to enter into a financed transaction by means of a misrepresentation,[65] the common law position of the financier[66] would appear to be influenced by the fact that the primary contractual relationship is between the financier and the consumer: in a directly financed transaction,[67] there is an instalment supply contract (see para 1.03) made between them; and in loan financing, there is a loan contract made between them. Now, we are postulating a case where the misrepresentation inducing the consumer to enter the financed transaction is made by a third party, the dealer. Leaving aside any rights which this may give the consumer against the dealer,[66] it can only affect the relationship between the financier and consumer if the dealer made the misrepresentation as agent of the financier (see para 16.06).

The problem first arose in connection with directly financed transactions, where the common law position was probably that the dealer was not the agent of the financier for the purposes of affecting the financier with liability in respect of misrepresentations made by the dealer in the course of negotiating the transaction

---

61　E.g. installation maintenance or insurance contracts—Goode, *Op. cit.*, para 32.19. What of part-exchange goods?

62　As to 'advertisement', see para 8.29. Does the advertisement have to play any part in inducing the debtor or hirer to enter into the transaction? Cf. the common law misrepresentation rule.

63　It would follow that oral statements after formation, e.g. during fitting or on delivery, are not within s 56 and hence will not attract s 67: see Goode, *Op. cit.*, para 31.93.

64　If there is a fresh contract each time the card is used (see para 7.11), oral statements preceding each use will be part of the 'antecedent negotiations': Goode, *Op. cit.*, Division IIB, para 5.106.

65　For the effect of misrepresentations at common law on contracts induced thereby, see para 26.12, *et seq.*; and for statutory intervention, see 17.10.

66　For the liability of the dealer in respect of such misrepresentations, see para 16.18.

67　As to the forms of financing, see paras 2.21–4.

with the customer (16.06). In their *Tenth Report* (on Innocent Misrepresentation), the Law Reform Committee thought that this was unjust, and recommended that the dealer should be deemed to be the agent of the financier for such purposes.[68] This proposal was adopted by the HPA 1965 (s 16); but its formulation was thought defective in that it concentrated on direct financing. Hence, this deemed agency provision was extended by the CCA to ensure coverage of both direct and loan financing. Moreover, whilst s 16 was restricted to 'representations with respect to the goods', the comparable s 56 of the CCA was not so restricted (see para 16.10). In a consumer supply, an express agency may be unfair.[69]

**[16.10] Statutory agency.** Having carefully defined 'antecedent negotiations' (see para 16.08), the CCA provides that (s 56(2)):

> 'Negotiations with the debtor in a case falling within subsection (1)(b) or (c) shall be deemed to be conducted by the negotiator in the capacity of agent of the creditor as well as in his actual capacity.'

Two points must be borne in mind in relation to this compulsory[70] deemed agency.

*First*, s 56(2) does not apply to **all** those 'antecedent negotiations' within s 56(1) which lead to any two- or three-party transaction involving a regulated agreement: s 56(2) probably does not touch consumer hirings;[71] nor does it extend to vendor credit; nor does it apply in favour of persons other that the debtor.[72] What s 56(2) clearly does cover is direct and loan-financed consumer credit transactions, where the dealer/negotiator and financier/creditor are engaged in a joint operation in financing the supply of goods or services on credit to the consumer:[73] direct financing is within s 56(1)(b) and loan financing within s 56(1)(c) (see para 16.08).

*Second*, provided only the negotiations are made, in the words of s 56(1), 'in relation' to the above transactions (presumably including any trade-in), the words 'in the capacity of' would seem to import a deemed authority whether or not the common law would regard the dealer as acting within the scope of his actual or apparent authority (see para 16.06). The result has been said to be that 'provided the debtor to whom the representations are made acts in good faith, he can treat the negotiator's representations as those of the creditor himself, however fanciful and extravagant they may be and whether or not they are of a kind which a person in the position of the negotiator would ordinarily be authorised to make by a person in the position of the creditor'.[74] It would seem that this will be so even where the agent making the representation does so overseas.[75] Indeed, the generosity with which the courts have interpreted this statutory deemed agency is exemplified in *Forthright Finance Ltd v Ingate*.[76]

---

68   (1962) Cmnd. 1782, paras 19–20.
69   [2005] *UTCCR Bulletin J/S, Forthright Finance*, citing reg 7 (see para 11.13).
70   By s 173(1): see further, para 18.11.
71   Because they remain outside s 56(1)(b) and (c): see para 16.10.
72   *Lombard North Central PLC v Gate* [1998] CLY 2491, Cty Ct (guarantor).
73   Within s 187: as to which, see para 5.33. Is the wording of s 56(1)(b) wide enough to produce the same result even where the consumer chooses and introduces the financier into the transaction?
74   Goode, *Consumer Credit Law & Practice*, para 32.12.
75   *Jarrett v Barclays Bank plc* [1999] QB 1, CA (timeshare).
76   [1997] 4 All ER 99, CA.

The consumer was the conditional buyer of an Austin Metro under an agreement made with F Ltd. Before she had completed the payments due under that agreement, the consumer decided to change the car for a Fiat Panda owned by a dealer. The dealer ascertained that the settlement figure[77] on the Metro was £1,992 and offered her £2,000 for it. That leaving virtually no surplus, the consumer put down a £1,000 deposit and entered a directly financed transaction, under which she agreed to buy the Panda under a regulated conditional sale from C Ltd. The dealer became insolvent without having paid the settlement figure to F Ltd; and F Ltd sued the consumer to recover that sum. The consumer brought in C Ltd as third party, arguing that anything said by the dealer was, under s 56, said as agent for C Ltd.

The Court of Appeal unanimously held as follows: the negotiations conducted by the dealer over the Metro and the Fiat were part of a single package within s 56(1)(b), relating to the regulated supply of the Fiat;[78] s 56(4) made it clear that a wide construction should be given to the words 'negotiations . . . in relation to' in s 56(1)(b);[79] so that under s 56(2) C Ltd was liable to discharge the dealer's debt in relation to the settlement figure. As to the effect of this deemed agency, see para 16.10A.

[16.10A] **The effect of the statutory agency**. Where there is such a statutory deemed agency (see para 16.10), it has a number of effects.

*First*, the effect of s 56(2) is that **both** the financier/creditor and the dealer/negotiator will be liable to the consumer/debtor for those acts or omissions of the dealer/negotiator as 'relate' to, and are made in the course of, 'antecedent negotiations'. Thus, the dealer/negotiator will remain liable at common law to the consumer/debtor in tort or under any collateral contract (see para 16.18); whilst by s 56(2) the dealer/negotiator is also deemed to be acting in these respects as agent of the financier/creditor, so that the latter takes on the—normally additional[80]—liability.[81] Such liability may 'relate' to the consumer credit agreement, as where the consumer/debtor is enabled by s 56(2) to invoke against the financier/creditor the remedies for misrepresentation (see para 26.12). Or that liability may be independent of the consumer credit agreement, as in the torts of negligence, negligent misstatement or deceit (see Chap 17).

*Second*, there is the question whether the financier/creditor may be fixed with s 56(2) liability where, after the dealer has completed the negotiations with the consumer, the creditor declines to accept the proposal: s 56(1) speaks of actual and

---

77   The 'settlement figure' is the amount needed to complete the payments due under the regulated conditional sale with F Ltd, less any statutory rebate: see para 26.19A.

78   *Per* Staughton LJ at 102. This is despite the fact that the part-exchange was only worth a net £8 (£2,000 – £1,992) and seems to have been ignored by the parties and the court. As to part-exchanges, see para 2.09.

79   Because s 56(4) was wide enough to comprehend the customer's discussions with the dealer, which the subsection described as 'other dealings': *per* Henry LJ at 106.

80   Additional, because at common law the dealer would not normally be the agent of the financier. It will thus be prudent for the financier to create full dealer recourse in respect of this liability (see para 16.21).

81   Does the imputed knowledge extend beyond this to the dealer's knowledge, e.g. that the transaction is a disguised bill of sale, that the dealer's title to the goods is defective, or that an agreement signed in blank has been wrongly completed by the dealer, or that the agreement is to be conditional on settlement of a trade-in? See Guest and Lloyd, *Encyclopedia of Consumer Credit*, para 2-057.

proposed transactions;[82] but it may be that 'proposed' refers here only to those cases where a consumer credit agreement is subsequently made.[83]

*Third*, the wide definition of 'representations' (see para 16.08) extends their scope far beyond the goods or credit supplied.[84] Building on this, the financier's s 56(2) liability comprehends not just the dealer's mere representations, but also those misrepresentations of the dealer which become express[85] contractual promises:[86] the latter may amount to, or be part of, a contract between the dealer and consumer at common law;[87] and by virtue of s 56(2) they may also become a term of an agreement between the financier and consumer.[88] This leads as regards loan financing to a very substantial overlap between s 56(2) and s 75 (see para 16.14).

*Fourth*, the creditor has no special right of indemnity in respect of the liability over against the dealer (cf. s 75(2): see para 16.17), but is left to his ordinary remedies.[89]

## Connected lender liability

**[16.11] Introduction**. The purpose of this section is to consider the liability of the financier for the financed supply of defective goods or services, or related misrepresentations.

1. *Direct financing.*[90] Where there is a directly financed transaction, the financier will, on the basis of principles already discussed, be liable to the consumer for misrepresentations and breaches of contract: as there is an instalment credit contract between them, the financier will as supplier be liable for breaches of express or implied terms of the supply contract or misrepresentations made by him.[91] Further, by reason of s 56(2) the financier has a deemed agency liability for any misrepresentation or express promise which the negotiator (dealer) might make during the antecedent negotiations (see para 16.10).

2. *Loan financing.*[90] As there is no initial supply contract between the financier and consumer, the financier will not on ordinary principles be liable for misrepresentations and breaches of the supply contract by the dealer, though there may be some liability under s 56(2) (see para 16.10). Accordingly, the Crowther

---

82 See Bennion, *Consumer Credit Manual*, 3rd edn, 25–7, 48–9, suggesting that this is only possible where the dealer is a connected-lender. *Sed quaere* in respect of his category (1)? This view could be significant also in relation to deposits.

83 Guest and Lloyd, *Op. cit.*, para 2-057.

84 Jones, *Credit Cards*, 198. *Contra*, s 75: see para 16.14.

85 But not the statutorily implied terms: see Chaps 12–15. *Contra* s 75 liability: see para 16.14.

86 A misrepresentation becomes a contractual promise when the parties so intend: see para 11.02. But how can the parties to a deemed agency have any intention? See Goode, *Consumer Credit Law & Practice*, para 32.12.

87 Where there is a contract between them for the supply of goods (i.e. loan financing), it may become a term of that contract; and in the case of both loan and direct financing, it may become part of a collateral contract between them.

88 It may become a term of the regulated agreement, or of a collateral contract between them. In the former case, does it make the contract improperly executed (see para 9.12)?

89 See the Civil Liability (Contribution) Act 1978.

90 For direct and loan financing, see paras 2.20–22.

91 *Renton v Hendersons Garage* [1994] CCLR 29 (S).

Report (see para 5.03) recommended that, where the financier was 'connected with' the dealer, the financier should be made so liable (para 6.6.28). This recommendation was adopted by s 75 of the CCA (see para 16.12). A threatened s 75 claim against the creditor may give the consumer/debtor a potent lever against a solvent supplier.

Section 75 does not create any new cause of action. Rather, it establishes a new defendant (the financier) for an existing cause of action against the dealer by introducing a new limited exception to the privity rule (see para 10.01). When first introduced, s 75 was primarily used with personal loans (usually fixed-sum) taken out to finance the purchase of a motor vehicle from a connected dealer.[92] However, more recently, its principal application has been in connection with credit cards (running-accounts) used to obtain goods or services within the United Kingdom, e.g. Master and Visa cards (see generally, para 2.28). The OFT have argued that the effect of s 75 is to spread the risk[93] and so act as a sort of insurance for card-users.[94] However, card issuers in particular have been so apprehensive as to their potential s 75 liability, e.g. for failure of a cash-back insurer (see para 8.13A), or inability to obtain s 75(2) recourse against an overseas supplier (whether or not by internet (see para 8.17A)); and they have therefore taken every opportunity to deny or restrict that liability whilst also charging a loading for it. The matter was tested in *OFT v Lloyds TSB Bank plc*,[95] where, in a claim for a declaration (see para 29.01) and on appeal from Gloster J,[96] the Court of Appeal unanimously decided that, as a matter of interpretation (see para 1.04), s 75 attaches to all regulated DCS consumer credit transactions within s 12(b), regardless of whether they:

(1) take place within a three- or four-party structure (see para 2.28). For the purposes of s 75, s 187 requires a business connection between the creditor and supplier (or their agents): whilst an arrangement made *directly* between them in a three-party structure satisfies s 187, the Court of Appeal agreed with Gloster J that it also applies *indirectly* to a four-party structure (at para 66: see para 5.33).

(2) are entered into within the UK or elsewhere. Contrary to Gloster J (see the CA at paras 68–70), the Court of Appeal dismissed all the following arguments: (a) because overseas card transactions were unusual in the 1970s, the Crowther Report (see para 5.03) did not intend what became s 75 to apply to them (at para 72); and (b) under the territoriality rule of construction (see paras 73–5)

---

92 OFT, *Second Report on Connected Lender Liability*, 1995, para 6. It also applies to trading checks (see para 15.17) and store cards (see para 2.24).

93 Because s 75 liability is passed back up the payment chain towards the original supplier (see para 16.17) and forms an element in the annual fee (see para 7.11): OFT, *Connected Lender Liability*, 1994, paras 3.18 and 4.4(8).

94 OFT, *Second Report on Connected Lender Liability*, 1995 recommends the following limitations to the s 75 liability of creditors: (a) second-in-line (see below); (b) limited to amount of credit (see para 16.15); (c) subrogation (see para 16.17). For criticism by LACORS (see para 28.03), see (1995) 16 CCA News 4/8.

95 [2006] 2 All ER 821; [2006] EWCA Civ 268; (2006) 156 NLJ 553, CA. The creditors were refused leave to appeal, but may petition the HL because they claim this decision effectively makes them insurers of some 29M foreign suppliers, whether terrestrial or internet-based.

96 [2005] 1 All ER 843; [2005] 1 All ER (Comm) 354. Speaking before the CA decision, the Government said that it will consider whether any alteration of the law is required when the litigation is completed (Minister (2005–6) HL GC, col. 318.

as applied to the wording of s 75,[97] the CCA more widely[98] and EU law,[99] the section was intended to be confined to domestic transactions (paras 81–2 and 102). If this is correct, it seems to follow that UK consumers will generally have the benefit of s 75 if they buy with their credit card whilst abroad, or even over the internet whilst sitting at home.

Nor was any change to a financier's s 75 liability made by the 1987 EC Consumer Credit Directive: that Directive only makes the financier second-in-line liable after the consumer has first pursued the supplier,[100] as would the Draft Directive (Art 19), though the latter would exclude credit card issuers from such liability altogether.[101] The 1987 Directive, but not the Draft Directive (see para 5.12), allows the UK to retain the greater first-in-line liability of the financier under s 75 (see para 16.17), a provision which could be enforced on behalf of consumers generally by Enforcement Orders (see para 6.08).

**[16.12] Ambit of s 75.** Section 75(1) of the CCA extended the liability of financiers for the acts of dealers with whom they were 'connected' in the following compulsory[102] guarantee:

> 'If the debtor under a debtor-creditor-supplier agreement falling within section 12(b) or (c) has, in relation to a transaction financed by the agreement, any claim against the supplier in respect of a misrepresentation or breach of contract, he shall have a like claim against the creditor, who, with the supplier, shall accordingly be jointly and severally liable to the debtor.'

Section 75(1) can come into operation **only** where **all** the following requirements are satisfied in relation to a supply of goods:[103]

(1) *There must be a regulated agreement* (see para 5.13). This requirement will exclude the following:[104]

   (a) All payment cards where there is no credit, which will exclude most cash cards, cheque guarantee cards and debit cards (see para 5.33).

   (b) All unregulated credit cards, as where the debtor is a limited company (see paras 5.23 and 5.24).

   (c) All exempt credit cards, e.g. charge cards (see para 5.13).

(2) *The claim must be by a debtor under that regulated agreement.* It seems that this

---

97 Paras 77–91. See s 75(2) and (5) (see para 16.17); and s 75(3)(b) (see para 16.13).

98 Paras 92–102. See s 9(2) (see para 5.23); s 16(5)(c) (see para 5.15); s 69 (see para 10.32).

99 Paras 110–19. See the Treaty of Rome, Arts 28–9 (see para 8.06); the Consumer Credit Directive (see below).

100 1987/102/EEC, as amended, Art 11: set out in Goode, *Consumer Credit Law & Practice*, Pt X, para 2312. As to the effect of this on EU supplies; see Gidney (1996) 146 NLJ 762.

101 This could be implemented (so as to avoid a Parliamentary vote on s 75) by way of delegated legislation under s 2(2) of the ECA (see para 1.03A) and repeal of the present s 75 under the Deregulation Acts (see para 5.10).

102 By s 173(1): see further, para 18.11.

103 Our concern is primarily with financing the supply of goods. However, it should be noticed that s 75 is also apt to cover the financing of supplies of services, e.g. holidays, or mixed goods and services, e.g. installation of double-glazing.

104 Insofar as payment cards fall outside s 75, there is no obligation under the Banking Code of Practice (see para 3.13) for card issuers voluntarily to apply similar rules.

extends the ambit of s 75 to joint debtors, but not to authorised users, because s 75(1) says 'if the debtor . . . has [a] claim'.

(3) *The transaction must fall outside the special exemptions* contained in s 75(3) (see para 16.13).

(4) *There must be a DCS agreement falling within s 12(b) or (c):*

  (a) As s 12 only refers to consumer credit agreements (see para 5.34), this must exclude from s 75 all consumer hirings.

  (b) As s 12 requires a s 187 connection between creditor and supplier, this will exclude from s 75 all DC loans, including credit card 'cheques'.[105]

  (c) As s 75 deliberately excludes DCS agreements falling within s 12(a), this seems to shut out any form of vendor credit.[106] Furthermore, s 75(1) seems to envisage that the creditor and supplier must be different persons, as does the definition of 'supplier' in s 189(1) (see below).

(5) *The particular types of claim* which the debtor may have against the supplier falls within the section (see para 16.14).

Loan financing (see para 2.23) will be the normal case where s 75 is invoked and it soon came to be of greatest importance in relation to credit cards (see para 2.28): where there were three parties, because the card-issuer was the merchant-acquirer, this requirement is clearly satisfied; and, where those two were separate parties (the so-called 'four-party transactions'), it was decided in *OFT v Lloyds TSB Bank PLC* (see para 16.11) that these requirements were also satisfied (see paras 5.29 and 5.33). However, difficulty has arisen with directly financed transactions (see para 2.21): whilst the goods originate so far as the three parties are concerned with the dealer and are physically supplied by him to the consumer, it has been pointed out that in law the goods are supplied to the consumer by the financier; and, on the assumption that 'supplier' in s 75 means supplier in the eyes of the law to the consumer,[107] it has therefore been concluded that s 75 has no application to direct financing.[108]

**[16.13] Special exemptions**. Section 75(3) contains a special regime of exemptions, laying down that s 75(1) (as to which, see para 16.12) does not apply to a claim:

  '(a) under a non-commercial agreement, or

  (b) so far as the claim relates to any single item to which the supplier has attached a cash price not exceeding [£x] or more than [£y].'

*Paragraph (a)* will save from s 75 liability a creditor in respect of an agreement

---

105 See para 7.28. Can they really be cheques within the Bills of Exchange Act 1882, when there are conditions attached to their usage (see para 7.24)? Are these 'cheques' credit tokens within s 14 of the CCA (see para 5.30)?

106 As to vendor credit, see para 2.19. For discussion of s 12(b), see para 5.34; and as to pleading such claims as against the dealer, see para 16.18.

107 See para 5.34. *Sed quaere*? Alternatively, it could mean (i) supplier in fact to the consumer, or (ii) supplier into the transaction, i.e. seller to the financier = dealer.

108 *Renton v Hendersons Garage* [1994] CCLR 29 (S). Goode, *Consumer Credit Law & Practice*, para 33.147. But see *Porter v General Guarantee Corpn Ltd* [1982] RTR 384, criticised by MacQueen 1984 SLT 65. See also Guest and Lloyd, *Encyclopedia of Consumer Credit*, para 2-076; and paras 16.17 and 16.21.

entered into by him which is not made by him 'in the course of a business carried on by him'.[109]

*Paragraph (b)* exempts from the attentions of s 75 those regulated consumer credit agreements where the sterling[110] **cash price**[111] of 'any single item' (see below) is either:

(1) *very small*, which is now defined as 'not exceeding **£100**', which will save from s 75(1) many credit card and check trading transactions; or

(2) *very large*, which is now defined as 'more that **£30,000**', e.g. the purchase of an expensive new car with a credit card.

It is anticipated that the phrase 'any single item' may cause difficulty.[112] Even supposing it means any single item due under a single contract, e.g. a set of golf clubs, can the effect of s 75 be avoided by assigning separate prices of less than £100 to various parts of the goods?[113] Or what if some parts are priced less than £100, some more than £100, the loss being caused by defects in some of each class?[114] In respect of misrepresentations, it may be that these limitations can be avoided by suing under s 56 (see para 16.10).

As the effect of s 75 is to make the creditor liable co-extensively with the supplier (see para 16.15), however great the claim asserted (including consequential loss), there may be advantages to the debtor in taking out a minimum regulated DCS loan regardless of his financial needs, e.g. to pay a deposit by credit card (see para 7.12): presently, this may fall within s 75 however small the amount of credit, provided the cash price is within s 75(3)(b);[115] but the OFT have recommended that the liability of a card-issuer be limited to the amount of the credit (see para 16.11).

**[16.14] The debtor's claim against the supplier.** Section 75(1) (see para 16.12) is applicable only where the debtor has a particular sort of claim.

(1) The section only applies where the debtor has 'any claim against the supplier'. Opposed by the OFT, card-issuers sometimes argued that this category does not extend to overseas suppliers where the card is used abroad. In *OFT v Lloyds TSB*

---

109 See s 189(1): see para 5.16.

110 Where goods are purchased abroad using a UK credit card, the system of law governing the supply contract is determined by the conflict of laws (see para 10.01); but the credit contract is governed by the CCA, for the purposes of which the foreign currency price is translated into sterling by s 9(2) (see para 5.23): see *OFT v Lloyds TSB Bank plc* (see para 16.11), *obiter* at para 90.

111 For a general discussion of 'price', see para 2.07. The power to increase these limits was included in s 181; and the level as stated in the text was introduced by the Consumer Credit (Increase in Monetary Limits) Order, 1983 SI 1878. For a recommendation that the limit should be expressed in terms of the amount of credit, see OFT, *Second Report on Connected Lender Liability*, 1995, paras 19–21.

112 See generally Goode, *Consumer Credit Law & Practice*, para 33.183; Campbell (1994) 13 Tr L 18 at 20–21. Cf. the concept of a 'commercial unit' in the SGA, new s 35(7): see para 29.08.

113 As to the ordinary test of when there are either (a) separate contracts or (b) a single severable contract, see para 23.23. Are those tests apposite here, when s 75(3) talks of the supplier having 'attached a cash price'?

114 The exception is only 'so far as' the claim relates to items below £100. How is the loss to be apportioned?

115 The s 75 protection continues even after the credit has been paid off: Campbell, *op. cit.*, 24.

*Bank PLC*[116] the fifth declaration made by Glosters J was that, as a matter of interpretation, this phrase does not extend to foreign contracts for the following reasons:[117] besides general principles of statutory interpretation (paras 47–8: see para 1.04), especially in relation to extra-territoriality (para 45), there is no reference in the Crowther Report to extra-territoriality (paras 44 and 49: see para 5.03); the contrary implication seems to arise from the real difficulties that would otherwise arise both from operating the statutory recourse in s 75(2) and (5) (paras 50–1: see para 16.17) and from proceeding in the English courts with a 'like claim' governed by foreign law (para 52: see para 16.16); the absence from s 75(3)(b) of any provision for the cash price to be denominated in a foreign currency (paras 53–4: see para 16.13). A unanimous court of appeal disagreed (at para 80). Again, it is sometimes argued that, in relation to the travel trade, card-issuers will be under no s 75 liability where the travel agent is the agent of the consumer/card-holder.[118]

(2) 'In respect of a misrepresentation or breach of contract'.[119] In a loan-financed transaction (see paras 2.23–6), it is clear that this expression comprehends breaches by the dealer/supplier of express or implied terms of his supply contract with the consumer: this will include express guarantees by the supplier, e.g. a 10-year guarantee on double glazing; and the statutory implied terms (see Chaps 12–15). Further, a s 75 claim would also lie on the grounds that the consumer was induced to enter that sale contract by the misrepresentation of the dealer/supplier[119]—which will include actions for deceit or negligent misstatement (see generally, paras 17.18–20); and in this context there is a substantial overlap as regards loan financing with s 56(2) (see para 16.10). However, it would seem that s 75 does **not** comprehend other torts committed by the dealer/supplier in the course of negotiating the transaction, e.g. negligent acts,[120] or statutory product liability.[121] On the other hand, it would appear to extend to a quasi-contractual claim by a buyer who has rightly rescinded the sale contract to recover his price on grounds of total failure of consideration.[122]

(3) The claim referred to above must be made 'in relation to a transaction financed by the [regulated] agreement'. Accordingly, s 75 does not extend to claims made in relation to ancillary contracts, e.g. maintenance, extended warranties, unless that ancillary contract is also financed by the creditor, e.g. free gifts.[123]

---

116 See para 16.11, where Gloster J sought (at para 55) to distinguish the CA decision in *Jarrett v Barclays Bank plc* on the basis that the s 75 point was not there argued (see para 16.16).

117 At para 59. Her Ladyship noted that academic writers were divided over the issue (at para 56) and also dismissed any possible EU impediment to her decision (at para 57).

118 If the misrepresentation was made by a professional agent, there may be difficulty in showing that he was the supplier in law: see Samuels (1993) 10 Tr L at 92; OFT, *Op. cit.*, paras 5.11 and 5.14; Rutherford (1994) 144 NLJ 668.

119 What if the debtor is making a contract on behalf of a club?

120 Goode, *Consumer Credit Law & Practice*, para 33.161. What of torts committed in performing the contracts, e.g. wrongful refusal to deliver the goods, or wrongful recaption?

121 Under Pt I of the CPA (see para 17.24): Guest and Lloyd, *Encyclopedia of Consumer Credit*, para 2-076.

122 For this claim, see para 16.16. For quasi-contractual remedies generally, see para 29.12, *et seq.*

123 Goode, *Op. cit.*, para 33.161. Is his test whether the transaction is a linked one (see para 5.31)?

It is not clear what is the position in relation to cashbacks (see para 8.13A) or replacements (see para 16.15).

For the effect of s 75, see para 16.15.

**[16.15]  The effect of s 75**. Where the conditions for the application of s 75 are all satisfied (as set out above), s 75(1) provides that the debtor:

'shall have a like claim against the creditor, who, with the supplier, shall accordingly be jointly and severally liable to the debtor'.

Leaving aside what amounts to 'a like claim' (see para 16.16),[124] this liability in the creditor towards the debtor is co-terminous with the liability of the supplier to the debtor,[125] and may far exceed the amount of the credit (see para 16.13), or perhaps its duration.[126] Most such claims are made against credit card issuers when the supplier is insolvent; and card-issuers have argued that the extent of the liability is unreasonable particularly when consequential loss is taken into account, e.g. air travel, where claims arise from death or injury in a major crash. The OFT have recommended that the liability of the card issuer should be limited to the amount charged to the card account (see para 16.11).

To the extent only that the supplier effectively excludes or restricts his liability towards the debtor (see Chap 18), that exclusion or restriction enures for the protection of the creditor facing a s 75 claim; but the creditor cannot rely as against a s 75 claim[127] on any term in the consumer credit agreement excluding or restricting his liability.[128] Moreover, the debtor may pursue his s 75 claim against either or both the supplier and creditor;[129] an unsatisfied judgment against one does not bar proceedings against the other;[130] nor does the CCA require the debtor to pursue first his remedies against the supplier (see para 16.11). Further, s 75(4) would appear to be intended to extend the scope of the creditor's s 75(1) liability, for it provides that:

'This section applies notwithstanding that the debtor, in entering into the transaction, exceeded the credit limit or otherwise contravened any term of the agreement.'

This is probably aimed at revolving credit agreements, e.g. credit cards, and refers to the 'credit-limit' fixed by such agreements.[131] If so, then the draftsman would

---

124 For the effect of limitation periods, see Guest and Lloyd, *Encyclopedia of Consumer Credit*, para 2-076.

125 It would seem to follow that the creditor can be under no s 75 liability in respect of items for which the supplier incurs no liability, e.g. where the supplier 'sells' a maintenance contract or 'extended warranty' by a third party who subsequently becomes insolvent (see generally, para 17.09).

126 What if a supplier's express guarantee is only repudiated by him after the term of the credit has expired? See Guest and Lloyd, *Op. cit.*, para 2-076.

127 *Aliter*, where the creditor is being sued for breach of a term of the credit agreement which the CCA does not make compulsory.

128 UCTA, s 10 (see para 18.16); CCA, s 173(1) (see para 18.11); UTCC Regulations, reg 8 (see para 11.15A). What is the effect of the differing scope of these sections?

129 Suppose the creditor factors the debt (see para 7.28). It has been argued that, notwithstanding s 189(1), 'creditor' does not here include his assignee: Goode, *Consumer Credit Law & Practice*, para 33.181. *Sed quaere*?

130 Civil Liability (Contribution) Act 1978, s 3; Guest and Lloyd, *Ibid*, para 2 076. As to this Act see generally, para 12.10.

131 See the definition of 'credit limit' in ss 189(1) and 10(2): for an explanation of such credit limits and of revolving credit generally, see para 5.28.

seem to have intended that a debtor should be able to take advantage of s 75 even in respect of a transaction which took his debit balance above his agreed credit limit,[132] and hence amounted to a breach of the revolving credit agreement.[133]

Finally, if the creditor is liable under s 75(1), he is given a subsidiary claim against the supplier (see para 16.17).

[16.16] 'A like claim'. Section 75 of the CCA does not create any additional ground of complaint: it simply adds a third party[134] against whom an existing complaint can be made. Where a transaction falls within the ambit of the section and the debtor has on ordinary principles a claim against his supplier (see paras 16.13–14), s 75 grants the debtor 'a like claim' against the creditor.[135] The obvious example is where the debtor has a claim for damages against the supplier on grounds of misrepresentation or breach of contract: s 75(1) will there enable the debtor to claim that sum from the creditor, e.g. a 10-year warranty on a double-glazing installation; and this may even extends to where the UK 'like claim' is as regards a complaint in respect of a foreign supply governed by foreign law.[136]

However, suppose the debtor's claim against the supplier is for rescission *ab initio* or *de futuro* of the supply contract (see para 26.11). If the debtor in a loan-financed transaction rescinds the linked **sale** agreement with the supplier,[137] then the creditor is jointly and severally liable in respect of any restitutionary claim which the debtor may have against the supplier for any sums paid by the debtor to the supplier under the rescinded **sale** agreement, e.g. for the return of part of the price. On the other hand, the fact that the debtor in a loan-financed transaction is entitled to rescind the **sale** agreement would not by a combination of s 75 and ordinary principles give the debtor a right to rescind the **credit** agreement,[138] because the words 'a like claim' refer back to the transaction financed by the agreement (the **sale**).[139] However, such a result may be achievable by paying in aid s 56(2) (see para 16.10) as well:[140] by s 56(2) the supplier is deemed to make any representation as agent of the creditor, so enabling the debtor to rescind the regulated **credit** agreement on grounds, e.g. of a misrepresentation inducing entry

---

132  Goode, *Op. cit.*, para 33.167.

133  Does s 75(4) prevent the creditor suing the debtor for this breach? And if not, do the creditor's damages for breach of the revolving credit agreement include the sums he has to pay the debtor by reason of s 75(4)—thus nullifying the effect of s 75(4)? See Goode, *Op. cit.*, Division IIB, annotation to s 75(4).

134  What if a debtor uses two different cards to effect payment under a single transaction?

135  As to the position where the creditor has assigned his rights under the credit agreement, e.g. *Re Charge Card Services Ltd* (set out at para 2.27), see Guest and Lloyd, *Encyclopedia of Consumer Credit*, para 2-076.

136  *OFT v Lloyds TSB Bank PLC* (see para 16.11), CA, at paras 80-1, 121.

137  The sale agreement will be a linked transaction within s 19(1)(b): see para 5.31. As to who is entitled to the goods (supplier or creditor?), see Jones, *Credit Cards*, 208.

138  Davidson (1980) 96 LQR 343, criticising *UDT v Taylor* 1980 SLT 28 (Sh. Ct). Of course, the debtor could recover his price from the supplier, and then exercise his statutory right to make early payment of sums due under the credit agreement: as to early payment, see para 26.19A. See also Guest and Lloyd, *Ibid*.

139  Goode, *Consumer Credit Law & Practice*, para 33.165.

140  For an alternative argument via a claim for damages see Lowe (1981) 97 LQR 532, Dobson [1981] JBL 179.

into the linked sale.[141] Where there is a consumer supply of goods within Pt 5A of the SGA (see para 29.09A), the position in respect of the additional consumer remedies would appear to be this: there would seem no difficulty in granting the consumer a full or partial refund under the principles discussed above; but perhaps the courts will exercise their discretion not to grant him repair or replacement as against the card-issuer on the grounds that it would be a disproportionate remedy.

It seems likely that s 75 does not interfere with the ordinary common law right of set-off (see generally, para 23.14). Thus, a creditor sued under s 75 can reduce his liability by exercising any right of set-off vested in the supplier.[142] Likewise, a debtor sued under the consumer credit agreement may set off by way of s 75 any sum owed to him by the supplier which he could have set off against a claim by the supplier. So, reliance on s 75 by a debtor may be either offensive or defensive: he may sue on the section to recover a sum of money from the creditor; or he may wait until sued by the creditor and then plead a s 75 set-off by way of a defence.[143]

**[16.17] Statutory recourse**. Because it is recognised that the real fault in cases falling within s 75(1) lies in the supplier, s 75(2) allows the financier/creditor full statutory recourse[144] to the supplier in the following terms:

> 'Subject to any agreement between them, the creditor shall be entitled to be indemni-fied by the supplier for loss suffered by the creditor in satisfying his liability under subsection (1), including costs reasonably incurred by him in defending proceedings instituted by the debtor.'

And so that the creditor may obtain judgment against the supplier in the same proceedings, s 75(5) enables the creditor sued under s 75(1)[145] to make the supplier a party to those proceedings.[146] In practice, that liability may be enhanced by chargeback arrangements, particularly where the card-issuer and merchant acquirer are separate businesses.[147] There remains the following dangers: the sup-plier may be insolvent, or recourse liability excluded,[148] in which case the creditor is left to foot the bill,[149] even where the supplier is insured;[150] or the creditor may be unable to sue a foreign supplier.[151]

---

141  Goode, *Op. cit.*, para 33.165. *Contra* Guest and Lloyd, *Ibid*. Cf. the rule that withdrawal or can-cellation of the regulated agreement has the same effect on the linked transaction.

142  Goode, *Op. cit.*, para 33.163; Guest and Lloyd, *Ibid*.

143  Goode, *Op. cit.*, paras 33.169–70; Lowe (1981) 97 LQR 533. This would indirectly produce the same result as *UDT v Taylor* (above).

144  For recourse agreements, see para 16.21.

145  *Quaere* whether s 75(2) is applicable where the liability of the financier/creditor is otherwise than under s 75(1): see 16.21.

146  E.g. *Porter v General Guarantee Corpn Ltd* [1982] RTR 384 (a directly financed transaction: see fn 145, above; and para 16.12). For third-party proceedings, see Guest and Lloyd, *Encyclopedia of Consumer Credit*, para 2-076.

147  OFT, *Connected Lender Liability* (1994), para 4.4(d). See generally, para 2.28.

148  Such exclusion is not prohibited by CCA, s 173 (see para 18.11); nor will it fall within the ambit of the UTCC Regulations because both parties are in business (see para 11.12). But it might be subject to UCTA, s 3 (see para 18.20).

149  Unless he has a right of contribution against another party; e.g. manufacturer, under the Civil Liability (Contribution) Act 1978.

150  The OFT has recommended that the creditor have a right of subrogation, so that he may claim under the insurance policy: *Second Report on Connected Lender Liability*, 1996, paras 22.

151  Dismissed by the CA in *OFT v Lloyds TSB Bank plc* (see para 16.11): see above, para 16.16.

The justification for imposing this risk on a creditor is that the creditor and supplier are engaged in a joint business enterprise within the meaning of s 187 (see para 5.33). However, it may be that the supplier has put the consumer's deposit in a trust account or insured it.[152] Will this allow a creditor to claim on that fund in the hands of a third party?[153]

## LIABILITY OF THE DEALER

### To the consumer

[16.18] Where there is a loan-financed transaction, the primary contract in respect of the goods is between the dealer and the consumer; and the fact that a finance company may be involved does not alter this. The position is very different in a directly financed transaction, where there is ordinarily no primary contractual relationship between the dealer and consumer.[154] Frequently, the consumer will allege that he was induced to enter into the directly financed transaction by some misrepresentation on the part of the dealer, e.g. deceit (see para 17.18). The question arises whether the consumer has any redress against the dealer. The leading case is *Andrews v Hopkinson*:[155]

> The dealer said to the consumer in respect of one of his vehicles: 'it is a good little bus; I would stake my life on it'. The following day, the consumer signed an hp proposal form in respect of the vehicle; and he subsequently took delivery of it. About a week later, the steering failed, and the consumer was involved in an accident. The consumer's action against the dealer succeeded before McNair J.

All the grounds of the consumer's claim were accepted by McNair J as follows:

(1) *Express warranty.* 'For breach of an express warranty that the car was in good condition . . . whereby he was induced to enter into a hire-purchase agreement in respect thereof'.[156] In practice, it is usually the signature of the consumer on the proposal form that is induced by the misrepresentation.[157] Furthermore, it has rightly been pointed out that the term 'warranty' is a misnomer in this context:[158] that the allegation must be of a collateral contract of warranty; and the representation made by the dealer is at most evidence of such a collateral contract.[159]

---

152  See para 23.22. Can the creditor get at trust funds?

153  See para 23.22. Can the creditor get at an insurance fund? See above, fn 150.

154  *Drury v Victor Buckland Ltd* [1941] 1 All ER 269, CA; *Alpha Chauffeurs Ltd v Citygate* (set out at para 14.26), at paras 30–3. But see *Polsky v S & A Services Ltd* [1951] 1 All ER 1062, CA. But for use of the Contracts Act 1999, see para 16.22.

155  [1957] 1 QB 229, [1956] 3 All ER 422. See also *MacKenzie Patten & Co v British Olivetti Ltd* (1984), reported in 48 MLR 344.

156  At 235. For the measure of damages, see *Yeoman Credit Ltd v Odgers* [1962] 1 All ER 789, CA; *Wells Merstham Ltd v Buckland Sand and Silica Co Ltd* [1965] 2 QB 170, and below, para 29.34.

157  E.g. *Astley Industrial Trust Ltd v Grimley* [1963] 2 All ER 33, CA: see Goode, *HP Law & Practice*, 2nd edn, 639, fn 3.

158  Goode, *HP Law & Practice*, 2nd edn, 640.

159  See *per* Pearson LJ *Astley Industrial Trust Ltd v Grimley* (above) at 45. Compare *Alpha Chauffeurs Ltd v Citygate* (above) at para 27.

(2) *Implied warranty.* 'For breach of an implied warranty that the car was reasonably fit for driving on the public highway'.[160] There appears to be few subsequent cases where this idea has been taken up (see para 15.26); and it has been doubted whether an intention to contract would be inferred where there was no express representation.[161]

(3) *Negligence.* 'For negligence in that the defendant knew or ought to have known that the car was dangerous'.[162]

**[16.19] CCA controls.** A credit-broker (see paras 5.38–41) is subject to a number of restrictions.

1. *Licensing.* A credit-broker needs a category C licence, together (if he so requires) with special permission to canvass.[163] He may also need to be licensed for some other ancillary credit services.[164]

2. *Seeking business.* It was seen in Chap 8 that the Act places a considerable number of restrictions on the creditor or owner with regard to his seeking business; and the Act also imposes these restrictions on credit-brokers,[165] including in relation to credit status enquiries.[166]

3. *Entry into agreements.* It was seen in Chaps 9 and 10 that there are considerable powers to make regulations controlling the entry into credit or hire agreements. Section 156 contains similar powers in relation to credit-brokerage.[167]

4. *Brokerage fees.* One of the complaints considered by the Crowther Report concerned brokers' fees (para 6.4.22) and this led to the following restrictions:

    (a) No fees can be charged by an unlicensed ancillary credit business (see para 6.27).

    (b) Section 155 provides that, where no credit or hire agreement results from the introduction by the licensed credit-broker, brokerage fees chargeable to the individual must in most cases be kept to a purely nominal amount,[168] whatever the costs incurred. Attempts to circumvent this rule, e.g. by mortgage brokers giving advice by premium-rate phone, are more likely to be dealt with under the CCA licensing provisions (see para 6.11, *et seq.*) than as an unfair term.[169] Further, the dealer will usually be the debtor's agent,

---

160 At 237. His Lordship distinguished earlier cases refusing an implied warranty on the grounds that the point was not argued in them.
161 Cf. Goode, *Op. cit.*, 1st edn, 198 and, 2nd edn, 640. But for analogous terms, see generally, para 15.26.
162 At 237. As failure to act, see para 17.14; and as to failure to warn, see para 18.29.
163 As to licences, see para 6.15; and as to canvassing indorsements, see para 6.14.
164 E.g. credit information services (see para 5.44).
165 See ss 151–2 (as amended by s 25 of the 2006 Act). Moreover, even though licensed to canvass credit or hire agreements (see above), s 154 forbids the credit-broker from canvassing his own services (see para 7.07).
166 S 157 actually casts the duty on 'the negotiator': see para 8.37.
167 The power also extends to debt-adjusting, debt-counselling (see para 5.43) and credit information services (by s 25 of the 2006 Act: see above). No regulations have yet been made.
168 There is power to increase the £1 of the original provision by statutory order (s 181); and this has been exercised to increase it to £5: Consumer Credit (Further Increase in Monetary Limits) Order, 1998 SI 997.
169 OFT, *Bulletin No. 6*, para 1.21; *AR–2000*, 109, e.g. (2001) *Fair Trading* 4. But see *UCT Bulletin No. 22*, case 31, relying on grey terms (b) and (f): see para 11.16.

so that any commission paid to the broker by the creditor may amount to a secret commission.[170]

(c) If any regulated agreement is validly cancelled by the debtor or hirer, the maximum fee is similarly limited (see para 10.33).

## To the financier

[16.20/1] The liability of the dealer to the company financing his retail trade may arise in two separate and distinct phases of that trade:

(1) *Stocking plans* when the dealer is acquiring his stock are beyond the scope of this work.[171]

(2) *Dealer recourse* when he is disposing of it by retail (see para 16.22).

[16.22] **Dealer recourse**. The techniques used to achieve dealer recourse in financed transaction (see para 16.20) are as follows:

(1) *Directly financed transactions*. The contract of sale from the dealer to the finance company will, of course, subject the dealer to all the implied undertakings discussed in Pt 4;[172] and, in addition, that contract may provide that the dealer warrants the truth of all the information contained in the proposal form,[173] or is liable for any misrepresentation it contains.[174] Apart from these types of liability, dealer recourse is usually achieved in one of three ways. *First*, the dealer may be required, as part of the consideration for the finance company agreeing to accept the transaction and purchase the goods, to promise that in the event of default by the consumer he will **repurchase** the goods at a price (see SGA, s 49: see paras 27.17–18) which covers the finance company's 'loss'.[175] In the event of repurchase, the finance company will usually have promised to assign all its rights against the consumer and the goods to the dealer,[176] so that the latter is left to enforce the supply agreement against the consumer.[177] This form of recourse provision suffers from the disadvantage that it cannot be enforced against the dealer unless all the conditions of the repurchase clause are satisfied to the letter[178] and the company is able to redeliver the goods to the

---

170 *Industries & General Mortgage Co Ltd v Lewis* [1949] 2 All ER 573 (see (2001) 61 *Quarterly Account* 11).

171 See Macleod, *Consumer Sales Law*, 1st edn, paras 16.20–1.

172 E.g. *Warman v Southern Counties Finance Corpn Ltd* (set out at para 12.07); the *Alpha Chauffeurs* case (set out at para 14.12).

173 E.g. *Liverpool and County Discount Ltd v AB Motors Ltd* [1963] 2 All ER 396, CA. Alternatively, an action may lie for deceit: *United Motor Finance Co v Addison & Co Ltd* [1937] 1 All ER 425, PC.

174 *Royscot Trust Ltd v Rogerson* (set out at para 27.28).

175 Is this such a case that it would be reasonable for the seller (finance company) to exclude the implied terms: see Sched 2 of UCTA (see para 18.26)? As the repurchase is for money or money's worth, there will be no question of the CCA treating it as a consumer credit agreement.

176 This assignment is unlikely to savour of maintenance: see para 7.26. If the finance company is in breach of the reassignment provision, the measure of damages is the value of the goods: *Bowmaker (Commercial) Ltd v Smith* [1965] 2 All ER 304, CA.

177 E.g. *Karsales (Harrow) Ltd v Wallis* (set out at para 15.23). It would seem that the dealer does not in those circumstances have to be a licensed debt-collector: see para 5.42.

178 See *United Dominions Trust (Commercial) Ltd v Eagle Aircraft Ltd* [1968] 1 All ER 104, CA; *GMAC Commercial Credit Development Ltd v Sandhu* [2001] 2 All ER (Comm) 782, CA.

dealer.[179] *Second*, as the primary vehicle for achieving recourse,[180] the dealer may simply agree to **indemnify** the finance company against all loss it may incur in the transaction,[181] in return for which the dealer has the option of calling for an assignment of the finance company's rights against the consumer and the goods.[176] Whilst such recourse provisions are usually expressed as indemnities, they have often been interpreted by the courts as being in reality contracts of guarantee, in which case the finance company can have no greater rights against the dealer than it has against the consumer and the dealer will be discharged if the company impairs the security (see para 25.06). Further, it may even be possible in these circumstances to invoke the statutory recourse provision to be found in s 75 of the CCA.[182] *Third*, the consumer may be encouraged to sue the dealer direct by introducing an aptly granted right in the contract under which the dealer supplies the goods to the financier: whereas at common law there would normally be no privity of supply contract between dealer and consumer (see para 16.18), that problem can be overcome by use of the Contracts Act 1999 (see para 17.08).

(2) *Loan-financed transactions.* Whilst there will be no question of any re-purchase clause because the financier is not the legal supplier of the goods, there may be an express recourse provision (**indemnity**) similar to that found in direct financing (above). Furthermore, where the loan is a regulated DCS agreement, then the financier may have the advantage of a statutory right of recourse where the financier (creditor) has been held liable to the consumer (debtor) under s 75 of the CCA (see para 16.17).

---

179 Because non-delivery will lead to a total failure of consideration: *Watling Trust Ltd v Briffault Range Co Ltd* [1938] 1 All ER 525, CA; and generally, para 29.13.

180 There may also be an auxiliary right of repurchase exercisable by the dealer (at his own expense) if and when the financier has achieved full recourse, but without any obligation on the financier of either delivery or implied terms.

181 E.g. *Southern Industrial Ltd v Brooke House Motors Ltd* (1968) 112 Sol Jo 798, CA (retailer and hirer conspired to enter false figures, the agreement being illegal).

182 *Porter v General Guarantee Corpn Ltd* [1982] RTR 384, criticised by MacQueen 1984 SLT 65. For consideration of the issue of whether s 75 is applicable to directly financed transactions, see para 16.12.

# CHAPTER 17

# PRODUCT LIABILITY[1]

## INTRODUCTION

**[17.01] The chain of distribution**. This chapter is concerned with the legal position of parties in the chain of distribution of goods in this country to their eventual consumption. The goods may be imported;[2] or they may commence their existence in this country by growth or by manufacture such as to create a new identity.[3] Further, in relation to the last category, already-created goods may lose their separate identity by alteration, accession or intermixture.[4] Take the typical case of manufactured consumer durables, such as a motor car: the person who in common parlance is described as the 'manufacturer' (Z)[5] will actually create some parts of the vehicle, e.g. the body shell; but he will buy some components, e.g. electrical, from a components manufacturer or grower (X) or component wholesaler/importer (Y); and Z will wholly or in part act as an assembler or canner of those products.[6] The assembled goods will then be supplied by Z to the retail seller (B),[7] either directly, e.g. own brand goods,[5] or by way of one or more wholesalers (A1, A2, A3).[8] The retail buyer (C)[9] may use or consume the goods himself, or he may donate (see para 2.08) them to a donee/consumer (D). If the goods prove defective, the donee (D) may have a right of action against B or C in the tort of negligence (see para 15.29), or perhaps in contract against B on the basis of agency or assignment (see para 17.12). This whole sequence of events may be rendered diagrammatically as follows:[10]

---

1 See generally Miller, *Product Liability Encyclopedia*; Waddams, *Product Liability*; Mildred, *Products Liability: Law and Insurance* (2000).
2 International trade is beyond the scope of this work: see para 1.01.
3 E.g. *Borden (UK) Ltd v Scottish Timber Products* (manufacture of chipboard: see para 25.32).
4 See generally Crossley Vaines, *Personal Property*, 5th edn, Chap 9.
5 It is Z's name and brand which will normally appear on assembled goods. In other cases, the retailer may be sufficiently strong commercially to insist that the goods are supplied for retail sale under the retailer's name and own or exclusive brand (= own brand goods).
6 In some cases, Z will seal the goods in such a manner that they are obviously intended to be unsealed only by their end-consumer. In other cases, trade usage may require inspection and adjustment by some intermediate trade party in the chain of distribution (A, B) or member of the public (C, D).
7 A 'retailer' is the common description of the person who is usually intended to be the last business purchaser for resale unused: his sale will therefore be the one that effectively bears VAT and any car tax (see para 2.06). Cf. *Chappell & Co Ltd v Nestle & Co Ltd* [1960] AC 87, HL.
8 The expression 'wholesaler' is usually reserved for those who make a business of purchasing goods for resale in their purchased form in bulk.
9 For legislative attempts to distinguish retail (C) from trade (Z, A, B) purchasers, see paras 18.18 and 21.56.
10 Each of the contracting parties may act in person, or *via* an agent who may be disclosed, e.g. trader's employee, or undisclosed, e.g. many retail purchases (see para 17.07).

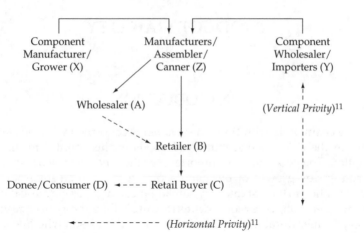

[17.02]  **Product liability**. The rationale of what the Americans term 'product liability' is to allocate within the chain of distribution (see para 17.01) any loss caused by using a defective product, presumably with the following inter-related objectives:[12]

(a)  To achieve the optimum balance between the interests of the person injured in recovering compensation and that of other uninjured consumers in minimising the price of the product.[13]

(b)  To encourage accident prevention by good design and quality control in production,[14] clear warning labels[15] and an effective recall system where dangers subsequently appear. If the defective goods are dangerous, failure to mount an effective recall[16] may amount to an offence under the GPS Regulations (see para 4.36A); and it may also give rise to civil liability, either strict (CPA, s 3: see para 17.28) or negligence (see para 17.13). The easiest way for a manufacturer to mount a recall is by instituting a registration system on retail supply, so

11  For the notions of 'horizontal' and 'vertical' privity, see para 17.08.

12  See generally Harris, *Compensation and Support for Illness and Injury*, 17–25; Winfield and Jolowicz, *Tort*, 16th edn, para 1.1-3; *The Royal Commission on Civil Liability and Compensation for Personal Injury* (1978, Cmnd. 7054), paras 1199–1204; Clark, *Product Liability*, 183; Mildred, *Product Liability: Law and Insurance*, Chap 7.

13  As to the risk-benefit analysis of tort, see Clark, *Op. cit.*, 30–4; Harvey, *Consumer Protection and Fair Trading*, 6th edn, 23–8; Mildred, *Product Liability*, 2000, para 7.146. As to welfare weighting, see OFT, *1999-AR*, 103.

14  What about goods which are inherently dangerous to the consumer or others, e.g. medicine, motor vehicles? Does it make any difference if the goods are regarded as of little social utility, e.g. alcoholic beverages, tobacco, cannabis? What if a manufacturer is warned that a criminal has poisoned his products? But see [1995] 2 *Which?* 14 (cars).

15  This is part of the general product safety requirement: see para 4.34. Warnings may not always be effective: see (1992) 142 NLJ 83. It has been argued that it is undesirable for warnings to be effective as a substitute for redesign, and that warnings should be reserved for those circumstances where it is not possible to eliminate risk: Clark, *Op. cit.*, 103.

16  Under a Code of Practice (see para 3.13), which will be monitored by the DTI: see DTI, *Consumer Product Recall: a Good Practice Guide* (1999); Mildred, *Op. cit.*, paras 7.81–4 and 419, *et seq*. For the 2000 vehicle recall figures, see [2001] 7 *Which?* 17. Cf. *Carroll v Fearon* (set out at para 17.16); the *Bacardi* case (see para 11.08).

enabling direct communication to consumers;[17] but, failing direct communication, reliance may have to be placed on public advertisement.[18]

(c) To minimise loss to the economy, whether in the form of junked defective products, personal or property loss to purchasers and users, or loss of productive labour occasioned by injury to the consumer or others.[19]

(d) To institute a morally and politically acceptable form of compensation for injury.

(e) To achieve all this in as cost-efficient a manner as possible,[20] both as regards the cost of the compensation system to the parties[21] and any effect which the consequently enhanced price of the product may have on its circulation,[22] perhaps through higher product liability insurance premiums.[23]

**[17.03] Criminal proceedings.** Some types of behaviour connected with the distribution of products and some defects in products are covered by statutes imposing strict criminal liability, usually for unsafe goods (see Chap 4), further enhanced by vicarious criminal liability (see para 28.09). Theoretically, a conviction under one of these statutes could be used to achieve civil compensation under the Powers of Criminal Courts Act 2000.[24] However, there would appear to have been a conscious decision to make this route difficult as follows: by statutory limitation;[24] by judicial caution in using even the power granted (see para 3.20); and by the reluctance of prosecuting authorities.[25] Nevertheless, such convictions may still be of interest to the injured user. From his personal viewpoint, not only is there the emotional element,[26] but the conviction is useful evidence in any subsequent civil litigation.[27] From the viewpoint of society, prosecution under central guidance is more likely to achieve uniform enforcement free from the vagaries of private litigation.[28]

---

17 Maintaining or accessing a list of retail purchasers may raise data protection issues (see para 3.27). As to tracing ownership of motor vehicles, see para 21.60.

18 Tracing consumers directly may be more effective than public advertising, but is subject to the DPA (see above).

19 See Abbott, *Safe Enough to Sell?* (1980, Design Council). For BSI standards, see para 3.08.

20 For group actions, see Mildred, *Op. cit.*, Chap 10; and see generally, para 3.18.

21 In some cases, product liability insurance will be taken out by some parties in the chain of distribution, e.g. *Zurich Insurance Co v FW Martin & Son* (1984) 134 NLJ 38. If the insured then becomes insolvent, his rights under the policy are 'transferred' to any claimant whose injury falls within the terms of that policy: Third Parties (Rights Against Insurers) Act 1930, s 1; *M/S Aswan Engineering Establishment Co v Iron Trader Mutual Insurance Co* [1987] 1 Lloyd's Rep 289. But this procedure cannot be used after the insured company is dissolved: see (1989) 139 NLJ 571.

22 Cf. the approach to contractual allocation of loss by Milner in (1979) 42 MLR 508. It has long been claimed that a no-fault liability system would be far more cost-effective than any tort-based system: Brahams (1988) 138 NLJ 678.

23 This is unlikely to be significant: Clark, *Op. cit.*, 74. *Sed quaere*? See generally Mildred, *Op. cit.*, Chap 5.

24 However, the 2000 Act provision is itself hedged around with restrictions (see para 3.20). Moreover, many of the statutes imposing criminal liability expressly deny any action for breach of statutory duty (see para 3.21): does that deny use of the 2000 Act?

25 There is a reluctance to prosecute simply to facilitate civil compensation for what is really product liability: see para 3.19.

26 Besides the element of retribution, he will be saved the emotional (and financial) cost of enforcement.

27 Under s 11 of the Civil Evidence Act 1968: see para 3.21.

28 For enforcement by the public authorities of the strict liability offences considered in Chap 4, see Chap 28.

However, in relation to safety, the (criminal) general safety requirement (see para 4.34) plus safety regulations[29] and (civil) strict product liability (see para 17.24) are seen as complementary: the former can be used as a preventative device, aimed at keeping very unsafe goods off the market;[29] whereas the latter provides compensation in respect of items which are not necessarily all that unsafe.[30]

**[17.04] Substantive civil law.** This chapter is chiefly concerned with the substantive rules of civil law applicable to product liability in the possibly lengthy chain of distribution (see paras 17.01–02) further extended by financing (see Chap 16), whilst leaving aside any complication arising from the presence of exclusion clauses or instructions for use (see Chap 18).

From the late sixteenth century, the common law began to make consideration the touchstone of an enforceable promise (*assumpsit*), with these results:

(a) The distinction between contract and tort developed on the basis of whether or not a cause of action was supported by consideration.[31]

(b) The doctrine of privity was treated as a logically inevitable outcome from the requirement of consideration in contract.[32]

(c) The development of strict liability in contracts for the supply of goods[33] versus *mens rea* liability in tort, the latter chiefly through the tort of negligence.[34]

All these developments may be seen in the English common law tests of product liability,[35] which in modern times have begun to blur once more the contract/tort dichotomy.[36] *First*, the courts have allowed an action from a single set of facts to succeed in both contract and tort.[37] *Second*, they have permitted an action in tort for failure to provide a benefit promised under a contract to which the plaintiff was not a party.[38] *Third*, there are the statutory contribution rules.[39] *Fourth*, to supplement the common law rules of privity,[40] there has been introduced a statutory

---

29  E.g. the statutory instrument requiring consumer durables to be fitted with electrical plugs by manufacturers. As to safety regulations, see generally, para 4.33.

30  See Wright, *Product Liability*, 90.

31  It would seem that NHS drugs are not supplied to the consumer under contract (see para 1.07), which enhances the importance of the non-contractual remedies.

32  It follows that warranties do not run with the goods: see para 2.13. For the effect of privity on exclusion clauses, see para 18.05.

33  See Chaps 12–14. *Quaere* contracts for the supply of services (see para 15.15)?

34  There may also be difficulty in determining whether liability is in contract or tort in respect of matters ancillary to the supply of goods, e.g. a cloakroom in a restaurant, though this may be obscured if there is a contractual duty of care, e.g. under a bailment.

35  The contract (suitability) test concerns consumer expectations, whereas the tort (negligence) test is about 'social standards of acceptable safety': Clark (1985) 48 MLR at 338. See also the development of the writ of deceit (see para 17.18); and generally Goode, *Commercial Law*, 3rd edn, 184–6.

36  In the United States, this process has been taken much further by deleting the requirement of consideration from the action for breach of warranty (see para 17.22) and by making tort liability strict (see para 17.23).

37  *Esso Petroleum Co Ltd v Mardon* [1975] QB 819, CA.

38  See the interesting argument by Jaffey (1985) 5 LS 77, especially at 89, *et seq.*

39  As between defendants, it may be possible to claim a contribution regardless of whether their respective liability to the plaintiff is in contract or tort: see generally, para 12.10.

40  For the extent to which contract-based liability can be extended without breaching the privity rules, see para 17.07, *et seq.*; and for the scope of common law tort liability, see para 17.12, *et seq.*

extension of privity to third parties expressly named in the contract (see para 17.08). *Fifth*, statute has introduced strict civil liability for unsafe goods (CPA: see para 17.24).

The result is to draw a sharp distinction for civil law purposes between shoddy and unsafe goods: there is strict statutory liability with regard to unsafe goods, whether by way of an implied term under the supply contract (see Chap 14) or the CPA (see above); but with regard to shoddy goods outside the privity rule, there is only common law negligence liability (see para 17.13).

**[17.05] Problems**. The major problems faced by the injured product user in obtaining compensation in civil proceedings within the jurisdiction of the English courts[41] are as follows:

1. *The state-of-the-art issue*. Whereas it is no defence in a contract-based action that the state of scientific knowledge at the relevant time did not allow for any possibility of precautions,[42] such a defence is normally available outside the contractual nexus.[43] Such a defence has been criticised as making consumers guinea pigs.[44]

2. *Burden of proof*. The difficulties of proving that an injury was caused by a defect in a product include the following: obtaining expert evidence,[45] including the lack of access to substantial government information acquired from indigenous producers[46] and importers;[47] but the Freedom of Information Act 2000 is unlikely to help in this regard.[48] The multiplicity of parties involved in the chain of distribution (see para 17.01) itself exacerbates the problem,[49] as do the restrictions on private access to government information contained in Pt 9 of the EA (see para 28.06).

3. *The cost of civil litigation*. Notwithstanding modern improvements in redress systems (see paras 3.15, *et seq*.), the sheer cost of litigation at both the High Court and County Court level will tend to raise the stakes so high that most injured private consumers are likely to be deterred from litigation. First, there is the apparently conscious restriction in our courts of trial by paper (see para 3.23). Second, there is the propensity of the present substantive law

---

41 Especially in the case of personal injury caused in circumstances with an international flavour, e.g. crash of a foreign manufactured aircraft, there may be attempts to bring civil proceedings in the jurisdiction likely to award the largest damages (forum shopping): see *SNI Aerospatale v Lee Kui Jak* [1987] 3 All ER 510, PC; and Geddes (1988) NLJ 542.

42 E.g. the *Ashington Piggeries* case (set out at para 13.13); *Frost v Aylesbury Dairy* (set out at para 14.08).

43 As in the tort of negligence: see paras 17.14 and 17.19. For the position in relation to statutory product liability, see para 17.30.

44 For the significance of this defence to the pharmaceutical industry, see Newdick (1985) 101 LQR 405; and para 17.30.

45 See Harris, *Compensation and Support for Illness and Injury*, 110–12.

46 E.g. Medicines Act 1968, s 118; Deregulation Act 1994, s 75 and Sched 15 (see para 28.06).

47 For discussion of the issue of public access to Government information, see Baxter [1997] JBL 199.

48 Because it exempts commercially sensitive information: s 43. See also ss 29, 40 and 41; and generally Johnson (2001) 151 NLJ 1030; [2006] 5 *Which?* 22.

49 For the difficulties this has caused in tort claims, see para 17.16. But note the burden of proof in negligent representation: see para 17.10.

of product liability to inflate costs, in particular by reason of its complexity and uncertainty;[50] and the advantage which the foregoing gives to economically powerful litigants.

4. *Liability for acts of another*. As the transaction will frequently be arranged by a salesman on behalf of a stockist of goods, there may well be involved the different rules as to the latter's liability for the former: if the transferee's action is in contract, it will introduce the rules of agency, whereas in tort vicarious liability is involved;[51] and, if criminal proceedings are undertaken, yet another set of rules is involved (see para 28.12).

5. *The international dimension* (see para 10.01), nowadays common in internet sales (see para 8.17B).

**[17.06]** Many of the legal problems in this area are neatly exemplified in the case of *Lambert v Lewis*:[52]

> The plaintiff family were travelling along the highway in a car. Coming the other way was a Landrover, owned by a farmer (C) and driven by his employee, towing a trailer. The trailer became detached, slewed across the road and crashed into the plaintiffs' car, killing two of them and injuring the other two. The unhitching occurred by reason of a defective coupling between the Landrover and trailer: it had a defectively designed locking mechanism allowing the spindle to sheer; but C must have known about this for some months. The coupling had been supplied and fitted by a retailer (B), who had indirectly obtained it from the manufacturer (Z).

*The plaintiff's claim for negligence.* The plaintiff sued all the identified parties in the chain of distribution in the tort of negligence. Stocker J found that the coupling was of an unsafe design, that C was negligent in not noticing this and he apportioned liability 25% to C and 75% to Z; but he dismissed the plaintiff's claim against B, on the grounds that B had not been negligent in obtaining the coupling with no apparent defects from a reputable dealer.[53]

*Third party proceedings.* The farmer (C) sought to recover his share of the damages from B for breach of the undertaking as to fitness (see para 14.07). The Court of Appeal held B liable for all the damage which flowed from his undoubted breach of the undertaking,[54] but this was unanimously reversed by the House of Lords on the grounds that the loss was caused, not by B's breach, but by C's failure to remedy the breach.[55]

*Fourth party proceedings.* The retailer (B) could not prove from which of two wholesalers (A1 or A2) he had obtained the offending coupling and therefore could

---

50 See para 17.12. Bear in mind also the complexity which may arise simply from the length of the chain of distribution (as to which, see para 17.01).

51 See para 17.12. For the possibility of a contribution, see the Civil Liability (Contribution) Act 1978.

52 [1982] AC 225, [1981] 1 All ER 1185, HL (discussed by Harvey and Parry, *The Law of Consumer Protection and Fair Trading*, 6th edn, 165–70. It has been pointed out that the incidence of loss depends on the inability to identify A and the plaintiff's choice of defendant: Schofield [1981] JBL at 213.

53 [1978] 1 Lloyd's Rep 810, [1979] RTR 61. The events occurred before the Civil Liability (Contribution) Act 1978 came into force.

54 [1980] 1 All ER 978, [1980] 2 WLR 299, CA.

55 For discussion of the causation issue, see below, paras 27.29 and 29.37.

not sue either of them in contract. Accordingly, he chose to sue Z, and lost in the Court of Appeal[54] on all the following grounds:

(1) There was no express collateral warranty on the basis of statements made in Z's sales literature,[56] because the claims it contained were not made to specific individuals and hence not intended to be acted upon.[57] This defect would not be cured by a statutory extension to the privity rule (see para 17.08); but the decision might now be reversed by the statutory liability under manufacturers' guarantees (see para 17.09B).

(2) There was no negligent misstatement liability in respect of that sales literature because there was no special relationship between the parties (see generally, para 17.13).

(3) There was no liability for the negligent act of design because B's loss was wholly financial. Though in the House of Lords, Lord Diplock *obiter* cast serious doubts on this argument (at 278), it has subsequently been affirmed (see para 17.13). However, as regards such dangerous goods, there might now be liability under statutory product liability (see para 17.23).

## WITHIN THE CONTRACTUAL NEXUS

Where there is a contractual nexus between the parties, it is important to distinguish whether or not there are any contractual promises between the parties as to the state of the product. If not, other remedies must be sought (see para 17.10, *et seq.*).

Assuming that there is such a contractual promise, the discussion may be conveniently sub-divided according to whether that promise became: (1) a term of a supply contract, (2) under an extension of the privity doctrine, or (3) a term of a collateral or other contract.

**[17.07] A supply contract.** Within the privity rule (see para 10.01), there should first be considered the identity of the person who is in law the supplier of the goods to the retail customer. The retail supplier may act through a servant or agent (see para 10.06); the salesman will not necessarily be an employee of the occupier of the premises, as may happen where there is a franchise system (sometimes termed 'a shop-within-a-shop': see para 1.07) or the salesman is the manufacturer's representative, e.g. the beauty preparations counter in a retail store; that apparent retailer may not even be the person who in law contracts to supply the goods to the retail cash customer, as where the salesman acts for an undisclosed principal, e.g. where the salesman is simply taking orders subsequently fulfilled by supply direct from the manufacturer to the retail consumer; and the picture is further altered where the transaction is directly financed, in which case the financier will in law be the supplier to the retail consumer (see para 2.21).

---

56 'Requires no maintenance, it is foolproof, once pin home—locked absolutely.' See generally, para 8.05.

57 The CA explicitly distinguished the cases cited in fns 83 and 84. But see *E Hobbs (Farms) v The Baxenden Chemical Co* [1992] 1 Lloyd's Rep 54; and generally, para 8.05.

Assuming that the identity of the supplier in law of the goods to the retail customer is established, there are two possible types of promise in that supply contract upon which the retail customer[58] may *prima facie*[59] sue:[60]

1. *Express promises.* The supplier's express promises[61] may be termed 'guarantees'[62] or 'warranties'.[63] Sometimes, the benefit of the promise is expressed to be transferable,[64] and sometimes not; but a prohibition on assignment by the consumer may be an unfair term (OFT, *Bulletin No. 12*, case 19).

2. *Implied promises.* In the previous chapters of Pt 4, the various implied undertakings which may be imported into contracts for the supply of goods were considered,[60] and it was seen that the major protection of the buyer or hirer rests on the undertakings as to title, description, fitness and quality.

*A chain of supply contracts.* Where a chain of supply contracts can be traced (see para 17.01), it may be possible for each buyer to bring a similar action for breach of express or implied terms (see above) against his supplier, all the actions being joined together in a single set of proceedings;[65] and this technique may even be available where there is an impecunious intermediate buyer.[66] In such a case, a commercial end-buyer will *prima facie* have a right to rescind for breach of condition; but rescission is less likely to be available to previous commercial transferees (see s 35 of the SGA, which is discussed at para 29.05), nor to any consumer transferees (see Pt 5A of the SGA: see para 29.02B). To the extent that any transferee can only claim damages,[67] as under an express indemnity, e.g. in a recourse provision (see para 16.22), his position is similar to that of a person suing under a collateral contract (see para 17.09). Finally, it should be borne in mind that any person in the chain of distribution found liable may claim a contribution from any other person in that chain 'liable in respect of the same damage', whether the latter's liability be in contract or tort;[68] and that, where there is a 'consumer

---

58  As to the position of the family of the retail purchaser, see paras 17.12 and 17.22.
59  Even if the retail consumer enters into a product insurance increasing his rights in respect of defective goods (see para 17.09), UCTA would prevent the retail supplier excluding his liability: see para 18.19. *Contra*, where subsequent to breach, the retail consumer enters into a contract of compromise: see para 26.18.
60  What if the retail consumer has in fact donated the goods to another? Will he thereupon lose any right to rescind (see para 29.06); and what damages will he suffer?
61  E.g. *Parker v Oloxo Ltd* [1937] 3 All ER 524; *Carlill v Carbolic Smoke Ball Co* (see para 8.05). See generally, para 11.07.
62  E.g. 'money-back guarantees': see para 20.24. Distinguish contracts of guarantee: see para 17.09.
63  As against the suppliers, the label 'warranty' will not necessarily be given its technical meaning: see para 18.06. For warranties, see generally, para 11.04.
64  As to where a transferable express promise is purportedly transferred to a donee, see equitable assignments (see para 7.18); or transferred to one expressly mentioned in the contract (see para 17.08). For the effect of the assignment of rights and duties, see generally, para 7.23, *et seq*.
65  E.g. *Kasler and Cohen v Slovouski* [1928] 1 KB 78 (see para 29.36); *Parker v Oloxo Ltd* (above); *Butterworth v Kingsway Motors Ltd* (set out at para 12.06); *Lambert v Lewis* (above); and see further Macleod, *Consumer Sales Law*, 1st edn, para 17.08.
66  He may assign his rights to his sub-buyer: *Total Liban SA v Vitol Energy SA* [2000] 1 All ER 267.
67  Any attempt by contract to reduce the consumer's remedies so that they matched those of earlier commercial parties in the chain may be unfair: OFT, *Bulletin No. 23*, cases 16, 21; and para 11.16.
68  Civil Liability (Contribution) Act 1978, s 6(1). For this Act, see generally, para 12.10.

supply', the SGG Directive reinforces the rights of suppliers to sue back up the chain.[69]

On the other hand, even supposing there is a chain of *prima facie* contractual liability, there are several weaknesses in that chain from the viewpoint of a consumer (say) pursuing an original substantial supplier. An intermediate contract may contain a valid exclusion clause (see Chap 18). An intermediate party may be insolvent (see Chap 19), or his identity uncertain, e.g. *Lambert v Lewis* (set out at para 17.06). In any event, such chain litigation may be protracted and expensive.

**[17.08] Extension of privity.** No doubt, the common law has already blurred the edges of the privity doctrine in the field of product liability by both the device of the collateral contract (see para 17.09) and 'astute manipulation' of the rules of the agency or assignment (see para 17.12). *Inter alia*, the latter will include the undisclosed principal doctrine, though development here is limited by the rule that an undisclosed principal cannot ratify (see para 10.06). Additionally, important extensions have been made by the CCA, with the making of further defendants liable for misrepresentation or on the basis of being a connected lender (CCA, ss 56 and 75: see Chap 16). However, in the United States there has been developed two new exceptions to the privity doctrine specifically to impose strict contractual liability in favour of consumers.

1. *'Horizontal privity'*.[70] To obviate artificial arguments as to whether the retail buyer (C) purchased as agent for the injured consumer (D), the United States have come up with the idea of a limited waiver of the privity rule in favour of all in the household of the retail buyer (Uniform Commercial Code, Art 2-318, alternative c). Something similar might now be achievable in England by use of a statutory extension to the privity rule (see below).

2. *'Vertical privity': a 'leapfrog' action.*[70] At common law, instead of a chain of supply contract actions (see para 17.07), in some US jurisdictions an injured retail consumer (C or D) has been allowed to 'leapfrog' the 'innocent' retailer (B) and sue the 'guilty' producer (X, Y, Z) in just the same way as if the consumer had purchased the goods direct from the producer: this has particularly been the case where unsafe goods caused physical damage. Something similar might now be achievable in England in respect of manufacturers' express warranties (see para 17.09B).

*The extension of English privity.* Besides his rights under all the other exceptions to the privity rule (s 7), s 1 of the Contracts (Rights of Third Parties) Act 1999[71] introduces a new general[72] statutory right for a third party (T) to enforce the benefit of a contractual term in a contract to which he is not a party (see below): T is then

---

69 Directive 99/44 (see para 14.01), Art 4, which has not been specifically implemented in English law.

70 For a diagrammatic portrayal of the ambit of these two concepts, see para 17.01. For an excellent exposition, see the Law Commission Working Paper on *Liability for Defective Products* (1975, WP No. 64), paras 119–33.

71 The Act is largely based upon the Report of the Law Commission, *Privity of Contract: Contracts for the Benefit of Third Parties* (1996, Law Com 242). See generally, Treitel, *Law of Contract*, 11th edn, 651, *et seq.*; Stevens (2004) 120 LQR 292.

72 Of the exceptional cases excluded from the Act by s 6, the only one likely to be relevant here is bills of exchange (s 6(1)). As to bills of exchange, see para 7.24.

entitled to exercise all those remedies which would have been available to him in an action for breach of contract had he been a contracting party;[73] and he may also take advantage of any exclusion or limitation clause in his favour (s 1(6)), e.g. excluding liability for negligently caused personal injury. However, T is to be in no better position than if he had been a party to the contract (s 1(4)), e.g. as to time limits; and his rights will therefore be subject to all defences and set-offs that the promisor may have against the other contracting party (s 3). The promisor's duty shall be owed to both the other contracting party (s 4) and the third party, though he should be protected from double liability.[74] T cannot usually be deprived of this new statutory right by subsequent agreement between the contracting parties (s 2; and see generally, para 26.18).

The above s 1 right is expressed in general terms, but is likely to have particular significance for product liability, where it would appear capable of extending both horizontal and vertical privity (see above). For T to take advantage of this *prima facie* rule, he 'must be expressly identified in the contract by name, as a member of a class or as answering a particular description but need not be in existence when the contract is entered into' (s 1(3)). Where he falls within s 1(3), T may enforce a term of the contract in either of the following situations (s 1(1)):

(1) The contract expressly provides that T, which it identifies by 'name, class or description', may enforce the promise,[75] e.g. where C purchases a gift for D and explicitly agrees with B that D shall be able to enforce the contract, or in a directly financed transaction the dealer's contract with the financier so provides (see para 16.22). This situation should be distinguished from that where the contract is made as agent for T (see para 10.06) and overlaps with manufacturers' guarantees (see para 17.09B).

(2) The contract purports to confer a benefit on T.[76] Here, the fact that T is identified by 'name, class or description' merely creates a rebuttable presumption that he may enforce the contract (s 1(2));[77] so, the ordinary retail purchaser of defective goods (C) would not, without more, normally have the right to sue under the contract between the retailer (B) and the wholesaler or manufacturer (A, Z);[78] but it would be quite possible to frame, e.g. a manufacturer's guarantee (see para 17.09A), so that it extended to C and D. Where C directs B to send a purchased gift direct to D and the gift is defective, D will have the benefit of the statutory implied terms in the SGA.[79]

---

73  S 1(5): 'action' would rule out use of the self-help remedies, e.g. recaption (see para 24.23); 'breach of contract' would preclude T's use of tort actions, e.g. wrongful interference with goods (see para 19.04); and restitutionary remedies (see para 29.12). S 1(5) also explicitly makes T's action subject to the ordinary rules relating to 'damages, injunctions, specific performance and other relief' (see para 27.27, *et seq*).

74  S 5: see para 27.39. However, it has been argued that this would not necessarily be the case where C purchases defective goods for D: see Stevens, *Op. cit.*, at 300–2.

75  S 1(1)(a). Cf. *Tweddle v Atkinson* (1861) 1 B & S 393; *The Eurymedon* [1975] AC 300, PC (not sale cases).

76  S 1(1)(b). For difficulties, see Stevens, *Op. cit.*, at 306–8.

77  S 1(2). Usually, there must be a positive intention to displace s 1(1)(b): *Nissin Shipping Co Ltd v Cleaves & Co Ltd* [2004] 1 All ER (Comm) 481; but this may be an unfair term (*Bulletin No. 26*, p 20: see para 11.15A).

78  The above Law Commission Report, para 7.18.

79  The above Law Commission Report, paras 7.41 and 7.54; and as to remedies, see generally, Chap 29.

**[17.09] Collateral or other contracts**. Whether there is a single contract for the supply of goods or a chain of such contracts (see para 17.07), there may also be one or more collateral[80] or other contracts. In the field of product liability, there are a number of situations where this device has been used to impose liability as between remote parties in the chain of distribution.[81]

1. *In direct financing.* To impose contractual liability on the dealer to the consumer (see para 16.18) and financier (see para 16.22).

2. *On manufacturers.*[82] The promise may be made personally to the consumer by the representative of the manufacturer,[83] distributor or wholesaler.[84] It is more likely, however, that the promise will be made to the consumer in a less personal way by sales literature,[85] or other advertisement, whether distributed at the point of retail sale, directly mailed or carried in newspapers or on television.[86] One particular device which requires special mention here is the manufacturer's 'guarantee' against defects in parts and workmanship discovered within a stipulated time (see para 17.09A), perhaps with an extended warranty as regards those discovered thereafter (insurance: see below). Further problems arise with network guarantees; ie where a manufacturer sets up a system that any accredited outlet will do warranty work, regardless of from which outlet the consumer obtained the goods.[87]

3. *After-sales service.* Manufacturers or retailers may offer after-sales service, e.g. the continued availability of replacement parts. As regards the promised after-sales service, whilst its absence might amount to an offence under s 14 of the TDA (see para 4.15) and a breach of the undertaking as to satisfactory quality, perhaps on the basis of lack of durability (para 14.06), all too often the service is available,[88] but at a seemingly disproportionate cost (but see s 15 of the SGSA: see para 15.15); and in any event it may depend on the continued solvency of the promisor (see para 19.18), unless bought by credit card (see para 16.11).

---

80 For collateral contracts, see generally, para 11.06. For cases where the necessary *animus contrahendi* was absent, see the cases cited below, fn 86; and *Jonathan Wren & Co Ltd v Microdec PLC* [2000] CLY 876.

81 For the chain of distribution, see para 17.01. Distinguish title-transferring collateral contracts: see para 15.26.

82 See generally, Atiyah, *Sale of Goods*, 10th edn, 266–7. For motor vehicle guarantees by manufacturers, see [2004] 5 *Which?* 48. Several industry codes of practice deal with such guarantees: see generally, para 3.13. For concern that Art 81 (ex 85) of the Treaty of Rome (see para 2.13) may require such a warranty to be honoured community-wide, see Fine (1989) 10 ECLR 233.

83 E.g. *Shanklin Pier Ltd v Detel Products Ltd* [1951] 2 KB 854; *Comyn Ching & Co (London) Ltd v Oriental Tube Co Ltd* [1981] Com LR 67, CA.

84 E.g. *Wells (Merstham) Ltd v Buckland Sand and Silica Ltd* [1965] 2 QB 170.

85 Which may be a separate document, or printed on packaging, e.g. chocolates. For EU avoidance of restrictions on guarantees, see para 2.13.

86 Liability is, perhaps, less likely here, because the advertising industry is usually very careful not to make any material representations of fact, e.g. *Lambert v Lewis* (set out at para 17.06); the *Howard Marine* case (set out at para 17.10). See Bradgate (1991) 20 Anglo-Am LR 334.

87 Twigg-Flesner [1999] JBL 568.The new car warranty scheme may be anti-competitive: see OFT, *AR-2003/4*, 73.

88 But its terms may be struck down as being unfair: OFT, *UCT Bulletin No. 23*, case 40; and see para 11.15.

4. *Insurance*. There are a number of circumstances where an insurance contract may be utilised in relation to the supply of goods; but, even where there is a regulated supply, these insurance contracts are exempt from the linked transaction rules (see para 5.31). First, there may be an extended warranty (see para 17.09C). A second range of risk is covered by the consumer's product loss insurance.[89] A third example is the cash-back insurer (see para 8.13A), where any regulated financier may incur liability under ss 56 or 75 of the CCA (see Chap 16). The OFT have had some success in controlling the terms of these insurances under the UTCCR.[90]

**[17.09A] Manufacturer's (producer's) guarantees**.[91] At common law, because the consumer's (C's) supply contract is usually with the retailer (B),[92] the manufacturer (Z) is not privy to that retail supply contract (see para 17.04), so that Z's 'guarantee' could only take effect as a collateral contract (see generally, paras 11.06 and 17.09). Such a guarantee is usually found in advertising and/or a document supplied with the goods and used normally to contain the following three elements: (i) the guarantee 'promise' by Z, e.g. that the goods will not fail within six months; (ii) the limited remedies available to C if the promise is not fulfilled, e.g. replacement of defective parts; (iii) the conditions under which the guarantee is provided, both as to C's reliance, e.g. return to Z of date-stamped registration card on purchase, and as to Z's performance, e.g. return of the defective goods. It is not a contract of guarantee in the traditional sense of the promise to answer for the default of another (see para 25.06), nor a money-back 'satisfaction' guarantee (see para 10.28); and in the motor vehicle industry it is usually termed a 'manufacturer's warranty' (for another use of the expression 'warranty', see para 11.06). At common law, these manufacturer's guarantees might not have the *animus contrahendi* to amount to collateral contracts, e.g. *Lambert v Lewis* (set out at para 17.06); but, insofar as they did so, these contracts behaved much like other consumer standard-form contracts (see para 11.08): they tended to be drafted so as to minimise the rights of C as compared with B and Z, but would be read *contra proferentem* (see para 18.06). It is legally possible for Z to make the benefit of a guarantee transferable to a second-hand purchaser or C's donee under the Contracts Act 1999,[93] or for C to assign the benefit of the guarantee (see para 7.15); but this *prima facie* depends on the terms of the guarantee drafted by Z as allowing transfer or assignment.[94] It seems likely that the statutory implied terms in supply contracts and manufacturers' guarantees will operate concurrently, yet independently.[95]

---

89 Long-term cover should normally be taken out via a household insurance policy; but interim cover may be automatically available where items are obtained by payment card.

90 See *UCT Bulletin No. 22*, case 39; *No. 23*, case 40; *No. 24*, cases 14 and 44.

91 See generally Twigg-Flesner, *Consumer Product Guarantees*, 2003, Chaps 2 and 5.

92 *Contra* guarantees given by B, or where the retail supply is by Z.

93 See para 17.08. It is thought unlikely that this will extend to network guarantees, so as to enable C to sue any member of the network, e.g. car dealer. See Twigg-Flesner, *Op. cit.*, para 8.6.

94 E.g. dry-rot guarantees, double-glazing or fitted kitchen guarantees. As to prohibitions on transfer and assignment, see respectively, paras 17.08 and 7.26; and generally Twigg-Flesner, *Op. cit.*, paras 8.5.1–3.

95 *Rogers v Parish* (set out at para 14.23), *per* Mustill LJ at All ER at 237e–h. Whilst his Lordship is correct that the guarantee cannot be in lieu of statutory rights, it does not follow that the guarantee cannot be taken into account in determining statutory rights: the existence of a guarantee may be a factor in determining whether goods are of satisfactory quality: see para 14.19.

However, the legal effect of such guarantees on private consumers is substantially affected by statute: as between B and C, B cannot adopt the words of the guarantee so as to exclude or restrict his statutory liability under the implied undertakings,[96] nor anything which amounts to misleading advertising (see para 8.12A); and, where the 'guarantee' refers to B, it must state positively that it does not affect C's statutory rights against B by reason of both criminal[97] and civil law,[98] though there are persistent reports of retailers (wrongly) denying remedies to consumers on the grounds that C should look instead to Z. As between Z and C, Z cannot employ such words to exclude or restrict his liability in the tort of negligence or for death;[99] and the contractual terms must be both fair under the UTCC Regulations[100] and reasonable under UCTA (s 3: see para 18.22) and are subject to the competition rules.[101]

For the private consumer (C), the result of the foregoing was frequently this: whilst the statutes prevent his losing his general rights, they may also remove the consideration which may support any promise (albeit limited) by Z,[102] so rendering the 'guarantee' without legal effect. However, such difficulties would now appear to have been circumvented, not only by a new statutory exception to the privity rule (see para 17.08), but also by the Directive (Art 6) applicable only to private consumers (see para 17.09B).

**[17.09B]  Consumer guarantees.**[103] Pursuant to Directive 99/44 (see para 14.01) the SSG Regulations 2002 only apply to guarantees given to private consumers.[104] Clearly, the Regulations do not require anybody to give that private consumer a guarantee; but, insofar as he may choose to give one, the Regulations make compulsorily[105] liable in the law of contract one who gives a **consumer guarantee**. This last expression is defined as (reg 2):

> 'any undertaking given by a seller or producer to the consumer, given without extra charge, to reimburse the price paid or to replace, repair or handle consumer goods in any way if they do not meet the specifications set out in the guarantee statement or in the relevant advertising'.

---

96  For the prohibition on exclusion, see UCTA, ss 6 and 7 (see para 18.19); and for the OFT guidelines, see para 3.11.

97  Consumer Transactions (Restrictions on Statements) Order 1976, Art 4: see para 4.22. Does this requirement produce sufficient clarity to satisfy Art 6(2)? The introduction of any further criminal sanctions has been rejected: Twigg-Flesner, *Op. cit.*, para 5.12.3.

98  A term which does not state this sufficiently clearly may be unfair under Grey Term (b): see *UCT Bulletin No. 10*, case 3; and para 11.16.

99  For Z's liability in the tort of negligence, see paras 17.13–7; and for the prohibition on exclusion, see UCTA, ss 2 and 5 (see paras 18.17 and 18.26); UTCC Grey Term (a) (see para 11.16).

100  See Twigg-Flesner, *Op. cit.*, paras 8.9.4–10. This might also encompass guarantee requirements that C, e.g. maintain the goods in a particular manner, return a registration card.

101  E.g. territorial restrictions on the availability of guarantees, an agreement between traders to offer similar guarantees (see Twigg-Flesner, *Op. cit.*, para 7.2.3; and generally, paras 2.13–14).

102  E.g. *Roscorla v Thomas* (1842) 3 QB 234 (goods); *Stewart v Reavell's Garage* [1952] 2 QB 545 (servicing); *Wartsila France SAS v Genergy PLC* (2003) 92 Con LR 112 (goods); and see para 10.01.

103  See generally Twigg-Flesner, *Consumer Product Guarantees*, 2003, Chaps 7 & 8. For comparison, see the US Magnuson-Moss Warranty Act 1975, discussed above, Chaps 3 and 6.

104  Distinguish business consumers, who are dealt with under para 17.09A. As to the definition of 'consumer', see the identical definition in UTCC, reg 3(1): see para 11.12A.

105  Art 6 recites that the guarantee 'shall be legally binding'; and there is an express prohibition in Art 7(2) against contracting out of this rule. But the Regulations are silent on the point.

Closely following Art 1(2)(e), this **consumer guarantee** comprehends not only the (frequently ornate) card provided with the goods by Z, but also any promise made in an 'associated advertisement'.[106] What if the two texts differ?[107] It will be noted that this definition only applies to undertakings 'given without charge', so that it will not apply to extended warranties (see para 17.09C); and, because of the reference to not meeting 'specifications', probably does not extend to satisfaction guarantees (see para 10.28). However, the present Regulations are not restricted to an 'undertaking' given by Z to private consumers and extends to any 'supplier' or 'producer': 'supplier' will include any retail supplier, whether by way of sale, lease, hire or hp (reg 2: see para 14.01); and 'producer' means any manufacturer or importer into the European Economic Area.[108] The Regulations collectively define that person as the **guarantor** (reg 2) and provide as follows (reg 15(1)):

> 'Where goods are sold or otherwise supplied to a consumer which are offered with a consumer guarantee, the consumer guarantee takes effect at the time the goods are delivered as a contractual obligation owed by the guarantor under the conditions set out in the guarantee statement and the associated advertising'.

This freely given guarantee is to be treated as an express contract even in the absence of consideration (unlike manufacturers' guarantees at common law: see para 17.09A), in addition to the consumer's rights under the supply contract or any collateral contract, e.g. an extended warranty (see para 17.09). It has been argued[109] that under these Regulations the guarantee could be enforceable by a second-hand purchaser or donee: whilst this is *prima facie* dependent on the drafting of the guarantee by Z (see para 17.09A), it will be subject to the UTCC Regulations[109] against prohibitions on assignment (see Grey Term (p): see para 11.18A). Further, the Regulations place the following burdens on the **guarantor** 'and any other person who offers to consumers the goods which are the subject of the guarantee for sale or supply' (reg 15(4)):

(1) He shall ensure that the guarantee sets out the contents of the guarantee and the essential particulars necessary for making claims under the guarantee, notably the duration[110] and its territorial scope, which is likely to be particularly significant with internet sales (see para 8.17A). Further, the guarantee must also contain the name and address of the guarantor (reg 15(2)), e.g. for return of goods carriage-paid to Z.

(2) These terms must be set out 'in plain intelligible language';[111] and, where the offer is made within the UK, it must be written in English (reg 15(5)).

(3) On request, within a reasonable time the consumer must be provided with a copy 'in writing or other durable medium' (reg 15(3)), a requirement which will

---

106 The phrase in the Directive (Arts 1(1) and 6(1)) is 'associated advertising', but in reg 2 (*contra* reg 15(1)) this is rendered as 'relevant advertising'. Does it matter?
107 See Twigg-Flesner, *Op. cit.*, para 7.2.2.
108 SGA, new s 61(1), SSGA, new s 18; and SOGIT, new s 15(1), as inserted by SSG, regs 6, 12 and 13.
109 See Twigg-Flesner, *Op. cit.*, para 8.5. This is less clear in the Directive, which refers to 'undertaking' (Art 1(2)(e)). See further, para 11.12, *et seq.*
110 E.g. 12-month guarantee. If Z wishes to obtain an Eco-label (see para 3.14), the guarantee must comply with a minimum duration.
111 Reg 15(2). Cf. UTCC, reg 7(1): set out at para 11.13.

usually result in paper copies of advertising material being held at the point-of-sale.[112] Further, if the goods were distance-sold, B must also supply C with details of the guarantee (see para 9.05A).

Breach of the above provisions will enable C to sue Z for breach of the guarantee, e.g. for repair/replacement; but this may also overlap with C's right to sue B under the supply contract for repair/replacement (see para 29.02A) and both sets of rights could even be exercisable against the same person, e.g. where Z makes the retail supply, or B adopts the guarantee as part of his retail contract. Furthermore, the regulations also empower an 'enforcement authority'[113] to apply for an Enforcement Order (reg 15(6) and (7): see generally, para 28.03).

**[17.09C] Extended warranties.**[114] In some cases, B and Z arrange to increase C's rights if the goods prove defective by offering a (say five-year) optional 'extended warranty'.[115] Such insurances do not always cover maintenance and are sometimes offered 'free' where purchases are made with a payment card.[116] This amounts to a product insurance for the stated period beyond the ordinary express (say for one year) manufacturer's guarantee:[117] it may offer a significant commission to the retailer on such business; and, in an attempt to curb hard-sell and excessive profits, further statutory control has been introduced by the Extended Warranties Order 2005.[118] This Order seems restricted to where a retail 'supplier' of 'domestic electrical goods' to a private consumer also supplies an 'extended warranty' providing 'cover' in relation to them.[119] The Order offers the following types of protection:[120]

(1) It imposes an obligation on the retail store usually to display the price and duration of the optional extended warranty (Art 3(1) and (2)), together with further relevant information, e.g. leaflets on the extended warranty (Art 3(1)(b)), information as to the consumer's rights (below), the obligation to provide a price

---

112 As to 'durable form', cf. Distance Selling Regulations, reg 8(1) (see para 9.05A). See generally, Twigg-Flesner, *Op. cit.*, para 7.3.2.

113 ' "Enforcement authority" means the Director General of Fair Trading (and) every local weights and measures authority' (reg 2): for the DG, see para 3.03; and for the LA, see para 28.02.

114 See Singleton [2005] Consumer Law Today 9. These extended warranties may be extremely profitable to retailers; and the OFT have referred them to the Competition Commission (see para 2.12): see OFT, *2002–3 AR*, 20.

115 For the duration of the statutory implied terms and retailer-promoted insurance, see para 14.06; and as to insolvency see para 19.18, *et seq*.

116 As to whether these insurances are worthwhile to consumers, see [2000] 4 *Which?* 35. Cf. prior payment insurance (see para 23.22). See generally, Twigg-Flesner, *Consumer Product Guarantees*, 2003, 46–50.

117 Recovery under the policy may be subject to onerous conditions: see [1998] 11 *Which?* 4. Moreover, if offered by B to C, the 'guarantee' may contravene insurance legislation: Twigg-Flesner [1999] JBL 279.

118 The Supply of Extended Warranties on Domestic Electrical Goods Order, 2005 SI 37, made under the FTA. This was made as a result of the report of the Competition Commission (see para 2.14). For a report as to how it is working, see [2005] 12 *Which?* 16.

119 Art 2 defines 'domestic electrical goods' as excluding watches and jewellery; 'cover' as a contract which includes the cost of repairing or replacing them; 'extended warranty' as the cover in respect of such goods; and 'supplier' as the retailer of such goods who also 'offers' such extended warranty either directly or on behalf of a third party.

120 The supplier or provider must give the OFT compliance information (Art 9); and the Secretary of State may give directions to secure compliance (Art 10).

quotation (Art 3(1)(c) and (3)) and a statement that the consumer need not purchase the warranty at the same time as the goods or at all (Art 3(4)).

(2) It usually requires the retail store which advertises the price of such electrical goods to also advertise adjacently the price and duration of the extended warranty, whether the advertisement be placed in a newspaper or other printed publicity (Art 4), catalogue (Art 5), or website (Art 6).

(3) Where the supplier has provided a price quotation (above), it must be kept open for at least thirty days (Art 7).

(4) Where a consumer has taken out an extended warranty of more than one year and it is not a distance contract (Art 2: see para 8.17), then, unless the warranty price is less than £20 and ignoring all discounts, under Art 8 the consumer:

   (a) if he has not made a claim on it, he has a 45-day right of cancellation by notice with full refund;[121]

   (b) even if he has made a claim, he has a 45-day right of termination by notice with *pro rata* refund[121] in the terms of Art 8(4), unless the warranty terminates on making a claim.

## Other remedies

Even though there is no breach of any contractual promise made to a party, **as against the other contracting party only** he may be able to rely on the law relating to misrepresentation, illegality, unenforceability or mistake (see para 10.18).

**[17.10] Misrepresentation.** At common law, a misstatement of fact which induced a contract is termed a 'misrepresentation' (see para 11.01), provided that it is made by a contracting party or his authorised agent.[122] Of course, at a later stage, that misrepresentation may become a term of the contract (see para 11.02); but, even though it does not, that 'mere representation' gives rise in the representee to a right to rescind (see paras 26.12–14), though at common law only an inferior right to damages: damages may lie in the torts of deceit or negligent misstatement (see para 17.18); but otherwise there is only the possibility of an indemnity. However, the Misrepresentation Act 1967 may enable the representee to recover damages from the other contracting party[123] in two extra situations (see below), though only where that party has made or authorised the representation.[124] There is no statutory definition of 'misrepresentation', so the common law definition presumably applies (see para 11.01); and the measure of those damages is tortious (see para 27.24).

---

121 Under Art 8(6), 'notice' may be given orally or in writing; and 'refund' does not usually extend to refund in vouchers or credit notes.

122 *MCI WorldCom International Inc v Primus Telecommunications Inc* [2004] 1 All ER (Comm) 138 (not a goods case).

123 But not against an agent authorised to make the representation: *The Skopas* [1983] 2 All ER 1. If the agent were acting outside his authority, he might instead be liable for breach of warranty of authority.

124 *Overbrooke Estates Ltd v Glencombe Properties Ltd* [1974] 3 All ER 511; *SW General Properties v Marton* [1983] 2 TrL 14. For a case where a retail supplier may adopt the misrepresentation of a manufacturer, see para 17.07; and for auctioneers, see para 10.10.

1. *Careless misrepresentations.* Where there is an innocent but careless misrepresentation, s 2(1) provides that the representor, 'if he would be liable to damages if the misrepresentation had been made fraudulently',[125] shall be so liable 'unless he proves that he had reasonable ground to believe and did believe up to the time the contract was made that the facts represented were true'. The effect of s 2(1) is thus to cast upon the **representor** the (legal?) burden of proof as to his state of mind: this should be compared with the representor's much lighter onus in the tort of deceit, where the legal and evidential burden is on the representee. The last phrase of s 2(1) spells out the state of mind which the representor must disprove, making him liable if he has *either* of the following states of mind:

   (i)  **The unreasonable believer** will refer to the more common, careless man.[126] In *Howard Marine & Dredging Co Ltd v A Ogden & Sons (Excavations) Ltd*,[127] where the majority of the Court of Appeal held P liable for damages for breach of s 2(1) on the grounds that P had failed to prove that they had reasonable grounds for believing the truth of the statement. However, the Court refused to allow D's claim on the basis of a collateral contract (see para 17.09) and disagreed over the tort of negligent misstatement.[128]

   (ii) **The non-believer.** There may here be an overlap with the tort of deceit (see para 17.18), though failure by the representor to prove his innocence does not make him liable for deceit.[129]

2. *Non-fraudulent misrepresentations.* Where there is an innocent misrepresentation, whether careless or not,[130] s 2(2) gives the court a discretion in a claim for rescission to award damages in lieu of rescission (see para 26.12).

**[17.11] Other vitiating factors.** These include the following:

1. *Illegality and unenforceability.* There are a number of statutory provisions which may taint a contract with illegality or render it unenforceable; and many of these were specifically designed for the protection of a particular group of persons (see Chap 4). The effect of these provisions on the contract has already been considered (see para 10.19).

2. *Mistake.* Frequently as a line of last resort, the buyer or hirer may claim to avoid his contractual liability on grounds of mistake. Immediately, it is vital to decide whether or not the parties have reached agreement. If they have, but are both labouring under the same fundamental mistake, such as where the goods have been destroyed, this raises the question of impossibility (see para 22.10). On the

---

125  The effect of this would appear to be to incorporate by reference the law of deceit (see generally, para 17.18): see Treitel, *Law of Contract*, 11th edn, 351–2.

126  See also *Thomas Witter Ltd v TBP Industries Ltd* (set out at para 26.14). By suing under s 2(1), P will gain the deceit test of remoteness rather than that applicable for common law negligence (see para 27.41).

127  [1978] QB 574, [1978] 2 All ER 1134, CA.

128  Shaw LJ for liability; Lord Denning MR against; and Bridge LJ *dubitante*. For negligent misstatement, see further, para 17.17.

129  Distinguish s 2(1) from actual claims for fraud, because under s 2(1) D is liable simply for lack of proof of innocence: Hooley (1991) 107 LQR 31.

130  S 2(3) enables the court to award damages under both s 2(1) and (2), provided that there is no element of double recovery: see generally, para 27.39.

other hand, it may be denied that the parties were ever *ad idem*, so that the alleged contract was void *ab initio*;[131] or alternatively, that a written contract should be rectified because it does not accurately represent the mutual intention of the parties.[132] It has been pointed out that such a plea is particularly likely to be raised by the buyer or hirer who finds that the contract goods are defective.[133] Within the English law of contract, there are only two possible solutions in such a case of mistake of quality:

(1) The goods are at the risk of the buyer or hirer, i.e. the rule of *caveat emptor* (see para 15.22) applies; or

(2) the goods are at the risk of the supplier for one of the following reasons:

  (a) there is a breach of an express or implied term which puts responsibility on the supplier (see Chaps 13–15), or

  (b) the contract is void, in which case the supplier as owner bears the risk in the sense of the reduced worth of the goods due to any defect (see para 22.01).

On this basis, it is clear that the plea by a buyer or hirer that the contract is void on grounds of mistake of quality is really an alternative method of trying to place the risk on the supplier.[134] Of course, there is a strong argument for saying that it is undesirable that the law should too frequently allow a buyer or hirer escape from his supply contract on a plea of mistake, on the grounds that this would unduly interfere with the interests of finality.[135] Indeed, there is only one reported case where a contract for the sale of goods has been held void on grounds of such a mistake.[136]

# OUTSIDE THE CONTRACTUAL NEXUS

**[17.12]** With a few limited exceptions, the common law takes an extremely strict view of contractual promises, the promisor being almost regarded as guaranteeing his promise (see para 26.02). Yet this strict contractual liability is limited by the doctrine of privity (see para 17.04), albeit extended by statute (see para 17.08, *et seq*.); and those who are not privy can only be civilly liable in tort, where liability at common law usually depends on fault (see below), except in the case of vicarious civil liability, e.g. that of an employer for the acts of his employee.[137]

---

131 E.g. *Scriven Bros & Co v Hindley & Co* [1913] 3 KB 564; *Hartog v Colin and Shields* [1939] 3 All ER 566. And see *Henkel v Pape* (1870) LR Ex 7, discussed by Treitel, *Law of Contract*, 11th edn, 28.

132 See *Frederick E Rose (London) Ltd v William H Pim Jnr Co Ltd* [1953] 2 QB 450, CA (rectification refused).

133 Where he has lost the right to reject for breach of contract: Atiyah, *Sale of Goods*, 10th edn, 210. See generally, paras 10.16–17.

134 E.g. *Smith v Hughes* (set out at para 10.17); *Oscar Chess Ltd v Williams* [1957] 1 All ER 325, CA; *Harrison and Jones Ltd v Bunten and Lancaster Ltd* [1953] 1 QB 646.

135 See *The Great Peace* case [2003] QB 679, CA (not a sale case).

136 *Nicholson and Venn v Smith-Marriott* (1947) 177 LT 189: but see the criticisms of that case in Atiyah, *Sale of Goods*, 10th edn, 211, fn 335; Treitel, *Op. cit.*, 292, fn 62.

137 For vicarious criminal liability, see para 28.09.

It has already been noted how the courts have sought to avoid this limitation of strict liability by the collateral contract of warranty (see para 17.09) and by the action for breach of statutory duty (see para 3.21); and the courts have also sought to mitigate the effects of the doctrine of privity by astute manipulation of the agency concept and a husband's or parent's claim in the case of injury or death to his wife or child.[138] For such a contractual claim, the argument must be within the laws of agency (see para 10.06), not vicarious liability.[139] Alternatively, it might be possible for a consumer to assign his contractual rights to a sub-buyer[140] donee[141] or to find an implied contract[142] or joint purchase.[143]

However, because there are so many claims that cannot be fitted within the framework of contract, we must consider, albeit briefly, the grounds of product liability in tort. In this discussion, it is convenient to distinguish product liability as between the following: (1) common law liability for acts and omissions (see para 17.13), which will be relevant as regards both design and production defects; (2) common law liability for statements (see para 17.17), which will include sales literature; and (3) statutory product liability for unsafe goods (see para 17.24). There should also be borne in mind any relevant instructions for use (see para 18.28, et seq.).

**[17.13/4] Common law liability for acts and omissions: (1).**[144] Outside the contractual nexus, the supplier of goods will seldom be under any strict liability at common law in relation to defects in the goods causing physical loss: the doctrine of *Rylands v Fletcher* (see para 17.22) probably has no application in this context;[145] and, except in respect of breach of safety regulations, an action for breach of statutory duty is seldom available;[146] and the possibility of an action in trespass will usually be ruled out because the act or omission of the supplier on which the complaint is based will generally have occurred whilst the goods were in the supplier's ownership or control.[147] Thus, recovery in tort will usually depend on the tort of negligence.[148] The difference between liability in contract, and that in the tort of negligence was neatly exemplified by *Daniels and Daniels v White & Sons Ltd:*[149]

---

138 E.g. *Lockett v Charles* (below); *Jackson v Horizon Holidays* [1975] 3 All ER 92, CA. See also the comments of the Law Commission in the *First Report on Exemption Clauses in Contracts* (Law Com No. 24), paras 60–3. For the rules as to when an agent may bind his principal, see generally, para 10.06.

139 *Director General of Fair Trading v Smiths Concrete Ltd* [1991] 4 All ER 150, CA.

140 *Total Liban SA v Vitol Energy SA* [2000] 1 All ER 267.

141 As to assignment of choses in action, see para 7.16, *et seq.* For a transmissible warranty of safety, see (1991) 107 LQR at 270–5.

142 *Lockett v AM Charles Ltd* [1938] 4 All ER 170.

143 Why is this not an answer when purchases are by spouses? Cf. *Daniels v White* (set out at para 17.13).

144 Fleming, *Torts*, 9th edn, Chap 23; Street on *Torts*, 10th edn, 340, *et seq.*; Winfield and Jolowicz, *Tort*, 16th edn, Chap 10; Clark, *Product Liability*, 1–8.

145 See the judgment of Scott LJ in *Read v Lyons Ltd* [1945] 1 KB 216, CA, decision affd [1947] AC 156, HL.

146 For breach of safety regulations, see para 4.33. As to actions for breach of statutory duty, see generally, para 3.21.

147 Now termed 'wrongful interference with goods': Torts (Interference with Goods) Act 1977, s 1(b) (see para 19.04).

148 For negligent loss of credit cards, see para 7.13.

149 [1938] 4 All ER 258. See also Street, *Op. cit.*, 346, fn 14.

The male plaintiff sued the retailer in contract and his wife sued the manufacturer in tort when they both suffered injury by reason of the fact that the sealed bottle of lemonade sold to them included a large element of carbolic acid.

Notwithstanding that it seemed extremely likely that the acid was introduced into the bottle whilst at the manufacturer's plant, Lewis J held that the manufacturer was not liable in negligence on the grounds that his process was foolproof, but that the innocent retailer was liable for breach of the undertaking as to merchantability (see para 14.18). Indeed, it was only with the decision of the House of Lords in *Donoghue v Stevenson*,[150] to the effect that a manufacturer owed a duty of care to the ultimate consumer, that it became clear that participation in the chain of distribution might involve a general liability in the tort of negligence and now also termed 'wrongful interference with goods'.[151] Even granted a duty of care owed to the consumer, the duty owed by each above business party in the chain of distribution to every subsequent party in the chain is merely to exercise reasonable care so as not to cause damage:[152] this could be to get it right in the first place, ie the design or manufacturing defects; or to recall the product when a defect is subsequently discovered (see para 17.02). Moreover, a defendant may be exonerated from liability, or that liability reduced, where the plaintiff himself knows of the danger and disregards it; or where the defect is due to wear and tear, inadequate maintenance, repair or warning;[153] or the plaintiff uses the goods for a purpose which is materially different from that for which it is designed, although it may be doubted whether this is so as regards a very young child who drinks furniture polish or sniffs solvent.[154] Negligence liability clearly comprehends physical damage done by the defective product, particularly personal injury. However, where the goods are shoddy or the defect discovered, the loss is then purely economic and the courts are reluctant to impose liability in the tort of negligence to do the work of a warranty of quality (see paras 11.03, *et seq.*), as it would amount to a transmissible warranty of quality.[155]

Nowadays, this sharp dichotomy between strict and negligence liability is only likely to obtain as regards **safe** but shoddy goods: this is because contract liability for shoddy goods is strict (see para 14.08), whereas tort liability usually depends on proof of negligence (see above). As regards **unsafe** goods, the position is otherwise: whilst contract liability continues to be strict, outside the contractual nexus there is frequently a sort of strict civil liability under the CPA (see para 17.21, *et seq.*); and there may also be strict criminal liability under the GPS Regulations (see para 4.32, *et seq.*).

**[17.15/6] Common law liability for acts and omissions: (2).** Frequently, the most vital matter in a product liability claim is proof of causation, a matter which

---

150 [1932] AC 562, [1932] All ER Rep 1, HL (see Rodger (1992) 108 LQR 236).

151 Torts (Interference with Goods) Act 1977, s 1(c): see para 19.04.

152 *The Aswan Engineering* case (set out at para 14.14); the *Bacardi* case (see at para 11.08). Compare the strict liability in contract (see para 17.13) and under statutory product liability (see para 17.24).

153 For warnings, see paras 18.04; 18.29. What of the dilemma that such a warning may suggest a new form of misuse to some, e.g. glue or aerosol spray sniffing?

154 *Evans v Souls Garages Ltd* [2001] 2 CL 458; *Times* 23.1 (petrol to a 13-yr-old).

155 *Per* Lord Keith in *Murphy v Brentwood DC* [1990] 2 All ER 908 at 921b, HL (not a goods case). E.g. *Lambert v Lewis* (set out at para 17.06; third-party proceedings); *Hamble Fisheries Ltd v L Gardner & Sons Ltd* [1999] CLY 3960, CA.

becomes more difficult to prove as more links exist in the chain of distribution between plaintiff and defendant.[156] *Prima facie*, it would seem that that burden is placed upon the party who affirmed, rather than the one who denied.[157] Whilst the burden of proving liability on the balance of probabilities is then a formidable task,[158] it is not impossible.[159] In *Carroll v Fearon*:[160]

> In 1988, there was a fatal collision between two cars, seemingly caused by a sudden and complete tread strip of a rear tyre of one of them. The tyre was manufactured in 1981 by Dunlop; and it was proved that Dunlop's manufacturing process had been defective as the radial tyre contained inadequate rubber penetration of the cords. The judge decided that Dunlop had been negligent, but apportioned 20% of the blame to the driver/owner. On appeal, Dunlop argued that no particular act of negligence by itself had been established.

Nevertheless, the Court of Appeal unanimously held Dunlop wholly liable at common law,[161] saying that the particular individual responsible for the manufacturing defect need not be identified, nor need the particular act of negligence be specified.[162] Judge LJ pointed out that the tyre had burst many years after it had left the factory and had been regularly used, so that its failure might have resulted from any one of a number of possible causes. Ignoring speculative considerations, e.g. that the driver was negligent, and focusing on the evidence, the judge was entitled to decide on the balance of probabilities that negligence had been established against Dunlop;[163] and there was no evidence upon which the drivers could have been held partly to blame.

However, it is in the nature of this type of situation that the defect may be caused by the default of any one of a number of people in the chain of distribution, so that it is very difficult to prove that only one person was at fault. As it will normally be impossible to say whose fault caused the defect, he who bears the burden of proof will normally lose.[164] On the other hand, it is sometimes possible to escape this dilemma by apportioning loss,[165] or because the evidence clearly establishes the innocence of all but one of the parties in the chain of distribution.[159] These proof problems will also arise with statutory product liability (see para 17.24).

**[17.17] Common law liability for statements**. Irrespective of any contractual nexus, there are a number of torts giving a partial, sometimes overlapping,

---

156 See Macleod, *Consumer Sales Law*, 1st edn, para 17.15; and generally Street on *Torts*, 10th edn, 343–4; Mildred, *Product Liability: Law and Insurance*, 128, *et seq.*

157 *BHP Billiton Petroleum Ltd v Delmine SPA* [2003] CLY 4354 (fraud).

158 See *Daniels and Daniels v White & Sons Ltd* (set out at para 17.13); and Street on *Torts*, 10th edn, 345–7.

159 See *res ipsa loquitur* and McInnes (1998) 114 LQR 547; Witting (2001) 117 LQR 392.

160 [1998] CLY 3995; [1998] PIQR P416, CA; discussed by Slapper (1998) 148 NLJ 345.

161 The CPA, Pt I (see para 17.24, *et seq.*) did not apply to goods manufactured in 1981.

162 Relying on a dictum by Lord Wright in *Grant v Australian Knitting Mills Ltd* [1936] AC 85 at 101.

163 In part, this was because, knowing of the manufacturing defect, Dunlop had decided not to institute a recall 'for commercial reasons'.

164 Normally the plaintiff: *Ng Chun Pui v Lee Chuen Tat* [1988] CLY 1582, PC.

165 Civil Liability (Contribution) Act 1978, s 1(1) (see generally, para 12.10); Law Reform (Contributory Negligence) Act 1945 (see para 27.39).

protection against loss arising by reason of the untrue statement of another. *First*, the law of torts offers some protection in respect of injury to the person or goods by way of defamation, injurious falsehood and passing off. *Second*, statements calculated to cause injury to the person may be actionable: for instance, there may be liability for inducing breach of contract. *Third*, where reliance on a statement causes injury, it may be possible to bring an action in deceit or negligence (see below).

Each tort is subject to its own rules and limited in its scope; and for the details reference must be made to the standard works on tort. However, some comments about the third category may be apposite here in relation to both the torts of deceit (see para 17.18) and negligent misstatement (see para 17.19), though attempts at exclusion will be left until later (see paras 18.17).

**[17.18] Deceit**. Where the defendant knowingly[166] or recklessly makes a false statement with the intention that the plaintiff should act on it,[167] then the plaintiff may at common law recover in respect of any loss caused by his reliance on it,[168] irrespective of whether or not the statement was made directly to him.[169] The independent tort of deceit is a relatively modern one, but its basis may be traced back to the writ of deceit in the thirteenth century.[170] This writ was the origin of two separate lines of development: the modern tort of deceit itself;[171] and, quite separately, the old writ, which had been used to give a remedy for breach of warranty, was absorbed into the action of *assumpsit*, as may be seen from the modern definition of a warranty (see para 11.03). With the passage of time, the two developments became quite distinct: so that liability for breach of warranty became strict, subject only to the privity rule (see para 17.04); but liability in deceit required proof of a fraudulent intent,[172] but no privity of contract between representor and representee, so that a deceitful company director might be personally liable to a person contracting with his company.[173]

Where there is no contractual liability and fraud cannot be proved, there may be a remedy in the tort of negligent misstatement (see para 17.19). However, where fraud can be shown, by suing instead under s 2(1) of the 1967 Act (see para 17.10) the plaintiff can not only reduce the burden of proof[174] whilst recovering the same measure of damages as for fraud, but also leave open the possibility of summary

---

166 What if the representation is made innocently, but its falsity is later discovered? See Fleming, *Torts*, 9th edn, 696. Cf. *Wings Ltd v Ellis* (set out at para 4.17).

167 *Goose v Wilson Sandford & Co (No. 2)* [2001] CLY 5356, CA.

168 To stop litigants avoiding the Statute of Frauds (see para 25.06) by suing in deceit, it was enacted that only written false statements as to creditworthiness were actionable: Statute of Frauds Amendment Act 1828, s 6. This provision does not apply to actions for negligent misstatement (see para 17.19): *Anderson v Rhodes* [1967] 2 All ER 850.

169 *Derry v Peek* (1889) 14 App Cas 337, HL; *GE Commercial Finance Ltd v Gee* [2006] 1 Lloyd's Rep 337, esp. paras 96–114. Cf. CCA, s 46: see para 8.27. For damages, see *Archer v Brown* [1985] QB 401; and *Gee* (above), paras 329–370.

170 For the effect of this on product liability generally, see para 17.04.

171 See *Pasley v Freeman* (1789) 3 Term Rep 51.

172 *Hornal v Neuberger Products* [1957] 1 QB 247, CA. For the measure of damages, see para 27.24.

173 *Thomas Saunders Partnership v Harvey* (1990) 9 Tr LR 78, DC. This avoids the *Saloman* rule (see para 19.25).

174 *Garden Neptune Shipping v Occidental etc Corpn* [1990] 1 Lloyd's Rep 330, CA (see 107 LQR 31).

judgment.[175] Nevertheless, it seems likely there remain a number of distinct benefits for a victim of fraud in pleading a claim in deceit, such as that no defence of contributory negligence (see para 27.39) is available,[176] whilst a claim may lie for a contribution.[177]

**[17.19/20] Negligent misstatement**. In 1963, the House of Lords for the first time accepted in principle that there might be liability for negligent misstatements which caused purely financial loss,[178] though their Lordships were there impressed by the need to confine liability for negligent misstatements within fairly narrow limits and said that normally the only duty should be to give an honest answer.[179] Within our field the courts have since accepted liability of negligent misstatement in all the following cases: as to creditworthiness;[180] or as seller's agent (see para 10.11) or buyer's agent;[181] or sometimes where the parties were in the process of contract negotiation;[182] or by piercing the corporate veil (see para 19.25); or the giving of a mortgage valuation or loan advice;[183] or where a local authority erroneously stipulated that expenditure must be incurred under the Food Safety Act 1990;[184] or where the originator fails to implement a direct debit mandate.[185] On the other hand, the courts have held a manufacturer was not liable for negligent misstatement contained in his sales literature to a retailer because there was no special relationship between them;[186] nor a finance company in respect of erroneous statements issued by HPI.[187]

Insofar as it results in damage to goods, under the Torts (Interference with Goods) Act 1977, this must now be termed 'wrongful interference with goods' (s 1(c): see para 19.04). It has since been held that the mere fact that there was a contract between the parties under which there was an implied term to exercise due care did not preclude the existence of a tortious duty of care between the same parties;[188] and that the tort liability was not necessarily co-extensive with the

---

175  *Newton Chemical v Arsenis* [1989] 1 WLR 1297, CA (for summary judgment, see para 27.03). See Hooley (1992) 142 NLJ 60.

176  *Standard Chartered Bank v Pakistan National Shipping Corpn (No. 2)* [2003] 1 AC 959, HL.

177  *AIC Ltd v ITS Testing Services (UK) Ltd* [2006] 1 Lloyd's Rep 1 (compliance certificate).

178  *Hedley Byrne & Co Ltd v Heller & Partners Ltd* [1964] AC 465, [1963] 2 All ER 575, HL (not a goods case; liability disclaimed). See further Street on *Torts*, 10th edn, 215, *et seq*.

179  *Per* Lords Reid, Morris, Hodson, and Devlin, at 483, 504, 513 and 514. But see *Intervention Board for Agricultural Products v Leidig* [2000] Lloyd's Rep PN 144, CA.

180  *Anderson Ltd v Rhodes Ltd* [1967] 2 All ER 850. Why did the plaintiff not plead a collateral contract?

181  *Chaudhry v Prabhakar* [1988] 3 All ER 718, CA. *Contra Gran Gelato Ltd v Richcliff (Group) Ltd* [1992] 1 All ER 865 (criticised 109 LQR 539).

182  *Esso Petroleum Co Ltd v Marden* [1976] QB 801, CA; *Howard Marine & Dredging Co Ltd v A Ogden & Sons (Excavations) Ltd* (set out at para 17.10). As to whether there could be liability in contract on the basis of a contract to negotiate, see para 10.03.

183  *Smith v Bush* [1990] 1 AC 831, HL (see 105 LQR at 511–13; 52 MLR at 845). As to advice to a lender, see Ross (2001) 151 NLJ 960.

184  *Welton v North Cornwall DC* [1997] 1 WLR 570, CA.

185  *Weldon v GRE Linked Life Assurance Ltd* [2000] 2 All ER (Comm) 914 (not a goods case). For direct debits, see para 23.14.

186  *Lambert v Lewis* (set out at para 17.06): this is *a fortiori* from a negligent act: see para 17.13.

187  *Moorgate Mercantile Co Ltd v Twitchings* (set out at para 21.17). In the HL, tort liability was expressly rejected by Lord Fraser (924, 663).

188  *Henderson v Merrett Syndicates Ltd* [1995] 2 AC 145, HL (not a goods case).

contract liability.[189] Where the negligent misrepresentation induces a contract between the parties, it may be more advantageous to the representee to proceed under s 2(1) of the Misrepresentation Act 1967, rather than at common law for negligent misstatement, because of the reversal of the burden of proof (see para 17.10). In any event, the representor is only liable for loss caused by the misrepresentation (see para 27.29).

## Statutory product liability[190]

**[17.21/2] Introduction**. The sharp distinction between contract and tort is clearly logical once it is settled that a contract requires consideration; and it may not have mattered so much when the chain of distribution was short. However, with the modern application of the techniques of mass production to an increasingly sophisticated range of products and greatly increased chains of distribution (see para 17.01), problems were bound to occur: they appeared to indicate the need for stricter product liability which reached beyond the doctrine of privity of contract.[191] Analytically, this might appear achievable in either of the following ways:

(1)  By extending the ambit of the privity doctrine (see para 17.08, *et seq.*).

(2)  By increasing strict liability in tort. Whilst in English common law there have been few extensions of strict tort liability beyond the doctrine of *Rylands v Fletcher*,[192] such a development occurred in the EU, spurred on by the Thalidomide tragedy of the 1960s. Following the tort rather than the contract route, the EU developed a Directive relating to liability for defective products. Eventually, the more important disagreements between Members were solved by making certain provisions optional[193] and the Directive was promulgated in 1985.[194] Its major impact seemed likely to be in relation to unsafe design defects, shifting the focus from (negligence-based) fault to strict liability founded on causation[195] and it may be that the European Court is now interpreting it as a maximum directive.[196]

The foregoing civil product liability regime extends Europe-wide: the Directive should be implemented in all EU countries; and its reach has later been extended

---

189  *Holt v Payne Skillington* [1996] PNLR 179, CA (not a goods case).

190  Clark, *Product Liability*; Stapleton, *Product Liability*; Mildred, *Product Liability: Law and Insurance*, Chaps 2 and 9.

191  Cf. the strict criminal liability introduced to protect the consumer: see the rules of liability in Chap 4 and the defences in Chap 28.

192  (1868) LR 3 HL 330, a doctrine beyond the scope of this work.

193  The areas of disagreement included: (i) the state-of-the-art defence (see para 17.30); (ii) whether the Directive should extend to primary agricultural products (see para 17.26); (iii) whether there should be an overall financial limit in respect of identically defective items (the UK Government decided not to introduce an overall financial limit for damage caused by identical items).

194  85/374. For the text of the Directive see Thomas and Clark, *Encyclopedia of Consumer Law*, para 5-163; Guest and Lloyd, *Encyclopedia of Consumer Credit*, para 9-001. For argument as to the legality of the Directive, see Stapleton, *Op. cit.*, 52, *et seq.*

195  Clark, *Op. cit.*, 215; (1991) 135 Sol J 245.

196  See Hodges (2006) 122 LQR 393–4. For maximum directives, see para 3.10.

to much of the rest of Europe.[197] However, it does not require the manufacturer to take out compulsory product insurance, cf. compulsory road traffic insurance, so it is possible for the manufacturer to avoid such civil liability by going into liquidation (see para 19.21), but not criminal liability for unsafe products (see para 4.32).

**[17.23]  Consumer Protection Act 1987, Part I.**[198] The Directive (see para 17.23) was enacted into English law by Part I of the Consumer Protection Act 1987 (CPA), which for the first time ever provides that:[199]

> 'This part shall have effect for the purpose of making such provision as is necessary in order to comply with the product liability Directive and shall be construed accordingly.'

It has already been seen that in the event of conflict, EU law prevails over national law (see para 1.03A); and this provision is simply explicit Westminster recognition of that fact. It has considerable practical importance: in interpreting Part I of the CPA, one should always cross-check for consistency with the Directive.[200]

Following the Directive, Part I makes it clear that the liability it contains cannot be excluded (s 7: see para 17.30), is additional to any other contract or tort-based product liability[201] and binds the Crown (s 9): this last provision will bring within the scheme medicine supplied under the NHS and may hence sidestep an SGA problem (see para 1.07). In the hope that the disagreements which led to the optional provisions will be resolved with the passage of time, s 8 provides that the whole scheme may be modified at a later date by the authorities.[202] On the other hand, Part I introduced a special limitation period[203] to deal with difficulties caused by the number of hands through which a product is likely to pass and the length of time it may retain the capacity to damage:[204] the rules contain an ordinary limitation period of three years,[205] with a long-stop of ten years.[206]

---

197 By Treaty: see the European Economic Area Act 1993. For a general discussion of Europe-wide product liability claims, see Cromie (1992) 142 NLJ 14 and 1423.

198 See generally Street on *Torts*, 10th edn, 348, *et seq.*; Clark, *Product Liability*; *Clerk and Lindsell on Tort*, 18th edn, para 9.37, *et seq.*; Stoppa (1992) 12 Legal Studies at 225; Howells (1990) 51 NILQ 22; Stapleton, *Product Liability*; Mildred, *Product Liability: Law and Insurance*, Chap 2.

199 S 1(1). Suppose a Pt 1 provision is clear but flatly contradicts the Directive: as to whether an individual disadvantaged by that contradiction could sue in the European Court, see para 1.03A; and for an attempt to avoid such a contradictory construction, see ECA, s 3(1) and *Von Colson* [1984] ECR 1891.

200 *A v National Blood Authority* (set out at para 17.28); and Mildred, *Op. cit.*, para 2.5.

201 S 2(6). *Contra* breaches of statutory duty (s 41(2)): see para 10.19.

202 The operation of the Directive is being monitored by the EU Commission.

203 S 6(6) and Sched 1, Pt 1, introducing a new s 11A to the Limitation Act 1980. See *Horne-Roberts v Smithkline Beecham plc* [2002] 1 WLR 1662, CA; and Street, *Op. cit.*, 356; McGee, *Limitation Periods*, Chap 7; Clerk and Lindsell, *Op. cit.*, paras 12–25 and 12–26. For the ordinary limitation periods, see para 26.17.

204 In respect of property damage, time begins to run when such loss 'occurred', which is defined as 'the earliest time at which a person with an interest in the property had knowledge of the material defect' (s 5(5)); and see further s 5(6) and (7).

205 Sched I, para 4. Pt 4 stipulates a normal limitation period of three years from whenever is the later: (a) the date on which the cause of action accrued; and (b) the date of knowledge of the defect.

206 Sched I, para 3. See *O'Byrne v Sanofi Pasteur MSD Ltd* [2006] Case C-127/04, ECJ (French 'producer'; UK distributor; discussed 156 NLJ 538; Hodges (2006) 122 LQR 394–8); and see further, para 17.26.

Across the EU, decided cases under the Directive have been rare.[207] Despite the possibility of class actions here,[208] many UK actions under Part 1 of the CPA have not proceeded to judgment, some because of settlement and others when claimants lost their legal aid certificates (see para 3.17).[207] On the other hand, the availability of conditional fees (see para 3.18) might encourage such actions.

**[17.24] The ambit of Part 1**. The key lies in s 2(1) of the CPA, which provides that:

'Subject to the following provisions of this Part, where any damage is caused wholly or partly by a defect in a product, every person to whom subsection (2) below applies shall be liable for the damage.'

The effect is that, even in the absence of fault, s 2(1) casts a new civil[209] liability:

(1)  in respect of any **'product'** (see para 17.25)

(2)  on the **'producer'** (see para 17.26) or other party in the supply chain (see para 17.27)

(3)  as regards any **defect** (see para 17.28) in that product which

(4)  the complainant must prove **causes** (see below) within the special limitation period (see para 17.23)

(5)  **damage** (see para 17.29).

To mount such an action, the person injured[210] must prove all the matters listed above,[211] upon which the defendant becomes strictly liable, unless he proves one of the defences.[212]

*Causation*. This is perhaps the single most important practical issue facing a claimant alleging product liability, especially in the field of allegedly defective drugs and drug abuse. It requires the claimant[213] to prove on the civil burden of proof (the balance of probabilities) that the product for which the defendant producer was responsible 'wholly or partly' **caused** the claimant's non-remote (see below) damage.[214] Even where the damage was caused wholly by the defendant, this link of causation may be a very difficult thing to prove and involves a two-part

---

207  Deards and Twigg-Flesner (2001) 10 Nottingham LJ 1–3.

208  E.g. *A v National Blood Authority* (above). For class actions, see generally, para 3.18.

209  Contrast Pts II and III of the CPA which primarily impose strict criminal liability: see paras 4.32, 8.09A–10A.

210  The claimant does not need to be a consumer in the restricted sense employed by the SSG Regs (see para 1.02), CCA (see para 5.24), or UTCC Regs (see para 11.12A), or at all; he may be a mere bystander injured by the defective product.

211  On the balance of probabilities. Contrast the criminal burden (beyond all reasonable doubt) applicable to Pts II and III of the CPA. As to the civil burden, see the following note.

212  S 4: see para 17.30. Cf. the standard-form criminal defences (see para 28.13). Insofar as any of the defences only require the defendant to be careful, the effect of Pt I is to shift the burden of proof, so that the defendant must prove that he took care: see Giliker [2003] 4 BLR 87.

213  A group or class action is possible: see *A v National Blood Authority* (set out at para 17.28); and generally, para 3.18.

214  S 2(1). Presumably the ordinary rules of causation apply? As to which, see Clark, *Op. cit.*, 194–6; Street on *Torts*, 10th edn, 355; Giliker [2003] 4 BLR 87 at 89–90; and para 27.29.

test:[215] first, was the damage caused by the product;[216] and second, would the damage have happened in any event?[217] But, where the damage is caused partly by a defect in the product and partly by the fault of the person suffering the damage, the rules dealing with contributory negligence 'shall have effect as if the defect were the fault of every person liable by virtue of this Part', a rule which may cause some difficulty in practice.[218] However, the burden of proof is reversed for the defences (s 4: see para 17.30). It is for consideration as to the extent to which the rules of remoteness (see para 27.41) apply to this statutory tort.[219] As to joint liability, see para 17.26.

**[17.25] A product**. Under Pt I of the CPA (see para 17.24), a producer (see para 17.26) is only liable in respect of a 'product', which last expression means (s 1(2)):

> 'any goods or electricity and (subject to subsection (3) . . .) includes a product which is comprised in another product, whether by virtue of being a component part or raw material or otherwise.'

The definition of 'product' thus embraces,[220] but is wider than, the notion of goods within the SGA (see para 2.02): electricity and components (see s 1(3): para 17.26) are specifically mentioned in s 1(2); the expression 'goods' is defined in s 45(1)[221] to include 'substances'; and 'substance' is itself defined in s 45(1) to include water and 'gas'.[222] The overall effect is to extend the scope of 'products' beyond what might be described as consumer goods, e.g. asbestos, train door locks.[223] However, it does not extend to those producing services,[224] e.g. advice,[225] as opposed to supplying services produced by another,[226] or where the service includes the provision of a defective spare part, e.g. a plumber replacing a tap; but the position of information products, e.g. a recipe book, software, is unclear.[227] The Act makes two special cases, one an extension, the other a restriction.

---

215 Mildred, *Product Liability: Law and Insurance*, para 1.91; and see also para 1.185, *et seq*. See generally, para 27.29.

216 *F v Bosil* [2001] CLY 918 (see (2000) 150 NLJ 1780).

217 *Richardson v LRC Products Ltd* [2000] CLY 851; [2000] PIQR P164 (condom burst in use: Deards and Twigg-Flesner (2001) 10 Nottingham LJ 1 at 8–10). For oral contraceptive litigation, see (2002) 152 NLJ 1393.

218 S 6(4) and (5), e.g. the goods-owner who carelessly fails to submit goods to a manufacturer's recall. See Street, *Op. cit.*, 354. As to contributory negligence, see generally, para 27.40.

219 See Bell (1991) 20 Anglo-Am LR 371 at 380–1.

220 For an unconvincing attempt to argue that some 'goods' are not 'products', see Stapleton, *Product Liability* 309.

221 ' "Goods" includes substances, growing crops and things comprised in land by virtue of being attached to it and any ship, aircraft or vehicle'. 'Ships', 'aircraft' and 'motor vehicles' are themselves defined by s 45(1).

222 'Gas' is itself defined by s 45(1). As to electricity, gas and water, see para 3.07. As to environmental products, e.g. chemical waste, see Mildred, *Product Liability: Law and Insurance*, para 2.19.

223 This wide definition will help extend the ambit of Pt I to some major disasters: Clark, *Product Liability*, 52. Human blood and organs may be products: in *A v National Blood Authority* (set out at para 17.28) the point was conceded (at 307a).

224 They remain liable to the ordinary negligence rules (see para 17.12, *et seq.*) *Contra* supplies of goods and services, which are both subject to strict liability under the SGA and SGSA.

225 Clerk and Lindsell, *Torts*, 18th edn, para 9-41.

226 Clark, *Op. cit.*, 64.

227 As to intellectual products, e.g. books, see Whittaker (1989) 105 LQR 125. As to misstatements in books, see Clark, *Product Liability*, 53. As to software, see (1989) 5 Comp. L & P 154; (1990), 6 Comp L & P 2.

*Buildings.* Whilst the CPA does not extend to a defective building itself,[228] Pt I does apply to building materials incorporated into land owned by another. However, it does not apply to defective goods incorporated by their installer into his own land (s 46(4)) which he then sells: this would be the position with regard to a 'spec'. builder erecting a building on his own land (*contra* on a developer's land), or a DIY householder. However, as regards land not owned by the installer, s 46(3) provides that:

> 'the performance of any contract by the erection of any building or structure on any land or by the carrying out of any other building work shall be treated for the purposes of this Act as a supply insofar as, but only insofar as, it involves the provision of any goods to any person by means of their incorporation into the building, structure or works'.

Thus, whilst the SGA applies only to property severed from land under the sale (see para 9.03), Pt I of the CPA extends not just to fixtures, e.g. child's swing or roundabout (for fixtures, see generally, para 25.23), but also to materials incorporated in a building,[229] whether initially[230] or subsequently. So, in relation to later-fitted double glazing, the injured house occupier can proceed under Pt I against only the producer of the units or perhaps the installer.

*Agriculture.* In sharp contrast, Pt I of the CPA was particularly restrictive over agriculture: following the 1985 Directive, it exempted 'game or agricultural produce' (s 2(4)). However, a 1999 amendment to the Directive repealed this exemption and both s 2(4) and the definition of 'agricultural produce' have been duly repealed.[231]

**[17.26] A producer.** The basic liability under s 2(1) is laid upon 'the producer of the product' (s 2(1)(a)). 'Producer' is widely defined by s 1(2) to include the following categories of persons involved in the production and marketing of goods:

(a) *'The person who manufactured it'.* Leaving aside imports and own-brands (s 2: see para 17.27), this establishes the primary liability on the manufacturer of the defective product (Z),[232] which expression may include a wholly-owned sales subsidiary.[233] Perhaps the most difficult issue concerns bought-in components. Suppose the retail purchase from B by C as a gift for D of a new car with a defective tyre which injures D, that tyre having been supplied to the car

---

228 For an explanation of why builders and building owners remain free of liability, see Stapleton, *Op. cit.*, 305–9.

229 Does s 46(3) extend Pt I liability to a builder erecting a 'building, structure or works' on his customer's green-field site? Or does s 46(3) imply that there must already be a 'building structure or works' on the site to which the complained of item is added? The Directive was intended to apply only to movables; and the building is already within the Defective Premises Act 1972. See further the *Current Law* annotation to 'product' in s 1(2).

230 Pt I thus applies to the sub-contractor's installation in a new building being erected on the consumer's land, e.g. wiring, plumbing, tiling. Such materials will also be covered by the SGA and SGSA.

231 Directive 1999/34; enacted in the UK by 2000 SI 2771.

232 E.g. the manufacturer of proprietary medicines, motor vehicles, machinery. But not a mere designer, researcher, tester or repairer: see Mildred, *Product Liability: Law and Insurance*, para 2.42.

233 See *O'Byrne v Sanofi Pasteur MSD Ltd* [2006] Case C-127/04, ECJ (French 'producer'; UK wholly-owned subsidiary distributor; the discussion by Hodges (2006) 122 LQR 394–6; and see further, para 17.23).

manufacturer (Z) by a component-supplier (X). Section 1(2) assumes that both the manufactured goods, e.g. car, and its bought-in components, e.g. tyres, are 'products' (see para 17.25). This will assist D in those circumstances where it may be more convenient to sue Z and X because he cannot identify whether the fault lies in the car or tyre.[234] If, on the other hand, it is clear that the tyre is at fault, the effect of s 1(3) is that Z is not the 'supplier' of the tyre he fitted on the car: so that as against the injured claimant, Z cannot off-load the liability under s 2(3) to X (see above); and Z is also liable under s 2 as 'producer'. For joint liability, see below.

(b) *Unmanufactured, unprocessed goods.* According to s 1(2)(b), 'producer' means:

> 'in the case of a substance which has not been manufactured but has been won or abstracted, the person who won or abstracted it'.

'Won' perhaps includes gold panned, rubber tapped, root crops harvested and salt mined; and 'abstracted' obviously refers to raw materials which are the products of mines or quarries, e.g. diamonds mined, slate quarried. This s 1(2)(b) category now extends to agricultural produce (see para 17.25).

(c) *Unmanufactured, processed goods.* In a cumbersome provision designed to mesh with the now-repealed exemption of primary agricultural products (see above), s 1(2)(c) lays down that:

> 'in the case of a product which has not been manufactured, won or abstracted but essential characteristics of which are attributable to an industrial or other process having been carried out (for example, in relation to agricultural produce), the person who carried out that process.'

Whilst 'essential characteristics' are not defined, the sense would appear to embrace goods whose characteristics are changed by an industrial or other process,[235] e.g. canning, freezing, crushing, filleting:[236] in which case, s 1(2)(c) covers both the processor of agricultural produce[237] and the industrialist subjecting any other goods to a non-manufacturing industrial process.[238] The effect of s 1(2)(c) seems to be to make the 'producer' liable even if the defect is traceable back to the farm. Whilst already within the Food Safety Act (see para 4.27-8), there would appear to be some doubt as to the position under the CPA of processed foodstuffs. What of cooked foods, e.g. cooked ham, pork pie, pickled onions?

Joint liability. Whilst the usual scheme of the CPA is to enable liability to D to be passed back up the chain to a single manufacturer (s 2(3): see above), in the case of

---

234 It shifts the evidential burden of proof off D's shoulders: see Stapleton, *Product Liability* (1994) 294. However, if the car is damaged, by suing X alone, D may be able to recover that property damage under s 5(2) (see para 17.29): Mildred, *Op. cit.*, para 2.11.

235 The Directive refers to 'initial process': insofar as they may differ from the CPA, see Clerk and Lindsell, *Torts*, 18th edn, para 9-43, fn 90.

236 *Contra* harvesting, picking, grading, slaughtering, packaging. What of mixing produce, e.g. muesli, or processes which do not change the characteristics of a product, e.g. bottled herbal medicines, sawn timber? See the criticism by Merkin, *Guide to the CPA*, para 2.2.3.

237 ' "Agricultural produce" means any produce of the soil, of stock farming or of fisheries' (s 1(2)). E.g. tinned or frozen foods, milled flour, granulated sugar. What about muesli? For criticism of the phrase, see Tiplady (1988) 132 Sol Jo 430 at 434.

238 E.g. smelted ore, refined oil. *Contra* Merkin, *Op. cit.*, para 2.2.1.2. Does the phrase extend to bulking of agriculture produce from several farms?

components the effect of the Act is that there may be more than one 'producer' liable under s 2 (see above): the justification for this has been said to be to give the injured claimant a solvent defendant.[239] Where this results in two or more persons being liable under s 2, the Act provides that they shall be jointly and severally liable. This will be likely to increase the cost of insurance and litigation.[240] However, the Act is silent as to how that liability is to be shared between the defendants.[241] As between X and Z, if the root cause of the problem is a defective component, Z will on ordinary principles be able to sue X under his supply contract (see para 17.07); whereas, wrongful design by Z will give X a CPA defence,[242] leaving Z to carry the CPA liability to D.

**[17.27] The supply chain.** Under s 2, the primary liability for breach of s 2(2) (see para 17.24) is laid upon the **producer** of the product (s 2(2)(a)), that is, the manufacturer (Z) or component manufacturer (X), which may include a wholly-owned subsidiary (see paras 17.25–6). However, the Act is anxious to ensure that persons injured can easily find a defendant within the jurisdiction and therefore extends the liability to three additional categories of persons (as to joint liability, see para 17.26).

1.  *Own-branders*. According to s 2(2)(b), the **producer's** liability applies to:

    'any person who by putting his name on the product or using a trade mark or other distinguishing mark in relation to the product, has held himself out to be the producer of the product.'

    This rule will cover both own-branders and sub-branders[243] and appears to be grounded in estoppel (cf. para 21.10). The own-brander will typically be the retailer (B): whilst B is already strictly liable in contract to C,[244] except in those cases where it is well known that he does not do his own manufacturing, s 2(2)(b) will make B strictly liable to the donee/consumer (D). What if the goods carry a logo of both a retailer (B) and manufacturer (Z)? Or if B or Z use the logo of manufacturer M under a licensing or franchising agreement (but see s 4(1)(b): para 17.30)? What of 'exclusive' brands?

2.  *Importers*. Section 2(2)(c) also extends **producer's** liability to:

    'any person who has imported the product into a member State from a place outside the member States in order, in the course of any business of his, to supply it to another.'

    It should be noticed that liability is here confined to the first importer[245] into any 'Member State' from outside the EU, so that an injured UK consumer may

---

239  Stapleton, *Product Liability*, 295, *et seq.*

240  S 2(5)). See also the Civil Liability Act 1978, s 1. As contributory negligence, see para 27.39.

241  Clark (1987) 50 MLR at 616. As to concurrent liability, see Merkin, *Op. cit.*, para 2.6. As to piercing the corporate veil, see para 19.25.

242  S 4(1)(f): see para 17.30.

243  Own-branders are retailers who put their own trading name on goods sold; whereas sub-branders use a different label of their own: see [1966] 3 *Which?* 10. For the borderline between manufacturer and own-brander, see Mildred, *Product Liability: Law and Insurance*, paras 2.47–8.

244  See para 17.07. As to chemists, see Merkin, *Guide to the CPA*, para 2.3. For a suggestion that this liability is avoidable by apt packaging, see Howells (1991) 20 Anglo-Am LR 204 at 208.

245  As to whether 'importer' includes both the transport agent and the person who instructs him, see Mildred, *Op. cit.*, paras 2.50–1.

have to sue a foreign EU national (Y) before a UK court and have any favourable judgment enforced in Y's country under the Civil Jurisdiction and Judgments Act 1982.[246] What if the goods carry the name of a Far East manufacturer, but the importer remains anonymous?[247]

3. *Suppliers*.[248] In potentially the most far-reaching extension of **producer's** liability, designed to combat the uncertainties of long distribution chains (see para 17.01), s 2(3) enables the person injured (D) to hold an effective supplier[249] liable where **all** the following conditions are satisfied:

  (a) D requests that supplier to identify any prior supplier in the distribution chain;[250] and

  (b) D's request is made within a reasonable time and whilst it is not reasonably practicable for D to identify **all** such suppliers;[251] and

  (c) The supplier to whom D's request is addressed fails within a reasonable time to identify at least one supplier.[252]

If, in response to a s 2(3) request by D, B identifies A, then D may repeat the procedure to make A identify manufacturer (Z):[253] if B cannot make any such identification, the policy of the Act is to make B liable, even if it is not his fault that he cannot identify his source;[254] but, if that process identifies an insolvent Z, it seems that A and B escape liability under the Act.[251] This whole s 2(3) procedure is a powerful incentive to good record-keeping by all commercial parties in the chain of distribution.

**[17.28] Defect.** Loosely following the Directive (Art 6(1)), Part I of the CPA is confined to **dangerous** goods; but, if the real complaint is of **shoddiness** or **unsuitability** of the goods, the usual remedy will remain an action for breach of contract.[255] Section 3(1) provides that, subject to s 3(2) (see para 17.28A):

---

246 Surprisingly, 'Member State' is not defined, but presumably refers to members of the EU for the time being. What about re-imports into the EU of goods manufactured within it? See the Civil Jurisdiction and Judgments Act 1991, which creates a virtually uniform system of civil jurisdiction and enforcement of judgments throughout Western Europe (EU and EFTA).

247 See Mildred, *Op. cit.*, para 2.58.

248 For 'supply', see s 46(1)(as amended). E.g. dangerous hire tools (see 7 Tr L 227). For this Part of the CPA only, 'supplier' is not confined to a business supplier (s 46(5)).

249 In a directly financed transaction, this will be the dealer rather than the financier (s 46(2)).

250 If D makes the request to B, B could identify Z, A or Y 'whether still in existence or not' (s 2(3)(a)). B could not identify a financier (see above), nor possibly X (see below).

251 Under s 2(3)(b), the reasonable time runs from damage to D, subject to the special limitation period (see para 17.24). As to ambiguities of when damage occurs, see Merkin, *Op. cit.*, para 2.5.2. For criticism of the drafting, see Tiplady (1988) 132 Sol Jo at 432.

252 Under s 2(3)(c). Will this cause difficulty, e.g. for chemists as regards generic drugs? Compare Street on *Torts*, 10th edn, 356 and para 17.16.

253 Bearing in mind s 1(3), can this procedure be used to require Z to identify X? Does s 2(3) apply to own-branders?

254 This is not vicarious liability because B can escape liability by identifying Z, whether or not Z is still in existence (see above). This will be so regardless of whether Z is liable to B, perhaps because there is some exclusion clause in the contract between them. It is thus a sort of secondary liability: Merkin, *Op. cit.*, paras 2.1 and 2.5.4.

255 Clark, *Product Liability*, 28–30. As to express and implied terms, see para 11.07; and as to statutorily implied terms, see Chaps 13–15. What of inherently dangerous goods, e.g. arsenic?

'there is a defect in a product for the purposes of this Part if the safety of the product is not such as persons generally are entitled to expect; and for those purposes 'safety', in relation to a product, shall include safety with respect to products comprised in that product and safety in the context of risks of damage to property, as well as in the context of risks of death or personal injury.'

In such a case, there may also be criminal liability under the GPS Regulations (see paras 4.32–5). Without distinguishing between manufacturing and design defects,[256] s 3(1) insists that, for the purposes of s 2(1) (see para 17.24), the goods contain a 'defect' only if the **safety** of the product, or its components, 'is not such as persons generally are entitled to expect'.[257] This test does not refer to either the particular claimant or particular producer: defectiveness is to be determined, not by fitness for use, but by the lack of safety to which the public at large were entitled to expect.[258] In short, s 3 'implies a standard of reasonable objectivity'.[259] The standard is applicable as regards both personal injury (such as in *Daniels v White*[260]) and limited property damage (see para 17.29); and there is a special defence for Z in respect of defective components (s 4(1)(e)): see para 17.30. In *A v National Blood Authority*:[261]

> The claimants were infected with Hepatitis C virus through blood transfusions with blood which NBA had obtained from infected donors. This risk with 1–3% of bags was known to the medical profession; but the Authority did not at the time have the technology to screen the virus. The risk was unknown to consumers. On a trial of preliminary issues in a class action test case, Burton J held that (a) the blood was defective, (b) the NBA were not protected by the state-of-the-art defence (see para 17.30) and (c) explained what damages were recoverable (see para 17.29).

On the first point and placing heavy reliance on the text of the underlying Directive (see para, 17.23), Burton J held that, whilst the NBA were not liable in negligence because the defect was unavoidable (see para 17.14), the blood used on the claimants was from the 1–3% defective blood-bags, which the judge termed 'non-standard': it would seem that this would approximate to a design defect. The Judge distinguished the standard product (the other 97–99%): these would seem to approximate to manufacturing defects, which Burton J thought should be compared with products from other manufacturers and price (para 71). His Lordship explained that this virus amounted to a 'defect' within s 3 (paras 66 and 79), because the NBA had not taken all steps legitimately expectable by the public to be free from infection as a standard product (para 80). In respect of such non-standard products (with a design defect), Burton J made the following points: the fact that the risk was known to

---

256 In practice, Pt I may operate quite differently in relation to manufacturing and design defects: see the Dobson annotation to s 3 in *Current Law Statutes*; Stoppa (1992) 12 LS 211–18. As to the Design Council, see para 3.08.

257 Does it matter whether 'generally' is read with 'persons' or 'entitled to expect'? Are they entitled to expect more than reasonable care, which would change the law hardly at all for design defects? See generally, Clark (1987) 50 MLR at 617; *Product Liability*, 40–1, 45, 213; Howells (1992) 20 Anglo-Am LR 211–18.

258 *Abouzaid v Mothercare (UK) Ltd* [2001] CLY 920; *Times* 20.2, CA (Cosytoes sleeping bag: see Hodges 151 NLJ 424); *Tesco Stores Ltd v Pollard* [2006] EWCA Civ 393, CA, at paras 17–18.

259 Mildred, *Product Liability Law* (2000) para 2.25. Cf. the general safety requirement: see para 4.32A.

260 Set out at para 17.13. But s 3(1) may rule out those suffering from some specific sensitivity or allergy: Lawson (1991) 141 NLJ 1103.

261 [2001] 3 All ER 289 (see McAdams 151 NLJ 647).

doctors is irrelevant because it was unknown to consumers (paras 56 and 65); this CPA liability should be distinguished from contract liability founded on fitness for use (see para 14.07) because the CPA liability emphasises safety (para 66: see para 14.20); and that the primary issue was 'whether the public at large accepted the non-standard nature of the product' (para 68).[262]

There is no explicit reference in s 3 to the cost of safety measures. In *A v National Blood Authority*, the court ignored the cost of safety measures in what approximated to a design defect; but, as regards general principles, it has been argued that a cost-benefit analysis should not be ignored in relation to manufacturing defects.[263] Additionally, it may be argued that blood-products should be exempt from Part I of the CPA on policy grounds.

**[17.28A] Section 3(2).** This directs that for the purposes of s 3(1) (see above) 'all the circumstances shall be taken into account'. In *A v National Blood Authority* (set out at para 17.28), Burton J explained that 'all circumstances' in s 3(2) meant all *relevant* circumstances (para 57: see below) and did not include the fact that the defect was unavoidable at the relevant time (para 63). Section 3(2) then directs the court to consider a number of non-exclusive factors, but only insofar as relevant:

(1) *Marketing circumstances.* Section 3(2)(a) refers to 'the manner in which, and purposes for which, the product has been marketed' and 'its get-up', e.g. styling. This would cover advertising and distribution, e.g. in a manner likely to attract children, drugs on prescription only. The reference to 'purposes' would appear to allow a cost-benefit analysis (see para 17.02), so that harmful side-effects may be tolerated in a life-saving medicine but not in something marketed exclusively for pleasure.[264]

(2) *Marks.* The reference in s 3(2)(a) to 'the use of any mark in relation to the product' would give a civil remedy for an improperly used mark,[265] whereas mere compliance with the mark would not of itself be a defence under this Act, though it may avert the commission of a safety offence (see paras 4.33–5).

(3) *Instructions.* The provision also refers to 'any instructions for, or warnings with respect to, doing or refraining from doing anything with or in relation to the product' (s 3(2)(a)). This will allow any such instructions (see generally, para 18.28, *et seq.*) to be taken into account in the absence of privity.[266] They are already relevant in discharging the common law duty of care (see para 17.14). Can Z rely on instructions being given by B? Can an adequate instruction ignored break the chain of causation or amount to contributory negligence?[267]

---

262 Following Burton J, in *B (A Child) v McDonald's Restaurants Ltd* [2002] EWHC 490, Field J held that, in applying s 3, the court, 'acting as an informed representative of the public, must objectively assess the legitimate expectations of persons generally' (at para 73).

263 See Giliker [2003] 4 BLR 87 at 89; and see s 3(2)(a): para 17.28A.

264 Cf. *Watson v Buckley Ltd* [1940] 1 All ER 174. What of contraceptives; or cigarettes; or alcoholic drinks? See Street on *Torts*, 10th edn, 352.

265 S 3(2)(a). E.g. *Richardson v LRC Products Ltd* [2000] CLY 851; [2000] PIQR P164 (BSI Mark: see para 3.08).

266 *Worsley v Tambrands Ltd* [2000] CLY 548; [2000] PIQR P95, CA (no liability because of sufficient warning).

267 See para 17.29. See generally Clark (1987) 50 MLR at 618; Merkin, *Guide to the CPA*, para 4.2.2.1; Clark, *Product Liability*, 98–100.

It is to be hoped that extra warnings will not be used as a substitute for producing safer goods.

(4) *Use.* Section 3(2)(b) directs attention to 'what might reasonably be expected to be done with or in relation to the product'. Whilst the test may have been intended to refer to reasonable use it would in fact appear to deal with reasonable expectation (even of unreasonable?) use, e.g. glue sniffing. Is the expectation that of a supplier or consumer?[268] The subsection may involve a risk/benefit analysis (see para 17.02) and may also link up marketing circumstances and instructions for use; but it could cause difficulty where adequate instructions are forseeably ignored, e.g. a toddler suffocated by instant glue or a polythene bag, or a bad car driver.[269]

(5) *Time of supply.* Section 3(2)(c) makes it clear that this test is to be applied at 'the time when the product is supplied by its producer' (see below), which for goods with a long shelf-life may be some time before they are supplied to the consumer.[270] Without such a rule, producers might be liable for fair wear and tear; and they could also be discouraged from making safety improvements in the light of experience or increased knowledge; and Parliament did not want a hind-sight test to discourage recalls or redesigns by manufacturers of unsafe goods, e.g. vehicles. Further, s 3(2)(c) goes on explicitly to refute the inference of defect from the fact that at a later date safer goods are supplied, e.g. new car supplied without seat belts before their fitting became compulsory. See also the state-of-the-art defence (para 17.30). What of a later supply of an earlier unsafe version?

**[17.29] Damage.** One of the constituent requirements of s 2 is that, in respect of any 'defect' which comes to light,[271] a party shall suffer 'damage' (see para 17.24). So 'damage' is an essential part of a cause of action under Pt I of the CPA, just as in the tort of negligence (see para 17.13). 'Damage' is defined by s 5(1) to mean 'death or personal injury or any loss of or damage[272] to any property (including land[273])'. In *A v National Blood Authority* (set out at para 17.28), Burton J rejected the NBA's attempt to assess damages on the basis of a breach of duty and said that 'the damage to be compensated to the claimant is the damage caused by the defect in a product' (para 178). His Lordship went on to discuss the available heads of damage in detail, a matter far too detailed for this work (at paras 211, 214–16, 219–25 and 226–31).

Whilst consequential financial loss is not here mentioned, it is submitted that it is recoverable as follows. *First*, as regards death or personal injury,[274] it will be recoverable as usual: claims for loss of earnings will frequently be a large part of

---

268  See Clark, *Op. cit.*, 93; Clerk and Lindsell, *Torts*, 18th edn, para 9.48.

269  As to where there are component manufacturers, see Clerk and Lindsell, *Ibid*.

270  As to the burden of proof, see s 4(1)(d) (see para 17.30). Safety improvements on later models are expressly disregarded (see below).

271  S 5(5)–(7). So a buyer of already-damaged goods is not covered: Tiplady (1988) 132 Sol Jo at 480.

272  The special rules for nuclear accidents are preserved (s 6(8)). But does this preclude action under the CPA in respect of irradiated food?

273  Because 'property' includes land, liability would extend to soil damaged by a defective weed-killer: Clark, *Product Liability*, 127.

274  'Personal injury' is defined by s 45(1). Does it extend to a temporary rash? As to congenital disabilities, see s 6(3). What about fear of contracting asbestosis?

any personal injuries claim;[275] and the Act expressly preserves such claims after death (s 6(1)–(5)). *Second*, whilst pure financial loss is probably not recoverable,[276] claims for consequential loss damage to property are allowed,[277] subject to the rules considered below. However, the foregoing definition of 'damage' is expressly made subject to all the following limitations:

(a) *The product itself*. If the product goes into self-destruct, s 5(2) provides that there will be no s 2 liability 'for the loss of or any damage to the product itself or for the loss of or any damage to the whole or any part of any product which has been supplied with the product in question comprised in it', e.g. packaging. Thus, if a new car contains a defective electrical component which causes the car to catch fire, the position is as follows:[278] the burnt driver (D) can under s 2 sue the manufacturer and component manufacturer (Z, X) in respect of burns to his person or clothing caused even before he had the opportunity to use the car; but Z and X will not be liable under s 2 in respect of damage to the car or defective component.[279] What about optional extras fitted to a car, e.g. an expensive stereo?[280]

(b) *Private property only*. The CPA intends to exclude business property. Thus, under s 5(3) there will be no liability in the above example for property loss unless **both** the following conditions are fulfilled: (i) the property is of description ordinarily intended for private use, occupation or consumption,[281] e.g. D's clothing, unless equipment supplied by D's employer, e.g. a commercial traveller's samples, stock, or uniform; **and** (ii) mainly so intended by the person suffering the loss, e.g. D's cigarettes, even though he occasionally offers one to a customer. *Contra* D's tools, where he is a self-employed plumber.

(c) *Trivial property damage*. Under s 5(4), no damages shall be awarded in respect of property damage where the total capital loss does not exceed £275;[282] but, if the total property loss does exceed £275, then that first £275 worth is also recoverable. So, if D in the above example lost only his clothing and cigarettes, he would probably have no s 2 claim (because below the financial limit); whereas he would do so if he lost a valuable fur coat (e.g. worth £300) as well. What if D, instead of losing the fur coat, had personal injuries and minor property damage?

---

275 *A v National Blood Authority* (above).

276 See para 17.14; and further Clark, *Product Liability*, 127; Clerk and Lindsell, *Torts*, 18th edn, para 9-63.

277 It seems such claims are generally permissible on ordinary principles: Bradgate and Savage (1987) 137 NLJ at 1026. *Contra* Dobson in the *Current Law Annotation* to s 5.

278 Apart from the CPA, the retail purchaser (C) could sue the retailer (B) under the supply contract (see para 17.07); but C and D could only sue X and/or Z in negligence where C's loss may be purely economic (see para 17.14). See Owles (1988) 138 NLJ 771; Tiplady, *Op. cit.*, 480; Clark, *Op. cit.*, 127–8; Clerk and Lindsell, *Ibid*.

279 The Commission have identified this as a key factor militating against use of the Directive and Pt I of the CPA: Beards and Twigg-Flesner (2001) 10 Nottm LJ 1, at 4, fn 33.

280 Or a second-hand car with a replacement battery: Howells (1991) 20 Anglo-Am LR 204 at 222.

281 Similarly excluded, is business property from the following Directives: distance selling, doorstep selling, unfair terms, sale of consumer goods (see respectively, paras 8.17, 10.36, 11.12A and 14.01).

282 It has been argued that in several respects s 5(4) does not adequately embody the Directive: see Mildred, *Product Liability Law*, 2000, para 2.39.

**[17.30] Defences**. In a **reversal** of the ordinary burden of proof (see para 17.16), the CPA provides that, 'in any civil proceedings by virtue of this Part against any person (the 'person proceeded against') in respect of a defect in a product it shall be a defence for him to show' any of the following (s 4(1)):

(a) *Legal requirements*. This defence will only save him if the defect was the inevitable result of compliance with mandatory[283] domestic or EU law (s 4(1)(a)), e.g. safety regulations (see para 4.33); food regulations (see para 4.27).

(b) *No supply*. Complete absence of 'supply' (see ss 45 and 46) to any person is a defence (s 4(1)(b)), which appears to cover both a franchiser specifying an approved supplier and a producer from whom goods are stolen.[284] The corresponding terminology of the Directive is if the defendant 'did not put the product into circulation' (Art 7(a)) and 'supply' is likely to be so read.

(c) *Non-profit activities*. Section 4(1)(c) protects a person where any 'supply' (see above) by him was **both** otherwise than in the course of his business, e.g. grandfather making toy for grandchild; private sale of home-made wine to a guest (cf. trade suppliers: see para 14.04) **and** not done with a view to profit, e.g. mother making batch of cakes for village fête.[285]

(d) *Subsequent defects*. It is a defence under s 4(1)(d) to show that the defect did not exist in the goods at the 'relevant time':[286] if the person proceeded against is the producer or importer, this will be the time he supplied the goods to another;[287] whereas it is the time of last business supply in other cases (s 4(2)(b), which actually refers to s 2(3): see para 17.27). Even in the exceptional case where B can use this defence, he remains liable to C under the supply contract (see para 14.08).

(e) *Components*. Whereas a component manufacturer (X) may *prima facie* be liable as producer of a defective product (see para 17.26), X will escape if he can show that the problem arose wholly from Z's fault in designing his own goods or specifying the design of the component (s 4(1)(f)). Presumably, if the fault is wholly attributable to Z's assembly of the product, X will also escape because he has not 'caused' the defect (see para 17.29); but perhaps it might have been wiser if this had been spelt out.

(f) *State-of-the-art*. According to s 4(1)(e), it is a good defence:[288]

---

283 Mere compliance with any rule of law, code of practice (see para 3.11) or private standard (e.g. BSI standard: see para 3.08) is insufficient: see Mildred, *Product Liability: Law and Insurance*, paras 2.64–5.

284 Also toxic waste dumped or omitted: Clark, *Product Liability*, 189.

285 *Contra* promotional gifts: see para 2.08. What about charity shops; or the fatal jam supplied to a Women's Institute sale of work? Note the different wording of the Directive, Art 7(c): instead of 'view to profit', it says 'in the course of his business'.

286 E.g. third party removes safety features or instructions, or poorly fits or services: Clark, *Op. cit.*, 191–2.

287 S 4(2)(a), which actually refers to s 2(2) (see para 17.27). E.g. sale of old stock by retailer will not render producer liable, as where the goods carry a 'sell by' date. If a blackmailer tampers with products of X whilst on a supermarket shelf (B), both X and Z can use this defence when sued by C or D. The hoax blackmailer may commit an offence under s 5 of the Public Order Act 1986.

288 See generally Clark, *Op. cit.*, Chap 6; Street on *Torts*, 10th edn, 354–5; Pugh and Pilgerstorfer [2004] 4 JPI Law 258. For its parliamentary history, see Merkin, *Guide to the CPA*, para 4.5.11. As to whether s 4(1)(e) complies with the Directive, see Crossick (1988) 138 NLJ 233; Clark, *Op. cit.*, 152–3; Mildred, *Product Liability Law*, 2000, paras 2.76–7.

'that the state of scientific and technical knowledge at the relevant time was not such that a producer of products of the same description as the product in question might be expected to have discovered the defect if it had existed in his products while they were under his control.'

This seemingly legally permissible but politically controversial defence of development risks known at the 'relevant time' (see above) requires the producer to prove two things: (i) that the defect unknown to him was also unknowable in the then state of scientific and technical knowledge (the knowledge element); and (ii) that his state of knowledge was not such as to enable him to discover the defect (the discoverability element).[289] Producers argued that, in the absence of such a defence, product innovation would be stifled,[290] whilst consumers pleaded that such a defence would re-introduce negligence by the back door.[291] However, it has been held that accident reports are not 'technical knowledge' for this purpose;[292] and that, once a defect is known, the defence is no longer available, even though that defect might remain unavoidable.[293]

However, if a defendant cannot bring himself within any of the above defences, he cannot escape liability to consumers by reliance on the printed word. Section 7 lays down that:

'The liability of a person by virtue of this Part to a person who has suffered damage caused wholly or partly by a defect in a product, or to a dependant or relative of such a person, shall not be limited or excluded by any contract term, by any notice or by any other provision.'

As with some UCTA restrictions (s 1(3): see para 18.22), s 7 enures only for the benefit of an injured consumer, or his 'dependent relative' (see s 1(2)); but it may be confined to written 'notices' (s 45(1)). On the other hand, a businessman or his workmen suffering personal injury may find his action blocked by a written or oral exclusion clause (s 5(3): see para 17.29). Nor does s 7 interfere with the freedom of parties prior to the retail supply regulating their rights *inter se* by contract, perhaps for use if they are found jointly and severally liable to the injured consumer.[294] If not so blocked, redress on behalf of consumers generally may be obtainable by Enforcement Orders (see para 6.08).

---

289 *European Commission v UK* [1997] All ER (EC) 481; discussed by Miller [1997] All ER LR Annual Review 81.

290 Yet most of our major trading competitors seem unlikely to introduce such a defence. Might this tend to make the UK a guinea-pig market (see para 17.05) and be discriminatory (see [1985] JBL at 437)? But does it add anything to s 3(2) (see para 17.28A)?

291 See Bradgate and Savage (1987) 137 NLJ at 1049–50; Clark, *Op. cit.*, 182–5 and 215–16; Pugh and Pilgerstorfer [2004] 4 JPI Law 258 at 263–9. This fear was shown to be groundless in *A v National Blood Authority* (set out at para 17.28).

292 So that the absence of such reports, e.g. DTI accident data-base, was no defence: *Abouzaid v Mothercare (UK) Ltd* [2001] CLY 920; *Times* 20.2, CA.

293 *A v National Blood Authority* (above; para 74), where Burton J observed that a non-standard (design-defective) product might qualify **once** for such a defence (para 77). See further Deards and Twigg-Flesner (2001) 10 Nottingham LJ 1 at 14–15.

294 But might the exclusion be unreasonable within s 3 of UCTA (see para 18.20) or be avoided by s 2(1) of UCTA (see above)?

# CHAPTER 18

# EXCLUSIONS AND DISCLAIMERS

**[18.01]** It is common, particularly in standard-form contracts (see para 11.08), to find that one of the parties (the *proferens*) has introduced into a transaction words purporting to avoid or restrict any liability that would otherwise accrue to him.[1] The *proferens* may purport to do so either by excluding or restricting his obligations, or by inserting a formula of words to discharge that obligation. Leaving aside the case of discharge by words (paras 18.28, *et seq.*), there must first be examined the effect of words designed to exclude or restrict either the obligation, or the liability of the *proferens* for failure to fulfil it.[2] This will begin with an examination of the effect of such clauses at common law (paras 18.02, *et seq.*) and then deal with statutory control of such clauses (paras 18.09, *et seq.*).

## EFFECT AT COMMON LAW[3]

**[18.02] Introduction.** In considering how the common law deals with attempts to avoid liability by way of disclaimer or exclusion clause, two questions arise in any action: first, what in fact happened; and second, is the defendant liable to the plaintiff/claimant in view of the facts which are proved to have occurred? The first question has very great practical significance: it may be extremely difficult to prove what happened;[4] but the problem of who bears the burden of proof is beyond the scope of this work.[5] The present discussion will concentrate on the second question, which involves the effectiveness of any disclaimer. The disclaimer may be oral, though a written form is usually favoured by those seeking to rely on it, because it is easier to prove, and may be drafted more comprehensively.[6] The disclaimer may originate from the retail seller (B), or from any prior party in the chain of distribution;[7] it is frequently printed on the goods, their packaging, or in a supply agreement; and it may purport to protect either B or any prior party in the chain of distribution—or even all of them.

**[18.03] Nature and effect of exclusion clauses.** Whether the attempt is to exclude tortious or contractual liability, the clause may or may not be embodied in a contract.

---

1   Distinguish penalty clauses, which attempt to increase the obligations of the other party, and are subject to different considerations: see para 27.25.
2   Clauses which achieve this object have been described by judges and text-writers as 'exemption', 'exclusion' or 'exception' clauses. These terms are used interchangeably; and this usage will be adopted here. See further *Benjamin's Sale of Goods*, 6th edn, para 13-001; and para 18.03.
3   See generally Coote, *Exception Clauses*; Yates, *Exclusion Clauses in Contracts*, 2nd edn; Macdonald, *Exemption Clauses and Unfair Terms*. For the *res ipsa loquitur* doctrine, see para 17.14.
4   As to the burden of proof, see paras 17.05 and 17.16.
5   See Treitel, *Law of Contract*, 11th edn, 240–1.
6   See the strictures of Lord Reid in the *Suisse Atlantique Societe D'Armement Maritime SA v NV Rotterdamsche Kolen Central* [1967] 1 AC 361, HL at 406.
7   For a description of chains of distribution, see para 17.01.

1. *Non-contractual disclaimers.* These clauses are here termed disclaimers[8] to distinguish them from contractual exclusion clauses (see below). A disclaimer cannot affect contractual liability, except by way of the doctrine of waiver (see para 26.23) or instructions (see para 18.28, *et seq.*), but may well defeat an action in tort.[9] Perhaps the most obvious example of the operation of a disclaimer in tort is where it either expressly or impliedly ousts liability in negligence, because the other party voluntarily assumes the risk,[10] or the disclaimer discharges a duty of care.[11] Here, however, the courts may try to restrict the ambit of the disclaimer so as to be free to apportion loss under the Law Reform (Contributory Negligence) Act 1945 (see para 27.40).

2. *Contractual exclusion clauses.* A party may seek by incorporation of an exclusion clause in a contract (see para 18.04) to exclude either his contractual or tortious liability, or both. The clause may be effective to exclude tortious liability by its express terms;[12] or it may do so impliedly, as where it purports to exclude an equivalent duty in contract;[13] or it may act as a sufficient warning to discharge or reduce tort liability in any of the ways suggested above.[14]

**[18.04] Incorporation**. Suppose that packaged goods descending a typical distribution chain (see para 17.01) bear a notice purporting to exempt the manufacturer and retailer from any liability (whether in contract or tort), the position is as follows: if the retailer (B) is sued by the person to whom he sold the goods (C), the issue will probably be the effect of the exclusion clause on the supply contract; but, if the manufacturer (Z) is sued by C, or by any person to whom C transfers the goods (D), the problem is more likely to be a tortious one. The question whether the exclusion clause is incorporated into the transaction may therefore arise both inside and outside the contractual context (see para 17.12).

*Prima facie*, at common law an exclusion clause may become incorporated in a contract in either of the following ways:[15]

1. *Incorporation by notice.* The incorporation of a clause excluding liability into a contract between two parties is a matter of intention: such an exclusion will become part of a contract so as to bind one of the parties (irrespective of whether he listened to, or read it) provided that, at the time of contracting,[16] he realised that the other party intended it to form part of the contract between them.[17] Alternatively, in the absence of actual knowledge, a party may be

---

8  For disclaimers of strict criminal liability, see para 4.09.
9  E.g. *Hurley v Dyke* [1979] RTR 265, HL. Subject to s 2 of UCTA: as to which, see para 18.17.
10 See *per* Lord Denning (dissenting) in *Scruttons Ltd v Midland Silicones Ltd* [1962] AC 446, HL at 488–9.
11 E.g. *Southern Water Authority v Carey* [1985] 2 All ER 1007. See generally, para 17.13, *et seq.*
12 E.g. *Hedley Byrne & Co Ltd v Heller Ltd* (see para 17.19).
13 Cf. *White v John Warwick & Co* [1953] 2 All ER 1021, CA; *Humming Bird Motors v Hobbs* [1986] CLY 2283, CA.
14 However, in relation to the application of UCTA, it has been held that the court must first establish *prima facie* liability in the absence of the exclusion clause: see para 18.12.
15 E.g. *Apioil Ltd v Kuwait Petroleum Italia SpA* [1995] 1 Lloyd's Rep 124 (variation).
16 *Contra* where he did not realise the intention of the *proferens* in that regard until after the contract was made: *Olley v Marlborough Court* [1949] 1 KB 532, CA (not a sale case).
17 *Parker v South Eastern Railway Co* (1877) 2 CPD 416, CA; and see also para 18.30. For the battle of the forms, see para 10.04.

bound by an exclusion clause where he ought to have realised that it was intended to have contractual force because the other party took reasonable steps to bring it to his attention,[18] as where there is a consistent course of dealings between the parties[19] or a trade usage,[20] or the incorporation of club rules for the time being.[21] Where an exclusion of liability does not become incorporated in a contract between the parties, it can usually only operate on adequate notice as a disclaimer of liability in tort.[22] Thus, in the example above, the disclaimer on the package may save the manufacturer (Z) from liability in the tort of negligence by 'discharging' the duty of care;[23] or, where C ignores the warning, it may give rise to a voluntary assumption of risk[24] or contributory negligence on C's part. As to contributory negligence, see para 27.40. As to warnings, see para 18.29.

2. *Incorporation by signed document.*[25] Where the exclusion clause is embodied in a signed contract, the general common law rule is that the signatory is bound by the contents of the document regardless of whether he has read or understood them.[26] On the other hand, the signed document may neither amount to, nor evidence, a contract: possibly, a disclaimer in that document will become binding on the signatory merely by signature, rather than only by notice.[24]

In respect of consumer supply contracts (see para 11.12A), terms so incorporated by notice or signature may be unfair simply because the consumer has not actually seen them (see Grey term (i): see para 11.17).

**[18.05] Attitude of the courts to exclusion clauses.** There are a number of legal rules[27] which will render an exclusion clause ineffective, even though the clause be incorporated in the transaction (see para 18.04) and whatever its meaning (see para 18.06):

---

18 *Interfoto Picture Library Ltd v Stiletto Ltd* [1988] 1 All ER 348, CA (Macdonald [1988] JBL 375); *Grogan v Robin Meredith Plant Hire* [1996] 15 Tr LR 371, CA; *Ocean Chemical Transport Inc v Exnor Craggs Ltd* [2000] 1 All ER (Comm) 519, CA.

19 *Kendall v Lillico* (set out at para 14.10: the sold notes); the *Vacwell Engineering* case (set out at para 18.29); *George Mitchell (Cheshire) Ltd v Finney Lock Seeds Ltd* (set out at para 18.08); and para 18.09. See Macdonald (1988) 8 Legal Studies 48.

20 See para 15.11. When does a course of dealing (see above) become a trade custom (see para 11.10)?

21 *Shearson Lehman Hutton Inc v Maclaine Watson & Co Inc* [1989] 2 Lloyd's Rep 570 ([1990] LMCLQ at 308). But this rule may be unfair in a consumer transaction: *UCT Bulletin No 27*, p. 104; and para 11.15A.

22 Adequate notice here is the same as in contract: *Ashdown v Samuel Williams Ltd* [1957] 1 QB 409, CA.

23 See *Hedley Byrne & Co Ltd v Heller Ltd* [1964] AC 465, where the HL thought that the effect of the disclaimer was to prevent the duty of care from arising; and generally John (1985–6) 5 Litigation 91.

24 *Ashdown v Samuel Williams Ltd* (above). There is considerable dispute as to the basis of the decision in this case: see Winfield and Jolowicz, *Tort*, 16th edn, paras 9.17–18.

25 At common law, signature includes not just writing of a name or initials, but also a facsimile stamp or other form of marking.

26 *L'Estrange v Graucob Ltd* [1934] 2 KB 394, DC. *Contra* if he can plead *non est factum* (see para 10.16); or the additional term on the back is unannounced (*Harvey v Ventilatorenfabrik Oelde GmbH* [1988] CLY 463, CA). As to unreasonable terms, see *Danka Rentals Ltd v Xi Software Ltd* (1998) 17 Tr LR 74 at 84–5. As to unusual terms, see *Montgomery Litho Ltd v Maxwell* 2000 SC 56.

27 These rules are generally framed in the law of contract, but there would appear to be no reason why they should be so confined.

(1) Where the exclusion of liability is contrary to statute[28] or unfair (see para 11.12, *et seq.*).

(2) Where the object of the clause is contrary to public policy, as where it purports to exclude liability for fraud.[29]

(3) Where the *proferens* gives an overriding oral undertaking[30] or misrepresents the contents of the clause.[31] Paradoxically, a clause in a consumer supply contract giving effect to these decisions may be unfair.[32]

(4) Where in a contractual action there is no privity of contract between the parties, whether the clause purports to confer a benefit[33] or a burden.[34] However, it should be borne in mind that the effect of the privity doctrine is mitigated in a number of statutory[35] and common law[36] rules.

**[18.06] The *contra proferentem* rule.** Where an exclusion clause cannot be struck down on one of the above grounds, at common law its effect will be a matter of construction. In seeking to ascertain the intention of the parties, the courts will, if the clause was inserted merely for the benefit of the *proferens*, construe the words against him (the *contra proferentem* rule). Where there is a consumer supply, a similar rule is imposed by UTCCR, reg 7 (see para 11.13).

This common law rule is a general one, but has achieved special prominence in the field of contractual exclusion clauses and tortious disclaimers, which the courts have consistently construed strictly against the *proferens*,[37] e.g. to prevent a party taking advantage of his own wrong.[38] Thus, where it is to the disadvantage of the *proferens*,[39] they have attributed precise legal meanings to technical terms, regardless of whether the parties understood the technicalities: clauses excluding warranties have been held ineffective to exclude conditions;[40] clauses excluding implied terms have been held not to affect liability for breach of express conditions;[41]

---

28  See the provisions considered later in this Chapter at para 18.09, *et seq.*

29  Cf. *Gordon v Selico* [1986] CLY 1877, CA; para 4.09. Can a clause be struck down purely on grounds of unreasonableness?

30  *Mendelssohn v Normand Ltd* [1970] 1 QB 177, CA; *Harling v Eddy* [1951] 2 KB 739, CA. Cf. *Pagnan Sp A v Tradex Ocean Transportation* [1987] 1 All ER 81 (overriding written provision).

31  *Curtis v Chemical Cleaning Co* [1951] 1 KB 805, CA; *Harvey v Ventilatorenfabrik Oelde* [1989] Tr LR 138, CA.

32  Grey Term (i): OFT, *UTCC Bulletin No 4*, p 51; and see generally, para 11.17.

33  *Scruttons Ltd v Midland Silicones Ltd* [1962] AC 446, HL.

34  *Dunlop Pneumatic Tyre Co Ltd v Selfridge & Co Ltd* [1915] AC 847, HL; and see generally, para 10.01.

35  E.g. the statutory deemed agency provisions (see para 16.04); Contracts (Rights of Third Parties) Act 1999 (see para 17.08).

36  E.g. the doctrines of agency and collateral contract (see respectively, paras 10.06 and 17.09).

37  E.g. *Henry Kendall & Sons Ltd v William Lillico & Sons Ltd* (set out at para 14.10). But see para 18.08. As to statutory formulations, see para 15.22.

38  *Alghussein Establishment v Eton College* [1991] 1 All ER 267, HL (not a goods case).

39  *Contra* where a strict construction would advantage the *proferens*: *Schuler AG v Wickman Machine Tool Sales Ltd* [1974] AC 235, HL.

40  E.g. *Wallis Sons and Wells v Pratt and Haynes* (set out at para 11.04); *Baldry v Marshall Ltd* [1925] 1 KB 260, CA; *Harling v Eddy* [1951] 2 KB 739, CA; *Lowe v Lombank Ltd* (below).

41  E.g. *Andrews Brothers (Bournemouth) Ltd v Singer & Co Ltd* [1934] 1 KB 17, CA.

and plain words are needed to exclude liability for negligence.[42] A striking illustration of the effectiveness of the *contra proferentem* rule is to be found in *Lowe v Lombank Ltd.*[43]

> P, a widow of 65, agreed to enter a directly financed hp transaction in respect of a second-hand car, and signed a proposal form at her home without reading it. Clause 8 purported to exclude all warranties; and clause 9 read as follows:
>
> > 'The hirer acknowledges that he has examined the goods and that there are no defects in the goods which such examination ought to have revealed and that the goods are of merchantable quality. The hirer further acknowledges and agrees that he has not made known to the owners expressly or by implication the particular purpose for which the goods are required, and that the goods are reasonably fit for the purpose for which they are in fact required.'
>
> On delivery, P signed a 'delivery receipt', in which she acknowledged that the goods were in good order; but the car was, in fact, completely unroadworthy owing to a number of serious, but latent, defects.

The Court of Appeal held that P was entitled to damages against the finance company for breach of the implied condition as to fitness in the HPA 1938 because:

(1) P impliedly made known that she required the car as a means of transport (see para 14.10).

(2) Clause 8 did not purport to exclude conditions;[40] nor had it been brought to P's attention and its effect made plain to her as the 1938 Act required. Nowadays, assuming P were found to be dealing as a consumer, such a clause would be avoided by UCTA (s 6(2)(b): see para 18.19).

(3) Clause 9 was merely a statement of past facts, not a contractual promise, and at common law could, at most, give rise to an estoppel; but that there was no estoppel here because (a) the clause did not unambiguously cover the latent defects and (b) there was no evidence either that P intended the statements to be acted upon, nor that the company signed the agreement on the basis of the truth of the statement.[44] The position might have been otherwise with regard to visible external defects.[45]

Similar rules apply to the interpretation of indemnities.[46] Moreover, in respect of consumer supply contracts such as that in *Lowe* (above), a similar view is likely

---

42  *Dorset CC v Southern Felt Roofing Co* [1990] Tr L 96, CA (words could refer to other events which did not include negligence); *Thomas Witter Ltd v T B P Industries Ltd* (set out at para 26.14) Tr LR at 167E–170a (111 LQR at 389).

43  [1960] 1 All ER 611, [1960] 1 WLR 196, CA. As to delivery notes, see generally, para 23.02. On the facts of the case, see now para 18.16.

44  For a discussion of the common law doctrine of estoppel, see para 21.10, *et seq.*; and for acceptance notes, see para 23.10. The statement in the agreement that clause 8 had been brought to the hirer's notice, and its effect made plain to her, was not relied on in this action: see Goode, *HP Law & Practice*, 2nd edn, 201–202, 252. Cf. certificate of quality: see para 14.02.

45  *Astley Industrial Trust Ltd v Grimley* [1963] 2 All ER 33, at 44–5, CA. Cf. *Farnworth Finance Facilities Ltd v Attryde* [1970] 2 All ER 774, CA; *Gill & Duffus SA v Berger & Co Inc* (set out at para 23.06).

46  *Smith v South Wales Switchgear Ltd* [1978] 1 All ER 18, HL; *EE Caledonia Ltd v Orbit Valve Co* [1993] 4 All ER 165 (service contracts). But cf. para 25.07A.

to be taken with clauses unfairly acknowledging that the consumer has read and understood terms.[47]

**[18.07] The doctrine of fundamental breach.**[48] Particularly in the period after 1945, there was an almost continuous battle of wits between the draftsmen of standard-form contracts (see para 11.08) and the Court of Appeal: the draftsmen devised exclusion clauses on behalf of the *proferens* which were ever-more sweeping; whereas the Court of Appeal defeated the draftsmen's intention by applying the *contra proferentem* doctrine (see para 18.06) to such clauses with increasing severity. Eventually, this begun to lead to the doctrine of fundamental breach, the notion that there may be some terms which are so fundamental to a contract that, as a matter of law, no exclusion clause can offer protection against breach.[49] In *Karsales (Harrow) Ltd v Wallis*[50] the Court of Appeal did this on the basis that the object delivered was not the car contracted for. Two years later, in *Yeoman Credit Ltd v Apps* (set out at para 29.25) a bolder court went further and held that in respect of a defective car:

(1) there was implied into the hp agreement a common law condition that the goods are reasonably fit for the purpose for which they were required;[51] and

(2) the accumulation (congeries) of defects when added together amounted to such a fundamental breach of contract as to disentitle the plaintiffs from relying on the exemption clause.[52]

**[18.08] A matter of construction.** Before 1977, Lord Denning MR in particular[53] maintained a judicial campaign that there was a rule of law that an exemption clause, no matter how widely drafted, could not protect the *proferens* against a fundamental breach by him (see para 18.07). However, few of the cases unambiguously sought to raise the *contra proferentem* rule (see para 18.06) into a rule of law concerning fundamental breaches (see para 18.07). With the enactment of UCTA in 1977 (see para 18.12, *et seq.*), not only were the courts freed from any such rule of law (s 9), but they were also given a statutory weapon for controlling exclusion clauses in general; and, when the other party dealt as consumer, many such clauses were deprived of all effect.[54] With the prime motivation for this line of development removed, the attitude of the courts, led by the House of Lords, began to change: not only did they deny that there was a rule of law concerning fundamental breaches, but they also began to apply the *contra proferentem* rule in a much more

---

47  See OFT, *Bulletin No. 18*, cases 5 and 16; *No. 22*, case 16; *No. 24*, case 19; [2005] *Bulletin J/M, GIS Windows* case; [2005] *Bulletin J/S, Forthright Finance*.

48  The history of the doctrine is traced by Coote (1967) 40 ALJ 336. See also Treitel, *Law of Contract*, 11th edn, 225, *et seq.*

49  *Per* Devlin J in *Smeaton Hanscomb & Co Ltd v Sassoon Setty Son & Co* [1953] 2 All ER 1471 at 1473.

50  [1956] 2 All ER 866, CA.

51  For the statutory undertaking as to fitness, see now, para 14.07.

52  It was so applied in *Farnworth Finance Facilities Ltd v Attryde* [1970] 2 All ER 33, CA; *Charterhouse Credit Ltd v Tolly* (set out at para 29.34). But see further, paras 14.02 and 18.08.

53  E.g. *Harbutt's Plasticine Ltd v Wayne Tank Ltd* [1970] 1 QB 447, CA (not a sale case). A position he later revised: see below.

54  See especially UCTA, ss 6–7: see para 18.18, *et seq.*

even-handed manner.[55] A striking case is *George Mitchell (Chesterhall) Ltd v Finney Lock Seeds Ltd.*[56]

> The plaintiff farmers orally ordered 30lbs of Late Dutch Spring Cabbage seed from the defendant seed merchants, from whom they had purchased seed for many years. The seed was delivered together with the defendant's customary invoice, which contained many conditions. The seed looked alright; but six months after planting there sprouted a lot of loose green leaves, which were found to be commercially useless. The price of the seed was £192, but the loss to the plaintiffs was over £61,000.

The sellers sought to protect themselves by relying on a wide-ranging exclusion clause of long-standing in the seed trade, which purported to limit their liability to refund of the price. The Court of Appeal held that the exclusion clause formed part of the contract by course of dealings;[57] but their decision in favour of the buyers was confirmed by the House of Lords on partially different grounds.

(1) Whilst a majority of the Court of Appeal held that, as a matter of construction, the limitation clause did not protect the sellers against the event which occurred,[58] the House of Lords held that it was apt to do so. In delivering the unanimous judgment of their Lordships, Lord Bridge declined to 'read an ambiguity into it by the process of strained construction', adding that 'the very strict principles . . . applicable to exclusion and indemnity clauses cannot be applied in their full rigour to limitation clauses'.[59]

(2) Although enforceable at common law, their Lordships affirmed the unanimous judgment of the Court of Appeal that the clause was rendered unenforceable by statute, because it would not be 'fair or reasonable to allow reliance' on it.[60]

# STATUTORY CONTROLS OF EXCLUSION CLAUSES

## Introduction

**[18.09] Contracts for the supply of goods**. The SGA 1893 allowed almost complete freedom of contract. Apart from the half-hearted limitation that express terms did not negative implied terms unless inconsistent,[61] many of its provisions were expressed to give way to a contrary intention.[62] Furthermore, s 55 (now replaced by s 55(1) of the SGA 1979) provides:

---

55 E.g. *Photo Production Ltd v Securicor Transport Ltd* [1980] AC 827, HL; *Ailsa Craig Fishing Co Ltd v Malvern Fishing Co Ltd* [1983] 1 All ER 101, HL(S) (not sale cases).

56 [1983] 2 AC 803, [1983] 2 All ER 737, HL.

57 [1983] QB 284, CA: see generally, para 18.04.

58 Oliver and Kerr LJJ, with a powerful dissent by Lord Denning MR.

59 At 742: his Lordship expressly agreed with Lord Denning MR on this point. See Atiyah, *Sale of Goods*, 10th edn, 245–6; and also para 1.04.

60 Under s 55 of the Sale of Goods Act as set out in para 11 of Sched 1 to the SGA 1979. This transitional provision is now replaced by that found in UCTA, ss 6(3) and 11(2): as to the latter see para 18.26.

61 For this rule, see now SGA, s 55(2), and its counterparts in SOGIT, s 12(1) as amended and SGSA, s 11(2).

62 For reinforcement of the *caveat emptor* rule, see para 15.22.

'Where any right, duty or liability would arise under a contract of sale of goods by implication of law, it may (subject to the Unfair Contract Terms Act 1977) be negatived or varied by express agreement, or by the course of dealing between the parties, or by usage if the usage is such as to bind both parties to the contract.'

Whilst SOGIT contains no counterpart to this provision for hp agreements, the SGSA does include a virtually identical provision for quasi-sales and simple hiring agreements (s 11(1)). The provision envisages three ways in which any 'right, duty, or liability' might be 'negatived or varied' at common law. *First*, it might be ousted by express agreement; and the rules for interpreting that express agreement are considered above (paras 18.06–08). *Second*, it might be impliedly displaced by the course of dealings between the parties, even though no term to such effect could be implied in any single contract standing alone.[63] *Third*, even where there was neither such an express term nor a course of dealings, it might be negatived by a trade usage to that effect.[64]

[18.10] Because it was thought that the dominant party had frequently taken unfair advantage of this freedom of contract, Parliament sometimes sought to modify it. In relation to instalment credit contracts, the HPA specified a detailed list of provisions which were avoided and this function has now been taken over by the CCA (see para 18.11). With regard to misrepresentations which induce entry into any type of contract, some restriction on contracting out was introduced by the Misrepresentation Act 1967 (see para 18.17). Subsequently, more generalised controls on attempts to exclude contractual and tortious liability were introduced by the Unfair Contract Terms Act 1977 (see para 18.12); and the CPA introduced restrictions on contracting out of product liability or safety regulations;[65] and Part 8 of the EA introduced an injunctive regime to protect consumers generally (see paras 6.06–8).

To this must be added EU-inspired interventions. The Unfair Terms Regulations have granted a court wide powers to interfere with unfair standard terms in consumer supply contracts (see para 11.12): just one of its Grey Terms attacks attempts to exclude or restrict the consumer's rights against his supplier other than the implied terms (para (b): see para 11.16A); and this may be used to reinforce those provisions.[66] Nor is it possible to contract out of some other specific protections, e.g. Doorstep-selling (reg 10: see para 10.22), Distance selling (reg 25(1): see para 8.17), implied terms and guarantees in consumer supplies.[67] Further, the UCP Directive will introduce another raft of consumer protections (see para 4.01A).

[18.11] **The Consumer Credit Act**. Whilst the HPA sought to achieve its object by avoiding certain specifically listed provisions (consolidated list in s 29 of the HPA

---

63   *Henry Kendall & Sons Ltd v William Lillico & Sons Ltd* (set out at para 14.10), *per* Lords Morris, Guest, and Pearce, at 90, 105 and 113, affirming the unanimous decision of the CA on this point; [1966] 1 All ER 309, CA, *per* Sellers, Davies and Diplock LJJ, at 322 and 331. See generally, para 18.04.

64   *Cointat v Myham* (1914) 84 LJKB 2253, CA; and see generally, para 15.11.

65   As to product liability, see CPA, s 7 (see para 17.30); and as to safety regulations, see CPA, s 41(4) (see para 4.33).

66   OFT, *UCT Bulletins, No. 4*, pp 29 and 30; *No. 5*, pp 43 and 46; *No. 21*, case 13.

67   As to consumer supplies, see generally, para 14.01; as to exclusion of product guarantees, see para 17.09B; and as to exclusion of implied terms in sale, see para 18.19.

1965), the CCA adopted a new technique—a blanket prohibition on contracting out. Thus, s 173(1) provides:

'A term contained in a regulated agreement or linked transaction, or in any other agreement relating to an actual or prospective regulated agreement or linked transaction, is void if, and to the extent that, it is inconsistent with a provision for the protection of the debtor or hirer or his relative or any surety contained in this Act or in any regulation made under this Act.'

This does not of itself prevent the regulated agreement containing any clause inconsistent with the CCA,[68] but only denies such clause effect.[69] Nor does s 173(1) render void all provisions inconsistent with the CCA: it only strikes down those inconsistent with such CCA provisions as are 'for the protection of the debtor or hirer or his relative or any surety'.[70] However, s 173(2) makes it clear that this avoidance refers to both sides of the coin: whilst s 173(1) avoids attempts by the creditor or owner to cut down his duties, s 173(2) similarly avoids any attempt by the creditor or owner to increase the duties of the debtor or hirer above any CCA duty 'in those circumstances'.

On the other hand, amended s 173(3) provides:

'Notwithstanding subsection (1), a provision of this Act under which a thing may be done in relation to any person on an order of the court or the OFT only shall not be taken to prevent its being done at any time with that person's consent given at that time, but the refusal of such consent shall not give rise to any liability.'

This is quite consistent with the policy of the Act: whilst the creditor or owner may not by clever language in the documentation of the transaction increase his rights, or reduce those of the debtor or hirer, he can do so if he can persuade the debtor or hirer to give consent thereto at the time. Thus, the debtor may waive his right to treat as unenforceable a regulated agreement entered into by an unlicensed trader,[71] or an improperly executed agreement,[72] or a regulated land mortgage;[73] or he may waive his right to resist repossession of protected goods,[74] or entry into his premises for the purposes of recapting them.[75] But the consent must be informed (see para 24.37).

---

68  Nor is such a statement prohibited by the Consumer Transactions Order: see para 4.22. But in a consumer supply it might be an unfair term (OFT, *Bulletin No. 15*, case 8; [2005] *Bulletin J/S, Forthright Finance*).

69  *Wilson v Robertsons (London) Ltd* (set out at para 5.22), *per* Laddie J at paras 18 and 24. What would be the effect (if any) of a change in a creditor's employment contracts prohibiting his employees from contravening the CCA?

70  E.g. on the death of the debtor or hirer—s 86(1): see para 24.47. Does this protection extend to a dealer acting as surety under a recourse provision (see para 16.22)?

71  S 40: see para 6.20. See also para 6.27.

72  S 65: see para 9.19.

73  S 126: see para 25.24.

74  S 90: see para 24.34.

75  S 92: see para 24.34.

# The Unfair Contract Terms Act[76]

*Introduction*

**[18.12]  History**. Sweeping limitations on attempts by suppliers to exclude liability in sale and hp contracts were first introduced in 1973 by SOGIT.[77] Partly as a result of subsequent recommendations by the Law Commission,[77] these and other limitations were later embodied in the Unfair Contract Terms Act 1977 (UCTA) and have since been extended by the SGSA (ss 11(1), 17(2) and (3)) to quasi-sale and simple hirings (see paras 2.10 and 12.01A). The title 'Unfair Contract Terms Act' is a misnomer: unlike the UTCC Regulations (see para 11.12, *et seq.*), the Act does not deal with unfair contract terms generally, but mostly with exclusion clauses in particular types of contract.

The UCTA (as amended) does not render it unlawful[78] to purport to incorporate an invalid exclusion clause in a contract, but simply avoids in some circumstances exclusion clauses within its ambit. In *Phillips Products Ltd v Hyland* (see para 18.16) the Court of Appeal decided that, in considering whether there had been a breach of obligation, the court 'has first to leave out of account, at this stage, the contract term which is relied upon by the defence as defeating the plaintiff's claim'.[79] But how does one distinguish the clause defining the duty[80] (outside UCTA) from the one excluding liability for breach of that duty (inside UCTA)?[81] Or the apparent contradiction where ss 3 and 6 overlap (see para 18.22)?

The scheme set up by UCTA draws a sharp distinction between those contracts with an international flavour (see para 18.13) and wholly domestic contracts, confining its restrictions substantially to the latter.[82] Restrictions on 'exemption clauses' in domestic contracts governed by English law are to be found in Part 1 of UCTA.[83] Major changes would be made to UCTA if a new Unfair Terms Bill proposed by the Law Commission were enacted (see para 18.27).

**[18.13/15]  International contracts**. The basic principle by which English law decides which system of law applies to a contract with an international flavour is to look for the proper or applicable law of the contract (see para 10.01). However, these rules

---

76　See generally *Benjamin's Sale of Goods*, 6th edn, para 13-053, *et seq.*; Treitel, *Law of Contract*, 11th edn, 246–67; Mildred, *Product Liability: Law and Insurance*, para 3.231, *et seq.*

77　See the *Second Report on Exemption Clauses* (1975, Law Com 69). For a discussion of the expression 'exemption clauses', see paras 160–8.

78　But inclusion of the exclusion clause may amount to an offence under the Restrictions on Statements Order: see para 4.22. Further, it may sometimes infringe one of the codes of practice (see paras 3.11–14).

79　*Per* Slade LJ at 625c, delivering the judgment of the court; and in *Smith v Bush* [1990] 1 AC 831, HL, Lord Griffiths described this as the 'but for' test. However, this view appears to be inconsistent with some academic views as to the manner in which exclusion clauses operate at common law: see para 18.03.

80　E.g. an instruction to use goods only in a specified manner is impliedly saying do not use them in any other manner (see further, para 18.31); 'sold as seen' (see Tiplady (1987) 137 NLJ at 428).

81　See Macdonald (1991) 107 LQR at 557–8; and *Photoprint Ltd v Forward Trust Ltd* (1993) 12 Tr LR 146.

82　Nor does the Act affect contractual provisions authorised by statute or made with a view to compliance with international obligations (s 29(1)).

83　Pt 2 of UCTA lays down separate rules for Scots law.

give way to any contrary intention expressed by the parties in their agreement;[84] and many foreigners making contracts which have little or nothing to do with England have included in their contract a provision that English law shall be the proper law of the contract. It is therefore common in commercial contracts to find that the parties have so provided in what has become known as a choice laws clause; and this may be enforced by an anti-suit injunction.[85] To safeguard this lucrative jurisdiction, UCTA excludes from its ambit those contracts which are only governed by English law by reason of a choice of laws clause (s 27(1)). At the same time, Parliament did not wish to allow parties to escape from the restrictions of UCTA simply by dressing up what was really a domestic contract as a foreign one. Accordingly, s 27(2) seeks to bring such sham transactions[86] within the rules for domestic contracts discussed below.[87]

Where a contract with an international flavour is governed by English law by reason of the above rules, Part III of UCTA saves it from the restrictive rules which Part I makes applicable to domestic contracts (see para 18.16, et seq.). Thus, Part III makes special provision for contracts for the international supply of goods (but not services)[88] and contracts complying with international agreements (s 29(1)(b)). However, the effect of this statutory scheme is to put foreign commercial buyers from an English seller at a considerable disadvantage as compared with English buyers, because any exclusion clause in the supply contract is not subject to the constraints of UCTA. If the commercial buyer is within the EU, an exclusion clause in the supply contract may contravene Art 25 [ex 12] of the Treaty of Rome, in which case an English court would have to 'disapply' the exclusion clause.[89] Of course, if the EU buyer is a consumer, e.g. in an e-mail contract, the exclusion clause may be an unfair term[90] and perhaps contravene the E-Commerce Directive.[91] The conclusion is likely to be that s 26 of UCTA can nowadays only apply to foreign non-EU business buyers;[91] and, in any event, it is beyond the scope of this work. As to 'consumer supplies', there is a similar provision in an EU Directive (Art 7(2): see para 17.09B).

**[18.16] Domestic contracts**. Generally speaking (see para 18.12), in domestic contracts[92] governed by English law (see para 18.13), Part I of UCTA precludes or restricts reliance on certain exclusion clauses and clauses of similar effect. In fact, UCTA does not comprehensively define exclusion clauses, a common law notion

---

84  *Centrax Ltd v Citibank NA* [1999] 1 All ER (Comm) 557, CA (proper law); Contracts (Applicable Law) Act 1990, Sched 1, Art 3.

85  *Donohue v Armco Inc* [2000] 1 All ER (Comm) 641, CA; and see generally, para 29.39.

86  S 27(2) operates in either or both of the following circumstances: (a) the contract contains a choice of laws clause 'wholly or mainly for the purpose' of evading UCTA; (b) one party to that contract dealt as consumer (see para 18.18) and was 'habitually resident' in the UK. This rule still stands after the 1990 Act (below): [1991] JBL at 214.

87  For reform proposals, see para 18.27.

88  *Ocean Chemical Transport Inc v Exnor Craggs Ltd* [2000] 1 All ER (Comm) 519, CA. Distinguish *Amiri Flight Authority v BAE Systems plc* [2003] 1 All ER (Comm) 385, CA.

89  See *Econoler v GEC Alsthom* [1999] Unreported (Burbridge 150 NLJ 1544).

90  *Oceano Grupo Editorial SA v Quintero* [2002] GCCR 4451, Eu Ct (Whittaker 117 LQR 215).

91  00/31. As to Internet buyers, see para 8.17A.

92  Are pre-payment meters supplied by gas and electricity undertakings supplied under contract or statutory obligation? See Fairest (1985) 135 NLJ 238; *Unfair Terms in Contracts* (2002, 166 Law Comm Consultation), para 3.106.

(see para 18.06). However, in *Phillips Products Ltd v Hyland*[93] the Court of Appeal first looked at the contract without the exclusion clause (see para 18.12) to determine whether H had been 'negligent' within the meaning of s 1(1) (see para 18.17). Turning to the exclusion clause, they held that the matter was one of substance, not form: whilst the form of clause 8 was a transfer of vicarious liability, its effect was to exclude X's vicarious liability,[94] so that the clause fell within s 2(2) (see para 18.17).

An extension to the common law concept of exclusion clauses is to be found in s 13(1), which provides as follows:

'To the extent that this Part of this Act prevents the exclusion or restriction of any liability it also prevents—

(a) making the liability or its enforcement subject to restrictive or onerous conditions;

(b) excluding or restricting any right or remedy in respect of liability, or subjecting a person to any prejudice in consequence of his pursuing any such right or remedy;

(c) excluding or restricting rules of evidence or procedure;

and (to that extent) sections 2 and 5 to 7 also prevent excluding or restricting liability by reference to terms and notices which exclude or restrict the relevant obligation or duty.'

Examples of such exclusion[95] or restriction[96] would be as follows:

*Para (a):* a term requiring notification of loss within a specified time or in a specified manner. What of a clause allowing the supplier to substitute any later model? Or onerous instructions for use (see para 18.31)? Or *force majeure* clauses (see para 22.13A)?

*Para (b):* as to exclusion of a remedy, a term denying the right to rescind for breach of a condition, or limiting liability to a specified amount.[97] Does it extend to the right of examination under s 34 of the SGA (as to which, see para 23.10)?

*Para (c):* for instance *Lowe v Lombank Ltd* (set out at para 18.06). Does s 13(1)(c) also cover certificates of compliance (as to which see paras 13.11, 14.02, 14.04 and 15.06).

In *Stewart Gill Ltd v Horatio Meyer & Co Ltd*,[98] a business-to-business contract, the Court of Appeal agreed with the buyer (B) that clause 12(4) was struck down by s 3 (see para 18.20). Whilst it was not a clause 'excluding or restricting liability', the Court thought that clause 12(4) fell within both s 13(1)(b)—by suppressing B's right of set-off,[99] and s 13(1)(c)—by making B pay the price in full and then mount a

---

93   [1987] 2 All ER 620, CA (see 108 LQR at 109–11).
94   See also *Thompson v T Lohan (Plant Hire) Ltd* [1987] 2 All ER 631, CA; and the discussion by Macdonald [1994] JBL 441, at 447–9.
95   E.g. *Andrews Bros Ltd v Singer & Co Ltd* [1934] 1 KB 17, CA. There is no objection to clauses preventing the duty from arising: see para 18.12.
96   E.g. *George Mitchell (Chesterhall) Ltd v Finney Lock Seeds Ltd* (set out at para 18.08).
97   E.g. *British Crane Hire Corpn Ltd v Ipswich Plant Hire Ltd* [1975] QB 303, CA (hired equipment at hirer's risk).
98   [1992] QB 600, [1992] 2 All ER 257, CA (see (1993) LQR 41; Macdonald [1994] JBL 441–4).
99   Such suppression is not at common law contrary to public policy: *Coca-Cola Financial Corpn v Finsat International Ltd* [1998] QB 43, CA.

separate action. The closing words of s 13(1) refer to 'terms or notices': it has been suggested that 'terms or notices' allows the approach to exclusion clause adopted in *Phillips v Hylands* (above);[100] but another suggestion was put forward in relation to 'notices' by Lord Donaldson MR in the *Stewart Gill* case (at 260j). His Lordship found the closing words of s 13(1) obscure, but thought that they were not intended to cover contractual exclusion clauses within paragraphs (a), (b) or (c), but instead to deal with non-contractual disclaimers (see para 18.03; and para 18.23), except in relation to ss 3 and 4 which deal with exclusions of strict contractual promises (see paras 18.20 and 18.23).

On the other hand, the scope of s 13(1) is narrowed by s 13(2): this expressly saves from s 13(1) arbitration clauses (see further, para 3.23-4), but is unclear as to liquidated damages clauses.[101] Further, it is regrettably unclear whether s 13(1)(b) extends to any compromise a consumer makes with regard to a claim;[102] nor to instructions for use (see para 18.28, *et seq.*); nor to 'card-not-present' transactions (see para 7.09). For secondary contracts, see para 18.16A.

**[18.16A] Secondary contracts**. Section 10 makes it clear that the Act cannot be evaded by means of a secondary contract.

> 'A person is not bound by any contract term prejudicing or taking away rights of his which arise under, or in connection with the performance of, another contract, so far as those rights extend to the enforcement of another's liability which this Part of this Act prevents that other from excluding or restricting.'

This section applies where a consumer contracting with X and Y in separate contracts agrees with X that he will not sue Y[103] in respect of *future* claims:[104] it has no application where both parties to the contract are the same (such cases fall within s 13: see para 18.16), or with regard to compromises of *existing* claims.[105] Instances within s 10 are where the consumer is entering a directly financed transaction and agrees with the dealer that he will not sue the financier;[106] or where the consumer agrees with a retailer that he will not sue a prior party in the chain of distribution for product liability; or agrees with a servicer under a maintenance contract that he will not sue the retailer.[107] This rule would be reproduced in the Unfair Terms Bill (see para 18.27).

**[18.17] Part I of UCTA**. This applies to exclusion clauses as above explained (see para 18.16), with the following limitations (s 1(2)): contracts with an international flavour (see paras 18.13–15) are wholly outside the Act; whereas those within

---

100 *Unfair Terms in Contracts* (above), para 4.130. See further (1992) 12 LS 277.
101 Treitel, *Law of Contract*, 11th edn, 248; and as to liquidated damages clauses, see generally, para 27.29.
102 The point is clarified (it does not) for Scots law by s 15(1).
103 At common law, such a clause could only be effective where X has agreed to indemnify Y: cf. *Gore v Van Der Lann* [1967] 2 QB 31, CA (not a sale case).
104 Could the ambit of s 10 be confined to indirect attempts to exclude ('prevent'), rather than restrict, liability (see Brown (1992) 108 LQR 223–4)?
105 *Tudor Grange Holdings Ltd v Citibank NA* [1991] 4 All ER 1, CA (108 LQR 223; [1994] JBL at 450–55). See *Unfair Terms in Contracts* (2002, 166 Law Comm Consultation), paras 3.114–15.
106 *Quaere* whether such a provision would anyway contravene the rules in paras 16.10 and 18.11?
107 *Per* Browne-Wilkinson VC in the *Tudor Grange* case (above) at 13 (*obiter*).

Sched 1 fall outside only some of its provisions. *Inter alia*, the latter category includes contracts for sale of land.[108]

Subject to this, Part I proceeds by dealing separately with every sort of transaction within its ambit applicable to each of the following types of business liability:[109]

(a)  *implied terms in domestic supply contracts* (ss 6–7: see para 18.18).

(b)  *against negligence liability*. Where a business purports to exclude or restrict (see para 18.16) liability for 'negligence', defined by s 1(1) to include contractual or tortious negligence, s 2 carefully distinguishes the following **consequences** of that negligence.

   (i)   *Death or personal injury*. Where the negligence leads to death or personal injury,[110] under s 2(1) liability cannot be excluded 'by reference to any contract term or to a notice'.[111] However, regardless of negligence, where such death or personal injury arises in connection with a 'consumer supply' of goods or services, any such exclusion clause may be an 'unfair term' (UTCC Regulations, Grey Term (a): see para 11.16).

   (ii)  *Other loss or damage*. 'In the case of other loss or damage, under s 2(2)[112] a person cannot so exclude or restrict his liability for negligence except insofar as the term or notice[111] satisfies the requirement of reasonableness.'[113]

The above s 2 rules would be reproduced in the Unfair Terms Bill (see para 18.27).

(c)  *express terms in contract* (s 3: see para 18.24).

(d)  *indemnity clauses and product liability* (see para 18.23).

(e)  *for misrepresentation*. Where a contract is induced by a misrepresentation (see para 11.01), *prima facie* that will give the contracting party representee certain rights in respect of the contract as against the contracting representor (see para 17.10). However, if that contract purports to exclude or restrict the representor's foregoing liability, new s 3 of the Misrepresentation Act 1967[114] makes that exclusion subject to UCTA's requirement of reasonableness.[113] However, where the misrepresentation induces a 'consumer supply' (see para 11.12) such a clause may be an 'unfair term'.[115]

---

108  E.g. *Electricity Supply Nominees Ltd v IAF Group plc* [1993] 3 All ER 372. As to the distinction between sales of goods and sales of an interest in land, see para 9.03.

109  Except in the case of s 6(4) (see para 18.19), Pt I is limited to attempts to exclude 'business liability' (s 1(3)). 'Business' includes a profession and the activities of any government department or local or public authority (s 14).

110  ' "Personal injury" includes any disease and any impairment of physical or mental condition' (s 14).

111  ' "Notice" includes an announcement, whether or not in writing, and any other communication or pretended communication' (s 14): *Smith v Bush* [1990] 1 AC 831, HL.

112  S 2(3) prevents circumvention of the foregoing rule by reliance on the *volenti* principle.

113  For the reasonableness test, see para 18.24.

114  As amended by s 8 of UCTA, which is not confined to business liability (s 1(3)): see above.

115  UTCC Regulations, Grey Term (n): see para 11.18.

**[18.18]  Dealing as consumer.**[116] Section 12(1) of UCTA 1977 sets out when a party to a contract 'deals as consumer'; and the expression was subsequently also employed in the Sale and Supply of Goods Act 1994 (see paras 11.05A; 13.02; and 29.05). The expression appears to extend to all types of supply contract: it obviously covers sale and quasi-sale, but probably also takes in hp and simple hiring (see below). However, the definition was out of alignment with the EU restriction to private consumers (see para 1.02); and, as a result of the SGG Directive (99/44), the SSG Regulations 2002 begun the process of assimilating the two definitions.[117] The present unsatisfactory situation is that there are in effect two different definitions of 'dealing as consumer' according to whether the transferee is a business or a private consumer as follows:

1. *The supplier* makes the contract 'in the course of a business' (s 12)(1)(b)).[118] This does not cover any supplies by a private supplier (cf. offences under the TDA, ss 1 and 14: see paras 4.03 and 4.15); nor is there any extension here to sales conducted on behalf of a private supplier by a business agent (cf. the implied undertakings as to fitness and quality: see para 14.04). Even where the supplier is involved in a business supplying goods, there must clearly be a connection between that business and the supply, as where items are turned over in the course of that business as stock-in-trade. But does s 12 comprehend any sales which go through the books of that business, including dispositions of its plant and equipment, e.g. of an electrician selling his van? In the *R & B Customs* case (see below) the Court of Appeal restricted the notion to stock-in-trade; but in *Stevenson v Rogers* (set out at para 14.04) a later Court of Appeal construed the same phrase in s 14(2) of the SGA to include such sales of plant (AER at 625–6).

2. *The consumer* does not take the goods 'in the course of a business' (s 12(1)(a)). As a result of the above changes made by the SSG Regulations to s 12(1)(a) of UCTA, a distinction must now be made according to whether there is a private or business consumer.[119]

   (i) *Private consumers*. In the case of a private consumer, the status of the goods (see below) must be ignored (new s 12(1)(A)); but, he is not to be regarded as 'dealing as consumer' where the goods are sold to him 'at public auction of second-hand goods where the individual has the opportunity of attending the auction in person' (new s 12(2)(a)). This leaves within this category internet auctions of new and second-hand goods (as to which, see para 8.17A) and terrestrial auctions of new goods.[120]

---

116 The concept of 'dealing as consumer' is relevant not only for exclusion of statutory undertakings (see para 18.19), but also within UCTA for standard-form contracts (see para 18.20) and indemnities (see para 18.23).

117 Reg 14: see generally, para 14.01. For complete assimilation of the UCTA definition to the UTCCR, see para 18.27.

118 'Business' includes a profession and the activities of any government department or local or public authority': s 14. Does 'business' comprehend a co-operative society, Oxfam, a students' union (see Kidner (1987) 38 NILQ 46 at 53–4)? Cf. CPA, s 45(1): see para 4.33.

119 New s 12(1)(A) of UCTA, introduced by reg 14 of the SSG Regulations 2002. 'Consumer' here has the meaning given to it by reg 2: see para 17.09B.

120 As to sale by auction, see para 10.10, *et seq*. If the goods fail to reach their reserve price and are subsequently sold by the auctioneer by private treaty, the position is unclear: *D & M Trailers (Halifax) v Sterling* [1978] RTR 468, CA.

(ii) *Business consumers*. In *R & B Customs Brokers Ltd v United Dominions Trust Ltd*[121] the Court of Appeal held that the same construction should be used for s 12(1)(a) and (b); and that this phrase should be interpreted in the same narrow manner as the House of Lords had employed in *Davies v Sumner* in relation to the criminal law (TDA: see para 4.03A). In the *R & B Customs* case the court reasoned that, as the conditional purchase of a car was only incidental to R & B Ltd's business activity, there was insufficient regularity of car purchase to make that purchase an *integral* part of R & B Ltd's business,[122] so that it dealt as consumer and the exclusion clause did not preclude their claim for breach of SGA, s 14(3).[123] Neill LJ suggested, *obiter*, that the same meaning should be given to the phrase 'in the course of a business' in both s 12(1)(a) and (b) (AER at 859g): it is for consideration whether this treatment is confined to plant (as opposed to stock-in-trade) supplied to a business.[124] In the case of a business consumer (but not now a private consumer: new s 12(1)(A), above), whilst s 12 is not confined to contracts for the supply of goods, s 12(1)(c) makes it clear that, if the contract is for the supply of goods, whether it be by way of sale, quasi-sale, hiring or hp,[125] the goods must be of 'a type ordinarily supplied for private use or consumption':[126] perhaps a saloon car as opposed to a van. Further, the Act expressly takes outside the concept of 'dealing as consumer' supply to a person who holds himself out as acquiring in the course of business (s 12(1)(a)), e.g. to get a trade discount. What if the supplier knows that the other party is really a private buyer?

Notwithstanding the foregoing, the essence of 'dealing as consumer' is relatively easy to grasp; and any difficulties as the borderline may be eased by s 12(3), which enacts that 'it is for those claiming that a party does not deal as consumer to show that he does not'. For simplification, see the Unfair Terms Bill (see para 18.27).

**[18.19] Exclusion of statutory undertakings**. In relation to domestic contracts (see para 18.16) for the supply of goods,[127] UCTA deals with attempts to exclude or restrict the undertakings **implied** by statute in favour of the transferee as follows:

---

121 [1988] 1 All ER 847, CA (Price 52 MLR 245; Pearce (1989) LMCLQ 371; Twigg-Flesner (2005) 121 LQR 43). Cf. the following definitions: 'debtor' in the CCA (see para 5.24); 'trade or finance purchaser' in Pt III of the HPA 1964 (see para 21.56).

122 *Per* Dillon LJ at 854g–h, treating a one-off sale as integral; and see Neil LJ at 859.

123 See para 14.13. Note that R & B Ltd would not be a 'consumer' for the purposes of the Unfair Terms Regulations: see para 11.12A.

124 The *R & B Customs* rule was applied to a public company hirer in *Feldarol Foundry Plc v Hermes Leasing (London) Ltd* [2004] EWCA Civ 747, CA.

125 By referring to ss 6 and 7 of UCTA, which themselves apply to all four types of supply contract: see para 18.19.

126 S 12(1)(c). See *Benjamin's Sale of Goods*, 6th edn, para 13-073.

127 'Goods' has the same meaning as in the SGA: UCTA, s 14 (as to which, see para 2.01). For the reasons why the blanket prohibition was not extended to services and the effect of this, see Woodroffe, *Goods and Services—The New Law*, paras 7.07–10. Exclusion clauses in service contracts are now controlled by ss 2 and 3 of UCTA (as to which, see paras 18.20; 18.23) and the UTCC Regulations (see para 11.12, *et seq*).

1.  *Undertakings as to title.*[128] Whilst those provisions themselves envisage that the undertakings in contracts for the supply of goods by way of sale, hp[129] or quasi-sale may be limited (see para 12.18), UCTA provides that those (possibly limited) undertakings cannot be excluded or restricted by reference to any contract term.[130] However, the SGSA makes separate provision for simple hiring agreements (see para 12.01A); and UCTA lays down that these cannot be excluded or restricted by any term 'except insofar as it satisfies the requirement of reasonableness' (s 7(4)),[131] a concept considered later (see para 18.24).

2.  *Undertakings as to description, quality, fitness and sample.* These implied undertakings are considered in Chaps 13–15.[132] Bear in mind that some of these undertakings themselves envisage a limited degree of contracting out, e.g. as regards specified defects (see para 14.25), and UCTA does not affect this.[133] In relation to attempts to exclude or restrict them, UCTA draws a distinction according to whether or not the transferee 'deals as consumer' (see para 18.18):

    (a) where he does, then in respect of sales, quasi-sales, hp and simple hiring agreements these undertakings 'cannot be excluded or restricted by reference to any contract term' (ss 6(2) and 7(2).[131] But see para 18.22).

    (b) Where the transferee deals otherwise than as consumer, these undertakings 'can be excluded or restricted by reference to a contract term, but only in so far as the term satisfies the requirement of reasonableness' (ss 6(3) and 7(3):[131] see para 18.24). This category will comprehend those situations where the supplier does not supply in the course of a business,[134] or where the transferee acquires the goods in the course of business,[135] or insofar as the contract is one for services.[136]

Apart from implied terms as to title, these rules would be abolished by the Unfair Terms Bill (see para 18.27).

**[18.20] Express terms: liability in standard form contracts**. Where a transaction falls within the ambit of Pt I (see para 18.16), s 3 introduces restrictions on

---

128 Whilst for most purposes Pt I of UCTA only applies to 'business liability' (see para 18.22), ss 6(4) and 7(3A) expressly extend to private suppliers by way of sale or hp the restrictions on contracting out. What about quasi-sales?

129 Hp is defined simply by reference to the CCA (UCTA, s 14): see para 1.24. For cases within s 7 of UCTA, see para 18.18.

130 Ss 6(1) and 7(3A), inserted by s 17(2) of the SGSA. As to the reason, see Woodroffe, *Op. cit.*, 7.04.

131 UCTA, s 6 applies to the exclusion of implied terms in sale or hp; and UCTA, s 7 applies to the exclusion in quasi-sale and simple hiring. This protection does not extend to third party consumers: Law Commission, *Unfair Terms in Contracts* (2002, Law Com Consult. No. 166), para 3.100.

132 The undertaking as to description (but not fitness/quality) applies to sales by a private seller. In the case of sale and hp, s 6(4) applies to it the UCTA provisions in this paragraph. But there is no comparable provision for quasi-sales and simple hirings in s 7 of UCTA: so it seems s 7 does not apply to exclusions of the implied terms in SGSA, ss 3 and 8, in the case of private sales. S 17(2) of the SGSA would seem to this extent defective.

133 For the effect of this in relation to instructions for use, see para 18.31.

134 S 6(4). E.g. breaches of undertakings as to the description of goods supplied, which apply to private supplies: see para 13.11.

135 E.g. the *Stewart Gill* case (see para 18.16); the *Bacardi* case (see para 11.08). All the implied undertakings considered in Chaps 13–15 are then applicable.

136 Even in instances in favour of one who 'deals as consumer'. See s 3, discussed at para 18.20.

attempts to exclude or restrict (see para 18.17) contractual liability. It applies **only** as between contracting parties and in favour of the weaker party in one or both of the following (sometimes overlapping) circumstances:

(a) *One party 'deals as consumer'*, where the protection will basically be offered to a private individual dealing with a business.[137] It will be noted that this does not require the contract to be on standard terms, nor that it be for the supply of goods, so that s 3 would extend to, e.g. consumer loans (see Chap 7). However, the normal case is likely to involve a standard-form contract for the supply of goods to a consumer; and, here, the transaction may **also** amount to a 'consumer supply contract' and hence attract the UTCC Regulations (see para 11.12): to remove this overlap, this provision would be abolished by the Unfair Terms Bill (see para 18.27).

(b) *'On another's written standard terms'*,[138] which will protect anybody (business or private) contracting on standard **written** terms produced by another (the *proferens*), e.g. the merchant acquirer's franchise contract (see para 2.28). Following the advice of the Law Commission,[139] the Act made no attempt either to apply the protection as against oral terms; nor to define standard terms. It is to be noted that the provision refers to **terms**, not **contracts**: this would appear to extend the ambit of the category to those situations where a standard form contract contains customised parts, e.g. blanks completed at the time,[140] and even where the standard terms were only altered 'without material variation'.[141] Broadly speaking, there would appear to be two possibilities:

(1) The *proferens* refers to his own standard terms. In *St. Albans DC v International Computers Ltd*,[142] the Court of Appeal unanimously confirmed that there was a breach of an express term[143] of ICL's standard terms: they held that the LA had **dealt on** ICL's standard terms within s 3(1)(b) because, notwithstanding the prior negotiations, the LA had entered into the contract on those terms.[144] The Court then proceeded to confirm the decision of Scott Baker J that the limitation clause failed to satisfy the requirement of reasonableness in s 3(2) (see para 18.21).

---

137 For 'dealing as consumer', see *Brigden v American Express Bank Ltd* [2000] IRLR 94 (not a goods case); and para 18.18.

138 *Shearson Lehman Hutton Inc v Maclaine Watson & Co Inc* [1989] 2 Lloyd's Rep. 570 (see [1990] LMCLQ at 309); the *Stewart Gill* case (below), *per* Lord Donaldson MR at 259g. For the unnecessary difficulties with this formulation, see Wilson and Bone (2002) 1 Jo of Obligations & Remedies 29.

139 *Second Report on Exemption Clauses* (1975, Law Com No. 69) para 157.

140 Cf. UTCC, reg 5(3): see para 11.14.

141 *Watford Electronics Ltd v Sanderson CFL Ltd* [2000] 2 All ER (Comm) 984, at para 113 (unappealed point).

142 [1996] 4 All E R 481, CA. See also Lawson (1998) 17 Tr L 487–8.

143 Glidewell LJ also found there to be a breach of an implied term, being expressly supported by Norse LJ (at 487j): whilst the SGA did not apply because the software was not 'goods' (see para 2.02), there was a common law implied term as to fitness (see para 15.22).

144 At 491. This was despite the fact that the negotiations began with the LA's formal invitation to tender.

(2) The *proferens* refers to the standard terms of a third party. In *British Fermentation Products Ltd v Compair Reavell Ltd*,[145] on a trial of preliminary issues and assuming that the IME terms were incorporated in the contract (see para 18.04), the Judge *inter alia* held as follows:

(i) s 3(1)(b) **may** be wide enough to cover third-party terms (here IME's), but only on 'proof that the model form is invariably or at least usually used by the party in question' (at 401b); that, in the absence of an express statutory provision, it was for the party alleging that the statute applied to prove that it applied (at 402b); but that he failed to do so.

(ii) In case he was wrong and s 3 was applicable, the Judge considered whether clause 11 was reasonable (see para 18.25); and in so doing he applied the Statutory guidelines (see para 18.26).

Section 3(1)(b) would be reproduced in the Unfair Terms Bill (see para 18.27).

**[18.21] The effect of s 3**. Where a case falls within s 3(1) (see para 18.20), s 3(2) provides that, as against the weaker party, the business or *proferens* (see para 18.06) contracting party[146] 'cannot by reference to any contract term' escape liability in either of the following two circumstances, 'except insofar as . . . the contract term satisfies the requirement of reasonableness' (see para 18.24, *et seq.*).

(a) When himself in breach of contract, exclude or restrict any liability of his in respect of the breach (s 3(2)(a)). This refers to clauses which 'exclude or restrict liability', a phrase given an extended meaning by s 13;[147] but it has been held that this does not extend to the exclusion of defences which would otherwise be available, e.g. contributory negligence.[148] According to the Law Commission, 'this paragraph does not impose any control over terms which lay down whether a breach of contract occurs';[147] but this suggestion would seem to contradict the approach taken by the Court of Appeal in *Phillips v Hyland* (see para 18.12).

(b) Claim to be entitled under s 3(2)(b) to reduce his liability in one of two ways. It is to be noted that s 3(2)(b) does not refer to clauses which exclude or restrict liability or fall within s 13[147] and is not limited thereto.[149] However, it is seemingly confined to attempted **reductions** in the duties of the business or *proferens* in either of two stated ways; and so presumably it could not touch clauses **increasing** the obligations of the other party.[150] These two ways of **reducing** liability are:

---

145 [1999] 2 All ER (Comm) 389.

146 Not any third party: *Unfair Terms in Contracts* (2002, Law Com. Consultation No. 166), paras 3.100 and 3.102.

147 *Second Report on Exemption Clauses* (1975, Law Com No. 69), para 119. S 3(2)(a) was applied at first instance (unappealed point) in the *Watford Electronics* case (see below), at para 10.

148 *Rolls-Royce Power Engineering plc v Ricardo Consulting Engineers Ltd* [2004] 2 All ER (Comm) 129, at para 75.

149 *Second Report on Exemption Clauses* (1975, Law Com No. 69), para 119; Benjamin's *Sale of Goods*, 6th edn, para 13-087. But see *Unfair Terms in Contracts*, para 3.21.

150 *Paragon Finance plc v Staunton & Nash* (set out at para 11.10), at para 75.

(1) 'To render a contractual performance substantially different from that which was reasonably expected of him',[151] e.g. switch selling (see para 8.13A).[152] So, where the supplier of a computer system delivered defective software, it was no answer for him to plead that there was nothing wrong with the hardware, which could not be used without the software.[153] On the other hand, unilateral variation of interest rates under the terms of a loan would not appear to be a different 'contractual performance'.[154] Perhaps this clause is likely to take over much of the work of the now defunct doctrine of fundamental breach (as to which, see para 18.08). How far beyond the express terms will the courts be prepared to look? Will the courts look to the normal terms in that trade, the relative bargaining power of parties, the extent to which the weaker party understood the term?

(2) 'In respect of the whole or any part of his contractual obligation, to render no performance at all', e.g. an express cancellation clause (see para 10.28), a *force majeure* clause (see para 22.13A). Some such clauses are clearly reasonable, e.g. subject to availability (see para 10.02). Does s 3(2)(b)(ii) apply to stipulations for a tolerance as to quality or quantity? What of provisions denying all contractual promises on one side, and so appearing to translate the arrangement into a unilateral contract?

In *Watford Electronics Ltd v Sanderson CFL Ltd*,[155] the Judge applied the reasonableness test under s 3, but was overturned on appeal. In the leading judgment, Chadwick LJ held as follows: whilst an appellate court should normally refrain from interfering with the trial judge's assessment of reasonableness (see para 18.25), here the first instance judge had misconstrued the legal effect of the exclusions (at paras 32, 37, 40 and 42–8). His Lordship thought the different parts of different exclusion clauses in the contract reasonable as follows:

(i) The entire agreement clause (see para 11.07) was simply an acknowledgement by the parties that their entire agreement was contained in the contract and they could not rely on anything said during their extensive prior negotiations.[156]

(ii) Limitation of direct loss for breach of contract to the contract price would *prima facie* fall within the first rule in *Hadley v Baxendale* (see para 27.41). His Lordship pointed out that the starting point for assessing this loss was the *prima facie* rule contained in s 53(3) of the SGA (see para 29.33), and the limitation clauses simply pegged that value (at para 34); in other words, it was just a liquidated damages clause (see para 27.24).

---

151 As to the possible application to card-not-present transactions, see para 7.09, fn 11. As to whether the provision might apply to 'all monies' *Romalpa* clauses (see para 20.29), see Lawson (1998) 17 Tr L 487 at 490.

152 Unless perhaps it allowed the substitution of more valuable goods: see Benjamin, *Ibid*.

153 *South West Water Services Ltd v ICL* [1999] BLR 420.

154 *Paragon Finance plc v Staunton & Nash* (above), at paras 75–7. For price adjustment formulae, see generally, para 10.05.

155 [2001] 1 All ER (Comm) 696, CA (see 117 LQR 545).

156 If that had been a consumer supply contract, such a clause would probably have been unfair: see Grey term (n); para 11.18.

(iii) Exclusion of indirect loss for breach of contract would *prima facie* fall within the second rule in *Hadley v Baxendale* (see para 27.41). His Lordship (at paras 52–4) applied the guidelines set out in Sched 2 of the 1977 Act (see para 18.26) and also s 11(4) (see para 18.25), adding that two experienced businessmen 'should be taken to be the best judge on the question whether the terms of the agreement are reasonable' (at para 55).

These rules would be largely reproduced in the Unfair Terms Bill (see para 18.27).

**[18.22] Statutory overlap**. Where the contract is one for the supply of goods, there appears to be a considerable overlap between s 3 of UCTA (see paras 18.24–24A) and two others:

(a) *The UTCC Regulations*. Where one party deals as consumer on the other's standard terms (s 3(i)(a) of UCTA: see para 18.20), it may be that the contract is also a 'consumer supply', in which case the claim by the business supplier to do one of the things listed in s 3(2) of UCTA (see para 18.24A) may also be an 'unfair term' within the UTCC Regulations (Sched 3, paras (c), (f): see para 11.16B). The Unfair Terms Bill proposes to abolish UCTA, s 3(I)(a), so removing the overlap (see para 18.27).

(b) *UCTA, ss 6 and 7* (see para 18.19). Where the transferee deals as consumer, the two sets of provisions appear inconsistent: s 3 subjects the terms to the reasonableness test, whereas ss 6 and 7 make them void. However, in *Photoprint Ltd v Forward Trust Ltd*,[157] the judge suggested that the financier's exclusion clause fell outside s 3(2) because its effect was that the statutory implied terms did not become part of FT's 'contractual obligation' (at 156F). Whilst this approach appears at variance with *Phillips Products Ltd v Hyland*,[158] it would avoid any clash with ss 6 and 7 by taking the statutory implied terms outside s 3.[159] The result would be that exclusion of **express** terms would be dealt with by s 3, but exclusion of **implied** terms by ss 6 and 7; and the Unfair Terms Bill may produce a similar result (see para 18.27).

**[18.23] Consumer indemnity clauses and product liability**. This paragraph refers to two UCTA provisions which the Law Commission argue are now pointless (see para 18.27).

1. *Consumer indemnity clauses*.[160] Whereas an exemption clause in respect of business liability for death or personal injury may be void under s 2(1),[161] a clause requiring one dealing as consumer[162] to indemnify another against such

---

157 (1993) 12 Tr LR 146.

158 [1987] 2 All ER 620, CA (see para 18.12).

159 See Macleod (1993) 13 Tr L 96 at 99–100.

160 See generally Adams and Brownsword [1982] JBL 200; and para 25.05. As to the interpretation of indemnity clauses, see para 18.06.

161 As to which, see para 18.17.

162 A business complaining of such an indemnity would proceed under s 2: *Thompson v T Lohan (Plant Hire) Ltd* [1987] 2 All ER 631, CA.

business liability[163] is only by s 4 subject to the test of reasonableness (see para 18.20); and it may be that an important factor here will be the relative ability of the parties to insure against the risk (see s 11(4)(b): set out at para 18.20).

2.   *Product guarantees.* Section 5 of UCTA renders void any provision which attempts to save a manufacturer from negligence liability in respect of a defective product (see para 17.14). However, the Law Commission have pointed out that such a provision already falls within s 2 of UCTA and Part 1 of the CPA.[164]

The above rules are not replicated in the Unfair Terms Bill (see para 18.27).

**[18.24]  The requirement of reasonableness (1).**[165] Pt I of UCTA permits a party to exclude or restrict his liability by a term which satisfies the requirement of reasonableness in all the following cases: (a) negligent damage to property (see para 18.17); (b) standard-form contracts (see para 18.20); (c) indemnities (see para 18.23); (d) some domestic contracts for the supply of goods (see para 18.19); and (e) liability for misrepresentation (see para 18.17). Whilst expressly deeming reasonable any contractual term put forward by a competent authority exercising any statutory jurisdiction,[166] in all other cases s 11(1) explains that the requirement of reasonableness:

> 'is that the term shall have been a fair and reasonable one to be included having regard to the circumstances which were, or ought reasonably to have been, known to or in the contemplation of the parties when the contract was made'.

Whereas under the previous law the issue was whether **reliance** on the objective of the clause was reasonable, e.g. the *George Mitchell* case (set out at para 18.08), the s 11(1) test concentrates on the reasonableness of the **term** in that particular contract rather than in general.[167]

Further, in testing reasonableness, reference cannot be made to circumstances arising **after** the making of the contract,[168] but is confined to matters existing **at the time of contracting.**[169] In the *Stewart Gill* case (see para 18.16) the seller argued that, if clause 12(4) did fall within s 13, the effect of s 3 (see para 18.20) was only to cut out the objectionable words from clause 12(4). The Court of Appeal disagreed, holding

---

163  The section applies whether the liability in question (a) is directly that of the person to be indemnified or is to be incurred by him vicariously (see s 1(4): para 18.22), or (b) is to the person dealing as a consumer or to someone else (s 4(2)). Note that s 4 does not apply to indemnity contracts between two consumers.

164  *Unfair Terms in Contracts* (2005, Law Com No. 292), para 3.48. See paras 11.21, 18.17 and 17.23.

165  See generally Adams and Brownsword (1988) 104 LQR 94.

166  S 29(2) and (3). E.g. terms approved by the Regulator (see para 3.06) under s 56 of the Water Industry Act 1991. But see *Timeload Ltd v British Telecommunications plc* [1995] EMLR 459, CA.

167  So an identical clause may be unreasonable in one contract (*Philips Products Ltd v Hyland* [1987] 2 All ER 620, CA) but not in another (*Thompson v T Lohan (Plant Hire) Ltd* [1987] 2 All ER 631, CA). See Adams and Brownsword, *Op. cit.*, at 114–16.

168  E.g. the *George Mitchell* case (above). Further examples may include a later unexpected event insufficiently serious to frustrate the contract, or situations where the doctrine of frustration cannot be pleaded because self-induced. See further *per* Slade LJ in the *Phillips* case (above), at 628. For frustration, see para 22.09, *et seq.*

169  E.g. how the *proferens* had used the clause in previous disputes with other buyers; or the blame-worthiness of either party: the *George Mitchell* case (see para 18.25). What about codes of practice (see generally, para 3.13) prohibiting the exclusion?

that the reasonableness test must be applied to the whole of clause 12(4): it failed,[170] so that the wider the clause the more likely it is to fail. Nor does the mere longevity of an exclusion clause or disclaimer appear to be any defence,[171] though widespread usage within an industry may indicate that it has been accepted as fair and reasonable by those in the trade.[172] In *Overseas Medical Supplies Ltd v Orient Transport Services Ltd*,[173] Potter LJ set out the following propositions as relevant to the question of reasonableness arising from previous authorities (at 986–7): (1) a significant consideration is the reality of the plaintiff's consent to OTS's clause, which he here doubted (at 991); (2) in the case of a limitation clause rather than an exclusion clause (here £600), the size of the limit as compared with other limits in widely used standard terms; and (3) whilst relevant, the availability of insurance is not conclusive (see para 18.25).

Of considerable practical importance is likely to be s 11(5), which shifts the burden of proof to the supplier.[174] In the *Lease Management* case, it was held that the burden of proof on the *proferens* (LMS) was not to be lightly discharged and certainly not by standard terms purporting to negative an express oral assurance.[175] The whole test would be varied to 'fair and reasonable' by the Unfair Terms Bill (see para 18.27).

**[18.25]  The requirement of reasonableness (2).** Further to the foregoing paragraph, s 11(4) of UCTA deals explicitly with certain special cases.

1.   *Restrictions to a specified sum.* Where a contract term or notice seeks to restrict liability to a specified sum of money, regard shall be had in particular to:

(a)   the resources which he could expect to be available to him for the purpose of meeting the liability should it arise;[176] and

(b)   how far it was open to him to cover himself by insurance.[177]

Both limbs of s 11(4) were applied in the *Watford Electronics* case in finding the exclusions reasonable.[178]

---

170  Lord Donaldson MR at 261e; Stuart-Smith LJ at 262e (see 109 LQR 41); *Overseas Medical Supplies Ltd v Orient Transport Services Ltd* (below). See also *Thomas Witter Ltd v TBP Industries Ltd* (set out at para 26.14). Whilst s 11(4) deliberately says that this is to be without prejudice to the guidelines for supply contracts, does s 11(4) in any other respect restrict consideration of other factors which might otherwise fall within s 11(1)? Cf. the *George Mitchell* case (see para 18.25).

171  E.g. *First National Commercial Bank plc v Loxleys* [1997] PNLR 211, CA (not a goods case).

172  *Overseas Medical Supplies Ltd v Orient Transport Services Ltd* (below).

173  [1999] 1 All ER (Comm) 981, CA (freight forwarding case).

174  Reversing the *George Mitchell* case (see para 18.26). In consumer cases, there may be a trend indicating that suppliers will have considerable difficulty overcoming this presumption: the *Phillips* case (above), at 628.

175  *Lease Management Services Ltd v Purnell Secretarial Services Ltd* (1994) 13 Tr LR 337, CA. Similarly, in the *Overseas Medical Supplies* case (see above) the court likewise held that the *proferens* had not discharged the burden of proof of reasonableness (at 992).

176  *St. Albans City and District Council v International Computers Ltd* [1996] 4 All E R 481, CA, at 492a, 492c, 492e. See the discussion in Atiyah, *Sale of Goods*, 10th edn, 251–2.

177  In the *Overseas Medical* case (see para 18.24), Potter LJ commented that the availability of insurance 'is by no means a decisive factor' (at AER 987f). Compare the *George Mitchell* case (above) where the HL thought the supplier could have insured (see para 18.26) with the *Photo Production* case [1980] AC 827, HL, discussed by Adams and Brownsword (1988) 104 LQR at 101–2.

178  *Watford Electronics Ltd v Sanderson CFL Ltd* (see para 18.21), at para 53.

2.   *Non-contractual disclaimers*. Section 11(3) provides that the rules also apply to non-contractual notices,[179] here termed disclaimers.[180]

3.   *Guidelines for supply contracts*. Section 11(2) provides:

> 'In determining for the purposes of section 6 or 7 above whether a contract term satisfies the requirement of reasonableness, regard shall be had in particular to the matters specified in Schedule 2 to this Act; but this subsection does not prevent the court or arbitrator from holding, in accordance with any rule of law, that a term which purports to exclude or restrict any relevant liability is not a term of the contract.'

These guidelines, which are expressed to be applicable in respect of contracts for the supply of goods,[181] will be considered later (see para 18.26). The latter part of s 11(2) makes it clear that these guidelines have no place in determining the issue of whether the exclusion clause was ever incorporated in the transaction, a matter still governed by the common law (see para 18.04).

It has already been suggested that the pre-1977 approach of the courts to exclusion clauses has begun to change from open hostility to greater even-handedness as the courts realised they could achieve most of their objectives under the 1977 Act (see para 18.08). Indeed, in the *George Mitchell* case (set out at para 18.08), the House in rejecting the clause took a much more neutral postion[182] and Lord Bridge said that an appellate court should refrain from interfering with the original decision on this point unless satisfied that it proceeded on some erroneous principle or was plainly and obviously wrong.[183] However, an appellate court has interfered on sufficient grounds.[178]

**[18.26]  The guidelines**. First introduced in 1973,[184] these guidelines were re-enacted by s 11(2) of UCTA and are expressed by the Act to be relevant for the purposes of ss 6(3), 7(3) and 7(4). The guidelines for the application of the reasonableness test must be applied to the whole of the exclusion clause (see para 18.24) and are now set out in Sched 2 of UCTA as follows:

> '(a)  the strength of the bargaining positions of the parties relative to each other, taking into account (among other things) alternative means by which the customer's requirements could have been met;[185]

---

179  As to the definition of 'notice', e.g. disclaiming negligence liability in tort, see para 18.17. Is a 'swing ticket' within s 11(1) or (3) where the consumer purports to relinquish common law rights in return for promise, e.g. of free replacement parts?

180  *Smith v Bush* [1990] 1 AC 831, HL (clause unreasonable).

181  E.g. *Shearson Lehman Hutton Inc v Maclaine Watson & Co Inc* [1989] 2 Lloyd's Rep. 570 (see [1990] LM & CLQ at 309). They have been applied beyond that context: see para 18.26.

182  See Adams and Brownsword, *Op. cit.*, at 103–4, 114.

183  At 816. See also the *Phillips* case (see para 18.16), at 629; *St. Albans D C v International Computers Ltd* (above), *per* Norse LJ at 491j–492b; the *Overseas Medical Supplies* case (above), *per* Potter LJ at 986g; the *Watford Electronics* case (above). See also Adams and Brownsword (1988) 104 LQR at 99, 113 and 116–19.

184  By SOGIT 1973, enacting the recommendations of the *First Report on Exemption Clauses* (1969, Law Com 24) para 113. See generally, Benjamin's *Sale of Goods*, 6th edn, para 13-081, *et seq*. For reform proposals, see para 18.27.

185  E.g. a two-tier pricing system; or a monopoly supplier. Does paragraph (a) clearly enable the court to take into account the terms on which the goods were supplied to the supplier?

(b)  whether the customer received an inducement to agree to the term, or in accepting it had an opportunity of entering into a similar contract with other persons, but without having to accept a similar term;[186]

(c)  whether the customer knew or ought reasonably to have known of the existence and extent of the term (having regard, among other things, to any custom of the trade and any previous course of dealing between the parties);[187]

(d)  where the term excludes or restricts any relevant liability if some condition is not complied with, whether it was reasonable at the time of the contract to expect that compliance with that condition would be practicable;[188]

(e)  whether the goods were manufactured, processed or adapted to the special order of the customer.'[189]

Plainly, in any particular case, various of these factors may come into play at varying strengths on one side or the other. What the court has to do is weigh the factors and strike a balance. Thus, in *George Mitchell (Chesterhall) Ltd v Finney Lock Seeds Ltd*, the House of Lords unanimously held that, whilst the limitation clause as a matter of construction was apt to protect the seller in respect of the event which occurred (see para 18.08), it would not be 'fair or reasonable to allow reliance' on it. Affirming a unanimous Court of Appeal on this point,[190] Lord Bridge in delivering the judgment of the House identified the following factors (at 817): (a) in other cases of seed failure, the seed merchants had recognised that reliance on the clause was unreasonable and had negotiated settlements of farmers' claims for damages rather than seeking to rely on the limitation clause;[191] (b) the supply of defective seed was due to the carelessness of the seed merchant's associate company; and (c) the seed merchants could have insured against claims arising from the supply of defective seed (see para 18.25).

In the *Stewart Gill* case concerning exclusion of a set-off (see para 18.16), there was both a quasi-sale within s 7 (see para 18.19) and a standard-form contract within s 3 (see para 18.20). Stuart-Smith LJ said that, although the Sched 2 guidelines were not strictly applicable to s 3, 'they are usually regarded as being of general application to the question of reasonableness'.[192] These Guidelines would be largely re-produced as an Indicative List in the Unfair Terms Bill (see para 18.27).

**[18.27]  The draft Unfair Terms Bill.** In response to Government worries about the overlap between the UTCC Regulations (see para 11.12, *et seq.*) and UCTA (see para 18.12, *et seq.*), the Law Commission proposed in their *Unfair Terms in*

---

186  Cf. the *Overseas Medical* case (see para 18.24), *per* Potter LJ in observation (2) at 986–7.

187  The *Watford Electronics* case (see para 18.21) at paras 54, 56 and 62.

188  E.g. notification of complaint within a reasonable time. It has been suggested that para (d) extends to whether a motor dealer carried out any pre-delivery check (see para 15.11).

189  E.g. factory-fitted options; adaptions for a handicapped buyer.

190  Lord Bridge was reluctant to review such a decision on appeal: [1983] 2 All ER at 743f. Contrast the position under the UTCCR (see para 11.15).

191  What has been described as the 'estoppel argument': see Adams and Brownsword (1988) 104 LQR at 100, 107. The moral appears to be that it is safer to be hard-nosed: Adams (1983) 46 MLR at 774. Might such a frequent relaxation take an exclusion clause outside s 3 (see para 18.21)?

192  At 262h. Applied in the *Watford Electronics Ltd* case (see para 18.21). See Adams and Brownsword (1988) 104 LQR at 113.

*Contracts*[193] a new Unfair Terms Bill, which would make the following major changes in the substantive law:

(1) The UTCC Regulations and the remnants of UCTA would be re-enacted in a single, handy, new Bill in clear, accessible terms (para 4.24).

(2) For supplies by business to private consumers, the UCTA prohibition on exclusion of statutory implied terms and the UTCCR protections (largely against express terms) should be re-enacted and enhanced in the Unfair Terms Bill (see para 11.21, items (2)–(4)).

(3) For supplies by business-to-business, UTCCR protections should not be extended to business contracts in general (paras 4.4 and 4.16: see (5) below), but most of them should apply to micro-businesses (para 4.17: see (4) below).

(4) For supplies where one or both parties are micro-businesses (para 5.33), meaning those businesses (or associates) who employed over the preceding year an average of nine or fewer full-time-equivalent employees.[194] Micro-businesses should not only have the same protection from the Bill as any other business (para 5.25: see below), but should be able to challenge (para 5.30) any 'non-core' standard term[195] under a 'fair and reasonable' test.[196] This test should include the same 'Indicative List' guidelines (para 5.84) as for consumers (see para 11.21), but without the consumer-orientated Grey List.[197]

(5) For supplies by business to all other businesses, the new Unfair Terms Bill should in general, but subject to the minor exceptions in (6) below, embody the UCTA rules amended as follows:

   (i) The rules in respect of business liability caused by negligence, either for death or personal injury (s 2(1)), or other damage (s 2(2)), should continue (paras 4.19, 4.21 and 4.40: see para 18.17),[198] this to include non-contractual notices.[199]

   (ii) The prohibition against exclusion of liability for lack of title (ss 6(1) and 7(3A): see para 18.19) should continue (paras 4.20 and 4.21); but the other statutory implied term (ss 6(3), 7(3) and 7(4): see para 18.19) should be freely excludable (paras 4.29 and 4.35).

   (iii) The equivalent of s 3 (see paras 18.22–4) should be retained for all business-to-business contracts other than micro-businesses (as to which, see (4) above), using the test of whether the complainant was dealing 'on

---

193 *Unfair Terms in Contracts* (2005, Law Com No. 292), para 3.48. For review of the Law Commission Consultation Paper ((2002) Law Com. Consult No. 166), see Macdonald (2004) 67 MLR 69.

194 Paras 5.40 and 5.46. There are exempted from the micro-business category: (a) quasi-subsidiaries (para 5.54); (b) the contract or series of contracts exceeds £500,000 (paras 5.59 and 5.61); (c) regulated financial services business (para 5.67); (d) the same savings and exemptions as other businesses (para 5.77: see below).

195 Which has not subsequently been changed in favour of the micro-business (para 5.75).

196 This is to be the same 'fair and reasonable' test as other businesses (para 5.81: see below).

197 The burden of proof should remain on the micro-business (para 5.86); but the effect of failing the test should be as for consumers (para 5.88: see para 11.21). It would not be feasible to introduce an official body (cf. OFT) to provide a preventative regime for micro-businesses (para 5.95).

198 For the position of employees, see paras 6.5 and 6.10.

199 Paras 6.29 and 6.32. This should include the OFT's preventative powers (para 6.35).

the other party's written standard terms of business' (s 3(1): para 4.57),[198] without any special provision for trade association terms (para 4.62).

(iv) The UCTA test of reasonableness should be amended to basically the same test of 'fair and reasonable' as applies to micro-businesses (para 4.70: see (4) above).[200]

(v) As regards international contracts for the sale of goods (s 26: see para 18.13), the Report recommends that the rule should not be replicated for consumer contracts (para 7.6).[201]

(vi) In respect of choice of laws clauses (s 27: see para 18.13), the Report recommends that in a consumer contract, s 27(1) should not be replicated (para 7.9), but that a stronger version of s 27(2) was needed.[202]

(vii) There should remain the UCTA savings and exemptions.[203]

(6) The following UCTA rules should be omitted:

(i) Some sections perform no useful function and should be omitted, in particular the subjection of the statutory implied terms to the reasonableness test (para 4.5; see above), those replicated elsewhere (ss 4 and 5: see para 11.21) and those no longer required.[204]

(ii) The concept of dealing as consumer should not extend to any business consumers (para 4.44).

(iii) As regards attempted exclusion of the statutory implied terms, the UCTA rule that a buyer of second-hand goods at public auction which he had the opportunity to attend in person should not be treated as a consumer (para 3.29: see para 18.18).

(iv) The rule that a consumer must obtain goods of a type ordinarily supplied for private use or consumption should not be replicated (para 3.31), whilst the secondary contract rule should be preserved (s 10: paras 3.142 and 5.90: see para 18.16A).

(7) Supplies of goods not related to the supplier's business comprehends supplies by a consumer both: (a) to a business (see para 11.21); and (b) to another consumer, e.g. private sale of a car. In the latter case, the Report recommends that with regard to the statutory implied promises given by the consumer-supplier to anyone, he remains liable to the present extent in respect of the implied terms as to title, description and sample (paras 6.19, 6.22 and 6.27).

Some, but not all, of these recommended changes could be accomplished without a new statute, but by statutory instrument, perhaps under the deregulation powers (see para 5.10).

---

200 The burden of proof (s 11(5)) should remain on the supplier (para 4.74); and the effect of failing the test as under the UCTA (s 3(2): para 4.77).

201 But for business-to-business contracts a new version was required (paras 7.58 and 7.61).

202 Paras 7.19, 7.21, 7.24 and 7.26. But, in business-to-business contracts, s 27-type controls should remain (paras 7.29, 7.34, 7.62 and 7.66).

203 With the UCTA s 29, there are savings of matters required by enactment, rule of law, international convention or competent authority (para 4.77). As to exemptions from UCTA, see Sched 1 (para 4.84).

204 Ss 9 and 28: see paras 6.38 and 6.42.

# DISCHARGE BY WORDS[205]

**[18.28] Introduction**. In modern times, many goods are supplied together with instructions or warnings as to their use or consumption. Such instructions may prescribe procedures for any one or more of the following purposes: (a) using the goods;[206] (b) maintaining the goods;[207] (c) constructing, erecting or preparing the goods;[208] (d) avoiding hazards in relation to, or emanating from, the goods.[209] They may be addressed to the generality of UK consumers;[210] or they may be customised.[211] And they may originate from any prior party in the chain of distribution (see para 17.01); or they may be introduced in pursuance of an industry-wide voluntary code.[212]

Sometimes warnings will be addressed to the consumer himself,[211] whilst on other occasions they may be addressed to an 'informed intermediary'.[213] Thus, in the case of medicines (see para 4.29), it has been argued that for prescription drugs the warning should be given to the prescriber, whereas for other products it should be given to the consumer.[214] Notwithstanding that there may be little evidence that warnings do change behaviour,[215] they sometimes have legal effect (see para 18.29).

**[18.29] Legal effect**. Particularly where it can be shown that the dangerous nature of the goods gives rise to personal injuries, there are a number of criminal offences to which instructions may be relevant, mostly imposing strict liability, e.g. as to consumer safety,[216] or medicine labels (see para 8.12), or labelling of dangerous goods,[217] or trade description for such as an out-of-date instruction book (see paras 4.06/7). In civil law, the first issue will be the interpretation of the

---

205  See generally Macleod (1981) 97 LQR 550; Clark [1983] JBL 130; Brown [1988] LMCLQ 502; HMSO, *Instructions for Consumer Products* (1988).

206  Besides the implied terms as to fitness and quality (see para 18.32), there may also be instructions as to the time-span within which goods should be used, e.g. 'use by' or 'best before' dates for food (see para 8.11), labels on medicines (see para 8.12).

207  E.g. *Wormell v RHM Agriculture (East) Ltd* (set out at para 18.34).

208  For the position of unprepared goods, see para 14.02. As to unsafe goods, see paras 4.32 and 4.34. As to criminal liability for unsafe goods, see paras 4.31–2; and as to civil liability in contract, see para 14.20.

209  Does this make them more or less objectionable or effective? How far should warnings go in stating the obvious—e.g. on microwaveable food 'Take care—product will be hot after heating'?

210  So that little account is taken of the foibles of particular classes of consumer, e.g. minors, elderly, illiterates, foreigners. For some examples, see [1987] *Which?* 242.

211  E.g. a retailer's verbal instruction, directions for use on medicines, manufacturer's letter to particular consumer.

212  E.g. categorising foods for microwave cooking. For voluntary codes, see generally, para 3.11, *et seq*.

213  E.g. *Holmes v Ashford* [1950] 2 All ER 76, CA.

214  See Ferguson (1992) 12 OJLS 59.

215  See Robinson and Brickle (1992) 142 NLJ 83. Yet the Government invests labels with significance: see DTI, *Modern Markets, Confident Consumers*, 1999, paras 3.4 and 3.5.

216  See the General Product Safety Regulations (para 4.36); *Janbo Trading v Dudley MBC* [1994] 12 Tr LR 190, DC.

217  There are Directives on the labelling of dangerous substances, e.g. 1999/45; 1999/77 (see 18 Tr L 276).

instructions,[218] which are presumably to be read *contra proferentem*.[219] Thus, in *Vacwell Engineering Ltd v BDH Chemicals Ltd*:[220]

> The manufacturers of plant (VE) devised a new method of manufacturing plant utilising the chemical, X, and requested that the defendants supply X to them, making known the purpose for which it was required. X was supplied in glass ampoules bearing the legend 'Harmful Vapour'. Unknown to either party, X was uniquely dangerous in that it exploded violently on contact with water. There having been such an explosion whilst VE's servant was washing some of the ampoules, VE claimed for damage to his premises and for loss of profit. Rees J held the defendants liable because their failure to warn of the explosive risk constituted (1) a breach of the undertakings implied (a) by s 14 of the SGA,[221] and (b) from the course of dealings between the parties (see generally, para 15.22); and (2) the tort of negligence (see generally, para 17.13).

However, it would seem that liability was on the basis that the danger had been pointed out in scientific literature. Without that factor, there could have been liability in contract;[221] but not in the tort of negligence,[222] or under the CPA (s 4(1)(f): see para 17.30).

As regards the tort of negligence, insofar as the action is based on a negligent act, e.g. design or production defects (see para 17.13), the duty of care may be adequately discharged by an aptly worded warning[223] or because the defect was in some way discoverable on reasonable inspection (which might give rise to contributory negligence: see para 27.40); and, if the action is based on negligently drafted instructions, there are the usual difficulties attendant on actions for negligent misstatement, e.g. misleading wiring instructions on an electrical appliance (see generally, para 17.17). Alternatively, where the statutory strict product liability is being considered, it will be relevant in deciding whether a product is defective to have regard to any instructions.[224] Is there a duty to warn of known dangers, either at common law or under the CPA?[225]

If there is a contractual relationship between the parties, this may be by reason of a supply contract, where it has been seen as a duty to inform,[226] or a collateral contract (see para 17.09).

---

218 Can instructions in a foreign language have any relevance to retail supply within the UK? What of Welsh?

219 For the *contra proferentem* rule, see para 18.06. Does it make any difference if the person seeking to rely on the instructions is not their trade originator? Cf. *Wormell v RHM Agriculture (East) Ltd* (set out at para 18.34). See generally Clark, *Product Liability*, Chap 4.

220 [1971] 1 QB 88, [1969] 3 All ER 1681. This case was settled during appeal [1970] 3 All ER 553. See Weaver (1970) 33 MLR 446. See generally, Mildred, *Product Liability*, 2000, paras 7.327–31 and 338–40; 356.

221 What is now s 14(3): see *Frost v Aylesbury Dairy* (set out at para 14.08).

222 See para 17.09. E.g. *Lambert v Lewis* (set out at para 17.06). As to manufacturers' guarantees, see para 17.09A.

223 *Holmes v Ashford* [1950] 2 All ER 76, CA; the *Vacwell Engineering* case (above); *Hurley v Dyke* [1979] RTR 265, HL. For the effect of such disclaimers, see generally, para 18.04.

224 CPA, s 3(2)(a): see para 17.28. But see the state-of-the-art defence (para 17.30)?

225 See Clarke, *Op. cit.*, 85–9. As to the ineffectiveness in fact of warnings, see (1992) 142 NLJ 83.

226 Hedley [2001] JBL 114, at 117, 122–4: see para 18.32.

## Contracts for the supply of goods

**[18.30] Incorporation.** Where there is a contract for the supply of goods between the party injured and the person seeking to rely on the instructions, the first question in determining civil liability[227] is whether the instructions have been incorporated in the contract (see para 18.04). If there is a signed supply contract, the instructions may be incorporated therein expressly,[228] or impliedly (see para 11.08), provided that this is done before the contract was made.[229] If there is no signed supply contract, then the instructions could be incorporated by actual or reasonable notice;[230] but, the more unusual the instructions, the more steps have to be taken to give such notice.[231] However, if the instructions have not been incorporated in either of these ways, then it would seem that they can only take effect as part of the goods supplied (see para 18.33). In the case of a consumer supply contract, the common law rules may be unfair.[232]

### Pre-contract instructions

**[18.31]** Where the instructions as to the use of goods supplied are served before formation of the supply contract (see para 18.30), they may *prima facie* amount to a promise (express or implied) by the transferee to use the goods in conformity with those instructions, e.g. 'Do not spray aerosol on naked flame or burn container'. Suppose those instructions are inconsistent with other terms of the contract. If the instructions and other inconsistent terms are both express, the position would appear to be this: insofar as both terms are embodied in a contractual document, it would presumably be read *contra proferentem* the supplier;[233] whereas, if one is embodied in the writing and the other in an oral undertaking, the latter may override the former at common law[234] or the whole fall within the UTCC Regulations (see UTCC Grey term (b): see para 11.16).

Leaving aside the special provisions in contracts by sample (see paras 15.03–10), it will be recalled that the major terms implied into contracts for the supply of goods are as to their description,[235] fitness[236] and satisfactory quality (see para 14.15, *et seq.*). Furthermore, under the provisions of UCTA, the extent to which these terms may be 'excluded or restricted' (see para 18.16) depends on whether or not the transferee is 'dealing as consumer' (see para 18.18): if he does, then the instructions will be void to the extent that they 'exclude or restrict' the statutory

---

227 An incorrect statement or instructions supplied with goods may amount to an offence under the TDA if the instructions can be said to induce entry into the supply contract: see para 4.03.
228 Express incorporation may be either directly (where the instructions form part of the signed contract) or by reference (see para 11.07).
229 *Olley v Marlborough Court* [1949] I KB 532, CA (not a sale case).
230 E.g. the *Vacwell Engineering* case (incorporation by course of dealings: set out at para 18.29).
231 *Interfoto Picture Library Ltd v Stiletto Ltd* [1988] 1 All ER 348, CA (Macdonald [1988] JBL 375).
232 Grey Term (i): see para 11.17.
233 E.g. the *Vacwell Engineering* case (set out at para 18.29). For the *contra proferentem* rule, see para 18.06.
234 *J Evans & Sons (Portsmouth) Ltd v Andrea Mezario Ltd* [1976] 2 All ER 930, CA (not a sale case).
235 See para 13.11, *et seq.*
236 See para 14.07, *et seq.*

implied terms (see para 18.19); whereas, if the transferee does not 'deal as consumer', the instructions may only take effect insofar as they satisfy the requirement of reasonableness.[237] The extent to which instructions for use may be compatible with these statutory implied terms is considered below (see para 18.32).

[18.32] **Compatibility with statutory terms**. Suppose the instructions are clearly part of the goods supplied.[238] There must now be considered the extent to which pre-contract instructions for use may be compatible with the statutory undertakings as to the goods supplied.

1.  *Undertakings as to description*. Pre-contract instructions may render obvious the contractual identity of the goods,[239] e.g. dismantling instructions may show that a machine was only supplied for scrap.

2.  *Undertakings as to fitness*. Insofar as the instructions originate from a remote party in the chain of distribution (see para 17.01), that may show that the transferee did not rely on the skill and judgment of his immediate supplier as regards matters falling within the ambit of the instructions;[240] or reasonable fitness may be judged in the light of the instructions,[241] e.g. a 'Dry-Clean Only' label on a garment whose fabrics shrink at different rates if washed.

3.  *Undertakings as to satisfactory quality*. In relation to this undertaking (see para 14.18), it may be 'reasonable' to fix the characteristics required of the goods by the statutory definition in the light of the instructions for their use: like any other label, instructions affixed to goods are to be taken into consideration in assessing their quality.[242] Further, it may be possible to construe pre-contract instructions as a specified defect (see para 14.25), e.g. where there is a warning printed on glass ampoules against careless submersion in water.[243]

*Post-contract instructions*

[18.33] Where instructions as to the use of goods supplied are only communicated *after* formation of the supply contract (see para 18.30), it would not usually seem possible for them to affect the formulation of the supplier's contractual duties in the manner above considered.[244] Nor can post-contract instructions have any effect as *modifying* the supply contract,[245] except in the (perhaps unlikely) event that they are supported by fresh consideration.[246] On the other hand, such post-contractual

---

237 See para 18.24. Alternatively, the instructions may be subject to the reasonableness test by reason of s 3 of UCTA: see generally, para 18.21.

238 *Per* Glidewell LJ in *St Albans DC v ICL* (see para 18.20), at 493f.

239 The test for this undertaking probably turns on any difference in the identity of the goods: see para 13.13.

240 For this limitation on the undertakings as to fitness, see paras 14.13–14.

241 *Wormell v RHM Agriculture Ltd* (set out at para 18.34).

242 *Niblett's* case (set out at para 12.03); and see generally, para 14.16/17. Alternatively, instructions may be considered as a relevant circumstance: see para 14.19.

243 *Vacwell Engineering Ltd v BDH Chemicals Ltd* (set out at para 18.29), *obiter*, at 104C–G.

244 See paras 18.31–2. Except perhaps by trade custom: see *Shearson Lehman Hutton Inc v Maclaine Watson & Co Ltd* [1989] 2 Lloyd's Rep. 570 (see [1990] LMCLQ at 309); and generally, para 15.11.

245 *Roscorla v Thomas* (1842) 3 QB 234.

246 For variation by subsequent contract, see para 26.18.

instructions, e.g. as part of a manufacturer's product recall, might have a legal effect as part of the goods supplied[247] in either of the following ways:

(a)  to discharge by performance the supplier's duties (see para 18.34); or

(b)  by reducing or extinguishing the damages flowing from the supplier's breach of those duties (see para 18.35).

**[18.34] Instructions performing duties**. Whilst post-contractual instructions cannot affect the **formulation** of the supplier's contractual duties (see para 18.33) they may be relevant to the **performance** of those duties, either in whole or in part. Thus, in *Wormall v RHM Agriculture (East) Ltd*:[248]

> The plaintiff farmer (P) telephoned the defendant dealer in agricultural produce (D) and enquired whether he had any herbicide designed to kill wild oats in fields of wheat so late in the 1983 season. D recommended Commando, which P duly ordered. The copious manufacturer's instructions on the canisters *inter alia* directed that Commando was to be applied only between particular stages of crop growth and during particular weather conditions and added 'Damage may occur to crops sprayed after the recommended growth stage'. Unfortunately, weather conditions were not suitable for application until the recommended growth stage had passed, when Commando was applied but had very little effect on either the wild oats or wheat. P sued for breach of SGA, s 14(3).

The first-instance judge held that these instructions were part of the contract goods;[249] that the whole package of chemicals with instructions must be looked at to determine whether it was fit; that P believed the instructions meant merely that there was a risk of damage to the wheat crop from late application (a risk he was prepared to take); and that Commando was not fit because P had interpreted the instructions as a reasonable farmer. On the last point, he was unanimously reversed by the Court of Appeal[250] because P had ignored the clear warning. The judge had found the instructions misleading as to the effect of disregarding the warning; but the CA held that this was irrelevant (at 80g; 82b). Whilst the goods were not absolutely fit, they were reasonably fit (see below).

The effect of post-contract instructions would therefore appear to be as follows:

1.  *Undertakings as to fitness*. Suppose the post-contract instructions specify the manner in which the goods are to be used, e.g. a garment to be dry-cleaned only. As the requirement of the undertakings is that the goods must be 'reasonably fit' (see para 14.09), the instructions are to be approached as evidence of what constitutes reasonable use.[251]

---

247  As to goods supplied under the contract, see further, para 14.03.

248  [1987] 3 All ER 75, [1987] 1 WLR 1091, CA. See Mildred, *Product Liability* (2000) paras 3.90, 7.26, 7.319 and 7.341.

249  [1986] 1 All ER 769 at 778. As to goods supplied for the purpose of these undertakings, see para 14.03.

250  During the 1983 season, there never was a time in P's locality when the weather conditions and crop development would have allowed application (*per* Dillon LJ at 77).

251  The *Wormall* case (see above). See also *Vacwell Engineering* case (set out at para 18.29), where the instructions suggested only precautions against inhaling the vapour.

2. *Undertakings as to satisfactory quality*. Likewise, in relation to this statutory undertaking (see para 14.19), post-contract instructions may be a 'relevant circumstance' (as to multi-purpose goods, see para 14.21).

In the case of pre-contract instructions, the common law does not require actual notice, so long as the *supplier* does what is reasonably necessary to bring them to the attention of the transferee (see para 18.04). Similarly, in the case of post-contract instructions, it seems likely from the *Wormell* case that constructive notice to the transferee could amount to performance of the supplier's contractual duties.[252] Does the matter turn at common law upon what a reasonable consumer should anticipate by way of instructions?[253] In any event, post-contract instructions may be affected by statute: first, they may amount to 'notice' within s 13(1) of UCTA (see para 18.16), in which case the instructions might be subject to the reasonableness test in s 3(2)(b) (see para 18.21); and second, whilst the UTCC Regulations only affect 'contractual terms' (reg 5(1): see para 11.15), the instructions might be included as having an effect on other terms within Grey Term (k) (see para 11.17).

Even if post-contractual instructions do not prevent liability arising, they may reduce or extinguish damages (see para 18.35).

**[18.35] Instructions reducing or extinguishing damage**. The damages flowing from a breach by the supplier of his duties under the supply contract is limited by the chain of causation (see para 27.29) and the doctrine of mitigation of damage (see para 27.44). Suppose a transferee discovers, but ignores, post-contract instructions. In *Dobell & Co Ltd v Barber & Garrett*:[254]

> Goods were sold with a compulsory warranty of quality,[255] but the seller expressly disclaimed responsibility for the defect in question. The majority of the Court of Appeal nevertheless held that the buyer was entitled to resell the goods in reliance on the statutory warranty, and recover damages paid to his sub-buyers.

Lawrence LJ pointed out that, were it otherwise, the seller could always protect himself against the full consequences naturally flowing from his breach of warranty by stating that he did not accept the responsibility which the Act cast upon him.[256] Greer LJ dissented on the grounds that, in the light of the seller's attempted disclaimer, it was 'unreasonable' for the buyer to resell the goods without having them analysed;[257] and it has subsequently been held by the House of Lords in another case that the chain of causation is broken where the buyer continued to use the goods with **actual** knowledge of the remediable breach as regards subsequent consequential loss.[258]

---

252 Dillon LJ pointed out that both P and D knew that the goods would be supplied with detailed instructions (at 77e). Contrast *Feuer Leather Corpn v Frank Johnstone & Sons* [1981] Com LR 251 (appealed on another point). But see generally Reynolds [1984] JBL 14; Goode (1983) 3 LS at 292. Cf. disclaimers as a defence to strict criminal liability: see para 4.09.

253 Is this to import a sort of constructive notice into commercial transactions, notwithstanding the general prohibition against so doing (see 109 LQR at 369–70).

254 [1931] 1 KB 219, CA. See also *Kendall v Lillico* (set out at para 14.10).

255 Under s 2 of the Fertilisers and Feeding Stuffs Act 1926 (now replaced by s 72 of the Agriculture Act 1970: see para 15.20).

256 At 237. Cited with approval by McGregor on *Damages*, 17th edn, para 20-069.

257 At 247. See also Roche J at first instance. Cf. the *Wormell* case (set out at para 18.34).

258 *Lambert v Lewis* (set out at para 17.06). See also *Worsley v Tambrands Ltd* [2000] CLY 548; [2000] PIQR P95, CA. Constructive notice is not enough at common law: see paras 21.41 and 21.49.

The position of post-contractual instructions which identify a defect in the goods but do not oust the implied undertakings[259] would appear to be this: in respect of the *prima facie* measure of damages flowing from the reduced value of the goods in the defective state,[260] the instructions appear to be no more than advance notice of breach;[254] but, as regards consequential loss,[261] the supplier is under no liability for such loss occurring subsequent to the transferee's discovery of the defect, whether or not such discovery arises from the instructions.[258] The difficult area seems to concern consequential loss arising **before** discovery of the defects.[262] The current view would appear to be that the supplier cannot plead the contributory negligence of his transferee in not discovering that instruction (see para 27.40), though the effect of such a defence is canvassed elsewhere.[263]

---

259 In the *Wormell* case (above), the CA do not appear to have addressed the issue of how, in a contract made by phone, unmentioned instructions can oust the undertakings. At any rate, it is submitted that the ruling cannot apply to totally unexpected instructions.

260 See paras 29.30 and 29.33.

261 See paras 29.23 and 29.36.

262 E.g. washing instructions on clothes; assembly instructions on goods supplied in kit-form.

263 Macleod (1981) 97 LQR 550, at 572–3.

# PART 5

# THE CONVEYANCE IN SUPPLY CONTRACTS

# CHAPTER 19

# THE EFFECTS OF THE CONTRACT

## CONTRACT AND CONVEYANCE

**[19.01] Introduction**. Leaving aside most simple bailments (see para 1.17), the object of the parties to the transaction of sale, quasi-sale or hp is normally to transfer the proprietary rights in the subject-matter of the contract; and the conveyancing aspect of the transaction must now be examined. The difference between contractual and proprietary rights (rights *in rem*) is traditionally this: a contractual right merely gives the party entitled a right against the other contracting party, whereas a proprietary right gives an interest in the goods which can also be asserted against third parties.

At a fairly early stage, the English law of sale rejected the idea that proprietary rights in goods sold automatically passed at the time of either contract or delivery:[1] instead, it was settled that the matter should be left to the agreement between the parties.[2] The SGA lays down rules as to the passing of proprietary rights where the parties do not evince any specific intent in this respect: these rules will be considered in Chap 20 and are presumably also applicable to quasi-sales[3] and to hp upon exercise of the option to purchase.[4]

Whilst, therefore, the actual conveyance may, but need not, take place at the time the contract is made, it remains true that the contract suffices to effect the conveyance.[5] Unlike certain other systems of laws, and even certain other branches of our own law,[6] the English law of sale does not require some legal act distinct from the contract to effect the conveyance. An apparently similar position is to be found in contracts of hp, though here the agreement usually provides that the option cannot be exercised—and the contract of sale made—until all the instalments of hire rent have been paid (see para 1.25).

**[19.02] Possession and ownership**. Having separated the contract from the conveyance, it is necessary to examine what is conveyed by the transaction. In common parlance, it is usually said that the parties intend to transfer the 'ownership' in the goods; but this is not a term of art and merely obscures the true position.[7] Early law tended to concentrate on possession, which was protected largely for two reasons, the one proprietary and the other tortious (delictual). Whilst the real actions in

---

1    For the permutations of the passing of property and delivery, see para 23.02.
2    See now the SGA, ss 2(6) and 17. For alternative solutions, see TB Smith, *Property Problems in Sale*, 53, *et seq*.
3    Because the common law rules were largely codified in the SGA 1893: see Chap 20. What should happen where there was a change, e.g. the requirement of notice in rules 2 and 3 of s 18 (see para 20.13).
4    Because the exercise of the option completes the sale: see para 1.22.
5    This is recognised by the statutory definition of sale to be found in the SGA, s 61(1). See also the distinction between 'sale' and 'agreement to sell', para 1.10.
6    A delivery, deed or special statutory form may be required in the case of all gifts, transfers for value of choses in action, mortgages or pledges of chattels.
7    See Crossley Vaines, *Personal Property*, 5th edn, Chap 4; Bell, *Personal Property*, Chap 1.

respect of land developed their proprietary side in their protection of seizen ('ownership'?),[8] in the case of chattels the law concentrated on the tortious element of taking possession.[9] The long-term effect of this development was the evolution of the dichotomy between real and personal property at common law: the former was governed by the law of 'real property', but the latter mostly developed through the law of crime and tort,[10] the proprietary rules remaining rudimentary (see para 19.03) until the efforts of Blackburn.[11]

In the field of personal property, possession has been protected by the action of trespass,[12] and title by the actions of conversion[13] and detinue,[14] these torts now all being subsumed into the statutory tort of 'wrongful interference with goods' (see para 19.04). However, the chief common law tort for the protection of an interest in goods was conversion (see para 19.05). The scope of conversion was even employed to protect the value in a piece of paper, e.g. a cheque;[15] but the tort has never extended to a mere chose in action,[16] such as rights under a contract (see para 7.15).

**[19.03] Personal property**. At the outset of the consideration of the notion of personal property, three points must be made.[17] *First*, whatever be the effect of the doctrine of seizen in the law of real property, our common law probably does not recognise any theory of absolute ownership in the case of personal property;[18] and, whilst ss 16–20 of the SGA would appear to recognise an absolute right,[19] when a remedy is sought the courts are only concerned with the relative question of which of the two parties before the court has the better right to the goods.[20] *Second*, the doctrine of estates in real property has no application to personal property:[21] generally speaking, *successive* interests, e.g. life interests, in personal property can only exist behind a trust;[22] and a mortgagor of personalty has only an equity of redemption (see paras 25.20 and 25.25). Thus, in one sense, the 'ownership' of personalty is

---

8   Holdsworth, *History of English Law*, 3rd edn, vii, 465.
9   Holdsworth, *Op. cit.*, vii, 466–8; TB Smith, *Property Problems in Sale*, 38; Bridge [1991] LM & CLQ 52 at 63, *et seq*.
10  For tortious developments, see para 19.04.
11  See *Blackburn on Sale*, 1845. Was this work partly responsible for Chalmers assigning such a central place to 'property' in his SGA 1893 (see para 19.08)?
12  *Wilson v Lombank Ltd* [1963] 1 All ER 740.
13  *The Winkfield* [1902] P 42.
14  *Kahler v Midland Bank Ltd* [1950] AC 24, HL.
15  See Paget on *Banking*, 12th edn, paras 21.2–3 and 23.15.
16  *OBG Ltd v Allan* [2005] 2 QB 762, CA (122 LQR 31).
17  See further Crossley Vaines, *Personal Property*, 5th edn, Chap 4; *Oxford Essays in Jurisprudence*, Chap V, *Ownership* (by Honore); Goode, *Property Rights and Insolvency in Sale Transactions*, Chap 1; Bell, *Personal Property*, Chap 2.
18  But see Maitland (1885) 1 LQR 324; Hudson (1984) 100 LQR at 118, fn 60; and para 19.08.
19  But see Chap 20. It has been argued that the SGA concept of the property in goods should be expanded into an absolute legal interest analogous to the fee simple in land: see para 19.08.
20  See the action in conversion (wrongful interference with goods) considered at para 19.04. For situations where a plaintiff in conversion may be entitled only to something less than the market value of goods, see para 27.30.
21  See Bell, *Op. cit.*, 75.
22  E.g. LPA 1925, s 130 (entailed interests in real and personal property); and as to conversion, see para 19.05. As to trusts of chattels, see para 19.23; and generally Crossley Vaines, *Op. cit.*, 30–2.

indivisible;[23] but there may be *concurrent* legal rights in personal property,[24] as for instance between a bailor and bailee[25] or co-owners,[26] though this rule does not seem to have been extended to instalment sales (see para 24.22). *Third*, the distinction between ownership and possession of goods is not always apparent, because the courts will normally accept possession as *prima facie* proof of ownership; and this lends some substance to the maxim that 'possession is nine-tenths of the law'.[27] This maxim may, for instance, conceal some nice problems in relation to motor vehicles.[28]

## The title to goods

**[19.04] Wrongful interference with goods.**[29] At common law, the buyer or hirer might wrongfully deprive the supplier of the goods supplied in various different ways, which amount to a number of separate and overlapping torts. However, the Torts (Interference with Goods) Act 1977 has made a welcome (albeit modest) start on the long overdue simplification of this excessively technical branch of the law, subsuming all the following different actions under one new statutory tort, termed 'wrongful interference with goods' (s 1):[30]

1. *Conversion.* The Act refers to any act that would have amounted to an act of conversion (trover) at common law (s 1(a)), thus incorporating rather than replacing all the old learning (see further, paras 19.05–06). At common law, a wrongful detention of goods,[31] evidenced by a refusal to deliver them up on demand, amounted to both the torts of detinue[32] and conversion;[33] but the tort of detinue has been abolished by the 1977 Act (s 2(1)), the one area where the two torts might not overlap[34] now being brought within the purview of conversion (s 2(2)).

2. *Trespass.* It is provided that the statutory tort extends to any taking of the goods

---

23   See the explanations in Crossley Vaines, *Personal Property*, 41; Bell, *Op. cit.*, 67.

24   For examples of co-ownership, see *Lloyds Bank Ltd v Bank of America* [1938] 2 KB 147, CA; *The Ypatianna* [1987] 3 All ER 893 (inseparably mixed goods); and Goode, *Commercial Law*, 3rd edn, 220–1. To transfer a good title to personal property, all persons with a concurrent interest must act together: see the *Lloyds Bank* case (above). What if one co-owner murdered the other?

25   See McMeel [2003] LMCLQ 169 at 186, *et seq*. As to simple bailment, see para 1.17; as to hp, see para 1.20; as to pledges, see para 25.15, *et seq*. The rule does not apply to liens, which create no proprietary interest: see para 25.02.

26   See Bell, *Op. cit.*, 74–5; and see para 20.22A.

27   See Bell, *Op. cit.*, 76–7. But matters of proof aside, the common law has long preferred ownership to possession: see *Hartrop v Hoare* (1743) Atk 44 (see 103 LQR 182); and para 21.13.

28   E.g. the accession or intermixture of spare parts (see para 19.05); the fixture of accessories (see para 25.23); the title to abandoned vehicles (see para 12.17).

29   See generally Winfield and Jolowicz, *Tort*, 16th edn, Chap 17; *Street on Torts*, 10th edn, Chap 4.

30   It should be borne in mind that some such tortious liability may be modified or excluded by the terms of any agreement between the parties (see para 18.03) and does not apply to rights under a contract (see para 19.02).

31   But there may be no duty on the bailee to return the goods to the bailor: see para 24.25.

32   *Strand Electric and Engineering Co Ltd v Brisford Entertainment Ltd* (see para 27.33) But see fn 34, below.

33   *Henderson & Co v Williams* (set out at para 21.11/12).

34   Where the refusal to return the goods did not amount to a denial of title, as where the bailee had negligently lost the bailed goods, it had never been decided whether there was a conversion.

out of the actual or constructive possession of the supplier (s 1(b)), which at common law would have amounted to trespass to goods.[35]

3. *Negligence*. The 1977 Act comprehends the tort of negligence (see para 17.13) 'so far as it results in damage to goods or an interest in goods' (s 1(c)). For instance, a bailee in possession of goods will owe a duty of care to his bailor (see para 1.17); and as to product liability, see paras 17.15 and 17.19.

4. *Residual torts*. The section also encompasses other torts so far as they result in damage to goods (s 1(d)). This category will include permanent damage by a third party to a bailor's residuary interest in goods,[36] which it has been suggested includes in some circumstances the bailor under an instalment credit contract.[37] It has been expressly extended to product liability claims.[38] Where a bailor at will has recovered in full for the loss from the third party, his bailee may not subsequently recover from that third party.[39]

**[19.05] Acts of conversion**. Acts of conversion have been summarised as any 'dealing with the goods which amounts to an unjustifiable denial of [P's] rights [in goods] or the assertion of rights inconsistent therewith'[40] and include the following:

1. *Wrongfully taking possession*. This comprehends taking possession in such a manner as to question P's title, as by taking possession under a contract to purchase the goods from a third party,[41] or wrongful seizure by a sheriff in purported execution.[42] On the other hand, the mere receipt of goods as an involuntary bailee is not conversion; and this rule has been extended by statute to the retention of unsolicited goods (see para 8.18). Wrongful repossession by the supplier from his transferee is conversion,[43] as is withholding of goods by an administrator.[44] For auctioneers, see para 10.11.

2. *Abusing possession*. This may take many forms, such as the sale and delivery to a third party of P's goods or documents of title;[45] or the use of a borrowed car to carry contraband;[46] or a negligent loss of goods by their bailee (see para 19.04); or where D's possession is adverse to P (see para 19.05A). On the other hand, a

---

35  *Wilson v Lombank Ltd* [1963] 1 All ER 740. See further, para 17.13.

36  *HSBC Rail (UK) Ltd v Network Rail etc Ltd* [2006] 1 All ER 343, CA.

37  See Street, *Op. cit.*, 72; Goode, *HP Law & Practice*, 2nd edn, 775–6.

38  CPA, Sched 4, para 5. See generally, para 17.24, *et seq*.

39  *O'Sullivan v Williams* [1992] 3 All ER 385, CA.

40  Winfield and Jolowicz, *Tort*, 16th edn, para 17.6.

41  *Ingram v Little* [1961] 1 QB 31, CA; *GE Capital Bank Ltd v Rushton* (set out at para 21.56), R. Taking possession of goods by way of pledge was not a conversion at common law; but it has been made so by the 1977 Act (s 11(2)) and see further, para 25.15.

42  *Neumann v Bakeaway Ltd* [1983] 2 All ER 935, CA. *Contra* if the seizure is within the terms of the writ: see para 19.20. As to wheel-clamping, see *Arthur v Anker* [1996] 3 All 783, CA.

43  *The Playa Larga* [1983] 2 Lloyd's Rep 171, CA; recaption (see para 24.23). It is also a breach of the undertaking as to quiet possession: see para 12.16.

44  *Barclays Mercantile Business Finance Ltd v Sibee Developments Ltd* [1993] 2 All ER 195 (see further, para 19.19).

45  *Hollins v Fowler* (1875) LR 7 HL 757; *Union Transport Finance Ltd v British Car Auctions Ltd* [1978] 2 All ER 385, CA; *Long v Jones* [1990] CLY 4033, DC; *GE Capital Bank Ltd v Rushton* (above), R. There is an exception in favour of a bailee of uncollected goods: Torts Act 1977, ss 12–13; *Jerry Juhan Developments SA v Avon Tyres Ltd* [1999] CLY 834; [2005] UTCC *Bulletin* A/J, Pratt.

46  *Moorgate Mercantile Co Ltd v Finch* [1962] 1 QB 701, CA (see Customs and Excise Management Act 1979, s 152(b)).

mere contract to sell P's goods to a third party without any transfer of possession does not amount to conversion,[47] though it might amount to an injurious falsehood (see para 17.17).

3.  *Residual acts.* Any other action inconsistent with P's rights to the goods may be conversion: this may include signing a delivery order for goods which are delivered under that order;[48] or refusing to hand over the log-book of a car;[49] or deprivation of title by reason of unauthorised accession[50] or intermixture.[51] However, it has now been settled by the Torts Act 1977 that a mere denial of P's title by a person who is not in possession will not without more amount to a conversion (s 11(3)). The Act also confirmed the rules for co-owners, who broadly must act together in dealing with goods (s 10); and, where there is disagreement, there should be application to the court (LPA 1925, s 188). For the exception as regards co-owners of an undivided bulk, see para 20.22B.

**[19.05A] Adverse possession**. The defendant (D) may commit conversion where his possession is adverse to the plaintiff owner (P). For instance, D may so commit conversion where he wrongfully refuses to return goods to P (see para 24.25), though this will depend upon the bailee being in breach of a duty to return the goods.[52] What amounts to an act of conversion (see para 19.05) was judicially considered in *Kuwait Airways Corp v Iraqi Airways Co (No. 3)*:[53]

> In 1990, Iraq annexed Kuwait, seized ten aircraft belonging to the Kuwaiti airline (KAC), took them to Iraq and purported to transfer them to the Iraqi airline (IAC). During the 1991 coalition military action against Iraq, four of the aircraft were flown to Mosul (the Mosul four), where they were destroyed by coalition action. The other six were evacuated to Iran on orders of the Iraqi government (the Iran six). After the liberation of Kuwait, the Iran six aircraft were returned to KAC, who had to pay Iran $US 20M for the cost of keeping, sheltering and maintaining them. KAC sued IAC in the tort of conversion. The House of Lords, refused to accept the validity of the transfer by the Iraqi State of the aircraft to IAC for reasons beyond the scope of this book: it then held IAC liable for conversion of the Iran six, but not the Mosul four.

In delivering the leading judgment (with which three other Law Lords agreed), Lord Nicholls, whilst warning that there was no precise definition of universal application, identified three basic feature of the tort of conversion (at para 39):

> 'First, [IAC's] conduct was inconsistent with the rights of the owner (or other person entitled to possession). Second, the conduct was deliberate, not accidental. Third, the

---

47  *Lancashire Wagon Co v Fitzhugh* (1861) 6 H & N 592.

48  See Winfield and Jolowicz, *Op. cit.*, para 17.13, fn 2.

49  *Bryanston Leasing Ltd v Principality Finance Ltd* [1977] RTR 45. Cf. *Douglas Valley Finance Co Ltd v S Hughes (Hirers) Ltd* [1969] 1 QB 738 (special transferable commercial vehicle licences).

50  *Glencore International AG v Metro Trading Inc* [2001] 1 All ER (Comm) 103. Alternatively, consider the removal of items attached to goods, e.g. severing fixtures (see para 25.23). As to cherished vehicle registration numbers, see *Naylor v Hutson* [1994] FSR 63.

51  E.g. fixtures (see para 25.23), the mixture of woodchips and resin to make chipboard in *Borden's* case [1981] Ch 25, CA. See generally Crossley Vaines, *Personal Property*, 5th edn, Chap 19; TB Smith, *Property Problems in Sale*, 197–213; Guest (1964) 27 MLR 505; McCormack (1990) 10 LS 293; 12 LS at 203; Hickey (2003) 66 MLR 368. As to ownership, see para 19.03.

52  See para 24.45. For regulated agreements, see CCA, s 134: see para 24.42.

53  [2002] 2 AC 883, [2002] 3 All ER 209, HL (see 118 LQR 544).

conduct was so extensive an encroachment on the rights of the owner as to exclude him from use and possession of the goods.'

In finding these tests all satisfied, Lord Nicholls commented as follows: (1) whilst the wrongdoer (the Iraqi State) will frequently deprive the owner of possession, this will not always be the case, as (here by IAC) where there are successive conversions (at para 40); (2) an exercise of dominion over goods may amount to a conversion (at para 41),[54] but a mere unauthorised retention of another's goods would not (at para 42); and (3) IAC, believing that the aircraft were now its property, acted accordingly and thus asserted rights inconsistent with KAC's rights as owner (at para 43). Thus, Lord Nicholls held that IAC were not liable for loss of the Mosul four aircraft, because their loss was caused by coalition bombing, not IAC's acts (see para 27.29); but IAC were liable for the $US 20m in respect of the Iran six, because, in the event of successive conversions by the Iraqi State and then IAC, the wrongful acts of the previous convertor (the Iraqi State) did not diminish claims against IAC (at para 82) and the appropriate remoteness test to apply to IAC was foreseeability (see para 27.41).

**[19.06] Some rules of conversion**. Whilst detailed discussion of the requirements of the tort of conversion—in its new statutory guise of 'wrongful interference with goods' (see para 19.04)—is beyond the scope of this work, several of the rules of this very technical tort must be borne in mind, for it is not enough that D has committed an act of conversion (see para 19.05). *First*, the action is not necessarily available to the owner:[55] it lies only at the suit of one who at the time of D's act of conversion either is in possession of the goods[56] or who has an immediate right to possess them;[57] and a person who has only an equitable interest is liable to be defeated by a *bona fide* purchaser of the legal title.[58] *Second*, even where P has a legal title, in all cases D may now plead that a third party has a better title to the goods than P (Torts Act 1977, s 8) which rule is intended to allow the court power to settle competing claims in one set of proceedings. *Third*, liability for an act of conversion is partially strict:[59] where D (including his agent) takes part in transferring the property in a chattel belonging to another (X), D is strictly liable and it is immaterial that D acted by mistake or in good faith;[60] but, where D's act is unconnected with title transfer

---

54 E.g. *GE Capital Bank Ltd v Rushton* (set out at para 21.56), R & J.

55 *Lord v Price* (1874) LR 9 Exch 54 (auction sale, goods neither removed nor paid for; so unpaid seller entitled to his lien (see para 24.10) and the buyer had no immediate right to possession, and thus could not sue a third party in conversion).

56 E.g. *The Winkfield* [1902] P 42, CA (Postmaster-General as bailee of mail); *The Jag-Shakti* [1986] 1 All ER 480, PC (pledgee); attornee (1989) 112 Law Com WP 17, fn 48; *Costello v Chief Constable of Derbyshire Constabulary* [2001] 3 All ER 150, CA (receiver of stolen goods); and para 23.03. Is the explanation of *North West Securities Ltd v Alexander Breckon Ltd* (see para 10.07; hp) that the financier under the intended transaction was in constructive possession?

57 E.g. a bailor where the bailment is at will, either under the terms of the bailment (*Manders v Williams* (1849) 4 Exch 339) or because the bailment has been terminated (see para 26.09); one who acquires title under one of the exceptions to the *nemo dat* rule (see Chap 21); and see para 25.15, fn 114.

58 *MCC Proceeds Inc v Lehman Bros International (Europe)* [1998] 4 All ER 675, CA (not a goods case).

59 At common law, conversion did not lie for negligent loss of goods by a bailee; but such conduct is now within the statutory tort: see para 19.04, fn 34; and the Torts Act, s 2(2).

60 *Hollins v Fowler* [1875] LR 7 HL 757 (innocent buyer from thief); *Consolidated Co v Curtis & Son* [1892] 1 QB 495 (innocent auctioneer); wrongful seizure in execution (see para 19.05, fn 42); *RH Willis & Son v British Car Auctions Ltd* [1978] 2 All ER 392, CA (innocent auctioneer); *Motis Exports*

(a 'ministerial act') and done without notice of X's rights, it does not amount to conversion.[61] Under the Torts Act 1977 (s 11(1)), P's contributory negligence is no defence (see further para 27.40). *Fourth*, at common law, the only remedy available in an action in conversion was damages, and this remains the general rule:[62] only where D is in 'possession or control of goods' does s 3 of the Torts Act give the court power to order delivery of the goods to P;[63] and in other cases, whether within or outside s 3, D will normally have the choice (see para 24.26) of either returning the goods or paying their assessed value (see para 27.30). *Fifth*, s 9 of the Torts Act makes provision for concurrent actions, so that proceedings may be heard together, whether they arise from concurrent interests in goods[64] or from successive acts of conversion. There may be concurrent actions of conversion for any or all of the following reasons: there are successive acts of conversion in respect of the same goods, e.g. a chain of sales; or there are concurrent interests in goods in respect of the same act of conversion;[65] or there is one or more claims for an improvement allowance under s 6 (see para 27.30).

## Property and title

**[19.07]** Originally, the common law failed to distinguish between the property in and possession of chattels (see para 19.02). As it began to draw such a distinction, the notion of the ownership (or 'general property' in goods) developed, perhaps for the following reasons: (a) in contradistinction to the 'special property' of a pledgee (see para 19.08); (b) with an eye to the developing bankruptcy law;[66] (c) the rule *res perit domino* now embodied in s 20(1) of the SGA (see para 19.10); and (d) (perhaps?) equitable rights, e.g. successive interests in goods, mortgages and charges of goods (see para 25.03). In practice the courts tended to concentrate on the availability of remedies rather than any *a priori* theory of rights, so that the concept of 'ownership' has tended to follow the remedies rather than lead them. However, none of these actions necessarily protects ownership (see para 19.06); and the expression 'owner', used by the SGA on a number of occasions, itself causes trouble.[67]

---

*Ltd v Dampskibsselskabet AF 1912, A/S* [1999] 1 All ER (Comm) 571 (carrier misdelivered goods against a forged bill of lading); *Kuwait Airways* case (see para 19.05A: IAC accept planes from the State).

61    *Marcq v Christie Manson & Woods Ltd* (set out at para 10.11).

62    For the value of the goods and any consequential loss. As to consequential loss, see claims for loss of profit by a supplier (para 27.33) or buyer (para 29.36). For the different tests for remoteness of damage, see para 27.41.

63    S 3(1) and (2)(a). As to the circumstances where an order for specific delivery is likely to be made: see para 24.26.

64    Where more than one person would be entitled to sue in respect of a single act of wrongful interference with goods by D, s 7 attempts to ensure that D does not have to pay out in total more than one *prima facie* measure of damage ('double liability'). *Quaere* whether s 7 applies to bailment: see Bell, *Op. cit.*, 83–4. For the relationship between ss 7 and 8, see Winfield and Jolowicz, *Tort*, 16th edn, para 17.19.

65    E.g. where there is a bailment. For the measure of damages available to the owner of goods let on hp, see para 27.30.

66    The early bankruptcy statutes, e.g. the Act of 1570, did not spell out the different types of matter which fall into an insolvency, but later Acts used the convenient and compendious term 'property' to describe them: see now, para 19.23.

67    Ss 2(2), 5(1), 21, 24 and 25. See also the Factors Act 1889, s 2. For the difficulties to which the expression 'owner' gives rise in relation to the transfer of title, see Chap 21.

The SGA also uses two other concepts involving 'ownership', those of 'property' and 'title' (see paras 19.08–9) and carefully explains the relationship between property and contract (see para 1.10). It insists that the objective of a sale is to transfer the property in goods[68] and makes the seller impliedly promise to do so.[69] As between the seller and buyer, the right to maintain an action for wrongful interference with goods[70] turns not on the whereabouts of the general property in them, but upon having a right to immediate possession (see para 19.06). Indeed, under the SGA, this in turn *prima facie* depends on payment of the price,[71] unless the seller assents to a subsale (see para 21.02).

**[19.08] The general property in goods.** 'Property' is defined by s 61(1) as *prima facie* meaning 'the general property in goods, and not merely a special property'. Perhaps because of its ambiguous origins (see para 19.07), it is difficult to grasp the concept of the general property in goods. However, the 'general property' in goods may be thought of as the nearest English law gets to the ownership of goods; and it has already been pointed out that this ownership is indivisible (see para 19.03). On the other hand, the Act also allows that there may exist at the same time a 'special property' in the same goods.[72] One theoretical view seeks to equate 'general property' with ownership and 'special property' with possession.[73] However, this 'special property' of a pledgee (see para 19.07) is the right of the pledgee-creditor to retain possession of goods as security for his loan and sell them in default (see para 25.02); and it is also appears to be an ownership right in property,[74] albeit one inferior to the general property, because the pledgee has the right to sue in conversion anybody who interferes with his right to possess.[75] Moreover, in the absence of a better title, even a receiver of stolen goods can succeed in an action of conversion.[76]

The explanation has been said to be that the concept of property is like an onion, coming in many layers: when the owner holding the general property pledges those goods, what he is doing is stripping off a layer of ownership and passing it to the pledgee; but the owner/pledgor is retaining the central core of the onion.[77] If this analogy is right, the general property is the central core of the onion—that which the owner retains after parting with some lesser ownership rights. It may be this core which is indivisible.

**[19.09] The concepts of 'property' and 'title'.** The notion of 'title' was built upon the availability of an action in conversion or detinue; but the concept of the 'property'

---

68  SGA, s 2(1): see paras 1.07–8.
69  SGA, s 12(1): see paras 12.02–3.
70  Torts Act 1977, s 1: see para 19.04.
71  *Lord v Price* (1874) LR 9 Ex 54.
72  E.g. for the special property of an Enforcement Officer, see para 19.16.
73  See the authorities cited in Curwen (2000) 20 LS 181 at 183.
74  See the discussion in *Donald v Suckling* (1866) LR 1 QB 585; and para 25.15. Cf. *Lee v Atkinson* (1609) 1 Yelv 172 (speaking of the 'special interest' of a bailee for reward).
75  *Gordon v Harper* (1796) 7 TR 9 (where a sheriff wrongfully seizes hired goods, it is the hirer, not the owner, who can sue the sheriff in conversion). *Aliter*, where the bailment is at will: see para 19.06.
76  *Costello v Chief Constable of Derbyshire Constabulary* [2001] 3 All ER 150, CA.
77  Curwen (2000) 20 LS 181 at 192.

in goods is peculiar in that there is no action upon which it is obviously founded.[78] A layman might be forgiven for asking whether it is necessary for our law of personal property to have two concepts of 'property' and 'title'. Yet the SGA draws a clear distinction between them. Part III of the Act is entitled 'Effects of the contract', and is further sub-divided into sections entitled 'Transfer of property as between seller and buyer' (ss 16–20A) and 'Transfer of title' (ss 21–26). 'Title' is nowhere defined in the Act, but at first sight, it is perhaps difficult to see what the Act intended to be the relationship between 'property' and 'title', though it is reasonably clear when the provisions of the two sub-divisions of the Act are to operate: the sections under the heading 'transfer of property as between seller and buyer' (ss 16–20A) are concerned with the very many situations where the dispute is solely between the seller and buyer, or persons standing in their shoes, e.g. trustee in bankruptcy or liquidator (see para 19.18); whereas the sections under the heading 'Transfer of title' (ss 21–26) provide for the cases where the title to goods is effectively transferred by a person who has no property in them.[79]

There have been academic disputes as to the relationship of property and title;[80] but the SGA seems to give no assistance.[81] The explanation may be that Chalmers adopted this terminology from the common law because he felt that it was not the place of a codifying statute to reverse completely the theoretical basis of the existing law (see para 1.02). The significance of the property in goods is discussed below (see para 19.10, *et seq.*).

## THE INCIDENTS OF PROPERTY

[19.10] From the practical point of view, perhaps the best way of looking at the concept of the general property in goods is as a bundle of legal consequences,[82] albeit that modern statute may have obscured the symmetry. In particular, where there is a consumer sale, the more important consequences which follow the general property in goods, are as follows:

1.  *Property as the core of the contract.* As the transfer of the property in goods is regarded as the core of a contract of sale (SGA, s 2(1): set out at para 1.07), a failure to transfer that property is regarded as a breach of the undertaking of a right to sell, regardless of any transfer of possession (see para 12.06). Further, it is a general rule that the buyer acquires no common law real rights in the goods short of his obtaining property or possession of them, as may be seen in regard to sales of a share in an undivided bulk before the 1995 changes (see para 20.22A).

2.  *Nemo dat quod non habet.* The general rule is that only the person with the general property in the goods can pass a good title to them (see para 19.11). It

---

78  See Kiralfy (1949) 12 MLR 424. Nevertheless it has been suggested that the two concepts bear a similar (but undefined) meaning: Davies (1987) 7 LS 1 at 7.
79  See Thornely (1958) CLJ 349.
80  See Macleod, *Consumer Sales Law*, 1st edn, para 19.09.
81  See *Powell v Wiltshire* (set out at para 12.08), the effect of a court declaration after disposition.
82  Atiyah, *Sale of Goods*, 10th edn, 313. See also Goode, *Commercial Law*, 3rd edn, 216–19.

follows that, where an owner makes successive sales of goods, the property *prima facie* passes under the first purported conveyance,[83] so that first buyer will have sufficient title to recover the value of the goods in an action in conversion (see para 27.30). However, there are many exceptional cases where an innocent person in possession of goods may, regardless of whether he has the property in goods, have a good title to them (see Chap 21).

3. *Debtors and creditors*. The general rule of insolvency is that all goods of which the insolvent has the general property will fall into his insolvency (see para 19.23). As against an insolvent buyer, it may be possible for his supplier to avoid this rule by employing a reservation of title clause (see para 20.29). However, the buyer from an insolvent seller usually acquires no interest in the goods prior to the passing of property.[84] There is a special rule for some co-owners (see para 20.22A).

It is clear, therefore, that there are important results which flow from the passing of property. On the other hand, some other common law jurisdictions, e.g. the United States,[85] have taken the view that it is too confusing to have so many of the above-listed issues turning on the passing of property and have instead introduced separate provisions to deal with them. However, the drawback to such a 'specific issue' approach lies in its inability to deal with new problems,[86] leaving some English commentators to cast doubts on the advantages which might be gained by such a change.[87]

**[19.11]** The *nemo dat* rule. The basic rule of common law is that nobody can transfer a better common law title than he himself possesses, a rule which is conveniently expressed by the Latin maxim *nemo dat quod non habet*:[88] in the context of priorities, this is usually expressed as 'the first in time prevails';[89] and it must be distinguished from the rule that a bfp will defeat one with an equitable interest, e.g. right to trace (see para 27.14). The operation of the *nemo dat* rule may be illustrated by the following example: suppose a chain of sales from A through B to C, where the title of B is defective in that he did not obtain the property in the goods from A. B can only pass a defective title to C; and A may successfully sue C in tort because he (A) has a better title than C.[90]

The *nemo dat* rule is embodied in s 21(1) of the SGA, which provides that, subject to certain exceptions (see Chap 21),

---

83 *Johnson v Credit Lyonnais* (1877) 3 CPD 32. This rule was substantially reversed by what is now s 8 of the Factors Act 1889: see para 21.38.

84 *Re Wait* (set out at para 20.22). For the difficulties with regard to part of a bulk on insolvency, see (1989) 112 Law Com WP 12–13, 19–21.

85 See the Uniform Commercial Code, Art 2-105(4). See the account by Burns in (1996) 59 MLR 260 at 264–6.

86 E.g. *The Span Terza (No. 2)* [1984] 1 WLR 27, HL (ownership of ship's bunkers as between charterer and mortgagee).

87 Atiyah, *Sale of Goods*, 10th edn, 315.

88 E.g. *Re St Mary's Barton-on-Humber* [1987] Fam 41, [1987] 2 All ER 861. See *per* Lord Cairns LC in *Cundy v Lindsay* (1878), 3 App Cas 459, HL at 463 and 464.

89 See *Powell v Wiltshire* (set out at para 12.08); Bell, *Personal Property*, 459; and para 7.21.

90 See *National Employers Mutual etc Ltd v Jones* (set out at para 21.54), where a longer chain included a thief.

'where goods are sold by a person who is not the owner thereof . . ., the buyer acquires no better title to the goods than the seller had'.

This section speaks of goods being 'sold' by B and it has been decided that this does not include a mere agreement to sell (SGA, s 2(4)–(5): see para 1.10). In *Shaw v Commissioner of Police*:[91]

> The owner of a Porsche car (A) entrusted it to B to find a buyer, but also signed a letter stating that he had 'sold' the car to B. Relying on that letter, C, a bfp, agreed to buy the car under a contract which did not pass property to C until B was paid. The court held that B never obtained a good title because, despite the terms of the letter, the evidence showed that B had in fact been acting only as an agent for sale until he was paid by C; and C never paid B. So, the court reasoned that C did not get a good title under the *nemo dat* rule[92] or two of its exceptions.

These exceptions could not apply for the following reasons: (a) the estoppel rule (see para 21.08) was inapplicable because B did not purport to 'sell' to C until B was paid by C (which never happened);[92]and (b) the buyer in possession rule did not apply because B had not 'bought or agreed to buy' the car from A as s 25 required (see further, para 21.44).

However, assuming a disposition of the property in goods by B, the common law rule would appear to be wider than s 21(1) both in respect of the disposition and the defect of title. Any disposition recognised by law may bring the principle into play, so that it is enough that the goods be pledged or given. As regards the defect of title, it is clear that the principle applies where B has no title whatsoever, or has merely a possessory title;[93] but it has been taken even beyond this.[94]

## DEBTORS AND CREDITORS[95]

**[19.12]** It has been pointed out that the whole body of English law could be contained in comparatively few rules had everyone sufficient money to meet the debts and obligations incurred by him.[96] Nowhere is this more obvious than in relation to the rules relating to the passing of property in goods. In principle, an unsatisfied creditor has available to him, since the Insolvency Act 1986 as amended (IA), the following strategies:

(a) To take a security interest in some appropriate property owned by the debtor, so allowing the secured creditor after default to pursue that property (see paras 19.13–7). Nothing requires a lender to follow this course of action, but it has been said that the banks follow it with 'apostolic zeal'.[97] It allows them to lend

---

91  [1987] 3 All ER 405, [1987] 1 WLR 1332, CA.

92  The reason was 'more fundamental' than the *nemo dat* rule in that B never purported to transfer the property in the goods to C: *per* Lloyd LJ at 410d.

93  *Cundy v Lindsay* (1878) 3 App Cas 459, HL (no title); *North West Securities Ltd v Alexander Breckon Ltd* (see para 10.07: possessory title in thief).

94  *Mercantile Bank of India Ltd v Central Bank of India Ltd*: [1938] AC 287, [1938] 1 All ER 52, PC. For criticism of this case, see Macleod, *Consumer Sales Law*, 1st edn, para 19.11.

95  See generally Goode, *Commercial Law*, 3rd edn, Chap 31.

96  See Crossley Vaines, *Personal Property*, 5th edn, 465.

97  See McCormack [2003] JBL 389 at 392.

solely on the value of the security rather than the financial worth of the borrower.[98] As to realisation of security, see para 19.14.

(b) To go against the debtor himself by way of insolvency proceedings (see paras 19.18–23); but the creditor cannot so petition whilst goods are included in a County Court administration order (see para 27.04). In the last resort, unsecured lending is against the financial worth of the borrower.[99]

In the UK, the traditional insolvency procedure embodied in the IA carried the stigma of failure; but the Enterprise Act 2002 (EA) was intended to move the ethos towards the 'rescue culture' so long the US approach to business failure (see para 19.19).

Sometimes, the debtor would still be solvent even after his creditor has successfully recovered certain property, e.g. where the creditor repossesses a car supplied on hp. However, suppose the debtor is insolvent, that is, for the foreseeable future his net debts exceed his net assets.[100] As will be seen later (see para 19.18), one of the principles of insolvency law is to achieve an equal distribution of the debtor's assets between all his creditors (see para 19.23). So, if the debtor is insolvent, that property recovered by one secured creditor will be to the detriment of other creditors. In this sense, the law allowing one creditor to recoup his debt from certain property derogates from this basic insolvency principle. The result is that there is a trade-off between these two branches of the law, as in the different treatment of fixed and floating charges (see para 19.13). As we shall see, Pt 10 of the EA[101] has altered the balance of that trade-off,[102] e.g. the portion of assets subject to a floating charge which are to be ringfenced for the benefit of unsecured creditors (EA, s 252: see para 19.14). There is an issue of principle as to why the law allows the taking of security.[103]

## Actions against property

**[19.13]** If the unsatisfied creditor is considering recouping his loss by action against the property of the debtor, his position depends on whether his debt is secured, meaning whether he has taken the precaution of 'reserving' a proprietary interest in the property of the debtor by way of security for repayment of that debt. Upon default by the debtor, the creditor's position is thus as follows:

(a) If the debt is secured from the outset, e.g. the creditor is the owner under a conditional sale, hp or simple hiring agreement, he may look to that security to recoup the debt (see para 19.14). However, if the debtor is insolvent, the creditor must hand over to the trustee or liquidator any surplus (see para 19.23), but

---

98 See McCormack, at 396–7.

99 As to pre-loan checks, see para 8.36; and as to credit-scoring, see para 8.39.

100 See SGA, s 61(4) (see para 24.04); IA, ss 123 and 268 (see para 19.18).

101 This is intended to implement the policy outlined in the White Paper, *Productivity and Enterprise: Insolvency—a Second Chance* (2001) Cm. 2001. See generally, para 2.12.

102 See generally McCormack [2003] JBL 389.

103 See McCormack, at 398–401.

may prove like any other unsecured creditor[104] for any balance due to him (see below). Alternatively,[105] he may surrender his security and prove for his whole debt,[106] just like the unsecured creditors (see below).

(b) If the debt is unsecured at the outset, he can obtain a judgment for that debt[107] and then as a judgment creditor levy execution on the property of the judgment debtor (see para 19.15). Exceptionally, some categories of creditor have a special right to seize (distrain) goods of the debtor without first obtaining a judgment e.g. a landlord distraining for rent (see para 19.17). Where there are multiple debts, the law takes a 'devil-take-the-hindmost' attitude: in the absence of insolvency (see para 19.18), the greatest advantage usually accrues to the creditor who first enforces his debt: so, it is no answer to third-party debt proceedings (see para 27.04) that the debtor is insolvent.[108]

**[19.14] Realisation of security**. This depends on whether the security is fixed on a designated property or floats over a class of property (see generally, para 25.02).

1. *Fixed security*. A loan may be secured against a particular piece of property[109] by way of mortgage,[110] fixed charge[110] or pledge (see paras 25.15–18); or a supplier may seek to reserve title in the goods supplied.[111] In all these cases, an unpaid creditor may seek to recoup his loss by selling that property and repaying himself out of the proceeds.[112]

2. *Floating security*. An individual debtor cannot grant a floating charge;[113] but a debtor company may do so (see para 25.02). Such a floating charge would normally at common law give the chargee the power in default to appoint a receiver and manager of property within the scope of that charge:[114] typically, a single large creditor, e.g. a bank, would upon the debtor's default appoint a receiver and manager to take control of most of the debtor's worthwhile assets which he had not granted away as fixed security (see above). This was thought to be fundamentally unfair; and the EA sought to modify the procedure.

---

104 *Whitehead v Household Mortgage Corp plc* [2003] 1 All ER 319, CA. In the case of realty, any such deficiency is termed 'negative equity'. For the effect of negative equity on the mortgagee's proprietary remedies, see para 25.20.

105 E.g. a conditional seller may either seize the goods or sue for their price (see para 27.19).

106 *Alliance and Leicester plc v Slayford* [2001] 1 All ER (Comm) 1, CA.

107 Distinguish an action for debt from one for damages (see para 27.21).

108 *Reed v Oury No. 1* [2000] WL 33122368, High Crt.

109 Distinguish personal security: see paras 25.04–14.

110 This will create in the debtor an equity of redemption: see para 25.20.

111 A supplier may achieve this by a reservation of a right of disposal (see para 20.28) or a reservation of the property in goods (see para 24.22).

112 If such a realisation produces a surplus after satisfaction of the debt, the right to that surplus depends on the type of security (see para 24.22).

113 Because the Bills of Sale Act 1882 insisted on transfer of ownership: see para 25.26.

114 If a chargee issues instructions to the directors of the debtor company that subsequently becomes insolvent, could the chargee be liable as a 'shadow director' for wrongful trading under s 214 of the Insolvency Act 1986? See ss 214(7) and 251; and generally Oditah, *Receivables Financing*, 67–8 and 102–3.

*Administrative receiver.* The common law receiver and manager (see above) appointed by a floating chargee may well come within the IA statutory definition of an 'administrative receiver'.[115] However, the re-balancing of the rights of secured and unsecured creditors effected by the Enterprise Act 2002 (see para 19.12) led to two changes, which significantly curtailed the rights of floating charge-holders. First, their ability to appoint an adminstrative receiver in respect of post-2003 charges is all but abolished, being virtually reserved to only the very largest public company debtors;[116] and most creditors holding floating charges will usually have to follow the procedure for administration (see para 19.19). Second, at the substantive level, the emphasis swings back towards collectivising the process in favour of the equal treatment of creditors: crown preference is abolished (see para 19.23); and it is planned that a prescribed part, e.g. 10%, of the debtor's net property in excess of a certain minimum, which would previously have been exclusively available to floating charge-holders, shall be re-distributed to unsecured creditors.[117]

**[19.15] Levying execution**. Where court judgment is handed down for payment of a sum of money, including a criminal compensation order (see para 3.20), it becomes a judgment debt (see para 3.22), upon which interest normally runs (see para 7.03A). The formal means to enforce this civil judgment of the law is termed 'levying execution' and may take different forms according to the nature of the property of the judgement debtor out of which the judgment creditor seeks to satisfy the judgment debt. The most common forms of execution are seizure and sale of goods (see below), charging orders on the debtor's house (see para 27.04) and attachment of debts and earnings,[118] though all forms of execution may be suspended by the insolvency of the judgment debtor.[119] Following a government report,[120] this whole area of the law is due to be replaced, with modernised terminology and reformed procedure, by the draft Tribunals, Courts and Enforcement Bill 2006 (the TCE Bill).[121]

*Seizure and sale of goods.* Executing judgment on the goods belonging to the judgment debtor will involve their seizure and sale:[122] this is usually effected by the High Court sheriff or County Court bailiff (under the TCE Bill to be termed

---

115 Insolvency Act 1986, s 29(2). The powers of an English receiver and manager are regulated by ss 28–49: see further Oditah [1991] JBL 49.

116 EA, s 250 (inserting a new s 72A into the IA 1986). Further discussion is beyond the scope of this work.

117 EA, s 252, which will be at a percentage to be fixed by statutory instrument: see McCormack [2003] JBL 389 at 390–2 and 416–19.

118 As to the effect of an earnings order on other forms of execution, see Administration of Justice Act 1970, s 17(2). For attachment of earnings, see para 27.05.

119 Insolvency Act 1986, ss 10(1)(c) and 11(3)(d) (administration order); s 128 (liquidation); s 285 (bankruptcy). As to the effect of insolvency on executed goods, see para 19.16.

120 LCD, *Effective Enforcement* (2003, Cm. 5744). The Lord Chancellor's Dept (LCD) has since been re-named the Dept. for Constitutional Affairs (DCA). The LCD launched a National Enforcement Office and 'National Standards for Enforcement Agents' as forerunners of proposals contained in a draft TCE Bill, clauses 45–6 and Sched 11.

121 See http://www.dca.gov.uk/legist/tribenforce.htm. For proposals to protect the over-indebted, see para 6.10.

122 Courts Act 2003, s 99 and Sched 7. The new procedure will be contained in clause 44 and Scheds 11 and 12 of the TCE Bill.

'enforcement agents');[122] but certain prescribed property cannot be seized (see below). In earlier times, this unpleasant procedure was more commonly used against business debtors; but more recently, there has been a growth of executions against private debtors, whether for public debts, e.g. fines, taxes; or for commercial debts, e.g. mortgages and/or instalment credit. The procedure should balance the needs of creditors, e.g. for quick action and fairness as between creditors,[123] with those of debtors, e.g. for delay. Execution involves two stages:[124]

1. *Seizure of the goods from the judgment debtor.* Certain goods in the possession of the judgment debtor are not available for this process: goods owned by a third party, e.g. TV on hp; and those goods owned by the debtor which are necessary for his 'employment, business or vocation' or 'basic domestic needs' (Courts and Legal Services Act 1990, s 15). In a typical non-business debtor case, the enforcement agent is likely to wheel-clamp the debtor's car and then invite him to pay the debt plus charges to prevent the car being taken away;[125] and, whilst the debtor prevaricates, the costs escalate. The enforcement agent also has a limited right of entry into the debtor's premises,[126] in practice usually only achieved with the debtor's 'consent'.[127] Once entered, he is to find and seize such of the debtor's goods as might be sold (see below) for the amount stipulated in the writ. In principle, he should seize and immediately physically remove those goods; but in practice, he may with the debtor's co-operation take only legal ('walking') possession, leaving the goods in the physical possession of the debtor (see para 19.16). In relation to the seized goods, the fundamental principle is that the judgment creditor is in no better position than the judgment debtor so far as the rights of third parties are concerned.[128] Thus, the execution creditor seizing goods held by the judgment debtor on conditional sale,[129] hp or simple hiring has no greater rights as against the supplier than the buyer or hirer has (see para 1.21).

2. *Sale of the seized goods.* Normally, the sale will be by public auction. However, the execution creditor will not necessarily be entitled to retain the benefit of the execution if the debtor becomes insolvent before the execution is completed.[130]

The effect of the above process on the title to goods seized and sold is considered below (para 19.16). Even where completed, apart from cars this process tends to produce very small sums (see para 27.04).

---

123 As to the priority as between writs of execution, see *Bankers Trust Co v Galadari* [1987] QB 222, CA. Under the TCE Bill, Sched 11, para 4, priority will be determined by the date and time the warrant is issued.

124 The new enforcement rules will be found in the TCE Bill, clauses 47–9 and Sched 11.

125 Sheriffs/bailiffs have access to the DVLA register: [2003] 9 *Credit Today* 9.

126 The power of entry is currently the same as for distress: see para 19.17.

127 [2003] 10 CT 23. Insofar as this is achieved only by reason of the debtor's ignorance of his right to refuse entry, cf. consent to repossession (see para 24.37).

128 *Holroyd v Marshall* (1862) 10 HLC 191. What of co-owned goods? See *Sale and Supply of Goods* (1993, Law Com. No. 215), para 4.35.

129 Including where there is a *Romalpa* clause (see para 25.30).

130 See the Insolvency Act 1986, ss 183 and 346. For completion of execution, see IA, ss 183(3) and 346(5). For incomplete executions, see para 19.16.

**[19.16] The title in executed goods.** Pending the enactment of the TCE Bill 2006, where goods are seized and sold in execution (see para 19.15), the effect of that process on the title to the goods seized may be divided into three stages.

(a) A writ, or warrant of execution binds the general property in the goods:[131] in the case of a High Court writ, from the moment it is delivered to the sheriff to be executed;[132] and in the case of a county court warrant, from the moment application is made for the warrant to the registrar.[133] The title of the execution debtor does not at this stage transfer to the court agent, the effect of the provision being to create a sort of charge over the goods;[134] and special arrangements are made to deal with the situation where the execution debtor becomes insolvent at this point.[135] Moreover, at this stage the execution debtor can still transfer such title as he has to a third party[136] and can pass a good title to a bfp without notice of the writ or warrant.[137]

(b) The execution of the writ. Once the enforcement agent takes possession of goods under a writ of execution, the writ becomes executed; the agent acquires a 'special property' in the goods;[138] and the foregoing exception in favour of the bfp can no longer operate. It has been decided that this will be so even where the sheriff/agent merely takes 'walking possession'.[139]

(c) The sale by the sheriff/agent. Where goods belonging to a third party, but in the possession of the execution debtor, are seized by the sheriff/agent, the interest of the third party is not thereby overridden.[140] However, the sheriff/agent is protected in his seizure and sale of the goods;[141] and a bfp from the sheriff/agent is protected as against the execution debtor's trustee in bankruptcy.[142]

**[19.17] Distress.** Originally a form of self-help, distress has survived as a statutory remedy by which, *inter alia*, a landlord letting unfurnished premises might without

---

131  These statutory rules used to be found in s 26 of the SGA 1893. However, it was considered more appropriate to transfer them to statutes dealing with the administration of justice as follows: for High Court proceedings, they are to be found in the Supreme Court Act 1981, s 138 (as amended); and for county court proceedings in s 99 of the County Courts Act 1984. See further Walton (2003) 32 CLWR 179, at 186–8.

132  Supreme Court Act 1981, s 138(1) and (3). For definitions, see s 138(4).

133  County Court Acts 1984, ss 99(1), (2) and 103(2). For definitions, see s 199(4).

134  *Woodland v Fuller* (1840) 11 Ad & El 859.

135  Insolvency Act 1986, ss 184 and 346; Walton (2003) 32 CLWR 179, at 188–94. See fn 139 below.

136  See per Danckwerts J in *Re Cooper* [1958] Ch 922, at 928–929.

137  Supreme Court Act 1981, s 138(2); County Courts Act 1984, s 99(2).

138  But the execution creditor obtained no title to the goods: *Giles v Grover* (1832) 6 Bligh NS 277. As to 'special property', see generally, para 19.08.

139  *Lloyds and Scottish Finance Ltd v Modern Cars Ltd* (set out at para 12.14). As to 'walking possession', see para 19.15.

140  The third party can claim the proceeds of sale from the execution creditor. As to interpleader by the sheriff, see para 21.06. As to the position where the execution debtor becomes insolvent before the execution is complete, see Oditah, *Receivables Financing*, 147–9; Walton (2003) 32 CLWR 179, at 199–206 and 208–10.

141  In his seizure by the writ; and in his sale by Statute (see Benjamin's *Sale of Goods*, 6th edn, para 7-107, fn 81). *Contra* if the seizure is outside the terms of the writ (see para 19.05); or if the sheriff might 'by making reasonable enquiry have ascertained' the third party's interest, e.g. by consulting HPI (see para 21.01).

142  Insolvency Act 1986, ss 183(2)(b) and 346(7).

taking court action recover arrears of rent from his tenant, as an alternative to insolvency.[143] The levying of distress for rent entails the landlord (or his bailiff) seizing from the rented premises personal property found there, provided that it is owned by the tenant;[144] and, in the event that the tenant does not pay off the arrears, there is a statutory right to sell the goods, usually exercised by auction.[145] Certain goods are privileged from distress;[146] and the Law of Distress Amendment Act 1908 lays down a procedure by which a third party whose goods are distrained whilst in the possession of the tenant might extricate those goods from the distress by serving a statutory declaration on the distrainor, assuming the goods-owner who supplied them learns of the distress in time.[147]

The Government have proposed that distress for rent should be abolished in respect of residential property.[148] The proposal would be implemented by the TCE Bill 2006.[149]

## Actions against the insolvent debtor

**[19.18] Insolvency**. At common law, a debtor could generally only be released from his debt by satisfaction (see para 26.18): from medieval times, fraudulent debtors might be hanged; and even innocent debtors might be imprisoned until that sanction was replaced by attachment of earnings (see para 27.05). However, this harsh common law position has been softened by the statutory notion of bankruptcy. First introduced by statute in respect of insolvent traders, by the time of the 1571 Act the law of bankruptcy had a twofold purpose.[150] *First*, it was to prevent fraud on creditors and secure an equal distribution of the bankrupt's property between them, rather than the common law devil-take-the-hindmost rule (see para 19.13). *Second*, to allow the person who had become insolvent due to genuine misfortune to make a fresh start by assigning his entire estate to his creditors:[151] that is, all debts provable in the insolvency are normally discharged, e.g. bank debts, whilst only non-provable debts survive that discharge.[152] In essence, these remain the rules for

---

143 As to the effect of bankruptcy on rent arrears, see Kruse (2003) 70 *Quarterly Account* 9.

144 Sometimes, it is possible for a third-party owner to avoid a seizure either by obtaining in advance a 'landlord's waiver', or by affixing a notice of ownership to goods.

145 Law of Distress Act 1689, s 1 (as amended). Provided there is a 'true sale', this will pass a good title to a bfp: see para 21.06. However, there is no true sale where the landlord himself purchases the goods: *Moore, Nettlefold & Co v Sugar Manufacturing Co* [1904] 1 KB 820.

146 E.g. fixtures: *Crossley v Lee* [1908] I KB 86, DC (gas engine on hp bolted to floor): and see generally, para 25.23.

147 E.g. *Lawrence Chemical Co Ltd v Rubenstein* [1982] 1 All ER 653, CA. For the details, see 1st edn, para 19.17.

148 LCD, *Effective Enforcement* (2003, Cm. 5744); and see generally, para 19.15.

149 Clause 53. The Bill creates a statutory system of distraint against commercial tenants (clauses 54–69), which will be beyond the scope of this work.

150 The policy behind the legislation is traced in *Halsbury's Statutes*, 2nd edn, vol 2, 284.

151 The procedure was adapted to deal with criminal bankruptcy under what are now known as confiscation orders: see Proceeds of Crime Act 2002, Pt 2.

152 In personal bankruptcy, non-provable debts include fines for parking offences, but not parking charges: (2001) 61 *Quarterly Account* 18. For non-provable debts, see para 19.23; and for student loans, see para 19.21A.

personal insolvency: they are untouched by the SGA (s 62(1)) and continue to cause controversy as to the extent to which the system ought to release the debtor from his debts.[153] In Victorian times, the provisions of the bankruptcy legislation were extended to non-traders and a not dissimilar procedure was introduced for the liquidation of insolvent companies registered under the Companies Acts. However, the latter procedures differed in that, whilst a bankrupt's property vests in his trustee and the bankrupt eventually walks free of most of his debts,[152] a liquidator simply assumes the functions of the directors of a company, administers its assets and eventually kills off the company. Considerable disquiet having been expressed at the parallel development of the insolvency rules for natural persons (in the Bankruptcy Acts) and registered companies (in the Companies Acts), the two branches of the law were deliberately brought together in the Insolvency Act 1985 and consolidated in the Insolvency Act 1986, as amended (IA).[154]

[19.19] Another innovation by the IA allows the unsatisfied creditor to take a view as to whether the insolvency of his debtor[155] is temporary or permanent:

(a) If he judges the embarrassment to be temporary, the creditor may institute the Administration or Individual Voluntary Arrangement (IVA) procedures, which, with the consent of the debtor, are designed to take over the running of the debtor's affairs for the benefit of creditors generally until the debt is repaid, with a fall-back position as below (known as Chapter 7 or 11 proceedings in the USA).[156] Administration Orders are the appropriate version for debtor companies and are beyond the scope of this work. IVAs are used for debtors who are natural persons (see paras 19.20): when introduced in 1986, IVAs were primarily devised for business-generated insolvency; but in the present century they have come to be used primarily for debtors who are non-traders.

(b) If he judges the case hopeless, the creditor may proceed to make the debtor formally insolvent (see para 19.21). In this case, he should bear in mind all the following: (i) the position of secured and unsecured creditors (see paras 19.22–3); (ii) the property available to the insolvency (see para 19.24); and (iii) rogue company directors (see para 19.25).

Under the Enterprise Act 2002,[157] there has been made the following changes relevant to this discussion: (1) as a result of the changes concerning most floating charges (see para 19.14) and leaving aside fixed securities, the debtor's assets will be administered for the benefit of creditors as a whole (see para 19.22); (2) abolishing crown preference (s 251: see para 19.22); (3) reducing the ordinary bankruptcy period for a bankrupt individual debtors (see para 19.21A); and (4) a general lightening in the weight of bankruptcy on bankrupts, e.g. fast-track IVAs post-bankruptcy (see para 19.20).

---

153 It is not quite true today: some liabilities remain with the insolvent (see para 19.21); there are restrictions on his obtaining credit (see para 19.21); and there may be an entry in a credit bureau file.
154 Except for the provisions relating to the disqualification of directors: see para 19.25.
155 For the definition of when a debtor is insolvent, see IA, ss 123 and 268; and see para 19.21.
156 Chapter 7 is for consumer protection and Chapter 11 for company protection.
157 See (2003) 153 NLJ 1113; and generally, para 2.12. Difficulty may be caused by the fact that Pt 10 of the EA is written in plain English, rather than in conformity with the traditional drafting of the IA.

*The debtor's perspective.* Perhaps with the aid of a debt-counsellor,[158] a debtor may seek to stave off or defer insolvency, perhaps by a DMP[159] or re-mortgage[160] or common law composition.[161] Failing that, he may himself choose to initiate one of the following insolvency proceedings:[162]

1. *An IVA.* This has the advantage to a debtor that he will not lose his home or professional job.[163] In return, he must agree to pay a proportion of his income into a trust account for the benefit of his creditors. An IVA may cost the debtor an outlay of £5,000, requires the agreement of 75% of his creditors[164] and usually lasts at least five years.

2. *Bankruptcy.* This has the advantage to the debtor that, for a much lower outlay, he can discharge his provable debts and can usually obtain his discharge within a year. The disadvantages are that the debtor will usually suffer the humiliation of losing his home[160] and valuable possessions, e.g. car, and may be debarred from a professional job.[163]

**[19.20] Individual Voluntary Arrangements for natural persons (IVAs).** If it is desired to bind the debtor and all his creditors, the IA offers the fairly popular formal system of IVAs[165] as a measure short of bankruptcy, provided the debtor maintains the agreed repayment schedule:[166] this system is more expensive than a County Court Administration order (see para 27.04), and for that reason less suitable for consumer debts. The procedure establishes a new form of Interim Order, under the protection of which an insolvent individual may negotiate a 'voluntary arrangement' of his affairs with his unsecured creditors (ss 252–63, as amended): the debtor must be in a position to petition for his own bankruptcy (see para 19.21), so he cannot seek the protection of an Interim Order simply to avoid paying debts he could meet. Whilst the Interim Order is in effect, no bankruptcy petition relating to the debtor may be progressed (s 252(2)(a)); nor may any other proceedings, execution or other legal process[167] be progressed except with leave of the court (ss 252(2)(b) and 254). This would seem to leave intact the effect of any *Smart* v *Holt* clauses (see para 26.09).

---

158 These are usually a type of ancillary credit business (see para 5.44), which will require a CCA licence (see para 6.27). They may be based on a Money Advice Centre (see para 3.08).

159 For Debt Management Plans, see para 5.42.

160 Assuming the debtor owns his home. For re-mortgages, see para 7.04A.

161 As to doubts as to whether such a composition is binding at common law, see Treitel, *Law of Contract*, 11th edn, 129–30.

162 As forecast, this has led to an enormous increase in the number of consumers seeking their own insolvency or IVA: see Ball [2006] 2 *Credit Today* 20; *The Times* 6.5.2006.

163 Some professions strike off bankrupts, e.g. solicitor.

164 But a SIVA (see para 19.20) would not require creditor consent.

165 IA, ss 252–63, as amended. This procedure is to be in addition to, rather than instead of, the rarely used Deeds of Arrangement Act 1914. There is a suggestion that the procedure might be varied by making it cheaper and more flexible to enhance debt management plans (see para 5.42): [2003] 3 *Credit Today* 7; and see the TCE Bill (below, para 27.04).

166 For simple descriptions, see Money Advice Services *Court Procedures*, 2nd edn, 62–4; Howells, *Consumer Debt*, Chap 10); Griffiths (1992) 46 CC5/at 25. See further, Pond [1995] JBL 118.

167 'Legal process' means court actions (see para 19.19); and it has since been extended to include distress (see para 19.17) by s 3 of the IA 2000. But it does not include recaption (see para 24.23). For execution and distress, see paras 19.15–17.

If the negotiations are successful, the court may replace the Interim Order by giving approval to an IVA:[168] this will bind all unsecured creditors who are parties to it,[169] but may not interfere with the rights of any secured or preferential creditors.[170] It has been said that the key to a successful IVA is a compromise between the interests of the debtor and creditors:[171] if an IVA is unsuccessful, the likely result is bankruptcy proceedings (see para 19.21). Notwithstanding the cost (see above) and concomitant non-status (see para 19.18), IVAs have in recent years become relatively popular with consumer-debtors.[172] The EA has introduced a fast-track IVA procedure post-bankruptcy supervised by the Official Receiver (s 264). This is aimed at small debtors and consumer bankrupts: it envisages that the bankruptcy be annulled in return for increased or speedier returns made to creditors under the new form of IVA.[173]

*Simple Individual Voluntary Arrangements (SIVAs).* Additionally[174], for non-culpable non-trader debtors with undisputed debts of less than (say) £75,000, a DTI Report[175] recommends the introduction of a new simplified statutory system. It is envisaged that this will only be used where the debtor is in regular employment and, after living expenses, has sufficient disposable income (or assets) to enable a dividend to be paid to his creditors in excess of what would be achievable on bankruptcy (see paras 19.21–4). The debtor's finances would be controlled (generally for 5 years) by a nominee/supervisor and the scheme could not be modified. The idea is to provide something more formal that the popular DMPs (see para 5.42) in two tiers:

(a) SIVA1. Where the debts are less than (say) £25,000, the debtor would be able to choose to enter a SIVA1 without the consent of his creditors. The key would be simplicity.

(b) SIVA2. Where the debts are in the range of (say) £25–75,000, the creditors could exert more influence on the procedure.

**[19.21] Insolvency.**[176] Under the Insolvency Act 1986 (as amended) (IA), a debtor company may be wound up (ss 73–251) or an individual made bankrupt (ss 264–385) broadly on the petition of creditor or debtor and payment of the Official Receiver's fees.

---

168 Under EA, s 264, it is also possible to make a 'fast-track' IVA without a preceding Interim Order.

169 S 260(2). But not unsecured creditors who were not parties (*Re A Debtor* [1994] 1 WLR 264); nor any creditors insofar as the debtor materially understates his assets (*Stanley v Phillips* [2004] CLY 2160).

170 Without their consent: s 258(4) and (5). As to the rights of secured and preferential creditors, see para 19.21.

171 Pond (1999) 54 CC4/4. For a suggestion that IVAs should be piloted by consumer advisers, see [2005] 2 *Credit Today* 5; and the TCE Bill (below, para 27.04).

172 Should IVAs be allowed to consumers on non-means-tested benefits (see [2006] 3 *Credit Today* 7 and 20)?

173 EA, Sched 22, introducing new ss 263A–G to the IA.

174 It is not clear from the Report whether this proposal is as well as/instead of the other proposal.

175 DTI, *Improving IVAs* (2005). Business is pressing for more simplification: [2006] 1 *CT* 10.

176 For a layman's outline, see Money Advice, *Court Procedures*, 2nd edn, 64–9; Howells, *Consumer Debt*, Chaps 10–13; Keen, *Life after debt*, 2003, Chap 6.

1.  *Creditor's petition.* In the case of an individual debtor, a creditor's bankruptcy petition may be presented only where **all** the following are satisfied:[177]

    (a) The amount of his undisputed net debt exceeds a minimum level, termed the 'bankruptcy level'.[178] A single creditor below this level may take steps to reach this threshold;[179] or instead of bankruptcy consider the alternative county court administration procedure (see para 27.04).

    (b) That debt remains payable to the petitioning creditor(s). So the debtor can always avoid the bankruptcy by paying off before service of the petition so much of the debt as exceeds the bankruptcy threshold.[180]

    (c) That debt is liquidated, any security being surrendered (see para 19.13).

    (d) The debtor appears to have no reasonable prospect of being able to pay that debt as it falls due (s 267(2)).

    To make the creditor's task easier by saving him from first having to obtain a judgment for debt (see para 3.22), the IA says that a debtor is deemed to be unable to pay his debts in either of the following circumstances: there has been an unsatisfied execution;[181] or non-compliance with a 'statutory demand' (s 268(1)(a)), where the debtor cannot demonstrate a triable issue as to whether the debt can be disputed or set-off, e.g. by a counter-claim.[182] Further, it had been decided that the statutory demand procedure may be used in respect of debts due under regulated agreements, thereby avoiding the CCA protections for defaulting debtors under regulated agreements.[183] In respect of a debtor company, a similar procedure is available by way of compulsory liquidation by the court where the company cannot meet its debts (ss 122(1)(f) and 123), or winding up is in the public interest (see para 19.25). Alternatively, the creditors of an insolvent company may oust the directors and wind up the company under the creditors' voluntary winding-up procedure (s 97).

2.  *Debtor's petition.* Especially in the absence of personal sureties (see para 25.05), a debtor may choose to petition for his own bankruptcy (s 272) in order to relieve himself of pressure from his creditors.[184] Given the requisite

---

177 S 267. The court has a general power to dismiss or stay the proceedings where appropriate (s 266(3)), e.g. where the creditor has behaved improperly.

178 The figure has initially been fixed at £750, which may be increased by statutory order (ss 123(1)(a), (3) and 267(4)). The gross debt may be reduced by any set-off or counterclaim (see para 29.26). The petition should not be founded in any debt(s) *bona fide* disputed on substantial grounds.

179 By acting jointly with other debtors whose debts aggregate to the bankruptcy level; or by buying other debts up to that level (for assignment, see generally, para 7.16, *et seq.*).

180 S 271 (as amended); *Re Marr* [1990] 2 All ER 880, CA.

181 S 268(1)(b); and see para 19.15. As to what amounts to an unsatisfied execution, see *Re a Debtor* [1996] 2 All ER 211, CA.

182 The matter is one of substance: *Re a Debtor* [1992] 2 All ER 664. On statutory demands, see generally [1991] JBL 70; (1992) 142 NLJ 1452. Cf. SGA, s 61(4): see para 24.04.

183 *Enid Mills v Grove Securities Ltd* [1996] CCLR 74, CA (see Lawson (1997) 16 Tr L 34). As to the CCA protections of the debtor following the service of a default notice, see para 24.39, *et seq.*

184 In the case of joint debtors, each must apply individually. If only one joint debtor applies, the creditor can pursue the other for the whole debt.

finance,[185] a debtor who is sufficiently desperate may be prepared to initiate such proceedings, notwithstanding the stigma of bankruptcy (see para 19.21A). The court is empowered (ss 273 and 274) instead to make a voluntary arrangement (see para 19.20) or order summary administration (s 275: see para 27.04). In respect of a debtor company, a similar procedure is available by way of a members' voluntary winding up (ss 91–6), e.g. a phoenix company (see para 19.25).

Where a court grants one of the above insolvency petitions, control of the debtor's assets passes to a liquidator or trustee (ss 91, 103, 144–5 and 306). The extent of those available assets is considered below (paras 19.23–4), together with the system of entitlement to claim on them (see para 19.22). Whilst the debtor thus loses control of his assets, he is at the same time protected from most creditors' proceedings (ss 126, 128, 285 and 345–7). However, any malpractice by the debtor before or during the insolvency may amount to a criminal offence;[186] there is a specially strengthened system in respect of company directors (see para 19.25); and it is expressly made an offence for an undischarged bankrupt to obtain credit without disclosing his status.[187]

**[19.21A]  The individual insolvent debtor**. To the individual consumer-debtor, the above proceedings have the disadvantage that he will be registered with a credit bureau, upon which the debtor is unlikely to be able to obtain fresh credit, except upon the disadvantageous terms available to 'non-status' debtors (see para 8.36) or perhaps criminally under a different name—so escaping credit searches (see para 8.36). Assuming the individual consumer-debtor is made bankrupt (see para 19.21), this has the following results:

(1)  After discharge from bankruptcy, he will walk away free of those debts provable in the bankruptcy (see para 19.23), but remains liable for those debts which are not provable, e.g. court fines, maintenance or child support, benefit overpayments, debts incurred through fraud. The Government is worried that students will use the procedure to shake off repayment obligations to the Student Loan Company.[188]

(2)  The EA reduced the ordinary bankruptcy period for a non-culpable (see below) bankrupt individual debtor from three years to one year, or in practice perhaps as little as eight weeks (s 256), though his obligation to make bankruptcy payments out of disposable income will continue for at least three years.[189]

---

185 In 2005, a debtor's petition cost £310, there also being court fees (£150), with a compulsory deposit payable at the outset. A petitioning debtor is not entitled to a waiver of the compulsory deposit against fees: *R v Lord Chancellor, ex p Lightfoot* [1999] 4 All ER 583, CA (income support claimant). For the overindebted especially, the petition and court costs may be a severe hurdle, though it may be possible to get these paid by the Government Social Fund (see para 2.15): (2005) 75 *Quarterly Account* 15. Debtors may now petition on-line at www.insolvency.gov.uk.

186 For bankruptcy offences, see ss 350–62. For offences by an insolvent company and its officers, see ss 206–19. Such offences will usually become apparent during the investigation of the insolvent's affairs: ss 131–4, 288–91 and 366–71.

187 S 360: see generally Goode, *Consumer Credit Law & Practice*, Pt IE, paras 71.110–22. As to credit within the CCA, see para 5.21.

188 It all depends whether student debts are, or are not, debts provable in bankruptcy (see para 19.22): for students commencing studies after Autumn 2001, see the Teaching and Higher Education Act 1998, s 22(3)(e) and 2001 SI 951, reg 40 (not provable); Higher Education Act 2004, s 42.

189 Under an Income Payments Order (IPOs: IA, s 310(6), as substituted by EA, s 259) or an Income Payments Agreement (IPAs: IA, s 310A, as inserted by EA, s 260).

(3) Where the debtor has been culpable, e.g. extravagant, s 257 of the EA enables the making against him of a Bankruptcy Restriction Order (BRO), which is modelled on the directors' disqualification orders (see para 19.25) and could curb his borrowings for up to 15 years.[190]

(4) During the bankruptcy period, the bankrupt generally commits a criminal offence if he engages in business, or obtains credit (IA, s 360). However, since the EA, there has been a general lightening in the weight of bankruptcy on bankrupts, for instance, investigation of all bankrupts by the Official Receiver is no longer obligatory and is likely to be restricted to culpable ones (s 258).

(5) As regards provable debts (see above), the most significant is likely to be the bankrupt's home; and it used to be normal for his trustee to apply to court for an order to sell that home for the benefit of creditors.[191] If the bankrupt lives there alone, his trustee may sell the property for the benefit of his creditors (s 305(2)); and if the property houses his spouse and dependants, the trustee can usually still sell,[192] or may alternatively take a charge on the property.[193] However, under the EA, the bankrupt's home may cease to form part of his bankrupt estate after three years.[194]

(6) As regards the debtor's personal assets, his bank account will be frozen on bankruptcy;[195] and his car will usually be sold;[196] but his personal belongings will be 'protected' from bankruptcy insofar as they are necessary for his domestic needs or employment (IA, ss 283(2) and 308).[196]

(7) In view of the fact that prior to the EA, more than half of all personal bankruptcies involved credit card debts, the consumer credit industry has serious misgivings as to whether the EA changes will make bankruptcy too attractive to over-indebted individuals.[197] Perhaps the greatest worry is that bankruptcy fees are so reduced that bankruptcy becomes an attractive and viable option for any debtor pressed for payment.[198]

**[19.22] Secured and unsecured creditors.** The debt may be secured by the grant or reservation of rights over the property of the debtor by way of 'mortgage, charge, lien or other security'.[199] Presumably, 'other security' includes rights under a

---

190 See McKenzie Skene [2004] JBL 171. BROs have been little-used: for current statistics, see www.insolvency.gov.uk.

191 This rule does not extend to domestic tenancies; but a clause in the tenancy may preclude an undischarged bankrupt from holding the tenancy.

192 See IA, s 335A; and *Dean v Stout* [2006] 3 CL 220.

193 IA, ss 313 (as amended), 332; and as to the Charging Orders Act 1979, see para 27.04. For the situation where the insolvent has died, see IA, s 421A (as inserted by IA 2000, s 12) and *Re Byford* [2003] CLY 3542.

194 S 261, inserting two new sections into the IA: see Miller (2006) 156 NLJ 534. For the insolvent's estate, see para 19.23.

195 He can apply for a basic bank account (see para 2.15), because it gives him no access to credit.

196 Following a County Court case, in 2006 the Insolvency Service issued a new notice as to when a vehicle is exempt from bankruptcy: see (2006) 1 QA 23.

197 In 2004, debtor's petitions (see para 19.21) reached a 40-year high, with consumer bankruptcies 70% of the total. As to over-indebted individuals, see paras 6.09–10.

198 The Government has instituted an enquiry into how individual debtors might be diverted into IVAs: *The Times* 27.12.03; and para 19.20. For argument that the changes will not help consumers much, see (2004) 72 *Quarterly Account* 6.

199 IA ss 248 and 383(2). For mortgages, charges and liens, see generally, Chap 25; and for the unpaid seller's lien, see para 24.10.

pledge (see para 25.15); but there is the question of whether a set-off (see generally, para 7.23) is an 'other security', and is hence preserved from the insolvency.[200] The safest security is a reservation of ownership, as where the creditor has supplied goods to the debtor by way of conditional sale,[201] hp, or simple hiring (see para 24.22). However, in the case of a mortgage, charge or lien, at common law as between themselves secured creditors normally rank in order of creation of their security (see para 25.22).

As against the liquidator (representing unsecured creditors), the secured creditor may, in principle, take any of the courses of action above outlined (see para 19.13). This has led to reprehensibly secret attempts by creditors to achieve for themselves the status of secured creditors, e.g. by a secret sale or mortgage from the debtor. The reply of the law has been to require such transactions to be registered: where the transferor is an individual, under the Bills of Sale Acts (see para 9.02). However, at this point a distinction must be drawn between two classes of secured creditors because only those with a fixed security can choose to remain outside the statutory scheme imposed by the IA.

1.  *Creditors with fixed security.* Such a creditor may indeed ignore the unsecured creditors and proceed to recoup the whole of his debt from the secured asset (see para 19.13). Thus, provided only that a secured creditor has taken a financially adequate security, he can normally ensure that he is paid in full regardless of the plight of unsecured creditors (see para 19.25). Moreover, particularly in equipment financing (see para 16.06), the very threat of repossession may put the secured creditor in *de facto* control.[202]

2.  *Creditors with floating security.* Under the IA, a floating charge over the assets of a debtor company was postponed to preferential creditors (IA, s 175(2)(b)) but could usually levy its debt from the secured property free of the ordinary creditors. However, under the EA, few floating chargees will be able to appoint an administrative receiver (see para 19.14); and, even in those few cases, a share of the assets subject to a floating charge may be diverted to unsecured creditors (see para 19.23). An individual debtor cannot grant a floating charge to any of his creditors (see para 19.14).

    The fact that a floating charge is normally more vulnerable to unsecured creditors than a fixed charge has led to attempts to convert the one into the other.[203] It may also lead banks to transfer more of their business to direct financing and factoring (see paras 2.21–2).

**[19.23] Unsecured creditors**. Insofar as a creditor is not a supplier able to rely on an effective reservation of title clause (see para 25.29), or is otherwise unsecured, it may be vital for him to determine what property has fallen into the buyer's insolvency (see para 19.24). Thus, an unpaid seller will be reduced to claiming a dividend on his price if he cannot lay claim to the goods supplied, as by exercising his seller's

---

200  See Oditah, *Receivables Financing*, 200.

201  For *Romalpa* clauses, see para 25.29.

202  See McCormack [2003] JBL 389 at 394–7.

203  See Goode (1994) 110 LQR 592 (criticised by Berg [1995] JBL 433); McCormack [2003] JBL 389 at 394.

lien or right of stoppage (as to which see paras 24.08 and 24.17); and this rule will extend to a buyer who has paid for rejected goods (see para 24.03). Whereas secured creditors usually take in order of priority of creation (see para 19.22), as between unsecured creditors there is a general principle of 'equality of misery'.[204] However, this is subject to first payment of the expenses of the trustee or liquidator;[205] and thereafter the unsecured creditors are divided into the following three classes of descending priority. Generally, unsecured creditors take available property rateably within those classes (s 107):

1. *Preferential creditors.* An IA Schedule lists certain types of debt as preferential.[206] It provides that these shall have priority over all other debts, including any floating charge created by an insolvent company (IA, ss 40(2), 175(2)(b) and 251); and it lays down that, after payment of the expenses of insolvency, these preferential debts shall rank equally amongst themselves (IA, ss 175, 328 and 386). In practice, it was usually found that the largest preferential creditor was the Crown in respect of unpaid taxes and that, when the expenses (see above) and the Crown had been paid in full, there was little or nothing remaining for the ordinary creditors. However, the EA has excluded Crown preference from the list of preferential creditors (s 251), with the result that, after payment of the preferential back-wages to employees, there is much more likely to be remaining assets available for ordinary creditors (see below).

2. *Ordinary creditors,* for instance, suppliers on unsecured credit, victims of the insolvent's torts. Apart from the special position of preferential creditors (above), distraining landlords,[207] execution creditors[207] and those with a right of set-off,[208] ordinary creditors rank equally and are paid in equal proportions between themselves.[209] The normal result is payment of a small proportion of his debt to each ordinary creditor, this usually being expressed as a 'dividend' of so-much-per-pound of debt;[210] and the average is a nil return.[211] As a matter of public policy, it may not be possible to contract out of this rule,[212] though there are said to be exceptions to it.[213] Under the EA, this category of unsecured creditors will usually include holders of a floating charge (see para 19.14), so

---

204 McCormack [2003] JBL 389 at 398.

205 See IA, ss 115, 156 and 324(1).

206 Preferential debts originally listed in Sched 6 included PAYE, VAT, 4 months' remuneration of employees. An unsuccessful attempt was made to add consumer prepayments: NCC, *1985/6 Annual Report*, 10.

207 See respectively, paras 19.17 and 19.15.

208 IA, s 323. As to set-offs, see generally, para 7.23. See comment by Goode [1986] JBL 431; and generally Derham (1992) 108 LQR 99.

209 IA, ss 107 and 328(3). If there is any surplus, there are provisions as to payment of interest due (ss 189 and 328(4)). As to the payment of interest on debts generally, see para 7.03A.

210 IA, s 324. It has been argued that the position of unsecured creditors should be improved generally rather than adjusted by *Romalpa* Clauses (above): see Goodhart and Jones (1980) 43 MLR 489, 511. But does not a purchase-money security deserve some preference?

211 See McCormack, *op. cit.*, at 394.

212 *British Eagle International Airlines Ltd v Compagnie Nationale Air France* [1975] 2 All ER 390, HL.

213 Oditah, *Op. cit.*, 172–7. See also *Re Charge Card Services Ltd* (set out at para 2.27); and Nolan [1995] JBL 485.

bringing their interest within the purview of the trustee or liquidator (who is acting for all the unsecured creditors).

3.  *Deferred debts*. Only when all the preferential and ordinary creditors have been paid in full is any surplus distributed equally between the insolvent's deferred creditors, e.g. spouses or company members (IA, ss 329 and 107). The effect is that deferred creditors are likely to recover only to the extent that the debtor was otherwise solvent all along.

Finally, it is important to remember that, in the case of personal bankruptcy, only debts which can be proved ('bankruptcy debts': s 382) may take the benefit of the above scheme and that the bankrupt's discharge will only expunge all bankruptcy debts: so, other unprovable debts e.g. fines, some rent arrears[214] and security rights, continue to subsist (s 281(5) and (2)), whereas unproven bankruptcy debts are extinguished,[215] e.g. the secured debt itself. As to the position of any surety, see para 25.04, *et seq.*

**[19.24] Available property**. The general rule is that there falls into the insolvency all property beneficially owned by the insolvent at the moment of insolvency (IA, ss 144 and 283(1)(a)) or acquired thereafter.[216] So, the person administering the insolvent estate (trustee or liquidator) steps into the shoes of the insolvent person or company and takes control of whatever interest the insolvent had in real or personal property, e.g. hire rent due under leases, surplus on any security (see para 19.13). In the case of a bankrupt individual, the personal property actually vests in the trustee (IA, s 306).

The foregoing principles are subject to any legal or equitable rights that any third party might have in the property.[217] As regards legal rights, the principle covers the SGA rules governing the passing of property (see Chap 20): so, in respect of sales of unascertained goods by description, apart from any legal interest in shared goods (see above), *prima facie* no property passes: *Re Goldcorp Exchange Ltd* (set out at para 20.22). As regards equitable rights, the insolvency rule extends to 'mere equities'[217] and to the important equitable principle that equity regards as complete an assignment of after-acquired property. In *Re Kayford Ltd*:[218]

> A mail order business was anxious, in the event of its insolvency, to protect customers who might have sent in money for goods. Their accountants advised the opening of a separate 'Customers' Trust Deposit Account' but the company instead instructed its bank to utilise a dormant deposit account for that purpose. The company subsequently being put into liquidation, it was held that a trust had been created and that the moneys were held in trust for those customers who had sent them.

---

214  See *Harlow DC v Hall* [2006] EWCA Civ 156, CA (occupation charges: see Kruse (2006) 1 QA 12).

215  Where a regulated agreement is improperly executed (see para 9.19), is there a 'bankrupt debt' (s 382(3)—contingent); and is that debt so extinguished? See Howells, *Consumer Debt*, para 12.40.

216  S 307. There are also powers under which the liquidator or trustee may disclaim onerous property: IA 1986, ss 178–83 and 315–21.

217  IA, s 283(3)(a); *Tilley v Bowmans Ltd* [1916] 1 KB 745 (right to rescind for misrepresentation: see generally, para 26.12). See generally Goode (1987) 103 LQR 433, at 438–47.

218  [1975] 1 All ER 604 (discussed [1985] JBL 456). See also *Carreras Rothmans Ltd v Freeman Mathews Treasure Ltd (in liq)* [1985] 1 All ER 155 (not a sale case); *Re EVTR* (1987) 3 BCC 389, CA.

Megarry J explained:[219]

> 'No doubt the general rule is that if you send money to a company for goods which are not delivered, you are merely a creditor of the company unless a trust has been created. The sender may create a trust by using appropriate words when he sends the money . . ., or the company may do it by taking suitable steps on or before receiving the money'.

These cautionary words refer to the heavy burden of proof required to show the existence of an express trust:[220] it has been suggested that this is more easily achieved in respect of consumers than trade creditors;[221] and that this could be done by codes of conduct.[222]

The above general rules are subject to a number of qualifications:

1. *Subsequent dispositions.* Subject to the consent of the court, any disposition of property owned by the insolvent made after the relevant date is *prima facie* void.[223]

2. *Statutory registration.* In order to prevent one creditor secretly obtaining the status of secured creditor, statute provides compulsory registration systems (see para 19.22).

3. *Swelling the assets.* Besides allowing the trustee or liquidator to avoid incomplete executions (see para 19.16), the IA also recognises certain actions which can be brought to swell the assets of a liquidation (IA, ss 112 and 213–14: see para 19.25).

4. *Ultra vires contracts.* Like any other third party dealing with a debtor company in good faith, a creditor can enforce a debt against the company 'free of any limitation under the company's constitution' (Companies Act 1985, s 35A(1) (as inserted)).

5. *Avoidable transactions.* The property available to the unsecured creditors on insolvency is increased by setting aside for their benefit a number of types of unsecured transaction thought to have potential for causing inequality. These include transactions defrauding creditors (IA, ss 238–41, 245, 339–42 and 423(2)); transactions at an undervalue (IA, ss 238(2) and 340(2)); general assignments of book debts by a natural person (IA, s 344(2)); and extortionate credit transactions.[224] Where, in the three years before insolvency, the insolvent company or natural person borrowed money, the liquidator or trustee may claim that the transaction is, or was, extortionate[225] or an unfair credit

---

219 At 607. It is insufficient if the debtor fails to fulfill his promise to set up a trust: *Mac-Jordan Construction v Brookmount Erostin* [1992] BCLC 350, CA ([1992] JBL at 420–1). As to prior payment, see para 23.22.

220 Ulph [1996] JBL 482, at 486–7. But such a trust may be struck down by statute as amounting to an undue preference: see below.

221 Ulph, *Op. cit.*, 491–3.

222 Suggestion by DTI: see (1996) 14 *Fair Trading* 2.

223 IA, ss 127 and 284. But remember the rule in *Tailby v Official Receiver* (see para 7.18). See further, Oditah, *Receivables Financing*, 63–5.

224 The IA defines extortionate (ss 244(3) and 343(3)) in terms which are very similar to the now-repealed CCA definition (s 138(1)): as to the latter, see para 29.42.

225 The liquidator or trustee may now bring proceedings: IA, s 343 (as amended by the CCA 2006).

relationship.[226] Unless the creditor disproves this, the court has power to set aside or vary the transaction, recover any money paid to the creditor, or any security held by him, or to direct a taking of accounts (IA, ss 244(4) and 343(4)).

6.    *Student loans* (see para 19.21A).

**[19.25] Rogue company directors**. Many of the problems which the law has encountered in this respect may be traced back to the decision of the House of Lords in *Salomon v Salomon*.[227]

> S was the sole proprietor of a boot manufacturing business. In 1892, after some 30 years trading, he decided to incorporate the business as a limited liability company under the Companies Acts. He sold the business to the company, the purchase price being partly satisfied by the issue of paid-up shares and partly left on loan secured by a floating charge over the business. The company became insolvent in 1893, S having three roles: director of a liquidated company, principal shareholder and secured creditor. It was held that on incorporation the business became in law an independent person; that S was liable for the debts of the business neither as director nor shareholder; and that his secured loan ranked before the unsecured creditors.

It will be observed that the decision to benefit S follows logically from the effects of incorporation and basically still stands with regard to the position of shareholders and fixed (but not floating) charges (see para 19.21). Exceptionally, the courts have been willing to 'pierce the corporate veil' and look to the person behind the registered company,[228] e.g. fraudulent or negligent misstatement (see paras 17.18, 17.20), pre-incorporation contracts (see para 10.15), on insolvency (see para 19.18, *et seq*.). Take the example of a small, one-man company: normally, the acts or words of even the dominant director will have been on behalf of the corporate entity, so that only the company will be liable for them;[229] but exceptionally that director may have so acted as to give rise to his personal liability in either the torts of negligence[230] or deceit,[231] or in contract,[232] or from giving a personal indemnity (see para 25.05).

Another example is the so-called 'phoenix business', where an unscrupulous businessman sets up a company, incurring substantial debts and obligations in the name of the company, and then walks away to incorporate a new company to carry on a sometimes almost identical business.[233] It was thought unfair that the moving

---

226 In due course, the liquidator or trustee will be able to plead the debtor's unfair credit relationship, standing in the shoes of the debtor: see para 29.47.

227 [1897] AC 22, [1895–6] All ER Rep 33, HL.

228 E.g. *Trustor AB v Smallbone (No. 2)* [2001] 3 All ER 987 (see 119 LQR 13). See generally Gower, *Company Law*, 6th edn, Chap 8, esp 124, *et seq*.

229 *Williams v Natural Life Health Foods Ltd* [1998] 2 All ER 577, HL (not liable for negligent misstatement: see Griffin 115 LQR 36).

230 Different considerations apply as regards negligent misstatement, where the director must so act as to create the clear impression that he was holding himself personally answerable: the *Williams* case (above), *per* Lord Steyn (*obiter*); and see Watson and Willekes [2001] JBL 217; Noonan and Watson [2004] JBL 539.

231 *Standard Chartered Bank v Pakistan National Shipping Corpn (No. 2)* [2003] 1 AC 959, HL (director liable in deceit: see 119 LQR 199).

232 *Ojjeh v Waller* [1999] CLY 4405 (making a director personally liable for warranties in respect of goods sold by his company).

233 Fletcher [1989] JBL at 368; [2002] 3 *Which?* 6. For voluntary liquidations, see para 19.21.

spirit behind such a business should so triumph: not only have the courts been willing in these circumstances to lift the corporate veil;[234] but there is also a statutory prohibition on a director in most cases resuming trading under a new company with a similar name.[235] The IA 1986 also allows for a director to be penalised with regard to the previous business: first, there may be a misfeasance action against a delinquent director to remedy any breach of a duty that director owes to the company (s 112). Second, he may be sued for fraudulent or wrongful trading (ss 213 and 214). Other statutes allow for the possibility of disqualification of the director.[236] Thirdly, the Secretary of State may cause a company to be compulsorily wound up in the public interest, following a DTI investigation;[237] and, in this situation, the OFT have also sometimes taken out Enforcement Orders against its directors.[238]

---

234 E.g. *Creasey v Breachwood Motors* [1993] CLY 383 (making the new company liable for the obligations of the old company; but perhaps overruled in *Ord v Belhaven Pubs Ltd* [1998] CLY 377, CA); Clark, *Product Liability*, 67–70.

235 Insolvency Act 1986, s 216. Contravention is both an offence (s 216(4)) and leads to his personal responsibility for any debts incurred by the new company (s 217), e.g. *Ricketts v Ad Valorem Factors Ltd* [2004] 1 All ER 894, CA. These provisions have not been altogether effective: Brickman (1993) 143 NLJ 1614. See also Milman [1997] JBL 224; Griffiths (2006) 156 NLJ 530.

236 See the Company Directors Disqualification Act 1986 (as amended). A list of disqualified directors is available. Those trading through unincorporated businesses can be similarly dealt with by BROs (see para 19.21A).

237 IA, s 124A. See *Re Equity & Provident Ltd* [2002] EWHC 186; *Re Supporting Link Alliance Ltd* [2004] 1 WLR 1549 (unsolicited directory entries: see para 8.18).

238 OFT, *2002–3 AR* 36. For Enforcement Orders, see para 28.04.

# CHAPTER 20

# THE PASSING OF PROPERTY

## INTRODUCTION

[20.01] There are a number of circumstances in which it may be important to determine whether the property in goods has passed from the seller to the buyer (see para 19.10). In such cases, the first question to ask is whether, under the contract, the goods are specific or unascertained (see para 20.02); because this important question will determine in relation to the diagram set out below on which side of the bold line the contract falls. Once that issue is determined, except by novation a contract will **never** cross the bold line in the diagram below.[1] That issue being settled, the rules for the passing of property provide for carefully defined stages. *Stage 1* is that the legislature has laid down in s 16 of the SGA the earliest moment at which a contract for the sale of unascertained goods may pass the property in goods (see para 20.05). However, the s 16 rule is cast in such a manner that it is automatically satisfied with regard to specific goods. *Stage 2* is that, once the previous requirement is met, the property in the goods will pass when the parties so intend (SGA, s 17: see para 20.06). *Stage 3* is that, where the parties do not provide for the passing of property in their contract, s 18 of the SGA lays down a number of different rules, basically[2] according to whether the goods are specific (see para 20.08, *et seq.*) or unascertained (see para 20.15, *et seq.*). This pattern may be represented diagrammatically as follows:[3]

|  | Specific Goods | Unascertained Goods |
|---|---|---|
| *Stage 1* | – | s 16 (unascertained) |
| *Stage 2* | s 17 | s 17 (ascertained) |
| *Stage 3* | s 18, rr 1–4 | s 18, r 5 |

Special rules are laid down for the passing of property in (a) sale or return transactions, where the goods may be specific[4] or unascertained[5] and (b) sales of an unascertained part of a specific bulk (see para 20.22).

---

1    Thus, unascertained goods do **not** become specific when later identified: they become ascertained at stage 2.
2    As to the special rules for sale or return transactions, see para 20.23, *et seq.*
3    There cannot be appropriation before ascertainment (see para 20.05); but there may be ascertainment before appropriation (see para 20.21).
4    E.g. supply of an item of clothing on sale or return.
5    E.g. supply of cans of beer for a party on sale or return.

## Specific and unascertained or future goods

**[20.02/3] Specific/unascertained dichotomy**. Section 18 carefully distinguishes between sales of specific and unascertained goods, applying different rules as to the passing of property in the two situations:

(1)  Sales of specific goods (see paras 20.08–14).

(2)  Sales of unascertained goods (see paras 20.15–22).

Leaving aside sale or return transactions (see paras 20.23–7), the position is this: the term 'specific goods' occurs in the first three rules of s 18 and it presumably has the same meaning in each of them; whereas 'unascertained goods' are dealt with by rule 5. It has already been seen (see para 2.04) that the SGA expressly defines 'specific goods', subject to a contrary intention and leaving aside sales of an undivided share, as 'goods identified and agreed upon at the time a contract of sale is made'; and inferentially defines 'unascertained goods' as those which are not specific. Several points may be made at the outset:

(a)  The expression 'specific goods' is also employed in several other sections of the SGA;[6] and, especially in view of the express disclaimer, it does not necessarily have precisely the same meaning in all of those contexts.[7]

(b)  In the context of the passing of property, it is clear that the test of whether or not the goods are 'specific' is to be applied at the moment of contracting.[8] Goods which do not meet the test are initially unascertained, but may thereafter become 'identified and agreed upon'—at which point they are said to become 'ascertained'.[9]

(c)  At the precise moment of contracting, the SGA directs one to see if the goods are 'identified and agreed upon'; that is, whether only those particular goods will satisfy the contract, so that there is no room under the contract for further selection or substitution.[10] Thus, the test of specific goods is not whether the goods are within eye-shot of the contracting parties:[11] the retail purchase of 'one of those widgets on the shelf' may be a sale of unascertained goods; but a buyer who takes one widget from the self-service shelf to the checkout is buying specific goods. Nor do the goods fail to be specific simply because they are not within eye-shot of the parties at the time of their contracting: the upstairs sale of 'the only bottle of wine in my cellar' is specific;[12] whereas the upstairs sale of 'any one of the six identical bottles of wine in my cellar' is a sale of unascertained goods.

(d)  The matter is one of substance, not form: where what the parties say differs

---

6   Ss 6 and 7 (see paras 22.10–16); ss 17 and 18; s 19 (see para 20.28-9); s 29(2) (see para 23.04); s 52(1) (see para 29.38).

7   The substance of the test may differ for some other purposes, e.g. ss 6 and 7 (see para 22.15).

8   As to present and future goods, see para 2.03.

9   Under ordinary circumstances, unascertained goods **never** become specific: see para 20.01.

10  *Benjamin's Sale of Goods*, 6th edn, para 1-114; Goode, *Commercial Law*, 3rd edn, 208, the suit example.

11  So, a tin with a label saying baked beans may be sold as specific goods, notwithstanding that the tin may contain rhubarb.

12  Benjamin, *Op. cit.*, para 1-114, the black horse example.

from reality, the test of specificity follows substance rather than form.[13] Thus, to continue with the example of the upstairs sale of a bottle of wine in the cellar, if the parties mistakenly think there is only one bottle when there are several identical ones, the contract **is not** for the sale of specific goods; whereas, if they think there are several when there is in fact only one, the contract **is** for specific goods.[14]

For the completely different categories established by s 5, see paras 2.03/4.

**[20.04] Identifiable goods**. This concept was considered by the Court of Appeal in *Kursell v Timber Operators Ltd*.[15]

> A contract for the sale of uncut timber then standing in a Latvian forest provided that the buyer might cut and remove all timber of certain minimum specifications within the period of the next 15 years. The buyer paid a first instalment of the price, £30,000.00; but before the buyer could cut much timber, the forest was nationalised, and thereafter performance of the contract became illegal. The arbitrator found that the contract had been frustrated, so that no further part of the price was payable.

This finding was unanimously affirmed by the Court of Appeal, who held that the property in the timber had not passed to the buyer, and that the risk remained in the seller. Several reasons were given for the decision:

(1) The trees were *fructus naturales*, so that the property did not pass until severance.[16]

(2) Notwithstanding a clause in the contract that, if the buyer were prevented by the Latvian Government from cutting any timber, the 15 years was to be extended by the length of the interruption, the commercial object of the contract was frustrated (see the judgment, at 306–12 and 314–15. See further, para 22.14).

(3) Section 18, r 1 did not apply to this case. Lord Hanworth MR was content to find a contrary intention (at 309–10. See further, para 20.06); but his brethren examined the matter in rather more detail, and concluded that, for two reasons, there was not a sale of specific goods.

*First*, they thought that it was really a contract for the sale of a right of severance, that the trees did not become 'specific or ascertained' for the purposes of s 17 until put in a deliverable state (see para 20.12), and that they were not in a deliverable state until cut.[17] *Second*, they thought that the trees were not specific goods because the contract intended the trees to be measured at the date of cutting, rather than at the date of contracting;[18] but, even if the requisite date was the date of contracting, Sargant LJ said (at 314):

> 'I cannot think that the timber sold was at the date of the contract identified, or more than identifiable; and in order that the goods may be specific they must . . . be

---

13 Goode, *Op. cit.*, 215–6, the cellar wine example.
14 For the application of the rules to identifiable goods, see para 20.04.
15 [1927] 1 KB 298, CA.
16 *Per* Lord Hanworth MR at 309–10; and Sargant LJ at 314. As to *fructus naturales*, see para 9.03. Another example might be PYO strawberries.
17 *Per* Scrutton and Sargant LJJ at 312, 314, who both expressly adopted the reasoning in the Scots case of *Morison v Lockhard* 1912, SC 1017. 'Deliverable state' is considered further, para 20.12.
18 *Per* Scrutton and Sargant LJJ at 311 and 313–14. See also Lord Hanworth MR at 307–8.

identified and not merely identifiable . . . For the purpose of the passing of the actual
property in goods as distinguished from a right to ultimately claim a title to the goods
as against the vendor or volunteers under him, a present identification of the goods
as specific goods appears to be required by the statute.'

The last view that the goods are not specific where only identifiable at the moment
of contracting is difficult to reconcile with some of the other cases.[19] The better view
may be that, where **all** the contract goods are then owned by the seller and also
identified or identifiable[20] at the time of contracting,[21] they are specific;[22] but not
where measurement is at the date of cutting.[23]

## Stages in the passing of property

**[20.05] Stage 1: ascertainment**. The basic thesis of the law in respect of the passing
of property is to be found in s 16 of the SGA, which provides that, subject to s 20A
(see para 20.22B),

> 'Where there is a contract for the sale of unascertained goods no property in goods is
> transferred to the buyer unless and until the goods are ascertained.'

This section is concerned with the single issue of the passing of the sole general
property in the goods. In form negative[24] and mandatory,[25] its justification is that
otherwise there is no method of identifying (ascertaining) the contract goods.[26] In
fact, s 16 deals with two possibilities with regard to goods which are unascertained
at the time of contracting, e.g. a sale of 500 tons of wheat of a certain description:[27]

(1) The goods are purely generic, e.g. a contract for the sale of any 500 tons of
    such wheat.[28] Lacking identification,[26] s 16 continues to prevent the passing of
    property in such generic goods. Distinguish the sale of an undivided share
    of specific goods e.g. sale of half a race-horse, which can amount to a sale of
    specific goods: see para 2.02.

(2) There is a contract for the sale of 500 tons of wheat out of a cargo of 1,000 tons

---

19   E.g. *Varley v Whipp* (set out at para 13.14); *Lord Eldon v Hedley Brothers* [1935] 2 KB 1, CA.
20   E.g. a contract to sell all the black-faced lambs in the seller's flock, that number then being
     unknown to the parties; the single bottle of wine now in the seller's cellar, the parties not then
     being in the cellar.
21   Even if the goods cease to be identifiable thereafter: see *Re Stapylton Fletcher Ltd* (set out at para
     20.05A; ESV).
22   As to goods not owned by the seller, see para 20.02.
23   Because at least 15 years would have to be awaited before all the contract goods could be
     identified: see fn 21, above. Compare para 22.15.
24   This is not to say that the property in the goods will pass when they are specific or ascertained,
     for this depends on the intention of the parties: see Stage 2 (para 20.06).
25   The ascertainment of the goods is thus a condition precedent to the passing of property: SGA
     s 2(4)–(6); *Mischeff v Springett* [1942] 2 KB 331.
26   S 18, r 5: see para 20.15. If the bulk is possessed by a third party, e.g. a warehouseman, his mere
     attornment (see para 23.03) to the part-buyer is insufficient to pass the property in the part:
     *Laurie & Morewood v Dudin & Sons* [1926] 1 KB 223, CA. As to where the part is then separated
     from the bulk and sub-sold with consent, see para 21.02.
27   As to future goods (see para 20.03), e.g. goods to be manufactured or grown by the seller, see
     para 20.18.
28   As to generic goods and an unascertained part of a specific whole, see para 2.04.

on a particular ship.[28] Before the cargo is made up, the contract is for the sale of generic goods as in (1) above.[29] However, once the cargo is made up, the source of the contract goods is agreed, even if the particular grains of wheat due to our buyer are not. Nevertheless, the earlier versions of s 16 not only prevented the property passing,[30] it also prevented the purchaser from acquiring any interest in the contract goods. As this is thought sometimes to work unfairly, the law has been amended to allow for both positive and negative ascertainment (see paras 20.05A and 20.05B).

**[20.05A] Positive ascertainment.** The seller may, after making his contract of sale, do some act in relation to some goods which comply with the contract which clearly shows that he intends to use those goods to fulfill his contract. So he may ascertain the contract goods by physically setting them aside.[31] However, there may also be situations where the contract goods are fleetingly parted from a bulk and then merged back into a bulk. Thus, in *Re Stapylton Fletcher Ltd*[32]

> ESV and SFL were for many years two entirely separate wine merchant companies who both sold wines to customers and after payment held stocks of wine for them. Shortly before insolvency, the shares in both companies passed to a single owner, but this had not affected their different systems for dealing with wine stocks. Administrative receivers (see para 19.14), appointed by the bank under longstanding debentures securing overdrafts, claimed the stock.

The Judge dealt with the receivers' claims as against stocks held by the two companies as follows:

(a) ESV traded from two adjoining industrial units: the trading stock was put into unit 13; but, when (say) one case of a particular vintage was sold to a customer on the basis that ESV would store it for him, ESV would take a case of that description out of their stock in unit 13 and put it into the customer reserve in unit 12, where it would be stored unmarked together with identical wine held for other customers. The court held that, on such a removal from unit 13, a case became ascertained as that contracted to a particular buyer and appropriated, even though not delivered to him (see para 20.19); and, when merged in the bulk in unit 12, that buyer became an owner in common of a proportion of that bulk.[33]

(b) SFL had sold various quantities of wine held in a bonded warehouse to different buyers, but made no attempt to allocate that wine as between different customers. The court held that at common law this gave the individual buyers no proprietary rights in the wine.[34]

**[20.05B] Negative ascertainment (by exhaustion).** In one case, S agreed to sell to B 200 quarters of maize out of a parcel of 618 quarters then owned by him and lodged

---

29  *Re Goldcorp Exchange Ltd* (set out at para 20.20). See also Goode, *Proprietary Rights and Insolvency in Sales Transactions*, 2nd edn, 17.

30  E.g. *Re Wait* (set out at para 20.22).

31  *Pignataro v Gilroy* (set out at para 20.19).

32  [1995] 1 All ER 192; [1994] 1 WLR 1181 (see 110 LQR 509; [1996] JBL 199).

33  See also *Aldridge v Johnson* (set out at para 20.16).

34  See para 20.20. However, this has been achieved by adding two new sections to the SGA (see para 20.22B).

at a certain warehouse. Although S gave B a delivery order,[35] this was held to be a sale of unascertained goods, because the buyer could not point to any particular grain and say 'S agreed to sell that to me'.[36] On the other hand, if S had subsequently sold and delivered the remainder of the grain to a third party, it would have become clear which grains were to be delivered to B, so that they would become ascertained by being the only grains left. Following the recommendation of the Law Commission,[37] statutory effect was given to the latter rule by new s 18, rules 5(3) and (4),[38] which are subject to a contrary intention (see para 20.07). These new rules are restricted to the situation (new s 18, r 5(3))

> 'Where there is a contract for the sale of a specified quantity of unascertained goods in a deliverable state forming part of a bulk which is identified either in the contract or by subsequent agreement between the parties and the bulk is reduced to (or to less than) that quantity.'

Thus, the new rules do not apply where the goods are specific (as to where parties jointly buy specific goods, see para 2.02); nor unless there is an identified bulk,[39] so that the provision does not apply to generic goods (see para 2.04). Nor does it apply where goods forming part of a bulk are later delivered (the property may pass on delivery under r 5(2): see para 20.17); nor where there are other separate purchases without delivery from the undivided bulk;[40] nor where the bulk remains greater than the contract amount; nor where the goods are not in a deliverable state (as to when goods are in a deliverable state, see para 20.12). However, where there is a contract to sell a specified quantity of unascertained undelivered goods and the bulk is reduced to at most that quantity of deliverable goods, these new rules distinguish according to whether the single buyer is due the goods under one or more contracts.

1. *A single-contract buyer.* Confirming the common law,[41] where the single buyer is due all the remaining goods under a single contract, new s 18, r 5(3)[38] provides that, in the above circumstances, *prima facie*:[42]

   > if the buyer under that contract is the only buyer to whom goods are then due out of the bulk—
   >
   > (a) the remaining goods are to be taken as appropriated to that contract at the time when the bulk is so reduced; and
   >
   > (b) the property in those goods then passes to that buyer.

2. *A multi-contract buyer.* Largely confirming the common law,[43] where the single buyer is due all the remaining goods under more than one contract, new s 18, r 5(4),[38] provides that, in the above circumstances, *prima facie*:[42]

---

35   The delivery order was held not to be a document of title: see para 23.03. If it had been, B could have passed a good title: see para 21.49.

36   *Laurie & Morewood v Dudin & Sons* [1926] 1 KB 223, CA. See also *Healey v Howlett* (set out at para 22.06); and generally Nicol (1979) 42 MLR 129.

37   *Sale of Goods Forming Part of a Bulk* (1993), Law Com. No. 215), para 4.11.

38   As supplied by the Sale of Goods (Amendment) Act 1995, s 1(2).

39   'Bulk' is defined in s 61(1): see para 20.22B.

40   As to unascertained rights in an undivided share, see para 20.22B.

41   See *Wait and James v Midland Bank* (1926) 31 Com Cas 172.

42   See para 20.06.

43   *The Elafi* [1982] 1 All ER 208 (see Macleod, *Consumer Sales Law*, 1st edn, para 20.05B).

'Paragraph (3) above applies also (with necessary modifications) where a bulk is reduced to (or to less than) the aggregate of the quantities due to a single buyer under separate contracts relating to that bulk and he is the only buyer to whom goods are then due out of that bulk.'

**[20.06] Stage 2: actual intention**. Subject to *Stage 1* above, the Act confirms that the passing of property is a question of intention. Section 17(1) provides:

'Where there is a contract for the sale of specific or ascertained goods the property in them is transferred to the buyer at such time as the parties to the contract intend it to be transferred.'

Specific and ascertained goods are here coupled together, which seems to suggest that ascertained goods are those which are agreed upon[44] at some time **after** the contract is made.[45] Assuming that the goods are specific or ascertained, s 17(2) reiterates the common law rule[46] that:

'For the purpose of ascertaining the intention of the parties regard shall be had to them terms of the contract, the conduct of the parties, and the circumstances of the case.'

In the case of a written contract, the intention of the parties may become a matter of construction, as in *Re Anchor Line Ltd*:[47]

There was a contract for the sale of a crane, the price to be paid by instalments subsequent to delivery. Eve J held that the property passed when the contract was made under s 18, r 1 (see para 20.09); but the Court of Appeal pointed out that s 18 gives way to a contrary intention, and held that on a true construction of the written contract the parties had shown an intention that the property should not pass until the full price had been paid.

Similarly, the charterparty of a ship (a form of hiring: see para 1.18) may provide that, in relation to the oil on board for the operation of that ship (= bunkers), at the commencement of the charter the property in that oil shall pass under a sale from the shipowner to the charterer, whilst at the end of the charter the remaining bunkers shall be 'resold' to the shipowner.[48] Again, in the *Elafi*[49] where there was a sale of unascertained goods, Mustill J found that the contract goods had become ascertained,[50] but that s 18 had been ousted (for s 18, r 5, see para 20.15). Subsequent conduct may also provide evidence of intention.[51]

One example of an implied contrary intention to oust s 18 receives separate treatment in the SGA, namely where there is a reservation of a right of disposal (see para 20.28) and is the basis of *Romalpa* clauses (see para 25.30). This attitude has

---

44   See para 20.04; and further, para 20.22.
45   *Per* Atkin LJ in *Re Wait* (set out at para 20.20), at 630. See also Lord Blackburn in *Seath v Moore* (1886) 11 App Cas 350, HL, at 370.
46   See *Ogg v Shuter* (1875) LR 10 CP 159, CA at 162.
47   [1937] 1 Ch 1; [1936] 2 All ER 941, CA. See also *Davy Offshore v Emerald Field Contracting* [1992] 2 Lloyd's Rep. 142, CA.
48   See *The Span Terza (No. 2)* [1984] 1 WLR 27, HL; *The Saetta* [1994] 1 All ER 851.
49   [1982] 1 All ER 208.
50   Of course, the property could not pass when the documents were negotiated because the claimant's goods were not then identified: see para 20.19.
51   *The Filiatra Legacy* [1991] 2 Lloyd's Rep. 337, CA.

even been extended to an 'all monies' reservation in *Armour v Thyssen* (set out at para 20.29).

In the case of a consumer supply contract, an express provision as to the passing of property may be an unfair and unreasonable term; whereas in a business contract it may be merely an unreasonable term.[52]

**[20.07] Stage 3: deemed intention.** Whilst it may be possible in some cases to find a common intention, express[53] or implied,[54] as to the passing of property, most laymen do not act so as deliberately to satisfy such esoteric legal criteria; and, because the common law rejected any other objective test as to the passing of property (see para 19.01), the courts therefore had to lay down a series of more or less arbitrary rules for attributing such an intention (usually fictitious) to the parties. These rules have been embodied in s 18 of the SGA; and, in practice, they are very important simply because the parties so seldom evince any intention on this point. On the other hand, s 18 does make it clear that the intention of the parties is paramount, for the opening words of the section are as follows:[55]

> 'Unless a different intention appears, the following are rules for ascertaining the intention of the parties as to the time at which the property in the goods is to pass to the buyer.'

The rules that the section contains will apply not just to sales, but also to quasi-sales and hp transactions. As regards the latter, when the hirer exercises his option, a contract of sale comes into existence and the property passes in accordance with the intention of the parties or under the rules laid down in s 18.

## THE PASSING OF PROPERTY IN SPECIFIC GOODS

**[20.08]** Leaving aside sales on approval, which receive special treatment (see para 20.23, *et seq*.), the rules of s 18 with respect to the passing of property in specific goods differentiate between conditional and unconditional contracts, making special provision in r 1 for 'unconditional contracts'. The two major uses of the term 'condition' in the law of contract are that of conditions precedent (see para 1.11) and essential stipulations (see para 11.04); and, at first sight, it appears too obvious for argument that 'unconditional contract' in r 1 means a contract not subject to any conditions precedent as to the passing of property. This was the common law position;[56] but the courts have in several cases since 1893 suggested that 'unconditional contract' in r 1 means one without any essential stipulations.[57] Their motive for this apparently illogical attitude seems to have been to avoid the unfortunate effect of the combination of s 11(1)(c) and s 18, r 1 of the SGA 1893, which might in some circumstances have denied a buyer any right of rejection at

---

52   For unfair terms, see para 11.12, *et seq*.; and for unreasonable terms, see para 18.22, *et seq*.
53   Many standard-form contracts expressly deal with the point: for standard-form contracts, see generally, para 11.08.
54   E.g. trade custom: *Lord Eldon v Hedley Brothers* [1935] 2 KB 1, CA, especially *per* Greer LJ at 16–19.
55   Are these 'rules' in fact implied terms? See Bradgate [1988] JBL at 482.
56   See *Street v Blay* (1831) 2 B & Ad 456.
57   Only *Varley v Whipp* (set out at para 13.14) seems to have been decided on these grounds.

all.[58] However, this undesirable result has been removed from the law;[59] and it is submitted that it is now safe to regard 'unconditional' in r 1 as meaning 'without conditions precedent' as to the passing of property (see further, para 20.10).

**[20.09/10] Unconditional contracts**. Section 18, r 1 provides:

> 'Where there is an unconditional contract for the sale of specific goods in a deliverable state, the property in the goods passes to the buyer when the contract is made, and it is immaterial whether the time of payment or the time of delivery, or both, be postponed.'

It is usually said that this rule reiterates the position at common law;[60] and an example of the operation of the rule is to be found in *Dennant v Skinner*.[61]

> A rogue, X, attended an auction, and successfully bid for a van. Afterwards, he told the plaintiff auctioneer that his name was King and that he was the son of the proprietor of a well-known firm, King's of Oxford. The plaintiff then knocked down five more vehicles to X, including a Standard car. Afterwards, X went to the auctioneer's office, and asked to be allowed to pay by cheque, repeating that he was from King's of Oxford. The auctioneer allowed him to take the Standard away after he had signed a memorandum in the following terms: 'I agree that the ownership of the vehicles will not pass to me until such time as . . . my cheque . . . [is honoured]'. X disappeared, and the Standard found its way into the hands of the defendant, a bfp.

Hallett J held that there was a contract of sale between the auctioneer and X made 'by the fall of the hammer' under SGA, s 57(2) (set out at para 10.10), the identity of X being at that time irrelevant; and that the property passed under s 18, r 1 to X at the time the contract was made, this case being indistinguishable from *Phillips v Brooks*.[62] Nor did his Lordship think the memorandum aided the auctioneer: he pointed out that it merely stated a legal error. This case has given rise to controversy on several grounds not directly relevant to r 1. *First*, did the auctioneer's mistake as to the identity of X prevent there ever being a contract between the two of them in relation to the five vehicles (see para 21.19)? *Second*, assuming that there was a contract, why did the defendant not plead title under the SGA, s 25 (see para 21.43)? *Third*, why did the memorandum not impliedly revest the property in the auctioneer?[63]

So far as the actual wording of r 1 is concerned, the meaning of the terms 'unconditional contract' and 'specific goods' have already been discussed (see respectively, paras 20.08 and 20.02–4); and the meaning of 'deliverable state' will be dealt with later (see para 20.12). It only remains to consider the final words of the rule: 'it is immaterial whether the time of payment or the time of delivery, or both,

---

58   Where there was a contract for the sale of specific goods, the property in which passed to the buyer on formation of the contract: see further my Butterworth Edn, para 20.08.

59   By s 4 of the Misrepresentation Act 1967. The modern version of the limitation on the right to reject is to be found in s 11(4) of the SGA 1979: set out at para 29.04.

60   *Tarling v Baxter* (1827) 6 B & C 360 (sale of stacked hay. Payment February 4th; delivery May 1st. Held property passed on contracting). See criticism by Grieg, *Sale of Goods*, 32.

61   [1948] 2 KB 164; [1984] 2 All ER 29.

62   [1919] 2 KB 243 (the rogue North obtained a ring from a jeweller by misrepresenting his identity, and Horridge J held that the rogue obtained a voidable title to the ring).

63   Hallett J merely said that it had not revested the property, but it has been suggested (it is submitted wrongly) that even by appropriate wording it could not have done so. See Atiyah. *Sale of Goods*, 10th edn, 315.

be postponed'. Though immaterial as such, these events are clearly relevant as possibly giving some indication of a contrary intention which may exclude the operation of s 18 altogether. Thus, in *Ward Ltd v Bignall*[64] Diplock LJ commented:

'The governing rule . . . is in s 17, and in modern times very little is needed to give rise to the inference that the property in specific goods is to pass only on delivery or payment.'

In *Lacis v Cashmarts*, moreover, the Divisional Court held that in a supermarket or 'cash and carry' shop 'the intention . . . is that the property shall not pass until the price is paid';[65] and it may indeed be that s 18 is particularly likely to be ousted in consumer sales and auctions.[66]

**[20.11] Conditional contracts.** Rules 2 and 3 of s 18 deal with the passing of property in conditional contracts for the sale of specific goods;[67] and, apart from the question of notice (see para 20.13), they appear to embody the common law.[68]

*Rule 2* provides as follows:

'Where there is a contract for sale of specific goods and the seller is bound to do something to the goods, for the purpose of putting them into a deliverable state,[69] the property does not pass until such thing be done, and the buyer has notice thereof.'

This rule seems to be based on *Rugg v Minett*:[70]

There was a sale by auction as separate lots[71] of a number of casks containing different quantities of turpentine. The agreement provided that, before delivery, the seller was to top up the casks from two of their number, and the price was to be computed at so much for each full cask and a *pro rata* payment for the remainder. Halfway through the process of topping up, the seller stopped for the night, during which all the casks were destroyed by a fire which occurred without fault on the part of either seller or buyer. The court held that the property did not pass until the barrels were topped up; and hence the property and risk only passed to the buyer in respect of the barrels which had been topped up.

*Rule 3* provides as follows:

'Where there is a contract for the sale of specific goods in a deliverable state,[69] but the seller is bound to weigh, measure, test, or do some other act or thing with reference to the goods for the purpose of ascertaining the price, the property does not pass until such act or thing be done, and the buyer has notice thereof.'

This rule appears to be founded on *Hanson v Meyer*,[72] but has been little used (see para 20.14).

---

64   Set out at para 27.10; [1967] 1 QB 534 at 545.
65   At 407. Compare *Clarke v Reilly* (1962) 96 ILTR 96.
66   Harvey and Meisel, *Auctions*, 2nd edn, 172.
67   The conditions in rr 2 and 3 would appear to be both promissory on the part of the seller and conditional as to the obligations of the buyer: see generally, para 26.01.
68   As to whether reliance can be placed on pre-Act cases, see para 1.04.
69   For 'deliverable state', see para 20.12.
70   (1809) 11 East 210.
71   See now s 57(1), discussed at para 10.10. The fact that there were separate lots is important for the doctrine of total failure of consideration: see para 29.15.
72   (1805) 6 East 614.

**[20.12] Deliverable state**. It will be observed that under r 2 the property in goods does not pass until the goods are put in a 'deliverable state' by the seller, whereas rr 1 and 3 deal with situations where the goods are already in a deliverable state.[73] Presumably, the phrase 'deliverable state' means the same in each case, and is defined by s 61(5) as follows:

'Goods are in a "deliverable state", within the meaning of this Act when they are in such a state that the buyer would under the contract be bound to take delivery of them'.

The expression does not refer to the seller's duty of delivery under s 29 (as to which, see para 23.04), but to the state in which the contract requires those goods to be upon delivery. Its meaning was considered by the courts in *Underwood Ltd v Burgh Castle Brick and Cement Syndicate*:[74]

'There was a contract for the sale "free on rail" of a condensing engine weighing over 30 tons, then cemented to the floor of the seller's premises. It was envisaged by the parties that the process of detaching and loading the engine onto a railway truck would take about two weeks and cost about £100; and the contract provided that this was to be done by the seller at his own expense. The seller subsequently detached the engine; but it was severely damaged whilst being loaded, without any fault on the part of the seller, and, apparently, before the buyer had notice that it had been detached. The buyer refused to accept the damaged engine, and the seller argued that the property and risk had passed to the buyer at the time of the accident.

Rowlatt J thought that the parties intended the sale of a chattel, the severed engine, not of a fixture.[75] His decision in favour of the buyer was unanimously affirmed by the Court of Appeal, who stressed the time and money involved in the operation of loading. Bankes and Atkin LJJ were prepared to find a contractual intention that the property should not pass until the engine was loaded on rail;[76] but all three judges agreed that the engine was not in a deliverable state at the time of the accident because the contract was for the sale of an engine-loaded-on-rail. Bankes LJ explained (at 345):

'A "deliverable state" does not depend upon the mere completeness of the subject-matter in all its parts. It depends on the actual state of the goods at the date of the contract, and the state in which they are to be delivered by the terms of the contract.'

It would seem then that 'deliverable state' does not refer to whether or not the goods are deliverable in any literal sense.[77] Thus, if the buyer is not bound to take delivery, that does not necessarily show that the goods are not in a deliverable state, because the contract may contain conditions precedent to the passing of property other than the state of the goods, e.g. r 3.[78]

---

73  As to whether this refers only to the whole of the goods, see para 20.14.
74  [1922] 1 KB 343; [1921] All ER Rep 515, CA.
75  In a subsequent case, a contract was interpreted as a sale of a right of severance by two members of the CA: *Kursell v Timber Operators Ltd*, (set out at para 20.04).
76  At 345, 346. See also *Young v Matthews* (1866) LR 2 CP 127.
77  See *Phillip Head & Sons Ltd v Showfronts Ltd* [1970] 1 Lloyd's Rep 140 (a case under s 18, r 5).
78  Smith (1957–8) JSPTL, at 192; Thornely (1958) CLJ, at 126; and also Atiyah, *Sale of Goods*, 3rd edn, 108, fn 7. Thereafter, Atiyah changed his mind: see now *Op. cit.*, 10th edn, 319, fn 48, criticised by Goode, *Commercial Law*, 1st edn, 183, fn 83 (dropped from later editions).

**[20.13] Notice**. Where rr 2 or 3 are applicable (see para 20.11), they are subject to the requirement that something is done, and that the buyer has notice thereof, this last stipulation being an addition to the common law (see para 1.02). The Act does not provide that the seller shall give notice, merely that the buyer shall have notice;[79] and it may be that such notice is to be contrasted with the assent required under r 5.[80] This requirement of notice may provide another explanation of *Underwood's* case (set out at para 20.12): even if the engine was in a deliverable state at the time of the accident, the buyer did not know this.[81]

**[20.14] Effect of rr 2 and 3**. It should be noticed that both rr 2 and 3 are expressed in the negative, and are only applicable where something is to be done by the seller. Thus, it does not follow that once the rule is satisfied the property will pass, as there may be other conditions precedent to the passing of property: for instance, suppose A agrees to buy a second-hand car from B provided that (i) B executes certain repairs and (ii) A's wife likes the colour; when the car is repaired it is put in a deliverable state,[82] but the property will not pass until A's wife approves.[83] Even the negative effect of the rules has a fairly narrow scope: they do not apply where the act is to be done by the buyer;[84] and it has been suggested that they are only applicable where the act in relation to the goods is to be done by the seller before delivery.[85] Moreover, even where it is applicable, the presumption contained in rule 3 would appear to be weaker than that in r 2,[86] and has seldom been applied.[87]

Finally, there is the question whether rr 2 and 3 can operate to pass the property in part of the contract goods. At common law, the property could be passed in part only of the contract goods.[88] But s 18 would appear to be ambiguous on this point.[89] In *Underwood's* case (set out at para 20.12), the fact that a small part of the engine had already been delivered does not seem to have been considered significant. Even assuming that the property can pass in part of the contract goods, it would appear that this will not of itself prevent the buyer rejecting the goods under s 30(1) on the grounds that the contract quantity has not been delivered.[90] Could that condition be waived under SGA, s 11(2) (see para 26.24)?

---

79 It is suggested that 'notice' is here equivalent of 'knowledge': Benjamin's *Sale of Goods*, 6th edn, para 5-033.

80 This passive requirement of 'notice' may be compared with the active requirement of 'assent' needed in respect of ascertained goods: see para 20.22.

81 Cf. *Aldridge v Johnson* (set out at para 20.16).     82 *Contra* Atiyah, *Sale of Goods*, 10th edn, 322.

83 Insofar as the wife's approval is a condition precedent to contract, this raises other issues: see para 1.11.

84 Even if done on behalf of the seller?

85 Benjamin's *Sale of Goods*, 6th edn, para 5-032.

86 Atiyah, *Op. cit.*, 323; *Blackburn on Sale*, 3rd edn, 194.

87 *Eldon (Lord) v Hedley Bros* [1935] 2 KB 1, CA; *Nanka Bruce v Commonwealth Trust* [1926] AC 77, PC. Indeed, *The Napoli* (1898) 15 TLR 56 would appear to be the only reported post-1893 case where r 3 has been applied; and it is difficult to see why the buyer's action in conversion in that case should have depended on the passing of property.

88 See *Hanson v Meyer; Rugg v Minett* (for both cases, see para 20.11).

89 Can goods be in a 'deliverable state' where only part of them are in the contract state? Before the amendment of s 11(1)(c) of the SGA 1893 by the Misrepresentation Act 1967, s 4(1) (as to which see para 20.08), the operation of that subsection and s 18, r 2 appeared to conflict with s 30(1). Is this a reason for deducing that the Act did not intend to pass the property in part of the goods?

90 See *Barrow, Lane and Ballard Ltd v Phillip Phillips & Co Ltd* [1929] 1 KB 574 (discussed at para 22.12); and para 20.15, item 2.

## THE PASSING OF PROPERTY IN UNASCERTAINED GOODS

**[20.15] The rule**. If the contract is for the sale of unascertained goods, then it must initially be an agreement to sell, because s 16 prevents the property passing until the contract goods have been ascertained (see para 20.05). Once the goods have become ascertained, s 17 states that the property will pass when the parties so intend (see para 20.06); and, in the absence of a contrary intention, the property will pass according to r 5 of s 18, paragraph (1) of which states the general rule as follows:

> 'Where there is a contract for the sale of unascertained or future goods by description, and goods of that description and in a deliverable state are unconditionally appropriated to the contract, either by the seller with the assent of the buyer, or by the buyer with the assent of the seller, the property in the goods thereupon passes to the buyer. Such assent may be express or implied, and may be given either before or after the appropriation is made.'

Unlike rr 2 and 3 (see paras 20.09 and 20.11), r 5 is expressed in positive terms: it says that the property **will** pass when **all** the following requirements are fulfilled.

(1) The contract is for the sale of 'unascertained or future goods[91] by description'. It has already been suggested that today most sales will be by description (see para 13.09); and the concepts of unascertained and future goods have also been considered. It may therefore be that the passing of property in future specific goods (see para 2.03) is governed by this rule.[92]

(2) The goods appropriated to the contract are of the contract description and in a deliverable state. The latter expression presumably has the same meaning as under the other rules.[93] 'Contract description' certainly deals with (all?) matters of quality:[94] no purported appropriation, however, can pass the property in goods which do not comply with the contract description.[95] Nevertheless, it has been held that the property passed where there was appropriated to the contract of less (*Aldridge v Johnson*: set out para 20.16)) or more than the contract quantity of goods of the contract description,[96] though in the last case it would seem that it is always open to the buyer to reject for breach of s 30.[97]

(3) The appropriation is unconditional. As in the case of the other rules, it is submitted that this refers to the absence of any condition precedent:[98] it may be

---

91  As to future goods, SGA, s 5(1). The inclusion of future goods here amends the common law by adopting the equitable rule in *Holroyd v Marshall* (see para 9.05) that the buyer may automatically became the owner upon acquisition of the goods by the seller: Goode (1987) 103 LQR at 437, fn 5.

92  Goode, *Commercial Law*, 3rd edn, 234. But see para 20.04.

93  See para 20.12. For another view, see Goode, *Op. cit.*, 234.

94  *Healy v Howlett & Sons* (set out at para 22.06).

95  *Vigers Brothers v Sanderson Brothers* [1901] 1 KB 608. For comparison of the buyer's rights to reject appropriation and delivery in breach of s 13, see Goode, *Op. cit.*, 214, fn 35. For appropriation by mistake, see Benjamin's *Sale of Goods*, 6th edn, para 5-087.

96  *The Elafi* [1982] 1 All ER 208.

97  This would give the same answer as in the case of specific goods: see para 20.14. But it may be difficult to reconcile with the old cases such as: *Cunliffe v Harrison* (1851) 6 Exch 903; *Levy v Green* (1859) 1 E & E 969.

98  See para 20.08. *Contra Polar Refrigeration Ltd v Moldenhauer* (1967) 61 DLR (2d) 462; *Ollett v Jordan* [1918] 2 KB 41 (criminal case, said by Benjamin's *Sale of Goods*, 6th edn, para 5-073 to be wrong).

that such a condition precedent evinces an intention to oust s 18 altogether.[99] On the other hand, it has been suggested[100] that the position is analogous to that in relation to r 3 (see para 20.11): whilst the goods remain to be weighed, etc, by the seller, the property does not pass;[101] but, once that measuring has taken place, the property will pass.[102] An appropriation may be on terms (s 19: see para 20.28).

(4) There is appropriation with assent. It is this requirement which usually gives rise to the greatest difficulty; and the two constituent parts, 'appropriation' and 'assent' will be considered separately below (see paras 20.16–21). However, it must be remembered that there is little point in searching for an act of appropriation if there is no evidence of assent; and *vice versa*: both are required before the property will pass.

**[20.16] Appropriation**. In a contract for the sale of unascertained goods, an act done by one party in relation to certain goods which evinces an intention that the property in those goods should pass in pursuance of the contract is termed an 'appropriation'.[103] Two cases may be cited to illustrate the difficulty of determining whether there has been a sufficient appropriation. In *Aldridge v Johnson*:[104]

> There was a contract for the sale 'free on rail' of 100 quarters of barley from a larger bulk then situated in the seller's granary, the price of £215 to be paid as to £23 in cash and the rest in cattle (see para 2.09). It was agreed that the buyer was to send his own sacks, which the seller was to fill. The cattle were delivered, and the sacks sent to the seller. The seller filled most of the sacks, but emptied the barley back onto the pile of grain just before he became bankrupt. The buyer sued the seller's assignees in bankruptcy in conversion and detinue to recover the sacks and the barley.

The court held that the buyer was entitled to his sacks,[105] and also to so much of the barley as had been put into sacks,[106] because the property had passed when it was put into the sacks.[107] It has now been made clear that, when the barley was emptied back onto the pile, the buyer became an owner in common of part of that pile.[108]

On the other hand, in *Federspiel v Twigg Ltd*[109] the court came to the opposite conclusion:

---

99 E.g. *Stein, Forbes & Co v County Tailoring Co* (1916) 86 LJ KB 448.

100 Atiyah, *Sale of Goods*, 10th edn, 336.

101 *National Coal Board v Gamble* [1959] 1 QB 11, DC (prosecution in respect of coal loaded onto a lorry by hopper, priced by weighbridge).

102 *Edwards v Ddin* [1976] 3 All ER 705, DC (prosecution for theft in driving away without paying for petrol).

103 *Per* Pearson J in *Federspiel v Twigg* [1957] 1 Lloyd's Rep 240, at 255. See also *Denny v Skelton* (1916) 86 LJKB 280.

104 (1857) 26 LJQB 296. See also *Re Stapylton Fletcher Ltd* (set out at para 20.05A).

105 But the supplier could not identify which grains were his. This would not matter for conversion (see para 19.05); but was the detinue action therefore misplaced?

106 Cf. *Underwood Ltd v Burgh Castle Brick and Cement Syndicate* (set out at para 20.12).

107 It has been suggested that such an action will always result in specific recovery: *Williams on Bankruptcy*, 18th edn, 273. This is because the buyer is the co-owner of the bulk (see below), so that he may sue for wrongful interference with goods (see para 19.06).

108 See *Re Staplyton Fletcher Ltd* (above).

109 [1957] 1 Lloyd's Rep 240.

There was a contract for the sale of cycles by a British manufacturer to a foreign buyer, fob (see para 22.07) a British port. The seller packed and marked the goods in preparation for shipment, and the buyer paid the price. Before the goods could be dispatched to the port of shipment, the seller went into liquidation. The buyer sued the liquidator for conversion of the cycles, alleging that they had been appropriated to the contract and that the property had passed to him.

In rejecting this contention, Pearson J said (at 255–6):

'usually, but not necessarily, the appropriating act is the last act to be performed by the seller . . . If there is a further act, an important and decisive act to be done by the seller, then there is *prima facie* evidence that probably the property does not pass until the final act is done.'

His Lordship was of the opinion that the emphasis throughout was on shipment as the decisive act to be done by the seller, so that *prima facie* it appeared that the earliest time when the parties intended that the property should pass would be on shipment.[110] Nor could his Lordship find anything to displace this presumption.

[20.17] **Delivery.** Perhaps the most obvious example of appropriation (see para 20.16) is delivery,[111] a matter which receives special mention in paragraph (2) of r 5.

'Where, in pursuance of the contract, the seller delivers the goods to the buyer or to a carrier or other bailee . . . (whether named by the buyer or not) for the purpose of transmission to the buyer, and does not reserve the right of disposal,[112] he is deemed to have unconditionally appropriated the goods to the contract.'

Thus, in *Wardar's (Import and Export) Co Ltd v W Norwood & Sons Ltd*:[113]

There was a sale of 600 out of 6,500 cartons of frozen kidneys then stored in a cold store belonging to the seller's agent. When the buyer's carrier arrived to collect the goods, he found them already stacked on the pavement outside the coldstore. The loading took some four hours, towards the end of which the carrier noticed that the last cartons on the pavement were dripping. The goods were found unfit for human consumption.

The Court of Appeal held that, where a third person in possession of goods sold acknowledges them as the buyer's, there is an attornment which amounts to a delivery in law;[114] that upon such delivery the property passes to the buyer; and that the risk passed with the property.[115]

To satisfy r 5(2), the delivery must be made 'in pursuance of the contract', which implies that the goods must be of the contract description and in a deliverable state (see para 20.15); and, as we shall see later, 'delivery' is defined by the SGA in such a way as to include actual and constructive delivery (see para 23.03). Whilst

---

110 On the question of assent, see 20.22.
111 *Per* Parke B in *Wait v Baker* (1848) 2 Ex 1, at 7–8.
112 As to reservation of a right of disposal, see para 20.28.
113 [1968] 2 QB 663; [1968] 2 All ER 602, CA.
114 Attornment took place when the third party accepted the carrier's note and indicated the cartons on the pavement: see para 23.03.
115 See para 22.01. *Contra* if the seller had contracted to deliver the goods to the destination of the carrier's journey instead of its commencement: *Healey v Howlett & Sons* (set out at para 22.06). As to a sea transit, see *The Elafi* [1982] 1 All ER 208.

r 5(2) seems to be couched as if it were merely an example of r 5(1), there has been a tendency on the part of the courts to treat appropriation as being synonymous with an actual or constructive delivery.[116] Chalmers concludes that:[116] 'If the term "delivery" had been substituted for "appropriation", probably less difficulty would have arisen.' But would this be so? It may be that an actual delivery would clearly show when the property had passed;[117] but it is equally clear that there may be an appropriation notwithstanding that there has not been an actual delivery.[118] Thus, in *Aldridge v Johnson* (set out at para 20.16) it was held that the property passed when the grain was put into the buyer's sacks. To say that the difference between this case and *Federspiel v Twigg Ltd* is that in the former case there has been a constructive change of possession does not seem to advance matters much further, because this issue too turns on the intention of the parties.

As the position may vary according to the type of unascertained goods involved,[119] the cases on appropriation may be divided according to whether the goods are: (1) to be manufactured or grown by the seller, a situation beyond the scope of this work;[120] or (2) generic goods or an unascertained part of a specific whole (see para 20.18/9).

**[20.18/9]  Generic goods, or an unascertained part of a specific whole**. In *Aldridge v Johnson* (set out at para 20.16) the property was held to have passed when the seller put goods which conformed with the contract into containers supplied by the buyer.[121] Moreover, just as the goods may become ascertained by process of exhaustion (see para 20.05B), so they may become appropriated by being physically set aside.[122] Thus, in *Pignatoro v Gilroy*:[123]

> There was a contract for the sale by sample of 140 bags of rice to be delivered within 14 days in two lots—125 bags at a certain wharf, and 15 bags at the seller's premises. In response to the buyer's request, the seller sent the buyer a delivery order for the 125 bags, and also notified him that the 15 bags had been set aside ready for delivery. When the buyer eventually sent for the 15 bags nearly a month after the contractual delivery date, it was found that they had been stolen. The buyer's action to recover part of the price paid was dismissed on the grounds that the property and risk had passed to him.

A common situation which may cause some difficulty is the cash mail-order business. Where the seller posts goods of the type ordered, this would seem to be an act of appropriation.[124] But can any act prior to posting amount to an appropriation? Clearly, where the customer's order constitutes an offer and the posting an accept-

---

116  See Chalmers, *Sale of Goods*, 18th edn, 151.

117  E.g. *Edwards v Ddin* [1976] 3 All ER 705 (a criminal case).

118  E.g. the goods sold to FF in *The Elafi* (above).

119  A similar variation may be noticed in relation to the cases on the passing of risk, though there is no necessary connection between the two.

120  Compare *Federspiel v Twigg Ltd* (manufactured: set out at para 20.16) with *Langton v Higgins* (1859) 4 H & N 402 (grown); and see further Macleod, *Consumer Sales Law*, 1st edn, para 20.18).

121  As where petrol is irretrievably mixed with that already in the buyer's car: *Edwards v Ddin* [1976] 3 All ER 705.

122  Provided they conform with the contract description: *Healey v Howlett* (set out at para 22.06).

123  [1919] 1 KB 459, DC.

124  See *Badische Anilin und Soda-Fabrik v Basle Chemical Works, Bindschedler* [1898] AC 200, HL, which demonstrates the difficulty of trying to consider this in terms of constructive possession.

ance, posting is the earliest moment at which there may be an appropriation: the property may well pass when the contract is made.[125] But if the contract is made at some prior stage,[126] then it is arguable that the buyer may have conferred on the seller a power of selection (see para 20.20); and it would seem that the same considerations obtain with regard to appropriation as in the case of goods manufactured by the seller (see para 20.17).

[20.20] **Assent**. Section 18, r 5(1) infers that an act of appropriation by one party cannot pass the property in the goods without the assent of the other (see para 20.15) and adds:

> 'the assent may be express or implied, and may be given either before or after the appropriation is made'.

Thus, the rule requires a common intention to pass the property;[127] but in one case Lord Wright observed that this is generally to be inferred from the terms of the contract or the practice of the trade.[128] Thus, in *Pignatoro v Gilroy*[129] Rowlatt J thought that, by asking for a delivery order, the buyer had assented in advance to the seller's appropriation; but he was also prepared to find a subsequent assent in the fact that the buyer did nothing for a whole month in response to an appropriation made in consequence of his own request.

In considering the problem of implied assent, two situations have to be distinguished.

(1) Where the buyer appropriates with the assent of the seller. In these circumstances, the goods will usually be in the actual or constructive possession of the seller, in which case it will normally be fairly easy to see whether there has been a sufficient appropriation by the buyer and assent by the seller.

(2) Where the seller appropriates with the assent of the buyer. Because the goods will usually be in the actual or constructive possession of the seller, it may be rather more difficult in these circumstances to find an appropriation by the seller and assent by the buyer, as for instance in the mail-order business (see para 20.19). It is submitted that the buyer may impliedly assent in advance,[130] by conferring on the seller a power of selection, notwithstanding that the buyer has not seen the stock from which the goods are selected.[131] This might offer some protection against the insolvency of the mail-order trader,[132] who too

---

125 Compare s 18, r 1, considered at para 20.09.

126 Could such goods be in a deliverable state (see generally, para 20.12) before packaging is completed?

127 E.g. *Federspiel v Twigg* (set out at para 20.16). This active requirement of 'assent' may be compared with the passive requirement of notice required in respect of specific goods: see para 20.13.

128 *Ross T Smyth & Co Ltd v Bailey, Son & Co* [1940] 3 All ER 60, HL, at 66.

129 Set out at para 20.19. See also *Aldridge v Johnson* (set out at para 20.16).

130 *Contra* where unsolicited goods are supplied: for the formation of contract in such cases, see para 8.18.

131 E.g. *Pignatoro v Gilroy* (above); *Healey v Howlett* (set out at para 22.06). *Contra* Atiyah, *Sale of Goods*, 10th edn, 338.

132 As to the difficulties, see *Prepayments: Protecting Consumers' Deposits* (1984, National Federation of Consumer Groups); and further, paras 23.22; 23.27.

frequently appears to utilise the customer's advance payments as risk capital.[133] Payment by credit card may avoid the insolvency problem;[134] and changes in the law made by statute in 1995 my help (see para 20.22B).

**[20.21] Ascertainment and appropriation**. Neither of these processes is defined by the SGA; but appropriation is an act showing an intention that the property in certain goods should pass under the contract. It has been suggested above that ascertained goods are those identified and agreed upon after the contract is made (see para 20.04): this implies that ascertainment is the process of identification of the goods as being the contract goods.[135] Thus, both the acts of ascertainment and appropriation are acts evidencing an intention of a party to a contract of sale. However, an ascertainment shows an intention that certain goods be earmarked as the contract goods;[136] but appropriation evinces an intention that the property should pass in those goods under that contract. Of course, the distinction is rarely considered by the parties,[137] and the one act usually fulfils both purposes,[138] in which case the 'ascertainment' and 'appropriation' take place at the same moment. It is for this reason sometimes erroneously assumed that the two words, ascertainment and appropriation, are interchangeable; and confusion is worse confounded by the fact that the courts sometimes, understandably, use the two terms synonymously.

It would seem there cannot be appropriation before ascertainment;[136] but this rule has been altered as regards the undivided share in a bulk (see para 20.22B, *et seq.*).

## Undivided share in bulk

**[20.22] The effect of appropriation in equity**. At very least, the general effect of the cases seems to be that under the SGA 1893 the goods should be identified before they could be regarded as sufficiently appropriated for the property to pass. Thus, in *Re Wait*:[139]

> W contracted on November 20th to buy a cargo of 10,000 tons of wheat *ex Challenger*, the cargo to be made up the following month. On November 21st, W agreed to sell 500 tons of this cargo to X. The cargo was duly shipped, and, whilst the *Challenger* was at sea, X paid the price to W, who shortly afterwards became insolvent. W's trustee succeeded in claiming the entire cargo.

It was common ground that there had been no appropriation sufficient at law to pass the legal title in 500 tons of the wheat to X; and that X could not acquire any interest in the goods on 21 November, because the goods were then future goods

---

133 For other schemes to protect the consumer against the trader's insolvency see: (i) trusts (paras 23.22 and 27.14); (ii) the Newspaper Mail Order Protection Scheme.
134 CCA, s 75: see para 16.11, *et seq.*
135 Once ascertained, is it necessarily a breach of contract for the seller to dispose of the goods elsewhere?
136 *The Elafi* [1982] 1 All ER 208.
137 But it will be crucial where the contract evinces an intention as to the passing of property (s 17): see para 20.06.
138 *Per* Mustill J in *The Elafi* (above), at 215.
139 [1927] 1 Ch 606; [1926] All ER Rep 433, CA.

(see para 20.15). However, the majority thought that, before the SGA 1893, when the cargo was made up the buyer would have acquired an equitable lien which floated over the entire cargo.[140] Atkin LJ responded that, even if there had been such an equitable right, it could not have survived the SGA (at 635–6). At the same time, Atkin LJ argued that this did not preclude what he termed rights coming into existence 'dehors' the contract of sale for the following reason (at 636):

'A seller or a purchaser may ... create any equity he pleases by way of charge, equitable assignment or any other dealing with or disposition of the goods, the subject-matter of the sale; and he may, of course, create such an equity as one of the terms expressed in the contract of sale.[141] But the mere sale or agreement to sell or the acts in pursuance of such a contract mentioned in the Code will only produce the legal effects which the Code states.'

The views of Atkin LJ as to the effect of the sale itself appear to have been confirmed by the Privy Council in *Re Goldcorp Exchange Ltd*:[142]

G Ltd, gold dealers, purchased bullion on behalf of investors on terms that it would be stored and insured free of charge by G Ltd. Until about 1983, bullion purchased for customers was stored and recorded separately, but thereafter it was pooled. G Ltd became hopelessly insolvent, the bullion in its possession was claimed by the bank under a debenture and receivers were appointed in 1988 (see para 19.14).

This action was brought by two classes of investor, both of whom had paid G Ltd to purchase gold for them and would as unsecured creditors lose their money unless they could make a proprietary claim on some of the gold (see para 19.22). The New Zealand judge held that the effect was this: before 1983, bullion was ascertained and appropriated to individual customers; and thereafter, each pre-1983 customer had a shared interest in the pooled bullion.[143]

1. *Allocated (pre-1983) claimants*. As there was nothing left for the claimants to demand *in specie* and very little to trace, they unsuccessfully sought before the Privy Council an equitable lien on all the property of G Ltd at the time of receivership.[144]

2. *Unallocated (post-1983) claimants*. In respect of post–1983 investors, the Privy Council held that in this case there was a mere sale of generic goods so that there was no question of the property passing (see para 20.05), the case being in this respect even stronger than *Re Wait*.[145] As regards the above dictum of Atkin LJ concerning proprietary rights arising *dehors* the contract, the Privy Council held that G Ltd's collateral promise in respect of such generic goods could not

---

140 At 645 and 649. But Lord Hanworth MR took the view that such a right could not attach unless and until the contract goods became identifiable, which these never did (at 621–5). See Worthington [1999] JBL 1.

141 As to the creation of such equities as part of the financing of instalment supplies, see Chap 25.

142 [1994] 2 All ER 806 PC (see McKendrick 110 LQR 509).

143 See also *Re Staplyton Fletcher Ltd* (set out at para 20.05), ESV.

144 Subsequent English statutory changes (see para 20.20A) would, for us, reverse this result for allocated claimants (if they bought from 'bulk'), but not for the unallocated claimants.

145 It is simply to promise to maintain a fund of bullion to meet commitments to customers, whilst reserving freedom to use the bullion for other purposes. This attitude is supported by Ulph [1996] JBL 482, at 486.

amount to a declaration of trust, nor title by estoppel, nor give rise to a fiduciary relationship.[144] Nor did G Ltd's simple breach of contract impress the price paid with a beneficial interest in favour of the customer.[146]

**[20.22A] Co-owners**. In its Part entitled *'Transfer of Property as between Seller and Buyer'*, the SGA 1893 dealt with the transfer of the general property in the goods from one seller to one buyer (see para 19.08). However, it did envisage that ownership of the goods might be divided between more than one person, for it provided that one part owner might sell to another.[147] In 1993, the Law Commission sought to clarify the law as to sales and purchases by co-owners;[148] and its recommendations have been enacted in the Sale of Goods (Amendment) Act 1995 (SGAA):

1. *Sale by co-owner*. The SGAA has made clear that the sale of an undivided share by one co-owner to a third party is a sale of goods (see para 2.02). Moreover, the Commission thought that the law already allowed the sale of an undivided share in a larger bulk where that share was stated as a proportion,[149] rather than as a specified quantity (para 2.5): the buyer became a tenant in common of the bulk.[147] Accordingly, the SGAA provides that, if the undivided share is 'specified as a fraction (e.g. 1/2) or percentage (e.g. 50%)', this is a sale of specific goods (see para 2.04); and hence, it may pass a share in the general property in the goods under the ordinary rules for specific goods (see para 20.08).

2. *Purchases by a co-owner*. Similarly, a purchase of an undivided share 'by fraction or percentage' may pass the property in goods, the buyers becoming owners in common.[150] The SGAA has confirmed that, where there is a sale of a specified quantity of unascertained goods, the goods may subsequently become ascertained by exhaustion (see para 20.05A), so that the property in the remaining bulk may thereupon pass to the buyer.[151] Additionally, case law has decided that, where goods are fleetingly parted from bulk and then merged back into the bulk, the buyer becomes a co-owner of the general property in that bulk.[152]

It is thus clear that the general property in the goods may be divided between several owners. On the other hand, the basic thrust of s 16 is to prevent the general property in the goods passing until the contract goods have become ascertained; and the effect of this was to prevent a buyer of part of a bulk from acquiring any part of the general property in the goods (see para 20.05). The unfair result was that a pre-paying buyer of a specified quantity (not expressed by fraction or percentage) of an identified bulk might be reduced to the position of unsecured creditor in the event of his seller's insolvency, even where the buyer had obtained a delivery

---

146 See also *Re Staplyton Fletcher Ltd* (above), SFL. See further Ulph at 488–9 and 493–6.

147 SGA 1979, s 2(2): see para 1.09.

148 In its Report *Sale of Goods Forming Part of a Bulk* (1993, Law Com. No. 215). For actions in tort, see para 19.05.

149 Para 2.5. See Benjamin's *Sale of Goods*, 6th edn, paras 1.081 and 1.121.

150 E.g. *Re Goldcorp Exchange Ltd* (set out at para 20.22), pre-1983 position of allocated claimants; Goode, *Commercial Law*, 3rd edn, 221–2; Benjamin, *Op. cit.*, para 125.

151 The (above) Commission Report, para 2.4. E.g. goods bought jointly by spouses or a business consortium.

152 *Re Staplyton Fletcher Ltd* (set out at para 20.05), ESV.

order.[153] Accordingly, the above Law Commission Report recommended (para 4.1) that such a pre-paying buyer should be given an 'undivided share' in the bulk (see para 20.20B). If all went well with the transaction, in due course the contract goods would become ascertained (see para 20.05) and that rule would be superseded by the passing of property in the goods themselves under the rules previously considered.[154]

**[20.22B] Undivided share in bulk.** The problem just elicited (see para 20.22A) is primarily likely to arise in certain commodity trades,[155] but it could involve a pre-paying private consumers, e.g. a mail order buyer, or buyer of a length of carpet from an identified roll. To meet it, new ss 20A and 20B of the SGA[156] provide a new set of rules applicable only where **all** the following requirements are present (s 20A(1)):

(1) There is a sale of 'a specified quantity of unascertained goods'. This will exclude a sale of specific goods,[157] such as a sale of a share by 'fraction or percentage' (see para 20.22A).

(2) The unascertained goods are not generic,[157] but form an identified 'bulk'.[158] According to new s 61(1), ' "bulk" means a mass or collection of goods of the same kind which

   (a) is contained in a defined space or area; and

   (b) is such that any goods in the bulk are interchangeable with any other goods therein of the same number or quantity'.

   For the provision to operate, not only must there be a contractual bulk,[159] but the goods which compose it must be interchangeable (fungible), e.g. a designated model and type of electrical appliance (new s 20A(1)(a)). The bulk may be future goods (see para 2.03) or ever-changing, e.g. oil being drawn off from a tank and replenished.[159]

(3) The contract 'goods or some part of them form part of a bulk' (new s 20A(1)(a)); that is, the seller is contractually obliged to derive them from the bulk. This formula should also bring within new s 20A the situation where the buyer has obtained a part-delivery.[160]

(4) That bulk 'is identified either in the contract or by subsequent agreement between the parties'. The reference to 'subsequent agreement' will meet, for example, the case of the sale by a builder's merchant of a type of item, the consumer then to select one from the seller's stock.

---

153 See *Goods Forming Part of a Bulk* (above) paras 2.8, 3.2–4 and 3.6; and para 20.22.

154 So the buyer's co-ownership under new s 20A (see below) would merely be an interim stage: (above) Commission Report, para 4.9.

155 E.g. the facts of *Re Wait* (set out at para 20.22). See *Sale of Goods Forming Part of a Bulk* (1993, Law Com No. 215), para 4.3.

156 Introduced by s 1(3) of the SGAA 1995.

157 As to specific and generic goods, see para 2.04. See further Benjamin's *Sale of Goods*, 6th edn, para 5.112.

158 It is intended that this concept should not extend to the seller's general stock, but be limited to an identified bulk within that stock: see the (above) Commission Report, para 4.3.

159 See also the other examples set out in the (above) Commission Report, 4.3; Benjamin, *Op. cit.*, para 5.112.

160 See further the (above) Commission Report, para 4.5.

(5)  The buyer had paid the price.[161] This obviated some insolvency problems: as ordinarily a buyer cannot be forced to pay in advance of delivery (SGA, s 28: see para 23.16), new s 20A is restricted to the pre-paying cash buyer,[162] including part-payment.[163]

Where all the above conditions are satisfied, new s 20A may confer on the buyer an undivided share in the bulk (see para 20.22C). However, new s 20A(2) gives the parties the freedom to contract out of this rule, in which case the proprietary rights will only pass according to the traditional rules.[164]

**[20.22C]  The buyer's undivided share**. As soon as the conditions specified in new s 20A(1) are met (see para 20.22B), new s 20A(2) provides that, *prima facie*:[165]

'(a)  property in an undivided share in the bulk is transferred to the buyer, and

(b)  the buyer becomes an owner in common of the bulk.'

So, the buyer does not at that point become the legal owner of the goods themselves, the passing of the property in which remains governed by the ordinary rules (see para 20.05, *et seq*.). Instead, under new s 20A(1) the buyer becomes a proportionate owner of the bulk: para (a) describes the interest (see para 19.10) and perhaps the risk that is passed to a commercial buyer,[166] but presumably it is otherwise with regard to the passing of risk to a consumer buyer;[167] and para (b) explains how that interest is in principle to be reconciled to that of other co-owners in the bulk. In quantifying that interest, 'the basic idea is that the buyer's share is the share which the quantity bought and paid for bears to the quantity in the bulk'.[168] Suppose part sale(s) from a bulk of 9 widgets owned by S:

(1)  The buyer's undivided share 'shall be such share as the quantity of goods paid for and due to the buyer out of the bulk bear to the quantity of goods in the bulk at the time' (s 20A(3)). For instance, if B agrees to buy 2 widgets from the bulk and pays S for one, B owns an undivided 1/9 share in the bulk (= 9), whilst property and risk in the remaining 8/9 share (= 8) stays in S.

(2)  If the bulk is insufficient to meet in full the claims of all buyers from the bulk, *prima facie* the seller's claim is *pro tanto* ignored.[169] For example, if out of the bulk of 9 widgets, S sells 3 to B1 and 2 to B2, who each pay the full price: at first, B1 owns a 3/9 undivided share in the bulk (= 3), B2 owns a 2/9 share (= 2) and S

---

161  New s 20A(1)(b). As to what amounts to payment of the price, see para 23.14.

162  See the (above) Commission Report, para 4.6. As to an argument for extending this right to a buyer who has not pre-paid, see Goode, *Commercial Law*, 3rd edn, 223, fn 94.

163  S 20A(6). Thus, a 10% pre-payment was intended to be treated as payment for 10% of the goods agreed to be purchased: (above) Commission Report, para 4.7.

164  The (above) Commission Report, para 4.8. As to the traditional rules for the passing of property, see above, paras 20.15–21.

165  S 20A. E.g. on a later exchange of documents: see *Sale of Goods Forming Part of a Bulk* (1993, Law Com No. 215), para 4.8; Benjamin's *Sale of Goods*, 6th edn, para 5.116.

166  Notwithstanding s 20A(3), it is argued that the effect of s 20A(2) is to pass the risk to the buyer: see Benjamin, *Op. cit.*, para 6-006. Cf. *Sterns Ltd v Vickers Ltd* (see para 22.04).

167  Because of the compulsory SSGR rule that risk only passes to a consumer-buyer on delivery to him: see para 22.02A.

168  The (above) Law Commission Report (see para 20.22B), para 4.10; Benjamin, *Op. cit.*, para 5.118.

169  S 20A(4), which does not mention any seller's share.

a 4/9 share (4); if 4 are destroyed, that is S's loss and the shares of B1 and B2 remain the same; and if B2 removes his 2, the remaining 3 are appropriated by exhaustion to B1 (s 18, r 5(3): see para 20.05B).

Section 20A also deals with the following special cases:

(a) *Further reductions.* If, even leaving aside the seller's claim (see above), the bulk is insufficient to meet in full the claims of all the co-buyers of the bulk, the effect of s 20A(4) is that the claims of the co-buyer are 'reduced proportionally so that the total of their shares in the undivided bulk is equal to the whole bulk'.[170] Thus, if in the above example 5 are destroyed, of the remaining 4, B1 owns a 3/5 share and B2 owns a 2/5 share of the 4.

(b) *Part deliveries.* As s 20A only applies to undelivered pre-paid goods,[165] any part delivery[171] is first ascribed to the part-payment.[172] Further, any buyer who takes delivery before occurrence of the shortfall obtains the property in the delivered goods under s 18, r 5(2) (see para 20.17), so that the loss is shared between those buyers who have yet to take delivery.

*Rules to facilitate normal trading.* Whilst the ordinary rule is that co-owners must act in agreement (see para 19.05), the Law Commission recommended that both the seller and co-**owning** buyers should remain free to deal with their undivided share in the bulk by way of normal trading.[173] This was achieved in new s 20B(1), which is beyond the scope of this work.[174]

# 'SALE OR RETURN' TRANSACTIONS[175]

[20.23] Rule 4 of s 18 seeks to deal with the passing of property in sale or return transactions, e.g. retailers supplying goods by cash mail order (see para 8.19). However, the formation of a contract of sale must necessarily precede the passing of property, and there would appear to be two possible interpretations of the time of contracting.[176] *First*, the parties may intend to enter into a contract of sale immediately, but to give the buyer a unilateral right to discharge the contract if he does not approve of the goods after trial:[177] this may explain the decision in *P Edwards Ltd v Vaughan*;[178] but it might enable a supplier to side-step the unsolicited goods rules

---

170 See the (above) Commission Report, para 4.11; and the example there set out.

171 For the purposes of new ss 20A and 20B, the meaning of 'deliver' (see generally, para 23.03) has been extended by the SGAA, s 2(b).

172 S 20A(5). For the effect of this, see the (above) Commission Report, paras 4.7 and 4.12; Benjamin, *Op. cit.*, para 5.119.

173 Para 4.16. Distinguish co-buyers: see para 20.22A.

174 See Benjamin's *Sale of Goods*, 6th edn, paras 5–214/8.

175 See generally the essay by Adams in *Essays for Clive Schmitthoff* (1983), 1–13; Benjamin's *Sale of Goods*, 6th edn, para 5.039, *et seq*.

176 Is it relevant whether or not the person taking the goods on 'sale or return' upon delivery of the goods to him (a) pays the price, or (b) pays a sum expressed to be a 'deposit'? For other views, see Taylor [1985] JBL at 394–5.

177 *Mackay v Dick* (1881) 6 App Cas 251, HL(S). Is this an example of a condition subsequent (see para 1.11)? It must, in any event, be distinguished from the ordinary right of the buyer to rescind for breach: compare paras 26.02, 26.15 and 29.03. See also Taylor, *Op. cit.*, at 396.

178 (1910) 26 TLR 545, CA: see para 20.27.

(see para 8.18). *Second*, the goods may be delivered to the potential buyer only as bailee, in which case the bailor has merely made an offer to sell, and some later act of acceptance is required.[179] Thus, in *Atari Corpn (UK) Ltd v Electronics Boutique Stores (UK)*:[180]

> Atari supplied a quantity of Atari Jaguar computer games on sale or return to EB, a multiple retailer, which contract provided for payment by November 1995 and return until 31.1.96. In mid-January, EB wrote to Atari to say that the goods were selling too slowly; that EB had decided to withdraw all such stock from its branches; and that, when all stock had been returned to EB's central warehouse, EB would notify Atari of the precise stock to be returned.

The Court of Appeal held that this was a good notice by EB of rejection of unsold Atari Jaguar stock, notwithstanding that EB was not at that moment in a position to identify precisely the unsold stock, nor to return that stock to Atari. As from that notice, Waller LJ said that EB would commit conversion in selling any further stock within the notice (at 535B). Phillips LJ characterised the transaction as a contract of bailment with an irrevocable option in EB to buy (*per* Phillips LJ at 536C and 537B).

The distinction between the two alternatives is, of course, crucial in the period after delivery and before the transferee approves the purchase. If there is a contract of sale, the position is governed by the SGA; but, if there is merely a bailment, then the common law rules of bailment will apply (see para 1.17). The distinction may have important effects in the following respects:[181] (1) risk; (2) rejection; (3) resale; (4) insolvency of transferee; (5) negligence.

**[20.24] The passing of property**. The next difficulty is to ascertain the scope of r 4, which is expressed to take effect where a person takes possession of goods 'on approval', or 'on sale or return',[182] or 'other similar terms'. What are 'other similar terms'? There is some authority that it includes deliveries 'on free trial' or 'on approbation'.[183] But does it include hp agreements (see para 20.27) or unsolicited goods,[184] or money-back guarantees?[185]

As in the case of all the other rules of s 18, r 4 only applies in the absence of a contrary intention. Thus, in *Weiner v Gill*:[186]

> Jewellery was delivered to X, together with a memorandum which stated: 'On approbation. On sale for cash only or return . . . Goods had on approbation or on sale or return remain the property of [the transferor] until such goods are settled for or charged.' Without paying for the goods, X pledged them; but the Court held that

---

179  Alternatively, it might be argued that there is a contract of bailment plus an option to buy: see para 20.27.

180  [1998] QB 539; [1998] 1 All ER 1010; (1997) Tr LR 529, CA (see 114 LQR 198).

181  See Macleod, *Consumer Sales Law*, 1st edn, para 20.23.

182  It has been suggested by Taylor [1985] JBL, at 393, that there is a distinction in usage as follows: supply on 'approval' is usually to a consumer to try the goods; supply on 'sale or return' is usually to a businessman for resale. But what of drinks obtained for a party? See also Goode, *Commercial Law*, 3rd edn, 238.

183  See the list of authorities collected in Benjamin's *Sale of Goods*, 6th edn, para 5.041.

184  Rule 4 has been said to apply only to consensual arrangements and thus to be inapplicable to unsolicited goods (see para 8.18): Goode, *Op. cit.*, 238.

185  E.g. 'Your money returned if not absolutely satisfied'. See generally, para 11.07.

186  [1906] 2 KB 574; [1904–7] All ER Rep 773, CA. See also *Manders v Williams* (1849) 4 Exch 339.

X acquired no property in the goods, and could therefore transfer none to the pledgee.

However, assuming that a transaction falls within r 4 and that there is no contrary intention, that rule provides that the property passes to the transferee as follows:

'(a) When he signifies his approval or acceptance to the seller or does any other act adopting the transaction.

(b) If he does not signify his approval or acceptance to the seller but retains the goods without giving notice of rejection, then, if a time has been fixed for the return of the goods, on the expiration of such time, and, if no time has been fixed, on the expiration of a reasonable time.'

Thus, assuming that a transaction falls within r 4 and that there is no contrary intention, r 4 provides that the property passes to the transferee as follows:

1. *Approval or acceptance.* This appears to connote a making known of intention to the supplier.[187] Normally, this will present few problems; but difficult questions of fact may occur where the trial involves a partial consumption or destruction.

2. *Adoption* (see para 20.25).

3. *Retention* (see para 20.26).

**[20.25] Adoption.** In *Kirkham v Attenborough*:[188]

a manufacturing jeweller [P] entrusted some jewellery to W on sale or return. W pledged the goods with the defendant pawnbroker, and P claimed the return of the goods or their value.

The action was dismissed by the Court of Appeal, who held that in pledging the goods W had done an 'act adopting the transaction' within r 4, so that the property passed to him, and he passed a good title to the defendant. Lord Esher MR explained that the phrase 'act adopting the transaction' (at 203):

'cannot mean the delivery of the goods on sale or return, because that had been already done, and it must mean that part of the transaction which makes the buyer the purchaser of the goods . . . There must be some act which shews that he adopts the transaction; but any act which is consistent only with his being the purchaser is sufficient.'

He held that pawning was such an act, because it was 'inconsistent with his free power to return [the goods]'.[189] Presumably, the position is the same with regard to sales by the person in possession.

However, the concept of an act adopting the transaction may become unworkable if pushed too far.[190]

---

187 Compare the definition of acceptance for a normal sale in s 35 of the SGA: see para 29.05.

188 [1897] 1 QB 201; [1895–9] All ER Rep 450, CA. See also *London Jewellers Ltd v Attenborough* [1934] 2 KB 206, CA.

189 Would a gift be an act adopting the transaction because it passed the property in the goods (see para 2.08)? And what of a conditional gift, e.g. of a garment, provided it fitted?

190 See *Genn v Winkel* (1912) 107 LT 434; [1911–13] All ER Rep 910, CA; and Macleod, *Consumer Sales Law*, 1st edn, para 20.25.

**[20.26] Retention**. Rule 4(b) provides that the property will pass to the buyer if he 'retains the goods without giving notice of rejection'. This rule substantially reflects the common law position,[191] except that, whereas the common law probably required the transferee to return the goods, the Act only requires him to give notice of rejection.[192] Rule 4(b) assumes that, even without approval or acceptance on the part of the transferee, the property may pass in either of the following circumstances:

(a) The transferee retains the goods beyond any stipulated time limit. Even though the transferee retains the goods beyond the stipulated time, he will not be deemed to have accepted the goods where the transferor induced him to prolong the trial,[193] or his retention was involuntary.[194]

(b) Where there is no time-limit laid down, but the transferee retains the goods beyond a reasonable time. What is a reasonable time is a question of fact (s 59), and may depend on trade usage.[195]

**[20.27] The property/title borderline**. The effect of the operation of r 4 may well be to pass the property in the goods without the supplier realising it. This poses an obvious danger for the supplier and he may therefore oust the operation of r 4 altogether by reserving the property in the goods until the price is paid.[196] Such a precaution will usually be effective in the event of the transferee's insolvency; but it is less likely to defeat the bfp, who may, in particular, acquire a good title under one of the following exceptions to the *nemo dat* rule:

(1) *Estoppel*. Whilst the mere transfer of possession to the transferee will not of itself give rise to an estoppel,[197] there may be other circumstances which would do so (see para 21.14).

(2) *Agency*. It may be that the transferor goes further than merely reserving the property in the goods, and evinces an intention that the transferee is never to become the owner of them; that is, the transferee is not a buyer, but an agent with a power to sell on his principal's account. Thus, in *Weiner v Harris*:[198]

> a manufacturing jeweller sent jewellery to a retailer under a standing agreement whereby the property was to remain in the manufacturer until the goods were sold or paid for. The retailer pledged some of the jewellery.

The Court of Appeal unanimously held that the pledgee obtained a good title because the parties only intended the retailer to be an agent for sale, not a buyer:[199] their Lordships distinguished *Weiner v Gill*[196] on the grounds that in

---

191  See *Humphries v Carvalho* (1812) 6 East 45; *Moss v Sweet* (1851) 16 QB 493.

192  Though the agreement may show an intention that the goods actually be returned: *Ornstein v Alexandra Furnishing Co* (1895) 12 TLR 128; *Atari Corpn (UK) Ltd v Electronics Boutique Stores (UK)* (set out at para 20.23).

193  *Per* Bovill CJ in *Heilbutt v Hickson* (1872) LR 7 CP 438, at 452.

194  *Re Ferrier, ex p Trustee v Donald* [1944] Ch 295.

195  E.g. *Poole v Smith's Car Sales Ltd* [1962] 2 All ER 482, CA. Cf. s 35: see para 29.07.

196  E.g. *Weiner v Gill* (set out at para 20.24).

197  *Per* Bray J in *Weiner v Gill* (above) at 182. And see *Kempler v Bravingtons Ltd* (1925) 133 LT 680, CA.

198  [1910] 1 KB 285; [1908–10] All ER Rep 405, CA.

199  The retailer passed a good title as a mercantile agent: see para 21.24.

that case the property was only to pass to X when the goods were paid for, whereas in the present case the retailer was precluded by the terms of the agreement from ever becoming the owner of the goods under the transaction.

(3) *Buyers in possession.* As we shall see in the next Chapter, a person who has agreed to buy goods and is in possession of them may be able to pass a good title (see para 21.43). Whilst a mere bailee is not in such a position, one who has agreed to buy subject to a right to rescind after trial clearly could do so.[200] An analogous problem is whether an hp agreement falls within the ambit of r 4. There is a clear difference in function between the two types of transaction, which will be mirrored in the terms of the bailments. Perhaps the biggest difference concerns the effect of an act inconsistent with the ownership of the bailor: in a sale or return, such an act will usually cause the property to pass to the erstwhile bailee; whereas, in an hp agreement it will usually amount to an act of conversion, and prevent the bailee from becoming the owner of the goods.[201] Most commentators accept that hp agreements are not sale or return transactions; and *vice versa*.[202]

## RESERVATION OF A RIGHT OF DISPOSAL

[20.28] Section 19 of the SGA seems designed to deal with the situation where the parties are negotiating at a distance, and the unpaid seller wishes to safeguard himself against the insolvency of the buyer. The general rule is laid down in s 19(1) in the following terms:

> 'Where there is a contract for the sale of specific goods or where goods are sub-sequently appropriated to the contract, the seller may, by the terms of the contract or appropriation, reserve the right of disposal of the goods until certain conditions are fulfilled; and in such a case, notwithstanding the delivery of the goods to the buyer, or to a carrier or other bailee ... for the purposes of transmission to the buyer, the property in the goods does not pass to the buyer until the conditions imposed by the seller are fulfilled.'

It would seem that this poorly-drafted provision enables the seller to reserve a right of disposal (see below) in two circumstances,[203] which will both be examples of the operation of s 17 (see para 20.06): (1) in the case of specific goods, by the terms of the contract; and (2) as regards unascertained goods, by the terms of the contract or appropriation, so derogating from s 18, r 5(2).[204] Section 19 itself dealt expressly with two uses of the rule common in nineteenth century international trade, but

---

200 This may be the explanation of *P Edwards Ltd v Vaughan* (1910) 26 TLR 545, CA. See also *London Jewellers Ltd v Attenborough* [1934] 2 KB 206, CA, where the point may have been *obiter*. See the discussion by Adams in *Essays for Clive Schmitthoff* at 506.

201 *Helby v Matthews* (set out at para 1.22).

202 See Guest, *Law of HP*, 51; Goode, *HP Law & Practice*, 2nd edn, 60. It should follow that the CCA does not apply to sale or return transactions because there is no element of 'financial accommodation': see para 5.22.

203 Benjamin's *Sale of Goods*, 6th edn, para 5.132.

204 See above, para 20.17 and Benjamin, *Op. cit.*, paras 133–4. *Semble*, even if the reservation is a breach of contract: Benjamin, *Op. cit.*, para 5.127; Bradgate [1988] JBL 477.

beyond the scope of this work (ss 19(2) and (3)); but the most common modern use concerns *Romalpa* clauses (see para 20.29).

*The meaning of 'reservation of a right of disposal'*, Section 19(1) says that it will have the effect of reserving the property in the goods, e.g. a conditional sale (see para 1.14); and whether there has been such a reservation is a question of intention.[205] It might, therefore, be objected that, as s 18 is always subject to a contrary intention, s 19(1) seems superfluous. However, the explanation may be that businessmen do not usually think in terms of the passing of property in goods, but tend to express themselves with regard to risk (which is inconclusive as to the passing of property)[206] and the retention of control.[207] This retention of control must not be confused with the unpaid seller's real **rights**: the two sets of **rights** only overlap in the one case where goods are delivered to a carrier for the purposes of transmission to the buyer, and then the phrase 'reservation of a right of disposal' is used by the Act to describe both situations.[208] Nor must it be confused with the **power** of disposal.[209]

**[20.29] Romalpa clauses**. When *Romalpa* clauses were imported into English law (see para 25.29), it was found that their reservation of title in the goods supplied usually satisfied the 'conditions' referred to in s 19(1) (see para 20.28). In such a situation, it has been argued that there are two possible outcomes, depending on whether or not the seller has accepted the buyer's repudiation by non-payment:[210]

(1) If the contract remained on foot, the seller would only be able to sell so much of the goods as was necessary to pay the outstanding balance of the purchase price; and, if the seller resold more, he would be accountable to the buyer for the surplus (see para 27.10).

(2) If the contract was discharged, the seller could sell all the goods on his own account, keeping any surplus (see para 27.10), but having to restore any part-payment (see para 27.19).

However, the operation of s 19 has been extended to where the reservation of title clause was expressed to secure sums **greater** than that necessary to secure payment of the price of goods supplied under that contract. The attraction of this is that a supplier can bring forward past indebtedness and attach it to goods in the buyer's possession, even when paid for; but the ploy can only work when a similar clause is inserted in all supply contracts, because the seller will not know in what order the buyer will consume supplies.[211] In *Armour v Thyssen Edelstahlwerke AG*:[212]

---

205 *Re Shipton Anderson & Co and Harrison Brothers & Co* [1915] 3 KB 676, DC; *The Aliakmon* [1985] 2 All ER 44, CA (affirmed on other grounds).

206 *Per* Lords Westbury and Cairns in *Shepherd v Harrison* (1871) LR 5 HL 116, at 129, 131. See also paras 20.06 and 20.10.

207 The reservation cannot be effective where the goods are no longer identifiable, e.g. petrol put in a motorist's tank—*Edwards v Ddin* [1976] 3 All ER 705.

208 SGA, ss 19(1) and 43(1)(a): see further, para 24.13. The reservation of a right of disposal also acts as a deemed delivery to the buyer: s 32(1) (see para 23.03).

209 The buyer may be able to pass a good title, e.g. *Cahn v Pockett's Channel Ltd* [1899] 1 QB 643, CA.

210 Benjamin's *Sale of Goods*, 6th edn, para 5.146. But see Bridge, *Sale of Goods*, 107–8.

211 Bridge, *Op. cit.*, 107.

212 [1991] 2 AC 339; [1990] 3 All ER 481, HL(S).

a German manufacturer (T) sold to a Scottish engineering company (C Ltd) quantities of steel strip for use in C Ltd's manufacturing process. The contracts of sale were each subject to a condition that the property in the goods would not pass to C Ltd until all debts due from C Ltd to T under all contracts had been paid (the 'all monies' clause). At the time a receiver was appointed to C Ltd, part of the steel had been cut into sheets and part was in the course of being so cut, but most of it remained in the state in which it had been delivered by T. T successfully claimed ownership of all this steel, for which C Ltd had made no payment.

The House of Lords expressly applied s 19. It held that in Scottish law an all monies clause did not create a security in favour of T, but rather reserved the property in the goods to T under a genuine sale,[213] even in respect of the cut steel[214] and for debts due under other contracts.[215] Thus, their Lordships allowed T to avoid the problem of identifying which steel was supplied under which contract[216] and also the registration provisions for company charges (see para 25.28, *et seq*). It is for consideration whether such all monies clauses should require registration for the protection of the buyer's other creditors, especially if it can be shown that the seller has thereby made a substantial windfall beyond the contract price(s). In a consumer supply, an all monies clause may be unfair.[217]

---

213 It has been suggested that all monies clauses securing liabilities to third parties, e.g. associated companies, may be registrable: Hicks [1992] JBL 398 at 404–5.

214 Compare *Re Peachdart Ltd* [1984] Ch 131: see para 25.32.

215 It had previously been argued that reservation of title until payment due under other contracts amounted to a charge: Goode, *Commercial Law*, 1st edn, 718.

216 This may generate a surplus for the seller over the contract payments by reason of (a) previous part-payment by the buyer and (b) the proceeds of resale. The seller would not have to account for any surplus to the buyer, save in the unlikely event of a total failure of consideration: *per* Lord Keith at 485h. See Hicks [1992] JBL 398 at 404; and paras 24.22 and 27.19.

217 [2005] *UTCC Bulletin J/S, BP Oil*; and see para 11.15A.

# CHAPTER 21

# TRANSFER OF TITLE

## *NEMO DAT QUOD NON HABET*

**[21.01] The importance of good title**. The relationship between property and title was discussed in Chapter 19; and this Chapter will deal with the situation where goods belonging to A are transferred by B to C. Both the original owner (A) and the transferee (C) may be entirely blameless; and the problem is to determine which of the two is entitled to the goods. In theory, this should not make any difference, because the other will usually have the right to look to B for recompense: A could sue B in tort for wrongful interference with goods;[1] C could sue B for breach of the implied undertakings as to title.[2]

However, in practice a right of action against B may be worthless, so that the party left to seek recompense from B may himself have to bear the loss. Thus, the right to the goods may be of vital importance, and will usually be determined through the tort action for wrongful interference with goods.[1]A will argue that, as B had no title, he could pass none to C: this is known as the *nemo dat* rule (see para 19.11). C will argue that by way of one of the exceptions to that rule he has obtained a better title than B or A (see para 21.02). The burden of proof on the plaintiff/claimant to identify the disputed property should not be underestimated, few types of goods apart from motor vehicles being readily identifiable.[3]

*Hire Purchase Information Ltd (HPI)*[4]. Incorporated in 1938 as a company limited by guarantee, HPI was established to prevent financing fraud in the motor industry by a simple register of finance agreements on motor vehicles.[5] Subsequently, its service has been extended to other high-value identifiable mobile assets, e.g. caravans, boats, other types of instalment contract (see para 1.03) and insurance write-offs;[6] and the company itself has been taken over by a credit reference agency and the idea taken up by other agencies. Unfortunately, a trade survey in 2001 showed that only about half of the major finance companies bother to register their titles with HPI.[7]

As to Certificates of Title, see para 21.60.

---

1 Torts Act 1977, ss 1 and 2: see further, para 19.04, *et seq.*
2 See Chap 12. Or money handed to B may be traceable (see para 27.13). See generally Goode, *Commercial Law*, 3rd edn, 444–5.
3 This may lead to a battle between A and C to secure possession, and hence be defendant in any action: for recaption, see para 24.23. If the goods are in the physical possession of the police, their safest course may be to apply to the court under the Police (Property) Act 1897 (as amended). Any other third party in possession, e.g. a sheriff, should interplead (see para 21.06).
4 See further Goode, *Consumer Credit Law and Practice*, para 2.85.
5 In recent years, the DVLC have offered a number-plate transfer scheme to facilitate the trade in cherished number plates. This has engendered some plate transfer fraud and led to some system changes at HPI. One in three used cars checked had a 'hidden history': (1995) 50 CC 3/14; 50 CC5/21.
6 Vehicles written off by insurance companies have been re-built, or their identity transferred to stolen vehicles.
7 FLA, [2002] 11 *Update* 7. E.g. the *Twitchings* case (set out at para 21.15).

**[21.02/4]** **Exceptions**. Leaving aside the special rules for sales from a bulk (see para 20.22, *et seq*.) and all forms of bailment,[8] the SGA concentrates on the transfer of the general property in goods and the title to that property (see para 19.08). In fact, the SGA deals only with the title at law to goods, saying nothing about equitable titles:[9] a person with an equitable title to goods cannot sue in conversion (see para 19.06); and, under general principles any equitable title to goods gives way to a *bona fide* purchaser (bfp) of a legal interest in them in circumstances where A has parted with the property in the goods, but has an equitable right to rescind the contract and so recover that property, e.g. the voidable title rule (see paras 2.19–23).

So, let us concentrate on that title in law. In setting out the *nemo dat* rule (see para 19.11), s 21(1) of the SGA expressly makes it 'subject to the provisions of this Act' and also provides that it shall not apply where goods are sold by B 'under the authority or with the consent of the owner'. These reservations refer to the following cases:[10]

1. *Agency*. Section 21(1) recites that the *nemo dat* rule does not apply to a person (B) who sells 'under the authority' of the owner (A); and the common law rules of agency are expressly preserved by the SGA (s 62(2)). Those situations where the common law would allow B to act as agent of A, contracting on A's behalf to transfer A's title to C, have already been outlined (see para 10.06); and their extension in the Factors Acts[11] in respect of mercantile agents is dealt with below (see para 21.24, *et seq*.).

2. *Consent*. Whereas the agency exception (above) recognises that B will never become the owner of the goods, the present exception envisages that B will do so and resell to C 'with the consent of' A. In these circumstances, A would normally be secure in his unpaid seller's real rights because he has retained possession;[10] but s 47(1) provides that A loses those real rights if he assents to a subsale by B to C, presumably by way of waiver (see s 43(1)(c), considered at para 24 15). Section 47(1) would appear to go somewhat further than the common law,[12] in that it only requires A in some manner to communicate to B[13] his assent,[14] either expressly or impliedly. Thus, in *Mount Ltd v Jay Ltd*:[15]

---

8   SGA, s 62(4): set out at para 1.08.

9   See para 20.22. Any underlying policy behind these exceptions will be considered at para 21.07.

10  For the unpaid seller's rights of lien and stoppage, see para 24.04. For the overriding of these rights in favour of a bfp in possession, see para 21.43.

11  For the major FA exceptions to the *nemo dat* rule, see para 21.05.

12  A could not be estopped on ordinary principles from setting up his real rights where he repre-sents that he **will** not exercise these: see para 26.24. However, the courts were prepared to allow a delivery warrant to have such an effect, e.g. *Merchant Banking Co v Phoenix Bessemer Steel Co* (1877) 5 Ch D 205.

13  *DF Mount Ltd v Jay* (see below). In the pre-Act cases, knowledge of assent was obtained by B and C, and the courts sometimes talked in terms of estoppel: see *Benjamin on Sale*, 8th edn, 872, proposition 3a.

14  It is suggested that 'assent' here means actual assent, notwithstanding that it was obtained by fraud; cf. paras 21.19, 21.31 and 21.47.

15  [1960] 1 QB 159; [1959] 3 All ER 307.

A and B agreed that B should pay A out of the proceeds of subsale, and A gave B a delivery order addressed to the wharfingers who held the goods. B forwarded the orders to the wharfingers indorsed 'please transfer to our sub-buyer'. Salmond J held that C had obtained a good title on the grounds that:

(1)  A had impliedly assented to the subsale;[16] and

(2)  C obtained a good title under the SGA, s 25, but not s 47(2) (see para 21.49).

3.  *The SGA provisions.* The phrase 'subject to the provisions of this Act' in s 21(1) refers to the major SGA exceptions to the *nemo dat* rule (see para 21.05) and to s 21(2)(a), which lays down that:

> 'Nothing in this Act affects . . . the provisions of the Factors Acts, or any enactment enabling the apparent owner of goods to dispose of them as if he were the true owner thereof.'

Apart from the provisions of the FA,[11] which for many purposes must be treated with the SGA as a single code,[17] it is difficult to see to what s 21(2)(a) is referring.[18] Section 21(2)(b) refers to some miscellaneous powers of sale (see para 21.06).

**[21.05]  The major SGA, FA and HPA exceptions.**[19] The major exceptions to the *nemo dat* rule (see para 21.01) which are relevant to the disposition of goods to a *bona fide* transferee (C) are as follows:

(1)  *Estoppel.* A may be estopped from denying to C that B may pass a good title to C (see para 21.08).

(2)  *Voidable title.* If B obtains a voidable title from A, B may pass a good title to C at any time before A avoids B's title (see para 21.19).

(3)  *Mercantile agency.* If A entrusts his goods to B as mercantile agent, B may be able to pass a good title to C under the Factors Act 1889 (see para 21.24).

(4)  *Seller in possession.* If B has sold goods to A but retained possession of them, B may by statute pass a good title to C (see para 21.38).

(5)  *Buyer in possession.* If B has agreed to buy goods from A and obtained possession of them, B may by statute pass a good title to C (see para 21.43).

(6)  *Private sales of motor vehicles.* Under the HPA 1964, if B is in possession of a vehicle under an hp or conditional sale agreement, B may pass a good title to a private purchaser (see para 21.57).

*Sales in market overt.* This oldest exception to the *nemo dat* rule was part of the Law Merchant and incorporated into the law of many Western European States.[19] As developed by Elizabethan lawyers, it was a sensible attempt to balance the conflicting interests of the owner and the bfp. Notwithstanding that subsequent

---

16  *Distinguish Mordaunt v British Oil and Cake Mills Ltd* [1910] 2 KB 502: see 1st Cavendish edn, para 21.03.

17  *Per* Clarke J in *Forsythe International (UK) Ltd v Silver Shipping Co Ltd* [1994] 1 All ER 851, at 862.

18  Perhaps it includes the following: Pt III of the HPA (see para 21.55); the annexation of fixtures (see para 25.23).

19  See Murray (1960) 9 ICLQ 24.

developments left it a curious anomaly in English law,[20] Chalmers embodied it in the SGA,[21] whence it has now been abolished.[22] Nevertheless, for higher value goods, e.g. cars, antiques, the rule remains in a European context: where the value of the goods makes the cost of transit worthwhile, stolen goods can still be taken to the Continent, passed through say a Parisian *market overt* and then subsequently sold with a good title in England.[23]

**[21.06] Miscellaneous powers of sale**. Section 21(2)(b) of the SGA provides that 'nothing in this Act shall affect the validity of any contract of sale under any special common law or statutory power of sale or under the order of a court of competent jurisdiction'.

1. *Common law powers of sale*. Where these powers have not been absorbed by statute (see below), they are expressly preserved by the Act, e.g. the power of sale of a pledgee (see para 25.15) or of an agent (see para 10.06).

2. *Statutory powers*. From the very considerable list of statutory powers of sale,[24] several are worthy of mention for our purposes.

   (a) *Creditor's power of sale*. Unpaid sellers (see para 27.08, *et seq*.), distraining landlords (see para 19.17), pawnbrokers (see para 25.18) and repairers[25] all have varying statutory powers of sale.

   (b) *Insolvency*. The trustee in bankruptcy or liquidator has a statutory power of sale; but neither can normally pass a better title than the insolvent person has (see para 19.23), though an administrator may do so.[26]

   (c) *Execution*. The effect on the title to goods of execution and sale by a sheriff has already been considered (see para 19.16).

3. *Court orders*. There are a number of powers conferred on the courts to make an order for the sale of property. Particularly worthy of note are the power to order a sale or division of goods owned by co-owners who cannot reach agreement *inter se* with respect to the co-owned goods; the effect of satisfaction of a judgment in an action in conversion (see para 26.17); the power to order a sale under the Rules of Court where the sheriff interpleads because of a dispute as to the title of goods taken in execution;[27] or where the subject-matter of any litigation is perishable, or is likely to deteriorate if kept, or which 'for any other reason it is desirable to sell forthwith';[28] and the powers of the court to authorise sale by a bailee.[29]

---

20  See (1994) 114 NLJ 1014. *Contra* European law.

21  It was most recently to be found in s 22 of the SGA 1979. E.g. *Bishopsgate Motor Finance Corpn. Ltd v Transport Brakes Ltd* [1949] 1 KB 322, CA.

22  Sale of Goods (Amendment) Act 1994 (see Shears 14 Tr L 30).

23  E.g. *Winkworth v Christie Manson and Woods Ltd* [1980] Ch 496.

24  See further Benjamin's *Sale of Goods*, 6th edn, para 7.109. E.g. *Bulbruin Ltd v Romanyszyn* [1994] RTR 273, CA.

25  Torts Act 1977, s 12. If in doubt, the bailee may apply to the court, see below, fn 31.

26  Insolvency Act, 1986, s 15: see para 19.12; and generally, para 19.22.

27  See *Caldwell's* case (set out at para 21 22); and 19.05 and 19.20.

28  *On Demand Information plc v Michael Gerson plc* (set out at para 27.21), esp. *per* Lord Millett at paras 33–7. See also para 27.08.

29  Torts Act 1977, s 13.

**[21.07] The underlying policy.** It may be helpful at this point to consider the policy of the law in granting exceptions to the *nemo dat* rule. Generally speaking, the courts have tended to favour ownership and to uphold the *nemo dat* rule; and the history of this area of the law has largely been one where the pressure of the mercantile community has secured the adoption of statutory exceptions to the rule, and the courts have consistently interpreted those exceptions against C and in favour of A. As long ago as 1787, an attempt was made to ascribe a pattern to the rule and the counter-balancing exceptions by Ashhurst J in *Lickbarrow v Mason*,[30] where he said:

> 'We may lay it down as a broad general principle, that, wherever one of two innocent persons must suffer by the acts of a third, he who has enabled such a third person to occasion the loss must sustain it.'

This *dictum* was applied by the Privy Council in *Commonwealth Trust Ltd v Akotey*,[31] where that court appeared to hold that the mere handing over of possession of goods by A to B is sufficient to estop A from setting up his title against C. However, such a view was rejected by the Privy Council in the *Mercantile Bank of India Ltd* case.[32] Perhaps unfortunately, the latter case would seem to be correct: the issue between A and C does not turn on fault, but on the strict application of the *nemo dat* rule and the exceptions thereto; and the *dictum* by Ashhurst J remains no more than an aspiration. Moreover, Ashhurst J was talking about the common law, where there is, of course, no power to apportion. It has been judicially suggested that the courts should have a statutory power to apportion in these circumstances;[33] but this view was rejected by the Twelfth Report of the Law Reform Committee as 'unworkable'.[34] The position therefore remains that, unless C can bring his case within one (or more—for they overlap) of the exceptions, he will lose. Curiously, even if C can bring his case within one of the exceptions, he will normally get only such title as A has (see paras 21.09, 21.23, 21.37, 21.54 and 21.58).

## ESTOPPEL[35]

**[21.08] The rule.** According to the latter part of s 21(1) of the SGA, where A's goods are sold by B to C,[36] the *nemo dat* rule will apply:

> 'unless the owner of the goods is by his conduct precluded from denying the seller's authority to sell'.

---

30   (1787) 2 Term Rep 63, HL at 70.

31   [1926] AC 72; [1925] All ER Rep 270, PC. See also the dissenting judgment of Lord Denning MR in *Beverley Acceptances Ltd v Oakley* (see para 21.28) at 425E–F.

32   [1938] AC 287, HL, *per* Lord Wright at 298. See also *per* Cairns LJ in *J Sargent (Garages) Ltd v Motor Auctions (West Bromwich) Ltd* [1977] RTR 121, CA, at 128; and see para 21.13.

33   *Per* Devlin LJ in *Ingram v Little* [1961] 1 QB 31, CA at 74.

34   1966, Cmnd. 2958, paras 12, 40(1). For criticism of this Report, see Atiyah (1966) 29 MLR 541; Diamond 29 MLR 413.

35   See generally Spencer Bower, *Estoppel*, 4th edn; Pickering (1939) 55 LQR 400; *Cross and Tapper on Evidence*, 9th edn, 77, *et seq*.

36   So passing the property from B to C (see para 1.10). *Contra* where there is a mere agreement to sell from B to C so that this exception is inapplicable: *Shaw v Commissioner of Police* (set out at para 19.11).

Perhaps the leading case where this provision was applied is *Eastern Distributors Ltd v Goldring*:[37]

> Murphy (A) was the owner of a Bedford van; and he wished to purchase a car as well, but had no money to pay for it, not even enough for the deposit under an hp agreement. Dealer (B) suggested to A that he should raise the deposit in the following manner, and A acquiesced: B would pretend to the plaintiff finance company (C) that he (B) was letting on hp to A **both** the van and the car, so that the company would send B the balance of the price due to both vehicles. In pursuance of this scheme, A signed a blank hp proposal form in respect of both vehicles. B then filled in his own name as owner of both vehicles and submitted the proposals to C who rejected that in respect of the car. Nevertheless, B proceeded with that in respect of the van—which was really owned by A. C sent a memorandum of the agreement to A, who promptly told B that the whole transaction was cancelled, and shortly afterwards sold the van to the defendant, a bfp. Upon discovering the true state of affairs, C sued the defendants for conversion of the van, alleging title by estoppel,[38] and A was joined as third party.

The defendant pleaded that A had only given B a limited authority to sell, and that anyway they were not privy to the estoppel and were not bound by it. Alternatively, they pleaded that, even if C acquired title by estoppel, C could not recover the van because (i) A had conferred a good title on the defendants under what is now s 24 of the SGA (see para 21.39), and (ii) A had not signed the memorandum of the hp agreement as the HPA required;[39] and that that Act did not permit an action in conversion.[40] The Court of Appeal unanimously found that C had acquired a good title by estoppel, and rejected both defences.[41]

**[21.09] Effect of statutory exception**. *Prima facie*, the statutory formula in s 21(1) would appear to refer to the common law doctrine of issue estoppel,[42] though that doctrine is nowhere defined by the SGA. However, in *Goldring's* case (set out at para 21.08), this assumption was rejected as regards the title transferred, though it would appear that the Court of Appeal thought that the other rules of common law estoppel applied to this exception (see para 21.10, *et seq.*). The Court was clear that Murphy (A) was estopped and Devlin J explained the effect of a common law estoppel as follows:[43]

> 'An estoppel affects others besides the representor. The way it has always been put is that the estoppel binds the representor and his privies. But it is not easy to determine exactly who, for this purpose, is a privy. There can be no doubt that, although the representation was actually made by [B], [A] on the facts of this case was privy to the making and bound by it . . . It would also appear that anyone whose title is obtained

---

37  [1957] 2 QB 600, [1957] 2 All ER 525, CA; app *Stoneleigh Finance Ltd v Phillips* (see para 25.27).

38  The Factors Act, s 2(1), did not apply because the dealer was not in possession: see para 21.28. What if the hp documents had indicated that B was in possession?

39  For the modern rule contained in the CCA, s 61(1)(a): see para 9.18.

40  For the tort of conversion, now wrongful interference with goods, see para 19.04. For adverse possession, see the CCA, s 134: see para 19.05A.

41  What effect, if any, would s 56 of the CCA have on this decision? For discussion of this section, see para 16.10.

42  Distinguish estoppel *per rem judicatem*: see *Powell v Wiltshire* (set out at para 12.08), where there is a discussion of 'privies'.

43  At 606–7. Cf. *Henderson & Co Ltd v Williams* (set out at paras 21.11/12).

from the representor as a volunteer is a privy for this purpose. But it is very doubtful whether a purchaser for value without notice is bound by the estoppel.'

The defendant in this case was a bfp to whom A had purported to sell the van, so that, if s 21(1) merely embodied the common law of estoppel, it would seem that C's title could be defeated by a subsequent sale to a bfp.[44] Whatever the position with regard to the common law of estoppel, however, the Court of Appeal thought that s 21(1) referred rather to the wider common law doctrine of apparent authority resting on mercantile convenience.[45] Devlin J said (at 610–611):

'We doubt whether this principle ought really to be regarded as part of the law of estoppel ... The effect of its application is to transfer a real title and not merely a metaphorical title by estoppel ... The result is that [A] is, in the words of [the SGA, s 21(1)], precluded from denying [B's] authority to sell,[46] and consequently [C] acquired the title of the goods which [A] himself had and [A] has no title left to pass to the defendant.'

Of course, C could get no better title than A: if A had merely stolen the van from O, the plaintiff's title could still have been defeated by O.

## The common law doctrine of issue estoppel[47]

[21.10] The common law doctrine of estoppel requires an unambiguous[48] representation made **by** the person to be estopped (A),[49] or his privy,[50] **to** the person seeking to set it up (C).[51] In our context, this means that the representation relied upon to estop A from setting up his title to goods may be to the effect that another (B) is: (1) the owner of goods;[52] or (2) has A's authority to dispose of them.[53] It makes little difference whether the representation gives rise to apparent ownership or agency,[54] though in the latter situation this exception overlaps with that in respect of the apparent authority of an agent (see para 10.06).

However, before the requirements of this rule are examined (see para 21.12), there should be noted the difficulty in applying the doctrine (see para 21.11) and the words of caution sounded by Lord Wright in the *Mercantile Bank of India Ltd* case,[55] where his Lordship pointed out:

---

44 With or without delivery? Cf. Powell (1957) 20 MLR 650, 652.
45 See the criticism by Goodhart (1957) 73 LQR 455, 457; and the discussion in Powell, *Agency*, 2nd edn, 68–72.
46 Is this rule confined to dispositions by the agent by way of sale?
47 See generally Benjamin's *Sale of Goods*, 6th edn, 7-008, *et seq*.
48 Or one which may reasonably be taken as such: *Woodhouse AC Israel Cocoa SA v Nigerian Produce Marketing Co* [1972] AC 741, HL.
49 *Moorgate Mercantile Co Ltd* case (set out at para 21.17).
50 E.g. B in *Eastern Distributors Ltd v Goldring* (set out at para 21.08).
51 Distinguish the situation where A makes the representation only to B: see para 21.04.
52 E.g. *Eastern Distributors Ltd v Goldring* (above).
53 See Goode, *Commercial Law*, 3rd edn, 423–4; and the cases cited in Stoljar, *Agency* 26, fn 20. In *Pacifc Motor Auctions Pty Ltd v Motor Credits (Hire Finance) Ltd* [1965] AC 867, the Australian courts held that the finance company was estopped; but the point was expressly reserved by the PC.
54 Compare liens, para 1.23.
55 [1938] AC 287, PC, at 302.

'There are very few cases of actions for conversion in which a plea of estoppel by representation has succeeded.'

**[21.11]** The operation of common law estoppel may be illustrated by two similar cases, in which the courts contrived to reach different results.[56] In both cases, the owner (A) of goods lying in a warehouse instructed the warehousekeeper to transfer the goods to the order of a rogue (B), and B then sold the goods to a bfp (C), who paid the price to B in return for a delivery order made out to B. In *Henderson & Co v Williams*:[57]

C distrusted B and before paying him obtained confirmation from the warehouse-keeper that the sugar was held to B's order. C sued the warehousekeeper in conversion, and the Court of Appeal held that, although the property in the goods remained in A, the warehousekeeper was estopped as against C from denying C's title.[58]

However, in *Farquharson Brothers & Co v King & Co*:[59]

B, a confidential clerk of A, perpetrated a series of frauds over a period of about four years in the following manner: he instructed the warehousekeeper to transfer some of A's timber to the order of Brown; and, under the name of Brown, sold this timber to C and gave him delivery orders. C obtained delivery, and A sued him in conversion. The majority of the Court of Appeal held that A was estopped from setting up his title because he had enabled B to commit the fraud.[60] Sterling LJ dissented on the grounds that there had never been any holding out by A or the warehousekeeper to C as to B's authority; and the House of Lords adopted this dissenting opinion without hesitation.

It will be observed that in both cases the warehousekeeper was justified as far as A was concerned in delivering the goods to the order of B; and in both, B gave C a delivery order which at that moment the warehousekeeper was prepared to honour. However, in *Henderson v Williams* C took the precaution of getting the warehouse-keeper to confirm that he would honour the delivery order, which amounted to a representation by A (see para 21.13); but in *Farquharson v King* C did not take such a precaution.

**[21.12] Requirements**. Leaving aside the nature of the representation required (see para 21.13, *et seq.*), a common law estoppel will only operate where all the following requirements are present.

1. *The representation by A must concern an existing state of facts*. It is fundamental to the common law doctrine of estoppel that the representation must be as to existing facts, and not future intention.[61] A representation of future intention can only[62] take effect under the principles of equitable estoppel and waiver (see para 26.23, *et seq.*).

---

56   The following judges sat at different stages in both cases: Lords Halsbury and Lindley reached different conclusions in each case; AL Smith LJ decided that there was an estoppel in both.

57   [1895] 1 QB 521, CA. See also *Woodley v Coventry* (1863) 32 LJ Ex 185.

58   In this sort of situation, the safest course for the warehousekeeper is to interplead, though Lord Halsbury thought A would also be estopped as against the warehousekeeper from denying B's right of disposal.

59   [1902] AC 325; [1900–3] All ER Rep 120, HL. See also *Laurie and Morwood v Dudin* [1926] 1 KB 223, CA; *Moorgate Mercantile Co Ltd v Twitchings* (set out at para 21.17).

60   [1901] 2 KB 697, CA.

61   *Jorden v Money* (1854) 5 HL Cas 185. As to equitable estoppel, see para 26.25.

62   Unless it is that the representor has such an intention at the time of making the representation.

2. *The representation must be made to C.* The difficulties inherent in this are neatly illustrated by *Farquharson v King* (set out at para 21.11). The decision is intelligible, but makes no allowance for the carelessness of A over a four-year period (see para 21.15).

3. *The representation must be made with the intention that it be acted upon.* The test is objective. Thus, in *Eastern Distributors Ltd v Goldring* (set out at para 21.08) A was estopped from denying B's title to the van because he had signed documents which made it appear as if B were the owner of the van. On the other hand, in *Lowe v Lombank Ltd* (set out at para 18.06) one of the reasons given by the Court of Appeal for finding that the hirer was not estopped was that there was no evidence that the hirer intended her representations to be acted on.[63]

4. *The representee (C) must have a genuine belief in its truthfulness.* Another ground on which the Court of Appeal refused to find the hirer estopped in *Lowe v Lombank Ltd* was that there was no evidence that the finance company had a genuine belief in the truthfulness of the hirer's representation. On the other hand, in *Eastern Distributors Ltd v Goldring* the Court of Appeal held that the finance company did in fact act on the implied representation of ownership contained in the proposal form.[64]

5. *The representee (C) must act on the representation to his detriment.* In *Farquharson v King*[65] Lord Lindley said that A was not estopped because C was misled, not by anything done by or under the authority of A, but by B's fraud; and in *Lowe v Lombank Ltd* the Court of Appeal thought that the finance company inserted the relevant clause in the proposal form, not so that they might rely on the representation contained therein, but simply to preclude the hirer from invoking the implied undertakings of the HPA as to quality and fitness.[66]

## Representations, omissions and negligence

[21.13] The conduct relied upon as amounting to a representation of ownership or authority (see para 21.10) sufficient to found such an estoppel may itself make the representation,[67] or it may allow another to make a representation;[68] and, whilst there will usually be some active conduct, there may be a representation by omission.[69] However, once it is settled that there does not have to be active conduct on the part of the representor himself, it is difficult to decide what is necessary before there will be a representation sufficient to found an estoppel.[70] The *dictum* of

---

63 See also *Debs v Sibec Developments* [1990] RTR 91 ([1989] JBL 284); and settlement figures (see para 26.19A).

64 Perhaps the cases may be distinguished on the basis that the representation is in the very act of signing as opposed to being in the small print.

65 See also *Carr v L & NW Railway* (1875) LR 10 CP 307.

66 See now SOGIT, ss 9–11: see Chaps 13–15.

67 E.g. *Henderson & Co v Williams* (set out at para 21.11/2); *Eastern Distributors Ltd v Goldring* (set out at para 21.08).

68 *Coventry v GE Rail Co* (1883) 11 QBD 776, CA.

69 E.g. *Pickard v Sears* (1837) 6 Ad & El 469.

70 For an examination of whether possession plus or carelessness could raise an estoppel, see para 21.14, *et seq.*

Ashhurst J in *Lickbarrow v Mason* (set out at para 21.07) suggests that whenever the owner (A) has 'enabled' the rogue (B) to occasion the loss, he should be estopped. Thus, in handing possession of his goods to B, A in one sense enables B to dispose of them. However, it has been settled since *Johnson v Credit Lyonnais Co*[71] that the mere transfer of possession of goods to another will not generally raise an estoppel.[70] No doubt, this rule is convenient to owners: they would be in a difficult position if any repairer, cleaner, etc, with whom they deposited goods could pass a good title. Yet the rule obviously runs counter to the interests of the mercantile community, who have therefore secured a number of statutory exceptions, where a person in possession can pass a good title if he is either a seller, buyer or mercantile agent (see respectively, paras 21.38, 21.43 and 21.34).

**[21.14]  Possession plus**. If the mere possession of goods will not raise an estoppel (see para 21.13), what more is required? The issue was canvassed in *Central Newbury Car Auctions Ltd v Unity Finance Ltd:*[72]

> The plaintiff dealer (A) purchased a car, in the log-book of which the previous regis-tered owner, Ashley, had not signed his name. A did not register himself owner because he intended to resell the car. Subsequently, a rogue (B) tricked A into parting with possession of the car and log-book and then offered the car to C giving the name Ashley. By this time, B had signed the log-book in the name of Ashley. C compared the signature in the log-book with that which the rogue provided in his presence, and then completed the purchase. C sold the car to the defendant. The defendants pleaded that A was estopped by his negligence from denying B's authority to sell; and the County Court Judge agreed.

However, the decision was reversed by the Court of Appeal, where the majority thought that the result should turn, not upon fault, but upon whether the handing over of the log-book was sufficient to take the case outside the general rule. In deciding in favour of A, the majority pointed out that the log-book was not a document of title;[73] but in a strong dissenting judgment, Denning LJ adopted Ashhurst J's *dictum*, and pointed out that the log-book was best evidence of title.[74] On the other hand, in *Goldring's* case (set out at para 21.08), the Court of Appeal unanimously decided that the owner was estopped where he signed a document stating that the dealer was the owner of the vehicle. No doubt, there is an intelligible distinction between a positive statement of ownership and a mere careless transfer of possession, but it makes no allowance for the owner's culpability (see para 21.15).

**[21.15/8]  Carelessness**. Suppose an owner (A) has carelessly signed a document which appears to divest him of his property, and this document is utilised by a rogue (B) to enter into a transaction purporting to transfer the property to a bfp (C). In a contest between A and C as to the ownership of the goods, A may advance two separate lines of argument to escape from the effect of the document: a plea of *non*

---

71   (1877) 3 CPD 32, CA. See also *Jerome v Bentley* (set out at para 21.27); and generally Goode, *Commercial Law*, 2nd edn, 457–8.

72   [1957] 1 QB 371; [1956] 3 All ER 903, CA. Foll. *Sargent Ltd v Motor Auctions Ltd* (set out at para 27.30).

73   The log-book stated on every page 'The person in whose name a vehicle is registered may or may not be the legal owner of the vehicle'. There might have been an estoppel if it had been a document of title (see para 21.60).

74   Whilst the majority thought A's negligence irrelevant, Denning LJ was prepared to find a breach of a duty of care giving rise to an estoppel (at 385).

*est factum* (see para 10.16); and a denial of estoppel. The second point arose in *Moorgate Mercantile Co Ltd v Twitchings*:[75]

> The plaintiff finance company (A) was a member of HPI (see para 21.01). However, in letting a car on hp to B, A failed to inform HPI of the transaction. During the continuance of the hiring, B offered the car for sale to the defendant motor dealer (C), who was also a member of HPI. B falsely told C that he was the owner of the car and that it was not subject to any hp agreement. C contacted HPI, who informed him that the car was not registered with them. In consequence, C bought the car.

A's action for conversion succeeded before the House of Lords, who rejected C's argument of title by estoppel on the following grounds:

(1) HPI's communication to C did not amount to a representation on behalf of A that there was no outstanding agreement on the car: first, it was merely an assertion as to the state of HPI's records and not a positive assertion as to ownership; and second, in answering C's enquiry, HPI was not acting as agents for A, but in their own capacity.[76] It followed that it was not open to C to plead estoppel by representation (Lord Salmon dissenting).

(2) A bare majority[77] held that there was no legal duty owed by A to C to register or to take reasonable care in registering their hp agreements with HPI,[78] noting that the rules of HPI did not impose on members any contractual duty to register and that the search form sent to C expressly disclaimed any pretence that it was a complete record.[79] It followed that C could not plead estoppel by negligence.[80]

The *Twitchings* decision has subsequently been confirmed by the Court of Appeal.[81] However, if the minority view on above issue (2) in the House had prevailed, that might have established a sort of common law title registration system on HPI rules; and a similar result could be achieved by statutory reversal of *Twitchings* (see para 21.60).

# VOIDABLE TITLE

[21.19/20] **The exception**. Suppose A enters a **title-transferring** contract, proposing to sell, pledge or exchange[82] his car to B, that offer being induced by B's

---

75 [1977] AC 890; [1976] 2 All ER 641, HL.

76 Mr Twitchings seems to have been well aware of this fact: see *per* Lord Edmund-Davies 917. Even if HPI had been acting as an agent for A (see para 16.06), see *Freeman v Cooke* (1848) 2 Exch 654.

77 Lords Edmund-Davies, Fraser and Russell, affirming the dissenting judgment of Geoffrey Lane LJ in the CA. See also Atiyah, *Sale of Goods*, 10th edn, 379.

78 In the CA, Lord Denning MR would have extended such a duty to non-members, so apparently elevating the obligation into the tort of negligence: as to which, see para 17.20.

79 The rules of HPI have subsequently been changed so that members are now obliged to register. Does this strengthen the argument for a collateral contract between A and C (see Phillips (1976) 92 LQR 499) or an estoppel? HPI also offers a guarantee to searchers that the register is accurate: (1996) 51 CC1/10.

80 This attitude has even been taken where the owner of an aircraft let on hp was in breach of a statutory duty to register his title (see para 9.02): *Cadogan Finance Ltd v Lavery* [1982] Com LR 248. Compare Goode, *Commercial Law*, 3rd edn, 418.

81 *Dominion Credit & Finance Ltd v Marshall (Cambridge)* Ltd (1993) Lexis, CA (a test case supported by RMI).

82 *Anderson v Ryan* [1967] IR 34. Or quasi-sale?

misrepresentation. The distinction has already been drawn according to whether the outcome is a void or voidable contract between A and B (see para 10.15). If the contract is void, B will acquire no proprietary interest in the car; but, if the contract is merely voidable, he will acquire a defeasible proprietary interest in it. Suppose further, that B purports to dispose of the car to C. If the contract between A and B is void, B acquires no title to the goods, and under the *nemo dat* rule (see para 19.11) can therefore pass none,[83] though C might acquire a good title under one of the other exceptions to that rule, e.g. *Eastern Distributors Ltd v Goldring* (set out at para 21.08). Leaving aside this last possibility, the position is the same if the contract between A and B is voidable, and has been avoided by A before B purports to dispose of the goods.[84] On the other hand, if the voidable contract between A and B has not been avoided at the time of the disposition by B to C, C will at very least acquire that voidable title, e.g. if C is B's trustee in bankruptcy (see para 19.23), or a purchaser with notice (see X in *Caldwell's* case: set out at para 21.21). However, if C is a *bona fide* transferee for value without notice, he may acquire a good title indefeasible by A.[85] This common law rule only applies to title-transferring trans-actions:[82] it has no application to bailments.

As to where the disposition by B to C is by way of **sale**,[86] the exception has been encapsulated in s 23 of the SGA as follows:

> 'Where the seller of goods has a voidable title thereto, but his title has not been avoided at the time of the sale, the buyer acquires a good title to the goods, provided he buys them in good faith and without notice of the seller's defect of title.'

'Notice' is not defined in the SGA, but refers to C's knowledge of the defect in B's title.[87] According to s 61(3),

> 'A thing is deemed to be done "in good faith" within the meaning of the Act when it is in fact done honestly, whether it be done negligently or not'

To the cynical common law, 'good faith' is only the absence of proven dishonesty,[88] though it does extend beyond C's participation in B's wrongdoing (see para 21.36) to his own independent wrongdoing, e.g. C tries to defraud B. It is to be compared with the much wider continental concept of 'good faith' (see para 11.15).

The courts do not seem to regard s 23 as having made any changes in the com-mon law. In *Whitehorn Brothers v Davison*[89] the Court of Appeal were of the opinion that the common law exception still stands in respect of pledges by B to C;[90] and that,

---

83 *Cundy v Lindsay* (1878) 3 App Cas 459, HL; *Ingram v Little* [1961] 1 QB 31, CA; *Shogun Finance Ltd v Hudson* (set out at para 10.15).

84 *Car and Universal Finance Co Ltd v Caldwell* (above); *Newtons of Wembley Ltd v Williams* (set out at para 21.51).

85 This rule in respect of a bfp of goods does not apply in favour of a bfp of a chose in action: see para 7.23.

86 Presumably, s 23 does not apply where B has only agreed to sell to C: cf. *Shaw v Commissioner of Police* (set out at para 19.11). See Benjamin's *Sale of Goods*, 6th edn, para 7.026.

87 It is discussed in the context of another exception to the *nemo dat* rule, para 21.49.

88 The *Dodds* case (set out at para 21.57). See Chalmers, *Sale of Goods*, 18th edn, 272–3; Benjamin, *Op. cit.*, para 7.044.

89 [1911] 1 KB 463; [1908–10] All ER Rep 885, CA.

90 See also *Phillips v Brooks* [1919] 2 KB 243. And what if the disposition by A to B is by way of pledge? Or if there is only an agreement to pledge between B and C (see fn 86, above)?

under both statute and common law, if A seeks to recover the goods from C, the onus is on A to show that C did not purchase in good faith and without notice.[91] However, the onus is on C to show that his purchase was made before avoidance.[92]

**[21.21/2] Effect of the exception**. Assuming that the contract between A and B is voidable under the foregoing rules (see para 21.19), it is necessary to consider how A may rescind or avoid it.[93] Plainly, where A communicates his intention to rescind to B, that will be sufficient; but, for a long time it was thought that A could not effectively rescind by any means short of 'going to court',[94] except by actual communication with B[95] or recaption of the property (see para 24.23). Such a rule was perfectly adequate where B was innocent, but not if B was fraudulent. In the latter case, B would usually effectively dispose of the goods before A found him or the goods, with the result that it was assumed that B would usually be able to pass a good title to a bfp (C). However, this assumption was confounded by *Car and Universal Finance Co Ltd v Caldwell*:[96]

> On January 12th, Caldwell (A), contracted to sell his car to a rogue (B) for £975 and allowed B to take the car away in return for payment made as to £965 by cheque. The cheque was dishonoured the next morning; and A immediately went to the police, and also asked the AA to try to find his car. On January 15th, B sold the car to X, a *mala fide* purchaser, who immediately resold to C, a *bona fide* purchaser. On January 29th, A demanded the return of his car from X. In August, C sold the car to the plaintiff (D). Subsequently the car was seized by the sheriff, and the case arose on an interpleader summons. It was conceded that A had taken adequate steps to avoid the contract by January 29th, so that D could have no better title than C. The judge held best title was vested in A.

The Court of Appeal found that X was not the agent of C, so that C was not affected by X's *male fides*;[97] but they unanimously dismissed the appeal on the grounds that A had effectively avoided B's title on January 13th.[98] At first sight, *Caldwell's* case would appear to make substantial inroads into one of the principal exceptions to the *nemo dat* rule:[99] whereas the previous rule left very little chance of avoidance, the new one makes it a real possibility. Yet, it would seem that the Court of Appeal were careful to restrict themselves to cases where a contract was voidable by reason of B's fraud and B deliberately hides from A. Does the rule depend on (a) fraud in the sale, or (b) deliberate evasion, or both?

---

91  Is the position the same if A seizes possession, so that C is the plaintiff? The *Twelfth Report of the Law Reform Committee* (1966, Cmnd. 2958), para 25, recommended that the rule be reversed to achieve uniformity with the other exceptions to the *nemo dat* rule: see below and para 21.36.

92  *Thomas v Heelas* [1988] C & FLR 211, CA, distinguishing *Whitehorn Brothers v Davison* (above).

93  This will be rescission *ab initio:* see para 26.12.

94  See *per* Lord Pearson in *Garnac Grain Co Inc v HMF Faure and Fairclough Ltd* [1968] AC 1130 at 1140, HL.

95  *Per* Lord Clyde in *Macleod v Kerr* 1965 SLT 358, at 363.

96  [1965] 1 QB 525; [1964] 1 All ER 290, CA: see Cornish (1964) 27 MLR 472. Contra *Macleod v Kerr* (above).

97  The possible agency relationship between a finance company and dealer is considered at para 16.06.

98  '[B] would not expect to be communicated with as a matter of right or requirement . . . [A only] has to establish clearly and unequivocally that he terminates the contract' (*per* Sellers LJ at 550–1). See also Upjohn and Davies LJJ at 555, 558.

99  Atiyah [1965] JBL 130, 131.

Furthermore, another limitation on the effect of this case became apparent with the decision in *Newtons of Wembley Ltd v Williams* (set out at para 21.51). In somewhat similar circumstances to those in *Caldwell*, in *Newtons* it was accepted that A had avoided by doing all in his power to communicate with B; but the Court of Appeal nevertheless held that B had passed a good title as a buyer in possession: *Caldwell* was distinguished on the grounds that X was *male fide*.

**[21.23]** The implications of *Caldwell* (set out at para 21.22) may be illustrated by way of an example. Suppose X steals goods from O, and sells them to A; A resells to B under a contract voidable by A; B resells to C, who resells to D, who resells to E.

O

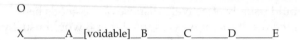

X_____A_[voidable]_B_____C_____D_____E

Several questions arise.

(1)  Suppose B sells to C before A avoids the contract. Is the effect of the exception to confer on C the title of O or A? It is submitted that C will only obtain A's title, with any defects it contains.[100]

(2)  Suppose B sells to C and C resells to D before A avoids his contract with B, but C is *male fide*. In *Caldwell*, the Court of Appeal seem to have thought that D would obtain a good title as being a bfp[101] before avoidance, cf. *Williams* case (set out at para 21.51).

(3)  Suppose further that the sale by D to E took place after A's avoidance of his contract with X.

It was conceded in *Caldwell* that E had no better title than D. If this is correct, the effect of the exception is that E will only succeed where he, or a prior party,[102] took *bona fide* and for value **before** A rescinds his contract with B.

Finally, it should be noted that the Law Reform Committee in 1966 recommended that the rule as to avoidance laid down in *Caldwell* should be reversed, and actual communication required:[103] if enacted, the recommendation would have reversed the result in *Caldwell*, but not that in *Williams*, i.e. the bfp in the *Williams* case would succeed on the basis of s 23 and would not need to rely on s 25. Nothing has been done.[104]

## MERCANTILE AGENCY[105]

**[21.24] Introduction.** In the series of nineteenth century Factors Acts, Parliament attempted to increase the protection of the bf purchasers and pledgees (C) who

---

100  Battersby and Preston (1972) 35 MLR at 280–1. This is the usual result: see para 21.07.
101  Is it important that he is the first bfp? See further, para 21.54. Cf. para 21.59.
102  *Peirce v London Horse and Carriage Repository Ltd* [1922] WN 170, CA.
103  *Twelfth Report* (1966, Cmnd. 2958), paras 16 and 40(4).
104  Commentators are reduced to minimising the scope of *Caldwell*: see Atiyah, *Sale of Goods*, 10th edn, 392; Treitel, *Law of Contract*, 11th edn, 372–3; Benjamin's *Sale of Goods*, 6th edn, para 7.023.
105  See Powell, *Agency*, 2nd edn, 216–36.

obtained goods from factors (B), to whom the goods had been entrusted by their owners (A). Begun in 1823, the history of the Acts is one of legislation in favour of the bfp followed by the courts adopting a restrictive interpretation in favour of the owner, followed by further legislation in favour of the bfp.[106] Curiously, the SGA then proceeded to repeat some of the more important provisions of the consolidating Factors Act 1889 (FA) in almost identical terms.[107] There are two major themes running through the FA: both are attempts to modify the common law rule that possession by B does not usually give rise to an apparent authority from A to dispose of the goods (see para 21.13).

(1) An intention to increase the power of professional agents, which the nineteenth century draftsman termed 'mercantile agents' (B). The object of the Act is not to derogate from the powers of an amateur agent,[108] but to increase the **powers** of the professional agent for the benefit of his transferee (C).[109] This it achieves as follows: it does not increase the **rights** of the agent *vis-à-vis* his principal (A);[110] but it does enable the agent to pass his principal's title to C, even though B is acting in excess of his authority from A.

(2) The Act lays down that a buyer or seller in possession may in certain circumstances pass a good title. These provisions will be considered later.[111]

Both these themes have certain similarities to the doctrine of estoppel (see para 21.54); and they do in fact cover some of the ground covered by estoppel in those situations where a person in possession (B) has an apparent or usual authority to dispose of goods.[108] But there the similarity ends: estoppel demands a representation made by A to C, whereas the FA requires instead that C's transferor (B) should be a mercantile agent, or a seller or a buyer in possession.[111]

[21.25] **The mercantile agency exception**. The key is to be found in s 2(1) of the FA, which provides:

> 'Where a mercantile agent[112] is with the consent of the owner,[113] in possession of goods or of documents of title to goods,[114] any sale, pledge, or other disposition of the goods, made by him when acting in the ordinary course of business of a mercantile agent,[115] shall, subject to the provisions of this Act, be as valid as if he were expressly authorised by the owner of the goods to make the same,[116] provided that the person taking under the disposition acts in good faith, and has not at the time of the disposition notice that the person making the disposition has not authority to make the same.'[117]

---

106 See Stoljar, *Agency*, 116–21.

107 Even whilst expressly preserving the Factors Acts: see SGA, s 21(2)(a). There are even discrepancies between the two: see paras 21.38 and 21.43.

108 The powers of an ordinary agent are outlined at paras 10.06 and 21.02.

109 S 13. If the transferee has not paid the price, the 'owner' may be able to recover it from him: s 12(3).

110 S 12(1). Nor of the agent's trustee in bankruptcy: s 12(2). Or liquidator?

111 See respectively, para 21.38, *et seq*. and para 21.43, *et seq*.

112 See para 21.26.

113 See para 21.31.

114 See para 21.28.

115 See para 21.33, *et seq*.

116 See para 21.37.

117 See para 21.36.

Since 1889, this subsection has become so encrusted with case law, that each phrase of it must be considered with some care. Indeed, the extent of the case law perhaps suggests the advisability of further statutory reform (see para 21.37). This analysis attempts to concentrate on the decisions particularly significant to private consumers.

**[21.26/7] A mercantile agent.** The FA requires that B should be a mercantile agent (ma).

1. *An agent.* The first requirement is that in acquiring the goods B must be acting as, or on behalf of, an agent: it is not sufficient if he acts as owner,[118] nor as any other type of custodian. Difficult questions may arise where he acts in more than one capacity as, for instance, where he is both a servant and an agent, e.g. a commercial traveller.

2. *A 'mercantile agent'.* Before 1889, the Acts merely used the term 'agent'; but this had been judicially interpreted to cover only those professional agents which were termed factors in the normal language of the time. The term 'mercantile agent' appeared for the first time in the 1889 Act. According to s 1(1) of the 1889 Act, the expression 'mercantile agent' shall mean (see also the SGA 1979, s 26):

   'a mercantile agent having in the customary course of his business as such agent authority either to sell goods, or to consign goods for the purpose of sale, or to buy goods, or to raise money on the security of goods'.

Thus, a 'mercantile agent' (ma) is one who by way of business is customarily entrusted with goods as agent for one of the purposes listed in s 1(1). This is commonly assumed to include a motor dealer: but, in the normal case, he will buy and sell on his own account; and the proposition would only seem to be true where he (perhaps unusually?) takes possession as agent for sale, etc.[119] On the other hand, the courts did somewhat stretch the notion of a mercantile agent in *Lowther v Harris*.[120]

   A installed some antiques he wished to sell in a house. He arranged with an antique dealer, B that B should take a flat in the house and sell the items on commission, but should first obtain the sanction of A. B fraudulently sold and delivered two tapestries to a bfp. As to one, there had clearly been no consent to its removal by a misrepresentation. A's action in conversion against the bfp succeeded in respect of the first tapestry (see para 21.31), but failed as to the second on the grounds that B was a mercantile agent and had passed a good title under the FA.

As B's function was not merely to deliver the goods, but also to collect the price and account for it to A, Wright J concluded that B was acting in the usual course of business of a fine art dealer,[121] albeit for one principal only.[122] It would seem to be

---

118 *Belvoir Finance Co Ltd v Cole Ltd* [1969] 2 All ER 904.
119 E.g. *Pearson v Rose & Young Ltd* (set out at para 21.35); *Stadium Finance Ltd v Robbins* (set out at para 21.29).
120 [1927] 1 KB 393; [1926] All ER Rep 352. See also *Weiner v Harris* (set out at para 20.27).
121 Would the answer have been the same if B had not already been an antique dealer?
122 Is this the effect of the word 'customary' in s 1(1)? And how is this reconcilable with the view of s 1(1) as a subjective test taken in *Oppenheimer v Attenborough* (set out at para 21.34)?

uncertain whether the entrusting of goods to another for the purposes of obtaining offers would fall within s 1(1).[123]

Now, in most of the cases where it has been held that the FA applied, the rogue has been working on a commission basis. This point was seized upon by Macnaughten J in *Budberg v Jerwood and Ward*,[124] where he held that the Act did not apply to defeat the title of the owner who had entrusted her jewellery to a friend for the purposes of sale, and relied upon the absence of any commission to negative any suggestion of a business relationship. However, *Jerome v Bentley*[125] would appear to deny that the presence or absence of commission is decisive, though it seems that the FA was not pleaded in this case.[126] It may be that the presence of commission does not conclusively show that an agent is a ma, but the cases other than *Jerome v Bentley* certainly seem to show that it is strong evidence to that effect.

**[21.28/30] Possession.** For the operation of this exception, B must be in possession of goods or documents of title. Under the FA, 'goods' are defined by s 1(3) to 'include wares and merchandise',[127] and documents of title by s 1(4), meaning documents which in commerce represent goods.[128] However, not only must B be in possession with A's knowledge that B is an ma,[129] but it has been held that B must also be in possession in his capacity as (**qua**) ma. In *Staffs Motor Guarantee Ltd v British Wagon Ltd*:[130]

> B, a dealer in motor lorries, agreed to sell a lorry to the defendant finance company (A) and to rehire it from them under an hp agreement with a view to sub-letting it to X. B then fraudulently sold the lorry, of which he had never relinquished possession, to C, a bfp. When B fell into arrears, A repossessed the lorry. In their action to recover the lorry, C pleaded that: (1) the hp agreement was void under the Bills of Sale Acts (see para 25.27), (2) B could pass a good title under what is now s 24 of the SGA (see para 21.40); and (3) B could pass a good title under s 2(1) of the FA. The action failed.

Mackinnon J rejected C's plea under s 2(1) of the FA on the grounds that, after B sold the lorry to A, it was entrusted by A to B, not in his capacity as ma, but as hirer (at 313). This view has been expressly accepted by the English courts.[131] However, such a distinction in capacity will obviously, if taken too far, nullify the effect of

---

123 Accepted without argument in: *Pearson v Rose and Young Ltd* (set out at para 21.35); *Stadium Finance Ltd v Robbins* (set out at para 21.29/30). But see *per* Salmon LJ in *Lloyds and Scottish Finance Ltd v Williamson* [1965] 1 All ER 641, CA at 644.

124 (1935) 51 TLR 99.

125 [1952] 2 All ER 114.

126 If it had been, the issue might well have turned on whether B was acting as an agent or principal because, if he were an agent, the commission arrangement would seem to indicate that he was an ma: see Parker (1952) 15 MLR 503; Powell, *Agency*, 2nd edn, 83, fn 6.

127 Compare the definition of goods in the SGA: para 2.02.

128 For the extended meaning given by s 1(4), see para 23.03.

129 *Lowther v Harris* (set out at para 21.26), the first tapestry; *Henderson v Prosser* [1982] CLY 21. As to the meaning of possession, see para 23.03.

130 [1934] 2 KB 305; [1934] All ER Rep 322.

131 See *per* Denning LJ in *Pearson v Rose and Young Ltd* (set out at para 21.35), at 288; *per* Willmer LJ in *Stadium Finance Ltd v Robbins* (set out at para 21.31) at 674.

s 2(1); and it has been rejected by the courts in the somewhat similar context of the exception relating to sellers in possession.[132]

Further, it must be remembered that s 2(1) only applies where a person is an ma at the time he is entrusted with the goods:[133] the mere fact that he later becomes an ma does not bring s 2(1) into operation,[134] unless the owner consents to his possession in that capacity (but see s 2(4): discussed at para 21.31).

**[21.31/2] Consent.** The ma (see paras 21.26–7) must be in possession (see para 2.28) with the consent (see below) of the owner. It has been decided that:[135]

'Where the right of ownership has become divided among two or more persons in such a way that the acts which the section is contemplating can never be authorised save by both or all of them, these persons together constitute the owner.'

The requirement of consent is also to be found in s 25 of the SGA (see para 21.47). The FA nowhere defines 'consent', but perhaps the sense of the term is conveyed by the word used in the previous FA, namely **'entrusts'**. It is clear that only consent to the fact of possession need be shown and any secret restrictions on the power of the ma are for this purpose irrelevant.[136] Whilst there must be actual consent to the ma's possession,[137] it is irrelevant that consent was obtained by trick.[138] Moreover, the legislature obviously intended to lessen the burden of the person seeking to prove consent by providing in s 2 as follows:

'(2) Where a mercantile agent has, with the consent of the owner, been in possession of goods or of documents of title to goods, any sale, pledge, or other disposition, which would have been valid if the consent had continued, shall be valid notwithstanding the determination[139] of the consent: provided that the person taking under the disposition has not at the time thereof notice that the consent has been determined.[140]

(3) Where a mercantile agent has obtained possession of any documents of title to goods by reason of his being, or having been, with the consent of the owner, in possession of the goods represented thereby, or of any other documents of title to the goods, his possession of the first-mentioned documents shall, for the purposes of this Act, be deemed to be with the consent of the owner.

(4) For the purposes of this Act the consent of the owner shall be presumed in the absence of evidence to the contrary.'

However, the courts have shown some reluctance to apply these provisions, except, curiously, in the context of sales by a buyer in possession (see para 21.47). Thus, it is difficult to see why the transfer of possession of the log-book to the dealer in *Pearson*

---

132 See below, para 21.40. But see *per* Chapman J in *Astley Industrial Trust Ltd v Miller* [1968] 2 All ER 36, at 41–42.

133 *Per* Lush J in *Heap v Motorists' Advisory Agency Ltd* [1923] 1 KB 577, at 588–9.

134 *Beverley Acceptances Ltd v Oakley* [1982] RTR 417, CA. See further, Butterworth edn at para 21.28.

135 *Lloyds Bank Ltd v Bank of America* [1938] 2 KB 147, CA, *per* Lord Greene MR at 162.

136 *Weiner v Harris* (set out at para 20.27); *Stadium Finance Ltd v Robbins* (see below).

137 *Lowther v Harris* (set out at para 21.26), the first tapestry: see para 21.26.

138 *Folkes v King* [1923] 1 KB 282, CA.

139 Whether that determination be by act of the owner or rule of law, e.g. his death?

140 E.g. *Newtons of Wembley Ltd v Williams* (set out at para 21.51).

*v Rose and Young Ltd* (set out at para 21.35) was not connected with the business of obtaining offers for sale;[141] or why this was not presumed under s 2(4); and, if it were so connected, why s 2(2) did not prevent such consent being withdrawn. Similarly, in *Stadium Finance Ltd v Robbins*:[142]

> The owner (A) of a Jaguar car left it with a car dealer (B) to see what offers to buy it B could obtain. A took away the ignition key, but accidentally left the log-book locked in the glove compartment. B opened the glove compartment with a duplicate key and found the log-book. B subsequently sold the car to the plaintiff finance company (C). A retook possession of the car and C's claim under s 2(1) failed on the grounds that the sale to C was not made in the ordinary course of business (see para 21.35).

The majority were of the opinion that the inference under s 2(4), that the owner had consented to possession by the dealer, had been rebutted as to the log-book, but not as to the car.[143] Willmer LJ went even further, and argued that (at 674):

> 'without either key or registration book, [the dealer] was not . . . in possession of the car in his capacity of [ma]'.

It is submitted that it would be undesirable if the view of Willmer LJ were to prevail, as it would unduly restrict the operation of s 2.[144]

**[21.33] Dispositions in the ordinary course of business to a *bona fide* purchaser (bfp).** The section requires all the following:

1. *A disposition*. Section 2(1) refers to 'a sale,[145] pledge[146] or other disposition'.[147] One of the major purposes of the FA was to deal with unauthorised pledges by an ma; and it tackles this subject in considerable detail. Section 5 provides that the pledgee's security extends only to the value of the consideration he gives;[148] and s 4 restricts this to consideration given by the pledgee at the time of the pledge (or subsequently?). However, leaving aside the question of pledges, the implication of s 5 seems to be that the disposition referred to in s 2(1) must be for valuable consideration.[149] But must there also be a delivery?[150]

2. *By a mercantile agent*. The FA envisages the possibility that the disposition may be made on behalf of a ma by his servant or agent (s 6).[151]

---

141  Powell, *Agency*, 2nd edn, 228, note 4.

142  [1962] 2 QB 664; [1962] 2 All ER 633, CA.

143  Ormerod and Danckwerts LJJ, at 670–71 and 676–77.

144  See Hornby (1962) 25 MLR 719.

145  The definition of 'sale' is discussed at para 1.06, *et seq*.

146  Pledges are defined in FA, s 1(5). For liens, pledges and mortgages, see generally, para 25.02. For another point, see para 21.41, fn 205.

147  Presumably, this includes hp. It has been doubted whether this includes a mortgage bill of sale (*Beverley Acceptances Ltd v Oakley* [1982] RTR 417, CA) or a mere agreement to dispose of goods (Goode, *Commercial Law*, 3rd edn, 429, fn 80).

148  The effect of the words 'pecuniary liability' in s 1(5) would appear to be that this covers antecedent liabilities.

149  See Powell, *Agency*, 2nd edn, 233–4; Goode, *Op. cit.*, fn 78. Cf. *Thomas Graham Ltd v Glenrothes Development Corpn* [1968] SLT 2.

150  Delivery is required for a pledge (see para 25.15), but not for a sale (see para 1.07). Compare s 8 of the FA, which expressly requires a delivery: see para 21.41.

151  See the criticism of s 6 in Powell, *Op. cit.*, 230.

3.   *In the ordinary course of business* (see para 21.34).

4.   *To a bf transferee* (see para 21.36).

**[21.34] In the ordinary course of business.** Plainly, this requirement cannot be taken literally, because it is never in the ordinary course of business (ocb) for any ma to dispose of goods contrary to his authority. This dilemma is present in the wording of the statute: according to s 1(1), an ma is one who in the ordinary course of **his** business has authority to sell, etc; but s 2(1) provides that an ma can pass a good title only when acting in the ocb of **an** ma (see para 21.25). In *Oppenheimer v Attenborough:*[152]

> The plaintiff (A) was induced to entrust a parcel of diamonds to a diamond broker (B) upon the representation that B could sell the diamonds to X at an agreed minimum price. Instead, the broker pledged the diamonds with C who took *bona fide* and for value. Evidence was given that a diamond broker (an ma) employed to sell diamonds had no authority to pledge them. A argued that an ma could only pass a good title under s 2(1) when acting in the ordinary course of *his* business, and that it was not in the ordinary course of a diamond broker's business to pledge diamonds.

Nevertheless, the Court of Appeal found in favour of C. The Court thought that it was irrelevant that C did not know that his pledgor (B) was not acting as a principal;[153] and it was further irrelevant that the broker (B) had brought the transaction within s 2(1) by acting in the ocb of **an** ma. Buckley LJ explained:[154]

> 'Section 1(1) is speaking of the arrangement made between the owner of the goods and his agent ... It deals with the circumstances under which the agent gets his authority; to satisfy the definition he must get [the goods] in the customary course of his business as a mercantile agent. Section 2(1) deals with another matter. It has to do with the stage at which the agent is going to deal with the goods in his possession with reference to some other person, and the form of the expression is here altered ... [to mean] 'acting in such a way as a mercantile agent acting in the ordinary course of business of a mercantile agent would act'; that is to say, within business hours,[155] at a proper place of business, and in other respects in the ordinary way in which a mercantile agent would act so that there is nothing to lead the pledgee to suppose that anything wrong is being done, or to give him notice that the disposition is one which the mercantile agent had no authority to make.'

This decision clearly accords with the purpose of the Act, namely, to reverse the rule that an apparent owner or factor cannot pledge goods;[156] but the courts have been careful not to extend s 2(1) too far (see para 21.35). Thus, it has been held that it is not in the ocb for an ma to ask a friend to pledge goods for him;[157] nor to ask his buyer to pay the price in part to a third party in satisfaction of a judgment debt

---

152  [1908] 1 KB 221; [1904–7] All ER Rep 1016, CA. Cf. *Waddington & Son v Neale & Sons* (1907) 97 LT 786, DC.

153  *Per* Lord Alverstone CJ and Kennedy LJ, at 228, 232. But see para 21.52.

154  At 230–1. But see criticisms in Powell, *Agency*, 2nd edn, 219.

155  See the *Pacific Motor Auctions* case [1965] AC 867, PC.

156  See paras 21.24 and 21.33. Would the decision have been otherwise if C had known (or suspected?) that B was a diamond broker? Would it be relevant to the ocb whether C was aware of the ordinary powers of a diamond broker; or does this last point rather go to *bona fides* (see para 21.36)?

157  *De Gorter v Attenborough* (1904) 21 TLR 19. But see s 6 of the FA.

against the ma;[158] nor where the operation was characterised as 'a very peculiar transaction'.[159]

**[21.35]** The question of whether a disposition for value of a motor vehicle by an ma has been in the ocb has caused the courts considerable difficulty. In *Pearson v Rose and Young Ltd*:[160]

> The owner (A) of a Morris car left it with a car dealer (B) to see if the latter could obtain any offers to buy it. At the same time, B tricked A into leaving the log-book with him. B sold the car plus log-book to C1, who resold to C2, who resold to C3. The owner sued C3 to recover the car, and Devlin J held that C3 obtained a good title by reason of s 2(1). His decision was reversed by the Court of Appeal.

Whilst the case was argued on the issue of whether B, an ma, obtained possession of the goods with the consent of the owner (see para 21.29), it also raised questions as to whether the sale by B to C1 was made in the ocb and whether C1 was a bfp (see para 21.36). The Court of Appeal unanimously held that a disposition of a car with its log-book was not in the ocb because the ma was in possession of the log-book without the consent of the owner, and the log-book must therefore be ignored for the purposes of the disposition.[161] It is difficult to accept this reasoning.

(1) It ignores the distinction drawn in *Oppenheimer v Attenborough* between the circumstances of (a) acquisition and (b) disposition by the ma: whilst the test of the owner's consent on acquisition is subjective, that of the ocb on disposition is objective.[162]

(2) Even assuming that the disposition was without the log-book, it is difficult to see why such a disposition was necessarily not in the ocb. Somervell LJ suggested that the price would be substantially reduced by the absence of the log-book;[163] Vaisey J argued that the reason is that a car without a log-book is like a car with only three wheels (at 291), though many cars sold in the ocb are defective[164] or without some parts;[165] and Denning LJ pointed out that it is not in the ocb to sell a second-hand car without a log-book.[166] In *Astley Industrial Trust Ltd v Miller*[167] Chapman J indicated that he thought that the two Court of Appeal decisions were wrong on this point; but he was prepared if necessary

---

158  *Biggs v Evans* [1894] 1 QB 88. But see *Lloyds and Scottish Finances Ltd v Williamson* [1965] 1 All ER 641, CA at 644.

159  *Heap v Motorists' Agency* [1923] 1 KB 577, at 589.

160  [1951] 1 KB 275; [1950] 2 All ER 1057, CA.

161  See also *Stadium Finance Ltd v Robbins* (set out at para 21.31), with respect to both log-book and ignition key.

162  See *per* Chapman J in *Astley Industrial Trust Ltd v Miller* (see below) at 42. See also Goodhart (1951) 67 LQR 6; Hornby (1962) 25 MLR 722; Schofield [1963] JBL 344, 350; Powell, *Agency*, 2nd edn, 232.

163  At 283. Cf. *Janesich v Attenborough* (1910) 102 LT 605, at 606. But there was no such reduction in *Pearson*; and, even if there were, this may only go to *bona fides* (see para 21.36).

164  See Powell, *Op. cit.*, 231; Lanerolle [1967] JBL 329, 331–2.

165  The easy availability of replacement parts renders their absence of little significance: Schofield [1963] JBL 344 at 349.

166  At 290. This argument was adopted *Stadium Finance Ltd v Robbins* (above), where financier C never asked for the log-book. Financiers do not normally do so, it being understood that the hirer will take care of such matters. Does it follow, that *prima facie* the ocb is that the hirer will take possession of the log-book?

167  [1968] 2 All ER 36.

to distinguish the two cases on the grounds that it is in the ocb to buy a new car without a log-book. It is submitted that, on the principle laid down in *Oppenheimer v Attenborough*, what should matter is how the transaction ought to appear to the transferee (C): if the ma can supply either a genuine, or a genuine-looking, vehicle registration document, or a good reason for its absence, or if that document is not ordinarily handed over, the transaction should be in the ocb.[168]

**[21.36] A *bona fide* transferee.** Neither good faith nor notice is defined by the FA;[169] but in *Heap v Motorists' Advisory Agency Ltd*,[170] Lush J held that the burden of proof in these matters lay on the transferee (C). Perhaps the most important issue here is the relationship between the ocb and the present requirement. It is clear from the decision in *Oppenheimer v Attenborough* that, if C thinks he is dealing with a principal, the fact that he is actually dealing with a ma who is not acting in the ocb is irrelevant.[171] However, if C realises that he is dealing with a particular type of ma, the fact that it is notorious that that type of ma never has authority to engage in the kind of transfer undertaken, e.g. a pledge, will usually destroy C's *bona fides*.[172] Similarly, the fact that the goods were bought at a gross under-valuation should not prevent the transaction being in the ocb, but may go to C's *bona fides*.[173] Again, the absence of the registration document or ignition key on the sale of a car should not necessarily prevent the transaction from being in the ocb, but may indicate that C is not acting *bona fide*.[174] It is submitted that there are sound reasons for the dual requirements that the transfer be in the ocb and that C act *bona fide* and without notice.[175]

**[21.37] Effect of the exception.** Where the requirements of s 2(1) are satisfied (see paras 21.26–36), that subsection provides that the disposition by the ma:

'shall, subject to the provisions of this Act, be as valid as if he were expressly authorised by the owner of the goods to make the same.'

Whilst s 2(1) uses the term 'owner', it is submitted that its effect is to transfer only such title as the ma's transferor (A) has.[176] Even this rule is subject to certain qualifications in the Act. First, it has already been seen how the FA restricts the rights of a pledgee to the extent of the value given by him at the time of the pledge (see para 21.33). Second, the FA enables the ma to create a lien over goods which he

---

168 See *Dreverton v Regal Garage Ltd* [1998] CLY 4382, Cty Ct. Does the present illogical position simply reflect a common law bias in favour of ownership that is likely to continue regardless?
169 See the discussions of good faith at para 21.20; and notice para 21.49. The two requirements are not synonymous: Goode, *Commercial Law*, 3rd edn, 430.
170 [1923] 1 KB 577, especially at 590.
171 See also *Lloyds and Scottish Finance Ltd v Williamson* [1965] 1 All ER 641, CA; *Pacific Motor Auctions Ltd v Motor Credit Ltd* [1965] AC 867, PC.
172 *Per* Kennedy LJ in *Oppenheimer v Attenborough & Sons* [1908] 1 KB 221, CA, at 231.
173 This may be the explanation of *Pearson v Rose and Young Ltd* (set out at para 21.35): see Thornely [1962] CLJ 139, 141.
174 The crucial factor may often be failure on the part of the transferee to ask for the item: *per* Scrutton LJ in *Folkes v King* [1923] 1 KB 282, CA at 300. But see *per* Ormerod and Willmer LJJ in *Stadium Finance Ltd v Robbins* (set out at para 21.31) at 672–6.
175 *Contra* Atiyah, *Sale of Goods*, 10th edn, 388.
176 *National Employers Mutual etc Ltd v Jones* (set out at para 21.54), *obiter per* Lord Goff at 431e, delivering the unanimous judgment of the HL and relying on the history of the section.

consigns to another in respect of 'advances made to or for the use of' the ma by the consignee (s 7).

In their *Twelfth Report*, the *Law Reform Committee* did not recommend any changes in this exception to the *nemo dat* rule;[177] but the changes they did recommend would appear to offer protection to transferees in the position of the buyers in both *Pearson* and *Robbins* (see para 21.52).

## SELLER IN POSSESSION[178]

**[21.38] The exception** The policy behind the provision about to be discussed is as follows: where the seller (B) has sold the same goods to a number of people in succession, the first buyer to get physical possession of the goods or documents of title (C) is to be preferred to the others, even though he may immediately part with possession again.[179] This new exception to the *nemo dat* rule was embodied in s 8 of the FA 1889 (see para 21.24). Unfortunately, the provision was repeated in the SGA 1893 in almost identical language, no attempt being made to repeal the earlier formulation. This provision, with the extra words of the FA italicised,[180] is now to be found in s 24 of the SGA 1979:

> 'Where a person, having sold goods, continues, or is, in possession of the goods or of the documents of title[181] to the goods, the delivery or transfer by that person, or by a mercantile agent[182] acting for him of the goods or documents of title under any sale, pledge[183] or other disposition[184] thereof, *or under any agreement for sale, pledge or other disposition thereof*,[180] to any person receiving the same in good faith and without notice of the previous sale, shall have the same effect as if the person making the delivery or transfer were expressly authorised by the owner of the goods to make the same.'

Once again, the statutory wording, and its judicial interpretation, needs careful analysis. In particular, the provision requires:

(1) A seller in possession (see para 21.39); and

(2) A delivery and disposition by him to a bf transferee (see para 21.41). However, if none of the successive transferees so qualifies, the first transferee (A) obtains title under the *nemo dat* rule.[185]

**[21.39] Seller in possession.** This exception to the *nemo dat* rule only applies where a seller is in possession.[186] Notice, first, the provision says 'sold', not 'agreed to sell':

---

177  Cmnd. 2958 (1966) paras 18; 40(5).

178  Compare the unpaid seller's powers and rights of resale: para 27.11.

179  This is effectively to reverse the decision in *Johnson v Credit Lyonnais* (see paras 19.10 and 21.13).

180  The extra words still stand by reason of the SGA, s 21(2)(a), which is set out at para 21.02; and note the difference in punctuation. See also sales by a buyer: para 21.34.

181  See the discussions of 'goods' and 'documents of title': para 23.03.

182  For the definition of ma, see SGA, s 26; and para 21.26.

183  For 'pledge' see paras 21.33 and 21.41.

184  The phrase 'sale, pledge, or other disposition' is considered in relation to s 2(1) of the FA: see para 21.33; and see para 21.49.

185  *Nicholson v Harper* [1895] 2 Ch 415.

186  *Anglo-Irish Asset Finance v DSG Financial Services* [1995] CLY 4491. For this purpose, there must be a contract of sale, so that a mortgagee is insufficient: see SGA, s 62(4), para 1.08.

in the latter case, the seller could still pass a good title by virtue of his property in the goods.[187] Second, 'possession' here has its ordinary commercial meaning, so that a seller may be in possession by an agent.[188] Third, the provision does not say that the seller need be in possession with the buyer's consent.[189]

Most of the litigation involving this provision has centred on the meaning of the phrase 'continues, or is, in possession'. In *Mitchell v Jones*:[190]

> B sold and delivered a horse to the appellant (A). Thirteen days later, B leased the horse from A and then sold and delivered it to C, a bfp. The New Zealand Supreme Court held that C was not protected by their equivalent of s 24.

Stout CJ explained that the meaning of the phrase is (at 935):

> 'first, that if a person sells goods and continues in possession, even though he has made a valid contract of sale, provided that he has not delivered them, he may to a *bona fide* buyer make a good title; and, secondly, the putting-in of the words "or is in possession of the goods" was meant to apply to a case of this character: If a vendor had not the goods when he sold them, but they came into his possession afterwards, then he would have possession of goods, and if he sold them to a *bona fide* purchaser he could make good title to them.'

The English courts have similarly insisted that the provision will only operate where the seller (B) remains in possession **qua** seller: but they extended this rule to cover the situation where there has been no actual delivery by the seller, merely a change in the nature of his possession. In *Staffs Motor Guarantee Ltd v British Wagon Co Ltd*[191] Mackinnon LJ held that the dealer (B) who had remained in physical possession, could not pass a good title under what is now s 24 because he was no longer in possession **qua** seller, but in the capacity of hirer. This development received the approval of the Court of Appeal in *Eastern Distributors Ltd v Goldring*.[192] Later, the courts had second thoughts on this matter (see para 21.40).

**[21.40]** Whilst paying lip-service to *Mitchell v Jones* (set out at para 21.39), the English decisions clearly went far beyond that case; and it would appear that they almost interpreted this exception to the *nemo dat* rule out of existence.[193] However, the Privy Council subsequently rejected the English case law on this point, and held that the disputed words refer, not to the nature of the seller's possession, but to the fact of his possession. In *Pacific Motor Auctions Ltd v Motor Credits Ltd*[194] a dealer unsuccessfully attempted to achieve a stocking plan by way of a sale and rehiring.

---

187 Even if the second buyer took with notice of the earlier agreement to sell: Goode, *Commercial Law*, 3rd edn, 431, fn 96. Compare buyers in possession at paras 21.44–6.

188 See s 1(2) of the FA set out at para 23.03; and *per* Branson J in *City Fur Manufacturing Co Ltd v Fureenbond (Brokers) London Ltd* [1937] 1 All ER 799, at 802 (see Bell, *Personal Property*, 56–7).

189 Cf. ss 2(1) and 9 of the FA: see para 21.31 and para 21.47.

190 (1905) 24 NZLR 932, SC.

191 Set out at para 21.28. See also *Olds Discount Ltd v Krett* [1940] 2 KB 117.

192 Set out at para 21.08, where the court accepted without question that A could not pass a good title under this exception because the character of his possession had changed from that of seller to bailee. See Goodhart (1957) 73 LQR 455, 459.

193 The only reported successful plea was a most unusual case: *Union Transport Finance Ltd v Ballardie* [1937] 1 KB 510.

194 [1965] AC 867; [1965] 2 All ER 105, PC.

Lord Pearce argued that what mattered was the dealer's physical possession.[195] His Lordship therefore concluded that the *Staffs Motor* case (set out at para 21.28), and *Goldring's* case (set out at para 21.08) *pro tanto*, were wrongly decided.[196] This lead was followed by the English Court of Appeal in *Worcester Works Finance Ltd v Cooden Engineering Co Ltd*:[197]

> The defendants (C) sold a car to B for £525, which was paid by cheque. B took delivery of the car and was registered as owner. Subsequently, B arranged a directly financed transaction whereunder the car was to be sold to the plaintiff finance company (A) who were to let it on hp terms to M. Whilst M signed a delivery receipt, he neither took delivery of the car nor paid any instalments. In the meantime, B's cheque to C had been dishonoured, and B relinquished possession of the car to C. To conceal his fraud from A, B for some time kept up payment of M's hire instalments.

The Court of Appeal unanimously agreed that B was a person who, having sold the car to A, *continued in possession* of it within the meaning of what is now s 24 of the SGA, because the italicised words referred to the **continuity of physical possession**, it being irrelevant that B remained in possession as bailee or trespasser; and the retaking of the car constituted a 'delivery' of it to C under a bf disposition (see para 21.41), so that C re-acquired a good title under this exception to the *nemo dat* rule. This new criterion of continuity of physical possession would seem both simpler and fairer, and will restore some worthwhile content to the provision; and it has been applied to a sale and rehiring transaction,[198] on the grounds that, as the sale and rehiring were a single transaction (para 17), there was under the sale a constructive transfer of possession from B to C1[199] and hence a constructive delivery to C1 within the SGA.[200]

**[21.41] Delivery and disposition to be a bf transferee.** The provision insists on all three of the following requirements.

(1) *Delivery or transfer.* As the intention of the legislature was to protect the first transferee to take possession (see para 21.38), the exception is only expressed to protect a person to whom there is a 'delivery or transfer'.[201] Thus, if the seller in possession (B) makes successive dispositions to different persons, the first to obtain physical possession obtains title under the exception:[202] for instance, the

---

195 'The object of the section is to protect an innocent purchaser who is deceived by the vendor's physical possession of the goods or documents and who is inevitably unaware of legal rights which follow the apparent power to dispose' (at 886). Part of this reasoning was cited with approval in the *Twelfth Report of the Law Reform Committee* (1966, Cmnd. 2958), para 20.

196 At 889. See also Atiyah, *Sale of Goods*, 10th edn, 393.

197 [1972] 1 QB 210; [1971] 3 All ER 708, CA (Goode 35 MLR 186).

198 *Michael Gerson (Leasing) Ltd v Wilkinson* (set out at para 21.41): A accepted that s 24 includes constructive delivery (at para 10).

199 So that B had a right to transfer possession to C1 under s 7(1) of the SGSA (para 20): see para 12.04A.

200 *Per* Clarke LJ at paras 21–31: see para 23.03. His Lordship expressly rejected the argument that, unless the case came within the definition of possession in s 1(2) of the FA (set out at para 23.03), there cannot have been a delivery within the SGA (paras 34–6). See also *per* Pill LJ at para 92.

201 'Delivery' seems to refer to goods, and 'transfer' to document of title: see para 21.49. It is doubtful whether a transfer of goods by deed falls within these expressions: *Kitto v Bilbie* (1895) 72 LT 266. See further Benjamin's *Sale of Goods*, 6th edn, paras 7.060 and 7.074.

202 If acting for the seller, must an ma have actual authority? Or is it sufficient that the ma is acting within the ocb within s 2(1) of FA (see para 21.25)?

*Worcester Works* case (see para 21.40), where C took physical possession of the car. However, the range of persons protected was extended in *Michael Gerson (Leasing) Ltd v Wilkinson.*[203]

> In March, B1 sought to raise money by a sale and leaseback of its plant and machinery, including the scheduled goods, to A; but B did not keep up the lease payments, though all the time retained physical possession of the goods. Subsequently, the goods were dealt with as follows:
>
> (1) In August, B1 sold and leased back the scheduled goods to C1; but, as B1 did not keep up the payments under this lease, C1 terminated the lease and sold the scheduled goods to C2. C1 and C2 successfully claimed title under s 24 of the SGA (see below).
>
> (2) Later, A terminated B1's March lease of all the goods, including the scheduled ones, and purported to sell them to B2, who resold them to C2. C2 unsuccessfully claimed title under s 25 of the SGA (see para 21.44).
>
> A claimed as owner all the plant and machinery in conversion. C1 and C2 were bf purchasers without notice.

As to the scheduled goods, the Court of Appeal unanimously agreed as follows: under the August sale and leaseback, there had been a constructive delivery of the goods to C1 (see para 21.40); and the result was that C1 obtained a good title under s 24 to the scheduled goods.

(2) *Disposition*. It is clear from the *Worcester Works* case (set out at para 21.40) that 'disposition' refers not to a transfer of legal possession, but of a proprietary interest in goods: B's transfer of legal (but not physical) possession to M was ignored, whilst his transfer of a proprietary interest to C satisfied this requirement. However, it would seem from the extra words in the FA that a mere agreement to dispose of the goods to C is sufficient for this purpose.[204] Four questions remain. *First*, since the formula 'under any sale, pledge or other disposition' is also found in ss 2(1) and 8 of the FA, does the formula have the same meaning in all three cases?[205] *Second*, does the express reference here to any 'pledge or other disposition' oust the general provision saving from the Act any transaction 'intended to operate by way of mortgage, pledge, charge or other security'?[206] *Third*, the rule requires a delivery under the disposition.[207] *Fourth*, by reason of the additional words in the FA referring to any agreement to sell etc, it may be that a conditional sub-buyer may obtain a good title provided his contract has matured into a sale, etc.[208]

---

203  [2001] QB 514; [2001] 1 All ER 148, CA.

204  See also ss 9 and 25(1) considered at para 21.49. *Contra* the estoppel exception: see para 21.08.

205  See para 21.33. Does it make any difference that ss 2–7 of the FA may not be applicable here? See para 21.47.

206  S 62(4): see further at para 1.08. *Contra Ladbroke Leasing (South West) Ltd v Reekie Plant Ltd* 1983 SLT 155.

207  Would a bailment for some other purpose be sufficient? Compare s 2(1) of FA, which does not expressly require a delivery: see para 21.33.

208  E.g. a *Romalpa* clause (see para 25.29) whose terms have been satisfied. *Aliter* if they have not: see the *Mills and Lawrence* case (set out at para 21.51).

(3)  Bona fide transferee. Both ss 8 and 24 are only expressed to operate in favour of:

> 'any[209] person receiving[210] the [goods] in good faith and without notice of the previous sale.'

A similar requirement was discussed in relation to mercantile agency, and here too raises questions as to the onus of proof (see para 21.36). Furthermore, in the *Worcester Works* case, where the Court of Appeal unanimously held that C had retaken the car 'in good faith and without notice',[211] Lord Denning MR said that the word 'notice' here meant actual notice, by which he meant actual knowledge on the part of C of the sale by B to A, or deliberately turning a blind eye to it.[212]

**[21.42]  The effect of the exception.** Where the requirements of ss 8 and 24 are satisfied, it is provided that the disposition with delivery to a bfp (C):

> 'shall have the same effect as if the person making the delivery or transfer were expressly authorised by the owner of the goods to make the same'.

Suppose B steals goods from O and sells them successively to A, C and D; and then B delivers them to C.

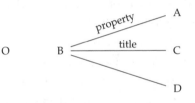

On ordinary common law principles (the first-in-time rule), B would pass his title to his first buyer (A: see para 21.38), retaining nothing to transfer to subsequent innocent buyers (C, D).[213] However, the effect of ss 8 and 24 is to transfer B's best title to his first purchaser to obtain possession (C).[214] Presumably, the term 'owner' refers to the person with the property in the goods under the disposition from B to A,[215] so that C acquires no better title than B had, and best title remains in O.[216]

---

209  To whom does 'any person', refer? See Rutherford and Todd [1979] CLJ 346, at 355–8.

210  It is submitted that C's state of mind is to be tested at the time of purported disposal of the goods to him, not delivery to him, so as to make sense of the reference to A's lien. *Contra* Goode, *Commercial Law*, 3rd edn, 433.

211  *Per* Megaw LJ, at 221, upholding the conclusion of the trial judge. See also the comments in the *Pacific Motor Auctions* case [1965] AC 867, PC.

212  Because 'our commercial law does not like constructive notice': *per* Lord Denning MR at 218E.

213  See Goode, *Commercial Law*, 3rd edn, 431.

214  Does it matter in what capacity C acquires possession? Or whether C acquires notice of the previous sales after his purchase but before taking delivery? See generally Rutherford and Todd [1979] CLJ 346.

215  *National Employers Mutual etc Ltd v Jones* (set out at para 21.54), *obiter per* Lord Goff at 432g–433a, delivering the unanimous judgment of the HL and relying on the history of the section.

216  Compare para 21.37 and para 21.54.

# BUYERS IN POSSESSION

**[21.43] The exception.** The converse situation to that of a seller in possession (see para 21.38) is covered by s 9 of the FA and s 25(1) of the SGA.[217] The provision, with the extra words of the FA italicised,[218] is as follows:

> 'Where a person, having bought or agreed to buy goods, obtains with the consent of the seller possession[219] of the goods or the documents of title to the goods,[220] the delivery or transfer by that person or by a mercantile agent[221] acting for him, of the goods or documents of title,[222] under any sale, pledge, or other disposition thereof,[223] *or under any agreement for sale, pledge, or other disposition thereof,*[218] to any person receiving the same in good faith and without notice of any lien or other right of the original seller in respect of the goods, shall have the same effect as if the person making the delivery or transfer were a mercantile agent in possession of the goods or documents of title with the consent of the owner.'

Amazingly, the bfp (C) taking a transfer of a document of title receives further statutory protection under both s 10 of the FA and s 47(2) of the SGA,[224] in terms which differ markedly from ss 9 and 25 and from each other as to effect,[225] but one beyond the scope of this work as involving business-to-business sales.

This extraordinary duplication of statutory provisions,[226] which have been restrictively interpreted,[227] require the following:

(1)  B to be in possession as buyer (see para 21.44);

(2)  With the consent of the seller (A) (see para 21.47); and

(3)  B to make a delivery and disposition to a bfp (C) (see para 21.49).

**[21.44] Bought or agreed to buy.** Sections 9 and 25 are only expressed to be applicable where a person in possession (B) has 'bought or agreed to buy'.[228] In *Michael Gerson (Leasing) Ltd v Wilkinson* (set out at para 21.41), C2 claimed all the plant and machinery on the basis that A had sold it to B2, who had resold it to C2: whilst the Court of Appeal were clear that there must at very least be a contract between

---

217 Care is required with the cases, since under the SGA 1893 this provision was numbered as s 25(2).
218 See para 21.38, fn 180.
219 See para 21.39.
220 See the discussion of 'goods' and 'documents of title', paras 21.29–30.
221 For the definition of ma, see SGA, s 26; and para 21.26.
222 For the transfer of documents of title, see s 10 of the FA and s 47(2) of the SGA; and further the 1st edn, para 21.48.
223 For 'pledge or other disposition', see para 21.41.
224 Even the ambit of ss 10 and 47 contains a small verbal discrepancy—'any' and 'a'. Does this matter?
225 Both are expressed to override A's rights of lien and stoppage, defeating them where B sells to C; but s 47(2) also expressly refers to a pledge by B to C. Does this make any difference?
226 All four versions were applied in the case of *Cahn v Pockett's Channel Ltd* [1899] 1 QB 643, CA.
227 They may even be confined to those circumstances where the true owner at least entered into a voidable contract to dispose of the goods: see para 21.54; and generally Goode, *Commercial Law*, 3rd edn, 434–5.
228 It is claimed that this emphasis on sale may cause anomalies where there is a contract to supply and fix: Atiyah, *Sale of Goods*, 10th edn, 398. But could not those difficulties be avoided by finding a hybrid contract: see para 2.05?

A and B2 before s 25 can operate,[229] the majority were prepared to find such a contract[230] under which B2 had agreed to buy (see para 21.45); but C2 seems to have failed at the next hurdle. By virtue of that contract, whilst B must obtain **possession** of the goods or documents of title to them,[231] such possession of goods may be actual or constructive (see para 23.03): it includes a temporary loan[232] and has even been held to extend to the situation where A delivers goods direct to C at the request of B.[233] The essence of the provision is that B, being in possession,[234] must as purchaser[235] satisfy one of the following criteria:[236]

(1) *'Bought'*. If B has bought goods, and obtained possession of them with the consent of the seller (A), then at first sight it seems that B should be able to pass a good title by virtue of his property and possession, no exception to the *nemo dat* rule being needed. However, it has been suggested that the effect of the exception is that the buyer (B) in possession of his own goods can only pass a good title in conformity with the terms of the exception.[237] Such a result would be startling; and there are two other possible explanations. First, just because a good title is passed under the exception where its terms are complied with, it does not follow that, where its terms are not complied with, a good title cannot be passed in any other way.[238] Second, it may be that the words 'bought or' are redundant, though it has been shown that there may be circumstances where these words are required to pass a good title under ss 9 and 25(1).[239]

(2) *'Agreed to buy'* (see para 21.45).

**[21.45/6] 'Agreed to buy'.** The phrase obviously comprehends ordinary conditional sales.[240] Now, it is tempting to assume that, where the seller (A) has agreed to sell, the buyer (B) must have agreed to buy; but this will not necessarily be so, because there can clearly be an agreement to sell without any agreement to buy, as where B purchases an option to buy.[241] The effect of this last distinction was to draw a sharp line between two very similar transactions on the basis of whether or not B has agreed to buy: if he has, there is a conditional sale within s 2(3) of the SGA, and B

---

229 The s 25 plea failed on a lack of consent to B2's possession: see para 21.47.
230 *Per* Bennett J at para 85, Pill LJ concurring at 93. Clarke LJ dissented on this point (para 57).
231 *Michael Gerson (Leasing) Ltd v Wilkinson* (above), *per* Clarke LJ at para 66, the other two judges agreeing (paras 82 and 88). As to the constructive delivery of goods, see para 21.40; and as to delivery of goods and transfer of documents of title, see generally, para 23.03.
232 *Marten v Whale* (set out at para 1.11).
233 *Four Point Garage Ltd v Carter* [1985] 3 All ER 12.
234 Must the possession be **qua** buyer, etc? Cf. para 21.40.
235 *Contra* if B only obtains the goods from A as agent for sale: *Shaw v Commissioner of Police* (set out at para 19.11).
236 The distinction between 'bought' and 'agreed to buy' is broadly whether the property in the goods has passed to the buyer: see para 1.10.
237 Atiyah, *Sale of Goods*, 3rd edn, 158; but see fn 238 below.
238 See Atiyah, *Sale of Goods*, 10th edn, 397.
239 Smith (1963) 7 SPTL 225–6; Rutherford and Todd [1976] JBL 262; Benjamin's *Sale of Goods*, 6th edn, para 7.069; Goode, *Commercial Law*, 3rd edn, 434.
240 E.g. *Lee v Butler* (set out at para 1.15); *Marten v Whale* (set out at para 1.11); *Michael Gerson (Leasing) Ltd v Wilkinson* (see para 21.44).
241 But see *Forthright Finance Ltd v Carlyle Finance Ltd* (set out at para 1.22). The question of whether 'sale or return' transactions fall within s 25(1) is discussed at para 20.27.

may therefore pass a good title to C under s 25(1) of the SGA;[240] but, if B has not agreed to buy,[242] the transaction is not a conditional sale and B cannot pass a good title under this exception to the *nemo dat* rule.[243]

Statute has settled doubts as to whether hp legislation applied to conditional sales by making express provision for such transactions.[244] However, in the course of a partial assimilation of conditional sales and hp transactions, s 25(2) of the SGA now provides that, for the purposes of s 25(1),[245] buyers under regulated conditional sales are not to be taken to be persons who have agreed to buy.[246] The effect of s 25(2) would appear to be that only the following contracts for the sale of goods are left within s 25(1): those under which the buyer has bought the goods (see para 21.44); or contracts where there is a reservation of property, but **either** the price is not payable by instaments,[247] **or** the transaction does not amount to a consumer credit agreement.[248]

Whilst it is true that the HPA 1964 did introduce an entirely new exception to the *nemo dat* rule (see para, 21.55, *et seq.*), the effect of s 25(2) is to reduce the statutory protection of the bfp by denying him the protection of the much wider exception in s 25(1). Not only does this run counter to the general trend of legislation, but it adds further complication to an already unduly difficult branch of the law.[249]

**[21.47/8] The seller's consent to disposal.** Unlike the provisions in respect of sellers in possession (see para 21.39), the present exception to the *nemo dat* rule is only expressed to operate where the buyer (B) obtains possession with the consent of the seller (A).[250] Leaving aside possession (see para 21.44), two questions arise:

(1) *What is the meaning of consent?* It will be recalled that consent to possession is similarly required in the case of the mercantile agency exception (see para 21.31). On the other hand, ss 2 and 9 do not fall under the same sub-heading of the FA,[251] which might imply that the provisions of s 2 do not apply to buyers in possession. This point was taken by the House of Lords in *Inglis v Robertson*,[252] an appeal from Scotland,[253] where a wine merchant (B) contracted to buy from

---

242 Or if his agreement to buy is void *ab initio*: see para 21.19.

243 E.g. *Helby v Matthews* (set out at para 1.22).

244 The development was to be found in the HP Acts, is now embodied in the CCA and expressly excludes conditional sales from the definition of hp: see para 1.24.

245 A similar limitation was introduced into s 9 of the FA by para 2 of Sched 4 of the CCA.

246 For conditional sales within the CCA, see paras 1.16 and 5.19. The result is to take outside s 25 of the SGA cases like *Lee v Butler* (above), the very decision which appeared to render necessary the invention of hp (see para 1.22).

247 E.g. *Marten v Whale* (above); *Newtons of Wembley Ltd v Williams* (set out at para 21.51); *Mount Ltd v Jay* [1960] 1 QB 159.

248 E.g. because B is a corporate buyer (see para 5.24) or the agreement exempt (see para 5.14).

249 The *Twelfth Report of the Law Reform Committee* (1966, Cmnd. 2958) para 28, thought it inappropriate for the Report to recommend any changes in this area.

250 Goode, *Commercial Law*, 3rd edn, 435–6.

251 Ss 2–7 are sub-headed 'Dispositions by Mercantile Agents', whilst ss 8–10 are sub-headed 'Dispositions by Sellers and Buyers of Goods'.

252 [1898] AC 616, HL(S).

253 The HL held that Scots law applied, but that the FA 1889 was applicable to Scotland by virtue of the Factors (Scotland) Act 1890.

A whisky then lying in a bonded warehouse and later pledged it to C. Their Lordships found for the unpaid seller (A) on the following grounds:

(a) that the pledge of the documents of title did not amount to a pledge of the goods under FA, s 3, because ss 2–7 of the FA were only applicable where the transferor was a ma (which B was not);[254] and

(b) that B had not 'obtained' the goods with consent within s 9 (see below).

However, the English Court of Appeal has twice held that the issue of consent in ss 9 and 25(1) is subject to ss 2(2), (3) and (4) of the FA;[255] and it is submitted that these decisions will probably be followed in England.[256]

(2) *What is meant by 'obtains'?* Sections 9 and 25(1) are expressed to cover only those situations where the buyer:

> 'obtains with the consent of the seller possession of the goods or the documents of title to the goods'.

The meaning of these words was considered by the House of Lords in *Inglis v Robertson*, where their Lordships concluded that s 9 did not confer on the pledgee (C) a title free from the rights of the unpaid seller (A), because B did not obtain the documents of title either from A or with his consent, but 'in his own right and in his own name'.[257]

**[21.49] Disposition by B**. The provision insists on all three of the following requirements.

(1) *Delivery or transfer*. Where C seeks to rely upon a delivery (see para 23.03) of the goods, or part of them,[258] he must show that B has voluntarily transferred possession of them to C. Thus, in *The Saetta*,[259] a charterparty case, Clarke J held that B had agreed to buy the bunkers and obtained possession of them with the consent of A (see para 21.44), but denied that the constructive transfer of possession of them to C amounted to the voluntary delivery required by s 25(1).[260]

(2) *Disposition*. Similar to the requirements in respect of dispositions, or agreements to dispose, by sellers in possession (see para 21.41), there is here the additional factor that ss 10 and 47(2) specifically require that the disposition by B should be for valuable consideration, but it is not clear that ss 9 and 25(1) impose a similar requirement.[261]

---

254 At 624, 628 and 630; and para 25.15. This result has been characterised as 'bizarre', because it allows an ma greater rights of disposal than an owner: Bell, *Personal Property*, 59–60.

255 See *Newtons of Wembley Ltd v Williams* (set out at para 21 51). See also *per* Sellers J in *Du Jardin v Beadman Bros Ltd* [1952] 2 QB 712 at 716.

256 Benjamin's *Sale of Goods*, 6th edn, para 7.072. But see the recommendations of the Law Reform Committee: para 22.52.

257 *Per* Lord Watson at 629. See also per Lord Herschel, at 630. Why was the warehousekeeper not treated as the agent of A to issue the documents, in which case it could be said that the documents were issued by and with the consent of A?

258 As to the effect of a sub-sale of an individual bulk, see Nicol (1979) 42 MLR 129.

259 [1994] 1 All ER 851; [1994] 1 WLR 1334.

260 Cf. *Michael Gerson (Leasing) Ltd v Wilkinson* (see para 21.40), *per* Clarke LJ at para 15.

261 See *Thomas Graham Ltd v Glenrothes Corporation* [1968] SLT 2; and also para 21.33.

(3)  *A 'bona fide' transferee*. Sections 9 and 25(1) speak of the goods or documents of title being delivered or transferred to:[262]

> 'any person receiving the same in good faith and without notice of any lien or other right of the original seller in respect of the goods'.

As in the cases of sellers in possession and mercantile agency, this raises the same issue as to the burden of proof (see paras 21.36 and 21.41). Neither the FA nor the SGA defines *notice*, so this matter is left to the common law.[263] In *The Saetta*, Clarke J said *obiter*[264] that 'notice' means actual notice and not constructive notice; that the issue is objective; that a person is deemed to have notice if he deliberately turns a blind eye, but that a commercial man has no general duty to make enquiries; and that the burden of proof lies on C.

**[21.50/1] The effect of the exception**. As regards the effect of the exception, the extra words of s 9 of FA seem to bring within the provision those transactions where the second disposition is only **an agreement** 'for the sale, pledge or other disposition'. It might be thought that the effect of these words is that C can acquire a good title where he has only agreed to buy.[265] But this was denied in *Mills and Lawrence v Harris (Wholesale Meat) Ltd*:[266]

> Wholesaler (A) agreed to sell meat (which turned out to be defective) to Highway Food Ltd (B), who in turn agreed to sub-sell and delivered it to a meat processor (C). Each contract contained a *Romalpa* clause (see para 25.29), reserving property until payment. Before payment under either contract, B's secured creditors appointed administrative receivers (see para 19.14). A contacted C, who had already processed some 10% of the meat, and they made the following arrangement: C returned the unprocessed meat directly to A who removed the defect and then sold that meat direct to C.

The judge held that the property in the goods never passed from A to B because of the retention of title clause (see para 20.28), so that the position with regard to the contract of sale from B to C was as follows:

(i)   *The unprocessed meat*. As between A and B, s 9 of the FA was satisfied, because B had 'agreed to buy' (see para 21.44). However, as between B and C, ss 9 and 25(1) are drafted so that, where they operate, the disposition by B 'shall have the same effect as if [B] were an ma in possession . . . with the consent of [A]';[267] that is, as if B were expressly authorised by A to dispose of the goods (see para 21.52). This last seems to require that B must actually sell the goods (as opposed to agree to see them) to C: as C had not paid the price to B, this had not happened; and so the judge argued that s 9 did not operate (at 279D).

---

262  As to good faith, see SGA, s 61(3). As to liens, see para 25.02. As to 'other rights', e.g. *Romalpa* clauses, see para 25.30; rights analogous to liens under SGA, s 39(2), see para 24.06. As to 'original seller', it is argued below that this refers to A (see para 21.54).

263  See *per* Tenterden LCJ in *Evans v Truman* (1831) I Mood & R 10.

264  The principles were laid down by Neill J in *Feuer Leather Corp v Frank Johnstone & Sons* [1981] Com. LR 251 at 253. They were accepted by the parties, and seem to have been applied by Clarke J in *The Saetta* (above).

265  Benjamin, *Sale of Goods*, 6th edn, para 5-156, fn 58.

266  (1995) 14 Tr LR 273; *sub nom Re Highway Foods International Ltd* [1994] CLY 4029.

267  Atiyah, *Sale of Goods*, 10th edn, 404, 471.

Accordingly, A retained title to the unprocessed meat which it repossessed (at 280D): this, it resold directly to C after removing the defect, so that A was entitled to the price due under the resale contract (at 280F). If the judge is correct, the extra italicised words in s 9 would seem to be of no effect whatever.

*(ii) The processed meat*. See para 25.33.

**[21.52/3] Sections 9 and 25(1)**. Where the conditions laid down by ss 9 and 25(1) are satisfied, it is provided thereby that the disposition by the buyer (B):

'shall have the same effect as if the person making the delivery or transfer were a mercantile agent in possession of the goods or documents of title with the consent of the owner'.

This is an obvious reference back to s 2(1) of the FA (set out at para 21.25), but gives no indication how much of that provision was being incorporated. There are at least two possibilities.

(1) *The lesser incorporation*. The effect might be to incorporate merely the result of s 2(1), so that the disposition by B:

'shall be as valid as if he were expressly authorised by the owner of the goods to make the same'.

If so, the result would be the same as in the case of sales by a seller in possession (see para 21.42).

(2) *The greater incorporation*. It might be read so that a disposition by B:

'made by him when acting in the ordinary course of business of a mercantile agent shall . . . be as valid as if he were expressly authorised by the owner of the goods to make the same'.

This would recognise the difference in wording from the exception in respect of sellers in possession (above).

The vital difference between the two is whether B is required to dispose of the goods in the ocb of an ma; and the Court of Appeal seems to have changed its mind on this point. In *Lee v Butler* (set out at para 1.15), the court appeared to take the first (lesser) view, there being no hint in that case of such a greater requirement. But in *Newtons of Wembley Ltd v Williams*[268] the court took the second (greater) view.

On June 15th, the plaintiff (A) sold and delivered a Sunbeam car to rogue B in return for a cheque, it being agreed that the property should not pass until B's cheque was cleared. On June 18th, A found that B's cheque would not be met, and immediately took steps to try to recover the car. In July, C *bona fide* agreed to buy the car from B in the Warren Street car market; and thereafter C sold the car to D. In A's action to recover the car, the issue thus turned on whether C had a good title to transfer to D.

It was held that B had only obtained a voidable title, which had been avoided within a few days of June 18th (see para 21.22); but the court nevertheless decided

---

268 [1965] 1 QB 560; [1964] 3 All ER 532, CA. Affirming the first instance decision of Davies LJ.

that C had acquired a good title under the FA. In the course of examining ss 2, 8 and 9 of that Act, Pearson LJ pointed out that B in possession might or might not be an ma and continued:[269]

> 'When the provisions of s 2 are applied to the s 9 position of [B] this is the *prima facie* result: if the transaction is made by the person concerned when acting in the ordinary course of the business of a mercantile agent, the transaction is validated: on the other hand, if the transaction is made by him when not acting in the ordinary course of business of a mercantile agent, the transaction is not validated.'

On this basis, the Court of Appeal agreed that the determination of A's consent was irrelevant under s 9 by reason of s 2(2) of the FA (set out at para 21.31); that the test of whether a disposition (see paras 21.34–35) was made in the ocb for the purposes of s 9 was the same as that under s 2 (see paras 21.34–35); and that the sale by B in Warren St, where there was an established second-hand car market, was made in the ocb.[270] In *The Saetta*,[271] Clarke J indicated that, had the matter been of first impression, he would not have introduced such a further requirement; but, feeling bound by *Newtons*, he found that C was acting in the ocb of ma.

There is no doubt that, if B is an ma disposing of the goods in the ocb, he can pass a good title under this exception.[272] However, if B is not an ma, are the courts required to ask what would have been the situation if he had been? This difficult task has been attempted by an English court;[273] and in *Newtons* the court were saved from the issue by the accident that B happened to dispose of the car in the Warren St car market, hence looking like an ma. However, *Newtons* has been rejected in the Commonwealth in favour of the above lesser incorporation.[274] *Newtons* would appear incompatible with *Oppenheimer v Attenborough*.[275] It would also severely restrict the operation of ss 9 and 25(1),[276] and would appear to have rendered unnecessary the development of hp on the basis of the device sanctioned in *Helby v Matthews* (set out at para 1.22).

**[21.54] The title transferred**. The range of operation of this exception came before the English courts in *National Employers Mutual etc Ltd v Jones*.[277]

---

269  At 578. He argued that the difference in wording between ss 8 and 9 must have been intended to bring about some difference in result because the difference was repeated in s 25 of the SGA. See also *per* Sellers LJ, at 574–5.

270  *Per* Sellers and Pearson LJJ, at 575, 580. Why was it not pleaded as a sale in market overt (as to which, see para 21.05)?

271  [1994] 1 All ER 851.

272  *Forthright Finance Ltd v Carlyle Finance Ltd* (set out at para 1.21).

273  *Lambert v G & C Finance Corpn* (1963) 107 SJ 666 (private seller B sold second-hand car without the log-book); but see para 21.35.

274  See Atiyah, *Sale of Goods*, 10th edn, 407.

275  Set out at para 21.34. The bfp thought that the broker was acting as principal, so that even if ss 9 and 25(1) do require the disposition to be in the ocb as in s 2(1), this should not unduly restrict the scope of the exception.

276  For arguments why this (surely *obiter?*) conclusion was wrong, see Goode, *HP Law and Practice*, 2nd edn, 613–14. For its reversal, see the recommendation of the *Twelfth Report of the Law Reform Committee* (1966 Cmnd. 2958), paras 23, 24; and Benjamin's *Sale of Goods*, 6th edn, para 7.079.

277  [1990] AC 24; [1988] 2 All ER 425, HL (see Brown 104 LQR 516; Tiplady [1988] LMCLQ 297).

A Fiesta car owned by Miss H was stolen and sold down a chain of buyers to L, to T, to A, to B, to C. Standing in the shoes of Miss H,[278] her insurer sued to recover from C the value of the car. C pleaded title under ss 9 and 25. It was agreed that C was completely honest.

The Court of Appeal decided that title remained in H under the *nemo dat* rule (see para 19.11); and this decision was unanimously affirmed by the House of Lords on different grounds.[279] In delivering the judgment of the House, Lord Goff traced the history of ss 9 and 25, arguing as follows (at 432C): the FA 1877 referred to the transaction taking effect as if B were entrusted by the 'vendor' (A) with the documents of title; whereas s 9 of the FA 1889 spoke instead of the 'consent of the owner'. He reasoned that, for this change in expression to entail an alteration in meaning so that **owner** referred to Miss H[280] instead of A,[281]

'would constitute a change in policy of a fundamental kind, of which there is no evidence whatsoever in the remainder of the 1889 Act'.

The result is to reaffirm the estoppel basis of the FA exceptions to the *nemo dat* rule (see para 21.24): A, who has done the entrusting to B, has his title barred as against C; and because title to goods is not normally traceable very far, this will often determine such a title dispute.[282]

## SUPPLIES OF MOTOR VEHICLES[283]

**[21.55] The exception.** The decision in *Helby v Matthews* (set out at para 1.22) to the effect that a hirer under an hp agreement could not pass a good title under ss 9 and 25(1) (see para 21.43) is particularly likely to work hardship on a bfp of a motor vehicle from the hirer. Accordingly, there was introduced a new exception to the *nemo dat* rule in Part III of the HPA 1964.[284] Unfortunately, in order to keep this new exception within the ambit of the mischief at which it was aimed, it proved necessary to draft it in extremely complex language, running to some four pages of the Statute Book.[285]

The exception is expressed to override the *nemo dat* rule but to be without

---

278 Having paid out Miss H, her insurer acquired her rights in the Fiesta by subrogation (cf. para 25.07).
279 For trenchant criticism of the majority reasoning of the CA, see Tiplady (1988) 51 MLR 240.
280 This was the dissenting CA view of Buckley LJ (at 440f).
281 At 432e. For academic support, see Atiyah, *Sale of Goods*, 10th edn, 408; Goode, *Commercial Law*, 3rd edn, 437–8; Dobson [1987] JBL at 306.
282 Unless a case is taken outside this exception as being a consumer credit agreement: see para 21.45.
283 See generally Goode, *HP Law & Practice*, 2nd edn, 617–30; Guest, *Law of HP*, paras 757–71; Benjamin's *Sale of Goods*, 6th edn, para 7.085, *et seq*.
284 As amended and set out in Sched 4 of the CCA. All subsequent references are to this amended version. Does the CCA version apply where the transaction is unregulated; or does the original version then apply?
285 The *Twelfth Report of the Law Reform Committee* (1966, Cmnd. 2958), para 27, asks whether it is necessary to distinguish between motor vehicles and other goods. One might go further, and ask whether it is necessary to have an exception of this complexity at all. Finance companies sometimes argue that this limited exception against them contravenes the European Convention of Human Rights (see generally, para 3.09A).

prejudice to the FA or any other Act enabling the apparent owner to dispose of goods (s 27(5)). Its scope is set out in s 27(1), which says that:

> 'This section applies where a motor vehicle has been bailed under a hire-purchase agreement, or has been agreed to be sold under a conditional sale agreement, and, before the property in the vehicle has become vested in the debtor, he disposes of the vehicle to another person.'

Whilst the terms **hire-purchase** and **conditional sale** are to have the meanings assigned to them by the CCA,[286] the other restrictions of the CCA are not applicable: so, it does not matter whether the agreement is exempt (see para 5.14); nor whether the buyer or hirer is a body corporate (see para 5.24). Further, it should be noticed that s 27(1) is only expressed to operate where a motor vehicle (see para 4.37) is disposed of by a debtor (hirer or buyer)[287] under an hp or conditional sale agreement:[288] it does not extend to leasing/simple hiring (see para 1.18) nor bills of sale (see para 25.26); and it is not needed in the case of credit sales (see para 1.13). The insistence on an **agreement** means that s 27 can have no application if the proposal form put forward by the hirer or buyer is not accepted (see para 10.02); nor where that agreement is illegal or void *ab initio*, as where the hirer gives a false identity to the finance company;[289] but that it can apply where the agreement is merely voidable,[290] or unenforceable under the CCA.[291]

It is unclear for how long a person is to be deemed a **debtor** for the purposes of s 27. Whilst s 29(4) seems to suggest that once a person has become a **debtor**, he is always deemed to be one for the purposes of s 27,[292] it has been argued that s 27 should no longer be applicable once the owner has resumed possession of the motor vehicle.[293]

**[21.56] Trade or finance purchaser.** Within the ambit of Part III (see para 21.55), Parliament intended to protect consumers ('private purchasers'), but not persons in the motor trade.[294] The latter category, it termed **'trade or finance purchasers'**,

---

286  S 29 does this by setting out definitions of 'conditional sale' and 'hp' in terms identical (except as regards omission of any reference to land with regard to the former) to those in the CCA: as to which, see respectively, paras 1.16 and 1.24.

287  *Keeble v Combined Lease Finance plc* [1998] CLY 5656; [1998] GCCR 2065, CA (disposition by one joint debtor).

288  E.g. *Carlyle Finance Ltd v Pallas Industrial Finance Ltd* (set out at para 10.08). It obviously does not apply to a disposal by a person who has stolen the goods from the hirer or buyer: see Atiyah, *Sale of Goods*, 10th edn, 411; Guest, *Law of HP*, 760. As to dispositions by an employee of the hirer, see (1992) 47 CC2/27.

289  *Shogun Finance Ltd v Hudson* (set out at para 10.15). Because they held that there was no contract between the finance company and the rogue (see para 10.15), a bare majority of the HL decided that the rogue was not the 'debtor' under an hp agreement, so that the case fell outside s 27(1) (at paras 44, 119 and 180). So, it is to the disadvantage of the finance company to make pre-contract identity checks which are too strenuous.

290  *Hitchens v General Guarantee Corpn Ltd* [2001] CLY 880, CA (directly financed agreement made orally; distinguishing *Financings Ltd v Stimson* (set out at para 10.08)).

291  *Majid v TMV Finance Ltd* [1999] CLY 2448, Cty Ct. What if the agreement has been avoided (see para 21.19)?

292  *Chartered Trust PLC v Conlay* [1998] CLY 2516, Cty Ct.

293  See Goode, *Op. cit.*, 620; Guest, *Law of HP*, para 759.

294  Persons in the motor trade were expected to protect themselves by prior checks with HPI: see para 8.35. It has been suggested that fresh attention should be given to the need to protect bf 'trade or finance purchasers': *per* Lord Edmund-Davies in *Moorgate Mercantile Co Ltd v Twitchings* (set out at paras 21.16/7), at 922C.

defined in s 29(2) as 'a purchaser who, at the time of the disposition to him, carries on a business[295] which consists, wholly or partly of' (a) dealing in motor vehicles[296] or (b) directly financing such business.[297] Any other purchaser is a *private purchaser* (s 29(2): see para 21.57), which distinction was considered in *Stevenson v Beverley Bentinck Ltd.*[298]

> A was the owner of a car let on hp to B. Before completing the payments, B purported to sell the car to C, who took bf and without notice of the hp agreement. At the time of the purchase, C was employed full-time as a tool-room inspector, but in his spare time bought and sold cars: in the previous 18 months he had some 37 dealings in cars, some on his own account and some on account of a principal. When A sued for conversion of the car, C pleaded title as a 'private purchaser' within Part III of the HPA.

Notwithstanding that C bought this car for his own personal use, the Court of Appeal unanimously held that he was a **trade or finance purchaser** within the foregoing provision, pointing out that the provision contains no such qualification as *acting* 'in the course of business',[299] so that the courts were concerned with status rather than capacity.[300] Thus, C could not acquire a Part III title (see para 21.58), though a multi-national corporation outside the motor trade could qualify as a *private purchaser*.[301] Without express reference to *Stevenson*, a similar answer was reached by a unanimous Court of Appeal in *GE Capital Bank Ltd v Rushton*.[302]

> By way of a stocking plan (see para 16.20), in 2002 the Bank (B) provided finance for a car dealer to buy seven cars on its behalf. In January 2004, to raise money, the dealer sold and delivered those seven cars to R, who admitted that he bought the cars as a matter of business. In February, B terminated the stocking plan; and the next day R sold one of the cars to J. On the basis that R and J had jointly removed the cars from the dealer, B sued them both in conversion (see para 19.05), both defendants alleging a Part III title. R's defence under s 27(2) failed (see below), but J's defence under s 27(3) succeeded (see para 21.59).

As to s 27(2), the Court concluded that R was a trade purchaser within s 29(2) because at the time of his purchase he came within the phrase 'carries on business' in s 29(2)[303] on the basis that his purchase was 'a one-off adventure in the nature of trade, carried through with a view to profit' (at para 40).

---

295 As to carrying on a business, cf. CCA, s 189(2): see paras 5.36 and 6.12.
296 What if he only repairs cars? Or is a scrap dealer?
297 For finance companies, see para 2.17; and for direct financing, see para 2.20.
298 [1976] 2 All ER 606; [1976] 1 WLR 483, CA.
299 Cf. the undertakings as to fitness and quality (see para 14.04) and exemption clauses (see para 18.18).
300 At All ER 608b, 609e and 610a. Is this confined to those who deal as principal rather than as agent or employee?
301 Nor is the provision confined to regulated agreements: see para 21.55.
302 [2006] 3 All ER 865; [2005] EWCA Civ 1556, CA.
303 At para 40. In delivering the judgment of the court, Moore-Blick LJ found support in authorities on 'in the course of business' in the following branches of the law: Moneylenders Act 1900, ss 2 and 6 (see para 5.36); TDA, s 1(1) (see para 4.03A); UCTA, s 12(1) (see para 18.18); SGA, s 14(2) (see para 14.04).

**[21.57] Dispositions to 'private purchasers'.** Where the disposition within s 27(1) (see para 21.55) is to a **private purchaser** (see para 21.56), s 27(2) provides that, if:

> 'he is a purchaser of the motor vehicle in good faith without notice of the hire-purchase or conditional sale agreement (the 'relevant agreement') that disposition shall have effect as if the creditor's title to the vehicle has been vested in the debtor immediately before that disposition'.

1.  *The disposition.* Section 29(1) carefully defines the term 'disposition' in a manner which includes certain types of contract.[304] In respect of such a 'disposition', s 27 has an effect which is both wider than s 25(1) of the SGA in that it does not require delivery, and narrower in that it does not cover pledges and liens (see paras 21.43–54). But it would not apply to gifts by the debtor, nor by the debtor's partner.

2.  *To a private purchaser.* Section 27(2) only operates where the disposition is to a **private purchaser** and s 29(3) explains that:

    > 'a person becomes a purchaser of a motor vehicle if, and at the time when, a disposition of the vehicle is made to him'.

    Moreover, it should be noted that **disposition** is defined in s 29(1) in such a way that there may be two dispositions in the case of an hp agreement with a **private purchaser**: (a) when the contract is made; and (b) when the option is exercised.[305]

3.  *In good faith and without notice.* A private purchaser[305] cannot obtain the benefit of s 27 unless he takes in good faith **and** without notice of the prior agreement. There are two separate requirements which must both be satisfied. It would appear that the underlying burden of proof of these above requirements is on the purchaser;[306] but the Act helps him by laying down certain presumptions in s 28 (see para 21.59). 'Notice' is defined by s 29(3) as actual notice at the time of disposition to him, e.g. where his seller said that he would pay off his car finance out of the price to be paid, or the buyer successfully searches the title register.[307] It would therefore appear that constructive notice does not prevent a person claiming the benefit of s 27.[308] Further, in *Barker v Bell*[309] it was held that the agreement referred to in s 29(3) was only a **relevant** agreement,[310] meaning one to which the goods were subject at the time of the disposition.[311]

---

304  S 29(1) includes ordinary and conditional sales and hp. Does it extend to the situation where goods are taken in part-exchange or swapped (see para 2.09)? See the unusual conditional sale in *Dodds* case (below).

305  What is the position if the purchaser is a motor dealer at the time he signs the agreement but not when he exercises his option; or *vice versa*? See Goode, *HP Law & Practice*, 2nd edn, 623.

306  See Benjamin's *Sale of Goods*, 6th edn, para 7-097.

307  See para 21.01. So, it is to the disadvantage of the bfp to make such checks and to the advantage of the finance company to encourage the bfp to make pre-contract checks.

308  E.g. where an hp agreement is registered with HPI (see para 21.01). There is no duty to search HPI (see para 21.15).

309  [1971] 2 All ER 867; [1971] 1 WLR 983 CA (private purchaser falsely informed that all hp instalments had been paid; obtained Pt III title).

310  'Or was' in s 27(3) was restricted to a relevant agreement which had automatically terminated on disposition (see para 26.09): *per* Lord Denning MR at 869d.

311  See s 27(2). As to the burden of proof, see Benjamin's *Sale of Goods*, 6th edn, para 7.097.

The effect of these provisions was considered in *Dodds v Yorkshire Bank Finance Ltd*.[312]

> A let a Porsche car on hp to a builder (B). When his business got into financial difficulties, B sought to raise money from X. X arranged for Miss Dodds (C) to purchase the Porsche from B. As C was suspicious, B gave her a receipt saying 'I confirm that there is no hp agreement on this vehicle'. A having repossessed the Porsche, C claimed a Part III title. It was accepted that she had no notice of the hp agreement.

The Court of Appeal unanimously held that the transaction with C was an unusual type of conditional sale. However, A argued that, as a suspicious purchaser, C was not in good faith: whilst good faith was not defined in Part III, A conceded that it had the same meaning as in the SGA (see para 21.20). Neill LJ commented:

> 'That means that good faith is equated with honesty and bad faith with dishonesty.'

His Lordship pointed out that C's suspicions were allayed by the receipt and that she was therefore acting in good faith and acquired a Part III title.[313] Factors relevant to good faith would appear to include the price paid, location of the transaction and absence of documents.

4. *Creditor and debtor.* Under s 27(2), the title of the 'creditor' (A)[314] will vest in the 'debtor' (C).[315]

**[21.58] Effect**. Section 27(2) provides that a disposition within its ambit:

> 'shall have effect as if the creditor's title to the vehicle had been vested in the debtor immediately before that disposition'.

However, s 29(5) explains that:

> 'any reference to the title of the creditor to a motor vehicle which has been bailed under a hire-purchase agreement, or agreed to be sold under a conditional sale agreement, and is disposed of by the debtor, is a reference to such title (if any) to the vehicle as, immediately before that disposition, was vested in the person who then was the creditor in relation to the agreement'.

Suppose A is in possession of a motor vehicle which has been stolen from O; A lets it on hp to B; B wrongfully sells it to C during the currency of the agreement; and C resells it to D:

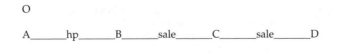

O

A_____hp_____B_____sale_____C_____sale_____D

---

312 [1992] GCCR 1621, CA (see 47 CC1/7).

313 Miss Dodds gave evidence that she thought the builder would not sign the receipt if untrue. Would a business buyer (a private purchaser within Pt III) likewise be in good faith when insisting on such a receipt?

314 'Creditor' is defined in s 29(1) as the bailor in hp or the seller in sale or his assignee. Cf. the CCA definitions: see para 5.25.

315 'Debtor' is defined in s 29(4) as the bailee under an hp agreement or the buyer in a sale (but not his assignee). Cf. the CCA definition: see para 5.24. As to s 29(4), see further, para 21.55.

If C acts *bona fide*,[316] the effect of ss 27 and 29(5) is to confer on him A's title (usually called a Part III title[317]), though best title remains in O.[318] Suppose A can claim title under one of the other exceptions to the *nemo dat* rule: does this imply that C may, if he wishes, affirm the supply to him and stand in A's shoes and similarly claim title under that exception?[319] If C acts *male fide*,[316] neither C nor D can claim the benefit of s 27, which is only expressed to apply where the **first** purchaser from B acts *bona fide*; but, provided C does act *bona fide*, D will have the benefit of s 27 even though he acts *male fide*[320] or is a dealer.[321] Finally, it should be noticed that s 27(6) explicitly saves any civil or criminal liability of A.[322] In *Barber v NWS Bank Plc* (set out at para 12.04), the Judge ignored C's Part III title on the basis that, even so, the effect of s 27(6) was to preserve C's action against the innocent finance company.[323]

**[21.59] Dispositions to trade or finance purchasers**. Suppose A is in possession of a motor vehicle which has been stolen from O; A lets it on hp to B and during the currency of the agreement B wrongfully sells it to C, a bf *trade or finance purchaser*; and C later resells to D, a bf *private purchaser*, who resells to E:[324]

O

A_____hp_____B_____sale_____C (op)_____sale_____D (fpp)_____sale_____E

Section 27(3) terms C *the original purchaser*, and provides that, where C is a *trade or finance purchaser* (see para 21.56):

> 'then if the person who is the first private purchaser of the motor vehicle after that disposition (the 'first private purchaser') is a purchaser of the vehicle in good faith without notice of the relevant agreement, the disposition of the vehicle to the first private purchaser shall have effect as if the title of the creditor to the vehicle had been vested in the debtor immediately before he disposed of it to the original purchaser'.

The effect of s 27(3) on the above example is that the title of A ('the creditor') is deemed to have vested in B ('the debtor') immediately before he disposed of the vehicle to C ('the original purchaser'), with the result that, utilising this fiction, C can pass A's title to D ('the first private purchaser': s 29(5): set out at para 21.58).[325] So long as D acts *bona fide*, D obtains, and can pass to E, A's title irrespective

---

316 The term *bona fide* purchaser is used to mean one who takes in good faith and without notice, and the term *mala fide* purchaser for one who does not.

317 See *Royscot Trust Ltd v Rogerson* (set out at para 27.28).

318 Under the *nemo dat* rule: see para 19.11. Cf. para 21.54.

319 See Goode, *HP Law & Practice*, 2nd edn, 624.

320 D will not then be guilty of handling stolen goods: Theft Act 1968, s 24(3).

321 D will as a dealer commonly discover that C has tendered him a Pt III title through a search of HPI (see para 2.18). As to whether this will amount to a breach by C of the SGA, s 12(1), see Goode, *Commercial Law*, 3rd edn, 441; and generally, para 12.03.

322 E.g. the tort of conversion (see para 19.04) or crime of theft.

323 This seems to beg the question: Does C have an action against NWS where C acquires a Pt III title? See *Freeman v Walker* [2002] GCCR 3025, CA (note severe criticism in the Comment).

324 Cf. *Butterworth's* case (set out at para 12.06).

325 *GE Capital Ltd v Rushton* (set out at para 21.56), J in purchasing one car from R (at para 55).

of whether E takes *bona fide*; but best title remains in O.[326] Notwithstanding that A's title passes through B and C to D, s 27(6) makes it clear that B and C are to remain both civilly and criminally liable.[326] Where the disposition to D is by way of a financed hp transaction,[327] s 27(4) provides that, when the property in the vehicle is transferred to D or E under the terms of the hp agreement,[328] D or E, as the case may be, will obtain A's title.[329]

Particularly where some trade or finance purchasers are involved, it is obvious that the chain of title may be lengthy. In such circumstances, it may be difficult to prove those requirements necessary for the operation of s 27. Parliament therefore enacted in s 28 an elaborate series of presumptions in favour of the person seeking to rely on s 27. They are applicable where a purchaser proves that in a chain of dispositions he[330] is a *bona fide* private purchaser of a vehicle previously supplied on hp or conditional sale.[331] In such circumstances, the effect of s 28 is that that purchaser will get a Part III title unless A can show that there is no bf first private purchaser in the chain.[332]

**[21.60] Certificates of title.** Because so many suppliers of motor vehicles (see para 4.37) on hp or conditional sale are being deprived of their ownership by Part III titles, their trade organisations (the FLA: see para 2.18) sponsored a failed Private Members Bill.[333] A second opportunity for statutory reform has appeared with an EU Directive aiming at a common vehicle registration scheme.[334] The Directive is in two parts:

*Part 1* is mandatory for all Member States and lays down that in each an Authority will issue certificates containing information as to first registration when the vehicle is new.[335]

*Part 2* is voluntary and designed to facilitate the checking of rightful ownership of a motor vehicle for the time being. The issue is whether the UK will adopt this title registration system.[336]

Subsequently, the industry has been in discussions with the DVLA about showing the hp owner's title on the registration documents.

---

326  See para 21.58.
327  Why did the draftsman not provide as well for the case where D takes under a conditional sale agreement?
328  The person exercising the option does not have to be bf at that moment also. What if D sells the motor vehicle to E during the currency of his agreement?
329  Why was it necessary for the draftsman to insert both s 27(4) and the definition of 'disposition' in s 29(1)?
330  Or a party through whom he is claiming (X); the purchaser or X (as the case may be) is described as the 'relevant purchaser'.
331  S 28(1). *Contra* where all the dispositions are known: *Soneco Ltd v Barcross Finance Ltd* [1978] RTR 444, CA (presumably supportable on the grounds that C, D and E were all shown to be *male fide*?).
332  See further Goode, *HP Law & Practice*, 2nd edn, 628–30.
333  The Vehicles (Ownership) Bill 1994. See Davies [1995] JBL 36; 15 Legal Studies 14.
334  1999/37/EC (see Davies [2001] JBL 489). It was due for implementation June 2004.
335  In the UK, the DVLA will presumably satisfy this requirement.
336  For a discussion of the effect of so doing, see Davies, *Op. cit.*, 499, *et seq.*

*The Law Commission.* Yet another statutory exception to the *nemo dat* rule might have been created in relation to dispositions by registered companies in respect of interests in their goods registered under the Companies legislation.[337] The transfer of title by non-owners has been included in the Commission's Ninth Programme of Law Reform.

---

337 See *Company Security Interests* (CP 176, 2004). This proposal has now been omitted from the Commission's proposals for the reform of company law (as to which, see para 25.28), as has title reservation (see para 25.30).

# CHAPTER 22

# RISK AND IMPOSSIBILITY

## RISK

### General rules

**[22.01] Risk**. Logically, the term 'risk' ought to cover both losses and gains as regards the goods which are the subject-matter of the supply contract; but the pessimistic lawyer will usually use 'risk' solely in the sense of risk of loss.[1] In this sense, the ordinary rule of risk is summed up by the Latin maxim *res perit domino* (risk falls on the owner): it refers to the physical deterioration or destruction,[2] or fall in financial value of, goods supplied happening without breach of the supply contract;[3] and its operation may *pro tanto* override other contractual obligations.[4] Whilst also relating to the subject-matter of the contract, the foregoing rule is to be distinguished from both the *nemo dat* rule (see para 19.11) and the rules applicable where one of the parties becomes insolvent (see paras 19.22–23).

In the case of sales,[5] the general assumption of the common law is that any risk of loss or chance of gain accrued to the owner,[2] and thus depended on the passing of property.[6] This rule is embodied in s 20(1) of the SGA, which provides that, unless otherwise agreed (see para 22.02):

'the goods remain at the seller's risk until the property therein is transferred to the buyer, but when the property therein is transferred to the buyer, the goods are at the buyer's risk whether delivery has been made or not'.

It has already been seen that delivery is the most obvious act of appropriation of unascertained goods (see para 20.17), so that in sales of unascertained goods the property and risk will usually pass on delivery.[7] However, if property and possession are separated, s 20 is a reminder that risk will follow property, not possession,[8]

---

1   See Sealey [1972B] 31 CLJ 225, especially 227–37.
2   The owner will thus remain liable to perform his side of the bargain, notwithstanding any deterioration in the goods, that would otherwise discharge both parties under the doctrine of frustration: see Goode, *Commercial Law*, 3rd edn, 243, and further, para 22.17.
3   Compare the situation where the loss is due to breach by the supplier of his contractual promises: see para 23.09.
4   Thus, an unpaid seller bearing the risk cannot after destruction of the goods sue for the price (*Healy v Howlett*: set out at para 22.06); but, unless the contract is frustrated (see para 22.14), he remains liable for non-delivery (see para 29.17).
5   Do these sale rules apply to the supply and fixing of goods (see para 1.08) and other quasi-sales (see para 2.10)?
6   See Chap 20. Does it matter in a commercial sale that property will not necessarily pass at delivery, which is the moment at which the implied terms are to be tested (see para 14.06)?
7   E.g. *Warder's Import and Export Co Ltd v Norwood* (set out at para 20.17). For mail order sales, see paras 8.19, 20.20 and 20.22B.
8   E.g. *Pignatoro v Gilroy* (set out at para 20.19). The rule is criticised by Atiyah, *Sale of Goods*, 10th edn, 350; and see the other solutions referred to at para 19.10.

and may determine the contractual rights of the parties.[9] In the case of co-owners, the risk is divided between them in proportion to their proprietary interest (SGA, new s 20A(2)(b): see para 20.22C).

The position in respect of sales may be compared with that in bailment and hp transactions. In both the latter cases, the maxim *res perit domino* also applies: risk of loss *prima facie* falls on the bailor. However, it is a well-established rule in bailment that any gains *prima facie* accrue to the bailee, on the grounds that the bailor should not be allowed the double benefit of rent and gains; and, in *Tucker v Farm and General Investments Trust Ltd*,[10] the Court of Appeal decided that this rule should apply to hp agreements, notwithstanding the element of sale they contained, so that the hirer could sue for conversion of the lambs (see generally, para 19.05).

[22.02] **Contrary intention**. It is clear that the presumption outlined above may give way to a contrary intention. It will be recalled that the same is the case with the rules relating to the passing of property (see para 20.06). But there is a practical difference between the two situations: the concept of risk is easier for a layman to understand, so that it is, perhaps, more common for a contract to make special provision as to risk,[11] than to deal expressly with the passing of property.[12] As with a provision as to the passing of property (see para 20.10), the obligation to insure is at best an ambiguous indication of the intention of the parties:[13] it may or may not show where the risk is to lie.[14] Of course, if the contract is a standard-form one (see para 11.08), then it is likely to make express provision for risk, property and insurance; and it will do so in the manner most advantageous to the *proferens*.[15] It is, therefore, unlikely that the ordinary standard-form instalment contract will leave the matter to the ordinary law. On the other hand, where there is a consumer supply contract (see para 11.12A), an express provision as to risk which favours the supplier may amount to an unfair term.[16]

Moreover, a special compulsory rule has been introduced as regards the transfer of risk in consumer sales (see para 22.02A); but, as regards commercial sales, the basic presumption remains *res perit domino* (see para 22.01), though there are certain special cases dealt with in ss 20(2) and (3) where the presumption is qualified[17] and these special cases must be outlined (see paras 22.03–8).

[22.02A] **Supplies to consumers**. The *res perit domino* rule (see para 20.01) was

---

9  E.g. if the property and risk is in the buyer, even destruction of the goods will probably not frustrate the contract (see para 22.17), so that the seller can sue for the price (see para 27.35), whilst the buyer cannot sue for non-delivery of those goods (see para 29.19).

10 [1966] 2 QB 421; [1966] 2 All ER 508, CA.

11 E.g. to pass on delivery: *Borden (UK) Ltd v Scottish Timber Products Ltd* (see para 25.32); Harvey and Meisel, *Auctions*, 2nd edn, 219.

12 For the situation where the parties split the risk, see Sealy [1972B] 31 CLJ 225, at 246–7.

13 The existence of insurance does not eliminate issues of risk, but merely shifts them from insured to insurer: Goode, *Commercial Law*, 3rd edn, 259.

14 See Atiyah, *Sale of Goods*, 10th edn, 321.

15 E.g. *Romalpa* clauses, *Borden* (see above); cif contracts (see para 22.07); maintenance of security clauses (see para 11.08).

16 OFT, *Bulletin No. 13*, case 1; *No. 15*, case 3; *No. 24*, cases 39, 46 and 48; *No. 27*, pp 16 and 27; [2005] *Bulletin J/M*, *Flogas* case.

17 Do s 20(2) and (3) give way to a contrary intention? The matter appears to have been rather clearer in the 1893 Act.

thought to produce a result unfair to consumers in those circumstances where property passed before possession. Suppose the face-to-face retail sale of a carton of six eggs, which were cracked after contract. If the consumer made the purchase in a shop, under the old rules the property and risk *prima facie* passed as follows:[18] in a sale of unascertained goods, the property might pass on appropriation;[19] and in a sale of specific goods, the property might pass when the contract was made.[20]

Accordingly, the SSG Regulations (see para 14.01) inserted a compulsory new s 20(4) into the SGA as follows:[21]

'In a case where the buyer deals as consumer . . ., subsections (1) to (3) must be ignored and the goods remain at the seller's risk until they are delivered to the buyer'.

The effect of new s 20(4) is to separate property from risk and postpone the passing of risk until delivery.[22] What amounts to a delivery will be considered later; but the most obvious example is the physical transfer of possession from seller to buyer:[23] up until the moment of delivery, under new s 20(4) the risk remains with the seller. However, this has a particularly significant effect where the seller agrees to deliver by a third-party carrier to the buyer's home and the goods are damaged during that carriage: under s 32(1) delivery to the carrier is deemed to be delivery to the buyer,[23] with the result that the seller had no liability for the damage and buyer was left to claim in negligence from the bailee/carrier (see para 19.10; and para 22.08); but this rule too was reversed for consumer sales by new s 32(4), so that the risk will not pass until the goods are physically delivered to the consumer.[23] The result is that, if the goods are lost, the seller will remain strictly liable for non-delivery (see para 29.19); and, if the goods are damaged, he may be strictly liable for breach of an undertaking as to quality (see para 29.32).

The following further points should be noticed about new s 20(4):

1. *It is compulsory.* Whilst the ordinary rules as to risk found in s 20 give way to a contrary intention (see para 22.02), it would seem that the Directive-inspired rule found in new s 20(4) is compulsory and applies irrespective of the terms of the agreement between the parties.[24]

2. *Distinguish commercial sales.* Whilst sales outside new s 20(4) follow the *prima facie* rules contained in ss 20(1)–(3) (see para 22.03), those within new s 20(4) do not.

3. *Dealing as consumer.* For the SGA, this concept has the same meaning as in s 12 of UCTA (SGA, s 61(5A)); and we have already seen that the concept extends beyond simple sales to quasi-sales (see para 18.18), so that these too are subject to the risk rule in new s 20(4).

---

18 There was nothing to prevent the seller agreeing to carry the risk; but in the retail context it would not be common for him to do so.

19 Under s 18, r 5(1): see para 20.15.

20 Under s 18, r 1: see para 20.09.

21 SGA, new s 20(4), as inserted by SSG, reg 4. The SGG Directive (99/44) does not require this change: recital 14.

22 Neither the Directive nor the SSG Regulations define 'delivery', so the matter is left to English law.

23 See para 23.03.

24 See OFT, *Bulletin No. 21*, case 9; and generally, para 1.03A.

However, there are a couple of difficulties. First, whilst new s 20(4) obviously applies to private consumers, it has already been seen that 'dealing as consumer' in s 12 also extends to business consumers (see para 18.18). Does new s 20(4) therefore extend to business consumers? Second, what about simple hiring and hp? We have already seen that at common law the basic risk rule in bailment is *res perit domino*, so that the risk of loss falls on the bailor/owner (see para 22.01). So, it would seem that new s 20(4) is not needed; and that is presumably why new s 20(4) is drafted with its express reference to 'seller' and 'buyer' so that it does not extend to bailments. However, unlike new s 20(4), the common law rule will give way to a contrary intention. To prevent exclusion of the *res perit domino* rule from hiring and hp, presumably reliance will have to be placed on the UTCC Regulations (see para 20.02).

**[22.03/4] Commercial sales.** This paragraph applies where the transaction does not amount to a consumer supply (see para 22.02A): this will usually be a business-to-business supply, but could be a consumer-to-consumer contract, or even perhaps a business supply to a business consumer (see above). In these cases, the basic presumption as to risk contained in s 20(1) of the SGA (*res perit domino*) may be ousted by any of the following factors, which may either cause the risk to remain in the supplier, or to revert to him upon some particular occurrence:

1. *Delay in delivery.* Whilst the contractual duties relating to delivery will be considered later (see para 23.05, *et seq.*), a distinction must immediately be drawn according to whether or not the delay in delivery amounts to a breach of the supply contract.

   *(A) Delay amounting to breach of contract.* Section 20(2) provides as follows:

   > 'But where a delivery has been delayed through the fault[25] of either buyer or seller the goods are at the risk of the party in fault as regards any loss which might not have occurred but for such fault.'

   The provision clearly requires a causal connection between the fault and the loss, and the test which the court seems to have applied was whether the seller acted reasonably after the default of the buyer.[26] Further, it should be noted that s 20(2) does not operate in respect of any breach of contract, but only those breaches relating to delivery;[25] and that it seems to assume that the property passes on delivery.[27] If s 20(2) is invoked upon default by the buyer, the risk affected by that delay passes to the buyer: the effect is that the contract probably cannot be frustrated by the occurrence of that risk (see para 22.17) and the buyer is liable for the price or damages for non-acceptance.[28] If s 20(2) is invoked upon default by the seller, that risk

---

25   S 61(1) provides that 'fault' means 'wrongful act of default'. See also para 2.06. 'Fault' seems to be confined in s 20(2) to delay-causing fault. See Goode: *Commercial Law*, 3rd edn, 248.

26   *Demby Hamilton Ltd v Barden* [1949] 1 All ER 435; [1949] WN 73.

27   As under s 18, r 5(2): set out at para 20.17. Can s 20(2) apply where property has already passed (as it might under s 18, r 5(1) before delivery: see para 20.17A)?

28   See respectively, paras 27.17–18 and 27.35. E.g. the *Borden* case (see para 25.32: it is not clear from the reports whether the seller recovered part of the price or damage). See generally Goode, *Op. cit.*, 250–1.

remains with the seller: the seller cannot plead frustration where self-induced (see para 22.14), but remains liable for damages for non-delivery.[29]

(B) *Delay not in breach of contract.* Where the buyer is entitled to, and does, delay in taking delivery, it may sometimes be inferred that the parties intend the risk to pass notwithstanding that property remains in the seller: see *Sterns Ltd v Vickers Ltd.*[30] This decision has subsequently received the approval of the House of Lords, though their Lordships stressed the exceptional nature of the case;[31] and it also seems to accord with the subsequently enacted s 20A of the SGA.[32] However, *Sterns Ltd v Vickers Ltd* gives rise to a number of problems;[33] and, whilst the rule could apply to specific goods, e.g. conditional sales (see para 1.14), it is submitted that it could not operate in respect of generic or future goods.[34]

2. *Transit* (see paras 22.05–6).

3. *Bailment* (see para 22.08).

**[22.05/6] Transit.** Where under a business-to-business contract of sale the goods are subject to a transit from seller to buyer,[35] we have already seen that the implied undertakings as to fitness and quality are tested at the end of the transit, so that the seller is impliedly promising that the goods will stand up to an ordinary transit (see para 14.06). Subject to this understanding that the goods are travelworthy, the SGA makes special provision for risks materialising during the course of transit.[36] Section 33 provides:

> 'Where the seller of goods agrees to deliver them at his own risk at a place other than that where they are when sold, the buyer must, nevertheless, unless otherwise agreed, take any risk of deterioration in the goods necessarily incident to the course of transit.'

This section is expressed to give way to a contrary intention. Moreover, it can only operate where (a) the contract ousts the ordinary assumption that delivery is to be at the seller's place of business,[37] **and** (b) the seller agrees to deliver at his own risk. The section is not expressed very clearly, but was probably intended to reflect the common law, where a distinction was drawn between an ordinary and an extraordinary deterioration.[38] In those circumstances where it operates, s 33 would appear to assume that the two business parties have agreed to allocate the risk of deterioration because of the contemplated transit as follows:

---

29 See para 29.20; and generally Goode, *Op. cit.*, 248–9.
30 [1923] 1 KB 78; [19221 All ER Rep 126, CA (see the discussions in Benjamin's *Sale of Goods*, 6th edn, paras 6-004 and 18-266; and Atiyah, *Sale of Goods*, 10th edn, 351).
31 *Per* Lords Porter and Normand in *Comptoir D'Achat v Luis de Ridder Limitada* [1949] AC 293, HL at 312, 319. But see Goode, *Commercial Law*, 3rd edn, 248.
32 The facts of *Sterns v Vickers* may fall within s 20A of the SGA; and that section, introduced in 1995, may transfer the risk: see para 20.22C.
33 See the 1st edn at para 22.04.
34 See Atiyah, *Sale of Goods*, 10th edn, 352.
35 Distinguish where the third party has possession of goods but not *qua* carrier: see para 22.04.
36 Delivery to the carrier (see para 23.03) *prima facie* marks the commencement of the transit (s 45(1)): see para 24.18) and appropriation of the goods (s 18, r 5(2): see para 20.17).
37 As in ex-ship contracts (see para 22.07). For the ordinary rule, see s 29(1): discussed at para 23.04.
38 See *per* Alderson B in *Bull v Robison* (1854) 10 Exch 342, at 346.

1. *Normal transit*. The buyer is to bear the risk under s 33 of any deterioration which all goods of the contract description would ordinarily suffer during that transit;[39] but the seller is to bear the risk of any deterioration due to some inherent vice peculiar to the contract goods which precludes their being travel-worthy (see above).

2. *Abnormal transit*. The owner—whether seller or buyer—bears the risk of any deterioration due to any abnormality of the transit under the ordinary principle *res perit domino* (see para 22.01). Thus, in *Healy v Howlett*:[40]

> The plaintiff fish exporter (P), who carried on business in Ireland, contracted to sell 20 boxes of mackerel to the defendant (D), a Billingsgate fish salesman, this being the first transaction between the parties. P consigned by railway 190 boxes of mackerel. He wired instructions to the railway officials at Holyhead to appor-tion the boxes between three of his customers, including D, and notified D by invoice that the fish was at his risk from the moment it was put on rail. Owing to delays in Ireland, the fish was no longer in a merchantable state by the time it reached D, and he refused to accept it. P's action for the price[41] failed before the Divisional Court, which held that the invoice could not transfer the risk because it was subsequent to the agreement,[42] that risk therefore went with property, and that the property had not passed.

The Court decided that the property had not passed because there had not been any effective appropriation: they argued that the earmarking took place after the delay, when the fish had already begun to deteriorate, and that the railway officials at Holyhead were then in the impossible position of having to decide who would get the deteriorated fish. It may be that in *Healy v Howlett* the deterioration had set in before delivery[43] and that this delay in transit took it outside s 33.[44]

**[22.07] Delivery to a carrier: commercial export sales**. Section 32 makes provision for those cases where a business-to-business contract envisages delivery to a carrier for transmission to the buyer; and s 32(1) provides that delivery to the carrier shall *prima facie* be deemed delivery to the buyer (see para 23.03). The importance of ss 32(2) and (3) is primarily in relation to export sales, which are beyond the scope of this work (see para 1.01); but it may be convenient if the major types of such contract are listed.[45]

1. *Ex-works or ex-store contracts*. The designation primarily refers to the place of delivery (see para 23.04), and all the ordinary rules as to the passing of property and risk apply.

---

39  S 33. Is this section *redundant*? Compare Greig, *Sale of Goods*, 217–18 with Goode, *Commercial Law*, 3rd edn, 254.

40  [1917] 1 KB 337, DC.

41  As to actions for the price, see para 27.16.

42  It might be otherwise if this were not the first transaction between the parties: see para 18.04.

43  Presumably delivery was to take place in London, thus ousting s 32(1): as to which, see para 23.03.

44  So distinguishing *Sterns Ltd v Vickers Ltd* [1923] 1 KB 78, CA: see 1st edn, para 22.06.

45  The question of the type to which a particular contract belongs is a matter of construing the intention of the parties: *Couturier v Hastie* (set out at para 22.10).

2. *Free on board (fob) contracts.* The expense of delivering the goods on board ship *prima facie* lies on the seller, who must have a cargo available.[46] It is unusual in an fob contract for the property to pass before shipment;[47] but the risk will usually do so,[48] subject to the following exceptions: (a) a reasonable contract of carriage (see SGA, s 32(2)); and (b) those (c and f) contracts where the buyer is left to take out any marine insurance (see SGA, s 32(3)).

3. *Cost, insurance and freight (cif) contracts.* Under this type of contract, the seller undertakes the following duties: (a) to deliver the goods to the port and to ship them under a contract for their carriage to the agreed destination; and (b) to insure the goods for the transit; and (c) to tender the buyer an invoice, bill of lading and insurance policy. In law, these documents together represent the goods, a rule which has several important effects on cif contracts. *First,* delivery of the documents amounts to delivery of the goods (see para 23.03). *Second,* because the seller is under an express obligation to insure, s 32(3) is inapplicable. *Third,* the risk usually passes on shipment,[49] unless the seller is in breach of s 32(2). *Fourth,* it is the transfer of the bill of lading (not delivery) which will usually transfer the property in the goods, once they are ascertained.[50] *Fifth,* the buyer has two rights to reject: he may usually reject the documents if they do not comply with the contract;[51] and reject subsequently arriving goods that do not comply with the contract (see para 29.03). *Sixth,* destruction of the goods after shipment cannot frustrate a cif contract.[52]

4. *Arrival or ex-ship contracts.* The seller's obligation is to deliver the goods from a ship on arrival at a named port, and not merely to ship goods for transit to that port, as in the case of fob and cif contracts. Section 32 can have no application to arrival contracts. The bill of lading only operates as a delivery order, so that its transfer does not pass the property in the goods; and the risk remains in the seller until arrival.[53]

**[22.08] Bailment.** It may be that the subject-matter of the business-to-business contract of supply is for some time in the possession of someone other than the owner of the goods; and that someone may be either one of the parties to the supply contract or a third party. Where the loss is not due to any breach of duty by that bailee,[54] the loss will *prima facie* fall on the owner; but, it is otherwise if the loss is due to a breach of duty by the bailee.[55]

---

46  *The Naxos* [1990] 3 All ER 641, HL.

47  See *Carlos Federspiel & Co v Twigg & Co Ltd* (set out at para 20.16).

48  *Inglis v Stock* (1885) 10 App Cas 263, HL.

49  *Tsakiroglou & Co Ltd v Noblee Thorl GmbH* [1962] AC 93, HL.

50  *Cheetham & Co Ltd v Thornham Spinning Co Ltd* [1964] 2 Lloyd's Rep 17. *Contra* arrival contracts: see below.

51  *Kwei Tek Chao v British Traders Ltd* (see para 29.30). *Contra* where the documents conform with the contract: *Gill & Duffus SA v Berger & Co Inc* (set out at para 23.06).

52  *Manbre Saccharine Co Ltd v Corn Products Ltd* [1919] 1 KB 198.

53  *Comptoir D'Achat v Luis de Ridder Limitada* [1949] AC 293, HL. Subject to s 33: see para 22.05.

54  The duties of a bailee are discussed in Crossley Vaines, *Personal Property*, 5th edn, 85, *et seq.*; and see para 1.17.

55  If both bailee and owner are negligent, does the Law Reform (Contributory Negligence) Act 1945 apply? As to this Act see para 27.40.

1. *A contracting party bailee.* Either the seller or buyer may be in possession as bailee whilst the property in the goods belongs to the other party; and in either case s 20(3) of the SGA simply preserves the common law rules of bailment and allows for two possibilities:

    (a) Property passes before delivery, in which case the seller may be in possession under a contract for value (the supply contract): unless otherwise agreed, his duty is to exercise reasonable care.[56] If the buyer fails to take delivery at the contract time, the supplier becomes either an involuntary or gratuitous bailee, with correspondingly lower duties of care.[57]

    (b) Property passes after delivery, in which case the buyer may be a bailee for value (see para 1.14) and *prima facie*[58] under a duty to exercise reasonable care during the continuance of the bailment.[59]

2. *A third-party bailee.* Where the goods are damaged or lost by the act of an independent third party, either of the parties to the contract for the supply of the goods may wish to maintain an action against the third party in contract or tort:

    (a) In tort. An action in negligence will be available to the buyer when the property in the goods has passed to him;[60] but it is unlikely to succeed prior to that event[61] whilst he is out of (actual) possession (see para 19.10).

    (b) In contract. Whilst an action in contract under the terms of the bill of lading may be available to the seller,[62] the buyer to whom the bill is transferred is prevented by his lack of privity from suing on the bill at common law[63] but has been given such a statutory right of action under the Carriage of Goods by Sea Act 1992, which is beyond the scope of this work.

## IMPOSSIBILITY

[22.09] Assuming that the parties to a contract for the supply of goods have reached an agreement,[64] that agreement may be, or become, impossible of performance in the manner envisaged in the contract. This impossibility may be caused by any number of events, ranging from the death, insolvency or imprisonment of a contracting party to the destruction of the subject-matter or illegality of the contract.

---

56  *Wiehe v Dennis Brothers* (1913) 29 TLR 250; *Nelson v Raphael* [1979] RTR 437, CA.

57  Benjamin's *Sale of Goods*, 6th edn, para 6-022. See para 1.17.

58  The typical conditional sale will probably specify the buyer's duties as bailee.

59  Presumably the position is the same in respect of a transferee under a sale or return transaction: see para 20.23.

60  *The Elafi* [1982] 1 All ER 208.

61  *The Aliakmon* [1986] 1 AC 785, HL, discussed by Goode (1987) 103 LQR 433, at 453–60; [1990] JBL 23; 107 LQR 264–6. As to claims in negligence for economic loss, see Markensis 103 LQR 354, at 384–95; and generally, para 17.14. Does this ruling extend to claims for wrongful interference with goods (see para 19.04)?

62  Once the property has passed, the seller suing a third-party bailee in contract may recover only nominal damages: *The Albazero* [1977] AC 774, HL.

63  *Scruttons Ltd v Midland Silicones Ltd* [1962] AC 446, HL. But the bailee may enter into a separate contract of carriage with the buyer: *The Albazero* (above).

64  For the rules as to formation of a supply contract, see para 10.02, *et seq.*

The question to be discussed in this section is whether the impossibility of performance will discharge either or both the parties from their contractual obligations; or whether the non-performance caused by the impossibility will constitute a breach of contract actionable by the other party.[65] Leaving aside void and illegal contracts,[66] the supply contract may *prima facie* be open to any one of the following interpretations in respect of a particular type of impossibility:

(1) The supplier promises that the particular type of impossibility has not occurred or will not occur, but the obligations of the other party (the buyer or hirer) will lapse by reason of the impossibility; or

(2) The buyer or hirer promises that the particular type of impossibility has not occurred or will not occur, but the obligations of the supplier will lapse by reason of the impossibility; or

(3) The obligations of both parties will lapse by reason of the impossibility; or

(4) The obligations of both parties are to remain binding despite the impossibility of performing the primary obligations,[67] because the contract stipulates in these circumstances for an alternative method of performance, e.g. *force majeure* (see para 23.13A).

At this point, it is necessary to distinguish between initial and subsequent impossibility: the contract may be impossible of performance at the time when it is made; or it may become impossible of performance at some later stage.

## Initial impossibility

[22.10] The supply contract may be initially impossible of performance owing to the act or omission of a contracting party, e.g. where the contract contemplates that the goods be obtained by the supplier from a third party, and he makes no attempt to obtain them from the third party; or by reason of the conduct of some third party, e.g. where the contract contemplates that the goods be obtained by the supplier from a third party who refuses to supply them; or because of the happening or non-happening of some event, e.g. the destruction or non-arrival of the goods respectively. The effect of such impossibility should *prima facie* be a question of interpretation; but in one case the matter is apparently dealt with prescriptively by statute. Section 6 of the SGA provides:

> 'Where there is a contract for the sale of specific goods,[68] and the goods without the knowledge of the seller have perished[68] at the time when the contract is made, the contract is void.'

Within its ambit,[69] s 6 would appear to admit of only one interpretation of the contract; namely, that neither party will be under any contractual liability, i.e.

---

65 'Nothing in this section affects a condition or warranty whose fulfilment is excused by law by reason of impossibility or otherwise': SGA, s 11(6).

66 As to which, see respectively, paras 10.14–17 and 10.18–20.

67 *The Safeer* [1994] 1 Lloyd's Rep 637. Distinguish secondary obligations: see para 26.16.

68 As to 'specific goods' and 'perished', see para 22.13.

69 The expression 'contract of sale' is apt to cover the situation whether or not that contract has purported to pass the property in the goods.

option (3) in para 22.09. The section was always thought to embody the House of Lords decision in *Couturier v Hastie*:[70]

> The seller shipped a cargo of corn at Salonica for delivery in England, and then employed a London corn-factor to sell it on a *del credere* commission. However, owing to inclement weather the cargo became unfit for further transit and was sold by the ship's master in Tunis. Unaware of this sale, the corn-factor shortly afterwards negotiated a sale of the cargo 'free on board, and including freight and insurance to a safe port in the United Kingdom'. On discovering the previous sale by the ship's master the buyer repudiated the contract.[71] As a *del credere* agent guarantees performance by the party he introduces, the seller sued the corn-factor for the price.

The liability of the corn-factor depended on that of his buyer; and accordingly the argument turned on whether the repudiation by the buyer had been wrongful. The Court of Exchequer held that the true meaning of the contract was that there was a sale of an adventure,[72] **the goods or documents**, so that the buyer, and therefore the corn-factor, remained liable for the price.[73] However, the Court of Exchequer Chamber[74] and the House of Lords took the contrary view; namely, that there was an fob contract for the sale of **goods** alone (see para 22.07), and the buyer, and therefore the corn-factor, was not liable for the price. Not only was this decision reached as a matter of construction, but strictly it only decided that the buyer was not liable for the price in the absence of delivery.[75] Thus, it did not decide whether the seller was liable for non-delivery, or whether both parties were discharged; but it seems to have been taken by Chalmers to have decided the latter.[76]

**[22.11]** More recently, the issue of *res extincta* has been canvassed in *McRae v The Commonwealth Disposals Commission*.[77]

> The Commission was charged with the task of disposing of the various wrecks lying abandoned in the Pacific at the end of World War Two. By accident, they offered for sale a non-existent tanker on a non-existent reef. The plaintiff, who had submitted the successful tender, incurred considerable expenditure in undertaking an abortive salvage expedition. The plaintiff's action for breach of contract, deceit and negligence succeeded before the High Court of Australia on the first ground.

The Court decided that the equivalent of s 6 in the State of Victoria did not apply because the goods had never existed; that the question was primarily one of construction; and that the Commission had impliedly warranted that the tanker existed, i.e. option (1) in para 22.09. On the basis of the cases, there are a number of possible interpretations of English law.[78]

(1) *Couturier v Hastie* (set out at para 22.10) indicates that the contract is void for mistake; and this rule is embodied in s 6. This implies that *McRae's* case does

---

70    (1856) 5 HL Cas 673; [1843–60] All ER Rep 280.
71    Because the insurance policy did not cover the loss: Treitel, *Law of Contract*, 11th edn, 295, fn 87.
72    Compare cif contracts (para 22.07); and the explanation by Treitel, *ibid*.
73    (1852) 8 Ex 40.
74    (1853) 9 Ex 102.
75    Slade (1954) 70 LQR 385, 396–7.
76    See Chalmers, *Sale of Goods*, 18th edn, 98.
77    (1951) 84 CLR 377, HC.        78    See Benjamin's *Sale of Goods*, 6th edn, paras 1.129–134.

not represent English law, and that a contract falling within the ambit of s 6 is always void for mistake.[79]

(2) *Couturier v Hastie* may be distinguished from *McRae's* case on the basis that in the latter the goods never existed, whereas in the former case the goods did have an existence once. If this view is adopted, then it may be that s 6 only applies where the goods once had an existence, which was the view taken by the High Court of Australia.

(3) *Couturier v Hastie* does not show that the contract is void for mistake; and s 6 embodies a mere presumption to that effect.[80] Such an argument may be bolstered by reference to ss 49 and 51(1) of the SGA.[81] On the other hand, s 6 is one of the few which is not expressed to give way to a contrary intention,[82] and the terminology of s 55(1) is difficult to reconcile with its application here.[83]

(4) The contract of supply will always be rendered void by the non-existence of the subject-matter, but that there may be a collateral contract whereby the seller warrants the existence of the goods.[84] Such a device would be of no avail if the contract of sale remained purely executory on both sides.[82] Alternatively, it may be that there is liability in tort for deceit or negligent misstatement.[85]

**[22.12]** **Effect of s 6**. The effect of the operation of s 6 of the SGA is illustrated by *Barrow, Lane & Ballard Ltd v Phillips Ltd*.[86]

> On October 7th, the plaintiff (P) purchased one lot of 700 bags of ground nuts then in the possession of a warehousekeeper (W), and inspected but did not count the bags. On October 11th, P agreed to sell the 700 bags to the defendant (D), and the next day handed D a delivery order, which D immediately presented to W. D agreed to resell the goods; but when D attempted to take delivery six weeks later it was discovered that W only had 150 bags in his warehouse. It was found that 109 bags had been stolen from, or irregularly delivered by, W before October 11th, and that 441 bags had similarly disappeared after that date. W being insolvent, P sued for the price of (150+441=) 591 bags, arguing that the property had passed in the goods then in store on contract (October 11th).

Wright J held that the 700 bags was an indivisible parcel;[87] that the present situation fell within s 6, and that the contract was therefore void; but that the seller was entitled to the 'price' of the 150 bags actually received.[88] His Lordship denied that the acceptance of the delivery order by W constituted an appropriation of the 591 bags, on the grounds that the parties only intended to appropriate the 700 bags (see para 20.14). The seller (P) further argued that the case was to be treated as a tender of the wrong quantity within s 30, and that the buyer (D) had accepted the

---

79  I.e. option (3) in para 22.09. See Glanville Williams (1954) 17 MLR 154, 155.

80  See *Bell v Lever Bros* [1932] AC 161, HL, *per* Lord Atkin at 217.

81  As to whether s 49 gives way to a contrary intent, see para 27.16. Section 55(1) is set out at para 18.09. See Atiyah, *Sale of Goods*, 10th edn, 96; Chalmers' *Sale of Goods*, 18th edn, 98–9.

82  Treitel, *Law of Contract*, 11th edn, 295.       83  Smith (1963) JSPTL 227.

84  Cheshire and Fifoot, *Law of Contract*, 11th edn, 223; but see 14th edn at 258.

85  See Treitel, *Law of Contract*, 11th edn, 295; and generally, para 17.17, *et seq*.

86  [1929] 1 KB 575; [1928] All ER Rep 74.

87  The answer might have been different if the contract had been divisible: see para 23.24.

88  Presumably in quasi-contract. But the buyer had already resold, so how could the quasi-contractual remedy be available? See para 29.15.

offer of 591 bags; but Wright J disagreed with this on the grounds that: (1) s 30 gives the buyer an option to reject and rescind when he knows the true facts (see para 13.04); and (2) the contract was void under s 6. Nor did his Lordship think that the property passed to D by reason of their sub-sale or delay in taking delivery, and pointed out that there was no contract under which the property could pass.[89]

**[22.13] Ambit of s 6.** In view of the apparently restricting effect which s 6 has on the ability of the courts to interpret the intention of the parties, it is important to delimit the ambit of the section, which is only expressed to be applicable where 'specific goods' have 'perished' under a contract of sale. Does s 6 apply to quasi-sales, sale or return, or hp?

1. *Specific goods.* Both ss 6 and 7 are limited to sales of 'specific goods'. This term presumably means the same in each case, and will be considered in connection with s 7 (see para 22.15).

2. *Perish.* Both ss 6 and 7 are only expressed to be applicable where the contract goods have 'perished'. Presumably, this term means the same in each case, though it is nowhere defined in the SGA. The term obviously covers physical destruction; and it would also seem to include those situations[90] where the goods are unavailable to the parties for completion of the contract for some reason which is beyond the control of the parties.[91] Can the goods be said to 'perish' whilst they remain identifiable in the hands of the parties? According to Benjamin,[92] goods have 'perished' where they have 'ceased to exist in a commercial sense', as where a cargo of cement is submerged, or dates saturated in sewage.[93] But can this be taken further? Can those situations be included where the goods have never existed,[94] or where they are requisitioned,[95] or where the contract is illegal?[96] What if only part of the goods suffer such a calamity?[97] Is it going too far to suggest that the goods have 'perished' where, subject to the *de minimis* rule, any part of them are commercially unavailable to the parties for the performance of the contract?

## Subsequent impossibility

**[22.13A]** The supply contract may become impossible of performance subsequent to its formation. In this situation, the rules of risk decide who bears the loss of the

---

89   Therefore the risk could not pass under *Sterns Ltd v Vickers Ltd* [1923] 1 KB 78, CA.

90   E.g. *Couturier v Hastie* (set out at para 22.10); *Barrow, Lane and Ballard Ltd v Phillips & Co Ltd* (set out at para 22.12).

91   E.g. lawful sale to third party—*Couturier v Hastie* (above). *Contra* where the supplier caused the non-availability, as by selling and delivering the goods to a third party: *Goode v Garriock* [1972] 2 Lloyd's Rep 369, at 372. What if the seller causes the unavailability, but is protected by an exclusion clause? Compare self-induced frustration: see para 22.14.

92   *Sale of Goods*, 6th edn, para 1-128.

93   Cf. *Asfar & Co v Blundell* [1896] 1 QB 123, CA. But see *obiter* to the contrary in *Horn v Minister of Food* [1948] 2 All ER 1036, which is usually thought to be wrong (Atiyah, *Sale of Goods*, 10th edn, 101; Chalmers, *Sale of Goods*, 18th edn, 99) but would provide another method of escaping ss 6 and 7. See also *Rendell v Turnbull* (1908) 27 NZLR 1067.

94   E.g. *McRae's* case (set out at para 22.11).

95   Cf. *Re Shipton Anderson & Co* [1915] 3 KB 676, DC.

96   Cf. *Re Badische Co Ltd* [1921] 2 Ch 331.

97   See the *Barrow, Lane* case (above); Benjamin, *Op. cit.*, para 1-128.

goods (see paras 22.01–08); but they will not determine whether the supervening impossibility from causes not expressly or impliedly dealt with by the allocation of risk (see above) discharges both parties from all their obligations under the contract. The parties will only be so discharged where the contract is frustrated. As with a breach discharging a contract (see para 26.16), it is thought that the effect of frustration is to bring to an end all the remaining indivisible executory obligations in a contract.[98] Particularly in international trade, the parties sometimes seek to deal with such difficulties by what have become known as *force majeure* clauses.[99] Whilst a simple provision that a contract shall be subject to *'force majeure* conditions' is void for uncertainty,[100] clauses spelling out the events causing difficulty in performance may lead to frustration of the contract (see below) by reason of impossibility.[101] In a commercial contract, such a clause may be subject to the reasonableness test (UCTA, s 3: see para 18.20); and in consumer contracts it may also be an unfair term.[102] Nor is it likely that a *force majeure* clause can be invoked merely because a contract is unexpectedly expensive.[103]

## When a contract may be frustrated

**[22.14]** *Prima facie*, a contract for the supply of goods may be frustrated by the destruction of the person or thing essential for its performance,[104] by legal impossibility[105] or illegality,[106] by serious delay inconsistent with the terms of the contract,[107] or by the disappearance of the purpose of the contract,[108] or other frustrating breach;[109] but it is clear that a party cannot rely on a self-induced frustrating event[110] or moral duties,[111] nor that a contract has become unexpectedly expensive to perform.[112]

---

98 As to the implications of this, see para 22.17.

99 As to which see Schmitthoff, *Export Trade*, 10th edn, 6-017/21; Atiyah, *Sale of Goods*, 10th edn, 359–60.

100 *British Electrical etc Ltd v Patley Pressings Ltd* [1953] 1 All ER 94; see generally Benjamin's *Sale of Goods*, 6th edn, para 8-087, *et seq.*, and para 10.03.

101 See *Mamidol-Jetoil Greek Petroleum Co SA v Okta Crude Oil Refinery AD (No. 2)* [2003] 2 All ER (Comm) 640, CA; and further Benjamin, *Op. cit.*, paras 6-050 and 18-320, *et seq.*

102 *Bulletin No. 27*, p 107: see Grey Term (e); and para 11.16.

103 *Thames Valley Power Ltd v Total etc Ltd* [2006] 1 Lloyd's Rep 441, para 50. This follows the frustration rule (see para 22.14).

104 E.g. *Taylor v Caldwell* (1863) 32 LJQB 164. But see cif contracts: para 22.07. As to the situation where there is part destruction of goods promised to several buyers, see para 22.16.

105 E.g. *Re Shipton Anderson & Co* [1915] 3 KB 676, DC.

106 *Re Badische* [1921] 2 Ch 331; *Kursell v Timber Operators Ltd* (set out at para 20.23).

107 E.g. *Jackson v Union Marine Insurance Co Ltd* (1874) LR 10 CP 125. Distinguish non-frustrating delays e.g. *Shearson Lehman Hutton Inc v Maclaine Watson & Co Inc* [1989] 2 Lloyd's Rep 570 (see [1990] LMCLQ at 308). For the effect of a non-frustrating delay on risk, see paras 22.03–4.

108 E.g. *Krell v Henry* [1903] 2 KB 740, CA (not a goods case).

109 *Harbutt's Plasticine Ltd v Wayne Tank Ltd* [1970] 1 QB 447, CA (not a goods case).

110 *Maritime National Fish Ltd v Ocean Trawlers Ltd* [1935] AC 524, PC. Does this rule cover all events falling within s 20(2) and (3) of the SGA (see paras 22.03 and 22.08)? See also *Goodey v Garriock* [1972] 2 Lloyd's Rep 369.

111 *Pancommerce SA v Veeckeema BV* [1983] 2 Lloyd's Rep 304, CA. Cf. the US Uniform Commercial Code, Art 2-615.

112 See Treitel, *Law of Contract*, 11th edn, 881.

Suppose the parties make specific provision in their contract for the *prima facie* frustrating event, e.g. *force majeure* clauses (see para 22.13A). Can reliance be placed on the possible interpretation of contractual intention analysed above (para 22.09); or does the doctrine of frustration prevent this? In part, the answer may depend on the theoretical basis of the doctrine of frustration;[113] but in one situation there has been statutory intervention. Section 7 of the SGA provides:

'Where there is an agreement to sell specific goods, and subsequently the goods, without any fault on the part of the seller or buyer,[114] perish before the risk passes to the buyer, the agreement is thereby avoided.'

This section expressly refers only to contracts for the sale of goods; and it is then restricted in that it is only applicable where the contract is for the sale of 'specific goods' (see para 22.15), the frustrating event is the 'perishing' of those goods (see para 22.13) and neither the property nor risk have passed (see further, para 22.18). In all other cases,[115] it is arguable that the matter should depend on the contractual intention of the parties. Even where s 7 is applicable, it is arguable that both ss 6 and 7 give way to a contrary intention (see para 22.11).

[22.15] **Specific goods**. It will be recalled that s 61(1) says that, 'unless the context or subject-matter otherwise requires', specific goods 'means goods identified and agreed upon at the time a contract of sale is made' (see generally, para 2.04). This concept has already caused difficulty in relation to the passing of property in identifiable goods (see para 20.03); and, with regard to the issue of risk, it has led to litigation in respect of future goods. There have been two cases, in both of which a farmer has agreed before his crops were grown to sell for delivery after harvest the estimated yield of his acreage; but the actual yield has, without fault on the part of either party, fallen substantially below the estimate. In the pre-1893 case of *Howell v Coupland*,[116] the Court of Appeal unanimously held that there was an implied term that both parties be excused performance in such an event. In *Sainsbury Ltd v Street*:[117]

The contract was made in July for the delivery to a corn merchant the following autumn of 275 tons of barley. The unexpectedly poor harvest produced only 140 tons which the seller sold for a higher price elsewhere. The corn merchant claimed damages for non-delivery, and the farmer pleaded there was a condition precedent that the land would yield 275 tons.

McKenna J held the farmer liable for damages for non-delivery of the 140 tons,[118] holding his duty to deliver 275 tons was *prima facie* subject to an implied condition precedent that the farmer should *pro tanto* be discharged with regard to the shortfall (135 tons). His Lordship put his decision on the following grounds:

---

113  See Treitel, *Law of Contract*, 11th edn, 920–3. And see *Clarke v Bates* [1913] LJCR 63, Cty Ct; affd by DC at 114.

114  It has been suggested that 'fault' here means the same as in s 20 (see para 22.03): Goode, *Commercial Law*, 3rd edn, 260, fn 113.

115  Ie other types of supply contract, e.g. hp, quasi-sales and sales outside the ambit of s 7, e.g. of unascertained goods (see para 22.16).

116  (1876) 1 QBD 258; [1874–80] All ER Rep 878, CA.

117  [1972] 3 All ER 1127; [1972] 1 WLR 834.

118  For the action for non-delivery, see generally, para 29.18.

(1) He applied the rule in *Howell v Coupland*, which was either embodied in s 5(2) of the SGA, or preserved by the general saving of the common law.[119]

(2) The case fell outside s 7, because ss 6 and 7 were dealing only with 'existing goods',[120] whereas a crop which had not yet grown does not fall within that category.[121]

**[22.16] Unascertained goods.** In *Blackburn Bobbin Ltd v TW Allen Ltd*:[122]

> There was a contract for the sale free on rail Hull of 70 standards of Finland birch timber. Unknown to the buyer, the seller was following the usual trade practice, namely, to then load timber in Finland for shipment to England. Before delivery commenced, the outbreak of war made such shipment impossible. The buyer's claim for damages succeeded before McCardie J who saw no reason why such 'a bare and unqualified contract for the sale of unascertained goods' should be frustrated by the outbreak of war; and the Court of Appeal agreed.[123]

This decision must be compared with the failed harvest cases already considered (see para 22.15). The explanation is that everything turns on the precise nature of the allegedly frustrating event in relation to the terms of the contract: in the harvest cases, it was impossible to perform the contracts from the contemplated sources; but in the *Allen* case, there was no source contemplated in the contract and performance could be from any such timber in the world.[124] Such a distinction has sometimes erroneously led to the conclusion that it is not possible to frustrate a contract for the sale of generic goods by their non-availability.[125]

Assuming the contract is frustratable, a further problem concerns the case where there are multiple buyers. Suppose the supplier without fault obtains sufficient goods to satisfy less than the contractual requirements of all his buyers. Subject to the express terms of the supply contracts, are they all frustrated, do they rank in delivery date order, should they be pro-rated, or what?[126]

**[22.17] Relationship of risk and frustration.** Unless the contract goods are at least ascertained (see para 20.21), the contract is unlikely to be frustratable (see para 22.16). Assuming that it is frustratable and leaving aside the effect of frustration (see para 22.18), this issue of the relationship of risk and frustration can only arise where the alleged frustrating event is the damage or destruction of the contract goods occurring whilst some of the promises under that contract remain executory, e.g. delivery and payment. Leaving aside any proprietary interest in an undivided

---

119 The common law is expressly preserved by SGA, s 62(2).

120 This varies from what Chalmers seems to have assumed was the law: see his *Sale of Goods*, 18th edn, 100. Such future goods are outside s 7, perhaps because the type of future goods is unascertained (see para 20.15).

121 Presumably he thought they were 'future goods' (as to which see para 2.03), and unascertained at the time of contracting. Compare para 20.04, and para 22.18.

122 [1918] 1 KB 540; affirmed [1918] 2 KB 467, CA.

123 It has been suggested that the CA decision seems to envisage a slightly wider field of operation for the doctrine of frustration: Atiyah, *Sale of Goods*, 10th edn, 358. *Sed quaere?*

124 *Aliter*, if performance of the contract were rendered illegal by the outbreak of war (see generally, para 10.20): Benjamin's *Sale of Goods*, 6th edn, para 6-036, *et seq*.

125 But see Benjamin, *Op. cit.*, para 6-035.

126 See Hudson (1968) 31 MLR 535; and also the discussion of supervening prohibition of export and import in Benjamin, *Op. cit.*, para 18-248, *et seq*.

share in a bulk (see para 20.22, *et seq.*), there are four possible permutations as to the incidence of property and risk.

|          | Seller | Buyer  |
|----------|--------|--------|
| *Case 1* | P + R  |        |
| *Case 2* |        | P + R  |
| *Case 3* | P      | R      |
| *Case 4* | R      | P      |

*Case 1*: the property and risk are in the seller, e.g. s 7 of the SGA (set out at para 22.14). This is, perhaps, the most obvious case where the contract may be frustrated by the destruction of the goods,[127] in which case the seller ceases to be liable for non-delivery,[128] and the buyer ceases to be liable for the price.[129]

*Case 2*: the property and risk are in the buyer. Once all promises made under a contract have been performed there remains nothing that could be frustrated (see para 22.13A). If we were to say that this contract were frustrated by the destruction of the goods, the effect would be that the buyer would no longer be liable for the price,[129] thereby effectively throwing the risk back on the seller. Does this show that such a contract cannot be frustrated by the destruction of the goods?

*Case 3*: the property is in the seller and the risk is in the buyer. In a consumer sale, the risk cannot pass before delivery (see para 22.02A), so that this category could only cover goods delivered under a conditional sale (see para 1.14). Now, a sale contract cannot be executed before the passing of property. But can it be frustrated by the destruction of the goods after delivery, so saving the buyer from liability for the price?[129]

*Case 4*: the risk is in the seller and the property is in the buyer, e.g. a sale to a consumer of specific goods destroyed before delivery. It has been argued that the contract cannot be frustrated by the destruction of the goods because its object, the transfer of property, has been carried out.[130] Yet, if the buyer is held liable for the price,[129] this is in effect to put the risk on him. Does it therefore follow that the contract can be frustrated?

It is tempting to simplify this rather difficult pattern by saying that, whether the contract can be frustrated by the destruction of the goods, depends on whether

---

127 Under the rules of risk the buyer is no longer liable for the price though the seller remains liable for non-delivery: see *Healy v Howlett* (set out at para 22.06).

128 For actions against a seller for non-delivery, see para 29.19.

129 For actions against a buyer for the price, see paras 27.16–18. If he has already paid the price, the buyer may be able to recover it on grounds of total failure of consideration: see para 29.13.

130 Atiyah, *Sale of Goods*, 10th edn, 356.

the risk has passed,[131] perhaps on the basis of the implied term theory of frustration: it would follow that it is possible to frustrate in *Cases 1* and *4*, but not in *Cases 2* and *3*. Yet this view assumes that a provision in the contract passing risk ousts the doctrine of frustration[132] and that frustration affects all the terms of the contract.[133] No doubt it is ordinarily true that only in *Cases 1* and *4* will the contract be frustrated; but this may not simply reflect the incidence of risk so much as the fact that within *Cases 2* and *3* there will rarely be any outstanding contractual obligations which survive the frustrating event other than payment.[129] If there were such a survival of terms, it would seem that at very least the contract could be frustrated where it fell within *Case 3*.[134] But is it possible to go further and say that a contract can be frustrated whilst any duty remains to be performed thereunder, in which case it would follow that even contracts within *Case 2* could be frustrated?[135] For instance, where goods have not yet been delivered.[128]

## *The effect of frustration*

[22.18] Assuming that the contract is frustrated, the effect of frustration is governed by the common law, as amended by the Law Reform (Frustrated Contracts) Act 1943 (FCA). That Act is expressed to be applicable to all contracts which have:

'become impossible of performance or been otherwise frustrated . . . subject to the provisions of section 2 of this Act' (s 2(1)).

The only important exception for our purposes is that contained in s 2(5)(c), which excludes from the operation of the FCA:

'any contract to which s 7 of the Sale of Goods Act 1979 . . . applies, or . . . any other contract for the sale, or for the sale and delivery, of specific goods, where the contract is frustrated by reason of the fact that the goods have perished'.

In cases falling within s 2(5)(c), only the unamended common law rules apply; and it is therefore necessary to determine the scope of this provision. The first part of s 2(5)(c) refers to contracts falling within s 7 of the SGA (set out at para 22.14); and it is often said that the second part of s 2(5)(c) does not add anything to the first part.[136] However, on the basis of the analysis set out above (para 22.17), it is submitted that the first part refers to contracts falling within *Case 1*, and the second part refers to contracts falling within *Cases 3* and *4*, and probably even *Case 2*. Both parts will only apply where there is a contract for the sale of 'specific goods' frustrated by reason of the fact that the goods have 'perished', both of which expressions appear in ss 6 and 7 of the SGA and s 2(5)(c) of the FCA; and they presumably mean the same in all three cases.[137] But what of the requirement of s 7 that the goods should

---

131 See Goff and Jones, *The Law of Restitution*, 6th edn, paras 20.080–1; Goode, *Commercial Law*, 3rd edn, 261. *Contra* Glanville Williams, *The Frustrated Contracts Act*, 82, fn 30.

132 This is consistent with the implied term theory, but not necessarily the just solution approach.

133 Atiyah, *Op. cit.*, 312. But see Glanville Williams, *Ibid*.

134 See Glanville Williams, *Op. cit.*, 84–85, and especially fn 35.

135 Doubted by Atiyah, *Op. cit.*, 361.

136 See Atiyah, *Sale of Goods*, 10th edn, 361; Treitel, *Law of Contract*, 11th edn, 918–19; Goff and Jones, *The Law of Restitution*, 6th edn, para 20.081.

137 As to 'specific goods', see para 22.15; and as to 'perish', see para 22.13.

perish **without fault** on the part of either party, and the absence of any such requirement from s 6 of the SGA and s 2(5)(c) of the FCA?[138]

**[22.19] The Frustrated Contracts Act.** The effect of frustration on contracts falling inside and outside s 2(5)(c) of the FCA is adequately discussed elsewhere;[139] but there would only seem to be any practical difference between the two situations in respect of advance payments and part delivery.

1.   *Advance payments.* Two situations must be distinguished:

   (a) Where the buyer has paid part or all of the price before the frustrating event. If there has been a total failure of consideration, the buyer may recover that sum at common law[140] or under the FCA. However, where the failure of consideration is only partial (see para 29.16), the buyer cannot recover at common law; but he may do so under the FCA (s 1(2)), subject to 1(b) below.

   (b) Where the contract provides for payment of part or all of the price before the frustrating event and the seller has incurred expenses before that event. The FCA allows the seller to claim reasonable expenses out of the sums paid or payable (s 1(2)); but he has no such right at common law.

2.   *Part delivery.* Again, a distinction must be drawn:

   (a) Where the buyer has paid the price and received part of the goods. At common law the buyer could not recover the price because there had been no total failure of consideration;[141] but under the FCA the seller can only claim to retain so much of the price as is attributable to any gain which has accrued to the buyer (s 1(3)) or any expenses incurred by the seller (s 1(2)) as above.

   (b) Where the seller has delivered part of the goods, but been paid nothing. Under the FCA the seller may be compensated for any benefit which has accrued to the buyer (s 1(3)), or may claim his expenses out of any sum payable by the buyer before the frustrating event (s 1(2)).[142] However, the seller cannot recover anything from the buyer at common law, unless he can show an implied contract from the fact that the buyer has voluntarily retained the goods after the frustrating event.[143]

---

138  See Glanville Williams, *The Frustrated Contracts Act*, 83, fn 30.

139  See Atiyah, *Sale of Goods*, 10th edn, 361–7; Treitel, *Law of Contract*, 11th edn, 909–20. See also *Clarke v Bates* [1913] LJCCR 63 and 114 DC; *British Berna Motor Lorries Ltd v Inter-Transport Co Ltd* (1915) 31 TLR 200; *Shepherd v Ready Mix Concrete (London)* (1968) 112 SJ 518; *BP (Exploration) Libya Ltd v Hunt* [1979] 1 WLR 232, substantially affirmed [1983] 2 AC 352, HL.

140  *Fibrosa Spolka Akeyjna v Fairbairn etc Ltd* [1943] AC 32, HL.

141  But he might recover a proportionate amount of the price on the grounds that the goods were still at the seller's risk: Atiyah, *Sale of Goods*, 10th edn, 363.

142  For an examination of the basis of the rules, see Haycroft and Waksman [1984] JBL 207.

143  The claim is quasi-contractual; and it is difficult to fit in with the requirement that the buyer's retention of the benefit be voluntary the decision in *Barrow, Lane and Ballard Ltd v Phillips & Co Ltd* (set out at para 22.12).

# PART 6

# PAYMENT IN SUPPLY CONTRACTS

# CHAPTER 23

# DELIVERY AND PAYMENT

**[23.01] Introduction**. Under the contract of sale, it is normally envisaged that there will be a delivery of goods (see para 2.01) in exchange for the price (see para 2.06); and, leaving aside all questions of what must be delivered and what must be paid,[1] this chapter is concerned with the acts of delivery and payment. As s 27 of the SGA states:

> 'It is the duty of the seller to deliver the goods, and of the buyer to accept and pay for them, in accordance with the terms of the contract of sale.'

Whilst this section is subject to a contrary intention (s 55: set out at para 18.09), it plainly expresses the normal expectation of the parties to a contract of sale.[2] By comparison, hp and simple hiring agreements are both forms of bailment (see para 1.17): the essence of the transaction is a transfer of possession for the payment of rent (see para 1.18).

The duties of delivery and payment will now be separately analysed (paras 23.02–15); and the time of performance of those duties, and performance by instalments, is reserved until later (para 23.16, *et seq.*). However, it should be noted that some retail sales on payment cards (see para 2.24), e.g. by supermarkets, also involve a payment of cash to the consumer (cashback),[3] which is in effect a loan by the retailer to the consumer (see para 7.02, *et seq.*).

## DELIVERY

**[23.02]** English law differentiates between the passing of **property** in, and **delivery** of, the contract goods (see para 19.01) and, because of the different incidents attached to the two, they must be carefully distinguished.[4] Four situations are possible:

(1) Property may pass after delivery, as in a conditional sale or hp agreement.[5]

(2) Property may pass at the moment of delivery, as where a delivery of unascertained goods to the buyer or a carrier constitutes an appropriation of them.[6]

---

1  It is one of the oddities of the SGA (and of the common law?) that delivery and payment are expressed as duties, whereas many other provisions are expressed as implied terms: Goode, *Commercial Law*, 3rd edn, 263–5.

2  Would there be a similar rule for quasi-sales?

3  About 20%: (2001) 55 CC6/10. For third-party cashbacks, see para 8.13A.

4  The incidents of property are analysed at para 19.10, *et seq.* and those of delivery below.

5  See respectively, paras 1.14, 1.20.

6  S 18, r 5(2): see para 20.17.

(3)  Property may pass before delivery, at the earliest when the contract is made.[7]

(4)  The property is never to pass under the contract, as with a simple hiring.[8]

In all cases, the cautious supplier may require his transferee to sign a delivery note acknowledging that he is satisfied with the delivery.[9] Any contractual provision to this effect may fail as being unreasonable[10] or unfair.[11] A sensible supplier may use a bar-code system (see para 2.06) to keep track of goods, prove delivery and reduce fraud.[12]

## Meaning and rules of delivery

**[23.03]  The meaning of delivery**. The CCA nowhere defines delivery; but the SGA provides that, unless the context otherwise requires,[13] ' "Delivery" means voluntary transfer of possession from one person to another.' The person making the delivery may be the seller or his agent, e.g. the *Albright & Wilson* case (set out at para 13.01); and the delivery may be to the buyer or the business premises designated in the contract.[14] The most obvious example of 'delivery' is the physical transfer of actual possession of goods; but possession clearly includes constructive possession, e.g. documents of title (FA, s 1(2)). Whilst detailed discussion of the common law concept of 'possession' is beyond the scope of this work,[15] certain common instances of a constructive transfer of possession may be noticed.

(1)  *Symbolic delivery*; that is, the handing over of the means of control, e.g. the keys to a room, or a left-luggage locker.[16]

(2)  *Delivery of the documents of title*. Whilst the general rule is that a transfer of documents of title is not a transfer of possession of the goods they represent,[17] there are exceptions, such as 'documents of title' within the SGA.[18]

(3)  *Delivery to the buyer's agent*. This may amount at common law to a transfer of possession from seller to buyer;[19] but the SGA makes special provision for

---

7   S 18, r 1 see para 20.09.

8   See para 1.18.

9   There may be two reasons for this procedure: to protect the supplier (see para 23.10) and to protect any carrier. For a possible limitation on the efficacy of delivery notes, see para 18.06; and for their effect on the buyer's right to rescind, see para 29.05.

10   Under UCTA, s 3: see para 18.22, *et seq*.

11   Under the UTCC Regulations: see para 11.12, *et seq*.

12   See [2002] 6 *Credit Today* 13.

13   S 61(1). Note that the concept of delivery is specially extended with regard to sales from a bulk: see para 20.22C.

14   *Computer 2000 Distribution Ltd v ICM Computer Solutions Plc* [2004] EWCA Civ 1634, CA (rogue persuaded buyer to order delivery to serviced office accommodation, where received by bf security guard and handed to rogue. Held: goods delivered so buyer must pay for them).

15   See generally Crossley Vaines, *Personal Property*, 5th edn, 4. Compare possession for the purposes of the exceptions to the *nemo dat* rule (see paras 21.28 and 21.39) with loss of possession on terminating the unpaid seller's lien (see para 24.14).

16   Benjamin's *Sale of Goods*, 6th edn, para 8-008; Bell, *Personal Property*, 57–61. But for criticism of the expression 'symbolic', see Crossley Vaines, *Op. cit.*, 307.

17   Bell, *Op. cit.*, 58.

18   The SGA definition (s 61(1)) cross-refers to s 1(4) of the FA. See further, 1st edn, para 23.03.

19   *The Saetta* (see para 21.49). But the goods may still be regarded as in the course of transit: see s 45(1) SGA, set out at para 24.18.

the circumstance where the contract requires or allows the seller to send the goods to the buyer, according to whether or not the buyer deals as consumer (see para 18.18). If so, compulsory new s 32(4) (as inserted by SSG, reg 4) provides that 'the delivery of the goods to the carrier is not delivery of the goods to the buyer'; and the result is that the retail seller retains possesssion and risk (new s 20(4): see para 22.02A) until delivery, e.g. to the consumer's home. This will be particularly significant where the seller and buyer are not dealing face-to-face, as where there is a distance sale, e.g. conducted by telephone, internet or mail order (see paras 8.17–19), so that the property (but not now the risk) will normally pass when the goods are posted (see para 20.20). However, where a sale falls outside new s 32(4), e.g. commercial sales or private sales, s 32(1) of the SGA provides a *prima facie*[20] rule that

> 'The delivery of goods to a carrier, whether named by the buyer or not, for the purposes of transmission to the buyer is . . . deemed to be a delivery of the goods to the buyer.'

With regard to commercial sales, ss 32(2) and (3) contain special rules for the export trade (see para 22.07). Remember also that delivery to a carrier may pass the property in goods (see para 23.02).

(4) *Attornment*; that is, acknowledgement by the person in physical possession of goods that he is holding the goods on behalf of another, upon which the law regards the former as having merely custody and the other as being in legal possession.[21] Attornment to the buyer or hirer could be by either of the following:

(a) the supplier, as where he agrees to retain possession as agent of the buyer or hirer.[22]

(b) a third party, e.g. a warehouseman or carrier. In such a case, s 29(4) of the SGA provides as follows:[23]

> 'Where the goods at the time of sale are in the possession of a third person, there is no delivery by seller to buyer unless and until the third person acknowledges to the buyer that he holds the goods on his behalf; but nothing in this section affects the operation of the issue or transfer of any document of title to goods.'

(5) *Delivery documents*. Delivery to the private consumer's premises may be the only option if ordering bulky items or distance buying, e.g. by telephone or internet; and in these cases the quality of the supplier's delivery service may be

---

20  E.g. *Galbraith and Grant Ltd v Block* [1922] 2 KB 155; and see para 22.05, fn 43. As to the scope of s 32(1), see Goode, *Commercial Law*, 3rd edn, 253–6. For the passing of property, see para 20.17.

21  *Michael Gerson (Leasing) Ltd v Wilkinson* (set out at para 21.41); and see para 21.40. See the definitions in Palmer, *Bailment*, 846; Bell, *Op. cit.*, 63; and para 20.17. Distinguish mere receipt of a delivery order by the person having custody of the goods, e.g. *Laurie & Morewood v Dudin* [1926] 1 KB 223, CA, from the situation where he 'attorns' to another, e.g. *Henderson v Williams* (set out at para 21.11).

22  As to the implications of this for the unpaid seller's rights of lien and stoppage, see paras 24.11 and 24.19. There can be no attornment in respect of an unidentified part of a larger bulk: Goode, *Op. cit.*, 44, 266.

23  E.g. *Inglis v Robertson* (see para 21.47); *Wardar's Co Ltd v Norwood & Sons Ltd* (set out at para 20.17). See also Reynolds [1984] JBL 151; McMeel [2003] LMCLQ 169 at 196–8.

important to the consumer.[24] In the ordinary course of business, a buyer is entitled to assume that non-title contractual documents, e.g. delivery notes, are correct and relevant to the goods to which they purport to relate (The *Albright & Wilson* case (set out at para 13.01), CA at para 13).

**[23.04] The rules of delivery**. The basic rule is to be found in SGA s 29(1):

> 'Whether it is for the buyer to take possession of the goods or for the seller to send them to the buyer is a question depending in each case on the contract, express or implied, between the parties.'

Thus the Act leaves it to the parties to decide the mode of delivery; and it has been regretted that there is no more definite *prima facie* rule.[25] However, this seems to reflect the common law that the seller's *prima facie* duty was merely to afford the buyer the opportunity of taking possession of the goods at the agreed place of delivery; and it is usually thought that these rules are also applicable to quasi-sales, hp and simple hiring.[26] The SGA lays down a *prima facie* rule that the expenses of, and incidental to, putting the goods in a deliverable state (see para 20.12) must be borne by the seller (s 29(6)) and then deals with the following aspects of delivery:

1.  *The place of delivery*. Section 29(2) provides that *prima facie*:

    > 'the place of delivery is the seller's place of business if he has one, and if not, his residence; except that, if the contract is for the sale of specific goods, which to the knowledge of the parties when the contract is made are in some other place, then that place is the place of delivery'.

    The underlying presumption is not that the seller will send the goods, but that the buyer will collect them; and this ties in with the buyer's duty to seek out his creditor, the seller (see para 23.13). However, this presumption may be displaced,[27] e.g. home and internet sales, mail order[28] and Interflora.

2.  *Demand or tender of delivery*. According to s 29(5), this 'may be treated as ineffectual unless made at a reasonable hour, and what is a reasonable hour is a question of fact'. Presumably, this will be related to the ordinary course of business (see paras 21.34–5).

3.  *The time of delivery*. The following rule as to the time of delivery is laid down by s 29(3):

    > 'Where under the contract of sale the seller is bound to send the goods to the buyer,[29] but no time for sending them is fixed, the seller is bound to send them within a reasonable time.'[30]

---

24  See [2003] 11 *Which?* 12.
25  Chalmers, *Sale of Goods*, 18th edn, 179.
26  As to hp, see Guest, *Law of HP*, para 321; Goode, *HP Law & Practice*, 2nd edn, 220.
27  *Zenziper Grains and Feed Stuffs v Bulk Trading Corp Ltd* [2001] 1 All ER (Comm) 385, CA (free on truck). See also fob, cif and ex-ship contracts: para 22.07.
28  The Post Office is offering a new service, allowing customers to collect undeliverable goods from a local post office: [2001] 5 *Credit Today* 7.
29  Thus ousting s 29(2). Even then, *prima facie* time of delivery is not usually of the essence: see para 23.18.
30  E.g. *Charles Rickards Ltd v Oppenheim* (set out at para 26.25); and *Thomas Borthwick (Glasgow) Ltd v Bunge & Co Ltd* [1969] 1 Lloyd's Rep 17. What is a reasonable time is a question of fact: SGA, s 59. Cf. SGSA, s 14: see para 15.15.

A clause allowing the supplier to delay delivery may be unreasonable (under s 3 of UCTA: see para 18.20) or unfair.[31] The effect of s 37 may be that time runs from the buyer's request for delivery (see para 23.09). As to whether time of delivery is of the essence, see para 23.16, *et seq.*

*Distance selling.* Where a consumer enters a distance contract (see para 8.17), the Distance Selling Regulations assume that *prima facie* the parties have agreed that the supplier 'shall perform the contract within a maximum of 30 days beginning with the day after the day the consumer sent his order to the supplier' (reg 19(1)). Subject to where the Regulations allow delivery of substitute goods[32] and the special rules for outdoor leisure events,[33] reg 19(2) provides that:

> 'where the supplier is unable to perform the contract because the goods or services ordered are not available, within the period of performance referred to in paragraph (1) or such other period as the parties agree ("the period of performance"), he shall:
>
> (a) inform the consumer; and
>
> (b) reimburse[34] any sum paid by or on behalf of the consumer[35] under or in relation to the contract to the person by whom it was made.'[33]

Where a contract has not been performed within the 'period of performance' (see above), it 'shall be treated as if it had not been made, save for any rights or remedies which the consumer has under it as a result of the non-performance' (reg 19(5)); any security shall be treated 'as never having had any effect' (reg 19(6)); and any credit agreement shall be cancelled (reg 20). As to the cancellation rules, see regs 15 and 16 (see para 10.38).

## Duties of delivery

There are two facets of the duty of delivery: the supplier is under a duty to tender delivery; and the buyer or hirer is under a duty to accept delivery.

### Tender of delivery

[23.05] Because delivery is the essence of bailment, the law puts great emphasis on the tender of delivery in hp and simple hiring transactions. The hiring does not commence until the owner tenders to the hirer goods which conform with the contract **and** the hirer accepts the same (see para 15.23). If the hirer does not accept the goods, he cannot be sued for the instalments of rent, even if expressed to be payable in advance (see para 27.21). However, in the case of sale, the seller's duty is

---

31  OFT, *UCT Bulletin No. 23*, case 16; and see generally, para 11.16. For a discussion of delivery times, see [2006] 5 *Which?* 20.

32  The supplier may supply substitute goods where **all** the following conditions are satisfied (reg 19(7)): (a) allowed by the contract; and (b) prior to the contract the consumer has been so informed under reg 7 (see para 9.04).

33  In the case of outdoor leisure events, the parties may agree that reg 19(2)(b) shall not apply: reg 19(8).

34  Reimbursement shall be as soon as possible and in any event within 30 days of expiry of the period of performance: reg 19(4).

35  This includes any sum paid by a third-party creditor: reg 19(3).

to tender delivery in accordance with the rules set out above (see para 23.04); and the buyer is under a duty to accept them (see para 23.08). As these duties are reciprocal, if the seller tenders non-conforming goods, the buyer is under no duty to accept them (see para 23.09). Suppose the buyer indicates to the seller that he will not accept delivery: if he repudiates on an actual tender, the question of whether it is a conforming tender, so that the buyer is liable for non-acceptance, can be tested against the actual tender; but, if the buyer repudiates in anticipation of tender, the seller is clearly entitled to accept the anticipatory breach (see para 26.15) and need not make an actual tender of delivery.[36] On principle, it might appear that, if the seller is not ready and willing to deliver, the contract will be discharged by mutual abandonment (see para 26.18). The courts have therefore held that, if he wishes to sue the buyer for non-acceptance, the seller must remain ready and willing to perform his side of the bargain.[37] However, in *British and Benningtons Ltd v North West Cacher Tea Co Ltd*:[38]

> The buyer agreed to buy the crop of tea to be produced on a certain Indian estate, delivery to be made in bonded warehouse in London, but no date for delivery being specified. In the seller's action for damages for non-acceptance, it was found that a reasonable time for delivery had not expired when the buyer repudiated.

The House of Lords held that, where there was such an anticipatory breach by the buyer, the seller need not tender actual delivery before commencing the action; nor need he **prove** that at the date of repudiation he was ready and willing to deliver in London; and they upheld the award of damages to the seller.[39] Lord Sumner accepted that a buyer could set up his seller's breach of contract in these circumstances,[40] but pointed out that in this case there was not yet a breach because the seller might still have tendered in London within the contract period.[41]

It would appear that the effect of the buyer's anticipatory repudiation upon the seller's duty of delivery depends on whether or not the seller elects[42] to accept that repudiation (see paras 23.06–07).

**[23.06] Repudiation by the buyer**. Where the buyer's anticipatory repudiation is accepted by the seller, the effect is to discharge both parties from any duty of further performance (see para 26.16), so that the seller is discharged from his duty of delivery. At the same time, a defaulting buyer remains liable for damages for non-acceptance.[43] Is it any answer for that buyer to show that, had the contract continued in existence up until the time for delivery, the seller would have been

---

36  *Levy & Co v Goldberg* [1922] 1 KB 688, at 692.
37  *Per* Lord Abinger CB in *De Medina v Norman* (1842) 9 M & W 820 at 827. See also Dawson (1981) 96 LQR 239.
38  [1923] AC 48; [1922] All ER Rep 224, HL, discussed in Benjamin's *Sale of Goods*, 6th edn, para 9-013.
39  For the seller's action for non-acceptance, see generally, para 27.24.
40  At 71–72. Three other Law Lords concurred with this judgment; and the relevant passage in Lord Sumner's judgment was cited with approval by Devlin J in *Universal Cargo Corporation v Citati* [1957] 2 QB 401, 445.
41  At 71. Does this rebut the argument that, as the seller was still in breach, the buyer was still entitled to rescind? See Stoljar (1957) 35 Can BR 485, 509; and para 26.26.
42  As to the effect of a repudiation, see generally, para 26.15.
43  *British and Benningtons Ltd v North West Cacher Tea Co Ltd* (set out at para 23.05); discussed by Treitel, *Law of Contract*, 11th edn, 767–8.

unable to deliver?[44] Benjamin[45] answers that it depends who has made the first, and therefore wrongful, repudiation; but, in applying that principle, two others must be borne in mind. *First*, a seller is not necessarily in breach of contract by making a defective tender, as the contract may allow him time to cure that defect by re-tendering.[46] *Second*, if at the time of his repudiation, the buyer (unknown to himself) has a good reason for repudiation and that repudiation is accepted (see para 26.16), his repudiation does not give rise to any liability in damages, because the fact that he gave no reason (or a bad one) for his repudiation is irrelevant (see para 26.26).

*Wrongful repudiation accepted by seller.* Suppose the buyer wrongfully repudiates and the seller accepts that repudiation (see para 26.15), the buyer cannot escape liability for that repudiation by showing that, had the contract continued in existence, the seller would have been unable to perform his promise. In *Gill & Duffus SA v Berger & Co Inc,*[47]

> There was a sale by sample of 500 tonnes of Argentine 'bolita' (white) beans cif Le Havre. Suspecting that some of the beans were coloured, the buyer rejected the documents on the grounds that they did not include a certificate of quality. The seller re-tendered the documents, together with such a certificate in respect of the 445 tonnes already unloaded. The buyer again rejected the documents.

The House of Lords accepted that in a cif contract the seller has two separate duties, first to submit conforming documents, second to deliver conforming goods (see para 29.30). However, the House unanimously agreed that, since conforming documents were tendered,[48] the buyer's rejection of them was a wrongful repudiation; and that the seller, having accepted that repudiation, was released from his obligation to deliver conforming goods.[49] It followed that the buyer could not plead as a defence to liability that part of the cargo consisted of coloured beans,[50] which issue went only to damages.[51]

**[23.07] Wrongful repudiation not accepted by the seller**. Where the buyer's wrongful anticipatory repudiation is not accepted by the seller, then on principle the contract is kept alive for the benefit of both parties (see para 26.12), so that a subsequent event may release both parties from liability.[52] It would follow that the seller would continue bound by his duty of delivery: whilst he need not tender actual delivery (see para 23.05), he ought to continue ready and willing to deliver;

---

44  The doctrine of frustration would no longer be available: *Avery v Bowden* (1855) 5 E & B 714 (charterparty).

45  *Sale of Goods*, 6th edn, para 9.017. Cf. Dawson (1980) 96 LQR 239.

46  See *Borrowman Phillips & Co v Free & Hollis* (see para 29.03).

47  [1984] AC 382; [1984] 1 All ER 438, HL.

48  HL held the certificate of quality was not part of the shipping documents required to be presented by the seller, so that the absence of a certificate in respect of 55 tons was irrelevant. See further below.

49  *Aliter*, if the buyer had accepted the documents: the *Kwei Tek Chao* case (see para 29.30).

50  On this point, the HL reversed the CA, who had held that the buyer was entitled to rely on s 30 to repudiate (see para 13.03).

51  HL held the buyer had not in fact proved that any cargo was defective and was therefore liable for non-acceptance of the whole 500 tons (see para 27.33). See generally Benjamin, *Op. cit.*, para 9-019.

52  E.g. *Avery v Bowden* (1855) 5 E & B 714 (frustration, as to which, see generally above, para 22.14).

and it should be a good defence for the buyer to show that the seller was unable to perform his obligations at the time appointed for performance.[53] These propositions would appear to run counter to the Court of Appeal decision in *Braithwaite v Foreign Hardwood Co Ltd*;[54] but, in the *Simona*, a charterparty case,[55] in delivering the judgment of the House of Lords, Lord Ackner indicated that, unless *Braithwaite* could be treated as a case where repudiation was accepted (see para 23.06), it was wrong (at 805, 751j).

Nevertheless, if the innocent seller elects to keep the contract alive after the buyer's wrongful repudiation, the seller may put himself in a difficult position.[56] Although not accepting the wrongful repudiation,[57] the innocent seller may, for instance, refrain from delivering; and he may consequently be met by the buyer's argument that the seller did not have the capacity to perform at the time of delivery. In the *Simona*, the House of Lords suggested the following answer: if the buyer has clearly represented to the seller that there is no point in the seller attempting to deliver the goods, in acting on that representation the seller raises an estoppel against the buyer.[58]

## Acceptance of delivery

**[23.08]  Conforming goods.** Only where the seller tenders goods in conformity with the contract is it the buyer's duty to accept them.[59] If the buyer then wrongfully refuses to accept delivery,[60] s 37(1) of the SGA provides as follows:

> 'Where the seller is ready and willing to deliver goods, and requests the buyer to take delivery, and the buyer does not within a reasonable time[61] after such request take delivery of the goods, he is liable to the seller for any loss occasioned by his neglect or refusal to take delivery, and also for a reasonable charge for the care and custody of the goods.'

Whilst s 37 is not expressed to give way to a contrary intention, it is submitted that it will *prima facie* do so with the following result: if the contract stipulates a time for **acceptance** of delivery, the section is ousted and delivery must be made at that time; but, if the contract merely stipulates a time for **tender** of delivery, acceptance of delivery need only be made within a reasonable time thereafter; and, if there is no stipulation as to the time of delivery, s 37(1) requires the buyer to accept delivery

---

53   *Per* Lord Ackner in *The Simona* (below), delivering the judgment with which his fellow judges agreed.
54   [1905] 2 KB 543, CA, discussed by Benjamin's *Sale of Goods*, 6th edn, paras 9-012 and 19-162, *et seq.*
55   *Fercometal SARL v Mediterranean Shipping Co SA* [1989] AC 788; [1988] 2 All ER 742, HL, discussed by Benjamin, *Op. cit.*, para 9-015.
56   Atiyah, *Sale of Goods*, 10th edn, 118.
57   But, as to the effect of the seller's resale under SGA, s 48(3) and (4), see paras 27.08–10.
58   See Benjamin, *Op. cit.*, para 9.018.
59   SGA, s 27. This is one of the reasons for getting the buyer to sign a delivery receipt acknowledging that he has received the goods in the contract state: see para 23.02.
60   *Aliter* if the seller delays delivery for his own ends, or by exercising his unpaid seller's lien (see para 24.04): Benjamin's *Sale of Goods*, 6th edn, para 9-009.
61   What is a reasonable time is a question of fact: SGA, s 59.

within a reasonable time of the seller's request that he should do so. Section 37(2) expressly recognises that the buyer's delay in taking delivery may be so great as to evince an intention to repudiate the contract,[62] in which case it is treated as a non-acceptance (s 50(1): see para 27.24). In the case of a consumer supply, if there is a statutory right of cancellation, the above rules may be over-ridden (see para 23.09).

**[23.09] Non-conforming goods.** Where the goods tendered by the seller are **not** in conformity with the contract, the buyer is *prima facie* entitled to refuse to accept them,[63] in which case s 36 provides:

> 'Unless otherwise agreed, where goods are delivered to the buyer, and he refuses to accept them, having the right to do so, he is not bound to return them to the seller, but it is sufficient if he intimates to the seller that he refuses to accept them.'

This section seems to assume that there is a contract of sale between the parties; but, if the delivery merely amounts to an offer to sell, the ordinary common law rules of acceptance apply.[64] Where there is a contract of sale, it is open to the buyer who rejects to return the goods to the seller; but s 36 reaffirms the common law rule that he need not do so, and that *prima facie* the buyer may reject the goods by 'any unequivocal act showing that he rejects them'.[65] Again following the common law, it would seem that the buyer who evinces an intention to reject becomes a mere involuntary bailee of the goods, and is only under a duty to exercise care of them as a gratuitous bailee:[66] the underlying risk is on the erstwhile seller,[67] in whom the property in the goods remains or revests;[68] and that seller acquires an immediate right to possession of the goods.[69] Whilst the buyer has no lien on the rejected goods for repayment of the price (see para 24.03), he may be able to recover the price in quasi-contract where the contract of sale is rescinded (see para 29.13); and he can maintain an action against the seller for non-delivery of the contract goods (see para 29.18).

*Consumer supplies.* In such cases, any promise by the consumer to pay return carriage may be unfair.[70] Moreover, where there is a statutory right of cancellation, the consumer is in a strengthened position, regardless of whether or not the goods conformed with the contract. Thus, where a regulated cancellable agreement is

---

62  For repudiation, see further, para 26.15.

63  For the restrictions on the buyer's right to reject, see para 29.04.

64  Chalmers, *Sale of Goods*, 18th edn, 198: see further, para 10.02. As to unsolicited goods, see para 8.18.

65  *Per* Brett J in *Grimoldby v Wells* (1875) LR 1O CP 391, at 395. For an express agreement to reject in a certain manner, see *Docker v Hyams* [1969] 3 All ER 808, CA.

66  Benjamin's *Sale of Goods*, 6th edn, para 12-065; and generally, para 1.17.

67  It has been argued that the ordinary rules as to risk do not operate where the buyer validly rescinds for breach: Atiyah, *Sale of Goods*, 10th edn, 352; Goode, *Commercial Law*, 3rd edn, 248, fn 35.

68  As to the retention in (or reversion to) the seller of the property in goods after the buyer's rescission for breach, see para 26.11; and as to the ordinary rule as to the passing of risk, see para 22.01.

69  *Per* Bankes LJ in *E Hardy & Co (London) v Hillerns and Fowler* [1923] 2 KB 490, CA, at 496. See also *Commission Car Sales Ltd v Saul* [1957] NZLR 144; and see generally, para 19.06.

70  Grey Term (b): see para 11.16.

cancelled, generally the debtor or hirer is only under a duty to make the agreement goods available for collection by the creditor or owner (CCA, s 72(5): see para 10.34). A similar position obtains where the consumer exercises a right of cancellation in respect of a doorstep[71] or distance[72] supply.

**[23.10] Examination.**[73] Obviously, it is very important to the buyer to determine whether or not he must accept the goods tendered by the seller; and the SGA therefore gave him a right to examine the tendered goods before he accepted delivery of them (s 34).[74] This formulation was thought insufficiently generous to the buyer[75] and new s 34 provides (as amended by SGSA, s 2):

> 'Unless otherwise agreed, when the seller tenders delivery of goods to the buyer, he is bound, on request, to afford the buyer a reasonable opportunity of examining the goods for the purpose of ascertaining whether they are in conformity with the contract and, in the case of a contract for sale by sample, of comparing the bulk with the sample.'

As will be seen later, the buyer loses his right to reject by accepting the goods (see para 29.05) and will normally be liable for the price when the property has passed (see para 27.17). However, subject to the terms of the contract, s 34 gives the buyer a right, **on request**, to a reasonable opportunity for examination (see para 23.11) **before** he accepts delivery or pays the price, so that he may ensure that the goods correspond with the contract, e.g. in matters of description,[76] quantity[77] or quality[78] or with any sample.[79]

*Delivery or acceptance notes.* Particularly in those circumstances where the seller effects delivery at the buyer's premises,[80] it is common for the seller's delivery agent to demand that the buyer sign a delivery or acceptance note. Sometimes, such a note simply recites that the buyer acknowledges delivery and it is commonly so understood. However, the note may go further. It may state that the delivered goods were in the state required by the contract, though it seems doubtful whether such a clause will bar subsequent complaint by the buyer.[81] Alternatively, the note may be intended to operate as an acceptance of the goods by the buyer, so reducing him to the lesser claim for damages for any breach (s 35). The Law Commission recommended that this latter device was unfair to both consumer and non-consumer buyers (para 5.21). This recommendation has been adopted by

---

71   Doorstep Selling Regulations 1987, reg 7(3); and see generally, para 10.37.
72   Distance Selling Regulations 2000, reg 17(4); and see generally, para 10.38.
73   This right to examine before acceptance of delivery must not be confused with examination before contract: see para 14.26.
74   Old s 34 embodied the common law: *Benjamin on Sale*, 8th edn, 741, 753.
75   By the Law Commission: see *Sale and Supply of Goods* (1987, Law Com 160), para 5.20. For an explanation, see Bridge [1995] JBL 405–6.
76   SGA, s 13: see para 13.11.
77   SGA, s 30: see para 13.04-5.
78   SGA, ss 14 and 15(2)(c): see paras 14.07, 14.15 and 15.11.
79   SGA, s 15(2)(a): see para 15.06. The overlapping special opportunity to compare bulk with sample is defectively repealed: see para 15.08.
80   Thus ousting the ordinary SGA presumption of delivery at the seller's premises (s 29(2)): see para 23.04.
81   See *Lowe v Lombank Ltd* (set out at para 18.06).

amendment to s 35 (see para 29.05). Further, where there is a consumer supply, such a deemed acceptance may be an unfair term.[82]

**[23.11] Reasonable examination**. What constitutes a reasonable examination must depend on the nature of the goods[83] and any agreement between the parties.[84] The place of examination is *prima facie* the place of delivery;[85] but, if a reasonable examination is not possible at that place, the courts will try to read the contract so that the place where an effective examination is first possible is the place the parties have agreed upon for the examination.[86] This will commonly be the buyer's place of business,[87] or the place of delivery to a sub-buyer;[88] but it has been said that the latter will only be the place of acceptance where:[89]

> 'the original vendor must know, either because he is told or by necessary inference, that the goods are going further on, and the place at which he delivers must either be unsuitable in itself or the nature or packing of the goods must make inspection at that place unreasonable.'

Such an approach has been adopted where the defect was a latent one not discoverable on delivery;[90] or where the delivery was to be made at a wharf where only a cursory inspection was possible;[87] or where the goods were specially packaged for carriage to a sub-buyer,[91] a rule which perhaps extends in the consumer context to gift-wrapped goods. It has been held that the conduct of the seller must be taken into account in determining what is a reasonable time.[92] Presumably, the same is true for the nature of the goods, e.g. the purchaser of a fitted carpet cannot effectively examine it until it has been fitted; the purchaser in January of a lawn mower cannot effectively test it until the Spring.

**[23.12] Bailees**. Whilst there is no authority on the point, it is thought that the position of a bailee under an hp or simple hiring agreement is similar to that of a buyer in respect of acceptance of delivery. Thus, it is the duty of the bailee to take delivery (see para 15.24); and failure to do so will render him liable to damages,[93] and may even evince an intention to repudiate (see para 26.15). Furthermore, it would seem that, before accepting delivery and rendering himself liable to pay instalments of rent, the hirer has a right of examination similar to that of the buyer under the SGA 1893.[94]

---

82  OFT, *Bulletin No. 14*, case 1; and see further, para 11.12, *et seq*. It has been recommended that consumers endorse the note 'unexamined': see Benjamin's *Sale of Goods*, 6th edn, para 13-095.

83  See, e.g. *Esmail & Sons v Rosenthal & Sons Ltd* [1964] 2 Lloyd's Rep 447, CA; reversed on other grounds [1965] 2 All ER 860, HL.

84  *W Potts & Co Ltd v Brown, Marfarlane & Co Ltd* (1924) 30 Com Cas 64, HL.

85  *Perkins v Bell* [1893] 1 QB 193, CA (pre-SGA 1893); and *per* Pearce LJ in *Long v Lloyd* (set out at para 26.13) at 407.

86  E.g. fob contracts: *Scaliaris v E Ofverberg* (1921) 37 TLR 307, CA; *Boks & Co v JH Rayner & Co* (1921) 37 TLR 800, CA; *Bragg v Villanova* (1923) 40 TLR 154, DC. See further Benjamin's *Sale of Goods*, 6th edn, paras 20–105/7.

87  *B and P Wholesale Distributors v Marko* [1953] CLY 3266.

88  E.g. *Heilbutt v Hickson* (1872) LR 7 CP 438; *Molling & Co v Dean & Son Ltd* (1901) 18 TLR 217, DC.

89  *Per* Bailhache J in *Saunt v Belcher and Gibbons Ltd* (1920) 26 Com Cas 115, at 119.

90  *Heilbutt v Hickson* (above).

91  *Molling & Co v Dean & Son Ltd* (above).

92  *Lucy v Mouflet* (1860) 29 LJ Ex 110.

93  But not to any instalments of hire-rent: see para 27.21.

94  *Farnworth Finance Facilities Ltd v Attyde* [1970] 2 All ER 774, CA (hp). See para 23.10.

# PAYMENT

The SGA makes it clear that it is the duty of the buyer to pay the price (s 27); an hp or a simple hiring agreement will usually impose a similar obligation on the hirer with respect to the instalments of hire-rent (see para 15.23); and a contract of loan will usually expressly provide for repayment, whether by lump sum or instalments (see para 7.03). This obligation to pay the price or other debt should be carefully distinguished from a claim for damages for breach of contract (see para 27.15A).

**[23.13] The duty to pay.**[95] At common law, payment is a consensual act requiring the consent of both creditor and debtor, whereas tender is a unilateral act by the debtor. The obligation of the buyer, hirer or debtor to pay or tender (see para 23.14) the debt is balanced by the obligation (implied if not express) on the part of the seller, owner or creditor not to refuse the whole or part of the debt where this is tendered in conformity with the contract (see para 24.14). At common law, it is *prima facie* the duty of the debtor or his authorised agent[96] to tender the exact nominal amount of his debt to the creditor,[97] or to such agent as the creditor author- ises to receive payment under the ordinary rules of agency (see para 10.06), which rules are expressly saved by s 62(2) SGA,[98] e.g. the Bank Giro (BACS) system,[99] the dealer in a financed transaction (see paras 2.21–2). Acceptance of that tender turns it into payment, whilst even an unaccepted valid tender produces certain legal effects: for instance, the seller is no longer 'unpaid' within the SGA, s 38(1)(a) (see para 24.03); the creditor's court proceedings may be adjourned on his receipt of a cheque;[100] and, in the case of regulated agreements, 'payment' includes a valid tender (CCA, s 189(1)). Default in payment may give rise to express remedies[101] and those implied by law, e.g. withholding performance (see SGA, s 28: set out at para 23.16); damages (see para 27.28, *et seq.*); termination (see para 26.08, *et seq.*); remedies of an unpaid seller (see para 24.03, *et seq*). Normally, payments made are irrecoverable[102] and the creditor may be bound by a mistakenly low settlement figure (see para 26.04).

---

95 See generally, Goode, *Payment Obligations in Commercial and Financial Transactions.*

96 E.g. *Bennett v Griffin Finance* [1967] 2 QB 46, CA. See generally, *Chitty on Contract*, 28th edn, para 22-041.

97 *Bradford Old Bank v Sutcliffe* [1918] 2 KB 833, CA. For the principle of nominalism, see Goode, *Op. cit.*, 33. For exact performance, see para 26.04.

98 See further, Chitty, *Op. cit.*, paras 22–043 and 22–096; Jones, *Credit Cards*, 158; Arora, *Electronic Banking*, 2nd edn, 10–12; Jacks, *Report on Banking Services* (1989, Cm. 622), paras 7.22–81. For the distinction between an agent and a stakeholder, see *Bank of Scotland v Trumen* [2005] EWHC 583, at paras 50–74.

99 *Commissioners of Customs & Excise v National Westminster Bank plc* [2003] 1 All ER (Comm) 327. The BACS system is steadily increasing in popularity: in 2003, it reported an 8% increase in use, largely at the expense of cheques: *The Times* 24.1.04.

100 *Coltrane v Day* [2003] 1 WLR 1379, CA.

101 E.g. *sometimes* interest on overdue payments (see para 7.03A); acceleration clauses (see paras 23.26 and 26.19); repossession (see para 24.23, *et seq.*); termination (see para 26.08 *et seq.*); liquidated damages (see para 27.29).

102 Exceptionally, payments may be recoverable, e.g. where there is a condition subsequent as on sale or return (see para 20.23, *et seq.*); where there is a total failure of consideration (see para 29.12); under the equitable rule for relief against forfeiture (see para 27.20); where money is paid under a mistake.

*Multiple debts to the same person.* If the buyer, hirer or debtor owes more than one debt to the same person, he is *prima facie* entitled when making a payment to appropriate that payment to a particular debt. If the debtor remains silent, the creditor is entitled at common law to make such appropriation as he thinks fit.[103] However, the creditor is usually deprived of this right by the CCA, s 81, where payments are due under two or more regulated agreements. *Prima facie*, the debtor or hirer is entitled to make the appropriation (s 81(1)): if he fails to do so, in the case of hp, conditional sales and consumer hirings, appropriation will usually be *pro rata* (s 81(2)); but, with other multiple consumer credit agreements, e.g. credit sale, loan and card debts, the creditor retains the residual power of appropriation.[104] Note that s 81 is limited to the situation where there is more than one regulated agreement between the parties, so that it does not interfere with the creditor's power of appropriation under a single regulated agreement, e.g. a single Visa card.[105] Special rules obtain where the creditor or debtor is insolvent (see para 19.12); or subject to a Third Party Order (see para 27.04); or the payment is to be made by instalments (see paras 23.26–27) or by post (see para 23.14); or the debtor is unlawfully harassed (see para 24.25); or the right to receive payment has been assigned (see para 7.16); or payment is of a lesser sum (see para 26.18); or unenforceable[106] or in respect of tracing (see para 27.13).

**[23.14] Valid tender.** What constitutes a valid tender will depend on the terms of the agreement creating the debt (see para 23.13) and the ordinary law.[107] *Prima facie*, in a contract governed by English law the debtor must seek out the creditor[108] and proffer his debt in pounds sterling, which is the legal tender.[109] The position may vary where such payment is sent by post[110] or the initial debt is later discharged by subsequent agreement or set off.[111] However, it may be that the supplier cannot be required to contract for cash;[112] and the agreement may instead provide another form of payment.

---

103 See *Chitty on Contract, Op. cit.*, para 22-059, *et seq.*

104 But the agreement must contain a statement explaining that: Agreement Regulations (see para 9.11), Sched 1, para 14A.

105 So the card-issuer offering 0% balance transfers is entitled to appropriate payments first to the balance transferred ('the balance transfer trap': see [2003] 5 *Which?* 12), which may be an offence under CCA, s 46 (see para 8.28).

106 As being a penalty (see paras 27.46 and 27.38); or under the doctrines of frustration (see para 22.14, *et seq.*) or unconscionable bargain (see para 29.40).

107 See generally *Chitty on Contract*, 28th edn, para 22-039. The EU plan to review the forms of consumer payment: [2002] 7 *Consumer Law Today* 8 at 10.

108 See Chitty, *Op. cit.*, para 22-054. This ties in with the duty of the seller to make delivery at his own premises (s 29(2)): see para 23.04.

109 For discussion of legal tender, see *Halsbury's Laws*, 4th edn rev, Vol 9(1), para 975; and see further, paras 2.06 and 7.24. If/when the UK joins the EMU, the Euro will presumably become the legal tender. For decimalisation, see para 4.24.

110 The express or implied authority by a creditor for his debtor to post a cheque to him may transfer the risk of loss in course of post on the creditor: Chalmers, *Bills of Exchange*, 15th edn, para 374. But this is not necessarily so: see (1994) 144 NLJ 419. Such possibility of loss may be obviated by using the 1992 Act cheque forms: see para 7.28.

111 See *Sinochem International Oil (London) Co Ltd v Mobil Sales and Supply Corpn* [2000] 1 All ER (Comm) 474, CA. As to variation, waiver or novation, see paras 26.18, *et seq.*; and as to set-off, see para 7.23; and *Hong Kong and Shanghai Banking Corpn v Kloeckner & Co AG* [1990] 2 QB 514 (contracting out of set-off—which may in other cases be subject to UCTA: see para 18.16).

112 White Paper on *Banking Services* (1990, Cm. 1026) Annexe 8.22.

In domestic transactions, where the obligations will normally be in sterling, instead of legal tender (see above), the debt to the supplier may instead be settled by 'digital money' (see para 2.24); or by Bank Giro (see para 23.13); or by payment card or voucher;[113] or by credit note;[114] or by gift voucher[115] or token, e.g. electricity tokens; or by debit card (see para 23.15), perhaps effected by telephone or internet (see para 8.16A); or by Postal Orders;[116] or increasingly rarely by cheque.[117] Further, where there is an instalment credit transaction (see para 1.03), the supplier may prefer to insist that payments are made by banker's standing order or by direct debit.[118] In such cases, the supplier may also require a deposit before delivery, perhaps partly as a test of creditworthiness: such a deposit may be paid by way of legal tender (see above), but frequently takes the form of a part-exchange. In the last case, the parties will usually themselves agree a price to be put on the part-exchanged goods (see para 2.09); and the CCA expressly includes such part-exchange allowance in the deposit (see para 2.07).

[23.15] **Debit cards.**[119] These are plastic payment cards used to effect a transmission of funds from the bank or other account of the debtor to the account of his creditor by way of EFT (see para 2.17) and have been likened to an electronic cheque (see para 2.25), although it would seem that the debit card arrangements make no provision for a debit to be stopped.[120] To operate one of these cards to transfer a sum of money from his account, the card-holder inserts it into an electronic reader, which connects it by telephone to his account and then authorises the transaction either by signature on a flimsy or by PIN.[121] Such cards may involve two or three parties: a two-party cash card is used by the holder to extract cash from his account via an ATM; whereas a three-party card is used by the holder for making retail payments for goods and services at the point of sale, so they are known as EFTPOS cards.[122]

Even at common law, the several different contracts necessary to effect debit card transactions[123] give rise to a number of problems. *First*, is payment by way of

---

113 For payment cards and vouchers, see generally, paras 2.24, *et seq*. Unlike payment by cheque, payment by credit or charge card *prima facie* amounts to absolute payment: *Re Charge Card Services Ltd* (set out at para 2.27).

114 As to which, see para 29.02. Is it an assignable (see para 7.21) promissory note (see para 7.24)?

115 For gift vouchers, see para 15.18. For early settlement, see para 26.19A.

116 The revamped Postal Orders are most used for sending money as gifts, paying for mail order purchases, household bills and purchases on eBay (see *The Times* 27.4.06). For the Post Office, see para 2.15.

117 The number of (almost always 'account payee': see para 7.28) cheques drawn is decreasing rapidly and now accounts for less than 8% of domestic purchases, commonly with a cheque guarantee card (see para 2.26). For the rules regarding payment by cheque, see 1st edn, para 23.14A. A Government Payments Systems Task Force is due to report in September 2006 see OFT, AR-2005/6, 9.

118 Giving a DD has been held equivalent to a cash payment: *Weldon v GRE Life Assurance Ltd* [2000] 2 All ER 914 (not a goods case). See also *Esso Petroleum Ltd v Milton* [1997] 2 All ER 593, CA.

119 See generally *Chitty on Contract*, 28th edn, paras 38.438/40.

120 Arora, *Electronic Banking*, 2nd edn, 74.

121 See para 2.24. Is a flimsy a negotiable instrument (see para 7.24)?

122 E(lectronic) F(und) T(ransfer) at P(oint) O(f) S(ale). For EFT generally, see para 2.17.

123 These follow a similar analysis to that in *Re Charge Card Services Ltd* (set out at para 2.27). If the debit card-issuer is not debiting a (bank) account which it holds, there may be an extra contract between the card-issuer and the card-holder's bank: see para 2.28.

debit card conditional payment like a cheque (see para 23.14A); or is it absolute payment like a charge card (see para 2.27)? It has been argued that it is absolute payment,[124] perhaps because it cannot be stopped (see above). *Second*, these systems are usually off-line, i.e. recorded by the bank and processed subsequently, so that the debtor has a similar delay between use of his debit card and debiting of his account to that which he would have had if payment had been made by cheque.[125]

In neither case is credit an essential element of the transaction, though use of the card may draw down credit facilities already established on that bank or other account (see para 7.03). As a significant deferment of payment is necessary for the credit essential for a transaction to fall within the CCA (see para 5.21), it has therefore been argued that debit cards are not *per se* regulated,[126] though there has been disagreement as to whether or not debit cards can amount to credit tokens within s 14 (see para 5.30). If, like charge cards (see para 5.15), debit cards are also outside the ambit of the CCA, this will mean that the legal rules applicable to charge and debit cards differ substantially from those governing regulated credit cards, even though they may all be dealt with in an identical way by the Banking Code (see para 3.12). It has been pointed out that this inconsistency of legal treatment is undesirable, as being unreasonable and confusing to customers;[127] and statutory reform should be considered.

## THE TIME OF DELIVERY AND PAYMENT

**[23.16]** Having analysed the duties of payment and delivery, the importance of the time element in their performance must now be examined.[128] *First*, reference must be made to the connection between payment and the right of the buyer or hirer to sue in conversion. It has been seen that a person can only maintain an action in conversion where he is entitled to the immediate possession of goods (see para 19.06); and this in turn depends on whether the supplier is bound to deliver immediately. *Second*, it must be remembered that each party has two obligations: it is for the supplier to tender delivery of the goods and accept payment of the price or rent; and for the buyer or hirer to accept delivery of the goods and tender payment of the price or rent. The basic rule for sale is laid down in s 28 of the SGA as follows:

> 'Unless otherwise agreed, delivery of the goods and payment of the price are concurrent conditions, that is to say, the seller must be ready and willing to give possession of the goods to the buyer in exchange for the price and the buyer must be ready and willing to pay the price in exchange for the possession of the goods.'

---

124 Arora, *Op. cit.*, 71.
125 For recent attempts to speed up electronic payments systems, see OFT (2006) *Fair Trading* 13. The Banks have promised same-day transfers by the end of 2007 (*The Times* 17.7.06).
126 Because it is purely a payment/debit mechanism: Goode, *Consumer Credit Law & Practice*, paras 3.43, 3.47 and 24.84.
127 The Jack's *Report on Banking Services* (1989, Cmnd. 622), paras 11.04–11, rejecting the call for a Payments Card Act; and the White Paper on *Banking Services* (1990, Cmnd. 1026), Annex 8.3.
128 SGA, s 10(3), defines a 'month' as *prima facie* a calendar month.

Two situations must be considered: (i) where the contract contemplates that the basic presumption of concurrent events applies (see below); and (ii) where it does not (see para 23.22). However, there should be noted the special rules for consumer distance contracts (see para 23.04).

## Where delivery and payment are concurrent terms

**[23.17]** Where the presumption in s 28 operates, delivery must be made in exchange for the price: that is, the SGA envisages that the seller will hold out the goods, the buyer will hold out the price, and price and goods will be exchanged simultaneously.[129] Thus, it is whilst the buyer is still holding out the price that the Act envisages that he will exercise his right under s 34 to inspect the goods (see para 23.10). However, where the contract contemplates delivery of documents of title, these documents are equivalent to the goods (see para 23.03), so that on delivery of the documents the seller is thereupon entitled to the price;[130] but the buyer retains the right to inspect and reject the goods,[131] so that a provision requiring a consumer to pay on delivery may be unfair.[132]

In order to appreciate the effect of delay in performance by either party, the status of the obligations of delivery and payment must first be examined. In *Bunge Corpn v Tradax*:[133]

> There was a chain of contracts, including one for the sale of 5,000 tons of soya bean meal fob at an American Gulf Port nominated by the sellers. Clause 17 stipulated that the buyers should 'give at least 15 consecutive days' notice' of the probable readiness of the buyer's vessel so that the sellers could arrange for the goods to be available at a Gulf Port they would then nominate. The buyers were four days late in giving the notice required by clause 17, which the sellers claimed amounted to a repudiation. The buyers argued that clause 17 was an innominate term; and the sellers conceded that, if so, the breach was not sufficiently serious to entitle them to treat the contract as being repudiated.

The House of Lords unanimously found for the seller, holding that clause 17 was a condition[134] for the following reasons: stipulations as to time in mercantile contracts were generally to be treated as conditions, even minor breaches of which might amount to repudiations,[135] both to enable each party to organise his affairs and to meet the need for certainty, especially necessary in the case of strings of contracts.[136] Of course, such stipulations may be waived (see paras 26.23–25); and anyway, it may be that the decision would not apply where a private buyer buys for consumption.

---

129  But see Oditah, *Legal Aspects of Accounts Receivable*, 1.
130  *Clements Horst v Biddell Brothers* [1912] AC 18, HL.
131  This dual right of rejection is explained at para 22.07.
132  OFT, *UCT Bulletin No. 22*, case 26.
133  [1981] 2 All ER 513, HL. See also *Gill & Duffus SA v Societe Pour L'Exploration des Sucres SA* [1986] 1 Lloyd's Rep 322, CA ('at latest').
134  For conditions and innominate terms, see para 11.05.
135  *Contra* delay in acceptance of delivery (see para 23.19) or tender of payment (see SGA, s 10(1): para 23.20).
136  For criticism of this doctrine, see Goode (1983) 3 Legal Studies at 285–6.

**[23.18]** **Tender of delivery**. In the case of hp agreements, the hiring does not commence until delivery (see para 15.23); but, subject to this, it is presumed that, insofar as the agreement does not cover delay in delivery, those rules of sale which relate to delivery apply by analogy. In fact, the SGA refrains from laying down any hard and fast rule as to whether the time of delivery is of the essence of the contract (s 10(2): set out at para 23.20), but does require that the 'demand or tender of delivery' be made at a reasonable hour (s 29(5): see para 23.04) and makes the duty to tender delivery subject to the unpaid seller's lien (see para 24.10). According to McCardie J:[137]

> 'In ordinary commercial contracts for the sale of goods the rule clearly is that time is *prima facie* of the essence with respect to delivery.'

This statement must obviously be read subject to the statutory rules just mentioned, and hides an ambiguity: the learned Judge may have been saying that delay is always fatal; or only such delay as causes serious loss amounts to a breach entitling the other side to rescind.[138] In fact, the courts have decided that, if a commercial contract stipulates a time for delivery,[139] any breach by the seller entitles the buyer to rescind,[140] even if he has suffered no damage.[141] However, if the contract is not a commercial one, or does not stipulate a time for delivery,[142] the SGA merely requires that the seller must deliver within a reasonable time (s 29(2): set out at para 23.04), though the seller's delay may be so great as to show an intention to repudiate,[143] or the buyer may give notice to the seller making 'time of the essence',[144] so making timely performance a condition.[144]

*Consumer sales*. It may seem a pity that there does not appear to be a *prima facie* rule for retail sales. Should they be regarded as a sort of 'spot' contract (see para 23.19)? However, in a distance sale the goods must be supplied within a maximum of thirty days,[145] otherwise the supply agreement and any related credit agreement shall be treated as if the supply agreement were cancellable;[146] and a provision allowing delay in delivery may be unfair.[147]

**[23.19]** **Acceptance of delivery**. Bearing in mind the foregoing rules for tender of delivery (see para 23.18), it might be thought that the law would impose reciprocal obligations with respect to acceptance of delivery. However, the law will only assume that acceptance of delivery is of the essence where the goods are

---

137 In *Hartley v Hymans* (set out at para 26.24), at 484. See also *Bunge Corpn v Tradax* (set out at para 23.17).

138 See Stoljar (1955) 71 LQR 527, at 532.

139 Unless waived: see *Hartley v Hymans* (above).

140 *The Naxos* [1990] 3 All ER 641, HL. As to damages for non-delivery, see para 29.19.

141 *Bowes v Shand* (1877) 2 App Cas 455, HL.

142 E.g. *McDougall v Aeromarine of Emsworth Ltd* [1958] 3 All ER 431 (seller to use his 'best endeavours').

143 Cf. *Pearl Mill Co v Ivy Tannery Co* [1919] 1 KB 78. For repudiation, see para 26.15.

144 If a non-commercial contract stipulates a time for delivery: *Charles Rickards Ltd v Oppenheim* (set out at para 26.25); and generally Stannard (2003) 120 LQR 137.

145 Distance Selling Regulations 2000, reg 19(1); and see generally, para 8.17.

146 Reg 20; and see para 10.38.

147 [2005] *UCT Bulletin* A/J, *Micro*; and para 11.16A.

perishable[148] or there is a 'spot' contract.[149] In all other cases, it is assumed that the time of acceptance of delivery is not of the essence;[150] that, if no time of acceptance is specified, the buyer is merely required to accept delivery within a reasonable time;[151] and that further delay merely gives the seller the right to damages,[152] unless it is so great as to show an intention to repudiate.[153] In a commercial contract, why should the time of tender of delivery normally amount to a condition, whilst the time of acceptance of delivery is only a warranty? It has been suggested that, apart from the cases of perishable goods and 'spot' contracts, the seller's prime interest is to obtain the price whereas that of the buyer is to obtain delivery, so that it is understandable that the tender of delivery is more important to the buyer than acceptance of delivery is to the seller.[154] Yet it ought to follow that the tender of the price by the buyer is also an essential term; but this is not so (see para 23.20).

[23.20] **Payment**. It is the duty of the buyer to tender the price and of the seller to accept the price at the time laid down in the contract,[155] or, if no time is stipulated, within a reasonable time.[156] Section 10 of the SGA provides as follows:

'(1)  Unless a different intention appears from the terms of the contract, stipulations as to time of payment are not of the essence of a contract of sale.

(2)  Whether any other stipulation as to time is or is not of the essence of the contract depends on the terms of the contract.'

However, s 10(1) appears to conflict with s 28 of the SGA, which states that payment and delivery shall be 'concurrent conditions'. Perhaps the explanation lies in the different usage of the word 'condition' (see para 11.04): it may be that s 28 is referring to 'condition' exclusively in the sense of condition precedent, and not in the sense of a contractual promise,[157] whereas s 10(1) is dealing with the importance of the contractual promise. Certainly, the courts have acted on s 10(1), and held that its effect is to create a presumption that stipulations as to the time of payment are only warranties,[158] and it has been said that this reflects a more general common law rule.[159]

Of course, this presumption may be displaced, as when the contract provides for the payment of a deposit (see para 23.27), or the exercise of an option,[160] or where the buyer contracts to open a banker's confirmed credit,[161] or the goods are

---

148 *Sharp v Christmas* (1892) 8 TLR 687, CA; cf. SGA, s 48(3): see para 27.08.
149 A 'spot' contract is one which envisages almost immediate delivery, e.g. *Thames Sack & Bag Co Ltd v Knowles & Co Ltd* (1919) 88 LJKB 585.
150 *Woolfe v Horn* (1877) 2 QBD 355.
151 *Shearson Lehman Hutton v Maclaine Watson & Co* [1990] 2 Lloyd's Rep 570.
152 *Penarth Dock Engineering Co Ltd v Pounds* [1963] 1 Lloyd's Rep 359.
153 *Pearl Mill Co v Ivy Tannery Co* [1919] 1 KB 78. For repudiation, see para 26.15.
154 Stoljar (1955), 71 LQR 527, at 538. *Sed quaere?*
155 See Goode, *Payment Obligations in Commercial and Financial Transaction*, 64–9.
156 See *Brighty v Norman* (1862) 3 B & S 305 (stipulation for payment on request).
157 See Smith & Thomas, *Casebook on Contract*, 11th edn, 424.
158 *Payzu Ltd v Saunders* (set out at para 27.44).
159 Goode, *Op. cit.*, 74.
160 *United Dominions Trust (Commercial) Ltd v Eagle Aircraft Services Ltd* [1968] 1 All ER 104, CA. See also credit cards (below).
161 *Trans Trust SPRL v Danubian Trading Ltd* [1952] 2 QB 297, CA.

perishable (SGA, s 48(3): discussed at para 27.08). It is fairly common to find time of payment expressly made of the essence in a standard-form contract:[162] but in a consumer supply this may be an unfair term;[163] and in any standard form it may be unreasonable (UCTA, s 3: see para 18.20).

Even where time is not of the essence of the original contract, the delay in payment may be so great as to show an intention to repudiate (see para 26.15); or the seller may by giving notice make time of the essence.[164] Thus, in the case of regulated credit cards, the debtor will usually have an option as to the amount payable;[160] but if he breaks the terms of that option, the agreement will usually make time of the essence as to the whole debt,[162] though it may not be able to require an increased **rate** of interest payable on default (default interest).[165] However, as with all regulated agreements, a notice making time of the essence will be subject to the default notice procedure (CCA, s 87: see para 24.30).

[23.21] **Delivery and payment**. The relative importance of the stipulations as to the time of delivery and payment can now be examined. Leaving aside such delays as manifest an intention to repudiate, s 28 of the SGA appears to create a statutory stalemate; but what it really means is that each of the parties must be ready and willing[166] to perform his part of the bargain before the other party performs his obligations.[167] Moreover, the effect of s 10 would appear to be to allow the time of delivery to remain an essential undertaking, whilst making the time of payment a warranty: if the seller does not deliver on time, the buyer may treat the contract as repudiated; but if the buyer does not pay the price on time, the seller is only entitled to damages.[168] This state of affairs has been criticised as extending 'compulsory credit to the buyer'.[169] But it must be remembered that the unpaid seller is entitled to retain possession of the goods until payment under two provisions of the SGA: s 28 makes payment of the price a condition precedent to the duty of the seller to deliver the goods; and s 39 gives the seller a lien on the goods for the price (see para 24.04).

## Where delivery and payment are not concurrent terms

[23.22] The parties to a contract for the supply of goods are quite at liberty to oust the presumption in s 28 (set out at para 23.16) and make performance on one side conditional on prior performance by the other, whether in whole or in part.

---

162 See para 26.08. For acceleration clauses, see para 7.03; and for standard-form contracts, see generally, para 11.08.
163 OFT, *UCT Bulletin No. 5*, p 121; and see generally, para 11.12.
164 E.g. under the SGA, s 48(3). See generally, Goode, *Op. cit.*, 76–9.
165 Where the agreement is regulated, by reason of CCA, s 93: see Jones, *Credit Cards*, 163–5; and generally, para 26.19.
166 And able? See para 23.06.
167 As to concurrent conditions, see further, para 26.01.
168 Because the only consequence is that he is deprived of the use of the money: Goode, *Commercial Law*, 3rd edn, 407.
169 Stoljar (1955) 71 LQR 527 at 540.

1.  *Prior payment.* Where the contract provides for payment in advance of delivery, the seller is entitled to sue for the price without tendering delivery (SGA, s 49(2): set out at para 27.18): he merely has to show an intention to continue with the contract (see para 23.05). In relation to consumer transactions, this form of business is common for mail order,[170] double glazing, goods made-to-measure, e.g. suits, and goods not held by a retailer in stock, e.g. furniture. Any substantial delay between payment and delivery increases the risk that the consumer will lose his pre-payments, e.g. on the seller's insolvency.[171] Whilst some protection is offered by voluntary codes,[172] present legal safeguards are somewhat inadequate: some redress is obtainable if dishonesty can be proved (see para 4.01), which may lead to a compensation order (see para 3.20); or if a supplying company is liquidated;[173] or the consumer may avoid the problem by paying by credit card and using CCA, s 75 (see para 16.11); or the supplier may help by putting such prior payments into a trust account,[174] or by insuring them.[175] Moreover, prior payment deprives the customer of the leverage of withholding payment where the goods supplied are defective, so it may amount to an unfair term;[176] but the OFT have negotiated a 'voluntary' scheme whereby on complaint a furniture retailer will deposit 20% of the price with Qualitas.[177]

2.  *Prior delivery.* Similarly, if the contract provides for delivery in advance of payment, e.g. credit or conditional sale (see paras 1.12–16), the buyer is entitled to sue for non-delivery without tendering the price (SGA, s 51(1): set out at para 29.19). Alternatively, the buyer in this last situation may maintain an action in conversion against the seller, as he is *prima facie* entitled to immediate possession;[178] but he will lose this right if insolvent, because the unpaid seller's lien will arise by reason of the insolvency (SGA, s 41(1): set out at para 24.10).

Finally, it must be borne in mind that delay in performance of the obligation to deliver or pay may show an intention to repudiate (see para 23.19).

---

170  In a distance contract, the consumer should be aware of the pre-payment by reason of the notification provisions in the Distance Selling Regulations: see para 9.04.

171  As to insolvency, see para 19.12, *et seq.* And see generally OFT, *Don't Wave Your Money Goodbye* (1987); (1990) 7 Tr L 229.

172  E.g. the Mail Order Protection and Double Glazing Schemes. See para 3.13.

173  On the grounds of carrying on a business with intent to defraud creditors: see Insolvency Act 1986, ss 213 and 215; and further, para 19.24.

174  See *Re Kayford* (set out at para 19.24). For a failed scheme, see [2001] 7 *Which?* 4. A false claim that money will be held in a trust fund may amount to a TDA offence: see para 4.16.

175  Cf. product liability insurance (see para 17.09). For creditors' rights, see para 16.17.

176  OFT, *Bulletin No. 13*, para 1.9; *No. 14*, case 16; *No. 15*, para 15 and case 1; and see generally, para 11.12, *et seq.*

177  See OFT, *UCT Bulletin No. 18*, p 43; and generally, para 3.11. The OFT have negotiated a similar scheme in respect of home improvements: OFT, *2001 A-R* 38.

178  *Per* Bayley J in *Bloxam v Sanders* (1825) 4 B & C 941, at 948–9. It is sometimes said that this case conflicts with *Chinery v Viall* (set out at para 29.24), though in both cases it was irrelevant whether the sale was on credit. See also *Healing (Sales) Ltd v Inglis Ltd* (1968) 42 ALJR 280; and generally, para 19.06.

# PERFORMANCE BY INSTALMENTS

**[23.23]** It is quite compatible with s 28 of the SGA that either or both of the obligations of delivery or payment may be discharged by instalments. Indeed, if the parties agree that both delivery and payment shall be by matching instalments, they are plainly adhering to the basic presumption of s 28, e.g. a book club. On the other hand, it is open to the parties to provide that only one of the obligations shall be performed by instalments. However, in a consumer supply, this must not be done in a manner unfair to consumers.[179]

## Delivery by instalments

**[23.24] General.** One consequence of the general duty to deliver the right quantity[180] is that after accepting a short delivery the buyer is *prima facie* not obliged to accept a subsequent tender of the balance.[181] Nor is he entitled to demand delivery by instalments.[182] Thus, to permit delivery by instalments, there must be some agreement between the parties to this effect. No doubt, the typical litigation situation where the parties agree to instalment deliveries involves a 'lengthy course of dealings and great quantities of goods';[183] but it should be remembered that the rules also cover cases such as a retail sale where the consumer takes some goods away with him and has the rest delivered.

Whether a contract provides for delivery by instalments is a question of construction;[184] and, where it does so, the contract may be susceptible of any one of the following interpretations:

(1) That the parties intend that there should be not one contract, but a series of contracts between them;[185] or

(2) That the parties intend that there should be a single contract, but that that contract should be divisible or severable in the sense that each instalment is to be paid for separately;[186] or

(3) That the parties intend that there should be a single contract, and that the price is to be paid as a single sum.[187]

Which interpretation is adopted may be important for several reasons:[188] first, in determining whether acceptance of part of the goods prevents the buyer

---

179 See OFT, *Bulletin No. 12*, case 13; *No. 13*, case 1; *No. 14*, case 3; *No. 26*, p 69; and generally, para 11.12, *et seq*.

180 Under the SGA, s 30: see paras 13.03–7. Cf. the common law rule of exact performance: see para 26.02.

181 SGA, s 31(1). E.g. *Behrend and Co v Produce Brokers Co* (set out at para 13.04).

182 Goode, *Commercial Law*, 2nd edn, 281.

183 Stoljar (1955) 71 LQR 527, at 543.

184 E.g. *Howell v Evans* (1926) 134 LT 570. See generally, Goode, *Op. cit.*, 3rd edn, 272.

185 See Benjamin's *Sale of Goods*, 6th edn, para 8-074. Cf. SGA, s 57(1): see para 10.10.

186 E.g. *Robert Munro & Co Ltd v Meyer* [1930] 2 KB 312; *Jackson v Rotax Motor and Cycle Co* (set out at para 14.05), CA; and para 23.25.

187 E.g. *Longbottom & Co Ltd v Bass, Walker & Co* [1922] WN 245, CA; *J Rosenthal Ltd v Esmail* [1965] 2 All ER 860, HL.

188 See further, Goode, *Op. cit.*, 275–6.

subsequently rejecting the remainder (see paras 29.08–09); second, in deciding whether breach by the seller or buyer in respect of one of the instalments amounts to a repudiation of the whole contract;[189] third, in establishing the unpaid seller's real rights (see para 24.08); and fourth, to decide whether delivery is subject to the strict rules of s 30 (see para 23.25).

Where there is a series of contracts, then, however serious the breach of one of them, it cannot, without more, amount to a repudiation of the others. But in practice, the courts seem reluctant to treat an instalment contract as a series of contracts; and even a provision that each delivery shall be treated as a separate contract tends to be construed as indicating that there is a single contract under which each instalment is to be paid for separately.[190] Assuming that there is a single contract, the next question is whether performance of that contract is divisible. Where performance is indivisible, a serious breach in respect of one instalment is treated as giving rise to a right to rescind in the same manner as partial breach of a non-instalment contract would do;[191] whereas a partial breach of a divisible contract will not necessarily have such an effect (see para 23.25). Whilst the foregoing rules were developed in relation to commercial buyers, they should also be applicable to consumer buyers, e.g. order on a single mail-order form of multiple items, only some of which the supplier has in stock.

**[23.25] Divisible contracts**. In this case, the 'question is whether the acts and conduct of the (guilty) party evince an intention no longer to be bound by the contract';[192] and in conducting this enquiry, the common law today generally assumes that the parties contemplated payment of damages rather than discharge, so that the guilty party can normally set up his willingness to perform the rest of the contract, subject to his compensating the innocent party for the breach.[193] Such divisible contracts are partly[194] covered by s 31(2) of the SGA, which provides:

'Where there is a contract for the sale of goods to be delivered by stated instalments, which are to be separately paid for, and the seller makes defective deliveries in respect of one or more instalments, or the buyer neglects or refuses to take delivery of or pay for one or more instalments, it is a question in each case depending on the terms of the contract and the circumstances of the case, whether the breach of contract is a repudiation of the whole contract or whether it is a severable breach giving rise to a claim for compensation but not to a right to treat the whole contract as repudiated.'

---

189 See below and para 23.25. For repudiation generally, see para 26.15. As to the position of previous instalments, see Atiyah, *Sale of Goods*, 10th edn, 506–7.
190 *Per* Lord Wright in *Ross T Smyth & Co Ltd v Bailey, Sons & Co* [1940] 3 All ER 60, at 73, HL.
191 *Longbottom & Co Ltd v Bass, Walker & Co* (above).
192 *Per* Lord Coleridge CJ in *Freeth v Burr* (1874) LR 9 CP 208, at 213. See also *per* Lord Blackburn in *Mersey Steel and Iron Co Ltd v Naylor Benzon & Co* (1884) 9 App Cas 434, HL at 443.
193 *Per* Lord Wright in *Ross T Smyth & Co Ltd v Bailey, Sons & Co* [1940] 3 All ER 60, at 71, HL. See, e.g. *James Shaffer Ltd v Findlay* [1953] 1 WLR 106, CA; *Peter Dumenil & Co Ltd v Ruddin Ltd* [1953] 2 All ER 294, CA.
194 Whilst s 31(2) mentions the common cases, a number of others are listed in Benjamin's *Sale of Goods*, 6th edn, 8-076.

In the case of short delivery in one instalment, this provision appears to overlap with, and to be preferred on grounds of flexibility to, s 30(1): the **short** delivery (s 30(1)) is treated as a **defective** delivery (s 31(2)).[195] However, even where it applies, s 31(2) poses rather than answers the question, and it is necessary to fall back on common law principles. In *Robert Munro & Co Ltd Meyer*,[196] Wright J found that the seller had no intention of breaking his contract to supply meat and bone meal, but nevertheless held that, as there was a persistent breach continuing for nearly half the contract total of goods, the buyer was entitled to rescind. He explained that (at 331):

'In such circumstances, the intention of the seller must be judged from his acts and from the deliveries which he in fact makes, and that being so, where the breach is substantial and so serious as the breach in this case and has continued so persistently, the buyer is entitled to say that he has the right to treat the whole contract as repudiated.'

In *Maple Flock Co Ltd v Universal Furniture Products (Wembley) Ltd*,[197] the Court of Appeal said that (at 157):

'the main tests to be considered in applying the subsection ... are, first, the ratio quantitatively which breach bears to the contract as a whole, and secondly the degree of probability or improbability that such a breach will be repeated'.

In that case, the Court of Appeal found that the delivery complained of amounted to no more than one and a half tons out of a contract for the sale of 100 tons of rag flock and that the chances of the breach being repeated was for all practical purposes negligible; and the court therefore concluded that there was 'no sufficient justification to entitle the (buyer) to refuse further deliveries' (at 158). Should it make any difference that the breach is in respect of the first instalment? The cases are conflicting,[198] and commentators disagree;[199] but the issue must be set against the modern background of reluctance on the part of the courts to find an intention to repudiate.

## Payment by instalments

[23.26] Whereas s 31(1) enacts that *prima facie* the buyer is not bound to accept delivery of the goods by instalments (see para 23.24), the SGA contains no counterpart to s 31(1) in relation to the obligation to pay the price. However, it may be that it is to be implied from s 31(1) that payment is *prima facie* to be made in a lump sum.[200] Certainly, where the time for payment has arrived, there is no room for

---

195 *Regent OHG Aisenstadt & Barig v Francesco of Jermyn St Ltd* [1981] 3 All ER 327, discussed by Atiyah, *Sale of Goods*, 10th edn, 506–7. As to s 30(1), see para 13.04.

196 [1930] 2 KB 312; [1930] All ER Rep 241 (5% adulteration with cocoa husks).

197 [1934] 1 KB 148; [1933] All ER Rep 15, CA (judgment of Hewart LCJ, Lord Wright and Slesser LJ delivered by the LCJ).

198 Compare *Hoare v Rennie* (1859) 5 H & N 19 and *Honck v Muller* (1881) 7 QBD 92, with *Simpson v Crippin* (1872) LR 8 QB 14.

199 Compare *Benjamin on Sale*, 8th edn, 734 with Stoljar (1955) 71 LQR 527, at 543–4 and Benjamin's *Sale of Goods*, 6th edn, para 8-080.

200 But if the contract provides for payment by instalments, would not s 28 (set out at para 23.16) imply that delivery should also be by matching instalments?

payment by instalments; but, where the contract provides for delivery by instalments, s 31(2) itself lays down no definite rule for the effect of non-payment of instalments (see para 23.25). Of course, there is nothing to prevent the parties from stipulating in the contract for payment by instalments; and in this event, the contract will commonly specify the times of payment, make time of the essence[201] and provide that on any such default all the outstanding instalments shall be payable immediately.[202]

Sometimes, all the instalments of the price are payable before delivery of the goods,[203] e.g. under certain types of retail 'Xmas Club', the goods being selected and set aside for delivery after completion of payment of the price by instalments; but the situation is rather more complicated where delivery is made in advance of payment of the whole or part of the price.[204] Naturally, the unpaid seller will lose his lien (see para 24.14); and, where the price is payable by instalments, the transaction might amount to a credit sale regulated by the CCA (see para 1.13). Moreover, if the seller attempts to protect himself by reserving the property in the goods until paid for, then the transaction may be a regulated 'conditional sale' within the CCA (see para 1.14). Thus, if the transaction is a regulated one within the CCA, the real choice available to the supplier is whether or not to reserve the property in the goods: without a reservation of property, the transaction is a credit sale and offers him less protection, but is subject to only some of the CCA restrictions; whereas a transaction with a reservation of property—be it conditional sale or hp—offers some security (see para 24.27, *et seq.*), but is subject to the full rigours of the CCA. Further problems connected with instalment payments are considered below (see para 23.27).

[23.27] In considering the position of the instalments to be paid under a sale, hp or simple hiring, a distinction must be drawn between the initial payment and the subsequent instalments.

1. *The initial payment.* The supplier sometimes requires the first payment to be made before delivery, or even before contract. If the transaction proceeds, it will usually be possible to spell out a mutual intention that the initial payment is to constitute a part payment of the debt.[205] However, if the supply contract does not proceed, then, ignoring the supplier's insolvency (see para 23.22), a distinction must be drawn in dealing with the initial payment:

    (a)   If the supply contract is never concluded, it may depend on whether the sum is simply an advance part-payment, or a deposit.[206] If it is a part-payment, the buyer or hirer can recover the sum on grounds of total failure

---

201  Thus reversing s 10(1): set out at para 23.20.
202  For such acceleration clauses, see para 7.03 and further, para 26.19.
203  E.g. *Hyundai Heavy Industries Ltd v Papadopoulos* [1980] 2 All ER 29, HL (ship-building contract).
204  Pre-contract credit enquiries have already been considered: see para 8.35, *et seq.*
205  See para 27.19. As to the ordinary rules regarding payment of a debt, see paras 23.13–15.
206  For the distinction between part-payments and deposit, see further, para 27.19; and for prior payments, see para 23.22.

of consideration.[207] If it is a deposit, or a deposit and part-payment,[208] the position is as follows: generally, a reasonable deposit is irrecoverable by the defaulting buyer or hirer,[209] being in the nature of a preliminary contract guaranteeing completion, though there may be relief against forfeiture (see para 27.20) and, in a consumer supply, a retention of deposit clause may be unfair;[210] whereas, if the supply contract is a prospective regulated one (see para 5.20), any preliminary contract is probably void under s 59 of the CCA, upon which the intended deposit becomes recoverable on grounds of total failure of consideration.[207]

(b) Where the supply contract has been concluded, the position depends on whether or not it is regulated. Where the agreement is unregulated, then with the possible exception of sale or return transactions (see para 20.23, *et seq.*), the buyer or hirer cannot, except by subsequent agreement or lawful discharge, e.g. rescission (see Chap 26), escape from his contract without breaking it, in which case the supplier may elect either to affirm and sue for the agreed sum,[211] or treat the contract as discharged and claim damages.[212] In the latter event, the buyer or hirer may counter-claim to recover a part-payment,[213] whereas the position of a deposit is different: a reasonable deposit already paid by the guilty buyer or hirer[209] probably remains irrecoverable (see above); but an innocent supplier can recover by way of damages such a deposit payable but not yet paid.[214] Where the agreement is regulated, it may be cancellable, in which case all sums paid are recoverable (CCA, s 70: see para 10.33); or the protected goods rules may intervene (CCA, s 91: see para 24.38).

2. *The subsequent instalments.* In the case of an instalment sale, the buyer cannot normally[215] unilaterally terminate his obligations, remaining liable for the outstanding instalments, possibly at an accelerated rate;[211] and, notwithstanding the *prima facie* rule (see SGA, s 10(1): para 23.20), the sale contract will frequently make time of payment of the essence, so giving the supplier the right to treat the contract as discharged (see para 26.15). On the other hand, a hirer under a periodic hiring will have a unilateral right to terminate the agreement at the end

---

207 For total failure of consideration, see para 29.12, *et seq.* As to the question from whom the sum is recoverable in a tripartite transaction, see para 16.05.

208 Unless expressed to be a 'returnable deposit', which presumably is treated as a simple part-payment.

209 *Contra* if the supplier is at fault, in which case the deposit ought to be recoverable by the buyer or hirer on grounds of total failure of consideration (as to which, see fn 206, above). This may be spelt out in a standard-form contract, e.g. a new vehicle order form.

210 OFT, *Bulletin No. 15*, cases 8 and 13. See generally, para 11.12, *et seq.*

211 Unless the agreement contains an acceleration clause (see para 23.26), he will have to await the dates of payment: see para 23.20.

212 As to whether non-payment of one instalment shows an intention to repudiate, cf. para 23.25; and as to repudiation generally see para 26.15.

213 *Dies v British and International Mining and Finance Corpn Ltd* [1939] 1 KB 724.

214 *The Blankenstein* [1985] 1 All ER 475, CA (criticised by Carter 104 LQR 207). As the deposit exceeded his actual loss, the supplier was entitled only to nominal damages for repudiation: see further, para 27.20. See also *Pollway Ltd v Abdullah* [1974] 2 All ER 381, CA (auction buyer sued on stopped deposit cheque).

215 *Contra* where the sale is subject to a suitable condition subsequent: see para 20.03.

of each period of the hiring: in this case, the hirer is *prima facie* not liable for hire-rent in respect of any future period (see para 25.21); *contra* an agreement to hire for a fixed term (see para 7.18). Moreover, attempts by suppliers to secure for themselves such payments under minimum payment clauses may amount to unfair terms (Grey Term (e): see para 11.16); and are also bedeviled by the rule relating to penalties (see para 27.25) as regards unregulated agreements, or the CCA restrictions (s 100: see para 27.49) as regards regulated agreements.

# CHAPTER 24

# POSSESSION AND REPOSSESSION BY THE SUPPLIER

**[24.01]** It was seen in Chapter 23 that the basic assumption of a sale of goods is that the goods will be exchanged for the price (see para 23.16), in which case the seller is secure in the knowledge that he will have either his goods or his price (see Chap 2). On the other hand, the demands of the market place will frequently indicate that a supplier by way of sale or bailment should relinquish possession of the goods before payment. Leaving aside the general question of security (see Chap 25), the purpose of this chapter is to compare the relative legal strength in the position of a supplier weighing the following alternative strategies:

(1) To retain possession until paid, relying on his possessory rights as an unpaid seller (see paras 24.02–20); or

(2) To relinquish possession by way of sale or bailment and instead rely on a right to recover possession in the event of default, what might be termed his 'ownership' rights (see paras 24.21–48).

## SECURITY THROUGH POSSESSION

**[24.02]** There is much truth in the old adage that possession is nine-tenths of the law: to retain possession of the goods to be supplied may well be the safest way in which the seller can ensure payment or, at least, minimise his loss. In part, this is because Part V of the SGA gives the unpaid seller in possession certain rights against those goods.

### The unpaid seller's rights

**[24.03] The unpaid seller**. Part V of the SGA is expressed to operate only in favour of an 'unpaid seller'. This expression is given a special meaning.

*1. A seller.* Section 61(1) defines a seller as 'a person who sells or agrees to sell goods';[1] but s 38(2) here extends the concept to include any person in the position of a seller, such as his agent[2] or assignee.[3] However, this does not include a buyer who justifiably rejects the goods after paying the price.[4] He should therefore reject (see para 29.03) only if satisfied of the seller's solvency, as rejection will revest the property in the seller (see para 26.11), so allowing it to

---

1   It has been proposed that these rules should not apply to conditional sellers whilst they retain possession: see para 25.36. Why should they not remain 'unpaid sellers' for any deposit?

2   See generally, para 10.06. S 38(2) explicitly extends the category to an agent who has made himself personally liable on the contract as if he were the seller.

3   See para 7.16, *et seq.* As to purely personal contracts and those expressed to be non-assignable, see para 7.26.

4   *JL Lyons & Co Ltd v May and Baker Ltd* [1923] 1 KB 685.

pass into an insolvent seller's estate (see para 19.23) and reducing the buyer to a claim in quasi-contract for the return of the price.[5]

2. *An unpaid seller.* According to s 38(1):

> 'The seller of goods is deemed to be an "unpaid seller" within the meaning of this Act—
>
> (a)     When the whole of the price has not been paid or tendered;
>
> (b)     When a bill of exchange or other negotiable instrument has been received as conditional payment, and the condition on which it was received has not been fulfilled by reason of the dishonour of the instrument or otherwise.'

Notwithstanding that stipulations as to the time of payment are only warranties,[6] Part V of the SGA allows an unpaid seller who has not granted credit to retain possession of the goods until payment.[7] This fits in neatly with his duty under s 28 to deliver when the buyer is ready and willing to pay the price (see para 23.21). Alternatively, where the seller has taken a cheque or negotiable instrument for the price,[8] his rights under Part V are suspended; but they revive if the cheque is not met, for s 38(1)(b) then deems him to be an 'unpaid seller' again.[9] It is for consideration whether s 38(1)(b) can apply where the consumer buyer 'pays' by giving the seller a modern cheque: as we have already seen (see para 7.28), it seems unlikely that one of these instruments can amount to a 'bill of exchange or other negotiable instrument'.

**[24.04] His rights against the goods.** The rights of the unpaid seller against the goods are set out in s 39(1) as follows:

> 'Subject to this and any other Act,[10] notwithstanding that the property in the goods may have passed to the buyer, the unpaid seller of goods, as such, has by implication of law:
>
> (a) A lien on the goods or right to retain them for the price while he is in possession of them;
>
> (b) In the case of the insolvency of the buyer, a right of stopping the goods in transit after he has parted with the possession of them;
>
> (c) A right of re-sale as limited by this Act.'

Thus, the rights of the unpaid seller are as follows:

1. *A right of lien.* At common law, a lien merely conferred a right to retain possession of goods until certain demands were met (see para 1.23). The common law lien of the unpaid seller of goods has now been embodied in the SGA (see

---

5   Atiyah, *Sale of Goods*, 10th edn, 450–1; and see generally, para 29.12.

6   See s 10(1), discussed at para 23.20.

7   As to payment or tender of the price, see para 23.14. As to identifying the unpaid balance of the price in an instalment contract, see *Stocznia Gdanska SA v Latvian Shipping Co No. 3* (set out at para 29.16A), *per* Lord Goff at 893h–j.

8   Distinguish the situation where the cheque is merely taken by way of collateral security: see 1st edn, para 23.14A.

9   As to cheque guarantee cards, see para 2.26.

10  The provisions of the SGA directly relevant are ss 24, 25 and 41–8. The most directly relevant other statute is the FA; and see further Benjamin's *Sale of Goods*, 6th edn, para 15-009.

para 24.08), which has been said to replace entirely the common law on the subject.[11] Generally speaking, once the unpaid seller relinquishes possession, his lien is lost (see paras 24.13–14); and it will not revive merely because he regains possession.[12] However, an exception to this rule is where the unpaid seller validly stops the goods in transit (see below).

2.  *A right of stoppage.* Whilst that lien was lost where the goods passed into the possession of the buyer, the common law recognised an intermediate stage whilst the goods were in transit from seller to buyer. In this situation, the unpaid seller was given a limited right to stop the goods and recover possession from the carrier, whereupon the unpaid seller's lien arose once more.[13] This right of stoppage in transit has now been enacted in the SGA (see para 24.17), but is still limited in that it is only available where the buyer is insolvent.[14]

3.  *A right of resale.* In some cases, the unpaid seller's rights of lien and stoppage will meet his primary object: they will exert enough pressure to ensure that he is paid the contract price for the goods sold. However, where the buyer is unable or unwilling to pay the price, the exercise of the rights of lien and stoppage is a mere preliminary to resale. The common law granted a limited right of resale to an unpaid seller in possession; and this right is now embodied in the SGA (see para 24.07).

It would seem that the exercise of the rights of lien or stoppage by the unpaid seller will not necessarily show an intention on his part to rescind the contract,[15] but it will defeat an action in tort against him by the buyer for what used to be detinue.[16] On the other hand, where the unpaid seller wrongfully purports to exercise a lien or to stop the goods, he will be liable in tort, but damages will only be the value of the buyer's actual interest in the goods.[17] The effect of the exercise of the right of resale is considered later (see paras 27.08–11).

**[24.05]** Section 39(1) says that the three rights enumerated (see para 24.04) are to arise 'by implication of law', thereby implying that they may be excluded or varied by the terms of the agreement.[18] Furthermore, care must be taken not to confuse two things: (1) the **powers** of the unpaid seller to pass a good title to a second buyer either by virtue of his property in the goods or one of the exceptions to the *nemo dat* rule (see Chap 21); and (2) the **rights** of the unpaid seller as against the first buyer, which are listed in s 39. In order to distinguish between the rights and powers of the unpaid seller, it is convenient to set out the four basic permutations of possession and property.

---

11  *Transport and General Credit Corpn Ltd v Morgan* [1939] 1 Ch 531, at 546.
12  Even though he does so with the consent of the buyer: see *Pennington v Reliance Motor Works Ltd* [1923] 1 KB 127.
13  *Per* Buller J in *Lickbarrow v Mason* (1793) 6 East 21, at 27n.
14  According to s 61(4) of the SGA (as amended), 'A person is deemed to be insolvent within the meaning of the Act if he has either ceased to pay his debts in the ordinary course of business or he cannot pay his debts as they become due'; and see para 19.21. See further, para 24.10.
15  See s 48(1): set out at para 27.09.
16  *Milgate v Kebble* (1841) 3 Man & G 100 (detinue has now been abolished/replaced: see para 19.04).
17  *Chiney v Viall* (set out at para 29.24).
18  See SGA, s 55(1): set out at para 18.09.

*Case 1.* The property has passed to the buyer, who has taken possession of the goods. In this situation, the unpaid seller can have no rights against the goods,[19] nor any power to sell them;[20] and he is reduced to a personal action against the buyer for the price (see para 27.16).

*Case 2.* The property has passed to the buyer, but the seller retains possession. The seller has power to pass title to a bfp under one of the exceptions to the *nemo dat* rule;[20] but whether he has a right, as against the first buyer, to resell is another question.[21]

*Case 3.* The seller retains the property in the goods, but transfers possession to the buyer. In this case, the seller has the power to pass a good title to a third party by reason of his property in the goods;[19] but it may be a breach of the original contract of sale to do so.[21]

*Case 4.* The seller retains the property in, and possession of, the goods. He can, of course, pass a good title to a third party by reason of his property in the goods;[19] and the resale could only be a breach of the first contract where it could be shown that the goods annexed to that contract had been resold (see para 20.05).

This may be set out diagrammatically as follows:

|  | **Seller** | **Buyer** |
|---|---|---|
| *Case 1* |  | Po + Pr |
| *Case 2* | Po | Pr |
| *Case 3* | Pr | Po |
| *Case 4* | Po + Pr |  |

**[24.06] Lien and stoppage**. Strictly speaking, at common law a man could not have a lien over his own goods.[22] It would follow that the first two rights enumerated in s 39(1) are appropriate only to a seller who has retained possession of, but parted with property in, goods.[22] Thus, where the property and possession have passed (*Case 1*), the unpaid seller can have no right of lien or stoppage under s 39(1); and the apparent object of s 39(1) is to confer on a seller who has parted with property but retained possession (*Case 2*) 'not merely the power to deal with the goods, but the right to do so as against the buyer'.[23] However, in the pre-1893 case of *Re Edwards, ex p Chalmers*,[24] the Court of Appeal in Chancery held that an unpaid seller who had retained both property and possession (*Case 4*) should not have any less right to retain possession than one who had merely retained possession (*Case 2*). Perhaps the draftsman intended to reflect this in s 39(2), which provides as follows:

---

19  As to the *nemo dat* rule, see para 19.11.
20  SGA, s 24: see para 21.38.
21  As to resale, see para 24.07.
22  *Per* Lord Wright in *Nippon Yusen Kaisha v Ramkiban Serowgge* [1938] AC 429, PC, at 444; and Goode (1998) 114 LQR at 180.
23  Atiyah, *Sale of Goods*, 10th edn, 449.
24  (1873) LR 8 Ch App 289.

'Where the property in goods has not passed to the buyer, the unpaid seller has, in addition to his other remedies, a right of withholding delivery similar to and co-extensive with his rights of lien and stoppage in transit where the property has passed to the buyer.'

The question arises whether s 39(2) has the effect of restricting the unpaid seller who has retained property and possession to what Benjamin terms this 'quasi-lien'.[25] Presumably only applicable to specific or ascertained goods,[26] perhaps the better view is that s 39(2) merely ensures that a seller who **has** retained the property in the goods (*Cases 3 and 4*) will be no worse off than one who **has not** done so as regards the rights of lien and stoppage.[27]

**[24.07] Resale.** The third right enumerated in s 39(1) (set out at para 24.04) is a right of resale. Clearly, the unpaid seller has a **power** of resale where he has retained either or both of possession and property (see para 27.11); and the question is whether s 39(1) gives him a **right** to do so as against the original buyer. The obvious case where s 39(1) confers on the unpaid seller a right of resale is where he has retained possession but parted with the property in the goods (*Case 2*).[28] However, it is sometimes deduced from the existence of s 39(2) that s 39(1) is only applicable where the property has passed; and then inferred from the absence of any mention of a right of resale in s 39(2) (set out at para 24.06) that an unpaid seller who has retained both possession and property (*Case 4*) has no right of resale.[29] It would be possible to avoid this undesirable result by denying that the absence of a right of resale from s 39(2) has such a significance; but in *Ward v Bignall* (set out at para 27.10) the Court of Appeal escaped from the dilemma by another route, deciding that the unpaid seller who retained property and possession had a right of resale under s 39(1).

Does the unpaid seller have any **right** of resale in *Cases 1 and 3*; that is, where possession of the goods has passed to the buyer? Section 39(1)(c) gives a 'right of resale as limited by this Act'; and these limitations are to be found in s 48(3) and (4).[30] In one case, Turner J said that the New Zealand equivalent of s 48 conferred a power only on 'those vendors who have never lost possession',[31] though the wording of s 48 does not appear to support this view. Where both property and possession have passed to the buyer (*Case 1*), clearly the unpaid seller has neither the **power** nor the **right** of resale. However, where the unpaid seller takes the precaution of reserving the property in the goods whilst parting with possession (*Case 3*), it is arguable that he has a statutory **right** of resale under s 39(2); he certainly has the **power** to do so by virtue of his retention of property.[32]

---

25   Benjamin's *Sale of Goods*, 6th edn, para 15-029.

26   It has been argued that it is 'inconceivable' that s 39(2) should fetter the seller's discretion to deal with goods not yet earmarked to the contract: Atiyah, *Op. cit.*, 450.

27   Perhaps the words 'in addition to his other remedies' in s 39(2) will allow s 61(2) to save any other rights which the seller may have in respect of the goods.

28   E.g. *Gallagher v Shilcock* (see para 27.10).

29   See Atiyah, *Sale of Goods*, 10th edn, 450, where the author suggests that the courts are likely to avoid such an incredible result.

30   S 48(3) and (4) are discussed at para 27.08.

31   *Commission Car Sales Ltd v Saul* [1957] NZLR 144, at 146.

32   For reservation of property, see para 25.29, *et seq.*

## The unpaid seller's lien

### Nature of the lien[33]

**[24.08] Part-delivery**. The ordinary rule is that the seller's lien is for the whole of the price; but the question arises as to the effect of a part-delivery. Leaving aside the situation where the non-payment manifests an intention to repudiate (see para 26.15), the seller's rights may depend on whether there is a single contract or a series of contracts (see para 23.24). Where there is a series of contracts, the unpaid seller's statutory rights against the goods attach to each instalment only in respect of the price attributable to it;[34] but it may be otherwise where there is a single contract. Assuming that part-delivery under a single contract does not constitute delivery of the whole,[35] and that the other requirements for the exercise of a lien are satisfied (see para 24.10), s 42 provides:[36]

> 'Where an unpaid seller has made part-delivery of the goods, he may exercise his right of lien ... on the remainder, unless such part delivery has been made under such circumstances as to show an agreement to waive the lien'.

Suppose there is a single contract for the sale of goods at a price of £100; the contract envisages payment on delivery; but the seller delivers half the goods, valued at £50, before receiving any payment. *Prima facie*, this part-delivery indicates a waiver by the seller of his lien.[37] However, there are three possible interpretations of the seller's conduct: (1) the seller has waived his lien for the £100 and converted the transaction into a sale on credit; or (2) the seller has waived his lien over the goods delivered, but still retains a lien for £50 over the goods in his possession; or (3) the seller has waived his lien over the goods delivered, but retains a lien for £100 over the goods in his possession. Where the seller's conduct is not such as to indicate the first interpretation, the common law appears to have assumed that the lien over the remainder of the goods was for the £100, even where the contract was divisible;[38] and this presumed 'indivisibleness of the lien seems to have been recognised by the Act'.[39]

**[24.09] Repairer's lien and storage charges**. Whilst the SGA twice says that the lien granted thereby is for the price (ss 39(1)(a) and 41(1)), it is submitted that this does not prevent the seller from exercising any other particular lien to which he may be entitled at common law.[40] Thus, a seller who agrees to repair goods for his buyer will have a lien in respect of the cost of those repairs:[41] where the sale and repair are

---

33   For liens generally, see para 25.02.
34   *Steinberger v Atkinson* (1914) 31 TLR 110. Distinguish an all-monies clause: see para 20.29.
35   As to which, see the cases cited in Benjamin's *Sale of Goods*, 6th edn, para 15-041.
36   Cf. the right of stoppage in transit, see s 45(7), set out at para 24.19.
37   See s 43(1)(c), discussed at para 24.15.
38   *Re Edwards, ex p Chalmers* (1873) 8 Ch App 289. For the distinction between divisible and indivisible contracts, see para 23.24.
39   *Benjamin on Sale*, 8th edn, 841. See also *Longbottom v Bass, Walker & Co* [1922] WN 245, CA. *Sed quaere?*
40   The rules of common law are expressly saved insofar as consistent with the SGA by s 62(2).
41   For the repairs's lien, see generally, para 1.23. Distinguish a lien from a pledge: see para 25.02.

two independent transactions, he will have two separate liens, one for the price and the other for the cost of repairs; but, where there is a contract for the sale of repaired goods, it may be that the cost of repairs is subsumed under his seller's lien. On the other hand, there is no common law lien for storage charges,[42] and the unpaid seller may therefore wish to subsume these under his seller's lien. However, *Somes v British Empire Shipping Co*[43] is sometimes said to rule out indirectly any possibility of including storage charges in the lien,[44] though it does not preclude a claim for damages for such charges.[45] Moreover, storage charges may fall within the seller's lien if bargained for in the price.[46]

## Conditions under which the lien is exercisable

**[24.10]** Section 41(1) provides as follows:

'Subject to the provisions of this Act,[47] the unpaid seller of goods who is in possession of them is entitled to retain possession of them until payment or tender of the price in the following cases, namely—

(a)  Where the goods have been sold without any stipulation as to credit.

(b)  Where the goods have been sold on credit, but the term of credit has expired.

(c)  Where the buyer becomes insolvent.'

Not only does the lien granted by the SGA only exist for the price of goods sold (see para 24.09), but s 41(1) insists that three conditions all be fulfilled before it is exercisable:

(1)  The person seeking to exercise the lien must be an 'unpaid seller' within the meaning of s 38 (see para 24.03).

(2)  The price must be due, or the buyer insolvent. Leaving aside the case where the buyer becomes insolvent (see below), the position where the unpaid seller refuses to deliver the goods would appear to be as follows: in the absence of credit terms, the seller's lien and s 28 will prevent the buyer from having a right to immediate possession sufficient to succeed in an action in conversion against the seller (see para 19.06); but, where the granting of credit terms shows an intention that delivery shall be made before payment (thereby ousting s 28),[48] the buyer may bring such an action.[49] However, even where the seller has agreed to deliver in advance of payment, the unpaid seller's lien arises once

---

42   See *Re Southern Livestock Producers Ltd* [1963] 3 All ER 801 (maintaining pigs).

43   (1860) 8 HL Cas 338; [1843–60] All ER Rep 844 (because he is detaining the goods for his own benefit).

44   See *Benjamin's Sale of Goods*, 6th edn, para 15-044; Atiyah, *Sale of Goods*, 10th edn, 454.

45   The seller has an action for damages under s 37: set out at para 23.08.

46   *The Winson* [1981] AC 939, HL, *per* Lord Diplock (obiter) at 962–3; Benjamin, *Ibid.*; Atiyah, *Ibid.*

47   Thus, this lien is subject to the express provisions of the contract (s 55(1): see para 18.09), and the provisions for its termination (ss 43 and 47: see paras 24.12–16).

48   S 28 is set out at para 23.16. If the granting of credit shows no more than that delivery and payment are to be postponed, but are to remain concurrent terms, the buyer has no right to immediate possession before tendering the price.

49   See *per* Bayley J in *Bloxam v Sanders* (1825) 4 B & C 941, at 948–9.

more when[50] and if the term of credit expires[51] or the buyer becomes insolvent.[52] Insolvency does not necessarily amount of itself to a repudiation of the
contract,[53] so that it is still open to the buyer, his representative, or a sub-buyer
to tender the price and claim delivery;[54] but the effect of s 41(1)(c) is that the
seller cannot, against his will, be reduced to claiming a dividend in the buyer's
insolvency.[55] Nor can he be forced to supply goods: he is entitled to refuse to
supply in the absence of payment at common law;[56] and such an application of
ordinary commercial pressure is not an abuse of dominant position contrary to
the Treaty of Rome.[57]

(3)  The person claiming the lien must be in possession of the goods (see para 24.11).

**[24.11]  Possession.** The seller's lien depends on one of the most difficult concepts
in English law, namely, 'possession'. Not only does this term have different meanings
in different branches of the law,[58] but the extent of the control necessary to exercise
an innkeeper's lien differs from that required for a repairer's lien;[59] and neither
may be applicable to the unpaid seller.[60] Whilst the SGA nowhere defines possession, that concept is important in three contexts within the Act: (1) the exceptions
to the *nemo dat* rule;[61] (2) the seller's duty of delivery (see paras 23.05–07); and (3)
the unpaid seller's rights of lien (see below) and stoppage (see para 24.17). In the
present context, difficult problems can arise where actual control and the legal
(right to) possession are separated. Leaving aside the situation where actual control
is being exercised by a third party,[62] possession may be divided between seller and
buyer as follows:

(a)  The seller is in actual control as agent for the buyer. Section 41(2) provides:

> 'The seller may exercise his right of lien notwithstanding that he is in possession
> of the goods as agent or bailee . . . for the buyer.'

On the other hand, these facts may be evidence that the seller has waived his
lien.[63]

(b)  The buyer is in actual control as agent of the seller. Whilst the common law rule
may have been that the seller with 'legal possession' retained his lien, the SGA

---

50  Presumably, the seller is liable in conversion for the period before payment fell due. For this
    action, see generally, paras 19.04–6.
51  But does not the granting of credit show an intention to contract out of the statutory lien?
52  And if the buyer is insolvent at the time of contracting? As to when a buyer is insolvent, see
    s 61(4), set out at para 24.04.
53  *Re Edwards, ex p Chalmers* (1873) LR 8 Ch App 289.
54  As to repudiation, see generally, para 26.15; and as to tender of price and delivery, see Chap 23.
55  As to the claim of the unsecured creditor for a dividend, see para 19.22.
56  *Re Edwards* (above), *per* Mellish LJ at 291.
57  *Leyland Daf Ltd v Automotive Products plc* [1993] BCC 389, CA (Art 82 (ex 86)); and see generally,
    para 2.12.
58  See generally, Crossley Vaines, *Personal Property*, 5th edn, Pt 2; *Oxford Essays in Jurisprudence, IV
    Possession* (by Harris); Bell, *Personal Property*, Chap 3.
59  See Atiyah, *Sale of Goods*, 10th edn, 453.
60  *Per* Lord MacNaghten in *Great Eastern Railway Co v Lord's Trustee* [1909] AC 109, HL, at 115.
61  See Chap 21, and especially paras 21.28 and 21.40.
62  The Act distinguishes different sorts of third party: (i) 'carrier or other bailee' (see para 24.13);
    (ii) other third party, e.g. a warehouse-keeper (see para 24.18).
63  Waiver of lien is considered at para 24.15.

seems to suggest that, at least where actual control passes to the buyer, the lien is lost.[64] In other words, more regard may now be paid to actual control than to the legal right to control.[65]

## Termination of the lien

[24.12] The seller may lose his right to exercise a lien for the price in any of the ways set out below.

1. *Where he ceases to be an 'unpaid seller'*. According to s 41(1), the seller's lien only lasts 'until payment or tender of the price';[66] but s 43(2) provides that the unpaid seller:

   'does not lose his lien . . . by reason only that he has obtained judgment . . . for the price of the goods'.

   One difficulty here is that s 41(1) appears to suggest that the seller's lien, and hence his right to retain possession, does not cease until the buyer at very least tenders the price,[67] whereas s 28 expressly says that payment and delivery are concurrent conditions (see para 23.16). Whilst the two provisions are usually reconciled by inferring that actual tender of the price is not necessary provided the buyer is ready and willing to pay the price,[68] it has been argued that it is difficult to avoid giving effect to the literal words of s 41(1).[69] It is submitted that a solution may be found as follows: that the buyer's duty to tender the price is similar to the seller's duty to tender delivery (as to which, see paras 23.05–7); and that actual tender is not usually required because it is presumed that the buyer will perform his contract.[70]

2. *Delivery to a carrier* (see para 24.13).

3. *The buyer obtains possession* (see para 24.14).

4. *Waiver* (see para 24.15).

5. *Dispositions by the buyer* (see para 24.16).

[24.13] **Delivery to a carrier**. Section 43(1)(a) provides that the seller will lose his lien:

   'When he delivers the goods to a carrier or other bailee. . . for the purpose of transmission to the buyer without reserving the right of disposal of the goods.'

The scheme of the Act is that the unpaid seller will have a right of lien whilst he retains possession of the goods, and a right of stoppage whilst they are in transit to the buyer.[71] Not surprisingly, the Act uses the same test both for the termination of

---

64  See s 43(1)(b), considered at para 24.14.
65  Schmitthoff, *Sale of Goods*, 2nd edn, 156. But see Benjamin's *Sale of Goods*, 6th edn, para 15-038.
66  And see s 38(1)(a), considered at para 24.03.
67  *Quaere* whether in these circumstances the lien extends only to the price, or also to the costs on the judgment?
68  See Chalmers, *Sale of Goods*, 18th edn, 176; Schmitthoff, *Sale of Goods*, 2nd edn, 121–2.
69  Atiyah, *Sale of Goods*, 7th edn, 344. But see fn 70, below.
70  See also Atiyah, *Sale of Goods*, 10th edn, 455, relying on Australian authority.
71  For the effect of successfully exercising a right of stoppage, see para 24.16.

the lien and the commencement of the transit, namely, 'delivery to a carrier or other bailee for the purposes of transmission to the buyer'; and this expression will be examined in the latter context (see para 24.18). However, s 43(1)(a) allows one exception to the rule which it lays down: where the seller reserves 'a right of disposal'. In the context of sections dealing with the passing of property, this expression clearly denotes a reservation of property (see para 20.28); but it has been argued that, to avoid any inconsistency with s 39(2), it must in s 43(1)(a) refer only to a reservation of possession.[72] Perhaps the better view is that in s 43 the phrase denotes a reservation of property **and** possession;[73] and that in s 43(1)(a) it is referring to the 'quasi-lien' under s 39(2) (see paras 24.05–06).

**[24.14] The buyer obtains possession**. Section 43(1)(b) lays down that the lien is lost:

> 'When the buyer or his agent lawfully obtains possession of the goods.'

The first issue here concerns the meaning of 'possession': there has already been explored the situation where 'legal possession' and control are divided between seller and buyer (see para 24.11); but in other cases it probably extends to legal possession,[74] except where the goods are in the hands of an independent carrier.[75] The other problem in this subsection concerns the meaning of the word 'lawfully', as to which there are several theories. *First*, it may refer to the absence of criminal conduct on the part of the buyer.[76] However, there has been some reluctance to import the law of theft into this branch of the civil law. *Second*, Atiyah has suggested another possible meaning; namely, that 'lawfully' in this context means 'with the consent of the seller', so as to bring it into line with the provisions in respect of dispositions by buyers in possession found in ss 25(1) and 9 of the SGA and FA respectively.[77] Perhaps the strongest argument in favour of this view is that the term 'lawfully' is also used in ss 47 and 10 of the respective Acts. However, it has been pointed out that (1) this view rather strains the language of s 43(1)(b), and (2) there is no reason why s 43(1)(b) needs to be brought into line with this exception to the *nemo dat* rule.[78] Furthermore, it is quite conceivable that 'lawfully' has a different meaning in ss 47 and 10 from that which it bears in s 43(1)(b) (see para 21.49); and it is submitted that it is logically possible that the seller's lien binds all except a bf transferee under one of the exceptions to the *nemo dat* rule. *Third*, Benjamin has suggested that 'lawfully' in s 43(1)(b) means that 'the possession must not be obtained tortiously as against the seller'.[79] Whilst this test may be circular if one thinks in terms of the tort of conversion, it does seem satisfactory in relation to the

---

72   Schmitthoff, *Sale of Goods*, 2nd edn, 157.
73   See *Benjamin's Sale of Goods*, 6th edn, para 15-046, citing *Saunders v Maclean* (1883) 11 QBD 327, CA at 341.
74   As where the goods are in the physical control of a third party, e.g. warehouseman, on behalf of the buyer or his agent.
75   In which case, the right of stoppage may arise: see para 24.18.
76   E.g. *Wallace v Woodgate* (1824) 1 C & P 575.
77   *Sale of Goods*, 10th edn, 456.
78   Smith (1963) JSPTL 225, at 226.
79   *Benjamin's Sale of Goods*, 6th edn, para 15-055.

tort of trespass.[80] In the last analysis, then, it may be that 'lawfully' in s 43(1)(b) denotes the absence of a trespassory taking by the buyer, irrespective of whether that taking amounts to theft.

**[24.15] Waiver.** Section 39(1) gives the unpaid seller a lien by implication of law (see para 24.04); s 55(1) allows such rights to be waived expressly or by implication (see para 18.09); and s 43(1)(c) expressly states that the lien may be lost by waiver. Thus, the unpaid seller may expressly waive his statutory lien, e.g. a sale on credit; or waiver of it may be inferred. Examples of implied waiver are where the contract includes the reservation of an express lien;[81] or where the seller takes a cheque for the price (see para 23.14); or where the seller wrongfully deals with the goods in a manner inconsistent with the rights of the buyer, e.g. by consuming or reselling them;[82] or where the seller agrees to retain possession as agent of the buyer.[83] Can the unpaid seller who is still in possession go back on any waiver of his statutory lien? The Act envisages that, notwithstanding that the seller accepts payment by bill of exchange or sells on credit, he may exercise his lien where the bill is not met,[84] or the term of credit expired;[85] and it is possible to see these two instances in terms of an initial waiver and subsequent exercise of the unpaid seller's lien.[86]

Moreover, the common law will normally allow a party to go back upon a waiver of his rights if he gives adequate notice;[87] and it was decided before the 1893 Act that the unpaid seller might revive his waived lien where he was still in possession.[88] The better view would therefore appear to be that the statutory lien may be revived after waiver by giving adequate notice.[89]

**[24.16] Dispositions by the buyer.** Under the *nemo dat* principle (see para 19.11), a sub-buyer will *prima facie* acquire title subject to the lien of the original unpaid seller.[90] However, the sub-buyer may claim title under one of the exceptions to the *nemo dat* rule (see para 21.03); and sometimes the facts which bring a case within an exception may also operate to terminate the unpaid seller's lien under one of the rules discussed above. However, two such exceptions to the *nemo dat* rule which are especially likely to defeat both the unpaid seller's lien and his right of stoppage in transit (see paras 24.17–20) receive express treatment in s 47:

---

80 Is the point academic since both torts are now subsumed under the heading of wrongful interference with goods (see para 19.04)?

81 See Chalmers, *Sale of Goods*, 18th edn, 207.

82 Chalmers, *Op. cit.*, 208; Atiyah, *Sale of Goods*, 10th edn, 457.

83 See Atiyah, *Ibid.*; and para 24.11.

84 S 38(1)(b): set out at para 24.03.

85 S 41(1)(b) and (c): set out at para 24.10. It seems to be sensible to read s 43(1)(c) subject to s 41(b) and (c): see Atiyah, *ibid.* But compare *Benjamin on Sale*, 8th edn, 853 and *Benjamin's Sale of Goods*, 6th edn, para 15-056.

86 Alternatively, it may be agreed that the lien arises *de novo* upon the happening of these two events.

87 *Charles Rickards Ltd v Oppenheim* (set out at para 26.25).

88 See *Townley v Crump* (1835) 4 Ed & El 58.

89 See Atiyah, *Ibid.* For waiver generally, see para 26.23.

90 S 47(1): see *Laurie and Morewood v Dudin* [1926] 1 KB 223, CA. S 47(1) is expressed to give way to a contrary intent: s 55(1)—see para 18.09.

(1) the original seller's rights are completely lost where he assents to the subsale;[91] and

(2) his rights are overridden *pro tanto* where he parts with a document of title relating to the goods.[92]

## The unpaid seller's right of stoppage in transit

[24.17] In the eighteenth and nineteenth centuries, the right of stoppage in transit was an extremely valuable weapon in the armoury of the unpaid seller in both domestic and international sales; but in the twentieth century the importance of this right declined.[93] However, the right of stoppage never applied to one of the largest carriers, the Post Office.[94] Modern treatment of the right of stoppage in domestic sales is therefore restricted to private carriers, and may be reduced to a minimum. The basic principle is set out in s 44 of the SGA, which provides that:

'Subject to the provisions of this Act,[95] when the buyer of goods becomes insolvent,[96] the unpaid seller[97] who has parted with possession of the goods has the right of stopping them in transit, that is to say, he may resume possession of the goods as long as they are in course of transit, and may retain them until payment or tender of the price'.[98]

The most difficult questions involved here are probably the meaning of 'possession' and the duration of the transit, matters upon which s 45 lays down a series of rules (see paras 24.18–19). The difficulty may be illustrated by the following facts: suppose the seller owns goods then in independent warehouse A; he agrees to sell them to the buyer, with delivery to independent warehouse C; and the transfer of the goods is to be undertaken by an independent carrier, during the course of which the goods will be temporarily lodged in independent warehouse B. The unpaid seller's real rights whilst the goods are being transferred depend on who has physical possession of them and may be illustrated diagrammatically as follows:

| Right of lien | Right of stoppage | No real rights |
|:---:|:---:|:---:|
| Seller | Carrier | Buyer |
| Warehouse A | Warehouse B | Warehouse C |

91  S 47(1): see para 21.04.

92  S 47(2). See also s 10 of the FA 1889. See further, 1st edn, para 24.16.

93  Perhaps partly because of better communications, speedier carriage, better credit control and a higher volume of trade compensating for occasional bad debts.

94  And now Parcelforce. The PO does not enter into any contract of carriage (*Whitfield v Le Despenser* (1778) 2 Comp 754); it is not generally liable for torts connected with the postal services (see now s 90 of the Postal Services Act 2000 and para 3.07) and would not act on an order to stop (s 83 of the 2000 Act).

95  This refers principally to ss 39, 45, 46 and 55(1).

96  Notice the rather wider grounds which s 39(1) allows for the exercise of the unpaid seller's lien: see paras 24.10–11. As to insolvency, see para 24.04.

97  See para 24.03.

98  See para 24.12.

**[24.18/9]  Course of transit.** According to s 45(1):

> 'Goods are deemed to be in course of transit from the time when they are delivered to a carrier by land or water, or other bailee . . . for the purpose of transmission.'

It is quite clear that, where goods are in the legal possession and actual control of the seller, he has the more efficacious right of lien (see para 24.11); and that, where the legal possession and actual control of the goods have passed to the buyer, the seller has lost his rights of lien (see para 24.14) and stoppage.[99] Thus, the right of stoppage can only exist in the intermediate situation, where the goods are in the hands of a third party, whom s 45 calls 'a carrier[100] or other bailee',[101] as agent for either seller or buyer. Difficulties immediately arise, however, if it is admitted that either the seller or the buyer may be in legal possession of goods under the actual control of an agent (see para 23.03). Leaving aside the situation where either seller or buyer is in actual control as agent of the other (see para 24.11), the ordinary rule is that the possession of the agent is regarded as being the possession of his principal in this context as elsewhere (see para 24.14): where the seller's agent has actual control, the seller has the more efficacious right of lien; but, where the buyer's agent obtains control, the seller loses his real rights entirely. However, if this rule were applied indiscriminately, there would be no room for a right of stoppage at all; and the law is therefore committed to distinguishing between the constructive possession of (1) 'a carrier or other bailee', and (2) any other agent in actual control of the goods, e.g. a warehousekeeper. Even more difficult, it must distinguish between two different types of constructive possession of 'a carrier or other bailee'. For instance, the delivery by the seller of the goods to a carrier for transmission to a commercial buyer may operate under s 32(1) as a constructive transfer of possession to the buyer so as to discharge the seller's duty to deliver (see paras 23.05–07); but that does not necessarily end the transit.[102] Support for this approach may be gained from s 45(5), which deals with one particular instance as follows:

> 'When the goods are delivered to a ship chartered by the buyer it is a question depending on the circumstances of the particular case, whether they are in the possession of the master as a carrier, or as agent to the buyer.'

As might be expected, the matter which appears to have caused particular difficulty at common law was not so much when the transit commenced as when it ceased;[103] and s 45 concentrates on this latter point, dealing explicitly with a number of difficult cases.[104] Clearly, the transit can at most only last until the goods reach the place at which the contract contemplates that the transit will end;[105] and it will in any case

---

99  E.g. on attornment by the carrier to the buyer: see s 45(3); and generally, para 23.03.

100  Presumably, the word 'carrier' is wide enough to cover a common carrier. What about an air freighter?

101  He has been variously described as a 'middleman' (*Schotsmans v Lancs & Yorks Ry Co* (1867) 2 Ch App 332 at 338) or an 'independent contractor': (Atiyah, *Sale of Goods*, 10th edn, 459).

102  This seems consistent with the views of Brett LJ in *Re Cock, ex parte Rosevear China Clay Co* (1879) 11 Ch D 560, CA, at 569. For another explanation, see Todd [1978] JBL at 40.

103  The moment of commencement of the transit would only be material where the buyer was not insolvent, in which case the unpaid seller would look to his ordinary remedies: see Chap 27.

104  S 45(2)–(7). See further Macleod, *Consumer Sales Law*, 1st edn, para 24.20.

105  *Jobson v Eppenheim* (1905) 21 TLR 468.

be brought to an end where the 'carrier or other bailee' hands the goods to the buyer or his agent (s 45(1): see further, para 24.19).

**[24.20] Exercise of right of stoppage.** According to s 46(1):

'The unpaid seller may exercise his right of stoppage in transit either by taking actual possession of the goods or by giving notice[106] of his claim to the carrier or other bailee . . . in whose possession the goods are.'

In the latter event, s 46(4) provides as follows:

'When notice of stoppage in transit is given by the seller to the carrier or other bailee . . . in possession of the goods, he must re-deliver the goods to, or according to the directions of, the seller; and the expenses of the re-delivery must be borne by the seller.'

If the seller has no right of stoppage, the seller issuing the order and the 'carrier or other bailee' who complies are both liable to the buyer in conversion;[107] but, if the seller has the right to stop, but the 'carrier or other bailee' refuses to comply with such an order, he is liable to the seller in conversion, or possibly for breach of statutory duty:[108] if in doubt, the safest course for the 'carrier or other bailee' is to interplead, or to make delivery dependent on an indemnity. Finally, whilst the Act does not define the relationship between the 'carrier or other bailee' and the seller, it has been decided that the stoppage of goods by the seller gives the 'carrier or other bailee' a prior lien over the goods for his charges;[109] and that, after stopping the goods, the seller is under a duty to give orders for their disposal.[110]

# SECURITY WITHOUT POSSESSION

## General rules

**[24.21] Title and repossession as security.** The previous section considered the advantage in terms of security which may accrue to an unpaid supplier who retains possession, delivering the goods only on payment.[111] The present section seeks to contrast that with the position of a supplier who delivers goods without payment of the price. If he delivers under a credit sale,[111] he will be an unsecured creditor[112] for the price.[113] However, there are a number of ways in which the unpaid supplier may seek to elevate himself to a status equal to a secured creditor:[112]

---

106 'The notice may be given either to the person in actual possession of the goods or his principal' (s 46(2)). In the latter event, see s 46(3) as to the time when the notice is effective.

107 E.g. *Taylor v Great Eastern Ry Co* (1901), as reported in 17 TLR 394. For conversion, see generally, para 19.04.

108 See SGA, s 60. As to the possible purpose of this section, see Chalmers, *Sale of Goods*, 18th edn, 261; and as to actions for breach of statutory duty, see generally, para 3.21.

109 See *United States Steel Products Co v Great Western Ry Co* [1916] 1 AC 189, HL.

110 *Booth Steamship Co Ltd v Cargo Fleetiron Co Ltd* [1916] 2 KB 570, CA. But see the comment by Atiyah, *Sale of Goods*, 10th edn, 464.

111 For cash and credit sales, see generally, paras 1.07–13.

112 For unsecured and secured creditors, see generally, para 19.14.

113 Additionally, the unpaid supplier may have taken out some bad-debt insurance, though in domestic supplies this tends to be unusual. Distinguish insurance taken out by or on behalf of the debtor or hirer (see para 24.30).

he may enter into a conditional sale,[114] an hp or a simple hiring agreement.[115] Under all three forms of contract, he will make early delivery of the goods, but reserve the property in them, which may give him priority in respect of his interest (see para 24.22) as against his transferee's insolvency,[116] or sub-transferee under the *nemo dat* rule (see para 19.11). However, as bailee in possession, the transferee may be able to override the unpaid supplier's interest in favour of some creditors[117] or a bfp.[118] The best way for the unpaid supplier to avoid such overriding interests is to terminate the bailment (see para 26.08) and seize the goods.[119] This he may seek to achieve by either (1) **recaption** (see para 24.22), possibly followed by court action for breach of contract (see para 27.33, *et seq.*), or (2) **court action in tort**.[120] Such actions will usually be in the defendant's county court (see para 3.22).

**[24.22] The supplier's common law interest in the goods.** In the case of a cash or credit sale (see paras 1.03–07), the supplier's entire proprietary interest in the goods passes to the buyer at latest on delivery (see Chap 20); but, at the other end of the scale, where goods are supplied under a simple hiring agreement, the supplier retains the entire proprietary interest.[121] In between these two extremes lie conditional sales and hp, where it has already been pointed out that the value of the supplier's interest diminishes *pro tanto* with every payment made (see para 1.14), though neither form of contract creates a mortgage.[122]

1. *Conditional sales*[123]. If the buyer defaults, the unpaid seller can repossess the goods,[124] exercise his real remedy of resale (see para 24.04), so rescinding the contract,[125] and sue the defaulting buyer for damages to recover any loss (see para 27.34). In this case, the common law will not allow the seller also to sue for unpaid instalments **due**; but in respect of instalments already **paid** draws and distinction between a reasonable deposit, which is irrecoverable and a part-payment which may, subject to the terms of the agreement, be recoverable (see para 27.19). However, conditional sale agreements almost always provide for

---

114  See generally, para 1.14. Such a conditional sale may contain a *Romalpa* clause (see para 25.30).
115  As to simple hiring agreements, see paras 1.17–19; and as to hp agreements, see paras 1.20–5.
116  Generally, the trustee or liquidator takes only property owned by the insolvent: see para 19.23.
117  See the special rules for distress (para 19.18) and execution (paras 19.19–20).
118  Amongst the exceptions to the *nemo dat* rule (see generally, Chap 21) especially relevant here are the power of a conditional buyer to pass title as one who has agreed to buy (see para 21.43) or of a conditional buyer or hirer on hp to confer a Pt III title (see para 21.55).
119  As to when the right of repossession would arise at common law by reason of arrears of rent, see para 27.38.
120  See para 24.25. As to the assessment of the value of the goods in a tort action, see para 27.30.
121  Thus, the owner entitled to immediate possession may sue in conversion for the full value of the goods: *Manders v Williams* (1848) 4 Exch 338; and see further, para 19.06. As to simple hiring agreements, see generally, paras 1.17–19.
122  Compare the position of a mortgagee exercising a power of sale: see para 25.20. It is for consideration whether it would not be better if conditional sale and hp (and finance leases?) were turned into forms of chattel mortgage: see para 1.26.
123  As to conditional sales, see generally, paras 1.14–16; and as to hp, see generally, paras 1.20. As to remedies of the supplier, see para 27.12, *et seq.*
124  As to reservation of a right of disposal, see para 20.28. As to recaption, see para 24.23; and as to unlawful harassment, see para 24.24.
125  As to 'resale' amounting to a rescission of the first contract, see para 27.12.

the forfeiture of instalments already paid and it seems that equity offers little relief to the defaulting buyer (see para 27.20). Further, it follows from the fact that a conditional buyer has no equity of redemption (see *McEntire v Crossley Bros*: see para 1.14) that, unless also suing for damages,[126] the conditional seller is under no duty of care to get the best price obtainable.[127]

2. *Hire purchase*[123]. If the hirer defaults, the unpaid supplier is entitled to repossess the goods,[128] rescind the contract, [125] sell at his own price and sue the defaulting hirer for damages to recoup any loss.[129] However, the position of the defaulting hirer is worse than that of the conditional buyer: as a matter of principle, whereas the **seller** is *prima facie* entitled to recover the goods *or* price (see above), the supplier of goods on hp is as **bailor** entitled to *both* goods *and* rent.[129] Unfortunately, it seems an *a fortiori* case that the defaulting hirer has no equity of redemption,[130] though equity may sometimes give relief against forfeiture (see para 27.22). It is this which provides the element of 'double recovery' that helps to give rise to the snatchback (see para 26.08): the hirer is prevented by the legal fiction of hp (see para 1.20) from pleading either that the owner/supplier has made a double recovery in the legal sense,[131] or that instalments paid are a part-payment of the price.[132]

## Repossession through self-help

The principal choice of an unpaid supplier who has reserved the property in goods is to **seize** (recaption) or **sue** to recover possession.

**[24.23] Recaption.** A rightful recaption (repossession/seizure) of goods by the owner[133] will not deprive him of his other remedies under the agreement,[134] but a wrongful recaption will constitute both a tort and a repudiation of the agreement.[135] Leaving aside special statutory restrictions,[136] a recaption gives rise to the following legal problems. *First*, is the owner entitled to use force to repossess the goods? The position would appear to be that, after a failure by the hirer[133] to return the

---

126 In suing for damages, he is under a duty to mitigate by seeking the best price obtainable: see para 27.44.

127 *Contra Forward Trust Ltd v Best* (1983) unreported, discussed in 38 CC 3/26.

128 *Lombard North Central plc v Butterworth* (see para 27.26).

129 *Alf Vaughan & Co Ltd v Royscot Trust plc* [1999] 1 All ER Comm 856; and see further, para 27.22.

130 *Cramer v Giles* (1883) Cab & El 151, affd (1884) *The Times*, 9th May; but see Oditah (1992) 108 LQR 459 at 487, esp. fn 159. Nor has the court any discretion where the creditor seeks a writ of execution: *TC Trustees Ltd v JS Darwen Ltd* [1969] 2 QB 295, CA.

131 For double recovery, see para 27.39. *Contra* if the supplier sues in conversion: see para 27.31. For the uncertain value of the hirer's interest, see para 1.25.

132 *Ellis v Rowbotham* [1900] 1 QB 740, CA; *Kelly v Lombard Banking Ltd* [1958] 3 All ER 713, CA.

133 The owner may have supplied the goods under a conditional sale, hp or simple hiring agreement, in each of which cases there will be a form of bailment so that the transferee may properly be described as hirer: see para 24.21.

134 *Overstone Ltd v Shipway* [1962] 1 All ER 52, CA: see para 27.21.

135 *Abingdon Finance Ltd v Champion* [1961] CLY 3931. See generally, para 19.05 and para 26.15.

136 See Guest, *Law of HP*, 531; and Goode, *HP Law and Practice*, 2nd edn, 19–20.

goods after a request, the owner may use reasonable force to recapt them,[137] but that unreasonable force may amount to an assault.[138] To avoid the uncertainty of what is reasonable force in a confrontation with a hirer, a recaption is sometimes achieved in the early hours, e.g. motor vehicles. *Second*, is the owner entitled to enter the hirer's premises to recapt the goods? Because the common law is uncertain, the agreement will usually confer on the owner a licence to enter the hirer's land and seize the goods. Such a contractual licence is probably irrevocable:[139] unless unfair,[140] it will give the owner immunity from an action in trespass where only reasonable force is used,[141] though entry to recapt may amount to a criminal offence.[142] *Third*, recaption might amount to an offence under the Administration of Justice Act 1970 (see para 24.24). *Fourth*, effective recaption is, of course, part of the technique of the 'snatchback' (see para 26.08); but it cannot be used in respect of chattels after-acquired by a non-corporate hirer.[143] *Fifth*, even peaceable re-entry may infringe human rights (see para 3.09). It is largely by reason of the foregoing legal difficulties that separate firms of repossession agents have flourished,[144] though their use might give rise to vicarious criminal liability (see para 28.09).

**[24.24] Unlawful harassment of debtors**. The Report of the Payne Committee recommended that the unlawful harassment of debtors be made a criminal offence;[145] and Parliament sought to give effect to this by the Administration of Justice Act 1970. Section 40(1) provides that:

'A person commits an offence if, with the object of coercing another person to pay money claimed from the other as a debt due under a contract he—[146]

(a) harasses the other with demands for payment which, in respect of their frequency or the manner or occasion of making any such demand, or of any threat or publicity by which any demand is accompanied, are calculated to subject him or members of his family or household to alarm, distress or humiliation;

(b) falsely represents, in relation to the money claimed, that criminal proceedings lie for failure to pay it;

(c) falsely represents himself to be authorised in some official capacity to claim or enforce payment; or

---

137 *Blades v Higgs* (1861) 10 CBNS 713, *obiter* at 720.

138 *Dyer v Munday* [1895] 1 QB 742, CA.

139 *Hurst v Picture Theatres Ltd* [1915] 1 KB 1, CA; cf. *Wood v Leadbitter* (1835) 13 M & W 838.

140 See OFT, *Bulletin No. 15*, case 4; *No. 17*, case 13; *No. 18*, case 9; *No. 20*, cases 8, 19; *No. 21*, case 19; *No. 22*, case 33; *No. 24*, case 48; *No. 26*, p 90; [2005] *Bulletin* J/M, *Flogas*; and para 11.12, *et seq.*

141 *Hemmings v Stoke Poges Golf Club* [1920] 1 KB 720, CA.

142 Violent entry without consent or a court order may be an offence under s 6 (as amended) of the Criminal Law Act 1977. Compare the entry powers of a bailiff/sheriff (see para 19.15) or of a tso (see para 28.05).

143 Because it would contravene the Bills of Sale Acts (see para 25.26). It follows that the ordinary consumer running-account credit gives no right of recaption: see para 7.08.

144 It will be a matter of commercial judgment as to whether the financier will seek repossession (either on his own account or via a repossession agent), or whether repossession is left to the goods supplier: see [2003] 8 *Credit Today* 15.

145 The Report of the Committee on the *Enforcement of Judgment Debts* (1969, Cmnd. 3909), para 1238 (see further, para 27.01).

146 S 40(2) extends the offence to any person who 'concerts with others in taking such action . . ., notwithstanding that his own course of conduct does not by itself amount to harassment'.

(d)  utters a document falsely represented by him to have some official character or purporting to have some official character which he knows it has not.'[147]

The offence created by s 40[148] is intended to protect two classes of debtors (but not any creditors): (1) those who do not owe any money under a contract, either because they were never so indebted, or have repaid it, and (2) those who are so indebted.[149] On the other hand, the scope of the offence is limited by s 40(3), which excludes:

'anything done by a person which is reasonable (and otherwise permissible in law) for the purpose—

(a)  securing the discharge of an obligation due, or believed by him to be due to himself or to persons for whom he acts, or protecting himself or them from future loss; or

(b)  of the enforcement of any liability by legal process.'

*Unlawful harassment.* Section 40(1)(a) makes it an offence if—(i) with the **object** of coercing payment, (ii) a person **harasses** another with demands for payment (see below), (iii) which are **calculated** to subject him or his family or household to alarm, distress or humiliation.[150] Some idea of the type of conduct s 40(1)(a) was intended to prohibit may be gathered from the Payne Report;[151] but it is to be regretted that the section is 'sadly lacking in precision'.[152] For instance, the Payne Report intended that the provision should cover 'visiting the home of the debtor . . . under the guise of collecting chattels let under an hp agreement' (para 1233(i)), though s 40 gives rise to several problems in this context. *First*, is the act of recaption done 'with the objecting of coercing another person to pay money claimed' contrary to s 40(1);[153] and is it a 'demand for payment' within s 40(1)(a)? Or is it only the threat[154] of recaption which is prohibited? The latter interpretation would produce the undesirable result of encouraging recaption without warning— because it would be safer to actually recapt than to threaten. *Second*, as s 40 is only expressed to be applicable where money is claimed 'as a debt due under a contract', can s 40 be avoided entirely by the expedient of obtaining a judgment for debt prior to recaption? *Third*, what is the criterion for the establishment by the recaptor of the defence that his action was 'reasonable' within the meaning of s 40(3)?[155]

---

147  E.g. the OFT has revoked a CCA licence for regularly issuing statutory demands (see para 19.21) without taking bankruptcy proceedings: 50 CC1/37.

148  For penalties, see s 40(4) (as amended)

149  S 40 probably does not extend to suppliers of gas, water and electricity due under statute rather than contract: *Norweb plc v Dixon* [1995] 3 All ER 952, DC; and see generally, para 3.07.

150  'Are calculated to' means 'likely to' not 'intended to': the *Norweb* case (above): see 50 CC1/36.

151  See generally, paras 1230–44. For inertia selling, see para 8.18. For 'look-alikes', see offences under the County Courts Act: para 5.42.

152  Borrie and Pyke (1970) 114 NLJ 588, at 589. E.g. at what times of day or night may such demands be made? Can a trader publish a 'debtor's list' on his premises? In seeking an absconded debtor, can a creditor tell third parties why he wishes to find the debtor?

153  Presumably, it is an offence to imply falsely that there is a legal right of recaption, e.g. where goods are protected (see para 24.34)?

154  See also Malicious Communications Act 1988; Protection from Harassment Act 1997.

155  See Borrie and Pyke (1970) 114 NLJ 588. For enquiries as to previous occupants, see (1992) 47 CC 3/12.

Breach of s 40 by a person licensed under the CCA could jeopardise his CCA licence[156] or lead to proceedings under Pt 8 of the EA (see para 6.07). In 2007, s 40 will have to be aligned with the UCP Directive (see para 4.21B).

*Repossession through court action*

**[24.25] Adverse possession**. As an alternative to recaption (see para 24.23), the owner[157] might seek to obtain judgment for the return of the goods and have that judgment executed by court officers.[158] Leaving aside the summary process of replevin,[159] and a claim for restitution in criminal proceedings (see para 3.20) or quasi-contract (see para 29.12), the only such cause of action which will normally be available to the owner is the statutory tort of wrongful interference with goods (see para 19.04). To succeed in such an action, it is not sufficient for the owner to plead that another, e.g. the hirer or buyer, has continued in possession of goods:[160] there must be shown a neglect or refusal to return the goods which is **adverse** to the owner's right to immediate possession (see para 19.05A). Normally, **adverse possession** is proved by showing that the owner demanded redelivery, but that the hirer or buyer unreasonably refused to comply.[161] The battle of wits to which this may give rise is well illustrated by *Capital Finance Ltd v Bray*;[162] but the burden of the creditor or owner in respect of regulated agreements may be eased by s 134 of the CCA (see para 24.32).

**[24.26] The forms of judgment**. At common law, even a defendant to the now abolished action in detinue might have the option whether to return the goods or pay their value.[163] Statute has now vested this power in the court, once it has assessed the value of the litigated goods (see paras 27.30–32). Besides the power to order up delivery of any goods by way of interim relief,[164] s 3 of the Torts (Interference with Goods) Act 1977 provides for final judgment where goods are wrongfully detained in any one of the following alternative (s 3(3)(a)) forms:[165]

1. *For specific delivery* of the goods and damages for any consequential loss (s 3(2)(a)). This form gives the defendant no option to pay their value; and the

156 E.g. the Allied Collection Agencies Affair: see (1989) 44 CC 2/24.
157 See para 24.23, fn 133.
158 For the commonly available forms of execution, see para 27.04.
159 See Guest, *Law of HP* 847; Winfield and Jolowicz, *Tort*, 16th edn, para 17.31. Replevin is now a form of interlocutory relief as to which, see para 24.26, fn 164.
160 Though such continued possession may amount to a breach of the supply contract: *Heskell v Continental Express Ltd* [1950] 1 All ER 1033. Where non-return is due to destruction of the goods without fault on the part of the hirer or buyer, the supply contract will usually make him strictly liable, and the goods will probably be insured as well.
161 The forms of judgment then available to an owner are considered at para 24.26.
162 [1964] 1 All ER 603; [1964] 1 WLR 323, CA.
163 *Crossfield v Such* (1852) 8 Exch 159. For the abolition of detinue see para 19.04.
164 Torts Act 1977, s 4. See *Howard E Perry & Co Ltd v BRB* [1980] 2 All ER 579.
165 S 3(2). These forms appear to be modelled on the common law remedies for detinue: as to which, see *General and Finance Facilities Ltd v Cook Cars (Romford) Ltd* [1963] 2 All ER 214. According to s 3(8), these forms of judgment are without prejudice to the remedies afforded by s 133 of the CCA (see para 24.43).

plaintiff is allowed to recover the goods by execution.[166] This form of judgment is wholly discretionary (s 3(3)(b)), likely only to be granted where the goods are unique[167], and even then the order may be conditional (s 3(6)).

2. *For goods or value.* This form of judgment orders, perhaps conditionally, delivery of the goods to the plaintiff **unless** there is payment of their value[168] made within a specified time, plus damages for their detention.[169] Before the time limit expires, the defendant may prevent the initiation of process for recovery of their assessed value by returning the goods (s 3(5)); but thereafter he must pay their assessed value.[170]

3. *Payment of the values*[168] of the goods to the plaintiff,[171] with damages for their detention.[172] A judgment in this form means that neither party can insist on the return of the goods;[173] but this does not prevent the owner from seizing the goods (see para 24.23), which continue to belong to him until the judgment is satisfied.[174] If the plaintiff does recapt the goods, he is deemed to have waived his right under the judgment to their assessed value.

In a typical case, a county court judge is likely to consider his choice as lying between forms of judgment (2) and (3): for instance, if he believes the defendant is unmeritorious he may prefer judgment (2); whereas, if his sympathies be with the defendant he is more likely to choose judgment (3). In any event, any order for payment of money is likely to be by instalments (see para 27.03). Default may lead to a warrant for delivery (see para 27.04).

## Regulated agreements[175]

**[24.27]** Even though the unpaid supplier may have reserved ownership of the goods supplied, statute has imposed a substantial number of restrictions on his power to recover possession of them. However, eschewing the simple course of setting out the unpaid supplier's rights, the draftsmen instead produced a series of special statutory restrictions on the general rules previously considered (see paras

---

166 But if the judgment is not satisfied, the court has power to revoke it (s 3(4)). As to execution, see para 27.04.

167 See *Cohen v Roche* [1927] 1 KB 169; and *per* Swinfen Eady MR in *Whiteley Ltd v Hilt* [1908] 2 KB 808, CA, at 319. See also *Howard E Perry & Co Ltd v BRB* (above). Cf. claims for specific performance: see para 29.38.

168 As to the value of goods, and improvement allowances see para 27.30. Where the bailee has made improvements to the goods, that may be deducted from the assessed value: s 3(6).

169 S 3(2)(b). As to whether the defendant must actually deliver the goods, see Winfield and Jolowicz, *Tort*, 16th edn, para 17.28, fn 37.

170 *Metals and Ropes Ltd v Tattersall* [1966] 3 All ER 401, CA; *Astley Industrial Trust Ltd v Miller* [1968] 2 All ER 36. But the court has power to stay execution, even out of time.

171 If the plaintiff claims only this form, judgment must be in this form (s 3(3)(b)): Thornely [1990] CLJ at 367.

172 The court must put a separate figure on the value of the goods: *General and Finance Facilities Ltd v Cook Cars (Romford) Ltd* (above).

173 However, by returning the goods before trial, the defendant may reduce the damages by their value: *Hillesden Securities Ltd v Ryjak Ltd* [1983] 2 All ER 184.

174 *Brinsmead v Harrison* (1872) LR 7 CP 547. If judgment is satisfied, the plaintiff's title passes to the defendant: see para 26.17.

175 For regulated agreements, see Chap 5.

24.21–26). The HPA 1938 forbad recaption after one-third of the hp price had been paid.[176] The HPA 1964 added the default notice procedure and death provisions, and made all three provisions applicable to conditional sales.[177] Following its normal practice (see para 5.07), the CCA 1974 adopted all three of the above restrictions and simply applied them to a larger range of contracts:[178] indeed, some of the restrictions were made applicable to all regulated agreements, including credit sales, loans and consumer hirings. Additionally, the CCA sought to ensure that the supplier did not side-step the default notice procedure by acting under the terms of the agreement (see para 24.28); and it laid down in Part IX general powers of judicial control over the enforcement of regulated agreements,[179] including enforcement orders.[180] To the foregoing pattern, the CCA 2006 has added a number of refinements dealing principally with the following:[181] default information sheets (ss 8–12); default interest (ss 13 and 18); default notices (s 14); and Time Orders (s 16).

**[24.27A] Arrears letters**. Whilst the CCA 1974 contains many rules designed to protect consumers who become indebted under regulated agreements, the weakness of these protections is that they were sometimes a stable-bolting exercise; that is, by the time they operated, the consumer was already in a financial position that was beyond repair. Hence, the 2006 Act has introduced extra provisions designed to ensure that all consumers going into arrears receive (via their lenders) 'clear, concise, independent information on debt management options, including debt advice'.[182] As a first step, s 8 of the 2006 Act introduces new s 86A of the 1974 Act, which casts upon the OFT a duty to prepare and publish 'Default Information Sheets' for debtors and hirers about arrears and default.[183] The plan is that these Sheets will be supported by regulations made by the Secretary of State,[184] which will specify the types of information to be included; and the form these Sheets will take is to be left to the OFT in General Notice.[185] Such Default Information Sheets must be included with each of the types of notice referred to below (new ss 86B(6) and 86C(3)).

Under the 2006 Act, as from April 2008 there are three extra types of notice the creditor or owner must at his own expense (new ss 86B(7), 86C(5) and 86E(6)) serve

---

176  As to the modern restrictions on the recaption of goods, see para 24.34.

177  As to the modern procedures in respect of default notices and death, see respectively, paras 24.30 and 24.44.

178  As recommended by the Crowther Report (see para 5.03), para 6.7.17.

179  See para 24.39, *et seq*. As to the special rules for extortionate credit bargains/unfair credit relationships, see para 29.40, *et seq.*; and for the financial relief of defaulting hirer, see para 27.23.

180  S 127: see para 9.20. For enforcement orders in respect of negotiable instruments and security agreements, see paras 25.09–11; and upon death, see para 24.47.

181  The CCA 2006 also refers to the following enforcement matters: enforceability (s 15: see para 9.20); and interest on judgments (s 17: see para 7.03A).

182  The Minister, originally introducing cl 8 in Session 2004–5 in the HC Standing Committee E (25.1.05), col. 32.

183  The Sheets 'shall include information to help debtors and hirers who receive' notices under new ss 86B or 86C or default notices (new s 86A(2) and (3)).

184  New s 86A(4).

185  New s 86A(5). There are provisions for future-proofing these rules by subsequent General Notices (new s 86A(6) and (7)).

on a debtor or hirer who has made at least two instalment payments (new ss 86B(1)(a) and 86C(1)(a)). Normally agreements provide for monthly payments: in this case,[186] the protection does not extend to the debtor or hirer who, having entered into a regulated agreement, makes only one or no payments under it. Where the protection is so applicable and the debtor or hirer has missed at least two payments, the following notices in prescribed form[187] are usually[188] required of the creditor or owner at regular intervals and whilst the default continues:[189]

(a) *Section 86B notices* as regards fixed-sum consumer credit or any consumer hire. In such cases, within fourteen days of the second missed payment, the creditor or owner must at his own expense (new s 86B(7)) give a s 86B notice and thereafter six-monthly notices (new s 86B(2)) whilst the default as to capital or interest continues and no debt judgment has been given (new s 86B(3)–(5)).

(b) *Section 86C notices* as regards running-account credit, e.g. bank overdrafts, credit cards. In such cases, under new s 86C(2) the creditor shall give a s 86C notice to the debtor 'no later than the end of the period within which he is next required to give a statement under s 78(4)'.[190]

(c) *Section 86E notices* of 'default sums'. According to new s 187A, 'default sums' means any sum which is payable by the debtor or hirer 'in connection with a breach of the agreement by him,' e.g. a charge imposed for late payment of an instalment, or for exceeding the credit limit on a credit card;[191] but it does not include interest, nor an acceleration clause. Where such a default sum becomes payable under the terms of the agreement, new s 86E requires the creditor or owner within a prescribed period to give notice to the debtor or hirer: he shall not be liable to any notice in respect of the first 28 days (new s 86E(4); and the interest must be limited to simple interest (new s 86F). There is power to exempt from s 86E default sums which are less than a prescribed amount (new 86E(7)(a)).

Where the creditor or owner fails to supply one of the above required notices then, whilst that failure continues,[192] under new ss 86D(4) and 86E(5) he shall not be entitled to enforce the regulated agreement, nor is he entitled to any interest or 'default sum'.[193]

---

186 In the case of a s 86B notice, where payments are required 'at intervals of one week or less', the minimum number of payments are increased to four within a 20 week period (s 86B(9)–(11)). This is to accommodate the home credit industry, where the lender commonly allows the borrower to miss some weekly payments without it being regarded as a default.

187 Regulations may make provision as to the form and content of these notices (new ss 86B(8), 86C(6) and 86E(7)).

188 Provided it is neither a non-commercial nor a small agreement (new ss 86B(12), 86C(7) and 87E(8)). For non-commercial and small agreements, see respectively, paras 5.18 and 5.17.

189 As inserted by ss 8–12 of the CCA 2006. Provided the creditor has not already been required to give notice nor there remains an outstanding judgment (new ss 86B(1) and 86C(1)). Receipt of notice is assumed under the Interpretation Act 1978, s 7.

190 For such notices, see para 15.16. This notice may be incorporated in another statutory notice (new s 86C(4)), e.g. a default notice (see para 24.28).

191 New s 86D(1)–(3). Cf. the rule against penalties (see para 27.25).

192 For the calculation of such 'period of non-compliance', see s 86D(5) and (6).

193 New s 86F. For definition of 'default sum', see new s 187A (as supplied by s 18 of the 2006 Act). This would seem wide enough to cover late payment fees, missed payment fees, legal fees and even court costs.

## Notice of enforcement by creditor or owner

**[24.28]** The contractual right of a creditor or owner under a regulated agreement to enforce that agreement may, subject to any arrears letter (see para 24.27A), arise not only upon breach by the debtor or hirer, but also in accordance with a number of terms of the agreement (see para 26.08). As it may obviously be a matter of accident whether a multiple debtor or hirer getting into financial difficulties ceases payments under his regulated or another agreement first, the CCA seeks to ensure that the debtor or hirer has prior notice before activation of the acceleration clause (see para 7.03) in both events. However, the Act makes separate provision for notice of enforcement according to whether it operates after default or in the absence of default for this reason: whereas the defaulting debtor or hirer is given the right to wipe the slate clean by remedying a default (see para 24.32), a non-default notice only suspends the rights of the creditor or owner.[194] On the other hand, where the regulated agreement involves a supply of goods, both notice requirements **suspend** the right of the creditor or owner to immediate possession of the goods, so temporarily preventing continued possession by the debtor or hirer from being adverse (see para 24.25). To the following extent, default and non-default notices share the same rules:

1.  *Co-debtors*. Where there is more than one debtor or hirer, s 185 requires that the notice must be served[195] on each of them (see para 25.08).

2.  *Form of notice*. Each of the provisions requires its notice to be in a prescribed form;[196] and regulations now provide in detail the form of such notices in a manner which allows default and non-default notices to be combined in one document,[197] and even to incorporate/include an arrears letter (see para 24.27A).

3.  *Period of notice*. Each of the provisions requires that, prior to taking one of the steps listed in the relevant provision, the creditor or owner must give the debtor or hirer[198] a minimum period of notice of his intention to do so: in the case of non-default notices, that period remains seven days;[199] but as regards default notices, as from April 2006 it has been extended to fourteen days.[200]

---

194  Ss 76 and 98: see para 24.29. Except that the debtor or hirer can always apply to the court for a Time Order (see para 24.40) or equitable relief against forfeiture: Goode, *Consumer Credit Law & Practice*, paras 45.17 and 40.23.

195  'Serve' means 'deliver or send by appropriate method' (s 189(1), as amended); and receipt is assumed under s 7 of the Interpretation Act 1978. S 176 lays down how such a document may be served and may be of considerable assistance if the debtor/hirer has 'done a moonlight' or denies receipt: see *Lombard North Central v Power-Hines* [1994] CLY 501, Cty Ct; and Goode, *Op. cit.*, para 45.33a.

196  Ss 76(3), 88(1) and 98(3). This refers to the forms prescribed by the Secretary of State (s 189(1)) by statutory instrument (s 182). The prescribed form must be in writing (2004 SI 3237), not electronic as is generally allowed (see para 9.05).

197  Consumer Credit (Enforcement, Default and Termination Notices) Regulations, 1983 SI 1561 (as amended).

198  As 'debtor' and 'hirer' are defined to include persons to whom their rights may have passed 'by operation of law' (s 189(1)), this obviates any problem relating to service of a notice where the debtor or hirer has died: notice may be served on his personal representative or at the last known address of the debtor or hirer. As to death, see further, para 24.44, *et seq*.

199  Ss 76(1), 88(2) and 98(1). In practice, a minimum of 12 days from posting is generally allowed: (1995) 50 CC 3/35.

200  S 88(2) and (3), as amended by s 14(1) of CCA 2006.

4. *Exemptions*. Each of the provisions requiring such notices lays down in identical form that (ss 76(4), 87(2) and 98(4)):

> 'it does not prevent a creditor from treating the right to draw on any credit as restricted or deferred and taking such steps as may be necessary to make the restriction or deferment effective'.

Thus, a bank may, without such a notice, put a temporary embargo on a credit card facility or overdraft. Additionally, other types of agreement may be exempted by regulations.[201]

5. *Acting without notice*. If the creditor or owner takes one of the steps listed in the relevant provision without giving the requisite notice, the effect is as follows: even if the creditor or owner is permitted to take such steps at common law, e.g. because the debtor's landlord has levied distress (see para 26.08), he is not 'entitled' to do so in the absence of the requisite notice,[202] so that his taking that step without such notice may (notwithstanding s 170: see para 10.19) be a breach of contract[203] or tortious.[204] Failure to inform the debtor or hirer in the agreement that he has a right to such a notice before steps are taken may be unfair.[205]

**[24.29] Non-default notices**. There are two notice provisions which may be applicable where the CCA requires the creditor or owner[206] to give notice (see para 24.28) before exercising certain rights granted to him by the regulated agreement in the absence of default by the debtor or hirer (ss 76(6) and 98(6)).

1. *Termination notices*. Where the right granted to the creditor or owner is to terminate the regulated agreement, the matter is governed by s 98; and, as a remedy, this is more properly considered later (para 26.10).

2. *Other notices*. Section 76(1) provides that:

> 'The creditor or owner is not entitled to enforce a term of a regulated agreement by[207]
>
> (a)    demanding earlier payment of any sum,[208] or
>
> (b)    recovering possession of any goods or land,[209] or

---

201  Ss 76(5), 87(4) and 98(5). See the regulations referred to above.

202  Ss 76(1), 87(1) and 98(2). E.g. even if a creditor was entitled under the terms of an agreement to 'demand earlier payment of any sum', he would not be so entitled under a regulated agreement so long as he failed to serve a s 76 notice (see below).

203  E.g. breach of warranty of quiet possession (see para 12.16).

204  For wrongful interference with goods, see para 19.04.

205  [2006] *Bulletin J/M, Log Book*.

206  Under any regulated agreement, whether by way of conditional or credit sale, hp, consumer hiring or loan.

207  Note that paras (a)–(c) correspond with s 87(1)(b)–(d) applicable where the debtor or hirer defaults: see para 24.30. S 76 does not refer to the enforcing of any personal security: *contra* s 87(1)(e).

208  E.g. loans to buy goods which are then destroyed; loans which may be called in on notice, though this may be an unfair term. For accelerated payments clauses, see generally, para 7.03. This will be subject to the Time Order procedure: see para 24.39. For loans repayable on demand, see below.

209  For the repossession action in respect of goods, see paras 24.42–3; and in respect of land, see para 25.23.

(c) treating any right conferred on the debtor or hirer by agreement as terminated, restricted or deferred,[210]

except by or after giving the debtor or hirer not less than seven days' notice of his intention to do so.'

As s 98(1) deals with termination of regulated agreements, it has been suggested that s 76(1)(c) only deals with some lesser termination, e.g. of the hiring, so that a creditor or owner who wishes to terminate both the hiring and the agreement should give a combined ss 76 and 98 notice.[211]

It is further provided that the requirements as to non-default notices do **not** apply to either of the following types of case:

(i) Facilities where the credit is in the circumstances repayable on demand (ss 76(4) and 98(4): set out at para 24.28);[212] or

(ii) Agreements where the whole of the specified credit period has expired.[213]

**[24.30] Default notices.** One of the most frequent causes of repossession at common law was default in payment of instalments: as neither the conditional buyer nor hirer under an hp nor simple hiring agreement had any equity of redemption (see para 24.22), the supplier was not required to give him any latitude in this respect,[214] though in practice the courts were very willing to find that the supplier had waived the default by accepting late payment.[215] However, this dependence of the buyer or hirer on the whim of the supplier was thought to be wrong; and the CCA therefore requires the creditor or owner to do two things:

(a) to give the debtor or hirer early warning of the default under new ss 86B, 86C and 86E (see para 24.27A); and

(b) if the debtor or hirer remains in default and the creditor or owner wishes to exercise certain listed rights granted to him by the regulated agreement after default,[216] to give fourteen days' notice (see para 24.28). According to s 87(1):

'Service of a notice on the debtor or hirer in accordance with section 88 (a 'default notice') is necessary before the creditor or owner can become entitled, by reason of any breach by the debtor or hirer of a regulated agreement—

(a) to terminate the agreement,[217] or

---

210 E.g. terminate the hiring (see para 26.09). Cf. s 87(1)(d).

211 Goode, *Consumer Credit Law & Practice*, para 45.16; and see para 26.09.

212 E.g. *Barclays Bank v Brillouet* [1990] GCCR 1541, CA. Thus, without such seven-day notice, these running accounts may be embargoed (see para 24.28) or terminated. *Contra* credit granted for a specified period with an overriding right to call it in: Goode, *Op. cit.*, para 28.66.

213 Ss 76(2) and 98(2). E.g. a credit sale where all instalments are now overdue.

214 However, the debtor or hirer might have been persuaded to take out insurance against this event (see para 24.45): in this case, the insurance payment will prevent the default. *Contra* where the creditor or owner has insured himself against default. As to multiple agreements, see para 5.27.

215 E.g. *Reynolds v General Finance Facilities Ltd* (1963), 107 Sol Jo 889, CA. See generally, para 26.23. For refinancing, see para 7.04A.

216 For non-default notices, see para 24.29. As to the types of agreement requiring default notices, see para 24.29, fn 206.

217 For termination of the agreement, see further, para 26.09.

    (b)   to demand earlier payment of any sum,[218] or

    (c)   to recover possession of any goods or land,[219] or

    (d)   to treat any right conferred on the debtor or hirer by the agreement as terminated, restricted or deferred,[220] or

    (e)   to enforce any security.'[221]

Observe that s 87(1) is only applicable where the creditor or owner wishes to take any of the steps there listed, **and** where he becomes entitled to do 'by reason of any breach by the debtor or hirer':[222] if the listed right arises otherwise than by reason of breach, the case falls outside s 87(1),[223] though a non-default notice may be required before its exercise;[216] and if, despite the breach, the creditor or owner does not wish to take any of the above-listed steps, no default notice is required.[224] The contents and effect of a default notice are considered below. Further, the supplier may register the default with a credit reference agency.[225]

**[24.31] Contents**. The required minimum contents[226] of a default notice (see para 24.30) are spelt out by s 88.[227] As expanded by the Regulations, it requires that the default notice must be in the prescribed form (see para 24.28) and contain the prescribed contents, including all the following:

1.   *The nature of the alleged breach.* Whilst at common law it may not matter that one gives the wrong reason for doing that which one is entitled to do (see para 26.26), s 88(1)(a) of the CCA requires specification of the correct reason relied on by the creditor or owner for taking action,[228] and it may be that a waived breach will not suffice (see generally, para 26.23). The notice may specify more than one breach.[229]

---

218  For accelerated payments clauses, see para 7.03. It has been said that the creditor or owner cannot rely on the default notice, but must instead make separate demand after its expiry: Goode, *Consumer Credit Law & Practice*, para 45.33. *Sed quaere?*

219  For repossession actions in respect of goods, see para 24.34; and for repossession actions in respect of land, see para 25.24.

220  Cf. s 76(1)(c): see para 24.29.

221  See para 25.14. According to s 87(3), 'The doing of an act by which a floating charge becomes fixed is not enforcement of a security'. This provision is only applicable in the exceptional case where an incorporated body is a joint debtor with an individual, and its effect there is explained by Goode, *Op. cit.*, para 45.35. As to floating charges, see para 19.14.

222  Whether that right is expressly granted by the agreement, or given by the general law: Goode, *Op. cit.*, para 45.32. However, if it is to the advantage of the debtor or hirer, his actions might be construed as an exercise of any statutory right of cancellation or termination (see respectively, para 10.29 and para 26.05) rather then a default.

223  E.g. where the debtor wrongfully disposes of goods: Goode, *Op. cit.*, 45.34; *sed quaere?*

224  E.g. recover arrears of rent or damages from the debtor, or rescind for misrepresentation (see Goode, *Op. cit.*, 45.32).

225  As to credit reference agencies, see para 8.36. Default information which may be filed is limited by DP Principles 1–5: see para 3.28.

226  There is no reason why the notice may not also include other information, e.g. a demand for the return of the goods (see para 24.25). See further s 88(5): para 24.32.

227  The drafting seems to follow closely that of the Law of Property Act 1925, s 146: see Goode, *Consumer Credit Law & Practice*, para 45.36, who suggests that the authorities on s 146 may therefore be useful in interpreting s 88.

228  If any amount owing is overstated, does this not only make the default notice bad (see below), but also amount to 'unlawful harassment' (as to which, see para 24.24)?

229  *Ropaigealach v Allied Irish Bank plc* [1996] CLY 416, CA (16 Tr L 32).

2. *The required information.* As strengthened by the 2006 Act, as from April 2008 the CCA requires the notice to include 'information in the prescribed terms about the consequences of failure to comply with it and any other prescribed matters related to it'.[230] Under new s 88(4A), it must also include a copy of the current default information sheet (see para 24.27A).

3. *The action required of the debtor or hirer.* This will vary, according to whether or not the breach is remediable,[231] as follows:

   (a) *Remediable breaches.* Section 88(1)(b) requires the default notice to specify:

   > 'if the breach is capable of remedy, what action is required to remedy it and the date before which that action is to be taken'.

   The obvious example is non-payment of an instalment; but the notice is bad if it stipulates for a sum greater than was actually due.[232] The Act makes special provision for the relatively common occurrence that such a primary default may be expressed to activate a secondary clause.[233] For instance, where a debtor fails to make the stipulated minimum payment due under a credit card, the creditor may not during the default period[234] demand payment of all arrears under an acceleration clause (see para 7.03); but he may demand return of the card.[235]

   (b) *Irremediable breaches.* Section 88(1)(c) requires the default notice to specify:

   > 'if the breach is not capable of remedy, the sum (if any) required to be paid as compensation for the breach, and the date before which it is to be paid'.

   Thus, after an irremediable breach, the creditor or owner may demand some action by the debtor or hirer such as the return of the goods, in which event the debtor or hirer may apply for a Time Order (s 129: see para 24.40). Alternatively, the creditor or owner may demand compensation: so, if the debtor wrongfully passed a good Part III title to a bf private purchaser of a motor vehicle (see para 21.55, *et seq.*), or if the debtor wrote the hired vehicle off, the creditor or owner may demand its value in tort (see para 24.26).

[24.32/3] **Effect**. On receipt of a default notice in prescribed form (see paras 24.30–31), the debtor or hirer may or may not comply with it.

1. *Compliance.* Within that statutory breathing space compulsorily granted to the debtor or hirer, s 89 lays down that:

---

230  S 88(4) of the 1974 Act, as amended by s 14(2) of the 2006 Act. E.g. information about whether the agreement includes a term providing for the charging of post-judgment interest (see para 7.03A).

231  For discussion as to what amounts to a remediable breach, see Goode, *Op. cit.*, para 45.37.

232  *Woodchester Lease Management Services Ltd v Swain & Co* [1999] 1 WLR 263, CA.

233  Only the breach of primary obligations (see para 26.16), e.g. payment, is to be taken into account for the purposes of a default notice, not any secondary obligation, e.g. an unrelated administrative charge: s 88(3); and see Goode, *Op. cit.*, paras 45.51a–b.

234  As to the effect of s 88(3) where the default period has expired without compliance, see para 24.32.

235  Because this is not an action referred to in s 89(1). The credit token agreement will normally provide that ownership of the card remains in the creditor, to whom it must be returned on demand: see para 7.09.

'If before the date specified for that purpose in the default notice the debtor or
hirer takes the action specified under section 88(1)(b) or (c) the breach shall be
treated as not having occurred.'

Unlike the case of non-default notices, where the effect of the notice is only
suspensory (see para 24.29), the defaulting debtor or hirer is thus given a right to
make good the breach: *pro tanto* there is a compulsory[236] variation of the
regulated agreement[237] on each default notice.[238]

2. *Non-compliance.* On the other hand, it may be that the debtor or hirer is not in a
position to avail himself of this statutory right to make good the default, e.g.
where he suffers a distress or is otherwise impecunious. In this case, the effect of
the default notice itself is only to suspend the listed rights of the creditor or
owner for the period there mentioned, though the court will have jurisdiction to
make a Time Order (see para 24.39). Moreover, s 88(5) makes it clear that a
default notice may activate a provision in a regulated agreement that the
agreement or hiring is terminable[239] for arrears by saying such as: 'If arrears of
£x is not paid within ten days, the creditor will terminate the agreement,
repossess the goods,[240] and levy a default charge';[241] but this default charge is
circumscribed.[242] By s 134, the continuing possession of the goods by the debtor
or hirer under s 88(5) or other CCA protections is adverse to the creditor or
owner (see para 24.25).

Additionally, the Act provides that, whilst the default notice may not require
the making good of some promise only activated by breach, e.g. an accelerated
payments clause (see paras 7.03 and 24.31), if the specified breach, e.g. arrears of
instalments, is not remedied, such other clause, e.g. the acceleration clause, may
then be relied upon free of the default notice procedure.[243]

## Repossession

[24.34] The HPA 1938 introduced two statutory restrictions on the supplier's right
to recover goods let on hp within the ambit of the Act. Today, they form just two
items on a longer list of CCA restrictions (see para 24.27).

---

236  S 173(1): see generally, para 18.11.
237  Might acceptance of part of any arrears amount to a waiver of breach (see para 24.30)? For
     compulsory variation of regulated agreements, see generally, para 26.22. Cf. mortgages of land:
     para 25.20.
238  The debtor or hirer must already have been served with a s 86E notice, which has expired
     unsatisfied (see para 24.27A).
239  For the situation where the agreement or hiring is terminable, see generally, para 26.09.
240  For repossession actions in respect of protected goods, see para 24.42.
241  The regular slow payer may be charged default interest if the agreement so provides: (1993) 48
     CC 4/13. But the rate of interest must not be increased (see below).
242  A default charge may amount to a penalty (see para 27.46) or an increased rate of interest
     (default interest): default interest is prohibited in the case of consumer credit agreements (see
     para 26.19), but not in the case of consumer hirings (see (1989) 43 CC 6/17).
243  S 88(3). Thus, if the third of ten instalments is in default beyond the default notice period the
     acceleration clause operates, so that the creditor becomes entitled to claim immediately all the
     remaining seven instalments. Similarly with an administrative charge, e.g. for sending out a
     default letter.

1. *Licences to enter premises*. Whilst at common law instalment credit agreements might contain a contractual licence for the supplier to enter premises to recapt goods (see para 24.23), such provisions in some hp agreements were avoided by the HPA 1938. However, that did not prevent the hirer from granting his supplier express permission to enter premises at the time of entry. Fundamentally, this would still appear to be the position, though the CCA protection has also been extended to include conditional sales and simple hirings.[244] Section 92(1) of the CCA provides:

> 'Except under an order of the court, the creditor or owner shall not be entitled to enter any premises to take possession of goods subject to a regulated hire-purchase agreement, regulated conditional sale agreement or regulated consumer hire agreement.'

Presumably, 'premises' connotes land to which the public does not have access as of right and extends to car-ports and private driveways, whether or not 'premises' occupied by the debtor or hirer.[245] Within its ambit,[246] contravention of s 92(1) will give rise to an action for breach of statutory duty (s 92(3): see para 3.21). Any common law right to recapt[247] protected goods is therefore only likely to remain of significance in relation to such goods in two circumstances: (a) where recaption is possible without entry on 'premises', e.g. in respect of motor vehicles, especially where the vehicle cannot be shown to have been garaged at the time of repossession; or (b) where consent to entry on 'premises' is given at the time of entry under s 173(3).[248]

2. *Protected goods*. Where the hirer had paid more than one-third of the hp price, the HPA 1938 termed them 'protected goods': in respect of these, the exercise of any common law right of recaption[247] was totally prohibited; and, if the owner alternatively sought to recover the goods through court action, the 1938 introduced a number of substantive and procedural protections. These provisions were subsequently extended to conditional sales and have now been re-formulated in the CCA:[249] not only are such actions subject to prior observance of the notice procedure (see paras 24.27A–32), but an action to recover protected goods (see paras 24.35–38) must be brought in the debtor's local county court (s 141: see para 24.39), where there are alterations in the forms of judgment. The court may simply re-schedule the payments under a Time Order (see para 24.40); and, even where that remedy is inappropriate, there are substantial

---

244 With a similar restriction being introduced in relation to recovery of land subject to a conditional sale (s 92(2): see para 25.24). For such conditional sales, see generally, para 1.16.

245 But does it include a private road, lock-up garage, a garage under a block of flats, a dormobile, a caravan, or any other structure not amounting to a dwelling-house? This restriction may extend to premises occupied by third parties: see Goode, *Consumer Credit Law & Practice*, para 38.4.

246 What about exercise of a contractual right of entry to inspect goods? Or where goods are no longer subject to the agreement, e.g. where the hiring has terminated?

247 For the common law right of recaption, see para 24.23. Under s 80 of the CCA, the debtor must disclose the whereabouts of the goods: see para 15.17. But what is to stop him then moving them?

248 See generally, para 18.11 and para 24.37. Whose consent is relevant if the debtor or hirer is not the occupier of the 'premises'? What if the debtor's trustee in bankruptcy consents? As to consent, see further, para 24.37.

249 The substantive provisions do not apply to consumer hirings in respect of which the hirer's only substantive protection on repossession is financial (s 132): see para 27.23.

restrictions (see paras 24.42–3) on the forms of judgment otherwise applicable (see para 24.26).

3.   *Unprotected goods.* Before the hirer had paid one-third of the hp price, under the 1938 Act the owner retained his power to recapt,[247] though modified by the removal of any contractual licence to enter premises (see above). This last rule has now been extended to consumer hirings (see para 1.19) and to any security (see para 25.13) or linked transaction (see para 5.31).

Finally, it should be remembered that, if the goods are not commercially worth repossessing, the supplier can always sue instead for the price or rent (see para 27.15A, *et seq.*); but any purported exclusion of the above consumer rights may be unfair.[250]

**[24.35] Protected goods.** According to s 90(1):

'At any time when—

(a)  the debtor is in breach of a regulated hire-purchase or a regulated conditional sale agreement relating to goods, and

(b)  the debtor has paid to the creditor one-third or more of the total price of the goods, and

(c)  the property in the goods remains in the creditor,

the creditor is not entitled to recover possession of the goods from the debtor except on an order from the court.'

Thus, goods only fall within s 90(1) where **all** three paragraphs are satisfied as follows:

*Paragraph (a).* The section does not extend to all regulated agreements,[251] but only a regulated hp or conditional sale (see paras 1.24 and 1.16). Further, s 90(5) makes it clear that the protection is lost where the debtor terminates the agreement (see para 24.37); but the sense of s 90(1) is that the creditor cannot escape its ambit by himself exercising any common law right of termination (see para 26.09). Finally, the creditor must be claiming repossession **after** a breach by the debtor,[252] though it does not require any connection between the debtor's breach and the creditor's claim.[253]

*Paragraph (b).* The concept of 'total price' is defined by s 189(1) as:

'the total sum payable[254] by the debtor under a hire-purchase agreement or a conditional sale agreement, including any sum payable on the exercise of an option to purchase,[255] but excluding any sum payable as a penalty[256] or as compensation or damages for a breach of the agreement.'[257]

---

250  OFT, *UCT Bulletin No. 23*, case 3.

251  So it does not extend to consumer hiring agreements. But see s 132: para 27.23.

252  The goods will not fall within s 90(1) where the debtor has not committed any breach and the creditor is terminating the agreement under a s 98 notice (as to which, see para 26.10). It has been remarked that this is a surprising reduction in the protection of the debtor: Goode, *Consumer Credit Law & Practice*, para 45.60.

253  What if there is no breach at the time a s 98 notice is served, but one occurs before expiry of the seven days—as is quite likely if the triggering event is, e.g. insolvency? For death, see para 24.48.

254  This presumably includes part-exchange allowances (as to which, see para 2.09). What if there is a variable finance charge?

255  See para 1.25.          256  See para 27.25.

257  This does not extend to extra interest and administration charges: *Julian Hodge Bank Ltd v Hall* [1998] CLY 2493, CA.

This paragraph requires that the 'total price of the goods' be compared with the sums paid[258] by the debtor:[259] the goods will fall within s 90 only if the latter is at least one-third of the former (see further, para 24.36). It may, however, be possible for a debtor in possession of unprotected goods even after termination of the agreement to claim protection from s 90 by making additional payments up to the one-third level,[260] e.g. through the bank giro system (see para 23.13), even though the creditor has validly terminated the agreement and the fourteen-day notice expired (see above).

*Paragraph (c).* Whilst perhaps unlikely, it would seem that the property could pass in goods held under a regulated hp or conditional sale (see above) agreement before completion of the payments, upon which the goods would be taken outside s 90(1) and might seem unprotected in the hands of the hirer or buyer,[261] whilst safe in the hands of his purchaser.[262]

**[24.36] The one-third rule.**[263] Section 90(1)(b) brings a regulated hp or conditional sale agreement within the protection of s 90 only if the debtor has paid one-third of the 'total price' (see para 24.35) 'of the goods'.[264] Suppose a total price of £900. In the ordinary case, the goods will fall within s 90 where the debtor has paid £900 × $1/3 = £300$,[265] including any deposit.[266] However, the section also makes provision for the following special cases:

1. *Installation charges.*[267] According to s 90(2):

   'Where under a hire-purchase or conditional sale agreement the creditor is required to carry out any installation and the agreement specifies, as part of the total price, the amount to be paid in respect of the installation (the 'installation charge') the reference in subsection (1)(b) to one-third of the total price shall be construed as a reference to the aggregate of the installation charge and one-third of the remainder of the total price.'

   Thus, suppose a total price of £900 plus a **compulsory** installation charge of £60, the goods will fall within s 90 where the debtor has paid £60 + (£900 × 1/3) = £360. On the other hand, if the installation charge was **not compulsory** under

---

258  Does 'paid' include tendered? S 189(1) provides that *prima facie* 'payment' includes tender; and as to tender, see generally, paras 23.14–15.

259  Or on his behalf, e.g. by a surety. For the common law rules of payment, see para 23.13.

260  See para 24.36, fn 265. As to appropriation of payment where the debtor has more than one agreement, see *Ibid.*

261  Is this a drafting slip? Would any contractual right of repossession then amount to a colourable licence to seize? See para 25.27.

262  The purchaser would have a title good enough to defeat a tort claim by the supplier: see para 19.06.

263  As to multiple agreements, see para 5.27.

264  Might the words 'of the goods' in s 90(1)(b) save from the section payments in respect of related services? The words do not appear in s 100 (see para 27.49), but are arguably assumed to cover services by s 90(2).

265  Even this simple rule may cause creditors practical difficulties, given that a payment may be made by or on behalf of the debtor at any of the creditor's branches, or even via the banking system: see para 23.12. Might it be avoidable by not authorising receipt of payments; or does payment here include tender (see para 23.13)? See Goode, *Payment Obligations*, 21–3.

266  Distinguish the concept of credit, from which the deposit is excluded: see paras 5.22–3.

267  'Installation charges' are elaborately defined in s 189(1).

the regulated agreement,[268] the goods will fall within s 90 where only £300 has been paid (see above).

2. *Successive agreements*. Between the two world wars, there became prevalent the device of linking one hp agreement to another in the following manner:[269] the hirer under an almost completed agreement was persuaded to abandon it and take the goods from the first agreement together with further goods under a second agreement; and in this manner the owner increased his security at no cost to himself.[270] The HPA 1964 sought to combat this device in controls subsequently re-enacted in the CCA: the result is that, where the first agreement falls within s 90, both the old and new goods will fall within s 90, regardless of the amount paid under the second agreement.[271]

**[24.37] Loss of protected goods status**. Goods which fall within s 90 as above explained (paras 24.35–36) are termed 'protected goods' (s 90(7)). However, there are a number of ways in which the status of protected goods may be lost by action on the part of the debtor, though he could still apply for a Time Order (s 129: see para 24.40).

1. *Consent to repossession*. At first sight, s 90(1) looks as though it prohibits any repossession by the creditor without court order (recaption), so ruling out voluntary surrender of the goods by the debtor. However, when read in conjunction with s 173(3) (see para 18.11), it is clear that what the CCA does is only to avoid any device whereby the debtor consents **in advance** to repossession by the creditor.[272] *De facto* consent is frequently given by the debtor in the hope that resale by the creditor will discharge the balance due; and the question may be whether that consent is informed, and therefore *de iure*, consent.[273] Is s 173(3) wide enough to cover the case where goods are abandoned by the debtor?[274] Is it then needed?[275]

2. *Termination*. According to s 90(5), where a debtor[276] exercises his common law or statutory right of termination (see para 26.04), he loses the protection of s 90,

---

268 What if it was made compulsory under a prior collateral contract?

269 This became part of the technique of the 'snatchback': see para 26.08.

270 E.g. furniture trade. Unfortunately, the practice was to term these 'linked transactions'. However, the CCA reserves that expression for an entirely different device (see para 5.31).

271 Where the second agreement entirely discharges the first one, this effect is achieved by s 90(3); and, where the second agreement only modifies the first one, by s 90(4). For modifying agreements, see generally, para 26.22.

272 *Mercantile Credit Ltd v Cross* [1965] 2 QB 205, CA.

273 No consent held: *FC Finance Ltd v Francis* (1970) 114 Sol Jo 568, CA (third party purported to consent on behalf of hirer); *Chartered Trust plc v Pitcher* [1988] RTR 72, CA (consent by hirer qualified and uninformed); *Hunter v Lex Vehicle Finance Ltd* [2005] CLY 671 (acquiescing in repossession was consent). Consent of one joint debtor is sufficient (s 185(1)(b)): set out at para 25.08.

274 *Bentinck Ltd v Cromwell Engineering Co Ltd* [1971] 1 QB 324, CA (six months). See Goode, *Consumer Credit Law & Practice*, para 45.77; and Hudson (1984) 100 LQR 110, esp. 116–17, and 119, fn 70.

275 Are abandoned goods repossessed **from** the debtor within the meaning of s 90(1)? See Goode, *ibid*, Division 11B, para 5.170.

276 Where the debtor is bankrupt, his position is taken by his trustee (see para 5.24), who may disclaim the agreement as onerous property (see para 19.22). Consider then the effect of s 92 (see para 24.34).

though this would seem to follow only where that exercise were truly voluntary:[273] this rule is an inducement to the court to find that the debtor's action amounts to a breach rather than the exercise of a right to terminate.[277]

3. *Transfer of possession.* Sometimes, a person taking goods on conditional sale or hp will transfer possession of those goods to a third party (as to the effect of such a transfer at common law, see para 1.22). The effect of this on the protected goods status is as follows:[278] if the transfer of possession is by way of assignment, the goods remain protected because the expression 'debtor' includes his assignee;[279] if the debtor bails goods to another for a temporary purpose, e.g. to a repairer, the goods remain protected because they can still be regarded as in the legal possession of the debtor;[280] but, where the goods are sold by the debtor, it would seem that they are no longer protected, because s 90(1) only prohibits the creditor recovering possession from the 'debtor'.[281] Where the creditor takes the goods into protective custody under s 131 (see para 24.43), the goods seem to have lost their protected status.[282]

**[24.38] The protection.** The effect of s 90 (see paras 24.34–37) is that 'the creditor[283] is not entitled to recover possession of [protected] goods from the debtor except by order of the court' (s 90(1)). The process for obtaining such a court order is examined below (see para 24.39, *et seq.*). Contravention of s 90 attracts the severe[284] penalty of s 91:[285]

'If goods are recovered by the creditor in contravention of section 90—

(a) the regulated agreement, if not previously terminated, shall terminate, and

(b) the debtor shall be released from all liability under the agreement, and shall be entitled to recover from the creditor all sums paid by the debtor under the agreement.'[286]

Not only is the effect of s 91(a) to terminate the regulated agreement forthwith,[287] but it also renders ineffective any security provided in relation to the agreement.[288]

---

277 See *Bridge v Campbell Discount Co Ltd* (see para 27.25). For repudiation, see para 26.15.

278 Bear in mind the prohibition against such transfers frequently found in conditional sales and hp agreements: see para 7.26.

279 S 189(1). As to where the debtor dies, see para 24.48.

280 Goode, *Op. cit.*, para 45.78.

281 E.g. a vehicle transfer agency (see para 7.26A). See *Kassam v Chartered Trust PLC* [1998] RTR 220, CA. What if the goods are innocently given away by the debtor, perhaps to somebody within his immediate family?

282 *Lombank v Dowdall* (1973) 118 Sol Jo 96, CA (under narrower HPA 1965, s 34(3)). *Contra* where the owner does not obtain a court order before purporting to take the goods into protective custody: *UDT (Commercial) v Kesler* (1962) Sol Jo 15.

283 'Creditor' includes his assignee: s 189(1).

284 The penalty originated in the HPA 1938, when there did not exist the modern, more flexible, licensing provisions (see para 6.11, *et seq.*).

285 If there is any doubt as to whether or not s 91 has operated, any 'interested party' may apply to the court for a declaration: s 142(2)(b).

286 E.g. *Humberclyde Finance Ltd v Thomson* (1997) Tr LR 242.

287 For the position where only part of the protected goods are repossessed, see Goode, *Consumer Credit Law & Practice*, para 45.93.

288 Ss 106 and 113(3)(b). E.g. a guarantor who has paid some instalments may recover them.

However, it gives rise to no further sanction.[289] The effect of a similar scheme in the HPA 1938 was considered by Goddard LJ in *Carr v James Broderick Ltd*:[290]

> The owners of goods let under an hp agreement seized them in contravention of the Act after one-third of the hp price had been paid. Subsequently, the owners admitted their error, and offered to repay the sums already paid by the hirer. The hirer refuses to accept the money, and sued to recover the goods.

His Lordship held that the agreement had been determined by the Act; and that the hirer was not entitled to claim the goods either in detinue or conversion (see para 19.04), but merely the sums paid under the agreement. Thus, once the owner recapts the goods (see para 24.23), the hirer cannot recover their possession by court action.[291] Nor will the agreement be revived simply because the goods are returned to the hirer.[292] However, for s 91 to operate, it seems that some positive act of recaption is required.[293]

## Powers of the court

**[24.39] Introduction.** Thus far, this section has concentrated on the CCA rules designed to place fetters (see paras 24.27–38) on the rights of the creditor or owner to exercise his ordinary proprietary rights (see paras 24.21–26); to channel disputes into the relevant County Court (s 141(1): see para 24.34); and to ensure that all parties are before the court.[294] Attention must now be turned to what happens when the dispute gets to court. Leaving aside the interim power of the court to make a Protection Order,[295] the CCA envisages that the normal situation will be this: the court will conclude that the sum claimed under the regulated agreement is due under the terms of the contract, but wish to allow the debtor or hirer time for payment; and the Act envisages that this is to be effected by means of Time Orders (see para 24.40, *et seq.*). However, some special rules are provided for the case where the regulated agreement includes the supply of goods with a reservation of title (see para 24.42, *et seq.*).

Where a case is instead brought in the High Court, it may be transferred to the relevant County Court;[296] or it may be struck out if the person bringing the proceedings ought to have known this.[297] However, there would appear to be a gap in the strategy of the CCA in its seeking to channel all disputes into the relevant

---

289 S 170(1): see para 10.19. See further Goode, *Op. cit.*, para 46.143.

290 [1942] 2 KB 275, [1942] 2 All ER 441.

291 What if the debtor seizes the goods? Is it conversion? Theft?

292 Because fresh documentation would be necessary to comply with the CCA: see Chap 9. Cf. unregulated agreements: see *Capital Finance Ltd v Bray* (see para 24.25).

293 *Black Horse Ltd v Smith* [2002] CLY 689, Cty Ct (owner 'releasing title' to repairer held not within s 91).

294 This will include all co-principals and any sureties (s 141(5)): see further, para 25.08.

295 Under s 131, the creditor may apply for a 'protection order' in respect of the goods if worried as to his interest in them, e.g. if the debtor or hirer is driving uninsured, or trying to sell them. Repossession would then seem possible even of protected goods (see s 90(1): set out at para 24.35); but the efficacy of the proceedings may be reduced by court delays. Cf. an injunction (see para 29.39).

296 CCA, s 141(2); *Sovereign Leasing v Ali* [1992] CLY 3457, Cty Crt.

297 S 40(1), County Court Act 1984 (as substituted); *Barclays Bank plc v Brooks* [1997] CCLR 60.

County Court: it assumes that the creditor or owner will commence a court action under the agreement. However, it has been decided that the creditor or owner is entitled instead to make a 'statutory demand' leading to High Court insolvency proceedings (see para 19.21); but has been pointed out that the High Court may then exercise its discretion to set aside the demand.[298]

**[24.40] Time Orders**. Amended s 129(1) empowers the court 'if it appears just to do so' to make a Time Order[299] in any of the following circumstances:

'(a) on an application for an enforcement order;[300] or

(b) on an application made by a debtor or hirer under this paragraph after service on him of—

   (i)   a default notice,[301] or

   (ii)  a notice under section 76(1)[302] or 98(1);[303] or

(ba) on an application made by a debtor or hirer under this paragraph after he has been given a notice under section 86B or 86C;[304] or

(c) in an action brought by a creditor or owner to enforce a regulated agreement[305] or any security,[306] or recover possession of any goods[307] or land[308] to which a regulated agreement relates.'

The 2003 White Paper[309] noted that insufficient use was being made of Time Orders, especially in relation to the variation power in s 136 (see para 9.20) and stated that the Government was discussing how to encourage their wider use, including 'allowing a debtor to apply for a Time Order before Notice of Default has been served'. Accordingly, new s 129A(1) provides that as from April 2008 'a debtor or hirer may make an application under above section 129(1)(ba) in relation to a regulated agreement only if' all the following conditions are satisfied:

(a) The creditor or owner gave him an arrears notice under ss 86B or 86C (see 24.27A). Distinguish a default notice (s 87: see para 24.30).

(b) In response, he has given a proposal notice to the creditor or owner.[310] A debtor's/hirer's proposal notice within this provision must satisfy new s 129A(2): it must identify itself as such, indicate that he 'wants to make a proposal to the creditor or owner in relation to his making of payments under the agreement'

---

298  Goode, *Consumer Credit Law & Practice*, para 46.23.
299  For the reasons why Time Orders are more potent than instalment orders under s 71(1) of the County Courts Act 1984, see Goode, *Consumer Credit Law & Practice*, para 46.174.
300  See para 9.20.
301  See para 24.30.
302  See para 24.29.
303  See para 26.10.
304  As inserted by s 16(1) of the 2006 Act.
305  E.g. the terms of a loan: see para 7.02, *et seq*.
306  For security agreements, see para 25.10.
307  See para 24.34.
308  See para 25.24.
309  *Fair, Clear and Competitive: the Consumer Credit Market in the 21st Century* (Dec 2003, Cm. 6040), paras 5.74–5.
310  The notice must be in writing (s 189(1)).

and 'give details of that proposal'. The insistence on a proposal was so that debtors/hirers do not use the process simply to delay the inevitable.

(c)  A period of at least 14 days has elapsed after the day on which that proposal notice was given to the creditor or owner.

The new scheme envisages this: after receiving notice of sums in arrears under ss 86B or 86C, the debtor or hirer (perhaps having consulted a consumer adviser) can by the above notice make a formal proposal to the creditor or owner; and the creditor or owner will know that, if it does not accept the proposal within 14 days, the debtor or hirer is likely to apply to court for a Time Order.

**[24.41] Powers of the court**. Given that the court has jurisdiction by reason of s 129(1) to make a Time Order in respect of a regulated agreement, s 129(2) provides that:

> 'A time order shall provide for one or both of the following, as the court considers just—
>
> (a)  the payment by the debtor or hirer or any surety of any sum owed under a regulated agreement or a security by such instalments, payable at such times as the court, having regard to the means of the debtor or hirer and any surety, considers reasonable;[311]
>
> (b)  the remedying by the debtor or hirer of any breach of a regulated agreement (other than non-payment of money) within such period as the court may specify'.

It will be observed that Time Orders under s 129(2) may be made in respect of either of the following types of default.[312]

1.  *Monetary default*. This is the more common type of default. Where the debtor or hirer makes an instalment offer, the court may make a Time Order without hearing evidence of means (s 130(1)). In other cases, s 129(2)(a) implies that the court must hear evidence of means—what if the debtor simply fails to appear in court? For those cases where the debtor or hirer appears and does not make an offer, Leggatt LJ explained[313] that 'the power to make a Time Order under s 129 is essentially a social provision to assist debtors who find themselves unable to repay loans through no fault of their own. I see no reason to construe such a provision narrowly'. It is considered below (para 24.42).

2.  *Non-monetary default*. The jurisdiction conferred in respect of this less common situation by s 129(2) is further regulated by s 130(5). The basic effect is to freeze the remedies of the creditor or owner for the period specified in the Time Order (as varied): if the debtor complies with the Time Order, then under s 130(4) he continues to enjoy his contractual right to retain possession[314] and expunge his default by compliance with the Time Order; but, if the debtor or hirer further

---

311  There is a special exemption for pledges (s 130(3): see generally, para 25.18). For powers to reduce the sums payable on grounds that it is extortionate/unfair, see para 29.40, *et seq*.

312  The Order can usually be made conditional or suspended (s 135: set out at para 9.20). But this power may not be exercised so as to extend the period of a consumer hiring (s 135(3)).

313  Delivering the judgment of the CA in *Southern District Finance plc v Barnes* (see para 24.42).

314  However, if the creditor has already recovered possession, the Order does not entitle the debtor to resume possession, its sole effect being to freeze remedies which the creditor has not yet exercised: Goode, *Op. cit.*, para 46.191.

defaults, the remedy of the creditor or owner is to apply for revocation of the Time Order,[315] upon which the restraints imposed by s 130(5) are removed and the position is as in the case of monetary default.

**[24.42] Time Order after monetary default.** Where a Time Order is sought in respect of monetary default, the position is governed by s 129(2)(a) set out above, which refers to 'any sum owed' by the debtor or hirer. In the case of hp and conditional sale agreements, the Act expressly permits the court to deal with sums not yet due (s 130(2)); but in other cases, it was not clear whether the phrase referred just to arrears, or the entire sum which would become payable under the agreement. The matter was considered in *Southern & District Finance plc v Barnes*,[316] where the Court of Appeal dealt with three separate appeals concerning loans secured on land. Leggatt LJ laid down six principles.

(1) The court must first consider whether it is just to make an Order, taking into account the position of both parties.[317]

(2) A Time Order should normally be for a stipulated period on account of temporary financial difficulty,[318] so that it is normally inappropriate if the debtor is unlikely to be able to resume paying at least the contractual instalments.[319]

(3) The 'sum owed' means every sum due and owing under the agreement, which, perhaps by reason of an acceleration clause (see para 7.03), may include not just the arrears, but the total indebtedness (*Lewis*). But, where possession proceedings are brought, that will normally comprise the total indebtedness (as to possession actions, see para 25.24). The court must consider what instalments would be reasonable, having regard to the debtor's means.[320]

(4) The court may include in a Time Order any amendment of the agreement which it considers just to both parties, and which is a consequence of a term of the Order. The interest rate may be amended under s 136 (see para 9.20); but, if the interest rate is not amended, it is relevant that the smaller instalments will result both in a liability to pay interest on accumulated arrears[321] and in an extended period of repayment.[322]

---

315 Under s 130(6). For the position then in relation to default notices (see para 24.30), see Goode, *Ibid*.

316 [1995] GCCR 1935, CA. The Court also considered appeals in the following cases: *J & J Securities v Ewart; Equity Home Loans v Lewis* (leave to appeal to HL refused). See generally Lawson (1995) 14 Tr 527; Goode, *Consumer Credit Law & Practice*, para 46.173.

317 So, this does not appear to offer an easy sanction against over-selling credit: see *First National Bank plc v Syed* [1991] 2 All ER 250, CA.

318 As by reducing the amount payable under each monthly instalment for a finite time, e.g. *Lewis; Ewart* (above).

319 It will then normally be more equitable to allow the regulated agreement to be enforced. But see the *Lewis* case (above). In *Lewis*, that 'temporary' period lasted for 15yrs; and, in the *First National Bank* case Lord Bingham (at para 28), whilst approving *Lewis*, said that TOs 'extending over very long periods of time are usually better avoided'.

320 See para 24.41; and para 24.43.

321 To prevent any additional interest being payable: see *Barnes; Lewis; Ewart* (above); and the analysis by Hickman, etc in (1995) 145 NLJ 691.

322 To some extent the high rate of interest usually payable under regulated agreements already takes account of the risk that difficulties in repayment will occur.

(5) If the Order is made when the whole of the outstanding balance is due, there will inevitably be consequences for the term of the loan or rate of interest or both.[323]

(6) If justice requires the making of a Time Order, the court should suspend any possession order (see above) that it also makes (see below), so long as there is compliance with the terms of the Time Order.

This s 129 power is quite distinct from the power under s 138 to rewrite the agreement where the interest rate is extortionate/unfair (see para 29.40, *et seq.*).

*Effect of such a Time Order.* With regard to a loan secured on land, the effect of a Time Order is considered later (see para 25.24). However, where a Time Order is granted in respect of a hp, conditional sale or consumer hiring agreement of goods, the effect of the CCA is to turn the debtor or hirer into a sort of statutory bailee of those goods, though preserving any contractual power to acquire the creditor's title.[324] Moreover, the Act allows the court to make alterations in the terms of the regulated agreement or any security, either upon first making a Time Order under s 136 (see *Barnes*), or by means of subsequent variations (s 130(6)), e.g. if debtor's financial situation subsequently improves. Whilst re-scheduling the instalments payable under an instalment credit agreement, a Time Order made solely[325] under this provision does not of itself restrict the creditor's remedies for default.[326] However, in relation to hp or conditional sales agreements, the court is empowered to make further orders under s 133 (see para 24.43), so that typically the court is likely to combine the Time Order with an order for the return of the goods to the creditor suspended whilst the debtor adheres to the re-scheduled payments. It has been argued that the courts should make more use of Time Orders.[327] An illustration of the sort of Time Order that might be made under the above principles is to be found in the suggestions of the County Court Judge in *London North Securities v Meadows* (set out at para 8.25; at para 74).

[24.43] **Special powers**. It has already been seen that the CCA takes special steps so that a creditor may maintain an action for the recovery of goods. The CCA enables the creditor or owner to demonstrate adverse possession (s 134: see para 24.32) and also provides for interim protection orders (s 131: see para 24.39). However, besides the ordinary forms of judgment available either under the ordinary law where the hirer or buyer defaults (see para 24.26) and the special powers granted to a creditor where a debtor exercises a statutory right of termination (s 100(5): see para 26.06), s 133(1) grants the court some overriding[328] powers in the following circumstances:

'If, in relation to a regulated hire-purchase or conditional sale agreement, it appears to the court just to do so—

(a)  on an application for an enforcement order or time order;[329] or

---

323  See the eight principles deduced by Hickman, etc, *Op. cit.*, 692.
324  Goode, *Op. cit.*, para 46.178. This will be so even if the agreement has been terminated: s 130(4).
325  *Contra* if there is **both** a monetary and non-monetary default, in which case s 130(5) operates as for non-monetary default (see para 24.41).
326  E.g. to recapt unprotected goods or bring an action to recover protected goods. See Goode, *Op. cit.*, para 46.192.
327  DTI, *Tackling Loan Sharks—and more!*, Consultation Paper (March 2003), para 4.2.5.
328  Torts (Interference with Goods) Act 1977, s 3(8).        329  See paras 9.20, 24.39 and 24.40.

(b)  in an action brought by the creditor to recover possession of goods to which the agreement relates.'[330]

These powers do not extend to consumer hire agreements;[331] but they are exercisable even where the creditor is seeking repossession after the debtor has terminated the agreement, though there is a special restriction on the power of the court to refuse specific delivery (s 100(5): see further, para 26.05). Section 133 envisages the two following types of Order,[332] which can themselves be subsequently revoked:[333]

1.  *Return Orders.* This is an order for 'the return to the creditor of the goods to which the agreement relates' (s 133(1)). It may be made conditional or suspended,[334] but may not be suspended unless the court is satisfied that the goods are in the debtor's possession or control.[335] The form of Return Order most commonly used is where the Order is suspended on condition that the debtor makes the rescheduled payments due under a Time Order (see paras 24.40–41). Where the debtor fulfils the terms of that Time Order or Return Order, he will automatically acquire the creditor's title to the goods (s 133(5)); but, where the debtor further defaults, the form of the Order may allow the creditor to execute judgment immediately, though this cannot deprive the debtor of the statutory option to pay the outstanding balance.[336]

2.  *Transfer Orders.* This is a Judgment of Solomon, ordering the transfer to the debtor of the creditor's title to certain of the goods to which the agreement relates ('the transfer goods') and the return to the creditor of the remainder of the goods,[337] again subject to the right of the debtor to pay off the outstanding balance. Transfer Orders are sometimes used for the furniture trade.

After service of the above Orders on the debtor, he sometimes wishes to negotiate so that he can keep the goods.[338]

## Death

**[24.44/6]** On the death of the borrower, buyer or hirer, the general rule is that most causes of action subsisting against, or vested in, him survive against his estate or for its benefit.[339] However, the death of the borrower, buyer or hirer must usually at best result in a temporary cessation of payments; and over the years suppliers have

---

330  See paras 24.34–8.

331  Transfer Orders would not be appropriate to consumer hirings; and Return Orders are unnecessary as the owner can always seek a judgment under the Torts Act 1977, s 3: see para 24.26.

332  The Orders can amend any agreement or security (s 136): set out at para 9.20.

333  Under s 133(6). This will be useful, e.g. where the debtor has since the date of the order sold the goods.

334  S 135(1): set out at para 9.20. There is a power of subsequent variation: s 135(4).

335  S 135(2). What if the debtor does not appear, or no evidence of possession is led? See Goode, *Consumer Credit Law & Practice*, para 46.217. Compare the position under the Torts Act 1977, s 3(6): see para 24.26.

336  'At any time before the goods enter the possession of the creditor': s 133(4).

337  S 133(1). S 133 contains special rules designed to compensate the creditor for having to accept the return of used goods: see further Goode, *Op. cit.*, paras 46.218–9.

338  Lunn (1995) 49 CC 6/20.

339  Law Reform (Miscellaneous Provisions) Act 1934, s 1(1) (as amended).

therefore taken steps to safeguard their interests. Sometimes, they have taken the benevolent step of providing that the agreement shall then be treated as fully paid: this may be done either under the terms of the loan or supply contract,[340] or, more frequently, under a separate insurance,[341] itself subject to a right of cancellation (see para 10.39). Unfortunately, it has been rather more common for instalment credit contracts to provide that the agreement shall terminate automatically upon the death of the borrower, buyer or hirer.[342] Such a provision tends to compound the distress caused by the bereavement.[343]

The only contribution made by the HPA 1938 to the above problem was to provide that 'hirer' should include the person to whom his rights or liabilities passed by operation of law; and this provision has been repeated in the CCA.[344] This has the effect of extending the statutory restrictions on recovery of possession in appropriate circumstances to the personal representative of the debtor or hirer;[345] but it did not prevent the operation of a clause providing in that event for the termination of the agreement, or the recovery of the goods. As a matter of grace, some suppliers were prepared to accept tender of the outstanding balance of the hp price from a personal representative or other interested party;[346] but it was felt that the hirer's interest should be given some measure of legal protection. However, statute has eschewed the simple, and benevolent, answer of a compulsory transfer of property and cessation of payments[347] in favour of another solution (see para 24.47), which itself causes difficulty over voluntary insurance premiums (see para 24.48).

[24.47] The CCA provisions. A distinction may conveniently be drawn between the effect of the death of the debtor or hirer on the payment obligations under a regulated agreement (see para 24.48) and the measures taken by the Act to combat clauses in the regulated agreement expressed to operate on death *simpliciter* (see paras 24.44–46). In the latter connection, s 86 provides as follows:

'(1) The creditor or owner under a regulated agreement is not entitled, by reason of the death of the debtor or hirer, to do an act specified in paragraphs (a) to (e) of section 87(1) if at the death the agreement is fully secured.

(2) If at the death of the debtor or hirer a regulated agreement is only partly secured or is unsecured, the creditor or owner is entitled, by reason of the death of the debtor or hirer, to do an act specified in paragraphs (a) to (e) of section 87(1) on an order of the court only.'

---

340 This effectively insures the life of the borrower, buyer or hirer at the expense of the lender or supplier who in fact sometimes take out credit protection insurance (see below).

341 Group insurance is normally offered as an optional extra with separate premiums payable by the borrower, buyer or hirer (Insurance Companies Amendment Act 1973, s 50). The modern Group Insurance frequently extends beyond death cover to embrace accident, illness and unemployment: see para 7.03; and (1988) 43 CC2/4; [2002] 7 *Which?* 12. For PPI insurance, see para 24.48.

342 For such automatic termination of agreement, see generally, para 26.08.

343 Commonly, the loan or supply agreement was in the name of the deceased breadwinner, so compounding the difficulties of the family caused by the cessation of income.

344 In the definitions of 'debtor' and 'hirer': see s 189(1). See para 5.24.

345 E.g. as to notices, repossession and court orders: see para 24.27, *et seq*.

346 Under s 97, a 'debtor' is entitled to notice of a settlement figure: see further, para 26.19A.

347 It would have saved much subtle learning if this provision had also applied on the insolvency of the buyer or hirer. However, matters have been improved by the Insolvency Act 1986: see para 19.12.

It will be noticed that, where s 86(1) applies because the agreement is 'fully secured', any such clause is void (s 173(1): set out at para 18.11); whereas, if the agreement is 'only partly secured or unsecured', the agreement may be enforced by court order (see para 24.27). Unfortunately, this dichotomy between 'fully secured', e.g. a pledge or mortgage of sufficient value to secure the debt, on the one hand and 'partly secured'[348] or 'unsecured'[349] on the other is not defined in the Act:[350] first, there is some doubt as to the meaning of the word 'secured';[351] and second, it is uncertain whether the fully/partially secured dichotomy refers to (i) whether the security extends to the full debt or (ii) the market value of the security, e.g. suppose the market value of the goods in less than the balance outstanding.[348]

However, the distinction is clearly important as determining the rights of the creditor or owner which may arise simply by reason of the death of the debtor or hirer. If the agreement is 'fully secured', s 86(1) deprives the creditor or owner of those rights, e.g. to accelerate payments; whereas, if the agreement is only partly secured or unsecured, s 86(2) allows the creditor or owner to apply for a court order to that effect, though s 128 adds the rider that:

'The court shall make an order under section 86(2) if, but only if, the creditor or owner proves that he has been unable to satisfy himself that the present and future obligations of the debtor or hirer under the agreement are likely to be discharged.'

However, in any event the scope of s 86 is somewhat limited. It basically applies to rights exercisable 'by reason of the death of the debtor or hirer';[352] and then only where the creditor or owner is entitled under the terms of the agreement to do one or more of the acts specified in s 87(1).[353] It neither prevents a creditor from 'treating the right to draw on any credit as restricted or deferred',[354] nor affects the operation of any agreement providing for payment of instalments out of any life insurance,[355] nor prevent repossession by reason of default (see para 24.48).

**[24.48] The effect of death on payment obligations.** Section 86 is directed solely towards rights of the creditor or owner arising by reason of the fact of death of the debtor or hirer (see para 24.47): it does not suspend any of the rights of the creditor or owner to payment of instalments.[356] Even supposing the debtor or hirer is up to date with his payments at death, there is a considerable likelihood that one or more instalments will fall into arrears before anyone can act on his behalf. The CCA therefore extends to the deceased's personal representatives all the protections conferred on the debtor or hirer as previously outlined in this Chapter (see para 24.27, *et seq.*), whilst allowing service of any requisite notice as if the debtor had

---

348 See Goode, *Consumer Credit Law & Practice*, Division 11B, para 5.166.

349 Presumably, this includes loans and credit sales. What about promissory notes?

350 See Guest and Lloyd, *Encyclopedia of Consumer Credit*, para 2-087.

351 Does it refer to the s 189(1) definition of 'security' (see para 25.11), which will exclude hp and conditional sale?

352 See s 86(6). Or, if there are joint debtors or hirers, the death of any of them: s 185(4).

353 See para 24.30. Thus, s 86 will not prevent the creditor or owner exercising any other right, e.g. to inspect the goods.

354 S 86(4). E.g. to prevent further withdrawals under an overdraft agreement. Cf. s 76(4): see para 24.28.

355 S 86(5). For insurance arrangements, see para 24.48.

356 But for the remarkable effect of s 86(6)(b), see Goode, *Consumer Credit Law & Practice*, para 45.96.

not died.[357] Where there are protected goods (see para 24.35) at the date of death, the CCA expressly provides that they shall continue to be so until the grant of probate or administration (s 90(6): see para 24.37), upon which the personal representative will fall to be treated as the 'debtor' or 'hirer'.[358]

Whilst the foregoing CCA provisions are no doubt a substantial improvement on their HPA counterparts, they would still appear to be open to the following criticism: it might have been much simpler and fairer if the CCA had deemed the agreement automatically paid up on the debtor's death, so effectively giving compulsory life insurance cover (see para 24.45). Instead, the present practice is to offer Payment Protection Insurance (PPI) as an optional extra.[359]

*PPI insurance.*[360] Unfortunately, this gives rise to some difficulties with the CCA;[361] and there may be problems on the cancellation of credit insurances which are linked transactions.[362] The CCA 1974 did not expressly deal with the negative option system used to maximise insurance sales:[363] profit margins are huge[364] and PPI is frequently missold to the ineligible, e.g. self-employed; and, as voluntary PPI premiums are not usually within the APR (see para 8.24), consumers are generally unaware of the high cost.[365] The following changes in the law may curb some of these excesses: first, the 2004 CCA amending Regulations require a separate signature box and consumer signature for PPI insurance (see para 9.13); second, it may fall within the Distance Selling of Financial Services (see para 9.06); and nowadays, to sell PPI insurance also requires an FSA licence (see para 3.02). In 2005, allegations of misselling PPI gave rise to a super-complaint (see paras 2.14; 4.19).[366] In 2007, these rules will have to be aligned with the UCP Directive (see para 4.20, item (r)).

## Conclusions

**[24.49]** The common law denied that a buyer or hirer under a conditional sale or hp agreement was a mortgagor with an equity of redemption (see para 24.22). It followed that, if the supplier managed to recover the goods either by recaption or

---

357  S 176(6). In practice, the requisite notices are likely to be received by the deceased's spouse.

358  Because 'debtor' and 'hirer' are defined by s 189(1) to include their assignees by operation of law. See para 5.24.

359  This enables the financier to give competitive quotations (excluding PPI) and collect valuable commission on the additional insurance: see [1994] 3 *Which?* 30. PPI insurance tends to be over-sold by reason of the high rates of commission. For an optional payment waiver clause, see *Humberclyde Finance Ltd v Thompson* (1997) Tr LR 242, CA.

360  For an account of PPI, see (2006) 1 QA 20. The FSA in enquiring whether PPI terms infringe the UTCCR (Report expected Sept 2006). For store card PPI, see para 2.12.

361  The PPI premium may turn the regulated transaction into a multiple agreement (see para 5.27).

362  Regulations made under s 19(4) (see para 5.31): Jones, *Credit Cards*, 71–2; (1993) 48 CC 1/13.

363  The OFT threatened (e.g. (1993) 10 Tr L 56) that, if inertia selling of PPI continued, the OFT would use its CCA licensing powers (see para 6.17) or Pt 8 of the EA (see para 6.07); and it also suggested that such a prohibition should be included in trade codes of practice (para 3.13).

364  E.g. on a £5,000 loan made in 2005, the PPI can cost £1,000.

365  The PPI premiums can add 35% to credit costs: *The Times* [2005] 9.12.

366  On 8.12.05, the OFT announced that it was to carry out a market study of PPI and the OFT Report is expected before the end of 2006 (see 43 *Fair Trading* 4; *AR-2005/6*, 61); [2006] 8 CT 197.

court action (see paras 24.22–26), he could keep for himself any surplus; and he was not answerable to the buyer or hirer where he realised less than the best price obtainable. Indeed, under the present system, there is little incentive for the supplier to dispose of the goods at any price in excess of his loss on the transaction; but *contra* where he needs to claim damages from the buyer or hirer in which case the duty to mitigate will go some way towards encouraging him to seek a good price (for the duty to mitigate, see para 27.44).

However, the CCA has created in respect of regulated conditional sale and hp agreements[367] an untidy approximation to a statutory equity of redemption.[368] This certainly accords with the policy of the Crowther Report,[369] and has substantially reduced the advantage of repossession. The logical result of this must be as follows:

(1) The total charge for credit will increase for all debtors and hirers—the good payers paying for the bad within each class of business, e.g. customers may be stratified into 'status' and 'non-status' (see para 7.04A).

(2) Wherever the domestic consumer is an adequate risk, the financier may prefer to divorce his loan from the supply of goods. Sometimes, he will enter into a Personal Loan,[370] which will deprive him of his security, but escape the 50% rule (s 100: see para 27.49). At other times, he may prefer running-account credit, e.g. a credit card (see also (4) below).

(3) Where security is indicated, a second mortgage or realty may be the preferred alternative,[371] with simple hiring agreements as a possible commercial alternative.[372] However, especially where the debtor is not a houseowner, the obvious form of security is a reservation of title, by way of conditional sale or hp, as discussed in this Chapter; and this is particularly likely to be the case in the subprime market (see para 7.04A). A major drawback to creditors in using conditional sale and hp as their security is their possible resale loss where the debtor exercises his statutory right to terminate the agreement (CCA, s 99: see para 26.05).

(4) Particularly in relation to goods of a small unit value, it may be that the advantages of repossession have been so reduced that suppliers will instead prefer the unsecured credit sale or loan;[373] and creditors will favour the commercial advantages of running-account credit, e.g. a credit card, especially for the possibility of repeat business. The danger is that this has been achieved by accident

---

367 But not consumer hiring agreements, where the only relief for the hirer is provided under s 132: see para 27.23.

368 See Bridge [1992] JBL at 16–17; and para 24.27-43.

369 Para 5.2.15. *Quaere* whether it would have been more satisfactory to convert all hp and conditional sales into chattel mortgages? See the Crowther Report, paras 5.2.5 7 and 5.4.3, and para 1.26.

370 Either taken out at the point of sale, or from an independent lender: see [2003] 2 *Credit Today* 39. As to personal loans, see para 2.17.

371 Where large sums are lent to householders to finance, e.g. central heating, double glazing. See generally, para 25.19. A similar result is achievable by making unsecured credit available to a householder, but on default placing a charging order on his house (see para 27.04).

372 Particularly favoured as regards goods with a high rate of obsolescence and servicing, e.g. computers, motor vehicles.

373 It must be remembered that retention of title is often regarded as important for psychological as much as legal reasons.

rather than conscious policy, thereby reducing the chance of marginal customers obtaining such credit or increasing the cost of that credit.

(5) Inevitably, with every extra statutory restriction, there will be an increase in the number of domestic consumers who are such bad financial risks that they cannot obtain financial accommodation within the law at any price.[374] For them, the illegal lender and the 'base-ball bat' method of collection.[375]

Currently, various different forms of chattel mortgage are being examined as potential alternatives (see para. 25.37).

---

374 As to over-indebtedness, see para 6.10; and as to extortionate/unfair credit bargains, see para 29.40, *et seq.*

375 Cayne and Trebilcock (1973) 23 UTLJ 396, at 418–9; OFT, *Vulnerable Consumers and Financial Services* (1999), para 400. As to loan-sharking, see para 6.20.

# CHAPTER 25

# SECURITY FOR PERFORMANCE

## SECURITY IN GENERAL

**[25.01]** This Chapter will deal with the ways in which the supplier of credit to facilitate the acquisition of goods can obtain security in respect of the performance by the private consumer of the latter's contractual obligations, which are principally to take delivery (see para 23.08, *et seq.*) and pay the price or rent (see para 27.16). Such security may be personal or real, and the various forms of security can often be used cumulatively.

1. *Personal security.* This offers the supplier a further action against a third party[1] and is fairly commonplace in instalment credit transactions, particularly when there is some doubt as to the efficacy of the legal obligation upon the private consumer, e.g. buyer, hirer or borrower, as where he is a minor (see para 10.18) or as to his financial status.[2] Personal security may take the form of requiring a third party to go surety for, or insure, the private consumer (see paras 25.04 and 25.14), or of a wage assignment;[3] and the supplier may insist on his accepting bills of exchange or giving post-dated cheques for the instalments.[4]

2. *Real security.* This offers the creditor the right to look to particular property for the satisfaction of his debt in preference to the consumer debtor's general creditors; and it is particularly useful in the debtor's insolvency (see para 19.22). However, from the legal viewpoint a clear distinction must be drawn between two types of secured credit:[5]

   (a) *Supply of goods on credit.* Whilst undoubtedly creating a debt,[6] price deferment or rental due has always been regarded by English law as essentially different from loan credit (see below).[7] The major methods by which the purchase-money 'lender' may seek to ensure payment of the deferred price or rent by *retaining* possession or property were considered in Chapter 24: they escaped the Bills of Sale Acts;[8] and, when property retention leads to resale, any surplus belongs to the supplier.[9]

---

1 Sometimes the supplier will separately buy the protection, as by taking out insurance against bad debts, e.g. with trade indemnity (for domestic supplies).
2 E.g. where the buyer or hirer is a student, or is not a householder. As to married women, this may cause trouble with the Sex Discrimination Act 1975: see para 4.23.
3 In the UK, wage assignments are more commonly used only after breach: see further, para 27.05.
4 For bills of exchange, see para 7.24; and for CCA regulation, see para 25.09. The advantage of taking a bill or cheque from the buyer or hirer lies in the simplified enforcement procedure available on default: see para 23.14.
5 See Goode, *Commercial Law*, 3rd edn, 579.
6 For contracts of loan, see generally Chap 7.
7 SGA, s 62(4) (see para 1.02) only applies to sham sales: see further, paras 25.29 and 25.35.
8 *McEntire v Crossley Bros* [1895] AC 457; see para 25.26.
9 See *Armour v Thyssen* (set out at para 20.29).

*(b)*   *Loan credit.* Where a debt[6] does not arise out of a contract for the supply of goods, the lender may seek by *taking* possession or property to ensure payment (see para 25.02); and where the lender's acquisition of property rights leads to sale, any surplus value belongs to the debtor.[9]

**[25.02] Consensual real security for loans**. These are rights over property granted by agreement[10] as a form of security for a loan:[11] they are not absolute rights, but conditional, collateral and outside the SGA (s 62(4): set out at para 1.08). The rights are **conditional** in the sense that they exist only to secure the payment of the debt, or the performance of some other obligation, and are discharged by that payment or performance. The rights are **collateral** in that they do not replace the primary obligation: if, for instance, the sale of an item pledged does not realise sufficient to pay off the secured debt, the debtor remains liable for the difference. Strictly, only three types of consensual real security are known to English law.[12]

1.   *A pledge* is made by the deposit of personal property by way of security.[13] It is essential to the validity of a pledge that possession should have passed to the secured party (pledgee): it follows that it is not possible to pledge a pure intangible such as a chose in action (see para 7.16). A pledge may be created where the goods are deposited before the sum to be loaned is agreed or advanced.[14] However, a mere agreement to pledge (hypothecation) creates only an equitable charge (see below): this does not operate as a pledge until delivery (see para 25.16); and it is inferior to a pledge in that it may be defeated under the *nemo dat* rule by a bfp.[15] Unlike a lien (see paras 1.23 and 24.09), a pledge is invariably created by agreement and gives the pledgee a special property in the goods pledged (see para 25.15). The normal remedy of a pledgee of goods is sale, not foreclosure.

2.   *A mortgage* involves a transfer by way of security of legal or equitable ownership in either realty or personalty by the owner/borrower (mortgagor) to another (the mortgagee) upon the express or implied condition that the asset be reconveyed when the sum secured has been paid. Initially, the mortgagee's ownership is subject to the mortgagor's equity of redemption; but after the mortgagor's default the mortgagee may extinguish (foreclose) that equity and become the absolute owner of the property (see para 25.20). Theoretically, it is this right of foreclosure which at common law distinguishes a mortgage from a pledge.[16] As the mortgagee was not required to take possession, the mortgage was an extremely flexible instrument: it could be applied to all classes of assets

---

10   Distinguish (a) purely **personal** rights, e.g. set-off (see para 7.23), retention of deposit (see para 27.20); (b) **reservation of title** and the rights it confers (see para 25.01); (c) rights granted by operation of law, e.g. liens (see below).

11   These rights against property have been described as rights of pursuit and preference: Goode, *Commercial Law*, 3rd edn, 623.

12   *Op. cit.*, 584.

13   See FA, s 1(5). As to the consideration necessary for a pledge, see FA, s 5: para 21.33.

14   *Blundell-Leigh v Attenborough* [1921] 3 KB 235, CA.

15   See *Harrold v Plenty* [1901] 2 Ch 314 (deposit of share certificate created only a charge). This equitable right will on principle give way to a bfp of the legal interest, notwithstanding the *nemo dat* rule (see para 19.11).

16   See para 25.26. But see the CCA, s 120(1)(a): para 25.18.

(land, goods and intangibles), and even to after-acquired property.[17] However, in practice a mortgagor will normally remain in possession of the mortgaged property during the currency of the mortgage, which has led to the following conclusion:[18] 'in short, the essence of a pledge is the transfer of possession; of a mortgage, the transfer of property'.

3. *A charge* does not depend on either delivery of possession (a pledge) or the transfer of ownership (a mortgage), but upon an agreement between the creditor and debtor that the creditor may look to the proceeds of a disposal of a particular asset owned by the debtor which he charges to discharge his indebtedness.[19] Such an encumbrance on goods cannot exist at common law (see para 2.14); but it can be created in relation to both real and personal property by statute or equity (see para 25.20), which recognise that a charge may be one of two sorts:[20] either a fixed (or specific) charge, or a floating charge (see para 19.14).

**[25.03] Regulated agreements**. The statutory restrictions on security rights (see para 25.02) were scattered all over the statute book. However, in respect of regulated agreements (para 5.13), the CCA for the first time attempted to collect those restrictions together in one place. Part VIII of the Act contains a coherent pattern of rules governing the taking and enforcement of security. It deals carefully with attempts to take both personal sureties (see paras 25.04–14) and pledges (see paras 25.15–18); but unfortunately, the pattern is a peculiarly lop-sided one. It will be recalled that the rules relating to rights against goods were to be left to the—as yet to be enacted—Lending and Security Act (see para 5.03). Apart from some special provisions for second mortgages of land (see para 25.24), the chattel mortgage rules to be considered later (see para 25.19, *et seq.*) therefore remain largely untouched by the CCA. Instead, the Act concentrates on ways in which the supplier may obtain personal rights against his transferee (see paras 24.21–48) or a third party (see para 25.04-14). For this purpose, it defines 'security' very widely, terms the person who gives that security 'a surety' and a document embodying that security a 'security instrument' (see paras 25.11 and 25.12).

## PERSONAL SECURITY

**[25.04] Introduction**. It is fairly common in instalment credit transactions for the 'lender' to insist on the security of some personal rights of action against a third party in the event of default by the hirer or buyer.[21] Whilst it is true that since 1970 there has been an apparently viable system for the attachment of earnings (see para 27.05), that system is only available in respect of debts where there is a court order following a default in payment. Hence, there seems little possibility of

---

17  *Holroyd v Marshall* (1862) 10 HLC 191.
18  Goode, *HP Law & Practice* (2nd edn) 536; and para 25.26.
19  This depends on the proper construction of the contract: *Smith v Bridgend CBC* [2002] 1 AC 336, HL.
20  *Re Atlantic Computer Systems plc* [1992] 1 All ER 476, CA, *per* Nicholls LJ at AER 493–4.
21  E.g. the provision of insurance (see para 24.21). The alternative strategy is to sell the bad debt: see para 27.02.

obtaining such an order as security for payment when the credit transaction is set up; and, as the system only has significance as a remedy, it is considered later (para 27.05, *et seq*.). This matter aside, the obvious form of personal security is a surety.

**[25.05] Types of surety**. Sureties of instalment credit transactions will usually fall into one of the following categories: (a) a friend or relative of the hirer or buyer; or (b) a dealer or supplier signing a recourse provision (see para 16.21); or (c) a director of the hiring or buying company;[22] or (d) one who makes a business of guaranteeing debts. In any particular transaction, there may be sureties from any or all of these classes; and the owner, seller or lender may use any of the following techniques to achieve his object:

1.  *Co-principals*. Particularly where the surety belongs to category (a), the 'lender' may make him a party to the supply or loan contract,[23] a device commonly employed in instalment contracts where the first 'borrower' is a minor (see para 10.18) and with credit cards.[24] It also makes it easier for the creditor to avoid having the transaction upset on grounds that he has constructive notice of any undue influence.[25] If the intention is that he should act as guarantor, the surety's liability is conditional on default by his co-principal;[26] but, if it is intended that he be a genuine principal, his liability may be joint only, or both joint and several,[27] e.g. category (d).

2.  *Indorsees*. A form more frequently used with sureties from categories (b), (c) and (d) is to require them to 'back' (indorse) a bill of exchange drawn by the debtor.[28] Since the Cheques Act 1992, this form is most unlikely to arise in consumer transactions, category (a) (see para 25.09).

3.  *Guarantors*. Into whatever category the surety may fall, a common technique is to require[29] the surety to guarantee[30] the principal contract.[31] On default by the

---

22  E.g. *Silverburn Finance (UK) Ltd v Salt* [2001] 2 All ER (Comm) 438, CA; and para 19.25. As to this class of surety unsuccessfully attempting to take advantage of UCTA and the UTCCR, see *Governor & Company of the Bank of Scotland v Reuben* (2005) 155 NLJ 1855.

23  E.g. *Royal Bank of Scotland PLC v Fielding* [2004] CLY 220. For joint obligations, see *Chitty on Contract*, 28th edn, 18.

24  For co-debtors on credit cards, see para 7.10. Co-debtors under regulated cards share the CCA protections: see paras 5.24; 7.12 and 25.08.

25  *CIBC Mortgages plc v Pitt* [1993] 4 All ER 433, HL (see 110 LQR at 169). Their Lordships distinguished this situation from that of a guarantee (see para 25.06) on the grounds that in the latter case there is an increased risk of undue influence over a co-habitee because the transaction does not involve a joint advance and hence is not for the surety's financial benefit (at 441j).

26  Equity may regard him as a surety: *Overend, Gurney & Co v Oriental Financial Corpn* (1874) LR 7 HL 348.

27  See further Goode, *HP Law & Practice*, 2nd edn, 471.

28  This would avoid the past consideration rule which might be troublesome with guarantors (see below): Bills of Exchange Act 1882, s 27(1)(b).

29  It will usually be safer for the lender to negotiate directly with the surety to avoid any taint of undue influence or fraud: see *Bank of Baroda v Shah* [1988] 3 All ER 24, CA.

30  E.g. cheque guarantee cards (see para 2.26). Distinguish the completely different 'manufacturer's guarantee': see see para 17.09A.

31  Beware of the past consideration rule: see *Astley Industrial Trust Ltd v Grimston Ltd* (1965) 109 Sol Jo 149. It could be side-stepped by getting the surety to: (a) back a bill of exchange (see above); or (b) enter a deed (see para 9.01).

principal 'debtor', the 'creditor' will then usually have the choice whether to sue the debtor and/or his guarantor (see para 25.06). Because guarantors of category (a) so frequently undertake guarantees for altruistic motives, the courts have adopted a protective attitude towards them, often insisting on precise compliance by the creditor with all relevant technical rules before he can succeed against the guarantor.[32] That aside, in recent years there has in domestic supply transactions been a significant increase in the activities of the above category (d) business, particularly in connection with the acceptance by retailers of cheques (see para 23.14). *First*, for cheques below a stipulated minimum size, the clearing banks have introduced cheque guarantee cards (see para 2.26). *Second*, above that figure a credit reference agency operates the following system: the retailer may obtain pre-approval, after which the agency guarantees the cheque.[33]

## Sureties generally[34]

**[25.06]** Many of the difficulties in this subject may be traced back to the Statute of Frauds 1677; and to the distinction drawn in consequence of that provision between a surety who **guarantees** performance by the principal debtor, and one who takes the primary obligation upon himself by agreeing to **indemnify** the creditor. The distinction between contracts of guarantee and of indemnity is a question which is both important in law and uncertain in practice. For instance, the courts have had some difficulty in deciding to which class a surety belongs, where he is a friend of the borrower, hirer or buyer, or a dealer under a recourse provision.[35] We must now examine the position of the surety.

1. *Liability.* The surety will not be liable unless the other party's loss is caused by the act in respect of which he has agreed to act as surety[36] and unless any condition precedent to which his promise is subject has been fulfilled.[37] Further, the liability of a guarantor, but not of an indemnifier[38] is also subject to the following restrictions: a guarantee must be evidenced by a signed note or memorandum;[39] it is necessary for the secured party first to call on the borrower, hirer or buyer to make good his default;[40] and at common law the guarantor's liability is co-extensive with that of the borrower, hirer or

---

32  E.g. *Levett v Barclays Bank plc* [1995] 2 All ER 615 (non-disclosure). The fact that this does not apply to types (b) and (c) obviously causes difficulty with precedents.

33  E.g. the Transax system offered by Equifax: see (1995) 49 CC 6/27.

34  See generally Treitel, *Law of Contract*, 11th edn, 181–6.

35  Cf. *Western Credit Ltd v Alberry* [1964] 2 All ER 938, CA (guarantee); and *Goulston Discount Ltd v Clark* [1967] 2 QB 493, CA (indemnity).

36  *Bentworth Finance Ltd v Lubert* (set out at para 15.23); *United Dominions Trust Ltd v Beech* [1972] 1 Lloyd's Rep 546; *Perrylease Ltd v Imecar AG* [1987] 2 All ER 373; *Dumford Trading AG v OAO Atlantrybflot* [2004] 2 Lloyd's Rep 157 (mistaken identity; and generally, para 10.15).

37  *Midland Counties Motor Finance Ltd v Slade* [1951] 1 KB 346, CA; *James Graham & Co (Timber) Ltd v Southgate Sands* [1985] 2 All ER 344, CA; *Associated Japanese Bank (International) Ltd v Credit du Nord* [1988] 3 All ER 902. E.g. cheque guarantee card conditions (see para 25.05).

38  Nor signatory on a bill of exchange: see para 25.05.

39  1677 Act, s 4; *The Maria D* [1992] 1 AC 21, HL; *Actionstrength Ltd v International Glass* [2003] 2 AC 541, HL (not a goods case); *Pereira Fernandes SA v Metha* [2006] 2 All ER 891 (e-mail).

40  *Moschi v Lep Air Services Ltd* [1973] AC 331, HL.

buyer.[41] However, the gap between guarantees and indemnities has been narrowed by statute, especially with regard to category (a) (see para 25.04): guarantees of minor's contracts have become more onerous, in that they are enforceable even though the minor's contract is not enforceable against him,[42] e.g. cheque guarantee card issued to a minor; and indemnities have been rendered less onerous generally in that, as against a surety 'dealing as consumer', they are subjected to the test of reasonableness (UCTA, s 4: see para 18.25) and equated with guarantees with regard to most regulated agreements (see para 25.07).

2.  *Rights* (see para 25.07).

3.  *Discharge* (see para 25.07A).

**[25.07] Rights of a surety**. The surety who meets his liability under a contract of suretyship (see para 25.05) has certain rights against the other parties.[43]

1.  *As against the buyer, hirer or borrower*, the surety has a right of indemnity[44] in respect of sums paid out in discharge of his obligations under the contract of surety.[45] This right of indemnity may be granted to the surety expressly; or it may be implied, as where the surety undertook the obligation at the request of the borrower, hirer or buyer. *Contra* where the suretyship is a form of dealer recourse (see para 16.21).

2.  *As against the supplier*, the surety has the right to secure his discharge by paying the amount due (see para 25.06); but he has no right to insist that the supplier first exercise any power of sale over mortgaged property.[46] However, the guarantor does have the right of exercising any set-off or counter-claim against a supplier that would have been available to a hirer or buyer.[47] When the surety pays the supplier, he is further entitled[48] to a right of subrogation;[49] that is, the supplier must assign (Mercantile Law Amendment Act 1856, s 5) to him all his rights against the hirer or buyer, including any securities,[50] insofar as those rights are not purely personal ones.[51]

---

41   E.g. *Stadium Finance Ltd v Helm* (1965) 109 SJ 471, CA. And see Steyn (1974) 90 LQR 246.

42   Minors' Contracts Act 1987, s 2: see para 10.18.

43   For the situation where the surety assumed the obligation without antecedent request from a party to the transaction, see *Owen v Tate* [1976] QB 402, CA.

44   And see his rights in equity: *Ascherson v Tredegar Dry Dock and Wharf Co Ltd* [1909] 2 Ch 401.

45   *Hampton v Minns* [2002] 1 All ER (Comm) 481. This right is not affected by the fact that the liability was not enforceable against the debtor because of an infringement of the Moneylenders Acts (now repealed: see para 6.09): *Re Chetwynd's Estate* [1938] Ch 13, CA. Would the same result follow under s 113 of the CCA (see para 25.14)? See *Chitty on Contract*, 29th edn, Vol 2, para 44-110, fn 528.

46   *China and South Sea Bank Ltd v Tan* [1990] AC 536, PC (a mortgagee of shares is under no duty to exercise his power of sale in a falling market: see generally, para 25.25).

47   *Sterling Industrial Facilities Ltd v Lydiate Textiles Ltd* (1962) 106 SJ 669, CA. Cf. *American Express International Banking Corpn v Hurley* [1985] 3 All ER 564. *Contra* a cross-claim: *Indrisie v General Credit* [1985] VR 251, SC of Vict.

48   Except insofar as he has expressly or impliedly waived such right: *Re Lord Churchill* (1888) 39 Ch D 174.

49   Much the same result may be achieved by taking a counter-indemnity: *Barclays Bank Ltd v TOSG Trust Fund Ltd* [1984] 1 All ER 628, CA.

50   *Prima facie*, any surplus realised from those securities must be paid over to the principal debtor: but see *L Lucas Ltd v Export Credit Guarantee Dept* [1974] 2 All ER 889, HL.

51   *Chatterton v Maclean* [1951] 1 All ER 761. Cf. para 7.26.

3.  *As against a co-surety*, the surety may have a right of contribution,[52] a rule which may operate between the different categories of surety above mentioned, even if unaware of each other's existence (see para 25.04).

**[25.07A]  Discharge of a surety**. The surety may be discharged from liability under his contract of guarantee in any of the ways in which a contract can normally be discharged (see Chap 26), including all the following: by a plea of *non est factum* (see para 10.16), by a variation (see para 26.21), by a misrepresentation (see paras 26.12–14). In the case of undue influence, whilst the surety may be discharged,[53] the debtor will remain liable, e.g. to the extent of his share of any joint security.[54] In addition, there are a number of situations where a surety may be discharged in pursuance of the rule that the creditor must not do anything to prejudice the rights of the surety (see para 25.07) without his consent: for example, where the supplier releases the borrower, hirer or buyer;[55] or there is a novation or material alteration in the terms of the supply agreement;[56] or possibly a waiver of its terms.[57] Where the supply agreement is terminated, a surety who has agreed to indemnify the creditor, owner or seller may be liable for the full debt or 'price'; but a guarantor is only liable to a maximum[58] of the accrued liabilities of the borrower, hirer or buyer.[59] Failure by the creditor to sell any security for its market value will be treated as if he had obtained that market value,[60] perhaps subject to the express terms of the guarantee.[61]

## Sureties of regulated agreements

**[25.08]**  Whilst the HPA 1938 offered little protection to sureties, their position was considerably improved by the HPA 1964, and further protected by the CCA. Of course, this protection is only available to persons who act as sureties of regulated agreements;[62] and in that context, it must be considered in relation to each of the following three surety techniques already explained (see para 25.04).

---

52  *Stimpson v Smith* (1999) 149 NLJ 414, CA. See generally Goode, *Commercial Law* (3rd Edn) 821–3.

53  *Royal Bank of Scotland v Etridge (No. 2)* [2002] 2 AC 773, HL; *UCB Corporate Services Ltd v Williams* [2002] CLY 3840, CA. See also para 29.40.

54  Under the Trust of Land and Appointment of Trustees Act 1996, ss 14 and 15: *First National Bank PLC v Achampong* [2004] CLY 3246, CA.

55  *Lloyd's TSB Bank plc v Shorney* [2001] CLY 4877, CA.

56  *Raiffeisen ZO AG v Crossseas Shipping Ltd* [2000] 1 All ER (Comm) 76, CA. But see *Lombard Finance Ltd v Brookplain Trading Ltd* [1991] 2 All ER 762, CA (immaterial); *Samuels Finance Group v Beechmanor* [1995] CLY 402, CA (variation clause).

57  *Triodos Bank NV v Dobbs* [2005] EWCA Civ 630. Distinguish a waiver by the surety of his right to discharge: see Goode, *Legal Problems of Credit and Security*, 66–8. The general effect of a waiver is considered, para 26.23.

58  See *Hewison v Ricketts* (set out at para 27.19).

59  *Western Credit Ltd v Alberry* (above: lawful termination by hirer); *Hyundai Heavy Industries Ltd v Papadopoulos* [1980] 2 All ER 29, HL (instalment of price due before cancellation). Difficulties have arisen over guarantees open-ended as to amount: Banking Ombudsman, *AR 1990/1*, Pt 6; and (2005) 122 LQR 42.

60  *Skipton BS v Stott* [2000] 2 All ER 779, CA. Cf. mitigation (see para 27.45).

61  *Barclays Bank Plc v Kingston* [2006] EWHC 533, paras 28–9. But cf. para 18.06.

62  Subject to the rules of court, all the parties to a regulated agreement must be before the court (s 141(5): see para 24 39).

1. *Co-principals*. In all cases where there is more than one debtor or hirer (see para 5.24), s 185(1) provides as follows:

> 'Where an actual or prospective regulated agreement has two or more debtors or hirers (not being a partnership or an unincorporated body of persons)—
>
> (a) anything required by or under this Act to be done in relation to the debtor or hirer shall be done in relation to each of them; and
>
> (b) anything done under this Act by or on behalf of one of them shall have effect as if done by or on behalf of all of them.'

It should be noticed that this provision does not apply where the debtor or hirer is a partnership or other unincorporated association:[63] in these cases, whether the act of one binds another depends on the ordinary law.[64] These aside, s 185 does two things. *First*, where the Act requires the doing of something **to** the debtors or hirers, it must be done in relation to all of them,[65] except where they have dispensed with the periodic notices prescribed under s 78(4) for running-account credit.[66] *Second*, when the Act allows something to be done **by** the debtors or hirers, any one of them may generally act on behalf of all of them;[67] but each debtor or hirer must usually sign the regulated agreement individually,[68] a rule extending to enforcement orders;[69] and the death of any of them triggers the death provisions.[70] Finally, the sections make special provision for the situation where one joint debtor or hirer is a body corporate,[71] with suitable amendment to the signature rule.[72]

2. *Indorsees* (see paras 25.09–10).

3. *Guarantors* (see paras 25.11–12).

**[25.09/10] Indorsees.** The use of bills of exchange to reinforce the consumer's payment obligations under instalment credit transactions had long been a cause of concern;[73] such bills were commonly negotiated even before the supply of the goods or services for which they were issued; and the consumer could then find himself committed to pay a holder in due course despite the supplier's breach, because such holder took free of any equities the consumer might have against his supplier.[74] The CCA sought to tackle this problem, not by attacking the concept of a

---

63　Even though the association may be an 'individual' within s 189(1): see para 5.24.

64　For partnership, see Partnership Act 1890, s 6; for unincorporated associations, see the law of agency; and further Goode, *Consumer Credit Law & Practice*, paras 44.9–10.

65　See para 5.24. For some difficult cases, see Goode, *Op. cit.*, paras 44.4–5.

66　S 185(2). So second joint credit card-holders may dispense with a second copy of the monthly statement: see para 7.12. For s 78(4), see para 7.08.

67　S 185(5): see para 5.24. E.g. consent to repossession (see para 24.37); statutory right of termination (see paras 26.06–7). For some difficult cases, see Goode, *Op. cit.*, para 44.7.

68　Ss 61(1)(a) and 185(3). Except in the case of a partnership or unincorporated association (s 61(4)): see para 9.13.

69　S 185(3): see para 9.13.

70　Ss 86 and 185(4): see para 24.48.

71　S 185(5): see para 5.24.

72　S 185(6), as amended.

73　E.g. in relation to central heating and double glazing: Goode, *Consumer Credit Law & Practice*, para 37.161.

74　For holders in due course, see para 7.24. *Contra* the position of an assignee: see para 7.23.

holder in due course, but by making it difficult for any bill or cheque issued in such circumstances ever to come into the hands of such a person (s 125(1)). Section 123 took the following two steps:[75]

(1) To prohibit the taking by way of payment of negotiable instruments in general (see para 7.24). Section 123(1) provides:

> 'A creditor or owner shall not take a negotiable instrument,[76] other than a bank note[77] or cheque,[78] in discharge of any sum payable—[79]
>
> (a) by the debtor or hirer under a regulated agreement, or
>
> (b) by any person as surety in relation to the agreement.[80]

(2) A general prohibition on negotiating cheques otherwise than to a banker.[81]

The consequence of non-compliance is that the instrument and any security are normally enforceable on an order of the court only.'[82]

Nowadays, it will be even less likely that the problems tackled by s 123 will arise. This is because, since the Cheques Act 1992, most banks no longer issue to their customers cheque-forms which are negotiable, but instead non-negotiable ones under the 1992 Act (see para 7.28).

[25.11] **Guarantors.** Whilst the HPA 1938 offered little protection to sureties of agreements within its ambit, their position was considerably improved by the HPA 1964, which assimilated the treatment of guarantees and indemnities as regards a limited range of safeguards. The CCA has gone much further, and now 'provides a reasonably comprehensive pattern of protection for guarantors and indemnifiers' of regulated agreements,[83] subsuming both these common law categories under the expression 'surety', which is defined as follows by s 189(1)):

> 'the person by whom any security[84] is provided, or the person to whom his rights and duties in relation to the security have passed by assignment or operation of law'.

However, the definition of 'security' is limited to that 'provided by the debtor or hirer or at his request',[84] which will effectively limit it to category (a) (see para 25.05). Within that limitation, s 113(1) prevents the creditor or owner side-stepping the protection of the CCA by laying down that a security:

> 'shall not be enforced so as to benefit the creditor or owner, directly or indirectly, to an extent greater . . . than would be the case if the security were not provided'.

---

75  S 123 does not apply to (i) non-commercial agreements (s 123(5): as to these, see para 5.18); (ii) international trade exempted by statutory order (s 123(6): cf. UCTA, s 26—see para 18.15).

76  It therefore does not apply to cheques worded 'not negotiable' or postal orders, where it is not needed because there cannot be a holder in due course (see para 7.24).

77  This will amount to legal tender: see para 23.13.

78  Does this include post-dated cheques? See Goode, *Op. cit.*, para 37.164.

79  Nor may this rule be circumvented by taking the negotiable instrument by way of security instead of payment: s 123(3) and (4); and Goode, *Op. cit.*, para 37.166.

80  See generally, para 25.11.

81  S 123(2). Usually a bank will only act as agent for collection and not itself become a holder of the cheque.

82  S 124. Is the effect that it is 'not properly executed' (see para 9.19)?

83  Goode, *Consumer Credit Law & Practice*, para 37.64.

84  'Security' is widely defined by s 189(1) to mean 'a mortgage, charge, pledge, bond, debenture, indemnity, guarantee, bill, note or other right'. For criticism of this definition, see Goode, *Ibid.*

Without this provision, a creditor could simply sue an indemnifier to extract his full common law rights, leaving the indemnifier to recoup his loss from the debtor (see para 25.07). However, the effect of s 113(1) is to deprive an indemnity of its principal advantage over a guarantee (see para 25.06) and restrict the creditor to amounts recoverable by him from the debtor,[85] whether that security is provided in relation to any actual or prospective regulated agreement[86] or linked transaction;[87] or the claim is by an assignee from the debtor.[88] Where a regulated agreement is enforceable only by court order, any security is not enforceable unless and until such enforcement order has been made.[89] However, there is an important saving from s 113(1) where the debtor or hirer is a minor, so that s 113(1) will not render the agreement unenforceable simply by reason of his minority.[90]

Besides making substantial provisions as to the formalities and enforcement of such 'securities' (see paras 25.12–14), the CCA also brings them within the following protections: the duty to provide information and copies during the continuance of the agreement;[91] service of default notice on the surety (s 87(1)(e): set out at para 24.30), together with copies of default or non-default[92] notices served on the debtor or hirer (s 111); Time Orders;[93] and extortionate credit bargains[94] or unfair credit relationships (new s 140B(2): see para 29.47).

[25.12] **Formalities.** In favour of a surety who has provided security in respect of a regulated agreement (see para 25.11), the CCA provides protection in relation to the formalities connected with the formation of the security agreement. Just as a regulated agreement must be in the prescribed form (see para 9.09), so must any security provided at the request of the debtor or hirer (see para 25.11) by a third party:[95] the 'security instrument' must be expressed in writing (s 105(1)) in the prescribed form (s 105(2)) containing the prescribed information (ss 105(2) and (3)). Further, ss 105(4) and (5) of the Act lay down that the security instrument is not properly executed unless it complies with the foregoing, embodies all the express terms of the security,[96] is signed 'by or on behalf of the surety'[97] 'in the prescribed manner',

---

85   Would the duty to mitigate (see para 27.44) enable a surety to make an offer for the repossessed goods (47 CC 6/25)?
86   S 113(1)). For examples of the operation of s 113(1), see Goode, *Op. cit.*, paras 37.196–9.
87   S 113(8). See *Citibank International PLC v Schleider* [1999] CLY 2505.
88   *Goshawk etc Ltd v Bank of Scotland* [2006] 2 All ER 610, paras 109–15.
89   S 113(2). As whether this might infringe the Human Rights Act, see *Wilson v First County Trust Ltd* (see para 3.09A).
90   S 113(7), as amended. Without this saving, it would be impossible for the creditor or owner to take an effective security in respect of minors' regulated agreements (see para 10.18), making it difficult for minors to obtain credit.
91   Ss 107, 108, 109 and 110. For the counterpart duties towards a debtor or hirer, see para 15.17.
92   S 111. For non-default notices, see para 24.29 and para 26.10.
93   S 129(1)(c): see para 24.40.
94   S 139: see para 29.40.
95   These rules do not apply to a security provided by the debtor or hirer (s 105(6)), which is governed by s 60(1): s 105(9); and para 9.10.
96   Under the Consumer Credit (Guarantees and Indemnities) Regulations, 1983 SI 1556, the security instruments must contain, *inter alia*, a statement alerting the surety to the fact that he may have to pay instead of the debtor and drawing his attention to the availability of advice from Trading Standards Depts and CABx.
97   S 105(4). Compare regulated agreements, which must be signed by the debtor or hirer personally (s 61(1)): see para 9.13.

i.e. in the Regulations, and that the debtor or hirer receives copies of both the security instrument and regulated agreement.[98] The sole (s 170(1): see para 10.19) penalty for non-compliance with the above rules is that (s 105(7)):

'the security, so far as provided in relation to a regulated agreement, is enforceable against the surety on an order of the court only'.

At any time before court action, a seven-day notice must be served on the surety.[99] When the case comes before the court, the position depends on whether or not the defect is on 'technical grounds only', a test already discussed (see para 9.19): if so, the position is governed by s 127 (see para 24.27); whereas, if there is a substantive infringement, then s 105(8) provides that the case shall fall within s 106 (see para 25.13).

**[25.13/4] Enforcement**. The scheme of the Act is to bring within s 106 any security which it wishes to invalidate. Section 106 provides as follows:[100]

'Where, under any provision of this Act, this section is applied to any security provided in relation to a regulated agreement, then, subject to section 177[101] . . .

(a)  the security, so far as it is so provided, shall be treated as never having effect;

(b)  any property lodged with the creditor or owner solely for the purposes of the security as so provided shall be returned by him forthwith;

(c)  the creditor or owner shall take any necessary action to remove or cancel an entry in any register, so far as the entry relates to the security as so provided; and

(d)  any amount received by the creditor or owner on realisation of the security shall, so far as it is referable to the agreement, be repaid to the surety.'

The section will be enforced by the courts even though it unfairly rewards the debtor.[102] Section 106 applies to securities in all the following cases (s 113(3)):

(1)  Where the regulated agreement is cancelled under s 69,[103] or terminated by s 91 because of the repossession of protected goods (see para 24.38).

(2)  Except on technical grounds only, where an application to a country court (see para 24.39) to enforce a security is dismissed for breach of s 105 (s 105(8): see further, para 25.11), because the agreement was made by an unlicensed trader[104] or credit broker,[105] by reason of the fact that it was improperly executed,[106] or that it involved a negotiable instrument in breach of s 123,[107] or upon refusal of an enforcement order under s 142(2) (see para 24.33. But see

---

98  Ss 105(4)(d) and (5). Cf. the rules for service of copies on the debtor or hirer: see para 9.14, *et seq.*

99  As to default notices, see ss 87(1)(e) and 111 (see paras 24.30 and 25.26). As to non-default notices, see Goode, *Consumer Credit Law & Practice*, 37.191.

100  Subject to the human rights point: see para 25.11, fn 87.

101  (As amended), which contains savings for registered land charges: see para 25.24.

102  *Wilson v Howard Pawnbrokers* [2005] EWCA Civ 147, CA (items re-pledged under unenforceable agreements: see para 25.18). As to the effect of s 106(d) in these circumstances, see *Wilson v Robertson (London) Ltd* (set out at para 10.19), *per* Cornwath LJ, at paras 15–34.

103  See further, para 10.32. But see s 113(5).

104  Under s 40(1): see further, para 6.20.

105  Under s 149(1): see further, para 6.28.

106  Under s 65(1): see further, para 9.19.

107  Under s 124: see para 25.09.

s 113(4)). As to where the security is a land mortgage, see s 126 (para 25.24); as to minors, see s 113(7) (para 25.11).

(3) According to s 113(6), a surety may withdraw[108] at any time before the making of the regulated agreement for which he was to stand surety by giving notice to the creditor or owner,[109] in which case the security is brought within s 106.[110] What if the surety does not withdraw, but the regulated agreement is never made?[111]

# POSSESSORY REAL SECURITY

[25.15/6] **Pledges at common law.**[112] A pledge (or pawn) is a special form of bailment (see generally, para 1.17), whereunder the bailor (pledgor) transfers possession of the goods to another (the pledgee) by way of security for a loan (see para 25.02). It being a species of bailment, the pledgor retains the general property in the goods (see para 19.08), which he is entitled to sell to a third party subject to the pledge.[113] However, a pledge grants the pledgee a special interest in the pledged goods, commonly referred to as a 'special property',[114] whose value equals the amount of the loan. During the continuance of the pledge, the pledgee may transfer that special property to another,[115] or sue for wrongful interference with the goods (see para 27.31); and on default by the pledgor/borrower, the pledgee has a power of sale to recoup his loan, holding any surplus for the pledgor.[116]

The essence of a pledge being a transfer of possession, only those species of personal property which admit of delivery may be pledged: so a chose in action, e.g. a contract debt such as instalments due under a credit sale, may not be pledged,[117] though a negotiable instrument may because title passes by delivery (see para 7.24). However, in relation to choses in possession (goods), the delivery may be actual[117] or constructive.[118] On the other hand, except in the case of

---

108  Cf. the protection of the debtor or hirer under s 59: see para 5.20.

109  The debtor or hirer who has given real security can also use s 113(6) to recover that security: see Goode, *Consumer Credit Law & Practice*, para 37.198; and para 10.26.

110  The complicated manner in which the draftsman has achieved this result is criticised by Goode, *Op. cit.*, Division IIB, para 5.223.

111  Must the surety give notice under s 113(6) to escape, or is his obligation automatically terminated on common law principles (see para 25.06)?

112  See generally Crossley Vaines, *Personal Property*, 5th edn, 23.

113  On tendering the amount of the pledge, the third party may sue for wrongful interference with the goods: *Franklin v Neate* (1844) 13 M & W 481; and generally, para 19.06.

114  Perhaps because of a tendency to extend the expression 'special property' to a lienee's interest (see para 25.02), the expression has been criticised: see Chalmers *Sale of Goods*, 18th edn, 269. Yet, if 'special property' is reserved for proprietary, rather than solely possessory interests (see para 19.08), its use to describe the interest of a pledge would seem appropriate.

115  *Donald v Suckling* (1866) LR 1 QB 585.

116  *Re Hardwick, ex p Hubbard* (1886) LR 17 QBD 699, CA. In equity, interest is due on that surplus until paid, as in a mortgage (see para 25.20): *Matthew v TM Sutton Ltd* [1994] 4 All ER 793; and generally, para 7.03A.

117  *Harrold v Plenty* [1901] 2 Ch 314. For choses in action, see generally, para 7.16.

118  *Wrightson v McArthur and Hutchinsons (1919) Ltd* [1921] 2 KB 807.

trust receipts of bills of lading,[119] a pledge of documents of title will not usually of itself amount to a pledge of the goods because it does not change the possession of the goods. It follows from this insistence on a transfer of possession that the owner/supplier of goods supplied on conditional sale, hp or simple hiring cannot create a pledge over those goods during the continuance of the agreement.[120] *Prima facie*, an attempted pledge by the conditional buyer or hirer will *ipso facto* determine the hiring,[121] though not an option to purchase (see para 1.22). As between the pledgor (buyer/hirer) and the pledgee, such a pledge may break the implied condition that the pledgor is the owner of the pledged goods, or has the authority of the owner to pledge them.[122] As between the owner who supplied the goods and the pledgee (lender), under the *nemo dat* rule the pledgee cannot obtain a good title (see para 21.02), except where one of the exceptions operates (see Chap 21); and his receipt of the goods will be a conversion (see para 19.05), as will his sale or refusal to deliver them to the owner.[123] Unfortunately, there have been reports that pawnbrokers are not accustomed to question the credit history of the pledgor and are unlikely to ask for proof of ownership.

## Regulated agreements

[25.17] **Pawnbroking**. The specialised pawnbroker, for whom lending money on the security of pledges (see para 25.15) was a principal form of business, has existed in this country for a long time, the first attempt at regulation being an Act of 1603.[124] In the eighteenth century, pawnbroking became a service principally utilised by the poor of the large cities, and a series of enactments aimed at the protection of that class was consolidated in the Pawnbrokers Acts 1872–1960.[125] The Crowther Report (see generally, para 5.03) recommended that the principles of those Acts should be retained and rationalised (para 6.2.60). However, the Report recognised that its general approach of restricting the taking of possession of the security[126] was inapplicable to pawnbroking, whose essence was a taking of possession (para 6.2.4). Accordingly, the Report recommended special provisions to regulate pawnbroking;[127] and these are now to be found in ss 114–22 of the CCA (see para 25.18), which replace the old Pawnbrokers Acts (above). More recently, there has been a renaissance in pawnbroking, which has even ventured into off trade premises business on the weekly collected credit model.[128] Moreover, the repeal of the wide statutory definition of 'pawnbroking' in the 1872 Act has seen a resurgence of activities which appear to fall just outside the common law notion of

---

119  For trust receipts, see 1st edn, para 25.16.
120  Goode, *HP Law & Practice*, 2nd edn, 537. Deposit of the instalment contracts will operate as a mortgage or charge.
121  But see Goode, *Op. cit.*, 540, fn 15.
122  *Sugar Manufacturing Co v Clark* (1879) 5 Ex D 37. See further Goode, *Op. cit.*, 538, fn 16.
123  *Belsize Motor Supply Co v Cox* [1914] 1 KB 244.
124  See the Crowther Report, paras 2.1.15–18. For that Report, see generally, para 5.03.
125  For the principal requirements of those Acts, see the Crowther Report, para 4.1.31.
126  For these restrictions, see para 24.27, *et seq*.
127  The Crowther Report, paras 6.2.37 and 6.13.19; and OFT, *UCT Bulletin No. 17*, case No. 18.
128  See (1990) 11 CCA News 5/20; 11 CCA News 6/5.

pawning.[129] The result would appear to be that such activities fell outside the specialist CCA control of pawnbroking and arguably outside the general CCA controls as well, depending on whether or not such activities amount to 'financial accommodation' (see para 5.22).

**[25.18] The CCA.** The modern business of pawnbroking is now likely to be regulated by the CCA (see above). The pawnbroker will then require a category A licence (see para 6.15); and his individual transactions will be governed by ss 114–22 of the CCA. According to s 114, these provisions apply to anyone 'who takes an article[130] in pawn[131] under a regulated agreement',[132] other than under a non-commercial agreement.[133] It may be an offence to take any article in pawn from a minor (s 114(2)) or to canvass such loans.[134] Unless the agreement to pledge complies with all the ordinary formalities for a regulated agreement (ss 62–4: see Chap 9), it is not properly executed, so that the creditor may be unable to enforce the security (s 113(2): see para 25.14). Further, the creditor (pawnbroker) must also issue a pawn receipt in the prescribed form to the debtor/pledgor.[135] Under the Act, the debtor may redeem the pledge[136] by surrender of the pawn-ticket[137] within the redemption period which expires upon the latest of the following events: expiry of six months or such greater period as the parties may agree;[138] or realisation by the pawnbroker (s 116(3)). Unreasonable refusal by the pawnbroker to redeliver the pawned goods amounts to an offence;[139] but the failure by the debtor to redeem the goods will allow the creditor to forfeit the pledge for a small sum, or sell to repay himself any sum,[140] or sometimes to seek a Time Order (see para 24.40). The burden of proving that he obtained the true market value lies on the pawnbroker;[141] and any surplus on sale by the creditor must be paid (plus interest) to the debtor (s 121(3)).

---

129  Sales agency, exchange and repurchase: see Macleod [1995] JBL 155, esp. 168–9.

130  The sections do not extend to pledges of documents of title or bearer bonds (CCA, s 114(3)(a), as amended). As to these, see para 25.15.

131  'Pawn' means any article subject to a pledge: s 189(1). For pledge, see para 25.15.

132  S 114(1). For regulated agreements, see para 5.13. Can a pledge ever amount to a consumer hire agreement (as to which, see para 1.19)?

133  S 114(3)(b). For non-commercial agreements, see para 5.18. Thus, strictly speaking, the provisions are not limited to pawnbrokers: Goode, *Consumer Credit Law & Practice*, para 37.126.

134  S 49(1). But it is still possible to conduct such business on the basis of solicited weekly home visits: see para 7.07.

135  S 114(1). However, the sanction for breach of s 114(1) is more powerful in that it amounts to a criminal offence (s 115). Home pawnbroking may lead to cancellable agreements (ss 67–73: see para 10.28, *et seq.*): (1990) 11 CCA News 4/3.

136  For redemption charges, see s 116(4); and for the redemption procedure, see s 117.

137  For the situation where the debtor has lost the pawn-ticket, see s 118.

138  S 116(1) and (2). The parties may not validly agree to reduce the redemption period below 6 months: *Wilson v Robertson (London) Ltd* (set out at para 5.22).

139  S 119. The onus lies on the pawnbroker to prove he had reasonable cause to refuse to allow redemption: s 171(6).

140  Ss 120(1)(a) and 121. Forfeiture of small pledges looks very much like foreclosure of mortgages: as to which, see para 25.20.

141  S 121(6). The OFT will usually require that the property is auctioned: see (1994/5) 9 *Fair Trading* 3. As to the pawnbroker's 'internal sales', see OFT, *1994 AR* 29.

# PROPRIETARY REAL SECURITY

**[25.19] Introduction**. This section is concerned with the situation where a debtor obtains or retains **possession** of real or personal property,[142] whilst his creditor retains or is granted **proprietary** rights therein by way of security for the payment or repayment of a sum of money. Such transactions have already been distinguished from both pledges and sales.[143]

*Legislation.* The statutory regimes which govern such transactions have to some extent been coloured by the typical circumstances in which they have been used. Mortgages or charges of land have tended to be associated with security for its purchase price, society's approval of the objective being mirrored by the evolution of a helpful legal framework.[144] On the other hand, mortgages or charges of chattels have frequently been given to secure cash loans; and the legislature has treated such loans with unsympathetic suspicion.[145] In more recent times, this dichotomy of usage has become less clear-cut, a shift reflected in statutory treatment: mortgages of choses in action have become acceptable[146] and charges of a company's stock-in-trade positively supported;[147] whereas second mortgages of land, often to secure home improvements, have achieved sufficient notoriety to ensure their inclusion in the CCA (see para 25.24). The outcome of this varied legislative treatment is a present position as follows:

(1) Where realty is mortgaged or charged to anyone, the system set up by the Law of Property Acts (LPA) must be followed;[144] and, if the borrower is a registered company, the transaction is **also** subject to the Companies Act.[147]

(2) Where goods are mortgaged or charged by an individual, the matter is governed by the Bills of Sale Act 1882;[145] but, if goods are mortgaged or charged by a company, the matter is **instead** dealt with by the Companies Act.[147]

(3) Where choses in action (see para 7.16) are mortgaged or charged, the transaction may be caught by the Companies Act,[147] but not by the Bills of Sale Acts.[145] **Additionally**, the transaction may in any event fall within some of the provisions of the LPA.[146]

## Mortgages and charges of realty

**[25.20] Introduction**.[148] The mortgage was originally a common law invention; but equity later intervened to mitigate the common law's harshness. By the seventeenth

---

142  For real and personal property, see generally, para 19.02. Distinguish the different sense of 'real' as opposed to personal security: see para 25.01.
143  See respectively, paras 25.02 and 25.01. How far, if at all, does the scheme that follows reflect the SGA rules?
144  See para 25.20, *et seq.*
145  See para 25.26, *et seq.*
146  See paras 7.20–1. E.g. factoring (see para 2.22).
147  See para 25.28, *et seq.*
148  See generally, Megarry and Wade, *Law of Real Property*, 6th edn, Chap 19.

century, the characteristics of a mortgage were clear. *First*, in the case of both real and personal property, a mortgage was effected by transfer of ownership: if the mortgagor (borrower) failed to redeem (repay) the mortgage, the property was forfeit to the mortgagee (lender), subject to the mortgagor's equity of redemption (see below). In the case of land, the usual form was a conveyance of land in fee simple with a covenant to reconvey if the money was paid by a fixed date;[149] but that rule was later changed by statute (see para 25.21). Equity allowed more informal modes of making mortgages.[150] *Second*, the rate of interest that could be charged was first governed by the usury laws, then by the Moneylenders Acts (now repealed: see para 6.09). In modern times, regulated mortgages of any property are governed by the CCA (see para 25.24), whilst the modern statutory rules relating to mortgages of real property are referred to below (para 25.21). *Third*, equity discouraged the mortgagee from taking possession, so leading to the modern form whereby the mortgagor remained in possession (see para 25.02). *Fourth*, the agreement commonly granted the mortgagee an express power to sell the security in default: in every modern mortgage by deed, such a power is now conferred by statute,[151] which also makes him a trustee of the proceeds of sale.[152] In any case, a mortgagee in exercising his power of sale is required to act in good faith and with reasonable care to obtain the best price reasonably obtainable.[153] *Fifth*, equity granted the mortgagor relief against forfeiture (see para 27.20) and a right to redeem (obtain reconveyance) even after the fixed date for repayment had long passed (the equity of redemption: see below), so compelling the mortgagee to treat the property as no more than security for the money actually owed.[149] Any attempt in the mortgage to restrict this right to redeem is ignored by equity, a rule which is usually expressed as there may be no clog on the equity of redemption.[154]

*Equity of redemption*. This mortgagor's equity of redemption was regarded as an equitable interest in property, exercisable by repayment, e.g. if property worth £50,000 is mortgaged to secure a loan of £40,000 the mortgagor's equity of redemption is worth £10,000 at the outset. However, if the money was not repaid, equity would foreclose (determine) the mortgagor's right of redemption, leaving the mortgagee with unfettered ownership,[155] but with an obligation to pay any

---

149 Equity regards the issue of a transfer of ownership by way of security instead of absolutely as a matter of substance rather than form: *Re Duke of Marlborough* [1894] 2 Ch 133 (transaction in form of conditional sale). Cf. the right of a debtor or hirer under a regulated agreement: see para 24.30.

150 E.g. by deposit of title deeds with the intention of creating a mortgage. Under s 2 of the LPA 1989, dispositions of an interest in land must be in signed writing (see para 9.03).

151 LPA 1925, ss 101–7; Administration of Justice Act 1970, ss 36–9 (as amended). See generally Megarry and Wade, *Op. cit.*, paras 19–056/66; Goode, *Commercial Law*, 3rd edn, 639–40. But see the *Syed* case (para 25.24).

152 LPA, s 105, including a statutory duty to pay interest on the surplus until paid over; and for interest payable in equity, see para 7.03A.

153 See *Den Norske Bank ASA v Acemex Management Co Ltd* [2003] 2 All ER (Comm) 318; *Bradford & Bingley PLC v Ross* [2005] EWCA Civ 394. Cf. the right of the hirer under the hiring or hp agreement: see para 24.22.

154 E.g. *Cityland and Property (Holdings) Ltd v Dabrah* [1968] Ch 166; *Jones v Morgan* [2001] CLY 4876, CA (see Berg [2002] JBL 335, discussing whether this allows the mortgagee to stipulate for a share of the profits; and Devenney [2002] JBL 539, examining the justification for the doctrine).

155 Because in the above example it would give the mortgagee a windfall of £10,000, the courts are reluctant in such cases to make foreclosure orders: Goode, *Op. cit.*, 641.

surplus obtained on sale to the mortgagor.[156] Thus, the market value of the equity is any excess obtained on such sale over the amount of the debt;[157] but any deficit is termed 'negative equity'.[158] A mortgage is enforceable not only as against the mortgagor, but also as against anyone to whom the mortgagor transfers his title, save only for a *bona fide* purchaser without notice. This infirmity of an equitable title may be compared with the common law exceptions to the *nemo dat* rule (see para 19.03).

**[25.21/2] Modern rules**. The modern rules relating to mortgages and charges of realty generally are set out in Part III of the LPA 1925 (as amended). This allows only two formal types of legal mortgage, of which the more common[159] is a charge[160] by deed expressed to be by way of legal mortgage.[161] However, where there is a land mortgage, by statute the borrower retains the estate.[159]

Nowadays, most formal transfers of interests in land fall within the registration system,[162] which abandons the *nemo dat* principle (see para 19.11) in favour of the indefeasibility of registered title. Where there is more than one mortgage or charge on the same property, there is generally no question of each of the secured lenders sharing any loss should the proceeds of realisation of the security be insufficient to pay them all out.[163] Each secured lender takes his claim in full in order of priority, and it is for a later secured lender to satisfy himself as to the value of the security before he takes his mortgage or charge.[164] The rules as to priority as between succeeding mortgages or charges depends on whether or not the borrower is a registered company.[165] Moreover, the 1925 legislation is displaced in respect of formally-created charges of equitable interests in land,[166] where priorities are usually[167] determined by the *Dearle v Hall* (first to register) rule.[168]

The only other matters which require special mention for our purposes are the following: the rules as to the tieing-in of services;[169] the position of fixtures

---

156 *Adamson v Halifax PLC* [2003] 4 All ER 423, CA.

157 *Bristol & West PLC v Bartlett* [2002] 4 All ER 544, CA. Compare the position of a hirer or conditional buyer: see para 24.22.

158 See *Palk v Mortgage Service Funding plc* [1993] 2 All ER 481, CA. If the sale or foreclosure leaves the mortgagor still indebted, this may be recorded in the credit register: see para 2.18.

159 The other form is a demise (lease) for a term of years absolute subject to a provision for cesser on redemption: LPA, ss 85(1) and 86(1).

160 For charges, see generally, para 25.02.

161 LPA, ss 85(1) and 86(1). This form involves no conveyance of any estate to the mortgagee, but grants him 'the same protection, powers and remedies' as if he had been granted a lease: s 87(1). This puts the chargee in much the same position as a mortgagee.

162 Under the Land Registration Act 2002, which is beyond the scope of this work.

163 *Contra* the unsecured lender: see para 19.13.

164 Goode, *Commercial Law*, 3rd edn, 582–4.

165 If the borrower is a registered company, the mortgage or charge will also require registration under the Companies Act: see para 25.29.

166 *Contra* goods: see para 25.25.

167 The rule in *Dearle v Hall* has not been applied to charging orders (see para 27.04): *United Bank of Kuwait plc v Sahib* [1995] 2 All ER 973, *ratio* 1 (affirmed on other grounds).

168 By the LPA 1925, s 137(1); and see Megarry and Wade, *Law of Real Property*, 6th edn, para 19-208, *et seq*. For the *Dearle v Hall* rule, see para 7.19.

169 Ss 104–7 of the Courts and Legal Services Act 1990 prohibit the lender under a 'residential property loan' from requiring the borrower to also take from him 'controlled services' e.g. conveyancing, surveying.

(see para 25.23); the restrictions on the right of a mortgagee of a dwelling house to recover possession;[170] those special rules pertaining to mortgages and charges which fall within the CCA (see para 25.24); and the realisation of charges over company realty (see para 25.28). For the mortgagee's remedies, see para 27.07.

**[25.23] The borderline between realty and personalty: fixtures and fittings**. English law draws a sharp distinction between land and chattels (see para 19.03). Where chattels are brought onto land, it has to be determined whether to apply to those chattels the law relating to realty or personalty (see para 9.03). Thus, materials used to build a house are thereby converted from personalty into realty.[171] On the other hand, 'fittings' are free-standing chattels which *prima facie* remain personalty, e.g. curtains, unfitted carpets. In between those two categories are 'fixtures', which are chattels annexed (attached) to the land in such a way that they may be later detached (severed).[172] Thus, on sale of a house, *prima facie* fixtures pass with the land, whereas fittings remain with the vendor.

The general rule is that where a hired chattel is annexed to land so as to become a fixture, at common law it *prima facie* becomes the property of the owner of the land.[173] Exceptions include the following:

1. *Landlord and tenant*. Generally speaking, a fixture becomes a landlord's and must be left for him; but, during the currency of a lease, it cannot be distrained (see para 19.17). Moreover, a fixture becomes the property of the landowner irrespective of the previous title to the chattel, in which case the *nemo dat* rule (see para 19.11) is defeated and the erstwhile owner of the chattel has an action in conversion (see para 19.05) against the person making the annexation, e.g. tenant. Thus, a person who supplied goods to a tenant by way of hire, hp or conditional sale would lose his security unless that fixture was removable under the agreement.[174]

2. *Mortgagor and mortgagee*. Where land is mortgaged, there will usually vest in the mortgagee all fixtures annexed to the land either at the date of the mortgage or thereafter,[175] whereas fittings remain in the ownership of the mortgagor.[176] This can lead to conflicts of priority in fixtures as between the mortgagee of the land and a third person having an interest in the chattel, e.g. as mortgagee[177] or supplier under a conditional sale. In modern times, this has caused particular

---

170 See Administration of Justice Act 1970, s 36 (as amended) and the cases decided thereunder. For the mortgagor's right to take possession generally, see Megarry and Wade, *Op. cit.*, paras 19–045/55.

171 *Elitestone Ltd v Morris* [1997] 2 All ER 513, HL; Wilkinson (1997) 147 NLJ 1031. See also Megarry and Wade, *Law of Real Property*, 6th edn, para 14-312. But such property might still be subject to Pt I of the CPA: see para 17.25.

172 E.g. 'shop fittings'; fitted carpets. Whether a chattel becomes a fixture depends on the degree and purpose of annexation: see Megarry and Wade, *Op. cit.*, paras 14–313/5; Gray, *Elements of Land Law*, 3rd edn, 44, *et seq*.

173 *Appleby v Myers* (1867) LR 2 CP 651; *Crossley v Lee* (1908) 1 KB 86; *Brookes Robinson Pty Ltd v Rothfield* [1951] VLR 405; *Aircool Installations v British Telecommunications* [1995] CLY 821, Cty Ct. There are similar rules with regard to the accession of goods (see para 19.05) e.g. a new gasket fitted to an engine. But what of a new car battery or radio telephone?

174 See Gray, *Op. cit.*, 54–5.

175 LPA, ss 62(1), 88(4), 89(4) and 205(1)(ii).

176 *Botham v TSB* [1996] CLY 4999, CA.

177 *Holland v Hodgson* (1872) 7 CP 328, Exch Ch; *Ellis v Glover & Hobson* [1908] 1 KB 388.

difficulty where the chattels which have been fixed to the land were supplied on simple hire (lease) or hp:[178] the mortgagee of the land may take priority over the lessor of the chattels;[179] but, if (as is usually the case) the chattel lease contains a licence to enter and seize the chattel on default, at common law[180] this would appear to create an equitable interest in the chattel good against all deriving title to the land from the goods-hirer except a bfp, which rule will include a mere mortgagee or chargee of the land.[181] The respective rights of chattel owner and land mortgagee may thus vary depending on whether the chattel is affixed to the land before or after the mortgage is created and whether that mortgage is legal or equitable.[182]

**[25.24] The Consumer Credit Act**. For the most part, first mortgages of domestic dwelling houses are outside the ambit of the CCA (see para 3.02), because the agreement is exempt.[183] Such CCA-unregulated mortgages are subject to different rules, e.g. as to powers to repossess in default (see para 25.21) and the Financial Services Authority (see para 3.02). On the other hand, there were serious abuses in the second mortgage market, in particular in relation to straightforward secured lending,[184] home improvements,[185] and more recently remortgages (see para 7.04A). Accordingly, the CCA regulates the second mortgage market, whilst taking regulated mortgages outside the ordinary (above) rules regarding repossession on default.[186]

Where a land mortgage[187] is undertaken to finance a regulated consumer credit agreement, it is subject to restrictions by the CCA in respect of all the following matters: advertising (see para 7.04A); withdrawal from a prospective land mortgage (see para 10.27); information during the currency of the agreement;[188] recovery of possession of land by the creditor under a conditional sale;[189] termination by the buyer (see para 26.06); and realisation of security.[190]

---

178 See Guest, *Law of HP*, Chap 18; Goode, *HP Law and Practice*, 2nd edn, Chap 32. It has been suggested that similar rules obtain in respect of *Romalpa* clauses (see para 25.30): Parris, *Retention of Title on the Sale of Goods*, 54; McCormack [1990] Conv 275 at 280–7.

179 Compare *Lyon & Co v London City and Midland Bank* [1903] 2 KB 135 (lease); and *Vaudeville Electric Cinema Ltd v Muriset* [1923] 2 Ch 74. The goods supplier may save himself by taking a waiver from an existing mortgagee: see Soper & Munro, *The Leasing Handbook*, 256 and Chap 21.

180 *Contra* where that licence contravenes the CCA, s 92: see para 24.34.

181 *Re Morrison, Jones & Taylor Ltd.* [1914] 1 Ch 50; and see Bennett and Davies (1994) 110 LQR 448 at 449–52. *Contra* a landlord.

182 See Giddins (1993) BJIBFL at 265; Bennet and Davies (1994) 110 LQR 448.

183 See para 5.15. Except for the extortionate credit bargain/unfair credit relationship provisions (see paras 29.41 and 29.44) and the advertising rules (see para 8.29).

184 The Crowther Report pointed particularly to the activities of mortgage brokers (paras 6.4.22–5).

185 The Crowther Report was particularly worried about the use of promissory notes in relation to financing central heating installations (para 6.6.35): see para 25.09.

186 S 38A, Administration of Justice Act 1970 (inserted by CCA, Sched 4, para 30). This seems to have been overlooked in *First National Bank plc v Syed* [1991] 2 All ER 250, CA (see Hickman (1994) 110 LQR 221).

187 'Land mortgage' includes any security charged on land: s 189(1).

188 Ss 77, 78 and 80: see para 15.17.

189 This may only be achieved by court order (s 92(2)), contravention being a breach of statutory duty (s 92(3); and generally, para 3.21).

190 S 113(6): see para 25.13. Whilst s 112 contains a general power to make regulations concerning the 'sale or other realisation' of any security, it must be primarily significant in relation to mortgage securities because the realisation of pledges is dealt with elsewhere (s 121): see para 25.18. No regulations have been made.

Furthermore, the CCA ousts the ordinary rules governing the rights of a mortgagee to take possession of land and sell it,[191] and provides that:[192]

> 'a land mortgage securing a regulated agreement is enforceable[193] (so far as provided in relation to the agreement) on an order of the court only'.

In such event, the court has jurisdiction to make a Time Order (see para 24.40), perhaps suspended (s 135), or the agreement may be varied (s 136). In *Barnes* (see para 24.41) the CA refused to allow separate actions for arrears (under s 129), holding that the s 129 proceedings covered the total indebtedness.

## Mortgages and charges of personalty

**[25.25] Introduction**. Personal property may be mortgaged or charged; but remember that a mortgagee or chargee of goods may lose his interest in them if they are annexed to land (see para 25.23).

1. *Mortgages of personalty.* This is a 'grant of an interest in an asset to secure payment of a debt or performance of some other obligation';[194] and it is subject to many of the same rules of common law and equity as a mortgage of realty.[195] However, whereas in a mortgage of land the borrower by statute retains the legal estate (see para 25.21), a legal mortgage of personalty can be effected only by a transfer of title;[196] and this leaves the mortgagor only an equity of redemption, whilst the mortgagee has powers of sale[197] and foreclosure (see para 25.20). As between competing legal mortgages, the common law rule is that interests rank in order to creation.[198] On the other hand, unlike a modern equitable mortgage of realty (see para 25.20), in an equitable mortgage of personalty the basic priority rule remains subject to the right of a bfp.[199] The written instrument recording the mortgage will be registrable: if the borrower is a natural person, such a mortgage may fall within the Bills of Sale Act 1882 (see para 25.27); and if he is a registered company, it may be governed by the Companies Acts (see para 25.28).

2. *Charges of personalty.* A charge of personalty conveys nothing and is necessarily equitable, giving the lender only a personal right of action against the borrower

---

191  S 177 (as amended): see para 25.20.

192  S 126. But no sanction is provided for breach: see s 170 (para 10.19), and Goode, *Consumer Credit Law & Practice*, para 38.7.

193  For difficulties as to whether enforcement includes repossession, see Guest and Lloyd, *Encyclopedia of Consumer Credit Law*, para 2-127.

194  Crowther Report, para 1.2.15. See also *per* Lord Lindley MR in *Santley v Wilde* [1899] 2 Ch 474 at 474.

195  See Holdsworth, *History of English Law*, vii, 80–1, 455–8, iii, 352, *et seq*.

196  Cf. mortgages of land before 1925; see para 25.20. In the case of a legal mortgage of a chose in action, there must also be notice to the debtor: see para 7.21.

197  *China and South Sea Bank Ltd v Tan* [1990] AC 536, PC.

198  Macleod [1995] JBL 155 at 156; Snell, *Principles of Equity*, 29th edn, 46. Because the first mortgage may be redeemed, this seems a better way to put it: see Thornely [1990] CLJ at 367. Cf. the *nemo dat* rule: see para 19.10.

199  The scope of the bfp rule in this context is limited by the statutory registration systems which may make it difficult for a purchaser to take without notice: see Goode, *Legal Problems of Credit and Security*, 3rd edn, paras 2.23–9.

and an encumbrance over the goods (see para 25.02), but no proprietary interest or right of foreclosure.[200] As usual with equitable rights (see para 7.17), no special form of words is required for the creation of an equitable charge over goods.[201] The personalty so charged may be either choses in possession (goods)[202] or choses in action. It is broadly subject to the same statutory control and priority rules as mortgages of personalty (see above), except as regards personal borrowers (see para 25.26). Where the borrower is a registered company, the charge may be fixed;[203] or it may float[203] over the assets for the time being falling within the generic description of the charge (see para 25.34) until crystallisation, upon which there occurs an equitable assignment to the chargee.[204] A floating charge is more vulnerable than a fixed charge on the insolvency of the chargor (see para 19.14).

**[25.26] Personal borrowers**. Generally speaking, a mortgage or charge of personalty by a natural person (the mortgagor) is subject to rules which are the same as, or analogous to, those governing mortgages of realty (see para 25.20). However, whereas the rights of a mortgagee of realty to enter into possession of, and sell, the mortgaged property are governed by the LPA (as varied), the position is not so simple with regard to personalty. Unlike choses in action (see para 25.19), a written[205] licence to seize goods by way of mortgage is governed by the Bills of Sale Act 1882: technically, this is because the written licence amounts to a 'bill of sale' of 'personal chattels' in the 'possession or apparent possession' of the grantor (seller) by way of security.[206] Designed to protect borrowers, the 1882 Act is almost commercially unworkable and is relatively little used.[207] Any mortgage bill falling within the 1882 Act was declared void as against all persons,[208] unless strictly in the form set out in the Schedule (s 9), which form precludes the granting of charges,[209] or any security over after-acquired property.[209] With regard to written chattel mortgages, even where the document complies with the formalities required by the 1882 Act, it severely limits the grounds upon which the goods may be seized[210]

---

200  Oditah, *Financing Receivables*, 95.

201  Megarry and Wade, *Law of Real Property*, 6th edn, para 19-040.

202  A charge on goods of which possession is retained by the chargor is sometimes called an hypothecation: see the Crowther Report, para 1.2.15; Goode, *Op. cit.*, 19–20; and further, para 25.16.

203  For fixed and floating charges, see para 19.14.

204  See Oditah, *Op. cit.*, 113, fn 37; and para 7.17. This prevents any subsequent arising of any set-off in respect of the debt: Grantham [1989] JBL 377 at 386.

205  A chattel mortgage can be made orally, in which case it is outside both the 1882 Act and the SGA (s 62(4)). Suppose the borrower/seller makes a subsequent sale, is the lender's title overridden by s 8 of the FA (see para 21.38)?

206  Bills of Sale (1878) Amendment Act 1882, s 3. For the definitions of 'bill of sale', 'personal chattels' and 'possession or apparent possession', see Macleod, *Consumer Sales Law*, 1st edn, para 9.04.

207  In recent years, there has been a developing market for loans to non-status borrowers secured by a bill of sale over his car: (2004) 73 *Quarterly Account* 6.

208  Including the parties: *Maas v Pepper* [1905] AC 102, HL.

209  It prevents charging by insisting on transfer of ownership; and it precludes the granting of security over after-acquired chattels because the security must be listed.

210  S 7. If contained in a regulated agreement, the licence to seize is subject to the default notice procedure (as to which, see para 24.30): Bills of Sale Act 1882, s 7A (added by the CCA, Sched 4, para 1). See the explanation in Goode, *Consumer Credit Law & Practice*, para 37.191. The seizure terms may also be subject to the UTCCR: [2006] *Bulletin J/M, Log Book*; and generally para 24.23.

and makes repossession difficult (s 13). Further, as few written transactions do accidentally comply with the requirements of the Act, such chattel mortgages are normally absolutely void (s 9). This has all caused difficulty in relation to both instalment supplies and pledges.

1. *Instalment supplies.* Quite early, there were worries as to whether the traditional conditional sale might fall within the 1882 Act by reason of the fact that it invariably **granted** the supplier a licence to seize in default. However, in *McEntire v Crossley Brothers*[211] the House of Lords confirmed that an ordinary two-party instalment supply transaction would escape the 1882 Act because the supplier had simply **reserved** a licence to seize. More difficulty was caused by sale and re-hiring transactions: after the passage of the 1882 Act, numerous attempts were made to disguise what were really chattel mortgages as sales and re-hirings on hp. To prevent such evasions of the 1882 Act, the courts laid down the rule that a sale and re-hiring would escape the Act if genuine, but not if it was a mere cloak for a loan.[212] It was one thing to lay down such a rule, but quite another to apply it; and the courts have experienced difficulty with both financed instalment credit (see para 25.27) and *Romalpa* clauses (see para 25.30, *et seq.*). However, in 2005 some motor financiers began to deliberately write secured instalment business as registered bills of sale, principally to avoid voluntary termination under the CCA (see para 26.06).

2. *Pledges.* In theory, a pledge is distinguished from a mortgage because the former depends on a special property, whilst the latter rests on a right of foreclosure.[213] However, faced with a written note of the transaction, the courts have found it more helpful to see whether the secured party goes into possession at the outset:[214] a change of possession at, or before, the moment of loan has been held to create a pledge outside the 1882 Act;[215] but where that right was deferred, the transaction was held to be a mortgage within the Act.[216]

**[25.27] Financed instalment supplies**. Suppose an owner of goods (C) wishes to raise money from B on the security of goods whilst retaining possession of them. One way of achieving this would be by way of a chattel mortgage (see para 25.25); but another would be for C to sell those goods to B and re-hire them on hp from B. As Lord MacNaughten said in one 1888 case:[217]

> 'there is all the difference in the world between a mortgage and a sale with a right of repurchase. But if the transaction is completed by redemption or repurchase as the case may be there is no difference in actual result.'

---

211 [1895] AC 457, HL. See the explanation in Macleod, *Op. cit.*, para 1.14A.

212 Compare *Yorkshire Railway Wagon G v Maclure* (1882) 21 Ch D 309, CA (genuine) with *Re Watson, ex p the Official Receiver* (1890) 25 QBD 27, CA (cloak for a loan).

213 *Charlesworth v Mills* [1892] AC 231, HL. For a summary of the different transactions under which money may be advanced upon the security of personal property, see Crossley Vaines, *Personal Property*, 5th edn, 449.

214 Whilst the essence of a pledge is a taking of possession (see para 25.02), it has been seen that a mortgagee may also go into possession (see para 25.20).

215 *Re Hall, ex p Close* (1884) 14 QBD 386; *Re Hardwick, ex p Hubbard* (1886) 17 QBD 690, CA.

216 *Re Townsend, ex p Parsons* (1886) 16 QBD 532. CA; *Dublin City Distillery Ltd v Doherty* [1914] AC 823, HL(I).

217 *Manchester, Sheffield and Lincolnshire Railway Co v North Central Wagon Co* (1888) 13 App Cas 554 at 567–8, HL.

It has already been seen that, whether a transaction amounts to a mortgage or a sale and re-hiring, is a matter of intention (see para 25.26). Within a few years, this attitude was used in a line of cases where an impecunious tenant (C) sought to raise money to pay his rent by the following device: there was held to be a chattel mortgage where C colluded with his landlord for the latter to levy distress for the rent on C's furniture, which was then sold to a third party (B), who let it to C under an hp agreement.[218] It was soon settled that similar circular transactions might amount to chattel mortgages.[219] However, the issues involved have arisen in a much more straight-forward manner in relation to directly financed transactions: if the customer (C) enters into a binding contract to purchase the goods from the dealer (A)[220] before the parties apply to the finance company (B), then the property in the goods may immediately pass from A to C; and there may subsequently be a colourable sale and re-hiring between B and C in order to re-imburse B for the price which he has advanced on behalf of C to A.[221]

More recently, the courts seem to have been less acute to find that a financed instalment credit transaction was a disguised chattel mortgage. In *Stoneleigh Finance Ltd v Phillips*,[222] a majority of the Court of Appeal held that B Ltd had obtained a good title to the vehicles for the following reasons: the refinancing transaction did not operate as a chattel mortgage, because there was no obligation on C Ltd to pay or repay any money to A Ltd[223] and B Ltd had no intention of lending money on the security of the documents.[224] Whilst it may be difficult to distinguish *Stoneleigh* from some of the earlier cases where the courts found a chattel mortgage, the distinction may be historical: perhaps pre-1960 suspicion of hp financing has been replaced by judicial familiarity with this modern financing. It has been argued[225] that in the last decade the above view has been circumvented by the creation by the courts of a new doctrine christened 'recharacterisation', allowing the courts for the purposes of some legislation to recognise that, for instance, a sale and re-hiring is really a secured loan registrable as a company charge (see para 25.28); and that such arrangements may in the future fall within the Law Commission's proposed definition of quasi-charges (see para 25.37).

**[25.28] Company borrowers**. Businesses frequently suffer from a shortage of working capital, and hence it is normal for them to raise as much money as they can on the security of their assets. Although the Bills of Sale Acts do not apply to incorporated companies,[226] Parliament has thought it important to keep a public

---

218 *Beckett v Tower Assets Co* [1891] 1 QB 638, CA.

219 *Maas v Pepper* [1905] AC 102, HL, where the facts were unusual.

220 Because his primary interest is to effect a 'sale', A may at an early stage give C a 'sold note' (see para 10.09). If that note was intended to evidence a contract of sale from A to C, with an option for C to take the goods on hp terms from B, then it might be contrary to *Scammell Ltd v Ouston* (set out at para 10.03) and also infringe s 59 of the CCA (set out at para 5.20).

221 *Polsky v S & A Services Ltd* [1951] 1 All ER 1062, CA; *North Central Wagon Co Ltd v Brailsford* [1962] 1 All ER 502.

222 [1965] 1 QB 537; [1965] 1 All ER 513, CA.

223 Davies LJ at 568. This echoes the reasoning of the HL in *Manchester Railway* case (see above, fn 215).

224 *Per* Davies and Russell LJJ at 572–3, 579–80; *contra* Sellers LJ at 564–66.

225 Berg [2003] JBL 205.

226 S 17 of the 1882 Act; and see *Re Standard Manufacturing Co* [1891] 1 Ch 627, CA.

record of these transactions so that persons lending money to registered companies have the means of ascertaining which of their borrower's assets are subject to mortgages or charges. The requirements originated in the Companies Act 1900 and were steadily elaborated in subsequent Companies Acts, reaching their ultimate implemented form in Part XII of the Companies Act 1985, even though substantial amendments have been on the statute book since 1989.[227] The essence of the 1985 scheme was this: although a **document** granting a mortgage or charge granted by an individual may fall within the Bills of Sale Act 1882 (see para 25.27), a similar **right** created by a company may fall within the Companies Act. The intended new scheme is not to be contained in the Companies Bill 2006, but instead to be embodied in regulations made under it. Following the recommendations of the Law Commission,[228] the scheme set out in the Regulations will be this:[229] the 1985 Act paper-based arrangements will be replaced with a new system for the electronic filing of fixed and floating charges (see para 25.02), usually at a Company Security Register. The lender will be responsible for the accuracy of the particulars which he voluntarily files against the company-debtor: that charge will be effective from the moment of registration against any subsequently appointed liquidator or administrator of the debtor-company;[230] and the lender may protect his position by filing in advance of making the loan. If the debtor-company becomes insolvent before registration, a charge will not be effective as against its liquidator or administrator. Priority as between competing charges will be governed by date of filing.[231]

In practice, an unpaid seller of goods to a company who has arranged a proprietary interest by way of security is most unlikely to register the price as such a secured debt, in which case the security will be avoided by the above provision.[232] Thus, the real issue is likely to be whether that secured interest is registrable (see para 25.29).

**[25.29] The ambit of registration**. For our purposes, the vital matter is normally the ambit of the registration provisions (see para 25.28), which do not necessarily encompass all charges within the common law notion (see para 25.02). Under the twentieth century scheme, it did not apply to absolute transfers, e.g. sales, or possessory security, whether granted by contract, e.g. pledges (see para 25.15, *et seq.*) or by law:[233] instead it refers exclusively to certain charges[234] granted by the debtor-company, which it listed; nor does it apply to simple title retention (see

---

227 By Pt IV of the Companies Act 1989, which was intended to insert new sections into the 1985 Act. It has never been implemented.

228 *Company Security Interests* (2005, Law Com. No. 296).

229 A draft of the Company Security Regulations 2006 is to be found set out in the above Law Commission Report, p 160, *et seq.*

230 Para 1.32. If the charged property is land, it can instead be registered at the Land Registry, which will automatically forward that registration to the Company Security Register.

231 Paras 1.28 and 1.33. Compare priorities in respect of the property of debtors outside this scheme: for choses in action, see para 7.19; and for choses in possession (goods), see para 19.11.

232 Instead, suppliers have relied on *Romalpa* clauses (see para 25.30).

233 E.g. liens: see *Re Hamlet International plc* [1998] CLY 3338; and para 1.23.

234 'Charge' includes mortgage: s 396(4); and used by itself the expression means a fixed (as opposed to a floating) charge.

para 25.29). Over the years, that list of charges became steadily more elaborate until the complete list to be found in s 396 of the 1985 Act, of which only three entries were within the scope of the present work:[235]

*Paragraph (c)* referred to 'a charge created or evidenced by an instrument which, if executed by an individual, would require registration as a bill of sale'. An absolute assignment of goods by a natural person falls within the Bills of Sale Act 1878 (see para 9.02); whereas an absolute assignment by a registered company fell outside s 396.[236] However, a written mortgage or charge granted by an individual comes within the 1882 Act; and one granted by a company was registrable under s 395, e.g. a *Romalpa* clause.[237]

*Paragraph (e)* spoke of 'a charge on book debts of the company'. This applied where book debts (see para 7.18) were charged;[238] but where a negotiable instrument, e.g. a post-dated cheque, was given to secure payment of any book debt, its deposit to secure an advance to the company was not for the purposes of s 396 to be treated as a charge on those book debts.[239] It had no counterpart in the Bills of Sale Acts, which do not apply to choses in action (see above). Its primary significance for us was in relation to tracing the proceeds of sale (see para 27.14) under a *Romalpa* clause.[237]

*Paragraph (f)* listed 'a floating charge on the company's undertaking or property'.[240] It had no counterpart in the Bills of Sale Act 1882 (s 17: see para 25.28); but it was highly relevant to *Romalpa* clauses.[237]

Under the Regulations implementing the new scheme (see para 25.28), it will be applicable where a debtor-company grants (reg 2(1)):

(1) Any 'charge', which includes a mortgage (reg 2(3)). The above old scheme under s 396 was considered by the Commission to be outdated; and, under their new scheme, all charges would be registrable unless specifically exempted.

(2) Any 'pledge', which includes contractual liens (reg 42), but not liens which arise by operation of law (reg 4(1)(a)).

(3) Any sale (or agreement to sell: reg 2(3)) of 'receivables', which expression means 'monetary obligations, whether or not earned by performance, arising from—(a) the supply of goods or services (other than insurance services)'.[241]

However, the Commission has reserved for further consideration the following issues significant for this work:

---

235 See further, Macleod, *Consumer Sales Law*, 1st edn, para 25.29.

236 *Stoneleigh Finance Ltd v Phillips* (see para 25.27).

237 See para 25.30, *et seq.*

238 *Smith v Bridgend CBC* [2002] 1 AC 336, HL, at para 41. Distinguish sums held in trust: see para 19.22; ECGD policies (*Paul and Frank Ltd v Discount Bank (Overseas) Ltd* [1967] Ch 348); attempts to charge a book debt to the debtor (*Re Charge Card Services Ltd* (on another point set out at para 2.27)); and set-offs (see [1988] JBL at 136, 225–8, 198).

239 S 396(2)). *Contra* where given by way of conditional payment: *Dawson v Isle* [1906] Ch 633.

240 As to floating charges, see generally, para 19.14. The charge may be over the whole or any part of the property: *Re Bond Worth Ltd* (see out at para 25.34).

241 E.g. the types of obligations companies sell to factors (see para 2.22). It does not apply to rent or payments under mortgage or credit card loans; nor to the various types of assigned listed in reg 4(1).

(A) Title retention devices, such as finance leases, hp and conditional sale agreements (para 1.29). This is considered later (see para 25.37).

(B) Charges granted by individual debtors, a matter which currently falls within the Bills of Sale Acts (see para 25.26) and is considered later (see para 25.37).

## Title reservation

**[25.30] Introduction**. As has already been pointed out (see para 25.01), with regard to proprietary rights to secure payment, English law has been accustomed to distinguish between those rights **granted** to a lender and those rights **reserved** by a supplier. Certainly, where common law rights in property were granted by an individual to a lender, the transaction was within the Bills of Sale Act 1882;[242] whereas common law rights reserved by a supplier were not, e.g. a bf conditional sale, hp or simple hiring agreement (see paras 1.14; 1.21; 25.27). However, the position was less clear where equitable rights were reserved: because equitable ownership in one person presupposes legal ownership in another, it might be presumed that the property in the goods has passed (as to proprietary interests, see generally, para 19.03); and so the transaction might be construed as a grant back of the equitable rights. The matter arose where suppliers of goods to businesses sought to obtain security for payment in respect of the goods supplied by taking or retaining an interest in those goods, products into which they were turned,[243] or proceeds of subsale.[244] In *Aluminium Industry Vaasen BV v Romalpa Aluminium Ltd*:[245]

> A manufacturer, B Ltd, bought from S some aluminium foil under a Dutch standard-form contract which provided:[246] (1) the ownership of the foil was only to pass from S to B when all debts between them had been settled; (2) until then, B agreed that the ownership of all products made with any of the foil should be transferred to S; (3) until then, insofar as B sold such products, the proceeds to be held for S. B became insolvent at a time when there were still debts owing to S. In an action between S and B's receiver, the Court of Appeal held—
>
> (a) By virtue of his property in the goods, S as (admitted) bailor was entitled to both the unworked and worked foil now in the possession of the receiver;[247] and
>
> (b) Insofar as B had sold such goods, he was accountable to S for the proceeds of sale, by virtue of their fiduciary relationship as agents and bailees.

---

242 Goode, *Legal Problems of Credit and Security*, 3rd edn, para 1.04; and generally, para 25.27.

243 For alteration, accession and intermixture, see generally Crossley Vaines, *Personal Property*, 5th edn, 19; *per* Staughton J in *Hendy Lennox Ltd v Graham Puttick Ltd* [1984] 2 All ER 152 at 159; Whittaker (1984) 100 LQR 25; and para 19.05.

244 On resale, a good title may be obtained under the SGA, s 25(1): set out at para 21.43.

245 [1976] 2 All ER 552; [1976] 1 WLR 676, CA. See generally (1976) 39 MLR 587; Eastway (1978) 128 NLJ 439; Atiyah *Sale of Goods*, 10th edn, 473–4; Smith, *Property Problems in Sale*, 126, *et seq.*; Parris, *Retention of Title on the Sale of Goods*, Chap 7; Goode, *Commercial Law*, 3rd edn, 720.

246 The standard terms were in Dutch. It was held that those terms were incorporated in this transaction and that Dutch law applied; but, there being no evidence to the contrary, it was assumed that Dutch law was the same as English law: see para 18.13.

247 For the bailment aspect of conditional sales, see para 1.14; and for tracing the price, see paras 27.13–14. It has been argued that B could not have been a bailee: Atiyah, *ibid*, 475; Williams (1991) 12 BCC at 57. But the real issue seems to have been whether he was a fiduciary bailee: McMeel [2003] LMCLQ 169 at 199.

Of course, the right to trace the proceeds depends on the finding of a fiduciary relationship (see para 27.14); and the case has been criticised for assuming that there will be a fiduciary relationship where a bailment exists, which will not necessarily be the case.[248] Moreover, as Mocatta J expressly recognised at first instance,[249] the effect of the decision was to by-pass the statutory system for the registration of charges on a company's property (see para 25.28); but the registration provisions were not mentioned by the Court of Appeal because it was notionally applying Dutch law and their effect left to be worked out in subsequent cases (see para 25.31). The decision has also been criticised for its artificiality: it resulted in S being entitled to all the value of the worked foil and proceeds, which will necessarily include the value added by B.[250]

The decision had the following practical result in the event of a company's (B's) insolvency: without such a clause, its bankers, who would normally have taken a first registered floating charge over its bank account and other property to secure its overdraft and therefore rank as a (prior) secured creditor; with such a clause, its bankers would be postponed to B's ordinary trade suppliers (S), even after delivery.[251] In practice, this proved far more useful to the suppliers of equipment than of raw materials or stock-in-trade.[252] In a consumer supply contract, a *Romalpa* clause may be unfair.[253]

**[25.31]** *Romalpa* **clauses at common law.**[254] The almost immediate popularity of what came to be called '*Romalpa* clauses' (see para 25.30) soon forced the courts to look with considerable care at the **incorporation** of such terms (see para 18.04, *et seq.*), their **interpretation** and the **effect** on them of the chattel mortgage legislation. In conducting this enquiry, it is convenient to distinguish the three major stages through which goods supplied to a manufacturer might pass, though it must be borne in mind that in this area so much turns on the precise wording of the *Romalpa* clause and of the facts in issue.[255]

1.  *The goods supplied.* In the *Romalpa* case itself, the court accepted almost without argument that the reservation of title escaped the chattel mortgage legislation (see paras 25.27–28). In *Clough Mills Ltd v Martin*,[256] the Court of Appeal explained how the chattel mortgage legislation was avoided as follows: the SGA allows for a reservation of property notwithstanding delivery (see para

---

248  Bridge, *Sale of Goods*, 109–10.
249  [1976] 2 All ER at 557; [1976] 1 WLR at 682–3. A similar result may be obtainable by supplying on sale or return: see para 20.23. See also Pollard [1988] JBL at 128–9.
250  Atiyah, *Op. cit.*, 473.
251  For enforcement, see *Lipe v Leyland Daf Ltd* [1993] CLY 2356, CA. Compare the rights of a supplier who has retained possession: see para 24.02.
252  Bridge [1992] JBL at 20. For discussion of the feasibility of such registrations, see Hicks [1992] JBL at 413–4.
253  OFT, *Unfair Contract Terms Bulletin No. 5*, p 121; *No 20*, case 19; and see generally, para 11.13, *et seq.*
254  See generally Parris, *Retention of Title on the Sale of Goods*; Goode, *Proprietary Rights and Insolvency in Sale Transactions*, Chap V; Spanier [1989] JBL 220; McCormack, *Reservation of Title*, 2nd edn; Davies, *Retention of Title Clauses* (1991); *Benjamin's Sale of Goods*, 6th edn, para 5.141, *et seq.*; Bridge, *Sale of Goods*, 104–10.
255  E.g. *Chaigley Farms Ltd v Crawford Kaye & Grayshire Ltd* [1997] CLY 4478.
256  [1984] 3 All ER 982; [1985] 1 WLR 111, CA. See Farrer and Chai [1985] JBL at 163–4; Goodhart 49 MLR 96; Webb [2000] JBL at 529–30.

20.06), a right of recaption (see para 24.23) and a right of disposal;[257] and the buyer was in no position to confer a valid charge on anyone.[258] Where a supplier/bailor validly retains legal title in the goods supplied, the goods are *prima facie* saved from the buyer's insolvency,[259] even where that retention is to support an 'all monies clause'.[260] On the other hand, notwithstanding the clause reserving the property in the goods, that property may pass to the buyer, as where the goods have become fixtures (see para 25.23) or cease to be identifiable;[261] or the buyer may pass a good title to a bfp under an exception to the *nemo dat* rule (see Chap 21). If so, then the unpaid seller must look to the products and proceeds.

2.  *Products* (see para 25.32).

3.  *Proceeds* (see para 25.33).

**[25.32]** *Romalpa* **clauses: products**. Where the goods supplied remain identifiable even after undergoing the buyer's manufacturing process,[262] the property in them may remain in the supplier, as where the goods supplied are merely worked, e.g. the worked foil in the *Romalpa* case, or **reversibly** attached to other goods owned by the buyer.[263] On the other hand, where the supplier's interest is expressed to extend to the products into which the goods are turned, this process may itself deprive the supplier of the property in the goods, as where the goods supplied are used or altered in the manufacturing process.[264] Thus, in *Re Peachdart Ltd*[265] this is because the property in the newly created goods (handbags) arises in the buyer, who then grants rights in that property to the seller of the original goods (leather). This case may be distinguished from *Hendry Lennox*[263] in that here the worked leather had been **irreversibly** altered; and the same principle has been applied to goods supplied and fitted by a repairer, which will usually become part of the repaired goods by *accession*.[266] Moreover, it would seem that the *Peachdart* rule has no application where the parties intend to be co-owners of goods.[267] As ever, everything turns on the precise drafting of the *Romalpa* clause and the circumstances of the case.

---

257 As to whether such a clause may be effective as a reservation of a right of disposal (see para 20.28) even though only included in a post-contract delivery note, see Bradgate [1988] JBL 477.

258 E.g. the unworked foil in the *Romalpa* case; the *Clough Mills* case (yarn remained unused and identifiable); *Re Peachdart Ltd* (see para 25.32; unworked leather).

259 For the rule that goods not owned by an insolvent normally escape his insolvency, see para 19.15.

260 *Armour v Thyssen*: set out at para 20.28.

261 For the reason explained at para 25.30. E.g. *Borden (UK) Ltd v Scottish Timber Products Ltd* [1981] Ch 25, CA (see para 27.13; and Macleod, *Consumer Sales Law*, 1st edn, para 25.31). Would priorities be subject to the rule in *Dearle v Hall* (set out at para 7.19)? For an argument that there might be an equitable tenancy in common, see Ulph [1996] JBL at 501–2.

262 *A fortiori* where the buyer is a wholesaler or importer who does not do anything to destroy the identify of the goods, e.g. *Re Interview Ltd* [1974] Ir 382.

263 *Hendy Lennox Ltd v Grahame Puttick Ltd* [1984] 2 All ER 152; and see Hicks [1993] JBL 485.

264 E.g. *Borden (UK) Ltd v Scottish Timber Products Ltd* [1981] Ch 25, CA; and see para 25.31.

265 [1984] Ch 131; discussed by Whittaker in (1984) 100 LQR at 38–41.

266 *Specialist Plant Services Ltd v Braithwaite Ltd* [1987] CLY 369, CA. This will amount to an act of conversion (see para 19.05).

267 E.g. *Re Stapleton Fletcher Ltd* (set out at para 20.05A); and as to co-owners, see para 20.22A.

**[25.33]** *Romalpa* **clauses: proceeds**. As a subsale by the buyer might in any event transfer either the property in the goods or products to a sub-buyer under the *nemo dat* rule,[268] or a good title to him under s 9 of the FA,[269] the *Romalpa* clause will normally attempt instead to confer on the original supplier rights in the proceeds of the sub-sale.[270] This will require proof of a fiduciary relationship: the mere reservation of the property in the proceeds (see para 25.31) will not create such a fiduciary relationship;[268] nor will a bailment necessarily do so.[268] A fiduciary relationship may be created expressly by the clause, as in the *Romalpa* case (set out at para 25.30); but it is unlikely that it will be implied.[271] Even where such a fiduciary relationship is created, it is unlikely to be over the entire proceeds of sale (an absolute interest), because it would be unlikely that the buyer would want to give his seller the right to the value which he has added to the product, e.g. by manufacture; instead, it is more likely to be construed as granting the unpaid seller just a floating charge over the proceeds of sale to the extent of his price. Such an interest by way of security will be registrable (see para 25.34). Take, for instance, the processed meat in *Mills and Lawrence v Harris (Wholesale Meat) Ltd* (set out at para 21.51): although the property in the meat had never passed from A to B, by the time it had been processed by C it had lost its identity and the property was thereupon vested in C (at 281F); and, by reason of s 9 of the FA, C had a good title to the meat as against A (at 281G). His Lordship held that the price of this processed meat must be treated as paid by C to B and then be subject at common law to A's reservation of title clause; but that this transaction was void for want of registration as amounting to a charge on the book debts of the buyer (see para 27.14).

**[25.34]** **Romalpa clauses as floating charges**.[272] Floating charges were invented to enable a borrowing company to grant security over the shifting assets, e.g. its trading stock of goods or receivables (trade debts), of its business by floating over them until the creditor needed to realise (crystallise) his security. Crystallisation operates as an equitable assignment to the chargee (see para 25.25). Whilst it is not possible for an individual to grant a floating charge,[273] an equitable floating charge over the assets of a registered company used to require registration by reason of s 396(1)(f) of the Companies Act 1985 (see para 25.29), which provision was considered in *Re Bond Worth Ltd*.[274] In a masterly judgment, Slade J held as follows:

---

268 E.g. *Hendy* case (see para 25.32).
269 E.g. *Four Point Garage Ltd v Carter* [1985] 3 All ER 12 (goods delivered direct to sub-buyer). Unless the sub-buyer has knowledge of the *Romalpa* clause: *Re Interview Ltd* [1974] IR Rep 382; and see para 21.49.
270 E.g. *Borden's* case [1981] Ch 25, CA; *Re Bond Worth Ltd* (see para 25.34); *Re Peachdart Ltd* (see para 25.32); *Hendy* case (see para 25.32).
271 See Benjamin's *Sale of Goods*, 6th edn, para 5.152.
272 See paras 25.02; 25.25; and generally Goode, *Commercial Law*, 3rd edn, Chap 25; Gower, *Company Law*, 6th edn, 362, *et seq.*; Oditah, *Accounts Receivable*, 110 *et seq.*
273 Bills of Sale Act 1882, s 17 (see para 25.28); but the charge may be void under s 344 of the IA 1986 (see para 19.24).
274 [1980] Ch 228; [1979] 3 All ER 919; discussed by Guest (1979) 95 LQR 477 and Parris, *Retention of Title on the Sale of Goods*, 113–23.

(1) The property and risk in the fibre passed to the manufacturer on delivery,[275] subject to the seller's (S) equitable interest, which amounted to a charge over the fibre, product or proceeds: the buyer had an equity of redemption.[276]

(2) This equitable charge was created by way of an implied grant back to S after the property in the goods had passed to the manufacturer under the sale;[277] and not by S reserving an interest out of the property passing.[278] Further, as the manufacturer had implied permission to use the fibre in his production, the charge must be a floating one rather than specific.

(3) S had therefore created a floating charge which was void for want of registration, the *Romalpa* case (set out at para 25.30) being distinguishable on all the following grounds: it was decided *per incuriam*; it involved an express reservation of property; the goods and proceeds remained identifiable; it gave rise to a fiduciary relationship generating a duty to account (see para 27.14); and, in the last resort, the effect of a reservation of title clause was always a matter of construction (see para 25.31).

## The future

**[25.35] Introduction**. It has already been seen that the essence of a mortgage is the equity of redemption (see para 25.20): this will distinguish mortgages of all types of property on the one hand, from conditional sales and hp on the other.[279] Whilst a first step would be to assimilate hp to conditional sales (see para 1.26), a second would be to establish a clear relationship between conditional sales and chattel mortgages.[280] With regard to individual debtors, there has already been demonstrated the difficulty of deciding whether a transaction falls within the Bills of Sale Acts; and in any event those Acts were designed to be difficult to operate (see paras 25.26–7). As to company debtors, a new scheme is being promulgated (see para 25.28–9).

**[25.36] The Crowther Report**.[281] Way back in 1971, that Report recommended the repeal of 'all existing legislation affecting the general law of lending and security in

---

275 Compare the position with regard to a purchase on mortgage of realty: see para 25.22. Personalty has been distinguished on the grounds that, at the time of its creation, the charge is of future property and is therefore registrable: Hicks [1992] JBL 398, at 405–9.

276 Distinguishing *Re George Inglefield Ltd* [1933] Ch 1, CA. Compare *Re Goldcorp Exchange Ltd* (see para 20.22 (the PC on allocated claimants).

277 It has been argued that this charging-back analysis has been overruled by a subsequent HL case on real property mortgages, which allows the seller to **grant** an equity of redemption: Gregory (1990) 106 LQR 550; Hicks [1992] JBL 398. But see Atiyah, *Sale of Goods*, 10th edn, 478, fn 130.

278 *Contra* reserving legal title: *McEntire v Crossley Bros* (set out at para 1.14); and *Clough Mills Ltd v Martin* (see para 25.31). See the criticism by Parris, *Op. cit.*, 72–82, 121–2; Gregory (1990) 106 LQR 550; and Ulph [1996] JBL 482 at 499–501.

279 The conditional buyer has no equity of redemption: see para 1 14. Nor does the hirer under an hp agreement: see para 24.22.

280 The US Uniform Commercial Code treats all conditional sales as subject to the chattel mortgage legislation rather than the sales legislation (Arts 2–102, 9–102; see further below). And see the Crowther Report, para 5.3.1.

281 See generally, paras 5.03–4. As to whether the law should allow security to stay outside the rules of insolvency, see para 19.12.

personal property' and its replacement by a Lending and Security Act,[282] which should be entirely separate from the then proposed statute (now enacted in the CCA 1974) to regulate consumer credit.[283] Faced with two alternative methods of achieving this, Crowther unhesitatingly recommended that the Act be drafted on the model of Art 9 of the Uniform Commercial Code.[284] As to what form the loan aspect of the transaction should take, Crowther recommended complete freedom of contract and the minimum of formality for non-consumer transactions (paras 5.2.15–16). As to the security aspect, Crowther envisaged the proposed Lending and Security Act applying to all security interests in pure personalty and fixtures, whether by way of hp or conditional sale,[285] finance leases, mortgages and charges of personalty, pledges and outright sales of accounts receivable (para 5.3.1). Its proposals extended to both the rights of the debtor and creditor *inter se* (para 5.6) and conflicts between the secured party and third parties, including a register of security interests (para 5.7). However, the Government, whilst accepting that there were aspects of the then existing law in this field (not substantially changed since) which cause difficulty, said they did 'not have sufficient evidence either of a need for such a major recasting of existing law on new principles or of general support for the particular solution proposed by the Committee'.[286] Nevertheless, the demand for reform continued.[287] The trouble is, there are conflicting opinions as to how to reconcile the interests of trade suppliers and the buyer's other creditors, e.g. bankers (see para 25.30): supporters of trade creditors argue for the unfettered recognition of *Romalpa* clauses;[288] whereas supporters of the banks argue for the fairness of making such clauses subject to the registration provisions.[289] Bearing in mind the practical unlikelihood of registration of *Romalpa* clauses by unpaid suppliers (see para 25.30), this debate is likely to settle the relative priority of suppliers and bankers.

**[25.37] The Law Commission Report.** In 2001, the terms of reference to the Law Commission requested that it look not only at the reform of company charges, but also at 'quasi-security' interests, such as conditional sales, title retention devices, hp agreements and finance leases. In 2002, the Law Commission supported a version of the *Crowther* proposal (see para 25.37) in their *Registration of Security Interests*.[290] However, after the Government has indicated that it was likely to introduce a Bill to

---

282 Para 5.3.4. The provisions which should be repealed are more particularly listed in para 5.3.7.

283 Para 5.2.18. See para 5.05.

284 Paras 1.3.9 and 5.5.6. For technical aspects of the proposed system, see Appendix III of the Report.

285 This would include taking conditional sales outside Pt V of the SGA (as to which see para 24.03 *et seq.*): Crowther Report, paras 5.2.3 and 19.

286 Reform of the Law on Consumer Credit (1973, Cmnd. 5427) para 14. But see the remarks of Lords Edmund Davies and Fraser in *Moorgate Mercantile Co Ltd v Twitchings* (set out at para 21.17) at 660–1 and 665e.

287 See Goode [1984] JBL 79; (1984) 100 LQR 234; Insolvency Law Review Committee (1982, Cmnd. 8558) paras 1623, 1639; Diamond, *A Review of Security Interests in Property* (DTI, 1989). A basis for a register of security interests might be provided by HPI: as to which, see para 21.01.

288 E.g. the draft Council of Europe Convention: see Latham [1983] JBL 81.

289 Atiyah, *Sale of Goods*, 10th edn, 478.

290 *Registration of Security Interests: Company Charges and Property other than Land* (2002, Law Com CP 164), Pts VI–XI. See also Law Com CP No. 176, paras 270–136.

amend only Company law, in its 2005 Report[291] the Law Commission reported only on company charges (see para 25.28-9), reserving for further work the following fields (para 1.45):

1. *Charges over the goods of individuals.* These fall within the Bills of Sale Act 1882 (see para 25.25). Whilst most observers agree that reform is needed (para 1.48), the Law Commission pointed to the advantages flowing from the fact that the security granted must be listed;[292] and it recommended that the DTI should examine the question of replacing the 1882 Act (see para 25.26) with a more efficient and effective scheme (para 1.53).

2. *Title retention devices.* These are practically possible over items which have unique serial numbers, e.g. motor vehicles. The Law Commission identified three critical issues:

   (a) *The public notice question*; that is, whether title retention devices and quasi-securities should be registrable, as they perform a similar economic function to charges (para 1.62).

   (b) *Default remedies* (para 1.63); that is, whether the debtor should have an equity of redemption like a chargee (see para 25.20), or the lender should keep any surplus from sale as with quasi-securities (see para 24.22).

   (c) *Protection of subsequent buyers and lenders*; that is, whether to amend the relevant exceptions to the *nemo dat* rule.[293] The Law Commission recommended that this should be considered as part of their Ninth Programme of law reform.[294]

3. *Security over personal property.* The issue is whether English law should have a provision setting out the law on the creation of security interests based on the overseas common law models (see para 25.36). The Law Commission has reserved its opinion (para 1.70).

---

291 *Company Security Interests* (2005, Law Com 296).

292 It prohibits the granting of floating charges and charges over after-acquired property (para 1.50); and it protects the borrower against repossession (para 1.51) in those circumstances when he cannot rely on the hp protected goods rule (see para 24.35).

293 In respect of buyers in possession (see para 21.43) and Pt III titles (see para 21.55).

294 Para 1.66. See para 21.60.

# PART 7

# DISCHARGE, ENFORCEMENT
# AND REMEDIES

# CHAPTER 26

# DISCHARGE OF CONTRACTUAL OBLIGATIONS

This Chapter is concerned with an examination of the ways in which contractual obligations may be discharged. Leaving aside such matters as discharge by frustration or illegality and rescission *ab initio* for mistake (as to frustration, see para 22.14, *et seq.*; as to illegality, see paras 10.19 and 22.14; and as to rescission *ab initio* for mistake, see paras 17.11 and 22.10), the subject may be divided on the basis of whether or not the discharge takes place in accordance with the terms of the contract.

## DISCHARGE IN ACCORDANCE WITH THE CONTRACT

In considering the discharge of contractual obligations in accordance with the contract, a distinction may be drawn as to whether that discharge is brought about by (a) performance, or (b) the happening of some other event.

### Discharge by performance[1]

**[26.01]** Performance by A of a contractual obligation owed to B may be important for two reasons: first, non-performance by A may prevent A enforcing B's promises to him; and second, performance will discharge A's obligations to B.

1. *Enforcement of B's obligations.* When sued by A, B may set up A's failure to perform as a defence; and the general rule is that A cannot succeed unless he can show that he has performed his side of the bargain to the letter (see para 26.02). This may be because performance by A is a condition precedent either to the existence of the contract or to performance by B (see para 15.21): if precedent to contract, A is not bound to perform, though neither party is bound unless he does so; but, if precedent merely to performance, there is a binding contract. In the latter case, it may be that A cannot enforce B's performance until he has performed his own side of the bargain;[2] or that the promises on each side are concurrent, e.g. s 28 of the SGA (set out at 23.16). However, it would seem that, notwithstanding the duty to mitigate (see para 27.45), A may be able to perform his promises against the wishes of B and then enforce B's obligations, e.g. to pay the price[3] or rent.[4] For the relationship of the duty to mitigate and the right of rescission, see para 26.16.

---

1   See generally Treitel, *Law of Contract*, 11th edn, Chap 18.
2   E.g. *Trans Trust SPRL v Danubian Trading Co Ltd* (see para 27.35). Cf. *State Trading Corpn of India v Golodetz* [1989] 2 Lloyd's Rep 277, CA.
3   *White and Carter (Councils) Ltd v McGregor* [1962] AC 431, HL(S) (action for price); discussed by Treitel, *Op. cit.*, 1015–19 (see esp. fn 11).
4   *The Odenfeld* [1978] 2 Lloyd's Rep 357 (charterparty—action for agreed hire).

2. *Discharge of A's obligations.* Generally speaking,[5] A will only be discharged by exact performance of his obligations;[6] and, if A's obligation is the payment of money, it is normally insufficient to pay a lesser sum (see para 26.18). If the contract gives A discretion as to the mode of performance, e.g. as to place of delivery, or time or amount of payment, he is entitled to perform in the manner least beneficial to B;[7] and, in giving up that discretion, A gives further consideration to support another promise.[8] The remedies available to B where A is in breach have already been discussed (see para 11.04, *et seq.*). What is A to do if B announces in advance that he **may** not be able to render due performance?[9]

**[26.02] Exact performance.** The common law normally takes an extremely strict view of contractual promises.[10] For instance, unless a supply contract is divisible (see para 23.24), it usually[11] insists that performance be exact, even if allowing for alternative methods of performance (see para 26.01). This principle may work particular hardship where A has partly performed his obligations under an 'entire contract'; that is, one where performance by A of **all** his obligations is a condition precedent to performance by B of **any** of his obligations. The effect may be unjustly to enrich B:[12] A cannot claim under the contract because he has not fully performed the condition;[13] nor may he claim in quasi-contract where B has no choice whether to accept/retain the benefit conferred.[14] Of course, sometimes contracts for the supply of goods will not give rise to such problems, as with deliveries of the wrong quantity or quality (see Chap 13), where B may either reject the goods delivered or is liable because he voluntarily accepted them.[15] However, where such escape is not possible, the common law has sometimes sought to avoid injustice by accepting a lower standard than exact performance and allowing A to sue B for breach of contract notwithstanding his own non-performance:

(1)  Where B has wrongfully[16] prevented A from completing performance.[17]

---

5   Alternatively, he may be discharged by a condition subsequent: see para 1.11.

6   As to exact performance, see para 26.02. In the case of a regulated agreement, the debtor or hirer may be entitled to a written confirmation ('termination statement') that he has discharged his indebtedness under the agreement: see para 26.04.

7   *The World Navigator* [1991] 2 Lloyd's Rep 23, CA.

8   May this be the explanation of *Williams v Roffey Bros & Nicholls (Contractors) Ltd* [1990] 1 All ER 512, CA?

9   B's statement being insufficiently unequivocal to amount to an anticipatory breach (see para 26.15): see Goode (1983) 3 Legal Studies 283 at 289–90.

10  E.g. *Arcos Ltd v Ronassen & Son Ltd* (set out at para 13.12). Cf. SGA, s 31(1): see para 23.24.

11  Although it has been suggested that in the case of an hp contract the obligations of hiring and option may sometimes be treated separately: see Goode, *HP Law and Practice*, 2nd edn, 328.

12  *Sumpter v Hedges* (below; the building. See McFarlane and Stevens (2002) 118 LQR 569). But see the recommendations of the Law Commission, *Pecuniary Restitution on Breach of Contract* (1983, Law Com No. 121, discussed by Burrows (1984) 47 MLR 76), which perhaps surprisingly excluded sales from its recommendations. What of other contracts for the supply of goods?

13  *Bolton v Mahadeva* [1972] 2 All ER 1322, CA (central heating installation).

14  *Forman & Co Pty Ltd v SS Liddesdale* [1900] AC 190, PC.

15  *Sumpter v Hedges* [1898] 1 QB 673, CA (building contract, materials left on site).

16  See Goode, *Payment Obligations in Commercial and Financial Transactions*, 40. *Contra* if B is entitled to prevent A performing, as where A has already repudiated the contract: *British and Bennington Ltd v Northwestern Cachar Tea Co Ltd* (set out at para 23.05).

17  Contrast the situation where A may complete performance against the wishes of B: see para 26.01.

(2) Where the contract provides for performance by B before performance by A, as where B sells on credit terms to A (see para 23.22).

(3) Where there are in fact a number of separate contracts, or where a single contract (or obligation) is divisible (see para 23.24). The effect of deciding that a particular obligation is divisible is that A may sue B for breach of contract notwithstanding his own non-performance of the divisible obligation, but is liable to a counter-claim for damages for non-performance.[18]

(4) Where B is only entitled to damages in respect of A's breach of contract (see para 11.03). In these circumstances, A may sue B for his non-performance, subject to a counter-claim for damages. The only real question is how to fit the doctrine of substantial performance into this scheme[19] and whether it applies to sales (see para 11.04).

(5) Where A has committed such a breach as would entitle B to rescind, but B elects to affirm and claim damages, as where a buyer voluntarily accepts goods of a different quality. For voluntary and statutory elections, see paras 26.17 and 29.04.

## Discharge by stipulated event

[26.03] The contract may provide for the discharge of one or both parties on the happening of some event other than performance.[20] Sometimes, that event is the unilateral choice of one of the parties, whether supplier[20] or transferee of the goods[21] or services;[22] and in a consumer supply, it should be remembered that, if there is no balance between the rights and duties of the two parties, the contract may be unfair (see para 11.14),[23] as may a clause which does not recognise the debtor's right to discharge by early payment under s 94 (see para 26.19A).[24] On other occasions, the event may be one outside the control of either party: an important example is to be found in the context of instalment credit contracts (see para 1.03), where it is common to find stipulated events upon the happening of which one or both parties are to be discharged from some or all of their contractual obligations.[25] Termination by transferee and by other stipulated event are considered separately below (paras 26.04–10).

---

18   It may be more accurate to speak of divisible obligations rather than divisible contracts, for one contract may contain both divisible and entire obligations: Treitel, *Law of Contract*, 11th edn, 785.

19   As to which, see Treitel, *Op. cit.*, 787; Beck (1975) 38 MLR 413.

20   E.g. SGA, s 48(4) provides that a contract of sale is discharged where the seller exercises an express power of sale: see para 27.08.

21   E.g. where a contract for the supply of goods envisages that the transferee may not complete a contract of purchase but instead return the goods, as with sale or return (see para 20.23) or hp (see para 1.22).

22   E.g. a running-account credit contract will normally allow the consumer to close the account unilaterally at any time by paying off the outstanding amount.

23   OFT, *Bulletin No. 12*, case 13, Grey Term (f): see para 11.16.

24   [2005] *UTCC Bulletin J/S, Forthright Finance*.

25   See para 26.08. As to revival and reinstatement of instalment credit agreements, see Goode, *HP Law & Practice*, 2nd edn, 346; and *St Margaret's Trust Ltd v Byrne* [1976] CLY 1342, CA.

In instalment contracts, it should be noted that the common law produces a different measure of damages according to the circumstances of termination (see para 27.37).

## Termination by the transferee (consumer)

[26.04] At common law, it was quite possible for a bailee under an instalment credit contract to be given the right to terminate or rescind the agreement at any time before all the instalments have been paid, even where the supplier was not in breach of the agreement. However, it was only in hp and simple hiring that the common law required that the bailee have a right to terminate without cause,[26] so that it was hardly ever available in other such cases.[27] Even in the context of hp and simple hiring, the right to terminate was almost always subject to some restrictions: sometimes these were merely designed to ensure that the owner recovered the goods, e.g. a requirement that the hirer give notice or return the goods to the supplier; but at other times the restrictions were intended to ensure that the owner did not make a loss on the transaction,[28] or to discourage the hirer from exercising his option to terminate,[29] or even primarily to increase the hirer's liability on a 'snatch-back' (see para 26.08).

With regard to contractual limitations on the right of the bailee to terminate a conditional sale or hp agreement without cause, the HPA restrictions were substantially re-enacted in the CCA with an extension to simple hiring agreements. They are threefold:[30]

1. *Agency.* Section 102(1) facilitates the exercise by the debtor or hirer under a regulated agreement of any common law right of 'rescission' (see paras 26.11–16) by deeming certain persons to be the agent of the creditor or owner for the purposes of receiving notice of that 'rescission' (see para 10.25). However, s 102(2) makes it clear that this is without prejudice to the exercise of any statutory right of cancellation (see para 10.29) or termination (see below).

2. *Termination.* The Act includes statutory rights of termination by the debtor (see para 26.05) or hirer (see para 26.07), which are in addition to any right of termination which may exist on general principles, e.g. under the terms of the agreement (see para 26.03), or by reason of breach by the creditor or owner (see para 26.15).

3. *Termination statements.* Except in the case of non-commercial agreements (see para 5.18), a debtor or hirer who has 'discharged his indebtedness' under a regulated agreement is entitled on written request[31] under s 103 on one

---

26   This is the essence of any bailment (see para 1.17); but its effect depends on whether or not the hiring is periodic (as to which, see para 7.18).

27   For statutory intervention in respect of pyramid selling, see para 1.09.

28   See the 'minimum payment clauses' discussed in Macleod, *Consumer Sales Law*, 1st edn, para 11.09; and para 27.50.

29   The transaction being viewed essentially as a secured loan of the price rather than a sale.

30   These rights of the debtor or hirer may not be ousted by the terms of the agreement: CCA, s 173(1), as to which, see para 18.11.

31   S 103 actually says by serving 'a notice'; and s 189(1) defines 'notice' as a 'written notice'.

occasion only to a statement from the creditor or owner ('trader') to that effect (s 103(1), (3) and (4)). Where the trader disputes that the indebtedness has been discharged, he must say so (s 103(2)): otherwise he is bound by the customer's version or his written confirmation.[32]

**[26.05] Termination of conditional sale or hp agreement.** Sections 99–100 of the CCA grant the debtor under a regulated conditional sale or hp agreement[33] an indefeasible[34] statutory right to terminate the agreement without cause. The key provision is s 99(1), which stipulates that:

'At any time before the final payment by the debtor under a regulated hire purchase or regulated conditional sale agreement falls due, the debtor shall be entitled to terminate the agreement by giving notice to any person entitled or authorised to receive the sums payable under the agreement.'

This statutory right to terminate by giving notice[35] lasts only whilst the agreement exists[36] and until the final payment 'falls due',[37] which moment may probably be advanced by the operation of any accelerated payments clause.[38] Moreover, its exercise is 'not to affect any liability under the agreement which has accrued before the termination' (s 99(2)): so the creditor is entitled after such termination to recover arrears of instalments[39] and damages for previous breaches, e.g. for failure to take reasonable care of the goods (see s 100(4); and para 27.24). The Act further provides that (s 100(5)):

'Where the debtor, on the termination of the agreement, wrongfully retains possession of goods to which the agreement relates, then, in any action brought by the creditor to recover possession of the goods from the debtor, the court, unless it is satisfied that having regard to the circumstances it would not be just to do so, shall order the goods to be delivered to the creditor without giving the debtor an option to pay the value of the goods.'

This s 99 right may be compared with all the following: the common law right to terminate, which may be exercised in accordance with s 102 (see para 26.04); the powers which a court will ordinarily have to order specific delivery in an action in tort (see para 24.26), or where the debtor is in breach (see para 24.43). As to the effect of ss 99–100, see para 26.06. Presumably, in respect of a non-cancellable agreement,

---

32 S 172(2). Delay in giving a termination statement beyond one month is an offence (s 103(5)); as to offences, see further, para 28.07, *et seq.*

33 For the definitions of regulated conditional sales and hp agreements, see respectively, paras 1.16 and 1.24.

34 S 173(1): set out at para 18.11. It seems to follow that the creditor cannot make this right subject to any conditions, e.g. such as the debtor make good any breach, the debtor pay any arrears, or repair the goods.

35 'Notice' means notice in writing: s 189(1). As to service of notice, see s 176. As to joint debtors, see s 185(1)(b): set out at para 25.08. It does not seem to include posting keys to a vehicle. What about e-mail notices? As to ambiguous notices, see *Bridge's* case [1962] AC 600, HL (see para 27.25).

36 As to termination by the supplier, see para 26.08. What if the supplier has already served a statutory notice of termination (see para 26.10)?

37 As to the persons entitled to payment, see para 23.13.

38 *Wadham Stringer Finance Ltd v Meaney* (set out at para 26.19).

39 E.g. hire rent (as to which, see paras 27.21; 27.50); contractual interest for late payment (see para 7.03A). This includes any instalments due by reason of an acceleration clause operating before the debtor terminates: the *Wadham Stringer* case (above).

a purported s 99 termination without cause which falls outside s 99, e.g. an oral termination of hp, or a written termination of a cash or credit sale, is likely to amount to a common law repudiation (see para 26.15). *Aliter*, if there are other good reasons for discharge of which the transferee is unaware (see para 26.26). Nothing is said by the Act as to the place to which the debtor must return the goods.[40] Whether such debtor termination causes loss to the creditor is likely to depend on the residual value of the repossessed goods and may be dealt with by adjustment of the terms as to the hirer's interest in the goods (see para 27.12).[41] Section 99 appears defective in that exercise by the debtor discharges only the main supply of goods agreement and not any linked transaction (see para 5.31), e.g. credit insurance, extended warranty insurance; but attempts by creditors faced with a loss on the supply contract to argue that the insurances nevertheless continue may be ineffective.[42]

[26.06] So far as hp agreements are concerned, the effect of ss 99–100 (see para 26.05) is simply to nullify any attempt to restrict the right of the hirer to terminate the agreement. However, in the case of a conditional sale, the provisions embody a right in the debtor to terminate without cause which would not necessarily exist at common law, thus taking yet another step towards the assimilation of conditional sales and hp. But this new right of the conditional buyer (debtor) to terminate without cause is a limited one: not only is there a special restriction in respect of conditional sales of land,[43] but s 99(4) provides that:

> 'In the case of a conditional sale agreement relating to goods, where the property in the goods, having become vested in the debtor, is transferred to a person who does not become the debtor under the agreement, the debtor shall 'not thereafter be entitled to terminate the agreement under subsection (1).'

Thus, a person [B] who as assignee stands in the shoes of the conditional buyer [A][44] may enjoy the benefit of ss 99–100; but, if A sells to B the goods of which he is conditional buyer,[45] A can only later exercise those s 99 rights provided the property in the goods has not passed to B;[46] and B has no statutory right of termination in any event.[47] Where a conditional buyer who has not resold exercises the statutory right to terminate, the position is as follows: normally, under the terms of the agreement the property will remain in the conditional seller until payment of the

---

40   The debtor's premises, or those of a trade party? An express term of the regulated agreement must be fair and reasonable (see paras 11.15 and 18.21). As to the LACORS advice on the issue of charging the debtor for the cost of delivering a vehicle to a car auction, see (2002) 63 *Quarterly Account* 15.

41   Or by refusing/amending hp terms to those credit risks likely to terminate: (2005) 60 CC4/4.

42   The inclusion of the insurances in the supply contract may render that contract unenforceable, which the debtor may demonstrate by asking for a declaration under s 142 (see para 9.19): Butler and Stonely (2004) 102 Adviser 49.

43   Section 99 does not apply after title to the land has passed to the debtor: s 99(3). For conditional sales of land, see further, para 25.23.

44   By reason of assignment or operation of law: see the definition of 'debtor' in s 189(1).

45   B cannot obtain a good title under s 25(2) of the SGA: see para 21.45.

46   It has been said this will include the case where B obtains title under one of the exceptions to the *nemo dat* rule (as to which see Chap 21): Goode, *Consumer Credit Law & Practice*, para 36.204. *Sed quaere?*

47   Whether A has sold the goods to B, or simply assigned his interest in them to B, is a matter of interpretation. Should A be assumed to do that which is to his greater advantage (see para 27.47)?

last instalment; but, to meet the unusual case where the property has already passed to the conditional buyer,[48] s 99(5) provides that generally:

> 'the property in the goods shall thereupon vest in the person (the 'previous owner') in whom it was vested immediately before it became vested in the debtor'.

Lobbying for repeal of this right of voluntary termination by the debtor or hirer, the motor finance industry argued that, what began as an understandable protection for overstretched borrowers[49] has become a ready means for motor dealers to increase turnover and customers to reduce the effect of a driving ban; and that this has led to massive and unpredictable losses to creditors (around £80M pa), especially in the motor business.[50] Presumably as a reaction, in 2005 some motor finance business shifted from hp to CCA-compliant loans (see para 7.04) plus bills of sale,[51] thereby avoiding both s 99 of the CCA[52] and Pt III titles (see para 21.55).

**[26.07]  Termination of consumer hiring.** Whilst the HPA gave no statutory right of termination to the bailee under a simple hiring agreement, the CCA sought to protect hirers under consumer hire agreements (see para 1.19) from being locked into burdensome contracts for long periods.[53] Accordingly, s 101(1) provides that:

> 'The hirer under a regulated consumer hire agreement is entitled to terminate the agreement by giving notice to any person entitled or authorised to receive the sums payable under the agreement.'

It will be observed that this provision nominates the same persons as eligible to receive such notice as does s 99;[54] and s 101(1) is likewise expressed to operate without prejudice to 'any liability under the agreement which has accrued before the termination' (s 101(2)). On the other hand, s 101 does not derogate from any common law right of termination;[55] 'shall not expire earlier than 18 months after the making of the agreement';[56] and is subject to a minimum period of notice.[57] However, it does not matter whether the hiring is for a fixed period or periodic (see para 7.18), so long as the hirer is an 'individual' (see para 5.24).

The foregoing provisions could have been made applicable to small equipment leases (see para 1.18A) made to sole traders and partnerships, in which event a minimum lease of only 18 months might have rendered this form of business

---

48  Under the terms of the agreement or operation of law, e.g. accession (see para 19.05). Note the proviso to s 99(5), which makes special provision for the situation when the 'previous owner' has died or become bankrupt, etc, in the meantime.

49  Vulnerable consumers who need this protection have been said to be about 5% of those so terminating.

50  See (2005–6) HL GC cols. 321–2.

51  *Company Security Interests* (2005, Law Com 296), para 1.52.

52  At the expense of more unwieldy formalities: see para 25.26

53  Goode, *Consumer Credit Law & Practice*, para 36.221. But note that s 101 is in addition to any more advantageous contractual right of termination not caught by s 173.

54  See para 26.05. 'Notice' means notice in writing: s 189(1). As to service of such notice, see s 176.

55  S 101(3). E.g. if the agreement provides for a minimum hiring period of only 12 months; or minimum notice of only one week.

56  S 101(3). Note that the period runs from the making of the original agreement: not from the commencement of the hiring; nor from the making of any modifying agreement (s 101(9)).

57  Expiring not earlier than the above 18 months, there must be a period of notice which is the lesser of the following (s 101(3) and (6)): the shortest payment interval or three months. See the example in Guest and Lloyd, *Encyclopedia of Consumer Credit*, para 2-102.

uneconomic.[58] Not wishing to give a blanket exemption to equipment leases, Parliament therefore exempted certain categories of lease which had been found not to generate abuse. Leaving aside those categories of exemption in respect of business hirers,[59] those exemption categories which might affect private hirers are as follows:

Category (a), where the minimum rental exceeded £x per year.[60]

Category (b), which empowers the OFT by General Notice to direct that there be exempt from s 101 any consumer hire agreement which falls within a specified description and conditions.[61]

As to the hirer's liability on termination, see para 27.49.

## Termination by other stipulated event

[26.08] Termination provisions. In order to protect the interests of the supplier, an instalment credit contract with a reservation of property, i.e. conditional sale, hp or simple hiring, would commonly stipulate a number of events that would either terminate the agreement or render it terminable.[62] Examples were death (see para 24.44), insolvency,[63] or levying of distress (see para 19.17) against the buyer or hirer, e.g. Smart v Holt (set out at para 26.09), or any attempt on his part to assign his rights (see para 1.22), or late payment of instalments.[64] Furthermore, to avoid any dispute as to whether the common law would allow the owner to terminate in the following situations, the agreement would usually expressly so provide in the case of: (a) any material inaccuracy in the proposal form (see para 8.35); (b) any arrears in payment of any instalments; and (C) any other breach of the agreement.[65] The insertion of an enormous variety of such stipulated events is, of course, part of the technique of the 'snatchback' (see below).

Snatchbacks. This is a form of business which flourished before 1939 as follows: there was an hp agreement, but the hirer was probably not told the cash price, so that he could not work out the finance charge (see now, para 9.11); it was frequently

---

58  For an explanation, see Goode, Op. cit., para 36.223.

59  These are: (a) business hirers in directly financed transactions (s 101(7)(b)); (b) business hirers for sub-leasing (s 101(7)(c)); and (c) business suppliers on hire who have obtained an OFT dispensation (s 101(8), as amended by s 63(2) of the 2006 Act). And see amended s 183.

60  S 101(7)(a). Originally fixed at £300, the minimum annual rental has now been raised to £1,500: Consumer Credit (Further Increase in Monetary Limits) Order, 1998 SI 997. The figure includes any deposit. But does it extend to 'balloon payments'? As to service payments, see Goode, Op. cit., III, para 102.

61  New s 101(8A), as supplied by s 63(1) of the 2006 Act.

62  See para 26.09. The invocation of an acceleration clause does not terminate the agreement: Wadham Stringer Finance Ltd v Meaney (set out at para 26.19). For termination of a loan facility, see para 7.03.

63  E.g. Granor Finance v Liquidator of Eastore 1974 SLT 296 (Sess), where the clause was held not to be operable on breach and therefore not a penalty (as to the latter, see para 27.25). As to whether such a condition is void as being a fraud on the bankruptcy law, see Oditah (1992) 108 LQR at 482–6. As to consumer supplies, see fn 69, below.

64  E.g. The Laconia [1977] AC 850, HL (charterparty); Lombard North Central plc v Butterworth [1987] QB 527, CA (lease).

65  See para 26.09. However, such a clause will not always be effective: compare Schuler AG v Wickham Machine Tool Sales Ltd [1974] AC 235, HL with Lombard North Central plc v Butterworth (above).

for shoddy goods, from which the supplier would be protected by wide-ranging exclusion clauses (see now, para 18.19); it would be signed in blank, with terms more onerous than those agreed inserted thereafter (see now, para 16.05); it would contain wide-ranging repossession clauses (as above), but, as the consumer had no copy, he would be unlikely to be aware of all the triggering events.[66] By ruthless use of these clauses, whose likelihood of operation was frequently enhanced by encouraging overindebtedness,[67] the supplier could almost ensure a right of repossession effected by recaption (see para 24.23); and, if the hirer sought to exercise his option to terminate, he was often faced with intimidation and an exorbitant minimum payment clause (see now, para 26.04). If the supplier delayed repossession until late in the day, he could usually obtain most of the 'price' by way of rent and still recover the goods, because the hirer had no equity of redemption;[68] and the supplier could then let the same goods again on similar terms, so recovering the 'price' of the goods several times over. Many of these ploys were outlawed by the HPA 1938 in provisions subsequently re-enacted in the CCA; and even where the agreement is unregulated, if the agreement is a consumer supply, it may nowadays infringe the Unfair Terms Regulations.[69]

**[26.09] Their effect**. In this paragraph there will be considered the effect at common law of the operation of termination provisions (see para 26.08). In the leading case of *Smart Bros Ltd v Holt*:[70]

> Clause 8 of the hp agreement provided that if the hirer was in breach the owner might alternatively—
>
> (a) without notice terminate the hiring, or
>
> (b) by written notice terminate both the hiring and the agreement.
>
> Acting under (b), the owner purported to terminate the agreement. Subsequently, the hirer's landlord levied distress on the hired goods. The owner successfully sued for illegal distress on the grounds that at the time levied the goods were no longer 'comprised in' the hp agreement for the purposes of s 4 of the Law of Distress Amendment Act 1908 (see para 19.17).

It will be noted that clause 8 is drafted around two distinct dichotomies. *First*, there is the distinction between the following:[71] (i) automatic termination clauses, which take effect *ipso facto* on the occurrence of the stipulated event;[72] and (ii) clauses granting the owner a right to terminate, which will not cause termination unless and until the owner so elects. Moreover, a terminable agreement will commonly impose some condition precedent to termination, for example, that the owner gives

---

66 For the modern copies rules, see para 9.14, *et seq*.

67 See para 6.09-10. This effect was compounded by the 'linked-on' agreement: see para 24.36, but now, para 26.22. Distinguish CCA linked agreements (see para 5.31) and running accounts (see para 5.28).

68 See para 24.22; but see now, para 24.34.

69 E.g. insolvency: see OFT, *Bulletin*, cases 1 and 11: Grey Terms (f) and (g): see paras 11.16–17.

70 [1929] 2 KB 303; [1929] All ER Rep 322, DC.

71 The matter is one of interpretation: for the difficulties this may cause, see *Jay's Furnishing Co v Brand & Co* [1915] 1 KB 458, CA; *Times Furnishing Co Ltd v Hutchings* [1938] 1 All ER 422; and Goode, *HP Law & Practice*, 2nd edn, 326.

72 Automatic termination is not possible with regulated agreements, because a termination notice is required: see para 26.10.

notice to the bailee: if it does so, there will be no termination until notice is given;[73] but, if it does not so stipulate, the supplier is not obliged to give notice before terminating.[74] *Second*, whilst the phrase 'termination of the agreement' has so far been used, it is necessary to distinguish between termination of the bailment and termination of the agreement, as it is possible to terminate the bailment without terminating the agreement for all purposes.

1. *Termination of the bailment. Prima facie*, the bailment will be determined by any act of the bailee inconsistent with the terms of the agreement, e.g. a sale or pledge of the goods; but in practice, it is normal for the agreement to make specific provision about this matter, e.g. *Smart Bros Ltd v Holt* (above). The question of whether the bailment is terminated automatically or merely terminable used to be important for the purposes of the reputed ownership doctrine;[75] and it remains important for the following reasons: (1) whether the supplier is entitled to immediate possession of the goods;[76] (2) whether the bailee can create a lien over the goods, e.g. a repairer's lien (see para 1.23); and (3) to determine the bailor's right to hire rent.[77]

2. *Termination of the agreement.* This will also necessarily terminate the bailment (see above); but, unless the agreement manifests a contrary intention, it will not discharge either party from any obligations which have already accrued under the agreement (see para 26.16). Once again, it may be important to know whether the specified event automatically terminates the agreement, or merely renders it terminable: (1) as regards the matters turning on termination of the bailment (see above); (2) whether the bailee has any proprietary interest which can be seized in execution or fall into his bankruptcy (see paras 19.15 and 19.23); and (3) whether the goods are still 'comprised in' any agreement for the purposes of the law of distress, e.g. *Smart Bros Ltd v Holt* (above).

**[26.10] Regulated agreements**. Where there is an instalment credit contract with a reservation of property, the plight of the bailee at common law (see paras 26.08–09) has to some extent been alleviated by statute. Perhaps the most significant innovations of the HPA, now elaborated by the CCA, are the interposition of default notices (see para 24.30) and the restrictions on the repossession of protected goods (see para 24.34, *et seq*.). In the case of the death of the debtor or hirer, the Act has partly struck out a common stipulated event (see para 24.47). In other cases, s 98 of the CCA has introduced a new restriction, applicable wherever the creditor or owner seeks to terminate an unexpired fixed-term regulated agreement otherwise than by reason of the default of the debtor or hirer (s 98(6)). Section 98(1) provides:

'The creditor or owner is not entitled to terminate a regulated agreement except by or after giving the debtor or hirer not less than seven days' notice of the termination.'

---

73  *Reliance Car Facilities Ltd v Roding Motors* [1952] 2 QB 844.
74  *Moorgate Mercantile Ltd v Finch and Read* [1962] 1 QB 70, CA; *Union Transport Finance Ltd v British Car Auctions Ltd* [19781 2 All ER 385, CA.
75  This doctrine no longer obtains in insolvency (see para 19.23) but still exists in the law of distress (see para 19.17).
76  To enable him to sue in conversion (see para 19.06). See the cases cited in fns 73 and 74 above.
77  Determination of the hiring extinguishes the owner's right to hire rent in respect of any period thereafter: see para 27.21. As to whether the owner may claim damages in respect of loss of future rentals, see para 27.38.

Like the notice required by s 76 before the creditor or owner can exercise one of the rights there listed (see para 24.29), the seven-day notice of termination required by s 98[78] is ineffective unless in the prescribed form (s 98(3)); there is the same saving with regard to credit repayable on demand (s 98(2)) and as to lines of credit;[79] and the OFT has a similar power to exempt from the provisions (s 98(5)). Like a s 76 notice (see para 24.29), a s 98 notice is **not** remediable by the debtor or hirer: whether the notice terminates the agreement or merely renders it terminable,[78] the debtor or hirer can only avoid its consequences by applying to the court for a Time Order.[80] If the creditor or owner wishes in the absence of breach both to terminate the agreement and repossess the goods, then he must give both s 76 and s 98 notices, though they can be combined in one document.[81]

## OTHER TYPES OF DISCHARGE

A party may be discharged from his contractual obligations otherwise than in accordance with the terms of the contract by (1) rescission of the contract, or (2) a subsequent act or event.

### Discharge by rescission

**[26.11] Introduction.** Rescission is a self-help remedy, being regarded by the law as an act of a party to a contract (see paras 27.02 and 29.02). A contract may be rescinded[82] on the grounds of (a) a misrepresentation or (b) a breach by the other party. However, it must be borne in mind that the 'rescissions' are of different sorts. Where a contract has been induced by misrepresentation (see para 17.10), the defect is in the **formation** of the contract and the innocent party may be able to rescind the contract *ab initio* (see para 26.12); that is, it may be annulled in every respect so as to produce a state of affairs as though the contract had never been entered into.[83] Where a contract has been broken by one party, the defect lies in his **performance** and the other party may be entitled to treat the contract as discharged, in which case the contract is usually terminated as from that moment (see para 26.15); and,

---

78  The s 98 notice need not necessarily terminate the agreement automatically on the expiry of the seven days: it is enough if it renders the agreement terminable: Goode, *Consumer Credit Law & Practice*, para 45.54.

79  S 98(4). E.g. a store withdrawing budget account facilities as to future transactions.

80  As to Time Orders, see para 24.40. If the debtor is in breach (although that breach is not relied upon by the creditor), the goods may in any event be protected goods: as to which, see para 24.35, *et seq*.

81  Consumer Credit (Enforcement, Default and Termination Notices) Regulations, 1983 SI 1561, reg 2(8).

82  Does 'rescission' refer to (a) the act of the party recognised by the court; or (b) the act of the court; or (c) neither? Insofar as it means (a), the CCA contains some deemed agency provisions for the purposes of receiving notice of rescission: see para 26.04.

83  *Per* Buckley LJ in *Buckland v Farmer & Moody* [1978] 3 All ER 929 at 938b (not a sale of goods case).

84  See generally Treitel, *Law of Contract*, 11th edn, 369–70 and 759–60.

85  E.g. *Rowland v Divall* (see para 12.05); and para 26.12.

86  *Per* Lord Atkinson in *Abram Steamship Co Ltd v Westville Steamship Co* [1923] AC 773, HL at 781. And see *Murray v Larsen* [1953] 2 Lloyd's Rep 453.

perhaps unfortunately, such discharge or termination of the contract for breach is likewise frequently described as 'rescission',[83] meaning rescission *de futuro*.[84] However, under both types of rescission, if the property in the goods has passed under the contract, upon rescission it revests in the supplier.[85]

## Rescission ab initio *for misrepresentation*

**[26.12]** Wherever a party is induced to enter into a contract by a material misrepresentation, whether innocent or fraudulent, *prima facie* he has a right to rescind, though the contract will continue in force until he so elects. This election may be made in court, either by asking the court to declare the contract rescinded (see para 26.17), or by setting up rescission as a defence to a claim for specific performance (see para 29.38); or it may be made at some earlier date, as by avoidance of a voidable contract (see para 21.21). Where the misrepresentation was fraudulent, the effect of rescission at common law was to avoid the contract *ab initio*;[86] and, whilst the common law would not allow rescission for innocent misrepresentation,[87] equity recognised a *prima facie* right to rescind *ab initio*.[88] However, it also accepted a number of ways in which that right may be lost (see para 26.13-4). Modern authorities accept that full rescission of a contract for the supply of goods will lead to a revesting of any property in the goods transferred by that fraudulent contract;[89] and it may be that full or partial rescission is available in respect of non-fraudulent misrepresentation.[90]

**[26.13] Bars to rescission *ab initio*.** Even assuming there is a *prima facie* right to rescind on grounds of innocent or fraudulent misrepresentation (see para 26.12), there are a number of ways in which that right to rescind may be lost,[91] though the list has been reduced by statute (see para 26.14).

1. *Restitutio in integrum impossible.* The common law took the strict view that there could be no rescission for misrepresentation unless there could be a complete handing back and taking back of benefits transferred under the contract; and it is for this reason that rescission was barred at common law where the representor had transferred a benefit gained under the contract to a bfp (see below). Whilst equity recognised the overriding claims of the bfp, it took a rather more realistic view of the situation: in the case of fraud, the victim did not have to make restitution insofar as this was impossible by reason of the fraud; and, in the case of innocent misrepresentation, equity was prepared, within reason, to accept substantial restitution and a financial allowance for depreciation of the subject-matter.[92]

---

87 *Kennedy v Panama Royal Mail Co* (1867) LR 2 QB 580.

88 *Car & Universal Finance Co Ltd v Caldwell* (set out at para 21.21).

89 *Car & Universal Finance Co Ltd v Caldwell* (above). Whilst this may have originally been a logical error (see Swadling (2005) 121 LQR 123), it would now seem to be firmly embedded in English law since the SGA 1893.

90 Poole and Keyser (2005) 121 LQR 273.

91 At one time, it was thought that the right to rescind for misrepresentation had not survived the SGA; but it is now clear that it has done so: see Howard (1963) 27 MLR 272, 282–5.

92 *Per* Bowen LJ in *Newbigging v Adam* (1886) 34 Ch D 582, CA at 594–5; and *per* Pearce LJ in *Long v Lloyd* (below), at 407.

2.  *Affirmation.* If the representee, with knowledge of the misrepresentation,[93] elects to affirm the contract, the election is determined forever.[94] For instance, in *Long v Lloyd*[95] the court held that the buyer had elected to affirm in accepting the seller's offer to pay half the cost of making good the defect (see below).

3.  *Lapse of time.* How short such a period of time may be is demonstrated by *Long v Lloyd.*[96]

> The seller of a lorry innocently misrepresented to the buyer that it was in 'exceptional condition', and capable of 40 mph and 11 mpg. The buyer paid part of the price, took delivery, and used the lorry in the course of his business for three days. Having discovered several defects after the first day's outing, the buyer complained to the seller, who offered to pay half the cost of some of the repairs. The buyer accepted this; but, after two further days' use, he purported to reject on grounds of misrepresentation (see para 29.11). The Court of Appeal unanimously held that, from the nature of the representation, it must have been intended that the buyer be allowed a reasonable trial after delivery; but that one day's trial was reasonable, so that sending the lorry on a further journey amounted to a 'final acceptance'; and that in any event he had lost the right to rescind by accepting the offer to pay half the cost of repairs (see above).

It would seem that, where there is an innocent misrepresentation, time *prima facie* begins to run from the date the contract is executed;[97] but it has been suggested that in the case of fraud time only runs from the date of discovery.[98] How much time must elapse is a question of fact, which will vary from case to case;[99] but in any event, it may be that it cannot exceed the time during which the innocent party might have rescinded *de futuro* for breach (see para 29.11).

4.  *Rights acquired by a* bona fide *purchaser* (see para 21.19).

**[26.14] The Misrepresentation Act 1967.** Where a person (A) has entered into a contract after a misrepresentation has been made[100] to him (A), but fraud[101] is not alleged, the Act made the following two types of change to the foregoing pattern.

1.  *Bars to rescission.* At common law, there were two further possible bars to rescission; but these have been removed by s 1 of the 1967 Act, which provides that where A would be entitled to rescind, he shall be so entitled notwithstanding either or both of the following matters:

> *Paragraph (a)*: 'the misrepresentation has become a term of the contract'. This resolves a conflict as to the effect of the incorporation in a contract of an

---

93  Or perhaps, if he ought to have known: see Treitel, *Law of Contract*, 11th edn, 384.

94  *Per* Mellor J in *Clough v London and North Western Railway Co* (1871) LR 7 Exch 26, at 34.

95  [1958] 2 All ER 402; [1958] 1 WLR 753, CA.

96  This must be because of a lapse of a reasonable time, not because it constituted an affirmation, as there does not appear to be the intimation to the seller necessary for an affirmation. Cf. *Butterworth v Kingsway Motors Ltd* (discussed at para 29.13).

97  *Leaf v International Galleries* (set out at para 29.11).

98  Treitel, *Op. cit.,* 385.

99  E.g. *Oscar Chess Ltd v Williams* [1957] 1 All ER 325, CA (eight months too long); *Leaf's* case (above, five years too long).

100  As to 'misrepresentation', and 'misrepresentation . . . made', see para 17.10.

101  It is usually assumed that the 1967 Act has not touched the common law action for deceit: as to which, see para 17.18.

innocent misrepresentation made before contract. Two situations are possible. *First*, the misrepresentee acquires the right to rescind for breach of contract. Two questions arise. (i) Does rescission for misrepresentation have the same effect as rescission for breach of contract (see para 26.16)? (ii) Is the right to rescind for misrepresentation lost when the right to rescind for breach of contract is lost (see para 29.11)?[102] *Second*, the misrepresentee only acquires a right to damages for breach of contract. Section 1 appears to grant him also a *prima facie* right to rescind for misrepresentation.[103]

*Paragraph (b)*: 'the contract has been performed'. This replaces the rule that rescission was barred by execution of a formal transfer.[104]

2.  *Damages in lieu of rescission.* It was thought unsatisfactory that the representee should be able to rescind, however minor the matter misrepresented.[105] Accordingly, s 2(2) of the Act now provides that where A:

    'would be entitled, by reason of the misrepresentation, to rescind the contract,[106] then, if it is claimed, in any proceedings arising out of the contract, that the contract ought to be or has been rescinded, the court or arbitrator may declare the contract subsisting and award damages[107] in lieu of rescission, if of the opinion that it would be equitable to do so, having regard to the nature of the misrepresentation and the loss that would be caused by it if the contract were upheld, as well as to the loss that rescission would cause to the other party.'

Unlike a claim under s 2(1) (see para 17.10), the claim for damages under s 2(2) is a discretionary alternative to rescission for innocent misrepresentation.[108] Unfortunately, the wording of the provision does not make it clear whether the power to award damages under s 2(2) exists where a *prima facie* right to rescind arose, but was lost by one of the bars above considered (see para 26.13). In *Thomas Witter Ltd v TBP Industries Ltd*:[109]

    During the negotiations for the sale of stock in trade by reference to its profitability, the seller (S) altered the basis upon which the management accounts were drafted. Four years later, the buyer (B) claimed rescission of the elaborate written contract and damages for misrepresentation and breach of contract. In finding S liable for damages, Jacob J held as follows:

---

102  As s 1(a) does not apply in the circumstances where there was no pre-contract misrepresentation, it may not be possible to grant rescission under s 1 in respect of a broken warranty which makes its first appearance in the contract.

103  E.g. the *Thomas Witter* case (below), at 167c.

104  The so-called rule in *Seddon v NE Salt Co* [1905] 1 Ch 326 (see Howard (1963) 23 MLR 272).

105  Law Reform Committee, 10th Report, *Innocent Misrepresentation* (1962, Cmnd. 1782), paras 11–12.

106  Does this mean right to rescind for (a) misrepresentation, or (b) misrepresentation or breach? Does it refer exclusively to the common law right to rescind; or to that right as enlarged by s 1 of the Misrepresentation Act 1967? See Atiyah and Treitel (1967) 30 MLR 369, 376–8.

107  The damages suffered must be substantial: *UCB Corporate Services Ltd v Thomason* [2005] 1 All ER (Comm) 601, CA (waiver of guarantee).

108  In *Huyton SA v Distribuidora Internacional etc CV* [2004] 1 All ER (Comm) 402, the CA refused any remedy under s 2, saying that the parties should be left to their remedies under the sale contract. See further Treitel, *Law of Contract*, 11th edn, 358–9. *Contra* Beale (1995) 111 LQR 385 at 386–8.

109  [1996] 2 All ER 573; (1995) 14 Tr LR 145 (Beale 111 LQR 385).

a)    S's 'rough estimate' of one cost was negligent (see para 17.20).

b)    Rescission for misrepresentation not available because *restitutio in integram* was no longer possible but that would not preclude a claim for damages under s 2(2) (see below).

c)    The profit forecasts were negligent misrepresentations within s 2(1) (see above), even though they were also (see below) breaches of contract.

d)    The generalised exclusions clause would not be read as excluding liability for misrepresentation (see para 18.06) and in any event contravened new s 3 as being unreasonable at the time the contract was made (at 170F). His Lordship refused to sever the clause to save part of it (see para 18.24).

e)    S was also liable for breach of several express warranties (see para 11.07).

Jacob J took the view that 'the power to award damages under s 2(2) does not depend upon an extant right to rescission—it only depends upon a right having existed in the past'.[110] As to the measure of damages, see para 27.27.

## *Rescission* de futuro *for breach of contract*

**[26.15]** B may be entitled to rescind the contract on grounds of breach by A as follows: where A without lawful excuse, e.g. frustration (see para 22.14), abandonment (see para 26.18), either performs his side of the bargain defectively or wrongfully repudiates his obligations under the contract; but where the agreement is regulated and B is the creditor or owner, he will first have to serve a default notice (see para 24.30). The effect of that 'rescission' will be considered later (see para 26.16).

1. *Defective performance.*[111] Whilst not every defective performance by A will justify B in refusing to continue with the contract,[112] it will do so in the following circumstances: where there is a breach of an essential stipulation (see para 11.04), which will include a self-induced frustration (see para 22.14); or a breach which deprives B of substantially the whole benefit of the contract (see para 11.05); or where the contract expressly entitles B to refuse to continue if A commits any breach of contract (see para 26.08); or where performance by A is a condition precedent to performance by B (see para 26.01).

2. *Wrongful repudiation.* Any unequivocal refusal by A to perform a contractual obligation without good cause may amount to a repudiation;[113] but it is otherwise where B is already in breach of an essential stipulation, when A's repudiation will be rightful (cf. s 11(3), SGA). It has been said that repudiation 'is a serious matter and not to be lightly inferred'.[114] Perhaps repudiation is

---

110   At 162c. *Contra Zanzibar v British Aerospace Ltd* [2000] 1 WLR 2333 (but see 117 LQR 524).

111   This should be distinguished from repudiation: *per* Lord Denning MR in *Harbutt's Plasticine Ltd v Wayne Tank Ltd* [1970] 1 QB at 464, CA.

112   E.g. *State Trading Corpn of India v Golodetz* [1989] 2 Lloyd's Rep 277, CA.

113   *Per* Lord Coleridge CJ in *Freeth v Burr* (1874) LR 9 CP at 213. For the difficulty this has caused with instalment contracts, see below and paras 23.24–5; and for failure to pay a deposit on time, see para 27.19. Does the rule even extend to refusal to perform a warranty?

114   *Per* Lord Wright *in Ross T Smyth & Co Ltd v Bailey, Son & Co* [1940] 3 All ER 60 at 71, HL. See *Lombard North Central plc v Butterworths* [1987] QB 527, CA; *Lloyds & Scottish Finance v Cyril Lord Carpet Sales* [1992] BCLC 609, HL; and para 27.47.

more likely to be inferred where A's conduct is covert and unfair to the innocent B.[115] The repudiation may be express, e.g. anticipatory breach (see below). Or it may be implied, either by statute (see s 11(3) of the SGA: above, para 11.04); or at common law, as where A incapacitates himself from performing his contractual obligations,[116] or becomes insolvent,[117] or otherwise completely fails to perform his side of the bargain.[118] However, it has been held that an unjustified attempted rescission by A will not necessarily amount to an implied repudiation;[119] nor will an unjustified attempted price escalation necessarily do so;[120] nor an erroneous reliance on one's own terms in a battle of the forms.[121] Obviously, A may repudiate at the time when performance is due; but the common law has accepted that A may alternatively sometimes repudiate before that time, in which case there is what is termed an 'anticipatory breach'.[122]

Whilst it is easy to draw the above distinctions in theory, it may be difficult to apply them in practice. This is particularly the case in instalment credit transactions, where an intimation by the borrower, buyer or hirer that he no longer intends to proceed with such a regulated transaction might amount to any of the following: (1) a notice of cancellation (see para 10.29); or (2) a notice exercising a right to terminate (see paras 26.05–07); or (3) a breach of contract or repudiation, though a clause entitling a supplier to treat a minor breach as repudiatory may be struck down as being unfair (UTCCR, reg 5: see above, para 11.15A).

[26.16] Effect of right to rescind *de futuro*. Assuming that B is *prima facie* entitled to rescind on the grounds of breach or repudiation by A, this does not automatically bring the contract to an end,[123] except possibly where further performance is impossible by reason of a frustrating breach (see para 22.14). It is thought that the general rule is that B merely has an option to treat the contract as discharged, the contract remaining binding on both parties unless and until B elects to rescind.[124] Nor is this option foreclosed by any express right to rescind,[125] nor the duty to

---

115 *Northern Foods PLC v Focal Foods Ltd* (set out at para 26.26), where A's breach damaged the profitability of the contract to B (at paras 7.18–23).

116 As by a supplier wrongfully reselling; but see the difficulties with *Smart v Holt* clauses (see para 26.09). Compare the supplier's right to resell: see para 27.09.

117 *Edinburgh Grain Ltd v Marshall Food Group Ltd* 1999 SLT 15.

118 E.g. *Gill & Duffus SA v Berger & Co Inc* (set out at para 23.06); The *Stocznia No. 3* case (see para 26.16A). Compare *Lombard North Central plc v Butterworth* [1987] QB 527, CA.

119 *Woodar Investment Development Ltd v Wimpey Construction UK Ltd* [1980] 1 All ER 571, HL (not a sale case; supported by Treitel, *Law of Contract*, 11th edn, 808). Contrast *The Nanfri* [1979] AC 757, HL (charterparty; also supported by Treitel, *Op. cit.*, 809).

120 *Vaswani v Italian Motors* [1996] I WLR 270, PC (genuine mistake). For price escalation clauses, see para 10.05.

121 *Northern Foods PLC v Focal Foods Ltd* (above), *obiter* at para 9.5. For the battle of the forms, see para 10.04.

122 E.g. *Tai Hing Cotton Mill Ltd v Kamsing Knitting Factory* (see para 29.21). The terminology has been criticised by Lord Wrenbury in *Bradley v Newsom, Sons & Co* [1919] AC 16 at 53–4, HL. See generally Carter (1984) 47 MLR 422. As to an equivocal statement, see para 26.01.

123 *Heyman v Darwins Ltd* [1942] AC 356, HL; *Decro-Wall International SA v Practitioners in Marketing Ltd* [1971] 2 All ER 216, CA (franchise agreements).

124 *Per* Diplock LJ in *Ward Ltd v Bignall* (set out at para 27.10) at 548. See also *Garnac Grain Co v HMF Faure & Fairclough Ltd* [1968] AC 1130, HL; The *Stocznia No. 3* case (see para 26.16A).

125 The *Stocznia No. 1* case (see para 26.16A).

mitigate.[126] Thus, it would appear that at common law[127] it is open to B to elect as to the following alternative rights.[127]

1. *To treat the contract as discharged*. It would now appear to be settled that the effect of discharge for breach is this: whether the discharge occurs automatically (upon a frustrating breach) or more commonly on unequivocal election by B,[128] the first effect is to discharge both parties from any duty of further performance of the ('primary') promises made under the contract, in a similar way to where the contract is frustrated (see para 22.14, *et seq.*). However, the two situations thereafter differ in that, whereas both parties to a frustrated contract walk free of any future contractual obligations (see para 23.06), if a contract is discharged by A's breach, it was explained by Lord Diplock in *Gill & Duffus SA v Berger & Co Inc* (set out at para 23.06; at 390) that B is totally discharged from any future ('primary') obligations, because performance by A was a condition precedent to performance by B (see para 26.01). However, with regard to all the other broken promises, the party in breach of that obligation remains liable to pay damages:[129] A remains liable for past and future breaches;[130] whereas B is only liable for past breaches[131] and can set these off when sued by A (SGA, s 53(1)(a): see generally, para 29.26). It follows that B escapes from more of his obligations by rescinding *ab initio* for misrepresentation than *de futuro* for breach; and by using the Misrepresentation Act 1967, s 2, he may be able to recover damages from A (see para 17.10; see further, para 26.14).

2. *Not to treat the contract as discharged*. If B elects to keep the contract alive, as in the *Stocznia No. 3* case (see para 26.16A), then it continues binding on both parties (see para 29.02), unless, perhaps, there is a 'continuing breach' (see para 29.10): each must perform his side of the contract (see para 26.01), but B may claim damages for that breach: *Wallis & Wells v Pratt & Haynes* (set out at para 11.04). In the case of an anticipatory breach, that election may operate to the advantage of either side in respect of subsequent impossibility[132] or the measure of damages.[133] Indeed, it may be that the right to rescind for breach is subject to the same bars as the right to rescind for misrepresentation (see para 26.13).[134]

**[26.16A] The *Stocznia* litigation.** Latco was a company owned by the State of Latvia. In 1992, Latco began to negotiate with Stocznia (the yard: S) for the latter to design and build six reefer vessels. Latco set up a subsidiary company (the

---

126 *Tredegar Iron Co Ltd v Hawthorn Brothers & Co* (1902) 18 TLR 716, CA. But see Goode, *Commercial Law*, 3rd edn, 126–7; and further, para 27.44.

127 *Per* Diplock LJ in *Ward Ltd v Bignall* (above) at 550. Election to treat the contract as discharged does not amount to a variation: *Moschi v Air Services* [1973] AC 331, HL. See also CCA, s 89: para 24.35.

128 *Vitol SA v Norelf Ltd, The Santa Clara* [1996] AC 800, HL.

129 What Lord Diplock termed 'substituted or secondary obligations' in *Photo Production Ltd v Securicor Transport Ltd* [19801 AC 827 at 848, HL. See also, para 27.29; and para 24.31.

130 See *Hyundai Heavy Industries Co Ltd v Papadopoulos* [1980] 2 All ER 29, HL; and the *Stocznia* case (see para 29.16A). As to future rentals, see para 27.38 and as to part-payments, see para 27.19.

131 *Northern Foods PLC v Focal Foods Ltd* (set out at para 26.26), at para 10.15.

132 E.g. *Avery v Bowden* (1855) 5 E & B 714. See generally, para 22.14.

133 E.g. *Roper v Johnson* (1873) LR 8 CP 167. See generally, para 29.21.

134 See *Alpha Chauffeurs Ltd v Citygate Dealership* (set out at para 14.12), at paras 42–4 and 47–8.

buyer: B) to buy the vessels. The yard did not request a guarantee from Latco, but proceeded on the assumption that Latco would fulfil its contractual promise to B to fund B. There were six contracts, each to design, build and supply a ship. In each contract, 5% of the price was payable at the outset; 20% on notice that the keel was laid; 25% on notice of launch; and 50% on delivery. The property was not to pass until delivery; and clause 5 of each contract provided that, if B defaulted on any instalment, S shall be entitled to rescind the contract. The first 5% was paid under each contract. The market for reefers hit a peak in 1992; but then declined and in 1994 collapsed. To bring pressure to bear on S to re-negotiate the contracts, Latco decided not to put B in funds; and consequently B took no steps with regard to the contract. S took the following proceedings:

(1) In contract against B. When S gave notice that the first two keels had been laid, the 20% payments were not made. S rescinded those contracts and sued for the two 20% payments as debts due before rescission. In preliminary proceedings, *Stocznia No. 1*,[135] the House of Lords held that the fact that the contract gave S an express right to rescind[136] did not show that he had abandoned his common law right to instalments due before rescission (see para 26.16); and that B had no right to recover the initial 5% payments in quasi-contract (see para 29.16). At the main trial, *Stocznia No. 3*, the Court of Appeal unanimously held B liable for repudiation of all the contracts as follows:[137] clause 5 was simply built on the common law remedies for breach of contract; at common law, actual non-payment of the 20% keel-laying instalments when due amounted to a repudiation by B of contracts 1 and 2;[138] and clause 5 simply defined when the period of grace expired and repudiation occurred (para 79). The court argued that the keel-laying notices by S were not an affirmation of the contract by S because they were equivocal, being mere attempts to get B to perform the contract,[139] explaining that there is (para 87):

> 'a middle ground between acceptance or repudiation and affirmation of the contract, and that is the period when the innocent party is making up his mind what to do'.

Even supposing the keel-laying notices were an affirmation by S, the Court of Appeal said *obiter* (para 101) that there was a continuing repudiation of contracts 3–6 by B's continued silence (para 96): Rix LJ[140] accepted that affirmation after actual repudiation may leave 'nothing outstanding for the future';[141] but, he argued that *prima facie* 'affirmation after anticipatory breach still leaves the future open' and concluded:

---

135 *Stocznia Gdanska SA v Latvian Shipping Co* [1998] 1 All ER 883, HL.
136 In some other contracts, termed a 'material breach': see Scott (2006) 156 NLJ 872.
137 *Stocznia Gdanska SA v Latvian Shipping Co (No. 3)* [2002] 2 All ER (Comm) 768, CA.
138 At para 76. See para 26.15.
139 At para 85. See para 26.16.
140 At para 99. His Lordship discussed the article by Treitel (1998) 114 LQR 22.
141 But even here, his Lordship thought that 'breach of a continuing notice, such as a failure to pay or deliver, might not necessarily be an irrevocable affirmation for all time in the future' (para 100).

'silence should not in this context be too readily regarded as equivocal; and that against the background of an earlier anticipatory repudiation it should not take much further to prove continuing repudiatory conduct'.

(2) Action in tort against Latco. In *Stocznia No. 2*, an unsuccessful attempt was made to stop the proceedings on the grounds that S was supported by champertous funding.[142] Subsequently, in *Stocznia No. 3*, S succeeded in his action on the grounds that Latco had indirectly induced B to break his contract with S.[143]

## Discharge by subsequent act or event

[26.17] Leaving aside discharge by breach, there are certain other acts or events occurring subsequent to the formation of the contract and irrespective of the terms which may bring about its discharge.

1.  *Subsequent agreement* (see para 26.18).

2.  *Election of remedies.* Where a man is entitled to one of two inconsistent rights, any unequivocal act of election to pursue one of them, made by him with knowledge of his rights, will shut him out from the other,[144] as where an owner under an hp agreement accepts hire-rent after breach (see para 27.22), or a seller exercises a licence to seize under a conditional sale.[145] However, normally it is not a question of choosing between two inconsistent rights, but merely of electing between two alternative remedies, in contract or tort, in which case the election is not *per se* irrevocable;[146] but a party will *prima facie* be bound by a final judgment of a court of competent jurisdiction,[147] e.g. rescission *ab initio* (see para 26.12).

3.  *Judgment. Prima facie*, final judgment in any suit has the effect of merging the original cause of action in the judgment, and the plaintiff must rely as against the defendant on the rights created by the judgment,[147] e.g. a judgment debt (see para 27.04). Judgment alone will normally extinguish any alternative claims against the defendant,[148] but not those claims which are cumulative, e.g. the right of an owner under an hp agreement to arrears of rentals and damages for breach (see para 27.21). Nor will judgment alone discharge the claim upon which that judgment was obtained, though satisfaction of the judgment will do so: for instance, a judgment in conversion for damages amounting to the assessed value of the goods claimed will vest the plaintiff's title in the defendant

---

142  *Stocznia Gdanska SA v Latvian Shipping Co (No. 2)* [1999] 3 All ER 822, Toulson J; and see para 7.26.

143  *Stocznia Gdanska SA v Latvian Shipping Co (No. 3)* (above), at paras 44–72, CA; and see para 17.17. A more normal arrangement would have been for Latco to act as surety for performance by B (its subsidiary) to S (for sureties, see generally, para 25.06).

144  Whether he has made such an election is a matter of fact: *Bremer Handelsgesellschaft mbH v Deutsche Conti Handelsgesellschaft mbH (No. 2)* [1983] 2 Lloyd's Rep 45, CA. For discussion of the use of the term 'waiver' in this context, see Spencer Bower, *Estoppel*, 2nd edn, 295.

145  *Hewison v Ricketts* (set out at para 27.19). Or where he sues for the price (see para 27.16).

146  But see *Meng Leong Development Pte Ltd v Jip Hong Trading Co Pte Ltd* [1985] AC 511, PC (specific performance sought on sale of land). For waiver, see para 26.23.

147  *Forward Trust Ltd v Whymark* [1990] 2 QB 670, CA, per Lord Donaldson MR, AER at 921d; *DG of FT v First National Bank plc* (set out at para 7.03A).

148  What of claims against third parties? Compare the two authorities cited in fn 147 above.

if satisfied,[149] but not if it remains unsatisfied.[150] Finally, it should be remembered that, where more than one person is liable in respect of the same damage, the position has been altered: whilst at common law even an unsatisfied judgment against one of them discharged the others,[151] by statute a contribution can now be claimed from 'any person liable in respect of the same damage'.[152]

4. *Repossession.* The recaption of 'protected goods' contrary to s 90 of the CCA terminates the agreement and releases the debtor from all liability thereunder (s 91: see para 24.38).

5. *Early payment* (see para 26.19).

6. *Limitation of actions.* Under the Limitation Act 1980 (as amended) the ordinary rule is that no **civil** action (as opposed to criminal proceedings) may be brought after the expiry of six years from the moment when the cause of action arose on a simple contract (ss 5 and 6),[153] or for a tort (ss 2 and 3), or for a sum recoverable by statute (s 9). However, there are many exceptions to this rule: for instance, there is a longer limitation period where a contract is made by deed (a specialty: s 8), or mortgage,[154] or the plaintiff suffers from a disability (s 28), or there is acknowledgment or part-payment of a debt,[155] or there is fraud, concealment or mistake (s 32), or in respect of product liability claims (see para 17.23); and the limitation period is reduced to three years for personal injuries (s 11). Further consideration of this complicated subject is beyond the scope of this work.

**[26.18] Subsequent agreement.** On ordinary principles, any duty created by one contract may be discharged by another contract between the same parties; and there may therefore be a total or partial discharge of liability.[156]

1. *Total discharge.* Where the parties expressly agree that each shall be discharged from his contractual liability, this may be seen almost as a mutual repudiation (see para 26.15); but a total discharge may also be brought about impliedly, as where the parties abandon the contract,[157] or both are simultaneously in serious breach.[158] If the first contract is still executory on both sides at the time

---

149 *USA v Dollfus Mieg* [1952] AC 582, HL (see now the Torts Act 1977, s 5, explained by *Benjamin on Sale,* 6th edn, paras 4.012–13). There is a similar rule under the CCA, s 133(5) in respect of a satisfied Time or Return Order (see para 24.43).

150 *Ellis v John Stenning & Son* [1932] 2 Ch 81.

151 E.g. *Kendall v Hamilton* (1879) 4 App Cas 504, HL (partnership case).

152 Civil Liability (Contribution) Act 1978, s 1(1); and see s 1(5). See further generally, para 12.10.

153 See *VAI Industries (UK) Ltd v Bostock & Bramley* [2003] BLR 359, CA.

154 S 20: see *West Bromwich BC v Wilkinson* [2005] 4 All ER 97, HL (cause of action arose on first default: see 79 QA 13).

155 Ss 29–31. Any acknowledgment must be in signed writing by the debtor or his agent (s 30). For the difficulty this may pose for a debt adviser trying to negotiate a compromise, see *Bradford & Bingley Plc v Rashid* [2006] 156 NLJ 1172, HL.

156 The common law rule that release of one joint tortfeasor or contractor releases all the others appears to have been left open by the silence of the Civil Liability (Contribution) Act 1978: see s 1(4), the *Current Law* Annotation thereto and Dugdale (1979) 42 MLR at 189.

157 E.g. *Pearl Mill Ltd v Ivy Tanneries Ltd* [1919] 1 KB 78, DC; *GW Fisher Ltd v Eastwoods Ltd* [1936] 1 All ER 421.

158 *Northern Foods PLC v Focal Foods Ltd* (set out at para 26.26), *obiter* at para 9.4, distinguished because S could here say his second breach was an acceptance of B's earlier breach.

of the subsequent agreement, it generates its own consideration;[159] but, if the first contract remains executory on one side only, it will usually be necessary for that party to give some fresh consideration for his release, in which case it is termed an 'accord and satisfaction'.[160] Several forms of total discharge as between the contracting parties require special mention; and it should be remembered that sometimes a third party may take the benefit of such promises (see para 17.08). *First*, the original contract may be replaced by an entirely new one: for instance, where the subject-matter of the first contract is 'traded-in' in part-exchange (see para 2.09); or taken with further goods under the second agreement (see para 26.08); or a fresh party is added to the agreement, an arrangement termed a 'novation' (see para 7.27). *Second*, where a lesser sum is tendered in satisfaction of a greater, *prima facie* that lesser payment is no satisfaction of the greater, and the difference is still owed.[161] However, sufficient consideration to discharge the first agreement may be generated, as where by agreement with the creditor[162] the lesser payment is made early or in kind (see para 26.19), or by a third party,[163] or in a different currency,[164] or the claim was of an uncertain amount (an unliquidated sum: see para 27.24), or bf disputed;[165] or it may be inequitable to claim the larger sum (see para 26.24). *Third*, after breach by a supplier in a sale to a business buyer, the parties may agree to replace the consumer's ordinary remedies (see para 11.04) with a credit note, replacement or cure (see para 29.02). *Fourth*, even in the absence of breach by the retailer, he may allow the return of goods and refund of the price,[166] sometimes even by a donee.[167]

2. *Partial discharge*. The terms of the original contract may be varied by contract or by mere waiver (see para 26.20). It is a question of intention whether there has been a total discharge and subsequent agreement or a contractual variation (see para 26.21).

**[26.19] Early payment.** Particularly in the case of a contract which provides for payment by instalments, there may be situations where either creditor or debtor seeks early payment; and a distinction must be drawn according to which party activated the early payment.

1. *Activated by creditor*. Especially in instalment sales on credit (see para 1.03), it is common to find an acceleration clause.[168] But distinguish a claim with regard

---

159 *Compagnie Noga D'Importation et D'Exportation SA v Abacha (No. 2)* [2003] 2 All ER (Comm) 915, CA.
160 See generally, Treitel, *Law of Contract*, 11th edn, 100–1; Goode, *HP Law & Practice*, 2nd edn, 329–30. But see s 62 of the Bills of Exchange Act 1882.
161 *D and C Builders Ltd v Rees* [1966] 2 QB 617, CA (payment by cheque); *Ferguson v Dawson* [1997] 1 All ER 315, CA (similar).
162 It is not sufficient simply to send a lesser sum unsolicited 'in final settlement': *IRC v Fry* [2002] CLY 722 (not a sale case).
163 *Hirachand Punamchand v Temple* [1911] 2 KB 330, CA.
164 *Alan & Co Ltd v El Nasr Export & Import Co* (set out at para 26.21).
165 *Re Warren* (1884) 53 LJ Ch 1016; *Auriema v Haigh and Ringrose* [1989] CLY 403.
166 Distinguish an express right of cancellation in the original supply contract: see para 10.28.
167 See [2003] 12 *Which?* 43.
168 See paras 7.03 and 23.26; and generally Goode [1982] JBL 148; Goode, *Payment Obligations in Commercial and Financial Transactions*, 51–3. As to damages for loss of future rentals, see para 27.38.

to future hire-rent: no hire-rent is due after termination of the bailment (see para 27.21); and an acceleration clause in an hp agreement may turn that agreement into a conditional sale (see para 1.22). In *Wadham Stringer Finance Ltd v Meaney*:[169]

> A conditional sale agreement within the HPA 1965 gave the seller an express right on the buyer's default to elect to accelerate payment of the price. The buyer having failed to pay any instalments, the seller successfully claimed the sum due under the accelerated payments clause, including charges.

Woolf J rejected all the following arguments by the buyer in trying to avoid that clause: (1) that it was void as being a restriction on his statutory right to terminate, because the sum payable under it was a 'final payment' for the purposes of what is now s 99(1) of the CCA (see para 26.05), or as seeking to impose an additional liability on him;[170] (2) that it was void as an attempt to impose on him liability after termination;[171] and (3) that it was void as being a penalty,[172] though nowadays such a clause might be attacked under other statutes as being unreasonable or unfair.[173] It is important to remember that reliance on an acceleration clause presupposes that the agreement is still in being, because the clause is treated (unrealistically?) as an alternative method of 'primary' performance (see para 26.16): if the clause become operable on breach, reliance on it by the supplier may be an election to affirm the contract.[174] Normally, the agreement will provide for payment of interest on sums accrued (including charges) but unpaid (see para 7.03A). However, sometimes an agreement will go further and provide for an **increase** in the rate of interest on default ('default interest'), supposedly to recompense the creditor for the extra administrative cost and increased risk.[175] In this regard, the CCA has in a number of respects altered the rules in favour of a debtor under a regulated consumer credit agreement: (a) it requires a prior seven-day notice (ss 76(1)(a); 87(1)(b): see para 24.28); (b) the agreement may be cancellable (s 67: see para 10.29) or amount to an unjust credit bargain (s 137: see para 29.44); (c) the buyer may seek a Time Order (s 129: see para 24.40) or statutory rebate;[176] (d) a court may suspend the operation of an acceleration clause (s 135(1)(b):

---

169 [1980] 3 All ER 789; [1981] 1 WLR 39; discussed by Davidson 1982 SLT 1.

170 The provision for the payment of interest was not an additional liability contrary to what is now s 100(1) of the CCA because it had accrued before termination under what is now s 99(2) of the CCA: see para 26.05 and para 27.50. But see now, para 26.19A.

171 Because the operation of the clause did not terminate the agreement (see paras 26.08; 26.10), which remained in force until the parties had performed all their obligations under it. For the rights of the innocent party upon serious breach, see para 26.16.

172 Because it contained provisions for rebate of charges on early settlement and was therefore a genuine pre-estimate of loss: see also *The Angelic Star* [1988] 1 Lloyd's Rep 122, CA; *Lordsvale Finance plc v Bank of Zambia* [1996] QB 752; and para 27.26.

173 Unreasonable under s 3 of UCTA (see para 18.24) or unfair under the UTCC Regulations, Grey Term (e) (see para 11.16). See (2005) 78 *QA* 4.

174 See *Hewison v Ricketts* (set out at para 27.19); and generally, para 26.16. In this sense, invocation of an acceleration clause may be seen at common law as an alternative to recaption: as to which see para 24.34.

175 E.g. *Mutual Loan Fund Association Ltd v Sanderson* [1937] 1 All ER 380. But this rule may be circumvented: see *Broadwick Financial Services v Spencer* (set out at para 8.22).

176 CCA, s 95: see para 26.19A. Judgment should be entered for the unrebated sum: *Forward Trust Ltd v Whymark* [1990] 2 QB 670, CA.

see para 9.20); and (e) directly protecting him against such default interest in a consumer credit (but not consumer hire) agreement,[177] though interest can still continue at the previous rate, and once again, the home credit trade does things differently.[178]

2.  *Activated by debtor* (see para 26.19A).

**[26.19A] Early payment by the debtor.** The debtor, buyer or hirer in a loan, instalment sale or hp agreement may seek to pay the whole outstanding sum ahead of time (some 70% do so). At common law, he is *prima facie* entitled to make early settlement by tender to the lender, seller or owner of the capital sum plus interest due to date of payment;[179] and this is commonly done in the case of personal loans, subject to any redemption charges, e.g. × months' interest. Where the lender/supplier mistakenly quotes too low a 'settlement figure' (see below) for this purpose, he may subsequently be estopped from claiming the difference.[180] Where there is a 'trade-in' (see para 2.09), 'payment' may be effected by the dealer paying the 'settlement figure' on the old goods out of their trade-in price[181] to their supplier on behalf of the buyer or hirer.[182] Suppose the dealer does not make that payment. On general principle, the buyer or hirer is responsible for seeing his debt paid to the creditor (see para 23.13) and it is not clear that the dealer is at common law the creditor's agent (see para 16.06). But see below.

*Rebates.* In confirmation of the common law rule (see para 27.29), the agreement will sometimes provide for,[183] or the supplier allow,[184] a rebate for early settlement, though this may cause him financial embarrassment if he has funded his operation at rates of interest higher than those prevailing at the time of settlement.[185] Nevertheless, when the agreement is regulated, the CCA requires the creditor to take this merciful line: on written request,[186] the debtor[185] has statutory rights to a

---

177  S 93. This does not preclude the charging of any extra administration costs actually caused by the default (see (1999) 54 CC 1/33), so that they cannot amount to a penalty (see para 27.26).

178  They tend to await the end of the credit period (say 20 weeks) and then renew the facility for a further such period at the same APR, claiming that this does not breach CCA, s 93 (see above).

179  *Lancashire Waggon Co v Nuttall* (1879) 42 LT 465, CA; and Goode, *HP Law and Practice*, 2nd edn, 268. Distinguish payment of a lesser sum on or after due date (see para 26.18); or where the creditor is entitled to terminate the agreement: *Alf Vaughan & Co Ltd v Royscot Trust plc* (set out at para 27.22).

180  *Lombard North Central plc v Stobart* (1990) 9 Tr LR 105, CA; CCA, s 172(1); and see generally, para 26.24.

181  If the settlement figure exceeds the trade-in and is added to the new agreement, this may create difficulties: (i) there may then be a multiple agreement—a dcs supply and a dc loan (see para 5.27); (2) there may be difficulty over the 'total price' (see para 24.35). See 46 CC1/26; 46 CC2/12.

182  See Goode, *Consumer Credit Law & Practice*, para 36.85.

183  If the interest is to be calculated daily, the debtor may be able to make an early 'capital repayment' and hence avoid any subsequent liability to interest on the sum repaid: [1990] *Which?* 492.

184  As to this displacing the prohibition on assignment, see para 7.26. For payment at an earlier date of a lesser sum, see para 26.18.

185  For the common law requirement of a rebate for accelerated payment made by way of the payment of damages, see para 27.29.

186  *Home Insulation v Wadsley* [1988] CCLR 25, DC. The notice does not need to be signed by the debtor, nor of any minimum duration: Goode, *Op. cit.*, para 36.13.

written statement of the sum outstanding;[187] once given, that information is binding on the creditor (s 172(1)); and, armed with it, the debtor may elect to exercise by written notice a right to make early payment of that sum to the creditor,[188] upon which actual payment he is entitled to a minimum statutory rebate in respect of future instalments (s 95). This 'early settlement rebate' is at a minimum figure prescribed by the regulations: for many years, the Regulations specified the traditional industry formula known as the 'Rule of 78'; but in 2004 this traditional formula was replaced by new Regulations.[189] These prescribe a maximum actuarial calculation (regs 4–6) and new settlement date capped at 28 days after the debtor's request is received deferred by one additional month (regs 5–6), both rules being much more advantageous to consumers; and, in the pre-contract information the consumer must have been given two representative examples (see Sched), so that he should be more aware of his early settlement rights (see para 9.08).

At the same time, such early payment will discharge any linked transaction (see para 5.31) as regards future obligations (s 96(1). There is power to exempt by regulation: s 96(3)). It would seem that the right to a statutory rebate is drafted widely enough to be applicable also on refinancing (see para 7.04A) or where it is the creditor who insists upon early payment by reason of the debtor's breach,[190] but not where there is no fixed date for repayment, e.g. a loan repayable on demand.

## Variation and waiver[191]

[26.20] The subject-matter of this section is the variation and waiver of obligations, whether or not those obligations arise from a contract.[192] Historically, this area is bedevilled by the Statute of Frauds 1677, though that body of law is no longer applicable to sales of goods,[193] and is only relevant here insofar as it relates to contracts of surety (see para 25.06). Ignoring the now largely irrelevant usage under the Statute of Frauds, the terms 'variation' and 'waiver' will be used to mean the following:[194] 'variation' will be reserved for those situations where contractual rights are

---

187 S 97. For the prescribed form, see the Consumer Credit (Settlement Information) Regulations, 1983 SI 1564. For the effect of the Data Protection Act 1998 (see para 8.36), see (1988) CC5/10.

188 S 94(1), together with any option to purchase (s 94(2)). Suppose the dealer never forwards payments to the creditor. Does s 56(1)(c) (see para 16.08) place the debtor in a stronger position than at common law (see fn 179, above)?

189 The Consumer Credit (Early Settlement) Regulations, 2004 SI 1483 (as amended). This followed recommendations in a DTI White Paper, *Fair, Clear and Competitive: the Consumer Credit Market in the 21st Century* (Dec 2003, Cm. 6040), paras 2.42–52.

190 Under an acceleration clause: see *Forward Trust Ltd v Whymark* [1990] 2 QB 670, CA. As to credit cards, see Jones, *Credit Cards*, 166–8.

191 See generally Stoljar (1957) 35 Can BR 484; Adams (1972) 36 Conv 245; Dugdale and Yates (1976) 39 MLR 680.

192 Distinguish the situation where the original contract itself allows alteration of its terms, e.g. price adjustment formulae (see para 10.05).

193 S 4 of the SGA 1893 was repealed by the Law Reform (Enforcement of Contracts) Act 1954, s 1: see para 9.02.

194 Unfortunately, the expression 'waiver' has not in practice been restricted as in the text, but has sometimes been used to mean rescission or variation: Treitel, *Law of Contract*, 11th edn, 102–4.

subsequently altered by another contract;[195] and any attempt to alter accrued rights otherwise than by contract will be called a 'waiver'.[196] Both variations and waivers bear some resemblance to the exclusion clauses and disclaimers considered in Chap 18; but they must be distinguished from the subject-matter of that Chapter in that variation and waiver take effect, if at all, only **after** the accrual of contractual or tortious liability. In a consumer supply, a requirement that any variation must be in writing may be an unfair term.[197]

## Variation of liability

**[26.21] Common law**. On ordinary principles, whilst an attempted unilateral variation of contract will usually only amount to a breach,[198] the parties may always make alterations to their contract by mutual agreement.[199] Thus, in *Alan & Co Ltd v El Nasr Export & Import Co*[200] the Court of Appeal held that the irrevocable credit should have been in Kenyan currency, because the money of account under the original contract was Kenyan currency; but that, in accepting a sterling irrevocable credit,[201] the sellers had either varied the original contract to substitute sterling for Kenyan currency[202] or waived the right to Kenyan currency (see generally, para 26.23).

*Prima facie*, even a written contract may be varied by oral agreement;[203] but a guarantee required to be evidenced in writing may only be varied by written agreement,[204] though it may be discharged by oral agreement.[205] Leaving that complication aside, the only matter likely to cause general difficulty in this context is the requirement of consideration. If neither or both of the parties are in breach of contract, then the variation generates its own consideration;[206] but, if only one party is in breach of the original agreement, consideration by that party is not so generated automatically.[207]

Several statutory interventions must be taken into account in respect of consumer contracts. First, any contractual variation may be unfair under the UTCC

---

195 The distinction is whether or not the promise to give up contractual rights is itself supported by consideration: see para 26.18.

196 In practice, it may be difficult to decide whether there has been a variation or a waiver: see Hoggett (1970) 33 MLR 518.

197 Grey Term (n): OFT, *Bulletin No. 13*, case 16; *No. 14*, case 16; and see generally, para 11.18.

198 See generally, para 26.15. With regard to payment of a lesser sum than the debt due, this will usually be no satisfaction (see para 26.18), except where there is a rebate (see para 26.19A).

199 See *D and C Builders Ltd v Rees* [1966] 2 QB 617, CA (not a sale case). For unilateral variations of price, rent or interest, see para 10.05.

200 [1972] 2 QB 189; [1972] 2 All ER 127, CA.

201 It was held that the giving of a credit was conditional payment, which became absolute when the credit was duly honoured: as to absolute and conditional payment, see 1st edn, para 23.14A.

202 See also *Hartley v Hymans* (set out at para 26.24). For a case where there was no variation because the parties were not *ad idem*, see *Woodhouse AC Israel Cocoa Ltd SA v Nigerian Produce Marketing Co Ltd* [1972] AC 741, HL.

203 A standard-form instalment credit contract may purport to exclude oral variations and waivers: see para 26.23. As to the formation in respect of a variation of a sale of land, see para 9.03.

204 *Goss v Nugent* (1833) 5 B & Ad 58.

205 *Morris v Baron* [1918] AC 1, HL. See further, para 25.06.

206 See para 26.18. It may be important to determine whether, in the case of non-performance of the varied agreement, the consideration is the promise to vary, or performance of that promise.

207 For a case where consideration was found, see *Tommey v Finextra Ltd* (1962) 106 Sol Jo 1012.

Regulations (see para 11.12, *et seq*.). Second, a doorstep or distance contract may be cancellable (see paras 10.36–8). Third, variation of regulated instalment credit transactions may give rise to particular difficulties in this context (see para 26.22).

**[26.22] Regulated agreements**. The CCA alters the general rules above considered with regard to both unilateral and consensual variations of regulated agreements.

1. *Unilateral variations.* The CCA allows one party to vary a regulated agreement without cause in several circumstances: cancellation (ss 67–73: see para 10.32); early payment (ss 94–6: see para 26.19A); remedying default (s 89: see para 24.32. For the position where the default arises upon the death of the debtor or hirer, see para 24.48); Time Orders (see para 24.41) or other court orders utilising s 136 (see para 9.20); and extortionate credit bargains/unfair credit relationships (see paras 29.41 and 29.44).

2. *Consensual variations.* Except in the case of non-commercial agreements (s 82(7). For non-commercial agreements, see para 5.18), s 82 (as amended) controls consensual variations of regulated agreements in a number of circumstances.

   (a) Section 82(1) envisages that the regulated agreement may confer on the creditor a power to vary the terms of the agreement. Such a power is common in relation to the rate of interest charged. In *Lombard Tricity Finance Ltd v Paton*:[208]

   > P was minded to obtain an Amstrad computer from a retailer, Dixons, for a price of £244.98. Instead of a credit sale from Dixons, he entered a loan transaction under which Lombard provided him with running-account credit within s 10 of the CCA (see para 5.28). A box on the face of that credit agreement stated that interest payable on the credit balance was 'subject to variation by the creditor from time to time on notification as required by law'. After an interest rate increase P defaulted and Lombard sued for the outstanding loan.

   P argued that the credit agreement was improperly executed because, contrary to Regulations made under s 60 (see para 9.10), the agreement did not indicate 'the circumstances in which any variation . . . may occur'. However, a unanimous Court of Appeal reasoned that, if it was lawful for a seller to vary unilaterally the price (see para 10.05), it was in principle permissible for the creditor to vary unilaterally the rate of interest charged;[209] that there was nothing in the CCA regulations to make that unlawful; and that this power was stated with sufficient clarity in the box on the face of the agreement (see para 9.11). As to the implementation of such rate changes,[210] s 82(1) insists that the variation does not take effect

---

208 [1989] 1 All ER 918; (1989) 8 Tr L 129, CA (criticised 105 LQR 524). It does not apply where the variation is automatic in the sense of being outside the control of the parties: as to which, see para 10.05.

209 If a lender treats old borrowers capriciously unfavourably, the OFT may take action under the CCA licensing provisions (see para 6.23): *per* Staughton LJ in *Paton* (below) at 923d; and see [2001] 3 *Credit Today* 7. As to new borrowers, if the loan is a consumer supply, the variation may also be unfair: OFT, *2000-AR* 35; and see para 11.12, *et seq*.

210 If the power is utilised to make too radical a variation of the agreement, it might be struck down by s 3(2)(b) of UCTA (see para 18.21). There being currently no statutory power to make minor alterations unilaterally, these are commonly effected by letters of waiver (see para 26.24): Rosenthal (1990) 45 CC1/10.

before notice is given to the debtor or hirer in the prescribed manner.[211] This rule does not apply to variations which are automatic in the sense of being outside the control of the parties.[212]

(b) Section 82(2) applies where, after the formation of a regulated agreement,[213] the parties subsequently agree[214] to 'vary or supplement' it;[215] but s 82(2) would not appear to extend to novations, e.g. where a new party is added (see para 7.27). The effect of s 82(2) on the modifying agreement is to revoke the earlier agreement and replace it with a new agreement combining the effect of the two agreements.[216] If the earlier agreement is regulated, the effect of s 82(3)[213] is that generally speaking the 'modifying agreement' is also regulated: so, once regulated always regulated,[217] though the variation may give rise to substantial extra CCA requirements, principally the Part V requirements (as to which, see generally Chap 9). Instead of first taking out a fixed-sum agreement and later varying it, it may therefore be simpler and more attractive to the creditor instead to propose from the outset a running-account credit.[218]

(c) Where the parties agree[213] to vary a non-regulated agreement,[214] s 82(2) spells out how to decide whether the 'modifying agreement' has become regulated,[219] but does not apply so as to render CCA-regulated first mortgages exempt by s 16(6C) (s 82(5A): see para 5.15).

## The doctrine of waiver

**[26.23]** A party may waive the right to sue in either tort or contract.

1. *Waiver of tort.*[220] Where a party indicates before the commission of a tort against him that he will waive any right of action in respect thereof, this may amount to

---

211 Consumer Credit (Notice of Variation of Agreements) Regulations, 1977 SI 328. See further Guest and Lloyd, *Encyclopedia of Consumer Credit*, paras 2–083 and 3–224; Jones, *Credit Cards*, 171–3.

212 See para 10.05. A newspaper advertisement announcing such variations would seem to be outside the advertising regulations (see paras 8.30), provided it referred only to existing (not potential) customers.

213 Could s 82(2) and (3) be avoided by inserting a general power of unilateral variation by the creditor? But see fn 210, above.

214 These provisions only apply where there is a contract of variation strictly so-called. They have no application to waivers, e.g. where the creditor unilaterally grants the debtor a 'payment holiday' (see para 26.24); nor to contracts which discharge earlier agreements, e.g. novations (see para 26.18). See Guest and Lloyd, *Op. cit.*, para 2-083.

215 E.g. linked-on agreements (see para 24.36); rescheduling of payments on default (see para 24.32); replacement of defective goods (see para 29.02); debtor or hirer wishes to assign his interest to a third party (see para 1.23); where an agreement is secured on land and the debtor moves house (see para 25.24).

216 Distinguish self-standing agreements: see Goode, *Consumer Credit Law & Practice*, para 35.62.

217 E.g. further loan advanced under a fixed-sum credit. But see the special rules for the modification of regulated running-account credit or house mortgages (s 82(3) (as amended), (4)) and cancellable agreements (s 82(5) and (6)): para 10.32. For protected goods, see para 24.36.

218 He would, of course, thereby give up any recaption rights (see para 24.23). For running-account credit, see para 7.08.

219 See Goode, *Op. cit.*, para 35.61, *et seq.* If so, matters become so complicated and expensive that such transactions are best avoided: Guest and Lloyd, *Op. cit.*, para 2-083. For the difficulties raised by further advances, see Ferran, *Mortgage Securitisation*, 122–3.

220 The expression 'waiver of tort' may be misleading: see Burrows (1983) 99 LQR at 236–7.

a consent to the commission of the tort against him, or a voluntary assumption of risk (see para 18.03). A waiver after commission of the tort may operate to discharge the right of action by way of an election of remedies, or by reason of a judgment (see para 26.17); but otherwise its effect is presumably similar to that in contract (see below).

2.  *Waiver of contractual rights.* The common law has long accepted that contractual rights may be expressly or impliedly waived before or after breach. The effect of a waiver may be to discharge the whole contract: it may evince a mutual intention to abandon the contract;[221] alternatively, a party who wrongfully repudiates his own obligations, or disables himself from performing them, may thereby impliedly waive his own rights.[222] However, we are concerned here with those waivers which do not discharge the whole contract, but merely purport to relinquish certain rights under it. Whether a contractual right has been waived is primarily a question of intention,[223] with this limitation: if the contractual provision is for the benefit of one party alone, he may waive it unilaterally; but, if it is inserted for the benefit of both parties, it can only be waived by mutual agreement.[224] Mere neglect or delay in enforcing an agreement does not *per se* amount to a waiver;[225] but, to avoid any doubt, standard-form agreements (see para 11.08) commonly provide that no relaxation or indulgence shall be construed as a waiver of rights. At any event, it is clear that a waiver has no effect unless unequivocal,[226] and perhaps then only where the representee acts on it to his detriment.[227] Examination of the basis of waiver in sale (see para 26.24) is followed by consideration of the general effect of such waiver (see para 26.25), and the relationship of waiver to rejection for the wrong reason (see para 26.26).

**[26.24] The basis of waiver**. The common law rules as to waiver of contractual rights (see para 26.23) would appear to have been partially embodied in s 11(2) of the SGA, which provides as follows:

> 'Where a contract of sale is subject to a condition to be fulfilled by the seller, the buyer may waive the condition, or may elect to treat the breach of the condition as a breach of warranty and not as a ground for treating the contract as repudiated.'

It should be noticed that the provision speaks of a 'waiver' of rights and an 'election' of remedies;[228] and the distinction between the two may become important

---

221 E.g. *Fisher Ltd v Eastwoods Ltd* [1936] 1 All ER 421.

222 See the cases collected in *Benjamin on Sale*, 8th edn, 1950, 560, fn (q).

223 See *per* Lord Denning LJ in *Charles Rickards Ltd v Oppenheim* (set out at para 26.25). See also *Finance for Shipping v Appledore* [1982] Com LR 49, CA.

224 See *per* Tucker J in the *Fibrosa* case [1942] 1 KB 12, at 20–21 (reversed by the HL on other grounds: [1943] AC 32); and *per* Buckley J in *Manchester Diocesan Council v Commercial and General Investments Ltd* [1969] 3 All ER 1593 at 1598.

225 *Perry v Davis* (1858) 3 CB NS 769 (not a sale case).

226 *Mardorf Peach & Co Ltd v Attica Sea Carriers Corpn* [1977] AC 850, HL (charterparty); *Woodhouse AC Israel Cocoa Ltd SA v Nigerian Produce Marketing Co Ltd* [1972] AC 741, HL (sale); *The Post Chaser* [1982] 1 All ER 19 (sale); *Bunge SA v Compagnie Europeene De Cereales* [1982] 1 Lloyd's Rep 306 (sale); *Peregrine Systems Ltd v Steria Ltd* [2005] EWCA 239, CA (services), para 23.

227 *The Post Chaser* (above). *Sed quaere?*

228 Are there (only?) two different sorts of waiver? See generally Treitel, *Law of Contract*, 11th edn, 811–6.

when deciding whether a buyer may go back on his waiver or election. Where the buyer has several alternative remedies at his disposal, the **election** may be or become irrevocable (see para 26.17); and in some circumstances the law may compel the buyer to accept damages rather than rescind for breach of condition (see para 29.05). On the other hand, the effect of a **waiver** of rights is illustrated by *Hartley v Hymans:*[229]

> A written contract for the sale of 11,000 lbs of cotton provided for delivery between September and November 15th, 1918. By the latter date, the seller had only delivered 500 lbs; and the buyer subsequently repeatedly complained and requested early delivery. Instalments totalling 3,704 lbs were delivered between November 15th, 1918 and February 27th, 1919. On March 13th, 1919 the buyer, without any previous notice, purported to cancel the order.

In the seller's action for non-acceptance (see para 27.24), McCardie J found that the time for tender of delivery was of the essence of the contract (see para 23.18); but he held that the buyer was not entitled to insist on delivery in the period ending November 15, 1918 for the following reasons:

(1) he had waived his rights under what is now s 11(2); and

(2) he was estopped from asserting that the contract ceased to be valid on that date;[230] and

(3) the parties had made a new agreement extending the period for delivery beyond November 15, 1918 (see para 26.21).

Each of the first two reasons appears to refer to a different line of authority, and 'reveals the incredible confusion of thought the law has now reached'.[231] The binding effect of a waiver at common law had already been recognised in the converse case where the buyer was in breach, and the seller waived the breach;[232] but in a later case Denning LJ explained the rule in terms of estoppel.[233] However, a promise as to future conduct cannot amount to an estoppel at common law (see para 21.12), and could only take effect under the alleged doctrine of equitable estoppel, a matter beyond the scope of this work.[234] The precise relationship of the doctrines of waiver and equitable estoppel are still being worked out.[235] In a common situation where a contract contained a provision that no variation (see para 26.21) would be valid unless in signed writing, it has been held that the provision may be waived/estopped.[236]

---

229 [1920] 3 KB 475; [1920] All ER Rep 328.

230 See also *Lombard North Central plc v Stobart* (1990) 9 Tr LR 105, CA. Compare *Societe Italo-Belge etc v Palm and Vegetable Oils etc* [1981] Com LR 249.

231 Stoljar (1957) 35 Can BR 485, 503.

232 *Panoutsos v Raymond Hadley Corporation* as reported in (1922) Com Cas 207, CA. Applied in *Plasticmoda Societe Per Azoine v Davidsons Ltd* [1952] 1 Lloyd's Rep 527.

233 *Charles Rickards Ltd v Oppenheim* (set out at para 26.25), at 623.

234 See Treitel, *Op. cit.*, 105–24; Stoljar (1957) 35 Can BR 485, 520–28; Spencer Bower, *Estoppel*, 2nd edn, Chap XIV.

235 See Treitel, *Op. cit.*, 115.

236 *MSAS Global Logistics Ltd v Power Packaging Inc* [2003] CLY 710 (not a goods case) where Davis J said that 'the precise label was unimportant'.

**[26.25] The effect**. Suppose A does waive a contractual duty owed to him by B, can either party later set up the subsequent non-performance of that waived term? It seems that the party for whose benefit the waiver was made (B) is estopped and cannot refuse to accept the varied performance.[237] Can A go back on his waiver? He cannot put the clock back; so that, if, for example, a delivery date is waived but the contract is not performed at all, damages are assessed on the footing that the breach took place at the end of the extended period.[238] On the other hand, the contractual promise still stands,[239] so A may go back on his waiver as regards future performance. Thus, in *Charles Rickards Ltd v Oppenheim*:[240]

> A ordered a Rolls Royce chassis from B and the latter agreed to build a body on it by March 20th. After B had failed to complete the work by that date A continued to press for delivery, but on June 29th gave notice that if the work was not completed within the next four weeks the contract was off.

The Court of Appeal unanimously held that time of delivery was of the essence of this contract (see para 23.18); that this stipulation was impliedly waived by A's requests for delivery after March 20th;[241] but that A was entitled to make time of the essence again by reasonable notice. It decided that A's notice of June 29 had made time of the essence again, so that B's failure to deliver within the four weeks amounted to a breach of condition, entitling A to rescind the contract. It would seem that a similar notice making time of the essence may be given in respect of contracts of services.[242]

**[26.26] Rejection for the wrong reason**. In *Taylor v Oakes*,[243] Greer J at first instance noted *obiter* the general[244]

> 'long-established rule of law that a contracting party who, after he has become entitled to refuse performance of his contractual obligations, gives a wrong reason for his refusal, does not thereby deprive himself of the justification which in fact existed, whether he was aware of it or not.'

For many years, there was no clear authority as to whether the foregoing general principle applied in the law of sale; and, indeed, there was disputed authority that it did not apply to cif sales.[245] However, the issue arose in relation to simple sales in *Northern Foods PLC v Focal Foods Ltd*.[246]

---

237 *Hickman v Haynes* (1875) LR 10 CP 598; *Levy & Co v Goldberg* [1922] 1 KB 688.

238 *Ogle v Earl of Vane* (1868) LR 3 QB 272, Ex Ch: see further, para 29.29. See also *The Eurometal* [1981] 3 All ER 533; and waiver of lien (para 24.15).

239 *British and Benningtons Ltd v North Western Cacher Tea Co Ltd* (set out at para 23.05).

240 [1950] 1 KB 616; [1950] 1 All ER 420, CA. See also *Tool Metal Manufacturing Co Ltd v Tungsten Electric Co Ltd* [1955] 2 All ER 657, HL; *Etablissements Chainbaux SARL v Harbormaster Ltd* [1955] 1 Lloyd's Rep 303.

241 Compare *Nichimen Corpn v Gatoil Overseas Inc* [1987] 2 Lloyd's Rep 46, CA.

242 *Shawton Engineering Ltd v DGP International Ltd* [2005] EWCA Civ 1359, CA (commercial case).

243 (1922) 27 Com Cas 261, CA. See also *per* Mocatta J in *The Mihalis Angelos* [1970] 1 All ER 673, at 676e; reversed on the other grounds [1970] 3 All ER 125, CA; and Benjamin's *Sale of Goods*, 6th edn, paras 9-016 and 19-154.

244 At 266. Applied *Glencore Grain Rotterdam BV v Lebanese Organisation for International Commerce* [1997] 4 All ER 514, CA.

245 *Panchaud Freres SA v Etablissements General Grain Co* [1970] 1 Lloyd's Rep 53, CA; but see the criticism in Benjamin's *Sale of Goods*, 6th edn, para 19-155.

246 [2003] 2 Lloyd's Rep 728.

B was a well-known food manufacturer. Wishing to put supplies on a long-term basis, in June 1997 B agreed with S a three-year written contract at a fixed price to supply a fixed proportion of B's daily needs, e.g. 50%: for about half each year, that fixed price would exceed the spot rate, whereas for the other half it would be less. Unbeknown to S, B largely only ordered from S when the agreed price was less than the spot rate and in total purchased more onions per year from third parties. Finding the contract uneconomic, after eight months S refused to supply any more onions at the agreed price, but continued to supply at the spot rate to a protesting B. In preliminary proceedings in B's action, the Court of Appeal held as follows: (1) B was under a logically implied continuing obligation throughout the year to source 50% supplies from S (see para 11.10); (2) B was in breach of that obligation, though S was unaware of that (para 1.19); but (3) S was in breach of contract in refusing in February 1998 further supplies at the contract price (para 1.5).

Upon the above findings, McGonigal J held as follows: (1) B regarded itself as entitled to disregard the 50% obligation as convenient (para 7.1); (2) that this was a sufficiently serious breach of an intermediate term as would entitle S to treat the contract as at an end (see para 11.05); (3) that this amounted to a repudiation by B (see para 26.15); and (4) that S could rely on this repudiation, notwithstanding that they gave no, or a wrong, reason for refusing to continue supplies (see paras 8.3 and 9.3; and above *obiter*). His Lordship explained that S's failure to supply at the contract price was therefore justified as an acceptance of B's prior repudiation;[247] and he refused to treat S's subsequent supply at the spot rate as an election to keep the contract alive because it was done in ignorance of B's repudiatory breaches (see para 10.4). So, in this case a party (S) sued for breach of contract was able to escape liability for breach because, in the course of proceedings there was revealed a prior repudiatory breach by the other side (B), which the defendant (S) was able to accept as bringing an end to the contract before the time for his breach arrived (see para 26.16).

*Anticipatory breach.* Suppose a seller intends to make a delivery which would be a breach of contract;[248] but, before he can tender the goods, the buyer, in ignorance of the seller's intention, intimates that he will not accept delivery and purports to repudiate for another reason insufficient in law. Can the buyer subsequently rely on the seller's intended breach as a waiver of performance so as to justify his refusal to accept delivery? Greer J sought to reconcile his above dictum with *Braithwaite's* case (see para 23.07) by suggesting that his rule applies where there is a refusal to accept an actual tender of delivery, whereas in *Braithwaite's* case there was a mere offer to tender delivery (at 267). The point seems to be that the valid ground for repudiation must actually exist at the time of rejection: in *British and Benningtons Ltd v North West Cacher Tea Co Ltd* (set out at para 23.05), the buyer committed an anticipatory breach which was accepted by the seller **before** the time when the seller was required to deliver.[249] Assuming that a valid ground for repudiation does exist at

---

247  At para 9.8. His Lordship distinguished the situation where there was mutual abandonment: see para 26.18.

248  For the duty of delivery, see para 23.05, *et seq*.

249  See also *Gill & Duffus SA v Berger & Co Inc* (set out at para 23.06).

the time the buyer gives the wrong reason, the above rule is only needed where the
buyer elects to treat the contract as repudiated: if the buyer had affirmed after what
he thought was a breach, the contract enures for the benefit of both parties, so that
when the buyer discovers the seller's actual breach, he can anyway rely upon it to
treat the contract as repudiated.[250]

---

250 *The Simona* (see para 23.07)

# CHAPTER 27

# REMEDIES OF THE SUPPLIER—'CREDITOR OR OWNER'

## INTRODUCTION

**[27.01]** In our modern society, the use by consumers of debt, and especially of instalment debt (see para 1.03), has become a widespread method of acquiring the life-style which our society assumes, this being particularly the case with young families (the 25- to 40-year-olds with children). The demand is fostered by advertising (see Chap 8), e.g. of interest-free, low-start and instant credit, whereas it is hoped that consumers will be helped to manage it by education (see para 3.01), consumer codes of practice (see para 3.13) and credit insurance (see para 24.48). Even assuming an initial ability to pay,[1] a proportion of those consumers will not pay their debts lawfully due. Those who will not pay include not only 'professional debtors', but also those who misguidedly cease payment because they have a valid complaint, e.g. about goods supplied (see Chaps 13–15) and those who cannot pay. This last group include the inadequate and a proportion of low-income families with unexpectedly reduced income, e.g. through illness or redundancy or divorce.[2]

Faced with a defaulting customer within the limitation period (see para 26.17), the supplier in principle has two basic choices open to him: (1) **self-help** (see para 27.02), in the pursuit of which the creditor may be restrained by the offences with regard to forcible entry of premises and unlawful harassment of debtors;[3] or (2) **court action** (see para 27.03), which in the case of insolvency proceedings only is carefully controlled (see para 19.18). Nevertheless, the present 'system' of enforcement by self-help and court action still gives significant advantages to the ordinary creditor who acts first as against other ordinary creditors, so unfortunately encouraging precipitate action rather than merciful forbearance.[4] To some extent, it is possible for the OFT to control the treatment of debtors by use of the CCA licensing system (see para 6.23).

As long ago as 1969 there were officially identified the following drawbacks to the enforcement system, still unremedied:[5] that in appropriate cases serial debtors should be restrained by court order from incurring further credit and creditors deterred from granting it by postponement to other creditors;[6] that the recovery of

---

1    This is assessed in the application process: see para 8.35, *et seq*.
2    See Dominy and Kempson for LCD, *Can't Pay or Won't Pay*, 2003, reviewed 69 *Quarterly Account* 9; [2005] CCA News, Autumn, 10–11.
3    See paras 24.23–24. But not by the Protection from Harassment Act 1997: *Tuppen v Microsoft Corpn Ltd* [2000] CLY 46.
4    For this 'Devil-take-the-hindmost' philosophy, see para 19.13.
5    The Payne Report on *The Enforcement of Judgment Debts* (1969, Cmnd. 3903). See especially paras 38, 44 and 78.
6    This might well result in lawful credit not being available to those who most need it. Is this desirable when the alternative is usually illegal lending (see para 27.02)?

debts should be undertaken jointly by an enforcement office administering all methods of enforcement;[7] and that the present harsh system should be displaced by the same priority system as on insolvency.[8] Alternatively, a debtor could go further and petition for his own insolvency (see para 19.21). Insofar as the serial debtor is inadequate, or simply overtaken by disaster, there are presently informal systems in the credit industry that may sometimes achieve some of these results. In 1998, the Lord Chancellor began a *Civil Enforcement Review*;[9] and his Department has since produced some interim reports (see paras 19.15 and 19.17; and para 27.04).

[27.02] **Self-help**. As a first step, the creditor or owner is likely to seek to encourage payment by filing a default with a credit reference bureau, which may effectively debar the debtor or hirer from obtaining further access to such facilities (see para 8.36) in his own name (for identity fraud, see para 10.15) and rescind the contract for breach (see para 26.11). Preferably before so doing (except in the case of fraud), the creditor or owner should serve on the debtor or hirer a notice of intention to file,[10] perhaps together with any Arrears Letter/Default Notice required (see paras 24.27A and 24.30) and do so in a manner which does not amount to unlawful harassment (see para 24.24). The information filed must comply with the DPA;[11] otherwise the IC may take enforcement action (see para 3.27) against the creditor or owner. Thereafter, the conduct of the creditor or owner against a solvent debtor depends on whether the debt is secured or unsecured.

1. *Unsecured debt.* The position here may depend on whether the unsecured debt is a 'priority' or ordinary debt.[12] This informal 'priority' category does not refer to priority on insolvency (see para 19.22), but to those unsecured creditors who have a greater power to make a debtor's life unpleasant than an ordinary creditor:[13] on the criminal side, by fines and court orders;[14] and on the civil side such as local authorities, who still have power to seek imprisonment in respect of some debts;[15] or the privatised utilities (see para 3.07) in recognition of their

---

7 Enforcement Offices were introduced for a trial period in Northern Ireland, but never on the mainland. They proved slow and costly. See further *Enforcement of Debt*, paras 69–74, 195–219.

8 See the Payne Report, paras 304, 1137; and *Enforcement of Debt*, paras 220–2.

9 For the terms of reference, see (1998) 53 CC2/5–6. See further 50 *Quarterly Account* 1.

10 Notice after filing would, if inaccurate, render the creditor or owner liable to pay compensation to the consumer (the 'data subject'): DPA, s 10: see para 3.27.

11 It must be, e.g. accurate, adequate, relevant and fair under the Data Protection Principles (see para 3.28); it must comply with any relevant Code of Practice (see para 3.13); and there must be no genuine dispute as to the existence of the debt. The IC has produced *Guidance Notes on Defaults*.

12 The expression 'priority debt' may come from the County Court Default Summons, which uses it to include also arrears on housing, community charge, tax and maintenance. More widely, it is used to describe unpaid debts which will cause the debtor a considerable degree of hardship (Keen, *Life After Debt* (2003) 31) and has even included hp of essential items (Keen, Chap 4).

13 Non-priority debts, e.g. overdrafts, payment cards, catalogue debts, which are only subject to lesser non-payment sanctions. See Keen, *Op. cit.*, Chap 4; Shields (2003) 99 Adviser 42.

14 Unpaid fines or court orders may be referred to the bailiffs (see para 19.15); or lead to attachment of earnings orders (see para 27.05); or wilful refusal to pay may lead to imprisonment. A Government crackdown on unpaid fines commenced in April 2004.

15 By applying to the Magistrates Court for a liability order. These orders do not appear to be recorded by the Registry Trust or credit reference agencies, so not spoiling the debtor's credit rating.

public regulation and that they provide essential services.[16] Where a consumer does not pay his gas or electricity bill (but not water)[17], the undertakings have power to install a pre-payment meter or disconnect the service.[18] Consumer debt advisers (see para 3.16) normally recommend that all priority debts are paid off before any non-priority debts.

2. *Secured debts.* The transaction may have been set up with some real security, which may take one of the traditional forms of pledge, mortgage or charge (see Chap 25); or a judgment creditor may obtain security after default by way of a charging order (see para 27.04). In relation to goods, security may be achieved by way of an instalment contract, i.e. conditional sale, hp or simple hiring. It remains to be noticed here the very small sums of money commonly realised on the sale of repossessed goods:[19] not only is the market price for second-hand goods frequently low,[20] but in the case of instalment contracts there is not even any duty on the repossessing supplier to secure the best price obtainable because there is no equity of redemption (see para 24.22), as compared with regulated pledges (CCA, s 121(6): see further para 25.18), mortgages and charges (see para 25.20).

Whether or not the creditor is secured, he may commonly resort to persuasion to get the debtor to pay up.[21] Whilst there is reasonable hope of retaining a customer, most creditors tend to keep early debt-recovery in-house, say when up to three instalments are in arrears and the debt 90 days old. Thereafter, creditors sometimes seek to distance themselves from the methods of collection employed by assigning[22] the (bad) debts to a debt-collection agency (see para 5.42), in which case it may be necessary to register the agency as a creditor to satisfy the DPA (see para 3.27). Moreover, the OFT has the negative and positive licensing powers considered in Chap 6, which should hopefully lead to the removal of the most undesirable creditors and debt-collectors from the legitimate trade.

**[27.03] Court action.** Leaving aside claims for restitution in criminal proceedings (see para 3.20), normally, the appropriate first step will be civil proceedings by a

---

16 A Water Board is statutorily required to supply, so the consumer has little need to provide his personal details: see [2002] 11 *Credit Today* 7. Water Boards lost their disconnection powers in 1999 (see para 3.07), which has led to their being treated as non-priority creditors and incurring record debts (+18%).

17 The water utilities also feel hampered by their difficulty, arising from the DPA (see para 3.27), in sharing information about defaulting customers: for a scheme, see Perkins (2006) 1 QA 10.

18 See para 3.07. Gas and Electricity Boards may not use these powers to collect other debts: *South Wales Electricity PLC v OFFER* [1999] CLY 2000; unless authorised under the Energy Act 2004, s 181. A ban on disconnection by all utilities has been called for: [2003] 12 *Credit Today* 5; and see (2005) 75 *Quarterly Account* 12; [2005] 4 CT 18; Bates (2005) 78 *QA* 12.

19 Cranston, *Op. cit.*, 273; Goode, *HP Law & Practice*, 2nd edn, 403–4. Cf. the effect of court action: para 27.04.

20 Sales of repossessed goods tend to take place either at local auctions or through second-hand dealers or specialist shops.

21 As to court action, see para 27.03. For collection strategies, see [2002] 11 *Credit Extra*. It is for consideration whether the law ought to put the creditor to his election—seize or sue. See Cranston, *Consumers and the Law*, 3rd edn, 282.

22 See (2006) 79 *QA* 7; and generally, para 7.17. Without more, such an assignment will not be struck down as maintenance or champerty (see para 7.26): *Camdex International Ltd v Bank of Zambia* [1998] QB 22, CA.

supplier against a consumer in the consumer's local county court[23] for any of the following: (1) **repossession** (see para 24.25); (2) **debt**, as for the price of goods sold[24] or arrears of rentals (see para 27.21) or money lent (see para 7.03); and (3) **damages** (see para 27.27). Frequently, such actions are undefended, in which case if the agreement is unregulated summary judgment may be obtained,[25] though it is sometimes more effective for the creditor to apply for adjournment and an order requiring the debtor's presence.[26] However, if the debtor puts in any sort of defence, e.g. that it is an unfair credit relationship (see para 29.44), or counter-claim for defective goods (see para 29.26), the creditor may have to choose between discontinuing the action because it is uneconomic, or continuing the proceedings to make an example of the debtor to encourage performance by other debtors.[27] If the creditor contemplates continuing proceedings, he will have to bear in mind the power of the county court to order payment by instalments as a way of redressing the inequality of bargaining power between creditors and debtors: such a general power has existed since 1846[28] and has been re-enforced as regards regulated debts by Time Orders (see para 24.40).

Assuming the unsecured creditor does succeed in obtaining judgment he is then said to be a **judgment creditor**: that judgment will be registered[29] and the judgment creditor has available to him the range of remedies considered below (para 27.04). However, a very large proportion of debt cases continue to be settled at a late stage in proceedings,[30] suggesting that in many cases the threat of judicial proceedings[31] secures payment.[32] Whence can the judgment debtor obtain funds to pay off such judgments, other than from unlicensed moneylenders (see para 6.09) or non-commercial sources?

---

23  See para 3.22. It should always be enforced as a judgment of the County, not High, Court: *per* Lord Donaldson in *Forward Trust Ltd v Whymark* [1989] 3 All ER 915, CA, at 921h.

24  See para 27.16. Where there is an instalment contract, instalments in arrears at the time of proceedings will be recoverable anyway; and the future instalments may become due immediately by reason of an acceleration clause (see para 26.19).

25  Under the CPR, Pt 12 (which is not available as regards regulated agreements), if no defence whatsoever is put in; or if the sum exceeds the arbitration limit (see para 3.23) and the reply put in is no real defence. See *Enforcement of Debt* (1987, LC's Dept), paras 13, 94–5.

26  These are known as 'Information Orders' (see CPR, Pt 71): for mechanics, see (2004) 72 *QA* 19. Failure to appear would be a contempt of court, which may lead to arrest of the debtor and hence pressurise him to pay: see (1991) 12 CCA News 5/11.

27  See *Consumer Credit* (Ed Goode) 302; and para 27.04. But some judgments are satisfied in whole or part: *Enforcement of Debt*, paras 96–100.

28  See now the County Courts Act 1984, s 71.

29  At the Registry Trust Ltd (see below). This may itself be a sanction in that the judgment debtor may find himself barred from further credit (see para 8.36); but it may be circumvented by a credit repair company (see fn 34, below). Entitlement to statutory interest may also commence: see para 7.03A.

30  See the Crowther Report, para 6.6.49; and para 27.04. Can attempts by the judgment creditor to pressure the debtor amount to unlawful harassment (see para 24.24)?

31  E.g. as a prior step to initiating bankruptcy proceedings, a judgment creditor may issue a Statutory Demand for payment (see para 19.21: and (1993) 47 CC 6/2).

32  See *Enforcement of Debt*, paras 228–33. However, from time to time financiers suggest that the security offered by conditional sale or hp has been so reduced (see para 24.49) that they might just as well rely upon a credit sale with acceleration clause, summary judgment and execution. See, e.g. the Crowther Report, para 6.6.46.

*Undefended claims.* In over 90% of unregulated debt cases no defence is made so that proceedings are administrative rather than judicial, in that application may be made for summary judgment (see above). As part of this process, a public registry of unsatisfied county court judgments is kept;[33] but, despite assertions to the contrary, these records cannot legitimately be 'repaired',[34] as by removing an adverse credit history so as to obtain a satisfactory credit score (see para 8.39).

**[27.04] The judgment creditor's remedies.** Where an unsecured judgment debt remains unsatisfied,[35] it should be borne in mind that, if the debtor is without assets, use of the following remedies will not lead to recovery of any money but simply add to the costs.[36] Hence, enquiry agents are sometimes used at an early stage in the proceedings to establish whether the debtor is worth suing.[37] The major remedies of such a judgment creditor, including where an instalment order, e.g. Time Order (see para 24.40) is in arrears,[38] are as follows,[39] it being for the creditor to choose his remedy (Civil Procedure Rules (CPR), r 70.2):

1. *Execution by sheriff or bailiff* (CPR, Sched 1, Ord 47). This ancient procedure under writ or warrant of execution may be used to carry out a judgment or an order for the payment of costs: it has already been outlined (see generally, paras 19.15) and is not normally used if the debt exceeds £5,000. In about half the cases, the likely return after payment of the officer's (relatively high) costs may be so small that the court officer simply notifies the execution creditor that the process has been abortive. Even where the requisite minimum level of debt makes the remedy available, forced sales of goods by way of execution tend to produce a very small financial return (see para 27.02), so that it may be more useful as a threat, or to trigger insolvency (IA, ss 123(1)(b) and 268(1)(b); see below).

---

33   County Courts Act 1984, ss 73 and 73A (as inserted by the Administration of Justice Act 1985, s 54). The Registry is a company limited by guarantee, Registry Trust Ltd (RTL). Its record of County and High Court judgments and criminal fines is computerised and routinely accessed by the major reference bureaux: see para 8.36. For an LCD review of RTL, see (2003) 58 CC3/4. In 2002, the EU adopted a Green Paper consultation on a harmonised procedure for uncontested court claims.

34   E.g. by applying to the county court to have judgments struck off the register using procedural excuses which lead to temporary removal. There have been warnings against these forms of activity by both the OFT (see (1992) 9 Tr L 102) and the Lord Chancellor (see 9 Tr L 229). See also (2005) 60 CC3/4. They now require a credit information licence (see para 5.44).

35   Distinguish a judgment for delivery of goods (see para 24.26): if unsatisfied, this may lead to a warrant for delivery of goods.

36   The pattern of debt-collecting is therefore likely to be affected by significant increases in court charges. The LCD has proposed in *Effective Enforcement* (2003, Cm. 5744) that creditors be helped to assess whether execution is worthwhile against a judgment debtor by the introduction of Data Disclosure Orders. On the LCD enforcement proposals, see the discussions in [2003] 5 *Credit Today* 15–18.

37   Under the draft TCE Bill 2006, clauses 77–85, the courts would have enhanced powers to obtain information as to the means of a judgment debtor. For this draft Bill, see generally, para 19.15.

38   *Ropaigealach v Allied Irish Bank PLC* [2002] CLY 314, CA. *Contra* where the instalment order is complied with: County Courts Act 1984, s 86(1). See generally Lett (2002) 66 *Quarterly Account* 23.

39   For the new rules, see CPR, Pts 70–73; and Walton (2003) 32 CLWR 179. The judgment creditor may *prima facie* use any of the available methods of enforcement and more than one of them (CPR, r 70(3)); but he must usually seek his enforcement order within the limitation period (see para 26.17): *Bennett v Bank of Scotland* [2004] CLY 263, CA.

2. *Charging orders.* In respect of land or investments owned by the judgment debtor,[40] the judgment creditor may apply for a 'charging order' securing the payment of money due or to become due under the judgment (Charging Orders Act 1979, ss 1 and 2). If granted, the effect is almost to turn the judgment creditor into a secured creditor,[41] though he will necessarily take subject to any prior charges, typically the judgment debtor's house mortgage. However, insofar as the judgment debtor has a significant equity of redemption in his home (see para 25.20) it is unlikely that the judgment creditor will have to go so far as to apply to a court order for sale of the charged property, making this form of execution attractive, which explains why credit proposal forms ask for details as to whether an applicant owns his own home (see generally, para 8.35). It is proposed that the law should be changed to allow a creditor to apply for a charging order even before default on the debt:[42] this would change him into a secured creditor (see para 27.02).

3. *Third-party (previously garnishee) orders (CPR, Pt 72).* The judgment debtor may himself be owed money, e.g. in a bank or building society account. Once aware of this, the judgment creditor may be able to ensure that the third-party debtor, e.g. bank, pays the judgment debt direct to the judgment creditor; and an interim order has been granted to a creditor who could show only that his judgment debtor had recently paid him money by a cheque drawn on that account.[43] Leaving aside the debtor's earnings (see below), this little-used process is sometimes effective against consumers,[44] more often against traders. The order binds the third party personally, not the debt.[45]

4. *Attachment of earnings.* In England, unlike the US, this procedure is not available when the contract is made (see para 25.04), but only when the creditor has become a judgment creditor (see para 27.05).

5. *Distress.* Whereas a house-owning debtor is subject to charging orders over his house (see above), a tenant debtor is subject to distress on his goods (see para 19.17).

6. *Insolvency.* This procedure is usually discretionary[46] and may not be used where the debtor genuinely disputes the debt. The summary administration procedure (IA, s 275) has been abolished (EA, s 269 and Sched 23).

7. *Debt administration orders.*[47] For NINAs (see para 6.10), the rules are contained in s 112 of the County Courts Act 1984. It was intended that they be replaced by

---

40  Ownership of land can now be cheaply checked: see para 2.18. In respect of land, even before an application for a Charging Order Nisi, it is possible to register a Caution at the Land Registry: (1993) 48 CC 2/12. For a consumer's view of the process, see Sullivan (1999) 52 *Quarterly Account* 4; Lett (2005) 76 *QA* 12. Compare the creditor's view: [2006] 3 *Credit Today* 17.

41  But see *Mercantile Credit Co v Ellis* [1987] CLY 2917, CA. *Effective Enforcement* (above) has recommended some procedural improvements to make these Orders more effective.

42  See the draft TCE Bill (above), clauses 75–6.

43  *Alawiye v Mahmood* [2006] 3 All ER 668; [2006] EWHC 277.

44  *SCF Finance Co Ltd v Masri (No. 3)* [1987] QB 1028, CA; *Fitzpatrick v DAF Sales* [1988] IR 464; and see generally *Enforcement of Debt*, paras 40, 125.

45  Grant of the order establishes priority as between different judgment creditors: see Robert-Tissot & Shepherd (2006) 156 NLJ 1119.

46  See para 19.18, *et seq*. It is not an abuse of process to file for insolvency against a solvent debtor wilfully failing to pay: *Cornhill Insurance v Improvement Services* [1986] 1 WLR 114.

47  See Fletcher, *Law of Insolvency*, 2nd edn, 60–61.

new provisions set out in s 13 of the Courts and Legal Services Act 1990; but it seems that s 13 is defective and cannot be implemented. Similar to Interim Orders in the High Court (see below) and often known the 'poor man's bankruptcy', this procedure was intended to allow a multiple debtor to apply to the County Court for an order consolidating personal judgment debts (up to a total of £5,000) under one payment arrangement to the court: the effect would usually be to discharge the debt by affordable instalments, either in full or by part-payment (composition: see para 19.20). This procedure may be seen as a more formal (court sanctioned) alternative to a negotiated DMP (see para 5.42) and generally precludes a petition for bankruptcy (see above) by any creditor named in the order. Perhaps negotiated by a money advice centre (see para 3.08) or other debt-counsellor or debt-adjuster (see para 5.43), it would be registered as a County Court judgment (see para 27.03). Under the draft TCE Bill 2006 (see generally, para 19.15), there should be introduced by clause 88 an elaborate new Pt 6 of the County Courts Act, which it is hoped will at last result in a viable court-based system.

8. *Enforcement Restriction Orders.* Besides the above court-based system, it is proposed in the draft TCE Bill that there should also be introduced two administrative schemes, the intention being to allow a consumer debtor to choose the most appropriate scheme for his circumstances, be it court (above) or administrative (below) based.

(1) Debt Relief Orders (DRO) to be administered by the Official Receiver (OR), e.g. for NINAs (above). On application by an individual debtor who meets specified criteria as regards his assets, income and liabilities, an OR could make a DRO, which would stay enforcement of his debts, the debts being discharged after one year.[48]

(2) Debt management schemes (DMS). For some years, the voluntary sector has supported consumer debtors by way of debt management plans for those with an adequate income stream (see para 5.42). However, their drawback is that such voluntary plans do not have any power of compulsion or composition. The draft TCE Bill sets out to remedy this deficiency by the introduction of DMS. Defined by clauses 91 and 109, DMS are restricted to approved scheme operators (clauses 93–5) supporting only consumer debtors (clause 96(1)), the details to be fleshed out by regulations.[49] Subject to a right of appeal to the county court by any affected creditor (clauses 99–100), a DMS is binding on all the consumer's creditors specified in the plan and *pro tanto* displaces the terms of their contract in both the following respects:

(a) *As to the amount of capital repayable.* Subject to the required payments (see below), the debtor is discharged from the debts specified in the plan (clause 96).

---

48 Under clauses 89–90 of the TCE Bill, there would be inserted a substantial new Pt 6A into the County Courts Act.

49 Clauses 96–8, 108. Supervised by the Lord Chancellor (clause 106) and subject to an elaborate scheme for termination of that approval (clauses 102–5), approved scheme operators are allowed to charge prescribed fees (clause 101) and to receive the LC's financial support (clause 107).

(b) *As to repayments.* The scheme operator may draw up a debt repayment plan (DRP) as to some or all of the consumer-debtor's debts, which must require the debtor to make payments in respect of each of the specified debts.[50]

**[27.05/6] Attachment of earnings.**[51] As a *quid pro quo* for the virtual abolition of imprisonment for judgment debt, in 1970 Parliament introduced attachment of earnings.[52] The new system was consolidated in the Attachment of Earnings Act 1971, whose orders may be made by the county court on application of either debtor[53] or creditor; but where application is made by the creditor, the court has slightly fewer powers. Under such an order, an amount will be deducted from the debtor's earnings which will not normally leave him with less than the basic level of Income Support;[54] and this is periodically paid into court, which may distribute the sums between multiple creditors.

Thus, where a judgment debtor continues in regular employment, this ought to be a procedure by which the creditor can depend on regular reduction of the debt in a simple and cheap manner.[55] However, the scope for an attachment of earnings order is limited: it only applies to judgment debts; even when a debtor continues in employment, it is only knowing failure by his employer to comply with an order which amounts to an offence;[56] the unemployed draw their social security in full; the scheme has no application to the self-employed;[57] and incomes paid by employers other than wages, salaries and pensions are immune from the process (s 24). If the debtor changes his job, the entire court process has to be started afresh;[58] and there is a minimum order.[59] The Lord Chancellor has proposed reform designed to strengthen the system.[60]

**[27.07] Secured creditor's remedies.** The powers of a pledgee to sell an unredeemed pledge depend on whether the pledge is regulated or not (see paras 25.15 and 25.18). The usual remedies of a mortgagee (foreclosure, sale, taking possession and appointment of a receiver) are beyond the scope of this work; but there are

---

50  Clause 92. These repayments will usually be of sums less than the contractual instalments; and clause 92(4) expressly says that it does not matter that the amount/time of payment varies, nor that the total instalments to be paid would only repay part of the debt.

51  See generally Cranston, *Consumers and the Law*, 3rd edn, 279–81; Crossley Vaines, *Personal Property*, 5th edn, 489–91; and para 19.18. Attachment is regarded as the most effective way to collect a debt: *Effective Enforcement* (2003, Cm. 5744).

52  Administration of Justice Act 1970, ss 11–12. See generally, para 27.01.

53  In which case the debtor is perhaps more likely to co-operate in its operation.

54  But there is now a statutory power to transfer collection functions to designated officers: Courts and Legal Services Act 1990, Sched 17, para 5.

55  For the mechanics, see (2004) 72 *Quarterly Account* 19.

56  S 23(2). But the employer is under no liability if he is unaware of the order; and there is no central register or provision for making employers aware of orders, e.g. to stamp them on the debtor's P45 (employment card).

57  The system requires the debtor to have an employer: s 6(2). Cf. whether the debtor is on PAYE.

58  S 9(4). Thus, an employer may avoid the obligations of the Act by sacking the debtor, whilst the debtor may make enforcement of such orders difficult, if not impossible, by frequently changing jobs.

59  Currently £50: (1991) 41 NLJ 887.

60  Following *Effective Enforcement* (above), the draft TCE Bill 2006 (see generally, para 19.15), clauses 73–4, proposes fixed table rates of deduction and a system for tracking employment.

additional restrictions in respect of a regulated mortgage (see para 25.24). In respect of conditional sale and hp the ordinary remedies of repossession and resale have already been considered (see paras 24.21–6), though there are substantial restrictions if the transaction is regulated (see para 24.27, *et seq.*). The position of a secured creditor upon the insolvency of his debtor has already been mentioned (see para 19.14).

## THE SUPPLIER'S REMEDIES AGAINST THE GOODS

### Remedies of an ordinary seller

This will cover cash and credit sales where the unpaid seller wishes to exercise his real rights of lien, stoppage and resale. It has already been pointed out that the SGA fails to draw a clear distinction between the power of sale and the right to resell (see para 24.05); that is, between the effect of resale on (1) the original contract of sale and (2) the title to the goods resold.

[27.08] **The original contract of sale**. Even a 'resale' by the seller will not be a breach of the original contract of sale in any of the following circumstances.[61]

1. *The goods are not ascertained.* The very expression 'resale' pre-supposes that the goods 'resold' have become the subject-matter of the prior contract of sale so that the original buyer has a contractual right to those goods, or to an as yet unascertained part of them (see para 20.05).

2. *Discharge of the seller.* Even if the goods 'resold' were specific or ascertained in relation to the original contract of sale, the seller is entitled to resell if the original contract, or the obligation to deliver those particular goods, is discharged, as by rescission *ab initio* or *de futuro* (see para 26.11). One instance of this receives special mention in s 48(4) of the SGA, which provides that:

   'Where the seller expressly reserves the right of resale in case the buyer should make default, and on the buyer making default, re-sells the goods, the original contract of sale is thereby rescinded, but without prejudice to any claim the seller may have for damages.'

   Typical examples here are contractual provisions for resale on non-acceptance or non-payment; but other types of default may also be stipulated.[62] However, in a consumer supply, such a clause may be unfair.[63]

3. *The statutory right of resale.* As the time for payment of the price is *prima facie* not of the essence (s 10(1): set out at para 23.20), the unpaid seller in possession may be in a quandary as to what to do with the goods;[64] so s 48(3) lays down that:

---

61   No comment on the passing of property is intended by the use of the term 'resale' in this context.
62   *Per* Diplock LJ in *Ward Ltd v Bignall* (set out at para 27.10), at 550.
63   OFT, *Bulletin No. 15*, case 13: Grey Term (d): see para 11.16.
64   As to whether a seller out of possession can resell under s 48(3), see Benjamin's *Sale of Goods*, 6th edn, para 15.123.

'Where the goods are of a perishable nature, or where the unpaid seller gives notice to the buyer of his intention to re-sell, and the buyer does not within a reasonable time pay or tender the price, the unpaid seller may re-sell the goods and recover from the original buyer damages for any loss occasioned by his breach of contract.'

This makes time of the essence in two situations:

(a) The goods are of 'a perishable nature'.[65] Where the price for goods of this type is not forthcoming within a reasonable time,[66] s 48(3) allows the seller to resell.[67]

(b) The seller gives notice. Whatever the type of goods, s 48(3) allows the seller to resell if the price is not paid or tendered within a reasonable time of receipt of that notice.[68] As will be seen later (para 27.10), the wording of s 48(3) is unfortunate; but presumably, at very least, its effect must be to prevent the resale from being a breach of the original contract of sale, as it envisages that the seller may still sue the buyer for damages for non-acceptance (as to which, see para 27.34).

**[27.09] Exercise of real rights**. It is necessary to consider the effect on the original contract of sale of the exercise by the unpaid seller of his real rights in respect of specific or ascertained goods.

1.  *Lien or stoppage.* Section 48(1) of the SGA provides that:

    'Subject to the provisions of this section, a contract of sale is not rescinded by the mere exercise by an unpaid seller of his rights of lien . . . or stoppage in transit.'

    It has been suggested that the object of this subsection was to protect the unpaid seller where time of delivery was of the essence;[69] but it actually only states the obvious fact that such an action by the seller does not, without more, demonstrate an unequivocal intention to repudiate the contract.[70]

2.  *Resale. Prima facie*, a seller with a right to rescind for breach by his buyer has the following alternatives (see para 26.16).

    (a) He may elect to rescind the contract,[71] in which case the property in the goods will, if it has already passed, revest in him (see para 26.11); and he may then resell the goods as his own,[72] and sue the first buyer for damages for non-acceptance (see para 27.24).

    (b) He may affirm the contract, in which case the property will pass under the terms of the contract to the buyer, whom he may sue for the balance of the

---

65  The expression 'perish' in the SGA was considered at para 22.13.
66  This is a question of fact: s 59. See *per* Finnemore J in *Gallagher v Shilcock* [1949] 2 KB 765, at 770.
67  The seller may also have a right to resell under the doctrine of agency of necessity (see para 10.06) or a court order (see para 21.06).
68  See Benjamin, *Op. cit.,* para 15.122.
69  *Per* Diplock LJ in *Ward Ltd v Bignall* [1967] 1 QB 534 at 549, CA.
70  As to repudiation, see para 26.15; as to the rights of lien and stoppage, see para 24.04.
71  See para 27.08. But note that his wrongful resale *may* amount to a repudiation (see para 26.15).
72  There appears to be no legal obligation on the seller as to the manner in which he exercises any right of resale, nor as to the price he accepts. However, if he also seeks damages, he is under a duty to mitigate his loss: see para 27.44.

purchase price (see para 27.16), and damages for non-acceptance, meanwhile exercising his unpaid seller's lien until judgment is satisfied.[73]

**[27.10] On whose behalf is a resale effected?** It is clear that, once the goods have been delivered to the first buyer and the property has passed to him, the seizure and resale by the seller can have no effect on the first sale because it is executed, the resale being merely tortious;[74] and in *Gallagher v Shilcock* Finnemore J took the same view with regard to the resale by an unpaid seller who had remained in possession after the property had passed.[75] However, the Court of Appeal unanimously took the opposite view of the effect of such a resale on the original sale in *Ward Ltd v Bignall*:[76]

> The buyer (B) contracted to buy two motor vehicles for a total purchase price of £850, and paid a £25 deposit; but he later wrongfully refused to take delivery. After giving due notice, the seller (S) attempted to resell the vehicles: he only succeeded in reselling one, for which he obtained £350; and sued B for £497 10s,[77] being the net balance of the purchase price.[78] At first instance, S was awarded the sum claimed; but the Court of Appeal deducted from the award the market value of the unsold car which S still retained (£450), and reduced the award to £47 10s.

The difference between the attitude of the two courts lay in the inference to be drawn from the fact that s 48(4) expressly states that the contract is rescinded by the resale, whereas s 48(3) is silent on this point (see para 27.08): in the earlier case, Finnemore J deduced that the resale under s 48(3) was therefore not intended to rescind the original contract of sale;[75] but in the later case, the Court of Appeal took the view that rescission was expressly referred to in s 48(4) to remove doubt, and to bring it into line with s 48(3), where on ordinary principles resale would rescind the first contract (see para 27.12). At the same time, Diplock LJ in *Ward Ltd v Bignall* pointed out that, if the seller had affirmed and sued for the balance of the purchase price, the first-instance award in the case before him would have been correct (at 547). The moral for an unpaid seller considering resale would appear to be as follows:[79] leaving aside the question of any deposit (see para 27.20), he should rescind and resell if he can thereby obtain a better price;[80] but he should affirm the contract if he cannot do better elsewhere.[81]

**[27.11] The title to the goods.** In discussing the effect of a resale by the seller on the title to the goods, it is convenient to distinguish according to whether or not the seller has ever delivered the goods to the first buyer.

---

73   *Per* Diplock LJ in *Ward Ltd v Bignall* (above) at 547.
74   See *Stephen v Wilkinson* (1831) 2 B & Ad 320; *Page v Cowasjee Edulijee* (1866) LR 1 PC 127.
75   [1949] 2 KB 765; [1949] 1 All ER 921. Cf. a mortgagee realising his security: see para 25.20.
76   [1967] 1 QB 534; [1967] 1 All ER 449, CA.
77   This was assumed by the CA to be for damages for non-acceptance.
78   I.e. £825, less £325, plus the expenses of attempting resale (£22 10s).
79   See also *per* Turner J in *Commission Car Sales v Saul* [1957] NZLR 144, at 146 (resale by seller after delivery and subsequent repudiation by buyer); and per Robert Goff LJ in *Clough Mills Ltd v Martin* (see para 25.31) at 987–8.
80   E.g. *Gallagher v Shilcock* (above).
81   E.g. *Ward Ltd v Bignall* (above).

1.  *Before delivery.* Where the resale by the seller before delivery does not amount to a breach of the first contract of sale, the seller can pass the property in the goods to the second buyer, either because the property never passed to the first buyer, or because it revested in him on resale.[82] However, where the resale is a breach of the first contract of sale,[83] it does not revest the property in the seller; and therefore he can only pass a good title to the second buyer, either because he has retained the property in the goods, or under one of the following exceptions to the *nemo dat* rule:

    (a) Sales by a seller in possession (see para 21.38, *et seq.*);

    (b) Section 48(2) of the SGA, which provides that:[84]

    > Where an unpaid seller who has exercised his right of lien . . . or stoppage in transit resells the goods, the buyer acquires a good title thereto as against the original buyer.

    It may be that s 48(2) is confined to the situation where the seller remains unpaid[85] and in possession.[86]

2.  *After delivery.* Once the goods have been delivered to the first buyer, the seller can only pass a good title to the second buyer where he has either retained the property in the goods (s 19: discussed at paras 20.28–9), or it has revested in him:[87] a mere bargain and sale changes neither property nor possession,[88] nor does it rescind the first contract of sale.[85] Nor should the seller have any greater power to pass title where he merely seizes the goods after delivery to the first buyer.[89] Thus, if the resale is a breach of the first contract of sale, the position is as follows: the seller does not ordinarily commit conversion by reselling without delivery,[90] though his seizure of the goods would be a trepass[91] and the resale an injurious falsehood (see para 17.17); but, if the seller resells and delivers to the second buyer, the seller commits conversion (see para 19.06), and the second buyer will do so unless he obtains good title under one of the exceptions to the *nemo dat* rule (see Chap 21).

---

82  *Ward Ltd v Bignall* (set out at para 27.10).

83  In which case the first buyer can sue the seller for non-delivery: see para 29.19, *et seq.*

84  S 48(2) differs from the *nemo dat* provisions: (1) it does **not** require a delivery or transfer to the second buyer; nor (2) does it require the original buyer to be in default; nor (3) insist that the second buyer act bf and without notice of the first sale. As to the title passed to the second buyer, see Goode, *Commercial Law*, 3rd edn, 412, fn 167.

85  If between exercise of the lien and resale the original buyer tenders the price, it has been argued that s 48(2) ceases to apply: Benjamin's *Sale of Goods*, 6th edn, para 15-102.

86  It is argued that s 48(2) requires the seller to be in possession at the time of resale: Goode, *Op. cit.*, 413.

87  E.g. on repudiation by the buyer: *Commission Car Sales Ltd v Saul* [1957] NZLR 144. Cf. *Jarvis v Williams* [1955] 1 All ER 108, CA (seller in whom property not revested could not sue in detinue).

88  *Lancashire Waggon Co v Fitzhugh* (1861) 6 H & N 502.

89  *Stephens v Wilkinson* (1831) 2 B & Ad 320.

90  *Lancashire Waggon Co v Fitzhugh* (above). But see para 19.05.

91  See para 19.04. If it is a conditional sale within the CCA there may also be a breach of s 90: see para 24.35, *et seq.*

## Remedies where there is a reservation of property

**[27.12]** Where the goods are supplied on conditional sale, hp or simple hiring,[92] the conventional strategy for the unpaid supplier is as follows:[93] to terminate any bailment (see para 26.09), repossess the goods (see para 24.21, *et seq.*) and resell or rehire them.[94] If a conditional seller legitimately resells whilst the contract subsists, he is entitled out of the proceeds only to the amount needed to discharge the outstanding balance;[95] but, where the conditional sale has been terminated, the conditional seller is entitled to retain the whole of any capital profit made on resale.[96] Presumably, the position is similar in relation to any hp or simple hiring, so making it important in all three cases to decide whether the instalment credit agreement has been terminated.[97]

Bearing in mind the foregoing process, when the original supply contract is made, the supplier should aim to ensure for himself sufficient real security over the life of the instalment contract (see para 1.25). To achieve this, he must estimate the likely resale value of the goods over the life of the instalment contract, and then arrange the repayments so that the estimated resale value always exceeds the outstanding instalments. Unlike a mortgagee (see para 25.20), the supplier is under no duty to get the best price obtainable, because the buyer or hirer has no equity of redemption (see para 24.22). However, in respect of creditors licensed under the CCA, the OFT has used its licensing powers (see para 6.23) to discourage creditors from claiming damages from the debtors in such circumstances.[98] However, insofar as the supplier does not realise enough from the resale to make good his loss, he may be thinking in terms of an action in damages against the buyer or hirer.[99]

**[27.13] Tracing generally.**[100] Whilst the common law and equitable doctrines of tracing are familiar in the context of trust property, such rights may arise whenever there exists a fiduciary relationship between the parties in relation to any type of property. Moreover, such a fiduciary relationship may be created by contract,[101] as

---

92  For the definitions of which, see Chap 1.

93  Where the buyer or hirer has disposed of the goods, there may be a right to trace: see para 27.13. For regulated agreements, see para 27.15.

94  If the repossession is in breach of the instalment contract, it will amount to a repudiation by the supplier (see para 26.15), enabling the buyer or hirer to rescind and/or claim damages: see Chap 29.

95  As to the small sums commonly realised, see para 27.02.

96  *Clough Mills Ltd v Martin* (see para 25.31), *per* Robert Goff LJ. (at 987j–988g), Oliver LJ (at 991–993g–h) and *per* Donaldson MR (at 994g–h). Compare resale by an ordinary unpaid seller: para 27.10.

97  As to the distinction between terminating the bailment and terminating the agreement, see para 26.09.

98  OFT, *1980-AR* 31.

99  In which case the duty to mitigate may require that the supplier resells for the best price obtainable: see para 27.45.

100  For the common law and equitable rules of tracing, see generally Pettit, *Equity*, 10th edn, Chap 25; Snell, *Equity*, 30th edn, para 13-29, *et seq.*; Goff and Jones, *Restitution*, 6th edn, 2.001, *et seq.*; Goode, *Commercial Law*, 3rd edn, 52–4.

101  But there will be no constructive trust without the clearest evidence of the assumption of equitable as against merely contractual obligations: *Feuer Leather Corpn v Johnstone & Sons* [1983] Com LR 12, CA; and generally, para 27.14.

was demonstrated with the introduction of *Romalpa* clauses into this country in 1976 (see para 25.30). This development dramatically drew the attention of lawyers to the potential of the doctrine of tracing in the commercial context,[102] where a clear distinction must be drawn according to whether or not the property in the goods had passed.

1. *Property in the supplier.* The simple case is where the supply contract reserves the property in the goods to the supplier, i.e. a contract of conditional sale, hp or simple hiring (see generally, para 27.12); and nothing is done to disturb this arrangement. For instance, in the *Romalpa* case itself, the unpaid supplier was held entitled at common law as against the receiver to the unworked aluminium in the possession of the conditional buyer.[103]

2. *Property in the buyer or hirer.* On the other hand, the unpaid supplier may lose both the property in, and possession of, the goods supplied. For instance, in *Borden v Timber Products Ltd*[104] the Court of Appeal held that, notwithstanding the express reservation of property, the property in the resin passed to the conditional buyer when the resin was irretrievably mixed with wood chips; and in *Re Bond Worth* (see para 25.34) one of the reasons the property passed was because the fibre became unidentifiable, even the unused yarn not remaining marked out in any way as the supplier's goods.[105] Where the property has so passed, the unpaid supplier has lost his rights to the goods at common law and is reduced to a claim in equity.[106]

**[27.14] Equitable tracing**. Notwithstanding any reservation of property by the supply contract, after the supplier has relinquished possession, he may also lose the property in the goods, either because of the way the goods have been dealt with by the buyer or hirer (see para 27.13), or because they have been disposed of to a bfp under exception to the *nemo dat* rule.[107] In such cases, the unpaid supplier has lost his right to the goods at common law, and is reduced to tracing his interest in equity insofar as the contract provides[108] and the law allows. Such interests may be avoided by the chattel mortgage legislation for non-registration (see para 25.28, *et seq.*).

1. *Tracing into products.* Where the unpaid supplier has lost his right to the goods supplied because they have been turned into other goods, the contract may purport to grant the supplier rights in such products. In the *Romalpa* case (set out at para 25.30), where there was both a reservation of property and an

---

102 See Goode (1976) 92 LQR 401 and 528; Goodhart and Jones (1980) 43 MLR 489.

103 It is argued that the seller is not then an undisclosed principal (see para 10.06) so as to render him liable to the sub-buyer for defects in the goods: McCormack (1990) 11 BLR 109.

104 [1981] Chap 25, CA (chipboard manufacture).

105 See also *Re Peachdart Ltd* (see para 25.32).

106 *Clough Mills Ltd v Martin* (see para 25.31), *per* Robert Goff LJ (at 989g–990e), Oliver LJ (at 993c–h) and Donaldson MR (at 994c–e). See further, para 27.14.

107 S 25 of the SGA (see para 21.43), as limited by the *Mills & Lawrence* case (set out at para 21.51): see [1996] JBL at 496, fn 78.

108 But not otherwise, the bailor-bailee relationship not necessarily being a fiduciary one: *Hendy Lennox (Industrial Engineer) Ltd v Grahame Puttick Ltd* (see para 25.32); *Re Andrabell Ltd* [1984] 3 All ER 407; and [1985] JBL at 161–2.

expressly created fiduciary relationship, the Court of Appeal held the unpaid supplier entitled to the worked aluminium into which the aluminium foil had been turned. On the other hand, in *Borden* (see para 27.13) the Court of Appeal held that the mere relationship of seller and buyer did not give rise to a fiduciary relationship between them, so that there was no right to trace; and it has subsequently been made clear that the question turns upon whether the parties expressly or impliedly intend to create such a fiduciary relationship.[109] Even if effective in equity, it has been suggested that such an interest is always registrable (see para 25.36).

2. *Tracing the proceeds.* Where the unpaid supplier has lost his rights to the goods supplied, the contract may purport to grant him rights in the proceeds of later disposal of the goods.[110] Thus, in the *Romalpa* case the receiver was held bound to account for proceeds of sale of the products under the first-in-time rule (see para 7.21), these being deposited along with other money in a mixed bank account which was in credit.[111] However, subsequent sellers have found it difficult to establish such a fiduciary relationship to the satisfaction of the courts (see para 25.32). Moreover, even assuming proof of the necessary fiduciary relationship, this interest may amount to a charge on the book debts of the buyer, in which case the equitable right to trace into proceeds is subject to any statutory duty to register that interest;[112] and the question may be whether there has been created a true beneficial interest or only a charge.[113] It has been recommended that all such *Romalpa* clauses should require registration to be effective (see para 25.36).

**[27.15] The CCA.** With regard to regulated conditional sale and hp agreements, the CCA makes the following alterations to the pattern observed above (para 27.12). Where the supplier wrongfully repossesses protected goods, the agreement automatically terminates, with the consequences spelt out in s 91 (see para 24.38). Where the debtor exercises his statutory right to terminate under s 99 (see para 26.05), his liability is limited by s 100 (see para 27.50). Upon the operation of either ss 91 or 99, the supplier has an unfettered right to dispose of the goods on his own account.

In the case of consumer hiring agreements, the rules relating to protected goods are inapplicable; but there is a parallel right under s 101 for the hirer to terminate the agreement (see para 26.07), the hirer's liability being considered later (see para 27.49).

---

109 *Per* Robert Goff LJ in *Clough Mills Ltd v Martin* (see para 25.31), at 987. This will not be lightly inferred: see para 27.13. For argument that there should be no such requirement, see Millett (1991) 107 LQR 71.

110 Either by the express provisions of the contract of sale, e.g. the *Romalpa* case (set out at para 25.30), or by operation of law, e.g. *Re Hallett's Estate* (above): see Williams (1991) 12 Company Lawyer at 57.

111 Under the doctrine in *Re Hallett's Estate* (1880) 13 Chap D 696, CA. See also *Re Kayford Ltd* (set out at para 19.24). Distinguish overdrawn bank accounts.

112 E.g. *Re Interview Ltd* [1975] Ir Rep 382; *Borden's* case (see para 27.13); *Re Bond Worth Ltd* (see para 25.34); *Re Peachdart Ltd* (see para 25.32); *Pfeiffer etc GmbH & Co v Arbuthnot Factors* [1987] BCLC 522.

113 See Goodhart and Jones (1980) 43 MLR at 513; Guest (1979) 95 LQR at 480.

## PERSONAL REMEDIES OF THE SUPPLIER

**[27.15A]** The supplier affirming the contract may also be able to maintain an action in debt against the buyer or hirer for the price or hire-rent;[114] but, if he recovers the price or hire-rent, this will be deducted from any damages awarded to avoid any double recovery (see para 27.39). Alternatively, the supplier may be suing for what his services are worth (*quantum meruit*) in the following circumstances:[115] (a) where there is a binding contract which does not stipulate the price or rent;[116] (b) where there is a binding contract which stipulates the price or rent, but that price or rent is not recoverable, either because of the contractual incapacity of the transferee,[117] or the buyer or hirer has wrongfully prevented the agreed price or rent becoming due (see para 26.02); or (c) the contract was void *ab initio*, e.g. for mistake (see para 10.14, *et seq.*), or the contract is frustrated.[118]

However, a clear distinction is drawn at common law between a claim in **debt**, as considered below, and a claim for **damages**:[119]

(1) An action in **debt** lies upon a primary obligation[120] to pay a definite sum of money fixed and made payable by the contract, e.g. the price or hire rent, or a loan. That debt obligation may arise upon the happening of some condition precedent,[121] or as liquidated damages upon breach (see para 27.24). It is normally recoverable regardless of loss, except for the rule against penalties (see para 27.25); and it is *prima facie* assignable (see para 1.23).

(2) A claim for **damages** for breach of contract is a secondary obligation arising from breach of a primary obligation.[120] To recover more than nominal damages, proof of loss is required (see para 27.29); transfer of such a claim may offend the rules against maintenance and champerty (see para 7.26); and the amount of damages recoverable is subject to a number of limitations (see para 27.39).

Being personal actions, both claims in debt and damages are subject to any restrictions applicable if the debtor/defendant is insolvent (see para 19.18, *et seq.*) and are subject to the rights of the court to order the sum to be paid either as a lump sum or by instalments in respect of a debt which is either regulated[122] or not.[123]

---

114  In electing to sue for the price or rent (as to election, see para 26.17), the unpaid supplier has generally speaking elected not to exercise any right of rescission (see para 26.16) and therefore cannot recover the goods: but see para 27.19.
115  *Benjamin on Sale*, 6th edn, para 12-067.
116  E.g. SGA, s 8(2): see para 2.06.
117  E.g. SGA, s 3: see para 10.18.
118  For benefits conferred before frustration: see the FCA 1943, s 1(3)—para 22.19.
119  See *Otis Vehicle Rentals Ltd v Ciceley Commercials Ltd* (set out at para 27.18).
120  For primary and secondary obligations, see para 26.16.
121  *Carlill v Carbolic Smoke Ball Co* [1893] 1 QB 256, CA (see para 8.05).
122  Consumer Credit Act 1974, s 129: see para 24.40.
123  County Courts Act 1984, s 71 (unsecured); Administration of Justice Act 1970, s 36 (mortgage).

## Action for price or rent

*Action for the price of goods sold*

**[27.16]** An action for the price (see para 2.06) may be available to the seller under the rules considered below in the case of a cash sale, or as to an instalment sale (credit or conditional) in respect of the instalments of the price which are due.[124] There are special rules for deposits and part-payments (see para 27.20).

*Prima facie*, a breach by the buyer of his duty to pay the price (see para 23.13) does not give rise to a right to rescind;[125] and, in considering the right of the unpaid seller to recover the price, two points must be borne in mind: first, the additional leverage provided by the rights of stoppage and lien are lost on delivery (see paras 24.18; 24.14); and second, for historical reasons a sharp distinction is drawn according to whether the property in the goods has passed to the buyer. Unfortunately, s 49 of the SGA has preserved the common law position that, generally speaking,[126] an action for the price is only maintainable where the property has passed (see paras 27.17–18); and that, if it has not passed, the seller is normally confined to an action for damages.[127] The significance of the distinction is as follows: not only may there be a substantial difference in monetary terms between the price and damages, but in an action for the price alone the seller is under no obligation to prove or mitigate his loss.[128] Further, he may apply for summary judgment for the price.

Rather than largely depending on the passing of property, Art 2 of the US Uniform Commercial Code uses the general yardstick of the transfer of possession.[129]

**[27.17] After the property has passed**. Section 49(1) of the SGA provides that:

'Where, under a contract of sale, the property in the goods has passed to the buyer, and the buyer wrongfully neglects or refuses to pay for the goods according to the terms of the contract, the seller may maintain an action against him for the price of the goods.'

Under this general rule, an action for the price is only maintainable on certain conditions.[130]

---

124 Where the period of credit has expired, the whole of the price will be due under an instalment sale; and the same result may follow upon the operation of an acceleration clause (see paras 7.03 and 23.26).

125 S 10(1): set out at para 23.20. For the situation where that *prima facie* rule is displaced, see para 27.19

126 It has been argued that this is only a *prima facie* rule, and that s 49 may be ousted by a contractual provision as to when the price shall be payable: Benjamin's *Sale of Goods*, 6th edn, para 16-027. Cf. para 22.11.

127 This apparent principle has been described as simply faulty drafting: Goode, *Commercial Law*, 3rd edn, 394.

128 *Aliter*, if there is also a claim for damages for consequential loss. For the duty to mitigate, see para 27.44.

129 Supported by Bridge [1991] LM & CLQ 52 at 68.

130 Nevertheless the unpaid seller who has parted with the property in the goods and is suing for the price may exceptionally be able to get an interlocutory injunction to restrain the buyer from disposing of the goods: *Flam Textiles (Canada) v McQueen of London Sportswear* [1976] CLY 2196, CA.

1.  *The property has passed to the buyer.* Unless the case falls within s 49(2) discussed below, no action for the price is possible before the passing of property, even where it is the buyer's fault that the property has not passed.[131] Thus, s 49(1) will typically be applicable where goods have been delivered under a cash sale.

2.  *The buyer wrongfully neglects or refuses to pay the price.* The duty to pay the price has already been examined (see para 23.13); and the most common cases where neglect or failure to pay the price is not wrongful are as follows: (1) where payment and delivery are concurrent terms and the seller has not yet tendered delivery;[132] and (2) where the goods have been delivered, but the sale is on credit terms which have not yet expired (see para 27.16). However, the unpaid seller under a credit sale will be able to sue for the full price where either the whole of the credit term has expired,[133] or an acceleration clause has operated.[134]

**[27.18] Before the property has passed**. The exceptional case where an action is maintainable for the price before the passing of property is embodied in s 49(2), which provides that:

> 'Where under a contract for sale, the price is payable on a day certain irrespective of delivery, and the buyer wrongfully neglects or refuses to pay such price, the seller may maintain an action for the price, although the property in the goods has not passed, and the goods have not been appropriated to the contract.'

Once again, the right of action is hedged around with restrictions: first, that the buyer wrongfully neglects or refuses to pay the price;[135] second, that the price is payable irrespective of delivery;[136] and third, that the price is payable on a day certain. With respect to this last requirement, the question arises as to whether it should be interpreted literally, or whether that literal meaning can be extended by invoking the maxim *certum est quod certum reddi potest.* Despite some doubt expressed by the Court of Appeal in 1908,[137] in *Shell Mex Ltd v Elton Cop Dying Co Ltd,*[138] whilst his Lordship was prepared to read into s 49(2) that 'the price is payable by instalments on days certain',[139] he was not willing to interpret it so that 'the price is payable **by** a day certain'. The better view would therefore appear to be that s 49(2) can only apply if the time for the payment of the price is 'fixed in advance by the contract in such a way that it can be determined independently of the action of either party or of any third person'.[140] In *Otis Vehicle Rentals Ltd v Ciceley Commercials Ltd*:[141]

---

131  *Colley v Overseas Exporters* [1921] 3 KB 302.

132  Where s 28 operates: set out at para 23.16.

133  Cf. SGA, s 41(1)(b): set out at para 24.10.

134  For acceleration clauses, see para 7.03; and for instalment sales see para 27.19.

135  As to payment by instalments, see para 27.19.

136  *Stein, Forbes & Co v County Tailoring Co* (1916) 86 LJKB 448 DC; *Colley v Overseas Exporters* [1921] 3 KB 320.

137  See *obiter* in *Workman Clark Ltd v Lloyd Brazileno* [1908] 1 KB 968, CA, esp at 977, 978, 981.

138  (1928) 34 Com Cas 39.

139  So that conditional sales may fall within s 49(2), as in *McEntire v Crossley Bros* [1895] AC 457, HL.

140  Benjamin's *Sale of Goods*, 6th edn, para 16-026; Goode, *Payment Obligations in Commercial and Financial Transactions*, 70.

141  [2002] EWCA Civ 1064, CA.

Otis wished to acquire 14 vehicles from a dealer; but, even using directly financed hp, Otis could not afford to do so without the following arrangements: the hp agreements contained end balloon payments (see para 1.25), to be financed by then selling the vehicles back to the dealer at an agreed price (the buy-back price). The dealer repudiated the repurchase agreement and Otis claimed the buy-back price. However, as the financier was pressing for the balloon payments, Otis sold the vehicles on the open market. The Court of Appeal held as follows: as the property in the vehicles had not passed to the dealer, s 49(2) was the appropriate provision; but the case fell outside s 49(2) as below; and that therefore Otis was only entitled to damages (see para 27.15A).

Their Lordships held that, even where the conditions mentioned in s 49(2) exist, s 49(2) will only be applicable where either the goods have been delivered to the buyer, or the seller remains willing and able to deliver them to the buyer.[142] Nowadays, it would seem that a seller could avoid this problem by selling under court order.[143]

**[27.19] Payment by instalments**. Where the *prima facie* rule is displaced and non-payment of the price shows an intention on the part of the buyer to repudiate the contract, the seller must elect between two mutually exclusive alternatives:[144] he can affirm the contract, and sue for the outstanding part of the price under s 49;[145] or he can rescind, in which case he is entitled to seize the goods, but not to recover the price. Thus, ordinarily the seller cannot have his cake and eat it too: he cannot have both the goods and their price. For instance, in *Hewison v Ricketts*:[146]

> The buyer under a conditional sale defaulted, whereupon the seller seized the goods and sued the defendant under his guarantee. The Court held that the seller could alternatively seize the goods or sue for the instalments; that in electing to seize the seller had therefore lost his right to the instalments; and that as the principal debt was extinguished, so was the liability of the guarantor (see para 25.06).

However, there is one instance where the seller may seek both to have his goods and the price; and that is where he recovers the goods and retains instalments of the price already paid.[147] In 1842, the common law rejected an attempt by a defaulting buyer to recover a sum already paid on account of the price;[148] but subsequently Stable J drew a distinction between a deposit and a part-payment, allowing recovery of the latter.[149] This decision is not easy to reconcile with the 1842 case; but the distinction between a deposit and a part-payment would appear at common law to depend on the intention of the parties and to have been accepted by the

---

142 *Per* Potter LJ at para 17, citing Benjamin's *Sale of Goods*, 5th edn, para 16-001.

143 *On Demand Information plc v Gerson* (set out at para 27.21).

144 See para 27.16. For recovery by an innocent depositor, see para 29.13.

145 See paras 27.17–18, in which case he may have to give credit for any deposit paid: *Gallagher v Shilcock* (see para 27.10); and para 23.27. Frequently, he will be able to sue for the whole of the price immediately by reason of an acceleration clause (see para 7.03).

146 (1894) 63 LJQB 711, DC.

147 As to what constitutes payment, see para 23.13, *et seq.*

148 *Fitt v Cassanet* (1842) 4 Man & G 898; and see *Cramer v Giles* (1883) 1 Cab & E1 151; affd (1884) May 9. See also paras 20.28 and 24.22; and para 29.15.

149 Treitel, *Law of Contract*, 11th edn, 1007.

courts.[150] Part-payments (or 'recoverable deposits') may be recoverable by the defaulting buyer if a contract goes off (see para 23.27); but in principle a deposit may be retained by the innocent seller.[151] However, the courts have since decided that that principle should be limited to a 'reasonable sum'; and that this connoted a sum which would not be penal (see para 27.26) under the rule against penalties.[152] The effect was to draw a sharp distinction between the following: a **reasonable** deposit, which the seller might at common law retain;[153] and an **unreasonable** (penal) deposit, which the rescinding seller must return.[152] At common law, the courts have even gone so far as to award damages for breach of a promise to pay a deposit (see para 23.27). On the other hand it seems clear that, if a seller retaining a deposit sues for damages, he must also bring into account that deposit.[154] It is another question as to whether equity or statute would intervene in relation to even a reasonable deposit (see para 27.20).

**[27.20] Recovery of deposits.**[155] At common law, after rescission an advance part-payment of the price was recoverable even by a party in default, but a **reasonable** (non-penal) deposit generally was not (see para 27.19). However, since that distinction between deposits and part-payments has become settled, attempts have been made to show that even a deposit may be recoverable in equity by the party in breach. In *Stockloser v Johnson*:[156]

> The plaintiff agreed to buy plant and machinery under a conditional sale contract which provided that the price was payable by instalments, and that if there was default for more than 28 days in payment of any instalment the seller could rescind, forfeit the instalments already paid and repossess the goods.[157] After the buyer's default the seller exercised these rights, and the buyer sued for the return of the instalments paid. The Court of Appeal unanimously held that the forfeiture did not constitute a penalty on the facts of the case (see para 27.19), but was of the opinion that in appropriate circumstances relief might be given.

Whilst the equitable power to grant relief against forfeiture is well established in relation to mortgages of land (see para 25.20), the courts have been more circumspect about extending the protection to personal property, even where the defaulting buyer was willing to pay, albeit late.[158] In *Stockloser v Johnson*, Romer LJ was prepared to give the defaulting buyer an opportunity (which the buyer did not want) to pay off the arrears;[159] but he added *obiter* that (at 501):

---

150 *Dies v British and International Mining and Finance Corpn Ltd* [1939] 1 KB 724. Cf. Salmond & Williams, *Contract*, 2nd edn, 569, fn (b); and Guest, *Law of HP* 596.

151 *Stockloser v Johnson* (set out at para 27.20).

152 *Workers Trust and Merchant Bank Ltd v Dojap Investments Ltd* [1993] AC 573, PC (sale of land case, where there may be special rule: Beale 109 LQR 524). See further Treitel, *Op. cit.*, 1008.

153 *Pye v British Automobile Commercial Syndicate Ltd* [1906] 1 KB 425.

154 Benjamin's *Sale of Goods*, 6th edn, para 15.132. Presumably, this is on the basis of the rule against double recovery: see para 27.39.

155 See generally Goff and Jones, *Law of Restitution*, 6th edn, 535–46; Treitel, *Law of Contract*, 11th edn, 1009–11; McGregor, *Law of Damages*, 17th edn, paras 13.075–88.

156 [1954] 1 QB 476; [1954] 1 All ER 630, CA. See Polack [1965] CLJ 17; Crawford (1966) 44 Can BR 142.

157 This was not a licence to seize within the Bills of Sale Acts because it was not granted **by** the owner (seller): see para 25.27.

158 *Goker v NWS Bank plc* (1990) [1999] GCCR 1507, CA (hp; relief denied to a persistent defaulter).

159 See also *BICC plc v Burndy Corpn* [1985] Chap 232, CA (not a sale case; noted 101 LQR 145).

'no relief of any other nature can properly be given, in the absence of some special circumstances such as fraud, sharp practice or other unconscionable conduct of the vendor to a purchaser after the vendor has rescinded the contract'.

However, the majority took a rather wider view; and Denning LJ said *obiter* that (only?) two things were necessary before equitable relief would be granted;[160]

'first, the forfeiture clause must be of a penal nature, in the sense that the sum forfeited must be out of all proportion to the damage,[161] and, secondly, it must be unconscionable for the seller to retain the money'.

Whilst the majority view may be desirable, it would appear that the weight of authority was on the side of Romer LJ. Since then similar issues have arisen in relation to bailments;[162] and, in relation to sales the Privy Council have held that at common law in sales of land it is only **reasonable** deposits which are forfeitable (see above), which ruling gives rise to considerable uncertainties in relation to supplies of goods.[163]

Upon the above pattern, there has been some statutory interference in relation to the recovery of deposits, whether reasonable or unreasonable: several types of relief have been offered in respect of regulated agreements (see para 27.23); and, in relation to consumer supplies, the requirement of a deposit may amount to an unfair term.[164] The consumer under a distance or doorstep supply may be able to avoid the above problems by exercising any statutory right of cancellation (see paras 10.35–9). For the position in relation to hp agreements, see para 27.22; and in relation to consumer hirings, see para 27.23; and for the action for damages, see para 27.37.

## Action for arrears of rentals

[27.21] There must here be considered the situation where there is an hp or simple hiring agreement. If the hirer refuses to accept delivery, the hiring does not commence; so that the owner is not entitled to any hire-rent,[165] but must sue for damages for non-acceptance (see para 27.27), and failure to pay any deposit (see para 23.27). On the other hand, once the hirer has taken possession under the agreement,[166] the owner is entitled, without any duty to mitigate (see para 27.16) to any hire-rent which accrues due by reason of the period during which the hirer is in possession under the terms of the agreement,[167] but not for any rentals in respect of

---

160 At 490. See also Somervell LJ at 485, 486 and 488. See Goode, *HP Law & Practice*, 2nd edn, 381.

161 This first test appears the same as that for penalties: see para 27.26.

162 See also the cases dealing with forfeiture of instalments due under a hiring contract: para 27.21. Cf. *Sport International Bussum BV v Inter-Footwear Ltd* [1984] 2 All ER 321, HL; *Jobson v Johnson* [1989] 1 All ER 621, CA.

163 E.g. does the same rule apply? See Beale (1993) 109 LQR 524 at 528–30; Ho (2003) 119 LQR 34.

164 Benjamin's *Sale of Goods*, 6th edn, 16-040; and see unfair term, Grey Term (e), para 11.16.

165 See para 15.23. Any rental paid in advance would be recoverable from the owner on grounds of tfc (see para 16.05); but a deposit would not (see para 27.20).

166 If no agreement is ever concluded, there is no liability to pay hire-rent: *Campbell Discount Co Ltd v Gall* [1961] 1 QB 431, CA (an hp case, overruled on other grounds: as to which, see para 16.05).

167 E.g. *Yeoman Credit Ltd v Apps* (set out at para 29.25); *Charterhouse Credit Ltd v Tolly* (set out at para 29.34) (hp cases).

any period thereafter.[168] This action for arrears of rental is an entirely separate one from the claim for damages for breach of contract.[169]

Because the essence of a hiring is payment of rent at an agreed rate in return for possession, the House of Lords have confirmed that at common law there is no power to order relief against forfeiture where a vessel is withdrawn by the owner upon failure by the time-charterer to make due payment of hire,[170] at least where the payments 'represent the agreed rate of hire and not a penny more' (at 703). Moreover, it follows from the very nature of bailment that at the end of its term the owner will both recover the goods and be entitled to retain or recover the hire-rent in respect of the period of the bailment. Whilst formally this involves no element of double recovery of goods and price (compare para 27.19), in practice it may do so (see also para 27.37). Thus, in *Galbraith v Mitchenall Estates Ltd*:[171]

> The plaintiff entered into a five-year simple hiring agreement in respect of a caravan, mistakenly thinking that it was an hp agreement, and paid a deposit of £550. The plaintiff failed to pay any instalments, whereupon the owner repossessed the caravan, and resold it for £775. The plaintiff's claim for the return of the deposit was dismissed.

Notwithstanding that he thought the agreement 'hideously harsh', Sachs J preferred the view of Romer LJ in relation to the recovery of deposits (see para 27.20); but his Lordship did recommend statutory intervention to protect such hirers (at 659). It would seem that the answer should be otherwise if the consumer hired on a trial basis, the supplier promising that, if satisfied, the consumer could convert to a purchase, putting the rent paid towards the purchase price. Is this hp?

However, in a sale the Privy Council have sanctioned relief against forfeiture of an unreasonable deposit (see para 27.19); and the question arises whether the equitable jurisdiction to relieve against forfeiture is applicable to finance leases (see para 1.18). In *On Demand Information plc v Gerson*:[172]

> There was a three-year finance lease of video equipment, which provided (Cl 9) for termination of the agreement if the lessee went into receivership (see para 26.08). However, after being appointed towards the end of the lease, the receiver was anxious to take advantage of another provision in the lease (Cl 12) allowing the lessee to sell the equipment at the end of the lease as agent of the lessor, but largely for his own benefit. To enable him to expedite matters and sell the leased equipment and business as a going concern, the receiver, having obtained the owner's permission, sold the equipment under court order. He then sought relief from Cl 9, so that he could take advantage of Cl 12. *Inter alia*, the lessor argued that the lessee was not entitled to relief

---

168 *Belsize Motor Supply Co v Cox* [1914] 1 KB 244 (hp case, where the hiring was for a fixed period). Would the answer be the same if there had been an acceleration clause (see para 26.19); or would such a clause be treated as a minimum payments provision (see para 27.49)? Cf. *IAC (Leasing) Ltd v Humphrey* (1972) 46 ALJR 106 (HC).

169 *Overstone Ltd v Shipway* [1962] 1 All ER 52, CA.

170 *The Scaptrade* [1983] 2 AC 694, HL (a time-charter is a mere contract for services and does not give the charterer any interest in the ship).

171 [1965] 2 QB 473; [1964] 2 All ER 653. But see *per* Pennycuick J in *Barton Thompson & Co Ltd v Stapling Machines Co* [1966] Chap 499 at 509; and also *San Pedro Compania Armadora SA v Henry Navigation Co Ltd* [1970] I Lloyd's Rep 32.

172 [2003] 1 AC 368; [2002] 2 All ER 949, HL.

against forfeiture because his rights in the goods were purely contactual; but the Judge disagreed.

On appeal as to whether the lessee was entitled to relief from the forfeiture provision (Cl 9), the House of Lords unanimously: (i) held the sale under court order (see para 21.06) did not affect the substantive position of the parties (at paras 8, 38–40, 46); and (ii) accepted that a finance lease granted such great rights to a lessee as to give him a proprietary right protected by the doctrine of relief against forfeiture (at paras 29, 31 and 41). On the latter point, the greater discussion took place in the Court of Appeal, where Robert Walker LJ explained that the forfeiture jurisdiction is in this context to deal with clauses designed to secure the payment of money (at 744b, 745h) and put it that the lessee's contractual right to indefinite possession gave him a right of a proprietary nature.[173]

**[27.22] Hire purchase.** As a species of bailment, an hp agreement entitles the owner to both the rentals and the goods at the end of the term: it does not matter whether he repossesses and then claims the arrears of rentals;[174] or *vice versa*.[175] However, under an hp agreement there is additionally an option to purchase, which makes it a hybrid (see para 1.25); and in fact the amount of the instalments will be calculated on the basis of an *aliquot* part of the price, e.g. if there are to be 20 instalments, each instalment will be one-twentieth of the price plus charges. Accordingly, if there is applied to hp the rule for simple hiring, the owner in recovering both the goods and the hire-rent will commonly obtain an element of double recovery (see para 24.22), which element would be reduced to the extent that the goods were worth less than the owner's loss. Of course, in some circumstances this result may be avoided on ordinary principles: firstly, the owner may affirm the contract with knowledge of the breach,[176] in which case he loses the right to repossess (see para 27.16); and secondly, the owner may rescind and recover a judgment in conversion, which is merely for the value of **his interest** in the goods.[177] However, where the owner rescinds and, either recapts the goods (see para 24.23), or obtains a judgment for their **full value** in conversion, there *prima facie* exists the potential element of double recovery (see para 27.39) which gave rise to the 'snatch-back' (see para 26.08).

It has already been seen that the nineteenth century case law discouraged any hope that the courts would grant the hirer under a hire-purchase agreement an equity of redemption (see para 24.22). However, there is some indication that the courts may sometimes be prepared to grant the hirer relief against forfeiture. In *Transag Haulage Ltd v Leyland Daf Finance plc*,[178] the Receiver argued that the hirer

---

173 [2000] 4 All ER 734, CA, at 750b. Stuart-Smith LJ also rejected a submission that the doctrine of forfeiture was confined to land (at 754j); and see also Pill LJ at 758b. See further McMeel [2003] LMCLQ 169 at 194–6.

174 *Brooks v Beirnstein* [1909] 1 KB 98 DC; *Overstone Ltd v Shipway* [1962] 1 All ER 52, CA; *Financings Ltd v Baldock* [1963] 2 QB 104, CA; *UCB Leasing Ltd v Haltom* (set out at para 29.10).

175 *South Bedfordshire Electrical Finance Ltd v Bryant* [1938] 3 All ER 580, CA.

176 E.g. *Keith Prowse & Co v National Telephone Co Ltd* [1894] 2 Ch 147; *Reynolds v General and Finance Facilities Ltd* (1963) 107 SJ 889, CA.

177 See para 27.30. And, if that judgment is satisfied, he will thereupon lose his title to the goods (see para 26.17).

178 (1994) 13 Tr LR 361; [1994] BCC 356.

on hp (T) was entitled to relief against repossession under the equitable doctrine of relief from penalties or forfeiture. Knox J accepted that, because the owners were not claiming a sum of money, the matter could not be decided by the common law rule against penalties (see para 27.25), but thought that T's loss of his option to purchase might amount to a forfeiture of property, even though it was contingent on completion of the payment of instalments (372G). His Lordship said that he had a discretionary jurisdiction[179] to grant exceptional relief against forfeiture: he listed the relevant factors to be taken into account (375C–376B); and said that relief would only be granted where, as here, the owner would otherwise obtain a substantial windfall over and above what he would have obtained if the agreement had run its course.[180] This equitable jurisdiction is confined to forfeiture of proprietary or possessory rights and does not extend to merely contractual rights,[181] e.g. an acceleration clause (see para 26.19) in an unsecured instalment loan; nor where the hirer has relinquished possession. In *Alf Vaughan & Co Ltd v Royscot Trust Ltd*:[182]

> RT owned a number of vehicles which had been supplied to AV on unregulated hp or finance leases. The Administrative Receiver (see para 19.14) appointed to AV wished to sell the business as a going concern and, to this end, exercise AV's rights under the agreements to pay all outstanding sums: he would then be able to sell the hp vehicles as owner and the leased vehicles as RT's agent. However, when the Receiver sought a settlement figure (about £34,000: see para 26.19A), RT responded that it was entitled to terminate the agreements upon appointment of a receiver (see para 26.08) and sent repossession agents to the site (see para 24.23). RT demanded £82,000 from the Receiver for not recapting the goods, which sum the Receiver paid under protest and then sold on the business with the vehicles.

As the Receiver had sold the vehicles, he could not ask for relief against forfeiture (see para 27.22). Instead, he claimed that the £82,000 had been paid under duress of goods (economic duress). The judge pointed out that a plea of economic duress was only available where the commercial pressure used to bring about a contract was illegitimate;[183] and he rejected the Receiver's claim on the grounds that, in the absence of exceptional circumstances amounting to unconscionable behaviour, the threat of recaption by the owner was not illegitimate (at 863–4).

For the position where the agreement is regulated, see para 27.23. For statutory protection by cancellation rights where there is a distance or doorstep supply, see paras 10.36–8.

**[27.23] Regulated agreements.** There is no general power in the CCA enabling the court to grant relief against forfeiture as such; but certain of the provisions of the

---

179 He made it clear that such relief would not be granted 'if the conduct of the hirer had disentitled it to receive it' (at 375C), e.g. *Goker v NWS* (1990)[1999] GCCR 1507, CA (repeated default by hirer).

180 He made an order for payment by the Receiver of the balance of the hp price within a week. If the agreement had had longer to run, would a discount for accelerated payment have been appropriate?

181 *The Scaptrade* [1983] 2 AC 694, HL. What about a restitutionary claim (cf. *Banque Financiere de la Cite v Parc (Battersea) Ltd* [1999] 1 AC 221, HL)?

182 [1999] 1 All ER (Comm) 856.

183 His Lordship (at 860 and 863) adopted passages from Goff and Jones, *Restitution*, 5th edn, 316. For duress, see generally, para 10.18.

Act will, where applicable, prevent the creditor or owner from having his cake and eating it too.[184]

1.  *Prohibition of preliminary agreements.* Section 59(1) will avoid any separate deposit agreement (see para 5.20), e.g. with a dealer who is to put forward a directly financed transaction.

2.  *The right of cancellation.* Where a hirer under an hp or simple hiring agreement, or a buyer under a conditional or credit sale agreement exercises his statutory right of cancellation, the creditor may recover the goods, but the debtor or hirer is under no further liability and may recover any payments made (s 70: see para 10.33).

3.  *Protected goods.* Where the creditor wrongfully repossess protected goods, the hirer on hp or conditional buyer is released from all further liability and may recover all sums already paid (s 91: set out at para 24.38). Even if the creditor does not recapt, where the debtor follows the procedure laid down for Time Orders, s 130(5) freezes the creditor's contractual rights arising by reason of the debtor's default (see para 24.41).

4.  *Extortionate credit bargains/unfair credit relationships.* A court may be persuaded to exercise the re-opening powers conferred by ss 137–140D (see paras 29.41 and 29.44).

5.  *Financial relief for hirers.* To combat the injustice evinced in *Galbraith v Mitchenall Estates Ltd* (set out at para 27.21), s 132(1) provides as follows:

    > 'Where the owner under a regulated consumer hire agreement[185] recovers possession of goods to which the agreement relates otherwise than by action, the hirer may apply to the court for an order that—
    > (a)  the whole or part of any sum paid by the hirer to the owner in respect of the goods shall be repaid,[186] and
    > (b)  the obligation to pay the whole or part of any sum owed by the hirer to the owner in respect of the goods shall cease,[187]
    >
    > and if it appears to the court just to do so, having regard to the extent of the enjoyment of the goods by the hirer, the court shall grant the application in full or in part.'

Whilst this provision applies where the owner recapts goods (see para 24.23), if the owner instead brings a successful action for repossession (see paras 24.25 and 25.16), similar powers to order release of the hirer are conferred on the court under s 132(2) or the court could reschedule those payments by way of a Time Order (see para 24.40). Compare the common law rule against penalties (see para 27.25).

---

184 Compare the position where the debtor or hirer makes a statutory election to terminate the agreement: see paras 26.05–7.
185 As to consumer hire agreements, see para 1.19.
186 This could include substantial deposits, as in *Galbraith's* case. But see *Automotive Financial Services v Henderson* 1992 SLT (Sh. Ct.) 63.
187 'Sum owed' appears to restrict s 132(1)(b) to rent arrears, and does not extend to sums payable: Guest and Lloyd, *Encyclopedia of Consumer Credit Law*, para 2-133. Presumably this would extend the subsection to rent accelerated by an acceleration clause, but does not touch claims for damages under minimum payment clauses (as to which see para 27.46).

## Liquidated damages and penalties

**[27.24] Liquidated damages.** As the quantification of damages can be a very difficult matter (see para 27.27, *et seq.*), the parties sometimes agree beforehand (usually in the contract) what sum shall be payable in the event of certain breaches or wrongs, e.g. an administration fee, the price.[188] Provided such a clause is a genuine pre-estimate of damage, then, irrespective of the precise amount of loss actually suffered, it is termed a 'liquidated damages' clause: without proof of actual loss, a liquidated damages clause will *prima facie* be given effect to by the courts,[189] unless it amounts to an unfair term.[190] However, if it works to the advantage of the innocent party, it may be struck down as being a penalty (see para 27.25); and, if it acts to protect the guilty party, it may amount to an exclusion clause (see Chap 18).

As a claim for an agreed sum (a debt), a liquidated damages clause is usually assignable (see para 27.15A). However, it will be free from the rules limiting the recovery of damages, such as those of causation, remoteness and mitigation.[191] Nor does it probably fall within the definition of an 'exclusion or restriction' of liability for the purposes of s 13 of UCTA,[192] nor amount to cancellation of a cancellable contract (see para 10.33).

**[27.25] The rule against penalties.**[193] Whilst a contractual promise to pay an agreed sum on default may take effect as a liquidated damages clause (see para 27.24), at common law it may be struck down by the rule against penalties, in which case the innocent party will only be able to recover damages which he **proves** represents his actual loss,[194] whether that be less[195] or more[196] than the sum stipulated in the penalty clause. However, it has been decided that this rule against penalties does not affect clauses providing for a deposit (see para 27.20), or accelerating payment,[197] or requiring entire performance by one side before performance by the other (see para 26.02), or liquidating damages,[198] or making time of the essence.[199]

In modern business-to-business contracts, it may be that the courts have not been astute to find that a clause amounts to a penalty. However, the same cannot be said in respect of business-to-private-consumer contracts, such as provisions for

---

188  E.g. the *George Mitchell* case (set out at para 18.08); the *Watford Electronics* case (see para 18.21).
189  *Robophone Facilities Ltd v Blank* [1966] 3 All ER 128, CA.
190  OFT, *Bulletin No. 14*, case 6: no refund of fees paid within Grey Term (d): see para 11.16.
191  See *Chitty On Contract*, 28th edn, para 27-08.
192  Treitel, *Law of Contract*, 11th edn, 248; and see generally, para 18.16.
193  See generally Treitel, *Law of Contract*, 11th edn, 999–1007.
194  *Financings Ltd v Baldock* [1963] 2 QB 104, CA; *Bridge* (see below); *Jobson v Johnson* [1989] 1 All ER 621, CA (not a sale of goods case; [1990] LM & CLQ 158).
195  E.g. *Clydebank Engineering and Shipbuilding Co* case [1905] AC 6, HL; *Jeancharm Ltd v Barnet FC Ltd* [2004] CLY 667, CA.
196  See Treitel, *Op. cit.*, 1033. Compare Hudson (1985) 101 LQR 480.
197  *Wallingford v Mutual Society* (1880) 5 App Cas 685, HL. But see *Wadham Stringer Finance Ltd v Meaney* (set out at para 26.19), at 796–7, discussed by Treitel, *Op. cit.*, 1001.
198  *Dunlop Pneumatic Tyre* case [1915] AC 79, HL.
199  *Lombard North Central plc v Butterworth* [1987] 1 All ER 267, CA, especially *per* Mustill LJ at 273d–275d. See generally, para 26.08.

compound interest in a non-status agreement[200] and the minimum payments clauses in instalment credit agreements.[201] Frequently, the largest element in this is the sum expressed to be 'compensation' for depreciation of the goods; and the real purpose of such a clause may be to allow the owner to recoup his 'loss of profit'. The leading case is *Bridge v Campbell Discount Co Ltd*, where two issues were involved, to both of which the House of Lords gave an affirmative answer: (1) whether the rule against penalties was applicable at all (see para 27.26); and (2) if so, whether clause 9 stipulated for a penal sum.[202] As to the latter issue, a modern example is provided by the County Court case of *Falco Finance Ltd v Gough*.[203]

> G, a non-status borrower (see para 8.35) entered into an unregulated mortgage with FF which contained all the following unusual features contravening the 'Non-Status Guidelines' (see para 7.04A): (i) the interest rate was calculated at a flat rate, rather than an APR (see para 8.25); (ii) the wording made it difficult for G to avoid default-ing and, if G defaulted by even one day, the interest rate for the remainder of the mortgage rose by a further 5% (the dual interest rate); (iii) if G sought to redeem, there was a redemption charge calculated under the 'Rule of 78' (see para 26.19A).

The County Court Judge refused to apply the terms of the mortgage because: the dual interest rate made the mortgage an extortionate credit bargain (see para 29.41); its terms were unfair under the UTCC Regulations;[204] and they amounted to a clog on the equity of redemption (see para 25.20) and a penalty at common law.

Presumably, the penalty rules also apply to the common practice by creditors granting running-account loans of charging fees for breach of the agreement, e.g. by exceeding credit limits, insufficient funds to meet direct debits.

**[27.26] The scope of the penalty rule.** On the traditional rule that the stipulated sum could only be a penalty if payable on breach,[205] it was at first held that a minimum payments clause could not be a penalty where the stipulated sum was payable not just on breach but also on certain other events, such as lawful termin-ation by the hirer.[206] However, this ruling offered such an obvious means by which a draftsman of a minimum payments clause could escape the rule against penalties that it was reversed: where the event which in fact brought the minimum payments clause into operation was a termination by the owner on grounds of breach by the hirer, the rule against penalties was held to be applicable.[207] Since then, the courts have sought to extend the operation of the rule against penalties. Notwithstanding

---

200  *London North Securities v Meadows* (set out at para 8.25), at para 69.

201  See the discussions in Goode, *HP Law & Practice*, 2nd edn, 385–409; Guest, *Law of HP*, 625–50; Ziegel [1964] CLJ 108; Hughes [1962] JBL 252.

202  See *Lombank Ltd v Excell* [1964] 1 QB 415, CA; the *Meadows* case (see above). See Thornley [1964] CLJ 108; Downey (1964) 27 MLR 100; Guest, *Law of HP*, 638.

203  (1998) 17 Tr LR 526 (see 115 LQR 360; 52 QA 9; [1999] *Credit Today* 18).

204  [2005] *Bulletin J/S, BP Oil; GE Capital; Lloyds TSB*; and para 11.16B.

205  *Associated Distributors Ltd v Hall* [1938] 2 KB 83, CA (determination by hirer; and as to determin-ation by transferee, see generally, para 26.04); *Re Apex Supply Co Ltd* [1942] Ch 108 (automatic termination on liquidation of hirer: see para 26.08); *Bank of Scotland v Truman* [2005] EWHC 583, at para 117 (charge-back clause: see para 7.09).

206  See *Lombard North Central plc v Butterworth* [1987] QB 527, [1987] 1 All ER 267, CA (discussed Treitel [1987] LMCLQ 143; Macassey 42 CC 1/2; Opeskin (1990) 106 LQR 293.

207  *Cooden Engineering Ltd v Stanford* [1953] 1 QB 86, CA.

the ordinary rule of interpretation that a party should *prima facie* be assumed to have intended to do that which is lawful, they have taken the view of the facts most advantageous to the hirer in deciding how the agreement has been terminated. In *Bridge v Campbell Discount Co Ltd*,[208] the hirer under an hp agreement wrote to the owner:

> 'Owing to unforeseen personal circumstances I am very sorry but I will not be able to pay any more payments.'

Faced with this ambiguous statement, the House of Lords held that the hirer had broken rather than lawfully terminated his agreement.[209]

*Statutory intervention.* The common law rules may be displaced in the case of regulated agreements: in hp or a conditional sale, there is a prohibition on default interest (CCA, s 93: see para 26.19) and the facts of *Bridge* would fall within s 100 of the CCA (see para 27.49); and in simple hiring there is power to give financial relief (CCA, s 132: see para 27.23). Further, whether or not regulated, in all consumer contracts a penalty clause may be subject to the unfair terms rules[210] or the statutory requirement reasonableness.[211]

# Action for damages[212]

**[27.27]** The common types of action for damages available to a supplier[213] against the hirer or buyer are for breach of contract, tort or misrepresentation.[214]

1. *For breach of contract.* The SGA partially covers the possibilities: besides expressly recognising the right of action for damages where the price is not forthcoming (s 48(3) and (4): set out at para 27.08), the Act in two places deals with the common situation where the buyer fails to take delivery,[215] on the basis of whether or not that delay is so great as to evince an intention to repudiate.[216] If not, s 37 (set out at para 23.08) expressly recognises the seller's right to damages for loss occasioned by the failure to take delivery and for storage charges. If so, s 50(1) provides that:

> 'Where the buyer wrongfully neglects or refuses to accept and pay for the goods, the seller may maintain an action against him for damages for non-acceptance.'

---

208 [1962] AC 600, [1962] 1 All ER 385, HL: see above and also *Chitty on Contract*, 28th edn, para 27-103.
209 See also *United Dominions Trust (Commercial) Ltd v Ennis* [1968] 1 QB 54, CA (hirer's letter treated as invitation to owner to terminate; or, if it were a repudiation, the owner had affirmed by suing on the minimum payments clause); *Chartered Trust v Pitcher* [1988] RTR 72, CA.
210 UTCC Regs, Grey Term (e) and see *UCT Bulletin No. 12*, case 6; *No. 21*, case 31; *No. 24*, case 48; *No. 26*, pp 41, 70 and 90; *No. 27*, pp 106, 109 and 110; and see para 11.16.
211 UCTA, s 3: see para 18.22.
212 See generally *McGregor on Damages*, 17th edn.
213 For damages actions by lenders, see para 7.03.
214 For declarations of non-liability, see para 29.01.
215 *Prima facie*, it is the buyer's duty to collect the goods (s 29(2)): see para 23.04.
216 This is the explanation of the apparent overlap between ss 37 and 50(1) preferred by Goode, *Commercial Law*, 3rd edn, 400.

It is usually assumed that these provisions apply by analogy where a hirer under an hp or simple hiring agreement fails to take delivery.[217] Under such a claim, the major head of *prima facie* loss is likely to be loss of profit (see paras 27.34–8). Claims for consequential loss are more likely to be made where it is the supplier who is in breach and will therefore be considered later (see Chap 29).

2.  *In tort.* The buyer or hirer might wrongfully deprive the supplier of the goods in several ways; and under the Torts Act 1977 these have all been subsumed under the new statutory tort of 'wrongful interference with goods' (see para 19.04). If the wrong amounts to conversion, the supplier is entitled to the value of the goods (see para 27.30).

3.  *For misrepresentation.* The common law offers a remedy for misrepresentation where it amounts to the torts of deceit or negligent misstatement (see paras 17.18–19); and in the former case the measure of damages is the same as in conversion,[218] i.e. the value of the goods (see above). Additionally, damages may now be awarded under s 2 of the Misrepresentation Act 1967 (see para 17.10), in which case the measure of damages is tortious: for breach of s 2(1), damages may be measured as for the tort of deceit;[219] whereas, damages granted under s 2(2) are presumably based on some lesser tortious measure,[220] so giving more meaning to s 2(3).[221] As to misrepresentations by the supplier, see para 29.18.

In English law, a cause of action for breach of contract is complete on breach: it is said to be actionable *per se*, so that nominal damages are recoverable without proof of loss.[222] On the other hand, in some torts,[223] loss or damage is an ingredient of the cause of action, i.e. there is no action without proof of loss.

## Quantification of damages

In pursuing the issue of damages, there will be examined first the object of damages and some special rules (see paras 27.28–9), then some of the more important heads of damage (see para 27.30, *et seq.*), and thereafter the restrictions on the amount recoverable (see para 27.39, *et seq.*).

---

217  See *Karsales Ltd v Wallis* [1956] 2 All ER 866, CA. See also Guest, *Op. cit.*, 321; Goode, *HP Law and Practice*, 2nd edn, 354–5.

218  *Smith Kline & French Laboratories Ltd v Long* [1988] 3 All ER 887, CA.

219  Including damages for unforeseeable loss: *Royscot Trust Ltd v Rogerson* (set out at para 27.28), *per* Balcombe and Ralph Gibson LJJ at AER 302e, 302c (criticised 107 LQR 547; [1992] JBL 311); and generally, para 27.41.

220  Perhaps on the basis of indemnity only: see Treitel, *Contract*, 11th edn, 366; *Chitty on Contract*, 28th edn, para 6-098. But why not as for negligent misstatement, i.e. subject to a foreseeability test of remoteness (see para 27.41)? See *Cemp Properties (UK) v Deutsply Corp* [1991] 2 EGLR 197, CA (not a goods case; consequential loss recovered).

221  I.e. that more damages are recoverable under s 2(1) than under s 2(2). For the double recovery point, see para 27.39.

222  *Charter v Sullivan* (set out at para 27.33). For the issues relevant to the recovery of substantial damages, see paras 27.28–9.

223  E.g. negligence (see para 17.14, *et seq.*); Misrepresentation Act 1967, s 2(1) (see para 17.10). *Contra* wrongful interference with goods (see para 19.04).

**[27.28] Object of damages.** It has been seen that a supplier will frequently have the choice of suing in either contract or tort in respect of damage caused by the wrong (see para 27.27). Sometimes such claims will lie in the alternative; but, insofar as they are concurrent,[224] there may be no double recovery (see para 27.39). In any event, the object of the award of damages in tort and contract are different.[225]

1.  *Damages in tort.* The object of damages in tort is *restitutio in integrum*; that is, so far as money can do it, to put the injured plaintiff/claimant back in the same position as if the wrong had not been sustained.[226] If the goods have been lost, this will *prima facie* be their value (see para 27.30), plus expenses, such as the cost of hiring a replacement: see *Dimond v Lovell* (set out at para 5.13); and support in hiring a replacement is unlikely to amount to champerty (see para 7.26). There may also be a claim for consequential loss, such as a loss of profit (see para 27.33). The same *prima facie* rule applies to claims for damages under the Misrepresentation Act 1967; and a similar result is obtained where there is a claim to recover money paid on grounds of total failure of consideration (see para 29.12). In *Royscot Trust Ltd v Rogerson*:[227]

    > The dealer (D) was arranging a directly financed hp transaction in respect of a Honda Prelude car, through a finance company (RT) to a hirer (H). D arranged with H an hp price of £7,600, a deposit of £1,200 and finance of £6,400. As this would not meet RT's stipulation for a 20% deposit, D misrepresented to RT that the hp price was £8,000 and that H had paid a deposit of £1,600, leaving a balance of £6,400. After paying instalments amounting to some £2,275, H dishonestly passed a Part III title to a bf private purchaser (see para 21.57). RT sued D for damages under s 2(1) of the 1967 Act for inducing RT to purchase the car by misrepresenting the financial arrangements.

    The Court of Appeal held that the measure of damages for breach of s 2(1) was that in tort for fraudulent misrepresentation (see para 27.27), which includes unforeseeable loss (see para 27.41); that H's sale was not a *novus actus*, such as would relieve D of all liability (see para 27.29), because it was foreseeable;[228] and that, as the essence of the transaction was for RT to finance H's instalments rather than purchase and resell to H, RT was therefore entitled to recover £3,652 from D, being the difference between the amount it paid D (£6,400) and that received from H (£2,775).

2.  *Damages in contract.* Whereas the object of damages in tort is to put the clock back, the object of damages in contract is to put it forward to the time when the

---

224 Is the plaintiff entitled to elect whichever cause of action will give him the greater damages? See Street, *Law of Damages*, 252–3.

225 *A v Bottrill* [2003] 1 AC 449, PC (119 LQR 24). As to whether exemplary damages should sometimes be available as a deterrence for breach of a consumer contract, see Edelman (2001) 117 LQR 539.

226 *Swingcastle Ltd v Alastair Gibson* [1991] 2 AC 223, HL (loan). See Fuller and Perdue (1936) 46 Yale LJ 52, at 71; Burrows (1983) 99 LQR 217, at 253; Holyoak (1983) 99 LQR at 593. See generally Stoljar (1975) 91 LQR 68. As to exemplary damages, see Bell (91) 20 Anglo-Am 371 at 372–6.

227 [1991] 2 QB 297; [1991] 3 All ER 294, CA (see Pugh (1993) 5 LN 20).

228 At AER 301d, 303a. Criticised by Hooley (1991) 107 LQR at 551. The fact that R's sale was foreseeable might lessen the force of the decision insofar as it suggests that unforeseeable loss was recoverable as in deceit: Cumberbatch [1992] JBL 311.

contemplated contract would be fully performed; that is, so far as money can do it, to put the injured plaintiff in the same situation as if the contract had been performed. In a supply contract,[229] *prima facie*, this will be the difference between the contract and market price (see para 27.34); but there may also be a claim for consequential loss, such as the business profit which could have been earned through the article bought (see para 27.33). This has been termed as giving the injured plaintiff 'the value of performance', or his 'expectancy interest'.[230] Of course, a business plaintiff, whilst expecting to make a profit from a venture, may not wish or be able to quantify that profit. In these circumstances, there is no objection to his simply claiming the wasted expenditure incurred in reliance on the contract;[231] that is, the expenses he would have set off against the gross profit of the venture to arrive at his net profit, what has been termed his 'reliance interest'.[232] However, except doubtfully in the case of pre-contract expenditure,[233] this should not enable the injured plaintiff to claim by way of his reliance interest expenses he would not have been able to recoup anyway, because it cannot then be said that the defendant **caused** the plaintiff's loss;[234] and this argument has been used to justify a refusal of expenses thrown away in the bad bargain cases.[235]

**[27.29] Some special considerations.** To recover more than nominal damages for breach of contract, the plaintiff must show that some loss has been sustained (*Thompson v Robinson* (set out at para 27.33)). Before proceeding to the rules by which the courts quantify damages (see para 27.30, *et seq.*) within the limitation period (see para 26.17), certain points of general application must be mentioned, though the impact of taxation or a foreign currency element are beyond the scope of this work.

1. There are the distinctions between general and special damage (see para 7.03A); and between damages and debt (see para 27.15A).

2. Generally, a party can only recover substantial damages in respect of a loss which he himself has sustained, except where one of the exceptions to the privity rule is present (see para 17.08).

3. There is the question of putting a monetary value on the time element: there are statutory provisions for the award of interest on debt or damages (SGA, s 54;

---

229 *Nimmo v Habton Farms* [2004] QB 1, CA, at paras 46, 120 (breach of warranty of buyer's authority: see para 10.12). But was not the loss caused by death of the horse rather than breach?

230 Waters (1958) 36 Can BR 360, 361. It is P's lost profit that is recoverable, not any extra profit accruing to D: *Surrey CC v Bredero Homes Ltd* [1993] 3 All ER 705, CA (not a goods case).

231 This will include the expenses of care and custody or resale (see para 27.24) and recompense for damage to the goods caused by a bailee's wrongful acts (*Brady v St Margaret's Trust Ltd* [1963] 2 QB 494, CA).

232 E.g. *Mason v Burningham* (see para 12.16); *Bacon v Cooper (Metals) Ltd* [1982] 1 All ER 397 (hp); interest (see para 7.03A); and generally, para 29.23. This has been seen as a completely separate principle: Treitel (1992) 108 LQR at 229.

233 See *Anglia Television Ltd v Reed* [1972] 1 QB 60, CA (not a sale case); but how can it be said that the defendant **caused** the plaintiff's pre-contract expenditure? See below; and Ogus (1972) 35 MLR 423; Trietel, *Op. cit.*, 226.

234 *C & P Haulage v Middleton* [1983] 3 All ER 94, CA (not a sale case). But the onus is on the defendant to show that the expenditure would not have been recouped: *CCC Films (London) Ltd v Impact Quadrant Films Ltd* [1984] 3 All ER 298 (licence and bailment).

235 *L Albert & Son v Armstrong Rubber Co* (1949) 178 F 2d 182 (US).

and para 7.03A); and the common law *prima facie* insists on a rebate for accelerated payment.[236]

4.  Where the defendant has the option of performing a contract in alternative ways, it is assumed that he would have performed in the manner most advantageous to himself.[237]

5.  The impecuniosity of the contract-breaker is no longer irrelevant,[238] whilst that of the innocent party is considered in relation to remoteness (see paras 27.41–2).

6.  In a commercial contract, no damages will be awarded for anguish, though the matter may be otherwise in a consumer contract to provide pleasure.[239]

7.  The agreement may actually spell out some of the heads of damages arising from the breach, e.g. reasonable expenses;[240] or it may go further and commute some or all of the damages into a liquidated damages clause, so turning them into a debt (see para 27.24).

8.  An exclusion clause may purport to limit recoverable damage (see Chap 18).

9.  There must always be borne in mind the extent to which express terms may be struck down on the basis that they are unreasonable or unfair (see UCTA, s 3 (para 18.20); and UTCCR (para 11.12, *et seq.*)).

*Causation.* Difficulty may sometimes be caused by questions of causation: the defendant is only liable for more than nominal damages where he caused a loss;[241] and, in an action in conversion, that is where he was 'the effective, natural and direct cause' of the loss.[242] Conversely, damages should only be diminished where he causes a benefit to accrue to the plaintiff.[243] Further, the test of whether the flow of damage has been interrupted by a *novus actus* is the same for contract and tort[244] and should be distinguished from the mitigation rule (see para 27.45). But, where the defendant's act is merely one of two or more causes of the plaintiff's harm, the

---

236 *Interoffice Telephones Ltd v Freeman* [1958] 1 QB 190, CA; *Overstone Ltd v Shipway* [1962] 1 All ER 52, CA. For express provisions and a statutory requirement, see para 26.19.

237 E.g. *Re Thornett and Fehr and Yuills Ltd* [1921] 1 KB 219; *Paula Lee Ltd v Robert Zehil and Co Ltd* [1983] 2 All ER 390. See also Hudson (1975) 91 LQR 20.

238 *Lagden v O'Conner* [2004] 1 AC 1067, HL (see Thompkinson 154 NLJ 424; Coote 120 LQR 382).

239 *Jackson v Chrysler Acceptances Ltd* [1978] RTR 474, CA; *Farley v Skinner* [2002] 2 AC 732, HL (house purchase; noise); and see para 29.37.

240 Large suppliers to consumers tend to take this as authority to levy standard charges: see (1998) 50 *Quarterly Account* 8–9; (2000) 54 CC6/32.

241 *Lambert v Lewis* (set out at para 17.06); *Dobell & Co Ltd v Barber and Garrett* (set out at para 18.35); *The Zinnia* [1984] 2 Lloyd's Rep 211 (repair contract); the bad bargain cases (see para 27.28), misrepresentations (see paras 17.10 and 17.20); *Ackerman v Protim Services Ltd* [1988] 2 EGLR 259, CA (guarantee); *Royscot Trust Ltd v Rogerson* (set out at para 27.28); *Dimond v Lovell* (set out at para 5.13; [1999] JBL at 464–6); para 17.24 and para 29.35. But see *Gran Gelato Ltd v Richcliff (Group) Ltd* [1992] 1 All ER 865 (criticised 109 LQR 539); *EE Caledonia Ltd v Orbit Value Co* [1993] 4 All ER 165.

242 *Kuwait Airways Corp v Iraqi Airways Co No. 3* (set out at para 19.05A; but see 118 LQR 548); *Nimmo v Habton Farms* [2004] QB 1, CA, at paras 95, 97 (breach of warranty of authority; and para 27.36).

243 E.g. subsales: *Slater v Hoyle* (see para 29.33). But see the difficult *British Westinghouse* case [1912] AC 673, HL; discussed by Treitel, *Law of Contract*, 11th edn, 891–2.

244 *Beoco Ltd v Alfa Laval Co Ltd* [1995] QB 137, CA. E.g. *The Theresa Navigation SA* [2001] 2 All ER (Comm) 243.

other cause is generally ignored,[245] unless it is subsequent to the defendant's act and involves questions of remoteness (see para 27.41), or there is the possibility of a contribution (see para 12.10).

**[27.30] Value in tort.** It has already been pointed out that a satisfied judgment in conversion is effectively a compulsory sale (see para 26.17); and, if the defendant destroys the goods, an action in negligence will have a rather similar effect.[246] But it is a 'sale' with a difference: the defendant in that tort action is not required to pay the contract price (see paras 27.16–19), but damages calculated by reference to the value of the goods.[247] *Prima facie*, the value is taken at the date of conversion, even where the value of the goods subsequently declines;[248] but, if the goods have increased in value by the date of trial, the plaintiff may be entitled to that increase.[249] However, where the increase is due to improvements made to the goods, the position is as follows: at common law an innocent improver was entitled to an allowance for his improvements;[250] and this rule has now been extended by s 6 of the Torts Act to protect a direct or indirect innocent purchaser (s 6(2)) or hirer (s 6(4)) from the improver, and also any intermediate purchaser sued in quasi-contract (s 6(3)). This will cover the situation where the end-purchaser (himself made an allowance for prior improvements) sues his supplier in quasi-contract to recover his price as on total failure of consideration (see para 12.06) and requires that a similar allowance be made to his supplier (for total failure of consideration generally, see para 29.12). Improvements aside, unless the defendant insists on returning the goods,[251] the plaintiff is entitled to the full value of the goods notwithstanding his own limited interest in them,[252] except where the defendant has a legal interest in them,[253] a rule which has caused difficulty with hp (see para 27.31).

For the purposes of the foregoing rules, the value of the goods in a tort action are assessed as follows: if the goods have a market value, that market value at the place of loss should *prima facie* be taken;[246] but, where the goods have no market value, the courts start with the assumption that the plaintiff should recover the replacement cost.[254] The effect of these rules in relation to second-hand cars was considered in *Sargent Ltd v Motor Auctions Ltd*:[255]

---

245 *Financings Ltd v Baldock* [1963] 2 QB 104, CA. Compare *Lombard North Central plc v Butterworth* [1987] QB 527, CA (discussed Treitel [1987] LMCLQ 143).

246 *Liesbosch Dredger v Edison Steamship (Owners)* [1933] AC 449, HL. Distinguish *Alcoa Minerals of Jamaica Inc v Broderick* [2002] 1 AC 371, PC.

247 *Dominion Mosaics and Tile Co Ltd v Trafalgar Trucking Co Ltd* [1990] 2 All ER 246, CA; *Ali Reza-Delta Transport Co Ltd v United Arab Shipping Co SAG (No. 1)* [2003] 2 All ER (Comm) 269, CA.

248 *BBMB Finance (Hong Kong) Ltd v Eda Holdings Ltd* [1991] 2 All ER 129, PC (shares).

249 *IBL Ltd v Coussens* [1991] 2 All ER 133, CA—is a trade plaintiff entitled to the trade or retail value?

250 *Greenwood v Bennett* [1973] QB 195, CA, discussed in (1973) 36 MLR 89 and (1977) 93 LQR 273. As to *accessio*, see para 19.05.

251 As the defendant may be entitled to do under s 3 of the Torts Act 1977: see para 24.26. But see the *BBMB* case (above); and there may be a duty to account: see para 1.17.

252 *The Winkfield* [1902] P 42, CA. For concurrent actions, see para 27.27.

253 E.g. co-owners, as to which see para 27.26; conditional buyers, as to which see para 27.31. Cf. *Chinery v Viall* (set out at para 29.24).

254 E.g. *J and E Hall Ltd v Barclay* [1937] 3 All ER 620, CA; *Harbutt's Plasticine Ltd v Wayne Tank Ltd* [1970] 1 QB 447, CA; *Lambeth LBC v Cumberbatch* [2006] RTR 2, CA; *Wilson v Robertson (London) Ltd* (set out at para 10.19).

255 [1977] RTR 121, CA. Cf. *Naughton v O'Callaghan* [1990] 3 All ER 191.

A rogue stole from a motor dealer (P) a second-hand Jaguar and sold it to an auctioneer (D1), who resold it to D2.[256] P had purchased the car only a few weeks before its theft for £1,975, paying £25 more than the Glass's Guide price because the car had some extras. In his action for conversion, P proved that he had every expectation of being able to sell the car for £2,650.

Applying the same reasoning as is used in actions between seller and buyer for non-acceptance (see para 27.36), the Court of Appeal decided that a second-hand car was a unique item, so that the market value of similar models (c£1,950) was not an appropriate measure, and P was entitled to what he could have got by selling it (£2,650).

[27.31/2] Valuing instalment contracts. This paragraph is concerned with the valuation of the supplier's interest in goods subject to a conditional sale, hp or simple hiring. In all three cases, the supplier retains the ownership of goods in the hands of another; but not until termination of the hiring (see para 26.09) does the owner have sufficient interest in the goods to maintain an action in conversion (see para 19.06). Where a simple bailment has been determined, the owner/supplier is entitled to recover in conversion[257] the full value of the goods as explained above (para 27.30). On the other hand, under a conditional sale the buyer has a contractual right to call for the property in the goods upon payment of the instalments; and on breach by the conditional buyer, if the supplier chooses to sue in conversion, he must make an allowance for that interest.[258]

Now, hp is a hybrid between bailment and sale (see para 1.20): whilst the right to sue in conversion arises upon termination of the bailment, there is still the question of the option to purchase (see para 26.09). Where the agreement still subsists, the hirer or assignee sued in conversion is entitled to have deducted from the value of the goods the value of that option.[259] However, where the agreement has been terminated, the supplier should on principle be entitled to the full value of the goods; and he has been held so entitled as against a third party.[260] However, when that value exceeds the amount outstanding, as against the hirer or his assignee the courts have restricted the supplier to the outstanding balance of the hp price. Some cases are explicable on the basis that the agreement has not in fact been terminated for breach. For instance, in *Wickham Holdings Ltd v Brooke House Motors Ltd*:[261]

A Rover car was let to a hirer under an hp agreement which contained a prohibition against assignment. When the hirer tried to trade in the Rover to obtain another model from a dealer, the dealer sought a settlement figure from the owner. The dealer accepted the trade-in, but forgot to pay the settlement figure (£270) to the owner. On

---

256 It was held that P was not precluded from denying the rogue's authority to sell: see para 21.14.

257 *Manders v Williams* (1849) 4 Exch 339.

258 See para 27.30. Cf. *Johnson v Stear* (1863) 15 CB (NS) 330 (owner suing pledgor). Compare the supplier's right to sue in contract for the outstanding instalments: see para 27.19.

259 *Whiteley Ltd v Hilt* [1918] 2 KB 808, CA; discussed in Goode, *HP Law and Practice*, 2nd edn, 586–8.

260 *North Central Wagon Co Ltd v Graham* [1950] 2 KB 7, CA (auctioneer); *Union Transport Finance Ltd v British Car Auctions Ltd* [1978] 2 All ER 385, CA (auctioneer); *Chubb Cash Ltd v John Crilly & Son* [1983] 2 All ER 294, CA (against bailiff levying execution).

261 [1967] 1 All ER 117, [1967] 1 WLR 295, CA. Discussed by Goode, *HP Law & Practice*, 2nd edn, 584–6; and para 27.31.

learning of the sale by way of trade-in of the Rover to the dealer, the owner terminated the hp agreement and sued the dealer for the return of the Rover or its value (£365).

The Court of Appeal restricted the owner to the settlement figure:[262] in rather unsatisfactory judgments, the majority appeared to say that, in quoting a settlement figure, the owner had waived the prohibition on assignment.[263] However, other cases are not so easily reconcilable,[264] and it may be that this hp rule is just *sui generis*.[265]

**[27.33] Loss of profit.** Whilst loss of profit is commonly thought of as an expectancy interest recoverable in an action for breach of contract, such a claim may arise out of a tort action.

1.  *Profit claims in tort.* Where a profit-earning chattel is destroyed, a claim for consequential loss of profit from a third party, e.g. by hiring out goods, is an alternative to claiming the cost of hiring a replacement.[266] A claim for loss of profit has been allowed in actions in detinue,[267] now wrongful interference with goods (para 19.04) and deceit.[268]

2.  *Profit claims in contract.* A claim for loss of profit for breach of s 50(1) of the SGA (set out at para 27.24) differs in two respects from that just considered: first, the plaintiff/claimant is not suing for a prospective profit that he might have made out of some third party, but the profit he would have made out of his contract with the defendant; and second, the plaintiff in contract must show that he has actually lost such a profit if he is to recover more than nominal damages.[269] The latter point may be neatly illustrated by reference to two cases, in both of which the defendant, a retail buyer of a new motor car at a price fixed by the manufacturer failed to take delivery of it; and the plaintiff, a retail seller, then disposed of the car and subsequently claimed for the loss of profit on the sale to the defendant. In *WL Thompson Ltd v Robinson (Gunmakers) Ltd*[270] it was found as a fact that the supply of that type of car exceeded demand in the area and Upjohn J held that the plaintiffs were entitled to recover the full sum, because they had lost a sale, and hence lost the profit they would otherwise have

---

262 For trade-ins by way of part-exchange, see para 2.09. For settlement figures, see para 26.19A.

263 For waiver, see para 26.23. See Diamond (1967) 30 MLR 322; Guest, *Law of HP*, para 700; Goode, *HP Law and Practice*, 2nd edn, 583, *et seq.*; Oditah (1992) 108 LQR at 484–5.

264 *Belsize Motor Supply Co v Cox* [1914] 1 KB 244, discussed by Goode, *Op. cit.*, 583–4; *Belvoir Finance Co Ltd v Stapleton* [1971] 1 QB 210, CA.

265 See *Street on Torts*, 10th edn, 48; and para 1.25. Cf. the recaption rule (see para 24.22) and the loss of profit rule (see para 27.37).

266 See Street, *Law of Damages*, 206–10.

267 *Strand Electric Ltd v Brisford Entertainments Ltd* [1952] 2 QB 246, CA. And see *Penarth Dock Ltd v Pounds* [1963] 1 Lloyd's Rep 359; *Astley Industrial Trust v Miller* [1968] 2 All ER 36; *Hillesden Securities Ltd v Ryjack Ltd* [1983] 2 All ER 184.

268 *East v Mauer* [1991] 2 All ER 733, CA (not a goods case; criticised 108 LQR 386; 55 MLR at 704–5; 20 Aust B LR 372); *Clef Aquitaine SARL v Laporte Materials Ltd* [2000] 3 All ER 493, CA (franchise case).

269 The same rule is applicable where there is an anticipatory breach: *The Mihalis Angelos* [1971] 1 QB 164, CA.

270 [1955] Ch 177; [1955] 1 All ER 154 (see Bridge, *Sale of Goods*, 585–7).

271 This may be an over-simplification: see Goode, *Commercial Law*, 3rd edn, 406–7.

made.[271] On the other hand, in *Charter v Sullivan*[272] it was shown that there was a shortage of cars of that type and the plaintiff could dispose of all he could obtain; and the Court of Appeal therefore awarded the plaintiff only nominal damages for loss of profit, because he had not lost a (profitable) sale. Of course, in other circumstances the disappointed seller may be under a duty to mitigate his loss;[273] and, in a consumer supply, a provision entitling the supplier to loss of profit may be unfair.[274] Assuming the plaintiff can show that he has lost a profit, how is that profit to be measured (see para 27.34)?

**[27.34] Assessing loss of profit in contract.** In the case of a sale (for bailments, see para 27.37), the unpaid seller will be able to sue in contract for either the price (see paras 27.16–18) or damages for loss of profit. However, it must be remembered that claims for damages differ from claims for the price (see para 27.15A) in that only the former are subject to the restrictions on damages (see para 27.39), e.g. as to remoteness.

As regards damages claims, the nineteenth century common law took the view that the value of performance in a contract for the sale of goods was the same whether the seller or buyer was in breach: the innocent party should go into the market;[275] and this artificial market rule has been adopted by the SGA.[276] However, whilst it may be that in some cases this market rule will normally provide the disappointed seller with an adequate level of compensation (see the *Shearson Lehman* case (below)), in practice the rule may be overridden by the remoteness rule contained in s 50(2).[277] Further, the two sections only lay down a *prima facie* rule to apply where there is an 'available market',[278] and there has been some judicial disagreement as to whether this refers to a market place (a geographical test),[279] or a level of supply and demand (an economic test);[280] but, if there is such a market, the rule also applies where it is deemed to be available. It may be thought that this last principle was tested nearly to destruction in *Shearson Lehman Hutton Inc v Maclaine Watson & Co Ltd (No. 2)*.[281]

**[27.35] Where there is an available market.**[282] In such cases (see para 27.34), the presumption is that the disappointed seller will go out into that market and resell

---

272  [1957] 2 QB 117; [1957] 1 All ER 809, CA.

273  Bridge, *Op. cit.*, 587–9.

274  [2005] *Bulletin J/S, Forthright Finance, GE Capital*.

275  *Per* Tindal CJ in *Barrow v Arnaud* (1846) 8 QB 604, at 609–10. See generally Bridge, *Sale of Goods* 568–70.

276  In respectively SGA, s 50(3) for sellers and s 51(3) for buyers. See Waters (1958) 36 Can BR 360, 370; Bridge, *Sale of Goods*, 561–4.

277  *Bem Dis A Turk Ticaret S/A TR v International Agri Trade Co Ltd* [1999] 1 All ER (Comm) 619, CA. The same thing may happen with a buyer's claim for damages: see *Bence Graphics International Ltd v Fasson UK Ltd* (see para 29.26).

278  See generally Waters (1958) 36 Can BR 360; Lawson (1969) 43 ALJ 52, 106; McGregor, *On Damages*, 17th edn, paras 20.108–17.

279  See *per* James LJ in *Dunkirk Colliery Co v Lever* (1878) Ch D 20 at 25, CA. It has even been extended to a black market: *Mouatt v Betts Motors Ltd* [1959] AC 71, PC.

280  See *per* Jenkins LJ in *Charter v Sullivan* [1957] 2 QB 117 at 128, CA.

281  [1990] 3 All ER 723; [1990] 1 Lloyd's Rep. 441 (see [1990] LMCLQ 305, esp. 310–14): see para 27.35.

282  Presumably, the terms of any sales franchise held by the innocent supplier ought to be relevant. But would this cause difficulties with the doctrine of remoteness (see para 27.41)?

the goods (s 50(3)); additionally, the supplier should be compensated for any expenses or other special damage under s 54, e.g. return carriage, storage (see generally, para 29.23). Section 50(3) of the SGA provides:

> 'Where there is an available market for the goods in question the measure of damages is *prima facie* to be ascertained by the difference between the contract price and the market or current price at the time or times when the goods ought to have been accepted or, if no time was fixed for acceptance, then at the time of the refusal to accept.'

This provision contains two rules: (a) the damages are to be established by the artificial market rule (see para 27.34); and (b) they are to be assessed at the time of breach (the 'breach date' rule), so that, if the seller chooses to speculate by staying out of the market, he does so at his own risk.[283] Further, it is only a *prima facie* measure: it may be increased by any consequential loss (cf. para 29.33) or reduced by any counter-claim by the buyer.[284] The onus of proving the selling price (where this differs from the buying price) in that market at the time of acceptance[285] is on the seller.[286] The assessment of damages may now be explained by reference to the simplest case, where the buyer is in breach at the time fixed for delivery and the seller resells immediately.[287] In this case, the amount recoverable from the buyer is as follows:

(1) If the **market price** is below the **contract price**, the seller is *prima facie* entitled under s 50(3) to the difference between the two:[288] if he resells below the market price, he is not entitled to that extra loss because he has not mitigated his loss (see para 27.44); and if he resells above that market price, he will only recover his actual loss.[289] The position on a notional resale was considered in the *Shearson* case (see para 27.34), where Webster J held that:

 (a) The appropriate price under s 50(3) is the fair market or current price at the moment of breach, not prices before or after that date.[290]

 (b) The duty to mitigate would only have been relevant had there been an actual, as opposed to notional, resale (at 731e).

 (c) The court has a discretion (perhaps by reason of the words '*prima facie*' in s 50(3)) to select as the appropriate price one that is not the average market price.[291]

---

283 The time element in fixing the price is examined later (see paras 29.20–21).

284 *Gill & Duffus SA v Berger & Co Inc* (set out at para 23.06).

285 'Acceptance' does not here refer to a s 34 acceptance (as to which see para 23.10) but rather to receipt of delivery: see Goode, *Commercial Law*, 3rd edn, 401–2.

286 *Per* Diplock LJ in *RV Ward Ltd v Bignall* (set out at para 27.10) at 547, CA. The resale price, if any, may be evidence of this.

287 If he delays beyond this time, the seller carries the risk of any fluctuation in the market price: *Campbell Mostyn (Provisions) Ltd v Barnett Trading Co* [1954] 1 Lloyd's Rep 65, CA. For anticipatory breach, see Atiyah, *Sale of Goods*, 10th edn, 534, *et seq.*

288 *Gebruder Metelmann GmbH & Co v NBR London* [1984] 1 Lloyd's Rep 614, CA.

289 But compare the position of the innocent buyer: see para 29.20.

290 At 728a. But prices obtaining in the market before or after that date were admitted as indirect evidence of what that price was (at 732a–c).

291 At 731g. His Lordship took a price somewhat below the midpoint of that range (at 732d–e). For the factors he took into account, see [1990] LMCLQ at 312–3.

(2) If the **market price** is equal to or above the **contract price**, presumably the intention of s 50(3) is that the seller will only be entitled to nominal damages. However, the courts may be willing to oust s 50(3), as in *Trans Trust SPRL v Danubian Trading Ltd*.[292] Similarly, the courts have shown very little enthusiasm for s 50(3) when dealing with fixed-price goods.[293]

**[27.36/8] Where there is no available market**. There may be no available market for a seller,[294] as where goods are specifically manufactured to order,[295] or supply exceeds demand;[296] and in such cases s 50(3) of the SGA is obviously inapplicable. *Prima facie*, such a seller will be entitled to be put in the same situation he would have been if the contract had been performed (see para 27.28). Thus, he has been held entitled to the profit he would have made, even where he does manage to resell the goods;[295] and the rule has even been used to justify the award to the seller of substantial damages for breach of a promise to pay a deposit.[297] The same principles have been applied to a simple hiring agreement: the supplier's right to rentals having been terminated with the hiring (see para 27.21), he has been awarded damages to compensate him for loss of future rentals.[298] Similarly, an available market has been ignored in an action for breach of warranty of buyer's authority (see para 10.12) where the innocent seller had not at the material time made up his mind what to do.[299]

On the other hand, it is clear that the defaulting buyer or hirer is entitled to adduce evidence to show that the supplier would not have made the second profit as well:[300] and if he does so, the supplier will receive only nominal damages for loss of profit.[301] In *Lazenby Garages Ltd v Wright*:[302]

> B agreed on February 19th to buy from S a second-hand BMW 2002 for £1,670. The next day, B changed his mind and repudiated the contract. S resold the car in April for £1,770. Nevertheless, S claimed from B £345 loss of profit, this being the difference between the price B had agreed to pay and that for which S had purchased the car in mid-February (£1,325). B replied that S had lost nothing, having resold the car for £100 more than he promised to pay. The Court of Appeal unanimously found for B.

Lord Denning MR pointed out that there could not automatically be applied to second-hand cars the rule for new goods;[301] second-hand goods may well (as here)

---

292  [1952] 2 QB 297; [1952] 1 All ER 970, CA.

293  See *WL Thompson Ltd v Robinson Ltd* and *Charter v Sullivan* (para 27.33).

294  As to available market, see para 27.34; and as to the *prima facie* measure of damages where there is such a market, see para 27.35.

295  E.g. *Re Vic Mills Ltd* [1913] 1 Ch 465, CA.

296  *Per* Upjohn J in *Thompson Ltd v Robinson Ltd* [1955] Chap 177 at 187.

297  See para 23.27. For deposits, see para 27.20. Why was this action not subject to the rule against penalties (as to which see para 27.25)? See also the UTCCR, Grey Term (e): see para 11.16B.

298  *Interoffice Telephones Ltd v Freeman Ltd* [1958] 1 QB 190, CA. Subsequently, this formula was reduced to take account of the accelerated payment: *Robophone Facilities Ltd v Blank* [1966] 3 All ER 128, CA (for another point, see para 27.26A).

299  *Nimmo v Habton Farms* [2004] QB 1, CA, at paras 55, 61.

300  *Hill and Sons v Showell* (1918) 87 LJKB 1106, HL.

301  See *Charter v Sullivan* (set out at para 27.33).

302  [1976] 2 All ER 770; [1976] 1 WLR 459, CA (criticised by Bridge, *Sale of Goods*, 589–90).

be unique, so that there was no available market;[303] and damages would have to be assessed on the basis of the reasonable contemplation of the parties (SGA, s 50(2): see further, para 27.42). However, the Court of Appeal thought that it was not within B's reasonable contemplation that S would lose a sale by B's repudiation, so that B would only have to make good S's loss; and there was none.

## Common law and statutory restrictions on damages

[27.39/40] Even where the damage caused to the supplier[304] has been quantified in accordance with the principles discussed above (see paras 27.24–38), there remain a number of rules which will restrict the sum recoverable below the amount indicated by those principles.

1. *Public policy.* There may be sums irrecoverable on grounds of public policy, e.g. fines (*Payne v Ministry of Food* [1953] CLY 3272, Cty Ct).

2. *The rule against double recovery.* As the primary function of the law of damages is to make good any loss (see para 27.28), it follows that the plaintiff can only recover once in respect of any particular loss, even though that loss may be recoverable by more than one cause of action.[305] For instance, a seller may be entitled to recover the value of goods in conversion from more than one person, but he can only recover it once because satisfaction of a judgment in conversion extinguishes the plaintiff's interest in the goods (see para 26.17); a conditional seller may be able at his option to sue the buyer for the price or recover the goods, but not both (see para 27.19); and in an action for damages for non-acceptance, the seller will have to give an allowance for the price paid, e.g. *Ward Ltd v Bignall* (set out at para 27.10); actions for loss of profit (see paras 27.33–6). Similarly, a disappointed buyer cannot recover his loss of profit twice over;[306] nor can he recover the price in contract and value in tort, e.g. *Chinery v Viall* (set out at para 29.24); and a misrepresentee will only be compensated once.[307] Further, where the Contracts Act 1999 applies, there is a provision to prevent double liability (s 5: see para 17.08).

3. *Contributory negligence.*[308] Whilst this was a complete defence at common law, the Law Reform (Contributory Negligence) Act 1945 provides for apportionment of damages with regard to the 'fault' (s 4) of the plaintiff (P) and defendant (D), except where there is an overriding contractual or statutory provision.[309] D's liability creating 'fault' includes his negligence or breach of

---

303 Cf. the argument in tort as to the valuation of the goods: see para 27.30.

304 As to causation, see para 27.29. In exceptional circumstances, the law may allow one who has not himself suffered loss to recover damages on behalf of another, e.g. the owner: *The Winkfield* (tort; see para 27.30). Compare the position in contract: see *The Albazero* [1977] AC 774, HL.

305 A further action may lead to the recovery of only nominal damages: *The Albazero* (above).

306 *Cullinane v British 'Rema' Manufacturing Co Ltd* (see para 29.35).

307 Even where more than one action may lie for damages under the Misrepresentation Act 1967: see s 2(3); and further, para 17.10.

308 See generally Glanville Williams, *Joint Torts and Contributory Negligence*, Pt 2; Winfield and Jolowicz, *Tort*, 16th edn, para 6.39, *et seq.*; Treitel, *Law of Contract*, 11th edn, 982–7.

309 As to contractual exclusion clauses, see para 18.03. What about a non-contractual disclaimer? As to statutory provisions, see, e.g. CCA, s 100 (see para 27.50); UCTA, s 3 (see para 18.20); CPA, s 6 (see para 17.29).

statutory duty (see respectively, paras 17.13 and 3.21), but does not extend to his wrongful interference with goods, nor to fraud.[310] As regards simple breach of contract, only where D's liability for negligence is independently co-extensive in contract and tort is the 1945 Act available to apportion damages in an action for breach of contract[311] or under s 2(1) of the 1967 Act.[312] Otherwise, the court must decide whether P or D caused the loss (see para 27.29). As to the statutory contribution rules, see para 12.10.

4. *Reasonableness*. In *Ruxley Electronics Ltd v Forsyth*[313] the House of Lords laid down the overriding principle that the damages must be reasonably pro-portionate to the loss suffered.[314]

5. *Remoteness of damage* (see paras 27.41–43).

6. *Mitigation of damage* (see paras 27.44–48).

7. *The CCA* (see para 27.49).

8. *Insolvency* (see para 19.18, *et seq.*).

**[27.41/2] Remoteness of damage.**[315] Whilst the criteria for quantifying damages have thus far been reasonably logical and scientific, the courts have always sought to retain an element of negative discretion, refusing compensation where damage was 'too remote', e.g. *ex gratia* payments to customers.[316] In a sense, the courts have been very successful in retaining an unfettered discretion: there remain consider-able doubts as to the tests of remoteness in tort and contract, and the extent to which they correspond (see para 27.43).

1. *Remoteness in tort*. Intended consequences cannot be too remote:[317] for this purpose, recklessness amounting to deceit (see para 17.18) is put on a par with intention;[318] and liability under s 2(1) of the Misrepresentation Act 1967 may be treated like deceit.[319] However, where the defendant did not intend the consequences of his act, it was decided that it was unreasonable to make him liable for more harm than he ought to have **foreseen** it would cause.[320]

---

310 See respectively Torts (Interference with Goods) Act 1977, s 11(1); and para 17.18.

311 The *Albright & Wilson* (set out at para 13.01), CA at para 13; *Rolls Royce Power Engineering plc v Ricardo Consulting Engineers Ltd* [2004] 2 All ER (Comm) 129, at paras 90–92. See also the White Paper on *Banking Services* (1990, Cm. 1026), Annexe 7. For a recommendation that the 1945 Act should be a defence to strict contractual duties, see *Contributory Negligence* (1990 Law Com WP No. 114), para 5(2)(c) and (e).

312 *Gran Gelato Ltd v Richcliff (Group) Ltd* [1992] 1 All ER 865 (not a goods case: criticised because of the connection with fraud—109 LQR 539).

313 [1996] AC 344, HL (not a goods case). See further, Treitel, *Op. cit.*, 947.

314 See also *Southampton Container Terminals Ltd v Hansa Schiffarts GmbH* [2001] CLY 4501, CA (negligent destruction of crane; reinstatement would be out of all proportion to loss).

315 See generally *Street on Torts*, 10th edn, 274, *et seq.*; Treitel, *Law of Contract*, 11th edn, 965–74.

316 *Anglian Water Services Ltd v Crawshaw Robbins & Co Ltd* [2001] BLR 173 (not a goods case).

317 *Scott v Shepherd* (1773) 2 WMB 1892; *Kuwait Airways Corp v Iraqi Airways Co (No. 3)* (set out at para 19.05A), at paras 100–105, HL (the strictly liable knowing converter: see para 19.06).

318 And see *per* Lord Denning MR in *Doyle v Olby Ltd* [1969] 2 All ER 119, CA at 122.

319 *Royscot Trust Ltd v Rogerson* (set out at para 27.28), at All ER 299 (see Wardsley 55 MLR at 701–4).

320 *The Wagon Mound* [1961] AC 388, PC; *Saleslease Ltd v Davis* [1999] 1 All ER (Comm) 883, CA; the innocent converter (see para 19.06). It is no answer that the precise mechanics by which the harm is caused, and the extent of the harm, is not foreseeable: *Vacwell Engineering Ltd v BDH Chemicals Ltd* (set out at para 18.29).

2. *Remoteness in contract.* The basic test of remoteness in contract laid down by Alderson B in *Hadley v Baxendale*[321] turned on what the guilty party could have **contemplated**; and as this depended on the state of his knowledge, it led to the formulation of two so-called rules.

*First rule.* The guilty party is assumed to have the knowledge that every person possesses and to contemplate all the damage which would arise according to the ordinary course of things.[322] In the case of sales, this rule has received statutory formulation in s 50(2) of the SGA, which provides:

> 'The measure of damages is the estimated loss directly and naturally resulting in the ordinary course of events, from the buyer's breach of contract.'

Is the statutory rule for sale[323] synonymous with the common law rule applicable in quasi-sale, hp and simple hiring?[324]

*Second rule.* If the guilty party has knowledge of some special circumstance which would increase the loss naturally arising from the breach, he may[325] be liable for that extra loss—what the SGA terms 'special damage' (s 54). Claims for special damage have rarely been successful, whether claimed by the sellers or buyers:[326] where successful, claims for special damage normally increase the recoverable loss; but this is not necessarily so (see the *Bence Graphics* case: see para 29.26).

**[27.43] Comparison of remoteness tests**. In *The Heron II*,[327] four members of the House of Lords *obiter* strongly took the view that the **foreseeability** test of remoteness in tort was far removed from the **contemplation** test of remoteness in contract (see para 27.41/2). This issue actually came before the court in *Vacwell Engineering Ltd v BDH Chemicals Ltd*,[328] where Rees J held that the damage was not too remote under either rule: as to the contractual claim,[329] he held (at 1696–7) that it was sufficient that some damage by explosion was reasonably contemplated within the rule in *The Heron II* and that the position was similar with regard to the claim in tort.[330] The matter was again considered *obiter* by the Court of Appeal in *Parsons Ltd v Uttley Ltd*:[331]

---

321  (1854) 9 Ex 341 at 354. For a modern formulation, see *The Heron II* [1969] 1 AC 350, HL (carriage of goods; discussed at para 27.43).
322  *Nimmo v Habton Farms* [2004] QB 1, CA (breach of warranty of authority); *Jackson v Royal Bank of Scotland* [2005] 2 All ER 71, HL (repeat business).
323  E.g. *Charter v Sullivan* (set out at para 27.33); *Lazenby Garages Ltd v Wright* (see para 27.36); *Victoria Laundry Ltd v Newman Industries Ltd* (set out at para 29.31).
324  E.g. *Liverpool and County Discount Ltd v AB Motors Ltd* [1963] 2 All ER 396, CA.
325  Liability depends on 'some knowledge and acceptance by one party of the purpose and intention of the other in entering the contract': *per* Lord Sumner in *Weld-Blundell v Stephens* [1920] AC 956 at 980, HL.
326  E.g. *Trans Trust SPRL v Danubian Trading Ltd* (seller: see para 27.35); *Victoria Laundry Ltd v Newman Industries Ltd* (buyer: see above).
327  [1969] AC 350; [1967] 3 All ER 686, HL.
328  Set out at para 18.29. This case was settled during appeal, [1970] 3 All ER 553. See Weaver (1970) 33 MLR 446.
329  Under (a) what is now s 14(3) (see para 14.07, *et seq.*) and (b) the course of dealings (see para 15.22).
330  At 1698. As to the negligence claim, see para 17.14.
331  [1978] QB 791; [1978] 1 All ER 525, CA. See (1978) 94 LQR 171; (1978) 41 MLR 483; Treitel, *Law of Contract*, 11th edn, 973. It was not very clear why this case was not also pleaded in tort: Winfield and Jolowicz, *Tort*, 16th edn, para 6.18, note 26.

S supplied B with a hopper for storing pig food, but failed to provide for proper ventilation so that the food became mouldy and many of B's pigs died from a rare intestinal disease. In an action mounted solely for breach of s 14 of the SGA, the Court of Appeal unanimously held S liable.

However, their Lordships gave differing reasons. Lord Denning MR based his judgment on the view that the stricter test stated in *The Heron II* applied where a claim was only for purely financial loss; and that where, as here, the claim was for physical damage the test of remoteness was the same in contract and tort, the difference between reasonably **foreseeable** (the test in tort) and reasonably **contemplated** (the test in contract) being 'a semantic exercise' (at 802B and 532b). However, Orr and Scarman LJJ expressly disagreed with this reasoning, though it is far from clear what that majority thought.[332] They appear to have taken the view that there was no distinction between financial loss and physical damage for the purposes of remoteness; and that S was liable under the test laid down in *The Heron* because he should have contemplated a 'serious possibility' that the pigs might, as a result of the breach, suffer that type of illness, albeit in a less serious form.[333] Subsequent cases have shed little light on the matter.[334]

However, even if the test of remoteness is the same in contract and tort, it is by no means clear that the rules of remoteness will produce the same result in those situations where actions in contract and tort are available concurrently.[335] *First*, the object of damages is different in the two cases (see para 27.28). *Second*, there is a difference in the time at which the remoteness test is directed: in contract, the material date is the time of contracting; and in tort, the time of the tort.[336] *Third*, there may be differences in attitude to concurrent causes.[337] *Fourth*, there may be differences in the degree of probability of consequences required.[338]

**[27.44] Mitigation of damage.**[339] Where an injured party makes a claim for damages, it is commonly said that he may be under a common law 'duty' to mitigate that damage, whether the claim be in tort[340] or for breach of contract.[341] Thus, in *Payzu Ltd v Saunders*:[342]

---

332 See para 27.42; and Treitel, *Op. cit.*, 967–8.
333 Before the CA, it was accepted that the loss had not been caused by B feeding the food to the pigs.
334 See *Jackson v Royal Bank of Scotland* [2005] 1 All ER (Comm) 337, HL (future business); and Bell (1991) 20 Anglo Am LR 371–9. It has been held that the *Hadley v Baxendale* rules (see para 27.42) are not applicable to tortious negligence: *Mortgage Corpn PLC v Halifax (SW) Ltd (No. 2)* [1999] Lloyd's Rep PN 159.
335 See *per* Lord Reid in *The Heron* [1969] 1 AC 350, at 385–6, HL.
336 On contract, see the *Jackson* case (above), at para 36. See generally Street, *Law of Damages*, 249.
337 See *McGregor on Damages*, 17th edn, paras 6.129–40 and 7.130–40.
338 See McGregor, *Op. cit.*, Chap 19; Pickering (1968) 31 MLR 203, 208.
339 See generally Treitel, *Law of Contract*, 11th edn, 976–82; *McGregor on Damages*, 17th edn, Chap 7. Does the duty to mitigate also apply to a claim for an agreed sum? See para 27.45. It has been said to be incorrect to express this rule as that the law places him under a duty to mitigate: *The Solholt*: [1983] 1 Lloyd's Rep 605 (and see below).
340 *Moore v DER Ltd* [1971] 3 All ER 517, CA (negligence); *Standard Chartered Bank v Pakistan National Shipping Corpn* [1999] 1 All ER (Comm) 417 (deceit; appealed on other grounds).
341 The damages rule in s 50(3) of the SGA is not an example of this rule: *Shearson Lehman Hutton Inc v Maclaine Watson & Co Ltd (No. 2)* (see paras 27.34–5).
342 [1919] 2 KB 581; [1918–19] All ER Rep 219, CA (criticised by Bridge (1989) 105 LQR 398, esp. at 412–16).

There was a contract for the sale of goods to be delivered by instalments, payment to be made within one month of each delivery. The buyer failed to make punctual payment for the first instalment. The seller claimed that this amounted to a repudiation, but offered to continue deliveries if the buyer would pay cash upon each delivery. Taking the view that this amounted to a repudiation by the seller, the buyer unsuccessfully sought to buy elsewhere on a rising market.

If there had been a repudiatory breach by the buyer, it seems that the doctrine of mitigation would not have interfered with the seller's right to treat the contract as discharged.[343] However, the Court of Appeal accepted that the buyer's delay in payment did not amount to a repudiation (see para 23.20) and that the seller was therefore liable to pay damages for non-delivery (see para 29.18); but the court took the view that the buyer should have mitigated his loss by accepting the seller's offer to deliver for cash and that damages must be limited to the loss the buyer would have suffered if he had accepted that offer (one month's credit).

However, what the injured party must do to mitigate his loss is a matter of fact, which will vary from case to case: so the above case may be compared with the ordinary situation with regard to non-acceptance or non-delivery, where the innocent party is expected to go into any available market and sell or buy as the case may be (see para 27.34; para 29.20). At very least, the duty to mitigate requires the injured party to consider whether he could take any reasonable steps to mitigate his loss; but the standard required of him is a fairly low one[344] and the burden of proof lies on the party in default.[345] Moreover, the injured party need not act so as to injure innocent persons and prejudice his commercial reputation,[346] nor risk his money too far,[347] nor accept a tender of goods of a lower quality than contracted for, even with an allowance for the inferiority.[348] Nor is the injured party required to mitigate if too financially impecunious to do so;[349] and it may be unfair by contract to oust the supplier's duty to mitigate.[350]

**[27.45/8] Effect of mitigation rule.** Where the injured party is required to take some steps to mitigate his loss (see para 27.44), the position is as follows: any advantages which he obtains by taking those steps is taken into account in assessing damages;[351] whilst, if he fails to mitigate, any loss occasioned by that failure is

---

343 See para 26.16. However, in *The Soholt* [1983] 1 Lloyd's Rep 605, the CA confirmed that, once the contract had been discharged, the mitigation rule required the buyer to accept late delivery (see below): but see the criticism by Bridge in (1989) 105 LQR 398 at 417–23.

344 Examples of breach of duty to mitigate include: *Payzu Ltd v Saunders* (above); *Nedd v Cox* (1940) 67 Ll LR 5, CA; *The Soholt* (above; discussed 99 LQR 497); *Dimond v Lovell* (set out at para 5.13).

345 The burden lies on the party in default to prove that the injured party has not discharged his duty to mitigate: *Garnac Grain Co Inc v Faure & Fairclough Ltd* [1968] AC 110, HL; *Regent OHG Aisenstadt & Barig v Francesco of Jermyn St Ltd* [1981] 3 All ER 327.

346 *James Finlay & Co Ltd v NV Kwik Hoo Tong* [1929] 1 KB 400, CA; *Banco de Portugal v Waterlow & Sons Ltd* [1932] AC 452, HL.

347 *Lester Leather and Skin Co v Home Brokers Ltd* (1948) 64 TLR 569, CA. And see *Jewelowski v Propp* [1944] 1 KB 510.

348 *Heaven & Kesterton Ltd v En Francois* [1956] 2 Lloyd's Rep 316, at 321.

349 *Lagden v O'Connor* [2004] 1 AC 1067, HL (see Coote 120 LQR 382).

350 *Bulletin No. 24*, case 6: see para 11.16. *Contra* the consumer's duty to mitigate: reg 5(1); and para 11.15A.

351 *Pagnan & Fratelli v Corbisa Industrial Agropacuaria Limitada* [1971] 1 All ER 165, CA.

irrecoverable.[352] On the other hand, the injured party can recover any extra expenses incurred in an unsuccessful attempt to mitigate if reasonable,[353] but not if unreasonable.[354] Three matters have caused particular difficulty: *first*, whether to take into account any reduction in the loss to the injured party brought about by his efforts to mitigate succeeding to a greater extent than required by the duty to mitigate;[355] *second*, the distinction between an act of mitigation and a *novus actus interveniens*;[356] and *third*, the relationship of the duty to mitigate to the doctrine of anticipatory breach. As to the last issue, if the innocent party accepts the anticipatory repudiation as bringing an end to the contract, then he will in claiming damages be under the ordinary duty to mitigate;[357] but, if he elects to keep the contract alive, it has been held that no question of mitigation arises.[358] This is consistent with the ordinary rule that the duty to mitigate does not interfere with any right of the innocent party after breach to elect whether to rescind or affirm (see para 26.16); but in the case of an anticipatory breach it appears to enable the injured party to continue with the contract and so increase his loss.[359] Finally, an act of mitigation must be carefully distinguished from an accord and satisfaction (see para 26.18).

It must be remembered that the common law mitigation rule may be displaced by a liquidated damages clause (see para 27.24).

**[27.49] The CCA and minimum payments clauses.** The Act interferes with a number of clauses in instalment credit contracts which seek to entitle the supplier to a sum of money on the happening of some event. Reference has already been made to clauses which accelerate payment or provide for default interest (see para 26.19) and the power to re-open extortionate credit bargains/unfair credit relationships will be examined later (see paras 29.41 and 29.44). In relation to minimum payment clauses, the common law rules[360] have been supplemented by CCA provisions which have tended to concentrate on the event triggering the minimum payment clause, such as the death of the debtor or hirer,[361] his default[362] or exercise of his statutory right of termination (see paras 26.05–07). In the last event, his liability is limited.

1. *Conditional sale and hp.* Where a debtor under a regulated conditional sale or hp agreement exercises his statutory right of termination, his further liability is limited by s 100. Whilst such termination does not affect any already accrued

---

352 *Payzu Ltd v Saunders* (set out at para 27.44); *Schering Agrochemicals Ltd v Resibel NVSA* [1993] Unreported, CA (109 LQR 175); *Standard Chartered Bank v Pakistan National Shipping Corpn* [2001] 1 All ER (Comm) 822, CA. But arguably not any loss due solely to inflation: Feldman and Libling (1979) 95 LQR 270.

353 *Lloyd's and Scottish Finance Ltd v Modern Cars Ltd* (set out at para 12.14); *Bacon v Cooper (Metals) Ltd* [1982] 1 All ER 397 (hp charges).

354 *The Borag* [1981] 1 All ER 856, CA (see para 27.42).

355 See the *British Westinghouse* case [1912] AC 673, HL: para 27.29.

356 *Mobil North Sea Ltd v PJ Pipe & Valve Co* [2001] 2 All ER (Comm) 289, CA; and see para 27.29.

357 *Gebruder Metelmann GmbH & Co KG v NBR (London)* [1984] 1 Lloyd's Rep 614, CA.

358 See para 26.16. But how can the extra loss then be said to be caused by the guilty party?

359 See further Treitel, *Law of Contract*, 11th edn, 1015–19.

360 See especially the rules as to causation (para 27.29) and penalties (see para 27.25).

361 Where the position depends on whether or not the agreement is fully secured: see paras 24.47–8.

362 The matter is subject to the default notice procedure (see para 24.30) and the debtor or hirer can ask for a Time Order (see paras 24.40–1).

liability for price/rent[363] or damages and the debtor must return the goods to the creditor (s 100(5): set out at para 26.05), s 100 limits his further liability to whichever is the least of the following sums:[364]

(a) *a maximum of 50%*. The maximum amount recoverable under s 100(1) is such sum (if any) as will bring the sums paid and payable up to half the 'total price',[365] plus damages if the debtor has in breach of contract not taken reasonable care of the goods (s 100(4). For the position at common law, see para 27.38).

(b) *actual loss*. Whilst the formula of 'loss sustained' in s 100(3) reproduces faithfully the HPA wording, it would unfortunately appear to be ambiguous.[366]

(c) *the specified amount*. The foregoing rule does not apply where the agreement 'provides for a smaller payment, or does not provide for any payment' (s 100(1)). Whilst the Act does not expressly state what shall be payable in the latter event, presumably the amount recoverable is left to the common law and the penalties rule is inapplicable (see para 27.26).

2. *Consumer hiring*. Where a hirer under a consumer hiring exercises his statutory right of termination (s 101(1): see para 26.07), he remains liable to return the goods to the owner and for 'any liability under the agreement which has accrued before the termination';[367] but he is discharged from any liability for future rentals (s 101(2)). However, it has been argued that a minimum payments clause stipulating for further payments would be void;[368] and, in any event if the owner recaps or recovers possession by court order, the court has power under s 132 to grant a defaulting hirer financial relief in respect of both sums paid and payable (see para 27.23).

---

363  S 99(2). E.g. arrears of rentals (as to which, see para 27.21). It has been argued that an acceleration clause could lead to the entire balance being due under this rule: Goode, *Consumer Credit Law and Practice*, para 36.203.

364  Is the debtor entitled to a Time Order (see para 24.40) in respect of this statutory sum, which does not appear to fall within s 129(1)?

365  As to 'total price' see para 24.35. Plus any compulsory installation charge: see s 100(2); and Goode, *Op. cit.*, 36.206.

366  *Booth & Phipps Garages Ltd v Milton* [2000] CLY 2601, Cty Ct. Compare Goode, *Op. cit.*, para 36.207; Guest, *Law of HP*, para 609; and Plattern (2003) 98 Adviser 41.

367  S 101(2). E.g. arrears of rentals. But see fn 360, above.

368  Under s 173 (see para 18.11): Guest and Lloyd, *Encyclopedia of Consumer Credit Law*, para 2-102; Goode, *Op. cit.*, para 36.222. *Sed quaere*? What about acceleration clauses (see fn 353, above)?

# CHAPTER 28

# ENFORCEMENT BY PUBLIC AUTHORITIES

## INTRODUCTION

### Enforcement authorities

**[28.01] Historical development**. At least from medieval times, it has been found necessary to regulate by criminal law the provision to consumers of bread, beer, fuel and credit.[1] It is therefore hardly surprising that during the nineteenth century we find major enactments, the direct predecessors of modern legislation, dealing with such matters as the following: weights and measures (see para 4.24); food and drugs (see para 4.26); merchandise marks (see para 4.02); and moneylending (see para 6.09).

The pattern which emerged over the centuries had a number of common characteristics.[2] *Firstly*, there was the imposition of statutory criminal offences of strict liability (see para 28.08): this process has continued apace during the last century (see Chaps 4 and 5). *Secondly*, enforcement of these criminal offences has for the most part been left to local authorities,[3] who have usually been granted a number of ancillary powers (see para 28.05). *Thirdly*, the harshness of these locally enforced strict liability offences has been moderated by an elaborate series of increasingly common-form defences (see para 28.13, *et seq.*). It is for consideration whether this whole pattern is now sufficiently uniform to merit consolidation in a single enactment. *Fourthly*, the piecemeal nature of the foregoing developments inevitably led to a haphazard machinery of enforcement;[4] but, following some official recommendations,[5] this has in more recent times been substantially rationalised (see para 28.02). *Fifthly*, in place of criminal proceedings,[6] it may now be possible for the Authorities to obtain Enforcement Orders (see para 28.03); and this change to civil proceedings for injunctions may be encouraged by the UCP Directive (see para 4.01A). *Sixthly*, the authorities tend to seek compliance from deviant traders rather than prosecute them.[7] *Seventhly*, for cross-border enforcement the EU is developing an International Marketing Supervision Network.[8]

**[28.02] Modern enforcement**. The modern pattern for the enforcement of statutory

---

1 See Harvey, *Consumer Protection and Fair Trading*, 6th edn, 1–7.

2 For enforcement strategies, see Cartwright, *Consumer Protection and the Criminal Law*, 2001, 212–30 and 241–3. But see the UCP Directive (below).

3 *R v Croydon Justices, ex p Holmberg* (1993) 12 Tr LR 10, DC. See para 28.02. It does not follow that there should necessarily be a prosecution in respect of every breach: *Smedley Ltd v Breed* [1974] AC 839, HL, *per* Viscount Dilhorne.

4 For a modern exception designating no prosecuting authority, see the Mock Auctions Act 1961 (see para 10.11).

5 Molony Report, 1962, Cmnd. 1781, paras 682–5, 719; the *Review of the TDA* (1976, Cmnd. 6628), Chap X.

6 See Tench, *Towards a Middle System of Law*, 1981.

7 Cartwright, *Op. cit.*, 213, *et seq.*

8 Singleton (2002) 25 *Consumer Law Today* 8, at 10–11. See OFT, *2001-AR*, 33.

crimes of strict liability designed as measures of consumer protection has established two tiers.

(1) *Central supervision.* Whilst enforcement is primarily in the hands of the LAs (see below), this is under the political supervision of Whitehall (see paras 3.02–03), which has also taken powers to make model enforcement provisions for the LAs (see para 5.10). Central co-ordination of the administration of these provisions is largely undertaken by the Office of Fair Trading (OFT). Besides its licensing register (see para 6.26), the OFT also keeps a register of convictions[9] and co-ordinates LA enforcement.[10] Under the GPS Regulations, there is a special system requiring the LAs to report to the Secretary of State, who must in turn report dangerous products to Parliament and the European Commission (regs 32–5).

(2) *Local authority (LA) enforcement.* There is no single provision imposing on local authorities a general duty of enforcement, but there are two major strands of responsibility. In some geographic areas the powers are divided between district authorities and the county councils, whilst in other areas they are all vested in district councils.

(a) *Food and drugs authorities.* The Food Safety Act 1990 designates certain bodies 'food authorities', which are in effect the LAs (s 5). These are under a duty to appoint a public analyst (s 27) and are made responsible for enforcing many of the provisions of the 1990 Act[11] and the GPS Regulations in relation to food.[12] Similar arrangements are made in relation to medicines (Medicines Act 1968, s 108). The powers tend to be delegated to environmental health departments. Some idea of the types of consumer complaint fielded by LA Environmental Health Departments may be gathered from the *Annual Reports* of the OFT (see para 3.03) and Food Standards Authority (see para 4.26).

(b) *Weights and measures authorities.* The Weights and Measures Act 1985 designated certain bodies as 'local weights and measures authorities',[13] an expression it defined as local authorities (ss 52 and 69). Additionally, local weights and measures authorities have been charged with the responsibility of enforcing certain other consumer protection statutes within their area,[14] such as the TDA (s 26(1)), CPA (s 27), CCA (s 161(1)) and the UTCC

---

9   For an account of this **private** register, see (1996) 15 Tr L 257.

10  E.g. by a secure consumer regulations website and LA training (*AR–2003/4*, 29).

11  S 6. For discussion of the work of these food authorities, which detects a greater emphasis on in-factory enforcement, see Bradgate and Howells [1991] JBL 320, esp. at 321, 323 and 331.

12  Safety of products supplied with services in e.g. hotels: DTI, *Consultation on the GPS Regulations*, 2004, para 3.10.

13  See further Harvey and Parry, *Consumer Protection and Fair Trading*, 6th edn, 445.

14  E.g. Prices Act 1974, Sched, paras 6 and 8; FTA 1973, s 27(1) (in relation to statutory orders made under s 22—see para 4.22); Video Recordings Act 1984 (as amended by s 162 of the Criminal Justice Act 1988); Doorstep-selling Regulations reg 4D—(see para 10.37); Estate Agents Act 1979, s 26 and Property Misdescriptions Act 1991, s 3 (see para 4.03); Distance Selling Regulations, reg 26 (see para 8.17); Tobacco Advertising and Promotion Act 2002, ss 13, 14(11) and (12) (see para 8.06A); GPS reg 10 (see para 4.36).

Regulations (as 'qualifying bodies': see para 11.19). Some of this work has been contracted out to CABx (see para 3.08), such as advising consumers as to the position under the TDA, CPA and CCA. Some idea of the modern balance of their work may be gained by looking in the *Annual Reports* of the OFT at the Appendix dealing with the classification of consumer complaints and details of convictions. The result was to so alter the burden of their work that they have tended to be re-named the Trading Standards Service (see para 3.05), with their designated officers termed 'trading standards officers' (TSOs). Their professional association is the Institute of Trading Standards Administration (ITSA).

Whilst the foregoing designated local authorities have cast upon them a **duty** of enforcement, it is not an exclusive duty. Other LAs still have a **power** of prosecution where they consider this is in 'the interests of the inhabitants of their area' (Local Government Act 1972, s 222); and in some cases the OFT or other body is given a concurrent **power** of prosecution so that it may act where it is felt that an incident has national implications (e.g. CCA, s 161(1)(a)). Nor is there usually any legal impediment to a private prosecution.[15] However, it is to be expected that prosecution by anybody other than the designated LAs will be unusual. In practice most proceedings are taken by LAs after complaints by members of the public: usually, an LA is only empowered to prosecute offences committed in its area;[16] but exceptionally it may be empowered to act out of area.[17] The duty of the prosecuting LA to report intended prosecutions to the OFT (see para 28.06) should encourage uniformity in administration throughout the country, as should the statutory duty cast on the designated local authorities to report their activities to the OFT (see TDA, s 26(2); CCA, s 161(3); GPS Regulation, reg 33). It should also ensure a more uniform observance of the law: the OFT might remove any CCA licence (see para 6.23) or seek an Enforcement Order under Pt 8 of the EA (see para 28.04).

A system has been set up by the OFT for it to co-ordinate action between local authorities (LACORS—previously LACOTS);[18] and to enhance uniform national standards there have been introduced uniform enforcement codes (see para 5.10) and powers for LAs to share information with other enforcement agencies (EA, Pt 9: see para 28.06). For instance, there is the Home Authority Principle to streamline matters where a trader operates within the jurisdiction of more than one LA: this principle determines which shall be the lead LA for the purposes of advising and controlling the trader.[19] There is concern that the current tier of local authority normally designated under the above legislation

---

15  E.g. the Pharmaceutical Society who have statutory recognition, or some wholly private trade or other body. But sometimes the statute allows no room for private prosecution, e.g. Weights and Measures Act 1985, s 83(1). Cf. CPA, s 11(3)(c).

16  *Brighton & Hove DC v Woolworths plc* [2002] EWHC 2565, DC.

17  E.g. Video Recordings Act 1984, s 16(1A) and (1B); GPS, reg 10(2) and 38.

18  Local Authorities Co-ordinating and Regulatory Services, previously Local Government Co-ordinating Body on Trading Standards, which was extended to food safety.

19  See Harvey and Parry, *The Law of Consumer Protection and Fair Trading*, 6th edn, 54.

is too small to provide a viable service, but there are proposals for a high-level Enforcement Forum.[20]

**[28.03] Criminal offences and injunctions**. Presumably for policy reasons (see para 28.01), many consumer protection statutes are not content to grant a civil right of action for breach[21] but (also?) make it a criminal offence[22] of strict liability (see para 28.08). Penalties usually depend on the method of prosecution: so, for conviction on indictment under the TDA, the penalty is up to two years imprisonment and/or an unlimited fine; whereas, on summary prosecution under the TDA, the penalty is a fine up to 'the prescribed sum'.[23] Typically, prison tends to be reserved for situations where there is *mens rea* or repeated infringement. However, these offences tend not to be absolute (see para 28.08), but to be subject to some wide-ranging defences (see para 28.13, *et seq.*) and, of course, the higher criminal burden of proof on the prosecution. Moreover, in practice the present system does not necessarily result in prosecution, except as a last resort;[24] but, on repeated conviction, the authorities sometimes seek an injunction, which may result in further criminal sanctions on default.

*Injunctions.*[25] Apart from criminal proceedings (above), there will be many occasions where the ordinary remedies of rescission and damages for breach of contract are insufficient protection for a consumer, the obvious example being where the loss is too small to make individual court action a suitable remedy. In such cases, it has always been possible for the injured consumer to take out an injunction under the ordinary rules (see para 29.39). But again, the cost of individual court action make the remedy unattractive. Much more attractive to consumers is the continental system that such actions for injunctions may be brought by a public official on behalf of the consumer.

*Injunctions by local authority.* The LA (see para 28.02) may be faced with a defendant who finds it worthwhile to breach repeatedly a criminal provision involving a relatively mild sanction, e.g. small financial penalty. In this case, the authority may consider seeking an injunction,[26] a course of action that has been much used by local authorities with regard to Sunday trading. In *Stoke on Trent City Council v B & Q (Retail) Ltd*[27] the House of Lords confirmed that this was a proper cause of action on the part of the local authority, that prior actual convictions were not required, but that the authority must show that the defendant was deliberately

---

20  DTI, *Modern Markets: Confident Consumers* (1999), para 7.24. See also Pointing (2004) 154 NLJ 1192.
21  On principle, an action for breach of statutory duty may be available to a person injured thereby, but consumer protection statutes commonly expressly exclude this: see para 3.21.
22  E.g. Prices Act 1974, Sched, para 5(1); TDA, s 18 (as amended by s 32(2) of the Magistrates Court Act 1980); DPA, s 19; FTA, ss 23 and 122; CCA, s 167; CPA, ss 12(5) and 20(4). See further, para 28.07.
23  This is level 5 on the standard scale (Criminal Justice Act 1982, s 37). For a discussion of sentencing policy, see Bragg, *Trade Descriptions*, 218–20.
24  See *Op. cit.*, 201–2; OFT, *AR-2005/6*, 32.
25  See generally Harper (1989) 139 NLJ 1016. For injunctions sought by a buyer or hirer, see para 29.39.
26  E.g. *Portsmouth City Council v Richards* (1989) 87 LGR 757, CA (against a sex-shop). For a statutory power of the OFT to seek an injunction, see para 8.12A.
27  [1984] AC 754; [1984] 2 All ER 332, HL.

and flagrantly flouting the law.[28] Subsequently, the Sunday trading lobby sought to avoid this decision by two arguments. *Firstly*, they unsuccessfully argued that the Sunday trading laws were invalidated by the Treaty of Rome (see para 2.13). *Secondly*, they unsuccessfully argued that, in the (usual) application for an interim injunction, the local authorities were automatically required to give a cross-undertaking as to damages.[29]

*Part 8 orders.* Similar to injunctions are the new Enforcement Orders to be found in Pt 8 of the EA (see para 28.04), implementing the Injunctions Directive (98/27). It may be that some regulators will see these Pt 8 powers as an effective route for side-stepping the carefully constructed Parliamentary restrictions on enforcement:[30] as a civil action, proceedings for such an Order will avoid the need to prove breach of consumer legislation to the criminal standard of proof, the carefully constructed tariff of penalties (see para 28.07) and the rules of interpretation of criminal statutes (see para 1.05).

**[28.04] Part 8 enforcement orders**. Where an enforcer brings Pt 8 proceedings against a trader before a civil court (see para 6.08: *stage 2*), Pt 8 allows of any or all of the following outcomes.[31]

A. *Undertakings given in court.* Whilst the trader could have given a voluntary undertaking before proceedings were commenced (see para 6.08), it may be that he only realises the strength of the case against him after the court finds that his conduct constitutes an infringement (ss 217(1), (2) and 218(10): see below). In these circumstances, under s 215(9) the court may accept an Undertaking from the trader:[32] this Undertaking may be in the same form as a court order would have been (see below); or he may undertake to take such steps as the court considers will prevent him doing anything an order would have prevented him from doing.[33]

B. *Interim enforcement order.* It maybe that an enforcer considers that matters are too urgent to await the ordinary processes leading up to an Enforcement Order (see below), e.g. imminent publication of a misleading advertisement, or forthcoming 'one-day sale' of unsatisfactory goods. In such a case, the ordinary period for prior consultation with the trader is reduced to seven days (s 214(4)(b): see para 6.08); or, in cases of emergency, the OFT may dispense with any prior consultation (s 214(3)) and even any prior notice of proceedings, stating to the court why no prior notice has been given (s 218(7)). In such cases, the court may grant an Interim Enforcement Order to the 'applicant'[34] at any time before the

---

28  Acting under s 222 of the Local Government Act 1972: see para 28.02.

29  *Kirklees MBC v Wickes Building Supplies* [1993] AC 227, HL (undertaking not required: see 109 LQR 27).

30  McCalla (2001) 151 NLJ 751 at 752.

31  See further OFT, *Enforcement of Consumer Protection Legislation*, 2003, paras 3.46–51.

32  E.g. OFT, *UCT Bulletin No. 23*, case 44 and Annexe C; *OFT v The Officers Club Ltd* (set out at para 8.10A).

33  This may include an undertaking by the trader to publish at his own expense the terms of the undertaking and a corrective statement (s 217(10)).

34  The 'applicant' does not have to be an 'enforcer'; but the application must refer to all the material matter known to the applicant (s 218(6)). There are special rules (s 221) in respect of community infringements (see para 6.07).

application for an Enforcement Order is determined (s 218(5)), provided that it appears to the court (s 218(1)) that: (i) an Enforcement Order would be likely to be granted (see below);[35] (ii) 'it is expedient'; and (iii) if no notice of the application has been given, that it is appropriate to make an Interim Enforcement Order without notice. An Interim Enforcement Order is effectively an injunction and must indicate the nature of the alleged conduct and direct a person that he (s 218(2), (3) and (4)) does not continue or repeat the conduct or do any of the other things which he could have given a voluntary undertaking not to do;[36] or the court could alternatively then accept a voluntary Undertaking (s 218(10): see above). An Interim Enforcement Order may be varied or discharged by the court (s 218(8)) and automatically expires on determination of the application for an Enforcement Order (s 218(9): see below).

C. *Full enforcement orders.* Whether or not there has been an Interim Enforcement Order (see above), the court has jurisdiction to make an Enforcement Order if there has been the following (s 217(1)–(3)): an application to court under s 215 (see para 6.08) or in respect of an infringement or community infringement (see para 6.07). In considering whether to make an Enforcement Order, the court must have regard as to whether the trader has given, and failed, to comply with any previously given voluntary Undertaking;[37] and, if the court now accepts a voluntary Undertaking, it must not make an Enforcement Order in respect of the same conduct (s 217(11)). Otherwise, the conditions upon which an Enforcement Order are granted (s 218(5), (6) and (7)) are the same as for an interim order (see above). Finally, the court may require the trader (but not the enforcer) at his own expense to publish the court order, together with any corrective statement (s 217(8)), e.g. a misleading advertisement; but presumably the OFT will also continue to publish such matters in its *Annual Report*.

For further proceedings, see para 28.04A

**[28.04A] Further proceedings**. Section 220 applies where an enforcer believes that a trader has breached a voluntary Undertaking given to the court,[38] or an Interim Enforcement Order, or an Enforcement Order (s 220(1): see para 28.04). In these circumstances, the enforcer may:[39]

(a) for a breached voluntary Undertaking, apply for an Interim or full Enforcement Order;[40] or

(b) invite the court to treat a breached Interim or full Enforcement Order as a contempt of court, in which case the court can impose a fine on the trader or, if

---

35  *OFT v MB Designs (Scotland) Ltd* 2005 SLT 691, OH.

36  S 219(4): see para 6.08. The Interim Order takes effect in all parts of the UK (ss 218(11) and 217(12)).

37  S 217(4). The Undertaking could have been given either before proceedings (see para 6.08) or during any interim proceedings (see above).

38  These powers do not exist where the voluntary undertaking was given to the enforcer (as to which, see para 6.08), in respect of which the enforcer must initiate proceedings under ss 217 or 218.

39  Unless the enforcer is the OFT, the enforcer must notify the OFT (s 220(6)).

40  S 220(3) and (4). This is without going through the normal consulation and notice procedures (s 220(5)).

the trader is an individual, impose a term of imprisonment not exceeding two years.[41]

The foregoing account is written on the basis of the simple case where the errant 'trader' is a sole trader. However, to be effective, Part 8 also has to deal with the following situations:

(1) the errant trader seeks to avoid the effect of the proceedings by incorporating (or re-incorporating) his business as a limited company, what are often called phoenix companies (see para 19.25). Not only does the Undertaking or Enforcement Order extend to the errant trader as regards any other business he may run (ss 217(6)(b), 218(3)(b) and 219(4)(b)), but if he sets up another business run by an 'associate' (see below), it may also be extended to the pheonix company and associate by further proceedings under s 220 (see above).

(2) the errant trader is a limited company, the real culprits being its directors (s 222(1)). Whether or not proceedings under Part 8 are taken against the company,[42] under s 222(2))

> 'If the conduct takes place with the consent or connivance of a person (an accessory) who has a special relationship with the body corporate, the consent or connivance is also conduct which constitutes an infringement.'

A person has a special relationship with that errant trader if he is (s 222(3)): (i) its controller (see below) or (ii) its officer;[43] and against him the enforcer may obtain an Undertaking or Enforcement Order.[44]

(3) the errant trader is a subsidiary company in a group of companies. Proceedings may similarly be taken against the errant trader's 'controller' (s 222(2): see above). 'Controller' is widely defined to include directors and shadow directors,[45] and any 'associate';[46] and against any other company in the group, including new ones (s 223).

A list of the assurances, undertakings, court orders and contempt orders given or made each year is to be found in the OFT *Annual Report*.[47] It seems that an injured consumer could not obtain a compensation order in any of the above proceedings, because there is no 'conviction' (see para 3.20).

## Powers of enforcing authorities

Where consumer protection statutes (see Chaps 4 and 5) are enforced by a designated local authority (see para 28.03), the law sometimes, noticeably as

---

41  E.g. (2003) 36 *Fair Trading* 5.
42  Whether for an Undertaking (s 222(7)), or an Interim or full Enforcement Order (s 222(6)).
43  S 222(3)(b) refers to 'a director, manager, secretary or other similar officer . . . or a person purporting to act in such a capacity'. See generally, para 28.11.
44  S 222(5) and (6). The terms are modified slightly: see s 222(8) and (9).
45  S 222(4). Group of companies is defined by s 222(12).
46  This principally covers family relationships (s 222(10) and (13)), partnerships (s 222(11)(a) and (b)) and groups of companies (see below).
47  E.g. OFT, *2001-AR*, 33–5. See also *R v DG, ex p FH Taylor & Co Ltd* [1981] I CR 292, DC (publicity). The text of assurances, etc, may be set out in OFT *Bulletins*, e.g. *Bulletin No. 20*, paras 1.4–7, No. 23 and Annexe A.

regards safety, confers a battery of enforcement powers backed up by the criminal law (see para 4.36). More commonly, statute simply imposes strict liability criminal offences, in respect of which there are a number of almost common-form powers (see para 28.05) and duties (see para 28.06). In laying these down, the parliamentary draftsman has tended to reflect the general common law presumption in favour of the liberty of the subject, with any derogation being set out in detail.

**[28.05] Powers in consumer protection statutes**. Over and above the powers of any prosecutor, the designated authorities tend to be granted by statute the following powers,[48] which are unlikely to infringe the Human Rights Act (see para 3.09A).[49]

1. *Test purchases*.[50] For the purposes of obtaining evidence of the commission of an offence, the authorised officer of a designated authority is empowered to purchase goods or obtain the provision of services at all reasonable hours (business hours?) and on production of his credentials. There is no requirement of reasonable cause, so that 'spot checks' may be made. In the case of the CCA, the Act also expressly deals with one particularly relevant exercise of the power, allowing the officer to enter as debtor or hirer into a regulated agreement (s 164(2)); and some other Acts allow the taking of samples.[51]

2. *Inspection and entry*.[52] For the purposes of ascertaining whether any offence has been committed under the relevant Act, the duly authorised officer is empowered (see above) 'at all reasonable hours' to inspect any goods and enter any premises other than those used only as a dwelling-house: if the premises are being used both as a dwelling and as business premises, the power exists; and failure to allow entry is an obstruction (see para 28.06. *Contra* a self-contained flat over a shop). Where entry is refused, or it is desired to enter a dwelling-house, a warrant must first be obtained.[53]

---

48  Similar powers are granted under the Estate Agents Act 1979, s 11; Data Protection Act 1984, Sched 4; Property Misdescriptions Act 1991, Sched. For discussion of the Codes of Practice under the Food Safety Act 1990, s 40, see Roberts (1991) 8 Tr L 212. For reasoning as to the GPS provisions, see DTI, *Consultation on the GPS Regulations*, 2004, para 3.51.

49  *OFT v X* [2003] 2 All ER (Comm) 183 (competition proceedings: see para 2.12).

50  Prices Act 1974, Sched, para 7; TDA, s 27; FTA, s 28; CCA, s 164(1) and (3); Weights and Measures Act 1985, s 42; CPA, s 28(1); Food Safety Act 1990, s 29(a); Tobacco Advertising and Promotion Act 2002, s 14(2); GPS, reg 22. Can a trader refuse to sell? As to entrapment, see Roberts (1992) 9 TR L 158.

51  E.g. Prices Act 1974, Sched, para 9(2); Medicines Act 1968, s 112(2); Food Safety Act 1990, ss 29–31.

52  TDA, s 28(1)(a); Prices Act 1974, Sched, para 9(1); Medicines Act 1968, s 111(1); CCA, s 162(1)(a); Video Recording Act 1984, s 17; Weights and Measures Act 1985, s 79(1); CPA s 29(2) and (3); Tobacco Advertising and Promotion Act 2002, s 14(1), (4)–(6); Licensing Act 2003, ss 179–80; GPS, reg 23(1), (2) and (3). See generally Feldman, *Law Relating to Entry Search and Seizure*.

53  TDA, s 28(3); Prices Act 1974, Sched, para 9(1); CCA, s 162(3), as amended; Weights and Measures Act 1985, s 79(2); CPA, s 29(2); Food Safety Act 1990, s 32; GPS, reg 24(2), (3) and (4). There are strict conditions on the issue of a warrant which *inter alia* do not allow its use for conducting spot checks unless perhaps entry has been refused. If in doubt as to whether a business is being carried on, it may be wiser to apply for a warrant.

3. *Production and copy of documents.*[54] Where he has a reasonable cause to **suspect** that an offence has been committed, the authorised officer may require the production of books and documents[55] by any person carrying on a trade or business[56] and take copies thereof, though there are special protections for documents in the hands of legal advisers, e.g. TDA, s 28(7); GPS, reg 45. The Secretary of State has special powers to obtain information under GPS, reg 20, which are explained by the DTI (*Consultation* (2004) para 3.29).

4. *Seizure and detention of material.* Where he has reasonable cause to **believe** that an offence has been committed under the relevant Act, the authorised officer may seize and detain **goods** to ascertain by test or otherwise whether an offence has been committed;[57] he may detain goods and documents which he has reasonable cause to **believe** may be required as evidence;[58] and he has power to break open containers to obtain that test or evidential material.[59] This last power does not extend to breaking open containers to inspect goods; and in any case, it is subject to the condition precedent that any person authorised to do so must first be invited to break open the container. Finally, there is provision for compensation in respect of goods seized (see para 28.06).

5. *Enhanced powers under the CCA 2006* (see para 28.05A).

**[28.05A] Extra CCA powers.** In addition to the ordinary enforcement in the field of consumer protection (see para 28.05), where there is business regulated by the CCA, the CCA 2006 grants to the prosecuting authorities the following extra powers to inspect the operation of the regulated business (ss 47–9).

1. *By notice.* Whereas the ordinary enforcement powers are aimed at the collection of evidence after possible breach, new s 36C of the 1974 Act grants the OFT powers to inspect the business of holders of group and standard licenses (see paras 6.14–16) to make routine monitoring visits in advance of breach.[60] Upon its issuing a notice stating the reasons why access is sought (new s 36C(2)), the OFT may require the licensee to give to an officer of the enforcement

---

54  Prices Act 1974, Sched, para 9(1); TDA, s 28(1)(b); CCA, s 162(1)(b) (as amended by s 51 of the 2006 Act); the Doorstep-selling Regulations 1987, reg 4E; Tobacco Advertising and Promotion Act 2002, s 14(1) and (3); EA, ss 224 and 225; GPS reg 23(4) and (6). Cf. Medicines Act 1968, s 112(3)(b); CPA, s 29(4) and (5). The power to take a copy does not authorise the taking away of the original: *Barge v British Gas Corpn* (1983) 81 LGR 53, DC.

55  The CCA and CPA extend to computer-held information. The drafting of CPA, s 29(4) is criticised in 50 MLR 626–8. See also the Bankers' Books Evidence Act 1879, s 7. There is sometimes protection against self-incrimination, e.g. Doorstep Selling Regulations 1987, reg 4H; and *Walkers Snack Foods Ltd v Coventry CC* [1998] 3 All ER 163, DC (Food Safety Act 1990, s 33).

56  This need not be the suspected trade or business, e.g. accountant. As to 'trade or business', see para 4.03. But the officer must have grounds to suspect that an offence has been committed: *Dudley MBC v Debenhams plc* (1995) 14 TR LR 182, DC.

57  Prices Act 1974, Sched, paras 9(2) and 10; TDA, s 28(1)(c); CCA, s 162(1)(c); CPA, ss 29(6) and 33; Tobacco Advertising and Promotion Act 2002, s 14(1) and (7); GPS, reg 23(5), (6) and 26. Cf. Medicines Act 1968, s 112(4).

58  Prices Act 1974, Sched, para 9(2). Books are expressly mentioned only in some of the Acts: TDA, s 28(1)(d); CCA, s 162(1)(d), as amended. Cf. Medicines Act 1968, s 112(4); CPA, s 29(4). As to 'suspect' and 'believe', see Bragg, *Trade Descriptions*, 207.

59  But some Acts expressly give permission only to open vending machines: TDA, s 28(1)(e); FTA, s 29(1)(e); CCA, s 162(1)(e), as amended; CPA, s 29(7).

60  In the case of group licence, this power applies to the original applicant for the licence, e.g. a trade body; and it will also cover those operating under the group licence, e.g. trader-members (new s 36C(10)).

authority[61] reasonable access[62] to business[63] premises[64] in order for the officer (new s 36C(1)):

'(a) to observe the carrying on of a business under the licence by the licensee; or

(b) to inspect such documents of the licensee relating to such a business as are—

(i) specified or described in the notice; and

(ii) situated on the premises.'

The licensee shall also secure that persons on those premises give the officer reasonable assistance, specific information and documents[65] in connection with his enquiries.[66] But the foregoing powers are limited to 'purposes connected with the OFT's functions under this Act' (new s 36C(8)); and there are even tighter restrictions where the information is sought from a third party under new s 36B(6).[67]

2.  *By warrant (a dawn raid).* Under new s 36D(1), a justice of the peace may issue a warrant authorising an officer of an enforcement authority[65] as below if all the following conditions are satisfied (new s 36D(2)):

(a) there is on the premises information or documents which could be the subject of a notice under new s 36C (see above); and

(b) if such a requirement were imposed, it would not be complied with, or the information or documents would be tampered with.

Such a warrant may authorise the officer to do any of the following:[68] (i) enter the specified premises; (ii) search the premises and seize specified information and documents; (iii) take any other reasonably necessary steps for the preservation intact of that information or documents; (iv) use such force as may be reasonably necessary.

In the event of failure to comply with the above notice or warrant, the OFT may apply for a court order under s 36E;[69] and breach would be a contempt of court. It has been questioned whether there is such a lack of accountability in relation to these new OFT powers that their use might give rise to HRA proceedings (see para 3.09A).

---

61  As defined by s 161 of the CCA, e.g. tso: see para 28.02. The officer must act by arrangement with the OFT (new s 36F(1)).

62  At such times as the OFT reasonably require (new s 36C(4)), the OFT giving reasonable notice of those times (new s 36C(5)).

63  Entry to a dwelling-house requires a warrant under new s 36D: see below.

64  This includes any premises at which the licensed business is conducted, but not premises used 'only' as a dwelling (new s 36C(3)). What about a licensee having an office at home?

65  New s 174A (as inserted by s 51(5) of the 2006 Act) spells out the power of a 'relevant authority' (s 174A(5)) to seize or copy documents in such a way that it does not override legal professional privilege.

66  New s 36C(6). This includes an explanation of documents the officer is inspecting (new s 36C(7)).

67  New s 36C(9). For s 36B(6), see above, para 6.26.

68  New s 36D(3). The officer may take with him such persons and equipment as he thinks necessary (new s 36D(4)).

69  See new s 36E(2). If the information defaulter is a body corporate, partnership or other unincorporated body, the court may require any responsible officer to meet the costs (new s 36E(3)–(5)).

**[28.06] Duties**. In the exercise of the foregoing statutory powers by designated authorities for the purpose of enforcing these Acts (see para 28.05), both sides are subject to a number of statutory duties.

1.  *The general public*. There are a number of offences of obstructing the designated authorities in the exercise of their enforcement powers, such as wilfully obstructing, or failure without reasonable cause to supply information, or giving false information.[70] A convicted person may have to pay the expenses of enforcement (see CPA, s 35). What more than the general power of convicting courts as to costs, does this confer?

2.  *The designated authorities*. An officer[71] seizing any goods or documents must give the person from whom they were seized notice of seizure (e.g. TDA, s 28(2); FTA, s 29(2); CCA, s 162(2); CPA, s 30(1); GPS, reg 24(1)) and of the results of any test.[72] He must also give notice of intended prosecution to the OFT (e.g. FTA, s 130 (as amended); CCA, s 161(2);[73] Medicines Act 1968, s 125(4)), and sometimes also to the defendant.[74] On conviction, the authority is sometimes entitled to recover the special expenses arising from any seizure (e.g. CPA, s 35; GPS, reg 28). However, if the 'owner' of goods seized is not convicted, the goods must be returned and he must be compensated for any loss or damage to the goods during their detention,[75] a provision which may deter seizure in case of doubt.[76]

3.  *Public authorities: disclosure of information*. The piecemeal previous provisions have now been largely replaced by a new scheme under Part 9 of the EA. This applies to public authorities[77] which are under a duty to gather information under a series of statutes which include most of the important ones considered in this work.[78] The general principle is that such information, unless already

---

70  TDA, s 29; FTA, s 30; CCA, s 165 (as amended by s 51(4) of the 2006 Act); Prices Act 1974, Sched, para 9(3); Medicines Act 1968, s 114(2) and (3); Weights and Measures Act 1985, s 81; CPA, s 32; Food Safety Act 1990, s 33; Doorstep Selling Regulations 1987, reg 4F; Tobacco Advertising and Promotion Act 2002, ss 14(12), 15; GPS, reg 25. See Bragg, *Trade Descriptions*, 210–12.

71  Any person impersonating an officer commits an offence: TDA, s 28(6); FTA, s 30(4); CCA, s 162(6); CPA, s 30(5); GPS, reg 24(5).

72  TDA, s 30(1); FTA, s 31; CCA, s 164(4); CPA, s 30(6). As to the failure to give test results, see Bragg, *Op. cit.*, 202–3.

73  For civil law only (new s 36F(3)), the officer (commonly a tso) shall be treated as an officer of the OFT (new s 36F(2)).

74  E.g. where there is an offence under the Weights and Measures Act 1985 (s 83(3)) or also under the TDA (s 22(1), as amended) or the GPS, reg 24(6).

75  TDA, s 33; FTA, s 32; CCA, s 163; Food Act 1984, ss 9(4) and 28(5), CPA, ss 14 and 34; GPS reg 27. For the explanation as to why this rule (which is not in the Directive) has been inserted, see DTI, *Consultation on the GPS Regulations*, 2004, para 3.47. Cf. *Hobbs v Winchester Corpn* [1910] 2 KB 471, CA. The compensation powers do not extend to loss caused by breaking open containers. Do they extend to the seizure of documents? See generally Cardwell (1988) 6 TR L 212.

76  See Cardwell (1987) 50 MLR 634–7; Bragg, *Op. cit.*, 208–9.

77  E.g. the OFT. According to s 238(3), 'public authority' must usually be construed in accordance with s 6 of the Human Rights Act 1998: see para 3.09A.

78  These enactments are specified in Sched 14, which may be amended by statutory order by the Secretary of State (s 238(5)), e.g. 2003 SI 2580; 2004 SI 693; the GPS Regulations (reg 39(3)), which have their own regime governing making information available to the public (regs 39 and 40(4); and see recital 13).

properly in the public domain (s 237(3)), may not be disclosed if it relates to the affairs of a 'live' individual or business (s 237(1) and (2)). Apart from disclosure which contravenes the Data Protection Act 1998 (s 237(4): see para 3.27), this rule is not to 'affect any power or duty to disclose information which exists apart from this Part' (s 237(6)) and disclosure is permitted with the consent of the individual or business (s 239), or insofar as disclosure is only to facilitate any of the following cases:[79] (a) to meet a community obligation;[80] (b) to facilitate a statutory function under the EA or listed in Sched 15 (ss 241 and 246), these being an even broader range of consumer protection statutes;[81] (c) in connection with criminal proceedings (s 242). Otherwise, disclosure of such information is a criminal offence (s 245), which may inhibit both naming-and-shaming and any feedback to consumer organisations trying to access the efficacy of consumer protection measures. The DTI are consulting as to whether the authorities should also be permitted to release information to individual consumers pursuing civil proceedings (*Consultation on Part 9 of the EA* (Aug 2005)).

# OFFENCES[82]

**[28.07] Introduction**. The persons permitted to prosecute in respect of an offence against one of the consumer protection statutes have already been mentioned.[83] There are also provisions to deal with activities which amount to an offence under more than one of the Acts, e.g. TDA, s 22 (as amended). Time limits for prosecution tend to some extent to depend on the manner of prosecution (see para 28.02).

(a) *Summary prosecution*. The ordinary time limit for summary offences is six months.[84] However, where offences are triable either summarily or on indict-ment, the 1980 statute abolishes the special time limits, leaving most such prosecutions subject to the indictable time limits below.[85] A new system to administer fine defaults was introduced in 2005.[86]

(b) *Indictments*. Consumer protection statutes commonly require prosecution on indictment to be commenced before the expiry of the lesser of three years from the commission of the offence, or one year of its discovery by the

---

79    This disclosure must be made with regard to the following issues (s 244): the public interest; significance of the harm of disclosure to the individual or business; extent to which disclosure necessary.

80    S 240. For overseas disclosure, see s 243. Presumably, disclosure will be made in accordance with any enforcement codes (see para 5.10).

81    Including subsequent Acts, e.g. CCA, new s 36F(4)–(5); and subordinate legislation made under the EA, e.g. 2003 SI 1400; 2004 SI 693.

82    See generally Cartwright, *Consumer Protection and the Criminal Law*, 2002, esp. 82–5 and 111–25.

83    See para 28.03. For sentencing under the TDA, see Roberts (1991) 8 Tr L 36, 9 Tr L 205; *R v Hewitt* [1991] CLY 1122, CA; *R v Dobson Ltd* [1994] *The Times* 8.3, CA.

84    Magistrates' Courts Act 1980, s 127(1). Nor can the time limit for summary trial exceed that for trial on indictment: s 127(4). For the purposes of the time limit, it has been held that the latest moment at which goods are 'supplied' is on delivery (cf. para 23.03): *Rees v Munday* [1974] 3 All ER 506, DC (TDA).

85    S 127. See Bragg, *Trade Descriptions*, 214. For an exception, see GPS, reg 43.

86    Under the Courts Act 2003, ss 95–7. See (2005) 77 *Quarterly Account* 9.

prosecutor.[87] However, with regard to some consumer protection statutes the courts have side-stepped such limitations by holding that offences are continuing ones.[88]

At the trial of offences under consumer protection statutes, there are sometimes special rules as to the onus of proof[89] and evidence of sample analysis[90] or by certificate (TDA, s 31). A long chain of distribution (see para 17.01) may cause problems,[91] as may an insistence that the interpretation of words used are matters of fact rather than law.[92] The tribunal may also take into account compliance by the prosecuting authority with any enforcement code (see para 5.10) and previous acquittals in other regions.[93]

There must now be considered the liability for these offences created by consumer protection statutes (see para 28.08, *et seq*.) and the statutory defences available (see para 28.13, *et seq*.).

## Liability

**[28.08] Strict liability**. Whilst the presumption of the common law is that *mens rea* (a guilty mind) is normally required for the commission of a criminal offence, it is often said that consumer protection statutes tend to contain 'absolute prohibitions'.[94] However, this last expression is a misnomer in two senses: *firstly*, it is usually with regard only to a key element rather than all constituents of the offence that no *mens rea* is required;[95] and *secondly*, there is commonly a statutory defence where a person charged proves lack of negligence (see para 28.13, *et seq*.). On these grounds, the expression 'strict liability' has been preferred.[96]

Whilst the imposition of strict liability has become common in this context,[97] this is only partly attributable to the statutory language, as it often arises from judicial

---

87  TDA, s 19(1); FTA, s 129(1); FSA, ss 34–5. See *R v Beaconsfield Justices, ex p Johnston & Sons* (1985) 4 Tr L 212, DC (TDA); *Tesco Stores Ltd v Harrow LBC* [2004] CLY 1599 (Food Safety Act).

88  See Clayson (1995) 14 Tr L 6.

89  E.g. CCA, ss 171 and 172, discussed by Goode, *Consumer Credit Law & Practice*, paras 52.1–2. See further Glanville Williams, *Criminal Law: The General Part*, 2nd edn, para 292, *et seq*. The issue must always be left to the jury: *R v Wang* [2005] 1 All ER 782, HL.

90  TDA, s 22(3). For sample analysis, see para 28.05.

91  An earlier party in the chain of distribution, brought in because his act or default caused the offence by another (see para 28.12), is also entitled to the benefit of the time limit: *R v Bicester Justices, ex p Unigate Ltd* [1975] 1 All ER 449, DC.

92  So preventing the appellate courts from curing inconsistencies between the sentences of magistrates courts: Bragg, *Op. cit.*, 148.

93  As to whether an abuse of process, see *R (on the application of North Yorkshire TS) v Coleman* [2002] CLY 282.

94  E.g. *R v Bradish* [1990] 1 QB 981, CA. As to the rationale for imposing strict criminal liability under consumer protection statutes, see *Hobbs v Winchester Corpn* [1910] 2 KB 471 at 483, *per* Kennedy LJ. Contrast the continuing judicial reluctance to do so as exemplified in *Tesco Supermarkets Ltd v Nattrass* [1972] AC 153 at 194, *per* Lord Diplock.

95  Thus, on a charge of selling unfit meat, innocence of unfitness is irrelevant, whilst knowledge of sale is probably still required: Smith and Hogan, *Criminal Law*, 5th edn, 87; and see generally, 11th edn, 137–8.

96  Smith and Hogan, *Criminal Law*, 11th edn, 139. See also Cartwright, *Consumer Protection and the Criminal Law*, 2000, 87–91.

97  E.g. *Sherras v De Rutzen* [1895] 1 QB 918 (liquor); *R v St Margaret's Trust Ltd* [1958] 2 All ER 289, CA (credit terms); *Sweet v Parsley* [1970] AC 132, HL (drugs).

interpretation, claiming to be based on the implied intention of Parliament.[98] For example, it has been said of the TDA that 'trading standards, not criminal behaviour, are its concern'.[99] However, it has been questioned whether this requires the imposition of strict criminal liability,[100] or even criminal liability at all (see para 28.01). Yet Parliament has even gone beyond the imposition of strict liability on the principal actor,[101] be he an employee or agent:[102] that liability has been extended to third parties, such as the actor's employer or principal (see para 28.09), or corporations (see para 28.10) and other persons (see para 28.11), or sometimes 'by-passed' the actor to that third party (see para 28.12).

**[28.09] Vicarious criminal liability**.[103] Whilst in the law of tort a master may be vicariously liable for the acts of his servants or agents, this doctrine usually has no place in the criminal law (see para 28.10). However, if such an attitude were applied to consumer protection statutes, it would largely defeat their object, because the person whose conduct the statutes were designed to influence will frequently secure performance through another. After considerable hesitation, the courts therefore sought to uphold the purpose of such statutes by three means. *Firstly*, principally in relation to liquor licensing, they held that, where the person upon whom the statute cast a duty delegated performance of that duty to another, the former was liable for the offence committed by the latter.[104] *Secondly*, where the central feature of the offence is some act such as selling, the courts have had little difficulty in convicting under the relevant statute the person who is the seller in law;[105] and the person who conducts the sale has also been held liable either as an abettor[106] or co-principal,[107] even though the seller in law escapes conviction by pleading a statutory defence (see para 28.13). *Thirdly*, there are special rules provided where a corporation is involved,[108] under which there may be convicted the corporation (see para 28.10), its officers (see para 28.11) or another (see para 28.12).

---

98  Smith and Hogan, *Op. cit.*, 141.

99  *Per* Lord Scarman in *Wings Ltd v Ellis* [1985] AC 272 at 293, HL. See generally Peiris (1983) 3 Legal Studies 117.

100  Smith and Hogan, *Op. cit.*, 157, *et seq*. But see Stephenson, *Criminal Law and Consumer Protection*, 101–7.

101  There may be more than one such actor, as where there is a partnership, e.g. *Clode v Barnes* [1974] 1 All ER 1166, DC. A sleeping partner may have a defence under s. 24 (see para 28.13): Bragg, *Trade Descriptions*, 11n. 23.

102  E.g. auctioneer. As to clubs, see Bragg, *Op. cit.*, 11–12.

103  See generally Smith and Hogan, *Criminal Law*, 11th edn, 224, *et seq*.; Stephenson, *Criminal Law and Consumer Protection*, 109–11; Cartwright, *Consumer Protection and the Criminal Law*, 2000, 91–6.

104  *Howker v Robinson* [1972] 2 All ER 786, DC; and see further Smith and Hogan, *Op. cit.*, 201–2. Contrast *Jordan v White* (1945) 44 LGR 12 (club).

105  E.g. *Slatcher v George Mence Smith Ltd* [1951] 2 KB 631, DC (sells); *Evans v Clifton Inns* (1987) 85 LGR 119, DC (uses).

106  Even though he is in fact the only person present at the commission of the offence: *Ross v Moss* [1965] 2 QB 396, DC. Although the offence might be strict, the abettor requires *mens rea*: Smith and Hogan, *Op. cit.*, 233.

107  E.g. *Preston v Albury* [1963] 3 All ER 897, DC (sale by employee); *Clode v Barnes* [1974] 1 All ER 1166 (sale by partner); *Melias Ltd v Preston* [1957] 2 QB 380, DC (possession by employee).

108  Cf. *Saloman v Saloman Ltd* (set out at para 19.25).

**[28.10]  Corporate criminal liability.**[109] As consumer protection statutes commonly impose criminal liability on a 'person', which expression includes bodies corporate (Interpretation Act 1978, s 5 and Sched 2), there would *prima facie* appear to be no difficulty in charging a limited company with breach in the same manner as a natural person, notwithstanding that as an artificial person the company cannot perform the prohibited act or form the requisite intent.

1. *Vicarious liability.* In the same manner as a natural person (see para 28.09), a corporation may be held vicariously liable for the torts of its servants or agents; but the common law has made no parallel extension of liability in the criminal law.[110] In relation to statutory offences, the courts have occasionally accepted that a statute intended to fix a corporation with vicarious criminal responsibility for the acts of its employees.[111] More commonly, a statute will expressly provide an innocent corporation with a good defence (see para 28.14), from which it has been deduced that Parliament did not intend to introduce vicarious criminal liability: the *Nattrass* case (see below).

2. *Corporate brains.* Where the actor is part of the brains of the corporation, his act is held to be that of the corporation. In *Tesco Supermarkets Ltd v Nattrass:*[112]

> In operating their chain of several hundred supermarkets, T Ltd set up a careful and elaborate system for the supervision of its employees in order to avoid the commission of offences under the TDA. Because a store manager failed to check the work of his staff in accordance with his duties under this system, a 'special offer' poster was displayed at a time when no goods were available at the special price, so that a TDA s 11(2) offence (now repealed: see para 8.09) was committed by T Ltd.

The House of Lords held as follows:

(1) The store manager was insufficiently senior for his acts to be regarded as those of T Ltd (see below) so as to render liable its corporate officers (see para 28.11), though he himself might have been liable.[113]

(2) T Ltd was not vicariously liable for the acts of its store manager[114] as s 24(1) provided a good defence (see para 28.14).

---

109 See generally Smith and Hogan, *Criminal Law*, 11th edn, 234, *et seq.*; Stephenson, *Criminal Law and Consumer Protection*, 107, *et seq.*; Cartwright, *Consumer Protection and the Criminal Law*, 2000, 96, *et seq.*

110 As to the difficulty with corporate manslaughter, see *Involuntary Manslaughter* (1996) Law Com 237; Smith and Hogan, *Op. cit.,* 245. The Government published a Draft Bill, which was considered by a HC Select Committee; but no Bill looks likely in the 2006 Session: see Forlin (2005) 155 NLJ 720; 156 NLJ 363 and 907.

111 *Mousell Bros v LNWR Co* [1917] 2 KB 836, DC.

112 [1972] AC 153; [1971] 2 All ER 127, HL (discussed 34 MLR 676; and by Tench, *Towards A Middle System of Law*, 16–17; Cartwright, *Consumer Protection and the Criminal Law*, 2000, 94–5, 97–8.

113 See para 28.12. But compare *Bellerby v Carle* [1983] 2 AC 101, HL (discussed 99 LQR 360).

114 On the basis that the store manager was 'another person': see para 28.14. Does this allow the corporate employer a greater defence than a non-corporate employer? See Stephenson, *Op. cit.,* 112–13.

As to point (1), their Lordships explained that the store manager is not the company's 'brains' and does not act as the company;[115] and Lord Reid indicated that a company would be criminally liable for the acts only of:[116]

'the board of directors, the managing director and perhaps other supervisor officers of [the] company [who] carry out the functions of management and speak and act as the company'.

It is thus a question of law whether a company servant or agent in doing particular things is to be regarded as the 'brains' of the company (in the sense of a controlling officer), or merely as its 'hands'.[117] However, the decision has been criticised as requiring only a very low standard of supervision by the 'brains' of the company, seemingly concentrating on a paper system rather than looking at its implementation.[118] However, there are some more recent cases which suggest that, where a consumer protection defence requires knowledge, the knowledge of a more junior employee may be imputed to the employer/company.[119]

Finally, it should be borne in mind that, where the prohibited act is in fact done by a servant or agent of the corporation, there are two provisions under which the actor may be held liable, depending on whether he amounts to the 'brains'[113] or mere 'hands'[114] of the company.

**[28.11] Corporate officers: the 'brains' of the company**. Normally speaking, one employee could not possibly be criminally vicariously liable for the act of another employee. However, where a corporation is found criminally liable under one of the consumer protection statutes (see para 28.10), that will generally be due to the action or inaction of an employee (see para 28.12). In such circumstances, it has been thought right that criminal responsibility should also be visited on those senior employees who amount to the 'brains' of the corporation in what amounts to a limited lifting of the corporate veil (see generally, para 19.25). Seemingly based on a similar provision in the Companies Act 1985, s 733(2)), such almost common-form provisions[120] are to be found in the TDA (s 20), FTA (s 132), CPA (s 40(2)) and the CCA, this last providing as follows (s 169):

---

115 *Per* Lords Reid (171), Dilhorne (187), Diplock (200).
116 At 171. Lords Dilhorne and Diplock drew an analogy from the statutory provisions rendering liable 'any director, manager, secretary or other similar officer': see para 28.11.
117 Smith and Hogan, *Op. cit.*, 237. For the unreality of this test, see Stephenson, *Op. cit.*, 109.
118 Bragg, *Trade Descriptions*, 186–8, pointing out that, because the HL gave no guidance as to the required degree of supervision, there have been inconsistent cases in inferior courts. See also Bergman (2000) 150 NLJ 316.
119 *Tesco Stores Ltd v Brent LBC* [1993] 2 All ER 718, DC (Video Recordings Act 1984, s 11: see further, para 28.17); *Bank of India v BCCI* (2005) 155 NLJ 1357, CA. See also [1997] JBL 467–71; Wickens and Ong [1997] JBL 524; Cartwright, *Consumer Protection and the Criminal Law* (2000) 99–111; Talwar and Dawson (2003) 153 NLJ 908; Forlin and Appleby (2004) 154 NLJ 11; Forlin (2004) 154 NLJ 326.
120 See also Mock Auctions Act 1961, s 2; Prices Act 1974, Sched, para 13; Medicines Act 1968, s 124; Unsolicited Goods and Services Act 1971, s 5; British Telecommunications Act 1981, s 51; Food Act 1984, s 94 (as amended); Video Recordings Act 1984, s 15(1); Weights and Measures Act 1985, s 82; Health and Medicine Act 1988, s 23(5); DPA, s 20; Estate Agents Act 1979, s 28(2); Gas Act 1986, s 45; IA 1986, s 432; Doorstep Selling Regulations 1987, regs 4C(2) and (3); Electricity Act 1989, s 108; Property Misdescriptions Act 1991, s 4; FSA 1990, s 36; Water Industry Act 1991, s 210; Children and YP (Protection from Tobacco) Act 1991, s 4(6); Data Protection Act 1998, s 61;

'Where at any time a body corporate[121] commits an offence under this Act with the consent or connivance of, or because of neglect by, any individual,[122] the individual commits the like offence if at that time—

(a)  he is a director,[123] manager, secretary or similar officer[124] of the body corporate, or

(b)  he is purporting to act as such an officer,[125] or

(c)  the body corporate is managed by its members of whom he is one.'

It is to be noticed that the officer is not vicariously liable to quite the same extent as his corporation (see also CPA, s 40(3)). In proceedings against an officer under this section, it would appear that the prosecution must prove the 'consent' etc. of the officer, whereas in proceedings against the corporation, the latter must prove the facts necessary to make a good defence (see para 28.13). The reference to the officer's 'consent or connivance'[126] adds little to the ordinary rules of aiding and abetting (see generally, para 28.10); but the reference to his 'neglect' extends liability to his careless failure to prevent the offence.[127] However conviction of an officer under this provision also requires the commission of an offence by the corporation;[128] and it was made clear by the Divisional Court in *Tesco Supermarkets Ltd v Nattrass* that 'manager' in this context refers to one who manages the affairs of the company, not a mere store manager or other junior employee.[129]

Finally, it should be noted that in some cases statute expressly penalises any person who in the UK helps another person outside the UK to do an act which, if committed within the UK, would be an offence.[130]

**[28.12] Act of another (by-pass provisions), e.g. the 'hands' of a company.** Sometimes, the transgression under a consumer protection statute by A may be due to the conduct of B, e.g. a retailer's offence may be due to the act of his employee, agent or supplier. In these circumstances, A may be entitled to an acquittal under one of the statutory general defences (see para 28.13) and the policy of the Act may

---

Competition Act 1998, s 72; EA, s 222; Tobacco Advertising and Promotion Act 2002, s 18; Licensing Act 2003, s 187; Financial Services (Distance Selling) Regulations, 2004 SI 2095, reg 22; GPS, reg 31(2) and (3). Cf. Companies Act 1985, s 733(2).

121  Could this expression include a partnership? See *Douglas v Phoenix Motors* 1970 SLT 57, Sheriff Ct.

122  As to consent, connivance or neglect, see *R v Roussel Laboratories* (1989) 88 Crim App R 140, CA; *Southern BC v White* (1991) 11 Tr LR 65, DC.

123  E.g. *Elliott v DG* (set out at para 5.30). See generally the Companies Act 1985, s 741(1).

124  Cf. *Registrar of Restrictive Trading Agreements v WH Smith & Sons Ltd* [1969] 3 All ER 1065, CA.

125  Cf. 'shadow directors' (see Companies Act 1985, s 741(2)); *R v Boal* [1992] 1 QB 591, CA (Fire Precautions Act 1971).

126  E.g. *OFT v MB Designs (Scotland) Ltd* 2005 SLT 691, OH. Some statutes refer to 'consent and connivance', e.g. TDA, s 20; Medicines Act 1968, s 124. Does this make any difference?

127  See *Lewis v Bland* [1985] RTR 171, DC (delegation); *Hirschler v Birch* [1987] RTR 13, DC (co-director). Does it require *mens rea*?

128  But see Bragg, *Trade Descriptions*, 11.

129  [1971] 1 QB 133, at 142 (DC view unchallenged on this point. As to the facts, see para 28.10). For the rationale, see Cartwright (1996) 59 MLR 225 at 235–6. A culpable junior employee can be prosecuted under another provision: see para 28.12.

130  TDA, s 21, e.g. to help another outside the UK to give a false indication of Royal Approval (see para 4.10).

be better implemented by convicting B. Sometimes, B may be liable to be convicted of the same offence as A on the basis that B acted as co-principal or abettor (see para 28.09). To cover those cases where B is not so liable, the TDA provides as follows (s 23):

> 'Where the commission by any person of an offence under this Act is due to the act of default of some other person, that other person shall be guilty of the offence, and a person may be charged with and convicted of the offence by virtue of this section whether or not proceedings are taken against the first mentioned person.'

With the notable exception of the CCA, comparable by-pass provisions are to be found in a number of consumer protection statutes.[131] Thus, in *Nattrass v Timpson Shoes*:[132]

> A, owners of multiple shoe shops, issued to branch managers a warning against committing offences under the TDA and a procedure for re-pricing goods. In one of the shops where the manager (B) re-dressed the window, one pair of shoes in the display was by mistake left displaying the old price. A was charged with an offence under s 11(2), and B with an offence under s 23 on the grounds that it was due to his act or default. Held: A was rightly acquitted on the ground that the offence was due to B's default under s 24(1); but B's plea that it was due to the fault of his five assistants was rejected because he had not checked their work (see para 28.15).

However, the conviction of B is subject to the following limitations:

1. *Commission of an offence by A*. Whilst proceedings need not necessarily be taken against A,[133] the substantive position is as follows: it is sufficient if A commits only a *prima facie* offence, e.g. through the actions of servant B, whilst able to plead one of the statutory defences;[134] but B cannot be convicted under this section where A has committed no offence whatsoever.[135]

2. *Act or default of B*.[136] This will commonly be carelessness by B in fulfilling his duties as, for example, junior employee or wholesaler.[137] However, for B to be so convicted, his act or default must **cause** the commission of the offence by A,[138]

---

131 E.g. Prices Act 1974, Sched, para 5(3); Medicines Act 1968, s 121; FTA, s 24; Weights and Measures Act 1985, s 32; CPA, s 40(1); Doorstep-selling Regulations 1987, reg 4C(1); FSA 1990, s 20; GPS, reg 31(1). See generally Roberts (1991) 8 Tr L 145; and para 8.09.

132 [1973] Crim LR 197, DC.

133 Thus, A or B or both may be prosecuted, perhaps depending on whom the prosecutor thinks is really responsible for the infringement: see *Meah v Roberts* [1978] 1 All ER 97, DC (both A & B convicted). A must disclose his reliance on B's fault before trial: see para 28.14.

134 *Tesco Supermarkets Ltd v Nattrass* (set out at para 28.10); *Nattrass v Timpson Shoes* (above). Contrast *K Lill Holdings (Trading as Stratford Motor Co) v White* [1979] RTR 120, DC (criticised Roberts, *Op. cit.*, 149); Bragg, *Trade Descriptions*, 80–1 and 197–8.

135 *Cottee v Douglas Seaton (Used Cars) Ltd* [1972] 3 All ER 750, DC; *Coupe v Guyett* [1973] 2 All ER 1058, DC (A was a sleeping partner).

136 As to whether B's act or default must be wrongful, see Stephenson, *Criminal Law and Consumer Protection*, 136–7. For the raising of this plea as a defence by A, see para 28.14. For B's use of the time limit, see para 28.07.

137 E.g. *Hicks v Grewal* (1985) 4 Tr L 92, DC (supplier). For the policy issues concerning the prosecution of employees, see Cartwright (1996) 59 MLR 225 at 237–8.

138 *Tarleton Engineering Co Ltd v Nattrass* [1973] 3 All ER 699, DC; the *Lill Holdings* case (above). B does not have to be **the** cause to be convicted: see 17 Tr L 403.

though perhaps B does not always need to be a trader[139] unless the statute so requires.[140] Nor does B himself need to commit a separate offence.[134]

When charged, presumably B can raise the general defence (see para 28.13).

## Defences

Where under one of the consumer protection statutes there has *prima facie* been the commission of an offence (see paras 28.07–12), there may be available a statutory defence as follows:[141] the general defence (see paras 28.13–5); or one of the special defences (see para 28.16, *et seq.*).

### *The general defence*

**[28.13] The rule.** Most of the offences created by consumer protection statutes being ones of strict liability (see para 28.04), it is normal to ameliorate their effect by a provision which in effect entitles the defendant to be acquitted if he shows on the balance of probabilities that he took due care.[141] The traditional, almost common-form, general defence was laid down in the TDA (s 24(1)) and repeated in the CCA in the following terms:[142]

'In any proceedings for an offence under this Act it is a defence for the person charged to prove—

(a) that his act or omission was due to a mistake or to reliance on information supplied to him, or to an act or omission by another person, or to an accident or some other cause beyond his control, and

(b) that he took all reasonable precautions and exercised all due diligence to avoid such an act or omission by himself or any person under his control.'

To succeed in this defence, a defendant must on the balance of probabilities prove[143] **both**:

(1) that the commission of the *prima facie* offence was due to one of the statutory reasons specified in paragraph (a) (see para 28.14); **and**

(2) the two matters specified in paragraph (b) (see para 28.15).

---

139 *Olgeirsson v Kitching* [1986] 1 All ER 746, DC (see Roberts, *Op. cit.*, 145; Bragg, *Op. cit.*, 63; Cartwright, *Op. cit.*, 238–9). It has been recommended that it should remain possible to convict under this provision fraudulent private individuals: *Review of the TDA* (1976, Cmnd. 6628), paras 36–8.

140 *Warwickshire CC v Johnson* (set out at para 8.09). For support for this exemption of junior employees, see Cartwright, *Consumer Protection and the Criminal Law*, 2000, 149.

141 The defendant must discharge the civil burden of proof: *R v Carr-Briant* [1943] KB 607, CCA (Prevention of Corruption Act 1906); *Whitehead v Collett* [1975] Crim LR 53, DC (TDA).

142 S 168(1). See also FTA, s 25(1); Cf. Medicines Act 1968, s 121(2); Weights and Measures Act 1985, s 34(1); CPA, s 39; DPA, s 47(3); FSA, s 20; Property Misdescriptions Act 1991, s 2; Children & YP (Protection from Tobacco) Act 1991, s 4(5).

143 *Coventry CC v Ackerman Group PLC* [1996] CLY 1189, DC. See also *Waltham Forest LBC v TG Wheatley (No 2)* [1978] RTR 33, DC (Defendant offered no evidence on defence).

If he satisfies all the above requirements, a defendant is entitled to an acquittal[144] for the following reasons: as Lord Reid observed, if a defendant has done all that can reasonably be expected of him, how can he do more?[145] He has 'done his best'.[146] Any disclaimer must be at the time of the *prima facie* offence.[147] It has been said[148] that this traditional general defence can also apply to offences under s 14 of the TDA (see para 4.15, *et seq.*). However, it seems likely that it could only apply to those parts of the s 14 offence which do not require *mens rea*: if so, then the defence can apply to making a statement under s 14(1)(a), but not to doing so under s 14(1)(b).[149]

Experience with the above double-barrelled defence showed that defendants had little difficulty in overcoming paragraph (a), usually by claiming reliance or act of another, so that the real problem for defendants lay in paragraph (b).[150] Accordingly, more recent statutes have tended to dispense entirely with paragraph (a) (see para 28.17).

[28.14] **Paragraph (a)**. In order for the defendant to plead successfully the general defence (see para 28.13), he must prove *inter alia* that his act or omission was due to **one** of the matters specified in paragraph (a).

1. *Mistake*. This unusual[151] defence does not refer to ignorance of the statutory provision creating the offence, but to mistakes by the defendant personally (**not** by a third party) as to matters of fact known to him.[152] Thus, where a corporation is charged, the 'mistake' must be that of its 'brains' and not its 'hands' (see para 28.10); and a mistake by its 'hands' is properly dealt with in (3) below.

2. *Reliance on information supplied*. It has been held that the odometer-reading of a motor vehicle is 'information' for this purpose and statements printed on packaging or containers is also covered.[153] However, this defence will usually be dependent on the precautions taken by the defendant and may even extend to the reliance on legal advice.[154] It is in any event subject to the requirement of prior notice.[155] It has been suggested that this defence should be narrowly

---

144 E.g. *Beckett v Kingston Bros (Butchers) Ltd* [1970] 1 QB 606, DC; *Naish v Gore* [1971] 3 All ER 737, DC; *R v Glen Adaway* [2004] EWCA 2831, CA (for another point, see para 3.19); and see Fidler (1998) 148 NLJ 379.

145 *Tesco Supermarkets Ltd v Nattrass* (set out at para 28.10) at 174.

146 Compare (civil) product liability and development risks (see para 17.30).

147 *Lewin v Fuell* (1991) 10 Tr LR 126, DC (see para 4.09).

148 In *Wings Ltd v Ellis* (set out at para 4.17), *per* Lords Hailsham and Scarman.

149 Stephenson (1985) 135 NLJ 160, 162.

150 Lawson (1993) 137 SJ 144.

151 It seems to require proof of absence of *mens rea*, and anyway is usually inconsistent with due diligence (see para 28.15): Bragg, *Trade Descriptions*, 178–9.

152 If the mistake is by another employee, the proper defence would be 'act or default of another' (see below): *Birkenhead Co-op Ltd v Roberts* [1970] 3 All ER 391, DC. See also *Butler v Keenway Supermarkets* [1974] Crim LR 560, DC (TDA).

153 See the case discussed in Bragg, *Op. cit.*, 180–5. As to disclaimer of odometer, see para 4.09.

154 *Coventry CC v Lazerus* (1994 unreported); see Lawson (1995) 139 SJ 826. Can a defendant rely under this defence on advice sought from a tso? What of LA non-compliance with an enforcement code (see para 5.10)?

155 Prior notice to the prosecutor identifying the supplier of information is normally required so that he can pursue the person really responsible (see para 28.12): TDA, s 24(2); FTA, s 25(2);

construed by restricting it to information from an apparently authoritative source.[156]

3. *Act or default of another.* This will clearly cover both persons working within the same enterprise as the defendant, e.g. employees,[157] and those outside, e.g. suppliers;[158] and it may give rise to the opportunity to prosecute others (see para 28.12). As regards employees, the effect of the decision in *Tesco Supermarkets Ltd v Nattrass* is to draw a distinction between those senior corporate officers who might be liable along with the corporation (see para 28.11) and more junior employees. Where the senior officer is the 'brains' of the corporation, it may be vicariously liable for his conduct (see para 28.10); whereas if he is only part of its 'hands', the corporation may escape criminal liability under the general defence, and the authorities may be reluctant to prosecute the 'hands' under the by-pass provision (see para 28.12) for mis-operating a system designed by the 'brains'.[159] This defence is subject to the requirement of prior notice.[155]

4. *Accident, etc.* The defendant may escape if he can show that the prohibited act was the result of an 'accident or some other cause beyond his control'. Thus, the trader does not have to have a perfect system,[160] but it has been said that an employee cannot be beyond his control[161] and that some explanation must be given of an accident.[162]

**[28.15] Paragraph (b).** In order for the defendant to plead successfully the general defence (see para 28.13), he must prove that before the event he also took **both** the steps specified in paragraph (b) in order to 'avoid such an act or omission by himself or any person under his control'.

1. *All reasonable precautions.* In showing that he has taken all reasonable precautions, it may be a necessary, though not sufficient, precaution for a

---

CCA, s 168(2); Weights and Measures Act 1985, s 34(2); CPA, s 39(2); e.g. *Wings Ltd v Ellis* (absence of notice precluded defence: see para 4.17); *Kilhey Court Hotels Ltd v Wigan BC* (2005) 169 JP 1. But see *McGuire v Sittingbourne Co-op Society* [1976] Crim LR 268, DC (defence allowed although precise identification impossible; discussed Cmnd. 6628, para 59). For argument that the defendant should himself be required to prosecute the third party, see Cmnd. 6628, paras 64–6.

156 Stephenson, *Criminal Law and Consumer Protection*, 129. But see *Barker v Hargreaves* [1981] RTR 197 (reliance on MOT not allowed for this defence; but latency of defect allowed in another defence: see para 28.17). See now CPA, s 39(4).

157 *Tesco Supermarkets Ltd v Nattrass* (set out at para 28.10; store manager); *Nattrass v Timpson Shoes* (set out at para 28.12).

158 *Naish v Gore* [1971] 3 All ER 737, DC (TDA); *Sherratt v Gerald's the American Jewellers Ltd* (1970) 68 LGR 256, DC (TDA).

159 The effect may be that multiple traders are only effectively subject to *mens rea* liability, whereas single shops are strictly liable; and possible statutory amendments have therefore been considered: Cmnd. 6628, paras 52–63; Cartwright (1991) 141 NLJ at 889–90. As to the possible significance of codes of practice (see paras 3.11–4), see Bragg, *Op. cit.*, 189.

160 E.g. *Marshall v Herbert* [1963] Crim LR 506, DC (staff sickness); *Bibby-Cheshire v Golden Wonder Ltd* [1972] 3 All ER 738, DC (machine malfunction); *R v Swaysland* [1987] BTLC 299 (newspaper picture captions reversed).

161 *Hall v Farmer* [1970] 1 All ER 729, DC (Weights and Measures Act). What if the employee is on a frolic of his own? Cf. *McGuire v Sittingbourne Co-op Society* (above); and Stephenson, *Op. cit.*, 131–2.

162 *Urwin v Toole* (1976) 75 LGR 98, DC (weight labels missing from sacks).

retailer to show that he obtained his stock from a reputable source;[163] that he relied on an assurance from his supplier, or a British Standard;[164] or that he had adequate expertise in the type of products sold;[165] or that, if he cannot verify the facts, that he made an adequate disclaimer of them, or adequately consulted a tso.[166] Where the defendant is a large business, this will require him to lay down an adequate system for avoiding the commission of offences by persons under his control: in *Tesco Supermarkets Ltd v Nattrass* (set out at para 28.10), Lord Diplock pointed out that in a large organisation personal supervision of all employees by the 'brains' of the organisation was impractical, but an effective system operated by supervisory grades was required (at 197–8). Further, the business would require an adequate sampling system with regard to products manufactured beyond his control.[167]

2. *All due diligence.* Nor may the defendant rest on his laurels after showing that he took all reasonable precautions at the outset, but must continue to be vigilant.[168] As Lord Diplock explained in the *Nattrass* case (see above), at 199D,

> 'Due diligence is in law the converse of negligence . . . To establish a defence . . . a principal need only show that he personally acted without negligence.'

For instance, buying from a reputable source does not necessarily preclude his taking 'elementary precautions' for himself, such as asking his supplier meaningful questions,[169] or check-weighing goods supplied, or adequate random sampling.[170] Where the defendant is a large business, it is not sufficient just to lay down a proper system: the staff must be adequately trained in its operation,[171] the staff must apply it and the system itself must be able to cope

---

163 *Sherratt v Gerald's, The American Jewellers Ltd* (1970) 68 LGR 256, DC; *Riley v Webb* [1987] CLY 3321, DC; *Hurley v Martinez & Co* [1990] TLR 189, DC. See also *Gale v Dixons Stores Group* [1995] CLY 751, DC (resold without testing goods returned as defective); *Bilon v WH Smith Trading Ltd* [2002] CLY 837 (Video Recordings Act 1984).

164 *Sherratt* (above) and *Taylor v Lawrence Fraser* [1978] Crim LR 43, DC (supplier assurances); *Ealing LBC v Taylor* (1995) 159 JP 460, DC (no enquiry from supplier); *Balding v Lew Ways Ltd* (1995) Tr LR 344, DC (British Standard: see para 3.08).

165 *Aitchison v Reith and Anderson Ltd* [1974] SLT 282 (auctioneer with no previous experience of auctioning vehicles). Cf. *Naish v Gore* [1971] 3 All ER 737, DC (car examined by independent expert).

166 *Zawardski v Sleigh* [1975] RTR 113, DC; *Simmons v Potter* [1975] RTR 347, DC (disclaimers: see para 4.09). *A fortiori*, if he gives a warranty: *Norman (Alec) Garages v Phillips* [1985] RTR 164, DC; *Coventry CC v Lazerus* (1994, unreported; see Lawson (1995) 140 SJ 690).

167 *Rotherham MBC v Raysun (UK) Ltd* [1988] C & F LR 316, DC (importer of Hong Kong products). See also *Haringey LBC v Piro Shoes* [1976] Crim LR 462, DC; *Baxters (Butchers) v Manley* (1985) 4 Tr L 219, DC; and Roberts (1994) 13 Tr L 50.

168 *Denard v Smith & Dixons* (1991) 10 TLR 86, DC; *Turlington v United Co-operatives* [1993] Crim LR 376, DC. See also Cotter (1992) 142 NLJ 133 and 170; Lawson (1995) 14 Tr L 2.

169 *Richmond upon Thames LBC v Motors Sales (Hounslow) Ltd* [1971] RTR 116, DC; *Simmons v Potter* (above); *Riley v Webb* [1987] CLY 3321, DC; and see further Stephenson, *Criminal Law and Consumer Protection*, 133–4.

170 *Nattrass v Timpson Shoes Ltd* (set out at para 28.12); *Rotherham* (above; discussed by Weatherill [1990] JBL 36; *P & M Supplies v Devon CC* (1992) 11 Tr LR 52, DC. Cf. *Hurley v Martinez & Co* (above).

171 *Tesco Supermarkets Ltd v Nattrass* (above); *Knowsley MBC v Cowan* (1992) 11 Tr LR 44, DC. It must be more than a mere paper scheme: Stephenson, *Op. cit.*, 133.

with mistakes,[172] before such a defendant can rely on the 'act of another'.[173] Further, the phrase 'any other person under his control' (TDA, s 24(1)(b)) has been omitted from some later statutes.[174]

*Special defences*

**[28.16]** Besides what is here termed the general defence to offences laid down in consumer protection statutes (see paras 28.13–15), there are also to be found a number of special defences of more restricted application. These include the following:

1. *Reasonable diligence* (see para 28.17).

2. *Innocent publication.* For the owners of news media,[175] there is a special defence of innocent publication to some of the offences under the TDA and several other statutes.[176] The TDA provides that (s 25):

   'In proceedings for an offence under this Act, committed by the publication of an advertisement[177] it shall be a defence for the person charged to prove that he is a person whose business it is to publish or arrange for the publication of advertisements and that he received the advertisement for publication in the ordinary course of business and did not know and had no reason to suspect that its publication would amount to an offence under this Act.'

   Like the reasonable diligence defence (above), this s 25 defence is one of excusable ignorance rather than mistake: he must not know that publication amounts to an offence (subjective) nor have any reason to suspect that it does (objective). There is no provision for corrective advertisements.[178]

3. *Exempted exports, etc.* To save UK exporters from competitive disadvantage, the TDA allows a lower standard to be applied to goods being exported (s 32 (as amended)). The Act also allows some exemption from certain registered trade marks and genuine market research (ss 34 and 37), besides saving the wider defences available under some other Acts.[179]

4. *Wrong quantity.* Where the defendant is charged under the Weights and Measures Act 1985 in respect of goods marked with the wrong quantities (see

---

172  *Beckett v Kingston Bros (Butchers) Ltd* [1970] 1 QB 606, DC (chain store's remedial system omitted by one store manager); *Horner v Sherwoods of Darlington* (1990) 9 TLR 73, DC (staff did not apply system). But the business does not need to take **all practical** steps: *Berkshire CC v Olympic Holidays Ltd* (1994) 13 Tr LR 251, DC (computer malfunction).

173  It **may** be enough to rely on inspection by a tso: *Carrick DC v Taunton Vale Meat Traders Ltd* (1994) 13 Tr LR 258, DC.

174  As to the effect, see Bragg, *Trade Descriptions*, 146.

175  Possibly s 25 does not extend to advertising agents because they do not **receive** advertisements.

176  See Medicines Act 1968, s 93(6); FTA, s 121(1); CCA, s 47(2); Food Act, s 6(3); CPA, s 24(3); Tobacco Advertising and Promotion Act 2002, ss 5 and 17.

177  For the definition of 'advertisement', see para 8.07.

178  As to whether there should be power to require corrective advertising, see the *Review of the TDA* (1976, Cmnd. 6628), paras 194–7.

179  TDA, s 22 (as amended). Where the TDA overlaps with, e.g. the Food Act or the Weights and Measures Act, these other Acts provide some more generous defences, and s 22 saves these, e.g. the written warranty defence. As to prosecutions with regard to food, see Roberts (1993) 10 Tr L 93.

para 4.25), that Act provides special defences with regard to shrinkage after marking,[180] excess[181] or average quantity. As to the last, the 1985 Act lays down that, if other articles of the same type were available for testing, there shall be no conviction unless a reasonable number of those other articles were also tested.[182]

5.   *Written warranty* (see para 28.18).

6.   *Food Safety Act defences* (see para 28.19).

7.   *Pricing regulations* (see para 8.10).

8.   *Innocent supplier pyramid selling* (FTA, s 121(2). See further, para 1.09).

9.   *Dangerous antiques and other second-hand goods* (see para 4.36).

**[28.17] Reasonable diligence.** In relation to some of the less heinous offences, Parliament allows a rather more generous defence. For instance, where a defendant is charged with supplying goods to which another has applied a false trade description (see para 4.05), s 24(3) of the TDA provides that:

> 'it shall be a defence for the person charged to prove[183] that he did not know, and could not with reasonable diligence have ascertained, that the goods did not conform to the description or that the description had been applied to the goods'.

Similar provisions are to be commonly found in more modern consumer protection statutes.[184] In essence, this defence only requires excusable ignorance, whilst the general defence looks for proof of mistaken belief:[185] as the former appears to set a lower standard, it will clearly be preferred by the defendant in those many cases where the two defences appear to overlap;[186] but it may be that the defence considered in this paragraph should be confined to defective goods, whereas the general defence extends also to verbal misdescriptions.[187]

The present defence seems to envisage two different situations; namely, that the defendant did not know (a subjective test)[188] **and** could not with reasonable diligence have ascertained (an objective test)[189] that **either:**

---

180  S 35. This defence is available not only to the manufacturing packer, but also to the retailer: *FW Woolworth & Co Ltd v Gray* [1970] 1 All ER 953, DC.

181  S 36. This is to cover the situation where a machine is set to dispense a reasonable excess on average to try to avoid giving too little in any case.

182  S 37. E.g. *Ellis v Price* (1968) 66 LGR 404, DC. However, where a member of the public tenders one article in complaint, the authorities are under no duty to seek out others so that this defence may be established: *Sears v Smiths Food Group Ltd* [1968] 2 QB 288, DC.

183  On the balance of probabilities: *Wandsworth BC v Fontana* (1983) 146 JP 196, DC. As to food retailers, see para 28.19.

184  E.g. Weights and Measures Act 1985, s 34(1) (see *Bibby-Cheshire v Golden Wonder Ltd* [1972] 3 All ER 738, DC); CPA 1987, s 39(1); Doorstep Selling Regulations 1987, reg 4B(1); Food Safety Act 1990, s 21(1) (cf. *Benfall Farm Produce v Surrey CC* [1983] 1 WLR 1213, DC).

185  See *Barker v Hargreaves* [1981] RTR 197, DC (MOT certificated but latent corrosion).

186  As to whether the two defences do require different standards, see Bragg, *Trade Descriptions*, 194–6. See also *Tesco Stores Ltd v Brent LBC* [1993] 2 All ER 718, DC (Video Recordings Act 1984, s 11).

187  Bragg, *Op. cit.*, 195 fn 77.

188  *Furniss v Scott* [1973] RTR 314, DC (innocent; but culpability not considered).

189  This would appear to involve the same objective test as due diligence under the general defence (see para 28.15): *Taylor v Lawrence Fraser (Bristol)* [1978] Crim LR 43, DC (consumer safety); *Simmons v Ravenhill* [1983] Crim LR 749, DC (TDA); *Denard v Abbas* [1987] Crim LR 424, DC (TDA); *Texas Homecare v Stockport MBC* [1988] CLY 851, DC.

(i)  the goods did not conform to the description,[190] **or**

(ii)  the description had been applied to the goods, e.g. an importer has published a description.

Where the nub of the defence is the fault of an employee,[191] this may allow the possibility of prosecuting the latter (see para 28.12) but gives rise to the same reluctance to prosecute as in relation to the general defence (see para 28.14). In *Cottee v Douglas Seaton (Used Cars) Ltd*:[192]

> Trader B acquired a car with a suspension arm so rusted as to make in unroadworthy. Rather than weld it properly, B merely used a plastic filling material, so totally concealing the defect without repairing it. B sold the car to trader A, who sold it to S.

At first sight, it looked as though the plastic filler caused the car to be supplied to S with a false trade description contrary to s 1(1)(b) (see para 4.03). However the court held that A had committed no offence on the grounds that he had 'no knowledge' or means of knowledge of the defect (*per* Widgery LCJ, at 757f. See also Milmo J at 759b). It followed that B could not be convicted under the by-pass provision (see para 28.12). The decision has been criticised as defeating the intention of Parliament:[193] it is argued that A should have been found to have breached s 1(1)(b), as knowledge should be irrelevant, but that A had a reasonable diligence defence; and that consequently it would have been possible to convict B under the by-pass provision.[194]

**[28.18] Written warranty.** To prevent injustice to retailers, Parliament has sometimes thought it right to allow retailers charged with offences under consumer protection statutes to plead by way of defence that they reasonably relied on the written warranty of their supplier.[195] Provisions to this effect are to be found in the Medicines Act 1968 and the Weights and Measures Act 1985.[196] Reliance by the retailer on this defence is usually subject to prior notice to the prosecutor[197] and to proof by the retailer[198] of all the following conditions:

---

190  *Naish v Gore* [1971] 3 All ER 737, DC.

191  In some statutes it is provided that, if the defendant relies on the act or default of another, he must give prior notice: Food Safety Act 1990, s 21(5); para 28.14. Why is there not a similar requirement in relation to the TDA or CPA?

192  [1972] 3 All ER 750; [1972] 1 WLR 1408, DC.

193  Bragg, *Op. cit.*, 193–4, suggests the case was decided *per incuriam*. But the LCJ did point out that B could have been charged with supplying an unroadworthy car contrary to the RTA: see generally, para 4.37.

194  Instead of concentrating on the supply to S, the DC suggested B should have been charged under s 1(1)(1) in relation to his supply to A.

195  This defence also used to be available under the now-repealed Food Act 1984. Instead, s 21 of the Food Safety Act 1990 replaces it with two defences: (a) reasonable diligence (see para 28.17) and (b) innocent retailer (see para 28.19).

196  Respectively ss 122 and 33. In the latter case, the defence relates only to offences connected with the quantity or pre-packing of goods. Is there any reason why this type of defence should not be extended to offences created under other consumer protection statutes? Cf. the general defence of reliance on information supplied: see para 28.14.

197  And to the alleged warrantor: respectively ss 122(3) and 33(2). The alleged warrantor is entitled to appear in the proceedings: respectively ss 122(5) and 33(4) because the giving of the warranty may amount to an offence by him: respectively ss 123(2) and 33(6).

198  This defence is expressly extended to employees: respectively ss 122(5) and 33(3).

(1) the goods were lawfully supplied to him under their name or description and with a written warranty (see below) to that effect (respectively ss 122(1)(a), 33(1)(a) and (b)); and

(2) he had no reason to believe at the time of commission of the alleged offence that this was not the case (respectively ss 122(1)(b), 33(1)(c) and (d)); and

(3) the goods were in the same state as when purchased,[199] save for untampered natural deterioration.[200]

This defence requires a 'written warranty': whilst it must obviously be expressed,[201] this comprehends any contractual promise[202] and is specially extended to a name or description in an invoice.[203]

**[28.19] Innocent food retailer**. When the Food Safety Act 1990 was being enacted, food retailers were worried that it did not provide them with a defence of written warranty (see para 28.18). Not content with a new reasonable diligence defence (s 21(1): see para 28.17), they therefore insisted upon an additional (overlapping) defence with regard to the three types of offence most commonly charged under food legislation: viz selling food not complying with the food safety requirements (s 8: see para 4.27), selling food not of the nature, etc demanded (s 14: see para 4.28) and falsely describing food (s 15: see para 8.11). Retailers argued that the above reasonable diligence defence would be unduly burdensome where they had neither prepared the food nor imported it (s 21(2)). Accordingly, whether the retailed food was own-branded (s 21(4)(b)) or not (s 21(3)(b)), s 21(2) provided that the retailer shall be taken to have established the above reasonable diligence defence where he proves[204] **both** that:

(1) the commission of the offence was due to an act or default of another person who was not under his control, or to reliance on information supplied by such a person;[205] **and**

(2) he did not know and had no reason to suspect at the time of the commission of the alleged offence that his act or omission would amount to an offence under the relevant provision.[206]

---

199 Respectively ss 122(1)(c) and 33(1)(e). In the latter case, he must take all reasonable steps to ensure that the quantity remains unchanged: s 33(1)(e). But see *Gateway Foodmarkets v Simmonds* [1988] CLY 1698, DC.

200 *Watford BC v Maypole Ltd* [1970] 1 QB 573, DC (pre-packed perishable food). *Contra*, where goods have been processed: *Hall v Owen-Jones* [1967] 3 All ER 209, DC (pasteurised milk); *Tesco Stores Ltd v Roberts* [1974] 3 All ER 74, DC (liver bulk purchased, part-thawed, cut up and re-packaged). See generally Stephenson, *Criminal Law and Consumer Protection*, 123–6.

201 *Jeynes v Hindle* [1921] 2 KB 581 (sufficient that buyer stipulates in contract for warranty). As to express promises, see generally, para 11.07.

202 *Laidlaw v Wilson* [1894] 1 QB 74 (delivery note). But it may not extend to a mere representation (as to which, see generally, para 11.02).

203 Respectively ss 122(6) and 33(8). See *Rochdale MBC v FMC (Meat) Ltd* [1980] 2 All ER 303, DC (brand name on invoice).

204 S 21(3) and (4). So the burden of proof is on the retailer as in the reasonable diligence defence.

205 S 21(3)(a) and (4)(a).

206 S 21(3)(c) and (4)(c).

# CHAPTER 29

# REMEDIES OF THE TRANSFEREE—'DEBTOR OR HIRER'

**[29.01] Introduction**. Even assuming proof of purchase,[1] it must be borne in mind that there are a number of difficulties which a hirer or buyer may face when seeking to pursue his remedies. *First*, the sheer complexity of the legal rules discussed in this work may make ascertainment of his substantive rights a daunting experience; and even finding competent, affordable and timely advice may be difficult (see Chap 3). *Second*, a feasible way of avoiding the foregoing difficulties may be to identify a strict liability criminal offence in the supplier (see Chaps 4 and 5), persuade a public authority to prosecute (see para 28.03) and then use the conviction to obtain financial compensation (see paras 3.20–1). *Third*, turning to civil proceedings, it may be possible to simplify and cheapen proceedings by going to arbitration (see paras 3.23–24), or by complaining to an ombudsman (see para 3.25). *Fourth*, as regards the substantive civil law, there should be recalled the sharp distinction drawn in English law between remedies in contract and tort, which is often important in determining such issues as product liability (see Chap 17), particularly if the transaction is financed (see Chap 16); and there should also be remembered the differing limitation periods (see para 26.17). *Fifth*, there is the difficulty in enforcing legal rights[2] or judgment debts,[3] though even more important to the hirer or buyer is likely to be the cost of litigation (see para 3.22). However, consumers may avoid this by seeking enforcement on behalf of consumers generally by Enforcement Orders (see paras 6.08; 28.03).

The SSG Regulations have significantly improved the position of consumers as follows: (a) in relation to both breaches of statutory implied terms and manufacturers' guarantees (see para 14.01 and 17.09A); and (b) as regards the remedies available where the goods are not in conformity with the contract (see especially, para 29.01A). Further, it should be borne in mind that, in a consumer supply, any term which gives the supplier the right to decide whether the goods supplied conform with the contract may be void as being an unfair term (Grey Term (m): see para 11.18). Leaving aside termination of supply contracts (see para 26.04), actions for breach of a collateral contract (see para 17.09) or a court declaration either under statute[4] or common law,[5] loss caused by pricing and anti-competitive practices

---

1. Where the contract is not reduced to writing, this is a warning to bear in mind the possible need to prove purchase, as by keeping a receipt, or by paying by payment card or cheque.
2. As there is difficulty in identifying the seller by reason of, e.g. franchising (see para 1.07), eponymous subsidiaries (see para 16.06), or one-off sales events (see [1995] 2 *Which?* 5).
3. See Borrie, *The Development of Consumer Law and Policy*, 39–44, referring in particular to the difficulties of consumers facing insolvent limited liability suppliers (see para 19.25); and generally, para 27.04.
4. E.g. CCA, s 142 (see para 9.19); *OFT v Lloyds TSB Bank plc* (see para 16.11). See also *Wilson v First County Trust Ltd* (see para 3.09A; declaration under Human Rights Act). As to declarations in default of appearance, see Brehony (2002) 152 NLJ 1937.
5. *Garnac Grain Co Inc v Faure and Fairclough Ltd* [1968] AC 1130, HL (that contract valid); *Camilla Cotton Co v Granadex SA* [1975] 1 Lloyd's Rep 470, CA (of non-liability); *Rogers v Parish* (set out at para 14.23; validly rescinded); *The Gladys* [1990] 1 All ER 397, HL (existence of contract); *Manatee Towing Co v Oceanbulk Maritime SA* [1999] 2 All ER (Comm) 306; *Messier-Dowty Ltd v*

(see paras 2.12–4) and defective regulated agreements,[6] the major substantive remedies which may be available to the transferee-consumer under a valid supply contract are as follows: (1) the private consumer's right of repair or replacement (see para 29.02, *et seq*.); (2) rescission for breach of contract (see para 29.03, *et seq*.); (3) rescission for misrepresentation;[7] (4) restitution in quasi-contract;[8] (5) damages for breach of contract, tort or misrepresentation (see para 29.17, *et seq*.); (6) specific enforcement (see paras 29.38–9); (7) extortionate credit bargain/unfair credit relationship (see para 29.40, *et seq*.). Each of these remedies may be available alone; or more than one of them may be available alternatively or cumulatively,[9] depending on the duty broken and the nature of the breach.

Of great practical importance is the suspension of payments. Sometimes, there is a legal right of suspension because acting on the transferee's complaint is a condition precedent to the duty of payment, e.g. under SGA, s 28 (see para 23.16). However, there are also suggestions that disaffected consumers of goods supplied on credit be given both the explicit legal right to suspend payments,[10] a tactic frequently employed in any event.[11] In 2007, the UCP Directive will forbid a trader from systematically failing to respond to correspondence to dissuade the consumer from exercising his contractual rights (see para 4.20, item (r)).

**[29.01A]**  It has already been pointed out that the innocent party to the supply contract will be entitled to **rescind** it *de futuro* where the other party repudiates, or sometimes where he defectively performs the supply contract (see para 26.15); but that the innocent party may lose that right by waiver (see paras 26.23–25) or by electing to affirm the contract (see para 26.16). Of particular significance in the present context is the right of the hirer or buyer to reject the goods tendered and rescind on grounds of defective performance, and the fact that he may lose this right by accepting the goods with knowledge of the breach (see para 29.05, *et seq*.). Such an acceptance of the goods may amount to an election to affirm, in which event the hirer or buyer can only sue for damages; or it may even be treated as an acceptance of an offer to enter a contract to vary the previous contract, in which case all remedies for breach of the previous contract might be extinguished (see para 26.18).

*Where the buyer deals as private consumer.* Under the traditional English scheme reflected by Chalmers in the SGA 1893, for all buyers (whether business or private), the primary remedy for breach of condition is a *prima facie* right to **rescind** *de futuro* (see above), which is embodied in Pt 5 of the SGA 1979. However, where there has been a breach of ss 13–15 of the SGA and the buyer deals as private consumer, the

---

  *Sabena SA* [2000] 1 All ER (Comm) 833, CA (non-liability); *Powell v Wiltshire* (set out at para 12.08; ownership). And see generally Benjamin's *Sale of Goods*, 6th edn, para 17.100.

6  A regulated agreement may be unenforceable as not being properly executed; and both regulated and unregulated agreements may be cancellable or void for illegality: see Chaps 8–10.

7  See para 29.11. Possibly with recovery of any price already paid by way of tracing (see para 20.22); and generally, paras 27.13–14.

8  See paras 29.12–16. While refund is delayed, sums retained may be financing the supplier's business or earning interest for him: see *DG v All-wear Trading Ltd*, reported by OFT in *1980-AR*, 73. Cf. *The Manila* [1988] 3 All ER 843.

9  Subject to the rule against double recovery: see para 27.39.

10  NCC, *Buying Problems* (1984) 67; and see below.

11  There may already be a common law or statutory (CCA, s 75) right to set off payments due: see Chap 16.

SSG Regulations have introduced a new scheme of remedies. This is contained in new Pt 5A of the SGA 1979, which applies where goods 'do not conform with the contract . . . at the time of delivery';[12] that is, where the goods do not comply with an express terms of the contract or the implied undertakings as to description, quality and sample.[13] In these cases, the primary remedy of rescission is relegated behind replacement and cure (see para 29.02). Now, such Directive-inspired rules are compulsory (see para 1.03A), so that the traditional English system is *pro tanto* ousted: the result would appear to be that the new rules contained in the SSG Regulations (e.g. new Pt 5A of the SGA) apply to most contracts where the buyer deals as private consumer; whereas the traditional English rules (e.g. old Pt 5 of the SGA) alone apply to all commercial buyers and those (few?) consumer buyers outside the SSG Regulations, e.g. where there is a private seller, or breach of another implied term, e.g. the undertakings as to title and quantity.[14] A further problem concerns the relatively common situation where, after breach, buyer and seller vary their rights by subsequent agreement (see para 26.18). As it may be all too easy to persuade a consumer-buyer unsure of his rights to enter such subsequent agreement purporting to deprive him of his rights under the SSG Regulations, do such subsequent agreements fall foul of the (above) prohibition on contracting out of Directive-inspired rights introduced for the consumer's protection, e.g. elections to affirm (see above), credit notes (see para 29.02)?

## REPLACEMENT OR REPAIR

**[29.02] Subsequent agreement.** In the twentieth century, the traditional method by which English law allowed a buyer to achieve replacement or repair was this. Commonly, the seller might seek to stave off the buyer's rescission (see para 29.03) by offering one of the following two alternatives on the basis of subsequent agreement (see para 26.18):[15]

(A) *Replacement*. The seller might offer to replace free of charge the defective goods with an identical,[16] or even just a comparable, model. If the buyer agreed, the natural legal analysis of what transpired would appear to be this: the original contract of sale was mutually abandoned (see para 26.18); the property in the original goods, if it had already passed, revested in the seller (see para 29.06); and the parties made a second supply contract for the replacement goods, which would appear to be a barter or quasi-sale (see paras 2.09–10).

(B) *Cure/repair*. The seller might offer to cure the defect, whether by use of his own facilities, or by returning them to his supplier (the manufacturer, importer or wholesaler). If English law allowed the defaulting seller[17] a second tender (see

---

12   SGA, new s 48A(1)(b); SGSA, new s 11M(1)(b).
13   SGA, new s 48F; SGSA, new s 11S(1)(a). As to these implied terms, see Chaps 13, 14 and 15.
14   As to these implied terms, see Chaps 12 and 13.
15   Compare the rights of replacement and cure found in the US Uniform Commercial Code, Arts 2.508 and 2.608. See Benjamin's *Sale of Goods*, 6th edn, para 14-016. See also Bridge, *Sale of Goods*, 201.
16   See *VAI Industries (UK) Ltd v Bostock & Bramley* [2003] BLR 359, CA (replacement parts).
17   Distinguish cure in the absence of breach by the supplier: see para 17.09.

para 29.03), then the cure might be effected under the original contract of sale,[18] though the buyer's agreeing to repair would not itself amount to a deemed acceptance.[19] If not, the cure was effected under a second contract, which perhaps amounted to a contract of repair which varied the original sale (see para 26.21): the buyer would in effect bargain away his rights for breach of the original sale contract in return for the cure contract.

*Credit notes.* Retail suppliers frequently try to persuade complaining (usually) private consumers to accept a credit note. The intention is that this credit note (acknowledgement of indebtedness) will later be exchanged for other goods which the buyer will subsequently (perhaps within a time limit) choose from the seller's stock. However, two situations must be carefully distinguished: (i) where the buyer has no right to reject the goods, but is only acting on whim, in which case the seller is usually under no obligation to take the goods back[20] so that his doing so is properly effective as a subsequent agreement; and (ii) where the buyer is entitled to reject the goods, e.g. because they are defective, in which case the buyer is electing not to exercise his right to treat the contract as discharged and immediately recover any price he has already paid (see para 29.15). Any attempt by a retail supplier to provide in the supply contract that his consumer/buyer **must** in these circumstances accept a credit note suffers from the following defects: whether or not the buyer is a private consumer, it would be void,[21] unfair[22] and amounts to a criminal offence;[23] and, if the buyer is a private consumer, it would be a void attempt to contract out of the SSG Regulations (see above). However, it would seem that a private consumer might voluntarily accept a credit note, not by way of subsequent agreement (see para 29.03A), but as a waiver (see para 26.24) of his Pt 5A rights.

The above position reached by subsequent agreement may be compared with the **right** of a private consumer to insist on replacement/cure under SGA, Pt 5A (see para 29.02A), provided he proves his purchase (see para 29.01).

**[29.02A] The special remedies of a private consumer-buyer.** The rights of a disappointed consumer-buyer of defective goods have been significantly enhanced by the SSG Regulations, made pursuant to the SGG Directive (see para 14.01). This introduced a compulsory[24] new Pt 5A to the SGA (reg 5) and similar rules for quasi-sales and hirings in new Pt 1B of the SGSA (reg 9). Because of the reference to quasi-sales (see para 2.10), the new rules will extend to goods made to order,

---

18   *BMBF (No. 12) Ltd v Harland and Woolf Shipbuilding, etc Ltd* [2001] 2 All ER (Comm) 385, CA. It has been suggested that, in the case of supplies of new motor vehicles, the supplier may have a right to cure by reason of an implied term by trade usage: see para 15.11.

19   SGA, s 35(6)(a): see para 29.06.

20   Unless the consumer has a unilateral right of cancellation: see para 10.29. This right may be extended to donees/transferees (see para 17.08).

21   UCTA, ss 6 and 7: see para 18.19.

22   OFT, *Bulletin No. 12*, case 19; *No. 13*, case 13 (Grey Term (b): see para 11.16); Grey Term (m): see para 11.18.

23   It is void under s 6 of UCTA (see para 18.19) and an offence under the Restrictions on Statements Order (see para 4.22).

24   As these new rules are embodied in a Directive, they would seem to be compulsory (see paras 1.03A; 29.01A). But, it would appear that a consumer could waive his rights, as by voluntarily (but not compulsorily) taking a credit note: see para 29.02.

goods to be installed by a supplier (or his sub-contractor) and unsatisfactory installation instructions (see para 18.28).

Taking the new sale rules for simplicity, new Pt 5A of the SGA is **only** applicable where:[25] (i) the buyer 'deals as consumer' (see para 18.18); and (ii) the new, and (usually) second-hand, goods 'do not conform to the contract at the time of delivery' (new s 48F: see para 29.01A), an expression *prima facie* extended for six months after delivery (see para 14.06). Where the foregoing requirements are satisfied, the private consumer/buyer is granted by new Pt 5A the following **alternative** remedies,[26] exercisable by the buyer subject to the discretion of the court,[27] according to the following statutory order of preference:[28]

1.  *Repair or replacement.* New s 48A(2)(a) of the SGA introduces the following alternative limited new rights for the consumer/buyer, including a potentially revolutionary power enabling the court to order specific performance of them (see generally, para 29.38), requiring **either**:[29]

    (A) The seller to **replace** the non-conforming goods. 'Replacement' is not defined: it presumably means like-for-like, so that new goods cannot by 'replaced' by re-conditioned ones; and it remains to be seen whether second-hand goods are so unique (cf. the *Lazenby Garages* case; para 27.36) that they cannot be 'replaced'.[30] As to new goods, the inference is that the conforming replacement must be the same model,[31] so that this remedy is appropriate to mass-produced identical items, e.g. a production fault, or faulty component. It is not appropriate for unique goods, nor for mass-produced goods which suffer from a design fault. What about customised goods, e.g. wood or cloth cut to the buyer's order? As to property in the replaced goods, see para 29.02.

    **Or**

    (B) the seller to **repair** the non-conforming goods free of charge. As new s 61(1) of the SGA explains,[32]

    > '"repair" means, in cases where there is a lack of conformity in goods for the purposes of section 48F of this Act, to bring the goods into conformity with the contract.'

    These two remedies stipulate that the seller must replace or repair the goods 'within a reasonable time (see para 29.07) but without causing significant

---

25  New s 48A(1) of the SGA. For quasi-sales, see new s 11M(1) of the SGSA.

26  New s 48A(2) of the SGA. For quasi-sales, see new s 11M(2) of the SGSA. Must the buyer exercise these remedies in good faith (see the DTI, *Impact Assessment* (4.1.2001), Annex E, para 3)? For good faith, see para 11.15. Would this make any practical difference?

27  New s 48E(1), (3), (4) and (6) of the SGA. For quasi-sales, see new s 11R(1), (3), (4) and (6) of the SGSA.

28  New s 48C(1) and (2) of the SGA. For quasi-sales, see new s 11P(1) and (2) of the SGSA.

29  SGA, new s 48B(1). For quasi-sales, see new s 11N(1) of the SGSA.

30  Even in respect of conforming goods, the retailer may have granted the consumer a unilateral right of exchange without cause, e.g. if the colour does not match.

31  In the case of a regulated agreement, it would seem that a new or modifying agreement must be made: CCA (Agreement) Regulations 1983, First Sched, para 2(3).

32  As inserted by SSG, reg 6(2). For quasi-sales, see new s 18(1) of the SGSA.

inconvenience[33] to the buyer' and 'bear any necessary costs incurred in doing so (including in particular the costs of any labour, materials or postage)',[34] e.g. a new car needing a few minor adjustments. On the other hand, the buyer is not entitled to either of these remedies if they are: (a) impossible e.g. model discontinued, or (b) disproportionate with the other remedy, e.g. if repairs exceed the cost of replacement; or (c) disproportionate with the remedies considered below,[35] e.g. a new car needing seemingly endless adjustments.

2.   *A partial or full refund of purchase price* (see para 29.02B).

**[29.02B] Refunds**. Where the remedies of repair or replacement are either inappropriate or have not been completed by the seller (see para 29.02A), the buyer may either:[36]

(a)  require a **partial refund** of the price; that is, that the seller reduce the purchase price by an appropriate amount,[37] e.g. to take account of the reduced value of the goods, or loss of their use, or so that the buyer could himself commission third-party repairs; or

(b)  reject the goods, rescind the contract (see paras 29.03–4) and obtain a **full refund** of the price (see para 29.14), e.g. a Monday morning car (see para 14.23). When the references in the SSG Regulations to 'rescission' (SGA, new s 48A(1)(b); SGSA, new s 11P(1)(b)) are combined with the six-months-after-delivery rule (see para 14.06), it seems to point to a consumer right to rescission for breach[38] which is to last at least six months and hence ousts the ordinary rule that rescission is limited by acceptance.[39] Further, within the above scheme, rescission is only available to the consumer when he has given the seller a reasonable time to comply with any demand for replacement or repair;[40] but it does not depend on returning the goods in their pre-repaired state, nor in their original packaging, nor in accordance with the supplier's refund policy.

In the case of either partial or full refund, any reimbursement to the buyer may be reduced to take account of his use of the goods,[41] which rule presumably makes good the common law omission of use from a restitution claim (see para 29.15). What about goods which cannot be resold, e.g. medical devices?

---

33  'Reasonable time' and 'significant inconvenience' are both defined by SGA, new s 48B(5) as being determined by '(a) the nature of the goods and (b) the purpose for which the goods were acquired', e.g. a courtesy car. For quasi-sales, see new s 11N(5) of the SGSA.

34  SGA, new s 48B(2). For quasi-sales, see new s 11N(2) of the SGSA.

35  SGA, new s 48B(3); and 'disproportionate' is defined in terms of relative cost (new s 48B(4)). For quasi-sales, see new s 11N(3) and (4) of the SGSA. Cf. the mitigation rule: see para 27.44.

36  New s 48C(1) and (2) of the SGA. For quasi-sales, see new s 11P(1) and (2) of the SGSA.

37  This reduction does not appear to be classed as damages, so is not subject to the ordinary restrictions on damages, e.g. remoteness (see para 27.15A).

38  See para 26.11. Remember that a retail supplier may expressly take the more merciful line of offering consumers a unilateral right of rescission/cancellation without cause (see para 10.29).

39  Bridge (2003) 119 LQR 173 at 175. For the acceptance rule, see para 29.05.

40  SGA, new s 48D; but only if the buyer first requires repair/replacement. For quasi-sales, see new s 11Q of the SGSA.

41  SGA, new ss 48C(3) and 48E(5). For quasi-sales, see new ss 11P(3) and 11R(5) of the SGSA.

All the above remedies are subject to the ordinary limitation rules running from the time of contract;[42] but a consumer will in that case usually be able to bring proceedings in his local County Court or under an arbitration scheme (see paras 3.22–4). Any further consequential loss is claimable under the ordinary rules (see para 29.35).

# RESCISSION

This text will deal first with rescission by a buyer for breach of contract, starting with rejection (see para 29.03), and the rescission by a hirer for breach (see para 29.10), followed by rescission for misrepresentation (see para 29.11).

[29.03] **Rejection**. It will be recalled that it is the duty of the seller to tender goods in conformity with the contract (SGA, s 27: set out at para 23.01) and that the buyer has the right to inspect any goods tendered to ascertain whether they do so conform (s 34: set out at para 23.10). The buyer has a *prima facie* right to reject[43] the goods tendered on grounds of breach of contract in any of the following cases:[44] where there is an express or implied term of the contract to that effect;[45] where the seller has by defective tender or otherwise evinced an intention to repudiate the contract (see para 26.15); or where the seller has committed a breach of condition or innominate term giving a right to treat the contract as repudiated (see paras 11.04–5); or where a consumer buyer seeks a refund under Pt 5A of the SGA (see para 29.02B). A *prima facie* right to reject may be lost by acceptance of the goods (see para 29.04), which leaves a claim for damages available.[46] An improper rejection amounts to a repudiation by the buyer,[47] whilst a lawful rejection will at least nullify delivery and, if already passed, revest in the seller the property[48] and risk.[49] The position after rejection is considered below.

From the above right to reject for breach, there must be distinguished three things: (1) the right to rescind *ab initio* on grounds of misrepresentation (see paras

---

42   See para 26.17. In some trades, e.g. furniture, carpets, delivery may take place some months after contract (usually because the goods are only manufactured to order).

43   Rejection must be unequivocal: *SAM Business Systems Ltd v Hedley & Co* [2003] 1 All ER (Comm) 465.

44   Rejection may take place before or after delivery. As to delivery, see para 23.03. If there has been a delivery, it is the buyer's duty simply to hold rejected goods for collection: see para 23.09. As to rejection for the wrong reason, see para 26.26.

45   E.g. trade usage (see para 15.11); sale or return (see para 20.23), which may include 'money-back' guarantees (see para 20.24). Distinguish the common manufacturer's offer to replace goods with which the consumer is justifiably dissatisfied: see para 17.09. Cf. Codes of Practice (see para 3.13).

46   See para 29.17. Or a right to reject may be lost by waiver of all remedies: see para 26.25.

47   Even after *Woodar Investment Development Ltd v Wimpey Construction UK Ltd* [1980] 1 All ER 571, HL (not a sale case)? As to whether the improper rejection of one instalment constitutes a repudiation of an instalment contract, see para 23.25.

48   Before rejecting a defective tender, the buyer who has paid the price should first ensure his seller is solvent: otherwise he will be reduced to claiming a dividend—see para 19.15. As to the initial passing of property by appropriation, see para 20.15.

49   But might the right to reject be lost by accidental damage or part consumption by way of trial? See *Sale and Supply of Goods* (1987, Law Com No. 160), paras 5.39–40.

26.12–4); (2) a subsequent agreement between the parties to discharge the contract (see para 29.02); and (3) any unilateral right on the part of the transferee to cancel the contract. This last right may occasionally exist by reason of the terms of the original supply contract, or more commonly by statute (see para 10.28). For instance, sometimes the CCA gives him such a right without cause in respect of regulated conditional or credit sales (see para 26.22).

*After rejection.* Where the defective tender does not amount to a frustrating breach (see para 26.16), **must** the rejecting buyer (see above) also treat the contract as repudiated? Section 11(3) of the SGA runs together the notions of rejecting the goods and rescinding the contract, i.e. treat the contract as repudiated by reason of the seller's breach (see para 11.04); and it does so in a manner which seems to assume that the disappointed buyer will also want to rescind. No doubt, a buyer who can and does reject goods **may** also wish to rescind the contract (see para 29.04), in which case at common law there would be no question of the seller making a second tender of conforming goods. On the other hand, if the rejecting buyer did not also rescind, the common law allowed the defaulting seller to make a second tender;[50] and in a sale to a private consumer within SGA, Pt 5A, the defaulting seller will usually have the right to tender a replacement (see para 29.02A), irrespective of the fact that the first tender may have destroyed the buyer's confidence. Any replacement goods are *prima facie* supplied on the same terms as the originals.[51]

**[29.04] Rescission *de futuro*.** Even without any repudiation by the seller or espe-cially enhanced rights in the buyer, under the scheme adopted by the SGA 1893 many of the seller's duties were conditions (see Chaps 11–16). In such cases, even minor infringements of those conditions would *prima facie* give the buyer the right to reject the goods (see para 29.03), rescind the contract *de futuro*, even if the pro-perty had already passed to him,[52] reclaim the price if already paid[53] and sue for damages on the basis of non-delivery (see para 29.18). To counter-balance this very wide right of rescission, the draftsman of the SGA 1893 provided that the buyer could not exercise it unless he acted quickly (s 11(1)(c)). However, the last limitation has subsequently been whittled down by statute and new s 11(4) of the SGA lays down that (s 11(4) of the SGA 1979 was amended by s 3(2) of the SSGA 1994):

> 'Subject to section 35A below, where a contract of sale is not severable and the buyer has accepted the goods or part of them, the breach of a condition to be fulfilled by the seller can only be treated as a breach of warranty, and not as a ground for rejecting the goods and treating the contract as repudiated, unless there is an express or implied term of the contract to that effect.'

---

50  *Borrowman Phillips & Co v Free & Hollis*: (1878) 4 QBD 500, CA; and para 29.04. This rule certainly seems to be settled with regard to offers to tender the goods in cif sales (see para 22.07): see Benjamin's *Sale of Goods*, 6th edn, para 19-068; Bridge, *Sale of Goods*, 199.

51  *VAI Industries (UK) Ltd v Bostock & Bramley* [2003] BLR 359, CA, at para 40 (on the basis of an implied term: see para 11.10).

52  *McDougall v Aeromarine of Emsworth Ltd* [1958] 3 All ER 431. As to rescission, see para 26.15; and as to revesting of property, see para 29.06.

53  As on total failure of consideration: see para 29.12. Alternatively, he may accept a credit note: as to which, see para 29.02. As to the failure of credit traders to make refunds, see para 6.19; and as to refunds by credit or charge card, see para 7.09A.

New s 11(4) seems confined to those cases where (a) the contract is not severable[54] and (b) there is a breach of condition by the seller.[55] Even in those cases in which it is applicable, s 11(4) does not say that if a buyer can and does reject he must rescind the contract,[56] but merely imposes a *prima facie* restriction on his right to reject and rescind.[57] However, this does insert an important rigidity into the law, namely that the buyer's right to reject is lost by his acceptance of the goods.[58]

True, the rule can be ousted expressly,[59] or impliedly, e.g. by a contrary trade custom (see para 15.11) and is varied in respect of severable contracts (see para 23.24) and part-acceptance.[60] Further, the scope of s 11(4) was subsequently reduced by the provision that s 11(4) shall not apply to a conditional sale agreement[61] where the buyer deals as consumer within Pt I of UCTA (see para 18.18): in such cases, the right to reject and rescind is the same as for hp;[62] and this should also apply to consumer conditional buyers under new Pt 5A of the SGA (see para 29.02B). The position of quasi-sales (see para 2.10) in this respect remains unclear;[63] and similarly uncertain is the position of cash and credit buyers within new Pt 5A of the SGA.

**[29.05] Acceptance.** Under the scheme laid down in the SGA, after the buyer has acquired a right to reject the goods (see para 29.03), he will *prima facie* have a right to rescind the contract *de futuro*. However, he will lose that right to rescind and be reduced to claiming damages where he has accepted the whole of the goods (see para 29.04). Acceptance in this sense[64] is dealt with by new s 35 of the SGA, which deems the buyer to have accepted the goods in three situations,[65] though with special rules for sale or return transactions and breaches of the undertakings as to title or description (see respectively, paras 20.24, 12.08 and 13.04). Nowadays much hedged about with restrictions, the three situations of deemed acceptance by the buyer are these (new s 35(1) and (4)):

1.  *He intimates his acceptance* (new s 35(1)(a)). As a buyer has a statutory right of inspection (SGA, s 34: see para 23.10), even under the 1979 Act it followed

---

54  For a curious drafting argument, see Atiyah, *Sale of Goods*, 10th edn, 524. Why is that argument necessary?

55  As to whether s 11(4) is applicable to the implied condition as to title, see para 12.06A. As to s 35A, see para 29.09.

56  See para 29.03. This would deprive him of any right to specific performance. But see *per* Devlin J in *Kwei Tek Chao v British Traders and Shippers Ltd* [1954] 2 QB 459, at 480.

57  See *per* Salter J in *William Barker & Co Ltd v Agius Ltd* (1927) 33 Comm Cas 120, at 130.

58  As to which, see para 29.05. However, the earlier version of the rule (to be found in s 11(1)(c) of the SGA 1893) was significantly wider in effect: see para 20.08.

59  E.g. *WE Marshall v Lewis and Peat Ltd* [1963] 1 Lloyd's Rep 562 (reducing buyer's rights); retailer's guarantee 'money back if not entirely satisfied'.

60  See para 29.08. Suppose the desired goods are supplied along with a 'free gift' (as to which see para 2.08) and one of the items is defective. Is it possible to keep one and reject the other?

61  Conditional sales are defined by s 15(1) of SOGIT in a manner virtually identical to that in the CCA, except for the latter's reference to 'land': see para 1.16. However, the present rule applies whether or not a conditional sale is regulated.

62  SOGIT, ss 14(1), (2) and 15(3) as amended by the CCA, Sched 3. As to the effect, see para 29.10.

63  See Palmer (1983) 46 MLR at 622–3; and see *Jones v Gallagher* (set out at para 29.07A).

64  'Acceptance' seems to be used in different senses in ss 27, 35 and 50(3): Goode, *Commercial Law*, 3rd edn, 346.

65  Does new s 35 apply where the seller is fraudulent?

that mere receipt of the goods by the buyer would not *per se* amount to an acceptance. This was confirmed by new s 35(2), which lays down as follows:

> 'Where goods are delivered to the buyer, and he has not previously examined them, he is not deemed to have accepted them under subsection (1) above until he has had a reasonable opportunity of examining them for the purpose—
>
> (a) of ascertaining whether they are in conformity with the contract, and
>
> (b) in the case of a contract for sale by sample, of comparing the bulk with the sample.'

What was required before acceptance would bar the right to reject[66] was an intimation by the buyer to the seller that he had elected to accept the goods delivered as conforming with the contract.[67] Leaving aside sales by sample (see para 15.08/9) and inconsistent acts (see para 29.06), it will be realised that new s 35(2) does not preclude an actual acceptance by the buyer before he has inspected the goods. Now, the buyer's signature on an acceptance note (see para 23.10) might have acted as such an acceptance.[68] However, new s 35(3) provides that, where the buyer 'deals as consumer',[69] he cannot lose his right to rely on the new s 35(2) above 'by agreement, waiver or otherwise'. Accordingly, in a consumer sale, the buyer's acceptance can no longer be inferred just because he allows the seller to attempt a cure (new s 35(6)(a): set out at para 29.06), or uses the goods for a reasonable time to try to overcome teething problems.[70] On the other hand, in a non-consumer sale actual acceptance before inspection remains possible, either by a term of the sale contract,[71] signature of an acceptance note, allowing a cure,[72] or otherwise.

2.   *He does an inconsistent act* (see para 29.06).

3.   *Lapse of a reasonable time* (see para 29.07).

**[29.06] Inconsistent act.** The position at common law would appear to have been that the buyer was deemed to have accepted the goods if he did any act which clearly showed an intention to affirm.[73] The SGA 1893 amended this in a rule now to be found reproduced verbatim in new s 35(1)(b), namely that the buyer is deemed to have accepted the goods

---

66   It may be that much more is required before the buyer's acceptance will also act as a waiver of even his claim to damages (see para 26.24): Atiyah, *Sale of Goods*, 10th edn, 514.

67   E.g. *Rosenthal & Sons Ltd v Esmail* [1965] 2 All ER 860, HL; *Long v Lloyd* (set out at para 26.13); the *Kwei Tek Chao* case [1954] 2 QB 459; *Lee v York Coach and Marine* [1977] RTR 35, CA.

68   *Sale and Supply of Goods* (1987, Law Com. No. 160), paras 2.45 and 5.20–4.

69   'Reference in this Act to dealing as consumer are to be construed in accordance with Part I of UCTA; and, for the purposes of this Act, it is for a seller claiming that a buyer does not deal as consumer to show that he does not': SGA, new s 61(5A) (inserted by SSGA 1994, Sched 2, para 5(9)(c)). For 'dealing as consumer' in UCTA, see para 18.18.

70   See *Millicent v Hollick* [1956] CLY 7927, CA; and Whincup (1975) 38 MLR at 670–1. If the trial is prolonged beyond a reasonable time, that in itself is an act of acceptance: see para 29.07.

71   Such a clause may be subject to the UCTA reasonableness test (see para 18.24) by reason of UCTA, ss 3 and 6.

72   See *Jackson v Chysler Acceptances Ltd* [1978] RTR 474, CA; *Leaves v Wadham Stringer (Cliftons) Ltd* [1980] RTR 308. What if the same defect re-appears? What if another defect appears after acceptance? What if the supply contract contains a post-delivery maintenance provision?

73   It has been argued that the common law rule is preserved by the SGA, s 62(2), so saving other grounds of acceptance: Goode, *Commercial Law*, 3rd edn, 357.

'when the goods have been delivered to him and he does any act in relation to them which is inconsistent with the ownership of the seller'.

In the commercial context, the commonest example of an inconsistent act is a sub-sale by the buyer.[74] In *E Hardy & Co v Hillerns and Fowler*[75] the Court of Appeal took the view that any subsale must necessarily be inconsistent with the ownership of the seller; and the logical outcome of this was that a buyer who 'subsold' the goods before he purchased, or before the goods were delivered to him, or who ordered delivery direct to his sub-buyer, never had a right to inspect and reject.[76] Parliament has now dealt with the issue directly in new s 35(6), which provides as follows:

'The buyer is not by virtue of this section deemed to have accepted the goods merely because—

(a)  he asks for, or agrees to, their repair by or under an arrangement with the seller, or

(b)  the goods are delivered to another under a subsale or other disposition.'

So, the effect of a subsale would appear to depend on whether the buyer has a reasonable opportunity of inspection at the place of delivery (see para 23.04): where he does not, then after rejection by the sub-buyer he may himself in turn reject,[77] e.g. a finance company engaged in direct financing, whereas, if the buyer does have a reasonable chance of examination, he will lose his right to reject by dispatching the goods to his sub-buyer,[78] unless perhaps the defect is latent.[79]

In relation to consumer sales, there is little direct authority as to what may be an act by the consumer-buyer inconsistent with the rights of the (usually retail) seller.[80] However, it would now seem that the inconsistent act rule does not apply simply because the buyer makes a gift of his purchase (s 35(6)(b) 'other disposition') or has it repaired;[81] and the (retail) seller can in turn reject the goods back to his supplier.[82] As to whether a third party could himself reject the goods back to the retailer, see para 17.07A.

[29.07] **Lapse of time**. The mere fact that the goods remain in the buyer's possession cannot without more amount to an acceptance, because s 36 of the SGA

---

74  For analysis of the cases to find a rationale for the rule, see Benjamin, *Sale of Goods*, 6th edn, para 12-047, *et seq.*

75  [1923] 2 KB 490; [1923] 3 All ER Rep 275, CA. It has been said that a transfer of cif documents is not such an act: *per* Devlin J in the *Kwei Tek Chao* case [1954] 2 QB 459, at 488. Cf. *Barrow Lane & Ballard Ltd v Phillip Phillips Ltd* (set out at para 22.12).

76  *E and S Ruben Ltd v Faire Brothers & Co Ltd* [1949] 1 KB 254. But see *Rowland v Divall* (set out at para 12.05).

77  S 35(6)(b). Cf. *Molling v Dean* (1901) 18 TLR 215, DC; and see Atiyah, *Sale of Goods*, 10th edn, 517.

78  S 35(2). Cf. *Perkins v Bell* [1893] 1 QB 193, CA (common law: criticised by Atiyah, *Op. cit.*, 517).

79  *Truk (UK) Ltd v Tokmakidis* (see para 29.07, at 604j).

80  See *Sabir v Tiny Computers* [1999] CLY 840, Cty Ct (buyer installing upgraded software); *Clegg v Olle Andersson* (set out at para 14.18) at paras 59–60 (register and insure). See generally Atiyah, *Op. cit.*, 520–1; Benjamin, *Op. cit.*, para 12-051; *Sale and Supply of Goods* (1987, Law Com No. 160), para 2.47.

81  S 35(6)(a). *A fortiori* where the buyer has only conditionally agreed to repairs: *Clegg v Olle Andersson* (above) at paras 58 and 75.

82  S 35(6)(b): Law Commission *Sale and Supply of Goods* (above) para 5.38. Is this (possibly delayed) sub-buyer's rejection to be taken into account when deciding whether the retailer has rejected within a reasonable time (see para 29.07)?

provides that he is under no duty to return the goods (see para 23.09). However, assuming that the buyer has not rejected the goods, new s 35(4) lays down in the following terms:[83]

> 'The buyer is also deemed to have accepted the goods when after the lapse of a reasonable time he retains the goods without intimating to the seller that he has rejected them.'

What amounts to a reasonable time is a question of fact.[84] Certainly, the length of the reasonable time may vary according to the nature of the goods: in some cases, this will be indicated by a stated use-by date, e.g. food, medicines; in others it may be very short because of the nature of the goods, e.g. clothing, shoes. But the seller may extend the period of a reasonable time, either by a contractual term[85] or by conduct, for example by disregarding the time taken to negotiate a settlement,[86] or effect a cure.[87] New s 35(5) adds that:

> 'The questions that are material in determining for the purposes of subsection (4) above whether a reasonable time has elapsed include whether the buyer has had a reasonable opportunity of examining the goods for the purpose mentioned in subsection (2) above.'

The two statutory purposes of examining the goods contained in new s 35(2) have already been set out (see para 29.05); and in the commercial case of *Truk (UK) Ltd v Tokmakidis GmbH*[88] it was held that this enquiry involves a balancing of the opposing interests of the buyer and seller (at 603e–f) and cannot be less than the reasonable opportunity to examine (s 35(5)), though it may be more (s 35(6): see para 29.06).

However, the basic time limit may have been quite short (see para 29.07A), presenting a particular dilemma to consumers, the classic case being the expensive consumer durable in which a number of small defects appear over a period of time (see paras 14.23–4). To meet such problems, the SGG Directive stipulated a two year limit as from delivery (Art 5(1)); but the UK Government has not specifically enacted this provision in the SSG Regulations on the argument (see para 14.01) that the effect of Art 5(1) is already produced by our limitation of actions rule (see para 26.17). There may also be a different time limit under an express warranty by either the supplier or manufacturer (see paras 14.0A and 17.09); and, if it is too late to reject, it may still be possible to claim a repair or replacement (see paras 29.02A–B).

---

83  New s 35(4) was imported into the SGA 1979 by s 2 of the SSGA 1994. As recommended by the *Sale and Supply of Goods* (1987, Law Com No. 160), paras 5.14–19.

84  SGA 1979, s 59. This was to overcome previous uncertainty as to whether the matter was one of fact or law; and see the cases gathered by Benjamin's *Sale of Goods*, 6th edn, para 12-055, *et seq*. Distinguish acceptance of offer, where lapse of time does not *prima facie* amount to acceptance: see para 10.02.

85  As by auctioneer's conditions of sale allowing a finite period of rescission in respect of 'deliberate forgery': Harvey and Meisel, *Auctions*, 2nd edn, 164. In a consumer supply, this may be an unfair term: OFT, *Bulletin No. 14*, case 9: see generally, para 11.12, *et seq*.

86  *Manifatture Tossik Laniera Wooltex v JB Ashley Ltd* [1979] 2 Lloyd's Rep 28, CA, discussed at 43 MLR 463.

87  New s 35(6)(a): set out at para 29.06. See the Law Com, *Op. cit.*, para 5.31.

88  [2000] 2 All ER (Comm) 594; [2000] 1 Lloyd's Rep 543.

**[29.07A]  The running of time**. In drafting the SGA 1893, Chalmers took the view that the reasonable time rule would not unduly circumscribe the buyer of defective goods because the loss of right to reject (s 35) would not take place until the buyer had under s 34 (set out at para 23.10) had a reasonable time to inspect the goods.[89] Unfortunately, in *Hardy v Hillerns and Fowler* (see para 29.08), the Court of Appeal held that s 35 was not so subject to s 34; and the effect of this on consumers was to reduce the reasonable time 'solely to what is a reasonable practicable interval . . . [between the buyer] . . . receiving the goods and his ability to send them back';[90] that is, to ignore the buyer's inability to discover the defect. However, the wider protection of consumers was restored by new s 35(5), as has been explicitly confirmed by *Clegg v Olle Andersson* (set out at para 14.18). In this case, a unanimous Court of Appeal held that it was not too late for the buyer to reject: the court decided that the time taken for the buyer to obtain the information necessary to decide whether or not to attempt a repair (7 months from delivery) should be taken into account when deciding what is a reasonable time, so that time should not begin to run until the buyer had acquired this information, treating this as a matter of law (at para 63). However, in *Jones v Gallagher*,[91]

> Jones contracted with G for the supply and installation of a hand-made fitted pine kitchen 'to match the existing dresser'. The installation was completed by 2nd May 2000 and Jones paid the full price. Thereafter, Jones raised a number of complaints, including non-matching to the dresser. Whilst G returned several times to carry out other remedial work, the non-matching was not consistently raised but never satisfactorily resolved. In September 2000, Jones obtained an expert's report and sent a solicitor's letter threatening rescission. In October 2001, Jones commenced proceedings, and the trial judge found breaches of the undertakings as to description and satisfactory quality in the SGSA. Jones unsuccessfully appealed against a decision that he had lost the right to rescind by lapse of time.

A differently constituted Court of Appeal from *Clegg* unanimously held that a reasonable time had expired as a matter of fact; and that the effect of the 1994 reforms to s 35 was merely to confirm that a buyer who requests repairs does not automatically lose the right to reject (at para 34). Whereas the buyer in *Clegg* only waited three weeks after receiving the critical information from the seller, it was several months before Jones threatened proceedings. Yet, whilst Jones appeared to lose on the SGA acceptance rule (see para 29.04), it has been pointed out that that SGA rule does not purport to apply to quasi-sales;[92] but maybe *Jones* is implicit authority that the SGA acceptance rule will be so extended henceforth.

So, if it takes a consumer-buyer a number of days or weeks to test out the various cycles of his new washing-machine, he should still be able to reject if the last one he tests proves defective.[93] Further examples might be a lawnmower or skis

---

89   Cranston and Dehn [1990] JBL 346.

90   *Bernstein v Pamson Motors Ltd* [1987] 2 All ER 220, at 230g (discussed 104 LQR 16; [1988] JBL 56).

91   [2005] 1 Lloyd's Rep 377, CA. The facts arose before implementation of the modern consumer remedies as to replacement/repair (see paras 29.02A–B).

92   Bradgate (2004) 120 LQR 558 at 561–2, arguing that the right of rescission should instead be limited by the common law doctrines of affirmation and waiver, but that there had been none.

93   See the Law Commision, *Op. cit.*, para 5.16. 3–4 weeks have been suggested for a new car: [2006] 5 *Which?* 8.

bought at an end-of-season sale. On the other hand, new s 35(5) would not seem to preserve his right to reject where the delivered goods remain untested beyond a reasonable time,[94] e.g. where a consumer cannot test the goods within the usual reasonable time, as where he is going on holiday or into hospital. To meet such problems, the SGG Directive restricted the above two-year delivery rule (Art 5(1): see para 29.07) by stipulating that the buyer must inform the seller of the lack of conformity within two months from the date on which he detected this lack of conformity.[95]

**[29.08] Part acceptance**. Whilst not absolutely clear, it would appear that the effect of s 11(4) of the SGA 1979 was to extend the acceptance rule (see para 29.05) to partial acceptances.[96] However, the effect of this rule depends on the indivisibility of the contract (see para 23.24):

(1) Where there is in fact not one, but a series of contracts between the parties, each of that series is to be considered as a separate contract for the purposes of the acceptance rule.[97] It follows that acceptance of goods under one of those contracts[97] does not bar rejection of goods due under other contracts in the series, e.g. suppose a consumer on the same occasion makes a number of unconnected purchases in different parts of a department store. The position is the same where there is a single severable contract.[98]

(2) Where there is a single entire contract, different considerations generally apply (see para 28.09), except in the following case.

*A commercial unit*. The Law Commission recommended that there should be introduced into English law the notion of a 'commercial unit' of goods, with the idea that it should not be possible for a buyer to accept some of the goods within such a unit whilst rejecting others,[99] e.g. one shoe out of a pair. This recommendation was enacted by Parliament by means of new s 35(7):[100]

'Where the contract is for the sale of goods making one or more commercial units, a buyer accepting any goods included in a unit is deemed to have accepted all the goods making the unit; and in this subsection 'commercial unit' means a unit division of which would materially impair the value of the goods or the character of the unit.'

According to the Law Commission, the effect of this should be as follows:[101]

---

94 Cf. *Leaf v International Galleries* (set out at para 29.11). What if the retail-buyer keeps the goods for some time unopened, e.g. where intended for a gift? In Parliament, it was suggested that this period of non-use would be ignored as irrelevant (Standing Committee C, March 1994, col 37). *Sed quaere?*

95 Art 5(2). As to the Directive, see generally, para 14.01; and as to limitation periods, see generally, para 26.17.

96 See Atiyah, *Sale of Goods*, 10th edn, 524. *De minimis* partial acceptances are presumably ignored, e.g. the instruction book delivered in advance of a new car.

97 The courts seem reluctant to treat transactions as a series of contracts in the ordinary commercial context; and generally, paras 23.24–5.

98 *Jackson v Rotax Motor and Cycle Co* (set out at para 14.05): see new s 35A(2); and below, para 29.09.

99 *Sale and Supply of Goods* (1987, Law Com. 160) para 6.12, adopting a notion from the US Uniform Commercial Code, Arts 2-105(6) and 2-601.

100 As inserted s 2 of SSGA 1994.

101 Law Com, *Op. cit.*, para 6.13.

(i)  A buyer who accepted part only of a set, such as a single volume of an encyclopedia which is sold as a set, would normally be deemed to have accepted the whole set.

(ii)  A buyer who accepted part only of a sack or other unit (whether measured by weight or in some other way) by which goods of the type in question are customarily sold in the trade would be deemed to have accepted the whole unit. The buyer would not be so restricted if it was merely the seller (and not the trade in general) who chose to sell the goods in that particular way.

(iii)  A buyer who accepted one shoe of a pair would be deemed to have accepted the pair; but he would be entitled to accept one of a number of identical articles, even if more than one at a time was commonly bought, if each was in fact a self-contained unit.

**[29.09]  Partial rejection**. Where, under a single entire contract (see para 26.02), the buyer accepts one or more commercial units (see para 29.08), the law has been changed. Whereas the previous law did not normally[102] allow the buyer to reject any defective goods and keep the rest, the Law Commission recommended that there should be 'a general right of partial rejection in cases where some of the goods delivered to the buyer do not conform with the contract'.[103] This recommendation was adopted in the new s 35A of the SGA 1979 (as inserted by s 3(1) of the SGSA 1994). Subject to a contrary intention,[104] new s 35A(1) provides:

'(1)  If the buyer—

(a)  has the right to reject the goods by reason of a breach on the part of the seller that affects some or all of them, but

(b)  accepts some of the goods, including, where there are any goods unaffected by the breach, all such goods,

he does not by accepting them lose his right to reject the rest.'

It will be observed that this new right of partial rejection only applies where the buyer has a right to reject all the goods under the ordinary rules,[105] so is subject to the inability to reject part of a single commercial unit (s 35(7): set out at para 29.08). Where applicable, new s 35A(1) gives the buyer the additional choice of accepting 'some of the goods, including, where there are any goods unaffected by the breach, all such goods'. The new section makes it clear that the ordinary acceptance rule is subject to this new right of partial rejection;[106] that, in the case of an instalment contract, each instalment shall be treated separately for the purposes of this new rule;[107] and that this new right of partial rejection is no longer confined to 'mixed goods',[102] but applied wherever goods 'are not in conformity with the contract' (see para 29.01A), which expression will extend to matters of both quality and

---

102  Such a right had only existed where the contract goods had been 'mixed with' goods of a different description under the now repealed s 30(4) SGA 1979: see para 13.02.

103  *Sale and Supply of Goods* (1987, Law Com. 160), para 6.6.

104  New s 35(4): so this rule may be ousted for both consumer and non-consumer sales.

105  New s 35A(1)(a). So this new right is not available to a non-consumer buyer after a slight breach of condition (new s 15A): see para 29.03.

106  SSGA 1994, s 3(2). For the ordinary acceptance rule, see para 29.04. What if the buyer accepts only part of the conforming goods?

107  New s 35A(2). See generally, paras 23.24–5.

quantity.[108] The expected effect of the 1994 changes for a consumer who orders 100 objects were spelt out as follows:[109]

(a) If only one were defective, he could keep them all, reject them all, or keep the 99 and reject the defective one (and in all cases claim damages).

(b) If 50 are defective, he may reject 100, keep 100, or keep the 50 conforming objects and reject any or all of the 50 defective objects (and in all cases claim damages).

(c) If all are defective, he may reject all or any of them and claim damages.

(d) If the 100 objects in the previous examples comprised an instalment of a larger order, the result would be exactly the same as regards that instalment; the partial rejection rules do not affect any rights the buyer may have as regards other instalments.

**[29.10] Rescission by the consumer-hirer**. It is possible that a hirer under a simple hiring or hp agreement has a duty to accept delivery which is similar to that of a buyer (see para 27.27), counterbalanced by similar *prima facie* rights to reject and rescind where the owner is in serious breach.[110] However, the following matters need to be taken into consideration:

1. *Slight breaches of condition*. Following the recommendation of the Law Commission[111] that the rule should be the same as for sale (see para 29.03), a business hirer has no right of rejection for slight breaches under either an hp agreement[112] or simple hiring.[113]

2. *Continuous breaches*. In *Yeoman Credit Ltd v Apps* (set out at para 29.25) the hirer under an hp agreement paid instalments and retained the defective car for a total of five months. Nevertheless, the Court of Appeal unanimously agreed that the hirer was entitled to reject for breach of condition at the end of that five months. Holroyd Pearce LJ explained:[114]

   'Had this been a sale of goods on instalment payments, he could not, of course, have done so after payment of instalments and acceptance of goods. Had this been a simple hiring . . . he would have been entitled to reject [the goods] and end the hiring, since the owner's breach was a continuing one. The owner's conduct would constitute a continuing repudiation. This hire purchase agreement was, at the material time, more analogous to a simple hiring than to a purchase.'

   The oddity of the doctrine of continuous breach becomes apparent when the measure of damages is considered (see paras 29.25 and 29.34). The doctrine was subsequently rejected for simple hiring in *UCB Leasing Ltd v Holtom*:[115]

---

108 For defects of quality, see ss 13–15 (see Chaps 13, 14 and 15); and for defects of quantity, see s 30 (see paras 13.03–6).

109 Law Commission, *Op. cit.*, para 6.16.

110 E.g. *Ditchburn Equipment Co Ltd v Crich* (1966) 110 Sol Jo 266, CA (simple hiring).

111 *Sale and Supply of Goods* (1984, Law Com 160), para 4.21.

112 New s 11A of SOGIT 1973, as inserted by SSGA 1994, Sched 2, para 4(6).

113 New s 10A of SGSA 1982, as inserted by SSGA 1994, Sched 2, para 6(9).

114 At 552. As a conditional buyer is in possession of the goods as bailee (see para 1.14), why should he too not have the benefit of the doctrine of continuous breach?

115 [1987] RTR 362, CA.

Under a directly financed transaction, UCB leased a new Alfa Romeo car to H for 37 months. The car was found to have electrical faults rendering it unfit for the purpose supplied. After four months, H stopped paying rentals. The car was returned to UCB after seven months, when it had done nearly 8,000 miles. Held that UCB rather than H had rescinded after seven months (see below); and, in diminution of UCB's claim for rentals (see para 29.26), H was awarded damages as assessed in *Tolly's* case (see para 29.34).

In refusing H's claim that he was entitled to rescind after seven months,[116] the Court of Appeal expressly dismissed the above reasoning of Holroyd Pearce LJ as *obiter*. Has the *Apps* rule of continuous breaches survived for periodic hirings? If not, to what extent does the SGA, s 35 apply by analogy to limit rescission of bailment?

3. *Acceptance*. In the case of most sales, but not some conditional sales, any right to rescind is lost by acceptance of the goods (SGA, s 11(4): set out at para 29.04). It has been said that this acceptance rule has no place in hp,[117] where the hirer instead 'loses his right to termination only when he becomes aware of the defect in the good and then affirms the contract, or waives his right to terminate or is estopped from relying on his right to terminate'.[118] In 2004, the court held that a hirer had not accepted where he made a payment pending an attempt to 'roll over' the leasing contract by substitution of other goods.[119]

4. *Lapse of time*. This has caused problems in relation to defective motor vehicles obtained by consumers on hp, there being no doubt that the right to reject lapses on expiry of a reasonable time.[120] Frequently, there is a long history of attempts by the hirer to get his supplier to repair the goods before he finally rejects them. Sometimes the courts have ignored these periods of time on the grounds of the doctrine of continuous breach (see above) or whilst repairs were attempted or negotiations conducted.[121] However, unlike in sale (see para 29.07), the period itself seems to be measured by the opportunity to discover the defect.[122]

5. *Consumer hire*. New statutory remedies have now been introduced where the transferee 'deals as consumer' within the meaning of s 12 of UCTA; and it has already been seen that this expression extends beyond sale to include contracts of both simple hiring and hp (see para 18.18). It follows that such a consumer hirer has the same additional remedies of replacement, repair, reduction of the purchase price or rescission granted to a consumer buyer under new Pt 1B of the SGSA (see para 29.02B).

---

116  At 371, 375. The court adopted the argument by Goode, *HP Law & Practice*, 2nd edn, 456–8.

117  Law Commission, *Op. cit.*, para 5.43. The remark actually extends to 'other contracts for the supply of goods'. Presumably, this means simple hirings. What about quasi-sales (see para 29.04)?

118  *Ibid*; and see the *Alpha Chauffeurs* case (below), at para 46. As to whether SGA, s 11(4) might apply by analogy, see Palmer (1983) 46 MLR at 626–7.

119  *Feldarol Foundry Plc v Hermes Leasing (London) Ltd* [2004] EWCA Civ 747, CA.

120  *Jackson v Chrysler Acceptances Ltd* [1978] RTR 474, CA.

121  *Farnworth Finance Facilities Ltd v Attryde* [1970] 2 All ER 774, CA (repairs); *Porter v General Guarantee Corpn Ltd* [1982] RTR 384 (negotiations); and the *Alpha Chauffeurs* case (set out at para 14.12), at paras 44–5.

122  *Laurelgates v Lombard North Central* (1983) 133 NLJ 720; and see generally Mullan [1990] JBL 231. It has been recommended by the Law Commission that this position be allowed to continue: *Op. cit.*, para 5.46.

**[29.11] Rescission for misrepresentation**. The principles upon which a supply contract may be rescinded on the grounds that it was induced by misrepresentation have already been outlined (see paras 26.12–13). The effect of that misrepresentation subsequently becoming a term of the contract must now be considered. That incorporation will no longer *per se* bar the right to rescind for misrepresentation.[123] But will that right be lost where there is no right to rescind for breach of contract? The problem may arise (1) where there was never any right to rescind for the breach (see para 26.14), or (2) the right to rescind for breach has been lost by acceptance (see paras 29.05 and 29.10). In *Leaf v International Galleries Ltd*:[124]

> There was a misrepresentation that the painting sold was by Constable, and this became a term of the contract. Five years later the buyer discovered the truth, and immediately sought to rescind for misrepresentation. The Court of Appeal held that, even if there had been a right to rescind, it was barred by lapse of time.

Denning LJ assumed in the buyer's favour that the statement was a condition, pointed out that the right to reject for breach of condition had been lost by lapse of time (see para 29.07) and continued (at 90):

> 'An innocent misrepresentation is much less potent than a breach of condition; and a claim to rescission for innocent misrepresentation must at any rate be barred when the right to reject for breach of condition is barred'.

His Lordship was careful to confine his remarks to innocent misrepresentations which became conditions of that contract;[125] but in *Long v Lloyd* (set out at para 26.13) they were applied by the Court of Appeal to acts by the buyer which would have amounted to acceptance after breach,[126] although no breach of condition was alleged.[127] Even granted this, certain problems arise. *First*, does the rule apply to fraudulent misrepresentations[128] or to innominate terms (see para 11.05)? *Second*, does it follow that at common law, if the misrepresentation become a warranty, the right to rescind for misrepresentation is lost?[129] *Third*, does the rule apply to quasi-sale, hp and simple hiring transactions?

# RESTITUTION[130]

**[29.12]** Suppose one party (A) has performed his side of a 'contract' with B, so conferring a benefit B, but has not received the consideration for which he

---

123 S 1(a) of the Misrepresentation Act 1967: see para 26.14.
124 [1950] 2 KB 86; [1950] 1 All ER 693, CA. See also *Miljus v Yamazaki Machinery UK Ltd* [1997] CLY 992, OR.
125 The other members of the CA do not appear to have gone any further than to say that it was too late to rescind for misrepresentation. See further Treitel, *Law of Contract*, 11th edn, 384.
126 As to what would have amounted to acceptance by the buyer after breach, see generally, para 29.05.
127 Grunfeld (1958) 21 MLR 550, 555.
128 Treitel, *Op. cit.*, 384–5.
129 If so, s 1 of the Misrepresentation Act 1967 appears to grant the representee a new right of rescission: see para 26.14. But see Treitel, *Op. cit.*, 375–6.
130 See generally, Tettenborn, *Law of Restitution*, 3rd edn.

bargained. In the following circumstances, A may be able to seek restitution from B by an action in debt,[131] depending on the nature of that benefit conferred:[132]

1. *Benefit in money.* In our context, this situation will typically arise where A is a buyer or hirer who has paid the price or rent. Where A has obtained no part of that for which he bargained, he may be able to recover any money paid on grounds of total failure of consideration.[133] In relation to such claims by a buyer[134] or hirer of goods, two questions arise: (1) as to the relationship of this remedy to rescission (see para 29.13); and (2) as to what amounts to a total failure of consideration (see para 29.15).

2. *Benefit in kind.* In a contract for the supply of goods, such a situation may arise where the supplier (A) has supplied goods for which he cannot recover the agreed price or rent (see para 27.16, *et seq.*), but is instead suing for what the service is worth (*quantum meruit*: see para 27.15A).

**[29.13/14] Relationship to rescission.** Clearly, such a claim in debt by a buyer or hirer to recover sums paid will lie for total failure of consideration (see para 29.15) where the parties never reached agreement;[135] or where their agreement was rendered void *ab initio* on grounds of mistake or misrepresentation;[136] or sometimes where one party is a minor (see para 10.19). But what if the contract was valid when made but was subsequently terminated before it was fully executed? In the *Fibrosa* case,[137] the House of Lords said that the quasi-contractual test was not whether there had ever been a contract, but whether it had ever been performed: it followed that no such claim lay where a contract was illegal (see para 10.20); but it was available in the event of frustration,[138] or abandonment,[139] or rescission for breach,[140] whether or not the goods have been delivered to him (see para 29.18). Indeed, in the *Kwei Tek Chao* case[141] Devlin J said that (at 475):

> 'If the goods have been properly rejected, and the price has already been paid in advance, the proper way of recovering the money back is by an action for money paid for a consideration which has wholly failed . . .; but that form of action is governed by exactly the same rules with regard to affirming or avoiding the transaction as in any other case.'

It is, of course, logical that the innocent party must elect to rescind before he can recover the price paid on grounds of total failure of consideration; and that the

---

131 For the distinction between actions in debt and for damages, see para 27.15A.

132 This must be distinguished from the process of restitution on conviction: see para 24.25.

133 See generally Treitel, *Law of Contract*, 11th edn, 1049, *et seq.*; Chitty *On Contract*, 28th edn, para 30.048, *et seq.*; Goff and Jones, *Law of Restitution*, 6th edn, paras 20.10 and 20.35.

134 The SGA preserves the common law in this respect: s 54.

135 E.g. *Branwhite v Worcester Finance Ltd* [1969] 1 AC 552, HL: see para 16.05.

136 This would seem to follow from *Bell v Lever Brothers Ltd* [1932] AC 161, HL (not a goods case); and see Treitel, *Law of Contract*, 11th edn, 1057–61.

137 [1943] AC 32; [1942] 2 All ER 122, HL.

138 The decision in the *Fibrosa* case, (above); and see para 22.17.

139 Similarly, where a wholly executory contract is rescinded by mutual agreement: see generally, para 26.18.

140 See para 26.15. To secure his deposit against his seller's insolvency, a buyer should therefore insist on paying it into a joint trust account (see para 19.23).

141 The *Kwei Tek Chao* case [1954] 2 QB 459. This is accepted by most of the authorities as being the position: see Goff and Jones, *Law of Restitution*, 6th edn, paras 1.062 and 20.013.

quasi-contractual claim is not open to him if he affirms, or if he cannot rescind.[141] As such a view would entail making the availability of the quasi-contractual remedy dependent on the right to rescind,[142] it is difficulty to reconcile with the cases where the transferor has no title to the goods (see para 12.06A): in *Rowland v Divall*[143] the plaintiff had resold the car to X, who had been in possession for two months;[144] and in *Butterworth v Kingsway Motors Ltd* (set out at para 12.06) Pearson J held that the intermediate buyers had lost the right to rescind, but that Butterworth was entitled to rescind notwithstanding his eleven months' use of the car.[145]

So far, we have been considering the right of the innocent buyer or hirer to recover the price paid on grounds of total failure of consideration. Suppose the buyer or hirer were the guilty party. Assuming that the supplier elects to rescind (see para 29.16), can the buyer or hirer recover any sums paid on grounds of total failure of consideration? In bailment, the hirer's possession may preclude any failure of consideration being total.[146] In sale, the early cases refused to countenance such a claim; but we have seen that Stable J subsequently drew a distinction between a deposit and a part-payment, holding that the sum was recoverable in the latter case (see paras 27.19–20).

**[29.15] Total failure**.[147] The courts have always stressed that money paid under a contract can only be recovered under this ground if the failure of consideration was total. The vital thing is not whether there was rendered to the payee **any** benefit, but whether there was rendered to him any part of **that** benefit which he was entitled to expect by way of performance of the contract.[148] Thus, a buyer to whom no title is passed suffers a total failure of consideration;[149] as does a buyer of computer hardware to whom no software is delivered,[150] or a buyer who only uses goods long enough to discover that they are defective.[151] On the other hand, it has been held that a hirer under an hp agreement cannot so recover sums paid under the agreement where that agreement is subsequently determined but he has in the meantime enjoyed both possession of the goods under the bailment[152] and a valid option to purchase.[153] However, he may do so where there has never been any agreement,

---

142 The limitations on the right to rescind are considered at paras 26.13 and 29.11.

143 Set out at para 12.05. But compare *Linz v Electric Wire Co Ltd* [1948] AC 371, PC.

144 It is arguable that the resale should not bar rescission because it was cancelled by mutual agreement: see also para 29.06.

145 It is a little difficult to accept this in the light of other authorities, though the issue is essentially one of fact: see para 29.07.

146 But the problem is not so avoided where the hirer wrongfully refuses ever to take possession but has already paid a first instalment of rent. *Aliter* a deposit (see para 27.19).

147 See Treitel, *Law of Contract*, 11th edn, 1049, *et seq*. The rule that failure of consideration must be total may be re-considered: see *Chitty On Contract*, 28th edn, para 30-057.

148 *Rover International Ltd v Cannon Film Sales Ltd* (No. 3) [1989] 3 All ER 423, CA (not a sale case). See generally Samek (1959) 33 ALJ 392, 397; Chitty, *Op. cit.*, para 30-053. In the case of frustration, this rule has been modified by the Law Reform (Frustrated Contracts) Act 1943: see para 22.19. As to free gifts, see para 2.08.

149 *Rowland v Divall* (set out at para 12.05).

150 *South West Water Services Ltd v International Computers Ltd* [2000] CLY 870.

151 *Baldry v Marshall Ltd* [1925] 1 QB 260, CA.

152 *Yeoman Credit Ltd v Apps* (set out at para 29.25).

153 *Kelly v Lombard Banking Ltd* [1958] 3 All ER 713, CA.

notwithstanding his use of the goods for three months,[154] or where there is rescission of a consumer sale within new Pt 5A of the SGA (see para 20.02B).

However, the scope of the quasi-contractual remedy has been extended to several situations where the claimant has received part of the benefit for which he has bargained. *Firstly*, where the contract is divisible (see para 23.24), the courts have applied the doctrine to each part individually, so that there might be a total failure in respect of one or more parts notwithstanding that some other parts may have been performed.[155] *Secondly*, where under a single indivisible contract an obligation is entire (see para 26.02), there is a total failure of consideration although that obligation has been partially performed because the other party has bargained exclusively for a complete performance.[156] *Thirdly*, the parties can always agree that the partial failure of the whole consideration is to be treated as a total failure of part of the consideration;[157] and, where the partial performance of the seller shows an intention to repudiate (see para 23.25), the buyer will have an option to do so.[158] *Fourthly*, where a sum is paid in advance of delivery of the goods, it is recoverable if paid by way of part-payment rather than a deposit (see para 27.19). *Fifthly*, there is the matter of making restitution (see para 29.16).

**[29.16] Making restitution.** Even where the case cannot be brought within any of the above rules (see para 29.15), the law does not say that the receipt of part of the benefit for which the buyer or hirer has bargained must be fatal to his quasi-contractual claim, e.g. where defective goods are delivered.[159] As a first step, he must rescind the contract (see para 29.14), which will usually involve rejecting the goods (see para 29.03); but not, perhaps, where the goods are at the supplier's risk,[160] nor where the inability to return the goods is caused by the supplier's breach.[161] As it has been put, the claimant must make *restitutio* as a condition precedent to his claim.[162] On the other hand, making *restitutio* may not be sufficient, because the contract may require the supplier to do things other than transfer a returnable benefit, as where the contract involves the provision of services. In *Stocznia No. 1* case (see para 26.16A) the contractual consideration required of S was to design, build and supply one ship under each contract. Whilst the contracts had been rescinded before the property in the ships had passed to B, nevertheless S had already designed and started to build the ships, so there had been no total failure of consideration (see para 29.15). What mattered was not whether B had **received** any part of the contracted-for benefit, but whether S had **performed** any significant part of his duties. However, this causes difficulty with regard to both customised goods,

---

154 *Branwhite v Worcester Finance Ltd* [1969] 1 AC 552, HL: see para 16.05.

155 *Rugg v Minett* (set out at para 20.11). See also Chitty, *Op. cit.*, para 29.040.

156 *Giles v Edwards* (1797) 7 Term Rep 181: explained by Goff and Jones, *Law of Restitution*, 6th edn, para 20.10. *Contra* where the obligation broken is not an entire one.

157 See *Benjamin on Sale*, 8th edn, 1950, 419. See generally, para 26.18.

158 *Behrend & Co v Produce Brokers Ltd* (set out at para 13.04).

159 E.g. *Baldry v Marshall Ltd* [1925] 1 QB 260, CA.

160 See *Benjamin's Sale of Goods*, 6th edn, para 12-057.

161 A possible explanation of *Rowland v Divall* (below; see para 12.11).

162 *Towers v Barrett* (1786) 1 Term Rep 133.

e.g. a tailored suit, and intermediate enjoyment of possession. It is easy to see that the enjoyment should be ignored where it was induced by the supplier's fraud, but the courts have also adopted this approach where the supplier is innocently in breach of the implied condition as to title.[163]

# AN ACTION FOR DAMAGES

[29.17] A buyer or hirer may have at his disposal an action for damages against his supplier or some third party within the limitation period (see para 26.17) as follows: (1) as against the supplier for breach of the supply contract (see para 29.18) or some collateral contract, or in tort, or under the Misrepresentation Act;[164] and (2) as against a third party for breach of a collateral contract, or in tort.[164] Whilst the general principles for the measurement of damages have been previously outlined (see para 27.28, *et seq.*), two points may be made here concerning the measure of damages available to an innocent buyer induced to enter a contract by the misrepresentation of the seller: first, the *prima facie* measure of damages may be the difference between the contract price and value of the goods at the time any misrepresentation was discovered;[165] and second, the mitigation rule (see paras 27.44–5) will not require the innocent buyer to bring into account any profit made on an uncontemplated sub-sale.[166]

[29.18] **For breach of contract.** In this section it is proposed to concentrate on the right of the buyer or hirer to damages for breach of the supply contract. The rules in this regard will differ according to whether or not the breach amounts to a total failure to deliver the goods. *Prima facie*, the buyer or hirer will have a right of action for damages for non-delivery of the goods where no goods are delivered at all,[167] or where the goods tendered by the supplier are lawfully rejected and the contract rescinded on grounds that they do not conform with the contract in quantity or quality, or any other matter (see para 29.03); and he will also be able to recover any part of the price paid on grounds of total failure of consideration.[168] However, whereas the supplier has an action in contract for price or rent (see para 27.16, *et seq.*), an action to recover the contract goods themselves is seldom available to the buyer or hirer,[169] unless he deals as consumer (see para 29.02A); and to this extent he may be deprived of his so-called 'consumer surplus'.[170]

---

163 *Rowland v Divall* (set out at para 12.05); *Butterworth v Kingsway Motors Ltd* (set out at para 12.06).

164 For collateral contracts, see para 17.09; for tort actions, see para 29.24; and for the 1967 Act, see para 17.10.

165 *Naughton v O'Callaghan* [1990] 3 All ER 191 (55 MLR at 699–701; Bridge, *Sale of Goods*, 593–4).

166 *Hussey v Eels* [1990] 2 QB 227, CA (not a goods case; [1990] CLJ 394).

167 For the duty to deliver, see para 23.05, *et seq.*

168 *Comptoir D'Achat v Luis de Ridder* [1949] AC 293, HL: see generally, para 29.13.

169 Whether framed as an action for the specific performance of the contract or in tort: see paras 29.38 and 29.24. But, if the supplier has wrongfully resold, could the buyer trace the proceeds of the second sale (see para 27.14; cf. *Lake v Bayliss* [1974] 2 All ER 1114)?

170 His subjective element of enjoyment: see Harris, Ogus and Phillips (1979) 95 LQR 581; Macdonald (1996) 15 Tr L 239.

## Damages for non-delivery

**[29.19]  Sale: the cause of action**. The counterpart to the seller's action for damages for non-acceptance under s 50 of the SGA (see paras 27.24–27) is the buyer's action for non-delivery under s 51. Section 51(1) provides:

> 'Where the seller wrongfully neglects or refuses to deliver the goods to the buyer, the buyer may maintain an action against the seller for damages for non-delivery.'

This provision does not apply to a mere delay in tendering delivery, where damages will necessarily be assessed on different lines (see para 29.28); but it may be a nice question whether the delay is so great as to amount to a non-delivery.[171] Where there is a 'neglect or refusal to deliver' within the meaning of s 51(1), the SGA establishes a *prima facie* measure of damages in a manner similar to that used where the buyer is at fault in not taking delivery.[172] The law assumes that the buyer will mitigate his loss[173] if he can by going out into any available market and buying a substitute; so that, leaving aside the possibility of an express provision as to the amount payable by the seller,[174] the loss will *prima facie* be quantified by reference to whether there is at the place of delivery an available market (see para 27.34) in which the buyer may purchase substitute goods.[175] There may additionally be consequential loss (see para 29.23).

**[29.20]  Where there is an available market**. Section 51(3) of the SGA provides:

> 'Where there is an available market for the goods in question the measure of damages is *prima facie* to be ascertained by the difference between the contract price and the market or current price of the goods at the time or times when they ought to be delivered, or, if no time was fixed, then at the time of the refusal to deliver.'

This 'duty' on the disappointed buyer to shop around is the converse of the position of an innocent seller faced with a buyer's breach (see SGA, s 50(3): para 27.35); and it should be compared with the position as regards a late delivery (see para 29.28). The onus of proving the buying price in that market is on the buyer and the amount recoverable is as follows:

(1)  If the market price is above the contract price, the buyer is *prima facie* entitled under s 51(3) to the difference between the two;[176] and any subsales by the buyer must be ignored, so that it is irrelevant that he has resold at an intermediate[177] or even a higher[178] price. If the buyer buys on the market at above

---

171  For this reason it is illogical to use the delivery date in the market rule: the buyer may not then know whether he is facing a late delivery or a non-delivery.

172  The first rule in *Hadley v Baxendale* is set out in s 51(2) and the second rule referred to in s 54. Cf. s 50(2): see para 27.42. Cf. para 29.26.

173  As to the mitigation rule, see paras 27.44–5.

174  A liquidated damages clause (see para 27.24), which may amount to an exclusion clause (see Chap 18) or offend the rule against penalties: see para 27.25, *et seq*.

175  In practice, the courts have been fairly generous in deciding whether (a) the market is available and (b) what is a substitute: see generally Lawson (1969) 43 ALJ 52, 59–61. As to where there is no available market, see para 29.22.

176  *The Naxos* [1990] 3 All ER 641, HL.

177  *Williams Brothers v Agius Ltd* [1914] AC 510, HL.

178  *Williams v Reynolds* (1865) 6 B & S 495.

the market price, he cannot recover that extra expenditure because he has not mitigated his loss;[179] but, if he buys at below the market price, he will only recover his actual loss.[180]

(2) If the market price is equal to or below the contract price, the intention of s 51(3) is presumably that the buyer will only receive nominal damages because he would suffer no loss by buying in the market.[180] Unlike the predicament of the seller (see para 27.35), this result will usually be fair and is therefore normally adopted by the courts.

Thus, the *prima facie* measure of damages for non-delivery is the amount by which the **market price** exceeds the **contract price** at the stipulated date[181] and place for delivery of the goods.[182] If the contract provides for delivery within a specified period, the last possible moment at which the seller is entitled to tender delivery is taken;[183] and, if delivery is to be by instalments (see paras 23.24–25), the market price is fixed separately for each instalment at the time when it is due.[184] The provision that, if no time is fixed for delivery, the time of refusal to deliver is to be taken ought on principle to be relevant where delivery is to be made as required by the buyer;[185] but it is inapplicable where there is an anticipatory breach (see para 29.21). Finally, there is the question whether the buyer who has paid the price can be expected to go into the market and buy against the contract, which raises questions of remoteness and mitigation (see paras 27.42 and 27.44). If the buyer can be expected to buy a replacement, the above rules should apply; but otherwise, damages are presumably assessed on the basis that there is no market available to him.[186]

**[29.21] Anticipatory breach**. Where the supplier is in anticipatory breach (see para 26.01), the foregoing *prima facie* rule for assessing damages for non-delivery is altered in the following respects: (1) the final limb of s 51(3) is ignored, the market price always being taken when the goods ought to be delivered;[187] and (2) the operation of s 51(3) is suspended until the buyer elects to accept the repudiation,[188] so possibly enabling the buyer to prolong the seller's duty to deliver more or less indefinitely.[189] When the buyer does elect to accept the repudiation, the position is

---

179 *Gainsford v Carroll* (1824) 2 B & C 624; and para 27.44.

180 *Pagnan and Fratelli v Corbisa Industrial Agropacuaria Limitada* [1971] 1 All ER 165, CA (discussed by Atiyah, *Sale of Goods*, 10th edn, 492). For argument that this is difficult to apply to (commercial) buyers making multiple purchases, see Goode, *Commercial Law*, 3rd edn, 387–8.

181 *Toepfer v Cremer* [1975] 2 Lloyd's Rep 118, CA. This may be extended at the request of the seller (*Ogle v Earl of Vane* (1868) LR 3 QB 272, Ex Ch); or whilst there are negotiations for a settlement; or the seller reasonably considers his position (Atiyah, *Op. cit.*, 536).

182 *Melachrino v Nickoll and Knight* [1920] 1 KB 693; *ABD (Metal and Waste) Ltd v Anglo Chemical Co* [1955] 2 Lloyd's Rep 456. See further Goode, *Op. cit.*, 368–70. If this is a foreign country, there will be a foreign currency element involved: see para 27.29.

183 See *Leigh v Paterson* (1818) 8 Taunt 540.

184 See *Brown v Muller* (1872) LR 7 Exch 319; *Roper v Johnson* (1873) LR 8 CP 167.

185 However, a tendency to ignore the last words of ss 50(3) and 51(3) has been noted: Atiyah, *Op. cit.*, 493–4.

186 But see *McGregor on Damages*, 16th edn, para 831; Street, *Law of Damages*, 217–18.

187 *Millett v Van Heek & Co* [1921] 2 KB 369, CA; the *Tai Hing Cotton Mill* case (see below).

188 There is no duty to mitigate by buying in before the delivery date: *Brown v Muller* (1872) LR Exch 319, DC.

189 The *Tai Hing Cotton Mill* case [1979] AC 91, [1978] 1 All ER 515, PC.

as follows:[190] if the market is rising and the buyer elects to rescind, either immediately on repudiation or at a later time prior to the time of performance, he is then under a duty to mitigate his loss from the date of his election by purchasing substitute goods in the market at that date;[191] but, if the market is falling and the buyer similarly elects to rescind either immediately or at an intermediate date, he is only entitled to the amount by which that price then exceeds the contract price as that is his actual loss.[192]

[29.22] **Where there is no available market**. There may be no available market, perhaps because the buyer has specifically subsold the same goods, or demand exceeds supply, or no reasonable substitute was available.[193] In such cases, s 51(3) is inapplicable,[194] and the court must make the best estimate it can with a view to putting the disappointed buyer in the situation in which he would have been if the contract had been performed (see para 27.28). To some extent, this depends on the non-remote purpose for which the goods were required;[195] so a wholesale buyer has been given a normal trade mark-up.[196] In other cases, it may be appropriate to award the buyer the amount by which the value at the date of breach exceeds the contract price; and, if the buyer has effected a subsale, the subsale price is evidence of that value,[197] but not conclusive of that value.[198] Even the realisable scrap value has been given.[199]

[29.23] **Consequential loss**. This will be 'special damage' under s 54. Under his reliance interest (see para 27.28), the disappointed buyer could recover his expenses, such as those for carriage of the goods[200] and administration.[201] However, the more typical situation is one where the buyer is looking to recover his actual loss of the profit he expected to make on a subsale. The major difficulty here is whether the subsale is too remote (see generally, paras 27.41–43); and, where the buyer is a consumer, the circumstances where his seller should contemplate such a subsale would seem to be too unusual to be pursued here.[202]

[29.24] **An action in tort**. Besides amounting to a breach of contract, non-delivery by the seller may also enable the buyer to maintain an action in tort for wrongful interference with goods (see paras 19.04–06). Where the buyer is suing a third party in tort, the measure of his damages is *prima facie* the value of the goods (see

---

190 These qualifications apply conversely where the buyer is in anticipatory breach: see *McGregor on Damages*, 16th edn, para 930.

191 *Melachrino v Nickoll and Knight* [1920] 1 KB 693, at 697. See also *Kaines (UK) v Osterreichische etc* [1993] 2 Lloyd's Rep 1, CA ([1994] JBL 152).

192 *Melachrino v Nickoll and Knight* (above). Cf. *Rother v Taysen* (1896) 12 TLR 211, CA.

193 As to available market, see generally, para 27.34.

194 As to s 51(3), see para 29.20.

195 Goode, *Commercial Law*, 3rd edn, 371. For remoteness, see para 27.42.

196 *Household Machines Ltd v Cosmos Exporters Ltd* [1947] KB 217.

197 *France v Gaudet* (1871) LR 6 QB 199, Ex Ch.

198 *The Arpad* [1934] P 189, CA; *Heskell v Continental Express Ltd* [1959] 1 All ER 1033.

199 *The Alecos* [1991] 1 Lloyd's Rep. 120, CA (criticised 107 LQR 364).

200 *Braude (London) Ltd v Porter* [1959] 2 Lloyd's Rep 161 (freight).

201 *Robert Stewart & Sons Ltd v Carapanayoti Ltd* [1962] 1 All ER 418.

202 For the rules, see Macleod, *Consumer Sales Law*, 1st edn, para 29.23.

para 27.30); but, where he is suing the unpaid seller, the damages will be reduced by the unpaid price. Thus, in *Chinery v Viall*:[203]

S sold some sheep on credit to B, but before delivery wrongfully resold and delivered them to X. B sued in contract and tort; and the court held—

(1) in contract, B was entitled to damages for non-delivery calculated on the excess of the market value over the contract price (£5);

(2) in tort, B was not entitled to the whole value of the sheep without deducting the unpaid price, but only the actual loss sustained (£5).

Since this case, it has become well established that a buyer suing for non-delivery cannot recover more in compensatory damages[204] by suing in tort than in contract.[205] Whilst it is clear that the buyer suing in tort is *prima facie* able to recover a non-remote loss of profit on a subsale,[206] it may be that the heads of damage in respect of which recovery may be made in a tort action are limited to the types of loss which would be non-remote in a contractual action,[207] so that to this extent it is irrelevant that the rules of remoteness may differ as between contract and tort.[208] Nor can the buyer suing in tort obtain an order for specific restitution (see para 24.26) where he could not obtain a decree of specific performance of the contract (see para 29.38).

**[29.25] Hire purchase and hiring**. If the contract is one of simple hiring, the hirer will *prima facie* be entitled by way of damages to the amount by which the contract rate of hire is exceeded by the market rate at which the hirer could hire similar goods under similar terms. Logically, in the case of hp, the *prima facie* measure of damages should likewise be the amount by which the market hp price exceeds the contract hp price.[209] Whilst there has been no reported case where the measure of damages for physical non-delivery to a hirer under an hp agreement has been discussed,[210] the matter has been considered in relation to continuous breaches by the owner (see para 29.10). Clearly, a hirer who lawfully rejects the goods tendered and rescinds the contract is entitled to sue on the basis of non-delivery.[211] But what of a hirer who has accepted delivery? In *Yeoman Credit Ltd v Apps*:[212]

The consumer (C) entered into a directly financed hp transaction upon the dealer agreeing to do some repairs before delivery. After the car had been delivered, C ascertained that the repairs had not been done; and the car was found to have

---

203 (1869) 5 H & N 288.

204 What of exemplary damages, which are only available in torts?

205 See the authorities collected in Benjamin's *Sale of Goods*, 6th edn, para 17-101, fn 44.

206 See *France v Gaudet* (1871) LR 6 QB 199, Ex Ch.

207 *The Arpad* [1934] P 189, CA. See Goodhart (1937) 2 Univ of Tor LJ 1; *McGregor on Damages*, 17th edn, paras 6.097 and 33.065.

208 See para 27.43. Is the same true if contract damages would exceed tort damages?

209 Goode, *HP Law and Practice*, 2nd edn, 451–52. Even though the hirer could elect to terminate the agreement?

210 The issue arose in *Tommey v Finextra Ltd* (1962) 106 SJ 1012. See also *Kelly v Sovereign Leasing* [1995] CLY 720, Cty Ct.

211 But see *Farnworth Finance Facilities v Attryde* [1970] 2 All ER 774, CA.

212 [1962] 2 QB 508, [1961] 2 All ER 281, CA, discussed Goode, *HP Law & Practice*, 2nd edn, 456–8.

such an accumulation of latent defects as to render it unsafe and unroadworthy. C complained, but kept the car for five months and paid some instalments, hoping he could persuade the dealer to meet half the cost of the repairs. The plaintiff finance company (P) sued for arrears of instalments and C counterclaimed to recover the money he had paid on grounds of total failure of consideration.

The Court of Appeal implied into the hp agreement a common law condition as to fitness,[213] whose fundamental breach it said was outside the exclusion clause (see para 18.07) and held:

(1) That since C had approbated the contract by paying some instalments, there was no total failure of consideration (see para 29.15); and that P was therefore entitled to the hire-rent up to the moment of C's rejection of the goods (see para 27.21); but that

(2) C's rejection was lawful because there was a continuing breach of contract by P (but see para 29.10) and that C was also entitled to recover by way of damages the estimated sum that would be necessary to put the car into repair.[214]

However, this measure of damages appears closer to the measure applicable to breach of warranty than non-delivery; and the decision has been criticised on the grounds that the hirer could have no possible interest in repairing the goods after rescinding the contract.[215] Of course, this very dilemma spotlights the oddity of the doctrine of continuous breach; and the measure of damages where the hirer affirms is discussed below (see para 29.34).

## Damages for other breaches of contract

[29.26] In respect of sales, the rules governing actions by the buyer for damages for breaches of contract other than non-delivery have partially been given statutory form in s 53 of the SGA; and, insofar as s 53 reflects the common law, it is also applicable in quasi-sale, hp and simple hiring.[216] Section 53(1) provides:

'Where there is a breach of warranty by the seller, or where the buyer elects (or is compelled) to treat any breach of a condition on the part of the seller as a breach of warranty,[217] the buyer is not by reason only[218] of such breach of warranty entitled to reject the goods; but he may—

(a) set up against the seller the breach of warranty in diminution or extinction of the price, or

(b) maintain an action against the seller for damages for breach of warranty.'

---

213 For the statutory undertaking as to fitness, see para 14.07.

214 Harman and Davies LJJ had some doubts about the matter (at 524, 526). Compare *Porter v General Guarantee Corpn Ltd* [1982] RTR 384 (value of car and expenses).

215 Goode, *Op. cit.*, 456, 458; Guest, *Law of HP*, 283. *Contra* repair costs incurred whilst in possession: see para 29.34.

216 *UCB Leasing Ltd v Holtom* (set out at para 29.10).

217 This suggests that the draftsman thought that a condition became a warranty if the buyer only claimed damages; but this is not so: *Wallis, Son and Wells v Pratt and Haynes* (set out at para 11.04).

218 He may be able to reject for some other cause: see Chalmers, *Sale of Goods*, 18th edn, 242.

Section 53(1) envisages that the buyer may *prima facie*[219] be able to do one of two things:

(a) Set up the seller's breach of contract by way of an answer to the seller's action for the price. Technically, this is not a defence (set-off), but a cross-action (counterclaim),[220] and therefore must arise in respect of the same contract.[221]

(b) Maintain an action against the seller for breach of contract or tort,[222] in which case the mere existence of a potential counterclaim by the unpaid seller for the price will not *per se* justify reducing the damages by the price.[223]

These two are alternative, in the sense that the buyer cannot recover compensation in respect of the seller's breach and then set up that breach when sued for the price; and a decision that there was no warranty or no breach operates as *res judicata* (see para 26.17). However, in case the buyer's loss should exceed the price, s 53(4) says that:

> 'The fact that the buyer has set up the breach of warranty in diminution or extinction of the price does not prevent him from maintaining an action for the same breach of warranty if he has suffered further damage.'

The SGA also deals with the question of remoteness of damage in contract in a manner similar to that used in the other sections: the first rule in *Hadley v Baxendale* is set out in s 53(2) and the second rule referred to in s 54.[224] In relation to this remoteness issue, the courts have had difficulty in deciding whether subsales by the buyer were too remote to be taken into account in assessing his damages;[225] but, where the buyer is a consumer, the circumstances where his seller should contemplate such a subsale would seem to be too unusual to be pursued here.

In applying these rules, it is convenient to distinguish between the claims of the buyer or hirer in respect of the following: (a) defective title (see para 29.27); (b) late delivery (see para 29.28, *et seq.*); and (c) defective quality (see, para 29.32, *et seq*).

**[29.27] Actions in respect of a defective title**. Where the supplier is in breach of the implied undertaking that he has the right to sell the goods under a sale, quasi-sale or hp agreement,[226] the buyer or hirer who is evicted from possession by a person with a superior title[227] has a right of election as to the remedy he pursues (see paras 12.05–07): he may rescind the contract, recover the price on grounds of total failure of consideration and have his damages assessed on the basis of non-delivery (see below); or he may affirm the contract and recover by way of damages

---

219 In a consumer supply, ouster of this rule may be an unfair term: OFT, *Bulletin No. 14*, case 22: Grey Term (b): see para 11.16.
220 *Bright v Rogers* [1917] 1 KB 917, DC. For set-offs, see paras 7.23 and 23.14.
221 See *Bow McLacklan & Co v Ship Camosun* [1909] AC 597, PC.
222 See Benjamin's *Sale of Goods*, 6th edn, para 17-048.
223 *Gillard v Brittan* (1841) 8 M & W 575; *Healing (Sales) Pty Ltd v Inglis Electrix Pty Ltd* [1969] ALJR 533, HC. Compare non-delivery: para 29.12.
224 Cf. ss 50(2) and 51(2): set out at paras 27.24 and 29.19.
225 *Bence Graphics International Ltd v Fasson UK Ltd* [1998] QB 87; [1997] 1 All ER 979, CA (criticised by Bridge [1998] JBL 259).
226 See para 12.02. There is a necessarily different undertaking in respect of simple hiring agreements: see para 12.04A.
227 What if he is not evicted? See para 12.11.

under his 'reliance' interest the purchase or hp price[228] and any expenses.[229] Even where the supplier is merely in breach of warranty as to quiet possession or as to freedom from encumbrances, if the buyer or hirer is rightfully evicted from possession by a third party, the buyer or hirer is similarly entitled to recover under his 'reliance' interest the purchase or hp price[230] and any expenditure thrown away.[231]

Where the buyer or hirer might have made a profit from the goods, he may alternatively claim under his 'expectancy' interest.[232] If he can and does rescind, then damages are measured on the basis of non-delivery (see para 29.18). If not, it would appear that damages are assessed on the same basis as where the goods are defective in quality in respect of both the *prima facie* rule[233] and consequential loss (see para 29.35) flowing from the breach of an undertaking as to title.

## Actions in respect of a late delivery

[29.28] If the late delivery of goods supplied amounts to a repudiation (see para 26.15), the buyer may elect to rescind, in which case damages will be assessed on the basis of non-delivery (see para 29.18), though the duty to mitigate (see paras 27.44–45) may reduce these damages if the buyer or hirer has acted unreasonably.[234] On the other hand, where the buyer cannot or does not rescind, the action for damages is something of a hybrid: the *prima facie* measure of damages has much in common with claims for breach of warranty because there has been a delivery,[235] whereas the measure of damages for consequential loss is akin to that for non-delivery.[236] Presumably, the rules are similar in the case of late delivery of goods supplied under a quasi-sale, hp agreement or simple hiring.

*Prima facie measure on late delivery.* Whilst there is no statutory formulation in the SGA which specifically refers to the measure of damages recoverable for late delivery of goods sold, it would appear that once again the *prima facie* measure of damages depends on whether there is an available market (see para 27.34), though this time the assumption is that the buyer will sell the goods in such a market (see paras 29.29–30). Where an hp or simple hiring agreement contains the usual prohibition of sale by the hirer (see para 7.26), presumably there is no available market in which the hirer can sell the goods during the continuance of the agreement. Claims for consequential loss will be considered later (see para 29.31).

---

228 *Warman v Southern Counties Finance Corpn Ltd* (set out at para 12.07).
229 *Warman's* case (above); and *per* Singleton LJ in *Mason v Burningham* [1949] 2 KB 545, CA, at 560. And see Treitel, *Law of Contract*, 11th edn, 948.
230 *Lloyds and Scottish Finance Ltd v Modern Cars Ltd* (set out at para 12.14).
231 The *Lloyds & Scottish* case (above); *Mason v Burningham* (above).
232 The relationship of claims under the 'reliance' and 'expectancy' interest is explained at para 27.28.
233 *Louis Dreyfus Trading Ltd v Reliance Trading Ltd* [2004] 2 Lloyd's Rep 243. The *prima facie* rule for defective quality is considered at para 29.33.
234 *The Solholt* [1983] 1 Lloyd's Rep 605 (failure to accept the late tender of the ship reducing the damages to nil). This may always be a factor where the buyer has not already gone into the market and obtained a replacement: Atiyah, *Sale of Goods*, 10th edn, 542.
235 *Per* Lord Dunedin in *Williams Brothers v ET Agius Ltd* [1914] AC 550, HL at 522.
236 See *McGregor on Damages*, 17th edn, para 20.035.

*Distinction from non-delivery.* A significant difference between the two formulae for measuring damages in the event of a non-delivery or late delivery (see above) appears where the buyer or hirer made a bad bargain,[237] from which he can effectively escape by taking any opportunity to rescind. What is to happen where the buyer has lost the right to rescind through no fault of his own?[238]

**[29.29/30] Whether there is an available market**. The buyer or hirer will eventually obtain possession of the goods, so that his position is analogous to that where there is a breach of warranty of quality (see para 29.28). Where there is an available market, what the buyer or hirer has lost depends on the purpose for which he is acquiring the goods[239] and the duty to mitigate.[240] In the case of a private consumer, he will be obtaining the goods for use:[241] in this case, the appropriate measure of damages may be the loss of **use**, or cost of **hiring** a replacement, for the period of the delay.[242]

*Where there is no available market.* In this case, the measure of damages is *prima facie* the amount by which the **contract price** exceeds the **actual value** at the contractual time for delivery. In *Kwei Tek Chao v British Traders Ltd*,[243] Devlin J held as follows:

(a) *Prima facie*, the measure of damages for late delivery is the difference between the market values at the contractual and actual time of goods delivery (at 478) and document delivery.[244] In both cases, it is assumed that the buyer on discovering the breach will resell the goods on delivery to mitigate his loss, so that the relevant price is the selling price then (at 495, 497).

(b) Because of the Chinese embargo, there was no market in which the goods could be sold, so that the salvage value of the goods must be taken.

**[29.31] Consequential loss**. Naturally, the buyer may recover any money expended in reliance on the seller's promise, such as extra delivery charges,[245] or losses resulting from currency changes.[246] However, where he would have made a profit, the buyer may alternatively claim in respect of his expectancy interest;[247] and the major issue here is whether he may recover anything beyond the *prima facie* measure in respect of his intended use or subsale of the goods, subject always to the duty to mitigate (see paras 27.44–45).

---

237 Either because the market price falls, or he agreed to pay too much in the first place: see para 27.28.

238 A *fortiori* where it is the act of the seller which has deprived him of the right to rescind.

239 Goode, *Commercial Law*, 3rd edn, 374. Cf. para 29.34.

240 *The Solholt* [1983] 1 Lloyd's Rep 605, CA, as explained by Atiyah, *Sale of Goods*, 10th edn, 542.

241 *Contra* a commercial buyer buying for resale, where the *prima facie* measure is the amount by which the market value at the contractual time of delivery exceeds the market value at the actual time of delivery: see Goode, *Op. cit.*, 375–6.

242 The *Victoria Laundry* case (loss of profit: set out at para 29.31); and see Goode, *Op. cit.*, 376.

243 [1954] 2 QB 459; [1954] 3 All ER 165.

244 As the buyer had not rejected, the price at which he could have bought substitute goods in Hong Kong was irrelevant (at 479). Compare non-delivery: para 29.20.

245 *Borries v Hutchinson* (1865) 18 CBNS 445 (freight).

246 *Aruna Mills Ltd v Dhanrajmal Gobindram* [1968] 1 All ER 113.

247 The relationship of claims under the 'reliance' and 'expectancy' interest is explained at para 27.28.

1. *Loss of use.* Obviously, the buyer may recover in respect of any expenses incurred as a result of the loss of use;[248] but he may also recover in respect of loss of profit he would have made from use of the goods. In *Victoria Laundry Ltd v Newman Industries Ltd:*[249]

> B decided to obtain a larger boiler to expand their laundry business in view of the prevailing shortage of laundry facilities. B contracted to buy one from S, who agreed to deliver and install it on B's premises. S knew that B needed the boiler in connection with their laundry business, though not the exact use to which it was to be put. When the boiler was delivered some five months late, B claimed damages for loss of profit as follows: (1) £16 per week for the new customers he would have taken on; and (2) £262 per week which he would have earned on a specially lucrative dyeing contract with the Ministry of Supply.

The Court of Appeal unanimously held that the seller could have foreseen that loss of business profits would be liable to result from the delay,[250] but did not know of the contract with the Ministry of Supply; and they therefore held that the buyer could recover (1) but not (2).

2. *Loss on a subsale.* Where the seller knew of the subsale of the goods *per se* and the sub-contract delivery date, he has been held liable for the loss of profit on the subsale.[251] However, where the buyer is a consumer, the circumstances where his seller should contemplate such a subsale would seem to be too unusual to be pursued here.

## Actions in respect of a defect in quality

**[29.32]** The present discussion is concerned with the situation where the goods delivered by the supplier do not comply with the contract description as to quality or undertakings as to quality (see Chaps 13 and 14), but the buyer or hirer elects, or is required (see para 29.03), to accept the goods and claim damages.[252] This situation must be distinguished from the following cases: *firstly*, where the buyer or hirer accepts the goods delivered in full satisfaction of his rights under the contract, in which case those rights are thereby extinguished (see para 26.18); and *secondly*, where the buyer or hirer properly rejects the goods, this is treated in law as a non-delivery (see para 29.18). The *prima facie* measure of damages for contractual defects of quality[253] is the shortfall between the **warranted** and **actual value** of the goods in the hands of the buyer or hirer. Additionally, claims for consequential loss are perhaps more common in this context than in respect of non-delivery (see para 29.35).

---

248  *Henderson v Meyer* (1941) 46 Com Cas 209.

249  [1949] 2 KB 528, [1949] 1 All ER 997, CA.

250  For criticism of this test of remoteness, see para 27.42.

251  *Hydraulic Engineering G v McHaffie* (1878) 4 QBD 670, CA.

252  The ordinary common law rules of remoteness and measure of damage obtain: see generally, para 27.24, *et seq.*

253  SGA, s 53(3): set out below. As to the calculation of the *prima facie* measure of damages in the case of supply contracts, see paras 29.33–4. As to misrepresentations, see para 29.17.

The *prima facie* measure must be contrasted with that available in non-delivery claims, the latter being the amount by which the **market price** exceeds the **contract price** (see para 29.20), if any.[254] A significant difference between the two formulae for measuring damages in the event of a non-delivery or defective delivery (see above) appears where the buyer or hirer made a bad bargain (see para 27.28), from which he can effectively escape by taking any opportunity to rescind (see para 29.28). However, it is clear that where the buyer with knowledge of the breach accepts the goods, he will recover only the normal measure of damages for breach of warranty;[255] but it has been argued that this should not be the case where he accepts the goods without knowledge of the breach.[256]

**[29.33] The *prima facie* measure in sale.** Where in a contract of sale (or presumably quasi-sale?) the price has been paid, s 53(3) of the SGA provides as follows:

> 'In the case of a breach of warranty of quality such loss is *prima facie*[257] the difference between the value of the goods at the time of delivery to the buyer and the value they would have had if they had fulfilled the warranty.'

1. *The warranted value.* As in actions for non-delivery or late delivery, the process of ascertaining the warranted value depends on whether or not there is an available market.[258] The contract price and any subsale price[259] are merely evidence of the value of the goods as warranted.[260]

2. *The actual value.* There may be evidence of the actual value of the goods to a hypothetical buyer with knowledge of the breach, e.g. where there is a recognised price for 'seconds'; and the courts may accept this in supporting the common commercial practice of taking defective goods at an allowance, perhaps fixed by an arbitrator.[261] Where the actual value cannot be ascertained, the courts may award damages based on the cost of repairs needed to bring the goods up to the contractual standard;[262] and, if that exceeds the warranted value, the actual value will be nil.[263] The buyer may sometimes be entitled to the cost of buying a substitute;[264] but, where this purchase exceeds the duty

---

254 The *Bernstein* case [1987] 2 All ER 220: nil difference.

255 *Vargas Pena Apezteguia y Cia Saic v Peter Cremer GmbH* [1987] 1 Lloyd's Rep 394.

256 Atiyah, *Sale of Goods*, 10th edn, 547.

257 But the rule may be ousted, as by a liquidated damages clause (see para 27.24): the *Watford Electronics* case (see para 18.21).

258 As to the *prima facie* measure for non-delivery, see paras 29.20–2; and as to late delivery, see paras 29.29–30.

259 *Loder v Kefak* (1857) 3 CBNS 128 (contract price); *Clare v Maynard* (1835) 6 Ad & El 519 (subsale price).

260 *Slater v Hoyle & Smith Ltd* [1920] 2 KB 11, CA; discussed by Benjamin, *Sale of Goods*, 6th edn, paras 17.056–7.

261 *Biggin & Co Ltd v Permanite Ltd* [1951] 1 KB 422 (affd on different grounds). But the courts are wary of such evidence: Benjamin, *Op. cit.*, para 17-052; and see *Jones v Just* (below).

262 *Minster Trust Ltd v Traps Tractors Ltd* [1954] 3 All ER 136; *Keeley v Guy McDonald* (1984) 134 NLJ 552. As to where the cost of repairs exceeds the value of the goods, see Bridge, *Sale of Goods*, 593.

263 *Bridge v Wain* (1816) 1 Star 504. So the buyer will then be awarded as *prima facie* damages the market value of the goods in their warranted state. Cf. motor insurance 'write-offs'.

264 *British Westinghouse Electric and Manufacturing Co Ltd v Underground Electric Co Ltd* [1912] AC 673, HL. As to buying a substitute part, see *Bacon v Cooper (Metals) Ltd* [1982] 1 All ER 397. As to an allowance for use, see *Kanakaris v Furniture Land Ltd* [2006] 1 CL 474, Cty Ct.

to mitigate (see para 27.44), the question arises whether his damages should be reduced to take account of any extra profit (see para 27.29). Where the defect in the goods is a legal one (see para 14.21), the courts have rejected the argument that an illegal motor vehicle had a nil value.[265]

In providing that these two values are to be taken at the contractual time and place of delivery, SGA, s 53(3) is clearly reflecting the common law.[266] However, this does not always make good sense and may be displaced, as where the defect is only discovered by a sub-buyer,[267] or the breached warranty refers to a future state.[268]

**[29.34] The *prima facie* measure in hiring and hp**. In the case of a simple hiring (leasing), the *prima facie* measure of damages should be like that for late delivery (see para 29.29); that is, what the buyer or hirer has lost should depends on the purpose for which he is acquiring the goods and the duty to mitigate.

(1) Where a buyer or hirer is obtaining the goods for **use**, the appropriate measure of damages may be the loss of **use**, or cost of **hiring** a replacement.

(2) Where a buyer is **buying** for resale, the normal *prima facie* measure is the amount by which the **market value** at the contractual time for delivery exceeds the **market value** at the actual time of delivery, the relevant price being the selling price.[269]

However, in the case of hp allowance has to be made for the option to purchase; and, at first sight, it might appear that the *prima facie* measure should be the amount by which the hp price of the goods in their **warranted** condition exceeds the hp price obtainable in their **actual** condition.[270] Whilst this may be appropriate where the hirer is suing a third party under a collateral contract,[271] it ignores the possibility that the hiring may be determined, in which case the hirer would retain damages for a loss he has not suffered. All too commonly, this dilemma will arise because the hirer ceases payment of instalments on discovering the defects and the owner thereupon terminates the agreement.[272] Thus, in *Charterhouse Credit Ltd v Tolly*:[273]

> The hirer under an hp agreement elected to affirm the agreement after discovering the owner's breach (in providing an unroadworthy vehicle). He paid £50 in repairs, but failed to pay any instalments. The owner therefore terminated the agreement, and claimed damages for breach; and the hirer counterclaimed for damages in respect of the defective state of the vehicle. The Court of Appeal unanimously held:

265 *Bramhill v Edwards* (set out at para 14.21), *per* Auld LJ at para 60, *obiter*.

266 *Jones v Just* (1868) LR 3 QB 197 (after contract date market rose so that buyer able to resell damaged lamp at almost warranted value at delivery date). See Benjamin, *Op. cit.*, para 17.053.

267 *Van den Hurk v Martens & Co Ltd* [1920] 1 KB 850 (chemicals packed in drums and contemplated will not be examined until reach sub-buyer).

268 *Ashworth v Wells* (1898) 14 TLR 227, CA (orchid sold warranted to flower purple: two years later first flowering white).

269 *McGregor on Damages*, 17th edn, para 21.03. Cf. the sale rule: see 29.33.

270 Atiyah, *Sale of Goods*, 6th edn, 411 (chapter dropped from later editions).

271 *Brown v Sheen and Richmond Car Sales Ltd* [1950] 1 All ER 1102: para 16.13; *Yeoman Credit Ltd v Odgers* [1962] 1 All ER 789, CA.

272 Arguably, the hirer's action arises from impecuniosity due to the need to meet repair bills and might be ignored: see para 27.29.

273 [1963] 2 QB 683; [1963] 2 All ER 433, CA; *UCB Leasing Ltd v Holtom* (set out at para 29.10).

(1)  As the owner had terminated, the hirer was only liable for arrears of instalments because he only caused the loss of those instalments (see para 27.29);

(2)  The appropriate measure of the hirer's damages was not the cost of repairs,[274] but the cost of hiring a similar car on similar terms.[275]

Actually, Upjohn LJ suggested that, if the owner had not terminated, the hirer would only have been entitled to the amount required to put the vehicle in a proper state of repair, plus damages for loss of use.[276] However, in this circumstance repair will not always be a realistic option: so in *Doobey v Mohabeer*,[277] where the machine was useless in its defective condition, the Privy Council held that, after affirming the hp agreement, the hirer was entitled to recover by way of damages all the sums paid or payable under the agreement.[278] Yet where the contract remains afoot, the basic dilemma outlined remains.[279] A form of apportionment has been suggested.[280]

**[29.35/6] Consequential loss**. Naturally, the buyer or hirer may recover any money thrown away in reliance on the promise of the supplier.[281] However, when he would have made a profit, the buyer or hirer may, alternatively, claim the value of performance.[282] Here, he may have less opportunity to mitigate his loss as the breach may be less obvious than in the case of non-delivery or late delivery (see respectively, paras 29.23 and 29.31); and to this extent there may be greater scope for recovery in respect of consequential loss. Three difficulties have arisen: *firstly*, whether the supplier's breach has caused the loss;[283] *secondly*, following on from this, whether the buyer or hirer is under any duty to examine the goods with a view to discovering any patent or latent defects;[284] and *thirdly*, whether the buyer or hirer who takes steps to protect himself which go beyond the duty to mitigate is to have his damages diminished by way of any benefit accruing to him from such further steps, e.g. the profit on a subsale (see para 27.29).

There are several types of consequential loss commonly caused by the defective quality of the goods delivered.

---

274  Distinguish the situation where the hirer is not claiming recovery of repair costs incurred during the period of his possession, but future repair costs after he has relinquished possession: see para 29.25.

275  The present agreement may be a good guide as to value: *per* Donovan LJ at 705–6.

276  At 711–12. His Lordship also suggested that each case should be judged on its own facts, and no general rule laid down (at 711). As to loss of use, see para 29.35.

277  [1967] 2 AC 278; [1967] 2 All ER 760, PC.

278  For criticism of the decision, see Goode, *HP Law and Practice*, 2nd edn, 463.

279  It was said that the hirer should not be in any worse position with regard to his claim for damages where he affirmed than where he rescinded: *per* Ormerod LJ in *Tolly's* case, at 715. See also *per* Lord Wilberforce in *Doobay v Mohabeer*, at 289.

280  Goode, *Op. cit.*, 459–60.

281  E.g. *Bernstein v Pamson Motors Ltd* [1987] 2 All ER 220 (cost of car breakdown recovery + spoilt day); *Doobay v Mohabeer* [1967] 2 AC 278, PC (cost of installing engine); *Molling v Dean* (1902) 18 TLR 216 (cost of delivery).

282  The relationship of claims under the 'reliance' and 'expectancy' interest is explained, see para 27.28.

283  *Beoco Ltd v Alfa Laval Co* [1995] QB 137, CA (buyer carelessly failed to check third-party repair); and see generally, para 27.29.

284  *McGregor on Damages*, 17th edn, para 20.067.

1. *Loss of use. Firstly*, the defect may deprive the buyer or hirer of the enjoyment of using the goods for which he must be compensated.[285] *Secondly*, he may recover any non-remote loss of profit[286] he would have made by utilising the goods to make some product for resale.[287]

2. *Loss on a subsale of goods*. Whilst liability in respect of a non-remote subsale on identical terms is not in question,[288] where the buyer is a consumer, the circumstances where his seller should contemplate such a subsale would seem to be too unusual to be pursued here.

3. *Loss caused by the defect* (see para 29.37).

**[29.37] Loss caused by the defect**. Normally, damage which the defect does to the goods themselves will be included in the *prima facie* measure of damages because it will reduce the value of the goods; but it is otherwise where the defective goods damage persons or other property. If such loss is caused to the buyer or hirer then, subject to the rules of causation[289] and remoteness (see para 27.41, *et seq*.), it is possible that an action will lie for the tort of negligence;[290] but it is more likely that he will sue for breach of contract, because liability is strict. Where the goods have been put to their contemplated use and the defect amounts to a breach of the contract of sale, it has been held that the buyer may recover in respect of personal injury,[291] death of his wife[292] and injury to his other property;[293] and in a consumer supply he may also sometimes recover in respect of disappointment and distress.[294] The position is the same with regard to actions by a hirer under a simple hiring or hp agreement against the owner;[295] and it has been held that a dealer in a directly financed hp transaction is liable to the hirer both for breach of a collateral contract of warranty and the tort of negligence (*Andrews v Hopkinson*: set out at para 16.18).

Finally, it is necessary to consider the liability of the supplier for loss caused to any third party. Possibly that third party can sue the supplier directly under a

---

285 *Jackson v Chrysler Acceptances Ltd* [1978] RTR 474, CA (defective car spoilt French touring holiday); *Bernstein v Pamson Motors Ltd* (above); and see generally, *Street on Torts*, 10th edn, 552.

286 But see the difficult case of *Cullinane v British 'Rema' Manufacturing Co Ltd* [1954] 1 QB 292, [1953] 2 All ER 1257, CA. See Macleod [1970] JBL 19; Fuller & Perdue (1936) 46 Yale LJ 52; Stoljar (1975) 91 LQR 68. See also Benjamin's *Sale of Goods*, 6th edn, para 17-069.

287 *Holden Ltd v Bostock Ltd* (1902) 18 TLR 317, CA. See also *Ashworth v Wells* (1898) 78 LT 136, CA; *Central Meat Products Ltd v McDaniel Ltd* [1952] 1 Lloyd's Rep 562; *Hotel Services Ltd v Hilton International Ltd* [2000] 1 All ER (Comm) 750, CA.

288 See *per* Scrutton LJ in *Dexters Ltd v Hill Crest Oil Co Ltd* [1926] 1 KB 348 at 359, CA.

289 *Commercial Fibres (Ireland) Ltd v Zabaida* [1975] 1 Lloyd's Rep 27 (buyer received yarn in damaged cartons; but shipped it and so caused much more damage to yarn).

290 E.g. *Lambert v Lewis* (set out at para 17.06; fourth-party proceedings).

291 E.g. *Geddling v Marsh* (set out at para 14.03); *Griffiths v Peter Conway Ltd* (set out at para 14.09); *Godley v Perry* [1960] 1 All ER 36; *Grant v Australian Knitting Mills Ltd* [1936] AC 85, PC.

292 E.g. *Jackson v Watson & Sons* [1919] 2 KB 193, CA.

293 E.g. *Bostock & Co Ltd v Nicholson & Sons Ltd* [1904] 1 KB 725; *Wilson v Rickett Cockerell & Co Ltd* (set out at para 14.03).

294 *Jackson v Chrysler Acceptances Ltd* [1978] RTR 474, CA; *Bernstein v Pamson Motors Ltd* [1987] 2 All ER 220; and Atiyah, *Sale of Goods*, 10th edn, 551–2. See also Campbell and Harris (2002) 22 LS 208 at 226, fn 100.

295 *White v John Warwick & Co Ltd* [1953] 1 All ER 1021, CA (simple hire); *Jackson v Chrysler Acceptances Ltd* (above; hp).

collateral contract (see para 17.09) or in the tort of negligence.[296] Alternatively, that third party may successfully sue the buyer or hirer in the tort of negligence;[296] and, in either case, the buyer or hirer may be able to pass that loss back to his supplier. Leaving aside the possibility that the buyer or hirer and his supplier are joint tort-feasors (see para 17.16), it may be that such a claim is a non-remote loss flowing from the breach of contract by the supplier; and in this event, the supplier[297] will be liable for the damages and costs paid by the buyer or hirer to a third party under a judgment[298] or a reasonable settlement,[299] or for any costs reasonably incurred in successfully defending such an action.[300]

# SPECIFIC ENFORCEMENT[301]

**[29.38] Specific enforcement**. Whilst detailed discussion of the common law principles on which a decree of specific performance is granted or refused are beyond the scope of this work, it will be recalled that the remedy is discretionary; it is an **alternative** to damages and will only be granted where damages are not an adequate remedy;[302] and may not available in the case of fraud.[303] Moreover, in relation to contracts for the disposition of goods, the buyer or hirer will usually only be able to obtain specific performance of the contract where the subject-matter is unique in some way.[304] Nor can he avoid this restriction by suing in tort.[305]

In the case of sales, the remedy of specific performance was put in statutory form by s 52 of the SGA. This provides as follows (s 52(1)):[305]

'In any action for breach of contract to deliver specific or ascertained goods the court may, if it thinks fit, on the plaintiff's application,[306] by its judgment . . . direct that the contract shall be performed specifically, without giving the defendant the option of retaining the goods on payment of damages.'[307]

---

296 E.g. *Lambert v Lewis* (above; plaintiff's claim).

297 But as to causation, see *Lambert v Lewis* (above; third-party proceedings); and para 27.29.

298 *Vogan & Co v Oulton* (1899) 81 LT 435, CA (simple hire). Cf. *Hadley v Droitwich Construction Ltd* [1967] 3 All ER 911, CA (simple hire).

299 *Kendall v Lillico* (set out at para 14.10).

300 *Britannia Hygienic Laundry Ltd v Thornycroft Ltd* (1925) 41 TLR 667. Reversed on facts: (1926) 42 TLR 198, CA.

301 See Treitel, *Law of Contract*, 11th edn, 1019, *et seq.*; Bridge, *Sale of Goods*, 531–7.

302 *Societie des Industries Metallurgiques SA v Bronx Engineering Co Ltd* [1975] 1 Lloyd's Rep 465, CA; and the criticism by Goode, *Commercial Law*, 3rd edn, 387–8. What if the parties bargain for specific performance (see Ogus (1985) 5 Legal Studies at 114)?

303 See *Geest plc v Fyffes plc* [1999] 1 All ER (Comm) 672, *obiter* (not a goods case).

304 E.g. *Behnke v Bede Shipbuilding Co Ltd* [1927] 1 KB 649; *Clarke v Reilly* [1962] ILTR 96 (part-exchange goods—see para 2.09). Compare *The Stena Nautica (No. 2)* [1982] 2 Lloyd's Rep 336, CA (damages only).

305 S 3 of the Torts (Interference with Goods) Act 1977: see para 24.26.

306 This means the buyer: *per* Wright J in *Shell Mex Ltd v Elton Cop Dying Co Ltd* (1928) 34 Com Cas 39, at 46.

307 The order may be conditional, e.g. *BICC plc v Burndy Corpn* [1985] Ch 232, CA. Compare the powers of the court in a tort action: see para 24.26.

In the unlikely event of unique goods being supplied under a quasi-sale or hired, this provision would presumably apply by analogy. At any event, s 52 only applies where the contract goods are identified and agreed upon either at the time of contracting (specific goods) or subsequently (ascertained goods);[308] and it does not apply to an unascertained part of a specific whole.[309]

The above general principles have been amended by the SSG Regulations in favour of private consumers: introducing new first-choice statutory rights of repair/ replacement (see para 29.03B), the Regulations allow the court the potentially revo-lutionary power to award specific performance of them,[310] notwithstanding that on ordinary common law principles damages would be an adequate remedy.[311]

**[29.39] Injunctions benefiting private consumers**. Just as the buyer or hirer of unique goods may be able to obtain a decree of specific performance requiring his supplier to deliver the specific or ascertained goods to himself (see above), so he may be able to obtain an injunction preventing his supplier disposing of those goods to a third party,[312] perhaps on an interlocutory basis.[313] However, an injunc-tion would appear to be available in somewhat wider circumstances, it being no defence to show that damages would be an adequate remedy,[314] nor that the goods remain unascertained.[315] But it has been refused to prevent presentation of a post-dated cheque.[316] As to anti-suit injunctions, see para 18.13.

Additionally, an injunction may be available to a stranger to a supply contract. *First*, where the formation or performance of a supply contract amounts to a crim-inal offence whose penalty is an insufficient deterrent, a public authority may seek an injunction against a contracting party (see para 28.03). *Second*, where perform-ance of a supply contract would amount to a tort, an injunction may be sought.[317] *Third*, an injunction may be obtained to enforce EU Competition law;[318] and the Competition Act 1998 has its own system of court orders for enforcement (see para 2.14). *Fourth*, whilst a consumer may always apply for an injunction under the above rules, qualified entities may in certain circumstances apply for injunctions on their behalf (see below). *Fifth*, where a Local Authority takes action to enforce consumer protection statutes by way of seeking an injunction or Enforcement Order (see paras 28.03–4), unlike a private plaintiff, it was usually under no obligation to give a cross-undertaking as to damages.[319]

---

308 *Per* Atkin LJ in *Re Wait* (below), at 630.
309 *Re Wait* (set out at para 20.22). But see para 29.39.
310 New s 48E(2) of the SGA. For quasi-sales, see new s 11R(2) of the SGSA.
311 As to the potentially revolutionary nature of this new power, see Harris (2003) 119 LQR 541.
312 *Contra* where statute prohibits further remedies, e.g. CCA, s 170.
313 The specialised interlocutory injunctions to prevent his removing assets from the jurisdiction by what have become known as *Mareva* (or freezing) injunctions are used in business-to-business disputes and are beyond the scope of this work.
314 *Redler Grain Silos Ltd v BICC Ltd* [1982] 1 Lloyd's Rep 435, CA.
315 *Sky Petroleum Ltd v VIP Petroleum Ltd* [1974] 1 All ER 954 (P would be forced out of business if contract to deliver petrol not performed).
316 *Eldan Services Ltd v Chandag Motors Ltd* [1990] 3 All ER 459.
317 E.g. *Morris Motors Ltd v Lilley* [1959] 3 All ER 737 (passing-off); *BBC Enterprises Ltd v Hi-Tech Xtravision Ltd* [1991] 2 AC 327, HL (breach of copyright).
318 *R v Secretary of State for Transport, ex p Factortame No. 2* [1991] 1 AC 658, HL (allowing injunction against Crown following ECJ's judgment); and see generally para 2.13.
319 *Coventry CC v Finnie* [1996] CLY 841.

Moreover, as against a third party an injunction may be available to a contracting party to prevent the third party interfering with that contract.[320]

## EXTORTIONATE CREDIT BARGAINS/ UNFAIR CREDIT RELATIONSHIPS

[29.40] **Introduction**. The old usury laws dealt with the problem of extortion by fixing a maximum rate of interest which a lender might charge—a rate ceiling (see para 6.09). However, after the repeal of the usuary laws and prior to the CCA,[321] the law had only very meagre weapons at its disposal with which to attack extortionate credit bargains. *First*, leaving aside the common law doctrine of duress,[322] equity was sometimes prepared to intervene in unconscionable bargains. Besides the well-established equity of redemption in respect of mortgaged land (see para 25.22), equity might grant some relief in respect of forfeiture of goods (see para 27.20 and 27.22) or where a contract was procured by undue influence;[323] but it would seem that there is not yet any general principle that relief may be granted simply because of unconscionability and inequality of bargaining power.[324] *Second*, there was a limited statutory power under the Moneylenders Acts 1900 to 1927 to 're-open' loans charging excessive interest, this being presumed if the rate of interest exceeded 48%.[325] In fact, this statutory jurisdiction led to the confusion of two separate policies:[326]

(a) the terms of the loan, including the interest rate, may be harsh and unconscionable in the light of the risks the lender was undertaking; and

(b) the re-introduction of a rate ceiling which would 'prohibit' lenders granting loans to bad credit risks even on terms reasonable in the light of that risk.[327]

The *Crowther Report* (see para 5.03) considered whether a rate-ceiling should be re-introduced on the grounds that such socially harmful lending should be prohibited (para 6.6.3–6); but the Report rejected the idea (para 6.6.9), perhaps because of the tendency of such a rule to force that class of borrower onto the illegal, 'loanshark',

---

320 E.g. *Cutsforth v Mansfield Inns Ltd* [1986] 1 All ER 577 (for inducing breach of the supply contract—see para 17.17); or amounting to an unlawful restraint of trade (see para 2.13); *The Messiniaki Tolme* [1982] QB 1248, CA (against a banker under a documentary credit—see further [1983] 2 AC 787, HL); *The Iran Bohonar* [1983] 2 Lloyd's Rep 620, CA (against carrier).

321 Doorstep transactions may now be cancelled without cause, whether made on a cash or credit basis: see respectively, paras 10.36 and 10.28.

322 Including economic duress: see para 10.18.

323 Compare *Lloyds Bank Ltd v Bundy* [1975] QB 326, CA and *Goldsworthy v Brickell* [1987] Ch 378, CA with *Coldunell Ltd v Gallon* [1986] QB 1184, CA and *Woodstead Finance Ltd v Petrou* (1986) 136 NLJ 188, CA. See generally Treitel, *Law of Contract*, 11th edn, 408, *et seq.*; *Chitty on Contract*, 28th edn, Vol I, para 7-041, *et seq.*

324 *Lloyd's Bank Ltd v Bundy* [1975] QB 326, CA, *per* Lord Denning MR (discussed in the authorities cited above; Treitel, *Op. cit.*, 420–3; Chitty, *Op. cit.*, para 7-088; Goode, *Consumer Credit Law & Practice*, para 47.91; OFT, *Trading Malpractices* (1990), Appendix 3). Cf. UCC, Art 2–302.

325 1900 Act, s 1; 1927 Act, s 10 (both now repealed). There was also a statutory tariff of charges laid down under the Pawnbrokers Acts (now repealed).

326 But the Moneylenders Acts did not themselves make this mistake: see the Crowther Report, para 6.6.3.

327 See Cayne and Trebilcock (1973) UTLJ 396, at 411–18; Johnson (1997) 51 CC6/2, at 5–6.

market.[328] But, the Report did recommend continuation of the existing presumption that a rate in excess of 48% was *prima facie* harsh and unconscionable (para 6.6.9). However, in repealing the Moneylenders Acts, the CCA varied these proposals by abandoning the 48% rule, whilst confirming and extending the court jurisdiction to re-open what it termed 'extortionate credit bargains' (see para 29.41). Inevitably, these rules are chiefly measured against sub-prime business (see para 7.04A). Additionally, the OFT may exercise its licensing powers (see para 6.11, *et seq.*). In the last resort, only the Government has sufficient resources and reach to offer uniform country-wide provision, in the form of the Social Fund.[329]

**[29.41] Extortionate credit bargains: (1)**.[330] Abandoning the former 48% rule of thumb (see para 29.40), the CCA, ss 137–40, introduced a new jurisdiction for the court to attack extortionate credit bargains.[331] This jurisdiction may be invoked by any debtor or any surety[332] so as to reduce his obligations: it may be compared with Time Orders, which do not allow reduction of the sum owed, but only stretch the repayment period (see para 24.40). Under it, the court might, if 'extortionate' (see below), re-open a 'credit agreement' (s 137(1)), which expression is defined by s 137(2)(a) as:

> any agreement between an individual (the 'debtor') and any other person (the 'creditor') by which the creditor provides the debtor with credit of any amount.

In ambit, this not only precluded entirely consumer hire agreements,[333] but was both narrower and wider than consumer credit agreements (see para 5.19): whilst both were only applicable to individual debtors, the notion of a 'credit agreement' was regardless of financial limit,[334] and whether the agreement was exempt (s 16(7): see para 5.15), or the creditor in business.[335] However, the court was empowered to look beyond the four corners of the credit agreement to what the Act conveniently termed the 'credit bargain', which was defined in s 137(2)(b) to include the host of ancillary agreements in which the creditor might have hidden his excessive charges, e.g. maintenance or insurance contracts taken out by the debtor; or surety contracts by a third party. It was for the creditor to prove[336] that his was not an extortionate credit bargain.[337]

---

328 For the CCA licensing penalties against loan-sharking, see para 6.20. The legal alternative would appear to be social lending, e.g. Government social loans (see para 1.15; and below); credit unions (see para 15.19).

329 See Collard and Kempson, *Affordable Credit*, 2005, 31–7.

330 See further Macleod, *Consumer Sales Law*, 1st edn, para 29.40, *et seq.*

331 But not so as to alter the effect of any judgment (s 138(4)); nor where the debtor is insolvent (see para 19.24).

332 S 139(1). As to whether a court can raise the issue, see *per* Dillon LJ in *First National Bank plc v Syed* [1991] 2 All ER 250, CA, at 252e.

333 See para 1.19. For the power to grant financial relief to consumer hirers under s 132, see para 27.23.

334 It has been held that 'credit agreement' does not include a sale and re-hiring on hp transaction: *Lavin v Johnson* [2002] EWCA Civ 1138, CA; and see generally, para 25.27.

335 The agreement might be non-commercial, so that even a loan between friends is caught.

336 S 171(7) (repealed by Sched 4 of 2006 Act), e.g. *Coldunell Ltd v Gallon* [1986] QB 1184, CA. But the debtor must first raise the issue (s 139(1)) so as to discharge an evidential burden: *Bank of Baroda v Shah* [1988] 3 All ER 24, CA. For the complicated process the debtor must follow, see Rosenberg (1999) 53 *Quarterly Account* 4; 54 *QA* 11.

337 This is so, however low the interest rate, even if it is a low-cost exempt agreement: see para 5.15. Cf. the definition of 'extortionate' in the Insolvency Act 1986: see para 19.16.

Section 138(1) explained that a credit bargain was extortionate if it required the debtor to make payments which were 'grossly exorbitant', or 'otherwise grossly contravenes ordinary principles of fair dealing;' and this has been interpreted ignoring any concessions granted by the creditor[338] and any changes in interest rates **after** the agreement is made.[339] Thus, a bargain is not 'extortionate' merely because it is harsh or even unconscionable;[340] nor even because it is unfair (see para 11.15). Before a transaction could be struck down, it must not only be exorbitant, but **grossly** so. Thus, in *Broadwick Financial Services Ltd v Spencer* (set out at para 8.22), Dyson LJ in the Court of Appeal made the following points in finding that the credit bargain was not extortionate: (a) the statutory test of 'grossly exorbitant' was a high one, so that the payments required to be made must be **grossly** exorbitant (at para 80); (b) the judge was correct to ignore standard interest rates at the time of contracting, the proper comparators being other lenders in the non-status market (at para 35); (c) subject to (d), the manner in which the variable interest rate clause was operated would certainly not be a relevant factor because occurring after the contract was made;[341] (d) nor was the failure to disclose that policy to S before contract here unfair, as there was no evidence that S would not then have proceeded with the transaction (at para 57); (e) nor was the fact that the loan allowed early settlement on the statutory basis (see para 78; and para 26.19A); and (f) failure to follow OFT Guidelines did not of itself render the loan extortionate (at paras 78 and 81).

**[29.42] Extortionate credit bargains: (2)**. The test of 'grossly exorbitant applies not just to the primary obligations of the debtor, or his 'relative' (see para 5.33), but also to any secondary ones operating on default and linked transactions (s 138(5)). Such sums will mostly already be included in the total charge for credit (see para 8.24). To help a court decide whether a credit bargain was grossly exorbitant, the Act laid down a number of guidelines (s 138), most of them based on decisions under the Moneylenders Acts.[342] However, these criteria failed in that very few cases were found to be extortionate: seemingly, this was not because the tests were impractical, but rather because the modern sub-prime market is very competitive, so that such lenders rarely have the opportunity to lend on harsher terms than the market average for that class of business. A court is not obliged to take only these factors into account,[343] but they do provide a useful checklist.[344]

---

338 *Broadwick Financial Services Ltd v Spencer* (below), CA at para 60.

339 *Paragon Finance plc v Staughton & Nash* (set out at para 11.10), CA at para 64.

340 *Davies v Directloans Ltd* [1986] 2 All ER 783. It has been pointed out that the expression is 'extortionate' not 'unwise', connoting a 'substantial imbalance of bargaining power of which one party has taken advantage': *per* Donaldson MR in *Wills v Wood* (1984) 3 Tr L 93 at 98, CA.

341 At para 56. The debtor pleaded that these were 'other relevant considerations' within s 138(2)(c) (see *per* Dyson LJ at para 40); but Dyson LJ rejected this use of the provision (at para 55); and see para 29.42.

342 See Meston, *Moneylenders*, 5th edn, Chap 12. But see *per* Foster J in *Ketley Ltd v Scott* [1981] ICR 241, at 245.

343 E.g. switch-selling. The factors are also relevant to linked transactions (see para 5.31): s 138(5).

344 So warning the creditor of the sorts of things on which he should lead evidence: *Woodstead Finance Ltd v Petrou* (1986) 136 NLJ 188, CA. Can there be taken into account the defective state of any goods supplied under the regulated or any linked agreement? For a discussion of the statutory factors, see Bently and Howells [1989] Conv 164.

1. **Interest rates** prevailing at the time the bargain was made (s 138(2)(a)), which means exclusively APRs.[345] As interest rates will differ for different classes of business and borrowers, much may depend on how a particular bargain is classified.[346] The reference to rates prevailing at the time of contracting will exclude later falls in general interest rates.[347]

2. The **debtor's** (a) 'age, experience, business capacity and state of health' and (b) the degree and nature of any financial pressure he was then under (s 138(3)).

3. The degree of risk accepted by the **creditor** having regard to (a) the value of any security and (b) his relationship to the debtor.[348]

4. Whether a colourable cash price was quoted, this being an anti-avoidance device (s 138(4)(c)), e.g. by inflating the cash price and shrinking the credit charge.

5. 'Any other relevant considerations' (s 138(2)(c)). Whilst this provision has been relied upon to find a bargain not extortionate,[349] when a debtor relied upon these words in the *Broadwick Financial* case (set out at para 8.22), Dyson LJ denied his argument by giving the words a very narrow construction.[350]

In *London North Securities v Meadows* (set out at para 8.25) the County Court Judge could have decided the issue simply on the basis that the 1989 loan was not properly executed because it did not state the tcc (see para 8.25). However, in relation to the issue of extortionate credit, he also held as follows: in the 1989 non-status market, a charge of 34.9% APR on the capital outstanding was not by itself extortionate (at para 61); but to charge that rate compound on arrears might be extortionate (at para 62) and certainly was so in respect of a defaulting non-status loan such as this (at para 64), though this would not be the case with regard to a performing non-status loan (at para 66).

**[29.43] Reform of 1974 Act**. Interest rates charged by back street lenders have been recorded as high as 17.9 billion % (OFT, July 87). In 1989, it was suggested that ss 137–9 had failed for three reasons:[351] (i) the onus placed on the debtor to raise the

---

345 *Broadwick Financial Services Ltd v Spencer* (above), CA at para 34; *Batooneh v Asombang* [2004] CLY 629 (creditor delayed demanding repayment). A high interest rate in the original contract will be saved from the UTCCR as being a core term (see para 11.14).

346 So presumably it will not catch a standard commercial rate which is just not geared to the personal characteristics of a particular debtor: Goode, *Consumer Credit Law & Practice*, para 47.43.

347 *Paragon Finance plc v Staunon and Nash* (set out at para 11.10). The fact that the implied term is that the creditor must act reasonably may make it more difficult to argue that it is unfair (see para 11.15). See further *Broadwick Financial Services Ltd v Spencer* (above); *Paragon Finance plc v Pender* [2005] GCCR 5331, [2005] EWCA Civ 760, CA, at para 126.

348 S 138(4)(a), (b). See *Ketley Ltd v Scott* (above); *Davies v Direct Loans Ltd* (above). Does this encourage secured lending on the basis of the equity in the property rather than the debtor's ability to repay?

349 The expression was utilised in *Ketley Ltd v Scott* (above) so as not to re-open a transaction in view of the debtor's business experience, deceitful conduct and the rate of interest balanced against the risk.

350 See para 29.41. His Lordship read those words (at para 55) strictly in the context of the other matters listed in s 138: this seems to be a *eiusdem generis* interpretation.

351 Bently and Howells [1989] Conv 164 & 234; and further Howells, *Aspects of Credit & Debt*, Chap 6.

issue; (ii) the statutory formulation employed; and (iii) judicial reticence to interfere with agreements voluntarily entered into by the parties. The statutory provisions were reviewed in 1991 by the OFT, who identified particular difficulty with non-status borrowers and roll-over loans (see para 7.04A) and recommended that ss 137–9 should be recast as '**unjust** credit transactions'.[352] In its 2003 *White Paper*,[353] the Government pointed out (paras 3.29–30) that under CCA, ss 137–40, only about 30 extortionate credit cases had reached the courts (only 10 proven), so that the provisions had not operated effectively (see also para 3.31). It therefore promised legislation, *inter alia*: to make it easier for consumers to challenge unfair credit agreements by introducing new legislative factors and guidance to be applicable both when the agreement was made and subsequently (paras 3.32–6), including dealing with unfair practices, unfair credit costs, irresponsible lending and other relevant circumstances (para 3.37). However, if the new law increased the uncertainty faced by responsible lenders too much, it warned that there was always the danger that they will withdraw from the most marginal markets, thereby increasing the scope for illegal loansharks (see para 6.20). Seeking to steer a middle line between these two considerations, the CCA 2006 prospectively entirely repealed the extortionate credit bargain rules[354] and as from April 2007 replaced them[355] with a new jurisdiction for the courts to re-open credit transactions where there is an **unfair** credit relationship (see para 29.44). The new provisions will apply to new agreements made on or after 6 April 2007; and also to agreements previously made which do not expire by April 2008.[354]

**[29.44] Definition of unfair credit relationships.** Introducing a new set of numeration for the 1974 Act (presumably to minimise confusion) and significant new terminology, new s 140A(1) of the CCA 1974[356] provides that the court may make an order under s 140B (see para 29.47) in connection with a credit agreement[357] if it determines that the **credit relationship** between the creditor[358] and the debtor[358] arising out of the agreement (or the agreement taken with any related agreement)[359] is **unfair** (see para 29.45) to the debtor because of one or more of the following (new s 140A(1)):

(a)  Any of the terms of the agreement[357] or of any related agreement.[359]

---

352  *Unjust Credit Transactions* (1991), para 1.9. The Government largely accepted the Report: see (1992) 9 Tr L 105 and the OFT continued to press for its implementation: *1998 AR*, 12, 24.

353  *Fair, Clear and Competitive: the Consumer Credit Market in the 21st century* (Cm 6040, Dec 2003). It rejected for the present interest-rate ceilings (para 3.51).

354  S 22(3) of the 2006 Act repeals ss 137–40 of the 1974 Act; but these sections continue to apply to existing credit bargains that are not caught by the rules as to unfair credit relationships (see below): Sched 3, para 15.

355  The date ss 19–22 of the 2006 Act is to come into force.

356  As inserted by s 19 of the 2006 Act.

357  As to 'credit agreement', see new s 140C(1): see para 29.46. Would it extend to minimum repayments too low to pay off the capital?

358  'Creditor' and 'debtor' include their assignees and multiple creditor/debtors: new s 140C(2). As to 'creditor' and 'debtor', see paras 5.24–5.

359  As to 'related agreement', see new s 140C(4): see para 29.46. Would this extend to roll-over loans?

(b) The way in which the creditor has exercised or enforced any of his rights under the agreement[357] or any related agreement.[359] The Act explicitly extends this to conduct of the creditor's 'associate'.[360]

(c) Any other thing done (or not done) by, or on behalf of, the creditor (either before or after the making of the agreement or any related agreement). The Act explicitly extends this to conduct of the creditor's 'associate'.[360] The OFT considers that this category is wider than the others, including pre-contract business practices, e.g. advertising, and post-contract actions not based on rights, e.g. demanding sums of money that the consumer has not agreed to pay, plus acts or omissions which are non-commercial or do not amount to a practice.[361]

Taken together, the scope of the powers in new s 140A(1) would appear to be much wider than the reopening powers in relation to extortionate credit bargains, which latter largely concentrated on the terms of the agreement itself (see para 29.41). In relation to such unfairness, the 2006 Act places the burden of proof on the creditor[362] and new s 140A(2) provides that:

> 'In deciding whether to make a determination under this section the court shall have regard to all matters it thinks relevant (including matters relating to the creditor and matters relating to the debtor).'

This jurisdiction exists not only whilst the credit agreement is running, but also 'notwithstanding that the relationship has ended'.[363] However, it is anticipated that the new ss 140A–C jurisdiction will not come into force for some years yet;[364] and in the meantime all transactions remain subject to the present ss 137–40 rules (see paras 29.41–2). When the new rules come into force, they apply not just to all agreements made thereafter, but also to some existing agreements which are still running at the end of a specified period after commencement.[365] This last provision will be particularly relevant in relation to some existing (but not completed) long-term credit agreements, e.g. 20yrs. It follows that for some years yet, some of these long-term agreements will be governed by the extortionate credit bargain provisions (ss 137–40), whilst others will be determined under the new unfair credit relationship rules (new ss 140A–D), perhaps retrospectively.[366]

---

360 By new s 140A(3), 'the court shall treat anything done (or not done) by, or on behalf of, or in relation to, an associate or a former associate of the creditor as if done (or not done) by, or on behalf of, or in relation to, the creditor'. 'Credit relationship' presumably connotes mutual dealings involving credit.

361 OFT, *Unfair Relationships* (2006, OFT 854 con) para 4.14. These practices do not themselves need to contravene the law (para 4.29), e.g. irresponsible lending (see para 6.19).

362 New s 140B(10) where debtor is alleging unfairness. But not otherwise?

363 New s 140A(4); i.e., 'when all or any of the parties had no further duties under the credit agreement': Minister (2004–5) HC Deb on 3rd Reading, col. 1160.

364 Even after the 2006 Act is brought into force (s 71(2) of the 2006 Act: see para 5.11), it is anticipated that there will be a transitional period (see Sched 3) for ss 140A–C lasting at least 12 months: Minister (2004–5) HC Deb on 3rd Reading, cols. 1161–2; and see above, para 29.43.

365 See Sched 3, paras 14–7. See the Minister in (2005–6) HC Deb, R3, col.1023.

366 It was understood in Parliament that the intended target of the retrospective application was loansharks: (2005–6) HL Deb, R, col.1050.

**[29.45] 'Unfair' under the 2006 Act.** In its 2003 Consultation Document,[367] there were indications that the DTI favoured replacing CCA, s 138(1)(a) with a fair and reasonable test.[368] In its White Paper that year, the DTI reached the following conclusions about the new scheme:[369] it should be easier for consumers to challenge unfair agreements and for individual consumers to seek redress through an ADR scheme (para 3.32); and this should be achieved by widening the current 'extortionate' test (para 3.33) which would include legislative factors and guidance from the OFT (para 3.34). Whilst there were some indications that the Government was contemplating introducing a more comprehensive list of unfair factors in place of extortionate ones contained in s 138, perhaps it was frightened off by the strict application of the *eiusdem generis* rule in the *Broadwick Financial* case (see para 29.42).[370] In any event, the Bill was intentionally drafted with a new unfair test without listing any legislative factors, so as not to give undue emphasis to some factors. The Government justified this on the basis that the object was to lower the hurdle[371] so as to shift the balance of power towards the borrower;[372] to avoid being over-prescriptive so as to afford the courts maximum flexibility;[373] and to encourage creditors to adhere to the spirit of the Act, rather than merely complying with its technical requirements.[374] Industry was particularly worried that the vague 'unfair' test, combined with the burden of proof on the creditor (s 140B(9): see para 29.46) would prove too onerous,[375] but the Minister refused (as with so many concerns with this Bill raised in Parliament) to embroider the test, beyond referring to the following comparators: the CCA; the UTCCR; the Unfair Commercial Practices Directive; and the TDA.[376] But he did suggest that the terms of codes of practice, such as the Banking Code, might be helpful.[377] The Minister proffered the olive branch that the OFT might publish guidelines as to when it might intervene on behalf of consumers generally under Pt 8 of the EA (see above, paras 6.06–8), but he was careful to point out that these would not be binding on the

---

367 *Tackling Loan Sharks—and more!* (March 2003). By way of contrast, see the following submissions on this Consultation Document: by CCA (dated 18.6.03); by CCTA (2003) 57 CC6/34; by DOOD (dated June 2003); and by OFT (dated 12.6.03). See also the DTI, *Summary of Responses* (Dec 2003).

368 Cf. UTCCR (see para 11.15). For house mortgages regulated by the FSMA (see para 3.02), there is a prohibition on excessive charges: see 2001 SI 1177.

369 *Fair, Clear and Competitive: the Consumer Credit Market in the 21st Century* (Cm 6040, Dec 2003).

370 The Minister in (2005–6) HC Standing Committee D, col. 55; HL GC col. 160.

371 Minister (2004–5) HC Deb on 3rd Reading, cols. 1161.

372 Minister (2004–5) HC Standing Committee E, col. 54. Does this breach the requirement of certainty in the Human Rights Convention (see para 3.09A)? See Rosenthal (2006) 61 CC2/17.

373 Minister (2005) HC Standing Committee E, col. 51, 52, 70. But for argument that there should be a rate-ceiling, see para 6.09.

374 Minister (2005–6) HL Deb, R2, col. 1054. Described as a 'tick-box mentality': Minister (2005–6) HL GC col. 160; HL Report col. 725.

375 (2005) HC Deb on 3rd Reading, cols. 1158, 1172.

376 (2005–6) HL GC col. 160. In the Third Reading, the Minister did suggest as an example of unfairness where the creditor knowingly disregards the inability of the debtor to understand the documents: (2005–6) HC Deb, R3, col. 1001. Also suggested during the debates as comparators were the following: unfair dismissal in employment; and the FSA's fair treatment of customers (see para 3.02).

377 Minister (2004–5) HC Standing Committee E, cols. 71–2; (2005–6) HC Standing Committee D, cols. 59–61. For codes of conduct, see paras 3.11–13.

courts and did not define unfair relationships.[378] The guidance[379] does not seek to define what is an 'unfair relationship', but rather to indicate how the OFT expects Pt 8 enforcement powers to be used in this area (para 2.2; and see para 29.47); and later versions are planned to include subsequent relevant court judgments (para 3.11).

Accordingly, the 2006 Act adopts the test of 'unfair', but makes no attempt to define 'unfair'. In effect, Parliament was passing the buck to the courts. Perhaps the courts will start with the earlier case law on unconscionability and extortionate credit bargains (see paras 29.40–2) and then be more generous to debtors. By way of illustrating the uncertainty, would the rules extend to repayment schedules reasonable in themselves, but wildly unrealistic in the light of the debtor's ability to pay? An affirmative may have data protection implications (see para 3.29), may make credit scoring (see para 8.39) compulsory and reinforce the responsible lending requirement (CCA, new s 25(2B): see para 6.19). Might the concept extend to late payment charges which amount to common law penalties (see paras 27.25–6)? Particularly as against the sub-prime sector (see para 7.04A), trade sources have forecast that issues likely to arise include price, transparency of information, roll-over agreements ('churning'), car finance, home credit and cheque cashing.

**[29.46] Ambit of unfair credit relationships**. The extortionate credit bargain jurisdiction may be invoked by the debtor or any surety; but the drawback of so doing is that the sub-prime market is quite small (see para 7.04A): if the debtor does invoke the jurisdiction, he may find it difficult ever to get such credit again. Fortunately, the new unfair credit relationships jurisdiction does not adopt the same rule: so the court may raise the matter of its own volition.

The matter having been raised, new s 140C[380] contains some jurisdiction provisions, mostly in favour of the debtor. *First*, 'credit agreement' 'means any agreement between an individual (the 'debtor') and any other person (the 'creditor') by which the creditor provides the debtor with credit of any amount' (new s 140C(1)): like the extortionate credit bargain provisions (see para 29.41), this precludes consumer hire agreements (see para 1.19), but applies to agreements to grant credit to individuals usually regardless of financial limit (see para 5.23) and covers both fixed and running-account credit. *Second*, also like the extortionate credit bargain provisions,[381]

> 'If, in any proceedings, the debtor or surety alleges that the relationship between the creditor and the debtor is unfair to the debtor, it is for the creditor to prove to the contrary.'

*Third*, unlike the extortionate credit bargain provisions, the new jurisdiction does not apply to all exempt agreements,[382] so that agreements secured on land will

---

378 (2005–6) HC Deb, R3, col. 1021; HL GC col. 325.
379 HL Report col 327. In June 2006, the OFT published draft guidance entitled *Unfair Relationships* (2006, OFT 854 con), promising final guidance by the end of 2006.
380 As inserted by s 21 of the 2006 Act.
381 New s 140B(8) (inserted by s 20 of the 2006 Act), which closely follows s 171(7) of the 1974 Act: see para 29.41.
382 New s 140A(5), as supplied by s 19 of the 2006 Act.

continue to be regulated by the FSA under the FSMA.[383] *Fourth*, the new jurisdiction ousts the ordinary definition of 'court' as county court (new s 140C(3)), so allowing these disputes to be heard by the Ombudsman (see para 3.25), but thereby depriving decisions of precedent-value. *Fifth*, the new provisions tackle the practice where a creditor enters into successive credit agreements with the debtor to, e.g. increase the total amount of debt or generate multiple fees. It does so by terming the current credit agreement the 'main agreement' and providing in new s 140C(4) that references in ss 140A–B to 'credit agreement' shall include all the following: (a) a credit agreement consolidated by the main agreement;[384] (b) a linked transaction to either of them;[385] and (c) a security provided in relation to any of them.[386]

**[29.47] Powers of the court.** Where an unfair credit relationship (see para 29.46) is found, new s 140B sets out the types of order that the court or Ombudsman may make.[387] However, under new s 140B(2) these orders may only be made in one of the following circumstances:[388] (i) on an application made to the county court[389] by the debtor or by a surety (new s 140B(2)(a));[390] or (ii) at the instance of the debtor or surety[390] in any court proceedings[389] where either the proceedings are to enforce the main agreement or any related agreement (see para 29.44), or in any other proceedings 'where the amount paid or payable under the agreement is relevant'. Where the foregoing requirements are satisfied, under new s 140B(1) 'in connection with a credit agreement only' (see para 29.43) and within the limitation period (LA 1980, s 9: see para 26.17), the court is empowered to do any one or more of the following:

(a) require the creditor, or any associate or former associate of his,[391] to repay (in whole or in part) any sum paid by the debtor or by a surety by virtue of the agreement or any related agreement (whether paid to the creditor, the associate or the former associate or to any other person);

(b) require the creditor, or any associate or former associate of his, to do or not to do (or to cease doing) anything specified in the order in connection with the agreement or any related agreement;

(c) reduce any sum payable by the debtor or by a surety by virtue of the agreement or any related agreement;

(d) direct the return to a surety of any property provided by him for the purposes of a security;

---

383 See s 16(6C) of the 1974 Act: para 5.15. For the FSA, see para 3.02.
384 For the definition of 'consolidated', see new s 140C(7)–(8).
385 New s 140C(6)(b), which extends the expression 'linked transaction' to where the credit agreement is unregulated.
386 The expressions 'security' and 'surety' are extended to where the credit agreement is unregulated: new s 140C(6)(a).
387 As inserted by s 20 of the CCA 2006.
388 By new s 140B(9), 'a party to any proceedings mentioned in subsection (2) shall be entitled, in accordance with rules of court, to have any person who might be the subject of an order under this section made a party to the proceedings'.
389 As to the county court, see para 24.39.
390 As to the debtor, see para 5.24; and as to a surety, see para 25.11. If the debtor/surety is insolvent, application may instead be made by the Official Receiver or trustee in bankruptcy: Minister (2005–6) HL GC col. 164.
391 'Associate' is widely defined by s 184: see para 5.32.

(e) otherwise set aside (in whole or in part) any duty imposed on the debtor or on a surety by virtue of the agreement or any related agreement;

(f) alter the terms of the agreement or of any related agreement;

(g) direct accounts to be taken.

The section further provides that the above orders 'may be made notwithstanding that its effect is to place on the creditor, or any associate or former associate of his, a burden in respect of an advantage enjoyed by another person' (new s 140B(3)), e.g. a credit-broker. Further, it would seem that the above orders may alter the effect of any preceding judgment,[392] a position which is likely to be particularly important because such debtors tend to delay taking advice until the last moment.

Finally, the draftsman anticipates that the foregoing individual jurisdiction initiated by, e.g. the debtor or surety, may 'interact' with the collective jurisdiction under Pt 8 of the EA supervised by the OFT (see para 6.06A): the reason for this is that, where an unfair relationship also affects consumers generally, e.g. it arises from the use of particular standard terms, the OFT may wish to take Pt 8 action. Accordingly, new s 140D[393] requires the OFT to indicate in its published advice and information how it expects that interaction to work.[394] This may include examples of the circumstances, conduct or practices that, in the opinion of the OFT, could give rise to an unfair relationship between creditors and debtors.[395] A detailed scheme is to be found in the subsequently published draft guidance.[396]

---

392 At a late stage in the Parliamentary process, a provision to the opposite effect was dropped from s 20 of the 2006 Act: see (2005–6) HC Deb, col. 987.

393 As inserted by s 22 of the 2006 Act.

394 That advice and information is published under s 229 of the EA: see para 6.06A.

395 Explanatory memorandum to the 2005 Bill, para 51.

396 *Unfair Relationships* (2006, OFT 854 con), paras 3.1–5.32. The OFT intends to publicise court judgments (para 5.24) and they may impinge on subsequent licensing decisions (paras 5.30–2: see para 6.17, *et seq.*).

# INDEX